MOVIE STILL IDENTIFICATION BOOK
Ultimate Edition

Volume I - Letters

By
Ed and Susan Poole

2015 Edition

*A Must Reference Tool For Anyone
Who Handles Movie Studio Production, Short,
Portrait, Studio and Television Stills*

A Publication by
LearnAboutMoviePosters.com
of the
Learn About Network, L.L.C.

Movie Still Identification Book
Ultimate Edition
Volume I - Letters

2015 Edition

Published by:
Ed and Susan Poole
P. O. Box 3181
Harvey, LA 70059
edp@LearnAboutMoviePosters.com

ISBN: 978-0-9965015-0-7

© 2015 by Ed and Susan Poole
All Rights Reserved.

No part of this publication may be reproduced, stored in a database, or transmitted in any form, or by any means, electronic, mechanical, photocopying, recording, or otherwise, without prior written permission of the Authors/Publishers.

LIMIT OF LIABILITY/DISCLAIMER OF WARRANTY

The Authors/Publishers have used their best efforts in preparing this publication. Authors/Publishers make no representation or warranties with respect to the accuracy or completeness of the contents of this publication and specifically disclaim any implied warranties of merchantability or fitness for any particular purpose and shall in no event be liable for any loss of profit or any other commercial damage, including but not limited to special, incidental, consequential, or other damages.

ADDITIONAL COPIES:

Additional copies of this publication are available through the authors.

Ed Poole
P. O. Box 3181
Harvey, LA 70059
(504) 298-LAMP
Email: edp@LearnAboutMoviePosters.com

or online at www.MovieStillID.com or www.LearnAboutMoviePosters.com

DO YOU want to buy vintage movie paper?

There is NO auctioneer of vintage movie paper who auctions more items than eMoviePoster.com, and we auction every type of movie paper, including tens of thousands of stills per year. Go to our website to start bidding!

eMoviePoster.com - P.O. Box 874 - West Plains, MO 65775 - phone +1 (417) 256-9616
e-mail: mail@eMoviePoster.com - web: http://www.eMoviePoster.com

DOMINIQUE BESSON AFFICHES

220 Chemin de la Blanchère - 84270 Vedène - France

TEL : 33.613.451.355   -   FAX : 33.442.634.188
WEB : www.dominiquebesson.com
E-MAIL : info@dominiquebesson.com

CATALOGUE

ON

REQUEST

High quality shipping tubes for Vintage Posters.

95 sizes in stock. Immediate Shipment.
End Plugs included. One box minimum.
Credit Cards Accepted.

YAZOO MILLS, INC.
MANUFACTURERS OF PAPER TUBES AND CORES
P.O. BOX 369 • NEW OXFORD, PA 17350

CALL TOLL FREE 1-800-242-5216   FAX 717-624-4420

ORDER ONLINE
www.yazoomills.com

The Original Movie Poster Specialist
01494 432816

The Original Movie Poster Specialists

Trade Address

Vintage Movie Posters (UK) Limited

14 Chiltern Business Centre
63-65 Woodside Rd
Amersham, Bucks
HP6 6AA

Email: shop@vintagemovieposters.co.uk

Phone number: 01494 432 816

JOHN REID
VINTAGE MOVIE MEMORABILIA

**ORIGINAL MOVIE POSTERS,
LOBBY CARDS,
MOVIE STILLS
AND MEMORABILIA**

JOHN REID VINTAGE MOVIE MEMORABILIA
PO Box 92 -- Elanora -- Qld 4221 -- Australia

info@moviemem.com
http://www.moviemem.com
ebay userid: johnwr

James Bond — THE MOVIE POSTER PAGE — Disney
Tarzan — Godzilla

A Major Internet Presence
Since 1994
www.musicman.com/mp/mp.html
734 973 7303 (John)
****
*JUST What you want—no hype! *
****
classic posters from everywhere

We have Arabic
posters from Egypt
نحن متخصصين فيي افيشات مصريّة للسينما

---

kinoart.net

original movie posters — arthouse cult cinema horror/scifi classic movies (s)exploitation

Online-gallery with more than 20.000 selected international movieposters
Searchable database with multiple search options
Posters from the 30s to 90s from all major countries available

US . German . Italian . French . British . Polish . Czech . Australian
Belgian . Japanese . Mexican . East German . Danish . Swedish etc

Visit us online - We ship worldwide - In business since 12 years

US Stills available on request! We have many stills from the 30s to the 80s.

www.kinoart.net   Wolfgang Jahn
Sülzburgstr.126 D-50937 Cologne Germany
mail@kinoart.net Fon (+49) (0)221 1698728

ABOUT THE AUTHORS

Ed and Susan Poole
Film Accessory Researchers

For almost 40 years Ed and Susan Poole have been involved with documenting, recording and preserving film accessories (i.e., press books, movie stills, movie posters, general press materials, etc.). Their path has evolved from being just collectors to retail and wholesale dealers and eventually to full time researchers. They have been featured in dozens of newspaper and magazine articles.

Their accomplishments on a national and international level include:

- **Published the** first reference book on movie posters, *Collecting Movie Posters*, released in 1997 by McFarland Publishers.

- Published 19 additional reference books including: *Learn About Movie Posters; Learn About International Movie Posters; Movie Still Identification Book; Legality of U.S. Movie Posters; Movie Trailer Identification Codes; National Screen Service Accessory Codes; Production Code Basics; and the Silent Studio Directory.*

- In 2001, developed the first reference website on movie posters designed for novice to intermediate level collectors: *LearnAboutMoviePosters.com*.

- In 2005, developed the first and only cross referenced research film accessory database with 100,000 images online: *MoviePosterDataBase.com*.

- In 2009, developed the first and only advance research website for documenting press still codes, lithographer plate numbers, etc. – now in a member only research site.

In 2010, the Pooles realized that documentation of local film history was basically non-existent. The Pooles are firm believers that the research and documentation of this history is a necessary foundation for development of many associated industries such as tourism and education.

The Pooles have been on a quest to BUILD that foundation for Louisiana through:

Books: In 2011, by using film accessories, the Pooles used their research to create ***Hollywood On The Bayou***, documenting 1170 films made in or about Louisiana. They then went to work on local background stories and filming locations and the following year released ***Louisiana Film History: A Comprehensive Overview Beginning 1896.*** Since then, they have released ***Crescent City Cinema Movie Posters, Heroine to Hussy: Women in Louisiana Films*** and ***Louisiana Plantations: Real to Reel.***

Exhibits: In February 2012, the first exhibit on Louisiana Film History was opened at Ellender Memorial Library at Nicholls State University and ran for 4 months during their Jubilee. Since that time, numerous exhibits have been shown throughout the southern part of the state including a 6 month exhibit in the Louisiana section of the State Library of Louisiana.

Film Prints: Some of the most iconic films ever put on the screen have been made in Louisiana. The Pooles have recreated over 75 vintage movie posters on 12"x18" glossy card stock. These are professionally printed and made available to "friends" organizations and fund raising groups to bring more awareness to Louisiana's wonderful film history and to help fund expansion projects to a wider area. You can find these in the *HollywoodOnTheBayou.com* store, in the Historic New Orleans Collection gift shop and several galleries in New Orleans.

Lectures/Presentations: Powerpoint presentations are available on different phases of Louisiana Film History and include clips of vintage film trailers, newspaper clippings and behind the scenes stories plus an exclusive 7 minute documentary on Vitascope Hall (the first seated indoor theater in the U.S. opened in New Orleans in 1896).

Research: Expansion of research information on ALL films made in or about Louisiana is being created and compiled to be available for research students, film makers, industry professionals and the general public. The Pooles have also been actively campaigning for the placing of markers of the first cinema in the United States which opened in New Orleans in 1896, making Louisiana the Birthplace of the Movie Theater in the United States.

Websites: HollywoodOnTheBayou.com is online and has over 50 vintage Louisiana trailers and lists of Louisiana films by time period AND by Parish. This is a sister site for their larger research websites *LearnAboutMoviePosters.com*; *MoviePosterDataBase.com* and *MovieStillID.com*.

Currently: The Pooles are using their research, books and websites to expand in 3 major directions: using what has been created for Louisiana as a template for other states; create training material to help develop programs for the academic community for film accessory documentation; and the creation of the first Film Accessory Museum and Research Center to document, preserve and use film accessories to recreate national and international film history that has been considered LOST.

What good is preservation, if you can't identify or verify it?

THE LAST MOVING PICTURE COMPANY

Morris Everett, Jr
10535 Chillicothe Rd.
Kirtland, OH 44094
Phone: 440-256-3660
Email: lastmo@aol.com
Web: www.hollywoodposterauction.com

MovieArt GmbH

one of Europe's largest
selection of movie posters
- silent to present -
over 6000 titles online

Walchestrasse 17
8006 Zurich Switzerland
phone ++41 44 363 50 26
fax ++ 41 44 363 50 27

www.movieart.ch

LIMITED RUNS
WWW.LIMITEDRUNS.COM

ORIGINAL VINTAGE POSTERS, PRINT ART & PHOTOGRAPHY

pastposters.com

Jamie at pastposters specializies in
Original British Quad Posters
Titles from the 1950's until present day.

Also stocking One Sheets, Lobby Cards
F.O.H and Press Stills
Plus Press Kits, Press Books
and Other Memorabilia

UK based but ships to over
50 countries worlwide.
Ships Daily To the U.S.A.,
Australia and Europe

Thousands of Vintage Movie Posters
instantly available on a secure website
ask to join my weekly mailing list.
support @ pastposters.com
www.pastposters.com

Conway's Vintage Treasures

Vintage Movie Posters * Rare Vintage Stills
Rare Autographs * Classic Sports Artifacts
Historical Memorabilia * Fine Art

www.CVTreasures.com
Kevin@CVTreasures.com
866-499-8112

CINEMARETRO

BRINGING CINEMA OF THE PAST INTO THE FUTURE IN A NEW MAGAZINE DEVOTED TO 60'S & 70'S

http://www.cinemaretro.com

CINEMA RETRO
PO Box 1570
Christchurch
Dorset BH23 4XS England
Tel: + 44 (0) 870 4423 007
Fax: + 44 (0) 1425 273068
solopublishing@firenet.uk.com

USA OFFICE:
PO Box 152
Dunellen, NJ 08812
USA
Tel: + 001 732 752 7257
Fax: + 001 732 752 6959
cinemaretro@hotmail.com

SIMON DWYER!

GENUINE VINTAGE MOVIE POSTERS
DATING FROM THE 1920's
TO THE 1970'S BROUGHT
FROM CINEMA HOARDINGS
AROUND THE WORLD TO
YOUR FRONT DOOR

Simon Dwyer
7 Epirus Mews
London SW6 7UP
United Kingdom

www.SimonDwyer.com
SIMON.DWYER@LAKESVILLE.COM

ACKNOWLEDGMENTS

As we moved from collectors to dealers to retailers, and finally 14 years ago to full time researchers, we have been surrounded by some really fantastic people. So, when you stop and start to think about acknowledging the ones who helped you, it's like following a line of fallen dominoes, each one an important piece that is needed to reach that projected outcome.

This journey couldn't have taken place without the first steps of learning about how the various departments worked. For the specific details handling stills, we have to give a special thanks to a long-time friend, Rudy Franchi, whose job it was to handle the keybook material for a major studio.

Then if it wasn't for our sponsors, we wouldn't have the time to do the research and compiling. Some of our sponsors have been with us over a decade and we truly thank them for their continued support. See their ads throughout the book.
For this specific book, we have to give special thanks to Grey Smith at Heritage Auction, Barry Gilliam at Everett Collections, Gene Arnold (retired dealer), Jim Episale at Unshredded Nostalgia, and Craig Heller for their tremendous help with this project.

And finally, we must mention our family, who puts up with our fanatical ways.
If we forgot to mention anyone in particular, we are sorry. We sincerely apologize; however, please remember that we too are "vintage" and plead temporary memory loss.

MOVIEART.COM

U.S. and International Film Posters

phone: 512 479 6680 / email: posters@movieart.com

MovieArt.com / Kirby McDaniel / P.O. Box 4419, Austin, Texas 78765-4419

LETTER FROM THE AUTHORS

On our 2006 visit to Cinevent in Columbus, we asked dealers and collectors what areas needed research that would be the most helpful to the industry. We had an overwhelming response pointing us towards stills identification.

The following year, we released the first stills code reference book with 18,000 codes. This is our 6th and final edition toward helping resolve that problem, with each edition making huge leaps forward by focusing on the weaknesses of the previous edition. Each edition has taken a massive amount of time to research and document, and this book is no different with the expansion to 2 volumes and over 50,000 codes.

The focus on this edition has been on filling in the previously uncovered areas of shorts, independents, mid-range distributors and international films while expanding coverage of studios and celebrity portraits. In this edition we also utilized more of our own codes to help expand the information on specific titles. We marked thousands of titles with country of origin and hundreds with original titles. We also included aka's and more notes to help with the verification of titles.

The problem is that this edition has grown so massive that it has placed us at a crossroads on how to expand and present our research in print form. There is no room for all the tutorials that are needed for anyone unfamiliar with the use of production codes. With each studio, category and expanding variation needing more samples and explanations, the tutorials have become large enough that they are in a separate publication. If you purchased this set directly from us, we provided our companion book "*Production Code Basics*" with your set. If you purchased the set somewhere else, contact us and we will give you a special price to acquire your copy.

Whether you are a novice or well advanced, there are so many oddities and variations that we believe that it can definitely help get a better grasp of their usage, no matter what level you are.

We hope our book is useful in your quest to solve your unknown stills dilemma. We would appreciate any questions, comments, suggestions or criticisms, which we use to help us improve. For those needing beyond this edition, we have created MovieStillID.com with specialty sorts and additional information without the publication limitations. You can email (edp@LearnAboutMoviePosters.com) or call us (504-298-5267) for more info.

Ed and Susan Poole

COMMON PROBLEMS WITH ALL STUDIOS

If you acquired your *Movie Still Identification Book* from the publisher, you also received a small book called *Production Code Basics* which covers the creation and history of production codes, analysis of use by different departments and studios, problems and then a look at individual studio use.

The following is a slightly edited version of Chapter 8 from that book, so if you have it, you can skip this section.

When we created our first production code book in 2007, it had 18,000 codes and was developed completely from lists that we had acquired from several reputable sources. Since that time, we have been continually modifying and expanding the original lists because we were USING THEM as we were going through literally tens of thousands of stills.

Our *Movie Still Identification Book* Ultimate Edition has 50,030 production codes and the VAST majority were taken directly from the stills. And I can tell you that taking them DIRECTLY from the images has shown every kind of crazy variation imaginable.

Because of this, we think it would be beneficial for YOU to see a couple of the oddities that were common to all studios and might help you understand some of the unusual marks that you might see.

When you first start using production code numbers, you will immediately recognize the huge amount of inconsistencies.

We gathered these codes from a WIDE variety of sources, such as studio records, lists from dealers and collectors, Library of Congress records AND going through tens of thousands of stills. BUT, the problem isn't from the wide variety of sources; the problem is within the studio system.

These codes were used for control at THAT particular time for THAT particular purpose. They didn't take into consideration that maybe different people who created different stills from the Key Set would write the numbers differently, OR that when the distributor remade the stills for press releases, they would write it a different way, OR, if it was redistributed later by a different distributor, or even a distributor in a different country, that the codes would become slightly different.

You have to remember that at the time these stills were originally released, people were just doing their job and there was NEVER EVER a single thought that MAYBE... 40... 50... 60 ... or more years down the road someone might have trouble figuring out what this still was. Their only thought was to do their job and promote the film.
When oddities arise, you basically have to be a detective to search for clues. Sometimes it is written one way and then another. If you don't find it under one listing, try it under a slight variation, etc.

When we first started, I thought that when problems arose that I would just contact the studio archives and they could quickly clear up any problems. So, my first encounter was trying to identify some cast members on some early stills from the teens.

The stills had the studio stamp, the title, a recognizable star, a well-known director and a good production code number, so we "thought" this wouldn't be too much of a problem.

After our initial search, none of the regular sources had the cast members, so we contacted the studio archivist. We sent over the title and production code and received a shocking report: **THEY HAD NO RECORD OF THAT PRODUCTION EVER BEING MADE THERE.**

We said: "Wait, here's a copy of the stills with the studio stamp and you can see the production codes!" The studio archivist said: **"We have no record of that."**

After some additional discussions, we came to the conclusion that it was fairly common for the production company to use their own system and THEN the studio or distributor would completely re-number and quite often re-title the project.

The problem is that once the film moved to distribution, the documentation during production was basically eliminated and NO records kept. Sometimes, identifying pre-release stills CAN GIVE YOU NIGHTMARES!

Here are some other examples common to all studios:

Problems With NSS Number Confusion

Let's start off with an NSS problem:

The still on the previous page is a nice shot from the *Sound of Music*. The following image is a close up of the bottom right of the still.

```
79/7   Maria (JULIE ANDREWS), governess of the
 ↑     seven Von Trapp children, calms them during
       a thunderstorm by singing "My Favorite
       Things."
```

If you asked poster collectors, the majority would say that the 79/7 is the NSS number.

That is until you showed them another one, such as this one:

A close-up of the bottom of this still follows on the next page.

> 79/44 Julie Andrews, Christopher Plummer and the
> seven children sing at the Salzburg Music
> Festival prior to their escape from the
> Nazis.

It shows the number 79/44. That's right. 79 is the production code number and NOT the NSS number.

In the 1960s, some studios started "printing" production codes with still descriptions on **some** of the stills. It wasn't consistent, but occasional. This practice gained in popularity and is now the norm for a lot of newer stills distributors.

Mistakes In Studio Issued Information

Here is a problem that happens often and is rarely caught except for major films. When studios send out their press materials, it would be expected that their employees would know what they are doing, or at least know when something is blatantly wrong. Collectors rely on the studio tag and rarely double check the production code number to make sure.
Below we have a WONDERFUL shot of Spencer Tracy and Sidney Poitier from the Academy Award winning film, *Guess Who's Coming to Dinner*.

Sidney Poitier looked a lot different when he was younger! According to the production code, this still is from the film *Captain's Courageous*.

OK, let's try that again. Here is another WONDERFUL shot of Spencer Tracy and Sidney Poitier from *Guess Who's Coming to Dinner*.

Well, Sidney has grown a little but still doesn't look like himself. Maybe he had a rough day at the office. The production code on this still clearly states that it is *Boy's Town*. Anyway, you get the point.

When mistakes like this occur on a major title that everyone knows, it is easy to spot the wrong still. But this is not the case when it involves a lesser known title. These stills are normally just passed through because we have a tendency to think that the studio would know their own material.

The point is this. Just because it is issued by the studio doesn't automatically make the information correct. So, it's good to always check the production code as well.

Multiple Production Code Numbers on Stills

We touched early on a problem of multiple numbers under independent distributors. Let's revisit this point, as it was not just an independent distributor problem, but a problem for ALL distributors that handled imports. While we are at it, with our next sample, we can also cover copyright tags.

Shown below and on the next page are some stills for the 1972 re-release of Charlie Chaplin's *Limelight*.

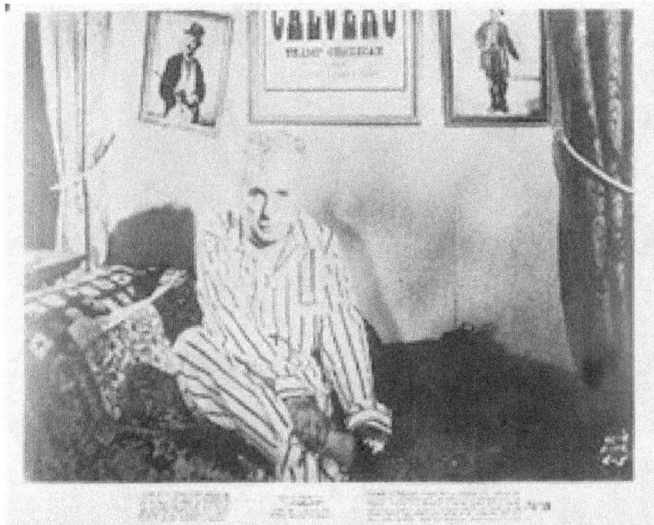

What you can't see is that three of the six have a 1956 copyright on the left with no studio (which is odd since the original release came out in 1952). The other three stills have a 1972 copyright by Columbia Pictures.

REMEMBER: ALL 6 have the 1972 NSS tag and number.

Now let's look closer at the top left still on the preceding page, which you can plainly see has 3 production codes in the right corner.

72/26

L-5 is the production code for *Limelight*; CC-8 is bound to be Charlie Chaplin -8, but P-116 – No clue.

We have already learned that every time the stills were handled by a different distributor, the production codes were added and/or taken away at the discretion of that distributor. But now we can add that the copyright tags went along with it also.

Original vs. Reissued Stills

One of the biggest problems with production codes is identifying reissues from originals. When a studio reissues their own film, they just pull the material and send it out again. So, it is almost impossible to tell which release it is from. You can hope that they put different copyright tags on them, but as you saw in the last example, that's not that accurate either. Only one major studio went out of their way to renumber their reissues. We cover that in the next chapter on individual studios. The best hope that we currently have is that the reissue was by a different distributor leaving their own mark.

There have been rumors for several years now that a company in New York trying to come up with a way of dating newer stills by the chemicals that were used to develop them, but I haven't heard any real results yet that could be used on the open market.

Handwriting Mistakes

Here are a couple of clips from the film, *Hannie Caulder*. The production code for Hannie Caulder is "HC." "HC" = **H**annie **C**aulder - that seems fairly simple. We have gone through a lot of Hannie Caulder stills and they were all the same with one exception.

The samples below represent the bottom information on two different stills for Hannie Caulder. The first sample shows the "HC." The second still clearly has the code "MC."

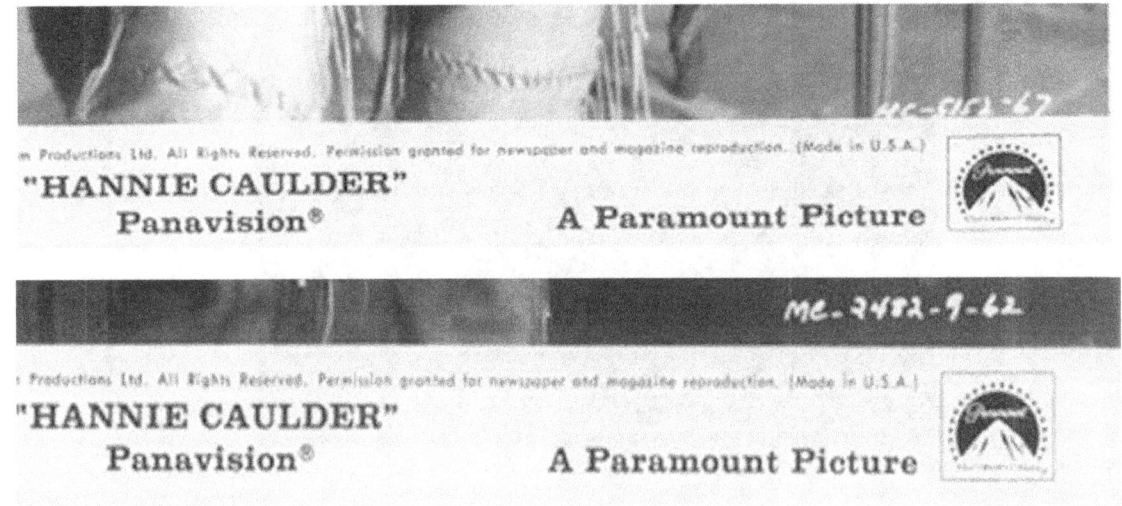

Reverse Printing

Here's a clip of a still from the film *The Bride Wore Red*.

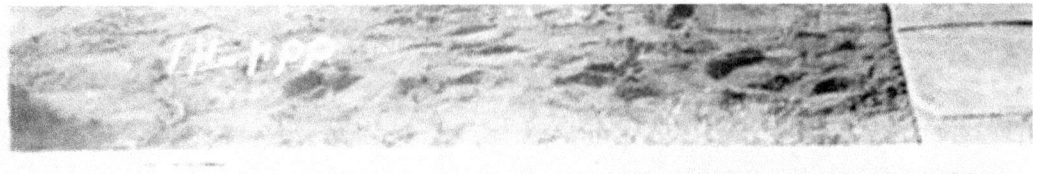

The production code number is actually "997," which you would see if you hold the still up to a mirror. The still was developed backward and then the tag line added.

Numbers Chopped

The next clip is taken from a still for the film The *Incredible Shrinking Man*. Fortunately, this is a popular film and should be recognizable to most. However, there is NO identification on the front of the still, and all you have is the production code. (which you can see is 828)

Unfortunately, if the identification of THIS particular still was based solely on the production code, it would remain unidentified. Here's why.

The production code on the still, "828" was actually **chopped** at printing. The actual production code, as seen on the snipe that was attached to the back of the still, is "1828." Fortunately, in this particular instance, there was a studio clip on the back side.

Always beware when the production code is very close to the edge, as there is no telling how much could be **CHOPPED!**

That Little Black Box

We have been asked many times about the little black boxes found on some stills. Here is a sample of a still from the Marilyn Monroe film, *Don't Bother to Knock*. Notice the black box at the bottom right of the still, which has the production code in it.

OK, now here is another still from the same film, BUT NOTICE, the black box is on the top right.

We constantly get asked WHY the black box and does the placement mean anything, i.e. produced in different locations or edited for different reasons, etc?
Let's first address the black box.

Occasionally, the publicity department would have to make changes to a production code on a still AFTER it had been etched. The best way to make these changes was to create a black background and make a new one. Yes, these black boxes were initially created to make changes.

Some studios picked up the process to become a regular spot instead of scratching them into the still. Then if there was a need to make a change, there was already a space to do it.

And as for the placement, I wanted to make sure so I asked an employee who worked in the publicity department creating key sets. I was told that it was placed where they had more room. There was NO reason other than that.

Let's look at one last area of concern that involves re-makes of films using different actors BUT the SAME codes.

Warner Brothers was one of the worse to do this. Numerous times Warner Brothers would remake a film 5 to 10 years later and then use the same production code for BOTH films.

For example *Two Against the World* was released in 1932 starring Constance Bennett with the working title of *Higher Ups*. In 1936, Warner Brothers released *Two Against the World* starring Humphrey Bogart.

It was also released under the TV title *One Fatal Hour* and the British title *Case of Mrs. Pembroke*. BOTH the 1932 and the 1936 films used the SAME PRODUCTION CODE.

For this reason, when possible, always try to reconfirm the identification by a second source. For example, if you identify a still by the production code, if there are actors in the still, if possible, try to confirm their identity.

If you are a veteran at production stills, then you know that you will run into every scenario imaginable. You basically have to be a detective looking for clues to the identity of THAT still. So any information that can be gleaned from the still, such as distributors, markings on the back, scene explanations, magazine stamps, etc., are potential clues.

NOTICE! SPECIAL OFFER

For those that did not acquire your Movie Still Identification Books from the publisher and therefore did not get a copy of Production Code Basics AND would like to learn more about production codes... **We have a special offer for you.**

Email us where you purchased your Movie Still Identification Books Ultimate Edition and we will make you a **SPECIAL HALF PRICE OFFER** (plus shipping of course).

Our email is:
edp@LearnAboutMoviePosters.com

Our direct line is:
504-298-LAMP (5267)

And ask for our special ½ Price Offer.

Craig's Curios
Silent and Golden Age Movie Stars

We specialize in original vintage postcards and photographs

http://stores.ebay.com/Craigs-Curios-and-Other-Junque

Movie Poster Frames
Direct from Studio Supplier

Specializing in framing your collectibles since 1984

Made to order custom frames
At Wholesale Prices
~ Delivered to your door ~

www.hollywoodposterframes.com
(800) 463-2994

9260 Deering Ave
Chatsworth, CA 91311

Open to public:
Thur-Fri: 10-5 p.m.
Sat: 9-2 p.m.

ILLUSTRACTION GALLERY

ART THAT POPS!

VINTAGE AND RARE POSTERS
MOVIES, MUSIC, COMIC BOOK ART,
ADVERTISING AND OLYMPIC POSTERS
FROM THE 1960's AND BEYOND

illustractiongallery.com • 1 646 801 27 88 • hello@illustractiongallery.com

---

L'imagerie gallery

- ♥ ORIGINAL VINTAGE MOVIE POSTERS
- ♥ RARE FILM POSTERS BOUGHT AND SOLD
- ♥ LINENBACKING AND RESTORATION SERVICES
- ♥ EXPERT CUSTOM FRAMING

L'IMAGERIE ART GALLERY
In Business Since 1973

www.limageriegallery.com

PHONE: 818-762-8488   FAX: 818-762-8499   EMAIL: limageriegallery@gmail.com

10555 Victory Boulevard - North Hollywood, CA 91606
Tuesday through Saturday from 11:30 to 6:00

HOW TO USE THIS BOOK

Movie stills fall into several categories depending on who took the images, why they were taken and how they were going to be used. Our focus is upon stills that were created either during the production of the film OR re-marked during distribution of the film. In other words, those that had a control code on them. We do NOT cover pre-production, promotional, publicity, paparazzi, photographer, celebrity, autographed or homemade stills as these do not have production or distribution markings.

In this 2-volume set, we are presenting over 50,000 codes covering production codes, portrait codes, serial codes, series codes, tv codes, and studio codes. To help you identify such a wide variety of codes AND present it in a simplified fashion, we also had to use our own type of codes. **Please read this section carefully** -- it explains how we present each column to help with your identification as no explanations are presented in the remainder of the book.

We have tried to simplify every phase that we could. The first step is to look at your code. If the code **starts** with a LETTER, use the LETTER volume. If it **starts** with a NUMBER, use the NUMBER volume. Many codes are alpha-numeric but that does not matter. Simply look at what the code starts with.

You will see the same 5 columns in each volume:

1. Code
2. Title/Name
3. Director/Type
4. Studio/Distributor
5. Year

Let's take a look at each column.

Code: Whether it is a production code, portrait code, series code, serial code or studio code, all codes are together.

> In the NUMBERS volume, all will start with a number. We DO HAVE some codes starting with the number "0" and they precede "1." Codes are in numeric order. When a letter is used in the middle of the code, they will be in alphabetic order and then any numbers afterwards starting over in numeric order.

> In the LETTERS volume, following the initial letter, we used the general rule of numbers before letters, so A400 would come BEFORE AA.

Also, because the majority of the codes listed are taken directly from the stills, numerous oddities occur. IMPORTANT: When checking multiple stills from the same title, we noticed that the codes were NOT consistent and written in a variety of ways.

For example, a code such as MC42 could be found on the stills as M C42; MC-42; or MC4/2. We tried to place them in the most common form that we found. BUT, for this reason, **ONLY IN THIS COLUMN**, we have ignored ALL **spaces, dashes, slashes and dots**. The codes are presented in order as if they were not there.

Title/Name - This column has the film title, personality name or studio name (plus a LOT more information). This is the most complex column with the majority of OUR codes to try to help you with that identification, so PLEASE read this section carefully.

ALL TITLES, NAMES AND STUDIOS ARE IN ALL CAPITAL LETTERS.

If the code was identified as a "Working Title," we placed an asterisk (*) behind it. If we also had the release title, we placed the working title BEHIND the release title and in parenthesis.

For non-US titles that we identified, we placed a code for the country of origin. Here are the country codes that are used in the edition:

(ARG) – ARGENTINA	(GR) – GREECE	(POL) – POLAND
(AUS) – AUSTRALIA	(HK) – HONG KONG	(RUS) – RUSSIA
(BRA) – BRAZIL	(IND) – INDIA	(SP) – SPAIN
(CAN) – CANADA	(IS) – ISRAEL	(SWE) – SWEDEN
(CZ) – CZECH REPUBLIC	(IT) – ITALY	(SWIT) – SWITZERLAND
(DEN) – DENMARK	(JAP) – JAPAN	(UK) –UNITED KINGDOM
(FR) – FRANCE	(MEX) – MEXICO	(YUGO) – YUGOSLAVIA
(GER) - GERMANY	(NETH) - NETHERLANDS	Combos divided with (/)

If there was a time difference between the original release title and distribution, we placed the year behind the title of origin.

For rereleases, we put them behind the title and in () parenthesis. We put as many as space allowed and the year behind it.

Instructions, variations and additional information are written in small letters.

The standards are: (t) for toon or animation; (sh) for shorts; (tv) for tv movies; (serial); and (series) are as stated.

Other instructions include: an (aka) was used if it was a portrait code for an alias used (Not used on film titles); (changed to...) was used when the studio made changes in the code.

When we found mistakes in the coding or pieces mis-marked, we marked it as (mistake) and put the correct code if we had it.

If it was a portrait code for multiple people, we placed an (*) behind the names.

If there was a distribution oddity, we placed it in [ ] brackets.

Director/Type - The primary director is listed in all caps by last name only. If multiple directors were used, we place both divided by a comma when possible. When it is a portrait, series, serial or studio code, they are shown in small letters.

Studio/Distributor - The major distributor is listed (NOT the production company) for production codes. For major studios, they are the same so no problem.

For smaller, independent distributors and import/export distributor, check the date and title columns for more information.

For portrait, series, serials, tv or studio codes, we tried to list the major distributor when available.

Year - Year of release is shown for production codes. When it is a reissue, the year is shown as "R" plus a 2 digit reissue year.

If the film was in import, also look to the title line for original country, title and release year.

Some series and portrait codes have ranges shown by decade.

ENTERTAINMENT MEMORABILIA
Consignments now invited for upcoming auctions

+1 (323) 436 5467
entertainment.us@bonhams.com

THE PIANO FROM *CASABLANCA* ON WHICH SAM PLAYS "AS TIME GOES BY"
Sold for $3,413,000

Bonhams

bonhams.com/entertainment

© 2015 Bonhams & Butterfields Auctioneers Corp. All rights reserved.
Principal Auctioneer: Patrick Meade. NYC License No. 1183066-DCA

.co.uk

Original Vintage Film Posters - For Sale.

British quads, US & UK one sheets, animation art, front of house and lobby cards.

Over 7,000 posters and lobby cards available online!

info@originalposter.co.uk
UK Callers 01905 620 370
Int Callers +44 1905 620370

Award winning & on TV

Store Information:

Based in Lancashire, England

07530862046

mail@thebestlittlefilmhouse.com

www.thebestlittlefilmhouse.com

channingposters

ORIGINAL MOVIE POSTERS, LOBBY CARDS, AND AUTOGRAPHED ITEMS

CHANNING THOMSON
P. O. BOX 330232
SAN FRANCISCO, CA 94133-0232

Email: channinglylethomson@att.net
ebay: http://stores.ebay.com/CHANNINGPOSTERS

Leading UK Entertainment & Memorabilia Auctioneers

Regular Entertainment & Memorabilia auctions throughout 2015.

Including Movie / TV, Music, Sporting Memorabilia and Posters, Photography and Autograph Auctions.

Consignments welcome.
Contact the Auctioneer: 00 (1) 483 223 101   valuations@ewbankauctions.co.uk

583 Pacific Street - Stanford CT 06902
203.324.9750
www.posterconservation.com

Before

After

LINEN BACKING AND RESTORATION SERVICES

Also the home of PosterParty.com!

Movie Posters ~ Music Posters
TV Posters ~ Celebrity Posters
Star Wars & James Bond
Harry Potter

Collectormania
17892 Cottonwood Dr
Parker, CO 80134

1-866-630-1648

questions@posterplanet.net
posterplanetfile@aol.com

Posters ~ Comics
Comic Art ~ Books
Magazines ~ Memorabilia

Four Color Comics LLC
Robert Rogovin

P.O. Box 1399
Scarsdale, NY 10583
TEL: (914) 722-4696
FAX: (914) 722-7656

WEB: www.fourcolorcomics.com

EMAIL: rob@fourcolorcomics.com

Femmes Fatales & Fantasies

Visit our Museum/Gallery
Femmes Fatales &
Fantasies
7013 E. Main Street
Scottsdale, AZ 85251
480.429.6800

FILM/ART
Original Film Posters

Hollywood, CA

323.363.2969

filmartgallery.com

FRENCH MOVIE POSTER

THOUSANDS OF ORIGINAL FRENCH MOVIE POSTERS
FROM 1960'S TO NOW DAYS

contact@frenchmovieposter.com
www.frenchmovieposter.com

Movie Still Identification Book Ultimate Edition - Letters

CODE	TITLE/NAME	DIRECTOR/TYPE	STUDIO/DISTRIBUTOR	YEAR
A	ACCURSED (UK: TRAITOR 1957)	MCCARTHY	ALLIED ARTISTS	1960
A	ACCUSED	FREELAND	UNITED ARTISTS	1936
A	ADVENTURERS	GILBERT	PARAMOUNT	1970
A	AGENT 8 3/4 (UK: HOT ENOUGH FOR JUNE 1964)	THOMAS	CONSOLIDATED	1965
A	ALADDIN (IT: SUPERFANTAGENIO)	CORBUCCI	CANNON	1986
A	ALAMO	WAYNE	UNITED ARTISTS	1960
A	ALCATRAZ ISLAND	MCGANN	WARNER BROS	1937
A	ALIBI (UK)	HURST	REPUBLIC	1943
A	ALICE IN WONDERLAND (t)	GERONIMI, JACKSON	RKO	1951
A	ALIEN 3	FINCHER	20th CENTURY FOX	1992
A	ALIENS	CAMERON	20th CENTURY FOX	1986
A	ALIMONY	HORNE	FILM BOOKING OFF	1924
A	AMERICANO	CASTLE	RKO	1955
A	ANNA	LATTUADA	LUX FILM	1951
A	ANZIO (IT)	DMYTRYK, COLETTI	COLUMBIA	1968
A	APARAJITO (IND 1957)	RAY	EDWARD HARRISON	1959
A	ARTCRAFT PRODUCTIONS	studio		
A	ASHANTI	FLEISCHER	WARNER BROS	1979
A	ASSASSINATION	HUNT	CANNON	1986
A	ASSAULT	RADEMAKERS	CANNON	1986
A	ASSIGNMENT REDHEAD (UK: UNDERCOVER GIRL)	SEARLE	UNITED ARTISTS	1958
A	AVIATOR	DEL RUTH	WARNER BROS	1929
A	DEATH OF AN ANGEL (UK)	SAUNDERS	HAMMER-EXCLUSIVE	1952
A	FRENZY (UK: LATIN QUARTER)	SEWELL	FOUR CONTINENTS	1945
A	HAPPY-GO-LOVELY (UK)	HUMBERSTONE	RKO	1950
A	I'LL STICK TO YOU (UK)	HISCOTT	BRITISH LION	1933
A	KANSAS CITY CONFIDENTIAL	KARLSON	UNITED ARTISTS	1952
A	LASH	LLOYD	WARNER BROS	1930
A	LOSS OF INNOCENCE (UK: GREENGAGE SUMMER)	GILBERT	COLUMBIA	1961
A	MYSTERIANS (JAP)	HONDA	MGM	1959
A	RAMONA	CAREWE	UNITED ARTISTS	1928
A	REVENGE	CAREWE	UNITED ARTISTS	1928
A	ROMOLA	KING	METRO GOLDWYN	1924
A	STOLEN PARADISE	GASNIER	MONOGRAM	1941
A	SWEET ADELINE	LEROY	WARNER BROS	1934
A	WE'RE RICH AGAIN	SEITER	RKO	1934
A-1	CATCH AS CATCH CAN (sh)	NEILAN	MGM	1931
A-1	LUKE RIDES ROUGHSHOD (sh)	ROACH	PATHE EXCHANGE	1916
A-1	ONE NIGHT OF LOVE	SCHERTZINGER	COLUMBIA	1934
A-1	OUR GANG (sh)	MCGOWAN	PATHE EXCHANGE	1922
A1	TAILOR-MADE MAN	DE GRASSE	UNITED ARTISTS	1922
A-2	BROADWAY BILL	CAPRA	COLUMBIA	1934
A-2	FIRE FIGHTERS (sh)	MCGOWAN	PATHE EXCHANGE	1922
A-2	HOOP-LA	CHAUDET	EXHIBITOR'S	1919
A-2	LUKE, CRYSTAL GAZER (sh)	ROACH	PATHE EXCHANGE	1916
A-2	PAJAMA PARTY (sh)	ROACH	MGM	1931
A3	ALIEN 3	FINCHER	20th CENTURY FOX	1992
A-3	GIRL FRIEND	BUZZELL	COLUMBIA	1935
A-3	LUKE'S LOST LAMB (sh)	ROACH	PATHE EXCHANGE	1916
A-3	WAR MAMAS (sh)	NEILAN	MGM	1931
A-3	YOUNG SHERLOCKS (sh)	MCGOWAN	PATHE EXCHANGE	1922
A-4	LUKE DOES THE MIDWAY (sh)	ROACH	PATHE EXCHANGE	1916
A-4	ON THE LOOSE (sh)	ROACH	MGM	1931
A-4	ONE TERRIBLE DAY (sh)	MCGOWAN	PATHE EXCHANGE	1922
A4	POOR LITTLE RICH GIRL	TOURNEUR	PARAMOUNT	1917
A-4	THAT'S GRATITUDE	CRAVEN	COLUMBIA	1934
A-5	A QUIET STREET (sh)	MCGOWAN	PATHE EXCHANGE	1922
A5	IN AGAIN, OUT AGAIN	EMERSON	ARTCRAFT	1917
A-5	JEALOUSY	NEILL	COLUMBIA	1934
A-5	LUKE AND THE BANGTAILS (sh)	ROACH	PATHE EXCHANGE	1916
A-5	SEAL SKINS (sh)	LIGHTFOOT	MGM	1932
A-6	CHAMPAGNE FOR BREAKFAST	BROWN	COLUMBIA	1935
A-6	LUKE JOINS THE NAVY (sh)	ROACH	PATHE EXCHANGE	1916
A-6	RED NOSES (sh)	HORNE	MGM	1932
A-6	SATURDAY MORNING (sh)	MCGOWAN	PATHE EXCHANGE	1922
A-7	BIG SHOW (sh)	MCGOWAN	PATHE EXCHANGE	1923
A-7	EIGHT BELLS	NEILL	COLUMBIA	1935
A7	LITTLE AMERICAN	MACPHERSON	PARAMOUNT	1917
A-7	LUKE AND THE MERMAIDS (sh)	ROACH	PATHE EXCHANGE	1916
A-7	STRICTLY UNRELIABLE (sh)	MARSHALL	MGM	1932

Movie Still Identification Book Ultimate Edition - Letters

CODE	TITLE/NAME	DIRECTOR/TYPE	STUDIO/DISTRIBUTOR	YEAR
A-8	COBBLER (sh)	MCNAMARA	PATHE EXCHANGE	1923
A-8	LUKE'S SPEEDY CLUB LIFE (sh)	ROACH	PATHE EXCHANGE	1916
A-8	OLD BULL (sh)	MARSHALL	MGM	1932
A-8	WHITE LIES	BULGAKOV	COLUMBIA	1934
A-9	CHAMPEEN (sh)	MCGOWAN	PATHE EXCHANGE	1923
A-9	LUKE THE CHAUFFEUR (sh)	ROACH	PATHE EXCHANGE	1916
A-9	SHOW BUSINESS (sh)	WHITE	MGM	1932
A-9	WHOLE TOWN'S TALKING	FORD	COLUMBIA	1935
A-10	ALUM AND EVE (sh)	MARSHALL	MGM	1932
A-10	BOYS TO BOARD (sh)	MCNAMARA	PATHE EXCHANGE	1923
A-10	LUKE'S PREPAREDNESS PREPARATIONS (sh)	ROACH	PATHE EXCHANGE	1916
A-10	MILLS OF THE GODS	NEILL	COLUMBIA	1935
A-11	BEST MAN WINS	KENTON	COLUMBIA	1935
A-11	LUKE THE GLADIATOR (sh)	ROACH	PATHE EXCHANGE	1916
A-11	PLEASANT JOURNEY (sh)	MCGOWAN	PATHE EXCHANGE	1923
A-11	SOILERS (sh)	MARSHALL	MGM	1932
A12	BARBARY SHEEP	TOURNEUR	PARAMOUNT	1917
A-12	CARNIVAL	LANG	COLUMBIA	1935
A-12	GIANTS VS. YANKS (sh)	MCGOWAN	PATHE EXCHANGE	1923
A-12	LUKE, PATIENT PROVIDER (sh)	ROACH	PATHE EXCHANGE	1916
A-12	SNEAK EASILY (sh)	MEINS	MGM	1932
A-13	ASLEEP IN THE FLEET (sh)	MEINS	MGM	1933
A-13	BACK STAGE (sh)	MCGOWAN	PATHE EXCHANGE	1923
A-13	I'LL LOVE YOU ALWAYS	BULGAKOV	COLUMBIA	1935
A14	NARROW TRAIL	HART, HILLYER	PARAMOUNT	1917
A-14	DOGS OF WAR (sh)	MCGOWAN	PATHE EXCHANGE	1923
A-14	LET'S LIVE TONIGHT	SCHERTZINGER	COLUMBIA	1935
A-14	LUKE'S NEWSIE KNOCKOUT (sh)	ROACH	PATHE EXCHANGE	1916
A-14	MAIDS A LA MODE (sh)	MEINS	MGM	1933
A-15	BARGAIN OF THE CENTURY (sh)	CHASE	MGM	1933
A-15	DEATH FLIES EAST	ROSEN	COLUMBIA	1935
A-15	LODGE NIGHT	MCGOWAN	PATHE EXCHANGE	1923
A-15	LUKE'S MOVIE MUDDLE - LUKE'S MODEL MOVIE (sh)	ROACH	PATHE EXCHANGE	1916
A15	RISE OF JENNIE CUSHING	TOURNEUR	PARAMOUNT	1917
A-16	FAST COMPANY (sh)	MCGOWAN	PATHE EXCHANGE	1924
A-16	LUKE'S RANK IMPERSONATOR (sh)	ROACH	PATHE EXCHANGE	1916
A-16	ONE TRACK MINDS (sh)	MEINS	MGM	1933
A-16	UNWELCOME STRANGER	ROSEN	COLUMBIA	1935
A-17	BEAUTY AND THE BUS (sh)	MEINS	MGM	1933
A-17	LUKE'S FIREWORKS FIZZLE (sh)	ROACH	PATHE EXCHANGE	1916
A-17	PARTY WIRE	KENTON	COLUMBIA	1935
A17	REBECCA OF SUNNYBROOK FARM	NEILAN	PARAMOUNT	1917
A-17	STAGE FRIGHT (sh)	MCGOWAN	PATHE EXCHANGE	1923
A-18	BACK TO NATURE (sh)	MEINS	MGM	1933
A-18	JULY DAYS (sh)	MCGOWAN	PATHE EXCHANGE	1923
A-18	LOVE ME FOREVER	SCHERTZINGER	COLUMBIA	1935
A-18	LUKE LOCATES THE LOOT (sh)	ROACH	PATHE EXCHANGE	1916
A-19	AIR FRIGHT (sh)	MEINS	MGM	1933
A-19	AIR HAWKS	ROGELL	COLUMBIA	1935
A-19	LUKE'S SHATTERED SLEEP (sh)	ROACH	PATHE EXCHANGE	1916
A19	ROSE OF THE WORLD	TOURNEUR	PARAMOUNT	1918
A-19	SUNDAY CALM (sh)	MCGOWAN	PATHE EXCHANGE	1923
A-20	AWAKENING OF JIM BURKE	HILLYER	COLUMBIA	1935
A-20	BABES IN THE GOODS (sh)	MEINS	MGM	1934
A-20	LUKE'S LOST LIBERTY (sh)	ROACH	PATHE EXCHANGE	1917
A-20	NO NOISE (sh)	MCGOWAN	PATHE EXCHANGE	1923
A-21	DERBY DAY (sh)	MCGOWAN	PATHE EXCHANGE	1923
A-21	LUKE'S BUSY DAY (sh)	ROACH	PATHE EXCHANGE	1917
A21	SILENT MAN	HART	PARAMOUNT	1918
A-21	SOUP AND FISH (sh)	MEINS	MGM	1934
A-22	LUKE'S TROLLEY TROUBLES (sh)	ROACH	PATHE EXCHANGE	1917
A-22	MAID IN HOLLYWOOD (sh)	MEINS	MGM	1934
A22	STELLA MARIS	NEILAN	PARAMOUNT	1918
A-22	TIRE TROUBLE (sh)	MCGOWAN	PATHE EXCHANGE	1924
A-22	UNKNOWN WOMAN	ROGELL	COLUMBIA	1935
A-23	AFTER THE DANCE	BULGAKOV	COLUMBIA	1935
A-23	BIG BUSINESS (sh)	MCGOWAN	PATHE EXCHANGE	1924
A-23	I'LL BE SUING YOU (sh)	MEINS	MGM	1934
A-23	LONESOME LUKE, LAWYER (sh)	ROACH	PATHE EXCHANGE	1917
A23	SONG OF SONGS	KAUFMAN	PARAMOUNT	1918

Movie Still Identification Book Ultimate Edition - Letters

CODE	TITLE/NAME	DIRECTOR/TYPE	STUDIO/DISTRIBUTOR	YEAR
A24	MODERN MUSKETEER	DWAN	PARAMOUNT	1918
A-24	BUCCANEERS (sh)	MCGOWAN, GOLDAINE	PATHE EXCHANGE	1924
A-24	FEATHER IN HER HAT	SANTELL	COLUMBIA	1935
A-24	LUKE WINS YE LADYE FAIRE (sh)	ROACH	PATHE EXCHANGE	1917
A-24	THREE CHUMPS AHEAD (sh)	MEINS	MGM	1934
A-25	BLACK ROOM	NEILL	COLUMBIA	1935
A-25	DONE IN OIL (sh)	MEINS	MGM	1934
A-25	LONESOME LUKE'S LIVELY LIFE (sh)	ROACH	PATHE EXCHANGE	1917
A-25	SEEIN' THINGS (sh)	MCGOWAN	PATHE EXCHANGE	1924
A25	WOLVES OF THE RAIL	HART	PARAMOUNT	1918
A26	BLUE BIRD	TOURNEUR	PARAMOUNT	1918
A-26	COMMENCEMENT DAY (sh)	MCGOWAN, GOLDAINE	PATHE EXCHANGE	1924
A-26	LONESOME LUKE, MECHANIC (sh)	ROACH	PATHE EXCHANGE	1917
A-26	ONE HORSE FARMERS (sh)	MEINS	MGM	1934
A-26	SHE MARRIED HER BOSS	LA CAVA	COLUMBIA	1935
A27	BLUE BLAZES RAWDEN	HART	PARAMOUNT	1918
A-27	FIGHTING TEXAN	ABBOTT	AMBASSADOR	1937
A-27	IT'S A BEAR (sh)	MCGOWAN	PATHE EXCHANGE	1924
A-27	LONESOME LUKE'S HONEYMOON (sh)	ROACH	PATHE EXCHANGE	1917
A-27	OPENED BY MISTAKE (sh)	PARROTT	MGM	1934
A-28	ATLANTIC ADVENTURE	ROGELL	COLUMBIA	1935
A-28	BUM VOYAGE (sh)	GRINDE	MGM	1934
A-28	CRADLE ROBBERS (sh)	MCGOWAN	PATHE EXCHANGE	1924
A-28	LONESOME LUKE, PLUMBER (sh)	ROACH	PATHE EXCHANGE	1917
A28	WHISPERING CHORUS	DEMILLE	PARAMOUNT	1918
A-29	JUBLIO, JR. (sh)	MCGOWAN	PATHE EXCHANGE	1924
A29	LIE	DAWLEY	PARAMOUNT	1918
A-29	PUBLIC MENACE	KENTON	COLUMBIA	1935
A-29	STOP! LUKE! LISTEN! (sh)	ROACH	PATHE EXCHANGE	1917
A-29	TREASURE BLUES (sh)	PARROTT	MGM	1935
A-30	HIGH SOCIETY (sh)	MCGOWAN	PATHE EXCHANGE	1924
A-30	LONESOME LUKE'S WILD WOMEN (sh)	ROACH	PATHE EXCHANGE	1917
A30	TIGER MAN	HART	PARAMOUNT	1918
A-30	TIN MAN (sh)	PARROTT	MGM	1935
A31	AMARILLY OF CLOTHESLINE ALLEY	NEILAN	PARAMOUNT	1918
A-31	LONESOME LUKE ON TIN CAN ALLEY (sh)	ROACH	PATHE EXCHANGE	1917
A-31	MISSES STOOGE (sh)	PARROTT	MGM	1935
A-31	SUN DOWN LIMITED (sh)	MCGOWAN	PATHE EXCHANGE	1924
A-32	EVERY MAN FOR HIMSELF (sh)	MCGOWAN	PATHE EXCHANGE	1924
A32	HEADIN' SOUTH	DWAN, ROSSON	PARAMOUNT	1918
A-32	LONESOME LUKE LOSES PATIENTS (sh)	ROACH	PATHE EXCHANGE	1917
A-32	SING, SISTER, SING (sh)	PARROTT	MGM	1935
A-33	LONESOME LUKE IN LOVE, LAUGHS AND LATHER (sh)	ROACH	PATHE EXCHANGE	1917
A-33	MYSTERIOUS MYSTERY! (sh)	MCGOWAN	PATHE EXCHANGE	1924
A33	SELFISH YATES	HART	PARAMOUNT	1918
A-33	SLIGHTLY STATIC (sh)	TERHUNE	MGM	1935
A-34	BIG TOWN (sh)	MCGOWAN	PATHE EXCHANGE	1925
A34	DOLL'S HOUSE	TOURNEUR	PARAMOUNT	1918
A-34	LONESOME LUKE, MESSENGER (sh)	ROACH	PATHE EXCHANGE	1917
A-34	TWIN TRIPLETS (sh)	TERHUNE	MGM	1935
A-35	CIRCUS FEVER (sh)	MCGOWAN	PATHE EXCHANGE	1925
A-35	HOT MONEY (sh)	HORNE	MGM	1935
A-35	LONESOME LUKE IN FROM LONDON TO LARAMIE (sh)	ROACH	PATHE EXCHANGE	1917
A35	MR. FIX-IT	DWAN	PARAMOUNT	1918
A-36	DOG DAYS (sh)	MCGOWAN	PATHE EXCHANGE	1925
A-36	LONESOME LUKE IN BIRDS OF A FEATHER (sh)	ROACH	PATHE EXCHANGE	1917
A36	M'LISS	NEILAN	PARAMOUNT	1918
A-36	TOP FLAT (sh)	JEVNE, TERHUNE	MGM	1935
A-37	ALL AMERICAN TOOTHACHE (sh)	MEINS	MGM	1936
A37	HOW COULD YOU JEAN?	TAYLOR	PARAMOUNT	1918
A-37	LOVE BUG (sh)	MCGOWAN	PATHE EXCHANGE	1925
A-37	TRUMPS (sh)	ROACH	PATHE EXCHANGE	1917
A-38	ASK GRANDMA (sh)	MCGOWAN	PATHE EXCHANGE	1925
A38	HIT THE TRAIL HOLLIDAY	NEILAN	PARAMOUNT	1918
A-38	LONESOME LUKE IN WE NEVER SLEEP (sh)	ROACH	PATHE EXCHANGE	1917
A-38	PAN HANDLERS (sh)	TERHUNE	MGM	1936
A-39	AT SEA ASHORE (sh)	TERHUNE	MGM	1936
A39	SAY! YOUNG FELLOW	HENABERY	PARAMOUNT	1918
A-39	SHOOTIN' INJUNS (sh)	MCGOWAN	PATHE EXCHANGE	1925
A-40	AGAINST THE LAW	HILLYER	COLUMBIA	1934

Movie Still Identification Book Ultimate Edition - Letters

CODE	TITLE/NAME	DIRECTOR/TYPE	STUDIO/DISTRIBUTOR	YEAR
A40	DANGER MARK	FORD	PARAMOUNT	1918
A-40	HILL TILLIES (sh)	MEINS	MGM	1936
A-40	OFFICIAL OFFICERS (sh)	MCGOWAN	PATHE EXCHANGE	1925
A-41	MARY, QUEEN OF TOTS (sh)	MCGOWAN	PATHE EXCHANGE	1925
A-41	MEN OF THE NIGHT	HILLYER	COLUMBIA	1934
A-42	BEHIND THE EVIDENCE	HILLYER	COLUMBIA	1935
A-42	BOYS WILL BE JOYS (sh)	MCGOWAN	PATHE EXCHANGE	1925
A42	SHARK MONROE	HART	PARAMOUNT	1918
A-43	BETTER MOVIES (sh)	MCGOWAN	PATHE EXCHANGE	1925
A-43	IN SPITE OF DANGER	HILLYER	COLUMBIA	1935
A44	HEART OF THE WILDS	NEILAN	PARAMOUNT	1918
A-44	MEN OF THE HOUR	HILLYER	COLUMBIA	1935
A45	GREAT LOVE	GRIFFITH	PARAMOUNT	1918
A46	CAPTAIN KIDD, JR.	TAYLOR	PARAMOUNT	1919
A-46	SWELL HEAD	STOLOFF	COLUMBIA	1935
A47	RIDDLE GAWNE	HART, HILLYER	PARAMOUNT	1918
A-47	TOGETHER WE LIVE	MACK	COLUMBIA	1935
A48	BOUND IN MOROCCO	DWAN	PARAMOUNT	1918
A-48	SUPERSPEED	HILLYER	COLUMBIA	1935
A49	HUN WITHIN	WITHEY	PARAMOUNT	1918
A50	CAR OF DREAMS (UK)	CUTTS, MELFORD	GAUMONT BRITISH	1935
A-50	PRESCOTT KID	SELMAN	COLUMBIA	1934
A-50	UNDER THE TOP	CRISP	PARAMOUNT	1919
A51	JOHANNA ENLISTS	TAYLOR	PARAMOUNT	1919
A-51	WESTERNER	SELMAN	COLUMBIA	1934
A-52	SQUARE SHOOTER	SELMAN	COLUMBIA	1935
A52	TILL I COME BACK TO YOU	DEMILLE	PARAMOUNT	1918
A53	FIRST A GIRL (UK)	SAVILLE	GAUMONT BRITISH AMERICA	1935
A53	JOHNNY GET YOUR GUN	CRISP	PARAMOUNT	1919
A-53	LAW BEYOND THE RANGE	BEEBE	COLUMBIA	1935
A54	BORDER WIRELESS	HART	PARAMOUNT	1919
A-54	REVENGE RIDER	SELMAN	COLUMBIA	1935
A-55	FIGHTING SHADOWS	SELMAN	COLUMBIA	1935
A-56	RIDING WILD	SELMAN	COLUMBIA	1935
A-57	JUSTICE OF THE RANGE	SELMAN	COLUMBIA	1935
A57	RHODES (UK: RHODES OF AFRICA)	VIERTEL	GAUMONT BRITISH AMERICA	1936
A57	ROMANCE OF HAPPY VALLEY	GRIFFITH	PARAMOUNT	1919
A58	GOAT	CRISP	PARAMOUNT	1918
A59	SECRET AGENT (UK)	HITCHCOCK	GAUMONT BRITISH AMERICA	1936
A59	UNDER THE GREENWOOD TREE	CHAUTARD	PARAMOUNT	1919
A60	BRANDING BROADWAY	HART	PARAMOUNT	1919
A60	IT'S LOVE AGAIN (UK)	SAVILLE	GAUMONT BRITISH AMERICA	1936
A61	DOOMED CARGO (UK: SEVEN SINNERS)	DE COURVILLE	GAUMONT BRITISH AMERICA	1936
A62	EVERYTHING IS THUNDER (UK)	ROSMER	GAUMONT BRITISH	1936
A63	EAST MEETS WEST	MASON	GAUMONT BRITISH	1936
A-63	WAY OF A MAN WITH A MAID	CRISP	PARAMOUNT	1918
A64	SILENT BARRIERS (UK)	ROSMER	GAUMONT BRITISH	1937
A65	STRANGERS ON HONEYMOON (UK)	DE COURVILLE	GAUMONT BRITISH AMERICA	1936
A66	HIS PARISIAN WIFE	CHAUTARD	PARAMOUNT	1919
A66	SABOTAGE (WOMAN ALONE) (UK)	HITCHCOCK	UNITED ARTISTS	1936
A67	MAN OF AFFAIRS (UK: HIS LORDSHIP)	MASON	GAUMONT BRITISH AMERICA	1936
A68	GREATEST THING IN LIFE	GRIFFITH	PARAMOUNT	1918
A68	HEAD OVER HEELS IN LOVE (UK: HEAD OVER HEELS)	HALE	GAUMONT BRITISH AMERICA	1937
A-69	YOU'RE IN THE ARMY NOW	WALSH	GAUMONT BRITISH	1937
A70	BREED OF MEN	HILLYER	PARAMOUNT	1919
A70	KING SOLOMON'S MINES (UK)	STEVENSON	GAUMONT BRITISH AMERICA	1937
A71	MARRIAGE PRICE	CHAUTARD	PARAMOUNT	1919
A72	NON-STOP NEW YORK (UK: LISBON CLIPPER MYSTERY)	STEVENSON	GAUMONT BRITISH AMERICA	1937
A73	GANGWAY (UK)	HALE	GAUMONT BRITISH AMERICA	1937
A74	GIRL WAS YOUNG (UK: YOUNG AND INNOCENT)	HITCHCOCK	GAUMONT BRITISH AMERICA	1937
A74	KNICKERBOCKER BUCKAROO	PARKER	PARAMOUNT	1919
A75	SAILING ALONG (UK)	HALE	GAUMONT BRITISH AMERICA	1938
A76	GIRL WHO STAYED AT HOME	GRIFFITH	PARAMOUNT	1919
A77	MONEY CORRAL	HART	PARAMOUNT	1919
A79	SQUARE DEAL SANDERSON	HART, HILLYER	PARAMOUNT	1919
A80	AVALANCHE	FITZMAURICE	PARAMOUNT	1919
A81	TRUE HEART SUSIE	GRIFFITH	PARAMOUNT	1919
A82	DARK STAR	DWAN	PARAMOUNT	1919
A83	WHITE HEATHER	TOURNEUR	PARAMOUNT	1919
A84	WAGON TRACKS	HILLYER	PARAMOUNT	1919

Movie Still Identification Book Ultimate Edition - Letters

CODE	TITLE/NAME	DIRECTOR/TYPE	STUDIO/DISTRIBUTOR	YEAR
A85	SOCIETY EXILE	FITZMAURICE	PARAMOUNT	1919
A86	MALE AND FEMALE	DEMILLE	PARAMOUNT	1919
A88	MIRACLE MAN	TUCKER	PARAMOUNT	1919
A90	COUNTERFEIT	FITZMAURICE	PARAMOUNT	1919
A-90	ONE WAY OUT (sh)	HILLYER	COLUMBIA	1934
A-91	HIDDEN EVIDENCE	HILLYER	COLUMBIA	1934
A91	LIFELINE	TOURNEUR	PARAMOUNT	1919
A92	CINEMA MURDER	BAKER	PARAMOUNT	1919
A-92	SIMPLE SOLUTION (sh)	LEDERMAN	COLUMBIA	1934
A-93	BY PERSONS UNKNOWN (sh)	LEDERMAN	COLUMBIA	1934
A93	WHY CHANGE YOUR WIFE	DEMILLE	PARAMOUNT	1920
A-94	PROFESSOR GIVES A LESSON	HILLYER	COLUMBIA	1934
A95	SCARLET DAYS	GRIFFITH	PARAMOUNT	1919
A96	SAND	HILLYER	PARAMOUNT	1920
A97	JOHN PETTICOATS	HILLYER	PARAMOUNT	1919
A97	TREASURE ISLAND	TOURNEUR	PARAMOUNT	1919
A98	VICTORY	TOURNEUR	PARAMOUNT	1919
A99	HIS HOUSE IN ORDER	FORD	PARAMOUNT	1920
A100	TOLL GATE	HILLYER	PARAMOUNT	1920
A103	FIGHTING CHANCE	MAIGNE	PARAMOUNT	1920
A-103	RADIO DOUGH	BOASBERG	COLUMBIA	1934
A104	HUMORESQUE	BORZAGE	PARAMOUNT	1920
A-105	TEN BABY FINGERS (sh)	WHITE	COLUMBIA	1934
A106	INSIDE OF THE CUP	CAPELLANI	PARAMOUNT	1921
A-106	SCHOOL FOR ROMANCE (LESSONS IN LOVE*) (sh)	GOTTLER	COLUMBIA	1934
A-107	ELMER STEPS OUT (PLAYFUL HUSBANDS*) (sh)	WHITE	COLUMBIA	1934
A107	WORLD AND HIS WIFE	VIGNOLA	PARAMOUNT	1920
A-107	ELMER STEPS OUT (PLAYFUL HUSBANDS*) (sh)	WHITE	COLUMBIA	1934
A-108	LOVE DETECTIVES (sh)	GOTTLER	COLUMBIA	1934
A108	RESTLESS SEX	D'USSEAU, LEONARD	PARAMOUNT	1920
A109	FORBIDDEN FRUIT	DEMILLE	PARAMOUNT	1921
A-109	WHEN DO WE EAT? (SHOWMANSHIP*) (sh)	GOULDING	COLUMBIA	1934
A110	PASSIONATE PILGRIM	VIGNOLA	PARAMOUNT	1920
A-110	STABLE MATES (sh)	WHITE	COLUMBIA	1934
A111	BURIED TREASURE	BAKER	PARAMOUNT	1921
A-111	FISHING FOR TROUBLE (HOLY MACKERAL*) (sh)	WHITE	COLUMBIA	1934
A111	THAT LADY (UK)	YOUNG	20TH CENTURY FOX	1955
A112	STRAIGHT IS THE WAY	VIGNOLA	PARAMOUNT	1921
A-112	WOMAN HATERS (sh)	GOTTLER	COLUMBIA	1934
A-113	SUSIE'S AFFAIRS (sh)	GOTTLER	COLUMBIA	1934
A113	WILD GOOSE	CAPELLANI	PARAMOUNT	1921
A-114	GET ALONG LITTLE HUBBY (sh)	MCCAREY	COLUMBIA	1934
A-115	PLUMBING FOR GOLD (sh)	LAMONT	COLUMBIA	1934
A116	PROXIES	BAKER	PARAMOUNT	1921
A-116	PUNCH DRUNKS (sh)	BRESLOW	COLUMBIA	1934
A117	LIFE	VALE	PARAMOUNT	1921
A-117	TRIPPING THRU THE TROPICS (sh)	GOTTLER	COLUMBIA	1934
A-118	BACK TO THE SOIL (PAYDIRT*) (sh)	WHITE	COLUMBIA	1934
A118	BRIDE'S PLAY	TERWILLIGER	PARAMOUNT	1922
A-119	HOLLYWOOD HERE WE COME (sh)	GOTTLER	COLUMBIA	1934
A120	WOMAN GOD CHANGED	VIGNOLA	PARAMOUNT	1921
A121	GET RICH QUICK WALLINGFORD	BORZAGE	PARAMOUNT	1921
A-150	COUNSEL ON DE FENCE (sh)	RIPLEY	COLUMBIA	1934
A-151	IT'S THE CATS (sh)	RAY	COLUMBIA	1934
A-152	MEN IN BLACK (sh)	MCCAREY	COLUMBIA	1934
A-153	PERFECTLY MISMATED (SCRAMBLE WIVES*) (sh)	HORNE	COLUMBIA	1934
A-154	SHIVERS (sh)	RIPLEY	COLUMBIA	1934
A-155	IN THE DOG HOUSE (sh)	RIPLEY	COLUMBIA	1934
A-158	ONE TOO MANY (sh)	MCGOWAN	COLUMBIA	1934
A-161	I'M A FATHER (sh)	HORNE	COLUMBIA	1935
A-164	OLD SAWBONES (sh)	LORD	COLUMBIA	1935
A311	NO HIGHWAY IN THE SKY (UK: NO HIGHWAY)	KOSTER	20TH CENTURY FOX	1951
A-315	MY SON, THE HERO	ULMER	PRC	1943
A334	I'LL NEVER FORGET YOU (UK: HOUSE IN THE SQUARE)	BAKER	20TH CENTURY FOX	1951
A395	JUST AROUND THE CORNER	MARION	PARAMOUNT	1921
A399	BOOMERANG BILL	TERRISS	PARAMOUNT	1922
A-401	SILVER CITY KID	ENGLISH	REPUBLIC	1944
A-402	STAGE TO MONTEREY	SELANDER	REPUBLIC	1944
A-403	SHERIFF OF SUNDOWN	SELANDER	REPUBLIC	1944
A404	BACK PAY	BORZAGE	PARAMOUNT	1922

Movie Still Identification Book Ultimate Edition - Letters

CODE	TITLE/NAME	DIRECTOR/TYPE	STUDIO/DISTRIBUTOR	YEAR
A-404	TOPEKA TERROR	BRETHERTON	REPUBLIC	1945
A-405	CORPUS CHRISTI BANDITS	GRISSELL	REPUBLIC	1945
A-406	TRAIL OF KIT CARSON	SELANDER	REPUBLIC	1945
A416	ENCHANTMENT	VIGNOLA	PARAMOUNT	1921
A419	FIND THE WOMAN	TERRISS	PARAMOUNT	1922
A425	BEAUTY SHOP	DILLON	PARAMOUNT	1922
A427	YOUNG DIANA	CAPELLANI, VIGNOLA	PARAMOUNT	1922
A428	BEAUTY'S WORTH	VIGNOLA	PARAMOUNT	1922
A453	GOOD PROVIDER	BORZAGE	PARAMOUNT	1922
A472	VALLEY OF SILENT MEN	BORZAGE	PARAMOUNT	1922
A478	ANNA AND THE KING OF SIAM	CROMWELL	20th CENTURY FOX	1946
A486	WHEN KNIGHTHOOD WAS IN FLOWER	VIGNOLA	PARAMOUNT	1922
A-5092	AIRPLANE	ABRAHAMS, ZUCKER	PARAMOUNT	1980
AA	ACE OF ACES	RUBEN	RKO	1933
AA	ACTION IN THE NORTH ATLANTIC	BACON	WARNER BROS	1943
AA	AFRICAN ADVENTURE	RUARK	RKO	1954
AA	ALIVE ADAMS	STEVENS	RKO	1935
AA	ANNE AUBREY	portrait		1950s
AA	ANTHONY ADVERSE	LEROY	WARNER BROS	1936
AA	ARTHUR ARTHUR		MONOGRAM	
AA	GANGWAY FOR TOMORROW	AUER	RKO	1943
AA	RIDERS OF THE RANGE	SELANDER	RKO	1949
AA	SPRING AND PORT WINE (UK)	HAMMOND	ALLIED ARTISTS	1970
AA1	BLOOD OF THE VAMPIRE (UK)	CASS	UNIVERSAL	1958
AAA	ALMOST AN ANGEL	CORNELL	PARAMOUNT	1990
AAFP	ALL AROUND FRYING PAN	KIRKLAND	FBO (ROBERTSON-COLE)	1925
AAM	AGGIE APPLEBY MAKER OF MEN	SANDRICH	RKO	1933
AAN	AAN	KHAN	UNITED ARTISTS	1952
AAR	ALONE AGAINST ROME (IT: SOLO CONTRO ROMA 1962)	RICCI	MEDALLION	1963
AAV	ATOM AGE VAMPIRE (IT: SEDDOK, L'EREDE DI SATANA)	MAJANO	TOPAZ	1960
AAW	RUN FOR YOUR WIFE (IT)	POLIDORO	MONOGRAM	1966
AB	ABDUCTORS	MCLAGLAN	LIPPERT	1957
AB	ADRIAN BOOTH (LORNA GRAY)	portrait	REPUBLIC	1930s-50s
AB	ADVENTURE IN BLACKMAIL (UK: BREACH OF PROMISE)	HUTH, PERTWEE	ENGLISH	1942
AB	ADVENTUROUS BLONDE	MCDONALD	WARNER BROS	1937
AB	ALAMO BAY	MALLE	TRI STAR	1985
AB	ALAN BATES	portrait	MGM	1960s
AB	ALF'S BUTTON AFLOAT (UK)	VARNEL	GFD	1938
AB	ALICE BRADY	portrait	MGM, PAR, REALART	
AB	ALWAYS A BRIDE	SMITH	WARNER BROS	1940
AB	AMBUSH BAY	WINSTON	UNITED ARTISTS	1966
AB	ANGEL BABY	WENDKOS	ALLIED ARTISTS	1961
AB	ANN BLYTH	portrait	UNIVERSAL	1940s-50s
AB	ANNE BANCROFT	portrait	RKO	
AB	ANNE BAXTER	portrait	RKO	1940s-50s
AB	ANTHONY BUSHELL	portrait	WARNER BROS	1920s-30s
AB	ARRIVEDERCI, BABY! (UK: DROP DEAD DARLING)	HUGHES	PARAMOUNT	1966
AB	ASHER BROTHERS PRODUCTIONS (UK)	studio		
AB	ASSASSINATION BUREAU (UK)	DEARDEN	PARAMOUNT	1969
AB	BULLDOG SEES IT THROUGH (UK)	HUTH	PATHE	1940
AB	MAGIC BOW (UK)	KNOWLES	UNIVERSAL	1946
AB	SHADOW STRIKES	SHORES	GRAND	1937
AB6	MALE AND FEMALE	DEMILLE	PARAMOUNT	1919
ABB	FROM THIS DAY FORWARD	BERRY	RKO	1946
ABBB	ADVENTURES IN BABYSITTING	COLUMBUS	BUENA VISTA	1987
ABL	BUG'S LIFE	LASSETER	BUENA VISTA	1998
ABL8	WINSLOW BOY (UK)	ASQUITH	EAGLE-LION	1948
ABr	ALICE BRADY	portrait	REALART	early 1920s
AC	ABBOTT & COSTELLO	portrait	UNIVERSAL	1940s-50s
AC	ACE VENTURA: PET DETECTIVE	SHADYAC	WARNER BROS	1994
AC	ADV. OF ROBINSON CRUSOE (MEX: ROBINSON CRUSOE)	BUNUEL	UNITED ARTISTS	1954
AC	AGE OF CONSENT (AUS)	POWELL	COLUMBIA	1964
AC	ALAN CURTIS	portrait	UNIVERSAL	1940s
AC	ALAN CURTIS	portrait	MGM	
AC	ALICE CALHOUN	portrait	WARNER BROS	1920s
AC	AMERICAN CYBORG	DAVIDSON	CANNON	1993
AC	ANITA COLBY	portrait	UNIVERSAL	
AC	ANJANETTE COMER	portrait	UNIVERSAL	
AC	ANTHONY CURTIS/TONY CURTIS	portrait	UNIVERSAL	1948-1953
AC	APACHE CHIEF	MCDONALD	LIPPERT	1949

Movie Still Identification Book Ultimate Edition - Letters

CODE	TITLE/NAME	DIRECTOR/TYPE	STUDIO/DISTRIBUTOR	YEAR
AC	APACHE GOLD (GER)	REINL	COLUMBIA	1965
AC	ARGYLE CASE	BRETHERTON	WARNER BROS	1929
AC	ATLANTIC CITY	MALLE	PARAMOUNT	1980
AC	SECOND FLOOR MYSTERY	DEL RUTH	WARNER BROS	1930
AC-105	UNNAMED DIPPY DOO DADS (sh)		PATHE EXCHANGE	1923
AC-113	KNOCKOUT (sh)	POWERS	PATHE EXCHANGE	1923
AC-124	BAR-FLY (sh)	POWERS	PATHE EXCHANGE	1924
AC-128	MAN PAYS (sh)	POWERS	PATHE EXCHANGE	1924
ACF	ADVENTURES OF CAPTAIN FABIAN	MARSHALL	REPUBLIC	1951
ACJ	ALONG CAME JONES	HEISLER	RKO	1945
ACK	ALIEN	SCOTT	20th CENTURY FOX	1979
ACK	MAN UPSTAIRS	DEL RUTH	WARNER BROS	1926
ACL	A CHORUS LINE	ATTENBOROUGH	COLUMBIA	1985
ACM	A CHANGE OF MIND	STEVENS	CINERAMA	1969
ACM	AMAZING COLOSSAL MAN	GORDON	AIP	1957
ACM	ATTACK OF THE CRAB MONSTER	CORMAN	ALLIED ARTISTS	1957
A COL-1	ONE NIGHT OF LOVE	SCHERTZINGER	COLUMBIA	1934
A COL-2	BROADWAY BILL	CAPRA	COLUMBIA	1934
A COL-3	GIRL FRIEND	BUZZELL	COLUMBIA	1935
A COL-4	THAT'S GRATITUDE	CRAVEN	COLUMBIA	1934
A COL-5	JEALOUSY	NEILL	COLUMBIA	1934
A COL-6	CHAMPAGNE FOR BREAKFAST	BROWN	COLUMBIA	1935
A COL-7	EIGHT BELLS	NEILL	COLUMBIA	1935
A COL-8	WHITE LIES	BULGAKOV	COLUMBIA	1934
A COL-10	MILLS OF THE GODS	NEILL	COLUMBIA	1935
A COL-11	BEST MAN WINS	KENTON	COLUMBIA	1935
A COL-12	CARNIVAL	LANG	COLUMBIA	1935
A COL-14	LET'S LIVE TONIGHT	SCHERTZINGER	COLUMBIA	1935
A COL-15	DEATH FLIES EAST	ROSEN	COLUMBIA	1935
A COL-16	UNWELCOME STRANGER	ROSEN	COLUMBIA	1935
A COL 17	PARTY WIRE	KENTON	COLUMBIA	1935
A COL-18	LOVE ME FOREVER	SCHERTZINGER	COLUMBIA	1935
A COL-19	AIR HAWKS	ROGELL	COLUMBIA	1935
A COL-20	AWAKENING OF JIM BURKE	HILLYER	COLUMBIA	1935
A COL-22	UNKNOWN WOMAN	ROGELL	COLUMBIA	1935
A COL-23	AFTER THE DANCE	BULGAKOV	COLUMBIA	1935
A COL-24	FEATHER IN HER HAT	SANTELL	COLUMBIA	1935
A COL-25	BLACK ROOM	NEILL	COLUMBIA	1935
A COL-26	SHE MARRIED HER BOSS	LA CAVA	COLUMBIA	1935
A COL-28	ATLANTIC ADVENTURE	ROGELL	COLUMBIA	1935
A COL-29	PUBLIC MENACE	KENTON	COLUMBIA	1935
A COL-40	AGAINST THE LAW	HILLYER	COLUMBIA	1934
A COL-41	MEN OF THE NIGHT	HILLYER	COLUMBIA	1934
A COL-42	BEHIND THE EVIDENCE	HILLYER	COLUMBIA	1935
A COL-43	IN SPITE OF DANGER	HILLYER	COLUMBIA	1935
A COL-44	MEN OF THE HOUR	HILLYER	COLUMBIA	1935
A COL-46	SWELL HEAD	STOLOFF	COLUMBIA	1935
A COL-47	TOGETHER WE LIVE	MACK	COLUMBIA	1935
A COL-48	SUPERSPEED	HILLYER	COLUMBIA	1935
A COL-50	PRESCOTT KID	SELMAN	COLUMBIA	1934
A COL-51	WESTERNER	SELMAN	COLUMBIA	1934
A COL-52	SQUARE SHOOTER	SELMAN	COLUMBIA	1935
A COL-53	LAW BEYOND THE RANGE	BEEBE	COLUMBIA	1935
A COL-54	REVENGE RIDER	SELMAN	COLUMBIA	1935
A COL-55	FIGHTING SHADOWS	SELMAN	COLUMBIA	1935
A COL-56	RIDING WILD	SELMAN	COLUMBIA	1935
A COL-57	JUSTICE OF THE RANGE	SELMAN	COLUMBIA	1935
ACP	ANYONE CAN PLAY (IT/FR: DOLCE SIGNORE)	ZAMPA	PARAMOUNT	1968
ACP	COUNTERFEIT PLAN (UK)	TULLY	WARNER BROS	1957
ACR	ACROSS 110TH STREET	SHEAR	UNITED ARTISTS	1972
ACS	CROOKED SKY (UK)	CASS	UNITED ARTISTS	1957
ACT	GUNS OF DARKNESS (UK)	ASQUITH	WARNER BROS.	1962
ACT	GUNS OF NAVARONE (UK)	THOMPSON	COLUMBIA	1961
ACT-1	ACT ONE	SCHARY	WARNER BROS	1963
ACT-1	GREEN GROW THE RUSHES (UK)	TWIST	BRITISH LION	1951
ACT-5	KITCHEN (UK)	HILL	KINGSLEY INTERNATIONAL	1961
ACT-6	HER THREE BACHELORS (UK: ALF'S BABY)	ROGERS	ADELPHI	1953
ACT-9	BLUE PARROT (UK)	HARLOW	MONARCH	1953
ACT-11	BURNT EVIDENCE (UK)	BIRT	MONARCH	1954
ACT-22	DON'T PANIC CHAPS (UK)	POLLOCK	COLUMBIA	1959

Movie Still Identification Book Ultimate Edition - Letters

CODE	TITLE/NAME	DIRECTOR/TYPE	STUDIO/DISTRIBUTOR	YEAR
AD	ADRIENNE DORE	portrait	WARNER BROS	
AD	AFTER DARK (UK)	PARKER	FOX	1932
AD	ALIAS THE DOCTOR	CURTIZ	WARNER BROS	1932
AD	ALL DOGS GO TO HEAVEN	BLUTH, GOLDMAN	UNITED ARTISTS	1989
AD	AMBASSADOR'S DAUGHTER	KRASNA	UNITED ARTISTS	1956
AD	ANDY DEVINE	portrait	UNIVERSAL	1920s-40s
AD	ANDY DEVINE	portrait	REPUBLIC	1940s-50s
AD	ANGELS WITH DIRTY FACES	CURTIZ	WARNER BROS	1938
AD	ANGIE DICKINSON	portrait	UA, UNIVERSAL, WARNER	
AD	ANN DVORAK	portrait	RKO, REPUBLIC	1930s-40s
AD	ANNE DARLING (aka ANN OR ANNA DARLING)	portrait	UNIVERSAL	1930s
AD	ANOTHER DAWN	DIETERLE	WARNER BROS	1937
AD	ARLENE DAHL	portrait	RKO, UNIV	
AD	ARLENE DAHL	portrait	WARNER BROS	
AD	ASHES AND DIAMONDS (POL: POPOL I DIAMENT)	WAJDA	JANUS	1958
AD	DATE WITH THE FALCON	REIS	RKO	1942
AD	DIAMONDS	GOLAN	AVCO EMBASSY	1975
AD	SLEUTH	MANKIEWICZ	20th CENTURY FOX	1972
AD	THREE CAME TO KILL	CAHN	UNITED ARTISTS	1960
AD	WELCOME HOME SOLDIER BOYS	COMPTON	20th CENTURY FOX	1971
AD-371	PRISON BREAK	LUBIN	UNIVERSAL	1938
AD-372	STATE POLICE	RAWLINS	UNIVERSAL	1938
ADM	DAVID MANNERS	portrait	FN/WARNER BROS	
ADS	DIFFERENT STORY	AARON	AVCO EMBASSY	1978
ADX3	JOHNNY HINES	portrait	AFFILIATED DIST	1920s
AE	ALICE EDEN	portrait	RKO	
AE	ANITA EKBERG	portrait	UNITED ARTISTS, UNIVERSAL	
AE	ANN EDMONDS	portrait	WARNER BROS	early 40s
AE	LUCKY STIFF	FOSTER	UNITED ARTISTS	1949
AE	STRANGE JUSTICE	SCHERTZINGER	RKO	1932
AE	WIND ACROSS THE EVERGLADES	RAY	WARNER BROS	1958
AE-6	HONOR BOUND	GREEN	FOX FILM	1928
AF	ADDAMS FAMILY	SONNENFELD	PARAMOUNT	1991
AF	AFTER THE FOX (IT/UK)	DE SICA	UNITED ARTISTS	1966
AF	AIR FORCE	HAWKS	WARNER BROS	1943
AF	ALBERT FINNEY	portrait	UNIVERSAL	1960s
AF	ALLEGHENY RISING	SEITER	RKO	1939
AF	ANIMAL FARM (t) (UK)	BATCHELOR, HALAS	LOUIS DE ROCHEMONT	1954
AF	ANN FORREST	portrait		
AF	ANNETTE FUNICELLO	portrait	AIP	
AF	ARCTIC FURY	DAWN, FEITSHANS JR.	RKO	1949
AF	AUDREY FERRIS	portrait	WARNER BROS	1920s
AF	AVENGING FORCE	FIRSTENBERG	CANNON	1986
AF	DAUGHTERS COURAGEOUS	CURTIZ	WARNER BROS	1939
AF	WORKING MAN	ADOLFI	WARNER BROS	1933
AF-1	(UK)THUNDER IN THE CITY	GERING	COLUMBIA	1937
AF1	UNSTOPPABLE MAN (UK)	BISHOP	SUTTON	1961
AF-2	SHERIFF OF FRACTURED JAW	WALSH	20th CENTURY FOX	1959
AFI	KING IN NEW YORK	CHAPLIN	ARCHWAY	1957
AFP	SOCIAL REGISTER	NEILAN	COLUMBIA	1934
AG	ADVENTURES OF GERARD	SKOLIMOWSKI	UNITED ARTISTS	1970
AG	ALEXANDER THE GREAT	ROSSEN	UNITED ARTISTS	1956
AG	AMAZING GRACE	LATHAN	UNITED ARTISTS	1974
AG	AMAZING GRACE AND CHUCK (SILENT VOICE*)	NEWELL	TRI STAR	1987
AG	AMERICAN GIGOLO	SCHRADER	PARAMOUNT	1980
AG	ANDY GRIFFITH	portrait	UNIVERSAL	
AG	ANGELA GREENE (aka ANGELA GREEN)	portrait	WARNER BROS	
AG	ANGRY GOD	HEILNER	UNITED ARTISTS	1948
AG	ANNE GWYNNE	portrait	UNIVERSAL	1930s-40s
AG	ANNE OF GREEN GABLES	NICHOLAS JR.	RKO	1934
AG	AVA GARDNER	portrait	RKO, UA, UNIVERSAL	
AG	BRING ME THE HEAD OF ALFREDO GARCIA	PECKINPAH	UNITED ARTISTS	1974
AG-2	AUCTIONEER	GREEN	FOX FILM	1927
AG-3	IS ZAT SO?	GREEN	FOX FILM	1927
AG-3	PLUNDERERS OF PAINTED FLATS	GANNAWAY	REPUBLIC	1959
AG-4	TWO GIRLS WANTED	GREEN	FOX FILM	1927
AG-5	COME TO MY HOUSE	GREEN	FOX FILM	1927
AGCW	AND GOD CREATED WOMAN	VADIM	KINGSLEY INT'L	1957
AGE	AGE OF INNOCENCE	RUGGLES	WARNER BROS	1924
AGP	CAESAR AND CLEOPATRA (UK)	PASCAL	UNITED ARTISTS	1945

Movie Still Identification Book Ultimate Edition - Letters

CODE	TITLE/NAME	DIRECTOR/TYPE	STUDIO/DISTRIBUTOR	YEAR
AH	ACE HIGH (IT)	COLIZZI	PARAMOUNT	1968
AH	AFTER HOURS	SCORSESE	WARNER BROS	1985
AH	AIRHEADS	LEHMANN	20th CENTURY FOX	1994
AH	ALAN HALE	portrait	WARNER BROS	
AH	ALEXANDER HAMILTON	ADOLFI	WARNER BROS	1931
AH	ALFRED HITCHCOCK	portrait	UNIVERSAL	1930s-70s
AH	ALLISON HAYES	portrait	UNIVERSAL	1950s
AH	ALMOST A HONEYMOON (UK)	LEE	PATHE	1938
AH	ALWAYS IN MY HEART	GRAHAM	WARNER BROS	1942
AH	ANGEL HEART	PARKER	TRI STAR	1987
AH	ANN HARDING	portrait	RKO	1930s, '45
AH	ANN HARDING	portrait	PATHE, PDC	
AH	ANN HOVEY	portrait	RKO	1930s
AH	ANNABELLE HAYES	portrait	RKO	
AH	ANNIE HALL	ALLEN	UNITED ARTISTS	1977
AH	ARLENE HOWELL	portrait	WARNER BROS TV	1950s-60s
AH	ARTHUR HUNNICUTT	portrait	RKO	
AH	ASSASSIN FOR HIRE (UK)	MCCARTHY	HORNE & DIETZ	1951
AH	AUDREY HEPBURN	portrait	PARAMOUNT	
AH	STORY OF ADELE H (FR: L'HISTOIRE D'ADELE H)	TRUFFANT	NEW WORLD	1976
AH-4100	LOTTERY BRIDE	STEIN	UNITED ARTISTS	1930
AHW	AMONG HUMAN WOLVES (UK: SECRET JOURNEY)	BAXTER	FILM ALLIANCE	1939
AI	ADVENTURE IN IRAQ	LEDERMAN	WARNER BROS	1943
AI	AGE OF INNOCENCE	MOELLER	RKO	1934
AI	ALIBI IKE	ENRIGHT	WARNER BROS	1935
AI	RIDING ON AIR	SEDGWICK	RKO	1937
AIN	AUTUMN IN NEW YORK	CHEN	MGM	2000
AIT	GYPSY MELODY (UK)	GREVILLE	WARDOUR	1936
AJ	ADELE JERGENS	portrait	WARNER BROS	1950s
AJ	ALICE JANS	portrait	WARNER BROS	1930s
AJ	ALICE JOYCE	portrait	METRO GOLDWYN	mid 1920s
AJ	ALLAN JONES	portrait	UNIVERSAL	
AJ	ALLEN JENKINS	portrait	WARNER BROS	1930s-40s
AJ	ANNE JEFFREYS	portrait	RKO	1940s
AJ	ARLINE JUDGE	portrait	RKO	1930s-40s
AJ	EYES OF ANNIE JONES (UK)	LE BORG	20TH CENTURY FOX	1964
AJJ	ALIAS JESSE JAMES	MCLEOD	UNITED ARTISTS	1959
AK	ALEXANDER KORDA PRODUCTIONS	studio		
AK	ALICE KELLEY	portrait	UNIV	
AK	ANDREA KING	portrait	WARNER BROS	1940s, 50s
AK	ANDREA KING	portrait	UNIV	
AK	ANIMAL KINGDOM	GRIFFITH	RKO	1932
AK	APRIL KENT	portrait		
AK	ARTHUR KENNEDY	portrait	RKO, UNIV	
AK	ASSIGNMENT K	GUEST	COLUMBIA	1968
AK	ONE MORE TOMORROW	GODFREY	WARNER BROS	1946
AK	TROUBLE IN SUNDOWN	HOWARD	RKO	1939
AK-1	ONE OF OUR AIRCRAFT IS MISSING (UK)	POWELL, PRESSBURGER	UNITED ARTISTS	1942
AK2	THIEF OF BAGDAD (UK)	BERGER, POWELL	UNITED ARTISTS	1940
AK02	THIEF OF BAGDAD (UK)	BERGER, POWELL,	UNITED ARTISTS	1940
AK04	LION HAS WINGS (UK)	BRUNEL, HURST, POWELL	UNITED ARTISTS	1939
AK06	LION HAS WINGS (UK)	BRUNEL, HURST,	UNITED ARTISTS	1939
AK-8000	TO BE OR NOT TO BE	LUBITSCH	UNITED ARTISTS	1942
AK-55600	THAT HAMILTON WOMAN (UK: LADY HAMILTON)	KORDA	UNITED ARTISTS	1941
AK-57500	LYDIA	DUVIVIER	UNITED ARTISTS	1941
AK-57900	JUNGLE BOOK (UK)	KORDA	UNITED ARTISTS	1942
AKO-AW	THIEF OF BAGDAD (UK)	BERGER, POWELL, WHALEN	UNITED ARTISTS	1940
AL	ABBE LANE	portrait	UNIVERSAL	
AL	ABE LYMAN (& HIS ORCHESTRA)	portrait	MCA	
AL	ADDICTED TO LOVE	DUNNE	WARNER BROS	1997
AL	ADMIRAL WAS A LADY	ROGELL	UNITED ARTISTS	1950
AL	AGNES LAURENT	portrait	UNITED ARTISTS	
AL	ALAN LADD	portrait	RKO, WARNER BROS	
AL	ALAN LADD	portrait	UNITED ARTISTS, UNIVERSAL	
A-L	ALEXANDER THE GREAT	ROSSEN	UNITED ARTISTS	1956
AL	ALLAN LANE	portrait	REP	
AL	ALLAN 'ROCKY' LANE	portrait	RKO	
AL	ANDREA LEEDS	portrait	GOLDWYN, UNIVERSAL	late 30s
AL	ANGEL LEVINE	KADAR	UNITED ARTISTS	1970
AL	ANITA LOUISE	portrait	WARNER BROS	1930s

Movie Still Identification Book Ultimate Edition - Letters

CODE	TITLE/NAME	DIRECTOR/TYPE	STUDIO/DISTRIBUTOR	YEAR
AL	ANITA LOUISE	portrait	TIFFANY, UNIV	
AL	ANNA LEE	portrait	GAUMONT BRITISH	1930s
AL	ANNA LEE	portrait	UNIVERSAL	1940s, '59
AL	ANNA LUCASTA	LAVEN	UNITED ARTISTS	1958
AL	ARIZONA LEGION	HOWARD	RKO	1939
AL	ARSENIC AND OLD LACE	CAPRA	WARNER BROS	1944
AL	ARTHUR LUBIN	portrait		
AL	AUDRA LINDLEY	portrait	WARNER BROS	
AL	AUDREY LONG	portrait	RKO	
AL	BREAKFAST FOR TWO	SANTELL	RKO	1937
ALA	ALIEN FROM L.A.	PYUN	CANNON	1988
ALA	ME TRAES DE UN ALA	SOLARES	FILMEX	1953
ALC	ALL THE LOVING COUPLES	BING	U-M FILM	1969
ALBB	ALIVE	MARSHALL	BUENA VISTA	1993
ALC/X	AL LICHTMAN CORPORATION			1920s
ALCX33	RICHARD TUCKER	portrait	AL LICHTMAN	early '20s
ALF	ALFIE (UK)	GILBERT	PARAMOUNT	1966
ALLL	THAT LADY (UK)	YOUNG	20th CENTURY FOX	1955
ALN	ABOUT LAST NIGHT	ZWICK	TRI STAR	1986
A.Lo	ANITA LOUISE	portrait	UNIVERSAL	
ALP	APPOINTMENT IN HONDURAS	TOURNEUR	RKO	1953
ALS	A LIKELY STORY	POTTER	RKO	1947
ALS	AL ST. JOHN PRODUCTIONS	studio	FOX	
ALX	ANN LORING	portrait	MGM	mid 1930s
AM	ADELE MARA	portrait	REP	
AM	ADOLPHE MENJOU	portrait	RKO	1930s-50s
AM	AGNES MOOREHEAD	portrait	UNITED ARTISTS	1940s
AM	AGNES MOOREHEAD	portrait	RKO	1940s-50s
AM	AGNES MOOREHEAD	portrait	UNIVERSAL	1940s-
AM	ALAN MARSHAL	portrait	RKO	
AM	ALINE MACMAHON	portrait	WARNER BROS	1930s-50s
AM	ALINE MACMAHON	portrait	UNITED ARTISTS	
AM	ALLYN (ANN) MCLERIE	portrait	WARNER BROS	early 1950s
AM	AMERICATHON	ISRAEL	UNITED ARTISTS	1979
AM	ANATOMY OF A MURDER	PREMINGER	COLUMBIA	1959
AM	ANDRA MARTIN	portrait	UNIVERSAL	late 1950s
AM	ANN MILLER	portrait	RKO	
AM	ANNA MAGNANI	portrait		
AM	ANN-MARGRET	portrait	UNIVERSAL	1960s
AM	ANN-MARGRET	portrait	FOX	1960s-70s
AM	ANTONIO MORENO	portrait	RKO	1930s-40s
AM	ARSENAL STADIUM MYSTERY (UK)	DICKINSON	GFD	1939
AM	ATOMIC MAN (UK: TIMESLIP)	HUGHES	ALLIED ARTISTS	1955
AM	AUDIE MURPHY	portrait	UNIVERSAL	1950s-60s
AM	MAGNETIC MONSTER	SIODMAK	UNITED ARTISTS	1953
AM	MAN OF IRON		RKO	1938
AM-201	HARD GUY	CLIFTON	PRC	1941
AM-207	TODAY I HANG	DRAKE	PRC	1942
AM-439	ATOMIC MAN (UK: TIMESLIP)	HUGHES	ALLIED ARTISTS	1956
AMAC	ANOTHER MAN, ANOTHER CHANCE	LELOUCH	UNITED ARTISTS	1977
AMC	AFFAIR IN MONTE CARLO (UK: 24 HRS WOMAN'S LIFE)	SAVILLE	ALLIED ARTISTS	1952
AMC	AMARCORD	FELLINI	NEW WORLD	1974
AMF	ANNA MARIA FERRERO	portrait	IFE (ITALIAN FILMS EXPORT)	
AML	ALIKI (UK: ALIKI MY LOVE)	MATE	LIONEX	1963
AMOT	A MATTER OF TIME	MINNELLI	AIP	1976
AMP	ANOTHER MAN'S POISON (UK)	RAPPER	UNITED ARTISTS	1951
AMWD	AND MILLIONS WILL DIE		MONOGRAM	
AN	ALL NEAT IN BLACK STOCKINGS (UK)	MORAHAN	NATIONAL GENERAL	1969
AN	ALL THROUGH THE NIGHT	SHERMAN	WARNER BROS	1941
AN	AMERICAN NINJA	FIRSTENBERG	CANNON	1985
AN	ANASTASIA (t)	BLUTH	20th CENTURY FOX	1997
AN	ANNA NEAGLE	portrait	RKO	
AN	ANNE NAGEL	portrait	FN/WARNER BROS	late '30s
AN	ANNE NAGEL	portrait	UNIVERSAL	
AN	APOLCALYPSE NOW	COPPOLA	UNITED ARTISTS	1980
AN	ARABIAN NIGHTS (IT)	PASOLINI	UNITED ARTISTS	1974
AN	CRACKED NUTS	CLINE	RKO	1930
AN	SWEETHEARTS AND WIVES	BADGER	WARNER BROS	1930
AN2	AMERICAN NINJA 2	FIRSTENBERG	CANNON	1987
AN3	AMERICAN NINJA 3	SUNDSTROM	CANNON	1989

Movie Still Identification Book Ultimate Edition - Letters

CODE	TITLE/NAME	DIRECTOR/TYPE	STUDIO/DISTRIBUTOR	YEAR
AN4	AMERICAN NINJA 4	SUNDSTROM	CANNON	1990
AN5	AMERICAN NINJA 5 (video)	BRALVER	CANNON	1993
ANBS	ALL NEAT IN BLACK STOCKINGS (UK)	MORAHAN	NATIONAL GENERAL	1969
ANG-9100	SUMMER STORM	SIRK	UNITED ARTISTS	1944
ANJ	THERE AIN'T NO JUSTICE (UK)	TENNYSON	ABFD	1939
ANV	ANNIVERSARY (UK)	BAKER	20TH CENTURY FOX	1968
AO	ANNE OF WINDY POPLARS	HIVELY	RKO	1940
AO	ANNIE OAKLEY	STEVENS	RKO	1935
AO	DEVIL'S CANYON	WERKER	RKO	1953
AO	OUTLAND	HYAMS	WARNER BROS	1981
AOG-192	MILLIONAIRESS (UK)	ASQUITH	20TH CENTURY FOX	1960
AOPP	ATTACK OF THE PUPPET PEOPLE	GORDON	AIP	1958
AOR	ADVENTURES OF A ROOKIE	GOODWINS	RKO	1943
AOS	ASSIGNMENT OUTER SPACE (IT)	MARGHERITI	AIP	1962
AOT	IT'S ALL OVER TOWN (UK)	HICKOX	BRITISH LION	1963
AP	ABILENE TOWN	MARIN	UNITED ARTISTS	1946
AP	ABSENT MINDED PROFESSOR	STVENSON	BUENA VISTA	1961
AP	ACROSS THE PACIFIC	HUSTON	WARNER BROS	1942
AP	AILEEN PRINGLE	portrait	MGM	
AP	AIR PATROL	DEXTER	20th CENTURY FOX	1962
AP	ALASKA PASSAGE	BERNDS	20th CENTURY FOX	1959
AP	AMOROUS MR. PRAWN (UK: AMOROUS PRAWN)	KIMMINS	MEDALLION	1962
AP	ANATOMY OF A PSYCHO	PETROFF	UNITED OF CALIFORNIA	1961
AP	ANN PEARCE (aka ANNE KRAMER)	portrait	UNIVERSAL	1940s-50s
AP	ANN PENNINGTON	portrait		
AP	ARNOLD PRESSBURGER PROD. AT UA		UNITED ARTISTS	
AP	ASK A POLICEMAN (UK)	VARNEL	MGM	1939
AP	KANSAS CITY CONFIDENTIAL	KARLSON	UNITED ARTISTS	1952
A-P	MACOMBER AFFAIR (aka GREAT WHITE HUNTER 1953)	Z. KORDA	UNITED ARTISTS	1947
AP	PAMELA BLAKE (NÉE ADELE PEARCE)	portrait	RKO	1930s-40s
AP	SHIPMATES FOREVER	BORZAGE	WARNER BROS	1935
AP-1	SHAKE HANDS WITH MURDER	HERMAN	PRC	1944
AP 7700	SHANGHAI GESTURE	VON STERNBERG	UNITED ARTISTS	1941
AP 7800	HANGMEN ALSO DIE	LANG	UNITED ARTISTS	1943
AP-11900	IT HAPPENED TOMORROW	CLAIR	UNITED ARTISTS	1944
AP-15300	SCANDAL IN PARIS	SIRK	UNITED ARTISTS	1946
APBB	ARACHNOPHOBIA	MARSHALL	BUENA VISTA	1990
APBB	FLUBBER	MAYFIELD	BUENA VISTA	1997
AP-F	ROLLING HOME	BERKE	SCREEN GUILD	1946
APOC	FOUR HORSEMEN OF THE APOCALYPSE	INGRAM, BROWNLOW	METRO	1921
APT	APARTMENT	WILDER	UNITED ARTISTS	1960
APX	ANITA PAGE	portrait	MGM	1920s-30s
AQ	ALLAN QUATERMAIN AND THE LOST CITY OF GOLD	NELSON	CANNON	1986
AQ	ASSAULT ON A QUEEN	DONOHUE	PARAMOUNT	1966
AQN	ANNA Q. NILSSON	portrait	FN	
AR	AFFAIRS OF A ROGUE (UK: FIRST GENTLEMEN)	CAVALCANTI	COLUMBIA	1948
AR	ALICE'S RESTAURANT	PENN	UNITED ARTISTS	1969
AR	ANDY RUSSELL	portrait	UNITED ARTISTS	1940s
AR	ANN RICHARDS	portrait	RKO	1940s
AR	ANN RUTHERFORD	portrait	RKO, REPUBLIC	
AR	ANNE ROONEY	portrait	UNIVERSAL	1940s
AR	AUDREY ROSE	WISE	UNITED ARTISTS	1977
AR	LITTLE ANNIE ROONEY	BEAUDINE	UNITED ARTISTS	1925
AR	MILLION DOLLAR MANHUNT (UK: ASSIGNMENT REDHEAD)	ROGERS	TUDOR	1956
AR	RED RIVER ROBIN HOOD	SELANDER	RKO	1942
ARBB	ARMAGEDDON	BAY	BUENA VISTA	1998
ARG	3 GODFATHERS	FORD	MGM	1948
ARGO-1	SON OF ROBIN HOOD (UK)	SHERMAN	20TH CENTURY FOX	1958
ARM	ALL THE RIGHT NOISES	O'HARA	20th CENTURY FOX	1971
AROS-6	PLAY GIRL	A. ROSSON	FOX FILM	1928
ARR	ADVENTURES OF REX AND RINTY (serial)	BEEBE, EASON	MASCOT	1935
AR-R	BADMAN'S TERRITORY	WHELAN	RKO	1946
ART	ARTCRAFT PRODUCTIONS	studio		
ART	DOROTHY GISH (NEW ART FILMS)	portrait	PARAMOUNT	
ART 1	BATTLING JANE	CLIFTON	PARAMOUNT	1918
ART 2	HOPE CHEST	CLIFTON	PARAMOUNT	1919
ART 3	BOOTS	CLIFTON	PARAMOUNT	1919
ART 4	PEPPY POLLY	CLIFTON	PARAMOUNT	1919
ART 5	I'LL GET HIM YET	CLIFTON	PARAMOUNT	1919
ART 6	NUGGET NELL	CLIFTON	PARAMOUNT	1919

Movie Still Identification Book Ultimate Edition - Letters

CODE	TITLE/NAME	DIRECTOR/TYPE	STUDIO/DISTRIBUTOR	YEAR
ART 7	NOBODY'S HOME (OUT OF LUCK*)	CLIFTON	PARAMOUNT	1919
ART 8	TURNING THE TABLES	CLIFTON	PARAMOUNT	1919
ART 9	MARY ELLEN COMES TO TOWN	CLIFTON	PARAMOUNT	1920
ART 10	REMODELING HER HUSBAND	GISH	PARAMOUNT	1920
ART 11	LITTLE MISS REBELLION	FAWCETT	PARAMOUNT	1920
ART 12	FLYING PAT	JONES	PARAMOUNT	1920
ART 13	GHOST IN THE GARRET	JONES	PARAMOUNT	1921
ARWIN	JULIE	STONE	MGM	1956
AS	ABOMINABLE SNOWMAN OF THE HIMALAYAS (UK)	GUEST	20th CENTURY FOX	1957
AS	AFRICA SCREAMS	BARTON	UNITED ARTISTS	1949
AS	AIR STRIKE	ROTH	LIPPERT	1955
AS	ALONG CAME SALLY (UK: AUNT SALLY)	WHELAN	GAUMONT BRITISH AMERICA	1934
AS	AMERICAN SUCCESS COMPANY	RICHERT	COLUMBIA	1980
AS	ANDREW STONE PRODUCTIONS	studio		
AS	ANDREWS SISTERS	portrait	UNIVERSAL	1940s
AS	ANITA STEWART	portrait	MGM	
AS	ANN SAVAGE	portrait	UNIVERSAL	
AS	ANN SAVAGE	portrait		
AS	ANN SHERIDAN	portrait	UNIVERSAL	30s,50s,60s
AS	ANN SHERIDAN	portrait	WARNER BROS	1930s-40s
AS	ANN SHERIDAN	portrait	RKO	1940s-50s
AS	ANN SOTHERN	portrait	RKO	1930s,'49
AS	ANNAPOLIS SALUTE	CABANNE	RKO	1937
AS	ANNE SHIRLEY	portrait	RKO	1930s-40s
AS	ANOTHER SKY (UK)	LAMBERT		1954
AS	BACK IN CIRCULATION	ENRIGHT	WARNER BROS	1937
A.S.	BACHELOR'S DAUGHTERS	STONE	UNITED ARTISTS	1946
AS	BEDSIDE MANNER	STONE	UNITED ARTISTS	1944
AS	GIRL SAID NO	STONE	GRAND	1937
AS	GRIP OF THE STRANGLER (UK: HAUNTED STRANGLER)	DAY	AMALGAMATED	1957
A-S	MACOMBER AFFAIR (portraits)	Z. KORDA	UNITED ARTISTS	1947
AS	RACING LADY	FOX	RKO	1937
AS10900	HI DIDDLE DIDDLE	STONE	UNITED ARTISTS	1943
AS-12600	SENSATION OF 1945	STONE	UNITED ARTISTS	1944
ASG	BEYOND CHRISTMAS (BEYOND TOMORROW)	SUTHERLAND	RKO	1940
ASM	ASTOUNDING SHE MONSTER	ASHCROFT	AIP	1958
ASP	SAFE PLACE	JAGLOM	COLUMBIA	1971
ASR	AS THE SEA RAGES	HACHLER	COLUMBIA	1959
ASS	AND NOW THE SCREAMING STARTS (UK)	BAKER	CINERAMA RELEASING	1973
ASU	ALL SCREWED UP (IT)	WERTMULLER	NEW LINE CINEMA	1976
ASX4	MILDRED HARRIS	portrait		
AT	ACCIDENTAL TOURIST	KASDAN	WARNER BROS	1988
AT	ACTION OF THE TIGER (UK)	YOUNG	MGM	1957
AT	ALICE TERRY	portrait	MGM	1920s
AT	ALIX TILTON	portrait	WARNER BROS	
AT	AN ANGEL FROM TEXAS	ENRIGHT	WARNER BROS	1940
AT	ANDERSON TAPES	LUMET	COLUMBIA	1971
AT	ANGEL TOMPKINS	portrait	UNIVERSAL	early '70s
AT	ANNABELLE TAKES A TOUR	LANDERS	RKO	1938
AT	ARCH OF TRIUMPH	MILESTONE	UNITED ARTISTS	1948
AT	ARIZONA THOROUGHBRED			
AT	ASKING FOR TROUBLE (UK)	MITCHELL	ANGLO-AMERICAN	1942
AT	ATTACK ON THE IRON COAST (UK)	WENDKOS	UNITED ARTISTS	1968
AT	ATTILA	FRANCISCI	EMBASSY	1958
AT	AUDREY TOTTER	portrait	UNIVERSAL, RKO	
AT	GENTLEMAN FROM ARIZONA (ARIZONA THOROUGHBRED)	HALEY	ASTOR	1939
AT	IT ALL CAME TRUE	SEILER	WARNER BROS	1940
AT	LONE GUN	NAZARRO	UNITED ARTISTS	1954
ATG	ALEX THE GREAT	MURPHY	FILM BOOKING OFF (FBO)	1928
ATG	ALFRED THE GREAT (UK)	DONNER	MGM	1969
ATL	ANDROCLES AND THE LION	ERSKINE	RKO	1953
ATO	YOUTH RUNS WILD	ROBSON	RKO	1944
ATOC	ARE THESE OUR CHILDREN	RUGGLES	RKO	1931
ATR	ALONG THE RIO GRANDE	KILLY	RKO	1941
ATS	STROMBOLI	ROSSELLINI	RKO	1950
ATW	ALL THESE WOMEN (SWE)	BERGMAN	JANUS	1964
ATW	AROUND THE WORLD	DWAN	RKO	1943
ATX	AVONNE TAYLOR	portrait	MGM	
AU	GAMBLER WORE A GUN	CAHN	UNITED ARTISTS	1961
AV	ALIDA VALLI	portrait	RKO	1950

Movie Still Identification Book Ultimate Edition - Letters

CODE	TITLE/NAME	DIRECTOR/TYPE	STUDIO/DISTRIBUTOR	YEAR
AV	ALIDA VALLI	portrait	IFE	
AV	ANN VICKERS	CROMWELL	RKO	1933
AV	ANONYMOUS VENETIAN (IT)	SALERNO	ALLIED ARTISTS	1971
AV	AVANTI!	WILDER	UNITED ARTISTS	1972
AV	AVIATOR	MILLER	MGM/UA	1985
AV1	EIGHT O'CLOCK WALK (UK)	COMFORT	AAP	1954
AW	ALICE IN WONDERLAND (UK)	BOWER	SOUVAINE SELECTIVE	1949
AW	ALICE IN WONDERLAND (t)	GERONIMI, JACKSON	RKO (DISNEY)	1951
AW	ALICE IN WONDERLAND (x)	TOWNSEND		1976
AW	ALICE WHITE	portrait	FIRST NAT'L/WARNER BROS	1920s-30s
AW	AMELITA WARD	portrait		1940s
AW	ANDY WILLIAMS	portrait	UNIV	
AW	ANTON WALBROOK	portrait	RKO	
AW	APACHE WARRIOR	WILLIAMS	20TH CENTURY FOX	1957
AW	APACHE WOMAN (ARC)	CORMAN	AIP	1955
AW	ARLEEN WHELAN	portrait	UNIVERSAL	1940s
AW	AROUND THE WORLD IN 80 DAYS	ANDERSON	UNITED ARTISTS	1956
AW	ASH WEDNESDAY	PEERCE	PARAMOUNT	1973
AW-80	AROUND THE WORLD IN 80 DAYS	ANDERSON	UNITED ARTISTS	1956
AWC	ALL I WANT FOR CHRISTMAS	LIEBERMAN	PARAMOUNT	1991
AWN	ACE VENTURA: WHEN NATURE CALLS	OEDEKERK	WARNER BROS	1995
AWNO	AROUND THE WORLD WITH NOTHING ON (SWIT)	KUNZ	BARCLAY	1961
AX105	ELSIE FERGUSON	portrait	ARTCRAFT	
AXJX	ALLAN JONES	portrait	MGM	1930s
AXR	ANN RUTHERFORD	portrait	MGM	
AXS	ANN SOTHERN	portrait	MGM	
AY	AFFECTIONATELY YOURS	BACON	WARNER BROS	1941
AYO	KING SOLOMON'S MINES (UK)	STEVENSON	GAUMONT	1937
B	ABDICATION	HARVEY	WARNER BROS	1974
B	ALIAS BULLDOG DRUMMOND (UK: BULLDOG JACK)	FORDE	GAUMONT BRITISH AMERICA	1935
B	AWAKENING	NEWELL	ORION	1980
B	BABETTE GOES TO WAR (FRANCE)	JAQUE	COLUMBIA	1959
B	BACK ROADS	RITT	WARNER BROS	1981
B	BACKFIRE (FR: ECHAPPEMENT LIBRE)	BECKER	ROYAL	1962
B	BADLANDS	MALICK	WARNER BROS	1973
B	BAIT	HAAS	COLUMBIA	1954
B	BAMBI (t)	ALGAR, ARMSTRONG	RKO	1942
B	BANDIDO	FLEISCHER	UNITED ARTISTS	1956
B	BANJO	FLEISCHER	RKO	1947
B	BARBARELLA	VADIM	PARAMOUNT	1968
B	BARQUERO	DOUGLAS	UNITED ARTISTS	1970
B	BARRABUS	FLEISCHER	COLUMBIA	1962
B	BARTLEBY (UK)	FRIEDMAN	MARON	1970
B	BAYOU	DANIELS	UNITED ARTISTS	1957
B	BEACHHEAD	HEISLER	UNITED ARTISTS	1954
B	BEAR (FR: L'OURS 1960)	SECHAN	EMBASSY	1963
B	BECKET	GLENVILLE	PARAMOUNT	1964
B	BEDAZZLED (UK)	DONEN	20TH CENTURY FOX	1967
B	BEDELIA (UK)	COMFORT	EAGLE-LION	1946
B	BEDSIDE	FLOREY	WARNER BROS	1934
B	BELLE DE JOUR (FR) (BELLE OF THE DAY)	BUNUEL	ALLIED ARTISTS	1968
B	BENGAZI	BRAHM	RKO	1955
B	BERSERK	O'CONNOLLY	COLUMBIA	1967
B	BETRAYED	GAVRAS	UNITED ARTISTS	1988
B	BIG NOISE	MCDONALD	WARNER BROS	1936
B	BILLIE	WEIS	UNITED ARTISTS	1965
B	BIRD	EASTWOOD	WARNER BROS	1988
B	BLAZING SADDLES	BROOKS	WARNER BROS	1974
B	BOMBARDIER	WALLACE	RKO	1943
B	BORDER TOWN	MAYO	WARNER BROS	1935
B	BOSS	HASKIN	UNITED ARTISTS	1956
B	BOUGHT	MAYO	WARNER BROS	1931
B	BOY AND THE BRIDGE (UK)	MCCLORY	COLUMBIA	1959
B	BRAIN (GER: TOTER SUCHT SEINEN MORDER 1962)	FRANCIS	GOVERNOR	1964
B	BRAIN (FR/IT: LE CERVEAU)	OURY	PARAMOUNT	1969
B	BRASS	FRANKLIN	WARNER BROS	1923
B	BRAVEHEART	GIBSON	20TH CENTURY FOX	1995
B	BREAKAWAY (UK)	CASS	AAP	1955
B	BREAKOUT (UK: DANGER WITHIN)	CHAFFEY	CONTINENTAL	1959
B	BREATHLESS	GODARD	FILMS AROUND WORLD	1960

- 13 -

Movie Still Identification Book Ultimate Edition - Letters

CODE	TITLE/NAME	DIRECTOR/TYPE	STUDIO/DISTRIBUTOR	YEAR
B	BREWSTER'S MILLIONS (UK)	FREELAND	UNITED ARTISTS	1935
B	BROADMINDED	LEROY	WARNER BROS	1931
B	BRUTE	CUMMINGS	WARNER BROS	1927
B	BURGLAR	WENDKOS	COLUMBIA	1957
B	BUSHBABY (UK)	TRENT	MGM	1969
B	BUSHWHACKED	BEEMAN	20th CENTURY FOX	1995
B	BUSTING	HYAMS	UNITED ARTISTS	1974
B	BUTTERFLY	NEVE	AUDUBON	1970
B	CLARENCE SINCLAIR BULL PORTRAITS		MGM	
B	CRYSTAL CUP	DILLON	WARNER BROS	1927
B	ENFORCER	FARGO	WARNER BROS	1976
B	FIND THE BLACKMAILER	LEDERMAN	WARNER BROS	1943
B	FIREFOX	EASTWOOD	WARNER BROS	1982
B	FRIENDLY ENEMIES	MELFORD	PRODUCERS DIST (PDC)	1925
B	GIRL I LOVED	DE GRASSE	UNITED ARTISTS	1923
B	GLADYS BROCKWELL PRODUCTIONS	studio	FOX	
B	HEROES FOR SALE	WELLMAN	WARNER BROS	1933
B	HIGH ROAD TO CHINA	HUTTON	WARNER BROS	1983
B	JEALOUS HUSBANDS		WARNER BROS	
B	LET'S SING AGAIN	NEUMANN	RKO	1936
B	MAGNUM FORCE	POST	WARNER BROS	1973
B	MAN OF IRON	MCGANN	WARNER BROS	1935
B	MILLION BID	CURTIZ	WARNER BROS	1927
B	PERMISSION TO KILL (EXECUTIONER)	FRANKEL	AVCO EMBASSY	1975
B	STEEL AGAINST THE SKY	SUTHERLAND	WARNER BROS	1941
B	UPTOWN SATURDAY NIGHT	POITIER	WARNER BROS	1974
B	ZEPPELIN	PERIER	WARNER BROS	1971
B+B	BUTCH & BUDDY (LENHART, BROWN)	portrait	UNIVERSAL	
B&R	BATMAN AND ROBIN	SCHUMACHER	WARNER BROS	1997
B&S	BLOOD AND SAND	NIBLO	PARAMOUNT	R-ONLY
B&S	BODY AND SOUL	BOWERS	CANNON	1981
B&T-105	BILL AND TED'S EXCELLENT ADVENTURE	HEREK	ORION	1989
B-1	365 DAYS (sh)	CHASE	PATHE EXCHANGE	1922
B1	BATTLE OF THE SEXES (UK)	CRICHTON	CONTINENTAL	1960
B-1	CARETAKER'S DAUGHTER (sh)	MCCAREY	PATHE EXCHANGE	1925
B-1	GO GET 'EM HUTCH (sh)	SEITZ	PATHE EXCHANGE	1922
B-1	MICKEY	JONES	W. H. PRODUCTIONS	1918
B-1	MOVIE DAZE (sh)	MEINS	MGM	1934
B-1	PLEASE BE CAREFUL	BUCKINGHAM	FOX FILM	1922
B-1	SCHEMER SKINNY'S SCHEMES (sh)		PATHE EXCHANGE	1917
B-1	SHE COULDN'T TAKE IT	GARNETT	COLUMBIA	1935
B2	BASKETBALL FIX	FEIST	REALART	1951
B-2	BEFORE THE PUBLIC (sh)	CHASE	PATHE EXCHANGE	1923
B2	BELOVED ROGUE	CROSLAND	UNITED ARTISTS	1927
B-2	CROOK'S TOUR (sh)	MCGOWAN	MGM	1933
B2	ENTERTAINER (UK)	RICHARDSON	CONTINENTAL	1960
B-2	MUSIC GOES ROUND	SCHERTZINGER	COLUMBIA	1936
B-2	SKINNY'S LOVE TRIANGLE (sh)		PATHE EXCHANGE	1917
B-2	SPIDER AND THE ROSE	MCDERMOTT	PRINCIPAL PICTURES	1923
B-2	UNEASY THREE (sh)	CHASE	PATHE EXCHANGE	1925
B-2	VERY TRULY YOURS	DIETERLE	FOX FILM	1922
B-3	CHASING RAINBOWS	BEAL	FOX FILM	1919
B-3	CRIME AND PUNISHMENT	VON STERNBERG	COLUMBIA	1935
B-3	HIS WOODEN WEDDING (sh)	MCCAREY	PATHE EXCHANGE	1925
B-3	LA BELLE RUSSE	BRABIN	FOX FILM	1919
B-3	LIGHTS OF THE DESERT	BEAUMONT	FOX FILM	1922
B-3	NEWLY RICH (sh)	CHASE	PATHE EXCHANGE	1922
B-3	SCHEEMER SKINNY'S SCHEMES (sh)		PATHE EXCHANGE	1917
B-3	TWIN SCREWS (sh)	PARROTT	MGM	1933
B-4	BROKEN COMMANDMENT	BEAL	FOX FILM	1919
B-4	CHARLEY MY BOY (sh)	MCCAREY	PATHE EXCHANGE	1926
B-4	DRAMA'S DREADFUL DEAL (sh)		PATHE EXCHANGE	1917
B-4	GRAND EXIT	KENTON	COLUMBIA	1935
B-4	GREEN CAT (sh)	CHASE	PATHE EXCHANGE	1922
B-4	HIGH POCKETS	LOWRY	GOLDWYN	1919
B-4	KATHLEEN MAVOURNEEN	BRABIN	FOX FILM	1919
B-4	MIXED NUTS (sh)	PARROTT	MGM	1934
B4	SKYWATCH (UK: LIGHT UP THE SKY)	GILBERT	CONTINENTAL	1960
B-5	BALLAD OF A SOLDIER (RUS: BALLADA O SOLDATE 1959)	CHUKHRAY	UNION FILM	1960
B5	BOY WHO STOLE A MILLION (UK)	CRICHTON	PARAMOUNT	1960

Movie Still Identification Book Ultimate Edition - Letters

CODE	TITLE/NAME	DIRECTOR/TYPE	STUDIO/DISTRIBUTOR	YEAR
B-5	BRIAN'S SONG	KULIK	COLUMBIA	1971
B-5	BROKEN SABER	MCEVEETY	SENTINEL	1965
B-5	ESCAPE FROM DEVIL'S ISLAND	ROGELL	COLUMBIA	1935
B-5	MAMA BEHAVE (sh)	CHASE	PATHE EXCHANGE	1926
B-5	NEXT WEEKEND (sh)	DUNN	MGM	1934
B-5	SKINNY GETS A GOAT (sh)	ROACH	PATHE EXCHANGE	1917
B-5	THIEVES	BEAL	FOX FILM	1919
B-5	WHERE AM I? (sh)	CHASE	PATHE EXCHANGE	1923
B-6	BLIND WIVES	BRABIN	FOX FILM	1920
B-6	CARETAKER'S DAUGHTER (sh)	FRENCH	MGM	1934
B-6	DOG SHY (sh)	MCCAREY	PATHE EXCHANGE	1926
B-6	OLD SEA DOG (sh)	CHASE	PATHE EXCHANGE	1922
B-6	ONE WAY TICKET	BIBERMAN	COLUMBIA	1935
B-6	SKINNY'S FALSE ALARM (sh)	ROACH	PATHE EXCHANGE	1917
B-7	DIG UP (sh)	HUTCHINSON	PATHE EXCHANGE	1923
B-7	LONE WOLF RETURNS	NEILL	COLUMBIA	1935
B-7	MRS. BARNACLE BILL (sh)	FRENCH	MGM	1934
B-7	MUM'S THE WORD (sh)	McCAREY	PATHE EXCHANGE	1926
B-7	SKINNY'S SHIP-WRECKED SAND-WITCH (sh)	ROACH	PATHE EXCHANGE	1917
B-8	HOOK, LINE AND SINKER (sh)	CHASE	PATHE EXCHANGE	1922
B-8	IF YOU COULD ONLY COOK	SEITER	COLUMBIA	1935
B-8	LONG FLIV THE KING (sh)	MCCAREY	PATHE EXCHANGE	1926
B-8	MIDNIGHT PATROL	CABANNE	MONOGRAM	1932
B-8	SKINNY ROUTS A ROBBER (sh)		PATHE EXCHANGE	1917
B-8	SPEAKING OF RELATIONS (sh)	YATES	MGM	1934
B-9	BOARDER BUSTERS (sh)		PATHE EXCHANGE	1917
B-9	CALIFORNIA OR BUST (sh)	HUTCHINSON	PATHE EXCHANGE	1923
B-9	HELL-SHIP MORGAN	LEDERMAN	COLUMBIA	1936
B9	LINDA (UK)	SHARP	BRYANSTON	1960
B-9	MIGHTY LIKE A MOOSE (sh)	MCCAREY	PATHE EXCHANGE	1926
B-10	CRAZY LIKE A FOX (sh)	MCCAREY	PATHE EXCHANGE	1926
B10	DOUBLE BUNK (UK)	PENNINGTON-RICHARDS	SHOWCORPORATION	1961
B-10	ETERNAL STRUGGLE	BARKER	METRO	1923
B-10	TOUGH WINTER (sh)	CHASE	PATHE EXCHANGE	1923
B-10	YOU MAY BE NEXT	ROGELL	COLUMBIA	1936
B-11	BROMO AND JULIET (sh)	MCCAREY	PATHE EXCHANGE	1926
B-11	IT'S A GIFT (sh)	FAY	PATHE EXCHANGE	1923
B-11	KING STEPS OUT	VON STERNBERG	COLUMBIA	1936
B11	SPARE THE ROD (UK)	NORMAN	BRYANSTON	1961
B-12	LADY OF SECRETS	GERING	COLUMBIA	1936
B-12	NOTORIOUS MRS. SANDS	CABANNE	ROBERTSON COLE	1920
B-12	SOLD AT AUCTION (sh)	CHASE	PATHE EXCHANGE	1923
B-12	TELL 'EM NOTHING (sh)	MCCAREY	PATHE EXCHANGE	1926
B-13	BE YOUR AGE (sh)	CHASE	PATHE EXCHANGE	1926
B-13	CALLING OF DAN MATHEWS	ROSEN	COLUMBIA	1935
B-13	WALKOUT (sh)	JESKE	PATHE EXCHANGE	1923
B-13	WHY WORRY? (sh)	TAYLOR, NEWMEYER	PATHE EXCHANGE	1923
B-14	DEVIL'S SQUADRON	KENTON	COLUMBIA	1936
B-14	MANY SCRAPY RETURNS (sh)	PARROTT	PATHE EXCHANGE	1927
B-14	MYSTERY MAN (sh)	FAY	PATHE EXCHANGE	1923
B-15	DON'T GAMBLE WITH LOVE	MURPHY	COLUMBIA	1936
B-15	JACK FROST (sh)	CHASE	PATHE EXCHANGE	1923
B-15	THERE AIN'T NO SANTA CLAUS (sh)	PARROTT	PATHE EXCHANGE	1926
B-16	ARE BRUNETTES SAFE? (sh)	PARROTT	PATHE EXCHANGE	1927
B-16	COURTSHIP OF MILES SANDWICH (sh)	CHASE	PATHE EXCHANGE	1923
B16	GIRL ON APPROVAL (UK)	FREND	CONTINENTAL	1961
B-16	PRIDE OF THE MARINES	LEDERMAN	COLUMBIA	1936
B-17	END OF THE TRAIL	KENTON	COLUMBIA	1936
B-17	ONE MAMA MAN (sh)	PARROTT	PATHE EXCHANGE	1927
B17	STRONGROOM (UK)	SEWELL	UNION	1962
B-18	FORGOTTEN SWEETIES (sh)	PARROTT	PATHE EXCHANGE	1927
B18	QUARE FELLOW (UK)	DREIFUSS	ASTOR	1962
B-18	ROAMING LADY	ROGELL	COLUMBIA	1936
B-19	BIGGER AND BETTER BLONDS (sh)	PARROTT	PATHE EXCHANGE	1927
B-19	MINE WITH THE IRON DOOR	HOWARD	COLUMBIA	1936
B-20	AND SO THEY WERE MARRIED	NUGENT	COLUMBIA	1936
B-20	FLUTTERING HEARTS (sh)	PARROTT	PATHE EXCHANGE	1927
B20	LONELINESS OF THE LONG DISTANCE RUNNER (UK)	RICHARDSON	CONTINENTAL	1962
B-21	LOST HORIZON	CAPRA	COLUMBIA	1937
B-21	WHAT WOMEN DID FOR ME (sh)	PARROTT	PATHE EXCHANGE	1927

Movie Still Identification Book Ultimate Edition - Letters

CODE	TITLE/NAME	DIRECTOR/TYPE	STUDIO/DISTRIBUTOR	YEAR
B22	DON'T TALK TO STRANGE MEN (UK)	JACKSON	BRYANSTON	1962
B-22	NOW I'LL TELL ONE (sh)	PARROTT	PATHE EXCHANGE	1927
B-22	TRAPPED BY TELEVISION	LORD	COLUMBIA	1936
B-23	ASSISTANT WIVES (sh)	PARROTT	PATHE EXCHANGE	1927
B-23	BLACKMAILER	WILES	COLUMBIA	1936
B-25	COUNTERFEIT	KENTON	COLUMBIA	1936
B25	LUNCH HOUR (UK)	HILL	BRYANSTON	1961
B26	CALCULATED RISK (UK)	HARRISON	BRYANSTON	1963
B-27	MEET NERO WOLFE	BIBERMAN	COLUMBIA	1936
B-27	MR. DEEDS GOES TO TOWN	CAPRA	COLUMBIA	1936
B28	MODEL MURDER CASE (UK: GIRL IN THE HEADLINES)	TRUMAN	CINEMA V	1963
B-29	LADIES WHO DO (UK)	PENNINGTON-RICHARDS	CONTINENTAL	1963
B-29	THEODORA GOES WILD	BOLESLAWSKI	COLUMBIA	1936
B-30	ADVENTURE IN MANHATTAN	LUDWIG	COLUMBIA	1936
B-32	TWO FISTED GENTLEMAN	WILES	COLUMBIA	1936
B-33	THEY MET IN A TAXI	GREEN	COLUMBIA	1936
B-34	MAN WHO LIVED TWICE	LACHMAN	COLUMBIA	1936
B-35	LAWLESS RIDERS	BENNET	COLUMBIA	1935
B-35	WHEN YOU'RE IN LOVE	RISKIN	COLUMBIA	1937
B-60	GUARD THAT GIRL	HILLYER	COLUMBIA	1935
B-61	CASE OF THE MISSING MAN	LEDERMAN	COLUMBIA	1935
B-62	TOO TOUGH TO KILL	LEDERMAN	COLUMBIA	1935
B-63	DANGEROUS INTRIGUE	SELMAN	COLUMBIA	1936
B-64	PANIC ON THE AIR	LEDERMAN	COLUMBIA	1936
B-65	FINAL HOUR	LEDERMAN	COLUMBIA	1936
B-66	SHAKEDOWN	SELMAN	COLUMBIA	1936
B-67	ALIBI FOR MURDER	LEDERMAN	COLUMBIA	1936
B-68	KILLER AT LARGE	SELMAN	COLUMBIA	1936
B-70	WESTERN FRONTIER	HERMAN	COLUMBIA	1935
B-74	CATTLE THIEF	BENNET	COLUMBIA	1936
B-75	HEROES OF THE RANGE	BENNET	COLUMBIA	1936
B-76	AVENGING WATERS	BENNET	COLUMBIA	1936
B-77	FUGITIVE SHERIFF	BENNET	COLUMBIA	1936
B-80	GALLANT DEFENDER	SELMAN	COLUMBIA	1935
B-81	MYSTERIOUS AVENGER	SELMAN	COLUMBIA	1936
B-82	STAMPEDE	BEEBE	COLUMBIA	1936
B-83	SECRET PATROL	SELMAN	COLUMBIA	1936
B-84	TUGBOAT PRINCESS	SELMAN	COLUMBIA	1936
B-85	LUCKY FUGITIVES (CAN: STOP, LOOK AND LOVE)	GRINDE	COLUMBIA	1936
B-090	SO FINE	BERGMAN	WARNER BROS	1981
B113	HIS PEST FRIEND (sh)	GOODWINS	RKO	1938
B121	BERTH QUAKES (sh)	YARBROUGH	RKO	1938
B129	JITTERS (sh)	GOODWINS	RKO	1938
B131	HERE COME THE JETS	FOWLER JR.	20th CENTURY FOX	1959
B132	RETURN OF THE FLY	BERNDS	20th CENTURY FOX	1959
B134	ALLIGATOR PEOPLE	DEL RUTH	20th CENTURY FOX	1959
B135	OREGON TRAIL	FOWLER JR.	20th CENTURY FOX	1959
B148	STAGE FRIGHT (sh)	GOODWINS	RKO	1938
B152	MAJOR DIFFICULTIES (sh)	BROCK	RKO	1938
B176	CRIME RAVE (sh)	YARBROUGH	RKO	1939
B184	MOVING VANITIES (sh)	BROCK	RKO	1939
B187	RING MADNESS (sh)	D'ARCY	RKO	1939
B212	MYRNA LOY	portrait		
B215	WRONG ROOM (sh)	BROCK	RKO	1939
B225	ROLAND YOUNG	portrait		
B225	TRUTH ACHES (sh)	ROBERTS	RKO	1939
B228	SCRAPPILY MARRIED (sh)	RIPLEY	RKO	1939
B262	BESTED BY A BEARD (sh)	ROBERTS	RKO	1940
B268	HE ASKED FOR IT (sh)	D'ARCY	RKO	1940
B278	WHEN WIFE'S AWAY		RKO	1940
B286	TATTLE TELEVISION (sh)	D'ARCY	RKO	1940
B291	FIRED MAN (sh)	ROBERTS	RKO	1941
B302	PANIC IN THE PARLOR (sh)	ROBERTS	RKO	1941
B304	POLO PHONY (sh)	D'ARCY	RKO	1941
B-326	HIGHWAY DRAGNET	JURAN	ALLIED ARTISTS	1954
B-327	YUKON VENGEANCE	BEAUDINE	ALLIED ARTISTS	1954
B331	MAN-I-CURED (sh)	D'ARCY	RKO	1941
B336	WHO'S A DUMMY? (sh)	D'ARCY	RKO	1941
B344	HOME WORK (sh)	D'ARCY	RKO	1942
B360	WEDDED BLITZ (sh)	EDWARDS	RKO	1942

Movie Still Identification Book Ultimate Edition - Letters

CODE	TITLE/NAME	DIRECTOR/TYPE	STUDIO/DISTRIBUTOR	YEAR
B361	FRAMING FATHER (sh)	ROBERTS	RKO	1942
B370	HOLD 'EM JAIL (shy)	FRENCH	RKO	1942
B375	MAIL TROUBLE (sh)	FRENCH	RKO	1942
B381	TWO FOR THE MONEY (sh)	FRENCH	RKO	1942
B387	DEAR! DEER! (sh)	HOLMES	RKO	1942
B391	PRETTY DOLLY (sh)	HOLMES	RKO	1942
B399	DOUBLE UP (sh)	HOLMES	RKO	1943
B406	GEM JAMS (sh)	HILLYER	RKO	1943
B411	RADIO RUNAROUND (sh)	HILLYER	RKO	1943
B422	CUTIE ON DUTY (sh)	HOLMES	RKO	1943
B425	WEDTIME STORIES (sh)	HOLMES	RKO	1943
B427	SEEING NELLIE HOME (sh)	HOLMES	RKO	1943
B-429	SECURITY RISK	SCHUSTER	ALLIED ARTISTS	1954
B-434	PORT OF HELL	SCHUSTER	ALLIED ARTISTS	1954
B439	SAY UNCLE (sh)	HOLMES	RKO	1943
B442	POPPA KNOWS WORST (sh)	HOLMES	RKO	1943
B-444	TREASURE OF RUBY HILLS	MCDONALD	ALLIED ARTISTS	1955
B-447	BIG TIP-OFF	MCDONALD	ALLIED ARTISTS	1955
B459	GIRLS! GIRLS! GIRLS! (sh)		RKO	1944
B462	TRIPLE TROUBLE (sh)	D'ARCY	RKO	1944
B478	HE FORGOT TO REMEMBER (sh)	YATES	RKO	1944
B479	LUISE RAINER	portrait	MGM	
B489	BIRTHDAY BLUES (sh)	YATES	RKO	1945
B492	LET'S GO STEPPING (sh)	YATES	RKO	1945
B499	IT SHOULDN'T HAPPEN TO A DOG (sh)		RKO	1945
B510	DOUBLE HONEYMOON (sh)	YATES	RKO	1945
B513	BEWARE OF REDHEADS (sh)	YATES	RKO	1945
B530	BUDDY EBSEN	portrait		
B531	BUDDY EBSEN	portrait		
B531	MAID TROUBLE (sh)	EDWARDS	RKO	1945
B534	OH! PROFESSOR BEHAVE (sh)	YATES	RKO	1946
B543	TWIN HUSBANDS (sh)	YATES	RKO	1946
B547	I'LL TAKE MILK (sh)	YATES	RKO	1946
B-548	LAS VEGAS SHAKEDOWN	SALKOW	ALLIED ARTISTS	1955
B549	MARIE DRESSLER	portrait		
B552	FOLLOW THAT BLONDE (sh)	YATES	RKO	1946
B-555	BETRAYED WOMEN	CAHN	ALLIED ARTISTS	1955
B-556	TOUGHEST MAN ALIVE	SALKOW	ALLIED ARTISTS	1955
B559	DOROTHY SEBASTIAN	portrait		
B578	BORROWED BLONDE (sh)	YATES	RKO	1947
B585	HIRED HUSBAND (sh)	YATES	RKO	1947
B586	IN ROOM 303 (sh)	YATES	RKO	1947
B599	BLONDES AWAY (sh)	YATES	RKO	1947
B-613	YAQUI DRUMS	YARBROUGH	ALLIED ARTISTS	1956
B618	SPOOK SPEAKS (sh)	YATES	RKO	1947
B619	BET YOUR LIFE (sh)	YATES	RKO	1948
B620	LIONEL BARRYMORE	portrait		
B625	DON'T FOOL YOUR WIFE (sh)	YATES	RKO	1948
B626	SECRETARY TROUBLE (sh)	YATES	RKO	1948
B646	BACHELOR BLUES (sh)	GOODWINS	RKO	1948
B647	UNINVITED BLONDE (sh)	YATES	RKO	1948
B648	BACKSTAGE FOLLIES (sh)	YATES	RKO	1948
B649	ELEANOR POWELL	portrait		
B650	ELEANOR POWELL	portrait		
B652	ELEANOR POWELL	portrait	MGM	
B656	FATHER'S DAY (sh)		RKO	1948
B657	CACTUS CUT-UP (sh)	ROBERTS	RKO	1949
B658	ELEANOR POWELL	portrait		
B664	OIL'S WELL THAT ENDS WELL (sh)	YATES	RKO	1949
B665	I CAN'T REMEMBER (sh)	YATES	RKO	1949
B676	SWEET CHEAT (sh)	YATES	RKO	1949
B679	SHOCKING AFFAIR (sh)	YATES	RKO	1949
B693	HIGH AND DIZZY (sh)	YATES	RKO	1950
B-702	SEVEN GUNS TO MESA	DEIN	ALLIED ARTISTS	1958
B705	ROBERT TAYLOR	portrait		
B710	ROBERT TAYLOR	portrait		
B714	ROBERT TAYLOR	portrait		
B721	TEXAS TOUGH GUY (sh)	YATES	RKO	1950
B726	SPOOKY WOOKY (sh)	YATES	RKO	1950
B729	CHINA TOWN CHUMPS (sh)	YATES	RKO	1951

Movie Still Identification Book Ultimate Edition - Letters

CODE	TITLE/NAME	DIRECTOR/TYPE	STUDIO/DISTRIBUTOR	YEAR
B-752	BULLWHIP	JONES	ALLIED ARTISTS	1958
B756	LORD EPPING RETURNS (sh)	GOODWINS	RKO	1951
B-801	LEGION OF THE DOOMED	BROOKS	ALLIED ARTISTS	1958
B-802	ARSON FOR HIRE	BROOKS	ALLIED ARTISTS	1959
B1124	TED HEALY	portrait		
B1284	JAMES STEWART	portrait		
B1294	JAMES STEWART	portrait		
B1333	GRETA GARBO	portrait	MGM	
B1335	ERNESTINE SCHUMANN-HEINK	portrait		
B1337	GRETA GARBO	portrait	MGM	
B1361	GRETA GARBO	portrait	MGM	
B1397	ROBERT YOUNG	portrait		
B1583	CLARK GABLE	portrait		
B1913	EDMUND LOWE	portrait		
B1942	JEANETTE MACDONALD	portrait		
B1969	GRETA GARBO	portrait	MGM	
B1971	GRETA GARBO	portrait	MGM	
B2006	LILIAN BOND	portrait		
B2113	MYRNA LOY	portrait		
B2115	MYRNA LOY	portrait		
B2125	MYRNA LOY	portrait		
B2163	CHARLES BOYER	portrait		
B2189	LILIAN BOND	portrait	MGM	
B2198	MAUREEN O'SULLIVAN	portrait		
B2201	MAUREEN O'SULLIVAN	portrait		
B2203	MAUREEN O'SULLIVAN	portrait		
B2224	MAUREEN O'SULLIVAN	portrait		
B2254	CLARK GABLE	portrait		
B2259	CLARK GABLE	portrait		
B2276	ELEANOR POWELL	portrait	MGM	
B2442	FREDDIE BARTHOLOMEW	portrait		
B2517	LYNNE CARVER	portrait	MGM	
B2555	CLARK GABLE	portrait		
B2559	MYRNA LOY	portrait		
B2561	MYRNA LOY	portrait		
B2656	BERT LAHR	portrait		
B2741	GRETA GARBO	portrait	MGM	
B2754	GRETA GARBO	portrait	MGM	
B-2800	COPACABANA	GREEN	UNITED ARTISTS	1947
B2838	MAUREEN O'SULLIVAN	portrait		
B2933	NELSON EDDY	portrait		
B3023	MYRNA LOY	portrait		
B3082	CLARK GABLE	portrait		
B3103	JOHN BARRYMORE	portrait		
B3208	GRETA GARBO	portrait	MGM	
B3223	GRETA GARBO	portrait	MGM	
B3234	GRETA GARBO	portrait	MGM	
B3255	GRETA GARBO	portrait	MGM	
B3290	KAREN MORLEY	portrait		
B3297	GRETA GARBO	portrait	MGM	
B3319	GRETA GARBO	portrait	MGM	
B3479	FRANK MORGAN	portrait		
B3543	ROBERT MONTGOMERY	portrait		
B3547	ROBERT MONTGOMERY	portrait		
B3575	MYRNA LOY	portrait		
B3584	GRETA GARBO	portrait	MGM	
B3593	GRETA GARBO	portrait	MGM	
B3608	ROBERT YOUNG	portrait		
B3617	ROBERT YOUNG	portrait		
B3618	ROBERT YOUNG	portrait		
B3620	ROBERT YOUNG	portrait		
B3674	LENORE BUSHMAN	portrait		
B3674	LENORE BUSHMAN	portrait	MGM	
B3694	KAREN MORLEY	portrait		
B3830	HEDY LAMARR	portrait		
B3891	FAY HOLDEN	portrait		
B3960	LYNNE CARVER	portrait		
B4016	MARION DAVIES	portrait	MGM	
B4058	HEDY LAMARR	portrait		
B4073	RICHARD THORPE	portrait		

Movie Still Identification Book Ultimate Edition - Letters

CODE	TITLE/NAME	DIRECTOR/TYPE	STUDIO/DISTRIBUTOR	YEAR
B4078	SARA HADEN	portrait		
B4120	REGINALD OWEN	portrait		
B4181	MARIE DRESSLER	portrait		
B4189	MARIE DRESSLER	portrait		
B4207	FAY HOLDEN	portrait		
B4209	GREER GARSON	portrait		
B4213	GREER GARSON	portrait		
B4343	POLLY MORAN	portrait		
B4344	POLLY MORAN	portrait		
B4351	POLLY MORAN	portrait		
B4359	LIONEL BARRYMORE	portrait		
B4378	VEREE TEASDALE	portrait		
B4527	MAUREEN O'SULLIVAN	portrait		
B4533	MAUREEN O'SULLIVAN	portrait		
B4608	CLARK GABLE	portrait		
B4609	CLARK GABLE	portrait		
B4631	GREER GARSON	portrait		
B4637	GREER GARSON	portrait		
B4686	GREER GARSON	portrait		
B4713	GREER GARSON	portrait		
B4760	GRETA GARBO	portrait	MGM	
B4765	GRETA GARBO	portrait	MGM	
B4811	ILONA MASSEY	portrait		
B4954	HEDY LAMARR	portrait		
B4973	GRETA GARBO	portrait	MGM	
B4986	GRETA GARBO	portrait	MGM	
B4988	GRETA GARBO	portrait	MGM	
B5063	WALTER HUSTON	portrait		
B5071	ROBERT MONTGOMERY	portrait		
B5158	JEANETTE MACDONALD	portrait		
B5208	MARGARET SULLAVAN	portrait	MGM	
B5211	MARGARET SULLAVAN	portrait	MGM	
B5258	SHIRLEY TEMPLE	portrait		
B5291	LANA TURNER	portrait		
B5343	FAY HOLDEN	portrait	MGM	
B5460	MARGARET SULLAVAN	portrait	MGM	
B5463	MARGARET SULLAVAN	portrait	MGM	
B5464	MARGARET SULLAVAN	portrait	MGM	
B5465	MARGARET SULLAVAN	portrait	MGM	
B5473	MARGARET SULLAVAN	portrait		
B5497	GRETA GARBO	portrait	MGM	
B-5501	SHACK OUT ON 101	DEIN	ALLIED ARTISTS	1955
B5517	ELEANOR POWELL	portrait		
B5519	ELEANOR POWELL	portrait		
B5523	ANN SOTHERN	portrait		
B5539	ELEANOR POWELL	portrait		
B5542	ELEANOR POWELL	portrait		
B5552	JEANETTE MACDONALD	portrait		
B5566	KATHARINE HEPBURN	portrait	MGM	
B5614	BASIL RATHBONE	portrait		
B5617	VIRGINIA WEIDLER	portrait		
B5651	SUSAN PETERS	portrait		
B5722	MARJORIE MAIN	portrait		
B5723	MARJORIE MAIN	portrait		
B5724	MARJORIE MAIN	portrait		
B5876	NELSON EDDY	portrait		
B5882	MAUREEN O'SULLIVAN	portrait		
B5900	BARBARA STANWYCK/ROBERT TAYLOR	portrait	MGM	
B5917	KATHRYN GRAYSON	portrait		
B6260	LEWIS STONE	portrait		
B6558	MYRNA LOY	portrait		
B6710	LIONEL BARRYMORE	portrait		
B6835	CLARK GABLE	portrait		
B7108	FRANK MORGAN	portrait		
B7230	LUPE VELEZ	portrait		
B7291	LEWIS STONE	portrait		
B7343	FLORINE MCKINNEY	portrait		
B7472	POLLY MORAN	portrait		
B7482	POLLY MORAN	portrait		
B7923	GRETA GARBO	portrait	MGM	

Movie Still Identification Book Ultimate Edition - Letters

CODE	TITLE/NAME	DIRECTOR/TYPE	STUDIO/DISTRIBUTOR	YEAR
B7970	JIMMY DURANTE	portrait	MGM	
B7991	JIMMY DURANTE	portrait	MGM	
B8021	OTTO KRUGER	portrait		
B8227	LEWIS STONE	portrait		
B8230	LEWIS STONE	portrait		
B8284	MURIEL EVANS	portrait		
B8477	MAURICE CHEVALIER	portrait	MGM	
B8677	GWEN LEE	portrait		
B8836	FRANK MORGAN	portrait		
B8837	FRANK MORGAN	portrait		
B8846	FRANK MORGAN	portrait		
B8942	CLARK GABLE	portrait		
B9015	LUPE VELEZ	portrait		
B9069	MYRNA LOY	portrait		
B9630	ANITA PAGE	portrait		
B9678	POLLY MORAN	portrait		
B9800	ROSALIND RUSSELL	portrait	MGM	
B9843	BASIL RATHBONE	portrait		
B9896	JACKIE COOPER	portrait		
B9946	JEANETTE MACDONALD	portrait		
B9953	JEANETTE MACDONALD	portrait		
B9963	JEANETTE MACDONALD	portrait		
B10036	LIONEL BARRYMORE	portrait		
B10847	ROBERT MONTGOMERY	portrait		
B10902	GWEN LEE	portrait		
B11075	GRETA GARBO	portrait	MGM	
B11084	GRETA GARBO	portrait	MGM	
BA	ACQUANETTA (BURNU ACQUANETTA)	portrait	UNIVERSAL	1940s
BA	B&A PROD. (BERTIES OSTRER ALBERT FENNELL)	studio		UK
BA	BACHELOR APARTMENT	SHERMAN	RKO	1931
BA	BARON OF ARIZONA	FULLER	LIPPERT	1950
BA	BATTLE OF ALGIERS (ITALY: BATTAGLIA DI ALGERI)	PONTECORVO	ALLIED ARTISTS	1968
BA	BERMUDA AFFAIR (UK)	SUTHERLAND	COLUMBIA	1956
BA	BETTE/BETTY ARLEN	portrait	RKO	1950s
BA	BETTY ALEXANDER	portrait	RKO, WARNER BROS.	1940s
BA	BEULAH BONDI	portrait		
BA	BILLY ANDREWS	portrait	RKO	1950s
BA	BIRDMAN OF ALCATRAZ	FRANKENHEIMER	UNITED ARTISTS	1962
ba	BLOOD ARROW	WARREN	20th CENTURY FOX	1958
BA	BORN AGAIN	RAPPER	AVCO EMBASSY	1978
BA	BREAKING AWAY	YATES	20th CENTURY FOX	1979
BA	BRIAN AHERNE	portrait		
BA	BRITISH AGENT	CURTIZ	WARNER BROS	1934
BA	BROKEN ARROW	WOO	20th CENTURY FOX	1996
BA	BUD ABBOTT	portrait	UNIVERSAL	1940s
BA	EVERY WHICH WAY BUT LOOSE	FARGO	WARNER BROS	1978
BA	JULIE ADAMS (NEE BETTY ADAMS)	portrait	UNIVERSAL	1950s
BA	NIGHT SPOT	CABANNE	RKO	1938
BA	SHADOW OF FEAR (UK: BEFORE I WAKE)	ROGELL	UNITED ARTISTS	1954
BA	SHADOW OF FEAR (UK)	MORRIS	BUTCHER'S	1963
BA1	GREEN SCARF (UK)	O'FERRALL	AAP	1954
BAB	BEAUTY AND THE BARGE (UK)	EDWARDS	WARDOUR	1937
BAB	BEAUTY AND THE BEAST	CAHN	UNITED ARTISTS	1962
B-AE	8 1/2	FELLINI	EMBASSY	1963
BAF	BUTTERFLIES ARE FREE	KATSELAS	COLUMBIA	1972
BAL	BALCONY	STRICK	CONTINENTAL	1963
BALL	FIVE WEEKS IN A BALLOON	ALLEN	20th CENTURY FOX	1962
BAN	BANDIT OF ZHOBE	GILLING	COLUMBIA	1959
BAN	ZARAK	YOUNG	COLUMBIA	1956
BAP	PRIVATE POTTER (UK)	WREDE	MGM	1962
BAR	BARBARIANS	DEODATO	CANNON	1987
BAR	BIRDMAN OF ALCATRAZ	FRANKENHEIMER	UNITED ARTISTS	1962
BARKER1	WHEN THE DOOR OPENED	BARKER	FOX FILM	1925
BAT	BATMAN	BURTON	WARNER BROS	1989
BAT	GUNFIGHT AT DODGE CITY	NEWMAN	UNITED ARTISTS	1959
BAT 21	BAT 21	MARKLE	TRI STAR	1988
BAU	BUSINESS AS USUAL	AN-BARRETT	CANNON	1988
BB	ADV OF BUCKAROO BANZAI	RICHTER	20th CENTURY FOX	1984
BB	AND THE SAME TO YOU (UK)	POLLOCK	MONARCH	1960
BB	BABES IN BAGDAD	ULMER	UNITED ARTISTS	1952

Movie Still Identification Book Ultimate Edition - Letters

CODE	TITLE/NAME	DIRECTOR/TYPE	STUDIO/DISTRIBUTOR	YEAR
BB	BABY AND THE BATTLESHIP (UK)	LEWIS	DCA	1956
BB	BABY BOOM	SHYER	UNITED ARTISTS	1987
BB	BACHELOR BAIT	STEVENS	RKO	1934
BB	BACK-ROOM BOY (UK)	MASON	GFD	1942
BB	BALLAD IN BLUE (BLUES FOR LOVERS)	HENREID	20th CENTURY FOX	1964
BB	BALTIMORE BULLET	MILLER	AVCO EMBASSY	1980
BB	BAMBOO BLONDE	MANN	RKO	1946
BB	BARBARA BATES	portrait	WARNER BROS	
BB	BARBARA BEDFORD	portrait	FIRST NAT'L, METRO	
BB	BARBARA BEL GEDDES	portrait	RKO	late 40s
BB	BARBARA BRITTON	portrait	UNITED ARTISTS	
BB	BATTLE AT BLOODY BEACH	COLEMAN	20th CENTURY FOX	1961
BB	BATTLE OF THE BULGE	ANNAKIN	WARNER BROS	1965
BB	BEAST OF BLOOD	ROMERO	HEMISPHERE	1971
BB	BEAU BANDIT	HILLYER	RKO	1930
BB	BEAU BRUMMEL	BEAUMONT	WARNER BROS	1924
BB	BECKY BROWN	portrait	WARNER BROS	1940s
BB	BENEDICT BOGEAUS PRODUCTIONS	studio		
BB	BERNARD BUFFET	portrait		
BB	BETTY BLYTHE	portrait		
BB	BEVERLY BAYNE	portrait	WARNER BROS	
BB	BIG BLOCKADE (UK)	FREND	UNITED ARTISTS	1942
BB	BIG BLUFF	DENNY	TOWER PROD. (states rights)	1933
BB	BIG BLUFF	W. L. WILDER	UNITED ARTISTS	1955
BB	BIG BOODLE	WILSON	UNITED ARTISTS	1957
BB	BIG BOY	CROSLAND	WARNER BROS	1930
BB	BIG BREAK	STRICK	MADISON	1953
BB	BILLIE BURKE	portrait	RKO	1930s-40s
BB	BILLY & BOBBY MAUCH	portrait	WARNER BROS	
BB	BINNIE BARNES	portrait	UNIVERSAL	1930s-40s
BB	BITE THE BULLET	BROOKS	COLUMBIA	1975
BB	BLACK BIRD	GILER	COLUMBIA	1975
BB	BLACKBEARD THE PIRATE	WALSH	RKO	1952
BB	BLISS OF MRS. BLOSSOM (UK)	MCGRATH	PARAMOUNT	1968
BB	BLONDE BAIT	WILLIAMS	ASSOCIATED FILM	1956
BB	BOBBY BREEN	portrait	RKO	late 30s
BB	BOEING BOEING	RICH	PARAMOUNT	1965
BB	BOLD AND THE BRAVE	FOSTER	RKO	1956
BB	BOY IN BLUE	JARROTT	20th CENTURY FOX	1985
BB	BOYS FROM BRAZIL	SCHAFFNER	20th CENTURY FOX	1978
BB	BRIGITTE BARDOT	portrait	UNITED ARTISTS	
BB	BROADWAY BUTTERFLY	BEAUDINE	WARNER BROS	1925
BB	BROKEN BLOSSOMS (UK)	BRAHM	TWICKENHAM (UK)	1936
BB	BRONCO BULLFROG (UK)	PLATTS-MILLS	NEW YORKER	1969
BB	BROTHER RAT AND A BABY	ENRIGHT	WARNER BROS	1940
BB	BRUCE BENNETT	portrait	UA, WARNER BROS	
BB	BUFFALO BILL IN TOMAHAWK TERRITORY	RAY	UNITED ARTISTS	1952
BB	BUSTER AND BILLIE	PETRIE	COLUMBIA	1974
BB	RETURN OF BOSTON BLACKIE	HOYT	FILMS DIVISION	1927
BB	TIMES SQUARE PLAYBOY	MCGANN	WARNER BROS	1936
BB	YOUNG DONOVAN'S KID	NIBLO	RKO	1931
BB	WILLIAM BOYD	portrait	PARAMOUNT	
BB1	BRIDGE OF SAN LUIS REY	LEE	UNITED ARTISTS	1944
BB1	KID FOR TWO FARTHINGS (UK)	REED	LOPERT	1955
BB2	RICHARD THE 3RD (UK)	OLIVIER	LOPPERT	1955
BB-3	STORM OVER THE NILE	ZORDA, YOUNG	COLUMBIA	1955
BB-13-400	DARK WATERS	DE TOTH	UNITED ARTISTS	1944
BB-14-400	CAPTAIN KIDD	LEE	UNITED ARTISTS	1945
BB-14-900	DIARY OF A CHAMBERMAID	RENOIR	UNITED ARTISTS	1946
BB-210	TOO MANY WOMEN	RAY	PRC	1942
BB-212	HOUSE OF ERRORS	RAY	PRC	1942
BBA	BRING 'EM BACK ALIVE	ELLIOTT	RKO	1932
BBC	BLESS THE BEASTS AND CHILDREN	KRAMER	COLUMBIA	1971
BBD	SHE COULDN'T SAY NO	BACON	RKO	1954
BBE	BATTLE BENEATH THE EARTH (UK)	TULLY	MGM	1967
BBG	BELL-BOTTOM GEORGE (UK)	VARNEL	COLUMBIA	1944
BBG	BIG BUSINESS GIRL	SEITER	WARNER BROS	1931
BBH	BEAVIS & BUTTHEAD DO AMERICA	JUDGE	GEFFEN	1996
BBI	A KID FOR TWO FARTHINGS	REED	LOPERT	1956
BBI	BIRDS, BEES AND THE ITALIANS (IT)	GERMI	WARNER BROS	1965

- 21 -

Movie Still Identification Book Ultimate Edition - Letters

CODE	TITLE/NAME	DIRECTOR/TYPE	STUDIO/DISTRIBUTOR	YEAR
BB1	BRIDGE OF SAN LUIS REY	LEE	UNITED ARTISTS	1944
BBI	BUFFALO BILL AND THE INDIANS	ALTMAN	UNITED ARTISTS	1976
BBL	BLOOD AND BLACK LACE (IT)	BAVA	MONOGRAM	1965
BBL	BYE BYE LOVE	WEISMAN	20th CENTURY FOX	1995
BBM	BEST OF THE BADMEN	RUSSELL	RKO	1951
BBS	BACHELOR AND THE BOBBYSOXER	REIS	RKO	1946
BBS	BATTLE BEYOND THE SUN (RUS)	KARZHUKOV	AIP	1962
BBS	DANGEROUS PROFESSION	TETZLAFF	RKO	1949
BB-X	BOYS FROM BRAZIL	SCHAFFNER	20th CENTURY FOX	1978
BC	BAD COMPANY	BENTON	PARAMOUNT	1972
BC	BANDITS OF CORSICA	NAZARRO	UNITED ARTISTS	1953
BC	BARBARA CHALLIS	portrait	UNIVERSAL	
BC	BAREFOOT CONTESSA	MANKIEWICZ	UNITED ARTISTS	1954
BC	BENJAMIN CHRISTENSEN OR CHRISTIANSEN	portrait	MGM	1920s
BC	BERNICE CLAIRE	portrait	FN	
BC	BETTY COMPSON	portrait	WARNER BROS	1920s-30s
BC	BIG CAPER	STEVENS	UNITED ARTISTS	1957
BC	BIG COUNTRY	WYLER	UNITED ARTISTS	1958
BC	BILL CODY	portrait		
BC	BING CROSBY	portrait		
BC	BIRDCAGE	NICHOLS	UNITED ARTISTS	1996
BC	BLIND CORNER/US: MAN IN THE DARK (UK)	COMFORT	UNIVERSAL	1965
BC	BOB CROSBY	portrait	RKO	1940s-50s
BC	BREAK IN THE CIRCLE (UK)	GUEST	20TH CENTURY FOX	1955
BC	BRODERICK CRAWFORD	portrait	UNIVERSAL	
BC	BRUCE CABOT	portrait	FOX, PAR, RKO, UA, UNI	
BC	BULLET CODE	HOWARD	RKO	1940
BC	BUSH CHRISTMAS (UK)	SMART	UNIVERSAL	1947
BC	BUSTER COLLIER	portrait		
BC	BUSTER CRABBE	portrait	UNIV	
BC	KID FROM KOKOMO	SEILER	WARNER BROS	1939
BC	ROBERT CONRAD	portrait	WARNER BROS	
BC	SUNDAYS AND CYBELE (FR)	BOURGUIGNON	COLUMBIA	1963
BC-1	GREAT JOHN L.	TUTTLE	UNITED ARTISTS	1945
BC-1	RETURN OF THE SCARLET PIMPERNEL	SCHWARZ	UNITED ARTISTS	1937
BC-72	BILLY THE KID WANTED	NEWFIELD	PRC	1941
BC-74	BILLY THE KID ROUNDUP	NEWFIELD	PRC	1941
BC-78	BILLY THE KID TRAPPED	NEWFIELD	PRC	1942
BC-82	BILLY THE KID SMOKING GUNS	NEWFIELD	PRC	1943
BC-83	SHERIFF OF SAGE VALLEY	NEWFIELD	PRC	1943
BC-86	LAW AND ORDER	NEWFIELD	PRC	1942
BC-93	BILLY THE KID - THE MYSTERIOUS RIDER	NEWFIELD	PRC	1943
BC-95	BILLY THE KID - THE KID RIDES AGAIN	NEWFIELD	PRC	1943
BC-96	BILLY THE KID - FUGITIVE OF THE PLAINS	NEWFIELD	PRC	1943
BC-97	WILD HORSE RUSTLERS	NEWFIELD	TIFFANY	1943
BC-98	BILLY THE KID - WESTERN CYCLONE	NEWFIELD	PRC	1943
BC-101	BILLY THE KID - RENEGADES	NEWFIELD	PRC	1943
BC-102	BILLY THE KID - BLAZING FRONTIER	NEWFIELD	PRC	1943
BC-104	BILLY THE KID - CATTLE STAMPEDE	NEWFIELD	PRC	1943
BC-107	DEVIL RIDERS	NEWFIELD	PRC	1943
BC-110	NABONGA	NEWFIELD	PRC	1944
BC-111	FRONTIER OUTLAWS	NEWFIELD	PRC	1944
BC-111	DEVIL RIDERS (mistake? BC-107)	NEWFIELD	PRC	1943
BC-112	THUNDERING GUN STINGERS	NEWFIELD	PRC	1944
BC-114	VALLEY OF VENGEANCE	NEWFIELD	PRC	1944
BC-115	FUZZY SETTLES DOWN	NEWFIELD	PRC	1944
BC-116	RUSTLERS HIDEOUT	NEWFIELD	PRC	1944
BC-118	WILD HORSE PHANTOM	NEWFIELD	PRC	1944
BC-119	OATH OF VENGEANCE	NEWFIELD	PRC	1944
BCC	BOYS OF COMPANY C	FURIE	COLUMBIA	1978
B-COL-1	SHE COULDN'T TAKE IT	GARNETT	COLUMBIA	1935
B-COL-2	MUSIC GOES ROUND	SCHERTZINGER	COLUMBIA	1936
B-COL-3	CRIME AND PUNISHMENT	STERNBERG	COLUMBIA	1935
B-COL-4	GRAND EXIT	KENTON	COLUMBIA	1935
B-COL-5	ESCAPE FROM DEVIL'S ISLAND	ROGELL	COLUMBIA	1935
B-COL-6	ONE WAY TICKET	BIBERMAN	COLUMBIA	1935
B-COL-7	LONE WOLF RETURNS	NEILL	COLUMBIA	1935
B-COL-8	IF YOU COULD ONLY COOK	SEITER	COLUMBIA	1935
B-COL-9	HELL-SHIP MORGAN	LEDERMAN	COLUMBIA	1936
B-COL-10	YOU MAY BE NEXT	ROGELL	COLUMBIA	1936

Movie Still Identification Book Ultimate Edition - Letters

CODE	TITLE/NAME	DIRECTOR/TYPE	STUDIO/DISTRIBUTOR	YEAR
B-COL-11	KING STEPS OUT	VON STERNBERG	COLUMBIA	1936
B-COL-12	LADY OF SECRETS	GERING	COLUMBIA	1936
B-COL-13	CALLING OF DAN MATHEWS	ROSEN	COLUMBIA	1935
B-COL-14	DEVIL'S SQUADRON	KENTON	COLUMBIA	1936
B-COL-15	DON'T GAMBLE WITH LOVE	MURPHY	COLUMBIA	1936
B-COL-16	PRIDE OF THE MARINES	LEDERMAN	COLUMBIA	1936
B-COL-17	END OF THE TRAIL	KENTON	COLUMBIA	1936
B-COL-18	ROAMING LADY	ROGELL	COLUMBIA	1936
B-COL-19	MINE WITH THE IRON DOOR	HOWARD	COLUMBIA	1936
B-COL-20	AND SO THEY WERE MARRIED	NUGENT	COLUMBIA	1936
B-COL-21	LOST HORIZON	CAPRA	COLUMBIA	1937
B-COL-22	TRAPPED BY TELEVISION	LORD	COLUMBIA	1936
B-COL-23	BLACKMAILER	WILES	COLUMBIA	1936
B-COL-25	COUNTERFEIT	KENTON	COLUMBIA	1936
B-COL-27	MEET NERO WOLFE	BIBERMAN	COLUMBIA	1936
B-COL-27	MR. DEEDS GOES TO TOWN	CAPRA	COLUMBIA	1936
B-COL-29	THEODORA GOES WILD	BOLESLAWSKI	COLUMBIA	1936
B-COL-32	TWO FISTED GENTLEMAN	WILES	COLUMBIA	1936
B-COL-33	THEY MET IN A TAXI	GREEN	COLUMBIA	1936
B-COL-35	LAWLESS RIDERS	BENNET	COLUMBIA	1935
B-COL-35	WHEN YOU'RE IN LOVE	RISKIN	COLUMBIA	1937
B-COL-60	GUARD THAT GIRL	HILLYER	COLUMBIA	1935
B-COL-61	CASE OF THE MISSING MAN	LEDERMAN	COLUMBIA	1935
B-COL-62	TOO TOUGH TO KILL	LEDERMAN	COLUMBIA	1935
B-COL-63	DANGEROUS INTRIGUE	SELMAN	COLUMBIA	1936
B-COL-64	PANIC ON THE AIR	LEDERMAN	COLUMBIA	1936
B-COL-65	FINAL HOUR	LEDERMAN	COLUMBIA	1936
B-COL-66	SHAKEDOWN	SELMAN	COLUMBIA	1936
B-COL-67	ALIBI FOR MURDER	LEDERMAN	COLUMBIA	1936
B-COL-68	KILLER AT LARGE	SELMAN	COLUMBIA	1936
B-COL-70	WESTERN FRONTIER	HERMAN	COLUMBIA	1935
B-COL-74	CATTLE THIEF	BENNET	COLUMBIA	1936
B-COL-75	HEROES OF THE RANGE	BENNET	COLUMBIA	1936
B-COL-76	AVENGING WATERS	BENNET	COLUMBIA	1936
B-COL-77	FUGITIVE SHERIFF	BENNET	COLUMBIA	1936
B-COL-80	GALLANT DEFENDER	SELMAN	COLUMBIA	1935
B-COL-81	MYSTERIOUS AVENGER	SELMAN	COLUMBIA	1936
B-COL-82	STAMPEDE	BEEBE	COLUMBIA	1936
B-COL-83	SECRET PATROL	SELMAN	COLUMBIA	1936
B-COL-84	TUGBOAT PRINCESS	SELMAN	COLUMBIA	1936
B-COL-85	LUCKY FUGITIVES - CAN: STOP, LOOK AND LOVE)	GRINDE	COLUMBIA	1936
B-COL-157	HIS OLD FLAME (sh)	HORNE	COLUMBIA	1935
B-COL-159	HORSE COLLARS (sh)	BRUCKMAN	COLUMBIA	1935
B-COL-160	RESTLESS KNIGHTS (sh)	LAMONT	COLUMBIA	1935
B-COL-161	I'M A FATHER (sh)	HORNE	COLUMBIA	1935
B-COL-162	HIS BRIDAL SWEET (sh)	GOULDING	COLUMBIA	1935
B-COL-163	POP GOES THE EASEL (sh)	LORD	COLUMBIA	1935
B-COL-165	UNCIVIL WARRIORS (sh)	LORD	COLUMBIA	1935
B-COL-166	LEATHER NECKER (sh)	RIPLEY	COLUMBIA	1935
B-COL-167	GUM SHOES (sh)	LORD	COLUMBIA	1935
B-COL-168	PARDON MY SCOTCH (sh) (changed)	LORD	COLUMBIA	1935
B-COL-169	TRAMP TRAMP TRAMP (sh)	LAMONT	COLUMBIA	1935
B-COL-171	ALIMONY ACHES (sh)	LAMONT	COLUMBIA	1935
B-COL-172	STAGE FRIGHTS (sh)	RAY	COLUMBIA	1935
B-COL-173	DO YOUR STUFF (sh)	PARROTT	COLUMBIA	1935
B-COL-174	CAPTAIN HITS THE CEILING (sh)	LAMONT	COLUMBIA	1935
B-COL-175	GOBS OF TROUBLE (sh)	LORD	COLUMBIA	1935
B-COL-200	OH, MY NERVES! (sh)	LORD	COLUMBIA	1935
B-COL-202	IT ALWAYS HAPPENS (sh)	LORD	COLUMBIA	1935
B-COL-203	HIS MARRIAGE MIX-UP (sh)	WHITE	COLUMBIA	1935
B-COL-204	STAR GAZING (sh)	RUBIN	COLUMBIA	1935
B-COL-205	YOO HOO HOLLYWOOD (sh)	RUBIN	COLUMBIA	1935
B-COL-206	PARDON MY SCOTCH (sh)	LORD	COLUMBIA	1935
B-COL-207	HOI POLLOI (sh)	LORD	COLUMBIA	1935
B-COL-208	HONEYMOON BRIDGE (sh)	LORD	COLUMBIA	1935
B-COL-209	HOT PAPRIKA (sh)	WHITE	COLUMBIA	1935
B-COL-210	THREE LITTLE BEERS (sh)	LORD	COLUMBIA	1935
B-COL-211	I DON'T REMEMBER (sh)	WHITE	COLUMBIA	1935
B-COL-213	MOVIE MANIACS (sh)	LORD	COLUMBIA	1936
B COL-217	DISORDER IN THE COURT (sh)	WHITE	COLUMBIA	1936

Movie Still Identification Book Ultimate Edition - Letters

CODE	TITLE/NAME	DIRECTOR/TYPE	STUDIO/DISTRIBUTOR	YEAR
B-COL-219	CHAMP'S A CHUMP (sh)	WHITE	COLUMBIA	1936
B-COL-220	MISTER SMARTY (sh)	WHITE	COLUMBIA	1936
B-COL-221	SLIPPERY SILKS (changed to 252)	WHITE	COLUMBIA	1936
B-COL-222	CAUGHT IN THE ACT	LORD	COLUMBIA	1936
B-COL-223	PAIN IN THE PULLMAN (sh)	WHITE	COLUMBIA	1936
B-COL-224	FALSE ALARMS (sh) (changed to 250)	LORD	COLUMBIA	1936
B-COL-225	HALF SHOT SHOOTERS (sh)	WHITE	COLUMBIA	1936
B-COL-226	WHOOPS, I'M AN INDIAN! (sh) (changed to 251)	WHITE	COLUMBIA	1936
B-COL-250	FALSE ALARMS (sh)	LORD	COLUMBIA	1936
B-COL-251	WHOOPS, I'M AN INDIAN! (sh)	WHITE	COLUMBIA	1936
B-COL-252	SLIPPERY SILKS	WHITE	COLUMBIA	1936
B-COL-253	AM I HAVING FUN! (sh)	WHITE	COLUMBIA	1936
B-COL-254	AY TANK AY GO (sh)	LORD	COLUMBIA	1936
B-COL-255	OH, DUCHESS! (sh)	LAMONT	COLUMBIA	1936
B-COL-256	LOVE COMES TO MOONEYVILLE (sh)	WHITE	COLUMBIA	1936
B-COL-257	FIBBING FIBBERS (sh)	WHITE	COLUMBIA	1936
BCP	ABIE'S IRISH ROSE	SUTHERLAND	UNITED ARTISTS	1946
BCP	BIRD WITH THE CRYSTAL PLUMAGE (IT)	ARGENTO	UNIVERSAL MARION	1970
BCT	ELIZABETH THREATT	portrait	RKO	
BCTA	BOB AND CAROL AND TED AND ALICE	MAZURSKI	COLUMBIA	1970
BCX	BRUCE CABOT	portrait	MGM	
BD	ARIZONIAN	VIDOR	RKO	1935
BD	BACK FROM THE DEAD	WARREN	20th CENTURY FOX	1957
BD	BACKGROUND TO DANGER	WALSH	WARNER BROS	1943
BD	BARBARA DARROW	portrait	RKO	1950s
BD	BEAUTIFUL AND THE DAMNED	SEITER	WARNER BROS	1922
BD	BEBE DANIELS	portrait	FN, WARNER BROS,	
BD	BEBE DANIELS FILMS		REALART	early 1920s
BD	BELLA DONNA (UK)	MILTON	OLYMPIC	1934
BD	BEST DEFENSE	HUYCK	PARAMOUNT	1984
BD	BETSY DRAKE	portrait	RKO	
BD	BETTE DAVIS	portrait	WARNER BROS	
BD	BILLIE DOVE	portrait	FIRST NATIONAL, METRO	
BD	BLIND DATE	EDWARDS	TRI STAR	1987
BD	BLONDES FOR DANGER (UK)	RAYMOND	BRITISH LION	1938
BD	BLOOD OF DRACULA	STROCK	AIP	1957
BD	BOBBY DARIN	portrait	UNIVERSAL	
BD	BRIAN DONLEVY	portrait		
BD	BROADWAY DANNY ROSE	ALLEN	ORION	1984
BD	BROWN DERBY	HINES	FIRST NATIONAL	1926
BD	BULLET FOR JOEY	ALLEN	UNITED ARTISTS	1955
BD	BWANA DEVIL	OBOLER	UNITED ARTISTS	1952
BD	OH LADY, LADY	CAMPBELL	REALART	1920
BD	TEMPTATION	PICHEL	UNIVERSAL	1946
BD	TOO YOUNG TO MARRY	LEROY	WARNER BROS	1931
BD2	OH, LADY, LADY	CAMPBELL	REALART	1920
BDB	BILLION DOLLAR BRAIN (UK)	RUSSELL	UNITED ARTISTS	1967
BDE	BROADWAY AFTER DARK	BELL	WARNER BROS	1924
BDF	BOBBY DEERFIELD	POLLACK	WARNER BROS	1977
BDG	BADGE 373	KOCH	PARAMOUNT	1973
BDH	BACKDOOR TO HELL	HELLMAN	20th CENTURY FOX	1964
BDH	BIG DOLL HOUSE	HILL	NEW WORLD	1971
BDMS	BIG DEAL ON MADONNA STREET (IT: I SOLITI IGNOTI)	MONICELLI	UMPO	1958
BDR	BORDER RANGERS	BERKE	LIPPERT	1950
BDR	BROADWAY DANNY ROSE	ALLEN	ORION	1984
BDS	BANG THE DRUMS SLOWLY	HANCOCK	PARAMOUNT	1973
BE	BEGINNING OF THE END	GORDON	REPUBLIC	1957
BE	BERLIN EXPRESS	TOURNEUR	RKO	1948
BE	BLESSED EVENT	DEL RUTH	WARNER BROS	1932
BE	BRAIN EATERS	VESOTA	AIP	1958
BE	FIRST TIME	NEILSON	UNITED ARTISTS	1968
BE	WILL BILL ELLIOTT	portrait	REP	
BE-1	IN EARLY ARIZONA (ELLIOTT series)	LEVERING	COLUMBIA	1938
BE-2	FRONTIERS OF '49	LEVERING	COLUMBIA	1939
BE-3	LONESTAR PIONEERS	LEVERING	COLUMBIA	1939
BE-4	LAW COMES TO TEXAS	LEVERING	COLUMBIA	1939
BE-399	PHOENIX CITY STORY	KARLSON	ALLIED ARTISTS	1955
BEA	BLESS 'EM ALL (UK)	HILL	ADELPHI	1949
BEAU 1	ONE INCREASING PURPOSE	BEAUMONT	FOX FILM	1927
BEAU 2	FUGITIVES	BEAUDINE	FOX FILM	1929

Movie Still Identification Book Ultimate Edition - Letters

CODE	TITLE/NAME	DIRECTOR/TYPE	STUDIO/DISTRIBUTOR	YEAR
BEAU-4	SANDY	BEAUMONT	FOX FILM	1926
BEAU-7	SECRET STUDIO	BEAUMONT	FOX FILM	1927
B-E-COL 4	LAW COMES TO TEXAS	LEVERING	COLUMBIA	1939
BEL	BELLISSIMA (IT)	VISCONTI	IFE	1952
BEN-4	HONESTY - THE BEST POLICY	BENNETT	FOX FILM	1926
BF	BABY FACE	GREEN	WARNER BROS	1933
BF	BARBARA FULLER	portrait	REPUBLIC	1940s-50s
BF	BARFLY	SCHROEDER	CANNON	1987
BF	BARRY FITZGERALD	portrait	UNIVERSAL	
BF	BARTON FINK	COEN BROS	20th CENTURY FOX	1991
BF	BATMAN FOREVER	SCHUMACHER	WARNER BROS	1995
BF	BETTY FIELD	portrait	UA, UNIVERSAL, WB	
BF	BETTY FURNESS	portrait	MGM, RKO	
BF	BEYOND THE TIME BARRIER	ULMER	AIP	1960
BF	BIG FOOT	SLATZER	UNIVERSAL	1971
BF	BLOOD FEAST	LEWIS	BOX OFFICE SPECTACULARS	1963
BF	BLOOD FIEND (UK: THEATRE OF DEATH)	GALLU	HEMISPHERE	1967
BF	BORN FREE (UK)	HILL	COLUMBIA	1966
BF	BOULDER DAM	MCDONALD	WARNER BROS	1936
BF	BOY WHO CAUGHT A CROOK	CAHN	UNITED ARTISTS	1961
BF	BOYFRIEND (UK)	RUSSELL	MGM	1971
BF	BULLET AND THE FLESH		COLUMBIA	1972
BF1	TRUTH ABOUT WOMEN (UK)	BOX	CONTINENTAL	1957
BF3	MAN IN THE ROAD (UK)	COMFORT	REPUBLIC	1956
BF3	ROCK AROUND THE WORLD (UK: TOMMY STEELE STORY)	BRYANT	AIP	1957
BF4	TOO YOUNG TO LOVE (UK)	BOX	GO	1960
BF5	MAILBAG ROBBERY (UK: FLYING SCOT)	BENNETT	TUDOR	1957
BF-507	HOUSE OF INTRIGUE (IT)	COLETTI	MONOGRAM	1956
BFA	BEAUTY FOR THE ASKING	TRYON	RKO	1939
BFE	BACK FROM ETERNITY	FARROW	RKO	1956
BFE	BETRAYAL FROM THE EAST	BERKE	RKO	1945
BFG	BOUND FOR GLORY	ASHBY	UNITED ARTISTS	1976
BFL1	CARRY ON SERGEANT (UK)	THOMAS	GOVERNOR	1958
BFL-9	PLEASE TURN OVER (UK)	THOMAS	COLUMBIA	1959
BFM	BRIDES OF FU MANCHU (UK)	SHARP	SEVEN ARTS	1966
BFM6	ON APPROVAL (UK)	BROOK	ENGLISH	1944
BFPI	CARRY ON SERGEANT	THOMAS	ANGLO AMALGAMATED (UK)	1958
BFS	ADVENTURE IN BALTIMORE	WALLACE	RKO	1949
BFW	WATERLOO ROAD (UK)	GILLIAT	EAGLE-LION	1945
BG	BAD GIRLS	KAPLAN	20th CENTURY FOX	1994
BG	BADGER'S GREEN (UK)	BRUNEL	PARAMOUNT BRITISH	1934
BG	BADGER'S GREEN (UK)	IRWIN	GFD	1949
BG	BENNY GOODMAN	portrait	MCA MUSIC	
BG	BETTY GILLETTE	portrait	FN/WARNER BROS	
BG	BETTY GRABLE	portrait	RKO	
BG	BIG GAME	NICHOLS JR., KILLY	RKO	1936
BG	BIG GUNDOWN (SP)	SOLLIMA	COLUMBIA	1966
BG	BILLY GILBERT	portrait	RKO	
BG	BLACK GLOVE (UK: FACE THE MUSIC)	FISHER	LIPPERT	1954
BG	BLACK GUNN	HARTFORD-DAVIS	COLUMBIA	1973
BG	BLUE GARDENIA	LANG	WARNER BROS	1953
BG	BODYGUARD	FLEISCHER	RKO	1948
BG	BODYGUARD	JACKSON	WARNER BROS	1992
BG	BONITA GRANVILLE	portrait	MGM, RKO, UNIV, WB	1930s-40s
BG	BONITA GRANVILLE	portrait	WARNER BROS	
BG	BOP GIRL GOES CALYPSO	KOCH	UNITED ARTISTS	1957
BG	BOY MEETS GIRL	BACON	WARNER BROS	1938
BG	BROADWAY GONDOLIER	BACON	WARNER BROS	1935
BG	BRUCE GUERIN	portrait	WARNER BROS	
BG	DOWN IN SAN DIEGO	SINCLAIR	MGM	1941
BG	GIRL FROM GAY PAREE	GOLDSTONE, GREGOR	TIFFANY	1927
BG	PRIDE OF THE BLUE GRASS	MCGANN	WARNER BROS	1939
BG1	RETURN OF THE SCARLET PIMPERNEL (UK)	SCHWARZ	UNITED ARTISTS	1937
BGD	BELLS GO DOWN (UK)	DEARDEN	UNITED ARTISTS	1943
BGM	BORDER G-MAN	HOWARD	RKO	1938
BH	(CC) BURR & (JOHNNY) HINES ENTERPRISES		FN	1920s
BH	BAND OF THE HAND	GLASER	TRI STAR	1986
BH	BARBARA HALE	portrait	RKO	1940s
BH	BEAST OF HOLLOW MOUNTAIN	NASSOUR, RODRIGUEZ	UNITED ARTISTS	1956
BH	BENITA HUME	portrait	MGM	1930s

Movie Still Identification Book Ultimate Edition - Letters

CODE	TITLE/NAME	DIRECTOR/TYPE	STUDIO/DISTRIBUTOR	YEAR
BH	BENITA HUME	portrait	RKO	
BH	BEVERLY HILLBILLIES	SPHEERIS	20th CENTURY FOX	1993
BH	BIG HEARTED HERBERT	KEIGHLEY	WARNER BROS	1934
BH	BIG HOUSE, U.S.A.	KOCH	UNITED ARTISTS	1955
BH	BILLY HALOP	portrait	WARNER BROS	
BH	BILLY TWO HATS	KOTCHEFF	UNITED ARTISTS	1974
BH	BLACK FURY	CURTIZ	WARNER BROS	1935
BH	BOBBED HAIR	CROSLAND	WARNER BROS	1925
BH	BREAK OF HEARTS	MOELLER	RKO	1935
BH	BRITANNIA HOSPITAL	ANDERSON	UNITED ARTISTS	1982
BH	BROADWAY HOSTESS	MCDONALD	WARNER BROS	1935
BH	BROKEN HEARTS OF HOLLYWOOD	BACON	WARNER BROS	1926
BH	BROTHERHOOD	RITT	PARAMOUNT	1968
BH	BUCKSKIN LADY	HITTLEMAN	UNITED ARTISTS	1957
BH	CYCLOPS	GORDON	ALLIED ARTISTS	1957
BH	HORROR MANIACS (UK: GREED OF WILLIAM HART)	MITCHELL	JH HOFFBERG	1948
BH	ROBERT (BOB) HUTTON	portrait	WARNER BROS	1940s
BH	SHOWDOWN AT BOOT HILL	FOWLER	20th CENTURY FOX	1958
BH	THREE ON A WEEKEND (UK: BANK HOLIDAY)	REED	GAUMONT BRITISH AMERICA	1938
BH-1	BUSY BARCELONA		MGM	1931
BH-1	LIVE WIRE	HINES	WARNER BROS	1925
BH-2	RAINBOW RILEY	HINES	WARNER BROS	1926
BH-2	SPAIN'S MADDEST FIESTA		MGM	1930
BH-3	MODERN MADRID		MGM	1930
BH-4	SPANISH SPORTS		MGM	
BH-5	ALL ABOARD	HINES	WARNER BROS	1927
BH-5	SEVILLE'S MERRIEST PILGRIMAGE		MGM	
BH-6	THAT LITTLE BIT OF HEAVEN		MGM	1931
BH-7	DUBLIN AND NEARBY		MGM	1930
BH-7	HOMEMADE		WARNER BROS	1927
BH-8	FEZ		MGM	
BH-8	WHITE PANTS WILLIE	HINES	WARNER BROS	1927
BH-9	SULTAN'S CAMP OF VICTORY		MGM	1931
BH-9	WRIGHT IDEA	HINES	WARNER BROS	1928
BH-10	TANGIERS		MGM	
BH-11	INTO MOROCCO		MGM	1930
BH-12	TALE OF THE ALHAMBRA		MGM	1931
BH-13	MADIERA, GIBRALTAR, AND MALTA		MGM	
BH-14	KOBO AND KYOTO		MGM	
BH-15	CHINA'S OLD MAN RIVER		MGM	1930
BH-16	THROUGH THE YANGTZE GORGES		MGM	1930
BH-17	KOCHI		MGM	
BH-18	MATSUE		MGM	
BHC	BEVERLY HILLS COP	BREST	PARAMOUNT	1984
BI	BEDFORD INCIDENT (UK)	HARRIS	COLUMBIA	1965
BI	BLACKWELL'S ISLAND	MCGANN	WARNER BROS	1939
BI	CAMP ON BLOOD ISLAND (UK)	GUEST	COLUMBIA	1958
BIB	BLUES FOR LOVERS (BALLAD IN BLUE)	HENREID	20th CENTURY FOX	1965
BIL	BILLY THE KID VS DRACULA	BEAUDINE	EMBASSY	1965
BIS	BROTHERS IN THE SADDLE	SELANDER	RKO	1948
BIW	A BULLET IS WAITING	FARROW	COLUMBIA	1954
BIY	BABY ITS YOU	SAYLES	PARAMOUNT	1983
BJ	BENJAMIN	DEVILLE	PARAMOUNT	1968
BJ	BETTY JAYNES	portrait	MGM	
BJ	BIG JIM MCLAIN	LUDWIG	WARNER BROS	1952
BJ	BILLY JACK	LAUGHLIN	WARNER BROS	1971
BJ	BLIND JUSTICE (UK)	VORHAUS	OLYMPIC	1934
BJ	BONJOUR TRISTESSE	PREMINGER	COLUMBIA	1958
BJ	BRAD (BRADFORD) JACKSON	portrait	UNIVERSAL	
BJ	BRENDA JOYCE	portrait	UNIVERSAL	late 40s
BJ	BRIGHT LIGHTS	BERKELEY	WARNER BROS	1935
BJ	BROADWAY JONES	KAUFMAN	PARAMOUNT (ARTCRAFT)	1917
BJ	BROTHER JOHN	GOLDSTONE	COLUMBIA	1971
BJ	BUCK JONES	portrait		
BJ	BUCK JONES WESTERNS		COL, UNIVERSAL	
BJ	WHATEVER HAPPENED TO BABY JANE?	ALDRICH	WARNER BROS	1962
BJ-1	HOLLYWOOD ROUNDUP	SCOTT	COLUMBIA	1937
BJ-2	HEADING EAST	SCOTT	COLUMBIA	1937
BJ-2	WHEN A MAN SEES RED	JAMES	UNIVERSAL	1934
BJ-3	OVERLAND EXPRESS	EVERSON	COLUMBIA	1938

Movie Still Identification Book Ultimate Edition - Letters

CODE	TITLE/NAME	DIRECTOR/TYPE	STUDIO/DISTRIBUTOR	YEAR
BJ-4	STONE OF SILVER CREEK	GRINDE	UNIVERSAL	1935
BJ-4	STRANGER FROM ARIZONA	CLIFTON	COLUMBIA	1938
BJ-5	LAW OF THE TEXAN	CLIFTON	COLUMBIA	1938
BJ-6	CALIFORNIA FRONTIER	CLIFTON	COLUMBIA	1938
BJ-6	OUTLAWED GUNS	TAYLOR	REALART	R48
BJ-17	LAW FOR TOMBSTONE	JONES	UNIVERSAL	1937
BJ-COL-1	HOLLYWOOD ROUNDUP	SCOTT	COLUMBIA	1937
BJ-COL-2	HEADING EAST	SCOTT	COLUMBIA	1937
BJ-COL-3	OVERLAND EXPRESS	EVERSON	COLUMBIA	1938
BJ-COL-4	STRANGER FROM ARIZONA	CLIFTON	COLUMBIA	1938
BJ-COL-5	LAW OF THE TEXAN	CLIFTON	COLUMBIA	1938
BJ-COL-6	CALIFORNIA FRONTIER	CLIFTON	COLUMBIA	1938
BJG	JANE GREER (NÉE BETTEJANE GREER)	portrait	RKO	
BJH	JANE HOWARD (NÉE BETTY JANE HOWARTH)	portrait	UNIVERSAL	1950s
BK	8 1/2	FELLINI	EMBASSY	1963
BK	BARBARA KNUDSON	portrait	UNIV	
BK	BEBE'S KIDS (t)	SMITH	PARAMOUNT	1992
BK	BENGAL TIGER	KING	WARNER BROS	1936
BK	BEST FRIENDS	JEWISON	WARNER BROS	1982
BK	BETTY KEAN	portrait	REPUBLICUBLIC	
BK	BIG KNIFE	ALDRICH	UNITED ARTISTS	1955
BK	BILL KENNEDY	portrait	WARNER BROS	
BK	BILLY THE KID VS DRACULA	BEAUDINE	EMBASSY	1965
BK	BIRD	EASTWOOD	WARNER BROS	1988
BK	BLACK KNIGHT (UK)	GARNETT	COLUMBIA	1954
BK	BLADERUNNER	SCOTT	WARNER BROS	1982
BK	BORIS KARLOFF	portrait	WARNER BROS	1930s-40s
BK	BRETT KING	portrait	RKO	
BK	BRIGAND OF KANDAHAR (UK)	GILLING	COLUMBIA	1965
BK	BRUBAKER	ROSENBERG	20th CENTURY FOX	1980
BK	BUSTER KEATON	portrait	MGM	1920s-60s
BK	CANNONBALL RUN II	NEEDHAM	WARNER BROS	1984
BK	COBRA	COSMATOS	WARNER BROS	1986
BK	DEAD POOL	VAN HORN	WARNER BROS	1988
BK	DEAL OF THE CENTURY	FRIEDKIN	WARNER BROS	1983
BK	ELENI	YATES	WARNER BROS	1985
BK	EVERYBODY'S ALL AMERICAN	HACKFORD	WARNER BROS	1988
BK	GREAT SANTINI	CARLINO	WARNER BROS	1979
BK	HONKYTONK MAN	EASTWOOD	WARNER BROS	1982
BK	I SHOT BILLY THE KID	BERKE	LIPPERT	1950
BK	LOOKER	CRICHTON	WARNER BROS	1981
BK	LOST BOYS	SCHUMACHER	WARNER BROS	1987
BK	POLICE ACADEMY	WILSON	WARNER BROS	1984
BK	RISKY BUSINESS	BRICKMAN	WARNER BROS	1983
BK	SUDDEN IMPACT	EASTWOOD	WARNER BROS	1983
BK	UGLY ONES (BOUNTY KILLER)	MARTIN	UNITED ARTISTS	1967
BK	WHO'S THAT GIRL	FOLEY	WARNER BROS	1987
BK	WITCHES OF EASTWICK	MILLER	WARNER BROS	1987
BK	WOLFEN	WADLEIGH	WARNER BROS	1981
BK 4	DEVIL'S ISLAND	FRANCE	WARNER BORS	1939
BK-A	HONKY TONK MAN	EASTWOOD	WARNER BROS	1982
BL	BABY LOVE (UK)	REID	AVCO EMBASSY	1968
BL	BAD LANDS	LANDERS	RKO	1939
BL	BEA LILLIE	portrait	UNIV	
BL	BELOW THE LINE	RAYMAKER	WARNER BROS	1925
BL	BEN LYON	portrait	FN	
BL	BERT LYTELL	portrait	TIFFANY	
BL	BESSIE LOVE	portrait	MGM	
BL	BILLY LIAR (UK)	SCHLESINGER	CONTINENTAL	1963
BL	BLACK LEGION	MAYO	WARNER BROS	1937
BL	BLOB	YEAWORTH, DOUGHTEN	PARAMOUNT	1958
BL	BLOODLINE	YOUNG	PARAMOUNT	1979
BL	BOMBS OVER LONDON (UK: MIDNIGHT MENACE)	HILL	FILM ALLIANCE	1937
BL	BRASS LEGEND	OSWALD	UNITED ARTISTS	1956
BL	BRIGHT LIGHTS	CURTIZ	WARNER BROS	1930
BL	BRINK OF LIFE (SWE: NARA LIVET)	BERGMAN	AJAY	1958
BL	BRITISH LION	studio		
BL	BROKEN LAND	BUSHELMAN	20th CENTURY FOX	1962
BL	BURT LANCASTER	portrait	UNIV, WARNER BROS	
BL	DOWN THE STRETCH	CLEMENS	WARNER BROS	1936

Movie Still Identification Book Ultimate Edition - Letters

CODE	TITLE/NAME	DIRECTOR/TYPE	STUDIO/DISTRIBUTOR	YEAR
BL	JOAN BLONDELL	portrait	WARNER BROS	
BL	LEO THE LAST	BOORMAN	UNITED ARTISTS	1970
BL	LOVE AT STAKE	MOFFITT	TRI STAR	1987
BL	WILLIAM LUNDIGAN	portrait	UNITED ARTISTS	
BL-1	BONNIE PRINCE CHARLIE (UK)	KIMMINS, KORDA	SNADER	1948
BL-2	MAN ABOUT THE HOUSE (UK)	ARLISS	20TH CENTURY FOX	1947
BL-7	NIGHT BEAT (UK)	HUTH	BRITISH LION	1947
BL-8	WINSLOW BOY (UK)	ASQUITH	EAGLE-LION	1948
BL-9	HOUR OF GLORY (UK: SMALL BACK ROOM)	POWELL, PRESSBURGER	SNADER	1949
BL-10	WOMEN OF DOLWYN (UK: LAST DAYS OF DOLWYN)	WILLIAMS	LOPERT	1949
BL-12	WILD HEART (UK: GONE TO EARTH)	POWELL, PRESSBURGER	RKO	1950
BL-14	SEVEN DAYS TO NOON (UK)	BOULTING, BOULTING	MAYER-KINGLSEY	1950
BL-15	HAPPIEST DAYS OF YOUR LIFE (UK)	LAUNDER	BRITISH LION	1950
BL-16	WOODEN HORSE (UK)	LEE	SNADER	1950
BL-17	WONDER BOY (UK: WONDER KID)	HARTL	SNADER	1951
BL-18	CRY, THE BELOVED COUNTRY (UK)	KORDA	LOPERT	1951
BL-19	TALES OF HOFFMANN (UK)	POWELL, PRESSBURGER	LOPERT	1951
BL-20	OUTCAST OF THE ISLANDS (UK)	REED	LOPERT	1951
BL-21	BIKINI BABY (UK: LADY GODIVA RIDES AGAIN)	LAUNDER	CARROLL	1951
BL-22	BREAKING THE SOUND BARRIER (UK)	LEAN	UNITED ARTISTS	1952
BL-23	MR. DENNING DRIVES NORTH (UK)	KIMMINS	CARROLL	1951
BL-24	MURDER ON MONDAY (UK: HOME AT SEVEN)	RICHARDSON	MAYER-KINGLSEY	1952
BL-25	HOLLY AND THE IVY (UK)	O'FERRALL	PACEMAKER	1952
BL-26	PASSIONATE SENTRY (UK: WHO GOES THERE!)	KIMMINS	FINE ARTS	1952
BL-27	TWICE UPON A TIME (UK)	PRESSBURGER	BRITISH LION	1953
BL-28	RINGER (UK)	HAMILTON	BRITISH LION	1952
BL-29	GILBERT AND SULLIVAN (UK)	GILLIAT	UNITED ARTISTS	1953
BL-30	FOLLY TO BE WISE (UK)	LAUNDER	FINE ARTS	1953
BL-31	HEART OF THE MATTER (UK)	O'FERRALL	AAP	1953
BL-32	CAPTAIN'S PARADISE (UK)	KIMMINS	LLOPERT	1953
BL-33	MAN BETWEEN (UK)	REED	UNITED ARTISTS	1953
BL34	HOBSON'S CHOICE (UK)	LEAN	UNITED ARTISTS	1954
BL-35	THREE CASES OF MURDER (UK)	EADY, O'FERRALL, TOYE	AAP	1955
BL-35A	THREE CASES OF MURDER: YOU KILLED ELIZABETH (UK)	EADY	AAP	1955
BL-35B	THREE CASES OF MURDER: THE PICTURE (UK)	TOYE	AAP	1955
BL-35C	THREE CASES OF MURDER: LORD MOUNTDRAGO (UK)	O'FERRALL	AAP	1955
BL36	BELLES OF ST. TRINIANS (UK)	LAUNDER	ASSOC. ARTISTS	1955
BL37	MAN WHO LOVED REDHEADS (UK)	FRENCH	UNITED ARTISTS	1955
BL-38	MARRIAGE A LA MODE (UK: CONSTANT HUSBAND)	GILLIAT	STRATFORD	1955
BL-97	WILD HORSE RUSTLERS (mistake? See BC-97)	NEWFIELD	TIFFANY	1943
BL-100	DEATH RIDES THE PLAINS (LONE RIDER)	NEWFIELD	PRC	1943
BLA	BLIND ALIBI	LANDERS	RKO	1938
BLACK	BLACK CHRISTMAS	CLARK	WARNER BROS	1975
BLBC	WINSLOW BOY (UK - 1948)	ASQUITH	EAGLE LION	1950
BLBC	BRIGHT LIGHTS, BIG CITY	BRIDGES	UNITED ARTISTS	1988
BLC	BLANCHE LE CLAIR	portrait	MGM	late 20s
BLD	BREAD, LOVE AND DREAMS (IT: PANE, AMORE E FANTASIA)	COMENCINI	IFE	1953
BLIG	TALES OF HOFFMAN	POWELL, PRESSBURGER	LOPERT	1951
BLL-6	BEYOND LONDON LIGHTS	TERRISS	FILM BOOKING OFF (FBO)	1928
BLM	BARBARA LAMARR	portrait	METRO	
BLM	BUNNY LAKE IS MISSING (UK)	PREMINGER	COLUMBIA	1965
BLP	BY LOVE POSSESSED	STURGES	UNITED ARTISTS	1961
BLT	BLACK BELT JONES	CLOUSE	WARNER BROS	1974
BLY-28	LADIES TO BOARD	BLYSTONE	FOX FILM	1924
BLY-30	LAST MAN ON EARTH	BLYSTONE	FOX FILM	1924
BLY-31	TEETH	BLYSTONE	FOX FILM	1924
BLY-32	DICK TURPIN	BLYSTONE	FOX FILM	1925
BLY-34	LUCKY HORSESHOE	BLYSTONE	FOX FILM	1925
BLY-35	BEST BAD MAN	BLYSTONE	FOX FILM	1925
BLY-36	MY OWN PAL	BLYSTONE	FOX FILM	1926
BLY-38	FAMILY UPSTAIRS	BLYSTONE	FOX FILM	1926
BLY-39	WINGS OF THE STORM	BLYSTONE	FOX FILM	1926
BLY-43	SHARP SHOOTERS	BLYSTONE	FOX FILM	1928
BLY-44	MOTHER KNOWS BEST	BLYSTONE	FOX FILM	1928
BLY-45	CAPTAIN LASH	BLYSTONE	FOX FILM	1929
BLY-46	THRU DIFFERENT EYES	BLYSTONE	FOX FILM	1929
BLY-47	SKY HAWK	BLYSTONE	FOX FILM	1929
BLY-48	BIG PARTY	BLYSTONE	FOX FILM	1930
BLY-49	SO THIS IS LONDON	BLYSTONE	FOX FILM	1930
BLY-50	MEN ON CALL	BLYSTONE	FOX FILM	1930

Movie Still Identification Book Ultimate Edition - Letters

CODE	TITLE/NAME	DIRECTOR/TYPE	STUDIO/DISTRIBUTOR	YEAR
BLY-51	MR. LEMON OF ORANGE	BLYSTONE	FOX FILM	1931
BLY-52	YOUNG SINNERS	BLYSTONE	FOX FILM	1931
BLY-53	SHE WANTED A MILLIONAIRE	BLYSTONE	FOX FILM	1932
BLY-54	CHARLIE CHAN'S CHANCE	BLYSTONE	FOX FILM	1932
BLY-55	AMATEUR DADDY	BLYSTONE	FOX FILM	1932
BLY-56	PAINTED WOMAN	BLYSTONE	FOX FILM	1932
BLY-57	TOO BUSY TO WORK	BLYSTONE	FOX FILM	1932
BLY-58	HOT PEPPER	BLYSTONE	FOX FILM	1933
BLY-SAN-50	MEN ON CALL	BLYSTONE	FOX FILM	1930
BLYSTONE-36	MY OWN PAL	BLYSTONE	FOX FILM	1926
BM	BAD MEDICINE	MILLER	20th CENTURY FOX	1985
BM	BAD MEN	BADGER	WARNER BROS	1930
BM	BAD MEN OF MISSOURI	ENRIGHT	WARNER BROS	1941
BM	BARRY MACKAY	portrait	GAUMONT BRITISH	
BM	BARTON MACLANE	portrait	WARNER BROS	
BM	BEAU MARRIAGE	ROHMER	UNITED ARTISTS	1982
BM	BEVERLY MICHAELS	portrait	UNIV	
BM	BODIL MILLER	portrait	UNIVERSAL	early 30s
BM	BRAIN MACHINE (UK)	HUGHES	RKO	1956
BM	BRASS MONKEY (UK)	FREELAND	UNITED ARTISTS	1948
BM	BRENDA MARSHALL	portrait	WARNER BROS	
BM	BRIDE OF THE MONSTER	WOOD	FILMAKERS REL.	1956
BM	BUGSY MALONE	PARKER	PARAMOUNT	1976
BM	BURGESS MEREDITH	portrait	RKO	1930s-40s
BM	FOUR DAUGHTERS	CURTIZ	WARNER BROS	1938
BM	GIANT OF MARATHON	TOURNEUR	MGM	1959
BM	GIRL MISSING	FLOREY	WARNER BROS	1933
BM	HORRORS OF THE BLACK MUSEUM (UK)	CRABTREE	AIP	1959
BM	VAGABOND VIOLINIST (UK: BROKEN MELODY)	VORHAUS	OLYMPIC	1934
BMG	OUT OF THE PAST	TOURNEUR	RKO	1946
BMIA3	BRADDOCK: MISSING IN ACTION 3	RICHARDS	CANNON	1987
BMS	BLACK MOSES OF SOUL	JOHNSON	AQUNITED ARTISTSRIUS REL.	1973
BMT	BADMAN'S TERRITORY	WHELAN	RKO	1946
BMT	BULL MONTANA	portrait	RKO	late 30s
BN	BARBARA NICHOLS	portrait	UNITED ARTISTS	
BN	BEAUTIES OF THE NIGHT (FR: LES BELLES DE NUIT 1952)	CLAIR	LOPERT	1954
BN	BIG MONEY (UK)	CARSTAIRS	LOPERT	1958
BN	BIG NIGHT	LOSEY	UNITED ARTISTS	1951
BN	BIRTH OF A NATION	GRIFFITH	EPOCH	1915
BN	BOSS NIGGER	ARNOLD	DIMENSION	1975
BN	BRITISH NATIONAL FILMS			
BN	THAT SPLENDID NOVEMBER (IT)	BOLOGNINI	UNITED ARTISTS	1969
BN3	PIMPERNEL SMITH (MISTER V) (UK)	HOWARD	UNITED ARTISTS	1942
BNBII	BAD NEWS BEARS IN BREAKING TRAINING	PRESSMAN	PARAMOUNT	1977
BNO	BOYS NIGHT OUT (SEXY)	GORDON	MGM	1962
BO	BAILOUT AT 43,000	LYON	UNITED ARTISTS	1957
BO	BARBARA O'NEIL	portrait	UNIVERSAL	
BO	BETTER OLE	REISNER	WARNER BROS	1926
BO	BLACK ORPHEUS (BRA: ORFEU NEGRO)	CAMUS	LOPERT	1959
BO	BLACKOUT (UK)	BAKER	EROS	1950
BO	BLACKOUT (UK: MURDER BY PROXY)	FISHER	LIPPERT	1954
BO	BOBO	PARRISH	WARNER BROS	1967
BO	BOIN-N-G	LEWIS	BOX OFFICE SPECTACULARS	1963
BO	BORSALINO	DERAY	PARAMOUNT	1970
BO	BROTHER ORCHID	BACON	WARNER BROS	1940
BO	BULLETS FOR O'HARA	HOWARD	WARNER BROS	1941
BO	BURNT OFFERINGS	CURTIS	UNITED ARTISTS	1976
BO	FUGITIVES FOR A NIGHT	GOODWINS	RKO	1938
BO	SANDERS OF THE RIVER (UK)	Z. KORDA	UNITED ARTISTS	1935
BOA	BLOOD ON THE ARROW	SALKOW	ALLIED ARTISTS	1964
BOA	CURACU BEAST AMAZON	SIODMAK	UNIVERSAL	1956
BOB	BATTLE OF BRITAIN (UK)	HAMILTON	UNITED ARTISTS	1969
BOB	BRIDES OF BLOOD	ROMERO	HEMISPHERE	1968
BOD	BILL OF DIVORCEMENT	CUKOR	RKO	1932
BOF	WHAT'S THE MATTER WITH HELEN?	HARRINGTON	UNITED ARTISTS	1971
BOG	HOW TO SAVE YOUR MARRIAGE AND RUIN YOUR LIFE	COOK	COLUMBIA	1968
BOJ	BUNDLE OF JOY	TAUROG	RKO	1956
BOK	BORDER RANGERS	BERKE	LIPPERT	1950
BOM	BLOOD ON THE MOON	WISE	RKO	1948
BOR	BORN TO BE BAD	RAY	RKO	1950

Movie Still Identification Book Ultimate Edition - Letters

CODE	TITLE/NAME	DIRECTOR/TYPE	STUDIO/DISTRIBUTOR	YEAR
BOR	BORZAGE PRODUCTIONS	studio	FOX	
BOR-5	EARLY TO WED	BORZAGE	FOX FILM	1926
BOR-6	MARRIAGE LICENSE?	BORZAGE	FOX FILM	1926
BOR-7	SEVENTH HEAVEN	BORZAGE	FOX FILM	1927
BOR-8	STREET ANGEL	BORZAGE	FOX FILM	1928
BOR-9	RIVER	BORZAGE	FOX FILM	1929
BOR-10	LUCKY STAR	BORZAGE	FOX FILM	1929
BOR-11	RIVER	BORZAGE	FOX FILM	1929
BOR-11	THEY HAD TO SEE PARIS	BORZAGE	FOX FILM	1929
BOR-12	SONG O' MY HEART	BORZAGE	FOX FILM	1930
BOR-13	LILIOM	BORZAGE	FOX FILM	1930
BOR-14	DOCTOR'S WIVES	BORZAGE	FOX FILM	1931
BOR-15	YOUNG AS YOU FEEL	BORZAGE	FOX FILM	1931
BOR-16	BAD GIRL	BORZAGE	FOX FILM	1931
BOR-17	AFTER TOMORROW	BORZAGE	FOX FILM	1932
BOR-18	YOUNG AMERICA	BORZAGE	FOX FILM	1932
BORDERLINE	BORDERLINE	SEITER	UNIVERSAL-INT'L	1950
BORZ-1	LAZYBONES	BORZAGE	FOX FILM	1925
BOS	BATTLE IN OUTER SPACE (JAP)	HONDA	COLUMBIA	1959
BOSD	BLOOD ORGY OF THE SHE DEVILS	MIKELS	GEMINI	1972
BOV	BONFIRE OF THE VANITIES	DE PALMA	WARNER BROS	1990
BP	BABY PEGGY	portrait	UNIVERSAL	1930s
BP	BACHELOR PARTY	MANN	UNITED ARTISTS	1957
BP	BACHELOR PARTY	ISRAEL	20th CENTURY FOX	1984
BP	BARBARA PAYTON	portrait	WARNER BROS	
BP	BARBARA PEPPER	portrait	RKO	
BP	BATTLE FOR THE PLANET OF THE APES	THOMPSON	20th CENTURY FOX	1973
BP	BEES IN PARADISE (UK)	GUEST	GFD	1944
BP	BELSAM PRODUCTIONS	studio	FOX	
BP	BIKINI PARADISE	TALLAS	ALLIED ARTISTS	1967
BP	BIRD OF PARADISE	VIDOR	RKO	1932
BP	BIRTHDAY PARTY (UK)	FRIEDKIN	CONTINENTAL	1968
BP	BLACK PATCH	MINER	WARNER BROS	1957
BP	BLACK PIRATE	PARKER	UNITED ARTISTS	1926
BP	BLACK PIT OF DR. M	MENDEZ	UNITED PRODUCERS	1961
BP	BODY PARTS	DICKERSON	PARAMOUNT	1991
BP	BOY AND THE PIRATES	GORDON	UNITED ARTISTS	1960
BP	BREAKHEART PASS	GRIES	UNITED ARTISTS	1975
BP	BRIDAL PATH (UK)	LAUNDER	KINGSLEY-UNION	1959
BP	BRIDE OF PENNACOOK (sh)		TIFFANY	1927
BP	BUCK AND THE PREACHER	POITIER	COLUMBIA	1972
BP	BUREAU OF MISSING PERSONS	DEL RUTH	WARNER BROS	1933
BP	OPERATION BOTTLENECK	CAHN	UNITED ARTISTS	1961
BP1	MY SISTER AND I (UK)	HUTH	GFD	1948
BP1	NAKED EARTH (UK)	SHERMAN	20TH CENTURY FOX	1958
BP1	REACH FOR GLORY (UK)	LEACOCK	ROYAL	1962
BP-1	VIRGIN LIPS	CLIFTON	COLUMBIA	1928
BP2	COUNT FIVE AND DIE (UK)	VICAS	20TH CENTURY FOX	1957
BP2	LOOK BEFORE YOU LOVE (UK)	HUTH	GFD	1948
BP3	PRESCRIPTION FOR MURDER (UK: RX FOR MURDER)	TWIST	20TH CENTURY FOX	1958
BP7	BOBBIKINS (UK)	DAY	20TH CENTURY FOX	1959
BP-101	CHECKERED COAT	CAHN	20th CENTURY FOX	1948
BP-102	BUNGALOW 13	CAHN	20th CENTURY FOX	1948
BPH	BEHOLD A PALE HORSE	ZINNEMANN	COLUMBIA	1964
BPS	BONNIE PARKER STORY	WITNEY	AIP	1958
BQ	BANDIT QUEEN	BERKE	LIPPERT	1950
BQ	MURDER ON APPROVAL (UK: BARBADOS QUEST)	KNOWLES	RKO	1956
BR	BANANA RIDGE (UK)	MYCROFT	PATHE	1942
BR	BARBARA READ	portrait	RKO, UNIVERSAL	
BR	BARBARA RUSH	portrait	UNIV	
BR	BARBARA RUSH	portrait		
BR	BATMAN RETURNS	BURTON	WARNER BROS	1992
BR	BEACH RED	WILDE	UNITED ARTISTS	1967
BR	BED OF ROSES	LA CAVA	RKO	1933
BR	BEING RESPECTABLE	ROSEN	WARNER BROS	1924
BR	BEVERLY ROBERTS	portrait	UNIVERSAL, WARNER BROS	
BR	BIG RISK (FR)	SAUDET	UNITED ARTISTS	1960
BR	BLOOD ROSE (FR)	MULOT	MONOGRAM	1970
BR	BRANNIGAN	HICKOX	UNITED ARTISTS	1975
BR	BREATHLESS	MCBRIDE	ORION	1983

- 30 -

Movie Still Identification Book Ultimate Edition - Letters

CODE	TITLE/NAME	DIRECTOR/TYPE	STUDIO/DISTRIBUTOR	YEAR
BR	BRIGHTON ROCK (UK)	BOULTING	A. MAYER-E. KINGSLEY	1947
BR	BROTHER RAT	KEIGHLEY	WARNER BROS	1938
BR	BUSSES ROAR	LEDERMAN	WARNER BROS	1942
BR	CHARLES 'BUDDY' ROGERS	portrait	RKO	
BR	GIVE MY REGARDS TO BROAD ST	WEBB	20th CENTURY FOX	1984
BR	MONKEY ON MY BACK	DE TOTH	UNITED ARTISTS	1957
BR	NAKED STREET (aka BRASS RING)	SHANE	UNITED ARTIST	1955
BR	OLD BONES OF THE RIVER (UK)	VARNEL	GFD	1938
BR	REX REASON (aka BART ROBERTS)	portrait	UNIVERSAL	
BR	ROCCO AND HIS BROTHERS (IT: ROCCO E I SUOI FRATELLI)	VISCONTI	ASTOR	1961
BR	UNDERWATER	STURGES	RKO	1955
BR-1	MARSHALL OF HELDORADO	CARR	LIPPERT	1950
BR-1	QUICK MILLIONS	BROWN	FOX FILM	1931
BR-2	WEST OF THE BRAZOS	CARR	LIPPERT	1950
BR-4	HOSTILE COUNTRY	CARR	LIPPERT	1950
BR-5	WHILE NEW YORK SLEEPS	BRABIN	FOX FILM	1920
BR-6	BLIND WIVES	BRABIN	FOX FILM	1920
BR-7	LIGHTS OF NEW YORK	BRABIN	FOX FILM	1922
BRD	BEYOND A REASONABLE DOUBT	LANG	RKO	1956
BRENON-12	CUSTARD CUP	BRENON	FOX FILM	1923
BRO	BIG RED ONE	FULLER	UNITED ARTISTS	1980
B-RS	BOCCACCIO '70 (IT)	DE SICA, FELLINI	EMBASSY	1962
BRT	BREAKING THE ICE	CLINE	RKO	1938
BRX	BASIL RATHBONE	portrait	MGM	
BS	BALLAD OF A SOLDIER (USSR)	CHUKHRAJ	KINGSLEY INT'L	1961
BS	BANK SHOT	CHAMPION	UNITED ARTISTS	1974
BS	BARBARA STANWYCK	portrait	RKO, UA, UNIV, WARNER	
BS	BECKY SHARPE	MAMOULIAN	RKO	1935
BS	BELLE SOMMERS	SILVERSTEIN	COLUMBIA	1962
BS	BEST SELLER	FLYNN	ORION	1987
BS	BEVERLY SIMMONS	portrait		
BS	BIG SHOW	CLARK	20TH CENTURY FOX	1961
BS	BIG SLEEP	WINNER	UNITED ARTISTS	1978
BS	BITTER SWEET (UK)	WILCOX	UNITED ARTISTS	1933
BS	BLACK SLEEP	LE BORG	UNITED ARTISTS	1956
BS	BLACK SUNDAY	FRANKENHEIMER	PARAMOUNT	1977
BS	BLOOD ON SATAN'S CLAW (UK)	HAGGARD	CANNON	1971
BS	BLOODSPORT	ARNOLD	CANNON	1987
BS	BLUE STEEL	BIGELOW	MGM	1990
BS	BOB STEELE	portrait	TIFFANY	
BS	BODY AND SOUL	ROSSEN	UNITED ARTISTS	1947
BS	BODY SNATCHER	WISE	RKO	1945
BS	BOMB IN THE HIGH STREET (UK)	BEZENCENET, BISHOP	HEMISPHERE	1961
BS	BOND STREET (UK)	PARRY	STRATFORD	1948
BS	BRIEF SEASON (IT)	CASTELLANI	COLUMBIA	1969
BS	BROKEN STAR	SELANDER	UNITED ARTISTS	1956
BS	BULLET SCARS	LEDERMAN	WARNER BROS	1942
BS	SECRET FURY	FERRER	RKO	1950
BS	TWO MRS. CARROLLS	GODFREY	WARNER BROS	1947
BS-1	BILLY THE KID IN SANTA FE	NEWFIELD	PRC	1941
BS-1	SILVER STALLION	FINNEY	MONOGRAM	1941
BS-2	BILLY THE KID-GUN JUSTICE	NEWFIELD	PRC	1940
BS-3	BILLY THE KID IN TEXAS	NEWFIELD	PRC	1940
BS-4	BILLY THE KID – OUTLAWED	NEWFIELD	PRC	1940
BS-5	BILLY THE KID - RANGE WAR	NEWFIELD	PRC	1941
BS-6	BILLY THE KID – FIGHTING PALS	NEWFIELD	PRC	1941
BS-21	GENTLEMAN FROM DIXIE	HERMAN	MONOGRAM	1941
BS-22	RIOT SQUAD	FINNEY	MONOGRAM	1941
BS-23	KING OF THE STALLIONS	FINNEY	MONOGRAM	1942
BSB-1	GEORGE TAKES THE AIR (UK: IT'S IN THE AIR)	KIMMINS	SELECT ATTRACTIONS	1938
BSH	BARBER OF STAMFORD HILL (UK)	WREDE	BRITISH LION	1962
BSL	B.S. I LOVE YOU	STERN	20th CENTURY FOX	1971
BSL	BITTER SWEET LOVE	MILLER	AVCO EMBASSY	1976
BSM	BELLS OF ST. MARY'S	MCCAREY	RKO	1945
BSN	BODY SAID NO! (UK)	GUEST	EROS	1950
BSR	BED SITTING ROOM (UK)	LESTER	LOPERT	1969
BSSM	BROTHER SUN SISTER MOON (IT)	ZEFFIRELLI	PARAMOUNT	1973
BSW	BLACK SHEEP OF WHITEHALL (UK)	DEARDEN, HAY	UNITED ARTISTS	1942
BT	BABBITT	KEIGHLEY	WARNER BROS	1934
BT	BAND OF THIEVES (UK)	BEZENCENET	RANK	1962

Movie Still Identification Book Ultimate Edition - Letters

CODE	TITLE/NAME	DIRECTOR/TYPE	STUDIO/DISTRIBUTOR	YEAR
BT	BAWDY TALES (IT: STORIE SCELLERATE)	CITTI	UNITED ARTISTS	1973
BT	BEHIND THE RISING SUN	DMYTRYK	RKO	1943
BT	BEING THERE	ASHBY	UNITED ARTISTS	1979
BT	BEVERLY TYLER	portrait	UNIVERSAL	
BT	BILL THOMAS	portrait	UNIVERSAL	
BT	BITTER RICE (Riso Amaro)	DE SANTIS	LUX	1950
BT	BLACK 13 (UK)	HUGHES	20TH CENTURY FOX	1953
BT	BLACK TIDE (UK: STORMY CROSSING)	PENNINGTON-RICHARDS	ASTOR	1958
BT	BLACK TORMENT (UK)	HARTFORD-DAVIS	GOVERNOR	1964
BT	BLACK TUESDAY	FREGONESE	UNITED ARTISTS	1954
BT	BONJOUR TRISTESSE (FR)	PREMINGER	COLUMBIA	1958
BT	BRIMSTONE AND TREACLE	LONCRAINE	UNITED ARTISTS	1982
BT	CARNIVAL BOAT	ROGELL	RKO	1932
BT	LAND BEYOND THE LAW	EASON	WARNER BROS	1937
BT	SUSPICION	HITCHCOCK	RKO	1941
BT	YOU CAN'T BUY LUCK	LANDERS	RKO	1937
BT8	BACHELOR TOM AND HIS BIKINI PLAYMATES (BACHELOR	DEWAR	CORSICAN	1964
BTB	BEAT THE BAND	AUER	RKO	1947
BTB	BIGGER THAN BARNUMS	INCE	FILM BOOKING OFF (FBO)	1926
BTB	BRAVE ONE	RAPPER	RKO	1956
BTF	BRIDGE TOO FAR	ATTENBOROUGH	UNITED ARTISTS	1977
BTH	BLUEBEARD'S TEN HONEYMOONS	WILDER	ALLIED ARTISTS	1960
BT-NY	BONJOUR TRISTESSE (FR)	PREMINGER	COLUMBIA	1958
BTP	BACHELOR TOM PEEPING	DEWAR	CORSICAN	1964
BTR	UNDER THE TONTO RIM	LANDERS	RKO	1947
BTS	BELOW THE SAHARA	DENIS	RKO	1953
BTVS	BUFFY THE VAMPIRE SLAYER	KUZUI	20th CENTURY FOX	1992
BU	AFFAIR WITH A STRANGER	ROWLAND	RKO	1953
BU	BLOW-UP (UK)	ANTONIONI	PREMIER	1966
BU	BOB'S YOUR UNCLE (UK)	MITCHELL	BUTCHER'S	1942
BU	BRINGING UP BABY	HAWKS	RKO	1938
BU	BURGLARS (FR)	VERNEUIL	COLUMBIA	1972
BU15 S22	NO MAN'S LAND	(BU?) - SEILER	FOX FILM	1926
BUS	BIG BUS	FRAWLEY	PARAMOUNT	1976
BUS	BUNCO SQUAD	LEEDS	RKO	1950
BUT	BUTLER PRODUCTIONS	studio	FOX	
BUT-2	WIN THAT GIRL	BUTLER	FOX FILM	1928
BUT-4	PREP AND PEP	BUTLER	FOX FILM	1928
BUT 5 WER 2	CHASING THROUGH EUROPE	BUTLER - WERKER	FOX FILM	1929
BUT-7	SUNNYSIDE UP	BUTLER	FOX FILM	1929
BUT-8	HIGH SOCIETY BLUES	BUTLER	FOX FILM	1930
BUT-9	JUST IMAGINE	BUTLER	FOX FILM	1930
BUT-10	A CONNECTICUT YANKEE	BUTLER	FOX FILM	1931
BUT-11	BUSINESS AND PLEASURE	BUTLER	FOX FILM	1932
BUT-12	DELICIOUS	BUTLER	FOX FILM	1931
BUT-13	DOWN TO EARTH	BUTLER	FOX FILM	1932
BUT-14	HANDLE WITH CARE	BUTLER	FOX FILM	1932
BUT-H-6	MASKED EMOTIONS	BUTLER, HAWKS	FOX FILM	1929
BUT-SIL-3	FOX MOVIETONE FOLLIES OF 1929	BUTLER - SILVER	FOX FILM	1929
BV	BENAY VENUTA	portrait	REPUBLIC	
BV	BITTER VICTORY	RAY	COLUMBIA	1957
BV	BLUE VEIL	BERNHARDT	RKO	1951
BV	STOLEN KISSES (FR: BAISERS VOLES)	TRUFFAUT	UNITED ARTISTS	1968
BV1	WRONG ARM OF THE LAW (UK)	OWEN	CONTINENTAL	1963
BW	BACK TO THE WALL (FR: LE DOS AU MUR)	MOLINARO	ELLIS	1958
BW	BAND WAGGON (UK)	VARNEL	GFD	1940
BW	BARBARA WEEKS	portrait	WARNER BROS	early 30s
BW	BEAST WITHIN	MORA	UNITED ARTISTS	1982
BW	BEAUTIFUL BUT DANGEROUS	LEONARD	20th CENTURY FOX	1958
BW	BERT WHEELER	portrait	RKO	1920s-30s
BW	BIG WHEEL	LUDWIG	UNITED ARTISTS	1949
BW	BILL WILLIAMS	portrait	RKO	1940s-50s
BW	BLACK WHIP	WARREN	20th CENTURY FOX	1956
BW	BLACK WIDOW	RAFELSON	20th CENTURY FOX	1987
BW	BLONDES AT WORK	MCDONALD	WARNER BROS	1938
BW	BOSS' WIFE	STEINBERG	TRI STAR	1986
BW	BRAINWASHED (GER)	OSWALD	MONOGRAM	1960
BW	BRIDE WORE BLACK (FR)	TRUFFAUT	UNITED ARTISTS	1968
BW	BULWORTH	BEATTY	20th CENTURY FOX	1998
BW	BUTCHER'S WIFE	HUGHES	PARAMOUNT	1991

Movie Still Identification Book Ultimate Edition - Letters

CODE	TITLE/NAME	DIRECTOR/TYPE	STUDIO/DISTRIBUTOR	YEAR
BWC	BEFORE WINTER COMES	THOMPSON	COLUMBIA	1969
BWG	BOY WITH THE GREEN HAIR	LOSEY	RKO	1948
BWG	BOY, WHAT A GIRL	LEONARD	HERALD	1947
BWN	BOY, DID I GET A WRONG NUMBER!	MARSHALL	UNITED ARTISTS	1966
BWS	BUGS BUNNY'S WILD WORLD OF SPORTS (t)	FORD, LENNON	WARNER BROS	1989
BX	GOBUS	JEWISON	WARNER BROS	1996
BX	GRAND ESCAPADE (UK)	BAXTER	BRITISH LION	1946
BXB	BILLIE BURKE	portrait	MGM	
BY	BEHAVE YOURSELF	BECK	RKO	1951
BY	BEHAVE YOURSELF (sh)	WINNER	UNITED ARTISTS	1962
BY	BY YOUR LEAVE	CORRIGAN	RKO	1934
BY	INSPECTOR CLOUSEAU	YORKIN	UNITED ARTISTS	1968
BYE	BYE BYE BRAVERMAN	LUMET	WARNER BROS	1968
BYN	BEAST OF THE YELLOW NIGHT	ROMERO	NEW WORLD	1971
BZ	BEDAZZLED (UK)	DONEN	20th CENTURY FOX	1967
C	BLACKOUT (UK: CONTRABAND)	POWELL	UNITED ARTISTS	1940
C	CALL NORTHSIDE 777	HATHAWAY	20th CENTURY FOX	1948
C	CALTIKI THE IMMORTAL MONSTER (IT)	FREDA	MONOGRAM	1959
C	CAMILLE 2000	METZGER	AUDUBON	1969
C	CARAVAN (UK)	CRABTREE	EAGLE LION	1946
C	CARNIVAL STORY	NEUMANN	RKO	1954
C	CARTOUCHE (IT)	SEKELY, VERNUCCIO	RKO	1957
C	CASABLANCA	CURTIZ	WARNER BROS	1942
C	CHANCES	DWAN	WARNER BROS	1931
C	CHATTERBOX	NICHOLS JR.	RKO	1936
C	CHILD IS BORN	BACON	WARNER BROS	1939
C	CIMARRON	RUGGLES	RKO	1930
C	CIRCLE (UK: VICIOUS CIRCLE)	THOMAS	KASSLER	1957
C	CIRCUS	CHAPLIN	UNITED ARTISTS	1928
C	CLAIRVOYANT (UK)	ELVEY	GAUMONT BRITISH	1934
C	CLIMBERS	STEIN	WARNER BROS	1927
C	CLOUDBURST	SEARLE	UNITED ARTISTS	1951
C	COLLEEN	GREEN	WARNER BROS	1936
C	CONFIDENTIAL	CAHN	MASCOT	1935
C	CONFLICT	BERNHARDT	WARNER BROS	1945
C	CONQUERORS	WELLMAN	RKO	1932
C	CONQUEST	DEL RUTH	WARNER BROS	1928
C	CONTRABAND SPAIN (UK)	HUNTINGTON, SALVADOR	STRATFORD	1955
C	CONVENTION CITY	MAYO	WARNER BROS	1933
C	CONVOY (UK)	TENNYSON	RKO	1941
C	CORNERED	DMYTRYK	RKO	1946
C	CORRUPTION (UK) (CARNAGE)	HARTFORD-DAVIS	COLUMBIA	1968
C	COURAGE	MAYO	WARNER BROS	1930
C	COUSINS	SCHUMACHER (SH)	PARAMOUNT	1988
C	CRACKSMAN (UK)	SCOTT	PATHE	1963
C	CUBA	LESTER	UNITED ARTISTS	1979
C	ESCAPE FROM CRIME	LEDERMAN	WARNER BROS	1942
C	HEAT WAVE (CODE*) (UK)	ELVEY	GAUMONT BRITISH	1935
C	HELL'S KITCHEN	DUPONT, SEILER	WARNER BROS	1939
C	HOW TO MURDER A RICH UNCLE (UK)	PATRICK	COLUMBIA	1957
C	IN CALIENTE	BACON	WARNER BROS	1935
C	INTERNAL AFFAIRS	FIGGIS	PARAMOUNT	1990
C	INTERRUPTED JOURNEY (UK)	BIRT	LOPERT	1949
C	MAID'S NIGHT OUT	HOLMES	RKO	1938
C	MONSOON	AMATEAU	UNITED ARTISTS	1952
C	MOULIN ROUGE	LANFIELD	UNITED ARTISTS	1934
C	NO WAY BACK (UK)	OSIECKI	EROS	1949
C	OUTER GATE	CANNON	MONOGRAM	1937
C	POPEYE THE SAILOR (t)	FLEISCHER	PARAMOUNT	1933
C	PROFESSIONAL SWEETHEART	SEITER	RKO	1933
C	SECRET BRIDE	DIETERLE	WARNER BROS	1934
C	STORK BITES MAN	ENDFIELD	UNITED ARTISTS	1947
C	STRANGER IN TOWN	KENTON	WARNER BROS	1932
C	THEY MADE ME A CRIMINAL	BERKELEY	WARNER BROS	1939
C	TRIGGER PALS	NEWFIELD	GRAND	1939
C	TWO HEADED SPY (UK)	DE TOTH	COLUMBIA	1958
C	UNDERCOVER AGENT (UK: COUNTERSPY)	SEWELL	LIPPERT	1953
C	WAGON'S ROLL AT NIGHT	ENRIGHT	WARNER BROS	1941
C	WALK IN THE CLOUDS	ARAU	20th CENTURY FOX	1995
C&B	CUTTER AND BONE (CUTTER'S WAY)	PASSER	UNITED ARTISTS	1981

Movie Still Identification Book Ultimate Edition - Letters

CODE	TITLE/NAME	DIRECTOR/TYPE	STUDIO/DISTRIBUTOR	YEAR
C.B.DeM	CECIL B. DEMILLE		PATHE	
C&DC	CHECK AND DOUBLE CHECK	BROWN	RKO	1930
C.C.7	MONSIEUR VERDOUX	CHAPLIN	UNITED ARTISTS	1947
C.Mc	CATHERINE MCLEOD	portrait	REPUBLIC	1940s-50s
C-1	AMERICAN MADNESS	CAPRA	COLUMBIA	1932
C-1	BLOOD SHIP	SEITZ	COLUMBIA	1927
C-1	COUNSEL FOR CRIME	BRAHM	COLUMBIA	1937
C-1	COURT MARTIAL	SEITZ	COLUMBIA	1928
C-1	CRAIG'S WIFE	ARZNER	COLUMBIA	1936
C-1	FALSE ALARM	O'CONNOR	COLUMBIA	1926
C-1	FLIGHT	CAPRA	COLUMBIA	1929
C-1	GALLANT DEFENDER	SELMAN	COLUMBIA	1935
C-1	HE FORGOT TO REMEMBER (sh)	POWERS, BUCKINGHAM	PATHE EXCHANGE	1926
C-1	JUNE MADNESS (sh)	PEMBROKE	PATHE EXCHANGE	1920
C-1	LADY FOR A DAY	CAPRA	COLUMBIA	1933
C-1	LAW OF THE SEA	BROWER	MONOGRAM	1931
C-1	LIGHTER THAT FAILED (sh)	PARROTT	MGM	1927
C-1	ONE NIGHT OF LOVE	SCHERTZINGER	COLUMBIA	1934
C-1	PAGAN LADY	DILLON	COLUMBIA	1931
C-1	PANIC IS ON (sh)	PARROTT	MGM	1931
C-1	RAIN OR SHINE	CAPRA	COLUMBIA	1930
C-1	SCARLET LADY	CROSLAND	COLUMBIA	1928
C-1	SHE COULDN'T TAKE IT	GARNETT	COLUMBIA	1935
C-1	THUNDER IN THE CITY	GERING	COLUMBIA	1937
C-1	UNNAMED ROLIN PROJECT (sh)	WHITING	PATHE EXCHANGE	1915
C1C	BROTHERHOOD OF SATAN	MCEVEETY	COLUMBIA	1971
C-2	ALIAS THE LONE WOLF	GRIFFITH	COLUMBIA	1927
C-2	BROADWAY BILL	CAPRA	COLUMBIA	1934
C-2	BROADWAY SCANDALS	ARCHAINBAUD	COLUMBIA	1929
C-2	BUSTER	CAMPBELL	FOX FILM	1923
C-2	COURT MARTIAL	SEITZ	COLUMBIA	1928
C-2	DIRIGIBLE	CAPRA	COLUMBIA	1931
C2	IRON HEART	CLIFT, CAZENEUVE	FOX FILM	1920
C-2	LONE WOLF RETURNS	INCE	COLUMBIA	1926
C-2	MAN'S CASTLE	BORZAGE	COLUMBIA	1933
C-2	MICKEY'S TENT SHOW	DUFFY	COLUMBIA	1933
C-2	MURDER IN GREENWICH VILLAGE	ROGELL	COLUMBIA	1937
C-2	MUSIC GOES ROUND	SCHERTZINGER	COLUMBIA	1936
C-2	NIGHT CLUB LADY	CUMMINGS	COLUMBIA	1932
C-2	PENNIES FROM HEAVEN	MCLEOD	COLUMBIA	1936
C-2	SALLY IN OUR ALLEY	LANG	COLUMBIA	1927
C-2	SANDMAN (sh)	NEWMEYER	PATHE EXCHANGE	1920
C-2	SCARLET LADY	CROSLAND	COLUMBIA	1928
C-2	SHANGHAIED LOVE	SEITZ	COLUMBIA	1931
C-2	SHOULD SAILORS MARRY? (sh)	ROBBINS	PATHE EXCHANGE	1925
C-2	SKIP THE MALOO! (sh)	PARROTT	MGM	1931
C-2	SONG OF LOVE	KENTON	COLUMBIA	1929
C-2	STING OF STINGS (sh)	PARROTT	MGM	1927
C-2	UNNAMED ROLIN PROJECT (sh)	WHITING	PATHE EXCHANGE	1915
C-3	ABOVE THE CLOUDS	NEILL	COLUMBIA	1934
C-3	ALIAS ALADDIN (sh)	ROACH	PATHE EXCHANGE	1920
C-3	ALIAS THE LONE WOLF	GRIFFITH	COLUMBIA	1927
C-3	ARMORED CAR ROBBERY	FLEISCHER	RKO	1950
C-3	BITTER TEA OF GENERAL YEN	CAPRA	COLUMBIA	1933
C-3	BROTHERS	LANG	COLUMBIA	1930
C-3	BUCKING THE BARRIER	CAMPBELL	FOX FILM	1923
C-3	COME CLOSER FOLKS	LEDERMAN	COLUMBIA	1936
C-3	CRIME AND PUNISHMENT	STERNBERG	COLUMBIA	1935
C-3	FORBIDDEN	CAPRA	COLUMBIA	1932
C-3	GIRL FRIEND	BUZZELL	COLUMBIA	1935
C-3	MICKEY'S COVERED WAGON	DUFFY	COLUMBIA	1933
C-3	MOONLIGHT AND NOSES (sh)	LAUREL, JONES	PATHE EXCHANGE	1925
C-3	RUNAWAY GIRLS	SANDRICH	COLUMBIA	1928
C-3	SALLY IN OUR ALLEY	LANG	COLUMBIA	1927
C-3	SONG OF LOVE	KENTON	COLUMBIA	1929
C-3	TIMBER WAR	NEWFIELD	AMBASSADOR	1936
C-3	UNNAMED ROLIN PROJECT (sh)	WHITING	PATHE EXCHANGE	1915
C-3	WAY OF ALL PANTS (sh)	JONES, MCCAREY	MGM	1927
C-3	WHAT A BOZO (sh)	PARROTT	MGM	1931
C-3	WHEN THE WIFE'S AWAY	STRAYER	COLUMBIA	1926

Movie Still Identification Book Ultimate Edition - Letters

CODE	TITLE/NAME	DIRECTOR/TYPE	STUDIO/DISTRIBUTOR	YEAR
C-4	BELLE OF BROADWAY	HOYT	COLUMBIA	1926
C-4	BY WHOSE HAND?	LANG	COLUMBIA	1927
C-4	DEVIL'S PLAYGROUND	KENTON	COLUMBIA	1937
C-4	GRAND EXIT	KENTON	COLUMBIA	1935
C-4	HASTY MARRIAGE (sh)	PRATT	MGM	1931
C-4	LADY IS WILLING	MILLER	COLUMBIA	1934
C-4	LAW AND ORDER	CAHN	UNIVERSAL	1932
C-4	LIFE BEGINS WITH LOVE	MCCAREY	COLUMBIA	1937
C-4	MAMMA'S BOY (sh)	DORAN	PATHE EXCHANGE	1920
C-4	MICKEY'S MINSTRELS	DUFFY	COLUMBIA	1934
C-4	OLD DRACULA	DONNER	COLUMBIA	1975
C-4	PLATINUM BLONDE	CAPRA	COLUMBIA	1931
C4	PORT AFRIQUE (UK)	MATE	COLUMBIA	1956
C-4	STREET OF ILLUSION	KENTON	COLUMBIA	1928
C-4	THAT'S GRATITUDE	CRAVEN	COLUMBIA	1934
C-4	TOL'ABLE DAVID	BLYSTONE	COLUMBIA	1930
C-4	UNNAMED ROLIN PROJECT (sh)	WHITING	PATHE EXCHANGE	1915
C-4	US (sh)		MGM	1927
C-4	WALL STREET	NEILL	COLUMBIA	1929
C-4	WANDERING PAPAS (sh)	LAUREL	PATHE EXCHANGE	1926
C-4	WASHINGTON MERRY-GO-ROUND	CRUZE	COLUMBIA	1932
C-5	CRIMINAL CODE	HAWKS	COLUMBIA	1931
C-5	ESCAPE FROM DEVIL'S ISLAND	ROGELL	COLUMBIA	1935
C-5	FOG	ROGELL	COLUMBIA	1933
C-5	GUILTY GENERATION	LEE	COLUMBIA	1931
C-5	ISLE OF FORGOTTEN WOMEN	SEITZ	COLUMBIA	1927
C-5	JEALOUSY	NEILL	COLUMBIA	1934
C-5	MEXICALI ROSE	KENTON	COLUMBIA	1929
C-5	MICKEY'S RESCUE	DUFFY	COLUMBIA	1934
C-5	NEVER THE DAMES SHALL MEET (sh)	PARROTT	MGM	1927
C-5	POWDER MANKEYS (sh)	WHITING	PATHE EXCHANGE	1915
C-5	QUEEN'S UP! (sh)	NEWMEYER	PATHE EXCHANGE	1920
C-5	SINNER'S PARADE	ADOLFI	COLUMBIA	1928
C-5	SOS PERILS OF THE SEA	HOGAN	COLUMBIA	1925
C-5	STARVATION BLUES (sh)	WALLACE	PATHE EXCHANGE	1925
C-5	SWEET ROSIE O'GRADY	STRAYER	COLUMBIA	1926
C-5	TABASCO KID (sh)	HORNE	MGM	1932
C-5	THAT'S MY BOY	NEILL	COLUMBIA	1932
C-6	ALL FOR NOTHING (sh)	PARROTT	MGM	1928
C-6	CHAMPAGNE FOR BREAKFAST	BROWN	COLUMBIA	1935
C-6	COLLEGE HERO	LANG	COLUMBIA	1927
C-6	FASHION MADNESS (mistake)	GASNIER	COLUMBIA	1928
C-6	LION AND THE LAMB	SEITZ	COLUMBIA	1931
C-6	MAN AGAINST WOMAN	CUMMINGS	COLUMBIA	1932
C-6	MAN HATERS (sh)	BARROWS	PATHE EXCHANGE	1922
C-6	MEN IN HER LIFE	BEAUDINE	COLUMBIA	1931
C-6	MICKEY'S MEDICINE MAN	DUFFY	COLUMBIA	1934
C-6	MURDER ON THE ROOF	SEITZ	COLUMBIA	1930
C-6	NICKLE NURSER (sh)	DOANE	MGM	1932
C-6	OBEY THE LAW	RABOCH	COLUMBIA	1926
C-6	ONE WAY TICKET	BIBERMAN	COLUMBIA	1935
C-6	SHADOWS OF SING SING	ROSEN	COLUMBIA	1934
C-6	SHE MARRIED AN ARTIST	GERING	COLUMBIA	1937
C-6	SUBMARINE	CAPRA	COLUMBIA	1928
C-6	WHAT'S THE WORLD COMING TO? (sh)	JONES, WALLACE	PATHE EXCHANGE	1926
C-7	BETTER WAY	INCE	COLUMBIA	1926
C-7	DECEIVER	KING	COLUMBIA	1931
C-7	DRIFTWOOD	CABANNE	COLUMBIA	1928
C-7	EIGHT BELLS	NEILL	COLUMBIA	1935
C-7	GREEK MEETS GREEK (sh)	BARROWS	PATHE EXCHANGE	1920
C-7	I'M A FUGITIVE FROM A CHAIN STORE	NEILSON	COLUMBIA	1932
C-7	IN WALKED CHARLEY (sh)	DOANE	MGM	1932
C-7	LET'S FALL IN LOVE	BURTON	COLUMBIA	1934
C-7	LONE WOLF RETURNS	NEILL	COLUMBIA	1935
C-7	MADONNA OF THE STREETS	ROBERTSON	COLUMBIA	1930
C-7	MELODY MAN	NEILL	COLUMBIA	1930
C-7	MORE THAN A SECRETARY	GREEN	COLUMBIA	1936
C-7	MOVIE NIGHT (sh)	FOSTER	MGM	1929
C-7	NO MORE ORCHIDS	LANG	COLUMBIA	1932
C-7	SCARED STIFF (sh)	HORNE	PATHE EXCHANGE	1926

Movie Still Identification Book Ultimate Edition - Letters

CODE	TITLE/NAME	DIRECTOR/TYPE	STUDIO/DISTRIBUTOR	YEAR
C-7	TIGRESS	SEITZ	COLUMBIA	1927
C-8	AIR HOSTESS	ROGELL	COLUMBIA	1932
C-8	FAMILY GROUP (sh)	GUIOL, MCCAREY	MGM	1928
C-8	FIRST IN WAR (sh)	DOANE	MGM	1932
C-8	IF YOU COULD ONLY COOK	SEITER	COLUMBIA	1935
C-8	NO GREATER GLORY	BORZAGE	COLUMBIA	1934
C-8	PERSONALITY	HEERMAN	COLUMBIA	1930
C-8	REMEMBER	SELMAN	COLUMBIA	1926
C-8	SLEEPY HEAD (sh)	BARROWS	PATHE EXCHANGE	1920
C-8	STAGE KISSES	KELLEY	COLUMBIA	1927
C-8	STOOL PIGEON	HOFFMAN	COLUMBIA	1928
C-8	STRANGE CASE OF POISON IVY	NEILSON	COLUMBIA	1933
C-8	TEN CENTS A DANCE	BARRYMORE	COLUMBIA	1931
C-8	THREE WISE GIRLS	BEAUDINE	COLUMBIA	1932
C-8	WHITE LIES	BULGAKOV	COLUMBIA	1934
C-8	WIFE TAMERS (sh)	HORNE	PATHE EXCHANGE	1926
C-8	WOMEN OF GLAMOUR	WILES	COLUMBIA	1937
C-9	ACHING YOUTH (sh)	GUIOL	MGM	1928
C-9	BURGLARS BOLD (sh)	BARROWS	PATHE EXCHANGE	1921
C-9	GALLOPING GHOSTS (sh)	PARROTT	PATHE EXCHANGE	1928
C-9	HELL-SHIP MORGAN	LEDERMAN	COLUMBIA	1936
C-9	I PROMISE TO PAY	LEDERMAN	COLUMBIA	1937
C-9	LAST PARADE	KENTON	COLUMBIA	1931
C-9	LITTLE MISS ROUGHNECK	SCOTTO	COLUMBIA	1938
C-9	MAKER OF MEN	SEDGWICK	COLUMBIA	1931
C-9	MERRY WIDOWER (sh)	WALLACE	PATHE EXCHANGE	1926
C-9	ONCE TO EVERY WOMAN	HILLYER	COLUMBIA	1934
C-9	OPENING NIGHT	GRIFFITH	COLUMBIA	1927
C-9	POWER OF THE PRESS	CAPRA	COLUMBIA	1928
C-9	SO THIS IS AFRICA	CLINE	COLUMBIA	1933
C-9	STOLEN PLEASURE	ROSEN	COLUMBIA	1927
C-9	VENGEANCE	MAYO	COLUMBIA	1930
C-9	WHOLE TOWN'S TALKING	FORD	COLUMBIA	1935
C-9	YOUNG IRONSIDES (sh)	PARROTT	MGM	1932
C-10	DECEPTION	SEILER	COLUMBIA	1932
C-10	DISCONTENTED HUSBANDS	LESAINT	COLUMBIA	1924
C-10	GIRL GRIEF (sh)	PARROTT	MGM	1932
C-10	GUILTY?	SEITZ	COLUMBIA	1930
C-10	LIMOUSINE LOVE (sh)	GUIOL	MGM	1928
C-10	MENACE	NEILL	COLUMBIA	1932
C-10	MILLS OF THE GODS	NEILL	COLUMBIA	1934
C-10	NINTH GUEST	NEILL	COLUMBIA	1934
C-10	NO TIME TO MARRY	LACHMAN	COLUMBIA	1938
C-10	NOTHING TO WEAR	KENTON	COLUMBIA	1928
C-10	PINNING IT ON (sh)	BARROWS	PATHE EXCHANGE	1921
C-10	SHOULD HUSBANDS PAY? (sh)	JONES, LAUREL	PATHE EXCHANGE	1926
C-10	SUBWAY EXPRESS	NEWMEYER	COLUMBIA	1931
C-10	WANDERING GIRLS	INCE	COLUMBIA	1927
C-10	WARNING	SEITZ	COLUMBIA	1927
C-10	WOMAN IN DISTRESS	SHORES	COLUMBIA	1937
C-10	YOU MAY BE NEXT	ROGELL	COLUMBIA	1936
C-11	ACQUITTED	STRAYER	COLUMBIA	1929
C-11	APACHE	ROSEN	COLUMBIA	1928
C-11	AS THE DEVIL COMMANDS	NEILL	COLUMBIA	1933
C-11	BACHELOR'S BABY	STRAYER	COLUMBIA	1927
C-11	BEHIND THE MASK	DILLON	COLUMBIA	1932
C-11	BEST MAN WINS	KENTON	COLUMBIA	1935
C-11	CHILD OF MANHATTAN	BUZZELL	COLUMBIA	1933
C-11	FASHION MADNESS	GASNIER	COLUMBIA	1928
C-11	FIGHT PEST (sh)	GUIOL, MCCAREY	MGM	1928
C-11	FLOOD	TINLING	COLUMBIA	1931
C-11	IT HAPPENED ONE NIGHT	CAPRA	COLUMBIA	1934
C-11	IT'S ALL YOURS	NUGENT	COLUMBIA	1937
C-11	KING STEPS OUT	VON STERNBERG	COLUMBIA	1936
C-11	LADIES OF LEISURE	CAPRA	COLUMBIA	1930
C11	LITTLE MISS REBELLION	FAWCETT	PARAMOUNT	1920
C-11	NOW WE'LL TELL ONE (sh)	PARROTT	MGM	1932
C-11	OH, PROMISE ME (sh)	BARROWS	PATHE EXCHANGE	1921
C-11	PAL O'MINE	LESAINT	COLUMBIA	1924
C-12	CARNIVAL	LANG	COLUMBIA	1935

Movie Still Identification Book Ultimate Edition - Letters

CODE	TITLE/NAME	DIRECTOR/TYPE	STUDIO/DISTRIBUTOR	YEAR
C-12	FINAL EDITION	HIGGIN	COLUMBIA	1932
C-12	IMAGINE MY EMBARRASSMENT (sh)	YATES, MCCAREY	MGM	1928
C-12	LADY OF SECRETS	GERING	COLUMBIA	1936
C-12	LONE WOLF'S DAUGHTER	ROGELL	COLUMBIA	1929
C12	MAN FROM RED GULCH	MORTIMER	PRODUCER DIST. CORP	1925
C-12	MIRACLE WOMAN	CAPRA	COLUMBIA	1931
C-12	MR. BRIDE (sh)	PARROTT	MGM	1932
C-12	PENITENTIARY	BRAHM	COLUMBIA	1938
C-12	PRINCE PISTACHIO (sh)	BARROWS	PATHE EXCHANGE	1921
C12	REMODELING HER HUSBAND	GISH	ARTCRAFT	1920
C-12	ROYAL ROMANCE	KENTON	COLUMBIA	1930
C-12	SIREN	HASKIN	COLUMBIA	1928
C-12	SOCIAL REGISTER	NEILAN	COLUMBIA	1934
C-12	VALLEY OF VANISHING MEN (serial)	BENNET	COLUMBIA	1942
C-12	WRECK	CRAFT	COLUMBIA	1927
C-13	BELOW THE SEA	ROGELL	COLUMBIA	1933
C-13	CALL OF THE WEST	RAY	COLUMBIA	1930
C-13	CALLING OF DAN MATHEWS	ROSEN	COLUMBIA	1935
C-13	CARMEN, BABY	METZGER	AUDUBON	1967
C-13	FALLEN ARCHES (sh)	MEINS	MGM	1933
C-13	I'LL LOVE YOU ALWAYS	BULGAKOV	COLUMBIA	1935
C-13	IS EVERYBODY HAPPY? (sh)	YATES	MGM	1928
C-13	LINEUP	HIGGIN	COLUMBIA	1934
C-13	LONE WOLF RETURNS (mistake)	INCE	COLUMBIA	1926
C-13	MEET NERO WOLFE	BIBERMAN	COLUMBIA	1936
C-13	PAINT AND POWDER (sh)	ROACH	PATHE EXCHANGE	1921
C-13	PRICE OF HONOR	GRIFFITH	COLUMBIA	1927
C-13	RESTLESS YOUTH	CABANNE	COLUMBIA	1928
C-13	SHOPWORN	GRINDE	COLUMBIA	1932
C-13	THAT CERTAIN THING	CAPRA	COLUMBIA	1928
C-13	TOGETHER WE LIVE	MACK	COLUMBIA	1935
C-14	BIG TIMER	BUZZELL	COLUMBIA	1932
C-14	BIRDS OF PREY	CRAFT	COLUMBIA	1927
C-14	BOOSTER (sh)	YATES	MGM	1928
C-14	DEVIL'S SQUADRON	KENTON	COLUMBIA	1936
C-14	GOOD BAD GIRL	NEILL	COLUMBIA	1931
C-14	HURRY WEST (sh)	BARROWS	PATHE EXCHANGE	1921
C-14	LET'S GET MARRIED	GREEN	COLUMBIA	1937
C-14	LET'S LIVE TONIGHT	SCHERTZINGER	COLUMBIA	1935
C-14	LONE WOLF IN PARIS	ROGELL	COLUMBIA	1938
C-14	NATURE IN THE WRONG (sh)	CHASE	MGM	1933
C-14	PRINCE OF DIAMONDS	BROWN	COLUMBIA	1930
C-14	SISTERS UNDER THE SKIN	BURTON	COLUMBIA	1934
C-14	WHEN STRANGERS MARRY	BADGER	COLUMBIA	1933
C-14	WIFE'S RELATIONS	MARSHALL	COLUMBIA	1928
C-14	YOUNGER GENERATION	CAPRA	COLUMBIA	1929
C-15	ALL PARTS (sh)	YATES	MGM	1928
C-15	ARIZONA	SEITZ	COLUMBIA	1931
C-15	AROUND THE CORNER	GLENNON	COLUMBIA	1930
C-15	BRIEF MOMENT	BURTON	COLUMBIA	1933
C-15	DEATH FLIES EAST	ROSEN	COLUMBIA	1935
C-15	DON'T GAMBLE WITH LOVE	MURPHY	COLUMBIA	1936
C-15	HIS SILENT RACKET (sh)		MGM	1933
C-15	LADY RAFFLES	NEILL	COLUMBIA	1928
C-15	LOVE AFFAIR	FREELAND	COLUMBIA	1932
C-15	MOST PRECIOUS THING IN LIFE	HILLYER	COLUMBIA	1934
C-15	PLEASURE BEFORE BUSINESS	STRAYER	COLUMBIA	1927
C-15	RACKETEERS IN EXILE	KENTON	COLUMBIA	1937
C-15	RUNNING WILD (sh)	BARROWS	PATHE EXCHANGE	1921
C-15	SIDESHOW	KENTON	COLUMBIA	1928
C-15	THERE'S ALWAYS A WOMAN	HALL	COLUMBIA	1938
C-16	ARABIAN TIGHTS (sh)	ROACH	MGM	1933
C-16	ATTORNEY FOR THE DEFENSE	CUMMINGS	COLUMBIA	1932
C-16	CAPTAIN HATES THE SEA	MILESTONE	COLUMBIA	1934
C-16	CHASING HUSBANDS (sh)	PARROTT	MGM	1928
C-16	FIFTY FATHOMS DEEP	NEILL	COLUMBIA	1931
C-16	HOBGOBLINS (sh)	GORDON	PATHE EXCHANGE	1921
C-16	LADY RAFFLES	NEILL	COLUMBIA	1928
C-16	OBJECT: ALIMONY	DUNLAP	COLUMBIA	1928
C-16	PAROLE GIRL	CLINE	COLUMBIA	1933

Movie Still Identification Book Ultimate Edition - Letters

CODE	TITLE/NAME	DIRECTOR/TYPE	STUDIO/DISTRIBUTOR	YEAR
C-16	POOR GIRLS	CRAFT	COLUMBIA	1927
C-16	PRIDE OF THE MARINES	LEDERMAN	COLUMBIA	1936
C-16	SO THIS IS LOVE	CAPRA	COLUMBIA	1928
C-16	SOLDIERS AND WOMEN	SLOMAN	COLUMBIA	1930
C-16	UNWELCOME STRANGER	ROSEN	COLUMBIA	1935
C-16	YOU CAN'T TAKE IT WITH YOU	CAPRA	COLUMBIA	1938
C-17	AMERICAN MADNESS (see C-1)	CAPRA	COLUMBIA	1932
C-17	CIRCUS QUEEN MURDER	NEILL	COLUMBIA	1933
C-17	DANGEROUS AFFAIR	SEDGWICK	COLUMBIA	1931
C-17	END OF THE TRAIL	KENTON	COLUMBIA	1936
C-17	FAKER	ROSEN	COLUMBIA	1929
C-17	FATHER		COLUMBIA	1928
C-17	HOLIDAY	CUKOR	COLUMBIA	1938
C-17	LOVE LESSON (sh)	BARROWS	PATHE EXCHANGE	1921
C-17	PARTY WIRE	KENTON	COLUMBIA	1935
C-17	PAYING THE PRICE	SELMAN	COLUMBIA	1927
C-17	RUBY LIPS (sh)	PARROTT	MGM	1929
C-17	SHERMAN SAID IT (sh)	CHASE	MGM	1933
C-17	TEMPTATION	HOPPER	COLUMBIA	1930
C-17	TWENTIETH CENTURY	HAWKS	COLUMBIA	1934
C-17	VENUS MAKES TROUBLE	WILES	COLUMBIA	1937
C-17	WOMAN'S WAY	MORTIMER	COLUMBIA	1928
C-18	COCKTAIL HOUR	SCHERTZINGER	COLUMBIA	1933
C-18	HOLLYWOOD SPEAKS	BUZZELL	COLUMBIA	1932
C-18	LOVE ME FOREVER	SCHERTZINGER	COLUMBIA	1935
C-18	MIDSUMMER MUSH (sh)	CHASE	MGM	1933
C-18	NON SKID KID (sh)	GORDON	PATHE EXCHANGE	1922
C-18	OFF TO BUFFALO (sh)	HORNE	MGM	1929
C-18	ROAMING LADY	ROGELL	COLUMBIA	1936
C-18	SISTERS	FLOOD	COLUMBIA	1930
C-18	SPORTING AGE	KENTON	COLUMBIA	1928
C-18	TRIAL MARRIAGE	KENTON	COLUMBIA	1929
C-18	WHIRLPOOL	NEILL	COLUMBIA	1934
C-19	AIR HAWKS	ROGELL	COLUMBIA	1935
C-19	BEHIND CLOSED DOORS	NEILL	COLUMBIA	1929
C-19	BY WHOSE HAND?	STOLOFF	COLUMBIA	1932
C-19	CHARLEY'S AUNT	CHRISTIE	COLUMBIA	1931
C-19	CITY STREETS (CITY SHADOWS*)	ROGELL	COLUMBIA	1938
C-19	HELL'S ISLAND	SLOMAN	COLUMBIA	1930
C-19	LEAGUE OF FRIGHTENED MEN	GREEN	COLUMBIA	1937
C-19	LOUD SOUP (sh)	FOSTER	MGM	1929
C-19	LUNCHEON AT TWELVE (sh)	CHASE	MGM	1933
C-19	MATINEE IDOL	CAPRA	COLUMBIA	1928
C-19	MINE WITH THE IRON DOOR	HOWARD	COLUMBIA	1936
C-19	ROMANTIC AGE	FLOREY	COLUMBIA	1927
C-19	SPORTING AGE	KENTON	COLUMBIA	1928
C-19	STRAIGHT CROOK (sh)		PATHE EXCHANGE	1921
C-19	WHOM THE GODS DESTROY	LANG	COLUMBIA	1934
C-19	WOMAN I STOLE	CUMMINGS	COLUMBIA	1933
C-20	AND SO THEY WERE MARRIED	NUGENT	COLUMBIA	1936
C-20	ANN CARVER'S PROFESSION	BUZZELL	COLUMBIA	1933
C-20	AWAKENING OF JIM BURKE	HILLYER	COLUMBIA	1935
C-20	CHINK (sh)		PATHE EXCHANGE	1921
C-20	CRACKED ICEMAN (sh)	DUNN	MGM	1934
C-20	DESERT BRIDE	CAPRA	COLUMBIA	1928
C-20	GIRL'S SCHOOL	BRAHM	COLUMBIA	1938
C-20	LADIES MUST PLAY	CANNON	COLUMBIA	1930
C-20	MEET THE WIFE	PEARCE	COLUMBIA	1931
C-20	PARTY'S OVER	LANG	COLUMBIA	1934
C-20	QUITTER	HENABERY	COLUMBIA	1929
C-20	RICH MEN'S SONS	GRAVES	COLUMBIA	1927
C-20	SPLIT IMAGE (CAN)	KOTCHEFF	POLYGRAM	1982
C-20	THIN TWINS (sh)	HORNE	MGM	1929
C-20	WAR CORRESPONDENT	SLOANE	COLUMBIA	1932
C-21	BIG SQUAWK (sh)	DOANE	MGM	1929
C-21	BROADWAY DADDIES	WINDEMERE	COLUMBIA	1928
C-21	CLOWN	CRAFT	COLUMBIA	1927
C-21	DONOVAN AFFAIR	CAPRA	COLUMBIA	1929
C-21	FOUR PARTS (sh)	CHASE, DUNN	MGM	1934
C-21	HELLCAT	ROGELL	COLUMBIA	1934

Movie Still Identification Book Ultimate Edition - Letters

CODE	TITLE/NAME	DIRECTOR/TYPE	STUDIO/DISTRIBUTOR	YEAR
C-21	I AM THE LAW	HALL	COLUMBIA	1938
C-21	LATE HOURS (sh)	BARROWS	PATHE EXCHANGE	1921
C-21	NIGHTCLUB LADY	CUMMINGS	COLUMBIA	1932
C-21	SQUEALER	BROWN	COLUMBIA	1930
C-21	WHAT PRICE INNOCENCE?	MACK	COLUMBIA	1933
C-22	AFTER THE STORM	SEITZ	COLUMBIA	1928
C-22	BLACK MOON	NEILL	COLUMBIA	1934
C-22	BROADWAY DADDIES	WINDEMERE	COLUMBIA	1928
C-22	CATCH 22	NICHOLS	PARAMOUNT	1970
C-22	ETERNAL WOMAN	MCCARTHY	COLUMBIA	1929
C-22	I'LL TAKE VANILLA (sh)	DUNN	MGM	1934
C-22	IT HAPPENED IN HOLLYWOOD	LACHMAN	COLUMBIA	1937
C-22	KID SISTER	GRAVES	COLUMBIA	1927
C-22	LAST MAN	HIGGIN	COLUMBIA	1932
C-22	LAST OF THE LONE WOLF	BOLESLAWSKI	COLUMBIA	1930
C-22	LEAPING LOVE (sh)	DOANE	MGM	1929
C-22	STOP KIDDING (sh)	KERR, BARROWS	PATHE EXCHANGE	1921
C-22	TRAPPED BY TELEVISION	LORD	COLUMBIA	1936
C-22	UNKNOWN WOMAN	ROGELL	COLUMBIA	1935
C-22	WRECKER	ROGELL	COLUMBIA	1933
C-23	AFTER THE DANCE	BULGAKOV	COLUMBIA	1935
C-23	ANOTHER WILD IDEA (sh)	CHASE, DUNN	MGM	1934
C-23	BLACKMAILER	WILES	COLUMBIA	1936
C-23	BLIND DATE	NEILL	COLUMBIA	1934
C-23	FATHER AND SON	KENTON	COLUMBIA	1929
C-23	FOR LADIES ONLY	LEHRMAN, PEMBROKE	COLUMBIA	1927
C-23	FOR THE LOVE O' LIL	TINLING	COLUMBIA	1930
C-23	GOLF WIDOWS	KENTON	COLUMBIA	1928
C-23	GOOD MORNING JUDGE (sh)	ROACH	PATHE EXCHANGE	1922
C-23	LADY OBJECTS	KENTON	COLUMBIA	1938
C-23	MY WOMAN	SCHERTZINGER	COLUMBIA	1933
C-23	NIGHT MAYOR	STOLOFF	COLUMBIA	1932
C-23	SNAPPY SNEEZER (sh)	DOANE	MGM	1929
C-24	BACHELOR GIRL	THORPE	COLUMBIA	1929
C-24	CRAZY FEET (sh)	DOANE (SH)	MGM	1929
C-24	DEFENSE RESTS	HILLYER	COLUMBIA	1934
C-24	FEATHER IN HER HAT	SANTELL	COLUMBIA	1935
C-24	FLIGHT TO FAME	COLEMAN	COLUMBIA	1938
C-24	FURY OF THE JUNGLE	NEILL	COLUMBIA	1933
C-24	IT CAN'T LAST FOREVER	MACFADDEN	COLUMBIA	1937
C-24	IT HAPPENED ONE DAY (sh)	DUNN	MGM	1934
C-24	LATE LAMENTED (sh)	EDDY	PATHE EXCHANGE	1922
C-24	MODERN MOTHERS	ROSEN	COLUMBIA	1928
C-24	SWEETHEARTS ON PARADE	NEILAN	COLUMBIA	1930
C-24	SWELL HEAD	GRAVES	COLUMBIA	1927
C-24	THIS SPORTING AGE	BENNISON, ERICKSON	COLUMBIA	1932
C-25	BLACK ROOM	NEILL	COLUMBIA	1935
C-25	COUNTERFEIT	KENTON	COLUMBIA	1936
C-25	FLYING MARINE	ROGELL	COLUMBIA	1929
C-25	I'LL TAKE ROMANCE	GRIFFITH	COLUMBIA	1937
C-25	NAME THE WOMAN	KENTON	COLUMBIA	1928
C-25	NAME THE WOMAN	ROGELL	COLUMBIA	1934
C-25	ON THEIR WAY (sh)	BARROWS	PATHE EXCHANGE	1921
C-25	SOMETHING SIMPLE (sh)	CHASE, WEEMS	MGM	1934
C-25	STEPPING OUT (sh)	DOANE	MGM	1929
C-25	VANITY STREET	GRINDE	COLUMBIA	1932
C-25-A	FLIGHT	CAPRA	COLUMBIA	1929
C-26	FALL OF EVE	STRAYER	COLUMBIA	1929
C-26	GREAT GOBS! (sh)	DOANE	MGM	1929
C-26	LADY FROM NOWHERE	WILES	COLUMBIA	1936
C-26	MASTER OF MEN	HILLYER	COLUMBIA	1933
C-26	RANSOM	SEITZ	COLUMBIA	1928
C-26	SHE MARRIED HER BOSS	LA CAVA	COLUMBIA	1935
C-26	SWEET BY AND BY (sh)	KERR	PATHE EXCHANGE	1921
C-26	VIRTUE	BUZZELL	COLUMBIA	1932
C-26	YOU SAID A HATFUL! (sh)	CHASE	MGM	1934
C-27	AWFUL TRUTH	MCCAREY	COLUMBIA	1937
C-27	COLLEGE COQUETTE	ARCHAINBAUD	COLUMBIA	1929
C-27	FATE'S FATHEAD (sh)	CHASE	MGM	1934
C-27	FUGITIVE LADY	ROGELL	COLUMBIA	1934

Movie Still Identification Book Ultimate Edition - Letters

CODE	TITLE/NAME	DIRECTOR/TYPE	STUDIO/DISTRIBUTOR	YEAR
C-27	MANY HAPPY RETURNS (sh)	KERR	PATHE EXCHANGE	1922
C-27	MR. DEEDS GOES TO TOWN	CAPRA	COLUMBIA	1936
C-27	REAL MCCOY (sh)	DOANE	MGM	1930
C-27	WAY OF THE STRONG	CAPRA	COLUMBIA	1928
C-28	ALL TEED UP (sh)	KENNEDY	MGM	1930
C-28	ATLANTIC ADVENTURE	ROGELL	COLUMBIA	1935
C-28	BEWARE OF BLONDES	SEITZ	COLUMBIA	1928
C-28	BUSY BEES (sh)	KERR	PATHE EXCHANGE	1922
C-28	CHASES OF PIMPLE STREET (sh)	CHASE	MGM	1934
C-28	LADY BY CHOICE	BURTON	COLUMBIA	1934
C-28	LIGHT FINGERS	HENABERY	COLUMBIA	1929
C-28	THERE'S THAT WOMAN AGAIN	HALL	COLUMBIA	1939
C-28	WAY OF THE STRONG (MISTAKE)	CAPRA	COLUMBIA	1928
C-29	HIGH TIDE (sh)	BARROWS	PATHE EXCHANGE	1922
C-29	HURRICANE	INCE	COLUMBIA	1929
C-29	I'LL FIX IT	NEILL	COLUMBIA	1934
C-29	LITTLE ADVENTURESS	LEDERMAN	COLUMBIA	1938
C-29	OKAY TOOTS! (sh)	CHASE, TERHUNE	MGM	1935
C-29	PUBLIC MENACE	KENTON	COLUMBIA	1935
C-29	SAY IT WITH SABLES	CAPRA	COLUMBIA	1928
C-29	THEODORA GOES WILD	BOLESLAWSKI	COLUMBIA	1936
C-29	WHISPERING WHOOPEE (sh)	HORNE	MGM	1930
C-30	ACQUITTED	STRAYER	COLUMBIA	1929
C-30	ADVENTURE IN MANHATTAN	LUDWIG	COLUMBIA	1936
C-30	AMONG THE MISSING	ROGELL	COLUMBIA	1934
C-30	BETWEEN MEALS (sh)	GREY	PATHE EXCHANGE	1926
C-30	BLONDIE	STRAYER	COLUMBIA	1938
C-30	BROADWAY SCANDALS (mistake)	ARCHAINBAUD	COLUMBIA	1929
C-30	FAITH, HOPE AND CHARITY (sh)	BLAKE	COLUMBIA	1930
C-30	FIFTY MILLION HUSBANDS (sh)	HORNE, KENNEDY	MGM	1930
C-30	POKER AT EIGHT (sh)	CHASE	MGM	1935
C-30	SAY IT WITH SABLES	CAPRA	COLUMBIA	1927
C-30	VIRGIN LIPS	CLIFTON	COLUMBIA	1928
C-30-A	BROADWAY HOOFER	ARCHAINBAUD	COLUMBIA	1929
C-31	BROADWAY HOOFER	ARCHAINBAUD	COLUMBIA	1929
C-31	DEVIL IS DRIVING	LACHMAN	COLUMBIA	1937
C-31	DON'T BUTT IN (ROUSTABOUT) (sh)	GREY	PATHE EXCHANGE	1926
C-31	FAST WORK (sh)	HORNE	MGM	1930
C-31	NEVER STRIKE YOUR MOTHER (sh)	BLAKE	COLUMBIA	1930
C-31	SMASHING THE SPY RING	CABANNE	COLUMBIA	1939
C-31	SOUTHERN EXPOSURE (sh)	CHASE	MGM	1935
C-32	FOUR STAR BOARDER (sh)	CHASE	MGM	1935
C-32	GIRL SHOCK (sh)	HORNE	MGM	1930
C-32	HOT AND BOTHERED (sh)	BLAKE	COLUMBIA	1930
C-32	LADY AND THE MOB	STOLOFF	COLUMBIA	1938
C-32	LADY AND THE MOB	STOLOFF	COLUMBIA	1939
C-32	SECRETS	BORZAGE	UNITED ARTISTS	1933
C-32	TRY, TRY AGAIN (sh)	GREY	PATHE EXCHANGE	1922
C-32	TWO FISTED GENTLEMAN	WILES	COLUMBIA	1936
C-33	DOLLAR DIZZY (sh)	HORNE	MGM	1930
C-33	LONE WOLF SPY HUNT	GODFREY	COLUMBIA	1939
C-33	NURSE TO YOU! (sh)	CHASE, MOFFITT	MGM	1935
C-33	PRODIGAL DAUGHTER (sh)	BUZZELL	COLUMBIA	1930
C-33	SOFT PEDAL (sh)	GREY	PATHE EXCHANGE	1926
C-33	THEY MET IN A TAXI	GREEN	COLUMBIA	1936
C-34	CAME THE PAWN (sh)	BUZZELL	COLUMBIA	1930
C-34	LOOSER THAN LOOSE (sh)	HORNE	MGM	1930
C-34	MAN WHO LIVED TWICE	LACHMAN	COLUMBIA	1936
C-34	MANHATTAN MONKEY BUSINESS (sh)	CHASE, LAW	MGM	1935
C-35	HARD BOILED YEGGS (sh)	BUZZELL	COLUMBIA	1930
C-35	HIGH C'S (sh)	HORNE	MGM	1930
C-35	LAWLESS RIDERS	BENNET	COLUMBIA	1935
C-35	PAY THE CASHIER (sh)	GREY	PATHE EXCHANGE	1926
C-35	PUBLIC GHOST #1 (sh)	CHASE, LAW	MGM	1935
C-35	WHEN YOU'RE IN LOVE	RISKIN	COLUMBIA	1937
C-36	CRYSTAL GAZER	BUZZELL	COLUMBIA	1930
C-36	LIFE HESITATES AT 40 (sh)	CHASE, LAW	MGM	1936
C-36	ONLY ANGELS HAVE WINGS	HAWKS	COLUMBIA	1939
C-36	SLEUTH (sh)	GREY	PATHE EXCHANGE	1922
C-36	THUNDERING TENORS (sh)	HORNE	MGM	1931

Movie Still Identification Book Ultimate Edition - Letters

CODE	TITLE/NAME	DIRECTOR/TYPE	STUDIO/DISTRIBUTOR	YEAR
C-37	COAST GUARD	LUDWIG	COLUMBIA	1939
C-37	COUNT TAKES THE COUNT (sh)	LAW	MGM	1936
C-37	LONE STAR STRANGER (sh)	BUZZELL	COLUMBIA	1931
C-37	ONLY SON (sh)	GREY	PATHE EXCHANGE	1926
C-37	PIP FROM PITTSBURGH (sh)	PARROTT	MGM	1931
C-38	HIRED AND FIRED (sh)	GREY	PATHE EXCHANGE	1926
C-38	ROMANCE OF THE REDWOODS	VIDOR	COLUMBIA	1939
C-38	ROUGH SEAS (sh)	PARROTT	MGM	1931
C-38	VAMP TILL READY (sh)	CHASE, LAW	MGM	1936
C-38	WINE, WOMAN BUT NO SONG (sh)		COLUMBIA	1931
C-39	BLONDIE MEETS THE BOSS	STRAYER	COLUMBIA	1939
C-39	CHECK AND RUBBER CHECK (sh)	BUZZELL	COLUMBIA	1931
C-39	NEIGHBORHOOD HOUSE (sh)	CHASE, LAW	MGM	1936
C-39	ONE OF THE SMITHS (sh)	PARROTT	MGM	1931
C-39	RICH MAN, POOR MAN (sh)	CHASE	PATHE EXCHANGE	1922
C-40	AGAINST THE LAW	HILLYER	COLUMBIA	1934
C-40	GOLDEN BOY	MAMOULIAN	COLUMBIA	1939
C-40	KINGS OR BETTER (sh)	BUZZELL	COLUMBIA	1931
C-40	ON THE WRONG TREK (sh)	CHASE, LAW	MGM	1936
C-40	THRILL HUNTER	SEITZ	COLUMBIA	1933
C-41	ARE PARENTS PICKLES? (sh)	PRATT	PATHE EXCHANGE	1925
C-41	BLIND ALLEY	VIDOR	COLUMBIA	1939
C-41	FIGHTING CODE	HILLYER	COLUMBIA	1933
C-41	MEN OF THE NIGHT	HILLYER	COLUMBIA	1934
C-42	BEHIND THE EVIDENCE	HILLYER	COLUMBIA	1935
C-42	CHRIS-CROSSED (sh)	BUZZELL	COLUMBIA	1931
C-42	FIGHTING RANGER	SEITZ	COLUMBIA	1934
C-42	GOOD GIRLS GO TO PARIS	HALL	COLUMBIA	1939
C-42	WINNER TAKE ALL (sh)	SANTELL	PATHE EXCHANGE	1923
C-43	FRIDAY THE 13TH (sh)	DAVIS	PATHE EXCHANGE	1922
C-43	IN SPITE OF DANGER	HILLYER	COLUMBIA	1935
C-43	MAN TRAILER	HILLYER	COLUMBIA	1934
C-43	MR. SMITH GOES TO WASHINGTON	CAPRA	COLUMBIA	1939
C-43	RED MEN TELL NO TALES (sh)	BUZZELL	COLUMBIA	1931
C-44	MEN OF THE HOUR	HILLYER	COLUMBIA	1935
C-44	TRUTH JUGGLER (sh)	DAVIS	PATHE EXCHANGE	1922
C-44	WOLF IN CHEAP CLOTHING (sh)	BUZZELL	COLUMBIA	1932
C-45	BED OF ROSES (sh)	HOWE	PATHE EXCHANGE	1922
C-45	BLONDE PRESSURE (sh)	BUZZELL	COLUMBIA	1931
C-45	BLONDIE TAKES A VACATION	STRAYER	COLUMBIA	1939
C-46	BRIDE-TO-BE (sh)	DAVIS	PATHE EXCHANGE	1922
C-46	FIVE LITTLE PEPPERS AND HOW THEY GREW	BARTON	COLUMBIA	1939
C-46	SHE SERVED HIM RIGHT (sh)	BUZZELL	COLUMBIA	1931
C-46	SWELL HEAD	STOLOFF	COLUMBIA	1935
C-47	SOLDIER OF MISFORTUNE (sh)	BUZZELL	COLUMBIA	1931
C-47	TAKE THE NEXT CAR (sh)	HOWE	PATHE EXCHANGE	1922
C-47	THOSE HIGH GRAY WALLS	VIDOR	COLUMBIA	1939
C-47	TOGETHER WE LIVE	MACK	COLUMBIA	1935
C-48	CALL OF THE MOTH (sh)		COLUMBIA	1932
C-48	SUPERSPEED	HILLYER	COLUMBIA	1935
C-48	TOUCH ALL THE BASES (sh)	DAVIS	PATHE EXCHANGE	1922
C-49	BEWARE SPOOKS	SEDGWICK	COLUMBIA	1939
C-49	LOVE, HONOR AND HE PAYS (sh)	BUZZELL	COLUMBIA	1932
C-49	ROUGH ON ROMEO (sh)	DAVIS	PATHE EXCHANGE	1922
C-50	AFRICA SPEAKS	HOEFLER, FULLER	COLUMBIA	1930
C-50	PRESCOTT KID	SELMAN	COLUMBIA	1934
C-50	SPEED DEMON	LEDERMAN	COLUMBIA	1932
C-50	WET WEATHER (sh)	HOWE	PATHE EXCHANGE	1922
C-51	BLONDIE BRINGS UP BABY	STRAYER	COLUMBIA	1939
C-51	OUT ON BAIL (sh)	DAVIS	PATHE EXCHANGE	1922
C-51	STATE TROOPER	LEDERMAN	COLUMBIA	1933
C-51	WESTERNER	SELMAN	COLUMBIA	1934
C-52	ARIZONA	RUGGLES	COLUMBIA	1940
C-52	OBEY THE LAW	STOLOFF	COLUMBIA	1933
C-52	SHOOT STRAIGHT (sh)	HOWE	PATHE EXCHANGE	1923
C-52	SQUARE SHOOTER	SELMAN	COLUMBIA	1935
C-53	LANDLUBBER (sh)	DAVIS	PATHE EXCHANGE	1922
C-53	LAW BEYOND THE RANGE	BEEBE	COLUMBIA	1935
C-53	SCANDAL SHEET	GRINDE	COLUMBIA	1939
C-53	SOLDIERS OF THE STORM	LEDERMAN	COLUMBIA	1933

Movie Still Identification Book Ultimate Edition - Letters

CODE	TITLE/NAME	DIRECTOR/TYPE	STUDIO/DISTRIBUTOR	YEAR
C-54	AMAZING MR. WILLIAMS	HALL	COLUMBIA	1939
C-54	DANGEROUS CROSSROADS	HILLYER	COLUMBIA	1933
C-54	REVENGE RIDER	SELMAN	COLUMBIA	1935
C-54	SOAK THE SHEIK (sh)	HOWE	PATHE EXCHANGE	1922
C-55	BONE DRY (sh)	CHASE, DAVIS	PATHE EXCHANGE	1922
C-55	CAFE HOSTESS	SALKOW	COLUMBIA	1940
C-55	FIGHTING SHADOWS	SELMAN	COLUMBIA	1935
C-55	NIGHT OF TERROR	STOLOFF	COLUMBIA	1933
C-56	KING OF THE WILD HORSES	HALEY	COLUMBIA	1933
C-56	LOOSE TIGHT WAD (sh)	HOWE	PATHE EXCHANGE	1923
C-56	MY SON IS GUILTY	BARTON	COLUMBIA	1939
C-56	RIDING WILD	SELMAN	COLUMBIA	1935
C-57	JUSTICE OF THE RANGE	SELMAN	COLUMBIA	1935
C-57	MILITARY ACADEMY	LEDERMAN	COLUMBIA	1940
C-57	SHINE 'EM UP (sh)	DAVIS	PATHE EXCHANGE	1922
C-58	FACE THE CAMERA (sh)	HOWE	PATHE EXCHANGE	1922
C-58	FIVE LITTLE PEPPERS AT HOME	BARTON	COLUMBIA	1940
C-59	GOLF BUG (sh)	DAVIS	PATHE EXCHANGE	1922
C-60	CORNERED	EASON	COLUMBIA	1932
C-60	GUARD THAT GIRL	HILLYER	COLUMBIA	1935
C-60	LEGION OF TERROR	COLEMAN	COLUMBIA	1936
C-60	LONE RIDER	KING	COLUMBIA	1930
C-60	UPPERCUT (sh)	HOWE	PATHE EXCHANGE	1922
C-61	CASE OF THE MISSING MAN	LEDERMAN	COLUMBIA	1935
C-61	COUNTERFEIT LADY	LEDERMAN	COLUMBIA	1936
C-61	SHADOW RANCH	KING	COLUMBIA	1930
C-61	WESTERN CODE	MCCARTHY	COLUMBIA	1932
C-61	WHISTLING LIONS (sh)	PARROTT	PATHE EXCHANGE	1925
C-62	FIGHTING FOR JUSTICE	BROWER	COLUMBIA	1932
C-62	FIND THE WITNESS	SELMAN	COLUMBIA	1937
C-62	MEN WITHOUT LAW	KING	COLUMBIA	1930
C-62	SHIVER AND SHAKE (sh)	HOWE	PATHE EXCHANGE	1922
C-62	TOO TOUGH TO KILL	LEDERMAN	COLUMBIA	1935
C-63	BLONDIE ON A BUDGET	STRAYER	COLUMBIA	1940
C-63	DANGEROUS INTRIGUE	SELMAN	COLUMBIA	1936
C-63	DAWN TRAIL	CABANNE	COLUMBIA	1930
C-63	END OF THE TRAIL	LEDERMAN	COLUMBIA	1933
C-63	HARVEST HANDS (sh)	DAVIS	PATHE EXCHANGE	1922
C-63	PAROLE RACKET	COLEMAN	COLUMBIA	1937
C-64	DESERT VENGEANCE	KING	COLUMBIA	1931
C-64	FLIVVER (sh)	HOWE	PATHE EXCHANGE	1922
C-64	MAN OF ACTION	MELFORD	COLUMBIA	1933
C-64	PANIC ON THE AIR	LEDERMAN	COLUMBIA	1936
C-64	SPEED TO SPARE	HILLYER	COLUMBIA	1937
C-65	AVENGER	NEILL	COLUMBIA	1931
C-65	DOCTOR TAKES A WIFE	HALL	COLUMBIA	1940
C-65	FINAL HOUR	LEDERMAN	COLUMBIA	1936
C-65	I'LL TAKE VANILLA (sh)	DAVIS	PATHE EXCHANGE	1922
C-65	MOTOR MADNESS	LEDERMAN	COLUMBIA	1937
C-65	SILENT MEN	LEDERMAN	COLUMBIA	1933
C-66	CRIMINALS OF THE AIR	COLEMAN	COLUMBIA	1937
C-66	SHAKEDOWN	SELMAN	COLUMBIA	1936
C-66	TEXAS RANGER	LEDERMAN	COLUMBIA	1931
C-66	WASHED ASHORE (sh)	HOWE	PATHE EXCHANGE	1922
C-66	WHIRLWIND	LEDERMAN	COLUMBIA	1933
C-67	ALIBI FOR MURDER	LEDERMAN	COLUMBIA	1936
C-67	FAIR WEEK (sh)	DAVIS	PATHE EXCHANGE	1922
C-67	FIGHTING SHERIFF	KING	COLUMBIA	1931
C-67	GIRLS CAN PLAY	HILLYER	COLUMBIA	1937
C-67	RUSTY RIDES ALONE	LEDERMAN	COLUMBIA	1933
C-68	BLAZE AWAY (sh)	HOWE	PATHE EXCHANGE	1922
C-68	FRAMEUP	LEDERMAN	COLUMBIA	1937
C-68	KILLER AT LARGE	SELMAN	COLUMBIA	1936
C-69	FIRE THE FIREMAN (sh)	HOWE	PATHE EXCHANGE	1922
C-70	BRANDED	LEDERMAN	COLUMBIA	1931
C-70	DANGEROUS ADVENTURE	LEDERMAN	COLUMBIA	1937
C-70	JUNGLE FIGHTERS (UK: LONG AND SHORT AND TALL)	NORMAN	CONTINENTAL	1961
C-70	POLICE CAR 17	HILLYER	COLUMBIA	1933
C-70	WESTERN FRONTIER	HERMAN	COLUMBIA	1935
C-70	WHITE BLACKSMITH (sh)	JESKE	PATHE EXCHANGE	1922

Movie Still Identification Book Ultimate Edition - Letters

CODE	TITLE/NAME	DIRECTOR/TYPE	STUDIO/DISTRIBUTOR	YEAR
C-71	BORDER LAW	KING	COLUMBIA	1931
C-71	FIGHT TO THE FINISH	COLEMAN	COLUMBIA	1937
C-71	HOLD THE PRESS	ROSEN	COLUMBIA	1933
C-71	WATCH YOUR WIFE (sh)	HOWE	PATHE EXCHANGE	1923
C-72	GAME THAT KILLS	LEDERMAN	COLUMBIA	1937
C-72	PASTE AND PAPER (sh)	JESKE	PATHE EXCHANGE	1923
C-72	RANGE FEUD	LEDERMAN	COLUMBIA	1931
C-72	STRAIGHTAWAY	BROWER	COLUMBIA	1934
C-73	DEADLINE	HILLYER	COLUMBIA	1931
C-73	SPEED THE SWEDE (sh)	HOWE	PATHE EXCHANGE	1923
C-73	SPEED WINGS	BROWER	COLUMBIA	1934
C-74	CATTLE THIEF	BENNET	COLUMBIA	1936
C-74	MR. HYPPO (sh)	JESKE	PATHE EXCHANGE	1923
C-74	RIDIN' FOR JUSTICE	LEDERMAN	COLUMBIA	1932
C-74	VOICE IN THE NIGHT	COLEMAN	COLUMBIA	1934
C-75	DON'T SAY DIE (sh)	JESKE	PATHE EXCHANGE	1923
C-75	HELLBENT FOR LOVE	LEDERMAN	COLUMBIA	1934
C-75	HEROES OF THE RANGE	BENNET	COLUMBIA	1936
C-75	ONE MAN LAW	HILLYER	COLUMBIA	1932
C-76	AVENGING WATERS	BENNET	COLUMBIA	1936
C-76	HIGH SPEED	LEDERMAN	COLUMBIA	1932
C-76	MAN'S GAME	LEDERMAN	COLUMBIA	1934
C-76	ONCE OVER (sh)	JESKE	PATHE EXCHANGE	1923
C-77	BEYOND THE LAW	LEDERMAN	COLUMBIA	1934
C-77	FUGITIVE SHERIFF	BENNET	COLUMBIA	1936
C-77	JAILED AND BAILED (sh)	HOWE	PATHE EXCHANGE	1923
C-77	SOUTH OF THE RIO GRANDE	HILLYER	COLUMBIA	1932
C-78	TIGHT SHOES (sh)	JESKE	PATHE EXCHANGE	1923
C-79	DO YOUR STUFF (sh)	HOWE	PATHE EXCHANGE	1923
C-80	BEFORE MIDNIGHT	HILLYER	COLUMBIA	1933
C-80	BOWLED OVER (sh)	JESKE	PATHE EXCHANGE	1923
C-80	CODE OF THE RANGE	COLEMAN	COLUMBIA	1936
C-80	GALLANT DEFENDER	SELMAN	COLUMBIA	1935
C-80	HE STAYED FOR BREAKFAST	HALL	COLUMBIA	1940
C-80	LIGHTNING FLYER	NIGH	COLUMBIA	1931
C-80	SHOTGUN PASS	MCGOWAN	COLUMBIA	1932
C-81	COWBOY STAR	SELMAN	COLUMBIA	1936
C-81	GET YOUR MAN (sh)	JESKE	PATHE EXCHANGE	1923
C-81	MYSTERIOUS AVENGER	SELMAN	COLUMBIA	1936
C-81	ONE IS GUILTY	HILLYER	COLUMBIA	1934
C-81	ONE WAY TRAIL	TAYLOR	COLUMBIA	1931
C-81	SKY RAIDERS	BEEBE, TAYLOR	COLUMBIA	1931
C-82	ANGELS OVER BROADWAY	GARMES	COLUMBIA	1940
C-82	CRIME OF HELEN STANLEY	LEDERMAN	COLUMBIA	1934
C-82	DODGE CITY TRAIL	COLEMAN	COLUMBIA	1936
C-82	FIGHTING MARSHALL	LEDERMAN	COLUMBIA	1931
C-82	FOR SAFE KEEPING (sh)	JESKE	PATHE EXCHANGE	1923
C-82	GIRL IN DANGER	LEDERMAN	COLUMBIA	1934
C-82	STAMPEDE	BEEBE	COLUMBIA	1936
C-83	CRIME OF HELEN STANLEY	LEDERMAN	COLUMBIA	1934
C-83	FIGHTING FOOL	HILLYER	COLUMBIA	1932
C-83	GIRL IN DANGER	LEDERMAN	COLUMBIA	1934
C-83	SECRET PATROL	SELMAN	COLUMBIA	1936
C-83	SMILE WINS (sh)	JESKE	PATHE EXCHANGE	1923
C-83	WESTBOUND MAIL	BLANGSTED	COLUMBIA	1937
C-84	BEFORE I HANG	GRINDE	COLUMBIA	1940
C-84	DON'T FLIRT (sh)	POWERS	PATHE EXCHANGE	1923
C-84	TEXAS CYCLONE	LEDERMAN	COLUMBIA	1932
C-84	TRAPPED	BARSHA	COLUMBIA	1937
C-84	TUGBOAT PRINCESS	SELMAN	COLUMBIA	1936
C-85	DARING DANGER	LEDERMAN	COLUMBIA	1932
C-85	GOOD RIDDANCE (sh)	JESKE	PATHE EXCHANGE	1923
C-85	LUCKY FUGITIVES - (CAN: STOP, LOOK AND LOVE)	GRINDE	COLUMBIA	1936
C-86	RIDING TORNADO	LEDERMAN	COLUMBIA	1932
C-86	TWO GUN LAW	BARSHA	COLUMBIA	1937
C-86	UNDER TWO JAGS (sh)	JESKE	PATHE EXCHANGE	1923
C-87	SUNNY SPAIN (sh)	HOWE	PATHE EXCHANGE	1923
C-87	TWO FISTED LAW	LEDERMAN	COLUMBIA	1932
C-87	TWO FISTED SHERIFF	BARSHA	COLUMBIA	1937
C-88	CORNERED	EASON	COLUMBIA	1932

Movie Still Identification Book Ultimate Edition - Letters

CODE	TITLE/NAME	DIRECTOR/TYPE	STUDIO/DISTRIBUTOR	YEAR
C-88	ONE MAN JUSTICE	BARSHA	COLUMBIA	1937
C-88	SECRET PEOPLE	DICKINSON	LIPPERT	1952
C-88	WATCH DOG (sh)	POWERS	PATHE EXCHANGE	1923
C-89	NOON WHISTLE (sh)	JESKE	PATHE EXCHANGE	1923
C-90	FOR ART'S SAKE (sh)	CHASE	PATHE EXCHANGE	1923
C-90	HELLO TROUBLE	HILLYER	COLUMBIA	1932
C-90	LAND NOBODY KNOWS		COLUMBIA	1931
C-90	ONE WAY OUT (sh)	HILLYER	COLUMBIA	1934
C-90	SAY IT ISN'T SO	STAUB	COLUMBIA	1933
C-90	TIME OUT FOR RHYTHM (sh)	SALKOW	COLUMBIA	1941
C-91	GENTLEMEN PREFERRED		COLUMBIA	
C-91	HIDDEN EVIDENCE	HILLYER	COLUMBIA	1934
C-91	MCKENNA OF THE MOUNTIES	LEDERMAN	COLUMBIA	1932
C-91	WHITE WINGS (sh)	JESKE	PATHE EXCHANGE	1923
C-92	ENTERTAINER	STAUB	COLUMBIA	1933
C-92	PICK AND SHOVEL (sh)	JESKE	PATHE EXCHANGE	1923
C-92	SIMPLE SOLUTION (sh)	LEDERMAN	COLUMBIA	1934
C-92	WHITE EAGLE	HILLYER	COLUMBIA	1932
C-93	FORBIDDEN TRAIL	HILLYER	COLUMBIA	1932
C-93	FRESH EGGS (sh)	HOWE	PATHE EXCHANGE	1923
C-94	BE HONEST (sh)	POWERS	PATHE EXCHANGE	1923
C-94	PROFESSOR GIVES A LESSON	HILLYER	COLUMBIA	1934
C-94	SUNDOWN RACER		COLUMBIA	1933
C-95	KILL OR CURE (sh)	PEMBROKE	PATHE EXCHANGE	1923
C-95	TREASON	SEITZ	COLUMBIA	1933
C-96	CALIFORNIA TRAIL	HILLYER	COLUMBIA	1933
C-96	FINGER PRINTS (sh)	CEDER	PATHE EXCHANGE	1923
C-96	PENNY SERENADE	STEVENS	COLUMBIA	1941
C-97	COLLARS AND CUFFS (sh)	JESKE	PATHE EXCHANGE	1923
C-97	UNKNOWN VALLEY	HILLYER	COLUMBIA	1933
C-98	LIVE WIRES (sh)	HOWE	PATHE EXCHANGE	1923
C-99	GAS AND AIR (sh)	PEMBROKE	PATHE EXCHANGE	1923
C-100	HOT DAZE (sh)	MOORE	COLUMBIA	1933
C-100	POST NO BILLS (sh)	CEDER	PATHE EXCHANGE	1923
C-100	TWO ARABIAN KNIGHTS	MILESTONE	UNITED ARTISTS	1927
C-101	FOR GUESTS ONLY (sh)	HOWE	PATHE EXCHANGE	1923
C-101	UMPA	CONRAD, GOTTLER	COLUMBIA	1933
C-102	ORANGES AND LEMONS (sh)	JESKE	PATHE EXCHANGE	1923
C-102	ROAMIN' THRU THE ROSES	GOTTLER	COLUMBIA	1933
C-103	RADIO DOUGH	BOASBERG	COLUMBIA	1934
C-103	TAKE THE AIR (sh)	CEDER	PATHE EXCHANGE	1923
C-104	DUKE OF THE NAVY	BEAUDINE	PRC	1942
C-104	HOLD YOUR TEMPER	WHITE	COLUMBIA	1933
C-104	SHORT ORDERS	PEMBROKE	PATHE EXCHANGE	1923
C-105	ED CODIGO PENAL	ROSEN, VILLARREAL	COLUMBIA	1931
C-105	TEN BABY FINGERS (sh)	WHITE	COLUMBIA	1934
C-105	UNNAMED DIPPY DOO DADS (sh)		PATHE EXCHANGE	1923
C-106	SAVE THE SHIP (sh)	JESKE, ROACH	PATHE EXCHANGE	1923
C-106	SCHOOL FOR ROMANCE (LESSONS IN LOVE*) (sh)	GOTTLER	COLUMBIA	1934
C-107	ELMER STEPS OUT (PLAYFUL HUSBANDS*) (sh)	WHITE	COLUMBIA	1934
C-107	UNCOVERED WAGON (sh)	HOWE	PATHE EXCHANGE	1923
C-108	BATTLE OF GREED	HIGGIN	CRESCENT PICT	1937
C-108	CARNE DE CABARET	CABANNE	COLUMBIA	1931
C-108	LOVE DETECTIVES (sh)	GOTTLER	COLUMBIA	1934
C-109	NO PETS (sh)	HOWE	PATHE EXCHANGE	1923
C-109	WHEN DO WE EAT? (SHOWMANSHIP*) (sh)	GOULDING	COLUMBIA	1934
C-110	STABLE MATES (sh)	WHITE	COLUMBIA	1934
C-110	STABLEMATES	WOOD	COLUMBIA	1938
C-110	STEPPING OUT (sh)	POWERS	PATHE EXCHANGE	1923
C-111	FISHING FOR TROUBLE (HOLY MACKERAL*) (sh)	WHITE	COLUMBIA	1934
C-112	SCORCHING SANDS (sh)	WILLIAMSON, ROACH	PATHE EXCHANGE	1923
C-112	WOMAN HATERS (sh)	GOTTLER	COLUMBIA	1934
C-113	KNOCKOUT (sh)	POWERS	PATHE EXCHANGE	1923
C-113	SUSIE'S AFFAIRS (LA) (sh)	GOTTLER	COLUMBIA	1934
C-114	EL PASADO ACUSA	SELMAN, VILLARREAL	COLUMBIA	1931
C-114	GET ALONG LITTLE HUBBY (sh)	MCCAREY	COLUMBIA	1934
C-114	I WAS A PRISONER ON DEVIL'S ISLAND	LANDERS	COLUMBIA	1941
C-114	JOIN THE CIRCUS (sh)	JESKE	PATHE EXCHANGE	1923
C-115	PLUMBING FOR GOLD (sh)	LAMONT	COLUMBIA	1934
C-115	TWO IN A TAXI	FLOREY	COLUMBIA	1941

Movie Still Identification Book Ultimate Edition - Letters

CODE	TITLE/NAME	DIRECTOR/TYPE	STUDIO/DISTRIBUTOR	YEAR
C-115	WHOLE TRUTH (sh)	CEDER	PATHE EXCHANGE	1923
C-116	GO WEST (sh)	POWERS	PATHE EXCHANGE	1923
C-116	OUR WIFE	STAHL	COLUMBIA	1941
C-116	PUNCH DRUNKS (sh)	BRESLOW	COLUMBIA	1934
C-117	ADVENTURES OF DON COYOTE	LE BORG	UNITED ARTISTS	1947
C-117	HERE COMES MR. JORDAN	HALL	COLUMBIA	1941
C-117	LOVEY-DOVEY (sh)	POWERS	PATHE EXCHANGE	1923
C-117	TRIPPING THRU THE TROPICS (sh)	GOTTLER	COLUMBIA	1934
C-118	BACK TO THE SOIL (PAYDIRT*) (sh)	WHITE	COLUMBIA	1934
C-118	DEAR OLD PAL (sh)		PATHE EXCHANGE	1923
C-118	YOU'LL NEVER GET RICH	LANFIELD	COLUMBIA	1941
C-119	FROZEN HEARTS (sh)	HOWE	PATHE EXCHANGE	1923
C-119	HOLLYWOOD HERE WE COME (sh)	GOTTLER	COLUMBIA	1934
C-119	MYSTERY SHIP	LANDERS	COLUMBIA	1941
C-120	GET BUSY (sh)	HAYES	PATHE EXCHANGE	1924
C-120	TWO LATINS FROM MANHATTAN	BARTON	COLUMBIA	1941
C-121	OLD WAR HORSE (sh)	JESKE	PATHE EXCHANGE	1926
C-122	AT FIRST SIGHT (sh)	ROACH	PATHE EXCHANGE	1924
C-122	COUNTER-ESPIONAGE	DMYTRYK	COLUMBIA	1942
C-123	IT'S A JOY - (IT'S A BOY) (sh)	JESKE	PATHE EXCHANGE	1923
C-124	BAR-FLY (sh)	POWERS	PATHE EXCHANGE	1924
C-124	THREE GIRLS ABOUT TOWN	JASON	COLUMBIA	1941
C-125	FULLY INSURED (sh)	JESKE	PATHE EXCHANGE	1923
C-125	GO WEST YOUNG LADY	STRAYER	COLUMBIA	1941
C-126	FRIEND HUSBAND (WHY MARRY?) (sh)	HOWE	PATHE EXCHANGE	1924
C-126	HARMON OF MICHIGAN	BARTON	COLUMBIA	1941
C-127	BIG IDEA (sh)	JESKE	PATHE EXCHANGE	1924
C-127	STORK PAYS OFF	LANDERS	COLUMBIA	1941
C-128	MAN PAYS (sh)	POWERS	PATHE EXCHANGE	1924
C-128	SECRETS OF THE LONE WOLF	DMYTRYK	COLUMBIA	1941
C-129	HARD KNOCKS (sh)	PARROTT	PATHE EXCHANGE	1924
C-129	LADY IS WILLING	LEISEN	COLUMBIA	1942
C-129	PERFECT LADY (sh)	PARROTT	PATHE EXCHANGE	1924
C-130	JUST A MINUTE (sh)	PARROTT	PATHE EXCHANGE	1924
C-130	SING FOR YOUR SUPPER	BARTON	COLUMBIA	1941
C-131	ONE OF THE FAMILY (sh)	PEMBROKE	PATHE EXCHANGE	1924
C-132	HARVARD, HERE I COME	LANDERS	COLUMBIA	1941
C-132	LOVE'S REWARD (sh)	POWERS	PATHE EXCHANGE	1924
C-133	CONFESSIONS OF BOSTON BLACKIE	DMYTRYK	COLUMBIA	1941
C-133	POWDER AND SMOKE (sh)	PARROTT	PATHE EXCHANGE	1924
C-134	BLONDIE GOES TO COLLEGE	STRAYER	COLUMBIA	1942
C-134	LOVE'S DETOUR (sh)	PARROTT	PATHE EXCHANGE	1924
C-135	HONOLULU LU	BARTON	COLUMBIA	1941
C-135	OUR LITTLE NELL (sh)	POWERS	PATHE EXCHANGE	1924
C-136	CADETS ON PARADE	LANDERS	COLUMBIA	1942
C-136	HARD KNOCKS (sh)	PARROTT	PATHE EXCHANGE	1924
C-137	NORTH OF 50-50 (sh)	POWERS	PATHE EXCHANGE	1924
C-137	SHUT MY BIG MOUTH	BARTON	COLUMBIA	1942
C-138	DON'T FORGET (sh)	PARROTT	PATHE EXCHANGE	1924
C-138	TWO YANKS IN TRINIDAD	RATOFF	COLUMBIA	1942
C-139	MAN WHO RETURNED TO LIFE	LANDERS	COLUMBIA	1942
C-140	CANAL ZONE	LANDERS	COLUMBIA	1942
C-141	TRAMP TRAMP TRAMP	BARTON	COLUMBIA	1942
C-144	ALIAS BOSTON BLACKIE	LANDERS	COLUMBIA	1942
C-146	TALK OF THE TOWN	STEVENS	COLUMBIA	1942
C-147	NOT A LADIES MAN	LANDERS	COLUMBIA	1942
C-148	HELLO ANAPOLIS	BARTON	COLUMBIA	1942
C-150	COUNSEL ON DE FENCE (sh)	RIPLEY	COLUMBIA	1934
C-150	THEY ALL KISSED THE BRIDE	HALL	COLUMBIA	1942
C-151	IT'S THE CATS (sh)	RAY	COLUMBIA	1934
C-152	MEN IN BLACK (sh)	MCCAREY	COLUMBIA	1934
C-152	SWEETHEART OF THE FLEET	BARTON	COLUMBIA	1942
C-153	PERFECTLY MISMATED (SCRAMBLE WIVES*) (sh)	HORNE	COLUMBIA	1934
C-153	SUBMARINE RAIDER	LANDERS	COLUMBIA	1942
C-154	SHIVERS (sh)	RIPLEY	COLUMBIA	1934
C-154	YOU WERE NEVER LOVELIER	SEITER	COLUMBIA	1942
C-155	ATLANTIC CONVOY	LANDERS	COLUMBIA	1942
C-155	IN THE DOG HOUSE (sh)	RIPLEY	COLUMBIA	1934
C-155	NINE O'CLOCK TOWN		COLUMBIA	
C-156	FLIGHT LIEUTENANT	SALKOW	COLUMBIA	1942

Movie Still Identification Book Ultimate Edition - Letters

CODE	TITLE/NAME	DIRECTOR/TYPE	STUDIO/DISTRIBUTOR	YEAR
C-156	THREE LITTLE PIGSKINS (sh)	MCCAREY	COLUMBIA	1934
C-157	HIS OLD FLAME (sh)	HORNE	COLUMBIA	1935
C-157	ONE DANGEROUS NIGHT	GORDON	COLUMBIA	1943
C-158	BLONDIE FOR VICTORY	STRAYER	COLUMBIA	1942
C-158	ONE TOO MANY (sh)	MCGOWAN	COLUMBIA	1934
C-159	HORSE COLLARS (sh)	BRUCKMAN	COLUMBIA	1935
C-159	MAN'S WORLD	BARTON	COLUMBIA	1942
C-160	RESTLESS KNIGHTS (sh)	LAMONT	COLUMBIA	1935
C-160	SABOTAGE SQUAD	LANDERS	COLUMBIA	1942
C-161	I'M A FATHER (sh)	HORNE	COLUMBIA	1935
C-161	MY SISTER EILEEN	HALL	COLUMBIA	1942
C-162	HIS BRIDAL SWEET (sh)	GOULDING	COLUMBIA	1935
C-162	LUCKY LEGS	BARTON	COLUMBIA	1942
C-162	STORK BITES MAN	ENDFIELD	UNITED ARTISTS	1947
C-163	DESPERADOES	VIDOR	COLUMBIA	1943
C-163	POP GOES THE EASEL (sh)	LORD	COLUMBIA	1935
C-164	OLD SAWBONES (sh)	LORD	COLUMBIA	1935
C-164	STAND BY ALL NETWORKS	LANDERS	COLUMBIA	1942
C-165	SPIRIT OF STANFORD	BARTON	COLUMBIA	1942
C-165	UNCIVIL WARRIORS (sh)	LORD	COLUMBIA	1935
C-166	DESTROYER	SEITER	COLUMBIA	1943
C-166	LEATHER NECKER (sh)	RIPLEY	COLUMBIA	1935
C-167	GUM SHOES (sh)	LORD	COLUMBIA	1935
C-167	LET'S HAVE FUN	BARTON	COLUMBIA	1943
C-168	DARING YOUNG MAN	STRAYER	COLUMBIA	1942
C-168	PARDON MY SCOTCH (sh) CHANGED	LORD	COLUMBIA	1935
C-169	BOSTON BLACKIE GOES HOLLYWOOD	GORDON	COLUMBIA	1942
C-169	TRAMP TRAMP TRAMP (sh)	LAMONT	COLUMBIA	1935
C-170	SMITH OF MINNESOTA	LANDERS	COLUMBIA	1942
C-171	ALIMONY ACHES (sh)	LAMONT	COLUMBIA	1935
C-171	BOOGIE MAN WILL GET YOU	LANDERS	COLUMBIA	1942
C-172	STAGE FRIGHTS (sh)	RAY	COLUMBIA	1935
C-172	UNDERGROUND AGENT	GORDON	COLUMBIA	1942
C-173	DO YOUR STUFF (sh)	PARROTT	COLUMBIA	1935
C-173	NIGHT TO REMEMBER	WALLACE	COLUMBIA	1943
C-174	CAPTAIN HITS THE CEILING (sh)	LAMONT	COLUMBIA	1935
C-174	LAUGH YOUR BLUES AWAY	BARTON	COLUMBIA	1942
C-175	GOBS OF TROUBLE (sh)	LORD	COLUMBIA	1935
C-175	JUNIOR ARMY	LANDERS	COLUMBIA	1942
C-176	MORE THE MERRIER	STEVENS	COLUMBIA	1943
C-177	POWER OF THE PRESS	LANDERS	COLUMBIA	1943
C-178	WHAT'S BUZZIN COUSIN?	BARTON	COLUMBIA	1943
C-179	REVELIE WITH BEVERLY	BARTON	COLUMBIA	1943
C-180	MURDER IN TIMES SQUARE	LANDERS	COLUMBIA	1943
C-181	SAHARA	KORDA	COLUMBIA	1943
C-182	APPOINTMENT IN BERLIN	GREEN	COLUMBIA	1943
C-183	AFTER MIDNIGHT WITH BOSTON BLACKIE	LANDERS	COLUMBIA	1943
C-184	FIRST COMES COURAGE	ARZNER	COLUMBIA	1943
C-185	SHE HAS WHAT IT TAKES	BARTON	COLUMBIA	1943
C-186	IT'S A GREAT LIFE	STRAYER	COLUMBIA	1943
C-187	BOY FROM STALINGRAD	SALKOW	COLUMBIA	1943
C-188	REDHEAD FROM MANHATTAN	LANDERS	COLUMBIA	1943
C-189	ONCE UPON A TIME	HALL	COLUMBIA	1944
C-190	TWO SENORITAS FROM CHICAGO	WOODRUFF	COLUMBIA	1943
C-192	GOOD LUCK MR. YATES	ENRIGHT	COLUMBIA	1943
C-193	DOUGHBOYS IN IRELAND	LANDERS	COLUMBIA	1943
C-194	COVER GIRL	VIDOR	COLUMBIA	1944
C-195	MY KINGDOM FOR A COOK	WALLACE	COLUMBIA	1943
C-196	HOMBRES EN MI VIDA	SELMAN	COLUMBIA	1932
C-197	PASSPORT TO SUEZ	DE TOTH	COLUMBIA	1943
C-198	DANGEROUS BLONDES	JASON	COLUMBIA	1943
C-199	THERE'S SOMETHING ABOUT A SOLDIER	GREEN	COLUMBIA	1943
C-200	EXTORTION	HILLYER	COLUMBIA	1938
C-200	OH, MY NERVES! (sh)	LORD	COLUMBIA	1935
C-201	UNRELATED RELATIONS (sh)	LORD	COLUMBIA	1936
C-202	IT ALWAYS HAPPENS (sh)	LORD	COLUMBIA	1935
C-203	HIS MARRIAGE MIX-UP (sh)	WHITE	COLUMBIA	1935
C-203	MAIN EVENT	DARE	COLUMBIA	1938
C-204	PAID TO DANCE (HARD TO HOLD)	COLEMAN	COLUMBIA	1937
C-204	STAR GAZING (sh)	RUBIN	COLUMBIA	1935

Movie Still Identification Book Ultimate Edition - Letters

CODE	TITLE/NAME	DIRECTOR/TYPE	STUDIO/DISTRIBUTOR	YEAR
C-205	ALL AMERICAN SWEETHEART	HILLYER	COLUMBIA	1937
C-205	YOO HOO HOLLYWOOD (sh)	RUBIN	COLUMBIA	1935
C-206	PARDON MY SCOTCH (sh)	LORD	COLUMBIA	1935
C-206	SHADOW	COLEMAN	COLUMBIA	1937
C-207	HOI POLLOI (sh)	LORD	COLUMBIA	1935
C-207	SQUADRON OF HONOR	COLEMAN	COLUMBIA	1938
C-208	HONEYMOON BRIDGE (sh)	LORD	COLUMBIA	1935
C-208	WOMEN IN PRISON	HILLYER	COLUMBIA	1938
C-209	HOT PAPRIKA (sh)	WHITE	COLUMBIA	1935
C-209	WHO KILLED GAIL PRESTON?	BARSHA	COLUMBIA	1938
C-210	THREE LITTLE BEERS (sh)	LORD	COLUMBIA	1935
C-210	WHEN G-MEN STEP IN	COLEMAN	COLUMBIA	1938
C-211	HIGHWAY PATROL	COLEMAN	COLUMBIA	1938
C-211	I DON'T REMEMBER (sh)	WHITE	COLUMBIA	1935
C-212	HOMICIDE BUREAU	COLEMAN	COLUMBIA	1939
C-212	PEPPERY SALT (sh)	LORD	COLUMBIA	1936
C-213	JUVENILE COURT	LEDERMAN	COLUMBIA	1938
C-213	MOVIE MANIACS (sh)	LORD	COLUMBIA	1936
C-214	ADVENTURE IN SAHARA	LEDERMAN	COLUMBIA	1938
C-214	JUST SPEEDING (sh)	LORD	COLUMBIA	1936
C-215	NORTH OF SHANGHAI	LEDERMAN	COLUMBIA	1939
C-215	SHARE THE WEALTH (sh)	LORD	COLUMBIA	1936
C-216	MIDNIGHT BLUNDERS (sh)	LORD	COLUMBIA	1936
C-216	MY SON IS A CRIMINAL	COLEMAN	COLUMBIA	1939
C-217	DISORDER IN THE COURT (sh)	WHITE	COLUMBIA	1936
C-217	FIRST OFFENDERS	MCDONALD	COLUMBIA	1939
C-218	ANTS IN THE PANTRY (sh)	WHITE	COLUMBIA	1936
C-218	OUTSIDE THESE WALLS	MCCAREY	COLUMBIA	1939
C-219	CHAMP'S A CHUMP (sh)	WHITE	COLUMBIA	1936
C-219	MISSING DAUGHTERS	COLEMAN	COLUMBIA	1939
C-220	MISTER SMARTY (sh)	WHITE	COLUMBIA	1936
C-220	PARENTS ON TRIAL	NELSON	COLUMBIA	1939
C-221	SLIPPERY SILKS - CHANGE TO 252	WHITE	COLUMBIA	1936
C-221	WOMAN IS THE JUDGE	GRINDE	COLUMBIA	1939
C-222	BEHIND PRISON GATES	BARTON	COLUMBIA	1939
C-222	CAUGHT IN THE ACT	LORD	COLUMBIA	1936
C-223	MAN THEY COULD NOT HANG	GRINDE	COLUMBIA	1939
C-223	PAIN IN THE PULLMAN (sh)	WHITE	COLUMBIA	1936
C-224	FALSE ALARMS (sh) CHANGE TO 250	LORD	COLUMBIA	1936
C-224	KONGA, THE WILD STALLION	NELSON	COLUMBIA	1940
C-225	HALF SHOT SHOOTERS (sh)	WHITE	COLUMBIA	1936
C-226	WHOOPS, I'M AN INDIAN! (sh) CHANGE TO 251	WHITE	COLUMBIA	1936
C-250	FALSE ALARMS (sh)	LORD	COLUMBIA	1936
C-251	WHOOPS, I'M AN INDIAN! (sh)	WHITE	COLUMBIA	1936
C-252	SLIPPERY SILKS	WHITE	COLUMBIA	1936
C-253	AM I HAVING FUN! (sh)	WHITE	COLUMBIA	1936
C-254	AY TANK AY GO (sh)	LORD	COLUMBIA	1936
C-255	OH, DUCHESS! (sh)	LAMONT	COLUMBIA	1936
C-256	LOVE COMES TO MOONEYVILLE (sh)	WHITE	COLUMBIA	1936
C-257	FIBBING FIBBERS (sh)	WHITE	COLUMBIA	1936
C-258	FREE RENT (sh)	LORD	COLUMBIA	1936
C-259	GRIPS, GRUNTS AND GROANS (sh)	WHITE	COLUMBIA	1937
C-260	SAILOR MAID (sh)	LAMONT	COLUMBIA	1937
C-261	KNEE ACTION (sh)	LAMONT	COLUMBIA	1937
C-262	SUPER SNOOPER (sh)	WHITE	COLUMBIA	1937
C-263	DIZZY DOCTORS (sh)	LORD	COLUMBIA	1937
C-264	BURY THE HATCHET (sh)	LORD	COLUMBIA	1937
C-265	STUCK IN THE STICKS (sh)	WHITE	COLUMBIA	1937
C-266	3 DUMB CLUCKS (sh)	LORD	COLUMBIA	1937
C-267	NEW NEWS (sh)	LAMONT	COLUMBIA	1937
C-268	BACK TO THE WOODS (sh)	WHITE	COLUMBIA	1937
C-269	GRAND HOOTER (sh)	WHITE	COLUMBIA	1937
C-270	LODGE NIGHT (sh)	WHITE	COLUMBIA	1937
C-271	FROM BAD TO WORSE (sh)	LORD	COLUMBIA	1937
C-272	MY LITTLE FELLER (sh)	LAMONT	COLUMBIA	1937
C-273	WRONG MISS WRIGHT (sh)	LAMONT	COLUMBIA	1937
C-274	GOOFS AND SADDLES (sh)	LORD	COLUMBIA	1937
C-275	CALLING ALL DOCTORS (sh)	LAMONT	COLUMBIA	1937
C-280	COMMUNITY SING - #3	series	COLUMBIA	1937
C-281	COMMUNITY SING - #4	series	COLUMBIA	1937

Movie Still Identification Book Ultimate Edition - Letters

CODE	TITLE/NAME	DIRECTOR/TYPE	STUDIO/DISTRIBUTOR	YEAR
C-282	COMMUNITY SING - #5	series	COLUMBIA	1937
C-283	COMMUNITY SING - SERIES 2 #1	series	COLUMBIA	1937
C-284	COMMUNITY SING - SERIES 2 #2	series	COLUMBIA	1937
C-300	OUTLAWS OF THE PRAIRIE	NELSON	COLUMBIA	1937
C-301	CATTLE RAIDERS	NELSON	COLUMBIA	1938
C-302	OLD WYOMING TRAIL	BLANGSTED	COLUMBIA	1937
C-303	CALL OF THE ROCKIES	JAMES	COLUMBIA	1938
C-304	LAW OF THE PLAINS	NELSON	COLUMBIA	1938
C-305	WEST OF CHEYENNE	NELSON	COLUMBIA	1938
C-306	SOUTH OF ARIZONA	NELSON	COLUMBIA	1938
C-307	WEST OF SANTA FE	NELSON	COLUMBIA	1938
C-308	COLORADO TRAIL	NELSON	COLUMBIA	1938
C-309	RIO GRANDE	NELSON	COLUMBIA	1938
C-310	THUNDERING WEST	NELSON	COLUMBIA	1939
C-311	TEXAS STAMPEDE	NELSON	COLUMBIA	1939
C-312	NORTH OF THE YUKON	NELSON	COLUMBIA	1939
C-313	SPOILERS OF THE RANGE	COLEMAN	COLUMBIA	1939
C-314	WESTERN CARAVANS	NELSON	COLUMBIA	1939
C-315	MAN FROM SUNDOWN	NELSON	COLUMBIA	1939
C-316	OUTPOST OF THE MOUNTIES	COLEMAN	COLUMBIA	1939
C-317	STRANGER FROM TEXAS	NELSON	COLUMBIA	1939
C-318	RIDERS OF BLACK RIVER	DEMING	COLUMBIA	1939
C-319	TAMING OF THE WEST	DEMING	COLUMBIA	1939
C-320	MAN FROM TUMBLEWEEDS	LEWIS	COLUMBIA	1940
C-321	TWO FISTED RANGERS	LEWIS	COLUMBIA	1939
C-322	BULLETS FOR RUSTLERS	NELSON	COLUMBIA	1940
C-323	PIONEERS OF THE FRONTIER	NELSON	COLUMBIA	1940
C-324	BLAZING SIX SHOOTERS	LEWIS	COLUMBIA	1940
C-325	THUNDERING FRONTIER	LEDERMAN	COLUMBIA	1940
C-326	TEXAS STAGECOACH	LEWIS	COLUMBIA	1940
C-327	PINTO KID	HILLYER	COLUMBIA	1941
C-328	WEST OF ABILENE	CEDER	COLUMBIA	1940
C-329	RETURN OF WILD BILL	LEWIS	COLUMBIA	1940
C-330	DURANGO KID	HILLYER	COLUMBIA	1940
C-331	PRAIRIE SCHOONERS	NELSON	COLUMBIA	1940
C-332	OUTLAWS OF THE PANHANDLE	NELSON	COLUMBIA	1941
C-334	BEYOND THE SACRAMENTO	HILLYER	COLUMBIA	1940
C-335	ACROSS THE SIERRAS	LEDERMAN	COLUMBIA	1941
C-337	WILDCAT OF TUCSON	HILLYER	COLUMBIA	1940
C-338	NORTH FROM THE LONE STAR	HILLYER	COLUMBIA	1941
C-339	RETURN OF DANIEL BOONE	HILLYER	COLUMBIA	1941
C-340	HANDS ACROSS THE ROCKIES	HILLYER	COLUMBIA	1941
C-341	SON OF DAVY CROCKETT	HILLYER	COLUMBIA	1941
C-342	MEDICO OF PAINTED SPRINGS	HILLYER	COLUMBIA	1941
C-343	KING OF DODGE CITY	HILLYER	COLUMBIA	1941
C-344	THUNDER OVER THE PRAIRIE	HILLYER	COLUMBIA	1941
C-345	ROARING FRONTIERS	HILLYER	COLUMBIA	1941
C-346	PRAIRIE STRANGER	HILLYER	COLUMBIA	1941
C-347	LONE STAR VIGILANTES	FOX	COLUMBIA	1942
C-348	ROYAL MOUNTED PATROL	HILLYER	COLUMBIA	1941
C-349	BULLETS FOR BANDITS	FOX	COLUMBIA	1942
C-350	RIDERS OF THE BADLANDS	BRETHERTON	COLUMBIA	1941
C-351	NORTH OF THE ROCKIES	HILLYER	COLUMBIA	1942
C-352	DEVIL'S TRAIL	HILLYER	COLUMBIA	1942
C-353	WEST OF TOMBSTONE	BRETHERTON	COLUMBIA	1942
C-354	LAWLESS PLAINSMEN	BERKE	COLUMBIA	1942
C-355	DOWN RIO GRANDE WAY	BERKE	COLUMBIA	1942
C-356	PRAIRIE GUNSMOKE	HILLYER	COLUMBIA	1942
C-357	OVERLAND TO DEADWOOD	BERKE	COLUMBIA	1942
C-358	BADMEN OF THE HILLS	BERKE	COLUMBIA	1942
C-359	RIDERS OF THE NORTHLAND	BERKE	COLUMBIA	1942
C-360	VENGEANCE OF THE WEST	HILLYER	COLUMBIA	1942
C-362	RIDING THROUGH NEVADA	BERKE	COLUMBIA	1942
C-363	PARDON MY GUN	BERKE	COLUMBIA	1942
C-364	TORNADO IN THE SADDLE	BERKE	COLUMBIA	1942
C-365	LONE PRAIRIE	BERKE	COLUMBIA	1942
C-366	FIGHTING BUCKAROO	BERKE	COLUMBIA	1943
C-367	LAW OF THE NORTHWEST	BERKE	COLUMBIA	1943
C-368	SILVER CITY RAIDERS	BERKE	COLUMBIA	1943
C-369	RIDERS OF THE NORTHWEST MOUNTED	BERKE	COLUMBIA	1943

Movie Still Identification Book Ultimate Edition - Letters

CODE	TITLE/NAME	DIRECTOR/TYPE	STUDIO/DISTRIBUTOR	YEAR
C-370	HAIL TO THE RANGERS	BERKE	COLUMBIA	1943
C-371	ROBIN HOOD OF THE RANGE	BERKE	COLUMBIA	1943
C-372	SADDLES AND THE SAGEBRUSH	BERKE	COLUMBIA	1943
C-373	VIGILANTES RIDE	BERKE	COLUMBIA	1943
C-374	WYOMING HURRICANE	BERKE	COLUMBIA	1944
C-375	LAST HORSEMAN	BERKE	COLUMBIA	1944
C-376	RIDING WEST	BERKE	COLUMBIA	1944
C-377	FRONTIER FURY	BERKE	COLUMBIA	1943
C-400	CASH AND CARRY (sh)	LORD	COLUMBIA	1937
C-400	TARGET EARTH	ROSE	ALLIED ARTISTS	1954
C-401	PLAYING THE PONIES (sh)	LAMONT	COLUMBIA	1937
C-402	SITTER DOWNERS (sh)	LORD	COLUMBIA	1937
C-403	JUMP, CHUMP, JUMP! (sh)	LORD	COLUMBIA	1938
C-404	WEE WEE MONSIER (sh)	LORD	COLUMBIA	1938
C-405	DOGGONE MIXUP (sh)	LAMONT	COLUMBIA	1938
C-406	BIG SQUIRT (sh)	LORD	COLUMBIA	1937
C-407	GRACIE AT THE BAT (sh)	LORD	COLUMBIA	1937
C-408	OH, WHAT A KNIGHT! (sh)	CHASE	COLUMBIA	1937
C-409	CALLING ALL CURTAINS (sh)	LORD	COLUMBIA	1937
C-410	FIDDLING AROUND (sh)	LAMONT	COLUMBIA	1938
C-411	HE DONE HIS DUTY (sh)	LAMONT	COLUMBIA	1937
C-412	MIND NEEDER (sh)	LORD	COLUMBIA	1938
C-413	MANY SAPPY RETURNS (sh)	LORD	COLUMBIA	1938
C-414	MAN BITES LOVEBUG (sh)	LORD	COLUMBIA	1937
C-415	TIME OUT FOR TROUBLE (sh)	LORD	COLUMBIA	1938
C-416	TERMITES OF 1938 (sh)	LORD	COLUMBIA	1938
C-417	OLD RAID MULE (sh)	CHASE	COLUMBIA	1938
C-418	NIGHTSHIRT BANDIT (sh)	WHITE	COLUMBIA	1938
C-419	THREE LITTLE SEW AND SEWS (sh)	LORD	COLUMBIA	1939
C-420	TASSELS IN THE AIR (sh)	CHASE	COLUMBIA	1938
C-421	ANKLES AWAY (sh)	CHASE	COLUMBIA	1938
C-422	HEALTHY, WEALTHY AND DUMB (sh)	LORD	COLUMBIA	1938
C-423	VIOLENT IS THE WORD FOR CURLY (sh)	CHASE	COLUMBIA	1938
C-424	SOUL OF A HEEL (sh)	LORD	COLUMBIA	1938
C-425	HALF-WAY TO HOLLYWOOD (sh)	CHASE	COLUMBIA	1938
C-426	THREE MISSING LINKS (sh)	WHITE	COLUMBIA	1938
C-427	MUTTS TO YOU (sh)	CHASE	COLUMBIA	1938
C-428	SUE MY LAWYER (sh)	WHITE	COLUMBIA	1938
C-429	NAG IN THE BAG (sh)	CHASE	COLUMBIA	1938
C-430	SAVED BY THE BELLE (sh)	CHASE	COLUMBIA	1939
C-431	PIE A LA MAID (sh)	LORD	COLUMBIA	1938
C-432	NOT GUILTY ENOUGH (sh)	LORD	COLUMBIA	1938
C-433	MUTINY ON THE BODY (sh)	CHASE	COLUMBIA	1939
C-434	SWING YOU SWINGERS (sh)	WHITE	COLUMBIA	1939
C-435	SAP TAKES A WRAP (sh)	LORD	COLUMBIA	1939
C-436	HOME ON THE RAGE (sh)	LORD	COLUMBIA	1938
C-437	CHUMP TAKES A BUMP (sh)	LORD	COLUMBIA	1939
C-438	YES WE HAVE NO BONANZA (sh)	LORD	COLUMBIA	1939
C-439	FLAT FOOT STOOGES (sh)	CHASE	COLUMBIA	1938
C-440	BOOM GOES THE GROOM (sh)	CHASE	COLUMBIA	1939
C-441	STAR IS SHORN (sh)	LORD	COLUMBIA	1939
C-442	TROUBLE FINDS ANDY CLYDE (sh)	WHITE	COLUMBIA	1939
C-443	DEADLIEST SIN (UK: CONFESSION)	HUGHES	ALLIED ARTISTS	1956
C-443	WE WANT OUR MUMMY (sh)	LORD	COLUMBIA	1939
C-444	DUCKING THEY DID GO (sh)	LORD	COLUMBIA	1939
C-445	CALLING ALL CURS (sh)	WHITE	COLUMBIA	1939
C-446	RATTLING ROMEO (sh)	LORD	COLUMBIA	1939
C-448	NOW IT CAN BE SOLD (sh)	LORD	COLUMBIA	1939
C-449	OILY TO BED, OILY TO RISE (sh)	WHITE	COLUMBIA	1939
C-450	SKINNY THE MOOCHER (sh)	LORD	COLUMBIA	1939
C-451	THREE SAPPY PEOPLE (sh)	WHITE	COLUMBIA	1939
C-452	TEACHER'S PEST (sh)	KRAMER, ULLMAN	COLUMBIA	1939
C-453	STATIC IN THE ATTIC (sh)	CHASE	COLUMBIA	1939
C-454	PEST FROM THE WEST (sh)	LORD	COLUMBIA	1939
C-455	COOKOO CAVALIERS (sh)	WHITE	COLUMBIA	1940
C-456	MOOCHING THROUGH GEORGIA (sh)	WHITE	COLUMBIA	1939
C-457	GLOVE SLINGERS (sh)	WHITE	COLUMBIA	1939
C-458	HOW HIGH IS UP? (sh)	LORD	COLUMBIA	1940
C-459	MONEY SQUAWKS (sh)	WHITE	COLUMBIA	1940
C-460	ALL AMERICAN BLONDES (sh)	LORD	COLUMBIA	1939

Movie Still Identification Book Ultimate Edition - Letters

CODE	TITLE/NAME	DIRECTOR/TYPE	STUDIO/DISTRIBUTOR	YEAR
C-461	ROCKIN' THRU THE ROCKIES (sh)	WHITE	COLUMBIA	1940
C-462	PLUMBING WE WILL GO (sh)	LORD	COLUMBIA	1940
C-463	ANDY CLYDE GETS SPRING CHICKEN (sh)	WHITE	COLUMBIA	1939
C-464	AWFUL GOOF (sh)	LORD	COLUMBIA	1939
C-465	NUTTY BUT NICE (sh)	WHITE	COLUMBIA	1940
C-466	MR. CLYDE GOES TO BROADWAY (sh)	LORD	COLUMBIA	1940
C-467	HECKLER (sh)	LORD	COLUMBIA	1940
C-468	FROM NURSE TO WORSE (sh)	WHITE	COLUMBIA	1940
C469	BILL HAYWOOD, PRODUCER	PETERSON	GENERAL FILM (SELIG)	1915
C-469	HIS BRIDAL FRIGHT (sh)	LORD	COLUMBIA	1940
C-470	NOTHING BUT PLEASURE (sh)	WHITE	COLUMBIA	1940
C-471	YOU'RE NEXT (sh)	LORD	COLUMBIA	1940
C-472	YOU NAZTY SPY (sh)	WHITE	COLUMBIA	1940
C-473	SOUTH OF THE BOUDOIR (sh)	LORD	COLUMBIA	1940
C-474	NO CENSUS, NO FEELING (sh)	LORD	COLUMBIA	1940
C-475	PARDON MY BERTH MARKS (sh)	WHITE	COLUMBIA	1940
C-476	BOOBS IN THE WOODS (sh)	LORD	COLUMBIA	1940
C-477	TAMING OF THE SNOOD (sh)	WHITE	COLUMBIA	1940
C-478	FIREMAN, SAVE MY CHOO CHOO (sh)	LORD	COLUMBIA	1940
C-479	PLEASED TO MITT YOU (sh)	WHITE	COLUMBIA	1940
C-480	COLD TURKEY (sh)	LORD	COLUMBIA	1940
C-481	SPOOK SPEAKS (sh)	WHITE	COLUMBIA	1940
C-482	IN THE SWEET PIE AND PIE (sh)	WHITE	COLUMBIA	1941
C-483	BLONDES AND BLUNDERS (sh)	LORD	COLUMBIA	1940
C-484	SO LONG MR. CHUMPS (sh)	WHITE	COLUMBIA	1941
C-485	DUTIFUL BUT DUMB (sh)	LORD	COLUMBIA	1941
C-486	BOOBS IN ARMS (sh)	WHITE	COLUMBIA	1940
C-487	ALL THE WORLD'S A STOOGE (sh)	LORD	COLUMBIA	1941
C-488	ACHE IN EVERY STAKE (sh)	LORD	COLUMBIA	1941
C-489	WATCHMAN TAKES A WIFE (sh)	LORD	COLUMBIA	1941
C-490	BUNDLE OF BLISS (sh)	WHITE	COLUMBIA	1940
C-491	HIS EX MARKS THE SPOT (sh)	WHITE	COLUMBIA	1940
C-493	SO YOU WON'T SQUAWK (sh)	LORD	COLUMBIA	1941
C-494	RING AND THE BELLE (sh)	LORD	COLUMBIA	1941
C-495	FRESH AS A FRESHMAN (sh)	WHITE	COLUMBIA	1941
C-496	BLITZ KISS (sh)	LORD	COLUMBIA	1941
C-497	YUMPIN' YIMMINY!	WHITE	COLUMBIA	1941
C-498	YANKEE DOODLE ANDY (sh)	WHITE	COLUMBIA	1941
C-499	READY, WILLING BUT UNABLE (sh)	LORD	COLUMBIA	1941
C-500	I'LL NEVER HEIL AGAIN (sh)	WHITE	COLUMBIA	1941
C-501	LOVE AT FIRST FRIGHT (sh)	LORD	COLUMBIA	1941
C-502	THREE BLONDE MICE (sh)	WHITE	COLUMBIA	1942
C-503	FRENCH FRIED PATOOTIE (sh)	WHITE	COLUMBIA	1941
C-504	WHAT MAKES LIZZY DIZZY (sh)	WHITE	COLUMBIA	1942
C-505	BLACK EYES AND BLUES (sh)	WHITE	COLUMBIA	1941
C-506	HALF SHOT AT SUNRISE (sh)	LORD	COLUMBIA	1941
C-507	EVEN AS I.O.U. (sh)	LORD	COLUMBIA	1942
C-508	GENERAL NUISANCEE (sh)	WHITE	COLUMBIA	1941
C-509	HOST TO A GHOST (sh)	LORD	COLUMBIA	1941
C-510	LOCO BOY MAKES GOOD (sh)	WHITE	COLUMBIA	1942
C-511	SOME MORE OF SOMOA (sh)	LORD	COLUMBIA	1941
C-512	MITT ME TONIGHT (sh)	WHITE	COLUMBIA	1941
C-513	CACTUS MAKES PERFECT	LORD	COLUMBIA	1942
C-514	ALL WORK AND NO PAY (sh)	LORD	COLUMBIA	1942
C-515	PHONY CRONIES (sh)	EDWARDS	COLUMBIA	1942
C-516	LOVEABLE TROUBLE (sh)	LORD	COLUMBIA	1941
C-517	SAPPY BIRTHDAY (sh)	EDWARDS	COLUMBIA	1942
C-518	KINK OF THE CAMPUS (sh)	LORD	COLUMBIA	1941
C-519	WHAT'S THE MATADOR? (sh)	WHITE	COLUMBIA	1942
C-520	GLOVE BIRDS (sh)	WHITE	COLUMBIA	1942
C-521	SWEET SPIRITS OF NIGHTER (sh)	LORD	COLUMBIA	1941
C-522	BACK FROM THE FRONT (sh)	WHITE	COLUMBIA	1943
C-523	GROOM AND BORED (sh)	LORD	COLUMBIA	1942
C-524	HOW SPRY I AM (sh)	WHITE	COLUMBIA	1942
C-525	GLOVE AFFAIR (sh)	WHITE	COLUMBIA	1941
C-525	STUDY IN SOCKS (sh)	LORD	COLUMBIA	1942
C-526	SHE'S OIL MINE (sh)	WHITE	COLUMBIA	1941
C-527	MATRI-PHONY (sh)	EDWARDS	COLUMBIA	1942
C-528	OLAF LAUGHS LAST (sh)	WHITE	COLUMBIA	1942
C-529	DIZZY DETECTIVES (sh)	WHITE	COLUMBIA	1943

Movie Still Identification Book Ultimate Edition - Letters

CODE	TITLE/NAME	DIRECTOR/TYPE	STUDIO/DISTRIBUTOR	YEAR
C-530	KISS AND WAKE UP (sh)	WHITE	COLUMBIA	1942
C-531	QUACK SERVICE (sh)	EDWARDS	COLUMBIA	1943
C-532	THREE SMART SAPS (sh)	WHITE	COLUMBIA	1942
C-533	THEY STOOGE TO CONGA (sh)	LORD	COLUMBIA	1943
C-534	TIREMAN, SPARE MY TIRES (sh)	WHITE	COLUMBIA	1942
C-535	HAM AND YEGGS (sh)	WHITE	COLUMBIA	1942
C-536	CARRY HARRY (sh)	EDWARDS	COLUMBIA	1942
C-537	BLITZ ON THE FRITZ (sh)	WHITE	COLUMBIA	1943
C-538	WOLF IN THIEF'S CLOTHING (sh)	WHITE	COLUMBIA	1943
C-539	SOCK-A-BYE BABY (sh)	WHITE	COLUMBIA	1942
C-540	SAPPY PAPPY (sh)	EDWARDS	COLUMBIA	1942
C-541	HIS WEDDING SCARE (sh)	LORD	COLUMBIA	1943
C-543	PIANO MOONER (sh)	EDWARDS	COLUMBIA	1942
C-544	GREAT GLOVER (sh)	WHITE	COLUMBIA	1942
C-545	HIS GIRL'S WORST FRIEND (sh)	WHITE	COLUMBIA	1943
C-546	FARMER FOR A DAY (sh)	WHITE	COLUMBIA	1943
C-547	MAID MADE MAD (sh)	LORD	COLUMBIA	1943
C-548	SOCKS APPEAL (sh)	EDWARDS	COLUMBIA	1943
C-549	SPOOK LOUDER (sh)	LORD	COLUMBIA	1943
C-550	I SPIED FOR YOU (sh)	WHITE	COLUMBIA	1943
C-551	THREE LITTLE TWERPS (sh)	EDWARDS	COLUMBIA	1943
C-552	BLONDE AND GROOM (sh)	EDWARDS	COLUMBIA	1943
C-553	COLLEGE BELLES (sh)	EDWARDS	COLUMBIA	1942
C-554	HERE COMES MR. ZERK (sh)	EDWARDS	COLUMBIA	1943
C-555	DIZY PILOTS (sh)	WHITE	COLUMBIA	1943
C-556	TWO SAPLINGS (sh)	EDWARDS	COLUMBIA	1943
C-558	WHAT A SOLDIER (sh) not released		COLUMBIA	1943
C-559	SHOT IN THE ESCAPE (sh)	WHITE	COLUMBIA	1943
C-561	HE WAS ONLY FEUDIN' (sh)	EDWARDS	COLUMBIA	1943
C-562	ROOKIE'S COOKIE (sh)	WHITE	COLUMBIA	1943
C-563	BOOBS IN THE NIGHT (sh)	LORD	COLUMBIA	1943
C-564	NO DOUGH BOYS (sh)	WHITE	COLUMBIA	1944
C-565	HUGH HERBERT (sh)		COLUMBIA	
C-566	PITCHIN' IN THE KITCHEN (sh)	WHITE	COLUMBIA	1943
C-568	HIGHER THAN A KITE (sh)	LORD	COLUMBIA	1943
C-569	PHONEY EXPRESS (sh)	LORD	COLUMBIA	1943
C-570	I CAN HARDLY WAIT (sh)	WHITE	COLUMBIA	1943
C-571	YOKE'S ON ME (sh)	WHITE	COLUMBIA	1944
C-572	TO HEIR IS HUMAN (sh)	GODSOE	COLUMBIA	1944
C-573	GARDEN OF EATIN' (sh)	EDWARDS	COLUMBIA	1943
C-574	WHO'S HUGH (sh)	EDWARDS	COLUMBIA	1943
C-575	GEM OF A JAM (sh)	LORD	COLUMBIA	1943
C-595	STOOGES (sh)		COLUMBIA	
C-600	COMMUNITY SING - SERIES 2 #3	series	COLUMBIA	1937
C-602	COMMUNITY SING - SERIES 2 #4	series	COLUMBIA	1937
C-610	COMMUNITY SING - SERIES 2 #8	series	COLUMBIA	1938
C-611	COMMUNITY SING - SERIES 2 #9	series	COLUMBIA	1938
C-615	COMMUNITY SING - SERIES 2 #10	series	COLUMBIA	1938
C-620	COMMUNITY SING - SERIES 2 #11	series	COLUMBIA	1938
C-621	COMMUNITY SING - SERIES 2 #12	series	COLUMBIA	1938
C-622	COMMUNITY SING - SERIES 3 #1	series	COLUMBIA	1938
C-623	COMMUNITY SING - SERIES 3 #2	series	COLUMBIA	1938
C-624	COMMUNITY SING - SERIES 3 #3	series	COLUMBIA	1938
C-625	COMMUNITY SING - SERIES 3 #6	series	COLUMBIA	1938
C-631	COMMUNITY SING - SERIES 3 #4	series	COLUMBIA	1939
C-632	COMMUNITY SING - SERIES 3 #5	series	COLUMBIA	1939
C-635	COMMUNITY SING - SERIES 3 #7	series	COLUMBIA	1939
C-636	COMMUNITY SING - SERIES 3 #10	series	COLUMBIA	1939
C-637	COMMUNITY SING - SERIES 3 #8	series	COLUMBIA	1939
C-638	COMMUNITY SING - SERIES 4 #2	series	COLUMBIA	1939
C-639	COMMUNITY SING - SERIES 3 #9	series	COLUMBIA	1939
C-640	COMMUNITY SING - SERIES 4 #1	series	COLUMBIA	1939
C-646	FOOLS WHO MADE HISTORY-ELIAS HOWE	series	COLUMBIA	1939
C-647	FOOLS WHO MADE HISTORY-CHARLES GOODYEAR	series	COLUMBIA	1939
C-655	COMMUNITY SING - SERIES 4 #3	series	COLUMBIA	1939
C-656	COMMUNITY SING - SERIES 4 #4	series	COLUMBIA	1939
C-683	JUNIOR QUIZ PARADE		COLUMBIA	
C-697	MR. SMUG (sh)	CASTLE	COLUMBIA	1943
C-729	CITY WITHOUT MEN	SALKOW	COLUMBIA	1943
C-735	HEAT'S ON	RATOFF	COLUMBIA	1943

Movie Still Identification Book Ultimate Edition - Letters

CODE	TITLE/NAME	DIRECTOR/TYPE	STUDIO/DISTRIBUTOR	YEAR
C-749	(sh)		COLUMBIA	
C-751	CRY BABY KILLER	ADDISS	ALLIED ARTISTS	1958
C-753	WAR OF THE SATELLITES	CORMAN	ALLIED ARTISTS	1958
C-762	(sh)		COLUMBIA	
C-762	CRIME DR.'S STRANGEST CASE	FORDE	COLUMBIA	1943
C-766	(sh)		COLUMBIA	
C-770	SECRET COMMAND	SUTHERLAND	COLUMBIA	1944
C-773	ADDRESS UNKNOWN	MENZIES	COLUMBIA	1944
C-787	WHISTLER	CASTLE	COLUMBIA	1944
C-788	TEXAS	MARSHALL	COLUMBIA	1941
C-789	SHADOWS IN THE NIGHT	FORDE	COLUMBIA	1944
C-791	EVER SINCE VENUE	DREIFUSS	COLUMBIA	1944
C-803	MARK OF THE WHISTLER	CASTLE	COLUMBIA	1944
C-808	BRENDA STARR – REPORTER SERIAL	FOX	COLUMBIA	1945
C-811	RIDERS OF THE WHISTLING PINES	ENGLISH	COLUMBIA	1949
C-812	CRIME DR.'S COURAGE	SHERMAN	COLUMBIA	1945
C-813	POWER OF THE WHISTLER	LANDERS	COLUMBIA	1945
C-814	KISS AND TELL	WALLACE	COLUMBIA	1945
C-818	MONSTER AND THE APE	BRETHERTON	COLUMBIA	1945
C-822	OVER 21	VIDOR	COLUMBIA	1945
C-830	ADVENTURES OF RUSTY	BURNFORD	COLUMBIA	1945
C-834	SNAFU	MOSS	COLUMBIA	1945
C-835	JUNGLE RAIDERS - SERIAL	SELANDER	COLUMBIA	1945
C-838	CRIME DR.'S WARNING	CASTLE	COLUMBIA	1945
C-841	PERILOUS HOLIDAY	GRIFFITH	COLUMBIA	1946
C-844	WHO'S GUILTY?	BRETHERTON, GRISSELL	COLUMBIA	1945
C-850	JOHNNY O'CLOCK	ROSSEN	COLUMBIA	1947
C-851	MR. DISTRICT ATTORNEY	SINCLAIR	COLUMBIA	1947
C-855	HOP HARRIGAN	ABRAHAMS	COLUMBIA	1946
C-856	TO THE ENDS OF THE EARTH	STEVENSON	COLUMBIA	1948
C-862	CHICK CARTER DETECTIVE	ABRAHAMS	COLUMBIA	1946
C-863	RETURN OF MONTE CRISTO	LEVIN	COLUMBIA	1946
C-868	SON OF THE GUARDSMAN	ABRAHAMS	COLUMBIA	1946
C-869	LAST OF THE REDMEN	SHERMAN	COLUMBIA	1947
C-873	BETTY CO-ED	DREIFUSS	COLUMBIA	1946
C-876	CORPSE CAME C.O.D.	LEVIN	COLUMBIA	1947
C-878	JACK ARMSTRONG	FOX	COLUMBIA	1947
C-879	GUNFIGHTERS	WAGGNER	COLUMBIA	1947
C-882	VIGILANTE - SERIAL	FOX	COLUMBIA	1947
C-883	RELENTLESS	SHERMAN	COLUMBIA	1948
C-884	LITTLE MISS BROADWAY	DREIFUSS	COLUMBIA	1947
C-885	HER HUSBANDS AFFAIRS	SIMON	COLUMBIA	1947
C-886	SEA HOUND	EASON, WRIGHT	COLUMBIA	1947
C-887	PRINCE OF THIEVES	BRETHERTON	COLUMBIA	1948
C-888	I LOVE TROUBLE	SIMON	COLUMBIA	1948
C-889	MUSIC IN MY HEART	SANTLEY	COLUMBIA	1940
C-889	STRAWBERRY ROAN	ENGLISH	COLUMBIA	1948
C-890	SWEET GENEVIEVE	DREIFUSS	COLUMBIA	1947
C-891	TWO BLONDES AND A REDHEAD	DREIFUSS	COLUMBIA	1947
C-892	LAST ROUNDUP	ENGLISH	COLUMBIA	1947
C-893	BIG SOMBRERO	MCDONALD	COLUMBIA	1949
C-895	TEX GRANGER (serial)	ABRAHAMS	COLUMBIA	1948
C-896	SIGN OF THE RAM	STURGES	COLUMBIA	1948
C-897	BLACK ARROW	DOUGLAS	COLUMBIA	1948
C-899	BRICK BRADFORD (serial)	BENNET, CARR	COLUMBIA	1947
C-900	GREAT ADV OF WILD BILL HICKOK (serial)	NELSON, WRIGHT	COLUMBIA	1938
C-900	MARY LOU	DREIFUSS	COLUMBIA	1948
C-901	SPIDER'S WEB (SERIAL)	HORNE, TAYLOR	COLUMBIA	1938
C-902	ALL THE KING'S MEN	ROSSEN	COLUMBIA	1950
C-902	FLYING G-MEN (serial)	HORNE, TAYLOR	COLUMBIA	1939
C-903	MANDRAKE THE MAGICIAN (serial)	DEMING, NELSON	COLUMBIA	1939
C-904	OVERLAND WITH KIT CARSON	DEMING, NELSON	COLUMBIA	1939
C-905	LOADED PISTOLS	ENGLISH	COLUMBIA	1948
C-908	GLAMOUR GIRL	DREIFUSS	COLUMBIA	1948
C-908	HOWARDS OF VIRGINIA	LLOYD	COLUMBIA	1940
C-909	MANHATTAN ANGEL	DREIFUSS	COLUMBIA	1949
C-910	SUPERMAN (serial)	BENNET, CARR	COLUMBIA	1948
C-911	ADVENTURE IN WASHINGTON	GREEN	COLUMBIA	1941
C-912	I SURRENDER DEAR	DREIFUSS	COLUMBIA	1948
C-913	FULLER BRUSH MAN	SIMON	COLUMBIA	1948

Movie Still Identification Book Ultimate Edition - Letters

CODE	TITLE/NAME	DIRECTOR/TYPE	STUDIO/DISTRIBUTOR	YEAR
C-914	RACING LUCK	BERKE	COLUMBIA	1948
C-915	LOVES OF CARMEN	VIDOR	COLUMBIA	1948
C-916	SHE KNEW ALL THE ANSWERS	WALLACE	COLUMBIA	1941
C-918	MUTINEERS	YARBROUGH	COLUMBIA	1949
C-919	LULU BELLE	FENTON	COLUMBIA	1948
C-920	UNDERCOVER MAN	LEWIS	COLUMBIA	1949
C-921	SONS OF NEW MEXICO	ENGLISH	COLUMBIA	1949
C-923	ANNA LUCASTA	RAPPER	COLUMBIA	1949
C-924	COWBOY AND THE INDIANS	ENGLISH	COLUMBIA	1949
C-926	CONGO BILL	BENNET, CARR	COLUMBIA	1948
C-927	UNTAMED BREED	LAMONT	COLUMBIA	1948
C-928	LADIES OF THE CHORUS	KARLSON	COLUMBIA	1948
C-931	ADAM HAD FOUR SONS	RATOFF	COLUMBIA	1941
C-931	KNOCK ON ANY DOOR	RAY	COLUMBIA	1949
C-932	TOKYO JOE	HEISLER	COLUMBIA	1949
C-933	TRIPLE THREAT	YARBROUGH	COLUMBIA	1948
C-934	SONG OF INDIA	ROGELL	COLUMBIA	1949
C-935	JUNGLE JIM	BERKE	COLUMBIA	1948
C-937	BRUCE GENTRY	BENNET, CARR	COLUMBIA	1949
C-939	WE WERE STRANGERS	HUSTON	COLUMBIA	1949
C-942	LOST TRIBE	BERKE	COLUMBIA	1949
C-944	ADVENTURES OF BATMAN AND ROBIN	BENNET	COLUMBIA	1949
C-945	DOOLINS OF OKLAHOMA	DOUGLAS	COLUMBIA	1949
C-946	JOLSON SINGS AGAIN	LEVIN	COLUMBIA	1949
C-947	RIM OF THE CANYON	ENGLISH	COLUMBIA	1949
C-949	LADIES IN RETIREMENT	VIDOR	COLUMBIA	1941
C-950	STATE PENITENTIARY	LANDERS	COLUMBIA	1950
C-951	BARBARY PIRATE	LANDERS	COLUMBIA	1949
C-952	COW TOWN	ENGLISH	COLUMBIA	1950
C-953	ADVENTURES OF SIR GALAHAD	BENNET	COLUMBIA	1949
C-953	MEN IN HER LIFE	RATOFF	COLUMBIA	1941
C-954	CAPTIVE GIRL	BERKE	COLUMBIA	1950
C-955	MARK OF THE GORILLA	BERKE	COLUMBIA	1950
C-956	ATOM MAN VS. SUPERMAN	BENNET	COLUMBIA	1950
C-957	CODY OF THE PONY EXPRESS	BENNET	COLUMBIA	1950
C-958	CHINATOWN AT MIDNIGHT	FRIEDMAN	COLUMBIA	1949
C-962	TYRANT OF THE SEA	LANDERS	COLUMBIA	1950
C-964	ADVENTURES OF MARTIN EDEN	SALKOW	COLUMBIA	1942
C-964	RECKLESS MOMENT	OPHULS	COLUMBIA	1949
C-965	TRAVELING SALESWOMAN	REISNER	COLUMBIA	1950
C-966	AND BABY MAKES THREE	LEVIN	COLUMBIA	1949
C-967	BLAZING SUN	ENGLISH	COLUMBIA	1950
C-968	NEVADAN	DOUGLAS	COLUMBIA	1950
C-970	IN A LONELY PLACE	RAY	COLUMBIA	1950
C-971	RIDERS IN THE SKY	ENGLISH	COLUMBIA	1949
C-975	BRAVE BULLS	ROSSON	COLUMBIA	1951
C-976	MULE TRAIN	ENGLISH	COLUMBIA	1950
C-977	BEYOND THE PURPLE HILLS	ENGLISH	COLUMBIA	1950
C-981	INDIAN TERRITORY	ENGLISH	COLUMBIA	1950
C-982	SOMETHING TO SHOUT ABOUT	RATOFF	COLUMBIA	1943
C-986	LAST OF THE BUCCANEERS	LANDERS	COLUMBIA	1950
C-988	GENE AUTRY AND THE MOUNTIES	ENGLISH	COLUMBIA	1951
C-989	REVENUE AGENT	LANDERS	COLUMBIA	1950
C-990	PIRATES OF THE HIGH SEAS	BENNET, CARR	COLUMBIA	1950
C-991	SIROCCO	BERNHARDT	COLUMBIA	1951
C-992	HURRICANE ISLAND	LANDERS	COLUMBIA	1951
C-993	CHAIN GANG	LANDERS	COLUMBIA	1950
C-994	PYGMY ISLAND	BERKE	COLUMBIA	1950
C-995	FURY OF THE CONGO	BERKE	COLUMBIA	1951
C-996	COMMANDOES STRIKE AT DAWN	FARROW	COLUMBIA	1942
C-998	SATURDAY'S HERO	MILLER	COLUMBIA	1951
C-999	FAMILY SECRET	LEVIN	COLUMBIA	1951
C-1001	FOOTLIGHT GLAMOUR	STRAYER	COLUMBIA	1943
C-1002	IS EVERYBODY HAPPY?	BARTON	COLUMBIA	1943
C-1004	WHAT A WOMAN	CUMMINGS	COLUMBIA	1943
C-1005	NINE GIRLS	JASON	COLUMBIA	1944
C-1006	NONE SHALL ESCAPE	DE TOTH	COLUMBIA	1944
C-1009	RACKET MAN	LEDERMAN	COLUMBIA	1944
C-1010	RETURN OF THE VAMPIRE	LANDERS	COLUMBIA	1944
C-1011	SONG TO REMEMBER	VIDOR	COLUMBIA	1945

Movie Still Identification Book Ultimate Edition - Letters

CODE	TITLE/NAME	DIRECTOR/TYPE	STUDIO/DISTRIBUTOR	YEAR
C-1012	CHANCE OF A LIFETIME	CASTLE	COLUMBIA	1943
C-1014	MR. WINKLE GOES TO WAR	GREEN	COLUMBIA	1944
C-1015	KLONDIKE KATE	CASTLE	COLUMBIA	1943
C-1016	SWING OUT OF THE BLUES	ST. CLAIR	COLUMBIA	1943
C-1017	BEAUTIFUL BUT BROKE	BARTON	COLUMBIA	1944
C-1019	GHOST THAT WALKS ALONE	LANDERS	COLUMBIA	1944
C-1021	GIRL IN THE CASE	BERKE	COLUMBIA	1944
C-1022	TONIGHT AND EVERY NIGHT	SAVILLE	COLUMBIA	1945
C-1023	SAILOR'S HOLIDAY	BERKE	COLUMBIA	1944
C-1024	TOGETHER AGAIN	VIDOR	COLUMBIA	1944
C-1025	TWO MAN SUBMARINE	LANDERS	COLUMBIA	1944
C-1026	CAROLINA BLUES	JASON	COLUMBIA	1944
C-1027	STARS ON PARADE	LANDERS	COLUMBIA	1944
C-1028	BLACK PARACHUTE	LANDERS	COLUMBIA	1944
C-1029	SHE'S A SOLDIER TOO	CASTLE	COLUMBIA	1944
C-1030	JOLSON STORY (some marked 1130)	GREEN	COLUMBIA	1946
C-1031	COUNTER-ATTACK	KORDA	COLUMBIA	1945
C-1032	THEY LIVE IN FEAR	BERNE	COLUMBIA	1944
C-1033	U-BOAT PRISONER	LANDERS	COLUMBIA	1944
C-1035	LOUISIANA HAYRIDE	BARTON	COLUMBIA	1944
C-1036	IMPATIENT YEARS	CUMMINGS	COLUMBIA	1944
C-1037	CRY OF THE WEREWOLF	LEVIN	COLUMBIA	1944
C-1038	UNWRITTEN CODE	ROTSTEN	COLUMBIA	1944
C-1039	EVE KNEW HER APPLES	JASON	COLUMBIA	1945
C-1040	KANSAS CITY KITTY	LORD	COLUMBIA	1944
C-1042	MEET MISS BOBBY SOCKS	TRYON	COLUMBIA	1944
C-1043	STRANGE AFFAIR	GREEN	COLUMBIA	1944
C-1044	SOUL OF A MONSTER	JASON	COLUMBIA	1944
C-1045	ONE MYSTERIOUS NIGHT	BOETTICHER	COLUMBIA	1944
C-1046	SERGEANT MIKE	LEVIN	COLUMBIA	1944
C-1047	MISSING JUROR	BOETTICHER	COLUMBIA	1944
C-1048	ESCAPE IN THE FOG	BOETTICHER	COLUMBIA	1945
C-1049	SHE'S A SWEETHEART	LORD	COLUMBIA	1944
C-1050	TARS AND SPARS	GREEN	COLUMBIA	1946
C-1051	EADIE WAS A LADY	DREIFUSS	COLUMBIA	1945
C-1052	DANCING IN MANHATTAN	LEVIN	COLUMBIA	1944
C-1054	THOUSAND AND ONE NIGHTS	GREEN	COLUMBIA	1945
C-1055	TAHITI NIGHTS	JASON	COLUMBIA	1944
C-1056	LEAVE IT TO BLONDIE	BERLIN	COLUMBIA	1945
C-1057	LET'S GO STEADY	LORD	COLUMBIA	1945
C-1058	I LOVE A MYSTERY	LEVIN	COLUMBIA	1945
C-1059	YOUTH ON TRIAL	BOETTICHER	COLUMBIA	1945
C-1060	SHE WOULDN'T SAY YES	HALL	COLUMBIA	1945
C-1061	MEET ME ON BROADWAY	JASON	COLUMBIA	1946
C-1062	GUY, A GAL AND A PAL	BOETTICHER	COLUMBIA	1945
C-1063	ROUGH TOUGH AND READY	LORD	COLUMBIA	1945
C-1064	FIGHTING GUARDSMAN	LEVIN	COLUMBIA	1946
C-1066	TEN CENTS A DANCE	JASON	COLUMBIA	1945
C-1069	BOSTON BLACKIE HOOKED ON SUSPICION	DREIFUSS	COLUMBIA	1945
C-1070	BLONDE FROM BROOKLYN	LORD	COLUMBIA	1945
C-1071	GAY SENORITA	DREIFUSS	COLUMBIA	1945
C-1072	BOSTON BLACKIE'S RENDEZVOUS	DREIFUSS	COLUMBIA	1945
C-1074	BANDIT OF SHERWOOD FOREST	LEVIN, SHERMAN	COLUMBIA	1946
C-1075	I LOVE A BANDLEADER	LORD	COLUMBIA	1945
C-1076	VOICE OF THE WHISTLER	CASTLE	COLUMBIA	1945
C-1078	GIRL OF THE LIMBERLOST	FERRER	COLUMBIA	1945
C-1079	RENEGADES	SHERMAN	COLUMBIA	1946
C-1080	ONE WAY TO LOVE	ENRIGHT	COLUMBIA	1946
C-1081	HIT THE HAY	LORD	COLUMBIA	1945
C-1082	MY NAME IS JULIA ROSS	LEWIS	COLUMBIA	1945
C-1083	OUT OF THE DEPTHS	LEDERMAN	COLUMBIA	1945
C-1084	LIFE WITH BLONDIE	BERLIN	COLUMBIA	1945
C-1086	PRISON SHIP	DREIFUSS	COLUMBIA	1945
C-1087	GILDA	VIDOR	COLUMBIA	1946
C-1088	BLONDIE'S LUCKY DAY	BERLIN	COLUMBIA	1946
C-1089	CLOSE CALL FOR BOSTON BLACKIE	LANDERS	COLUMBIA	1946
C-1090	SO DARK THE NIGHT	LEWIS	COLUMBIA	1946
C-1091	NOTORIOUS LONE WOLF	LEDERMAN	COLUMBIA	1946
C-1092	GENTLEMEN MISBEHAVES	SHERMAN	COLUMBIA	1946
C-1093	JUST BEFORE DAWN	CASTLE	COLUMBIA	1946

Movie Still Identification Book Ultimate Edition - Letters

CODE	TITLE/NAME	DIRECTOR/TYPE	STUDIO/DISTRIBUTOR	YEAR
C-1094	WALLS CAME TUMBLING DOWN	MENDES	COLUMBIA	1946
C-1095	DEVIL'S MASK	LEVIN	COLUMBIA	1946
C-1096	DANGEROUS BUSINESS	LEDERMAN	COLUMBIA	1946
C-1097	TALK ABOUT A LADY	SHERMAN	COLUMBIA	1946
C-1098	MYSTERIOUS INTRUDER	CASTLE	COLUMBIA	1946
C-1099	NIGHT EDITOR	LEVIN	COLUMBIA	1946
C-1100	DOWN TO EARTH	HALL	COLUMBIA	1947
C-1101	PHANTOM THIEF	LEDERMAN	COLUMBIA	1946
C-1102	MAN WHO DARED	STURGES	COLUMBIA	1946
C-1103	GALLANT JOURNEY	WELLMAN	COLUMBIA	1946
C-1104	THRILL OF BRAZIL	SIMON	COLUMBIA	1946
C-1105	RETURN OF RUSTY	CASTLE	COLUMBIA	1946
C-1106	UNKNOWN	LEVIN	COLUMBIA	1946
C-1107	BLONDIE KNOWS BEST	BERLIN	COLUMBIA	1946
C-1108	SING WHILE YOU DANCE	LEDERMAN	COLUMBIA	1946
C-1109	PERSONALITY KID	SHERMAN	COLUMBIA	1946
C-1110	CRIME DR.'S MANHUNT	CASTLE	COLUMBIA	1946
C-1111	DEAD RECKONING	CROMWELL	COLUMBIA	1947
C-1112	IT'S GREAT TO BE YOUNG	LORD	COLUMBIA	1946
C-1113	FRAMED	WALLACE	COLUMBIA	1947
C-1114	SECRET OF THE WHISTLER	SHERMAN	COLUMBIA	1946
C-1115	GUILT OF JANET AMES	LEVIN	COLUMBIA	1947
C-1116	SHADOWED	STURGES	COLUMBIA	1946
C-1117	SWORDSMAN	LEWIS	COLUMBIA	1948
C-1118	SINGING IN THE CORN	LORD	COLUMBIA	1946
C-1119	BLONDIE'S BIG MOMENT	BERLIN	COLUMBIA	1947
C-1120	BOSTON BLACKIE AND THE LAW	LEDERMAN	COLUMBIA	1946
C-1121	RETURN OF OCTOBER	LEWIS	COLUMBIA	1948
C-1122	LONE WOLF IN MEXICO	LEDERMAN	COLUMBIA	1947
C-1123	ALIAS MR. TWILIGHT	STURGES	COLUMBIA	1946
C-1124	BLIND SPOT	GORDON	COLUMBIA	1947
C-1125	MILLIE'S DAUGHTER	SALKOW	COLUMBIA	1947
C-1126	LADY FROM SHANGHAI		COLUMBIA	1947
C-1127	CIGARETTE GIRL	VON FRITSCH	COLUMBIA	1947
C-1128	THIRTEENTH HOUR	CLEMENS	COLUMBIA	1947
C-1129	KING OF THE WILD HORSES	ARCHAINBAUD	COLUMBIA	1947
C-1130	BLONDIE'S HOLIDAY	BERLIN	COLUMBIA	1947
C-1130	JOLSON STORY (some marked 1030)	GREEN	COLUMBIA	1946
C-1131	MILLERSON CASE	ARCHAINBAUD	COLUMBIA	1947
C-1132	BULLDOG DRUMMOND AT BAY	SALKOW	COLUMBIA	1947
C-1133	FOR THE LOVE OF RUSTY	STURGES	COLUMBIA	1947
C-1135	MAN FROM COLORADO	LEVIN	COLUMBIA	1948
C-1136	BLONDIE IN THE DOUGH	BERLIN	COLUMBIA	1947
C-1137	SPORT OF KINGS	GORDON	COLUMBIA	1947
C-1138	IT HAD TO BE YOU	HARTMAN, MATE	COLUMBIA	1947
C-1139	KEEPER OF THE BEES	STURGES	COLUMBIA	1947
C-1140	SON OF RUSTY	LANDERS	COLUMBIA	1947
C-1141	KEY WITNESS	LEDERMAN	COLUMBIA	1947
C-1142	BULLDOG DRUMMOND STRIKES AGAIN	MCDONALD	COLUMBIA	1947
C-1143	MATING OF MILLIE	LEVIN	COLUMBIA	1948
C-1144	WHEN A GIRL'S BEAUTIFUL	MCDONALD	COLUMBIA	1947
C-1145	SLIGHTLY FRENCH	SIRK	COLUMBIA	1949
C-1146	LONE WOLF IN LONDON	GOODWINS	COLUMBIA	1947
C-1148	CRIME DR.'S GAMBLE	CASTLE	COLUMBIA	1947
C-1149	DEVIL SHIP	LANDERS	COLUMBIA	1947
C-1152	ADVENTURES IN SILVERADO	KARLSON	COLUMBIA	1948
C-1153	WRECK OF THE HESPERUS	HOFFMAN	COLUMBIA	1948
C-1154	PORT SAID	LE BORG	COLUMBIA	1948
C-1155	BLONDIE'S REWARD	BERLIN	COLUMBIA	1948
C-1156	BLONDIE'S ANNIVERSARY	BERLIN	COLUMBIA	1947
C-1157	WOMAN FROM TANGIER	DANIELS	COLUMBIA	1948
C-1159	RETURN OF THE WHISTLER	LEDERMAN	COLUMBIA	1948
C-1160	GALLANT BLADE	LEVIN	COLUMBIA	1948
C-1161	MY DOG RUSTY	LANDERS	COLUMBIA	1948
C-1162	BEST MAN WINS	STURGES	COLUMBIA	1948
C-1163	TRAPPED BY BOSTON BLACKIE	FRIEDMAN	COLUMBIA	1948
C-1164	THUNDERHOOF	KARLSON	COLUMBIA	1948
C-1165	LEATHER GLOVES	ASHER, QUINIE	COLUMBIA	1948
C-1166	RUSTY LEADS THE WAY	JASON	COLUMBIA	1948
C-1167	WALKING HILLS	STURGES	COLUMBIA	1949

Movie Still Identification Book Ultimate Edition - Letters

CODE	TITLE/NAME	DIRECTOR/TYPE	STUDIO/DISTRIBUTOR	YEAR
C-1168	DARK PAST	MATE	COLUMBIA	1948
C-1169	BLACK EAGLE	GORDON	COLUMBIA	1948
C-1170	GENTLEMEN FROM NOWHERE	CASTLE	COLUMBIA	1948
C-1171	RUSTY SAVES A LIFE	FRIEDMAN	COLUMBIA	1949
C-1172	BLONDIE'S SECRET	BERNDS	COLUMBIA	1948
C-1173	BOSTON BLACKIE'S CHINESE VENTURE	FRIEDMAN	COLUMBIA	1949
C-1174	SHOCKPROOF	SIRK	COLUMBIA	1949
C-1175	MR. SOFT TOUCH	DOUGLAS, LEVIN	COLUMBIA	1949
C-1176	HOLIDAY IN HAVANA	YARBROUGH	COLUMBIA	1949
C-1177	LAW OF THE BARBARY COAST	LANDERS	COLUMBIA	1949
C-1178	LONE WOLF AND HIS LADY	HOFFMAN	COLUMBIA	1949
C-1179	CRIME DR.'S DIARY	FRIEDMAN	COLUMBIA	1949
C-1180	BLONDIE'S BIG DEAL	BERNDS	COLUMBIA	1949
C-1181	AIR HOSTESS	LANDERS	COLUMBIA	1949
C-1182	MAKE BELIEVE BALLROOM	SANTLEY	COLUMBIA	1949
C-1183	LUST FOR GOLD	SIMON	COLUMBIA	1949
C-1185	BLONDIE HITS THE JACKPOT	BERNDS	COLUMBIA	1949
C-1186	DEVIL'S HENCHMEN	FRIEDMAN	COLUMBIA	1949
C-1187	JOHNNY ALLEGRO	TETZLAFF	COLUMBIA	1949
C-1188	SECRET OF ST. IVES	ROSEN	COLUMBIA	1949
C-1189	KAZAN	JASON	COLUMBIA	1949
C-1190	RUSTY'S BIRTHDAY	FRIEDMAN	COLUMBIA	1949
C-1191	MISS GRANT TAKES RICHMOND	BACON	COLUMBIA	1949
C-1192	TELL IT TO THE JUDGE	FOSTER	COLUMBIA	1949
C-1193	PALOMINO	NAZARRO	COLUMBIA	1950
C-1194	PRISON WARDEN	FRIEDMAN	COLUMBIA	1949
C-1195	BLONDIE'S HERO	BERNDS	COLUMBIA	1950
C-1196	GOOD HUMOR MAN	BACON	COLUMBIA	1950
C-1197	BORN YESTERDAY	CUKOR	COLUMBIA	1950
C-1198	CARGO TO CAPETOWN	MCEVOY	COLUMBIA	1950
C-1199	MARY RYAN, DETECTIVE	BERLIN	COLUMBIA	1949
C-1200	GIRL'S SCHOOL	BRAHM	COLUMBIA	1938
C-1201	ROGUES OF SHERWOOD FOREST	DOUGLAS	COLUMBIA	1950
C-1202	WOMAN OF DISTINCTION	BUZZELL	COLUMBIA	1950
C-1204	FATHER IS A BACHELOR	BERLIN, FOSTER	COLUMBIA	1950
C-1205	BODYHOLD	FRIEDMAN	COLUMBIA	1949
C-1206	FORTUNES OF CAPTAIN BLOOD	DOUGLAS	COLUMBIA	1950
C-1207	PETTY GIRL	LEVIN	COLUMBIA	1950
C-1208	BEWARE OF BLONDIE	BERNDS	COLUMBIA	1950
C-1209	KILL THE UMPIRE	BACON	COLUMBIA	1950
C-1210	MILITARY ACADEMY	LEDERMAN	COLUMBIA	1940
C-1211	FULLER BRUSH GIRL	BACON	COLUMBIA	1950
C-1212	FRIGHTENED CITY	MCEVOY	COLUMBIA	1950
C-1213	BEAUTY ON PARADE	LANDERS	COLUMBIA	1950
C-1214	NO SAD SONGS FOR ME	MATE	COLUMBIA	1950
C-1215	CUSTOMS AGENT	FREIDMAN	COLUMBIA	1950
C-1218	WHEN YOU'RE SMILING	SANTLEY	COLUMBIA	1950
C-1219	CONVICTED	LEVIN	COLUMBIA	1950
C-1220	ROOKIE FIREMAN	FRIEDMAN	COLUMBIA	1950
C-1221	DAVID HARDING – COUNTER SPY	NAZARRO	COLUMBIA	1950
C-1222	BETWEEN MIDNIGHT AND DAWN	DOUGLAS	COLUMBIA	1950
C-1223	HE'S A COCKEYED WONDER	GODFREY	COLUMBIA	1950
C-1224	HARRIET CRAIG	SHERMAN	COLUMBIA	1950
C-1225	ON THE ISLE OF SOMOA	BERKE	COLUMBIA	1950
C-1226	TWO OF A KIND	LEVIN	COLUMBIA	1951
C-1228	STAGE TO TUCSON	MURPHY	COLUMBIA	1950
C-1230	EMERGENCY WEDDING	BUZZELL	COLUMBIA	1950
C-1231	AL JENNINGS OF OKLAHOMA	NAZARRO	COLUMBIA	1951
C-1232	FLYING MISSING	LEVIN	COLUMBIA	1950
C-1233	MASK OF THE AVENGER	KARLSON	COLUMBIA	1951
C-1234	COUNTERSPY MEETS SCOTLAND YARD	FRIEDMAN	COLUMBIA	1950
C-1235	HER FIRST ROMANCE	FRIEDMAN	COLUMBIA	1951
C-1237	TOUGHER THEY COME	NAZARRO	COLUMBIA	1950
C-1238	FLAME OF STAMBOUL	NAZARRO	COLUMBIA	1951
C-1239	LADY AND THE BANDIT	MURPHY	COLUMBIA	1951
C-1240	GASOLINE ALLEY	BERNDS	COLUMBIA	1951
C-1241	BAREFOOT MAILMAN	MCEVOY	COLUMBIA	1951
C-1242	SUNNY SIDE OF THE STREET	QUINE	COLUMBIA	1951
C-1243	NEVER TRUST A GAMBLER	MURPHY	COLUMBIA	1951
C-1244	SMUGGLERS GOLD	BERKE	COLUMBIA	1951

Movie Still Identification Book Ultimate Edition - Letters

CODE	TITLE/NAME	DIRECTOR/TYPE	STUDIO/DISTRIBUTOR	YEAR
C-1245	MOB	PARRISH	COLUMBIA	1951
C-1246	CRIMINAL LAWYER	FRIEDMAN	COLUMBIA	1951
C-1248	PAULA	MATE	COLUMBIA	1952
C-1249	MY TRUE STORY	ROONEY	COLUMBIA	1951
C-1250	CHINA CORSAIR	NAZARRO	COLUMBIA	1951
C-1251	BIG GUSHER	LANDERS	COLUMBIA	1951
C-1252	SON OF DR. JEKYL	FRIEDMAN	COLUMBIA	1951
C-1253	ASSIGNMENT-PARIS	PARRISH	COLUMBIA	1952
C-1254	CHAIN OF CIRCUMSTANCES	JASON	COLUMBIA	1951
C-1255	CORKY OF GASOLINE ALLEY	BERNDS	COLUMBIA	1951
C-1256	SOUND OFF	QUINE	COLUMBIA	1952
C-1257	CAPT. PIRATE	MURPHY	COLUMBIA	1952
C-1258	MARRYING KIND	CUKOR	COLUMBIA	1952
C-1259	OKINAWA	JASON	COLUMBIA	1952
C-1260	MONTANA TERRITORY	NAZARRO	COLUMBIA	1952
C-1261	HAREM GIRL	BERNDS	COLUMBIA	1952
C-1263	LAST OF THE COMMANCHES	DE TOTH	COLUMBIA	1953
C-1264	RAINBOW 'ROUND MY SHOULDER	QUINE	COLUMBIA	1952
C-1265	TARGET HONG KONG	SEARS	COLUMBIA	1953
C-1266	ALL ASHORE	QUINE	COLUMBIA	1953
C-1267	AMBUSH AT TOMAHAWK GAP	SEARS	COLUMBIA	1953
C-1268	LET'S DO IT AGAIN	HALL	COLUMBIA	1953
C-1269	MISSION OVER KOREA	SEARS	COLUMBIA	1953
C-1270	LAST POSSE	WERKER	COLUMBIA	1953
C-1271	FROM HERE TO ETERNITY	ZINNEMANN	COLUMBIA	1953
C-1272	CRUISIN' DOWN THE RIVER	QUINE	COLUMBIA	1953
C-1273	EL ALAMEIN (GER: THAT WAS OUR ROMMEL)	WIGANKO	COLUMBIA	1953
C-1274	CHINA VENTURE	SIEGEL	COLUMBIA	1953
C-1276	BIG HEAT	LANG	COLUMBIA	1953
C-1278	GUN FURY	WALSH	COLUMBIA	1953
C-1280	MAN IN THE DARK	LANDERS	COLUMBIA	1953
C-1281	HUMAN DESIRE	LANG	COLUMBIA	1954
C-1283	NEBRASKAN	SEARS	COLUMBIA	1953
C-1284	BAD FOR EACH OTHER	RAPPER	COLUMBIA	1953
C-1285	IT SHOULD HAPPEN TO YOU	CUKOR	COLUMBIA	1954
C-1287	THREE FOR THE SHOW	POTTER	COLUMBIA	1955
C-1288	MASSACRE CANYON	SEARS	COLUMBIA	1954
C-1289	DRIVE A CROOKED MILE	QUINE	COLUMBIA	1954
C-1290	THEY RODE WEST	KARLSON	COLUMBIA	1954
C-1291	PUSHOVER	QUINE	COLUMBIA	1954
C-1292	OUTLAW STALLION	SEARS	COLUMBIA	1954
C-1293	THREE HOUSE TO FILL	WERKER	COLUMBIA	1954
C-1295	BLACK DAKOTAS	NAZARRO	COLUMBIA	1954
C-1296	VIOLENT MEN	MATE	COLUMBIA	1955
C-1298	PHFFT	ROBSON	COLUMBIA	1954
C-1299	WYOMING RENEGADES	SEARS	COLUMBIA	1954
C-1300	TIGHT SPOT	KARLSON	COLUMBIA	1955
C-1301	MY SISTER EILEEN	QUINE	COLUMBIA	1955
C-1302	CELL 2455-DEATH ROW	SEARS	COLUMBIA	1955
C-1303	THREE STRIPES IN THE SUN	MURPHY	COLUMBIA	1955
C-1305	BRING YOUR SMILE ALONG	EDWARDS	COLUMBIA	1955
C-1306	LAST FRONTIER	MANN	COLUMBIA	1955
C-1307	APACHE AMBUSH	SEARS	COLUMBIA	1955
C-1308	QUEEN BEE	MACDOUGALL	COLUMBIA	1955
C-1309	PICNIC	LOGAN	COLUMBIA	1955
C-1310	JUBAL	DAVES	COLUMBIA	1956
C-1311	EDDIE DUCHIN STORY	SIDNEY	COLUMBIA	1956
C-1313	FURY AT GUNSIGHT PASS	SEARS	COLUMBIA	1956
C-1314	YOU CAN'T RUN AWAY FROM IT	POWELL	COLUMBIA	1956
C-1315	HARDER THEY FALL	ROBSON	COLUMBIA	1956
C-1316	SECRET OF TREASURE MOUNTAIN	FRIEDMAN	COLUMBIA	1956
C-1318	SOLID GOLD CADILLAC	QUINE	COLUMBIA	1956
C-1319	OVER-EXPOSED	SEILER	COLUMBIA	1956
C-1320	HE LAUGHED LAST	EDWARDS	COLUMBIA	1956
C-1322	FULL OF LIFE	QUINE	COLUMBIA	1956
C-1323	SHADOW ON THE WINDOW	ASHER	COLUMBIA	1957
C-1329	GUNMAN'S WALK	KARLSON	COLUMBIA	1958
C-1332	GUNMEN FROM LAREDO	MACDONALD	COLUMBIA	1959
C-1334	GIDGET	WENDKOS	COLUMBIA	1959
C-1400	PIRATE	MINNELLI	MGM	1948

Movie Still Identification Book Ultimate Edition - Letters

CODE	TITLE/NAME	DIRECTOR/TYPE	STUDIO/DISTRIBUTOR	YEAR
C-1401	HUCKSTERS	CONWAY	MGM	1947
C-1402	SONG OF THE THIN MAN	BUZZELL	MGM	1947
C-1403	CASS TIMBERLANE	SIDNEY	MGM	1948
C-1404	GOOD NEWS	WALTERS	MGM	1947
C-1405	ALIAS A GENTLEMAN	BEAUMONT	MGM	1948
C-1406	KISSING BANDIT	BENEDEK	MGM	1949
C-1407	IF WINTER COMES	SAVILLE	MGM	1948
C-1408	KILLER MCCOY	ROWLAND	MGM	1948
C-1409	HIGH WALL	BERNHARDT	MGM	1948
C-1410	BRIDGE GOES WILD	TAUROG	MGM	1948
C-1411	ON AN ISLAND WITH YOU	THORPE	MGM	1948
C-1412	LUXURY LINER	WHORF	MGM	1948
C-1413	HOMECOMING	LEROY	MGM	1948
C-1414	STATE OF THE UNION	CAPRA	MGM	1948
C-1415	HILLS OF HOME	WILCOX	MGM	1948
C-1416	B.F.'S DAUGHTER	LEONARD	MGM	1948
C-1417	BIG CITY	TAUROG	MGM	1948
C-1418	EASTER PARADE	WALTERS	MGM	1948
C-1419	DATE WITH JUDY	THORPE	MGM	1948
C-1420	THREE MUSKETEERS	SIDNEY	MGM	1948
C-1421	SECRET LAND	NARRATED DOCUMENTARY	MGM	1948
C-1422	JULIA MISBEHAVES	CONWAY	MGM	1948
C-1423	SOUTHERN YANKEE	SEDGWICK	MGM	1948
C-1424	STRATTON STORY	WOOD	MGM	1949
C-1425	COMMAND DECISION	WOOD	MGM	1948
C-1426	SUN COMES UP	THORPE	MGM	1949
C-1427	WORDS AND MUSIC	TAUROG	MGM	1949
C-1428	ACT OF VIOLENCE	ZINNEMANN	MGM	1949
C-1429	NEPTUNE'S DAUGHTER	BUZZELL	MGM	1949
C-1430	LITTLE WOMEN	LEROY	MGM	1949
C-1431	BRIBE	LEONARD	MGM	1949
C-1432	TAKE ME OUT TO THE BALL GAME	BERKELEY	MGM	1949
C-1433	BARKLEYS OF BROADWAY	WALTERS	MGM	1949
C-1435	SECRET GARDEN	WILCOX	MGM	1949
C-1436	BIG JACK	THORPE	MGM	1949
C-1437	GREAT SINNER	SIODMAK	MGM	1949
C-1438	THAT FORSYTE WOMAN	BENNETT	MGM	1950
C-1439	RED DANUBE	SIDNEY	MGM	1950
C-1440	IN THE GOOD OLD SUMMERTIME	LEONARD	MGM	1949
C-1441	MADAME BOVARY	MINNELLI	MGM	1949
C-1442	CHALLENGE TO LASSIE	THORPE	MGM	1950
C-1443	THAT MIDNIGHT KISS	TAUROG	MGM	1949
C-1444	ANY NUMBER CAN PLAY	LEROY	MGM	1949
C-1445	EDWARD, MY SON (UK)	CUKOR	MGM	1949
C-1446	CONSPIRATOR (UK)	SAVILLE	MGM	1950
C-1447	SCENE OF THE CRIME	ROWLAND	MGM	1949
C-1448	BORDER INCIDENT	MANN	MGM	1949
C-1449	MALAYA	THORPE	MGM	1950
C-1450	ANNIE GET YOUR GUN	SIDNEY	MGM	1950
C-1451	INTRUDER IN THE DUST	BROWN	MGM	1949
C-1452	BATTLEGROUND	WELLMAN	MGM	1949
C-1453	ON THE TOWN	DONEN, KELLY	MGM	1949
C-1454	SIDE STREET	MANN	MGM	1950
C-1455	SHADOW ON THE WALL	JACKSON	MGM	1950
C-1456	DOCTOR AND THE GIRL	BERNHARDT	MGM	1949
C-1457	ADAM'S RIB	CUKOR	MGM	1950
C-1458	TENSION	BERRY	MGM	1950
C-1459	STARS IN MY CROWN	TOURNEUR	MGM	1950
C-1460	AMBUSH	WOOD	MGM	1950
C-1461	NANCY GOES TO RIO	LEONARD	MGM	1950
C-1462	PLEASE BELIEVE ME	TAUROG	MGM	1950
C-1463	KEY TO THE CITY	SIDNEY	MGM	1950
C-1464	EAST SIDE, WEST SIDE	LEROY	MGM	1949
C-1466	BLACK HAND	THORPE	MGM	1950
C-1467	KING SOLOMON'S MINES	BENNETT	MGM	1950
C-1468	DEVIL'S DOORWAY	MANN	MGM	1950
C-1469	OUTRIDERS	ROWLAND	MGM	1950
C-1470	BIG HANGOVER	KRASNA	MGM	1950
C-1471	YELLOW CAB MAN	DONOHUE	MGM	1950
C-1472	MINIVER STORY	POTTER	MGM	1950

Movie Still Identification Book Ultimate Edition - Letters

CODE	TITLE/NAME	DIRECTOR/TYPE	STUDIO/DISTRIBUTOR	YEAR
C-1473	HAPPY YEARS	WELLMAN	MGM	1950
C-1474	REFORMER AND THE REDHEAD	FRANK, PANAMA	MGM	1950
C-1475	DUCHESS OF IDAHO	LEONARD	MGM	1950
C-1476	KIM	SAVILLE	MGM	1951
C-1477	SUMMER STOCK	WALTERS	MGM	1950
C-1478	LADY WITHOUT A PASSPORT	LEWIS	MGM	1950
C-1479	ASPHAULT JUNGLE	HUSTON	MGM	1950
C-1480	SKIPPER SURPRISED HIS WIFE	NUGENT	MGM	1950
C-1481	MYSTERY STREET	STURGES	MGM	1950
C-1482	THREE LITTLE WORDS	THORPE	MGM	1950
C-1483	TOAST OF NEW ORLEANS	TAUROG	MGM	1950
C-1484	FATHER OF THE BRIDE	MINNELLI	MGM	1950
C-1485	LIFE OF HER OWN	CUKOR	MGM	1950
C-1486	CRISIS	BROOKS	MGM	1950
C-1487	RIGHT CROSS	STURGES	MGM	1950
C-1488	NEXT VOICE YOU HEAR	WELLMAN	MGM	1950
C-1489	PAGAN LOVE SONG	ALTON	MGM	1950
C-1490	DIAL 1119	MAYER	MGM	1950
C-1491	TWO WEEKS WITH LOVE (TENDER HOURS*)	ROWLAND	MGM	1950
C-1492	TO PLEASE A LADY	BROWN	MGM	1950
C-1494	CAUSE FOR ALARM	GARNETT	MGM	1951
C-1495	GROUNDS FOR MARRIAGE	LEONARD	MGM	1951
C-1496	VENGEANCE VALLEY	THORPE	MGM	1951
C-1497	WATCH THE BIRDIE	DONOHUE	MGM	1951
C-1498	IT'S A BIG COUNTRY - INTERRUPTIONS	series	MGM	1952
C-1499	IT'S A BIG COUNTRY - CENSUS TAKER	series	MGM	1952
C-1500	IT'S A BIG COUNTRY - FOUR EYES	series	MGM	1952
C-1501	IT'S A BIG COUNTRY - ROSIKA	series	MGM	1952
C-1502	ROYAL WEDDING	DONEN	MGM	1951
C-1503	MRS. O'MALLEY AND MR. MALONE	TAUROG	MGM	1951
C-1504	PAINTED HILLS	KRESS	MGM	1951
C-1505	IT'S A BIG COUNTRY - LOAD	series	MGM	1952
C-1506	MAGNIFICENT YANKEE	STURGES	MGM	1950
C-1507	AMERICAN IN PARIS	MINNELLI	MGM	1951
C-1508	ACROSS THE WIDE MISSOURI	WELLMAN	MGM	1951
C-1509	THREE GUYS NAMED MIKE	WALTERS	MGM	1951
C-1510	SHOWBOAT	SIDNEY	MGM	1951
C-1511	MR. IMPERIUM	HARTMAN	MGM	1951
C-1512	RED BADGE OF COURAGE	HUSTON	MGM	1951
C-1513	CALLING BULLDOG DRUMMOND	SAVILLE	MGM	1951
C-1514	GREAT CARUSO	THORPE	MGM	1951
C-1515	IT'S A BIG COUNTRY - TEXAS	series	MGM	1951
C-1516	GO FOR BROKE	PIROSH	MGM	1951
C-1517	SOLDIERS THREE	GARNETT	MGM	1951
C-1518	EXCUSE MY DUST	ROWLAND	MGM	1951
C-1519	FATHER'S LITTLE DIVIDEND	MINNELLI	MGM	1951
C-1520	SHOW BOAT	SIDNEY	MGM	1951
C-1521	KIND LADY	STURGES	MGM	1951
C-1522	RICH, YOUNG AND PRETTY	TAUROG	MGM	1951
C-1523	NIGHT INTO MORNING	MARKEL	MGM	1951
C-1524	LOVE IS BETTER THAN EVER	DONEN	MGM	1952
C-1525	IT'S A BIG COUNTRY - LETTER FROM KOREA	series	MGM	1952
C-1526	NO QUESTIONS ASKED	KRESS	MGM	1951
C-1527	TALL TARGET	MANN	MGM	1951
C-1528	STRIP	KARDOS	MGM	1951
C-1529	UNKNOWN MAN	THORPE	MGM	1951
C-1530	STRICTLY DISHONORABLE	FRANK, PANAMA	MGM	1951
C-1531	LAW AND THE LADY	KNOPF	MGM	1951
C-1532	TEXAS CARNIVAL	WALTERS	MGM	1951
C-1533	SCARAMOUCHE	SIDNEY	MGM	1952
C-1534	PEOPLE AGAINST O'HARA	STURGES	MGM	1951
C-1535	WILD NORTH	MARTON	MGM	1952
C-1536	WESTWARD THE WOMEN	WELLMAN	MGM	1951
C-1537	ANGELS IN THE OUTFIELD	BROWN	MGM	1951
C-1538	SHADOW IN THE SKY	WILCOX	MGM	1952
C-1539	BANNERLINE	WEIS	MGM	1951
C-1540	LIGHT TOUCH	BROOKS	MGM	1952
C-1541	TOO YOUNG TO KISS	LEONARD	MGM	1951
C-1542	CALLAWAY WENT THATAWAY	FRANK, PANAMA	MGM	1952
C-1544	MAN WITH A CLOAK	MARKLE	MGM	1951

Movie Still Identification Book Ultimate Edition - Letters

CODE	TITLE/NAME	DIRECTOR/TYPE	STUDIO/DISTRIBUTOR	YEAR
C-1545	BELLE OF NEW YORK	WALTERS	MGM	1952
C-1546	SINGIN' IN THE RAIN	DONEN, KELLY	MGM	1952
C-1547	LONE STAR	SHERMAN	MGM	1952
C-1548	WHEN IN ROME	BROWN	MGM	1952
C-1549	IVANHOE (UK)	THORPE	MGM	1952
C-1550	JUST THIS ONCE	WEIS	MGM	1952
C-1551	SELLOUT	MAYER	MGM	1952
C-1552	PLYMOUTH ADVENTURE	BROWN	MGM	1952
C-1553	BECAUSE YOU'RE MINE	HALL	MGM	1952
C-1554	TALK ABOUT A STRANGER	BRADLEY	MGM	1952
C-1555	LOVELY TO LOOK AT	LEROY	MGM	1952
C-1556	SKIRTS AHOY	LANFIELD	MGM	1952
C-1557	MERRY WIDOW	BERNHARDT	MGM	1952
C-1558	INVITATION	REINHARDT	MGM	1952
C-1559	YOUNG MAN WITH IDEAS	LEISEN	MGM	1952
C-1560	HOUR OF 13	FRENCH	MGM	1952
C-1561	GIRL IN WHITE	STURGES	MGM	1952
C-1564	GLORY ALLEY	WALSH	MGM	1952
C-1565	CARBINE WILLIAMS	THORPE	MGM	1952
C-1566	PAT AND MIKE	CUKOR	MGM	1952
C-1567	MILLION DOLLAR MERMAID	LEROY	MGM	1952
C-1568	WASHINGTON STORY	PIROSH	MGM	1952
C-1569	DEVIL MAKES THREE	MARTON	MGM	1952
C-1570	HOLIDAY FOR SINNERS	MAYER	MGM	1952
C-1571	STORY OF THREE LOVES	MINNELLI, REINHARDT	MGM	1953
C-1572	STORY OF THREE LOVES - MADEMOISELLE	MINNELLI, REINHARDT	MGM	1953
C-1573	FEARLESS FAGAN	DONEN	MGM	1952
C-1574	ABOVE AND BEYOND	FRANK, PANAMA	MGM	1953
C-1575	LILI	WALTERS	MGM	1953
C-1576	EVERYTHING I HAVE IS YOURS	LEONARD	MGM	1952
C-1577	STORY OF THREE LOVES (mistake 1571)	MINNELLI, REINHARDT	MGM	1953
C-1578	MY MAN AND I	WELLMAN	MGM	1952
C-1579	PRISONER OF ZENDA	THORPE	MGM	1952
C-1580	YOU FOR ME	WEIS	MGM	1952
C-1581	BAD AND THE BEAUTIFUL	MINNELLI	MGM	1952
C-1582	TERROR ON A TRAIN (TIME BOMB)	TETZLAFF	MGM	1953
C-1583	SKY FULL OF MOON	FOSTER	MGM	1952
C-1584	I LOVE MELVIN	WEIS	MGM	1953
C-1585	ROGUE'S MARCH	DAVIS	MGM	1953
C-1586	NAKED SPUR	MANN	MGM	1953
C-1587	APACHE WAR SMOKE	KRESS	MGM	1952
C-1588	SOMBRERO	FOSTER	MGM	1953
C-1589	SMALL TOWN GIRL	WELLMAN	MGM	1953
C-1590	DESPERATE SEARCH	LEWIS	MGM	1953
C-1591	SCANDAL AT SCOURIE	NEGULESCO	MGM	1953
C-1592	CONFIDENTIALLY CONNIE	BUZZELL	MGM	1953
C-1593	NEVER LET ME GO	DAVES	MGM	1953
C-1594	JEOPARDY	STURGES	MGM	1953
C-1595	BATTLE CIRCUS	BROOKS	MGM	1953
C-1596	STUDENT PRINCE	THORPE	MGM	1954
C-1597	RIDE, VAQUERO	FARROW	MGM	1953
C-1598	GIRL WHO HAD EVERYTHING	THORPE	MGM	1953
C-1599	JULIUS CAESAR	MANKIEWICZ	MGM	1953
C-1600	BRIGHT ROAD	MAYER	MGM	1953
C-1601	STORY OF THREE LOVES	MINNELLI, REINHARDT	MGM	1953
C-1602	DANGEROUS WHEN WET	WALTERS	MGM	1953
C-1603	CRY OF THE HUNTED	LEWIS	MGM	1953
C-1604	YOUNG BESS	SIDNEY	MGM	1953
C-1605	INVITATION TO THE DANCE	KELLY	MGM	1956
C-1606	HOAXTERS	HOFFMAN	MGM	1953
C-1607	DREAM WIFE	SHELDON	MGM	1953
C-1608	GIVE A GIRL A BREAK	DONEN	MGM	1954
C-1609	CODE TWO	WILCOX	MGM	1953
C-1610	BAND WAGON	MINNELLI	MGM	1953
C-1611	CLOWN	LEONARD	MGM	1953
C-1612	REMAINS TO BE SEEN	WEIS	MGM	1953
C-1613	FAST COMPANY	STURGES	MGM	1953
C-1614	ALL THE BROTHERS WERE VALIANT	THORPE	MGM	1953
C-1616	MOGAMBO	FORD	MGM	1953
C-1617	ACTRESS	CUKOR	MGM	1953

Movie Still Identification Book Ultimate Edition - Letters

CODE	TITLE/NAME	DIRECTOR/TYPE	STUDIO/DISTRIBUTOR	YEAR
C-1618	LATIN LOVERS	LEROY	MGM	1953
C-1619	SLIGHT CASE OF LARCENY	WEIS	MGM	1953
C-1620	GREAT DIAMOND ROBBERY	LEONARD	MGM	1954
C-1621	EASY TO LOVE	WALTERS	MGM	1954
C-1622	SAADIA	LEWIN	MGM	1954
C-1623	TAKE THE HIGH GROUND	BROOKS	MGM	1953
C-1624	AFFAIRS OF DOBIE GILLIS	WEIS	MGM	1953
C-1625	BIG LEAGUER	ALDRICH	MGM	1953
C-1626	ARENA	FLEISCHER	MGM	1953
C-1627	ESCAPE FROM FORT BRAVO	STURGES	MGM	1953
C-1628	RHAPSODY	VIDOR	MGM	1954
C-1629	KISS ME KATE	SIDNEY	MGM	1953
C-1630	HALF A HERO	WEIS	MGM	1953
C-1631	TORCH SONG	WALTERS	MGM	1953
C-1632	LONG, LONG TRAILER	MINNELLI	MGM	1954
C-1633	CREST OF THE WAVE	BOULTING, BOULTING	MGM	1954
C-1634	KNIGHTS OF THE ROUND TABLE	THORPE	MGM	1953
C-1635	FLAME AND THE FLESH	BROOKS	MGM	1954
C-1636	TENNESSEE CHAMP	WILCOX	MGM	1954
C-1637	ROSE MARIE	LEROY	MGM	1954
C-1638	GYPSY COLT	MARTON	MGM	1954
C-1639	HER TWELVE MEN	LEONARD	MGM	1954
C-1640	EXECUTIVE SUITE	WISE	MGM	1954
C-1641	MEN OF THE FIGHTING LADY	MARTON	MGM	1954
C-1642	VALLEY OF THE KINGS	PIROSH	MGM	1954
C-1643	SEVEN BRIDES FOR SEVEN BROTHERS	DONEN	MGM	1954
C-1644	BAD DAY AT BLACK ROCK	STURGES	MGM	1955
C-1645	BRIGADOON	MINNELLI	MGM	1954
C1646	BETRAYED	REINHARDT	MGM	1954
C-1647	BEAU BRUMMEL (UK)	BERNHARDT	MGM	1954
C-1648	PRISONER OF WAR	MARTON	MGM	1954
C-1649	LAST TIME I SAW PARIS	BROOKS	MGM	1954
C-1650	ATHENA	THORPE	MGM	1954
C-1651	GREEN FIRE	MARTON	MGM	1955
C-1652	JUPITER'S DARLING	SIDNEY	MGM	1955
C-1653	ROGUE COP	ROWLAND	MGM	1954
C-1654	DEEP IN MY HEART	DONEN	MGM	1954
C-1655	GLASS SLIPPER	WALTERS	MGM	1955
C-1656	MANY RIVERS TO CROSS	ROWLAND	MGM	1955
C-1657	INVITATION TO THE DANCE	KELLY	MGM	1957
C-1658	PRODIGAL	THORPE	MGM	1955
C-1659	HIT THE DECK	ROWLAND	MGM	1955
C-1660	MOONFLEET	LANG	MGM	1955
C-1661	INTERRUPTED MELODY	BERNHARDT	MGM	1955
C-1662	BEDEVILLED	LEISEN	MGM	1955
C1663	IT'S ALWAYS FAIR WEATHER	DONEN, KELLY	MGM	1955
C-1664	MARAUDERS	MAYER	MGM	1955
C-1665	SCARLET COAT	STURGES	MGM	1955
C-1666	BLACKBOARD JUNGLE	BROOKS	MGM	1955
C-1667	COBWEB	MINNELLI	MGM	1955
C-1668	LOVE ME OR LEAVE ME	VIDOR	MGM	1955
C-1669	KING'S THIEF	LEONARD	MGM	1955
C-1670	IT'S A DOG'S LIFE	HOFFMAN	MGM	1955
C-1671	FORBIDDEN PLANET	WILCOX	MGM	1956
C-1672	BHOWANI JUNCTION	CUKOR	MGM	1956
C-1673	TRIBUTE TO A BADMAN	WISE	MGM	1956
C-1674	QUENTIN DURWARD (UK)	THORPE	MGM	1955
C-1675	DIANE	MILLER	MGM	1956
C-1676	KISMET	MINNELLI	MGM	1955
C-1677	TRIAL	ROBSON	MGM	1955
C-1678	LAST HUNT	BROOKS	MGM	1956
C-1679	I'LL CRY TOMORROW	MANN	MGM	1955
C-1680	MEET ME IN LAS VEGAS	ROWLAND	MGM	1956
C-1681	TENDER TRAP	WALTERS	MGM	1955
C-1682	LUST FOR LIFE	MINNELLI	MGM	1956
C-1683	GABY	BERNHARDT	MGM	1956
C-1684	SWAN	VIDOR	MGM	1956
C-1685	RANSOM	SEGAL	MGM	1956
C-1686	RACK	LAVEN	MGM	1956
C-1687	CATERED AFFAIR	BROOKS	MGM	1956

Movie Still Identification Book Ultimate Edition - Letters

CODE	TITLE/NAME	DIRECTOR/TYPE	STUDIO/DISTRIBUTOR	YEAR
C-1688	OPPOSITE SEX	MILLER	MGM	1956
C-1689	FASTEST GUN ALIVE	ROUSE	MGM	1956
C-1690	HIGH SOCIETY	WALTERS	MGM	1956
C-1691	SOMEBODY UP THERE LIKES ME	WISE	MGM	1956
C-1692	RAINTREE COUNTY	DMYTRYK	MGM	1957
C-1693	TEAHOUSE OF THE AUGUST MOON	MANN	MGM	1956
C-1694	TEA AND SYMPATHY	MINNELLI	MGM	1956
C-1686	RACK	LAVEN	MGM	1956
C-1697	POWER AND THE PRIZE	KOSTER	MGM	1956
C-1698	BARRETTS OF WIMPOLE STREET	FRANKLIN	MGM	1957
C-1699	GREAT AMERICAN PASTIME	HOFFMAN	MGM	1956
C-1700	SOMETHING OF VALUE	BROOKS	MGM	1957
C-1701	WINGS OF EAGLES	FORD	MGM	1957
C-1702	VINTAGE	HAYDEN	MGM	1957
C-1703	HOT SUMMER NIGHT	FRIEDKIN	MGM	1957
C-1704	SLANDER	ROWLAND	MGM	1957
C-1705	TEN THOUSAND BEDROOMS	THORPE	MGM	1957
C-1706	DESIGNING WOMAN	MINNELLI	MGM	1957
C-1707	LES GIRLS	CUKOR	MGM	1957
C-1708	THIS COULD BE THE NIGHT	WISE	MGM	1957
C-1709	SILK STOCKINGS	MAMOULIAN	MGM	1957
C-1710	SEVENTH SIN	NEAME	MGM	1957
C-1711	GUN GLORY	ROWLAND	MGM	1957
C-1712	UNTIL THEY SAIL	WISE	MGM	1957
C-1713	MAN ON FIRE	MACDOUGALL	MGM	1957
C-1714	HOUSE OF NUMBERS	ROUSE	MGM	1957
C-1715	DON'T GO NEAR THE WATER	WALTERS	MGM	1957
C-1716	TIP ON A DEAD JOCKEY	THORPE	MGM	1957
C-1717	I ACCUSE!	FERRER	MGM	1958
C-1718	MERRY ANDREW	KIDD	MGM	1958
C-1719	JAILHOUSE ROCK	THORPE	MGM	1957
C-1720	BROTHERS KARAMAZOV	BROOKS	MGM	1958
C-1721	SADDLE THE WIND	PARRISH	MGM	1958
C-1722	HIRED GUN aka HOSTILE GUN	NAZARRO	MGM	1957
C-1723	GIGI	MINNELLI	MGM	1958
C-1724	BEN-HUR	WYLER	MGM	1959
C-1725	HIGH COST OF LOVING	FERRER	MGM	1958
C-1726	SHEEPMAN	MARSHALL	MGM	1958
C-1727	HANDLE WITH CARE	FRIEDKIN	MGM	1958
C-1728	LAW AND JAKE WADE	STURGES	MGM	1958
C-1729	TUNNEL OF LOVE	KELLY	MGM	1958
C-1730	RELUCTANT DEBUTANTE	MINNELLI	MGM	1958
C-1731	IMITATION GENERAL	MARSHALL	MGM	1958
C-1732	BADLANDERS	DAVES	MGM	1958
C-1733	HIGH SCHOOL CONFIDENTIAL	ARNOLD	MGM	1958
C-1734	GREEN MANSIONS	FERRER	MGM	1958
C-1735	CAT ON A HOT TIN ROOF	BROOKS	MGM	1958
C-1736	PARTY GIRL	RAY	MGM	1958
C-1737	WORLD, FLESH AND THE DEVIL	MACDOUGALL	MGM	1958
C-1739	ANDY HARDY COMES HOME	KOCH	MGM	1958
C-1740	WATUSI	NEUMANN	MGM	1959
C-1741	SOME CAME RUNNING	MINNELLI	MGM	1958
C-1742	COUNT YOUR BLESSINGS	NEGULESCO	MGM	1959
C-1743	NORTH BY NORTHWEST	HITCHCOCK	MGM	1959
C-1744	NIGHT OF THE QUARTER MOON	HAAS	MGM	1959
C-1746	BEAT GENERATION	HAAS	MGM	1959
C-1747	ASK ANY GIRL	WALTERS	MGM	1959
C-1748	NEVER SO FEW	STURGES	MGM	1959
C-1749	BIG OPERATOR	HAAS	MGM	1959
C-1750	WRECK OF THE MARY DEARE	ANDERSON	MGM	1959
C-1751	IT STARTED WITH A KISS	MARSHALL	MGM	1959
C-1752	TARZAN THE APE MAN	NEWMAN	MGM	1959
C-1753	GIRLS TOWN	HAAS	MGM	1960
C-1754	HOME FROM THE HILL	MINNELLI	MGM	1960
C-1755	TIME MACHINE	PAL	MGM	1960
C-1756	PLEASE DON'T EAT THE DAISIES	WALTERS	MGM	1960
C-1757	SUBTERRANEANS	MACDOUGALL	MGM	1960
C-1758	GAZEBO	MARSHALL	MGM	1959
C-1759	KEY WITNESS	KARLSON	MGM	1960
C-1760	BELLS ARE RINGING	MINNELLI	MGM	1960

Movie Still Identification Book Ultimate Edition - Letters

CODE	TITLE/NAME	DIRECTOR/TYPE	STUDIO/DISTRIBUTOR	YEAR
C-1761	ADVENTURES OF HUCKLEBERRY FINN	CURTIZ	MGM	1960
C-1762	PLATINUM HIGH SCHOOL	HAAS	MGM	1960
C-1763	CIMARRON	MANN	MGM	1960
C-1764	ALL THE FINE YOUNG CANNIBALS	ANDERSON	MGM	1960
C-1765	BUTTERFIELD 8	MANN	MGM	1960
C-1766	GO NAKED IN THE WORLD	MACDOUGALL	MGM	1961
C-1767	ATLANTIS, THE LOST CONTINENT	PAL	MGM	1961
C-1768	WHERE THE BOYS ARE	LEVIN	MGM	1960
C-1769	MUTINY ON THE BOUNTY	MILESTONE	MGM	1962
C-1770	TWO LOVES	WALTERS	MGM	1961
C-1771	FOUR HORSEMEN OF THE APOCALYPSE	MINNELLI	MGM	1962
C-1772	ADVENTURES OF TARTU (UK)	BUCQUET	MGM	1943
C-1773	ADA	MANN	MGM	1961
C-1774	HONEYMOON MACHINE	THORPE	MGM	1961
C-1775	THUNDER OF DRUMS	NEWMAN	MGM	1961
C-1776	HOW THE WEST WAS WON	FORD, HATHAWAY	MGM	1963
C-1783	BACHELOR IN PARADISE	ARNOLD	MGM	1961
C-1784	SWEET BIRD OF YOUTH	BROOKS	MGM	1962
C-1785	WONDERFUL WORLD BROTHERS GRIMM (t)	LEVIN, PAL	MGM	1962
C-1792	HORIZONTAL LIEUTENANT	THORPE	MGM	1962
C-1793	RIDE THE HIGH COUNTRY	PECKINPAH	MGM	1962
C-1794	TWO WEEKS IN ANOTHER TOWN	MINNELLI	MGM	1962
C-1795	BOYS' NIGHT OUT	GORDON	MGM	1962
C-1796	BILLY ROSES' JUMBO	WALTERS	MGM	1962
C-1797	PERIOD OF ADJUSTMENT	HILL	MGM	1962
C-1798	HOOK	SEATON	MGM	1963
C-1801	COURTSHIP OF EDDIE'S FATHER	MINNELLI	MGM	1963
C-1802	IT HAPPENED AT THE WORLD'S FAIR	TAUROG	MGM	1963
C-1803	DRUMS OF AFRICA	CLARK	MGM	1963
C-1804	TICKLISH AFFAIR	SIDNEY	MGM	1963
C-1805	WHEELER DEALERS	HILLER	MGM	1963
C-1806	TWILIGHT OF HONOR	SAGAL	MGM	1963
C-1807	SUNDAY IN NEW YORK	TEWKSBURY	MGM	1964
C-1808	PRIZE	ROBSON	MGM	1963
C-1809	GLOBAL AFFAIR	ARNOLD	MGM	1964
C-1810	ADVANCE TO THE REAR	MARSHALL	MGM	1964
C-1811	7 FACES OF DR LAO	PAL	MGM	1964
C-1812	VIVA LAS VEGAS	SIDNEY	MGM	1964
C-1813	MAIL ORDER BRIDE	KENNEDY	MGM	1964
C-1814	HOOTENANNY HOOT	NELSON	MGM	1963
C-1815	UNSINKABLE MOLLY BROWN	WALTERS	MGM	1963
C-1816	HONEYMOON HOTEL	LEVIN	MGM	1964
C-1817	LOOKING FOR LOVE	WEIS	MGM	1964
C-1818	SIGNPOST TO MURDER	ENGLUND	MGM	1964
C-1819	KISSIN' COUSINS	NELSON	MGM	1964
C-1820	AMERICANIZATION OF EMILY	HILLER	MGM	1964
C-1823	OUTRAGE	RITT	MGM	1964
C-1824	QUICK, BEFORE IT MELTS	MANN	MGM	1965
C-1825	ROUNDERS	KENNEDY	MGM	1965
C-1826	36 HOURS	SEATON	MGM	1965
C-1827	BARBARA KENT	portrait	MGM	
C-1828	JOY IN THE MORNING	SEGAL	MGM	1965
C-1829	GIRL HAPPY	SAGAL	MGM	1965
C-1830	GET YOURSELF A COLLEGE GIRL	MILLER	MGM	1964
C-1831	SANDPIPER	MINNELLI	MGM	1965
C-1832	ONCE A THIEF	NELSON	MGM	1965
C-1833	CINCINNATI KID	JEWISON	MGM	1965
C-1834	MONEY TRAP	KENNEDY	MGM	1966
C-1835	7 WOMEN	FORD	MGM	1966
C-1836	MISTER BUDDWING	MANN	MGM	1966
C-1837	PATCH OF BLUE	GREEN	MGM	1965
C-1838	HARUM SCARUM	NELSON	MGM	1965
C-1839	MADE IN PARIS	SAGAL	MGM	1966
C-1840	ICE STATION ZEBRA	STURGES	MGM	1968
C-1841	WHEN THE BOYS MEET THE GIRLS	GANZER	MGM	1965
C-1842	GLASS BOTTOM BOAT	TASHLIN	MGM	1966
C-1843	SINGING NUN	KOSTER	MGM	1966
C-1844	HOLD ON!	LUBIN	MGM	1966
C-1845	SPINOUT	TAUROG	MGM	1966
C-1846	DOCTOR, YOU'VE GOT TO BE KIDDING	TEWKSBURY	MGM	1967

Movie Still Identification Book Ultimate Edition - Letters

CODE	TITLE/NAME	DIRECTOR/TYPE	STUDIO/DISTRIBUTOR	YEAR
C-1847	VENETIAN AFFAIR	THORPE	MGM	1967
C-1848	PENELOPE	HILLER	MGM	1967
C-1849	DON'T MAKE WAVES	MACKENDRICK	MGM	1967
C-1850	DOUBLE TROUBLE	TAUROG	MGM	1967
C-1851	FASTEST GUITAR ALIVE	MOORE	MGM	1967
C-1852	LAST CHALLENGE	THORPE	MGM	1967
C-1853	POINT BLANK	BOORMAN	MGM	1967
C-1854	GUNS FOR SAN SEBASTIAN	VERNEUIL	MGM	1968
C-1855	EXTRAORDINARY SEAMAN	FRANKENHEIMER	MGM	1969
C-1856	POWER	HASKIN	MGM	1968
C-1857	SOL MADRID	HUTTON	MGM	1968
C-1858	PHANTOM TOLLBOOTH (t)	JONES, LEVITOW	MGM	1970
C-1859	LEGEND OF LYLAH CLARE	ALDRICH	MGM	1968
C-1860	SPEEDWAY	TAUROG	MGM	1968
C-1861	WHERE WERE YOU WHEN LIGHTS WENT OUT	AVERBACK	MGM	1968
C-1862	DAY OF THE EVIL GUN	THORPE	MGM	1968
C-1863	IMPOSSIBLE YEARS	GORDON	MGM	1969
C-1864	STAY AWAY, JOE	TEWKSBURY	MGM	1968
C-1866	TIME TO SING	DREIFUSS	MGM	1968
C-1867	SPLIT	FLEMYNG	MGM	1968
C-1868	LIVE A LITTLE, LOVE A LITTLE	TAUROG	MGM	1968
C-1869	HEAVEN WITH A GUN	KATZIN	MGM	1969
C-1870	YOUNG RUNAWAYS	DREIFUSS	MGM	1968
C-1871	GYPSY MOTHS	FRANKENHEIMER	MGM	1969
C-1872	MARLOWE	BOGART	MGM	1969
C-1873	ZABRISKIE POINT	ANTONIONI	MGM	1970
C-1875	TROUBLE WITH GIRLS	TEWKSBURY	MGM	1969
C-1876	MALTESE BIPPY	PANAMA	MGM	1969
C-1877	TICK-TICK-TICK	NELSON	MGM	1970
C-1878	MAGIC GARDEN STANLEY SWEETHEART	HORN	MGM	1970
C-1879	BAMBOLE (IT)	BOLOGNINI, COLOGINI	COLUMBIA	1965
C-1880	ZIGZAG	COLLA	MGM	1970
C-1881	STRAWBERRY STATEMENT	HAGMANN	MGM	1970
C-1884	DIRTY DINGUS MAGEE	KENNEDY	MGM	1970
C-1885	TRAVELING EXECUTIONER	SMIGHT	MGM	1970
C-1886	HOUSE OF DARK SHADOWS	CURTIS	MGM	1970
C-1887	ALEX IN WONDERLAND	MAZURSKY	MGM	1970
C-1888	BREWSTER MCCLOUD	ALTMAN	MGM	1971
C-1889	ELVIS- THAT'S THE WAY IT IS	SANDERS	MGM	1970
C-1890	PRETTY MAIDS ALL IN A ROW	VADIM	MGM	1971
C-1891	CORKY	HORN	MGM	1973
C-1892	BELIEVE IN ME	HAGMANN	MGM	1971
C-1893	FORTUNE AND MEN'S EYES	HART	MGM	1971
C-1894	WILD ROVERS	EDWARDS	MGM	1971
C-1895	SHAFT	PARKS	MGM	1971
C-1896	NIGHT OF DARK SHADOWS	CURTIS	MGM	1971
C-1897	GANG THAT COULDN'T SHOOT STRAIGHT	GOLDSTONE	MGM	1971
C-1898	GOING HOME	LEONARD	MGM	1971
C-1899	EVERY LITTLE CROOK AND NANNY	HOWARD	MGM	1972
C-1901	HORSING AROUND (sh)	WHITE	COLUMBIA	1957
C-1902	GUNS A POPPIN' (sh)	WHITE	COLUMBIA	1957
C-1902	MUSCLE UP A LITTLE CLOSER (sh) (SEE 4250)	WHITE	COLUMBIA	1957
C-1903	FIFI BLOWS HER TOP (sh)	WHITE	COLUMBIA	1958
C-1904	RUSTY ROMEOS (sh)	WHITE	COLUMBIA	1957
C-1905	PIES AND GUYS (sh) (SEE 1908)	WHITE	COLUMBIA	1958
C-1905	TRICKY CHICKS (sh)	WHITE	COLUMBIA	1957
C-1906	FLYING SAUCER DAFFY (sh)	WHITE	COLUMBIA	1958
C-1907	QUIZ WHIZZ (sh)	WHITE	COLUMBIA	1958
C-1908	OIL'S WELL THAT ENDS WELL (sh) (see 1911)	WHITE	COLUMBIA	1958
C-1908	PIES AND GUYS (sh)	WHITE	COLUMBIA	1958
C-1909	OUTER SPACE JITTERS (sh)	WHITE	COLUMBIA	1957
C-1910	SWEET AND HOT (sh)	WHITE	COLUMBIA	1958
C-1911	GUNS A POPPIN' (sh) (see1902)	WHITE	COLUMBIA	1957
C-1911	OIL'S WELL THAT ENDS WELL (sh)	WHITE	COLUMBIA	1958
C-1912	SAPPY BULLFIGHTERS (sh)	WHITE	COLUMBIA	1959
C-1913	TRIPLE CROSSED (sh)	WHITE	COLUMBIA	1959
C-3001	COWBOY FROM LONESOME RIVER	KLINE	COLUMBIA	1944
C-3002	CYCLONE PRAIRIE RANGERS	KLINE	COLUMBIA	1944
C-3003	COWBOY IN THE CLOUDS	KLINE	COLUMBIA	1943
C-3004	SUNDOWN VALLEY	KLINE	COLUMBIA	1944

Movie Still Identification Book Ultimate Edition - Letters

CODE	TITLE/NAME	DIRECTOR/TYPE	STUDIO/DISTRIBUTOR	YEAR
C-3005	COWBOY CANTEEN	LANDERS	COLUMBIA	1944
C-3006	SADDLE LEATHER LAW	KLINE	COLUMBIA	1944
C-3007	SAGEBRUSH HEROES	KLINE	COLUMBIA	1945
C-3008	ROUGH RIDING JUSTICE	ABRAHAMS	COLUMBIA	1945
C-3009	SWING IN THE SADDLE	LANDERS	COLUMBIA	1944
C-3010	RETURN OF THE DURANGO KID	ABRAHAMS	COLUMBIA	1945
C-3011	BOTH BARRELS BLAZING	ABRAHAMS	COLUMBIA	1945
C-3012	RUSTLERS OF THE BADLANDS	ABRAHAMS	COLUMBIA	1945
C-3013	FRONTIER GUNLAW	ABRAHAMS	COLUMBIA	1946
C-3014	SING ME A SONG OF TEXAS	KEAYS	COLUMBIA	1945
C-3015	BLAZING THE WESTERN TRAIL	KEAYS	COLUMBIA	1945
C-3016	LAWLESS EMPIRE	KEAYS	COLUMBIA	1945
C-3017	ROCKIN' IN THE ROCKIES	KEAYS	COLUMBIA	1945
C-3018	RHYTHM ROUNDUP	KEAYS	COLUMBIA	1945
C-3019	OUTLAWS OF THE ROCKIES	NAZARRO	COLUMBIA	1945
C-3020	TEXAS PANHANDLE	NAZARRO	COLUMBIA	1945
C-3021	SONG OF THE PRAIRIE	NAZARRO	COLUMBIA	1945
C-3022	DESERT HORSEMAN	NAZARRO	COLUMBIA	1946
C-3023	GUNNING FOR VENGEANCE	NAZARRO	COLUMBIA	1946
C-3024	ROARING RANGERS	NAZARRO	COLUMBIA	1946
C-3025	THROW A SADDLE ON A STAR	NAZARRO	COLUMBIA	1946
C-3026	HEADING WEST	NAZARRO	COLUMBIA	1946
C-3027	GALLOPING THUNDER	NAZARRO	COLUMBIA	1946
C-3028	TWO-FISTED STRANGER	NAZARRO	COLUMBIA	1946
C-3029	THAT TEXAS JAMBOREE	NAZARRO	COLUMBIA	1946
C-3030	TERROR TRAIL	NAZARRO	COLUMBIA	1946
C-3031	LANDRUSH	KEAYS	COLUMBIA	1946
C-3032	COWBOY BLUES	NAZARRO	COLUMBIA	1946
C-3033	SINGING ON THE TRAIL	NAZARRO	COLUMBIA	1946
C-3034	FIGHTING FRONTIERSMAN	ABRAHAMS	COLUMBIA	1946
C-3035	SOUTH OF THE CHISHOLM TRAIL	ABRAHAMS	COLUMBIA	1947
C-3036	LONE STAR MOONLIGHT	NAZARRO	COLUMBIA	1946
C-3037	OVER THE SANTA FE TRAIL	NAZARRO	COLUMBIA	1947
C-3038	WEST OF DODGE CITY	NAZARRO	COLUMBIA	1947
C-3039	LONE HAND TEXAS	NAZARRO	COLUMBIA	1947
C-3040	LAW OF THE CANYON	NAZARRO	COLUMBIA	1947
C-3041	PRAIRIE RAIDERS	ABRAHAMS	COLUMBIA	1947
C-3042	STRANGER FROM PONCA CITY	ABRAHAMS	COLUMBIA	1947
C-3043	RIDERS OF THE LONE STAR	ABRAHAMS	COLUMBIA	1947
C-3044	SWING THE WESTERN WAY	ABRAHAMS	COLUMBIA	1947
C-3045	SMOKEY RIVER SERENADE	ABRAHAMS	COLUMBIA	1947
C-3046	SIX GUN LAW	NAZARRO	COLUMBIA	1948
C-3047	BUCKAROO FROM POWDER RIVER	NAZARRO	COLUMBIA	1947
C-3048	PHANTOM VALLEY	NAZARRO	COLUMBIA	1948
C-3049	LAST DAYS OF BOOTHILL	NAZARRO	COLUMBIA	1947
C-3050	ROSE OF SANTA FE	NAZARRO	COLUMBIA	1947
C-3051	WHIRLWIND RAIDERS	KEAYS	COLUMBIA	1948
C-3052	WEST OF SONORA	NAZARRO	COLUMBIA	1948
C-3053	SONG OF IDAHO	NAZARRO	COLUMBIA	1948
C-3054	BLAZING ACROSS THE PECOS	NAZARRO	COLUMBIA	1948
C-3055	TRAIL TO LAREDO	NAZARRO	COLUMBIA	1948
C-3056	ARKANSAS SWING	NAZARRO	COLUMBIA	1948
C-3057	SINGIN' SPURS	NAZARRO	COLUMBIA	1948
C-3058	EL DORADO PASS	NAZARRO	COLUMBIA	1948
C-3059	QUICK ON THE TRIGGER	NAZARRO	COLUMBIA	1948
C-3060	CHALLENGE OF THE RANGE	NAZARRO	COLUMBIA	1949
C-3061	SMOKY MOUNTAIN MELODY	NAZARRO	COLUMBIA	1948
C-3062	SOUTH OF DEATH VALLEY	NAZARRO	COLUMBIA	1949
C-3063	DESERT VIGILANTE	SEARS	COLUMBIA	1949
C-3064	LARAMIE	NAZARRO	COLUMBIA	1949
C-3065	HOME IN SAN ANTONE	NAZARRO	COLUMBIA	1949
C-3066	BLAZING TRAIL	NAZARRO	COLUMBIA	1949
C-3067	HORSEMEN OF THE SIERRAS	SEARS	COLUMBIA	1949
C-3068	BANDITS OF EL DORADO	NAZARRO	COLUMBIA	1949
C-3069	RENEGADES OF THE SAGE	NAZARRO	COLUMBIA	1949
C-3070	HOEDOWN	NAZARRO	COLUMBIA	1950
C-3071	FEUDIN' RHYTHM	BERNDS	COLUMBIA	1949
C-3072	OUTCAST OF BLACK MESA	NAZARRO	COLUMBIA	1950
C-3073	FRONTIER OUTPOST	NAZARRO	COLUMBIA	1950
C-3074	TRAIL OF THE RUSTLERS	NAZARRO	COLUMBIA	1950

Movie Still Identification Book Ultimate Edition - Letters

CODE	TITLE/NAME	DIRECTOR/TYPE	STUDIO/DISTRIBUTOR	YEAR
C-3075	TEXAS DYNAMO	NAZARRO	COLUMBIA	1950
C-3076	STREETS OF GHOST TOWN	NAZARRO	COLUMBIA	1950
C-3077	ACROSS THE BADLANDS	SEARS	COLUMBIA	1950
C-3078	RAIDERS OF TOMAHAWK CREEK	SEARS	COLUMBIA	1950
C-3079	LIGHTNING GUNS	SEARS	COLUMBIA	1950
C-3080	PRAIRIE ROUNDUP	SEARS	COLUMBIA	1951
C-3081	RIDIN' THE OUTLAW TRAIL	SEARS	COLUMBIA	1951
C-3082	FORT SAVAGE RAIDERS	NAZARRO	COLUMBIA	1951
C-3083	SNAKE RIVER DESPERADOES	SEARS	COLUMBIA	1951
C-3084	BONANZA TOWN	SEARS	COLUMBIA	1951
C-3085	CYCLONE FURY	NAZARRO	COLUMBIA	1951
C-3086	KID FROM AMARILLO	NAZARRO	COLUMBIA	1951
C-3087	KID FROM AMARILLO	NAZARRO	COLUMBIA	1951
C-3087	PECOS RIVER	SEARS	COLUMBIA	1951
C-3088	SMOKY CANYON	SEARS	COLUMBIA	1952
C-3089	HAWK OF WILD RIVER	SEARS	COLUMBIA	1952
C-3090	LARAMIE MOUNTAINS	NAZARRO	COLUMBIA	1952
C-3091	ROUGH TOUGH WEST	NAZARRO	COLUMBIA	1952
C-3092	JUNCTION CITY	NAZARRO	COLUMBIA	1952
C-3093	KID FROM BROKEN GUN	SEARS	COLUMBIA	1952
C-3400	CORONER CREEK	ENRIGHT	COLUMBIA	1948
C-4001	BUSY BUDDIES (sh)	LORD	COLUMBIA	1944
C-4002	WEDDED BLISS (sh)	EDWARDS	COLUMBIA	1944
C-4003	BACHELOR DAZE (sh)	WHITE	COLUMBIA	1943
C-4004	YOU DEAR BOY (sh)	WHITE	COLUMBIA	1943
C-4005	DOCTOR, FEEL MY PULSE (sh)	WHITE	COLUMBIA	1944
C-4006	BOOBY DUPES (sh)	LORD	COLUMBIA	1945
C-4007	HIS TALE IS TOLD (sh)	EDWARDS	COLUMBIA	1944
C-4008	YOU WERE NEVER UGLIER (sh)	WHITE	COLUMBIA	1944
C-4009	GOLD IS WHERE YOU LOSE IT (sh)	WHITE	COLUMBIA	1944
C-4010	CRASH GOES THE HAS (sh)	WHITE	COLUMBIA	1944
C-4011	CRAZY LIKE A FOX (sh)	WHITE	COLUMBIA	1944
C-4012	HIS HOTEL SWEET (sh)	EDWARDS	COLUMBIA	1944
C-4013	IDLE ROOMERS (sh)	LORD	COLUMBIA	1943
C-4014	OH, BABY (sh)	WHITE	COLUMBIA	1944
C-4015	OFF AGAIN, ON AGAIN (sh)	WHITE	COLUMBIA	1945
C-4016	OPEN SEASON FOR SAPS (sh)	WHITE	COLUMBIA	1944
C-4017	DEFECTIVE DETECTIVES (sh)	EDWARDS	COLUMBIA	1944
C-4018	PICK A PECK OF PLUMBERS (sh)	WHITE	COLUMBIA	1944
C-4019	MOPEY DOPE (sh)	LORD	COLUMBIA	1944
C-4020	GENTS WITHOUT CENTS (sh)	WHITE	COLUMBIA	1944
C-4021	HEATHER AND YON (sh)	EDWARDS	COLUMBIA	1944
C-4022	THREE PESTS IN A MESS (sh)	LORD	COLUMBIA	1945
C-4023	WOO WOO (I SHOULD WORRY*)	WHITE	COLUMBIA	1945
C-4024	TWO LOCAL YOKELS (sh)	WHITE	COLUMBIA	1945
C-4025	KNIGHT AND A BLONDE (sh)	EDWARDS	COLUMBIA	1944
C-4025	WOO WOO (I SHOULD WORRY*)	WHITE	COLUMBIA	1945
C-4026	SHE SNOOPS TO CONQUER (sh)	WHITE	COLUMBIA	1944
C-4027	STRIFE OF THE PARTY (sh)	EDWARDS	COLUMBIA	1944
C-4028	DANCE DUNCE, DANCE (sh)	WHITE	COLUMBIA	1945
C-4029	SNOOPER SERVICE (sh)	EDWARDS	COLUMBIA	1945
C-4030	IDIOTS DELUXE (sh)	WHITE	COLUMBIA	1945
C-4031	JURY GOES ROUND AND ROUND (sh)	WHITE	COLUMBIA	1945
C-4032	HISS AND YELL (sh)	WHITE	COLUMBIA	1946
C-4033	IF A BODY MEETS A BODY (sh)	WHITE	COLUMBIA	1945
C-4035	PISTOL PACKIN' NITWITS (sh)	EDWARDS	COLUMBIA	1945
C-4036	WIFE DECOY (sh)	EDWARDS	COLUMBIA	1945
C-4037	SPOOK TO ME (sh)	EDWARDS	COLUMBIA	1945
C-4038	HIT WITH A MISS (sh)	WHITE	COLUMBIA	1945
C-4039	MAYOR'S HUSBAND (sh)	EDWARDS	COLUMBIA	1945
C-4040	MINER AFFAIR (sh)	WHITE	COLUMBIA	1945
C-4041	BLONDE STAYED ON (sh)	EDWARDS	COLUMBIA	1946
C-4042	CALLING ALL FIBBERS (sh)	WHITE	COLUMBIA	1945
C-4043	BIRD IN THE HEAD (sh)	BERNDS	COLUMBIA	1946
C-4044	MICRO-PHONIES (sh)	BERNDS	COLUMBIA	1945
C-4045	BEER BARREL POLECATS (sh)	WHITE	COLUMBIA	1946
C-4046	THREE TROUBLEDOERS (sh)	BERNDS	COLUMBIA	1946
C-4047	WHEN THE WIFE'S AWAY (sh)	BERNDS	COLUMBIA	1946
C-4048	JIGGERS, MY WIFE (sh)	WHITE	COLUMBIA	1946
C-4048	WHERE THE PEST BEGINS	EDWARDS	COLUMBIA	1945

Movie Still Identification Book Ultimate Edition - Letters

CODE	TITLE/NAME	DIRECTOR/TYPE	STUDIO/DISTRIBUTOR	YEAR
C-4049	YOU CAN'T FOOL A FOOL (sh)	WHITE	COLUMBIA	1946
C-4050	UNCIVIL WAR BIRDS (sh)	WHITE	COLUMBIA	1946
C-4051	HIGH BLOOD PLEASURE (sh)	WHITE	COLUMBIA	1945
C-4052	SOCIETY MUGS (sh)	BERNDS	COLUMBIA	1946
C-4053	THREE LOAN WOLVES (sh)	WHITE	COLUMBIA	1946
C-4054	MR. NOISY (sh)	BERNDS	COLUMBIA	1946
C-4055	GET ALONG LITTLE ZOMBIE (sh)	BERNDS	COLUMBIA	1946
C-4056	HALF-WITS HOLIDAY (sh)	WHITE	COLUMBIA	1947
C-4057	RHYTHM AND WEEP (sh)	WHITE	COLUMBIA	1946
C-4058	MONKEY BUSINESSMEN (sh)	BERNDS	COLUMBIA	1946
C-4059	ANDY PLAYS HOOKEY (sh)	BERNDS	COLUMBIA	1946
C-4060	HEADIN' FOR A WEDDIN' (sh)	WHITE	COLUMBIA	1946
C-4061	SCOOPER DOOPER (sh)	BERNDS	COLUMBIA	1947
C-4062	AIN'T LOVE CUCKOO (sh)	WHITE	COLUMBIA	1946
C-4063	G. I. WANNA HOME (sh)	WHITE	COLUMBIA	1946
C-4064	BRIDE AND GLOOM (sh)	BERNDS	COLUMBIA	1947
C-4065	MR. WRIGHT GOES WRONG (sh)	WHITE	COLUMBIA	1946
C-4066	HOT WATER (sh)	BERNDS	COLUMBIA	1946
C-4067	THREE LITTLE PIRATES (sh)	BERNDS	COLUMBIA	1946
C-4068	PARDON MY TERROR (sh)	BERNDS	COLUMBIA	1946
C-4069	SUNK IN THE SINK (sh)	WHITE	COLUMBIA	1949
C-4070	FIDDLERS THREE (sh)	WHITE	COLUMBIA	1948
C-4071	FRIGHT NIGHT	BERNDS	COLUMBIA	1947
C-4072	SHOULD HUSBANDS MARRY? (sh)	LORD	COLUMBIA	1947
C-4073	CRABBIN' IN THE CABIN (sh)	WHITE	COLUMBIA	1948
C-4074	HONEYMOON BLUES (sh)	BERNDS	COLUMBIA	1946
C-4075	HOT HEIR (sh)	BERNDS	COLUMBIA	1947
C-4076	HECTIC HONEYMOON (sh)	BERNDS	COLUMBIA	1947
C-4077	OUT WEST (sh)	BERNDS	COLUMBIA	1947
C-4078	SO'S YOUR ANTENNA (sh)	WHITE	COLUMBIA	1946
C-4079	TWO JILLS AND A JACK (sh)	WHITE	COLUMBIA	1947
C-4080	SLAPPILY MARRIED (sh)	BERNDS	COLUMBIA	1946
C-4081	MEET MR. MISCHIEF (sh)	BERNDS	COLUMBIA	1947
C-4082	SQUAREHEADS OF THE ROUND TABLE (sh)	BERNDS	COLUMBIA	1948
C-4083	RENO-VATED (sh)	WHITE	COLUMBIA	1946
C-4084	NERVOUS SHAKEDOWN (sh)	LORD	COLUMBIA	1947
C-4085	MORON THAN OFF (sh)	WHITE	COLUMBIA	1946
C-4086	GOOD BAD EGG (sh)	WHITE	COLUMBIA	1947
C-4087	HOLD THAT LION (sh)	WHITE	COLUMBIA	1947
C-4088	SING A SONG OF SIX PANTS (sh)	WHITE	COLUMBIA	1947
C-4089	ROLLING DOWN TO RENO (sh)	WHITE	COLUMBIA	1947
C-4091	I'M A MONKEY'S UNCLE (sh)	WHITE	COLUMBIA	1948
C-4093	PARDON MY CLUTCH (sh)	BERNDS	COLUMBIA	1948
C-4094	HOT SCOTS (sh)	BERNDS	COLUMBIA	1948
C-4095	BRIDELESS GROOM (sh)	BERNDS	COLUMBIA	1947
C-4096	WIFE TO SPARE (sh)	BERNDS	COLUMBIA	1947
C-4097	CUPID GOES NUTS (sh)	WHITE	COLUMBIA	1947
C-4098	TRAINING FOR TROUBLE (sh)	WHITE	COLUMBIA	1947
C-4099	WEDDING BELLE (sh)	BERNDS	COLUMBIA	1947
C-4100	TALL, DARK AND GRUESOME (sh)	LORD	COLUMBIA	1948
C-4101	WAITING IN THE LURCH (sh)	BERNDS	COLUMBIA	1949
C-4102	STOOGES (sh)		COLUMBIA	
C-4103	SHIVERING SHERLOCKS (sh)	LORD	COLUMBIA	1948
C-4104	ALL GUMMED UP (sh)	WHITE	COLUMBIA	1947
C-4105	MUMMY'S DUMMIES (sh)	BERNDS	COLUMBIA	1948
C-4106	WEDLOCK DEADLOCK (sh)	BERNDS	COLUMBIA	1947
C-4107	THREE HAMS ON RYE (sh)	WHITE	COLUMBIA	1950
C-4108	GHOST TALKS (sh)	WHITE	COLUMBIA	1949
C-4109	RADIO ROMEO (sh)	BERNDS	COLUMBIA	1947
C-4110	MAN OR MOUSE (sh)	WHITE	COLUMBIA	1948
C-4111	CRIME ON THEIR HANDS (sh)	BERNDS	COLUMBIA	1948
C-4112	WHO DONE IT? (sh)	BERNDS	COLUMBIA	1949
C-4113	EIGHT BALL ANDY (sh)	BERNDS	COLUMBIA	1948
C-4114	FUELIN' AROUND (sh)	BERNDS	COLUMBIA	1949
C-4115	HUGS AND MUGS (sh)	WHITE	COLUMBIA	1950
C-4116	HOKUS POKUS (sh)	WHITE	COLUMBIA	1949
C-4117	FLAT FEAT (sh)	BERNDS	COLUMBIA	1948
C-4118	GO CHASE YOURSELF (sh)	WHITE	COLUMBIA	1948
C-4119	MALICE IN THE PALACE (sh)	WHITE	COLUMBIA	1949
C-4120	JITTER BUGHOUSE (sh)	WHITE	COLUMBIA	1948

Movie Still Identification Book Ultimate Edition - Letters

CODE	TITLE/NAME	DIRECTOR/TYPE	STUDIO/DISTRIBUTOR	YEAR
C-4121	PARDON MY LAMBCHOP (sh)	WHITE	COLUMBIA	1948
C-4122	SILLY BILLY (sh)	WHITE	COLUMBIA	1948
C-4123	HE'S IN AGAIN (sh)	BERNDS	COLUMBIA	1949
C-4124	TWO NUTS IN A RUT (sh)	BERNDS	COLUMBIA	1948
C-4125	BILLIE GETS HER MAN (sh)	BERNDS	COLUMBIA	1948
C-4126	SHEEPISH WOLF (sh)	BERNDS	COLUMBIA	1948
C-4127	PARLOR, BEDROOM AND WRATH (sh)	WHITE	COLUMBIA	1948
C-4128	PINCH IN TIME (sh)	LORD	COLUMBIA	1948
C-4129	LOVE AT FIRST BITE (sh)	WHITE	COLUMBIA	1950
C-4130	MICROSPOOK (sh)	BERNDS	COLUMBIA	1949
C-4131	DOPEY DICKS (sh)	BERNDS	COLUMBIA	1950
C-4132	RADIO RIOT (sh)	BERNDS	COLUMBIA	1949
C-4133	TRAPPED BY A BLOND (sh)	LORD	COLUMBIA	1949
C-4134	FLUNG BY A FLING (sh)	BERNDS	COLUMBIA	1949
C-4135	CLUNKED IN THE CLINK (sh)	WHITE	COLUMBIA	1949
C-4136	MISS IN A MESS (sh)	WHITE	COLUMBIA	1949
C-4137	DUNKED IN THE DEEP (sh)	WHITE	COLUMBIA	1949
C-4138	DIZZY YARDBIRD (sh)	WHITE	COLUMBIA	1950
C-4139	SLAPHAPPY SLEUTHS (sh)	WHITE	COLUMBIA	1950
C-4140	VAGABOND LOAFERS (sh)	BERNDS	COLUMBIA	1949
C-4141	SELF MADE MAIDS (sh)	WHITE	COLUMBIA	1950
C-4142	PUNCHY COWPUNCHERS (sh)	BERNDS	COLUMBIA	1950
C-4143	STUDIO STOOPS (sh)	BERNDS	COLUMBIA	1950
C-4144	HOLD THAT MONKEY (sh)	WHITE	COLUMBIA	1950
C-4145	HIS BAITING BEAUTY (sh)	BERNDS	COLUMBIA	1950
C-4146	SUPER WOLF (sh)	LORD	COLUMBIA	1949
C-4147	LET DOWN YOUR AERIAL (sh)	BERNDS	COLUMBIA	1949
C-4148	ONE SHIVERY NIGHT (sh)	LORD	COLUMBIA	1950
C-4149	WHA' HAPPEN? (sh)	WHITE	COLUMBIA	1949
C-4150	NURSIE BEHAVE (sh)	WHITE	COLUMBIA	1950
C-4151	FRENCH FRIED FROLIC (sh)	WHITE	COLUMBIA	1949
C-4152	HOUSE ABOUT IT (sh)	WHITE	COLUMBIA	1950
C-4153	MARINATED MARINER (sh)	WHITE	COLUMBIA	1950
C-4154	SNITCH IN TIME (sh)	BERNDS	COLUMBIA	1950
C-4155	BABY SITTERS JITTERS (sh)	WHITE	COLUMBIA	1951
C-4156	THREE ARABIAN NUTS (sh)	BERNDS	COLUMBIA	1951
C-4157	SCRAMBLED BRAINS (sh)	WHITE	COLUMBIA	1951
C-4158	DON'T THROW THAT KNIFE (sh)	WHITE	COLUMBIA	1951
C-4159	MALICE IN THE PALACE (sh) (see 4119)	WHITE	COLUMBIA	1949
C-4159	MISSED FORTUNE (sh)	WHITE	COLUMBIA	1952
C-4160	BLUNDERFUL TIME (sh)	WHITE	COLUMBIA	1949
C-4161	MERRY MAVERICKS (sh)	BERNDS	COLUMBIA	1951
C-4162	TOOTH WILL OUT (sh)	BERNDS	COLUMBIA	1951
C-4163	PEST MAN WINS (sh)	WHITE	COLUMBIA	1951
C-4164	WINE, WOMEN AND BONG (sh)	WHITE	COLUMBIA	1951
C-4165	TWO ROAMING CHAMPS (sh)	BERNDS	COLUMBIA	1950
C-4166	HE FLEW THE SHREW (sh)	WHITE	COLUMBIA	1951
C-4167	FUN ON THE RUN (sh)	WHITE	COLUMBIA	1951
C-4168	SLIP AND A MISS (sh)	MCCOLLUM	COLUMBIA	1950
C-4169	WOO WOO BLUES (sh)	QUINE	COLUMBIA	1951
C-4170	BLONDE ATOM BOMB (sh)	WHITE	COLUMBIA	1951
C-4171	PLEASURE TREASURE (sh)	WHITE	COLUMBIA	1951
C-4172	INNOCENTLY GUILTY (sh)	WHITE	COLUMBIA	1950
C-4173	AWFUL SLEUTH (sh)	QUINE	COLUMBIA	1951
C-4174	FOY MEETS GIRL (sh)	ULLMAN	COLUMBIA	1950
C-4175	WEDDING YELLS (sh)	WHITE	COLUMBIA	1951
C-4176	HAPPY GO WACKY (sh)	WHITE	COLUMBIA	1952
C-4177	SHE TOOK A POWDER (sh)	WHITE	COLUMBIA	1951
C-4178	CORNY CASANOVAS (sh)	WHITE	COLUMBIA	1952
C-4179	HULA-LA-LA (sh)	MCCOLLUM	COLUMBIA	1951
C-4180	LISTEN, JUDGE (sh)	BERNDS	COLUMBIA	1952
C-4181	HE COOKED HIS GOOSE (sh)	WHITE	COLUMBIA	1952
C-4182	UP IN DAISY'S PENTHOUSE (sh)	WHITE	COLUMBIA	1953
C-4183	GENTS IN A JAM (sh)	BERNDS	COLUMBIA	1952
C-4184	TROUBLE IN-LAWS (sh)	MCCOLLUM	COLUMBIA	1951
C-4185	CHAMPS STEP OUT (sh)	BERNDS	COLUMBIA	1951
C-4186	ROOTIN' TOOTIN' TENDERFEET (sh)	WHITE	COLUMBIA	1952
C-4187	GINK AT THE SINK (sh)	WHITE	COLUMBIA	1952
C-4188	HEEBIE GEE-GEES (sh)	BERNDS	COLUMBIA	1952
C-4189	FOOL AND HIS HONEY (sh)	WHITE	COLUMBIA	1952

Movie Still Identification Book Ultimate Edition - Letters

CODE	TITLE/NAME	DIRECTOR/TYPE	STUDIO/DISTRIBUTOR	YEAR
C-4190	BLISSFUL BLUNDER (sh)	WHITE	COLUMBIA	1952
C-4191	HOOKED AND ROOKED (sh)	WHITE	COLUMBIA	1952
C-4192	FRAIDY CAT (sh)	WHITE	COLUMBIA	1951
C-4193	AIM, FIRE, SCOOT (sh)	WHITE	COLUMBIA	1952
C-4194	CUCKOO ON A CHOO CHOO (sh)	WHITE	COLUMBIA	1952
C-4195	CAUGHT ON THE BOUNCE (sh)	WHITE	COLUMBIA	1952
C-4196	BOOTY AND THE BEAST (sh)	WHITE	COLUMBIA	1953
C-4197	LOOSE LOOT (sh)	WHITE	COLUMBIA	1953
C-4198	STROP, LOOK AND LISTEN (sh)	WHITE	COLUMBIA	1952
C-4199	TRICKY DICKS (sh)	WHITE	COLUMBIA	1953
C-4200	THREE DARK HORSES (sh)	WHITE	COLUMBIA	1952
C-4201	BUBBLE TROUBLE (sh)	WHITE	COLUMBIA	1953
C-4201	RIP, SEW AND STITCH (sh)	WHITE	COLUMBIA	1953
C-4203	GOOF ON THE ROOF (sh)	WHITE	COLUMBIA	1953
C-4204	HE POPPED HIS PISTOL (sh)	WHITE	COLUMBIA	1953
C-4205	SPIES AND GUYS (sh)	WHITE	COLUMBIA	1953
C-4206	LOVE'S A POPPIN' (sh)	WHITE	COLUMBIA	1953
C-4207	OH, SAY CAN YOU SUE (sh)	WHITE	COLUMBIA	1953
C-4207	TWO JILLS AND A JACK (sh) (see 4079)	WHITE	COLUMBIA	1947
C-4208	INCOME TAX SAPPY (sh)	WHITE	COLUMBIA	1954
C-4209	MUSTY MUSKATEERS (sh)	WHITE	COLUMBIA	1954
C-4210	SPOOKS (sh)	WHITE	COLUMBIA	1953
C-4211	PALS AND GALS (sh)	WHITE	COLUMBIA	1954
C-4212	PARDON MY BACKFIRE (sh)	WHITE	COLUMBIA	1953
C-4213	A-HUNTING THEY DID GO	WHITE	COLUMBIA	1948
C-4214	DOGGIE IN THE BEDROOM (sh)	WHITE	COLUMBIA	1954
C-4215	DOWN THE HATCH (sh)	WHITE	COLUMBIA	1953
C-4216	SHOT IN THE FRONTIER (sh)	WHITE	COLUMBIA	1954
C-4217	KNUTZY KNIGHTS (sh)	WHITE	COLUMBIA	1954
C-4218	SCOTCHED IN SCOTLAND (sh)	WHITE	COLUMBIA	1954
C-4219	TOOTING TOOTERS (sh)	WHITE	COLUMBIA	1954
C-4220	MINER AFFAIR	WHITE	COLUMBIA	1945
C-4220	TWO APRIL FOOLS (sh)	WHITE	COLUMBIA	1954
C-4221	KIDS WILL BE KIDS (sh)	WHITE	COLUMBIA	1954
C-4222	BLUNDER BOYS (sh)	WHITE	COLUMBIA	1955
C-4223	FLING IN THE RING	WHITE	COLUMBIA	1955
C-4224	GYPPED IN THE PENTHOUSE (sh)	WHITE	COLUMBIA	1955
C-4225	OF CASH AND HASH (sh)	WHITE	COLUMBIA	1955
C-4226	FIRE CHASER (sh)	WHITE	COLUMBIA	1954
C-4227	CREEPS (sh)	WHITE	COLUMBIA	1956
C-4227	G. I. DOOD IT (sh)	WHITE	COLUMBIA	1955
C-4228	BEDLAM IN PARADISE (sh)	WHITE	COLUMBIA	1955
C-4228	HEAVENLY DAZE (sh)	WHITE	COLUMBIA	1948
C-4229	STONE AGE ROMEOS (sh)	WHITE	COLUMBIA	1955
C-4230	HIS PEST FRIEND (sh)	WHITE	COLUMBIA	1955
C-4231	NOBODY'S HOME (sh)	WHITE	COLUMBIA	1955
C-4232	WHAM-BAM-SLAM! (sh)	WHITE	COLUMBIA	1955
C-4233	HOT ICE (sh)	WHITE	COLUMBIA	1955
C-4234	ONE SPOOKY NIGHT (sh)	WHITE	COLUMBIA	1955
C-4235	SCRATCH SCRATCH SCRATCH	WHITE	COLUMBIA	1955
C-4236	HUSBANDS BEWARE (sh)	WHITE	COLUMBIA	1956
C-4238	FLAGPOLE JITTERS (sh)	WHITE	COLUMBIA	1956
C-4239	FOR CRIMIN' OUT LOUD (sh)	WHITE	COLUMBIA	1956
C-4240	HOOK A CROOK (sh)	WHITE	COLUMBIA	1955
C-4241	HE TOOK A POWDER (sh)	WHITE	COLUMBIA	1955
C-4242	ARMY DAZE (sh)	WHITE	COLUMBIA	1956
C-4243	COME ON SEVEN (sh)	WHITE	COLUMBIA	1956
C-4244	RUMPUS IN THE HAREM (sh)	WHITE	COLUMBIA	1956
C-4245	HOT STUFF (sh)	WHITE	COLUMBIA	1956
C-4246	SCHEMING SCHEMERS (sh)	WHITE	COLUMBIA	1956
C-4247	COMMOTION ON THE OCEAN (sh)	WHITE	COLUMBIA	1956
C-4248	ANDY GOES WILD (sh)	WHITE	COLUMBIA	1956
C-4249	PARDON MY NIGHTSHIRT (sh)	WHITE	COLUMBIA	1956
C-4250	MUSCLE UP A LITTLE CLOSER (sh)	WHITE	COLUMBIA	1957
C-4251	HOOFS AND GOOFS (sh)	WHITE	COLUMBIA	1957
C-4252	MERRY MIXUP (sh)	WHITE	COLUMBIA	1957
C-4253	SPACE SHIP SAPPY (sh)	WHITE	COLUMBIA	1957
C-8007	LORNA DOONE	KARLSON	COLUMBIA	1951
C-8008	ROAR OF THE IRON HORSE	BENNET, CARR	COLUMBIA	1951
C-8009	TEXANS NEVER CRY	MCDONALD	COLUMBIA	1951

Movie Still Identification Book Ultimate Edition - Letters

CODE	TITLE/NAME	DIRECTOR/TYPE	STUDIO/DISTRIBUTOR	YEAR
C-8010	VALLEY OF FIRE	ENGLISH	COLUMBIA	1951
C-8011	MAGIC CARPET	LANDERS	COLUMBIA	1951
C-8011	MYSTERIOUS ISLAND (serial)	BENNET	COLUMBIA	1951
C-8014	TEXAS RANGERS	LEDERMAN	COLUMBIA	1951
C-8015	BRIGAND	KARLSON	COLUMBIA	1952
C-8016	SILVER CANYON	ENGLISH	COLUMBIA	1951
C-8017	SCANDAL SHEET	KARLSON	COLUMBIA	1952
C-8026	WHIRLWIND	ENGLISH	COLUMBIA	1951
C-8029	INDIAN UPRISING	NAZARRO	COLUMBIA	1952
C-8030	CALIFORNIA CONQUEST	LANDERS	COLUMBIA	1952
C-8031	YANK IN KOREA	LANDERS	COLUMBIA	1951
C-8032	HILLS OF UTAH	ENGLISH	COLUMBIA	1951
C-8033	HARLEM GLOBETROTTERS	BROWN, JASON	COLUMBIA	1951
C-8035	MAN IN THE SADDLE	DE TOTH	COLUMBIA	1951
C-8036	PURPLE HEART DIARY	QUINE	COLUMBIA	1951
C-8037	JUNGLE JIM IN THE FORBIDDEN LAND	LANDERS	COLUMBIA	1952
C-8038	JUNGLE MAN-HUNT	LANDERS	COLUMBIA	1951
C-8039	KING OF THE CONGO (serial)	BENNET, GRISSELL	COLUMBIA	1952
C-8040	CAPTAIN VIDEO (serial)	BENNET, GRISSELL	COLUMBIA	1951
C-8041	BOOTS MALONE	DIETERLE	COLUMBIA	1952
C-8042	TEN TALL MEN	GOLDBECK	COLUMBIA	1951
C-8043	FIRST TIME	TASHLIN	COLUMBIA	1952
C-8044	BRAVE WARRIOR	BENNET	COLUMBIA	1952
C-8045	OLD WEST	ARCHAINBAUD	COLUMBIA	1952
C-8047	MEMBER OF THE WEDDING	ZINNEMANN	COLUMBIA	1952
C-8049	GOLDEN HAWK	SALKOW	COLUMBIA	1952
C-8053	PRINCE OF PIRATES	SALKOW	COLUMBIA	1953
C-8054	MY SIX CONVICTS	FREGONESE	COLUMBIA	1952
C-8055	BLACKHAWK	BENNET	COLUMBIA	1952
C-8056	DEATH OF A SALESMAN	BENEDEK	COLUMBIA	1951
C-8057	FOUR POSTER	REIS	COLUMBIA	1952
C-8061	CRIPPLE CREEK	NAZARRO	COLUMBIA	1952
C-8062	SNIPER	DMYTRYK	COLUMBIA	1952
C-8063	NIGHT STAGE TO GALVESTON	ARCHAINBAUD	COLUMBIA	1952
C-8064	5000 FINGERS OF DR. T	ROWLAND	COLUMBIA	1953
C-8066	AFFAIR IN TRINIDAD	SHERMAN	COLUMBIA	1952
C-8067	BLUE CANADIAN ROCKIES	ARCHAINBAUD	COLUMBIA	1952
C-8068	PRISONERS OF THE CASBAH	BARE	COLUMBIA	1953
C-8071	HAPPY TIME	FLEISCHER	COLUMBIA	1952
C-8072	APACHE COUNTRY	ARCHAINBAUD	COLUMBIA	1952
C-8074	MEMBER OF THE WEDDING	ZINNEMANN	COLUMBIA	1952
C-8078	EIGHT IRON MEN	DMYTRYK	COLUMBIA	1952
C-8079	BARBED WIRE	ARCHAINBAUD	COLUMBIA	1952
C-8082	CAINE MUTINY	DMYTRYK	COLUMBIA	1954
C-8085	YANK IN INDO-CHINA	GRISSELL	COLUMBIA	1952
C-8087	SERPENT OF THE NILE	CASTLE	COLUMBIA	1953
C-8088	LAST TRAIN FROM BOMBAY	SEARS	COLUMBIA	1952
C-8089	SAVAGE MUTINY	BENNET	COLUMBIA	1953
C-8090	VOODOO TIGER	BENNET	COLUMBIA	1952
C-8091	JUGGLER	DMYTRYK	COLUMBIA	1953
C-8092	JACK MCCALL – DESPERADO	SALKOW	COLUMBIA	1953
C-8093	PIRATES OF TRIPOLI	FEIST	COLUMBIA	1955
C-8094	WAGON TEAM	ARCHAINBAUD	COLUMBIA	1952
C-8095	LOST PLANET	BENNET	COLUMBIA	1953
C-8100	SON OF GERONIMO (serial)	BENNET	COLUMBIA	1952
C-8103	PATHFINDER	SALKOW	COLUMBIA	1952
C-8109	SLAVES OF BABYLON	CASTLE	COLUMBIA	1953
C-8115	SKY COMMANDS	SEARS	COLUMBIA	1953
C-8116	HANGMAN'S KNOT	HUGGINS	COLUMBIA	1952
C-8117	SALOME	DIETERLE	COLUMBIA	1953
C-8118	ON TOP OF OLD SMOKY	ARCHAINBAUD	COLUMBIA	1953
C-8120	FLAME OF CALCUTTA	FRIEDMAN	COLUMBIA	1953
C-8121	STRANGE FASCINATION	HAAS	COLUMBIA	1952
C-8122	SIREN OF BAGDAD	QUINE	COLUMBIA	1953
C-8125	WINNING OF THE WEST	ARCHAINBAUD	COLUMBIA	1953
C-8127	IRON GLOVE	CASTLE	COLUMBIA	1954
C-8128	GOLDTOWN GHOST RIDERS	ARCHAINBAUD	COLUMBIA	1953
C-8130	CONQUEST OF COCHISE	CASTLE	COLUMBIA	1953
C-8132	CHARGE OF THE LANCERS	CASTLE	COLUMBIA	1954
C-8140	ONE GIRL'S CONFESSION	HAAS	COLUMBIA	1953

Movie Still Identification Book Ultimate Edition - Letters

CODE	TITLE/NAME	DIRECTOR/TYPE	STUDIO/DISTRIBUTOR	YEAR
C-8146	PACK TRAIN	ARCHAINBAUD	COLUMBIA	1953
C-8149	GREAT ADV OF CAPTAIN KIDD (serial)	ABRAHAMS, GOULD	COLUMBIA	1953
C-8150	KILLER APE	BENNET	COLUMBIA	1953
C-8151	SAGINAW TRAIL	ARCHAINBAUD	COLUMBIA	1953
C-8157	49TH MAN	SEARS	COLUMBIA	1953
C-8170	MISS SADIE THOMPSON	BERNHARDT	COLUMBIA	1953
C-8173	FORT TI	CASTLE	COLUMBIA	1953
C-8178	STRANGER WORE A GUN	DE TOTH	COLUMBIA	1953
C-8188	LAST OF THE PONY RIDERS	ARCHAINBAUD	COLUMBIA	1953
C-8191	JESSE JAMES VS DALTSON	CASTLE	COLUMBIA	1954
C-8193	DRUMS OF TAHITI	CASTLE	COLUMBIA	1954
C-8194	GUNFIGHTERS OF THE NORTHWEST	BENNET, GOULD	COLUMBIA	1954
C-8197	SARACEN BLADE	CASTLE	COLUMBIA	1954
C-8204	JUNGLE MAN-EATERS	SHOLEM	COLUMBIA	1954
C-8205	RIDING WITH BUFFALO BILL (serial)	BENNET	COLUMBIA	1954
C-8206	LAW VS. BILLY THE KID	CASTLE	COLUMBIA	1954
C-8211	TEENAGE CRIME WAVE	SEARS	COLUMBIA	1955
C-8214	BATTLE OF ROGUE RIVER	CASTLE	COLUMBIA	1954
C-8247	MIAMI STORY	SEARS	COLUMBIA	1954
C-8249	CHICAGO SYNDICATE	SEARS	COLUMBIA	1955
C-8250	SEMINOLE UPRISING	BELLAMY	COLUMBIA	1955
C-8252	MASTERSON OF KANSAS	CASTLE	COLUMBIA	1954
C-8253	MAD MAGICIAN	BRAHM	COLUMBIA	1954
C-8257	ADVENTURES OF CAPTAIN AFRICA (serial)	BENNET	COLUMBIA	1955
C-8260	IT CAME FROM BENEATH THE SEA	GORDON	COLUMBIA	1955
C-8262	CANNIBAL ATTACK	SHOLEM	COLUMBIA	1954
C-8263	DEVIL GODDESS	BENNET	COLUMBIA	1955
C-8264	BAMBOO PRISON	SEILER	COLUMBIA	1954
C-8265	JUNGLE MOON-MEN	GOULD	COLUMBIA	1955
C-8271	MAN FROM LARAMIE	MANN	COLUMBIA	1955
C-8273	TEN WANTED MEN	HUMBERSTONE	COLUMBIA	1955
C-8274	WOMEN'S PRISON	SEILER	COLUMBIA	1955
C-8281	NEW ORLEANS UNCENSORED	CASTLE	COLUMBIA	1955
C-8284	GUN THAT WON THE WEST	CASTLE	COLUMBIA	1955
C-8285	CREATURE WITH THE ATOM BRAIN	CAHN	COLUMBIA	1955
C-8286	DUEL ON THE MISSISSIPPI	CASTLE	COLUMBIA	1955
C-8289	BATTLE STATIONS	SEILER	COLUMBIA	1956
C-8289	BROTHERS RICO	KARLSON	COLUMBIA	1957
C-8294	LONG GREY LINE	FORD	COLUMBIA	1955
C-8301	FIVE AGAINST THE HOUSE	KARLSON	COLUMBIA	1955
C-8305	NIGHT HOLDS TERROR	STONE	COLUMBIA	1955
C-8306	LAWLESS STREET	LEWIS	COLUMBIA	1955
C-8307	EARTH VS. THE FLYING SAUCERS	SEARS	COLUMBIA	1956
C-8308	COUNT THREE AND PRAY	SHERMAN	COLUMBIA	1955
C-8310	HOUSTON STORY	CASTLE	COLUMBIA	1956
C-8311	BLACKJACK KETCHUM-DESPERADO	BELLAMY	COLUMBIA	1956
C-8313	INSIDE DETROIT	SEARS	COLUMBIA	1956
C-8319	FLYING FONTAINES	SHERMAN	COLUMBIA	1959
C-8321	CROOKED WEB	JURAN	COLUMBIA	1955
C-8322	AUTUMN LEAVES	ALDRICH	COLUMBIA	1956
C-8323	BELL BOOK AND CANDLE	QUINE	COLUMBIA	1958
C-8330	NIGHTFALL	TOURNEUR	COLUMBIA	1957
C-8333	STORM CENTER	TARADASH	COLUMBIA	1956
C-8335	HOT BLOOD	RAY	COLUMBIA	1956
C-8336	BLAZING THE OVERLAND TRAIL (serial)	BENNET	COLUMBIA	1956
C-8342	GUNS OF FORT PETTICOAT	MARSHALL	COLUMBIA	1957
C-8344	SEVENTH CALVARY	LEWIS	COLUMBIA	1956
C-8346	REPRISAL	SHERMAN	COLUMBIA	1956
C-8352	ROCK AROUND THE CLOCK	SEARS	COLUMBIA	1956
C-8354	RUMBLE ON THE DOCKS	SEARS	COLUMBIA	1956
C-8355	MIAMI EXPOSE	SEARS	COLUMBIA	1956
C-8359	GIANT CLAW	SEARS	COLUMBIA	1957
C-8359	WHITE SQUAW	NAZARRO	COLUMBIA	1956
C-8363	CHA-CHA-CHA BOOM	SEARS	COLUMBIA	1956
C-8364	PHANTOM STAGECOACH	NAZARRO	COLUMBIA	1957
C-8365	20 MILLION MILES TO EARTH	JURAN	COLUMBIA	1957
C-8366	NIGHT THE WORLD EXPLODED	SEARS	COLUMBIA	1957
C-8368	CHA CHA CHA BOOM	SEARS	COLUMBIA	1956
C-8372	LINEUP	SIEGEL	COLUMBIA	1958
C-8373	MAN WHO TURNED TO STONE	KARDOS	COLUMBIA	1957

Movie Still Identification Book Ultimate Edition - Letters

CODE	TITLE/NAME	DIRECTOR/TYPE	STUDIO/DISTRIBUTOR	YEAR
C-8375	BRIDGE ON THE RIVER KWAI	LEAN	COLUMBIA	1957
C-8376	HELLCATS OF THE NAVY	JURAN	COLUMBIA	1957
C-8379	TALL T	BOATTICHER	COLUMBIA	1957
C-8381	UTAH BLAINE	SEARS	COLUMBIA	1957
C-8383	DON'T KNOCK THE ROCK	SEARS	COLUMBIA	1956
C-8394	RETURN TO WARBOW	NAZARRO	COLUMBIA	1958
C-8395	GARMENT JUNGLE	SHERMAN	COLUMBIA	1957
C-8396	NO TIME TO BE YOUNG	RICH	COLUMBIA	1957
C-8397	3:10 TO YUMA	DAVES	COLUMBIA	1957
C-8398	ESCAPE FROM SAN QUENTIN	SEARS	COLUMBIA	1957
C-8400	SEVENTH VOYAGE OF SINBAD	JURAN	COLUMBIA	1958
C-8403	JEANNE EAGELS	SIDNEY	COLUMBIA	1957
C-8406	CRASH LANDING	SEARS	COLUMBIA	1958
C-8407	PAL JOEY	SIDNEY	COLUMBIA	1957
C-8414	HARD MAN	SHERMAN	COLUMBIA	1957
C-8417	THIS ANGRY AGE	CLEMENT	COLUMBIA	1958
C-8418	DOMINO KID	NAZARRO	COLUMBIA	1957
C-8420	DECISION AT SUNDOWN	BOETTICHER	COLUMBIA	1957
C-8422	LIFE BEGINS AT 17	DREIFUSS	COLUMBIA	1958
C-8423	OPERATION MADBALL	QUINE	COLUMBIA	1957
C-8426	BATTLE OF THE CORAL SEA	WENDKOS	COLUMBIA	1959
C-8427	TARAWA BEACHHEAD	WENDKOS	COLUMBIA	1958
C-8428	CASE AGAINST BROOKLYN	WENDKOS	COLUMBIA	1958
C-8430	CALYPSO HEAT WAVE	SEARS	COLUMBIA	1957
C-8431	SCREAMING MIMI	OSWALD	COLUMBIA	1958
C-8449	TRUE STORY OF LYNN STUART	SEILER	COLUMBIA	1958
C-8453	COWBOY	DAVES	COLUMBIA	1958
C-8461	LAST BLITZKRIEG	DREIFUSS	COLUMBIA	1959
C-8462	1001 ARABIAN NIGHTS (t)	KINNEY	COLUMBIA	1959
C-8464	13 WEST STREET	LEACOCK	COLUMBIA	1962
C-8465	GODDESS	CROMWELL	COLUMBIA	1958
C-8468	JUKE BOX RHYTHM	DREIFUSS	COLUMBIA	1959
C-8470	FORBIDDEN ISLAND	GRIFFITH	COLUMBIA	1959
C-8472	APACHE TERRITORY	NAZARRO	COLUMBIA	1958
C-8475	ME AND THE COLONEL	GLENVILLE	COLUMBIA	1958
C-8476	PEPE	SIDNEY	COLUMBIA	1960
C-8485	LAST HURRAH	FORD	COLUMBIA	1958
C-8495	GOOD DAY FOR A HANGING	JURAN	COLUMBIA	1959
C-8496	IT HAPPENED TO JANE	QUINE	COLUMBIA	1959
C-8498	GENE KRUPA STORY	WEIS	COLUMBIA	1959
C-8500	CHASE		COLUMBIA	1958
C-8501	GUNS OF NAVARONE (UK)	THOMPSON	COLUMBIA	1961
C-8502	SONG WITHOUT END	VIDOR	COLUMBIA	1960
C-8503	THEY CAME TO CORDURA	ROSSEN	COLUMBIA	1959
C-8504	MOUNTAIN ROAD	MANN	COLUMBIA	1960
C-8506	RIDE LONESOME	BOETTICHER	COLUMBIA	1959
C-8507	SENIOR PROM	RICH	COLUMBIA	1958
C-8508	LET NO MAN WRITE MY EPITAPH	LEACOCK	COLUMBIA	1960
C-8511	I AIM AT THE STARS	THOMPSON	COLUMBIA	1960
C-8512	SURPRISE PACKAGE	DONEN	COLUMBIA	1960
C-8513	HEY BOY HEY GIRL	RICH	COLUMBIA	1959
C-8514	MAN ON A STRING	DE TOTH	COLUMBIA	1960
C-8515	MYSTERIOUS ISLAND	ENDFIELD	COLUMBIA	1962
C-8516	FACE OF A FUGITIVE	WENDKOS	COLUMBIA	1959
C-8518	WHO WAS THAT LADY?	SIDNEY	COLUMBIA	1960
C-8519	CRIMSON KIMONO	FULLER	COLUMBIA	1959
C-8520	LAST ANGRY MAN	MANN	COLUMBIA	1959
C-8525	DEVIL AT 4 O'CLOCK	LEROY	COLUMBIA	1961
C-8535	30 FOOT BRIDE OF CANDY ROCK	MILLER	COLUMBIA	1959
C-8536	MIDDLE OF THE NIGHT	MANN	COLUMBIA	1959
C-8539	STRANGERS WHEN WE MEET	QUINE	COLUMBIA	1960
C-8542	3 WORLDS OF GULLIVER (t)	SHERMAN	COLUMBIA	1960
C-8543	NOTORIOUS LANDLADY	QUINE	COLUMBIA	1962
C-8546	EDGE OF ETERNITY	SIEGEL	COLUMBIA	1959
C-8550	LEGEND OF TOM DOOLEY	POST	COLUMBIA	1959
C-8556	HAVE ROCKET WILL TRAVEL	RICH	COLUMBIA	1959
C-8557	COMANCHE STATION	BOETTICHER	COLUMBIA	1960
C-8559	TINGLER	CASTLE	COLUMBIA	1959
C-8566	CRY FOR HAPPY	MARSHALL	COLUMBIA	1961
C-8569	BECAUSE THEY'RE YOUNG	WENDKOS	COLUMBIA	1960

Movie Still Identification Book Ultimate Edition - Letters

CODE	TITLE/NAME	DIRECTOR/TYPE	STUDIO/DISTRIBUTOR	YEAR
C-8570	RAISIN IN THE SUN	PETRIE	COLUMBIA	1961
C-8572	ENEMY GENERAL	SHERMAN	COLUMBIA	1960
C-8573	ALL THE YOUNG MEN	BARTLETT	COLUMBIA	1960
C-8581	GIDGET GOES HAWAIIAN	WENDKOS	COLUMBIA	1961
C-8583	THIRTEEN GHOSTS	CASTLE	COLUMBIA	1960
C-8588	DIAMOND HEAD	GREEN	COLUMBIA	1963
C-8591	STOP, LOOK AND LAUGH	APPELL, BRANDT	COLUMBIA	1960
C-8594	HOMICIDAL	CASTLE	COLUMBIA	1961
C-8596	INTERNS	SWIFT	COLUMBIA	1962
C-8602	SAIL A CROOKED SHIP	BRECHER	COLUMBIA	1961
C-8603	FIVE FINGER EXERCISE	MANN	COLUMBIA	1962
C-8610	MR. SARDONICUS	CASTLE	COLUMBIA	1961
C-8617	THREE STOOGES MEET HERCULES	BERNDS	COLUMBIA	1962
C-8624	EVERYTHING'S DUCKY	TAYLOR	COLUMBIA	1961
C-8625	BYE BYE BIRDIE	SIDNEY	COLUMBIA	1963
C-8626	EXPERIMENT IN TERROR	EDWARDS	COLUMBIA	1962
C-8629	WALK ON THE WILD SIDE	DYMTRYK	COLUMBIA	1962
C-8633	MAN FROM THE DINER'S CLUB	TASHLIN	COLUMBIA	1963
C-8634	LOVE HAS MANY FACES	SINGER	COLUMBIA	1965
C-8650	13 FRIGHTENED GIRLS	CASTLE	COLUMBIA	1963
C-8652	WILD WESTERNERS	RUDOLPH	COLUMBIA	1962
C-8657	DON'T KNOCK THE TWIST	RUDOLPH	COLUMBIA	1962
C-8666	THREE STOOGES IN ORBIT	BERNDS	COLUMBIA	1962
C-8689	KING RAT	FORBES	COLUMBIA	1965
C-8691	STRAIGHT-JACKET	CASTLE	COLUMBIA	1964
C-8692	NEW INTERNS	RICH	COLUMBIA	1964
C-8699	GOOD NEIGHBOR SAM	SWIFT	COLUMBIA	1964
C-8701	CAT BALLOU	SILVERSTEIN	COLUMBIA	1965
C-8705	3 STOOGES GO AROUND THE WORLD IN A DAZE	MAURER	COLUMBIA	1963
C-8709	BABY THE RAIN MUST FALL	MULLIGAN	COLUMBIA	1965
C-8712	PROFESSIONALS	BROOKS	COLUMBIA	1966
C-8715	MAJOR DUNDEE	PECKINPAH	COLUMBIA	1965
C-8719	COLLECTOR	WYLER	COLUMBIA	1965
C-8720	HEY THERE IT'S YOGI BEAR (t)	HANNA, BARBERA	COLUMBIA	1964
C-8722	LIFE BEGINS AT 17	DREIFUSS	COLUMBIA	1958
C-8724	QUICK GUN	SALKOW	COLUMBIA	1964
C-8731	OUTLAWS IS COMING	MAURER	COLUMBIA	1965
C-8732	RIDE THE WILD SURF	TAYLOR	COLUMBIA	1964
C-8741	SILENCERS	KARLSON	COLUMBIA	1966
C-8744	ALVAREZ KELLY	DMYTRYK	COLUMBIA	1966
C-8755	WALK DON'T RUN	WALTERS	COLUMBIA	1966
C-8755	WALK DON'T RUN	WALTERS	COLUMBIA	1966
C-8761	ARIZONA RAIDERS	WITNEY	COLUMBIA	1965
C-8774	WINTER A GO-GO	BENEDICT	COLUMBIA	1965
C-8802	RIDE BEYOND VENGEANCE	MCEVEETY	COLUMBIA	1966
C-8817	THREE ON A COUCH	LEWIS	COLUMBIA	1966
C-8818	BIRDS DO IT	MARTON	COLUMBIA	1966
C-8826	RAGE	GAZCON	COLUMBIA	1966
CA	AFRICA: TEXAS STYLE (UK)	MARTON	PARAMOUNT	1967
CA	CABARET	FOSSE	MONOGRAM	1972
CA	CARRIE	DE PALMA	UNITED ARTISTS	1976
CA	CENTRAL AIRPORT	WELLMAN	WARNER BROS	1933
CA	CHANCES ARE	ARDOLINO	TRI STAR	1989
CA	CHARLEY'S AUNT (UK: CHARLEY'S BIG HEARTED AUNT)	FORDE	GFD	1940
CA	CHINA PASSAGE	KILLY	RKO	1937
CA	CLASS ACTION	APTED	20th CENTURY FOX	1991
CA	COCK OF THE AIR	BUCKINGHAM	UNITED ARTISTS	1932
CA	CONQUEST OF THE AIR (UK)	ESWAY, KORDA	UNITED ARTISTS	1936
CA	CROOKS ANONYMOUS (UK)	ANNAKIN	JANUS	1962
CA	QUESTION OF ADULTERY (UK)	CHAFFEY	EROS	1958
CA-1	HALF A SINNER		REPUBLIC	
CA-84	DON'T FLIRT (sh)	POWERS	PATHE EXCHANGE	1923
CA-88	WATCH DOG (sh)	POWERS	PATHE EXCHANGE	1923
CAA	QUESTION OF ADULTERY (UK)	CHAFFEY	EROS	1958
C-AA	GOODBYE GEMINI/ASK AGAMEMNON* (UK)	GIBSON	CINERAMA	1970
CAC	CAMELS ARE COMING (UK)	WHELAN	GAUMONT BRITISH	1934
CAF	CAGE AUX FOLLES (FR)	MOLINARO	UNITED ARTISTS	1978
CA-F	CANTERBURY TALES (IT)	PASOLINI	UNITED ARTISTS	1972
CAG-9800	BLOOD ON THE SUN	LLOYD	UNITED ARTISTS	1945
CAGE II	LA CAGE AUX FOLLES II (FR)	MOLINARO	UNITED ARTISTS	1980

Movie Still Identification Book Ultimate Edition - Letters

CODE	TITLE/NAME	DIRECTOR/TYPE	STUDIO/DISTRIBUTOR	YEAR
CAH	COMES A HORSEMAN	PAKULA	UNITED ARTISTS	1978
CAJ	CAPTAIN APPLEJACK	HENLEY	WARNER BROS	1931
CAL	CHANCE OF A LIFETIME (UK)	MILES	BALLANTINE	1950
CAL	CRIMINAL AT LARGE (UK: FRIGHTENED LADY)	HUNTER	HELBER	1932
CAN-1	RED WINE	CANNON	FOX FILM	1928
CAN-2	JOY STREET	CANNON	FOX FILM	1929
CAP	CAPRICORN ONE	HYAMS	WARNER BROS	1977
CAR	CAREER	JASON	RKO	1939
CAR	CARNY	KAYLOR	UNITED ARTISTS	1980
CAREW-1	SILVER WINGS	CAREWE	FOX FILM	1922
CAST	CASTILLIAN (SP)	SETO	WARNER BROS	1963
CAW	JOE/JOSEPH CAWTHORN(E)	portrait	WARNER BROS	
CB	BRASS KNUCKLES	BACON	WARNER BROS	1927
CB	CALLED BACK (UK)	DENHAM, HARRIS	RKO	1933
CB	CAPTAIN BLOOD	CURTIZ	FIRST NATIONAL	1935
CB	CARLA BALENDA	portrait	RKO	early 1950s
CB	CAROL BRUCE	portrait	UNIVERSAL	
CB	CASE OF THE CURIOUS BRIDE	CURTIZ	WARNER BROS	1935
CB	CAT BURGLAR	WITNEY	UNITED ARTISTS	1961
CB	CHARLES BOYER	portrait	RKO, UNIVERSAL	
CB	CHARLES BUTTERWORTH	portrait	FN, PARAMOUNT	
CB	CHINESE DEN (UK: CHINESE BUNGALOW)	KING	FILM ALLIANCE	1940
CB	CHITTY CHITTY BANG BANG (UK)	HUGHES	UNITED ARTISTS	1968
CB	CITIZEN'S BAND	DEMME	PARAMOUNT	1977
CB	CLARA BOW	portrait		
CB	COLONEL BLOOD (UK)	LIPSCOMB	MGM	1934
CB	CONSTANCE BENNETT	portrait	RKO	early 1930s
CB	CONSTANCE BENNETT	portrait	UNIVERSAL	
CB	CONSTANCE BINNEY	portrait	REALART	
CB	CORNELL BORCHERS	portrait	UNIVERSAL	
CB	CORRIDORS OF BLOOD (UK)	DAY	MGM	1958
CB	COUNTRY BOY	CAIN	HOWCO	1966
CB	COWBOY FROM BROOKLYN	BACON	WARNER BROS	1938
CB	CRIMSON BLADE (UK: SCARLET BLADE)	GILLING	COLUMBIA	1963
CB	CROOKED WAY	FLOREY	UNITED ARTISTS	1949
CB	IN COLD BLOOD	BROOKS	COLUMBIA	1967
CB	KILLING OF A CHINESE BOOKIE	CASAVETTES	FACES	1976
CB	ON MY WAY TO THE CRUSADES (IT)	CAMPANILE	WARNER BROS	1969
CB	PARIS UNDERGROUND	RATOFF	UNITED ARTISTS	1945
CB-1	GIDEON OF SCOTLAND YARD (UK)	FORD	COLUMBIA	1958
CBC	CHEER BOYS CHEER (UK)	FORDE	ABFD	1939
CBD	CECIL B. DEMILLE	portrait	MGM	
CBL	CLARE BOOTHE LUCE	portrait		
CBN	CLASH BY NIGHT	LANG	RKO	1952
C-BR-1	LADY IS WILLING	MILLER	COLUMBIA	1934
CBS	THEY CAME FROM BEYOND SPACE (UK)	FRANCIS	EMBASSY	1967
CBX	CHARLES BUTTERWORTH	portrait	MGM	
CBX	CLIVE BROOK	portrait	RKO	
CBXX	CLARENCE BROWN	portrait	MGM	
CC	A.K.A. CASSIUS CLAY	JACOBS	UNITED ARTISTS	1970
CC	BOAT FROM SHANGHAI (UK: CHIN CHIN CHINAMAN)	NEWALL	FIRST DIVISION	1931
CC	C. C. AND COMPANY	ROBBIE	AVCO EMBASSY	1970
CC	CABIN IN THE COTTON	CURTIZ	WARNER BROS	1932
CC	CAPTAINS OF THE CLOUDS	CURTIZ	WARNER BROS	1942
CC	CARBON COPY	SCHULTZ	AVCO EMBASSY	1981
CC	CHARLES CHAPLIN	portrait		
CC	CHARLES CHAPLIN PRODUCTIONS	studio		
CC	CHARLES COBURN	portrait	RKO	
CC	CHEROKEE STRIP	SELANDER	PARAMOUNT	1940
CC	CHICAGO CALLING	REINHARDT	UNITED ARTISTS	1952
CC	CHICKEN CHRONICLES	SIMON	AVCO EMBASSY	1977
CC	CHINA CLIPPER	ENRIGHT	WARNER BROS	1936
CC	CHRISTINE CARERE/CARRERE	portrait	FOX	
CC	CITY FOR CONQUEST	LITVAK	WARNER BROS	1940
CC	CLAIRE CARLETON	portrait	RKO	
CC	CLAUDETTE COLBERT	portrait	UNIVERSAL	
CC	CLAUDIA CARDINALE	portrait	UNIVERSAL	
CC	COAST TO COAST	SARGENT	PARAMOUNT	1980
CC	COCKEYED CAVALIERS	SANDRICH	RKO	1934
CC	COLIN CLIVE	portrait	WARNER BROS	

Movie Still Identification Book Ultimate Edition - Letters

CODE	TITLE/NAME	DIRECTOR/TYPE	STUDIO/DISTRIBUTOR	YEAR
CC	COLLEGE COACH	WELLMAN	WARNER BROS	1933
CC	COMET OVER BROADWAY	BERKELEY	WARNER BROS	1938
CC	CONSTANCE CUMMINGS	portrait	GAUMONT BRITISH	
CC	COOL AND THE CRAZY	WITNEY	AIP	1958
CC	COPYCAT	AMIEL	WARNER BROS	1995
CC	COTTON CLUB	COPPOLA	ORION	1984
CC	CURTAIN CALL	WOODRUFF	RKO	1940
CC	GIRL FROM MANHATTAN	GREEN	UNITED ARTISTS	1948
CC	HAVING A WILD WEEKEND (UK: CATCH US IF YOU CAN)	BOORMAN	WARNER BROS	1965
CC	SOPHIE'S PLACE (UK: CROOKS AND CORONETS)	O'CONNELLY	WARNER BROS.	1969
CC-8	LIMELIGHT	CHAPLIN	UNITED ARTISTS	1952
CC-129	HARD KNOCKS (sh)	PARROTT	PATHE EXCHANGE	1924
CC-131	ONE OF THE FAMILY (sh)	PEMBROKE	PATHE EXCHANGE	1924
CC-394	COTTON CLUB	COPPOLA	ORON	1984
CCC	CHU CHIN CHOW (UK)	WILCOX	METRO GOLDWYN	1923
CCC	CHU CHIN CHOW (UK)	FORDE	FOX FILM	1934
CC-K	CASSANDRA CROSSING	COSMATOS	AVCO EMBASSY	1976
C-COL-1	CRAIG'S WIFE	ARZNER	COLUMBIA	1936
C-COL-1	THUNDER IN THE CITY	GERING	COLUMBIA	1937
C-COL-2	PENNIES FROM HEAVEN	MCLEOD	COLUMBIA	1936
C-COL-3	COME CLOSER FOLKS	LEDERMAN	COLUMBIA	1936
C-COL-4	DEVIL'S PLAYGROUND	KENTON	COLUMBIA	1937
C-COL-7	MORE THAN A SECRETARY	GREEN	COLUMBIA	1936
C-COL-8	WOMEN OF GLAMOUR	WILES	COLUMBIA	1937
C-COL-9	I PROMISE TO PAY	LEDERMAN	COLUMBIA	1937
C-COL-10	WOMAN IN DISTRESS	SHORES	COLUMBIA	1937
C-COL-11	IT'S ALL YOURS	NUGENT	COLUMBIA	1937
C-COL-14	LET'S GET MARRIED	GREEN	COLUMBIA	1937
C-COL-15	RACKETEERS IN EXILE	KENTON	COLUMBIA	1937
C-COL-17	VENUS MAKES TROUBLE	WILES	COLUMBIA	1937
C-COL-19	LEAGUE OF FRIGHTENED MEN	GREEN	COLUMBIA	1937
C-COL-21	LOST HORIZON	CAPRA	COLUMBIA	1937
C-COL-22	IT HAPPENED IN HOLLYWOOD	LACHMAN	COLUMBIA	1937
C-COL-24	IT CAN'T LAST FOREVER	MACFADDEN	COLUMBIA	1937
C-COL-26	LADY FROM NOWHERE	WILES	COLUMBIA	1936
C-COL-30	ADVENTURE IN MANHATTAN	LUDWIG	COLUMBIA	1936
C-COL-31	DEVIL IS DRIVING	LACHMAN	COLUMBIA	1937
C-COL-34	MAN WHO LIVED TWICE	LACHMAN	COLUMBIA	1936
C-COL-60	LEGION OF TERROR	COLEMAN	COLUMBIA	1936
C-COL-61	COUNTERFEIT LADY	LEDERMAN	COLUMBIA	1936
C-COL-62	FIND THE WITNESS	SELMAN	COLUMBIA	1937
C-COL-63	PAROLE RACKET	COLEMAN	COLUMBIA	1937
C-COL-64	SPEED TO SPARE	HILLYER	COLUMBIA	1937
C-COL-65	MOTOR MADNESS	LEDERMAN	COLUMBIA	1937
C-COL-66	CRIMINALS OF THE AIR	COLEMAN	COLUMBIA	1937
C-COL-67	GIRLS CAN PLAY	HILLYER	COLUMBIA	1937
C-COL-68	FRAMEUP	LEDERMAN	COLUMBIA	1937
C-COL-70	DANGEROUS ADVENTURE	LEDERMAN	COLUMBIA	1937
C-COL-71	FIGHT TO THE FINISH	COLEMAN	COLUMBIA	1937
C-COL-72	GAME THAT KILLS	LEDERMAN	COLUMBIA	1937
C-COL-80	CODE OF THE RANGE	COLEMAN	COLUMBIA	1936
C-COL-81	COWBOY STAR	SELMAN	COLUMBIA	1936
C-COL-82	DODGE CITY TRAIL	COLEMAN	COLUMBIA	1936
C-COL-83	WESTBOUND MAIL	BLANGSTED	COLUMBIA	1937
C-COL-84	TRAPPED	BARSHA	COLUMBIA	1937
C-COL-86	TWO GUN LAW	BARSHA	COLUMBIA	1937
C-COL-87	TWO FISTED SHERIFF	BARSHA	COLUMBIA	1937
C-COL-88	ONE MAN JUSTICE	BARSHA	COLUMBIA	1937
C-COL-201	UNRELATED RELATIONS (sh)	LORD	COLUMBIA	1936
C-COL-212	PEPPERY SALT (sh)	LORD	COLUMBIA	1936
C-COL-214	JUST SPEEDING (sh)	LORD	COLUMBIA	1936
C-COL-215	SHARE THE WEALTH (sh)	LORD	COLUMBIA	1936
C-COL-216	MIDNIGHT BLUNDERS (sh)	LORD	COLUMBIA	1936
C-COL-218	ANTS IN THE PANTRY (sh)	WHITE	COLUMBIA	1936
C-COL-259	GRIPS, GRUNTS AND GROANS (sh)	WHITE	COLUMBIA	1937
C-COL-260	SAILOR MAID (sh)	LAMONT	COLUMBIA	1937
C-COL-261	KNEE ACTION (sh)	LAMONT	COLUMBIA	1937
C-COL-262	SUPER SNOOPER (sh)	WHITE	COLUMBIA	1937
C-COL-263	DIZZY DOCTORS (sh)	LORD	COLUMBIA	1937
C-COL-264	BURY THE HATCHET (sh)	LORD	COLUMBIA	1937

Movie Still Identification Book Ultimate Edition - Letters

CODE	TITLE/NAME	DIRECTOR/TYPE	STUDIO/DISTRIBUTOR	YEAR
C-COL-265	STUCK IN THE STICKS (sh)	WHITE	COLUMBIA	1937
C-COL-266	3 DUMB CLUCKS (sh)	LORD	COLUMBIA	1937
C-COL-267	NEW NEWS (sh)	LAMONT	COLUMBIA	1937
C-COL-268	BACK TO THE WOODS (sh)	WHITE	COLUMBIA	1937
C-COL-269	GRAND HOOTER (sh)	WHITE	COLUMBIA	1937
C-COL-270	LODGE NIGHT (sh)	WHITE	COLUMBIA	1937
C-COL-271	FROM BAD TO WORSE (sh)	LORD	COLUMBIA	1937
C-COL-273	WRONG MISS WRIGHT (sh)	LAMONT	COLUMBIA	1937
C-COL-274	GOOFS AND SADDLES (sh)	LORD	COLUMBIA	1937
C-COL-275	CALLING ALL DOCTORS (sh)	LAMONT	COLUMBIA	1937
C-COL-280	COMMUNITY SING - #3	series	COLUMBIA	1937
C-COL-281	COMMUNITY SING - #4	series	COLUMBIA	1937
C-COL-282	COMMUNITY SING - #5	series	COLUMBIA	1937
C-COL-400	CASH AND CARRY (sh)	LORD	COLUMBIA	1937
C-COL-401	PLAYING THE PONIES (sh)	LAMONT	COLUMBIA	1937
C-COL-402	SITTER DOWNERS (sh)	LORD	COLUMBIA	1937
C-COL-406	BIG SQUIRT (sh)	LORD	COLUMBIA	1937
C-COL-407	GRACIE AT THE BAT (sh)	LORD	COLUMBIA	1937
C-COL-408	OH, WHAT A KNIGHT! (sh)	CHASE	COLUMBIA	1937
C-COL-411	HE DONE HIS DUTY (sh)	LAMONT	COLUMBIA	1937
C-COL-414	MAN BITES LOVEBUG (sh)	LORD	COLUMBIA	1937
CCR	CANYON CROSSROADS	WERKER	UNITED ARTISTS	1955
CCS	CHASE A CROOKED SHADOW (UK)	ANDERSON	WARNER BROS	1958
CCS	KATHY'S LOVE AFFAIR (UK: COURTNEYS CURZON STREET)	WILCOX	SNADER	1947
CCX	CHARLEY/CHARLIE/CHARLES CHASE	portrait	MGM	
CD	CALL IT A DAY	MAYO	WARNER BROS	1937
CD	CATS AND DOGS	GUTERMAN	WARNER BROS	2001
CD	CHARLES DRAKE	portrait	UNIVERSAL	
CD	CHARLES DRAKE	portrait	WARNER BROS	
CD	CHARMING DECEIVER (UK)	BANKS	MAJESTIC	1933
CD	CHEAP DETECTIVE	MOORE	COLUMBIA	1978
CD	CHINA DOLL	BORZAGE	UNITED ARTISTS	1958
CD	CINDERELLA (t)	GERONIMI, JACKSON	RKO	1950
CD	CIRCLE OF DECEIT/GERMANY: DIE FALSCHUNG	SCHLONDORFF	UNITED ARTISTS	1981
CD	CLAIRE DODD	portrait	UNIVERSAL, WARNER BROS	
CD	CLAUDIA DELL	portrait	PEERLESS, WARNER BROS	
CD	CONSTANCE DOWLING	portrait	RKO	
CD	CONSTANCE DOWLING	portrait	UNIVERSAL	
CD	COUNTESS DRACULA	SASDY	20th CENTURY FOX	1971
CD	CRIME DOCTOR	ROBERTSON	RKO	1934
CD	CROCODILE DUNDEE	FAIMAN	PARAMOUNT	1986
CD	CROCODILE DUNDEE IN LOS ANGELES	WINCER	PARAMOUNT	2001
CD	CRY DANGER	PARRISH	RKO	1951
CD	OPERATION CONSPIRACY (UK: CLOAK WITHOUT DAGGER)	STERLING	REPUBLIC	1956
CD	PACE THAT KILLS		RKO	1952
CD	RETURN OF DRACULA (CURSE OF DRACULA)	LANDRES	UNITED ARTISTS	1958
CD-11	RETURN OF DRACULA (CURSE OF DRACULA)	LANDRES	UNITED ARTISTS	1958
CD1901	HORSING AROUND (sh)	WHITE	COLUMBIA	1957
CD8307	EARTH VS FLYING SAUCIERS	SEARS	COLUMBIA	1956
CDC	CRIME OF DR. CRESPI	AUER	REPUBLIC	1935
C-DC	DREYFUS CASE (UK)	KRAEMER, ROSMER	COLUMBIA	1931
C-DLB	DIRTY LITTLE BILLY	DRAGOTI	COLUMBIA	1972
CDO	CATHERINE DALE OWEN	portrait	MGM	
CDO	COURAGEOUS DR. CHRISTIAN	VORHAUS	RKO	1940
CDS	CAST A DARK SHADOW (UK 1955)	GILBERT	DCA	1957
CDVB	COUNT DRACULA AND HIS VAMPIRE BRIDE	GIBSON	WARNER BROS	1973
CE	CAGE OF EVIL	CAHN	UNITED ARTISTS	1960
CE	CAT'S EYE	TEAGUE	MGM	1985
CE	CATTLE EMPIRE	WARREN	20th CENTURY FOX	1958
CE	CHAD EVERETT	portrait	MGM	
CE	CHRISTMAS EVE	MARIN	UNITED ARTISTS	1947
CE	CLIFF EDWARDS	portrait	MGM	
CE	CLINT EASTWOOD	portrait	UNIVERSAL	
CE	CLOSE ENCOUNTERS OF THE THIRD KIND	SPIELBERG	COLUMBIA	1977
CE	CONQUEST OF EVEREST	LOWE	UNITED ARTISTS	1953
CE	CRAWLING EYE (UK: TROLLENBERG TERROR)	LAWRENCE	DCA	1958
CE	MY FORBIDDEN PAST	STEVENSON	RKO	1951
CE	SOLDIER'S PLAYTHING	CURTIZ	WARNER BROS	1930
CEF-2137	CASE OF THE MISSING SCENE (UK)	CHAFFEY	GFD	1951
CE-P	SINNER'S HOLIDAY	ADOLFI	ASTOR	1930

Movie Still Identification Book Ultimate Edition - Letters

CODE	TITLE/NAME	DIRECTOR/TYPE	STUDIO/DISTRIBUTOR	YEAR
CER	CEREMONY	HARVEY	UNITED ARTISTS	1963
CF	CACTUS FLOWER	SAKS	COLUMBIA	1969
CF	CALL OF THE FOREST	LINK SR.	LIPPERT	1949
CF	CAREFREE	SANDRICH	RKO	1938
CF	CAROL FORMAN	portrait	RKO	
CF	CARTHAGE IN FLAMES (IT: CARTAGINE IN FLAMME)	GALLONE	COLUMBIA	1961
CF	CITY OF FEAR (UK)	BEZENCENET	MONOGRAM	1965
CF	CONNIE FRANCIS	portrait	MGM	
CF	CRANES ARE FLYING (RUS)	KALATOZOV	WARNER BROS	1960
CF	CREEPING FLESH	FRANCIS	COLUMBIA	1973
CF	CROSSFIRE	DMYTRYK	RKO	1946
CF	CURSE OF THE FLY (UK)	SHARP	20th CENTURY FOX	1965
CF	DOWN THREE DARK STREETS	LAVEN	UNITED ARTISTS	1954
CF	ENTRE NOUS (FR: COUP DE FOUDRE)	KURY	UNITED ARTISTS	1983
CF	SPY SHIP	EASON	WARNER BROS	1942
CF1	QUIET WEDDING (UK)	ASQUITH	UNIVERSAL	1941
CF-2	TUGBOAT PRINCESS	SELMAN	COLUMBIA	1936
CF-3	STAMPEDE	BEEBE	COLUMBIA	1936
CF-4	SECRET PATROL	SELMAN	COLUMBIA	1936
CF-5	NIGHT OF TERROR	STOLOFF	COLUMBIA	1933
CF-6	WHAT PRICE VENGEANCE	LORD	COLUMBIA	1937
CF-10	MURDER IS NEWS		COLUMBIA	
CF-11	SPECIAL INSPECTOR	BARSHA	COLUMBIA	1938
CF-12	CONVICTED	BASHA	COLUMBIA	1938
CF-42	WOMAN AGAINST THE WORLD	SELMAN	COLUMBIA	1937
CFBL	CREATURE FROM BLACK LAKE	HOUCK JR	HOWCO INT'L	1976
CFF-11	SKID KIDS (UK)	CHAFFEY	ASSOCIATED BRITISH-PATHE	1953
CFF-APE	CLUE OF THE MISSING APE (UK)	HILL	ASSOCIATED BRITISH-PATHE	1953
CFF-CF	CIRCUS FRIENDS (UK)	THOMAS	CONTINENTAL	1956
CFF-DOG	DOG AND THE DIAMONDS (UK)	THOMAS	ASSOCIATED BRITISH-PATHE	1953
CFF-HD	HEIGHTS OF DANGER (UK)	BRADFORD	ASSOCIATED BRITISH-PATHE	1953
CFF-JOHN	JOHN OF THE FAIR (UK)	MCCARTHY	ASSOCIATED BRITISH	1954
CFF-PLAN	STOLEN PLANS (UK)	HILL	CONTINENTAL	1952
CFF S3	MURDER AT SITE 3 (UK)	SEARLE	EXCLUSIVE	1959
CFF-SA1	STOLEN AIRLINER (UK)	SHARP	BRITISH LION	1955
CFF-WISH	ONE WISH TOO MANY (UK)	DURST	STERLING	1956
CFMC	CASTLE OF FU MANCHU (UK)	FRANCO	INTERNATIONAL CINEMA	1969
CFP-168	DOCTOR'S DILEMMA (UK)	ASQUITH	MGM	1958
CFT	MUSIC IN MANHATTAN	AUER	RKO	1944
CG	CABINET OF CALIGARI	KAY	20th CENTURY FOX	1962
CG	CARMELITA GERAGHTY	portrait	TIFFANY	
CG	CARY GRANT	portrait	RKO, UNIVERSAL, WARNER	
CG	CAT GIRL (UK)	SHAUGHNESSY	AIP	1957
CG	CINDY GARNER	portrait	UNIVERSAL	
CG	CLARK GABLE	portrait	MGM	
CG	CONFIDENCE GIRL	STONE	UNITED ARTISTS	1952
CG	CONTEST GIRL (UK: BEAUTY JUNGLE)	GUEST	CONTINENTAL	1964
CG	CORINNE GRIFFITH	portrait	FN	
CG	CORPSE GRINDER	MIKELS	GENENI FILM	1972
CG	FRISCO JENNY	WELLMAN	WARNER BROS	1932
CG	HOLIDAY AFFAIR	HARTMAN	RKO	1949
CG	MILLIONAIRE FOR CHRISTY	MARSHALL	20th CENTURY FOX	1951
CG-900	GARDEN OF EDEN	MILESTONE	UNITED ARTISTS	1928
CGA	CHINA GATE	FULLER	20th CENTURY FOX	1957
CGNH	CAREER GIRLS ON A NAKED HOLIDAY	SUPPLEE		1960
CGX	CHARLOTTE GREENWOOD	portrait	MGM	
CH	ANGELS WASH THEIR FACES	ENRIGHT	WARNER BROS	1939
CH	CALLING ALL HUSBANDS	SMITH	WARNER BROS	1940
CH	CAPTAIN HURRICANE	ROBERTSON	RKO	1935
CH	CAROL HUGHES	portrait	WARNER BROS	
CH	CHANCE AT HEAVEN	SEITER	RKO	1933
CH	CHARGE OF THE LIGHT BRIGADE (UK)	RICHARDSON	UNITED ARTISTS	1968
CH	CHARLTON HESTON	portrait	UNIVERSAL	
CH	CHARLY	NELSON	CINERAMA RELEASING	1968
CH	CHILDREN'S HOUR	WYLER	UNITED ARTISTS	1961
CH	COMING HOME	ASHBY	UNITED ARTISTS	1978
CH	COP HATER	BERKE	UNITED ARTISTS	1958
CH	CRAWLING HAND	STROCK	AIP	1963
CH	CREIGHTON HALE	portrait	FN	
CH	FIRE WITH FIRE	GIBBINS	PARAMOUNT	1986

Movie Still Identification Book Ultimate Edition - Letters

CODE	TITLE/NAME	DIRECTOR/TYPE	STUDIO/DISTRIBUTOR	YEAR
CH	RANCHO NOTORIOUS	LANG	RKO	1952
CH	UNDERGROUND GUERRILLAS (UK: UNDERCOVER)	NOLBANDOV	COLUMBIA	1943
CHC	CHAMPAGNE CHARLIE (UK)	CAVALCANTI	BELL	1944
Ch.C.	CHICAGO CONFIDENTIAL	SALKOW	UNITED ARTISTS	1957
CH133	C.H.O.M.P.S.	CHAFFEY	AIP	1979
CHG	C. HENRY GORDON	portrait	MGM	
CHG	RUNAWAY BRIDE	CRISP	RKO	1930
CHS	CREATURE HAUNTED SEA	CORMAN	FILM GROUP	1961
CI	CROSS OF IRON	PECKINPAH	AVCO	1977
CI	CUTTHROAT ISLAND	HARLIN	CAROLCO	1995
CI	DRAEGERMAN COURAGE	KING	WARNER BROS	1937
CI	ISLAND WOMEN	BERKE	UNITED ARTISTS	1958
CIA	CHLOE IN THE AFTERNOON (FR: L'AMOUR L'APRES-MIDI)	ROHMER	COLUMBIA	1972
CIA	OPERATIONS CIA	NYBY	ALLIED ARTISTS	1965
CIM	MIDNIGHT	ERSKINE	UNIVERSAL	1934
C-INT	CAVEMAN	GOTTLIEB	UNITED ARTISTS	1981
CIS	CACTUS IN THE SNOW	ZWEIBACH	GENENI FILM	1971
CJ	CAROLYN JONES	portrait	UNITED ARTISTS	
CJ	CELIA JOHNSON	portrait		
CJ	CHRISTINE JORGENSEN STORY	RAPPER	UNITED ARTISTS	1970
CJ	CINDERELLA JONES	BERKELEY	WARNER BROS	1946
CJ	CLAUDE JADE	portrait	UNIV	
CJ	CLAUDE JARMAN JR.	portrait		
CJ	CONCRETE JUNGLE (UK: CRIMINAL)	LOSEY	FANFARE	1960
CJ	CRAZY JOE (IT)	LIZZANI	COLUMBIA	1974
CJ	CRIME AGAINST JOE	SHOLEM	UNITED ARTISTS	1956
CK	CAPTAIN KIDD AND THE SLAVE GIRL	LANDERS	UNITED ARTISTS	1954
CK	CAPTAIN KRONOS, VAMPIRE HUNTER	CLEMENS	PARAMOUNT	1974
CK	CARNAL KNOWLEDGE	NICHOLS	AVCO EMBASSY	1971
CK	CASTLE KEEP	POLLACK	COLUMBIA	1969
CK	CECIL KELLAWAY	portrait	SELZNICK	
CK	CHARLES KEMPER	portrait		
CK	CHARLES KORVIN	portrait	UNIVERSAL	
CK	CHARLES KULLMAN/KULLMANN	portrait	UNIV	
CK	CHRISTINE KAUFMANN	portrait	UNITED ARTISTS	1950s-60s
CK	CITIZEN KANE	WELLES	RKO	1941
CK	CLOWN AND THE KID	CAHN	UNITED ARTISTS	1961
CK	COVER GIRL KILLER (UK)	BISHOP	FANFARE	1960
CK3	DARING CABALLERO	FOX	UNITED ARTISTS	1949
CK5	GIRL FROM SAN LORENZO	ABRAHAMS	UNITED ARTISTS	1950
CK-A	VALIANT HOMBRE	FOX	UNITED ARTISTS	1948
CK-B	GAY AMIGO	FOX	UNITED ARTISTS	1949
CKX	CHARLES KING	portrait	MGM	
CKY	CLARA KIMBALL YOUNG	portrait	SELECT PICTURES	late 10s
C-K-Y10	CLAW	VIGNOLA	SELECT (SELZNICK)	1918
CL	BOMBSIGHT STOLEN (UK: COTTAGE TO LET)	ASQUITH	GFD	1941
CL	CAROLE LANDIS	portrait	RKO	
CL	CAROLE LOMBARD	portrait	RKO	1930s-40s
CL	CAROLE LOMBARD	portrait	PATHE	
CL	CASE OF THE LUCKY LEGS	MAYO	WARNER BROS	1935
CL	CHARLES LANG	portrait	RKO	
CL	CHARLES LAUGHTON	portrait	RKO	
CL	CHATO'S LAND	WINNER	UNITED ARTISTS	1972
CL	CHELSEA LIFE (UK)	MORGAN	PARAMOUNT BRITISH	1933
CL	CHILDREN OF LONELINESS (THIRD SEX)	KAHN	JEWEL	1934
CL	CIRCLE OF LOVE	VADIM	CONTINENTAL	1965
CL	CITY LIGHTS	CHAPLIN	UNITED ARTISTS	1931
CL	CLOPORTES	DEFERRE	20th CENTURY FOX	1965
CL	CLUE	LYNN	PARAMOUNT	1985
CL	COLLEGE LOVERS	ADOLFI	WARNER BROS	1930
CL	CRIMINAL LAWYER	CABANNE	RKO	1937
CL	CULLEN LANDIS	portrait	METRO	
CL	HE FOUND A STAR (UK)	CARSTAIRS	GFD	1941
CL	PROWLER	LOSEY	UNITED ARTISTS	1951
CL-3	DAUGHTERS OF THE NIGHT	CLIFTON	FOX FILM	1924
CL-257	MR AND MRS. SMITH	HITCHCOCK	RKO	1941
CLC	CURSE OF THE LIVING CORPSE	TENNEY	20th CENTURY FOX	1964
CLEO	CLEOPATRA	MANKIEWICZ	20TH CENTURY FOX	1963
CLIFT-7	PORTS OF CALL	CLIFT	FOX FILM	1925
CLIFTON-2548	STORMY KNIGHT	CLIFTON	UNIVERSAL	1917

Movie Still Identification Book Ultimate Edition - Letters

CODE	TITLE/NAME	DIRECTOR/TYPE	STUDIO/DISTRIBUTOR	YEAR
CLIFTON-2633	HIGH SIGN	CLIFTON	UNIVERSAL (BUTTERFLY)	1917
CLIFTON-2806	KISS OR KILL	CLIFTON	UNIVERSAL	1918
CLK	CLAIRE'S KNEE (FRANCE: GENOU DE CLAIRE)	ROHMER	COLUMBIA	1971
CM	BEAUTY AND THE BOSS	DEL RUTH	WARNER BROS	1932
CM	CAIN AND MABEL	BACON	WARNER BROS	1936
CM	CALL ME GENIUS (UK: REBEL)	DAY	CONTINENTAL	1961
CM	CAMPUS MAN	CASDEN	PARAMOUNT	1987
CM	CAPTAIN MILKSHAKE	CRAWFORD	TWI NATIONAL	1970
CM	CARMEL MYERS	portrait	MGM, UNITED ARTISTS	
CM	CATHERINE MCLEOD	portrait	REPUBLIC	1940s-50s
CM	CAVEMAN	MILESTONE	WARNER BROS	1926
CM	CAVEMAN	GOTTLIEB	UNITED ARTISTS	1981
CM	CHARLIE MURRAY	portrait		
CM	CHESTER MORRIS	portrait	RKO	1930s-40s
CM	CHRISTINE MARTEL	portrait	UNIV	
CM	CLEO MOORE	portrait	RKO	early 50s
CM	COLLEEN MILLER	portrait	RKO, UNIVERSAL	
CM	COLLEEN MOORE	portrait	FOX	early 30s
CM	COMEDY MAN (UK)	RAKOFF	BRITISH LION	1964
CM	CONSOLATION MARRIAGE	SLOANE	RKO	1931
CM	CONSTANCE MOORE	portrait	UNIVERSAL	
CM	COOL MIKADO (UK)	WINNER	UNITED ARTISTS	1963
CM	CORINNA MURA (aka CORINNE MURA)	portrait	RKO	1940s
CM	CORRIDOR OF MIRRORS (UK)	YOUNG	UNIVERSAL	1948
CM	COSMIC MAN	GREENE	ALLIED ARTISTS	1959
CM	COSMIC MONSTER (UK: STRANGE WORLD OF PLANET X)	GUNN	DCA	1958
CM	COURT MARTIAL (GER)	MEISEL	UNITED ARTISTS	1959
CM	DESPERATE MEN (UK: CAT AND MOUSE)	ROTHA	EROS	1958
CM	ESPIONAGE AGENT	BACON	WARNER BROS	1939
CMB	CALL ME BWANA	DOUGLAS	UNITED ARTISTS	1963
CMG	CHARLES MCGRAW	portrait	RKO	1940s-50s
CMH	COUNTRY MUSIC HOLIDAY	GANZER	PARAMOUNT	1958
C-MPS	SECRETS	BORZAGE	UNITED ARTISTS	1933
CMR	CANCEL MY RESERVATION	BOGART	WARNER BROS	1972
CMX	CHESTER MORRIS	portrait	MGM	
CMXX	COLLEEN MOORE	portrait	MGM	
CN	CAPTAIN NEMO AND THE UNDERWATER CITY (UK)	HILL	MGM-UK	1969
CN	CONRAD NAGEL	portrait	MGM	
CN	CONSTANT NYMPH	GOULDING	WARNER BROS	1943
CN	COSA NOSTRA - AN ARCH ENEMY OF THE FBI (tv)	MEDFORD	WARNER BROS	1967
CNT	CHANCE OF A LIFETIME (UK)	LYNN, WILCOX	WOOLF & FREEDMAN	1931
CO	BRIDE CAME C.O.D.	KEIGHLEY	WARNER BROS	1941
CO	CIRCLE OF DECEPTION (UK)	LEE	20TH CENTURY FOX	1960
CO	CLOCKWORK ORANGE	KUBRICK	WARNER BROS	1971
CO	CONTEMPT (LE MEPRIS) (FR)	GODARD	EMBASSY	1964
CO	CONVICT 99 (UK)	VARNEL	GFD	1938
CO	COP-OUT (UK: STRANGER IN THE HOUSE)	ROUVE	CINERAMA	1967
CO	CORRUPT ONES (FR)	HILL, WINTERSTEIN	WARNER BROS	1967
CO	COUNSEL'S OPINION (UK)	DWAN	PARAMOUNT BRITISH	1933
CO	CYCLONE ON HORSEBACK	KILLY	RKO	1941
COC	CARRY ON CABBY (UK)	THOMAS	GOVERNOR	1963
COC	CARRY ON CONSTABLE (UK)	THOMAS	GOVERNOR	1960
COD	CASH ON DELIVERY (UK: TO DOROTHY A SON)	BOX	RKO	1956
COD	CATHY O'DONNELL	portrait	RKO	late 40s
COD	CHILD OF DIVORCE	FLEISCHER	RKO	1946
COD	CHILDREN OF DREAMS	CROSLAND	WARNER BROS	1931
COD	COME ON DANGER	HILL	RKO	1932
COE	CHARLEY ONE EYE	CHAFFEY	PARAMOUNT	1973
COF	CITY ON FIRE	RAKOFF	AVCO EMBASSY	1979
COG	COME ON GEORGE! (UK)	KIMMINS	ABFD	1939
COH	BEDLAM	ROBSON	RKO	1946
COL-1	AMERICAN MADNESS	CAPRA	COLUMBIA	1932
COL-1	BLOOD SHIP	SEITZ	COLUMBIA	1927
COL-1	COURT MARTIAL	SEITZ	COLUMBIA	1928
COL-1	FALSE ALARM	O'CONNOR	COLUMBIA	1926
COL-1	FLIGHT	CAPRA	COLUMBIA	1929
COL1	GET CRACKING (UK)	VARNEL	COLUMBIA BRITISH	1943
COL-1	LADY FOR A DAY	CAPRA	COLUMBIA	1933
COL-1	PAGAN LADY	DILLON	COLUMBIA	1931
COL-1	RAIN OR SHINE	CAPRA	COLUMBIA	1930

Movie Still Identification Book Ultimate Edition - Letters

CODE	TITLE/NAME	DIRECTOR/TYPE	STUDIO/DISTRIBUTOR	YEAR
COL-1	UNKNOWN RANGER	BENNET	COLUMBIA	1936
COL-2	ALIAS THE LONE WOLF	GRIFFITH	COLUMBIA	1927
COL-2	BROADWAY SCANDALS	ARCHAINBAUD	COLUMBIA	1929
COL-2	DIRIGIBLE	CAPRA	COLUMBIA	1931
COL-2	LONE WOLF RETURNS	INCE	COLUMBIA	1926
COL-2	MAN'S CASTLE	BORZAGE	COLUMBIA	1933
COL-2	NIGHT CLUB LADY	CUMMINGS	COLUMBIA	1932
COL-2	RANGER COURAGE	GORDON	COLUMBIA	1936
COL-2	SALLY IN OUR ALLEY	LANG	COLUMBIA	1927
COL-2	SCARLET LADY	CROSLAND	COLUMBIA	1928
COL-2	SHANGHAIED LOVE	SEITZ	COLUMBIA	1931
COL-3	ABOVE THE CLOUDS	NEILL	COLUMBIA	1934
COL-3	BITTER TEA OF GENERAL YEN	CAPRA	COLUMBIA	1933
COL-3	BROTHERS	LANG	COLUMBIA	1930
COL-3	FORBIDDEN	CAPRA	COLUMBIA	1932
COL-3	RIO GRANDE RANGER (BOB ALLEN series)	BENNET	COLUMBIA	1936
COL-3	RUNAWAY GIRLS	SANDRICH	COLUMBIA	1928
COL-3	SALLY IN OUR ALLEY	LANG	COLUMBIA	1927
COL-3	SONG OF LOVE	KENTON	COLUMBIA	1929
COL-3	WHEN THE WIFE'S AWAY	STRAYER	COLUMBIA	1926
COL-4	BELLE OF BROADWAY	HOYT	COLUMBIA	1926
COL-4	BY WHOSE HAND?	LANG	COLUMBIA	1927
COL-4	LADY IS WILLING	MILLER	COLUMBIA	1934
COL-4	LAW OF THE RANGER (BOB ALLEN series)	BENNET	COLUMBIA	1937
COL-4	PLATINUM BLONDE	CAPRA	COLUMBIA	1931
COL-4	STREET OF ILLUSION	KENTON	COLUMBIA	1928
COL-4	TOL'ABLE DAVID	BLYSTONE	COLUMBIA	1930
COL-4	WALL STREET	NEILL	COLUMBIA	1929
COL-4	WASHINGTON MERRY-GO-ROUND	CRUZE	COLUMBIA	1932
COL-5	CRIMINAL CODE	HAWKS	COLUMBIA	1931
COL-5	FOG	ROGELL	COLUMBIA	1933
COL-5	GUILTY GENERATION	LEE	COLUMBIA	1931
COL-5	ISLE OF FORGOTTEN WOMEN	SEITZ	COLUMBIA	1927
COL-5	MEXICALI ROSE	KENTON	COLUMBIA	1929
COL-5	RECKLESS RANGER	BENNET	COLUMBIA	1937
COL-5	SINNER'S PARADE	ADOLFI	COLUMBIA	1928
COL-5	SOS PERILS OF THE SEA	HOGAN	COLUMBIA	1925
COL-5	SWEET ROSIE O'GRADY	STRAYER	COLUMBIA	1926
COL-5	THAT'S MY BOY	NEILL	COLUMBIA	1932
COL-6	COLLEGE HERO	LANG	COLUMBIA	1927
COL-6	LION AND THE LAMB	SEITZ	COLUMBIA	1931
COL-6	MAN AGAINST WOMAN	CUMMINGS	COLUMBIA	1932
COL-6	MEN IN HER LIFE	BEAUDINE	COLUMBIA	1931
COL-6	MURDER ON THE ROOF	SEITZ	COLUMBIA	1930
COL-6	OBEY THE LAW	RABOCH	COLUMBIA	1926
COL-6	RANGERS STEP IN	BENNET	COLUMBIA	1937
COL-6	SHADOWS OF SING SING	ROSEN	COLUMBIA	1934
COL-6	SUBMARINE	CAPRA	COLUMBIA	1928
COL-7	BETTER WAY	INCE	COLUMBIA	1926
COL-7	DECEIVER	KING	COLUMBIA	1931
COL-7	DRIFTWOOD	CABANNE	COLUMBIA	1928
COL-7	LET'S FALL IN LOVE	BURTON	COLUMBIA	1934
COL-7	MADONNA OF THE STREETS	ROBERTSON	COLUMBIA	1930
COL-7	MELODY MAN	NEILL	COLUMBIA	1930
COL-7	NO MORE ORCHIDS	LANG	COLUMBIA	1932
COL-7	TIGRESS	SEITZ	COLUMBIA	1927
COL-8	AIR HOSTESS	ROGELL	COLUMBIA	1932
COL-8	NO GREATER GLORY	BORZAGE	COLUMBIA	1934
COL-8	PERSONALITY	HEERMAN	COLUMBIA	1930
COL-8	REMEMBER	SELMAN	COLUMBIA	1926
COL-8	STAGE KISSES	KELLEY	COLUMBIA	1927
COL-8	STOOL PIGEON	HOFFMAN	COLUMBIA	1928
COL-8	TEN CENTS A DANCE	BARRYMORE	COLUMBIA	1931
COL-8	THREE WISE GIRLS	BEAUDINE	COLUMBIA	1932
COL-8	WHITE LIES	BULGAKOV	COLUMBIA	1935
COL-9	LAST PARADE	KENTON	COLUMBIA	1931
COL-9	MAKER OF MEN	SEDGWICK	COLUMBIA	1931
COL-9	ONCE TO EVERY WOMAN	HILLYER	COLUMBIA	1934
COL-9	OPENING NIGHT	GRIFFITH	COLUMBIA	1927
COL-9	POWER OF THE PRESS	CAPRA	COLUMBIA	1928

Movie Still Identification Book Ultimate Edition - Letters

CODE	TITLE/NAME	DIRECTOR/TYPE	STUDIO/DISTRIBUTOR	YEAR
COL-9	SO THIS IS AFRICA	CLINE	COLUMBIA	1933
COL-9	STOLEN PLEASURE	ROSEN	COLUMBIA	1927
COL-9	VENGEANCE	MAYO	COLUMBIA	1930
COL-9	WHOLE TOWN'S TALKING	FORD	COLUMBIA	1935
COL-10	DECEPTION	SEILER	COLUMBIA	1932
COL-10	DISCONTENTED HUSBANDS	LESAINT	COLUMBIA	1924
COL-10	GUILTY?	SEITZ	COLUMBIA	1930
COL-10	MENACE	NEILL	COLUMBIA	1932
COL-10	NINTH GUEST	NEILL	COLUMBIA	1934
COL-10	NOTHING TO WEAR	KENTON	COLUMBIA	1928
COL-10	SUBWAY EXPRESS	NEWMEYER	COLUMBIA	1931
COL-10	WANDERING GIRLS	INCE	COLUMBIA	1927
COL-10	WARNING	SEITZ	COLUMBIA	1927
COL-11	APACHE	ROSEN	COLUMBIA	1928
COL-11	AS THE DEVIL COMMANDS	NEILL	COLUMBIA	1933
COL-11	BACHELOR'S BABY	STRAYER	COLUMBIA	1927
COL-11	BEHIND THE MASK	DILLON	COLUMBIA	1932
COL-11	CHILD OF MANHATTAN	BUZZELL	COLUMBIA	1933
COL-11	FASHION MADNESS	GASNIER	COLUMBIA	1928
COL-11	FLOOD	TINLING	COLUMBIA	1931
COL-11	IT HAPPENED ONE NIGHT	CAPRA	COLUMBIA	1934
COL-11	LADIES OF LEISURE	CAPRA	COLUMBIA	1930
COL-11	PAL O'MINE	LESAINT	COLUMBIA	1924
COL-12	FINAL EDITION	HIGGIN	COLUMBIA	1932
COL-12	LONE WOLF'S DAUGHTER	ROGELL	COLUMBIA	1929
COL-12	MIRACLE WOMAN	CAPRA	COLUMBIA	1931
COL-12	ROYAL ROMANCE	KENTON	COLUMBIA	1930
COL-12	SIREN	HASKIN	COLUMBIA	1928
COL-12	SOCIAL REGISTER	NEILAN	COLUMBIA	1934
COL-12	WRECK	CRAFT	COLUMBIA	1927
COL-13	BELOW THE SEA	ROGELL	COLUMBIA	1933
COL-13	CALL OF THE WEST	RAY	COLUMBIA	1930
COL-13	LINEUP	HIGGIN	COLUMBIA	1934
COL-13	LOVER COME BACK	KENTON	COLUMBIA	1931
COL-13	PRICE OF HONOR	GRIFFITH	COLUMBIA	1927
COL-13	RESTLESS YOUTH	CABANNE	COLUMBIA	1928
COL-13	SHOPWORN	GRINDE	COLUMBIA	1932
COL-13	THAT CERTAIN THING	CAPRA	COLUMBIA	1928
COL-14	BIG TIMER	BUZZELL	COLUMBIA	1932
COL-14	BIRDS OF PREY	CRAFT	COLUMBIA	1927
COL-14	GOOD BAD GIRL	NEILL	COLUMBIA	1931
COL-14	SISTERS UNDER THE SKIN	BURTON	COLUMBIA	1934
COL-14	WHEN STRANGERS MARRY	BADGER	COLUMBIA	1933
COL-14	WIFE'S RELATIONS	MARSHALL	COLUMBIA	1928
COL-14	YOUNGER GENERATION	CAPRA	COLUMBIA	1929
COL-15	ARIZONA	SEITZ	COLUMBIA	1931
COL-15	AROUND THE CORNER	GLENNON	COLUMBIA	1930
COL-15	BRIEF MOMENT	BURTON	COLUMBIA	1933
COL-15	LADY RAFFLES	NEILL	COLUMBIA	1928
COL-15	LOVE AFFAIR	FREELAND	COLUMBIA	1932
COL-15	MOST PRECIOUS THING IN LIFE	HILLYER	COLUMBIA	1934
COL-15	PLEASURE BEFORE BUSINESS	STRAYER	COLUMBIA	1927
COL-15	SIDESHOW	KENTON	COLUMBIA	1928
COL-16	ATTORNEY FOR THE DEFENSE	CUMMINGS	COLUMBIA	1932
COL-16	CAPTAIN HATES THE SEA	MILESTONE	COLUMBIA	1934
COL-16	FIFTY FATHOMS DEEP	NEILL	COLUMBIA	1931
COL-16	OBJECT: ALIMONY	DUNLAP	COLUMBIA	1928
COL-16	PAROLE GIRL	CLINE	COLUMBIA	1933
COL-16	POOR GIRLS	CRAFT	COLUMBIA	1927
COL-16	SO THIS IS LOVE	CAPRA	COLUMBIA	1928
COL-16	SOLDIERS AND WOMEN	SLOMAN	COLUMBIA	1930
COL-17	CIRCUS QUEEN MURDER	NEILL	COLUMBIA	1933
COL-17	DANGEROUS AFFAIR	SEDGWICK	COLUMBIA	1931
COL-17	FATHER		COLUMBIA	1928
COL-17	PAYING THE PRICE	SELMAN	COLUMBIA	1927
COL-17	TEMPTATION	HOPPER	COLUMBIA	1930
COL-17	TWENTIETH CENTURY	HAWKS	COLUMBIA	1934
COL-17	WOMAN'S WAY	MORTIMER	COLUMBIA	1928
COL-18	COCKTAIL HOUR	SCHERTZINGER	COLUMBIA	1933
COL-18	HOLLYWOOD SPEAKS	BUZZELL	COLUMBIA	1932

Movie Still Identification Book Ultimate Edition - Letters

CODE	TITLE/NAME	DIRECTOR/TYPE	STUDIO/DISTRIBUTOR	YEAR
COL-18	SISTERS	FLOOD	COLUMBIA	1930
COL-18	SPORTING AGE	KENTON	COLUMBIA	1928
COL-18	TRIAL MARRIAGE	KENTON	COLUMBIA	1929
COL-18	WHIRLPOOL	NEILL	COLUMBIA	1934
COL-19	BEHIND CLOSED DOORS	NEILL	COLUMBIA	1929
COL-19	BY WHOSE HAND?	STOLOFF	COLUMBIA	1932
COL-19	CHARLEY'S AUNT	CHRISTIE	COLUMBIA	1931
COL-19	HELL'S ISLAND	SLOMAN	COLUMBIA	1930
COL-19	MATINEE IDOL	CAPRA	COLUMBIA	1928
COL-19	ROMANTIC AGE	FLOREY	COLUMBIA	1927
COL-19	WHOM THE GODS DESTROY	LANG	COLUMBIA	1934
COL-19	WOMAN I STOLE	CUMMINGS	COLUMBIA	1933
COL-20	ANN CARVER'S PROFESSION	BUZZELL	COLUMBIA	1933
COL-20	DESERT BRIDE	CAPRA	COLUMBIA	1928
COL-20	LADIES MUST PLAY	CANNON	COLUMBIA	1930
COL-20	MEET THE WIFE	PEARCE	COLUMBIA	1931
COL-20	PARTY'S OVER	LANG	COLUMBIA	1934
COL-20	QUITTER	HENABERY	COLUMBIA	1929
COL-20	RICH MEN'S SONS	GRAVES	COLUMBIA	1927
COL-20	WAR CORRESPONDENT	SLOANE	COLUMBIA	1932
COL-21	BROADWAY DADDIES	WINDEMERE	COLUMBIA	1928
COL-21	CLOWN	CRAFT	COLUMBIA	1927
COL-21	DONOVAN AFFAIR	CAPRA	COLUMBIA	1929
COL-21	HELLCAT	ROGELL	COLUMBIA	1934
COL-21	SQUEALER	BROWN	COLUMBIA	1930
COL-22	AFTER THE STORM	SEITZ	COLUMBIA	1928
COL-22	BLACK MOON	NEILL	COLUMBIA	1934
COL-22	ETERNAL WOMAN	MCCARTHY	COLUMBIA	1929
COL-22	KID SISTER	GRAVES	COLUMBIA	1927
COL-22	LAST MAN	HIGGIN	COLUMBIA	1932
COL-22	LAST OF THE LONE WOLF	BOLESLAWSKI	COLUMBIA	1930
COL-22	WRECKER	ROGELL	COLUMBIA	1933
COL-23	BLIND DATE	NEILL	COLUMBIA	1934
COL-23	FATHER AND SON	KENTON	COLUMBIA	1929
COL-23	FOR LADIES ONLY	LEHRMAN, PEMBROKE	COLUMBIA	1927
COL-23	FOR THE LOVE O' LIL	TINLING	COLUMBIA	1930
COL-23	GOLF WIDOWS	KENTON	COLUMBIA	1928
COL-23	MY WOMAN	SCHERTZINGER	COLUMBIA	1933
COL-23	NIGHT MAYOR	STOLOFF	COLUMBIA	1932
COL-24	BACHELOR GIRL	THORPE	COLUMBIA	1929
COL-24	DEFENSE RESTS	HILLYER	COLUMBIA	1934
COL-24	FURY OF THE JUNGLE	NEILL	COLUMBIA	1933
COL-24	MODERN MOTHERS	ROSEN	COLUMBIA	1928
COL-24	SWEETHEARTS ON PARADE	NEILAN	COLUMBIA	1930
COL-24	SWELL HEAD	GRAVES	COLUMBIA	1927
COL-24	THIS SPORTING AGE	BENNISON, ERICKSON	COLUMBIA	1932
COL-25	NAME THE WOMAN	KENTON	COLUMBIA	1928
COL-25	NAME THE WOMAN	ROGELL	COLUMBIA	1934
COL-25	VANITY STREET	GRINDE	COLUMBIA	1932
COL-26	FALL OF EVE	STRAYER	COLUMBIA	1929
COL-26	MASTER OF MEN	HILLYER	COLUMBIA	1933
COL-26	RANSOM	SEITZ	COLUMBIA	1928
COL-26	VIRTUE	BUZZELL	COLUMBIA	1932
COL-27	COLLEGE COQUETTE	ARCHAINBAUD	COLUMBIA	1929
COL-27	FUGITIVE LADY	ROGELL	COLUMBIA	1934
COL-27	WAY OF THE STRONG	CAPRA	COLUMBIA	1928
COL-28	BEWARE OF BLONDES	SEITZ	COLUMBIA	1928
COL-28	LADY BY CHOICE	BURTON	COLUMBIA	1934
COL-28	LIGHT FINGERS	HENABERY	COLUMBIA	1929
COL-29	HURRICANE	INCE	COLUMBIA	1929
COL-29	I'LL FIX IT	NEILL	COLUMBIA	1934
COL-29	SAY IT WITH SABLES	CAPRA	COLUMBIA	1928
COL-30	ACQUITTED	STRAYER	COLUMBIA	1929
COL-30	AMONG THE MISSING	ROGELL	COLUMBIA	1934
COL-30	FAITH, HOPE AND CHARITY (sh)	BLAKE	COLUMBIA	1930
COL-31	BROADWAY HOOFER	ARCHAINBAUD	COLUMBIA	1929
COL-31	NEVER STRIKE YOUR MOTHER (sh)	BLAKE	COLUMBIA	1930
COL-32	HOT AND BOTHERED (sh)	BLAKE	COLUMBIA	1930
COL-33	PRODIGAL DAUGHTER (sh)	BUZZELL	COLUMBIA	1930
COL-34	CAME THE PAWN (sh)	BUZZELL	COLUMBIA	1930

Movie Still Identification Book Ultimate Edition - Letters

CODE	TITLE/NAME	DIRECTOR/TYPE	STUDIO/DISTRIBUTOR	YEAR
COL-35	HARD BOILED YEGGS (sh)	BUZZELL	COLUMBIA	1930
COL-36	CRYSTAL GAZER	BUZZELL	COLUMBIA	1930
COL-37	LONE STAR STRANGER (sh)	BUZZELL	COLUMBIA	1931
COL-38	WINE, WOMAN BUT NO SONG (sh)		COLUMBIA	1931
COL-39	CHECK AND RUBBER CHECK (sh)	BUZZELL	COLUMBIA	1931
COL-40	KINGS OR BETTER (sh)	BUZZELL	COLUMBIA	1931
COL-40	THRILL HUNTER	SEITZ	COLUMBIA	1933
COL-41	FIGHTING CODE	HILLYER	COLUMBIA	1933
COL-41	LAST OF THE MOE HEE GINS (sh)	BUZZELL	COLUMBIA	1931
COL-42	CHRIS-CROSSED (sh)	BUZZELL	COLUMBIA	1931
COL-42	FIGHTING RANGER	SEITZ	COLUMBIA	1934
COL-43	MAN TRAILER	HILLYER	COLUMBIA	1934
COL-43	RED MEN TELL NO TALES (sh)	BUZZELL	COLUMBIA	1931
COL-44	WOLF IN CHEAP CLOTHING (sh)	BUZZELL	COLUMBIA	1932
COL-45	BLONDE PRESSURE (sh)	BUZZELL	COLUMBIA	1931
COL-46	SHE SERVED HIM RIGHT (sh)	BUZZELL	COLUMBIA	1931
COL-47	SOLDIER OF MISFORTUNE (sh)	BUZZELL	COLUMBIA	1931
COL-48	CALL OF THE MOTH (sh)		COLUMBIA	1932
COL-49	LOVE, HONOR AND HE PAYS (sh)	BUZZELL	COLUMBIA	1932
COL-50	AFRICA SPEAKS	HOEFLER, FULLER	COLUMBIA	1930
COL-50	SPEED DEMON	LEDERMAN	COLUMBIA	1932
COL-51	STATE TROOPER	LEDERMAN	COLUMBIA	1933
COL-52	OBEY THE LAW	STOLOFF	COLUMBIA	1933
COL-53	SOLDIERS OF THE STORM	LEDERMAN	COLUMBIA	1933
COL-54	DANGEROUS CROSSROADS	HILLYER	COLUMBIA	1933
COL-55	NIGHT OF TERROR	STOLOFF	COLUMBIA	1933
COL-56	KING OF THE WILD HORSES	HALEY	COLUMBIA	1933
COL-60	CORNERED	EASON	COLUMBIA	1932
COL-60	LONE RIDER	KING	COLUMBIA	1930
COL-61	SHADOW RANCH	KING	COLUMBIA	1930
COL-61	WESTERN CODE	MCCARTHY	COLUMBIA	1932
COL-62	FIGHTING FOR JUSTICE	BROWER	COLUMBIA	1932
COL-62	MEN WITHOUT LAW	KING	COLUMBIA	1930
COL-63	DAWN TRAIL	CABANNE	COLUMBIA	1930
COL-63	END OF THE TRAIL	LEDERMAN	COLUMBIA	1933
COL-64	DESERT VENGEANCE	KING	COLUMBIA	1931
COL-64	MAN OF ACTION	MELFORD	COLUMBIA	1933
COL-65	AVENGER	NEILL	COLUMBIA	1931
COL-65	SILENT MEN	LEDERMAN	COLUMBIA	1933
COL-66	TEXAS RANGER	LEDERMAN	COLUMBIA	1931
COL-66	WHIRLWIND	LEDERMAN	COLUMBIA	1933
COL-67	FIGHTING SHERIFF	KING	COLUMBIA	1931
COL-67	RUSTY RIDES ALONE	LEDERMAN	COLUMBIA	1933
COL-70	BRANDED	LEDERMAN	COLUMBIA	1931
COL-70	POLICE CAR 17	HILLYER	COLUMBIA	1933
COL-71	BORDER LAW	KING	COLUMBIA	1931
COL-71	HOLD THE PRESS	ROSEN	COLUMBIA	1933
COL-72	RANGE FEUD	LEDERMAN	COLUMBIA	1931
COL-72	STRAIGHTAWAY	BROWER	COLUMBIA	1934
COL-73	DEADLINE	HILLYER	COLUMBIA	1931
COL-73	SPEED WINGS	BROWER	COLUMBIA	1934
COL-74	RIDIN' FOR JUSTICE	LEDERMAN	COLUMBIA	1932
COL-74	VOICE IN THE NIGHT	COLEMAN	COLUMBIA	1934
COL-75	HELLBENT FOR LOVE	LEDERMAN	COLUMBIA	1934
COL-75	ONE MAN LAW	HILLYER	COLUMBIA	1932
COL-76	HIGH SPEED	LEDERMAN	COLUMBIA	1932
COL-76	MAN'S GAME	LEDERMAN	COLUMBIA	1934
COL-77	BEYOND THE LAW	LEDERMAN	COLUMBIA	1934
COL-77	SOUTH OF THE RIO GRANDE	HILLYER	COLUMBIA	1932
COL-80	BEFORE MIDNIGHT	HILLYER	COLUMBIA	1933
COL-80	LIGHTNING FLYER	NIGH	COLUMBIA	1931
COL-80	SHOTGUN PASS	MCGOWAN	COLUMBIA	1932
COL-81	ONE IS GUILTY	HILLYER	COLUMBIA	1934
COL-81	ONE WAY TRAIL	TAYLOR	COLUMBIA	1931
COL-81	SKY RAIDERS	BEEBE, TAYLOR	COLUMBIA	1931
COL-82	CRIME OF HELEN STANLEY	LEDERMAN	COLUMBIA	1934
COL-82	FIGHTING MARSHALL	LEDERMAN	COLUMBIA	1931
COL-83	FIGHTING FOOL	HILLYER	COLUMBIA	1932
COL-83	GIRL IN DANGER	LEDERMAN	COLUMBIA	1934
COL-84	TEXAS CYCLONE	LEDERMAN	COLUMBIA	1932

Movie Still Identification Book Ultimate Edition - Letters

CODE	TITLE/NAME	DIRECTOR/TYPE	STUDIO/DISTRIBUTOR	YEAR
COL-85	DARING DANGER	LEDERMAN	COLUMBIA	1932
COL-86	RIDING TORNADO	LEDERMAN	COLUMBIA	1932
COL-87	TWO FISTED LAW	LEDERMAN	COLUMBIA	1932
COL-90	HELLO TROUBLE	HILLYER	COLUMBIA	1932
COL-90	LAND NOBODY KNOWS	(DOCU)	COLUMBIA	1931
COL-91	MCKENNA OF THE MOUNTIES	LEDERMAN	COLUMBIA	1932
COL-92	WHITE EAGLE	HILLYER	COLUMBIA	1932
COL-93	FORBIDDEN TRAIL	HILLYER	COLUMBIA	1932
COL-94	SUNDOWN RACER		COLUMBIA	1933
COL-95	TREASON	SEITZ	COLUMBIA	1933
COL-96	CALIFORNIA TRAIL	HILLYER	COLUMBIA	1933
COL-97	UNKNOWN VALLEY	HILLYER	COLUMBIA	1933
COL-100	HOT DAZE (sh)	MOORE	COLUMBIA	1933
COL-101	UMPA	CONRAD, GOTTLER	COLUMBIA	1933
COL-102	ROAMIN' THRU THE ROSES	GOTTLER	COLUMBIA	1933
COL-104	HOLD YOUR TEMPER	WHITE	COLUMBIA	1933
COL-105	ED CODIGO PENAL	ROSEN, VILLARREAL	COLUMBIA	1931
COL-108	CARNE DE CABARET	CABANNE	COLUMBIA	1931
COL-114	EL PASADO ACUSA	SELMAN, VILLARREAL	COLUMBIA	1931
COL-114	I WAS A PRISONER ON DEVIL'S ISLAND	LANDERS	COLUMBIA	1941
COL-156	THREE LITTLE PIGSKINS (sh)	MCCAREY	COLUMBIA	1934
COL-196	HOMBRES EN MI VIDA	SELMAN	COLUMBIA	1932
COL-358	BADMEN OF THE HILLS	BERKE	COLUMBIA	1942
COL-423	VIOLENT IS THE WORD FOR CURLY (sh)	CHASE	COLUMBIA	1938
COL-541	HIS WEDDING SCARE (sh)	LORD	COLUMBIA	1943
COL-565	HUGH HERBERT (sh)	portrait	COLUMBIA	
COL-595	STOOGES (sh)		COLUMBIA	
COL-683	JUNIOR QUIZ PARADE		COLUMBIA	
COL-876	CORPSE CAME C.O.D.	LEVIN	COLUMBIA	1947
COL-976	MULE TRAIN	ENGLISH	COLUMBIA	1950
COL-1127	CIGARETTE GIRL	VON FRITSCH	COLUMBIA	1947
COL-1142	BULLDOG DRUMMOND STRIKES AGAIN	MCDONALD	COLUMBIA	1947
COL-1256	SOUND OFF	QUINE	COLUMBIA	1952
COL-1266	ALL ASHORE	QUINE	COLUMBIA	1953
COL-1267	AMBUSH AT TOMAHAWK GAP	SEARS	COLUMBIA	1953
COL-1274	CHINA VENTURE	SIEGEL	COLUMBIA	1953
COL-1276	BIG HEAT	LANG	COLUMBIA	1953
COL-1284	BAD FOR EACH OTHER	RAPPER	COLUMBIA	1953
COL-1285	IT SHOULD HAPPEN TO YOU	CUKOR	COLUMBIA	1954
COL-3003	COWBOY IN THE CLOUDS	KLINE	COLUMBIA	1943
COL-3087	PECOS RIVER	SEARS	COLUMBIA	1951
COL-4052	SOCIETY MUGS (sh)	BERNDS	COLUMBIA	1946
COL-4198	STROP, LOOK AND LISTEN (sh)	WHITE	COLUMBIA	1952
COL-4200	THREE DARK HORSES (sh)	WHITE	COLUMBIA	1952
COL-8062	SNIPER	DMYTRYK	COLUMBIA	1952
COL-8064	5000 FINGERS OF DR. T	ROWLAND	COLUMBIA	1953
COL-8085	YANK IN INDO-CHINA	GRISSELL	COLUMBIA	1952
COL-8090	VOODOO TIGER	BENNET	COLUMBIA	1952
COL-8094	WAGON TEAM	ARCHAINBAUD	COLUMBIA	1952
COL-8100	SON OF GERONIMO - SERIAL	BENNET	COLUMBIA	1952
COL-8121	STRANGE FASCINATION	HAAS	COLUMBIA	1952
COL-8157	49TH MAN	SEARS	COLUMBIA	1953
COL-8319	FLYING FONTAINES	SHERMAN	COLUMBIA	1959
COL-8426	BATTLE OF THE CORAL SEA	WENDKOS	COLUMBIA	1959
COL-8602	SAIL A CROOKED SHIP	BRECHER	COLUMBIA	1961
COL-8624	EVERYTHING'S DUCKY	TAYLOR	COLUMBIA	1961
COL-FR	VOICE IN THE NIGHT (UK: FREEDOM RADIO)	ASQUITH	COLUMBIA	1941
COL-IN	INVADERS (UK: 49TH PARALLEL)	POWELL, PRESSBURGER	COLUMBIA	1942
COL-MC	BELOVED VAGABOND (UK)	BERNHARDT	COLUMBIA	1936
COL-S-5	WHITE EAGLE (serial)	HILLYER	COLUMBIA	1932
COL-S-7	IRON CLAW	HORNE	COLUMBIA	1941
COM	COMANCHE	SHERMAN	UNITED ARTISTS	1956
COM	COMIC	REINER	COLUMBIA	1969
CON	CARRY ON NURSE (UK)	THOMAS	GOVERNOR	1959
CON	CONFORMIST (IT)	BERTOLUCCI	PARAMOUNT	1971
CON	CONSPIRACY	LANDERS	RKO	1939
CON	CONVERSATION	COPPOLA	PARAMOUNT	1974
CON-1	DISORDERLY CONDUCT	CONSIDINE	FOX FILM	1932
CON-3	ROUGHNECK	CONWAY	FOX FILM	1924
COP	COMING-OUT PARTY (UK: VERY IMPORTANT PERSON)	ANNAKIN	UNION	1961

Movie Still Identification Book Ultimate Edition - Letters

CODE	TITLE/NAME	DIRECTOR/TYPE	STUDIO/DISTRIBUTOR	YEAR
COP	CURSE OF THE CAT PEOPLE	FRITSCH, WISE	RKO	1944
COR	COME ON DANGER	KILLY	RKO	1942
COR-3	END OF THE AFFAIR (UK)	DMYTRYK	COLUMBIA	1955
COS	CARRY ON SARGEANT (UK: 1958)	THOMAS	GOVERNOR	1959
COS	CARRY ON SPYING (UK)	THOMAS	GOVERNOR	1964
C.O.S-12	VALLEY OF VANISHING MEN (serial)	BENNET	COLUMBIA	1942
COSG	CASE OF SERGEANT GRISCHA	BRENON	RKO	1929
COT	CALL OUT THE MARINES	HAMILTON, RYAN	RKO	1942
COT	CHILDREN ON TRIAL	LEE	ENGLISH	1946
COT	NIGHTMARE CASTLE (IT)	CAIANO	MONOGRAM	1966
CP	AMBUSH AT CIMMARON PASS	COPELAN	20th CENTURY FOX	1958
CP	CANADIAN PACIFIC	MARIN	20th CENTURY FOX	1949
CP	CAT PEOPLE	TOURNEUR	RKO	1942
CP	CECILIA PARKER	portrait	MGM	
CP	CHILD'S PLAY	LUMET	PARAMOUNT	1973
CP	CHILD'S PLAY	HOLLAND	UNITED ARTISTS	1988
CP	CISCO PIKE	NORTON	COLUMBIA	1972
CP	CLAY PIGEON	FLEISCHER	RKO	1948
CP	COUNTERFEIT PLAN (UK)	TULLY	WARNER BROS.	1957
CP	COUNTERPLOT	NEWMANN	UNITED ARTISTS	1959
CP	CRASH		WARNER BROS	
CP	DOCTOR BLOOD'S COFFIN (UK)	FURIE	UNITED ARTISTS	1961
CP	FLAT FOOT STOOGES (sh)	CHASE	COLUMBIA	1938
CP	HEADLINE (UK)	HARLOW	EALING	1943
CP	JOHNNY TROUBLE	AUER	WARNER BROS	1957
CP	SEA DEVILS	STOLOFF	RKO	1937
CP	WALKING ON AIR	SANTLEY	RKO	1936
CP-1	ABANDON SHIP	SALE	COLUMBIA	1957
CP-3	ALIAS THE LONE WOLF	GRIFFITH	COLUMBIA	1927
CP-3	LOVE TAKES FLIGHT	NAGEL	GRAND	1937
CP-101	HER FIRST ROMANCE	DMYTRYK	MONOGRAM	1940
CP-102	REDHEAD	CAHN	MONOGRAM	1941
CP-149	MEET THE STEWARTS	GREEN	COLUMBIA	1942
CP-151	PARACHUTE NURSE	BARTON	COLUMBIA	1942
CPA	CONQUEST OF THE PLANET OF THE APES	THOMPSON	20th CENTURY FOX	1972
CP-BB	BIRDS DO IT, BEES DO IT	NOXON, ROSTEN	COLUMBIA	1974
CP-BD	BIRDS DO IT, BEES DO IT	NOXON, ROSTEN	COLUMBIA	1974
CP BJ	BROTHER JOHN	GOLDSTONE	COLUMBIA	1971
CP-BP	BUCK AND THE PREACHER	POITIER	COLUMBIA	1972
CP-BS	BRIAN'S SONG	KULIK	COLUMBIA	1971
CPC-I	INTERLUDE	BILLINGTON	COLUMBIA	1968
CPC-2WH	HAPPENING	SILVERSTEIN	COLUMBIA	1967
CPC 129	LADY IF WILLING	LEISEN	COLUMBIA	1942
CPC-1322	FULL OF LIFE	QUINE	COLUMBIA	1957
CPC-1323	SHADOW ON THE WINDOW	ASHER	COLUMBIA	1957
CPC-1329	GUNMAN'S WALK	KARLSON	COLUMBIA	1958
CPC-1332	GUNMEN FROM LAREDO	MACDONALD	COLUMBIA	1959
CPC-1334	GIDGET	WENDKOS	COLUMBIA	1959
CPC-1902	GUNS A POPPIN' (sh)	WHITE	COLUMBIA	1957
CPC-1903	FIFI BLOWS HER TOP (sh)	WHITE	COLUMBIA	1958
CPC-1904	RUSTY ROMEOS (sh)	WHITE	COLUMBIA	1957
CPC-1905	TRICKY CHICKS (sh)	WHITE	COLUMBIA	1957
CPC-1906	FLYING SAUCER DAFFY (sh)	WHITE	COLUMBIA	1958
CPC-1907	QUIZ WHIZZ (sh)	WHITE	COLUMBIA	1958
CPC-1908	PIES AND GUYS (sh)	WHITE	COLUMBIA	1958
CPC-1909	OUTER SPACE JITTERS (sh)	WHITE	COLUMBIA	1957
CPC-1910	SWEET AND HOT (sh)	WHITE	COLUMBIA	1958
CPC-1911	OIL'S WELL THAT ENDS WELL (sh)	WHITE	COLUMBIA	1958
CPC-1912	SAPPY BULLFIGHTERS (sh)	WHITE	COLUMBIA	1959
CPC-1913	TRIPLE CROSSED (sh)	WHITE	COLUMBIA	1959
CPC-4250	MUSCLE UP A LITTLE CLOSER (sh)	WHITE	COLUMBIA	1957
CPC-4251	HOOFS AND GOOFS (sh)	WHITE	COLUMBIA	1957
CPC-4252	MERRY MIXUP (sh)	WHITE	COLUMBIA	1957
CPC-4253	SPACE SHIP SAPPY (sh)	WHITE	COLUMBIA	1957
CPC-8289	BROTHERS RICO	KARLSON	COLUMBIA	1957
CPC-8323	BELL BOOK AND CANDLE	QUINE	COLUMBIA	1958
CPC-8330	NIGHTFALL	TOURNEUR	COLUMBIA	1957
CPC-8342	GUNS OF FORT PETTICOAT	MARSHALL	COLUMBIA	1957
CPC-8357	27TH DAY	ASHER	COLUMBIA	1957
CPC-8359	GIANT CLAW	SEARS	COLUMBIA	1957

Movie Still Identification Book Ultimate Edition - Letters

CODE	TITLE/NAME	DIRECTOR/TYPE	STUDIO/DISTRIBUTOR	YEAR
CPC-8364	PHANTOM STAGECOACH	NAZARRO	COLUMBIA	1957
CPC-8365	20 MILLION MILES TO EARTH	JURAN	COLUMBIA	1957
CPC-8366	NIGHT THE WORLD EXPLODED	SEARS	COLUMBIA	1957
CPC-8372	LINEUP	SIEGEL	COLUMBIA	1958
CPC-8373	MAN WHO TURNED TO STONE	KARDOS	COLUMBIA	1957
CPC-8376	HELLCATS OF THE NAVY	JURAN	COLUMBIA	1957
CPC-8378	ZOMBIES OF MORA TAU	CAHN	CLOVER	1957
CPC-8379	TALL T	BOATTICHER	COLUMBIA	1957
CPC-8381	UTAH BLAINE	SEARS	COLUMBIA	1957
CPC-8385	YOUNG DON'T CRY	WERKER	COLUMBIA	1957
CPC-8395	GARMENT JUNGLE	SHERMAN	COLUMBIA	1957
CPC-8396	NO TIME TO BE YOUNG	RICH	COLUMBIA	1957
CPC-8397	3:10 TO YUMA	DAVES	COLUMBIA	1957
CPC-8398	ESCAPE FROM SAN QUENTIN	SEARS	COLUMBIA	1957
CPC-8403	JEANNE EAGELS	SIDNEY	COLUMBIA	1957
CPC-8406	CRASH LANDING	SEARS	COLUMBIA	1958
CPC-8407	PAL JOEY	SIDNEY	COLUMBIA	1957
CPC-8414	HARD MAN	SHERMAN	COLUMBIA	1957
CPC-8417	THIS ANGRY AGE	CLEMENT	COLUMBIA	1958
CPC-8418	DOMINO KID	NAZARRO	COLUMBIA	1957
CPC-8420	DECISION AT SUNDOWN	BOETTICHER	COLUMBIA	1957
CPC-8422	LIFE BEGINS AT 17	DREIFUSS	COLUMBIA	1958
CPC-8423	OPERATION MADBALL	QUINE	COLUMBIA	1957
CPC-8427	TARAWA BEACHHEAD	WENDKOS	COLUMBIA	1958
CPC-8428	CASE AGAINST BROOKLYN	WENDKOS	COLUMBIA	1958
CPC-8429	GOING STEADY	SEARS	COLUMBIA	1958
CPC-8430	CALYPSO HEAT WAVE	SEARS	COLUMBIA	1957
CPC-8431	SCREAMING MIMI	OSWALD	COLUMBIA	1958
CPC-8449	TRUE STORY OF LYNN STUART	SEILER	COLUMBIA	1958
CPC-8450	BUCHANAN RIDES ALONE	BOETTICHER	COLUMBIA	1958
CPC-8453	COWBOY	DAVES	COLUMBIA	1958
CPC-8461	LAST BLITZKRIEG	DREIFUSS	COLUMBIA	1959
CPC-8462	1001 ARABIAN NIGHTS (t)	KINNEY	COLUMBIA	1959
CPC-8464	13 WEST STREET	LEACOCK	COLUMBIA	1962
CPC-8465	GODDESS	CROMWELL	COLUMBIA	1958
CPC-8468	JUKE BOX RHYTHM	DREIFUSS	COLUMBIA	1959
CPC-8470	FORBIDDEN ISLAND	GRIFFITH	COLUMBIA	1959
CPC-8472	APACHE TERRITORY	NAZARRO	COLUMBIA	1958
CPC-8475	ME AND THE COLONEL	GLENVILLE	COLUMBIA	1958
CPC-8476	PEPE	SIDNEY	COLUMBIA	1960
CPC-8485	LAST HURRAH	FORD	COLUMBIA	1958
CPC-8495	GOOD DAY FOR A HANGING	JURAN	COLUMBIA	1959
CPC-8496	IT HAPPENED TO JANE	QUINE	COLUMBIA	1959
CPC-8498	GENE KRUPA STORY	WEIS	COLUMBIA	1959
CPC-8500	CHASE		COLUMBIA	1958
CPC-8501	GUNS OF NAVARONE (UK)	THOMPSON	COLUMBIA	1961
CPC-8502	SONG WITHOUT END	VIDOR	COLUMBIA	1960
CPC-8503	THEY CAME TO CORDURA	ROSSEN	COLUMBIA	1959
CPC-8504	MOUNTAIN ROAD	MANN	COLUMBIA	1960
CPC-8506	RIDE LONESOME	BOETTICHER	COLUMBIA	1959
CPC-8507	SENIOR PROM	RICH	COLUMBIA	1958
CPC-8508	LET NO MAN WRITE MY EPITAPH	LEACOCK	COLUMBIA	1960
CPC-8511	I AIM AT THE STARS	THOMPSON	COLUMBIA	1960
CPC-8512	SURPRISE PACKAGE	DONEN	COLUMBIA	1960
CPC-8513	HEY BOY HEY GIRL	RICH	COLUMBIA	1959
CPC-8514	MAN ON A STRING	DE TOTH	COLUMBIA	1960
CPC-8515	MYSTERIOUS ISLAND (UK)	ENDFIELD	COLUMBIA	1962
CPC-8516	FACE OF A FUGITIVE	WENDKOS	COLUMBIA	1959
CPC-8518	WHO WAS THAT LADY?	SIDNEY	COLUMBIA	1960
CPC-8519	CRIMSON KIMONO	FULLER	COLUMBIA	1959
CPC-8520	LAST ANGRY MAN	MANN	COLUMBIA	1959
CPC-8525	DEVIL AT 4 O'CLOCK	LEROY	COLUMBIA	1961
CPC-8535	30 FOOT BRIDE OF CANDY ROCK	MILLER	COLUMBIA	1959
CPC-8536	MIDDLE OF THE NIGHT	MANN	COLUMBIA	1959
CPC-8539	STRANGERS WHEN WE MEET	QUINE	COLUMBIA	1960
CPC-8543	NOTORIOUS LANDLADY	QUINE	COLUMBIA	1962
CPC-8546	EDGE OF ETERNITY	SIEGEL	COLUMBIA	1959
CPC-8550	LEGEND OF TOM DOOLEY	POST	COLUMBIA	1959
CPC-8556	HAVE ROCKET WILL TRAVEL	RICH	COLUMBIA	1959
CPC-8557	COMANCHE STATION	BOETTICHER	COLUMBIA	1960

Movie Still Identification Book Ultimate Edition - Letters

CODE	TITLE/NAME	DIRECTOR/TYPE	STUDIO/DISTRIBUTOR	YEAR
CPC-8559	TINGLER	CASTLE	COLUMBIA	1959
CPC-8566	CRY FOR HAPPY	MARSHALL	COLUMBIA	1961
CPC-8569	BECAUSE THEY'RE YOUNG	WENDKOS	COLUMBIA	1960
CPC-8570	RAISIN IN THE SUN	PETRIE	COLUMBIA	1961
CPC-8572	ENEMY GENERAL	SHERMAN	COLUMBIA	1960
CPC-8573	ALL THE YOUNG MEN	BARTLETT	COLUMBIA	1960
CPC-8581	GIDGET GOES HAWAIIAN	WENDKOS	COLUMBIA	1961
CPC-8583	THIRTEEN GHOSTS	CASTLE	COLUMBIA	1960
CPC-8588	DIAMOND HEAD	GREEN	COLUMBIA	1963
CPC-8591	STOP, LOOK AND LAUGH	APPELL, BRANDT	COLUMBIA	1960
CPC-8594	HOMICIDAL	CASTLE	COLUMBIA	1961
CPC-8596	INTERNS	SWIFT	COLUMBIA	1962
CPC-8603	FIVE FINGER EXERCISE	MANN	COLUMBIA	1962
CPC-8610	MR. SARDONICUS	CASTLE	COLUMBIA	1961
CPC-8617	THREE STOOGES MEET HERCULES	BERNDS	COLUMBIA	1962
CPC-8624	EVERYTHING'S DUCKY	TAYLOR	COLUMBIA	1962
CPC-8625	BYE BYE BIRDIE	SIDNEY	COLUMBIA	1963
CPC-8626	EXPERIMENT IN TERROR	EDWARDS	COLUMBIA	1962
CPC-8629	WALK ON THE WILD SIDE	DYMTRYK	COLUMBIA	1962
CPC-8633	MAN FROM THE DINER'S CLUB	TASHLIN	COLUMBIA	1963
CPC-8634	LOVE HAS MANY FACES	SINGER	COLUMBIA	1965
CPC-8650	13 FRIGHTENED GIRLS	CASTLE	COLUMBIA	1963
CPC-8652	WILD WESTERNERS	RUDOLPH	COLUMBIA	1962
CPC-8657	DON'T KNOCK THE TWIST	RUDOLPH	COLUMBIA	1962
CPC-8666	THREE STOOGES IN ORBIT	BERNDS	COLUMBIA	1962
CPC-8689	KING RAT	FORBES	COLUMBIA	1965
CPC-8691	STRAIGHT-JACKET	CASTLE	COLUMBIA	1964
CPC-8692	NEW INTERNS	RICH	COLUMBIA	1964
CPC-8699	GOOD NEIGHBOR SAM	SWIFT	COLUMBIA	1964
CPC-8701	CAT BALLOU	SILVERSTEIN	COLUMBIA	1965
CPC-8705	3 STOOGES GO AROUND THE WORLD IN A DAZE	MAURER	COLUMBIA	1963
CPC-8709	BABY THE RAIN MUST FALL	MULLIGAN	COLUMBIA	1965
CPC-8712	PROFESSIONALS	BROOKS	COLUMBIA	1966
CPC-8715	MAJOR DUNDEE	PECKINPAH	COLUMBIA	1965
CPC-8719	COLLECTOR (UK)	WYLER	COLUMBIA	1965
CPC-8720	HEY THERE IT'S YOGI BEAR (t)	HANNA, BARBERA	COLUMBIA	1964
CPC-8722	LIFE BEGINS AT 17	DREIFUSS	COLUMBIA	1958
CPC-8724	QUICK GUN	SALKOW	COLUMBIA	1964
CPC-8731	OUTLAWS IS COMING	MAURER	COLUMBIA	1965
CPC-8732	RIDE THE WILD SURF	TAYLOR	COLUMBIA	1964
CPC-8741	SILENCERS	KARLSON	COLUMBIA	1966
CPC-8744	ALVAREZ KELLY	DMYTRYK	COLUMBIA	1966
CPC-8755	WALK DON'T RUN	WALTERS	COLUMBIA	1966
CPC-8761	ARIZONA RAIDERS	WITNEY	COLUMBIA	1965
CPC-8802	RIDE BEYOND VENGEANCE	MCEVEETY	COLUMBIA	1966
CPC-8817	THREE ON A COUCH	LEWIS	COLUMBIA	1966
CPC-8818	BIRDS DO IT	MARTON	COLUMBIA	1966
CPC-8826	RAGE	GAZCON	COLUMBIA	1966
CPC-AK	ASSIGNMENT K (UK)	GUEST	COLUMBIA	1968
CPC-AR	SEVERED HEAD (UK)	CLEMENT	COLUMBIA	1970
CPC-B	BERSERK (UK)	O'CONNELLY	COLUMBIA	1967
CPC-BC	BUTTERCUP CHAIN (UK)	MILLER	COLUMBIA	1970
CPC-BWC	BEFORE WINTER COMES (UK)	THOMPSON	COLUMBIA	1969
CPC-CF	CACTUS FLOWER	SAKS	COLUMBIA	1969
CPC-CK	CASTLE KEEP	POLLACK	COLUMBIA	1969
CPC-CR	CASINO ROYALE	FELDMAN	COLUMBIA	1967
CPC-CROM	CROMWELL (UK)	HUGHES	COLUMBIA	1970
CPC-D	DUFFY (UK)	PARRISH	COLUMBIA	1968
CPC-DA	DANDY IN ASPIC (UK)	MANN	COLUMBIA	1968
CPC-DA	DEADLY AFFAIR	LUMET	COLUMBIA	1966
CPC-DBR	DON'T RAISE THE BRIDGE, LOWER THE RIVER (UK)	PARIS	COLUMBIA	1968
CPC-DF	DOCTOR FAUSTUS (UK)	BURTON, COGHILL	COLUMBIA	1967
CPC-EX	EXECUTIONER (UK)	WANAMAKER	COLUMBIA	1970
CPC-FG	FUNNY GIRL	WYLER	COLUMBIA	1968
CPC-FF	FRAGMENT OF FEAR (UK)	SARAFIAN	COLUMBIA	1970
CPC-GD	GUESS WHO'S COMING FOR DINNER	KRAMER	COLUMBIA	1967
CPC-GG	GEORGY GIRL (UK)	NARIZZANO	COLUMBIA	1966
CPC GS	GREENGAGE SUMMER (UK)	GILBERT	COLUMBIA	1961
CPC-H	HAMLET (UK)	RICHARDSON	COLUMBIA	1969
CPC-H	HAMMERHEAD (UK)	MILLER	COLUMBIA	1968

Movie Still Identification Book Ultimate Edition - Letters

CODE	TITLE/NAME	DIRECTOR/TYPE	STUDIO/DISTRIBUTOR	YEAR
CP-CIC	BROTHERHOOD OF SATAN	MCEVEETY	COLUMBIA	1970
CPC-KL	KING LEAR (UK)	BROOK	COLUMBIA	1971
CPC-LBJ	LIBERATION OF LB JONES	WYLER	COLUMBIA	1970
CPC-LGW	LOOKING GLASS WAR (UK)	PIERSON	COLUMBIA	1969
CPC-CLK	CLAIRE'S KNEE (FR: LE GENOU DE CLAIRE 1970)	ROHMER	COLUMBIA	1971
CPC-MDM	MOST DANGEROUS MAN ALIVE	DWAN	COLUMBIA	1961
CPC-MFAS	MAN FOR ALL SEASONS (UK)	ZINNEMANN	COLUMBIA	1967
CPC MMS	MIND OF MR. SOAMES	COOKE	COLUMBIA	1970
CPC MR	MAD ROOM	GIRARD	COLUMBIA	1968
CPC MS	MODEL SHOP	DEMY	COLUMBIA	1969
CPC-NOG	NIGHT OF THE GENERALS (UK)	LITVAK	COLUMBIA	1967
CPC-O	OLIVER! (UK)	REED	COLUMBIA	1968
CPC-O	OTLEY (UK)	CLEMENT	COLUMBIA	1969
CPC-OM	ONCE MORE, WITH FEELING! (UK)	DONEN	COLUMBIA	1960
CPCP	COTTONPICKIN' CHICKENPICKERS	JACKSON	SOUTHEASTERN PICTURES	1967
CPC-R	RECKONING (UK)	GOLD	COLUMBIA	1970
CPC-RH	REQUIEM FOR A HEAVYWEIGHT	NELSON	COLUMBIA	1962
CPC-SS	SOUTHERN STAR (UK)	HAYERS	COLUMBIA	1969
CPC-T	RING-A-DING RHYTHM! (UK: IT'S TRAD, DAD!)	LESTER	COLUMBIA	1962
CPC-TC	30 IS A DANGEROUS AGE, CYNTHIA (UK)	MCGRATH	COLUMBIA	1968
CPC-TG	TORTURE GARDEN (UK)	FRANCIS	COLUMBIA	1967
CPC-TMO	TIGER MAKES OUT	HILLER	COLUMBIA	1967
CPC-TSWL	TO SIR, WITH LOVE (UK)	CLAVELL	COLUMBIA	1967
CPC-TVM	THANK YOU ALL VERY MUCH	HUSSEIN	COLUMBIA	1969
CPC-TYM	THANK YOU ALL VERY MUCH (UK: TOUCH OF LOVE)	HUSSEIN	COLUMBIA	1969
CPC-WB	WRONG BOX (UK)	FORBES	COLUMBIA	1966
CPC-WC	RUN WILD, RUN FREE (UK)	SARAFIAN	COLUMBIA	1969
CPC-WM	WATERMELON MAN	VAN PEEBLES	COLUMBIA	1970
CPC-YCW	YOU CAN'T WIN 'EM ALL (UK)	COLLINSON	COLUMBIA	1970
CPD	CLEAR AND PRESENT DANGER	NOYCE	PARAMOUNT	1994
CP-DLB	DIRTY LITTLE BILLY	DRAGOTI	COLUMBIA	1972
CP-FEP	FIVE EASY PIECES	RAFELSON	COLUMBIA	1970
CP-GB	GO-BETWEEN (UK)	LOSEY	COLUMBIA	1971
CP-GVS	GOLDEN VOYAGE OF SINBAD	HESSLER	COLUMBIA	1974
CP-LD	LAST DETAIL	ASHBY	COLUMBIA	1973
CP-LH	LOST HORIZON	JARROTT	COLUMBIA	1973
CP-LOF	LORDS OF FLATBUSH	DAVIDSON, VERONA	COLUMBIA	1974
CP-NA	NICHOLAS AND ALEXANDRA	SCHAFFNER	COLUMBIA	1971
CP-OF	ODESSA FILE	NEAME	COLUMBIA	1974
CP-SK	STONE KILLER	WINNER	COLUMBIA	1973
CP/SW	SNAKE WOMAN (UK)	FURIE	UNITED ARTISTS	1961
CP-TGS	THERE'S A GIRL IN MY SOUP (UK)	BOULTING	COLUMBIA	1970
CP-VP	VALACCI PAPERS	CROMWELL	UNITED ARTISTS	1944
CP-WWW	WAY WE WERE	POLLACK	COLUMBIA	1973
CQ	CATTLE QUEEN OF MONTANA	DWAN	RKO	1954
CR	ANGEL ON MY SHOULDER	MAYO	UNITED ARTISTS	1946
CR	CASINO ROYALE (UK)	GUEST, HUGHES	COLUMBIA	1967
CR	CHAIN REACTION	DAVIS	20th CENTURY FOX	1996
CR	CHAPLIN REVIEW		UNITED ARTISTS	1972
CR	CHARLES R. ROGERS PRODUCTIONS	studio	UNITED ARTISTS	
CR	CHARLES RAY	portrait		
CR	CLAUDE RAINS	portrait	UNIV	
CR	COPS AND ROBBERS	AVAKIAN	UNITED ARTISTS	1973
CR	CRAIG REYNOLDS	portrait	RKO	mid 1940s
CR	CRAZE	FRANCIS	WARNER BROS	1974
CR	CRIMSON ROMANCE	HOWARD	MASCOT	1934
CR	CROOKED ROAD (UK)	CHAFFEY	GALA	1965
CR	CROSS PLOT (UK)	RAKOFF	UNITED ARTISTS	1969
CR	CRUISING	FRIEDKIN	UNITED ARTISTS	1980
CR	CYCLONE RANGER	HILLER	SPECTRUM	1935
CR	DELIGHTFULLY DANGEROUS	LUBIN	UNITED ARTISTS	1945
CR	FABULOUS DORSEYS	GREEN	UNITED ARTISTS	1947
CR	HEARTBREAK RIDGE (FR: CREVECOEUR)	DUPONT	TUDOR	1955
CR	LAW OF THE UNDERWORLD	LANDERS	RKO	1938
CR	MASTER OF BANKDAM/CROWTHERS OF BANKDAM* (UK)	FORDE	EAGLE-LION	1947
CR	POWERS GIRL	MCLEOD	UNITED ARTISTS	1943
CR	SANDERS OF THE RIVER/CONGO RAID* (UK)	KORDA	UNITED ARTISTS	1935
CR	SONG OF THE OPEN ROAD	SIMON	UNITED ARTISTS	1944
CR	YOU CAN'T GET AWAY WITH MURDER	SEILER	WARNER BROS	1939
CRISP	DONALD CRISP	portrait	WARNER BROS.	

Movie Still Identification Book Ultimate Edition - Letters

CODE	TITLE/NAME	DIRECTOR/TYPE	STUDIO/DISTRIBUTOR	YEAR
CRM	CASE OF THE RED MONKEY (UK: LITTLE RED MONKEY)	HUGHES	MONOGRAM	1955
CROM	CROMWELL	HUGHES	COLUMBIA	1970
CROS-1	WEEK ENDS ONLY	CROSLAND	FOX FILM	1932
CR-P	POWERS GIRL (SCENES)	MCLEOD	UNITED ARTISTS	1943
CR-T	POWERS GIRL (pubs + portraits)	MCLEOD	UNITED ARTISTS	1943
CR-X	POWERS GIRL (pubs + portraits)	MCLEOD	UNITED ARTISTS	1943
CS	BATTLE OF THE SEXES (UK)	CRICHTON	CONTINENTAL	1960
CS	CALIFORNIA SPLIT	ALTMAN	COLUMBIA	1974
CS	CALIFORNIA SUITE	ROSS	COLUMBIA	1978
CS	CAPTAIN SCARLETT	CARR	UNITED ARTISTS	1953
CS	CAST A LONG SHADOW	CARR	UNITED ARTISTS	1959
CS	CHINA SKY	ENRIGHT	RKO	1945
CS	CHINA SYNDROME	BRIDGES	COLUMBIA	1979
CS	CHOSEN SURVIVORS	ROLEY	COLUMBIA	1974
CS	COAST OF SKELETONS (UK)	LYNN	SEVEN ARTS	1965
CS	COLDITZ STORY (UK)	HAMILTON	DCA	1955
CS	CONFESSIONS OF A NAZI SPY	LITVAK	WARNER BROS	1939
CS	CONNIE STEVENS	portrait		
CS	CONVICT STAGE	SELANDER	20th CENTURY FOX	1965
CS	COPPER SKIES	WARREN	20th CENTURY FOX	1957
CS	CRAIG STEVENS	portrait	WARNER BROS	
CS	CRIME SCHOOL	SEILER	WARNER BROS	1938
CS	CROOKED SKY (UK)	CASS	TUDOR	1957
CS	GOING HIGHBROW	FLOREY	WARNER BROS	1935
CSB	CRIME SCHOOL BOYS*		WARNER BROS	
CSG	CONFESSIONS OF SORORITY GIRL		AIP	1957
CSH	CURSE OF THE STONE HAND	CHRISTENSEN, WARREN	ADP	1965
CSL	NEVER A DULL MOMENT	MARSHALL	RKO	1950
CSM	WHAT A BLONDE	GOODWINS	RKO	1945
CT	CARETAKERS	BARTLETT	UNITED ARTISTS	1963
CT	CARIBOO TRAIL	MARIN	20th CENTURY FOX	1950
CT	CAROL THURSTON	portrait	RKO	
CT	CHINATOWN	POLANSKI	PARAMOUNT	1974
CT	CLAIRE TREVOR	portrait	RKO, REPUBLIC, UNIVERSAL	
CT	CLAIRE TREVOR	portrait	WARNER BROS	
CT	CLAUDETTE THORNTON	portrait		
CT	COLD TURKEY	LEAR	UNITED ARTISTS	1971
CT	COME TOGETHER (IT)	ANTHONY, SWIMMER	MONOGRAM	1971
CT	CONSPIRACY THEORY	DONNER	WARNER BROS	1997
CT	CONSTANCE TALMADGE (AND FILM COMPANY)	portrait	FN, UA, WARNER BROS	
CT	CONWAY TEARLE	portrait		
CT	CRIME RING	GOODWINS	RKO	1938
CTC	CONSTANTINE AND THE CROSS	DE FELICE	EMBASSY	1961
CS	CRUEL SEA (UK)	FREND	UNIVERSAL	1953
CS	CRY FROM THE STREETS (UK)	GILBERT	TUDOR	1958
CS	CUL-DE-SAC (UK)	POLANSKI	COMPTON	1966
CT	CANTERBURY TALE (UK)	POWELL, PRESSBURGER	EAGLE-LION	1944
CT	CHRISTMAS TREE (UK)	CLARK	CHILDREN'S FILM FOUND.	1966
CT	COMMON TOUCH (UK)	BAXTER	ANGLO-AMERICAN	1941
CT	CROOK'S TOUR (UK)	BAXTER	ANGLO-AMERICAN	1941
CT	CRY TOUGH	STANLEY	UNITED ARTISTS	1959
CT	GUEST (UK: CARETAKER)	DONNER	JANUS	1963
CT	IT ALL CAME TRUE	SEILER	WARNER BROS.	1940
CT	TINTAN CONTRA EL HOMBRE LOBO (MEX)	SOLARES	PELMEX	1964
CT-3	STUDIO GIRL	GIBLYN	SELECT	1918
CT-6	GOOD NIGHT, PAUL	EDWARDS	SELECT	1918
CT-10	MRS. LEFFINGWELL'S BOOTS	EDWARDS	SELECT	1918
CT-14	PRIMITIVE LOVER	FRANKLIN	ASSOCIATED FIRST NATIONAL	1922
CT 14	SLEEPING PORCH	PEARCE	PARAMOUNT	1929
CT-15	EAST IS WEST	FRANKLIN	ASSOCIATED FIRST NATIONAL	1922
CT-17	DANGEROUS MAID	HEERMAN	ASSOCIATED FIRST NATIONAL	1923
CT-18	GOLDFISH	STORM	WARNER BROS	1924
CT-19	ONE NIGHT OF ROMANCE	FRANKLIN	FIRST NATIONAL	1924
CT-20	LEARNING TO LOVE	FRANKLIN	WARNER BROS	1926
CT-23	VENUS OF VENICE	NEILAN	WARNER BROS	1927
CT-35	HER SISTER FROM PARIS	FRANKLIN	FIRST NATIONAL	1925
CT-36	DUCHESS OF BUFFALO	FRANKLIN	FIRST NATIONAL	1926
CT-300	BREAKFAST AT SUNRISE	ST. CLAIR	WARNER BROS	1927
CT-3543A	THIN LINE BETWEEN LOVE AND HATE	LAWRENCE	NEW LINE CINEMA	1996
CTBB	COCKTAIL	DONALDSON	BUENA VISTA	1988

Movie Still Identification Book Ultimate Edition - Letters

CODE	TITLE/NAME	DIRECTOR/TYPE	STUDIO/DISTRIBUTOR	YEAR
CTW	CODE OF THE WEST	BERKE	RKO	1947
CU	CONDUCT UNBECOMING	ANDERSON	ALLIED ARTISTS	1975
CU	CRACKUP	REIS	RKO	1946
CU	GERT AND DAISY CLEAN UP (UK)	ROGERS	BUTCHER'S	1942
CUBE	BIG CUBE	DAVISON	WARNER BROS	1969
CUF	COURAGE UNDER FIRE	ZWICK	20th CENTURY FOX	1996
CUM-4	COUNTRY BEYOND	CUMMINGS	FOX FILM	1926
CUM-5	BERTHA THE SEWING MACHINE GIRL	CUMMINGS	FOX FILM	1926
CUM-6	DRESSED TO KILL	CUMMINGS	FOX FILM	1928
CUM-8	ROMANCE OF THE UNDERWORLD	CUMMINGS	FOX FILM	1928
CUM-9	NOT QUITE DECENT	CUMMINGS	FOX FILM	1929
CUM-10	BEHIND THAT CURTAIN	CUMMINGS	FOX FILM	1929
CUM-11	CAMEO KIRBY	CUMMINGS	FOX FILM	1930
CUM-12	ON THE LEVEL	CUMMINGS	FOX FILM	1930
CUM-13	A DEVIL WITH WOMEN	CUMMINGS	FOX FILM	1930
CUM-14	A HOLY TERROR	CUMMINGS	FOX FILM	1931
CUM-15	CISCO KID	CUMMINGS	FOX FILM	1931
CUMMINGS-3	MIDNIGHT KISS	CUMMINGS	FOX FILM	1926
CURWOOD-2	GOLD HUNTERS	HURST	DAVIS DISTRIBUTING	1925
CV	CODE 7, VICTIM 5 (UK: VICTIM 5)	LYNN	COLUMBIA	1964
CV	CONRAD VEIDT	portrait	GAUMONT BRITISH	1930s
CV	CURSE OF THE VAMPIRES (SP)	ELORRIETA	HEMISPHERE	1971
CV	CURSE OF THE VOODOO (VOODOO BLOOD BATH)	SHONTEFF	MONOGRAM	1965
CV	NATIONAL LAMPOON'S CHRISTMAS VACATION	CHECHIK	WARNER BROS	1989
CW	CAPTIVE WOMEN	GILMORE	RKO	1952
CW	CAROLE WELLS	portrait	UNIV	
CW	CHALLENGE THE WILD	GRAHAM	UNITED ARTISTS	1954
CW	CHARLOTTE'S WEB (t)	NICHOLS, TAKAMOTO	PARAMOUNT	1973
CW	CHILD IS WAITING	CASSAVETES	UNITED ARTISTS	1963
CW	CHILDREN OF THE WILD (TOPA TOPA 1938)	HUTCHISON, MOORE	GRAND	R39
CW	CHILI WILLIAMS	portrait	RKO	
CW	CHILL WILLS	portrait	UNIVERSAL	1940s-50s
CW	CIRCUS WORLD	HATHAWAY	PARAMOUNT	1965
CW	CLAIRE WINDSOR	portrait	METRO-GOLDWYN	
CW	CLINT WALKER	portrait	WARNER BROS	
CW	COLLEGE WIDOW	MAYO	WARNER BROS	1927
CW	CONDEMNED WOMEN	LANDERS	RKO	1938
CW	CONFESSIONS OF A WINDOW CLEANER	GUEST	COLUMBIA	1974
CW	CONSTANCE WORTH	portrait	RKO	1930s-40s
CW	CORNEL WILDE	portrait	RKO	1950s
CW	CRAWFORD WEAVER	portrait	RKO	
CW	CUSTER OF THE WEST (UK)	SIODMAK	CINERAMA	1967
CW	CUTTER'S WAY (CUTTER AND BONE)	PASSER	UNITED ARTISTS	1981
CW	IN SEARCH OF THE CASTAWAYS	STEVENSON	BUENA VISTA	1962
CW	SNOW TREASURE	JACOBY	ALLIED ARTISTS	1968
CW	SOUTHWEST PASSAGE (CAMELS WEST)	NAZARRO	UNITED ARTISTS	1954
CW-C	CHARLOTTE'S WEB (t)	NICHOLS, TAKAMOTO	PARAMOUNT	1973
CWF	CREATURES THE WORLD FORGOT	CHAFFEY	COLUMBIA	1971
CX	COVER GIRL KILLER	BISHOP	FANFARE	1960
CXB	CHARLES BICKFORD	portrait	MGM	
CXM	CONCHITA MONTENEGRO	portrait	MGM	
CY	CARELESS YEARS	HILLER	UNITED ARTISTS	1957
CY	CAROL YORKE	portrait	UNIVERSAL	late 40s
CY	CLIFTON YOUNG	portrait	WARNER BROS	
CY	COMIN AT YA! (IT)	BALDI	FILMWAYS	1981
CY	CONVOY	PECKINPAH	UNITED ARTISTS	1978
CY	CYBORG	PYUN	CANNON	1989
CZ	CEILING ZERO	HAWKS	WARNER BROS	1936
D	DAMES	BERKELEY, ENRIGHT	WARNER BROS	1934
D	DARLING	SCHLESINGER	WARNER BROS -PATHE (UK)	1965
D	DEMENTIA 13	COPPOLA	AIP	1963
D	DEMOBBED (UK)	BLAKELEY	BUTCHER'S	1946
D	DESPERADOES	VIDOR	COLUMBIA	1943
D	DESPERADOS ARE IN TOWN	NEWMANN	20th CENTURY FOX	1956
D	DEVOTION	BERNHARDT	WARNER BROS	1946
D	DINGAKA	UYS	EMBASSY	1965
D	DINKY	BRETHERTON, LEDERMAN	WARNER BROS	1935
D	DISCLOSURE	LEVINSON	WARNER BROS	1994
D	DISRAELI	GREEN	WARNER BROS	1929
D	DIXIANNA	REED	RKO	1930

Movie Still Identification Book Ultimate Edition - Letters

CODE	TITLE/NAME	DIRECTOR/TYPE	STUDIO/DISTRIBUTOR	YEAR
D	DREAMING (UK)	BAXTER	EALING	1944
D	DREAMS (SWE: KVINNODROM)	BERGMAN	JANUS	1955
D	DRIVE-IN	AMATEAU	COLUMBIA	1976
D	DUELLISTS	SCOTT	PARAMOUNT	1977
D	DUFFY	PARRISH	COLUMBIA	1968
D	DUMBO (t)	ARMSTRONG, FERGUSON	RKO	1941
D	DUTCHMAN (UK)	HARVEY	CONTINENTAL	1967
D	HEAVEN KNOWS, MR ALLISON	HUSTON	20th CENTURY FOX	1957
D	LES DIABOLIQUES	CLOUZOT	UNITED	1955
D	LOVER OF CAMILLE	BEAUMONT	WARNER BROS	1924
D	MAGNIFICENT MATADOR	BOETTICHER	20th CENTURY FOX	1955
D	THUNDERGATE	DE GRASSE	WARNER BROS	1923
D	TREACHERY ON THE HIGH SEAS (UK)	REINERT	FILM ALLIANCE	1936
D&B	DEAD AND BURIED	SHERMAN	AVCO EMBASSY	1981
D-1	COUNSEL FOR CRIME	BRAHM	COLUMBIA	1937
D-1	FOR ART'S SAKE (sh)	CHASE	PATHE EXCHANGE	1923
D1	KILL ME TOMORROW (UK)	FISHER	TUDOR	1957
D-1	TROLLEY TROUBLES (sh)	GOULDING	PATHE EXCHANGE	1921
D-1	UNNAMED ROLIN PROJECT (sh)	WHITING	PATHE EXCHANGE	1915
D-1	WHAT EVERY ICEMAN KNOWS (sh)	YATES, MCCAREY	MGM	1927
D-2	CALL OF THE CUCKOOS (sh)	BRUCKMAN	MGM	1927
D-2	MURDER IN GREENWICH VILLAGE	ROGELL	COLUMBIA	1937
D-2	ROUGH SEAS (sh)	GOULDING	PATHE EXCHANGE	1921
D-2	UNNAMED ROLIN PROJECT (sh)	WHITING	PATHE EXCHANGE	1915
D-2	WHITE WINGS (sh)	JESKE	PATHE EXCHANGE	1923
D3	CRIMSON RUNNER (VIENNESE MADNESS*)	FORMAN	PDC	1925
D-3	DODGE YOUR DEBTS (sh)	KENTON	PATHE EXCHANGE	1921
D-3	LOVE 'EM AND FEED 'EM (sh)	BRUCKMAN	MGM	1927
D-3	PICK AND SHOVEL (sh)	JESKE	PATHE EXCHANGE	1923
D-3	UNNAMED ROLIN PROJECT (sh)	WHITING	PATHE EXCHANGE	1915
D-3	YELLOW STAIN	DILLION	FOX FILM	1922
D-4	BROKEN BLOSSOMS	GRIFFITH	UNITED ARTISTS	1919
D-4	FIGHTING FATHERS (sh)	GUIOL	MGM	1927
D-4	FRESH EGGS (sh)	HOWE	PATHE EXCHANGE	1923
D-4	LIFE BEGINS WITH LOVE	MCCAREY	COLUMBIA	1937
D-4	ZERO HERO (sh)	KENTON	PATHE EXCHANGE	1921
D-5	KILL OR CURE (sh)	PEMBROKE	PATHE EXCHANGE	1923
D-5	LUCKY NUMBER (sh)	KENTON	PATHE EXCHANGE	1921
D-5	TELL IT TO THE JUDGE (sh)	MCCAREY, YATES	MGM	1928
D-6	FINGER PRINTS (sh)	CEDER	PATHE EXCHANGE	1923
D6	HELL SHIP	DUNLAP	FOX FILM	1920
D-6	PASS THE GRAVY (sh)	GUIOL, MCCAREY	MGM	1928
D-6	SHE MARRIED AN ARTIST	GERING	COLUMBIA	1937
D-7	COLLARS AND CUFFS (sh)	JESKE	PATHE EXCHANGE	1923
D-7	DUMB DADDIES (sh)	YATES	MGM	1928
D-7	HER ELEPHANT MAN	DUNLAP	FOX FILM	1920
D-8	CAME THE DAWN (sh)	HEATH, MCCAREY	MGM	1928
D-8	LIVE WIRES (sh)	HOWE	PATHE EXCHANGE	1923
D-9	BLOW BY BLOW (sh)	MCCAREY	MGM	1928
D-9	GAS AND AIR (sh)	PEMBROKE	PATHE EXCHANGE	1923
D-9	LITTLE MISS ROUGHNECK	SCOTTO	COLUMBIA	1938
D9	PROUD VALLEY (UK)	TENNYSON	SUPREME	1940
D-10	(sh)	CEDER	PATHE EXCHANGE	1923
D-10	NO TIME TO MARRY	LACHMAN	COLUMBIA	1938
D-10	SHOULD WOMEN DRIVE? (sh)	MCCAREY	MGM	1928
D-11	FOR GUESTS ONLY (sh)	HOWE	PATHE EXCHANGE	1923
D-12	IRON RIDER	DUNLAP	FOX FILM	1920
D-12	ORANGES AND LEMONS (sh)	JESKE	PATHE EXCHANGE	1923
D-12	PENITENTIARY	BRAHM	COLUMBIA	1938
D-13	CHEATER REFORMED	DUNLAP	FOX FILM	1920
D-13	TAKE THE AIR (sh)	CEDER	PATHE EXCHANGE	1923
D-14	SHORT ORDERS (sh)	PEMBROKE	PATHE EXCHANGE	1923
D-15	SAVE THE SHIP (sh)	JESKE, ROACH	PATHE EXCHANGE	1923
D-15	THERE'S ALWAYS A WOMAN	HALL	COLUMBIA	1938
D-16	UNCOVERED WAGON (sh)	HOWE	PATHE EXCHANGE	1923
D-16	YOU CAN'T TAKE IT WITH YOU	CAPRA	COLUMBIA	1938
D-17	HOLIDAY	CUKOR	COLUMBIA	1938
D-17	MAN ABOUT TOWN (sh)	JESKE	PATHE EXCHANGE	1923
D-18	NO PETS (sh)	HOWE	PATHE EXCHANGE	1923
D-19	CITY STREETS (CITY SHADOWS*)	ROGELL	COLUMBIA	1938

Movie Still Identification Book Ultimate Edition - Letters

CODE	TITLE/NAME	DIRECTOR/TYPE	STUDIO/DISTRIBUTOR	YEAR
D-19	SCORCHING SANDS (sh)	WILLIAMSON, ROACH	PATHE EXCHANGE	1923
D-20	GIRL'S SCHOOL	BRAHM	COLUMBIA	1938
D-20	KNOCKOUT (sh)	POWERS	PATHE EXCHANGE	1923
D-21	I AM THE LAW	HALL	COLUMBIA	1938
D-21	JOIN THE CIRCUS (sh)	JESKE	PATHE EXCHANGE	1923
D-22	WHOLE TRUTH (sh)	CEDER	PATHE EXCHANGE	1923
D-23	GO WEST (sh)	POWERS	PATHE EXCHANGE	1923
D-23	LADY OBJECTS	KENTON	COLUMBIA	1938
D-24	DEAR OLD PAL (sh)		PATHE EXCHANGE	1923
D-24	FLIGHT TO FAME	COLEMAN	COLUMBIA	1938
D-25	I'LL TAKE ROMANCE	GRIFFITH	COLUMBIA	1937
D-25	LOVEY-DOVEY (sh)	POWERS	PATHE EXCHANGE	1923
D-26	GET BUSY (sh)	HAYES	PATHE EXCHANGE	1924
D-27	OLD WAR HORSE (sh)	JESKE	PATHE EXCHANGE	1926
D-28	AT FIRST SIGHT (sh)	ROACH	PATHE EXCHANGE	1924
D-28	THERE'S THAT WOMAN AGAIN	HALL	COLUMBIA	1939
D-29	IT'S A JOY (IT'S A BOY) (sh)	JESKE	PATHE EXCHANGE	1923
D-29	LITTLE ADVENTURESS	LEDERMAN	COLUMBIA	1938
D-30	BAR-FLY (sh)	POWERS	PATHE EXCHANGE	1924
D-30	BLONDIE	STRAYER	COLUMBIA	1938
D-31	FULLY INSURED (sh)	JESKE	PATHE EXCHANGE	1923
D-31	SMASHING THE SPY RING	CABANNE	COLUMBIA	1939
D-32	FRIEND HUSBAND (WHY MARRY?) (sh)	HOWE	PATHE EXCHANGE	1924
D-32	LADY AND THE MOB	STOLOFF	COLUMBIA	1939
D-33	BIG IDEA (sh)	JESKE	PATHE EXCHANGE	1924
D-33	LONE WOLF SPY HUNT	GODFREY	COLUMBIA	1939
D-34	MAN PAYS (sh)	POWERS	PATHE EXCHANGE	1924
D-35	PERFECT LADY (sh)	PARROTT	PATHE EXCHANGE	1924
D-36	ONLY ANGELS HAVE WINGS	HAWKS	COLUMBIA	1939
D-36	POWDER AND SMOKE (sh)	PARROTT	PATHE EXCHANGE	1924
D-37	COAST GUARD	LUDWIG	COLUMBIA	1939
D-37	ONE OF THE FAMILY (sh)	PEMBROKE	PATHE EXCHANGE	1924
D-38	LOVE'S REWARD (sh)	POWERS	PATHE EXCHANGE	1924
D-38	ROMANCE OF THE REDWOODS	VIDOR	COLUMBIA	1939
D-39	BLONDIE MEETS THE BOSS	STRAYER	COLUMBIA	1939
D-39	JUST A MINUTE (sh)	PARROTT	PATHE EXCHANGE	1924
D-40	GOLDEN BOY	MAMOULIAN	COLUMBIA	1939
D-40	LOVE'S DETOUR (sh)	PARROTT	PATHE EXCHANGE	1924
D-41	BLIND ALLEY	VIDOR	COLUMBIA	1939
D-41	OUR LITTLE NELL (sh)	POWERS	PATHE EXCHANGE	1924
D-42	GOOD GIRLS GO TO PARIS	HALL	COLUMBIA	1939
D-42	HARD KNOCKS (sh)	PARROTT	PATHE EXCHANGE	1924
D-43	MR. SMITH GOES TO WASHINGTON	CAPRA	COLUMBIA	1939
D-43	NORTH OF 50-50 (sh)	POWERS	PATHE EXCHANGE	1924
D-44	DON'T FORGET (sh)	PARROTT	PATHE EXCHANGE	1924
D-45	BLONDIE TAKES A VACATION	STRAYER	COLUMBIA	1939
D-45	FRAIDY CAT (sh)	PARROTT	PATHE EXCHANGE	1924
D-46	FIVE LITTLE PEPPERS AND HOW THEY GREW	BARTON	COLUMBIA	1939
D-46	UP AND AT 'EM (sh)	POWERS	PATHE EXCHANGE	1924
D-47	PUBLICITY PAYS (sh)	MCCAREY	PATHE EXCHANGE	1924
D-47	THOSE HIGH GRAY WALLS	VIDOR	COLUMBIA	1939
D-48	POSITION WANTED (sh)	CEDER	PATHE EXCHANGE	1924
D-49	BEWARE SPOOKS	SEDGWICK	COLUMBIA	1939
D-49	BIG KICK (sh)	GUIOL, ROACH	PATHE EXCHANGE	1925
D-50	ONE AT A TIME (sh)	CEDER	PATHE EXCHANGE	1924
D-51	BLONDIE BRINGS UP BABY	STRAYER	COLUMBIA	1939
D-51	BOUNCER (sh)	CEDER, GUIOL	PATHE EXCHANGE	1925
D-52	APRIL FOOL (sh)	CEDER	PATHE EXCHANGE	1924
D-52	ARIZONA	RUGGLES	COLUMBIA	1940
D-53	SCANDAL SHEET	GRINDE	COLUMBIA	1939
D-53	SOLID IVORY (sh)	CEDER	PATHE EXCHANGE	1925
D-54	AMAZING MR. WILLIAMS	HALL	COLUMBIA	1939
D-54	STOLEN GOODS (sh)	MCCAREY	PATHE EXCHANGE	1924
D-55	BEFORE TAKING (sh)	CEDER	PATHE EXCHANGE	1924
D-55	CAFE HOSTESS	SALKOW	COLUMBIA	1940
D-56	MY SON IS GUILTY	BARTON	COLUMBIA	1939
D-56	YOUNG OLDFIELD (sh)	MCCAREY	PATHE EXCHANGE	1924
D-57	FAST BLACK (sh)	GARNETT	PATHE EXCHANGE	1924
D-57	MILITARY ACADEMY	LEDERMAN	COLUMBIA	1940
D-58	FIVE LITTLE PEPPERS AT HOME	BARTON	COLUMBIA	1940

Movie Still Identification Book Ultimate Edition - Letters

CODE	TITLE/NAME	DIRECTOR/TYPE	STUDIO/DISTRIBUTOR	YEAR
D-58	JEFFRIES JR. (sh)	MCCAREY	PATHE EXCHANGE	1924
D-59	RIDER OF THE KITCHEN RANGE (sh)	GARNETT, JESKE	PATHE EXCHANGE	1925
D-60	WHY HUSBANDS GO MAD (sh)	MCCAREY	PATHE EXCHANGE	1924
D-61	ALL WOOL (sh)	GARNETT	PATHE EXCHANGE	1925
D-62	SEEING NELLIE HOME (sh)	MCCAREY	PATHE EXCHANGE	1924
D-63	GRIEF OF BAGDAD (SHEIKS IN BAGDAD) (sh)	LEDERMAN	PATHE EXCHANGE	1925
D-64	TEN MINUTE EGG (sh)	MCCAREY	PATHE EXCHANGE	1924
D-65	ACCIDENTAL ACCIDENTS (sh)	MCCAREY	PATHE EXCHANGE	1924
D-66	(sh)BIG RED RIDING HOOD	MCCAREY	PATHE EXCHANGE	1925
D-67	BIG WEDNESDAY	MILIUS	WARNER BROS	1978
D-67	WHY MEN WORK (sh)	MCCAREY	PATHE EXCHANGE	1924
D-68	SWEET DADDY (sh)	MCCAREY	PATHE EXCHANGE	1924
D-69	OUTDOOR PAJAMAS (sh)	MCCAREY	PATHE EXCHANGE	1924
D-70	SITTIN' PRETTY (sh)	MCCAREY	PATHE EXCHANGE	1924
D-71	TOO MANY MAMMAS (sh)	MCCAREY	PATHE EXCHANGE	1924
D-72	BUNGALOW BOOBS (sh)	MCCAREY	PATHE EXCHANGE	1924
D-73	ALL WET (sh)	MCCAREY	PATHE EXCHANGE	1924
D-74	POOR FISH (sh)	MCCAREY	PATHE EXCHANGE	1924
D-75	ROYAL RAZZ (sh)	MCCAREY	PATHE EXCHANGE	1924
D-76	RAT'S KNUCKLES (sh)	MCCAREY	PATHE EXCHANGE	1925
D-77	HELLO BABY (sh)	MCCAREY	PATHE EXCHANGE	1925
D-78	FIGHTING FLUID (sh)	MCCAREY	PATHE EXCHANGE	1925
D-79	FAMILY ENTRANCE (sh)	MCCAREY	PATHE EXCHANGE	1925
D-80	SHOULD HUSBANDS BE WATCHED? (sh)	MCCAREY	PATHE EXCHANGE	1925
D-81	PLAIN AND FANCY GIRLS (sh)	MCCAREY	PATHE EXCHANGE	1925
D-82	IS MARRIAGE THE BUNK? (sh)	MCCAREY	PATHE EXCHANGE	1925
D-83	HOLD EVERYTHING (sh)	GUIOL, MCCAREY	PATHE EXCHANGE	1925
D-84	ARE HUSBANDS HUMAN? (sh)	BARROWS	PATHE EXCHANGE	1925
D-85	SURE MIKE (sh)	GUIOL	PATHE EXCHANGE	1925
D-86	TOL'ABLE ROMEO (sh)	ROBBINS	PATHE EXCHANGE	1925
D-87	IN THE GREASE (sh)	HOWE	PATHE EXCHANGE	1925
D-88	CHASING THE CHASER (sh)	LAUREL	PATHE EXCHANGE	1925
D-89	UNFRIENDLY ENEMIES (sh)	LAUREL	PATHE EXCHANGE	1925
D-90	TIME OUT FOR RHYTHM (sh)	SALKOW	COLUMBIA	1941
D-90	YES, YES NANETTE (sh)	HENNECKE, LAUREL	PATHE EXCHANGE	1925
D-115	TWO IN A TAXI	FLOREY	COLUMBIA	1941
D-116	OUR WIFE	STAHL	COLUMBIA	1941
D-117	HERE COMES MR. JORDAN	HALL	COLUMBIA	1941
D-118	YOU'LL NEVER GET RICH	LANFIELD	COLUMBIA	1941
D-119	MYSTERY SHIP	LANDERS	COLUMBIA	1941
D-120	TWO LATINS FROM MANHATTAN	BARTON	COLUMBIA	1941
D-122	COUNTER-ESPIONAGE	DMYTRYK	COLUMBIA	1942
D-124	THREE GIRLS ABOUT TOWN	JASON	COLUMBIA	1941
D-125	GO WEST YOUNG LADY	STRAYER	COLUMBIA	1941
D-126	HARMON OF MICHIGAN	BARTON	COLUMBIA	1941
D-127	STORK PAYS OFF	LANDERS	COLUMBIA	1941
D-128	SECRETS OF THE LONE WOLF	DMYTRYK	COLUMBIA	1941
D-129	LADY IS WILLING	LEISEN	COLUMBIA	1942
D-130	SING FOR YOUR SUPPER	BARTON	COLUMBIA	1941
D-132	HARVARD, HERE I COME	LANDERS	COLUMBIA	1941
D-133	CONFESSIONS OF BOSTON BLACKIE	DMYTRYK	COLUMBIA	1941
D-134	BLONDIE GOES TO COLLEGE	STRAYER	COLUMBIA	1942
D-135	HONOLULU LU	BARTON	COLUMBIA	1941
D-136	CADETS ON PARADE	LANDERS	COLUMBIA	1942
D-137	SHUT MY BIG MOUTH	BARTON	COLUMBIA	1942
D-138	TWO YANKS IN TRINIDAD	RATOFF	COLUMBIA	1942
D-139	MAN WHO RETURNED TO LIFE	LANDERS	COLUMBIA	1942
D-140	CANAL ZONE	LANDERS	COLUMBIA	1942
D-141	TRAMP TRAMP TRAMP	BARTON	COLUMBIA	1942
D-144	ALIAS BOSTON BLACKIE	LANDERS	COLUMBIA	1942
D-146	TALK OF THE TOWN	STEVENS	COLUMBIA	1942
D-147	NOT A LADIES MAN	LANDERS	COLUMBIA	1942
D-148	HELLO ANAPOLIS	BARTON	COLUMBIA	1942
D-149	MEET THE STEWARTS	GREEN	COLUMBIA	1942
D-150	THEY ALL KISSED THE BRIDE	HALL	COLUMBIA	1942
D-151	PARACHUTE NURSE	BARTON	COLUMBIA	1942
D-152	SWEETHEART OF THE FLEET	BARTON	COLUMBIA	1942
D-153	SUBMARINE RAIDER	LANDERS	COLUMBIA	1942
D-154	YOU WERE NEVER LOVELIER	SEITER	COLUMBIA	1942
D-155	ATLANTIC CONVOY	LANDERS	COLUMBIA	1942

Movie Still Identification Book Ultimate Edition - Letters

CODE	TITLE/NAME	DIRECTOR/TYPE	STUDIO/DISTRIBUTOR	YEAR
D-156	3 LITTLE PIGSKINS	MCCAREY	COLUMBIA	1934
D-156	FLIGHT LIEUTENANT	SALKOW	COLUMBIA	1942
D-156	THREE LITTLE PIGSKINS (sh)	MCCAREY	COLUMBIA	1934
D-157	ONE DANGEROUS NIGHT	GORDON	COLUMBIA	1943
D-158	BLONDIE FOR VICTORY	STRAYER	COLUMBIA	1942
D-159	MAN'S WORLD	BARTON	COLUMBIA	1942
D-160	SABOTAGE SQUAD	LANDERS	COLUMBIA	1942
D-161	MY SISTER EILEEN	HALL	COLUMBIA	1942
D-162	LUCKY LEGS	BARTON	COLUMBIA	1942
D-163	DESPERADOES	VIDOR	COLUMBIA	1943
D-164	STAND BY ALL NETWORKS	LANDERS	COLUMBIA	1942
D-165	SPIRIT OF STANFORD	BARTON	COLUMBIA	1942
D-166	DESTROYER	SEITER	COLUMBIA	1943
D-167	LET'S HAVE FUN	BARTON	COLUMBIA	1943
D-168	DARING YOUNG MAN	STRAYER	COLUMBIA	1942
D-169	BOSTON BLACKIE GOES HOLLYWOOD	GORDON	COLUMBIA	1942
D-170	SMITH OF MINNESOTA	LANDERS	COLUMBIA	1942
D-171	BOOGIE MAN WILL GET YOU	LANDERS	COLUMBIA	1942
D-172	UNDERGROUND AGENT	GORDON	COLUMBIA	1942
D-173	NIGHT TO REMEMBER	WALLACE	COLUMBIA	1943
D-174	LAUGH YOUR BLUES AWAY	BARTON	COLUMBIA	1942
D-175	JUNIOR ARMY	LANDERS	COLUMBIA	1942
D-176	MORE THE MERRIER	STEVENS	COLUMBIA	1943
D-177	POWER OF THE PRESS	LANDERS	COLUMBIA	1943
D-178	CLAUDINE AT SCHOOL (FR)	POLIGNY	PHOENIX FILM	1940
D-178	WHAT'S BUZZIN COUSIN?	BARTON	COLUMBIA	1943
D-179	REVELIE WITH BEVERLY	BARTON	COLUMBIA	1943
D-180	MURDER IN TIMES SQUARE	LANDERS	COLUMBIA	1943
D-181	SAHARA	KORDA	COLUMBIA	1943
D-182	APPOINTMENT IN BERLIN	GREEN	COLUMBIA	1943
D-183	AFTER MIDNIGHT WITH BOSTON BLACKIE	LANDERS	COLUMBIA	1943
D-184	FIRST COMES COURAGE	ARZNER	COLUMBIA	1943
D-185	SHE HAS WHAT IT TAKES	BARTON	COLUMBIA	1943
D-186	IT'S A GREAT LIFE	STRAYER	COLUMBIA	1943
D-187	BOY FROM STALINGRAD	SALKOW	COLUMBIA	1943
D-188	REDHEAD FROM MANHATTAN	LANDERS	COLUMBIA	1943
D-189	ONCE UPON A TIME	HALL	COLUMBIA	1944
D-190	TWO SENORITAS FROM CHICAGO	WOODRUFF	COLUMBIA	1943
D-192	GOOD LUCK MR. YATES	ENRIGHT	COLUMBIA	1943
D-193	DOUGHBOYS IN IRELAND	LANDERS	COLUMBIA	1943
D-194	COVER GIRL	VIDOR	COLUMBIA	1944
D-195	MY KINGDOM FOR A COOK	WALLACE	COLUMBIA	1943
D-197	PASSPORT TO SUEZ	DE TOTH	COLUMBIA	1943
D-198	DANGEROUS BLONDES	JASON	COLUMBIA	1943
D-199	THERE'S SOMETHING ABOUT A SOLDIER	GREEN	COLUMBIA	1943
D-200	EXTORTION	HILLYER	COLUMBIA	1938
D-203	MAIN EVENT	DARE	COLUMBIA	1938
D-204	PAID TO DANCE (HARD TO HOLD)	COLEMAN	COLUMBIA	1937
D-205	ALL AMERICAN SWEETHEART	HILLYER	COLUMBIA	1937
D-207	SQUADRON OF HONOR	COLEMAN	COLUMBIA	1938
D-208	WOMEN IN PRISON	HILLYER	COLUMBIA	1938
D-209	WHO KILLED GAIL PRESTON?	BARSHA	COLUMBIA	1938
D-210	WHEN G-MEN STEP IN	COLEMAN	COLUMBIA	1938
D-211	HIGHWAY PATROL	COLEMAN	COLUMBIA	1938
D-212	HOMICIDE BUREAU	COLEMAN	COLUMBIA	1939
D-213	JUVENILE COURT	LEDERMAN	COLUMBIA	1938
D-214	ADVENTURE IN SAHARA	LEDERMAN	COLUMBIA	1938
D-215	NORTH OF SHANGHAI	LEDERMAN	COLUMBIA	1939
D-216	MY SON IS A CRIMINAL	COLEMAN	COLUMBIA	1939
D-217	FIRST OFFENDERS	MCDONALD	COLUMBIA	1939
D-218	OUTSIDE THESE WALLS	MCCAREY	COLUMBIA	1939
D-219	MISSING DAUGHTERS	COLEMAN	COLUMBIA	1939
D-220	PARENTS ON TRIAL	NELSON	COLUMBIA	1939
D-221	WOMAN IS THE JUDGE	GRINDE	COLUMBIA	1939
D-222	BEHIND PRISON GATES	BARTON	COLUMBIA	1939
D-223	MAN THEY COULD NOT HANG	GRINDE	COLUMBIA	1939
D-224	KONGA, THE WILD STALLION	NELSON	COLUMBIA	1940
D-300	OUTLAWS OF THE PRAIRIE	NELSON	COLUMBIA	1937
D-301	CATTLE RAIDERS	NELSON	COLUMBIA	1938
D-302	OLD WYOMING TRAIL	BLANGSTED	COLUMBIA	1937

Movie Still Identification Book Ultimate Edition - Letters

CODE	TITLE/NAME	DIRECTOR/TYPE	STUDIO/DISTRIBUTOR	YEAR
D-303	CALL OF THE ROCKIES	JAMES	COLUMBIA	1938
D-304	LAW OF THE PLAINS	NELSON	COLUMBIA	1938
D-305	WEST OF CHEYENNE	NELSON	COLUMBIA	1938
D-306	SOUTH OF ARIZONA	NELSON	COLUMBIA	1938
D-307	WEST OF SANTA FE	NELSON	COLUMBIA	1938
D-308	COLORADO TRAIL	NELSON	COLUMBIA	1938
D-309	RIO GRANDE	NELSON	COLUMBIA	1938
D-310	THUNDERING WEST	NELSON	COLUMBIA	1939
D-311	TEXAS STAMPEDE	NELSON	COLUMBIA	1939
D-312	NORTH OF THE YUKON	NELSON	COLUMBIA	1939
D-313	SPOILERS OF THE RANGE	COLEMAN	COLUMBIA	1939
D-314	WESTERN CARAVANS	NELSON	COLUMBIA	1939
D-315	MAN FROM SUNDOWN	NELSON	COLUMBIA	1939
D-316	OUTPOST OF THE MOUNTIES	COLEMAN	COLUMBIA	1939
D-317	STRANGER FROM TEXAS	NELSON	COLUMBIA	1939
D-318	RIDERS OF BLACK RIVER	DEMING	COLUMBIA	1939
D-319	TAMING OF THE WEST	DEMING	COLUMBIA	1939
D-320	MAN FROM TUMBLEWEEDS	LEWIS	COLUMBIA	1940
D-321	TWO FISTED RANGERS	LEWIS	COLUMBIA	1939
D-322	BULLETS FOR RUSTLERS	NELSON	COLUMBIA	1940
D-323	PIONEERS OF THE FRONTIER	NELSON	COLUMBIA	1940
D-324	BLAZING SIX SHOOTERS	LEWIS	COLUMBIA	1940
D-325	THUNDERING FRONTIER	LEDERMAN	COLUMBIA	1940
D-326	TEXAS STAGECOACH	LEWIS	COLUMBIA	1940
D-327	PINTO KID	HILLYER	COLUMBIA	1941
D-328	WEST OF ABILENE	CEDER	COLUMBIA	1940
D-329	RETURN OF WILD BILL	LEWIS	COLUMBIA	1940
D-330	DURANGO KID	HILLYER	COLUMBIA	1940
D-331	PRAIRIE SCHOONERS	NELSON	COLUMBIA	1940
D-332	OUTLAWS OF THE PANHANDLE	NELSON	COLUMBIA	1941
D-334	BEYOND THE SACRAMENTO	HILLYER	COLUMBIA	1940
D-335	ACROSS THE SIERRAS	LEDERMAN	COLUMBIA	1941
D-337	WILDCAT OF TUCSON	HILLYER	COLUMBIA	1940
D-338	NORTH FROM THE LONE STAR	HILLYER	COLUMBIA	1941
D-340	HANDS ACROSS THE ROCKIES	HILLYER	COLUMBIA	1941
D-341	SON OF DAVY CROCKETT	HILLYER	COLUMBIA	1941
D-342	MEDICO OF PAINTED SPRINGS	HILLYER	COLUMBIA	1941
D-343	KING OF DODGE CITY	HILLYER	COLUMBIA	1941
D-344	THUNDER OVER THE PRAIRIE	HILLYER	COLUMBIA	1941
D-345	ROARING FRONTIERS	HILLYER	COLUMBIA	1941
D-346	PRAIRIE STRANGER	HILLYER	COLUMBIA	1941
D-347	LONE STAR VIGILANTES	FOX	COLUMBIA	1942
D-348	ROYAL MOUNTED PATROL	HILLYER	COLUMBIA	1941
D-349	BULLETS FOR BANDITS	FOX	COLUMBIA	1942
D-350	RIDERS OF THE BADLANDS	BRETHERTON	COLUMBIA	1941
D-351	NORTH OF THE ROCKIES	HILLYER	COLUMBIA	1942
D-352	DEVIL'S TRAIL	HILLYER	COLUMBIA	1942
D-353	WEST OF TOMBSTONE	BRETHERTON	COLUMBIA	1942
D-354	LAWLESS PLAINSMEN	BERKE	COLUMBIA	1942
D-355	DOWN RIO GRANDE WAY	BERKE	COLUMBIA	1942
D-356	PRAIRIE GUNSMOKE	HILLYER	COLUMBIA	1942
D-357	OVERLAND TO DEADWOOD	BERKE	COLUMBIA	1942
D-358	BADMEN OF THE HILLS	BERKE	COLUMBIA	1942
D-359	RIDERS OF THE NORTHLAND	BERKE	COLUMBIA	1942
D-360	VENGEANCE OF THE WEST	HILLYER	COLUMBIA	1942
D-362	RIDING THROUGH NEVADA	BERKE	COLUMBIA	1942
D-363	PARDON MY GUN	BERKE	COLUMBIA	1942
D-364	TORNADO IN THE SADDLE	BERKE	COLUMBIA	1942
D-365	LONE PRAIRIE	BERKE	COLUMBIA	1942
D-366	FIGHTING BUCKAROO	BERKE	COLUMBIA	1943
D-367	LAW OF THE NORTHWEST	BERKE	COLUMBIA	1943
D-368	SILVER CITY RAIDERS	BERKE	COLUMBIA	1943
D-369	RIDERS OF THE NORTHWEST MOUNTED	BERKE	COLUMBIA	1943
D-370	HAIL TO THE RANGERS	BERKE	COLUMBIA	1943
D-371	ROBIN HOOD OF THE RANGE	BERKE	COLUMBIA	1943
D-372	SADDLES AND THE SAGEBRUSH	BERKE	COLUMBIA	1943
D-373	VIGILANTES RIDE	BERKE	COLUMBIA	1943
D-374	WYOMING HURRICANE	BERKE	COLUMBIA	1944
D-375	LAST HORSEMAN	BERKE	COLUMBIA	1944
D-376	RIDING WEST	BERKE	COLUMBIA	1944

Movie Still Identification Book Ultimate Edition - Letters

CODE	TITLE/NAME	DIRECTOR/TYPE	STUDIO/DISTRIBUTOR	YEAR
D-377	FRONTIER FURY	BERKE	COLUMBIA	1943
D-400	CASH AND CARRY (sh)	LORD	COLUMBIA	1937
D-401	PLAYING THE PONIES (sh)	LAMONT	COLUMBIA	1937
D-404	WEE WEE MONSIER (sh)	LORD	COLUMBIA	1938
D-407	GRACIE AT THE BAT (sh)	LORD	COLUMBIA	1937
D-416	TERMITES OF 1938 (sh)	LORD	COLUMBIA	1938
D-422	HEALTHY, WEALTHY AND DUMB (sh)	LORD	COLUMBIA	1938
D-426	THREE MISSING LINKS (sh)	WHITE	COLUMBIA	1938
D-427	MUTTS TO YOU (sh)	CHASE	COLUMBIA	1938
D-430	SAVED BY THE BELLE (sh)	CHASE	COLUMBIA	1939
D-438	YES WE HAVE NO BONANZA (sh)	LORD	COLUMBIA	1939
D-439	FLAT FOOT STOOGES (sh)	CHASE	COLUMBIA	1938
D-443	WE WANT OUR MUMMY (sh)	LORD	COLUMBIA	1939
D-444	DUCKING THEY DID GO (sh)	LORD	COLUMBIA	1939
D-445	CALLING ALL CURS (sh)	WHITE	COLUMBIA	1939
D-446	RATTLING ROMEO (sh)	LORD	COLUMBIA	1939
D-448	NOW IT CAN BE SOLD (sh)	LORD	COLUMBIA	1939
D-449	OILY TO BED, OILY TO RISE (sh)	WHITE	COLUMBIA	1939
D-452	TEACHER'S PEST (sh)	KRAMER, ULLMAN	COLUMBIA	1939
D-453	STATIC IN THE ATTIC (sh)	CHASE	COLUMBIA	1939
D-454	PEST FROM THE WEST (sh)	LORD	COLUMBIA	1939
D-458	HOW HIGH IS UP? (sh)	LORD	COLUMBIA	1940
D-460	ALL AMERICAN BLONDES (sh)	LORD	COLUMBIA	1939
D-463	ANDY CLYDE GETS SPRING CHICKEN (sh)	WHITE	COLUMBIA	1939
D-467	HECKLER (sh)	LORD	COLUMBIA	1940
D-468	FROM NURSE TO WORSE (sh)	WHITE	COLUMBIA	1940
D-473	SOUTH OF THE BOUDOIR (sh)	LORD	COLUMBIA	1940
D-482	IN THE SWEET PIE AND PIE (sh)	WHITE	COLUMBIA	1941
D-483	BLONDES AND BLUNDERS (sh)	LORD	COLUMBIA	1940
D-484	SO LONG MR. CHUMPS (sh)	WHITE	COLUMBIA	1941
D-488	ACHE IN EVERY STAKE (sh)	LORD	COLUMBIA	1941
D492	GIANT BEHEMOTH (UK: BEHEMOTH THE SEA MONSTER)	HICKOX, LOURIE	ALLIED ARTISTS	1959
D-498	YANKEE DOODLE ANDY (sh)	WHITE	COLUMBIA	1941
D-500	I'LL NEVER HEIL AGAIN (sh)	WHITE	COLUMBIA	1941
D-501	LOVE AT FIRST FRIGHT (sh)	LORD	COLUMBIA	1941
D-503	FRENCH FRIED PATOOTIE (sh)	WHITE	COLUMBIA	1941
D-506	HALF SHOT AT SUNRISE (sh)	LORD	COLUMBIA	1941
D-507	EVEN AS I.O.U. (sh)	LORD	COLUMBIA	1942
D-508	GENERAL NUISANCEE (sh)	WHITE	COLUMBIA	1941
D-510	LOCO BOY MAKES GOOD (sh)	WHITE	COLUMBIA	1942
D-512	MITT ME TONIGHT (sh)	WHITE	COLUMBIA	1941
D-515	PHONY CRONIES (sh)	EDWARDS	COLUMBIA	1942
D-519	WHAT'S THE MATADOR? (sh)	WHITE	COLUMBIA	1942
D-521	SWEET SPIRITS OF NIGHTER (sh)	LORD	COLUMBIA	1941
D-522	BACK FROM THE FRONT (sh)	WHITE	COLUMBIA	1943
D-523	GROOM AND BORED (sh)	LORD	COLUMBIA	1942
D-525	GLOVE AFFAIR (sh)	WHITE	COLUMBIA	1941
D-528	OLAF LAUGHS LAST (sh)	WHITE	COLUMBIA	1942
D-529	DIZZY DETECTIVES (sh)	WHITE	COLUMBIA	1943
D-531	QUACK SERVICE (sh)	EDWARDS	COLUMBIA	1943
D-533	THEY STOOGE TO CONGA (sh)	LORD	COLUMBIA	1943
D-536	CARRY HARRY (sh)	EDWARDS	COLUMBIA	1942
D-537	BLITZ ON THE FRITZ (sh)	WHITE	COLUMBIA	1943
D-538	WOLF IN THIEF'S CLOTHING (sh)	WHITE	COLUMBIA	1943
D-541	HIS WEDDING SCARE (sh)	LORD	COLUMBIA	1943
D-545	HIS GIRL'S WORST FRIEND (sh)	WHITE	COLUMBIA	1943
D-546	FARMER FOR A DAY (sh)	WHITE	COLUMBIA	1943
D-547	MAID MADE MAD (sh)	LORD	COLUMBIA	1943
D-548	SOCKS APPEAL (sh)	EDWARDS	COLUMBIA	1943
D-549	SPOOK LOUDER (sh)	LORD	COLUMBIA	1943
D-550	I SPIED FOR YOU (sh)	WHITE	COLUMBIA	1943
D-551	THREE LITTLE TWERPS (sh)	EDWARDS	COLUMBIA	1943
D-552	BLONDE AND GROOM (sh)	EDWARDS	COLUMBIA	1943
D-554	HERE COMES MR. ZERK (sh)	EDWARDS	COLUMBIA	1943
D-555	DIZY PILOTS (sh)	WHITE	COLUMBIA	1943
D-556	TWO SAPLINGS (sh)	EDWARDS	COLUMBIA	1943
D-558	WHAT A SOLDIER (sh) NOT RELEASED		COLUMBIA	1943
D-559	SHOT IN THE ESCAPE (sh)	WHITE	COLUMBIA	1943
D-561	HE WAS ONLY FEUDIN' (sh)	EDWARDS	COLUMBIA	1943
D-562	ROOKIE'S COOKIE (sh)	WHITE	COLUMBIA	1943

Movie Still Identification Book Ultimate Edition - Letters

CODE	TITLE/NAME	DIRECTOR/TYPE	STUDIO/DISTRIBUTOR	YEAR
D-563	BOOBS IN THE NIGHT (sh)	LORD	COLUMBIA	1943
D-564	NO DOUGH BOYS (sh)	WHITE	COLUMBIA	1944
D-565	HUGH HERBERT (sh)		COLUMBIA	
D-566	PITCHIN' IN THE KITCHEN (sh)	WHITE	COLUMBIA	1943
D-568	HIGHER THAN A KITE (sh)	LORD	COLUMBIA	1943
D-569	PHONEY EXPRESS (sh)	LORD	COLUMBIA	1943
D-570	I CAN HARDLY WAIT (sh)	WHITE	COLUMBIA	1943
D-571	YOKE'S ON ME (sh)	WHITE	COLUMBIA	1944
D-572	TO HEIR IS HUMAN (sh)	GODSOE	COLUMBIA	1944
D-573	GARDEN OF EATIN' (sh)	EDWARDS	COLUMBIA	1943
D-574	WHO'S HUGH (sh)	EDWARDS	COLUMBIA	1943
D-575	GEM OF A JAM (sh)	LORD	COLUMBIA	1943
D-595	STOOGES (sh)		COLUMBIA	
D-646	FOOLS WHO MADE HISTORY-ELIAS HOWE	LEMAN	COLUMBIA	1939
D-647	FOOLS WHO MADE HISTORY-CHARLES GOODYEAR		COLUMBIA	1939
D-683	JUNIOR QUIZ PARADE		COLUMBIA	
D-697	MR. SMUG (sh)		COLUMBIA	1943
D-729	CITY WITHOUT MEN	SALKOW	COLUMBIA	1943
D-735	HEAT'S ON	RATOFF	COLUMBIA	1943
D-749	(sh)		COLUMBIA	
D-762	(sh)		COLUMBIA	
D-762	CRIME DR.'S STRANGEST CASE	FORDE	COLUMBIA	1943
D-766	(sh)		COLUMBIA	
D-770	SECRET COMMAND	SUTHERLAND	COLUMBIA	1944
D-773	ADDRESS UNKNOWN	MENZIES	COLUMBIA	1944
D-787	WHISTLER	CASTLE	COLUMBIA	1944
D-788	TEXAS	MARSHALL	COLUMBIA	1941
D-789	SHADOWS IN THE NIGHT	FORDE	COLUMBIA	1944
D-791	EVER SINCE VENUE	DREIFUSS	COLUMBIA	1944
D-803	MARK OF THE WHISTLER	CASTLE	COLUMBIA	1944
D-808	BRENDA STARR – REPORTER SERIAL	FOX	COLUMBIA	1945
D-811	RIDERS OF THE WHISTLING PINES	ENGLISH	COLUMBIA	1949
D-812	CRIME DR.'S COURAGE	SHERMAN	COLUMBIA	1945
D-813	POWER OF THE WHISTLER	LANDERS	COLUMBIA	1945
D-814	KISS AND TELL	WALLACE	COLUMBIA	1945
D-818	MONSTER AND THE APE	BRETHERTON	COLUMBIA	1945
D-822	OVER 21	VIDOR	COLUMBIA	1945
D-830	ADVENTURES OF RUSTY	BURNFORD	COLUMBIA	1945
D-834	SNAFU	MOSS	COLUMBIA	1945
D-835	JUNGLE RAIDERS – SERIAL	SELANDER	COLUMBIA	1945
D-838	CRIME DR.'S WARNING	CASTLE	COLUMBIA	1945
D-841	PERILOUS HOLIDAY	GRIFFITH	COLUMBIA	1946
D-844	WHO'S GUILTY?	BRETHERTON, GRISSELL	COLUMBIA	1945
D-850	JOHNNY O'CLOCK	ROSSEN	COLUMBIA	1947
D-851	MR. DISTRICT ATTORNEY	SINCLAIR	COLUMBIA	1947
D-855	HOP HARRIGAN	ABRAHAMS	COLUMBIA	1946
D-856	TO THE ENDS OF THE EARTH	STEVENSON	COLUMBIA	1948
D-862	CHICK CARTER DETECTIVE	ABRAHAMS	COLUMBIA	1946
D-863	RETURN OF MONTE CRISTO	LEVIN	COLUMBIA	1946
D-868	SON OF THE GUARDSMAN	ABRAHAMS	COLUMBIA	1946
D-869	LAST OF THE REDMEN	SHERMAN	COLUMBIA	1947
D-873	BETTY CO-ED	DREIFUSS	COLUMBIA	1946
D-876	CORPSE CAME C.O.D.	LEVIN	COLUMBIA	1947
D-878	JACK ARMSTRONG	FOX	COLUMBIA	1947
D-879	GUNFIGHTERS	WAGGNER	COLUMBIA	1947
D-882	VIGILANTE - SERIAL	FOX	COLUMBIA	1947
D-883	RELENTLESS	SHERMAN	COLUMBIA	1948
D-884	LITTLE MISS BROADWAY	DREIFUSS	COLUMBIA	1947
D-885	HER HUSBANDS AFFAIRS	SIMON	COLUMBIA	1947
D-886	SEA HOUND	EASON, WRIGHT	COLUMBIA	1947
D-887	PRINCE OF THIEVES	BRETHERTON	COLUMBIA	1948
D-888	I LOVE TROUBLE	SIMON	COLUMBIA	1948
D-889	MUSIC IN MY HEART	SANTLEY	COLUMBIA	1940
D-889	STRAWBERRY ROAN	ENGLISH	COLUMBIA	1948
D-890	SWEET GENEVIEVE	DREIFUSS	COLUMBIA	1947
D-891	TWO BLONDES AND A REDHEAD	DREIFUSS	COLUMBIA	1947
D-892	LAST ROUNDUP	ENGLISH	COLUMBIA	1947
D-893	BIG SOMBRERO	MCDONALD	COLUMBIA	1949
D-895	TEX GRANGER - SERIAL	ABRAHAMS	COLUMBIA	1948
D-896	SIGN OF THE RAM	STURGES	COLUMBIA	1948

Movie Still Identification Book Ultimate Edition - Letters

CODE	TITLE/NAME	DIRECTOR/TYPE	STUDIO/DISTRIBUTOR	YEAR
D-897	BLACK ARROW	DOUGLAS	COLUMBIA	1948
D-899	BRICK BRADFORD - SERIAL	BENNET, CARR	COLUMBIA	1947
D-900	GREAT ADV OF WILD BILL HICKOK - SERIAL	NELSON, WRIGHT	COLUMBIA	1938
D-900	MARY LOU	DREIFUSS	COLUMBIA	1948
D-901	SPIDER'S WEB (SERIAL)	HORNE, TAYLOR	COLUMBIA	1938
D-902	ALL THE KING'S MEN	ROSSEN	COLUMBIA	1950
D-902	FLYING G-MEN - SERIAL	HORNE, TAYLOR	COLUMBIA	1939
D-903	MANDRAKE THE MAGICIAN - SERIAL	DEMING, NELSON	COLUMBIA	1939
D-904	OVERLAND WITH KIT CARSON	DEMING, NELSON	COLUMBIA	1939
D-905	LOADED PISTOLS	ENGLISH	COLUMBIA	1948
D-908	GLAMOUR GIRL	DREIFUSS	COLUMBIA	1948
D-909	MANHATTAN ANGEL	DREIFUSS	COLUMBIA	1949
D-910	SUPERMAN - SERIAL	BENNET, CARR	COLUMBIA	1948
D-911	ADVENTURE IN WASHINGTON	GREEN	COLUMBIA	1941
D-912	I SURRENDER DEAR	DREIFUSS	COLUMBIA	1948
D-913	FULLER BRUSH MAN	SIMON	COLUMBIA	1948
D-914	RACING LUCK	BERKE	COLUMBIA	1948
D-915	LOVES OF CARMEN	VIDOR	COLUMBIA	1948
D-916	SHE KNEW ALL THE ANSWERS	WALLACE	COLUMBIA	1941
D-918	MUTINEERS	YARBROUGH	COLUMBIA	1949
D-919	LULU BELLE	FENTON	COLUMBIA	1948
D-920	UNDERCOVER MAN	LEWIS	COLUMBIA	1949
D-921	SONS OF NEW MEXICO	ENGLISH	COLUMBIA	1949
D-923	ANNA LUCASTA	RAPPER	COLUMBIA	1949
D-924	COWBOY AND THE INDIANS	ENGLISH	COLUMBIA	1949
D-926	CONGO BILL	BENNET, CARR	COLUMBIA	1948
D-927	UNTAMED BREED	LAMONT	COLUMBIA	1948
D-928	LADIES OF THE CHORUS	KARLSON	COLUMBIA	1948
D-931	ADAM HAD FOUR SONS	RATOFF	COLUMBIA	1941
D-931	KNOCK ON ANY DOOR	RAY	COLUMBIA	1949
D-932	TOKYO JOE	HEISLER	COLUMBIA	1949
D-933	TRIPLE THREAT	YARBROUGH	COLUMBIA	1948
D-934	SONG OF INDIA	ROGELL	COLUMBIA	1949
D-934	TRIPLE THREAT (mistake? 933)	YARBROUGH	COLUMBIA	1948
D-935	JUNGLE JIM	BERKE	COLUMBIA	1948
D-937	BRUCE GENTRY	BENNET, CARR	COLUMBIA	1949
D-939	WE WERE STRANGERS	HUSTON	COLUMBIA	1949
D-942	LOST TRIBE	BERKE	COLUMBIA	1949
D-944	ADVENTURES OF BATMAN AND ROBIN	BENNET	COLUMBIA	1949
D-945	DOOLINS OF OKLAHOMA	DOUGLAS	COLUMBIA	1949
D-946	JOLSON SINGS AGAIN	LEVIN	COLUMBIA	1949
D-947	RIM OF THE CANYON	ENGLISH	COLUMBIA	1949
D-949	LADIES IN RETIREMENT	VIDOR	COLUMBIA	1941
D-950	STATE PENITENTIARY	LANDERS	COLUMBIA	1950
D-951	BARBARY PIRATE	LANDERS	COLUMBIA	1949
D-952	COW TOWN	ENGLISH	COLUMBIA	1950
D-953	ADVENTURES OF SIR GALAHAD	BENNET	COLUMBIA	1949
D-953	MEN IN HER LIFE	RATOFF	COLUMBIA	1941
D-954	CAPTIVE GIRL	BERKE	COLUMBIA	1950
D-955	MARK OF THE GORILLA	BERKE	COLUMBIA	1950
D-956	ATOM MAN VS. SUPERMAN	BENNET	COLUMBIA	1950
D-957	CODY OF THE PONY EXPRESS	BENNET	COLUMBIA	1950
D-958	CHINATOWN AT MIDNIGHT	FRIEDMAN	COLUMBIA	1949
D-962	TYRANT OF THE SEA	LANDERS	COLUMBIA	1950
D-964	ADVENTURES OF MARTIN EDEN	SALKOW	COLUMBIA	1942
D-964	RECKLESS MOMENT	OPHULS	COLUMBIA	1949
D-965	TRAVELING SALESWOMAN	REISNER	COLUMBIA	1950
D-966	AND BABY MAKES THREE	LEVIN	COLUMBIA	1949
D-967	BLAZING SUN	ENGLISH	COLUMBIA	1950
D-968	NEVADAN	DOUGLAS	COLUMBIA	1950
D-970	IN A LONELY PLACE	RAY	COLUMBIA	1950
D-971	RIDERS IN THE SKY	ENGLISH	COLUMBIA	1949
D-975	BRAVE BULLS	ROSSON	COLUMBIA	1951
D-976	MULE TRAIN	ENGLISH	COLUMBIA	1950
D-977	BEYOND THE PURPLE HILLS	ENGLISH	COLUMBIA	1950
D-981	INDIAN TERRITORY	ENGLISH	COLUMBIA	1950
D-982	SOMETHING TO SHOUT ABOUT	RATOFF	COLUMBIA	1943
D-986	LAST OF THE BUCCANEERS	LANDERS	COLUMBIA	1950
D-988	GENE AUTRY AND THE MOUNTIES	ENGLISH	COLUMBIA	1951
D-989	REVENUE AGENT	LANDERS	COLUMBIA	1950

Movie Still Identification Book Ultimate Edition - Letters

CODE	TITLE/NAME	DIRECTOR/TYPE	STUDIO/DISTRIBUTOR	YEAR
D-990	PIRATES OF THE HIGH SEAS	BENNET, CARR	COLUMBIA	1950
D-991	SIROCCO	BERNHARDT	COLUMBIA	1951
D-992	HURRICANE ISLAND	LANDERS	COLUMBIA	1951
D-993	CHAIN GANG	LANDERS	COLUMBIA	1950
D-994	PYGMY ISLAND	BERKE	COLUMBIA	1950
D-995	FURY OF THE CONGO	BERKE	COLUMBIA	1951
D-996	COMMANDOES STRIKE AT DAWN	FARROW	COLUMBIA	1942
D-998	SATURDAY'S HERO	MILLER	COLUMBIA	1951
D-999	FAMILY SECRET	LEVIN	COLUMBIA	1951
D-1001	FOOTLIGHT GLAMOUR	STRAYER	COLUMBIA	1943
D-1002	IS EVERYBODY HAPPY?	BARTON	COLUMBIA	1943
D-1004	WHAT A WOMAN	CUMMINGS	COLUMBIA	1943
D-1005	NINE GIRLS	JASON	COLUMBIA	1944
D-1006	NONE SHALL ESCAPE	DE TOTH	COLUMBIA	1944
D-1009	RACKET MAN	LEDERMAN	COLUMBIA	1944
D-1010	RETURN OF THE VAMPIRE	LANDERS	COLUMBIA	1944
D-1011	SONG TO REMEMBER	VIDOR	COLUMBIA	1945
D-1012	CHANCE OF A LIFETIME	CASTLE	COLUMBIA	1943
D-1014	MR. WINKLE GOES TO WAR	GREEN	COLUMBIA	1944
D-1015	KLONDIKE KATE	CASTLE	COLUMBIA	1943
D-1016	SWING OUT OF THE BLUES	ST. CLAIR	COLUMBIA	1943
D-1017	BEAUTIFUL BUT BROKE	BARTON	COLUMBIA	1944
D-1019	GHOST THAT WALKS ALONE	LANDERS	COLUMBIA	1944
D-1021	GIRL IN THE CASE	BERKE	COLUMBIA	1944
D-1022	TONIGHT AND EVERY NIGHT	SAVILLE	COLUMBIA	1945
D-1023	SAILOR'S HOLIDAY	BERKE	COLUMBIA	1944
D-1024	TOGETHER AGAIN	VIDOR	COLUMBIA	1944
D-1025	TWO MAN SUBMARINE	LANDERS	COLUMBIA	1944
D-1026	CAROLINA BLUES	JASON	COLUMBIA	1944
D-1027	STARS ON PARADE	LANDERS	COLUMBIA	1944
D-1028	BLACK PARACHUTE	LANDERS	COLUMBIA	1944
D-1029	SHE'S A SOLDIER TOO	CASTLE	COLUMBIA	1944
D-1030	JOLSON STORY (SOME MARKED 1130)	GREEN	COLUMBIA	1946
D-1031	COUNTER-ATTACK	KORDA	COLUMBIA	1945
D-1032	THEY LIVE IN FEAR	BERNE	COLUMBIA	1944
D-1033	U-BOAT PRISONER	LANDERS	COLUMBIA	1944
D-1035	LOUISIANA HAYRIDE	BARTON	COLUMBIA	1944
D-1036	IMPATIENT YEARS	CUMMINGS	COLUMBIA	1944
D-1037	CRY OF THE WEREWOLF	LEVIN	COLUMBIA	1944
D-1038	UNWRITTEN CODE	ROTSTEN	COLUMBIA	1944
D-1039	EVE KNEW HER APPLES	JASON	COLUMBIA	1945
D-1040	KANSAS CITY KITTY	LORD	COLUMBIA	1944
D-1042	MEET MISS BOBBY SOCKS	TRYON	COLUMBIA	1944
D-1043	STRANGE AFFAIR	GREEN	COLUMBIA	1944
D-1044	SOUL OF A MONSTER	JASON	COLUMBIA	1944
D-1045	ONE MYSTERIOUS NIGHT	BOETTICHER	COLUMBIA	1944
D-1046	SERGEANT MIKE	LEVIN	COLUMBIA	1944
D-1047	MISSING JUROR	BOETTICHER	COLUMBIA	1944
D-1048	ESCAPE IN THE FOG	BOETTICHER	COLUMBIA	1945
D-1049	SHE'S A SWEETHEART	LORD	COLUMBIA	1944
D-1050	TARS AND SPARS	GREEN	COLUMBIA	1946
D-1051	EADIE WAS A LADY	DREIFUSS	COLUMBIA	1945
D-1052	DANCING IN MANHATTAN	LELVIN	COLUMBIA	1944
D-1054	THOUSAND AND ONE NIGHTS	GREEN	COLUMBIA	1945
D-1055	TAHITI NIGHTS	JASON	COLUMBIA	1944
D-1056	LEAVE IT TO BLONDIE	BERLIN	COLUMBIA	1945
D-1057	LET'S GO STEADY	LORD	COLUMBIA	1945
D-1058	I LOVE A MYSTERY	LEVIN	COLUMBIA	1945
D-1059	YOUTH ON TRIAL	BOETTICHER	COLUMBIA	1945
D-1060	SHE WOULDN'T SAY YES	HALL	COLUMBIA	1945
D-1061	MEET ME ON BROADWAY	JASON	COLUMBIA	1946
D-1062	GUY, A GAL AND A PAL	BOETTICHER	COLUMBIA	1945
D-1063	ROUGH TOUGH AND READY	LORD	COLUMBIA	1945
D-1064	FIGHTING GUARDSMAN	LEVIN	COLUMBIA	1946
D-1066	TEN CENTS A DANCE	JASON	COLUMBIA	1945
D-1069	BOSTON BLACKIE HOOKED ON SUSPICION	DREIFUSS	COLUMBIA	1945
D-1070	BLONDE FROM BROOKLYN	LORD	COLUMBIA	1945
D-1071	GAY SENORITA	DREIFUSS	COLUMBIA	1945
D-1072	BOSTON BLACKIE'S RENDEZVOUS	DREIFUSS	COLUMBIA	1945
D-1074	BANDIT OF SHERWOOD FOREST	LEVIN, SHERMAN	COLUMBIA	1946

Movie Still Identification Book Ultimate Edition - Letters

CODE	TITLE/NAME	DIRECTOR/TYPE	STUDIO/DISTRIBUTOR	YEAR
D-1075	I LOVE A BANDLEADER	LORD	COLUMBIA	1945
D-1076	VOICE OF THE WHISTLER	CASTLE	COLUMBIA	1945
D-1078	GIRL OF THE LIMBERLOST	FERRER	COLUMBIA	1945
D-1079	RENEGADES	SHERMAN	COLUMBIA	1946
D-1080	ONE WAY TO LOVE	ENRIGHT	COLUMBIA	1946
D-1081	HIT THE HAY	LORD	COLUMBIA	1945
D-1082	MY NAME IS JULIA ROSS	LEWIS	COLUMBIA	1945
D-1083	OUT OF THE DEPTHS	LEDERMAN	COLUMBIA	1945
D-1084	LIFE WITH BLONDIE	BERLIN	COLUMBIA	1945
D-1086	PRISON SHIP	DREIFUSS	COLUMBIA	1945
D-1087	GILDA	VIDOR	COLUMBIA	1946
D-1088	BLONDIE'S LUCKY DAY	BERLIN	COLUMBIA	1946
D-1089	CLOSE CALL FOR BOSTON BLACKIE	LANDERS	COLUMBIA	1946
D-1090	SO DARK THE NIGHT	LEWIS	COLUMBIA	1946
D-1091	NOTORIOUS LONE WOLF	LEDERMAN	COLUMBIA	1946
D-1092	GENTLEMEN MISBEHAVES	SHERMAN	COLUMBIA	1946
D-1093	JUST BEFORE DAWN	CASTLE	COLUMBIA	1946
D-1094	WALLS CAME TUMBLING DOWN	MENDES	COLUMBIA	1946
D-1095	DEVIL'S MASK	LEVIN	COLUMBIA	1946
D-1096	DANGEROUS BUSINESS	LEDERMAN	COLUMBIA	1946
D-1097	TALK ABOUT A LADY	SHERMAN	COLUMBIA	1946
D-1098	MYSTERIOUS INTRUDER	CASTLE	COLUMBIA	1946
D-1099	NIGHT EDITOR	LEVIN	COLUMBIA	1946
D-1100	DOWN TO EARTH	HALL	COLUMBIA	1947
D-1101	PHANTOM THIEF	LEDERMAN	COLUMBIA	1946
D-1102	MAN WHO DARED	STURGES	COLUMBIA	1946
D-1103	GALLANT JOURNEY	WELLMAN	COLUMBIA	1946
D-1104	THRILL OF BRAZIL	SIMON	COLUMBIA	1946
D-1105	RETURN OF RUSTY	CASTLE	COLUMBIA	1946
D-1106	UNKNOWN	LEVIN	COLUMBIA	1946
D-1107	BLONDIE KNOWS BEST	BERLIN	COLUMBIA	1946
D-1108	SING WHILE YOU DANCE	LEDERMAN	COLUMBIA	1946
D-1109	PERSONALITY KID	SHERMAN	COLUMBIA	1946
D-1110	CRIME DR.'S MANHUNT	CASTLE	COLUMBIA	1946
D-1111	DEAD RECKONING	CROMWELL	COLUMBIA	1947
D-1112	IT'S GREAT TO BE YOUNG	LORD	COLUMBIA	1946
D-1113	FRAMED	WALLACE	COLUMBIA	1947
D-1114	SECRET OF THE WHISTLER	SHERMAN	COLUMBIA	1946
D-1115	GUILT OF JANET AMES	LEVIN	COLUMBIA	1947
D-1116	SHADOWED	STURGES	COLUMBIA	1946
D-1117	SWORDSMAN	LEWIS	COLUMBIA	1948
D-1118	SINGING IN THE CORN	LORD	COLUMBIA	1946
D-1119	BLONDIE'S BIG MOMENT	BERLIN	COLUMBIA	1947
D-1120	BOSTON BLACKIE AND THE LAW	LEDERMAN	COLUMBIA	1946
D-1121	RETURN OF OCTOBER	LEWIS	COLUMBIA	1948
D-1122	LONE WOLF IN MEXICO	LEDERMAN	COLUMBIA	1947
D-1123	ALIAS MR. TWILIGHT	STURGES	COLUMBIA	1946
D-1124	BLIND SPOT	GORDON	COLUMBIA	1947
D-1125	MILLIE'S DAUGHTER	SALKOW	COLUMBIA	1947
D-1126	LADY FROM SHANGHAI		COLUMBIA	1947
D-1127	CIGARETTE GIRL	VON FRITSCH	COLUMBIA	1947
D-1128	THIRTEENTH HOUR	CLEMENS	COLUMBIA	1947
D-1129	KING OF THE WILD HORSES	ARCHAINBAUD	COLUMBIA	1947
D-1130	BLONDIE'S HOLIDAY	BERLIN	COLUMBIA	1947
D-1130	JOLSON STORY (SOME MARKED 1030)	GREEN	COLUMBIA	1946
D-1131	MILLERSON CASE	ARCHAINBAUD	COLUMBIA	1947
D-1132	BULLDOG DRUMMOND AT BAY	SALKOW	COLUMBIA	1947
D-1133	FOR THE LOVE OF RUSTY	STURGES	COLUMBIA	1947
D-1135	MAN FROM COLORADO	LEVIN	COLUMBIA	1948
D-1136	BLONDIE IN THE DOUGH	BERLIN	COLUMBIA	1947
D-1137	SPORT OF KINGS	GORDON	COLUMBIA	1947
D-1138	IT HAD TO BE YOU	HARTMAN, MATE	COLUMBIA	1947
D-1139	KEEPER OF THE BEES	STURGES	COLUMBIA	1947
D-1140	SON OF RUSTY	LANDERS	COLUMBIA	1947
D-1141	KEY WITNESS	LEDERMAN	COLUMBIA	1947
D-1142	BULLDOG DRUMMOND STRIKES AGAIN	MCDONALD	COLUMBIA	1947
D-1143	MATING OF MILLIE	LEVIN	COLUMBIA	1948
D-1144	WHEN A GIRL'S BEAUTIFUL	MCDONALD	COLUMBIA	1947
D-1145	SLIGHTLY FRENCH	SIRK	COLUMBIA	1949
D-1146	LONE WOLF IN LONDON	GOODWINS	COLUMBIA	1947

Movie Still Identification Book Ultimate Edition - Letters

CODE	TITLE/NAME	DIRECTOR/TYPE	STUDIO/DISTRIBUTOR	YEAR
D-1148	CRIME DR.'S GAMBLE	CASTLE	COLUMBIA	1947
D-1149	DEVIL SHIP	LANDERS	COLUMBIA	1947
D-1152	ADVENTURES IN SILVERADO	KARLSON	COLUMBIA	1948
D-1153	WRECK OF THE HESPERUS	HOFFMAN	COLUMBIA	1948
D-1154	PORT SAID	LE BORG	COLUMBIA	1948
D-1155	BLONDIE'S REWARD	BERLIN	COLUMBIA	1948
D-1156	BLONDIE'S ANNIVERSARY	BERLIN	COLUMBIA	1947
D-1157	WOMAN FROM TANGIER	DANIELS	COLUMBIA	1948
D-1159	RETURN OF THE WHISTLER	LEDERMAN	COLUMBIA	1948
D-1160	GALLANT BLADE	LEVIN	COLUMBIA	1948
D-1161	MY DOG RUSTY	LANDERS	COLUMBIA	1948
D-1162	BEST MAN WINS	STURGES	COLUMBIA	1948
D-1163	TRAPPED BY BOSTON BLACKIE	FRIEDMAN	COLUMBIA	1948
D-1164	THUNDERHOOF	KARLSON	COLUMBIA	1948
D-1165	LEATHER GLOVES	ASHER, QUINIE	COLUMBIA	1948
D-1166	RUSTY LEADS THE WAY	JASON	COLUMBIA	1948
D-1167	WALKING HILLS	STURGES	COLUMBIA	1949
D-1168	DARK PAST	MATE	COLUMBIA	1948
D-1169	BLACK EAGLE	GORDON	COLUMBIA	1948
D-1170	GENTLEMEN FROM NOWHERE	CASTLE	COLUMBIA	1948
D-1171	RUSTY SAVES A LIFE	FRIEDMAN	COLUMBIA	1949
D-1172	BLONDIE'S SECRET	BERNDS	COLUMBIA	1948
D-1173	BOSTON BLACKIE'S CHINESE VENTURE	FRIEDMAN	COLUMBIA	1949
D-1174	SHOCKPROOF	SIRK	COLUMBIA	1949
D-1175	MR. SOFT TOUCH	DOUGLAS, LEVIN	COLUMBIA	1949
D-1176	HOLIDAY IN HAVANA	YARBROUGH	COLUMBIA	1949
D-1177	LAW OF THE BARBARY COAST	LANDERS	COLUMBIA	1949
D-1178	LONE WOLF AND HIS LADY	HOFFMAN	COLUMBIA	1949
D-1179	CRIME DR.'S DIARY	FRIEDMAN	COLUMBIA	1949
D-1180	BLONDIE'S BIG DEAL	BERNDS	COLUMBIA	1949
D-1181	AIR HOSTESS	LANDERS	COLUMBIA	1949
D-1182	MAKE BELIEVE BALLROOM	SANTLEY	COLUMBIA	1949
D-1183	LUST FOR GOLD	SIMON	COLUMBIA	1949
D-1185	BLONDIE HITS THE JACKPOT	BERNDS	COLUMBIA	1949
D-1186	DEVIL'S HENCHMEN	FRIEDMAN	COLUMBIA	1949
D-1187	JOHNNY ALLEGRO	TETZLAFF	COLUMBIA	1949
D-1188	SECRET OF ST. IVES	ROSEN	COLUMBIA	1949
D-1189	KAZAN	JASON	COLUMBIA	1949
D-1190	RUSTY'S BIRTHDAY	FRIEDMAN	COLUMBIA	1949
D-1191	MISS GRANT TAKES RICHMOND	BACON	COLUMBIA	1949
D-1192	TELL IT TO THE JUDGE	FOSTER	COLUMBIA	1949
D-1193	PALOMINO	NAZARRO	COLUMBIA	1950
D-1194	PRISON WARDEN	FRIEDMAN	COLUMBIA	1949
D-1195	BLONDIE'S HERO	BERNDS	COLUMBIA	1950
D-1196	GOOD HUMOR MAN	BACON	COLUMBIA	1950
D-1197	BORN YESTERDAY	CUKOR	COLUMBIA	1950
D-1198	CARGO TO CAPETOWN	MCEVOY	COLUMBIA	1950
D-1199	MARY RYAN, DETECTIVE	BERLIN	COLUMBIA	1949
D-1200	GIRL'S SCHOOL	BRAHM	COLUMBIA	1938
D-1201	ROGUES OF SHERWOOD FOREST	DOUGLAS	COLUMBIA	1950
D-1202	WOMAN OF DISTINCTION	BUZZELL	COLUMBIA	1950
D-1204	FATHER IS A BACHELOR	BERLIN, FOSTER	COLUMBIA	1950
D-1205	BODYHOLD	FRIEDMAN	COLUMBIA	1949
D-1206	FORTUNES OF CAPTAIN BLOOD	DOUGLAS	COLUMBIA	1950
D-1207	PETTY GIRL	LEVIN	COLUMBIA	1950
D-1208	BEWARE OF BLONDIE	BERNDS	COLUMBIA	1950
D-1209	KILL THE UMPIRE	BACON	COLUMBIA	1950
D-1210	MILITARY ACADEMY	LEDERMAN	COLUMBIA	1940
D-1211	FULLER BRUSH GIRL	BACON	COLUMBIA	1950
D-1212	FRIGHTENED CITY (KILLER THAT STALKED NEW YORK)	MCEVOY	COLUMBIA	1950
D-1213	BEAUTY ON PARADE	LANDERS	COLUMBIA	1950
D-1214	NO SAD SONGS FOR ME	MATE	COLUMBIA	1950
D-1215	CUSTOMS AGENT	FRIEDMAN	COLUMBIA	1950
D-1218	WHEN YOU'RE SMILING	SANTLEY	COLUMBIA	1950
D-1219	CONVICTED	LEVIN	COLUMBIA	1950
D-1220	ROOKIE FIREMAN	FRIEDMAN	COLUMBIA	1950
D-1221	DAVID HARDING – COUNTER SPY	NAZARRO	COLUMBIA	1950
D-1222	BETWEEN MIDNIGHT AND DAWN	DOUGLAS	COLUMBIA	1950
D-1223	HE'S A COCKEYED WONDER	GODFREY	COLUMBIA	1950
D-1224	HARRIET CRAIG	SHERMAN	COLUMBIA	1950

Movie Still Identification Book Ultimate Edition - Letters

CODE	TITLE/NAME	DIRECTOR/TYPE	STUDIO/DISTRIBUTOR	YEAR
D-1225	ON THE ISLE OF SAMOA	BERKE	COLUMBIA	1950
D-1226	TWO OF A KIND	LEVIN	COLUMBIA	1951
D-1228	STAGE TO TUCSON	MURPHY	COLUMBIA	1950
D-1230	EMERGENCY WEDDING	BUZZELL	COLUMBIA	1950
D-1231	AL JENNINGS OF OKLAHOMA	NAZARRO	COLUMBIA	1951
D-1232	FLYING MISSING	LEVIN	COLUMBIA	1950
D-1233	MASK OF THE AVENGER	KARLSON	COLUMBIA	1951
D-1234	COUNTERSPY MEETS SCOTLAND YARD	FRIEDMAN	COLUMBIA	1950
D-1235	HER FIRST ROMANCE	FRIEDMAN	COLUMBIA	1951
D-1237	TOUGHER THEY COME	NAZARRO	COLUMBIA	1950
D-1238	FLAME OF STAMBOUL	NAZARRO	COLUMBIA	1951
D-1239	LADY AND THE BANDIT	MURPHY	COLUMBIA	1951
D-1240	GASOLINE ALLEY	BERNDS	COLUMBIA	1951
D-1241	BAREFOOT MAILMAN	MCEVOY	COLUMBIA	1951
D-1242	SUNNY SIDE OF THE STREET	QUINE	COLUMBIA	1951
D-1243	NEVER TRUST A GAMBLER	MURPHY	COLUMBIA	1951
D-1244	SMUGGLERS GOLD	BERKE	COLUMBIA	1951
D-1245	MOB	PARRISH	COLUMBIA	1951
D-1246	CRIMINAL LAWYER	FRIEDMAN	COLUMBIA	1951
D-1248	PAULA	MATE	COLUMBIA	1952
D-1249	MY TRUE STORY	ROONEY	COLUMBIA	1951
D-1250	CHINA CORSAIR	NAZARRO	COLUMBIA	1951
D-1251	BIG GUSHER	LANDERS	COLUMBIA	1951
D-1252	SON OF DR. JEKYL	FRIEDMAN	COLUMBIA	1951
D-1253	ASSIGNMENT-PARIS	PARRISH	COLUMBIA	1952
D-1254	CHAIN OF CIRCUMSTANCES	JASON	COLUMBIA	1951
D-1255	CORKY OF GASOLINE ALLEY	BERNDS	COLUMBIA	1951
D-1256	SOUND OFF	QUINE	COLUMBIA	1952
D-1257	CAPTAIN PIRATE (CAPTAIN BLOOD, FUGITIVE)	MURPHY	COLUMBIA	1952
D-1258	MARRYING KIND	CUKOR	COLUMBIA	1952
D-1259	OKINAWA	JASON	COLUMBIA	1952
D-1260	MONTANA TERRITORY	NAZARRO	COLUMBIA	1952
D-1261	HAREM GIRL	BERNDS	COLUMBIA	1952
D-1263	LAST OF THE COMMANCHES	DE TOTH	COLUMBIA	1953
D-1264	RAINBOW 'ROUND MY SHOULDER	QUINE	COLUMBIA	1952
D-1265	TARGET HONG KONG	SEARS	COLUMBIA	1953
D-1266	ALL ASHORE	QUINE	COLUMBIA	1953
D-1267	AMBUSH AT TOMAHAWK GAP	SEARS	COLUMBIA	1953
D-1268	LET'S DO IT AGAIN	HALL	COLUMBIA	1953
D-1269	MISSION OVER KOREA	SEARS	COLUMBIA	1953
D-1270	LAST POSSE	WERKER	COLUMBIA	1953
D-1271	FROM HERE TO ETERNITY	ZINNEMANN	COLUMBIA	1953
D-1272	CRUISIN' DOWN THE RIVER	QUINE	COLUMBIA	1953
D-1273	EL ALAMEIN (GER: THAT WAS OUR ROMMEL)	WIGANKO	COLUMBIA	1953
D-1274	CHINA VENTURE	SIEGEL	COLUMBIA	1953
D-1276	BIG HEAT	LANG	COLUMBIA	1953
D-1278	GUN FURY	WALSH	COLUMBIA	1953
D-1280	MAN IN THE DARK	LANDERS	COLUMBIA	1953
D-1281	HUMAN DESIRE	LANG	COLUMBIA	1954
D-1283	NEBRASKAN	SEARS	COLUMBIA	1953
D-1284	BAD FOR EACH OTHER	RAPPER	COLUMBIA	1953
D-1285	IT SHOULD HAPPEN TO YOU	CUKOR	COLUMBIA	1954
D-1287	THREE FOR THE SHOW	POTTER	COLUMBIA	1955
D-1288	MASSACRE CANYON	SEARS	COLUMBIA	1954
D-1289	DRIVE A CROOKED MILE	QUINE	COLUMBIA	1954
D-1290	THEY RODE WEST	KARLSON	COLUMBIA	1954
D-1291	PUSHOVER	QUINE	COLUMBIA	1954
D-1292	OUTLAW STALLION	SEARS	COLUMBIA	1954
D-1293	THREE HOUSE TO FILL	WERKER	COLUMBIA	1954
D-1295	BLACK DAKOTAS	NAZARRO	COLUMBIA	1954
D-1298	PHFFFT	ROBSON	COLUMBIA	1954
D-1299	WYOMING RENEGADES	SEARS	COLUMBIA	1954
D-1300	TIGHT SPOT	KARLSON	COLUMBIA	1955
D-1301	MY SISTER EILEEN	QUINE	COLUMBIA	1955
D-1302	CELL 2455-DEATH ROW	SEARS	COLUMBIA	1955
D-1303	THREE STRIPES IN THE SUN	MURPHY	COLUMBIA	1955
D-1305	BRING YOUR SMILE ALONG	EDWARDS	COLUMBIA	1955
D-1306	LAST FRONTIER	MANN	COLUMBIA	1955
D-1307	APACHE AMBUSH	SEARS	COLUMBIA	1955
D-1308	QUEEN BEE	MACDOUGALL	COLUMBIA	1955

Movie Still Identification Book Ultimate Edition - Letters

CODE	TITLE/NAME	DIRECTOR/TYPE	STUDIO/DISTRIBUTOR	YEAR
D-1309	PICNIC	LOGAN	COLUMBIA	1955
D-1310	JUBAL	DAVES	COLUMBIA	1956
D-1311	EDDIE DUCHIN STORY	SIDNEY	COLUMBIA	1956
D-1313	FURY AT GUNSIGHT PASS	SEARS	COLUMBIA	1956
D-1314	YOU CAN'T RUN AWAY FROM IT	POWELL	COLUMBIA	1956
D-1315	HARDER THEY FALL	ROBSON	COLUMBIA	1956
D-1316	SECRET OF TREASURE MOUNTAIN	FRIEDMAN	COLUMBIA	1956
D-1318	SOLID GOLD CADILLAC	QUINE	COLUMBIA	1956
D-1319	OVER-EXPOSED	SEILER	COLUMBIA	1956
D-1320	HE LAUGHED LAST	EDWARDS	COLUMBIA	1956
D-1322	FULL OF LIFE	QUINE	COLUMBIA	1956
D-1879	BAMBOLE (IT)	BOLOGNINI, COLOGINI	COLUMBIA	1965
D-3001	COWBOY FROM LONESOME RIVER	KLINE	COLUMBIA	1944
D-3002	CYCLONE PRAIRIE RANGERS	KLINE	COLUMBIA	1944
D-3003	COWBOY IN THE CLOUDS	KLINE	COLUMBIA	1943
D-3004	SUNDOWN VALLEY	KLINE	COLUMBIA	1944
D-3005	COWBOY CANTEEN	LANDERS	COLUMBIA	1944
D-3006	SADDLE LEATHER LAW	KLINE	COLUMBIA	1944
D-3007	SAGEBRUSH HEROES	KLINE	COLUMBIA	1945
D-3008	ROUGH RIDING JUSTICE	ABRAHAMS	COLUMBIA	1945
D-3009	SWING IN THE SADDLE	LANDERS	COLUMBIA	1944
D-3010	RETURN OF THE DURANGO KID	ABRAHAMS	COLUMBIA	1945
D-3011	BOTH BARRELS BLAZING	ABRAHAMS	COLUMBIA	1945
D-3012	RUSTLERS OF THE BADLANDS	ABRAHAMS	COLUMBIA	1945
D-3013	FRONTIER GUNLAW	ABRAHAMS	COLUMBIA	1946
D-3014	SING ME A SONG OF TEXAS	KEAYS	COLUMBIA	1945
D-3015	BLAZING THE WESTERN TRAIL	KEAYS	COLUMBIA	1945
D-3016	LAWLESS EMPIRE	KEAYS	COLUMBIA	1945
D-3017	ROCKIN' IN THE ROCKIES	KEAYS	COLUMBIA	1945
D-3018	RHYTHM ROUNDUP	KEAYS	COLUMBIA	1945
D-3019	OUTLAWS OF THE ROCKIES	NAZARRO	COLUMBIA	1945
D-3020	TEXAS PANHANDLE	NAZARRO	COLUMBIA	1945
D-3021	SONG OF THE PRAIRIE	NAZARRO	COLUMBIA	1945
D-3022	DESERT HORSEMAN	NAZARRO	COLUMBIA	1946
D-3023	GUNNING FOR VENGEANCE	NAZARRO	COLUMBIA	1946
D-3024	ROARING RANGERS	NAZARRO	COLUMBIA	1946
D-3025	THROW A SADDLE ON A STAR	NAZARRO	COLUMBIA	1946
D-3026	HEADING WEST	NAZARRO	COLUMBIA	1946
D-3027	GALLOPING THUNDER	NAZARRO	COLUMBIA	1946
D-3028	TWO-FISTED STRANGER	NAZARRO	COLUMBIA	1946
D-3029	THAT TEXAS JAMBOREE	NAZARRO	COLUMBIA	1946
D-3030	TERROR TRAIL	NAZARRO	COLUMBIA	1946
D-3031	LANDRUSH	KEAYS	COLUMBIA	1946
D-3032	COWBOY BLUES	NAZARRO	COLUMBIA	1946
D-3033	SINGING ON THE TRAIL	NAZARRO	COLUMBIA	1946
D-3034	FIGHTING FRONTIERSMAN	ABRAHAMS	COLUMBIA	1946
D-3035	SOUTH OF THE CHISHOLM TRAIL	ABRAHAMS	COLUMBIA	1947
D-3036	LONE STAR MOONLIGHT	NAZARRO	COLUMBIA	1946
D-3037	OVER THE SANTA FE TRAIL	NAZARRO	COLUMBIA	1947
D-3038	WEST OF DODGE CITY	NAZARRO	COLUMBIA	1947
D-3039	LONE HAND TEXAS	NAZARRO	COLUMBIA	1947
D-3040	LAW OF THE CANYON	NAZARRO	COLUMBIA	1947
D-3041	PRAIRIE RAIDERS	ABRAHAMS	COLUMBIA	1947
D-3042	STRANGER FROM PONCA CITY	ABRAHAMS	COLUMBIA	1947
D-3043	RIDERS OF THE LONE STAR	ABRAHAMS	COLUMBIA	1947
D-3044	SWING THE WESTERN WAY	ABRAHAMS	COLUMBIA	1947
D-3045	SMOKEY RIVER SERENADE	ABRAHAMS	COLUMBIA	1947
D-3046	SIX GUN LAW	NAZARRO	COLUMBIA	1948
D-3047	BUCKAROO FROM POWDER RIVER	NAZARRO	COLUMBIA	1947
D-3048	PHANTOM VALLEY	NAZARRO	COLUMBIA	1948
D-3049	LAST DAYS OF BOOTHILL	NAZARRO	COLUMBIA	1947
D-3050	ROSE OF SANTA FE	NAZARRO	COLUMBIA	1947
D-3051	WHIRLWIND RAIDERS	KEAYS	COLUMBIA	1948
D-3052	WEST OF SONORA	NAZARRO	COLUMBIA	1948
D-3053	SONG OF IDAHO	NAZARRO	COLUMBIA	1948
D-3054	BLAZING ACROSS THE PECOS	NAZARRO	COLUMBIA	1948
D-3055	TRAIL TO LAREDO	NAZARRO	COLUMBIA	1948
D-3056	ARKANSAS SWING	NAZARRO	COLUMBIA	1948
D-3057	SINGIN' SPURS	NAZARRO	COLUMBIA	1948
D-3058	EL DORADO PASS	NAZARRO	COLUMBIA	1948

Movie Still Identification Book Ultimate Edition - Letters

CODE	TITLE/NAME	DIRECTOR/TYPE	STUDIO/DISTRIBUTOR	YEAR
D-3059	QUICK ON THE TRIGGER	NAZARRO	COLUMBIA	1948
D-3060	CHALLENGE OF THE RANGE	NAZARRO	COLUMBIA	1949
D-3061	SMOKY MOUNTAIN MELODY	NAZARRO	COLUMBIA	1948
D-3062	SOUTH OF DEATH VALLEY	NAZARRO	COLUMBIA	1949
D-3063	DESERT VIGILANTE	SEARS	COLUMBIA	1949
D-3064	LARAMIE	NAZARRO	COLUMBIA	1949
D-3065	HOME IN SAN ANTONE	NAZARRO	COLUMBIA	1949
D-3066	BLAZING TRAIL	NAZARRO	COLUMBIA	1949
D-3067	HORSEMEN OF THE SIERRAS	SEARS	COLUMBIA	1949
D-3068	BANDITS OF EL DORADO	NAZARRO	COLUMBIA	1949
D-3069	RENEGADES OF THE SAGE	NAZARRO	COLUMBIA	1949
D-3070	HOEDOWN	NAZARRO	COLUMBIA	1950
D-3071	FEUDIN' RHYTHM	BERNDS	COLUMBIA	1949
D-3072	OUTCAST OF BLACK MESA	NAZARRO	COLUMBIA	1950
D-3073	FRONTIER OUTPOST	NAZARRO	COLUMBIA	1950
D-3074	TRAIL OF THE RUSTLERS	NAZARRO	COLUMBIA	1950
D-3075	TEXAS DYNAMO	NAZARRO	COLUMBIA	1950
D-3076	STREETS OF GHOST TOWN	NAZARRO	COLUMBIA	1950
D-3077	ACROSS THE BADLANDS	SEARS	COLUMBIA	1950
D-3078	RAIDERS OF TOMAHAWK CREEK	SEARS	COLUMBIA	1950
D-3079	LIGHTNING GUNS	SEARS	COLUMBIA	1950
D-3080	PRAIRIE ROUNDUP	SEARS	COLUMBIA	1951
D-3081	RIDIN' THE OUTLAW TRAIL	SEARS	COLUMBIA	1951
D-3082	FORT SAVAGE RAIDERS	NAZARRO	COLUMBIA	1951
D-3083	SNAKE RIVER DESPERADOES	SEARS	COLUMBIA	1951
D-3084	BONANZA TOWN	SEARS	COLUMBIA	1951
D-3085	CYCLONE FURY	NAZARRO	COLUMBIA	1951
D-3086	KID FROM AMARILLO	NAZARRO	COLUMBIA	1951
D-3087	KID FROM AMARILLO	NAZARRO	COLUMBIA	1951
D-3087	PECOS RIVER	SEARS	COLUMBIA	1951
D-3088	SMOKY CANYON	SEARS	COLUMBIA	1952
D-3089	HAWK OF WILD RIVER	SEARS	COLUMBIA	1952
D-3090	LARAMIE MOUNTAINS	NAZARRO	COLUMBIA	1952
D-3091	ROUGH TOUGH WEST	NAZARRO	COLUMBIA	1952
D-3092	JUNCTION CITY	NAZARRO	COLUMBIA	1952
D-3093	KID FROM BROKEN GUN	SEARS	COLUMBIA	1952
D-3400	CORONER CREEK	ENRIGHT	COLUMBIA	1948
D-4001	BUSY BUDDIES (sh)	LORD	COLUMBIA	1944
D-4002	WEDDED BLISS (sh)	EDWARDS	COLUMBIA	1944
D-4003	BACHELOR DAZE (sh)	WHITE	COLUMBIA	1943
D-4004	YOU DEAR BOY (sh)	WHITE	COLUMBIA	1943
D-4005	DOCTOR, FEEL MY PULSE (sh)	WHITE	COLUMBIA	1944
D-4006	BOOBY DUPES (sh)	LORD	COLUMBIA	1945
D-4007	HIS TALE IS TOLD (sh)	EDWARDS	COLUMBIA	1944
D-4008	YOU WERE NEVER UGLIER (sh)	WHITE	COLUMBIA	1944
D-4009	GOLD IS WHERE YOU LOSE IT (sh)	WHITE	COLUMBIA	1944
D-4010	CRASH GOES THE HAS (sh)	WHITE	COLUMBIA	1944
D-4011	CRAZY LIKE A FOX (sh)	WHITE	COLUMBIA	1944
D-4012	HIS HOTEL SWEET (sh)	EDWARDS	COLUMBIA	1944
D-4013	IDLE ROOMERS (sh)	LORD	COLUMBIA	1943
D-4014	OH, BABY (sh)	WHITE	COLUMBIA	1944
D-4015	OFF AGAIN, ON AGAIN (sh)	WHITE	COLUMBIA	1945
D-4016	OPEN SEASON FOR SAPS (sh)	WHITE	COLUMBIA	1944
D-4017	DEFECTIVE DETECTIVES (sh)	EDWARDS	COLUMBIA	1944
D-4018	PICK A PECK OF PLUMBERS (sh)	WHITE	COLUMBIA	1944
D-4019	MOPEY DOPE (sh)	LORD	COLUMBIA	1944
D-4020	GENTS WITHOUT CENTS (sh)	WHITE	COLUMBIA	1944
D-4021	HEATHER AND YON (sh)	EDWARDS	COLUMBIA	1944
D-4022	THREE PESTS IN A MESS (sh)	LORD	COLUMBIA	1945
D-4023	WOO WOO (I SHOULD WORRY*)	WHITE	COLUMBIA	1945
D-4024	TWO LOCAL YOKELS (sh)	WHITE	COLUMBIA	1945
D-4025	KNIGHT AND A BLONDE (sh)	EDWARDS	COLUMBIA	1944
D-4025	WOO WOO (I SHOULD WORRY*)	WHITE	COLUMBIA	1945
D-4026	SHE SNOOPS TO CONQUER (sh)	WHITE	COLUMBIA	1944
D-4027	STRIFE OF THE PARTY (sh)	EDWARDS	COLUMBIA	1944
D-4028	DANCE DUNCE, DANCE (sh)	WHITE	COLUMBIA	1945
D-4029	SNOOPER SERVICE (sh)	EDWARDS	COLUMBIA	1945
D-4030	IDIOTS DELUXE (sh)	WHITE	COLUMBIA	1945
D-4031	JURY GOES ROUND AND ROUND (sh)	WHITE	COLUMBIA	1945
D-4032	HISS AND YELL (sh)	WHITE	COLUMBIA	1946

Movie Still Identification Book Ultimate Edition - Letters

CODE	TITLE/NAME	DIRECTOR/TYPE	STUDIO/DISTRIBUTOR	YEAR
D-4033	IF A BODY MEETS A BODY (sh)	WHITE	COLUMBIA	1945
D-4035	PISTOL PACKIN' NITWITS (sh)	EDWARDS	COLUMBIA	1945
D-4036	WIFE DECOY (sh)	EDWARDS	COLUMBIA	1945
D-4037	SPOOK TO ME (sh)	EDWARDS	COLUMBIA	1945
D-4038	HIT WITH A MISS	EDWARDS, WHITE	COLUMBIA	1945
D-4038	HIT WITH A MISS (sh)	WHITE	COLUMBIA	1945
D-4039	MAYOR'S HUSBAND (sh)	EDWARDS	COLUMBIA	1945
D-4040	MINER AFFAIR (sh)	WHITE	COLUMBIA	1945
D-4041	BLONDE STAYED ON (sh)	EDWARDS	COLUMBIA	1946
D-4042	CALLING ALL FIBBERS (sh)	WHITE	COLUMBIA	1945
D-4043	BIRD IN THE HEAD (sh)	BERNDS	COLUMBIA	1946
D-4044	MICRO-PHONIES (sh)	BERNDS	COLUMBIA	1945
D-4045	BEER BARREL POLECATS (sh)	WHITE	COLUMBIA	1946
D-4046	THREE TROUBLEDOERS (sh)	BERNDS	COLUMBIA	1946
D-4047	WHEN THE WIFE'S AWAY (sh)	BERNDS	COLUMBIA	1946
D-4048	JIGGERS, MY WIFE (sh)	WHITE	COLUMBIA	1946
D-4048	WHERE THE PEST BEGINS	EDWARDS	COLUMBIA	1945
D-4049	YOU CAN'T FOOL A FOOL (sh)	WHITE	COLUMBIA	1946
D-4050	UNCIVIL WAR BIRDS (sh)	WHITE	COLUMBIA	1946
D-4051	HIGH BLOOD PLEASURE (sh)	WHITE	COLUMBIA	1945
D-4052	SOCIETY MUGS (sh)	BERNDS	COLUMBIA	1946
D-4053	THREE LOAN WOLVES (sh)	WHITE	COLUMBIA	1946
D-4054	MR. NOISY (sh)	BERNDS	COLUMBIA	1946
D-4055	GET ALONG LITTLE ZOMBIE (sh)	BERNDS	COLUMBIA	1946
D-4056	HALF-WITS HOLIDAY (sh)	WHITE	COLUMBIA	1947
D-4057	RHYTHM AND WEEP (sh)	WHITE	COLUMBIA	1946
D-4058	MONKEY BUSINESSMEN (sh)	BERNDS	COLUMBIA	1946
D-4059	ANDY PLAYS HOOKEY (sh)	BERNDS	COLUMBIA	1946
D-4060	HEADIN' FOR A WEDDIN' (sh)	WHITE	COLUMBIA	1946
D-4061	SCOOPER DOOPER (sh)	BERNDS	COLUMBIA	1947
D-4062	AIN'T LOVE CUCKOO (sh)	WHITE	COLUMBIA	1946
D-4063	G. I. WANNA HOME (sh)	WHITE	COLUMBIA	1946
D-4064	BRIDE AND GLOOM (sh)	BERNDS	COLUMBIA	1947
D-4065	MR. WRIGHT GOES WRONG (sh)	WHITE	COLUMBIA	1946
D-4066	HOT WATER (sh)	BERNDS	COLUMBIA	1946
D-4067	THREE LITTLE PIRATES (sh)	BERNDS	COLUMBIA	1946
D-4068	PARDON MY TERROR (sh)	BERNDS	COLUMBIA	1946
D-4069	SUNK IN THE SINK (sh)	WHITE	COLUMBIA	1949
D-4070	FIDDLERS THREE (sh)	WHITE	COLUMBIA	1948
D-4071	FRIGHT NIGHT	BERNDS	COLUMBIA	1947
D-4072	SHOULD HUSBANDS MARRY? (sh)	LORD	COLUMBIA	1947
D-4073	CRABBIN' IN THE CABIN (sh)	WHITE	COLUMBIA	1948
D-4074	HONEYMOON BLUES (sh)	BERNDS	COLUMBIA	1946
D-4075	HOT HEIR (sh)	BERNDS	COLUMBIA	1947
D-4076	HECTIC HONEYMOON (sh)	BERNDS	COLUMBIA	1947
D-4077	OUT WEST (sh)	BERNDS	COLUMBIA	1947
D-4078	SO'S YOUR ANTENNA	WHITE	COLUMBIA	1946
D-4079	TWO JILLS AND A JACK (sh)	WHITE	COLUMBIA	1947
D-4080	SLAPPILY MARRIED (sh)	BERNDS	COLUMBIA	1946
D-4081	MEET MR. MISCHIEF (sh)	BERNDS	COLUMBIA	1947
D-4082	SQUAREHEADS OF THE ROUND TABLE (sh)	BERNDS	COLUMBIA	1948
D-4083	RENO-VATED (sh)	WHITE	COLUMBIA	1946
D-4084	NERVOUS SHAKEDOWN (sh)	LORD	COLUMBIA	1947
D-4085	MORON THAN OFF (sh)	WHITE	COLUMBIA	1946
D-4086	GOOD BAD EGG (sh)	WHITE	COLUMBIA	1947
D-4087	HOLD THAT LION (sh)	WHITE	COLUMBIA	1947
D-4088	SING A SONG OF SIX PANTS (sh)	WHITE	COLUMBIA	1947
D-4089	ROLLING DOWN TO RENO (sh)	WHITE	COLUMBIA	1947
D-4091	I'M A MONKEY'S UNCLE (sh)	WHITE	COLUMBIA	1948
D-4093	PARDON MY CLUTCH (sh)	BERNDS	COLUMBIA	1948
D-4094	HOT SCOTS (sh)	BERNDS	COLUMBIA	1948
D-4095	BRIDELESS GROOM (sh)	BERNDS	COLUMBIA	1947
D-4096	WIFE TO SPARE (sh)	BERNDS	COLUMBIA	1947
D-4097	CUPID GOES NUTS (sh)	WHITE	COLUMBIA	1947
D-4098	TRAINING FOR TROUBLE (sh)	WHITE	COLUMBIA	1947
D-4099	WEDDING BELLE (sh)	BERNDS	COLUMBIA	1947
D-4100	TALL, DARK AND GRUESOME (sh)	LORD	COLUMBIA	1948
D-4101	WAITING IN THE LURCH (sh)	BERNDS	COLUMBIA	1949
D-4102	STOOGES (sh)		COLUMBIA	
D-4103	SHIVERING SHERLOCKS (sh)	LORD	COLUMBIA	1948

Movie Still Identification Book Ultimate Edition - Letters

CODE	TITLE/NAME	DIRECTOR/TYPE	STUDIO/DISTRIBUTOR	YEAR
D-4104	ALL GUMMED UP (sh)	WHITE	COLUMBIA	1947
D-4105	MUMMY'S DUMMIES (sh)	BERNDS	COLUMBIA	1948
D-4106	WEDLOCK DEADLOCK (sh)	BERNDS	COLUMBIA	1947
D-4107	THREE HAMS ON RYE (sh)	WHITE	COLUMBIA	1950
D-4108	GHOST TALKS (sh)	WHITE	COLUMBIA	1949
D-4109	RADIO ROMEO (sh)	BERNDS	COLUMBIA	1947
D-4110	MAN OR MOUSE (sh)	WHITE	COLUMBIA	1948
D-4111	CRIME ON THEIR HANDS (sh)	BERNDS	COLUMBIA	1948
D-4112	WHO DONE IT? (sh)	BERNDS	COLUMBIA	1949
D-4113	EIGHT BALL ANDY (sh)	BERNDS	COLUMBIA	1948
D-4114	FUELIN' AROUND (sh)	BERNDS	COLUMBIA	1949
D-4115	HUGS AND MUGS (sh)	WHITE	COLUMBIA	1950
D-4116	HOKUS POKUS (sh)	WHITE	COLUMBIA	1949
D-4117	FLAT FEAT (sh)	BERNDS	COLUMBIA	1948
D-4118	GO CHASE YOURSELF (sh)	WHITE	COLUMBIA	1948
D-4119	MALICE IN THE PALACE (sh)	WHITE	COLUMBIA	1949
D-4120	JITTER BUGHOUSE (sh)	WHITE	COLUMBIA	1948
D-4121	PARDON MY LAMBCHOP (sh)	WHITE	COLUMBIA	1948
D-4122	SILLY BILLY (sh)	WHITE	COLUMBIA	1948
D-4123	HE'S IN AGAIN (sh)	BERNDS	COLUMBIA	1949
D-4124	TWO NUTS IN A RUT (sh)	BERNDS	COLUMBIA	1948
D-4125	BILLIE GETS HER MAN (sh)	BERNDS	COLUMBIA	1948
D-4126	SHEEPISH WOLF (sh)	BERNDS	COLUMBIA	1948
D-4127	PARLOR, BEDROOM AND WRATH (sh)	WHITE	COLUMBIA	1948
D-4128	PINCH IN TIME (sh)	LORD	COLUMBIA	1948
D-4129	LOVE AT FIRST BITE (sh)	WHITE	COLUMBIA	1950
D-4130	MICROSPOOK (sh)	BERNDS	COLUMBIA	1949
D-4131	DOPEY DICKS (sh)	BERNDS	COLUMBIA	1950
D-4132	RADIO RIOT (sh)	BERNDS	COLUMBIA	1949
D-4133	TRAPPED BY A BLOND (sh)	LORD	COLUMBIA	1949
D-4134	FLUNG BY A FLING (sh)	BERNDS	COLUMBIA	1949
D-4135	CLUNKED IN THE CLINK (sh)	WHITE	COLUMBIA	1949
D-4136	MISS IN A MESS (sh)	WHITE	COLUMBIA	1949
D-4137	DUNKED IN THE DEEP (sh)	WHITE	COLUMBIA	1949
D-4138	DIZZY YARDBIRD (sh)	WHITE	COLUMBIA	1950
D-4139	SLAPHAPPY SLEUTHS (sh)	WHITE	COLUMBIA	1950
D-4140	VAGABOND LOAFERS (sh)	BERNDS	COLUMBIA	1949
D-4141	SELF MADE MAIDS (sh)	WHITE	COLUMBIA	1950
D-4142	PUNCHY COWPUNCHERS (sh)	BERNDS	COLUMBIA	1950
D-4143	STUDIO STOOPS (sh)	BERNDS	COLUMBIA	1950
D-4144	HOLD THAT MONKEY (sh)	WHITE	COLUMBIA	1950
D-4145	HIS BAITING BEAUTY (sh)	BERNDS	COLUMBIA	1950
D-4146	SUPER WOLF (sh)	LORD	COLUMBIA	1949
D-4147	LET DOWN YOUR AERIAL (sh)	BERNDS	COLUMBIA	1949
D-4148	ONE SHIVERY NIGHT (sh)	LORD	COLUMBIA	1950
D-4149	WHA' HAPPEN? (sh)	WHITE	COLUMBIA	1949
D-4150	NURSIE BEHAVE (sh)	WHITE	COLUMBIA	1950
D-4151	FRENCH FRIED FROLIC (sh)	WHITE	COLUMBIA	1949
D-4152	HOUSE ABOUT IT (sh)	WHITE	COLUMBIA	1950
D-4153	MARINATED MARINER (sh)	WHITE	COLUMBIA	1950
D-4154	SNITCH IN TIME (sh)	BERNDS	COLUMBIA	1950
D-4155	BABY SITTERS JITTERS (sh)	WHITE	COLUMBIA	1951
D-4156	THREE ARABIAN NUTS (sh)	BERNDS	COLUMBIA	1951
D-4157	SCRAMBLED BRAINS (sh)	WHITE	COLUMBIA	1951
D-4158	DON'T THROW THAT KNIFE (sh)	WHITE	COLUMBIA	1951
D-4159	MALICE IN THE PALACE (sh) (see 4119)	WHITE	COLUMBIA	1949
D-4159	MISSED FORTUNE (sh)	WHITE	COLUMBIA	1952
D-4160	BLUNDERFUL TIME (sh)	WHITE	COLUMBIA	1949
D-4161	MERRY MAVERICKS (sh)	BERNDS	COLUMBIA	1951
D-4162	TOOTH WILL OUT (sh)	BERNDS	COLUMBIA	1951
D-4163	PEST MAN WINS (sh)	WHITE	COLUMBIA	1951
D-4164	WINE, WOMEN AND BONG (sh)	WHITE	COLUMBIA	1951
D-4165	TWO ROAMING CHAMPS (sh)	BERNDS	COLUMBIA	1950
D-4166	HE FLEW THE SHREW (sh)	WHITE	COLUMBIA	1951
D-4167	FUN ON THE RUN (sh)	WHITE	COLUMBIA	1951
D-4168	SLIP AND A MISS (sh)	MCCOLLUM	COLUMBIA	1950
D-4169	WOO WOO BLUES (sh)	QUINE	COLUMBIA	1951
D-4170	BLONDE ATOM BOMB (sh)	WHITE	COLUMBIA	1951
D-4171	PLEASURE TREASURE (sh)	WHITE	COLUMBIA	1951
D-4172	INNOCENTLY GUILTY (sh)	WHITE	COLUMBIA	1950

Movie Still Identification Book Ultimate Edition - Letters

CODE	TITLE/NAME	DIRECTOR/TYPE	STUDIO/DISTRIBUTOR	YEAR
D-4173	AWFUL SLEUTH (sh)	QUINE	COLUMBIA	1951
D-4174	FOY MEETS GIRL (sh)	ULLMAN	COLUMBIA	1950
D-4175	WEDDING YELLS (sh)	WHITE	COLUMBIA	1951
D-4176	HAPPY GO WACKY (sh)	WHITE	COLUMBIA	1952
D-4177	SHE TOOK A POWDER (sh)	WHITE	COLUMBIA	1951
D-4178	CORNY CASANOVAS (sh)	WHITE	COLUMBIA	1952
D-4179	HULA-LA-LA (sh)	MCCOLLUM	COLUMBIA	1951
D-4180	LISTEN, JUDGE (sh)	BERNDS	COLUMBIA	1952
D-4181	HE COOKED HIS GOOSE (sh)	WHITE	COLUMBIA	1952
D-4182	UP IN DAISY'S PENTHOUSE (sh)	WHITE	COLUMBIA	1953
D-4183	GENTS IN A JAM (sh)	BERNDS	COLUMBIA	1952
D-4184	TROUBLE IN-LAWS (sh)	MCCOLLUM	COLUMBIA	1951
D-4185	CHAMPS STEP OUT (sh)	BERNDS	COLUMBIA	1951
D-4186	ROOTIN' TOOTIN' TENDERFEET (sh)	WHITE	COLUMBIA	1952
D-4187	GINK AT THE SINK (sh)	WHITE	COLUMBIA	1952
D-4188	HEEBIE GEE-GEES (sh)	BERNDS	COLUMBIA	1952
D-4189	FOOL AND HIS HONEY (sh)	WHITE	COLUMBIA	1952
D-4190	BLISSFUL BLUNDER (sh)	WHITE	COLUMBIA	1952
D-4191	HOOKED AND ROOKED (sh)	WHITE	COLUMBIA	1952
D-4192	FRAIDY CAT (sh)	WHITE	COLUMBIA	1951
D-4193	AIM, FIRE, SCOOT (sh)	WHITE	COLUMBIA	1952
D-4194	CUCKOO ON A CHOO CHOO (sh)	WHITE	COLUMBIA	1952
D-4195	CAUGHT ON THE BOUNCE (sh)	WHITE	COLUMBIA	1952
D-4197	LOOSE LOOT (sh)	WHITE	COLUMBIA	1953
D-4198	STROP, LOOK AND LISTEN (sh)	WHITE	COLUMBIA	1952
D-4199	TRICKY DICKS (sh)	WHITE	COLUMBIA	1953
D-4200	THREE DARK HORSES (sh)	WHITE	COLUMBIA	1952
D-4201	BUBBLE TROUBLE (sh)	WHITE	COLUMBIA	1953
D-4201	RIP, SEW AND STITCH (sh)	WHITE	COLUMBIA	1953
D-4203	GOOF ON THE ROOF (sh)	WHITE	COLUMBIA	1953
D-4204	HE POPPED HIS PISTOL (sh)	WHITE	COLUMBIA	1953
D-4205	SPIES AND GUYS (sh)	WHITE	COLUMBIA	1953
D-4206	LOVE'S A POPPIN' (sh)	WHITE	COLUMBIA	1953
D-4207	OH, SAY CAN YOU SUE (sh)	WHITE	COLUMBIA	1953
D-4207	TWO JILLS AND A JACK (sh) (see 4079)	WHITE	COLUMBIA	1947
D-4208	INCOME TAX SAPPY (sh)	WHITE	COLUMBIA	1954
D-4209	MUSTY MUSKATEERS (sh)	WHITE	COLUMBIA	1954
D-4210	SPOOKS (sh)	WHITE	COLUMBIA	1953
D-4211	PALS AND GALS (sh)	WHITE	COLUMBIA	1954
D-4212	PARDON MY BACKFIRE (sh)	WHITE	COLUMBIA	1953
D-4213	A-HUNTING THEY DID GO	WHITE	COLUMBIA	1948
D-4214	DOGGIE IN THE BEDROOM (sh)	WHITE	COLUMBIA	1954
D-4215	DOWN THE HATCH (sh)	WHITE	COLUMBIA	1953
D-4216	SHOT IN THE FRONTIER (sh)	WHITE	COLUMBIA	1954
D-4217	KNUTZY KNIGHTS (sh)	WHITE	COLUMBIA	1954
D-4218	SCOTCHED IN SCOTLAND (sh)	WHITE	COLUMBIA	1954
D-4219	TOOTING TOOTERS (sh)	WHITE	COLUMBIA	1954
D-4220	MINER AFFAIR	WHITE	COLUMBIA	1945
D-4220	TWO APRIL FOOLS (sh)	WHITE	COLUMBIA	1954
D-4221	KIDS WILL BE KIDS (sh)	WHITE	COLUMBIA	1954
D-4222	BLUNDER BOYS (sh)	WHITE	COLUMBIA	1955
D-4223	FLING IN THE RING	WHITE	COLUMBIA	1955
D-4224	GYPPED IN THE PENTHOUSE (sh)	WHITE	COLUMBIA	1955
D-4225	OF CASH AND HASH (sh)	WHITE	COLUMBIA	1955
D-4226	FIRE CHASER (sh)	WHITE	COLUMBIA	1954
D-4227	CREEPS (sh)	WHITE	COLUMBIA	1956
D-4227	G. I. DOOD IT (sh)	WHITE	COLUMBIA	1955
D-4228	BEDLAM IN PARADISE (sh)	WHITE	COLUMBIA	1955
D-4228	HEAVENLY DAZE (sh)	WHITE	COLUMBIA	1948
D-4229	STONE AGE ROMEOS (sh)	WHITE	COLUMBIA	1955
D-4230	HIS PEST FRIEND (sh)	WHITE	COLUMBIA	1955
D-4231	NOBODY'S HOME (sh)	WHITE	COLUMBIA	1955
D-4232	WHAM-BAM-SLAM! (sh)	WHITE	COLUMBIA	1955
D-4233	HOT ICE (sh)	WHITE	COLUMBIA	1955
D-4234	ONE SPOOKY NIGHT (sh)	WHITE	COLUMBIA	1955
D-4235	SCRATCH SCRATCH SCRATCH	WHITE	COLUMBIA	1955
D-4236	HUSBANDS BEWARE (sh)	WHITE	COLUMBIA	1956
D-4238	FLAGPOLE JITTERS (sh)	WHITE	COLUMBIA	1956
D-4239	FOR CRIMIN' OUT LOUD (sh)	WHITE	COLUMBIA	1956
D-4240	HOOK A CROOK (sh)	WHITE	COLUMBIA	1955

Movie Still Identification Book Ultimate Edition - Letters

CODE	TITLE/NAME	DIRECTOR/TYPE	STUDIO/DISTRIBUTOR	YEAR
D-4241	HE TOOK A POWDER (sh)	WHITE	COLUMBIA	1955
D-4242	ARMY DAZE (sh)	WHITE	COLUMBIA	1956
D-4243	COME ON SEVEN (sh)	WHITE	COLUMBIA	1956
D-4244	RUMPUS IN THE HAREM (sh)	WHITE	COLUMBIA	1956
D-4245	HOT STUFF (sh)	WHITE	COLUMBIA	1956
D-4246	SCHEMING SCHEMERS (sh)	WHITE	COLUMBIA	1956
D-4247	COMMOTION ON THE OCEAN (sh)	WHITE	COLUMBIA	1956
D-4248	ANDY GOES WILD (sh)	WHITE	COLUMBIA	1956
D-4249	PARDON MY NIGHTSHIRT (sh)	WHITE	COLUMBIA	1956
D-8007	LORNA DOONE	KARLSON	COLUMBIA	1951
D-8008	ROAR OF THE IRON HORSE	BENNET, CARR	COLUMBIA	1951
D-8009	TEXANS NEVER CRY	MCDONALD	COLUMBIA	1951
D-8010	VALLEY OF FIRE	ENGLISH	COLUMBIA	1951
D-8011	MAGIC CARPET	LANDERS	COLUMBIA	1951
D-8011	MYSTERIOUS ISLAND – SERIAL	BENNET	COLUMBIA	1951
D-8014	TEXAS RANGERS	KARLSON	COLUMBIA	1951
D-8015	BRIGAND	KARLSON	COLUMBIA	1952
D-8016	SILVER CANYON	ENGLISH	COLUMBIA	1951
D-8017	SCANDAL SHEET	KARLSON	COLUMBIA	1952
D-8026	WHIRLWIND	ENGLISH	COLUMBIA	1951
D-8029	INDIAN UPRISING	NAZARRO	COLUMBIA	1952
D-8030	CALIFORNIA CONQUEST	LANDERS	COLUMBIA	1952
D-8031	YANK IN KOREA	LANDERS	COLUMBIA	1951
D-8032	HILLS OF UTAH	ENGLISH	COLUMBIA	1951
D-8033	HARLEM GLOBETROTTERS	BROWN, JASON	COLUMBIA	1951
D-8035	MAN IN THE SADDLE	DE TOTH	COLUMBIA	1951
D-8036	PURPLE HEART DIARY	QUINE	COLUMBIA	1951
D-8037	JUNGLE JIM IN THE FORBIDDEN LAND	LANDERS	COLUMBIA	1952
D-8038	JUNGLE MAN-HUNT	LANDERS	COLUMBIA	1951
D-8039	KING OF THE CONGO SERIAL	BENNET, GRISSELL	COLUMBIA	1952
D-8040	CAPTAIN VIDEO - SERIAL	BENNET, GRISSELL	COLUMBIA	1951
D-8041	BOOTS MALONE	DIETERLE	COLUMBIA	1952
D-8042	TEN TALL MEN	GOLDBECK	COLUMBIA	1951
D-8043	FIRST TIME	TASHLIN	COLUMBIA	1952
D-8044	BRAVE WARRIOR	BENNET	COLUMBIA	1952
D-8045	OLD WEST	ARCHAINBAUD	COLUMBIA	1952
D-8047	MEMBER OF THE WEDDING	ZINNEMANN	COLUMBIA	1952
D-8049	GOLDEN HAWK	SALKOW	COLUMBIA	1952
D-8053	PRINCE OF PIRATES	SALKOW	COLUMBIA	1953
D-8054	MY SIX CONVICTS	FREGONESE	COLUMBIA	1952
D-8055	BLACKHAWK	BENNET	COLUMBIA	1952
D-8056	DEATH OF A SALESMAN	BENEDEK	COLUMBIA	1951
D-8057	FOUR POSTER	REIS	COLUMBIA	1952
D-8061	CRIPPLE CREEK	NAZARRO	COLUMBIA	1952
D-8062	SNIPER	DMYTRYK	COLUMBIA	1952
D-8063	NIGHT STAGE TO GALVESTON	ARCHAINBAUD	COLUMBIA	1952
D-8064	5000 FINGERS OF DR. T	ROWLAND	COLUMBIA	1953
D-8066	AFFAIR IN TRINIDAD	SHERMAN	COLUMBIA	1952
D-8067	BLUE CANADIAN ROCKIES	ARCHAINBAUD	COLUMBIA	1952
D-8068	PRISONERS OF THE CASBAH	BARE	COLUMBIA	1953
D-8071	HAPPY TIME	FLEISCHER	COLUMBIA	1952
D-8072	APACHE COUNTRY	ARCHAINBAUD	COLUMBIA	1952
D-8074	MEMBER OF THE WEDDING	ZINNEMANN	COLUMBIA	1952
D-8078	EIGHT IRON MEN	DMYTRYK	COLUMBIA	1952
D-8079	BARBED WIRE	ARCHAINBAUD	COLUMBIA	1952
D-8082	CAINE MUTINY	DMYTRYK	COLUMBIA	1954
D-8085	YANK IN INDO-CHINA	GRISSELL	COLUMBIA	1952
D-8087	SERPENT OF THE NILE	CASTLE	COLUMBIA	1953
D-8088	LAST TRAIN FROM BOMBAY	SEARS	COLUMBIA	1952
D-8089	SAVAGE MUTINY	BENNET	COLUMBIA	1953
D-8090	VOODOO TIGER	BENNET	COLUMBIA	1952
D-8091	JUGGLER	DMYTRYK	COLUMBIA	1953
D-8092	JACK MCCALL – DESPERADO	SALKOW	COLUMBIA	1953
D-8093	PIRATES OF TRIPOLI	FEIST	COLUMBIA	1955
D-8094	WAGON TEAM	ARCHAINBAUD	COLUMBIA	1952
D-8095	LOST PLANET	BENNET	COLUMBIA	1953
D-8100	SON OF GERONIMO - SERIAL	BENNET	COLUMBIA	1952
D-8103	PATHFINDER	SALKOW	COLUMBIA	1952
D-8109	SLAVES OF BABYLON	CASTLE	COLUMBIA	1953
D-8115	SKY COMMANDS	SEARS	COLUMBIA	1953

Movie Still Identification Book Ultimate Edition - Letters

CODE	TITLE/NAME	DIRECTOR/TYPE	STUDIO/DISTRIBUTOR	YEAR
D-8116	HANGMAN'S KNOT	HUGGINS	COLUMBIA	1952
D-8117	SALOME	DIETERLE	COLUMBIA	1953
D-8118	ON TOP OF OLD SMOKY	ARCHAINBAUD	COLUMBIA	1953
D-8120	FLAME OF CALCUTTA	FRIEDMAN	COLUMBIA	1953
D-8121	STRANGE FASCINATION	HAAS	COLUMBIA	1952
D-8122	SIREN OF BAGDAD	QUINE	COLUMBIA	1953
D-8125	WINNING OF THE WEST, THE	ARCHAINBAUD	COLUMBIA	1953
D-8127	IRON GLOVE	CASTLE	COLUMBIA	1954
D-8128	GOLDTOWN GHOST RIDERS	ARCHAINBAUD	COLUMBIA	1953
D-8130	CONQUEST OF COCHISE	CASTLE	COLUMBIA	1953
D-8132	CHARGE OF THE LANCERS	CASTLE	COLUMBIA	1954
D-8140	ONE GIRL'S CONFESSION	HAAS	COLUMBIA	1953
D-8146	PACK TRAIN	ARCHAINBAUD	COLUMBIA	1953
D-8149	GREAT ADV OF CAPTAIN KIDD - SERIAL	ABRAHAMS, GOULD	COLUMBIA	1953
D-8150	KILLER APE	BENNET	COLUMBIA	1953
D-8151	SAGINAW TRAIL	ARCHAINBAUD	COLUMBIA	1953
D-8157	49TH MAN	SEARS	COLUMBIA	1953
D-8170	MISS SADIE THOMPSON	BERNHARDT	COLUMBIA	1953
D-8172	VALLEY OF HEADHUNTERS	BERKE	COLUMBIA	1953
D-8173	FORT TI	CASTLE	COLUMBIA	1953
D-8178	STRANGER WORE A GUN	DE TOTH	COLUMBIA	1953
D-8188	LAST OF THE PONY RIDERS	ARCHAINBAUD	COLUMBIA	1953
D-8191	JESSE JAMES VS DALTONS	CASTLE	COLUMBIA	1954
D-8193	DRUMS OF TAHITI	CASTLE	COLUMBIA	1954
D-8194	GUNFIGHTERS OF THE NORTHWEST	BENNET, GOULD	COLUMBIA	1954
D-8197	SARACEN BLADE	CASTLE	COLUMBIA	1954
D-8204	JUNGLE MAN-EATERS	SHOLEM	COLUMBIA	1954
D-8205	RIDING WITH BUFFALO BILL (serial)	BENNET	COLUMBIA	1954
D-8206	LAW VS. BILLY THE KID	CASTLE	COLUMBIA	1954
D-8211	TEENAGE CRIME WAVE	SEARS	COLUMBIA	1955
D-8214	BATTLE OF ROGUE RIVER	CASTLE	COLUMBIA	1954
D-8247	MIAMI STORY	SEARS	COLUMBIA	1954
D-8249	CHICAGO SYNDICATE	SEARS	COLUMBIA	1955
D-8250	SEMINOLE UPRISING	BELLAMY	COLUMBIA	1955
D-8252	MASTERSON OF KANSAS	CASTLE	COLUMBIA	1954
D-8253	MAD MAGICIAN	BRAHM	COLUMBIA	1954
D-8257	ADVENTURES OF CAPTAIN AFRICA (serial)	BENNET	COLUMBIA	1955
D-8260	IT CAME FROM BENEATH THE SEA	GORDON	COLUMBIA	1955
D-8262	CANNIBAL ATTACK	SHOLEM	COLUMBIA	1954
D-8263	DEVIL GODDESS	BENNET	COLUMBIA	1955
D-8264	BAMBOO PRISON	SEILER	COLUMBIA	1954
D-8265	JUNGLE MOON-MEN	GOULD	COLUMBIA	1955
D-8271	MAN FROM LARAMIE	MANN	COLUMBIA	1955
D-8273	TEN WANTED MEN	HUMBERSTONE	COLUMBIA	1955
D-8274	WOMEN'S PRISON	SEILER	COLUMBIA	1955
D-8281	NEW ORLEANS UNCENSORED	CASTLE	COLUMBIA	1955
D-8284	GUN THAT WON THE WEST	CASTLE	COLUMBIA	1955
D-8285	CREATURE WITH THE ATOM BRAIN	CAHN	COLUMBIA	1955
D-8286	DUEL ON THE MISSISSIPPI	CASTLE	COLUMBIA	1955
D-8289	BATTLE STATIONS	SEILER	COLUMBIA	1956
D-8294	LONG GREY LINE	FORD	COLUMBIA	1955
D-8301	FIVE AGAINST THE HOUSE	KARLSON	COLUMBIA	1955
D-8305	NIGHT HOLDS TERROR	STONE	COLUMBIA	1955
D-8306	LAWLESS STREET	LEWIS	COLUMBIA	1955
D-8307	EARTH VS. THE FLYING SAUCERS	SEARS	COLUMBIA	1956
D-8308	COUNT THREE AND PRAY	SHERMAN	COLUMBIA	1955
D-8310	HOUSTON STORY	CASTLE	COLUMBIA	1956
D-8311	BLACKJACK KETCHUM-DESPERADO	BELLAMY	COLUMBIA	1956
D-8313	INSIDE DETROIT	SEARS	COLUMBIA	1956
D-8316	URANIUM BOOM	CASTLE	COLUMBIA	1956
D-8319	FLYING FONTAINES	SHERMAN	COLUMBIA	1959
D-8321	CROOKED WEB	JURAN	COLUMBIA	1955
D-8322	AUTUMN LEAVES	ALDRICH	COLUMBIA	1956
D-8333	STORM CENTER	TARADASH	COLUMBIA	1956
D-8335	HOT BLOOD	RAY	COLUMBIA	1956
D-8336	BLAZING THE OVERLAND TRAIL (serial)	BENNET	COLUMBIA	1956
D-8344	SEVENTH CALVARY	LEWIS	COLUMBIA	1956
D-8345	WEREWOLF	SEARS	COLUMBIA	1955
D-8346	REPRISAL	SHERMAN	COLUMBIA	1956
D-8352	ROCK AROUND THE CLOCK	SEARS	COLUMBIA	1956

Movie Still Identification Book Ultimate Edition - Letters

CODE	TITLE/NAME	DIRECTOR/TYPE	STUDIO/DISTRIBUTOR	YEAR
D-8354	RUMBLE ON THE DOCKS	SEARS	COLUMBIA	1956
D-8355	MIAMI EXPOSE	SEARS	COLUMBIA	1956
D-8359	WHITE SQUAW	NAZARRO	COLUMBIA	1956
D-8365	20 MILLION MILES TO EARTH	JURAN	COLUMBIA	1957
D-8368	CHA CHA CHA BOOM	SEARS	COLUMBIA	1956
D-8383	DON'T KNOCK THE ROCK	SEARS	COLUMBIA	1956
D-8394	RETURN TO WARBOW	NAZARRO	COLUMBIA	1958
D-8400	SEVENTH VOYAGE OF SINBAD	JURAN	COLUMBIA	1958
D-8426	BATTLE OF THE CORAL SEA	WENDKOS	COLUMBIA	1959
D-8476	PEPE	SIDNEY	COLUMBIA	1960
D-8519	CRIMSON KIMONO	FULLER	COLUMBIA	1959
D-8546	EDGE OF ETERNITY	SIEGEL	COLUMBIA	1959
D-8602	SAIL A CROOKED SHIP	BRECHER	COLUMBIA	1961
D-8624	EVERYTHING'S DUCKY	TAYLOR	COLUMBIA	1961
D HOW	HOWARD PRODUCTIONS	studio	FOX	
D HOW 9	RAINBOW TRAIL	HOWARD	FOX FILM	1932
D HOW 10	MYSTERY RANCH	HOWARD	FOX FILM	1932
D HOW 11	GOLDEN WEDT	HOWARD	FOX FILM	1932
D HOW 12	SMOKE AND LIGHTNING	HOWARD	FOX FILM	1933
D&S	DRACULA AND SON	MOLINARO	QUNITED ARTISTSRTET	1979
DA	DANDY IN ASPIC	MANN	COLUMBIA	1968
DA	DEAD AGAIN	BRANAGH	PARAMOUNT	1991
DA	DEADLY AFFAIR	LUMET	COLUMBIA	1966
DA	DEVIL'S ADVOCATE	HACKFORD	WARNER BROS	1997
DA	DOE AVEDON	portrait	WARNER BROS	
DA	DOROTHY ARNOLD	portrait		
DA	DUAL ALIBI (UK)	TRAVERS	PATHE	1947
DA	MAKE WAY FOR A LADY	BURTON	RKO	1936
DA	TORCHY PLAYS WITH DYNAMITE	SMITH	WARNER BROS	1939
D'A-1	DRY MARTINI	D'ARRAST	FOX FILM	1928
DA-C	101 DALMATIANS (t)	GERONIMI	BUENA VISTA	R69
DAD	DEADLINE AT DAWN	CLURMAN	RKO	1946
DAD	DRACULA A.D. 1972 (UK)	GIBSON	WARNER BROS	1972
DAF	DECLINE AND FALL OF A BIRD WATCHER (UK)	KRISH	20th CENTURY FOX	1968
DAN-1	DEVIL GIRL FROM MARS (UK)	MACDONALD	SPARTAN (DANZIGER)	1955
DAN-2	SATELLITE IN THE SKY (UK)	DICKSON	WARNER BROS (DANZIGER)	1956
DAR	DARBY O'GILL AND THE LITTLE PEOPLE	STEVENSON	BUENA VISTA	1959
DAR	DARLING (UK)	SCHLESINGER	EMBASSY	1965
DAS	DIVORCE AMERICAN STYLE	YORKIN	COLUMBIA	1967
DAW	WHO ARE MY PARENTS?	DAWLEY	FOX FILM	1922
DAW-3	WHO ARE MY PARENTS?	DAWLEY	FOX FILM	1922
DAY	DAYDREAMER	BASS	EMBASSY	1966
DAY	DOROTHY DAY	portrait	WARNER BROS	
DAY	SO THIS IS WASHINGTON	MCCAREY	RKO	1943
DB	ADVENTURES OF DUSTY BATES (UK: DUSTY BATES)	CATLING	GFD	1947
D-B	BAIT	HAAS	COLUMBIA	1954
DB	BEAU IDEAL	BRENON	RKO	1930
DB	BRIDE WALKS OUT	JASON	RKO	1936
DB	DANCE BAND (UK)	VARNEL	FIRST DIVISION	1935
DB	DANIEL BOONE	HOWARD	RKO	1936
DB	DANIEL BOONE	GANNAWAY, RODRIGUEZ	REPUBLIC	1956
DB	DANNY BOY (UK)	MITCHELL	BUTCHER'S	1941
DB	DAVID BRIAN	portrait	WARNER BROS	
DB	DAVID BRUCE	portrait	UNIVERSAL, WB	
DB	DAVID BUTLER	portrait	WARNER BROS	
DB	DEADLY BEES (UK)	FRANCIS	PARAMOUNT	1966
DB	DEADLY BLESSING	CRAVEN	UNITED ARTISTS	1981
DB	DEVIL RIDES OUT (UK: DEVIL'S BRIDE)	FISHER	20TH CENTURY FOX	1968
DB	DEVIL'S BRIGADE	MCLAGLEN	UNITED ARTISTS	1968
DB	DIAMONDS FOR BREAKFAST (UK)	MORAHAN	PARAMOUNT	1968
DB	DIANA BARRYMORE	portrait	UNIVERSAL	
DB	DIVE BOMBER	CURTIZ	WARNER BROS	1941
DB	DONOVAN'S BRAIN	FEIST	UNITED ARTISTS	1953
DB	DOROTHY BURGESS	portrait		
DB	DOUBLE BUNK (UK)	PENNINGTON-RICHARDS	SHOW CORPORATION	1961
DB	LOVE ON A BET	JASON	RKO	1936
DB	MADAME DUBARRY	DIETERLE	WARNER BROS	1934
DB	SWEENEY TODD, DEMON BARBER OF FLEET STREET (UK)	KING	SELECT ATTRACTIONS	1936
DB	THEY DIED WITH THEIR BOOTS ON	WALSH	WARNER BROS	1941
DB	TRIAL AND ERROR (UK: DOCK BRIEF)	HILL	MGM	1962

Movie Still Identification Book Ultimate Edition - Letters

CODE	TITLE/NAME	DIRECTOR/TYPE	STUDIO/DISTRIBUTOR	YEAR
DBH	DEATH AT BROADCAST (UK:DEATH BROADCASTING HOUSE)	DENHAM	FILM ALLIANCE	1934
DBK	DAYBREAK (UK)	BENNETT	UNIVERSAL	1948
DBK	WHY BOTHER TO KNOCK (UK: DON'T BOTHER TO KNOCK)	FRANKEL	SEVEN ARTS	1961
DBP80	ROLLING DOWN THE GREAT DIVIDE	NEWFIELD	PRODUCERS RELEASING	1942
DC	AMAZING DR. CLITTERHOUSE	LITVAK	WARNER BROS	1938
DC	COMBAT SQUAD	ROTH	COLUMBIA	1953
DC	DANE CLARK	portrait	WARNER BROS	
DC	DANGEROUS CORNER	ROSEN	RKO	1934
DC	DANGEROUSLY CLOSE	PYUN	CANNON	1986
DC	DANI CRAYNE	portrait	UNIVERSAL	
DC	DAVY CROCKETT, INDIAN SCOUT	LANDERS	UNITED ARTISTS	1950
DC	DECAMERON	PASOLINIi	UNITED ARTISTS	1971
DC	DIAHANN CARROLL	portrait	UNITED ARTISTS	
DC	DIANE CILENTO	portrait		
DC	DODGE CITY	CURTIZ	WARNER BROS	1939
DC	DOLORES COSTELLO	portrait	RKO	
DC	DON CHICAGO (UK)	ROGERS	ANGLO-AMERICAN	1945
DC	DONALD CRISP	portrait	FN/WARNER BROS	
DC	DOROTHY CHRISTY	portrait	TIFFANY	
DC	DOROTHY COMINGORE	portrait	RKO	early 40s
DC	DOROTHY COONAN (WELLMAN)	portrait	WARNER BROS	early 30s
DC	DOUGLAS CORRIGAN	portrait	RKO	late 30s
DC	DRAGON MURDER CASE	HUMBERSTONE	WARNER BROS	1934
DC	DRAUGHTSMAN'S CONTRACT	GREENWAY	UNITED ARTISTS	1982
DC	DUDE COWBOY	HOWARD	RKO	1941
DC	HIGH POWERED RIFLE	DEXTER	20th CENTURY FOX	1960
DC	ROBERT PAIGE/PAGE / DAVID CARLYLE/NEWELL	portrait	WARNER BROS	late 30s
DC	WINGS OF DANGER/US: DEAD ON COURSE (UK)	FISHER	LIPPERT	1952
DCD	BLAME THE WOMAN (UK: DIAMOND CUT DIAMOND)	ELVEY, NIBLO	PRINCIPAL	1932
D-COL-4	LIFE BEGINS WITH LOVE	MCCAREY	COLUMBIA	1937
D-COL-9	LITTLE MISS ROUGHNECK	SCOTTO	COLUMBIA	1938
D-COL-10	NO TIME TO MARRY	LACHMAN	COLUMBIA	1938
D-COL-12	VALLEY OF VANISHING MEN (serial)	BENNET	COLUMBIA	1942
D-COL-14	LONE WOLF IN PARIS	ROGELL	COLUMBIA	1938
D-COL-15	THERE'S ALWAYS A WOMAN	HALL	COLUMBIA	1938
D-COL-17	HOLIDAY	CUKOR	COLUMBIA	1938
D-COL-17	HOLIDAY (1938)	CUKOR	COLUMBIA	R48
D-COL-19	CITY STREETS (CITY SHADOWS*)	ROGELL	COLUMBIA	1938
D-COL-21	I AM THE LAW	HALL	COLUMBIA	1938
D-COL-23	LADY OBJECTS	KENTON	COLUMBIA	1938
D-COL-24	FLIGHT TO FAME	COLEMAN	COLUMBIA	1938
D-COL-27	AWFUL TRUTH	MCCAREY	COLUMBIA	1937
D-COL-28	THERE'S THAT WOMAN AGAIN	HALL	COLUMBIA	1939
D-COL-29	LITTLE ADVENTURESS	LEDERMAN	COLUMBIA	1938
D-COL-30	BLONDIE	STRAYER	COLUMBIA	1938
D-COL-31	SMASHING THE SPY RING	CABANNE	COLUMBIA	1939
D-COL-32	LADY AND THE MOB	STOLOFF	COLUMBIA	1938
D-COL-32	LADY AND THE MOB	STOLOFF	COLUMBIA	1939
D-COL-33	LONE WOLF SPY HUNT	GODFREY	COLUMBIA	1939
D-COL-36	ONLY ANGELS HAVE WINGS	HAWKS	COLUMBIA	1939
D-COL-37	COAST GUARD	LUDWIG	COLUMBIA	1939
D-COL-38	ROMANCE OF THE REDWOODS	VIDOR	COLUMBIA	1939
D-COL-39	BLONDIE MEETS THE BOSS	STRAYER	COLUMBIA	1939
D-COL-40	GOLDEN BOY	MAMOULIAN	COLUMBIA	1939
D-COL-41	BLIND ALLEY	VIDOR	COLUMBIA	1939
D-COL-42	GOOD GIRLS GO TO PARIS	HALL	COLUMBIA	1939
D-COL-43	MR. SMITH GOES TO WASHINGTON	CAPRA	COLUMBIA	1939
D-COL-45	BLONDIE TAKES A VACATION	STRAYER	COLUMBIA	1939
D-COL-46	FIVE LITTLE PEPPERS AND HOW THEY GREW	BARTON	COLUMBIA	1939
D-COL-47	THOSE HIGH GRAY WALLS	VIDOR	COLUMBIA	1939
D-COL-48	HIS GIRL FRIDAY	HAWKS	COLUMBIA	1939
D-COL-49	BEWARE SPOOKS	SEDGWICK	COLUMBIA	1939
D-COL-51	BLONDIE BRINGS UP BABY	STRAYER	COLUMBIA	1939
D-COL-52	ARIZONA	RUGGLES	COLUMBIA	1940
D-COL-53	SCANDAL SHEET	GRINDE	COLUMBIA	1939
D-COL-54	AMAZING MR. WILLIAMS	HALL	COLUMBIA	1939
D-COL-55	CAFE HOSTESS	SALKOW	COLUMBIA	1940
D-COL-56	MY SON IS GUILTY	BARTON	COLUMBIA	1939
D-COL-57	MILITARY ACADEMY	LEDERMAN	COLUMBIA	1940
D-COL-58	FIVE LITTLE PEPPERS AT HOME	BARTON	COLUMBIA	1940

Movie Still Identification Book Ultimate Edition - Letters

CODE	TITLE/NAME	DIRECTOR/TYPE	STUDIO/DISTRIBUTOR	YEAR
D-COL-62	MAN WITH NINE LIVES (1940)	GRINDE	COLUMBIA	R47
D-COL-63	BLONDIE ON A BUDGET	STRAYER	COLUMBIA	1940
D-COL-65	DOCTOR TAKES A WIFE	HALL	COLUMBIA	1940
D-COL-74	BLONDE FROM SINGAPORE	DMYTRYK	COLUMBIA	1941
D-COL-78	LADY IN QUESTION	VIDOR	COLUMBIA	1940
D-COL-79	THIS THING CALLED LOVE	HALL	COLUMBIA	1940
D-COL-80	HE STAYED FOR BREAKFAST	HALL	COLUMBIA	1940
D-COL-82	ANGELS OVER BROADWAY	GARMES	COLUMBIA	1940
D-COL-84	BEFORE I HANG	GRINDE	COLUMBIA	1940
D-COL-90	TIME OUT FOR RHYTHM (sh)	SALKOW	COLUMBIA	1941
D-COL-94	OVERLAND WITH KIT CARSON	DEMING, NELSON	COLUMBIA	1939
D-COL-96	PENNY SERENADE	STEVENS	COLUMBIA	1941
D-COL-100	FACE BEHIND THE MASK	FLOREY	COLUMBIA	R55
D-COL-102	DEVIL COMMANDS	DMYTRYK	COLUMBIA	R55
D-COL-114	I WAS A PRISONER ON DEVIL'S ISLAND	LANDERS	COLUMBIA	1941
D-COL-115	TWO IN A TAXI	FLOREY	COLUMBIA	1941
D-COL-116	OUR WIFE	STAHL	COLUMBIA	1941
D-COL-117	HERE COMES MR. JORDAN	HALL	COLUMBIA	1941
D-COL-118	YOU'LL NEVER GET RICH	LANFIELD	COLUMBIA	1941
D-COL-119	MYSTERY SHIP	LANDERS	COLUMBIA	1941
D-COL-120	TWO LATINS FROM MANHATTAN	BARTON	COLUMBIA	1941
D-COL-122	COUNTER-ESPIONAGE	DMYTRYK	COLUMBIA	1942
D-COL-124	THREE GIRLS ABOUT TOWN	JASON	COLUMBIA	1941
D-COL-125	GO WEST YOUNG LADY	STRAYER	COLUMBIA	1941
D-COL-126	HARMON OF MICHIGAN	BARTON	COLUMBIA	1941
D-COL-127	STORK PAYS OFF	LANDERS	COLUMBIA	1941
D-COL-128	SECRETS OF THE LONE WOLF	DMYTRYK	COLUMBIA	1941
D-COL-129	LADY IS WILLING	LEISEN	COLUMBIA	1942
D-COL-130	SING FOR YOUR SUPPER	BARTON	COLUMBIA	1941
D-COL-132	HARVARD, HERE I COME	LANDERS	COLUMBIA	1941
D-COL-133	CONFESSIONS OF BOSTON BLACKIE	DMYTRYK	COLUMBIA	1941
D-COL-134	BLONDIE GOES TO COLLEGE	STRAYER	COLUMBIA	1942
D-COL-135	HONOLULU LU	BARTON	COLUMBIA	1941
D-COL-136	CADETS ON PARADE	LANDERS	COLUMBIA	1942
D-COL-137	SHUT MY BIG MOUTH	BARTON	COLUMBIA	1942
D-COL-138	TWO YANKS IN TRINIDAD	RATOFF	COLUMBIA	1942
D-COL-139	MAN WHO RETURNED TO LIFE	LANDERS	COLUMBIA	1942
D-COL-140	CANAL ZONE	LANDERS	COLUMBIA	1942
D-COL-141	TRAMP TRAMP TRAMP	BARTON	COLUMBIA	1942
D-COL-144	ALIAS BOSTON BLACKIE	LANDERS	COLUMBIA	1942
D-COL-145	WIFE TAKES A FLYER (YANK IN DUTCH)	WALLACE	COLUMBIA	1942
D-COL-146	TALK OF THE TOWN	STEVENS	COLUMBIA	1942
D-COL-147	NOT A LADIES MAN	LANDERS	COLUMBIA	1942
D-COL-148	HELLO ANAPOLIS	BARTON	COLUMBIA	R42
D-COL-149	MEET THE STEWARTS	GREEN	COLUMBIA	1942
D-COL-150	THEY ALL KISSED THE BRIDE	HALL	COLUMBIA	1942
D-COL-151	PARACHUTE NURSE	BARTON	COLUMBIA	1942
D-COL-152	SWEETHEART OF THE FLEET	BARTON	COLUMBIA	1942
D-COL-153	SUBMARINE RAIDER	LANDERS	COLUMBIA	1942
D-COL-154	YOU WERE NEVER LOVELIER	SEITER	COLUMBIA	1942
D-COL-155	ATLANTIC CONVOY	LANDERS	COLUMBIA	1942
D-COL-156	FLIGHT LIEUTENANT	SALKOW	COLUMBIA	1942
D-COL-158	BLONDIE FOR VICTORY	STRAYER	COLUMBIA	1942
D-COL-159	MAN'S WORLD	BARTON	COLUMBIA	1942
D-COL-160	SABOTAGE SQUAD	LANDERS	COLUMBIA	1942
D-COL-161	MY SISTER EILEEN	HALL	COLUMBIA	1942
D-COL-162	LUCKY LEGS	BARTON	COLUMBIA	1942
D-COL-165	SPIRIT OF STANFORD	BARTON	COLUMBIA	1942
D-COL-168	DARING YOUNG MAN	STRAYER	COLUMBIA	1942
D-COL-169	BOSTON BLACKIE GOES HOLLYWOOD	GORDON	COLUMBIA	1942
D-COL-170	SMITH OF MINNESOTA	LANDERS	COLUMBIA	1942
D-COL-171	BOOGIE MAN WILL GET YOU	LANDERS	COLUMBIA	1942
D-COL-172	UNDERGROUND AGENT	GORDON	COLUMBIA	1942
D-COL-174	LAUGH YOUR BLUES AWAY	BARTON	COLUMBIA	1942
D-COL-175	JUNIOR ARMY	LANDERS	COLUMBIA	1942
D-COL-177	POWER OF THE PRESS	LANDERS	COLUMBIA	1943
D-COL-203	MAIN EVENT	DARE	COLUMBIA	1938
D-COL-206	SHADOW	COLEMAN	COLUMBIA	1937
D-COL-207	SQUADRON OF HONOR	COLEMAN	COLUMBIA	1938
D-COL-208	WOMEN IN PRISON	HILLYER	COLUMBIA	1938

Movie Still Identification Book Ultimate Edition - Letters

CODE	TITLE/NAME	DIRECTOR/TYPE	STUDIO/DISTRIBUTOR	YEAR
D-COL-209	WHO KILLED GAIL PRESTON?	BARSHA	COLUMBIA	1938
D-COL-210	WHEN G-MEN STEP IN	COLEMAN	COLUMBIA	1938
D-COL-211	HIGHWAY PATROL	COLEMAN	COLUMBIA	1938
D-COL-213	JUVENILE COURT	LEDERMAN	COLUMBIA	1938
D-COL-214	ADVENTURE IN SAHARA	LEDERMAN	COLUMBIA	1938
D-COL-215	NORTH OF SHANGHAI	LEDERMAN	COLUMBIA	1939
D-COL-216	MY SON IS A CRIMINAL	COLEMAN	COLUMBIA	1939
D-COL-217	FIRST OFFENDERS	MCDONALD	COLUMBIA	1939
D-COL-218	OUTSIDE THESE WALLS	MCCAREY	COLUMBIA	1939
D-COL-219	MISSING DAUGHTERS	COLEMAN	COLUMBIA	1939
D-COL-220	PARENTS ON TRIAL	NELSON	COLUMBIA	1939
D-COL-221	WOMAN IS THE JUDGE	GRINDE	COLUMBIA	1939
D-COL-222	BEHIND PRISON GATES	BARTON	COLUMBIA	1939
D-COL-223	MAN THEY COULD NOT HANG	GRINDE	COLUMBIA	1939
D-COL-223	MAN THEY COULD NOT KILL (1939)	GRINDE	COLUMBIA	R47
D-COL-224	KONGA, THE WILD STALLION	NELSON	COLUMBIA	1940
D-COL-283	COMMUNITY SING - SERIES 2 #1	series	COLUMBIA	1937
D-COL-284	COMMUNITY SING - SERIES 2 #2	series	COLUMBIA	1937
D-COL-301	CATTLE RAIDERS	NELSON	COLUMBIA	1938
D-COL-303	CALL OF THE ROCKIES	JAMES	COLUMBIA	1938
D-COL-304	LAW OF THE PLAINS	NELSON	COLUMBIA	1938
D-COL-305	WEST OF CHEYENNE	NELSON	COLUMBIA	1938
D-COL-306	SOUTH OF ARIZONA	NELSON	COLUMBIA	1938
D-COL-307	WEST OF SANTA FE	NELSON	COLUMBIA	1938
D-COL-308	COLORADO TRAIL	NELSON	COLUMBIA	1938
D-COL-309	RIO GRANDE	NELSON	COLUMBIA	1938
D-COL-310	THUNDERING WEST	NELSON	COLUMBIA	1939
D-COL-311	TEXAS STAMPEDE	NELSON	COLUMBIA	1939
D-COL-312	NORTH OF THE YUKON	NELSON	COLUMBIA	1939
D-COL-313	SPOILERS OF THE RANGE	COLEMAN	COLUMBIA	1939
D-COL-314	WESTERN CARAVANS	NELSON	COLUMBIA	1939
D-COL-315	MAN FROM SUNDOWN	NELSON	COLUMBIA	1939
D-COL-316	OUTPOST OF THE MOUNTIES	COLEMAN	COLUMBIA	1939
D-COL-317	STRANGER FROM TEXAS	NELSON	COLUMBIA	1939
D-COL-318	RIDERS OF BLACK RIVER	DEMING	COLUMBIA	1939
D-COL-319	TAMING OF THE WEST	DEMING	COLUMBIA	1939
D-COL-320	MAN FROM TUMBLEWEEDS	LEWIS	COLUMBIA	1940
D-COL-321	TWO FISTED RANGERS	LEWIS	COLUMBIA	1939
D-COL-322	BULLETS FOR RUSTLERS	NELSON	COLUMBIA	1940
D-COL-323	PIONEERS OF THE FRONTIER	NELSON	COLUMBIA	1940
D-COL-325	THUNDERING FRONTIER	LEDERMAN	COLUMBIA	1940
D-COL-326	TEXAS STAGECOACH	LEWIS	COLUMBIA	1940
D-COL-327	PINTO KID	HILLYER	COLUMBIA	1941
D-COL-328	WEST OF ABILENE	CEDER	COLUMBIA	1940
D-COL-329	RETURN OF WILD BILL	LEWIS	COLUMBIA	1940
D-COL-330	DURANGO KID	HILLYER	COLUMBIA	1940
D-COL-331	PRAIRIE SCHOONERS	NELSON	COLUMBIA	1940
D-COL-332	OUTLAWS OF THE PANHANDLE	NELSON	COLUMBIA	1941
D-COL-334	BEYOND THE SACRAMENTO	HILLYER	COLUMBIA	1941
D-COL-335	ACROSS THE SIERRAS	LEDERMAN	COLUMBIA	1941
D-COL-337	WILDCAT OF TUCSON	HILLYER	COLUMBIA	1940
D-COL-338	NORTH FROM THE LONE STAR	HILLYER	COLUMBIA	1941
D-COL-339	RETURN OF DANIEL BOONE	HILLYER	COLUMBIA	1941
D-COL-340	HANDS ACROSS THE ROCKIES	HILLYER	COLUMBIA	1941
D-COL-341	SON OF DAVY CROCKETT	HILLYER	COLUMBIA	1941
D-COL-342	MEDICO OF PAINTED SPRINGS	HILLYER	COLUMBIA	1941
D-COL-343	KING OF DODGE CITY	HILLYER	COLUMBIA	1941
D-COL-344	THUNDER OVER THE PRAIRIE	HILLYER	COLUMBIA	1941
D-COL-345	ROARING FRONTIERS	HILLYER	COLUMBIA	1941
D-COL-346	PRAIRIE STRANGER	HILLYER	COLUMBIA	1941
D-COL-347	LONE STAR VIGILANTES	FOX	COLUMBIA	1942
D-COL-348	ROYAL MOUNTED PATROL	HILLYER	COLUMBIA	1941
D-COL-349	BULLETS FOR BANDITS	FOX	COLUMBIA	1942
D-COL-350	RIDERS OF THE BADLANDS	BRETHERTON	COLUMBIA	1941
D-COL-351	NORTH OF THE ROCKIES	HILLYER	COLUMBIA	1942
D-COL-352	DEVIL'S TRAIL	HILLYER	COLUMBIA	1942
D-COL-353	WEST OF TOMBSTONE	BRETHERTON	COLUMBIA	1942
D-COL-354	LAWLESS PLAINSMEN	BERKE	COLUMBIA	1942
D-COL-355	DOWN RIO GRANDE WAY	BERKE	COLUMBIA	1942
D-COL-356	PRAIRIE GUNSMOKE	HILLYER	COLUMBIA	1942

Movie Still Identification Book Ultimate Edition - Letters

CODE	TITLE/NAME	DIRECTOR/TYPE	STUDIO/DISTRIBUTOR	YEAR
D-COL-357	OVERLAND TO DEADWOOD	BERKE	COLUMBIA	1942
D-COL-358	BADMEN OF THE HILLS	BERKE	COLUMBIA	1942
D-COL-359	RIDERS OF THE NORTHLAND	BERKE	COLUMBIA	1942
D-COL-360	VENGEANCE OF THE WEST	HILLYER	COLUMBIA	1942
D-COL-362	RIDING THROUGH NEVADA	BERKE	COLUMBIA	1942
D-COL-363	PARDON MY GUN	BERKE	COLUMBIA	1942
D-COL-364	TORNADO IN THE SADDLE	BERKE	COLUMBIA	1942
D-COL-365	LONE PRAIRIE	BERKE	COLUMBIA	1942
D-COL-403	JUMP, CHUMP, JUMP! (sh)	LORD	COLUMBIA	1938
D-COL-404	WEE WEE MONSIER (sh)	LORD	COLUMBIA	1938
D-COL-405	DOGGONE MIXUP (sh)	LAMONT	COLUMBIA	1938
D-COL-409	CALLING ALL CURTAINS (sh)	LORD	COLUMBIA	1937
D-COL-410	FIDDLING AROUND (sh)	LAMONT	COLUMBIA	1938
D-COL-412	MIND NEEDER (sh)	LORD	COLUMBIA	1938
D-COL-413	MANY SAPPY RETURNS (sh)	LORD	COLUMBIA	1938
D-COL-415	TIME OUT FOR TROUBLE (sh)	LORD	COLUMBIA	1938
D-COL-416	TERMITES OF 1938 (sh)	LORD	COLUMBIA	1938
D-COL-417	OLD RAID MULE (sh)	CHASE	COLUMBIA	1938
D-COL-418	NIGHTSHIRT BANDIT (sh)	WHITE	COLUMBIA	1938
D-COL-419	THREE LITTLE SEW AND SEWS (sh)	LORD	COLUMBIA	1939
D-COL-420	TASSELS IN THE AIR (sh)	CHASE	COLUMBIA	1938
D-COL-421	ANKLES AWAY (sh)	CHASE	COLUMBIA	1938
D-COL-422	HEALTHY, WEALTHY AND DUMB (sh)	LORD	COLUMBIA	1938
D-COL-423	VIOLENT IS THE WORD FOR CURLY (sh)	CHASE	COLUMBIA	1938
D-COL-424	SOUL OF A HEEL (sh)	LORD	COLUMBIA	1938
D-COL-425	HALF-WAY TO HOLLYWOOD (sh)	CHASE	COLUMBIA	1938
D-COL-426	THREE MISSING LINKS (sh)	WHITE	COLUMBIA	1938
D-COL-427	MUTTS TO YOU (sh)	CHASE	COLUMBIA	1938
D-COL-428	SUE MY LAWYER (sh)	WHITE	COLUMBIA	1938
D-COL-429	NAG IN THE BAG (sh)	CHASE	COLUMBIA	1938
D-COL-430	SAVED BY THE BELLE (sh)	CHASE	COLUMBIA	1939
D-COL-431	PIE A LA MAID (sh)	LORD	COLUMBIA	1938
D-COL-432	NOT GUILTY ENOUGH (sh)	LORD	COLUMBIA	1938
D-COL-433	MUTINY ON THE BODY (sh)	CHASE	COLUMBIA	1939
D-COL-434	SWING YOU SWINGERS (sh)	WHITE	COLUMBIA	1939
D-COL-435	SAP TAKES A WRAP (sh)	LORD	COLUMBIA	1939
D-COL-436	HOME ON THE RAGE (sh)	LORD	COLUMBIA	1938
D-COL-437	CHUMP TAKES A BUMP (sh)	LORD	COLUMBIA	1939
D-COL-438	YES WE HAVE NO BONANZA (sh)	LORD	COLUMBIA	1939
D-COL-439	FLAT FOOT STOOGES (sh)	CHASE	COLUMBIA	1938
D-COL-440	BOOM GOES THE GROOM (sh)	CHASE	COLUMBIA	1939
D-COL-441	STAR IS SHORN (sh)	LORD	COLUMBIA	1939
D-COL-442	TROUBLE FINDS ANDY CLYDE (sh)	WHITE	COLUMBIA	1939
D-COL-443	WE WANT OUR MUMMY (sh)	LORD	COLUMBIA	1939
D-COL-444	DUCKING THEY DID GO (sh)	LORD	COLUMBIA	1939
D-COL-445	CALLING ALL CURS (sh)	WHITE	COLUMBIA	1939
D-COL-446	RATTLING ROMEO (sh)	LORD	COLUMBIA	1939
D-COL-448	NOW IT CAN BE SOLD (sh)	LORD	COLUMBIA	1939
D-COL-449	OILY TO BED, OILY TO RISE (sh)	WHITE	COLUMBIA	1939
D-COL-450	SKINNY THE MOOCHER (sh)	LORD	COLUMBIA	1939
D-COL-451	THREE SAPPY PEOPLE (sh)	WHITE	COLUMBIA	1939
D-COL-452	TEACHER'S PEST (sh)	KRAMER, ULLMAN	COLUMBIA	1939
D-COL-453	STATIC IN THE ATTIC (sh)	CHASE	COLUMBIA	1939
D-COL-454	PEST FROM THE WEST (sh)	LORD	COLUMBIA	1939
D-COL-455	COOKOO CAVALIERS (sh)	WHITE	COLUMBIA	1940
D-COL-456	MOOCHING THROUGH GEORGIA (sh)	WHITE	COLUMBIA	1939
D-COL-457	GLOVE SLINGERS (sh)	WHITE	COLUMBIA	1939
D-COL-458	HOW HIGH IS UP? (sh)	LORD	COLUMBIA	1940
D-COL-459	MONEY SQUAWKS (sh)	WHITE	COLUMBIA	1940
D-COL-460	ALL AMERICAN BLONDES (sh)	LORD	COLUMBIA	1939
D-COL-461	ROCKIN' THRU THE ROCKIES (sh)	WHITE	COLUMBIA	1940
D-COL-462	PLUMBING WE WILL GO (sh)	LORD	COLUMBIA	1940
D-COL-463	ANDY CLYDE GETS SPRING CHICKEN (sh)	WHITE	COLUMBIA	1939
D-COL-464	AWFUL GOOF (sh)	LORD	COLUMBIA	1939
D-COL-465	NUTTY BUT NICE (sh)	WHITE	COLUMBIA	1940
D-COL-466	MR. CLYDE GOES TO BROADWAY (sh)	LORD	COLUMBIA	1940
D-COL-467	HECKLER (sh)	LORD	COLUMBIA	1940
D-COL-468	FROM NURSE TO WORSE (sh)	WHITE	COLUMBIA	1940
D-COL-469	HIS BRIDAL FRIGHT (sh)	LORD	COLUMBIA	1940
D-COL-470	NOTHING BUT PLEASURE (sh)	WHITE	COLUMBIA	1940

Movie Still Identification Book Ultimate Edition - Letters

CODE	TITLE/NAME	DIRECTOR/TYPE	STUDIO/DISTRIBUTOR	YEAR
D-COL-471	YOU'RE NEXT (sh)	LORD	COLUMBIA	1940
D-COL-472	YOU NAZTY SPY (sh)	WHITE	COLUMBIA	1940
D-COL-473	SOUTH OF THE BOUDOIR (sh)	LORD	COLUMBIA	1940
D-COL-474	NO CENSUS, NO FEELING (sh)	LORD	COLUMBIA	1940
D-COL-475	PARDON MY BERTH MARKS (sh)	WHITE	COLUMBIA	1940
D-COL-476	BOOBS IN THE WOODS (sh)	LORD	COLUMBIA	1940
D-COL-477	TAMING OF THE SNOOD (sh)	WHITE	COLUMBIA	1940
D-COL-478	FIREMAN, SAVE MY CHOO CHOO (sh)	LORD	COLUMBIA	1940
D-COL-479	PLEASED TO MITT YOU (sh)	WHITE	COLUMBIA	1940
D-COL-480	COLD TURKEY (sh)	LORD	COLUMBIA	1940
D-COL-481	SPOOK SPEAKS (sh)	WHITE	COLUMBIA	1940
D-COL-482	IN THE SWEET PIE AND PIE (sh)	WHITE	COLUMBIA	1941
D-COL-483	BLONDES AND BLUNDERS (sh)	LORD	COLUMBIA	1940
D-COL-484	SO LONG MR. CHUMPS (sh)	WHITE	COLUMBIA	1941
D-COL-485	DUTIFUL BUT DUMB (sh)	LORD	COLUMBIA	1941
D-COL-486	BOOBS IN ARMS (sh)	WHITE	COLUMBIA	1940
D-COL-487	ALL THE WORLD'S A STOOGE (sh)	LORD	COLUMBIA	1941
D-COL-488	ACHE IN EVERY STAKE (sh)	LORD	COLUMBIA	1941
D-COL-489	WATCHMAN TAKES A WIFE (sh)	LORD	COLUMBIA	1941
D-COL-490	BUNDLE OF BLISS (sh)	WHITE	COLUMBIA	1940
D-COL-491	HIS EX MARKS THE SPOT (sh)	WHITE	COLUMBIA	1940
D-COL-493	SO YOU WON'T SQUAWK (sh)	LORD	COLUMBIA	1941
D-COL-494	RING AND THE BELLE (sh)	LORD	COLUMBIA	1941
D-COL-495	FRESH AS A FRESHMAN (sh)	WHITE	COLUMBIA	1941
D-COL-496	BLITZ KISS (sh)	LORD	COLUMBIA	1941
D-COL-497	YUMPIN' YIMMINY!	WHITE	COLUMBIA	1941
D-COL-498	YANKEE DOODLE ANDY (sh)	WHITE	COLUMBIA	1941
D-COL-499	READY, WILLING BUT UNABLE (sh)	LORD	COLUMBIA	1941
D-COL-500	I'LL NEVER HEIL AGAIN (sh)	WHITE	COLUMBIA	1941
D-COL-501	LOVE AT FIRST FRIGHT (sh)	LORD	COLUMBIA	1941
D-COL-502	THREE BLONDE MICE (sh)	WHITE	COLUMBIA	1942
D-COL-503	FRENCH FRIED PATOOTIE (sh)	WHITE	COLUMBIA	1941
D-COL-504	WHAT MAKES LIZZY DIZZY (sh)	WHITE	COLUMBIA	1942
D-COL-505	BLACK EYES AND BLUES (sh)	WHITE	COLUMBIA	1941
D-COL-506	HALF SHOT AT SUNRISE (sh)	LORD	COLUMBIA	1941
D-COL-507	EVEN AS I.O.U. (sh)	LORD	COLUMBIA	1942
D-COL-508	GENERAL NUISANCEE (sh)	WHITE	COLUMBIA	1941
D-COL-509	HOST TO A GHOST (sh)	LORD	COLUMBIA	1941
D-COL-510	LOCO BOY MAKES GOOD (sh)	WHITE	COLUMBIA	1942
D-COL-511	SOME MORE OF SOMOA (sh)	LORD	COLUMBIA	1941
D-COL-512	MITT ME TONIGHT (sh)	WHITE	COLUMBIA	1941
D-COL-513	CACTUS MAKES PERFECT	LORD	COLUMBIA	1942
D-COL-514	ALL WORK AND NO PAY (sh)	LORD	COLUMBIA	1942
D-COL-515	PHONY CRONIES (sh)	EDWARDS	COLUMBIA	1942
D-COL-516	LOVEABLE TROUBLE (sh)	LORD	COLUMBIA	1941
D-COL-517	SAPPY BIRTHDAY (sh)	EDWARDS	COLUMBIA	1942
D-COL-518	KINK OF THE CAMPUS (sh)	LORD	COLUMBIA	1941
D-COL-519	WHAT'S THE MATADOR? (sh)	WHITE	COLUMBIA	1942
D-COL-520	GLOVE BIRDS (sh)	WHITE	COLUMBIA	1942
D-COL-521	SWEET SPIRITS OF NIGHTER (sh)	LORD	COLUMBIA	1941
D-COL-523	GROOM AND BORED (sh)	LORD	COLUMBIA	1942
D-COL-524	HOW SPRY I AM (sh)	WHITE	COLUMBIA	1942
D-COL-525	GLOVE AFFAIR (sh)	WHITE	COLUMBIA	1941
D-COL-525	STUDY IN SOCKS (sh)	LORD	COLUMBIA	1942
D-COL-526	SHE'S OIL MINE (sh)	WHITE	COLUMBIA	1941
D-COL-527	MATRI-PHONY (sh)	EDWARDS	COLUMBIA	1942
D-COL-528	OLAF LAUGHS LAST (sh)	WHITE	COLUMBIA	1942
D-COL-530	KISS AND WAKE UP (sh)	WHITE	COLUMBIA	1942
D-COL-532	THREE SMART SAPS (sh)	WHITE	COLUMBIA	1942
D-COL-534	TIREMAN, SPARE MY TIRES (sh)	WHITE	COLUMBIA	1942
D-COL-535	HAM AND YEGGS (sh)	WHITE	COLUMBIA	1942
D-COL-536	CARRY HARRY (sh)	EDWARDS	COLUMBIA	1942
D-COL-539	SOCK-A-BYE BABY (sh)	WHITE	COLUMBIA	1942
D-COL-540	SAPPY PAPPY (sh)	EDWARDS	COLUMBIA	1942
D-COL-543	PIANO MOONER (sh)	EDWARDS	COLUMBIA	1942
D-COL-544	GREAT GLOVER (sh)	WHITE	COLUMBIA	1942
D-COL-553	COLLEGE BELLES (sh)	EDWARDS	COLUMBIA	1942
D-COL-600	COMMUNITY SING - SERIES 2 #3	series	COLUMBIA	1937
D-COL-602	COMMUNITY SING - SERIES 2 #4	series	COLUMBIA	1937
D-COL-610	COMMUNITY SING - SERIES 2 #8	series	COLUMBIA	1938

Movie Still Identification Book Ultimate Edition - Letters

CODE	TITLE/NAME	DIRECTOR/TYPE	STUDIO/DISTRIBUTOR	YEAR
D-COL-611	COMMUNITY SING - SERIES 2 #9	series	COLUMBIA	1938
D-COL-615	COMMUNITY SING - SERIES 2 #10	series	COLUMBIA	1938
D-COL-620	COMMUNITY SING - SERIES 2 #11	series	COLUMBIA	1938
D-COL-621	COMMUNITY SING - SERIES 2 #12	series	COLUMBIA	1938
D-COL-622	COMMUNITY SING - SERIES 3 #1	series	COLUMBIA	1938
D-COL-623	COMMUNITY SING - SERIES 3 #2	series	COLUMBIA	1938
D-COL-624	COMMUNITY SING - SERIES 3 #3	series	COLUMBIA	1938
D-COL-625	COMMUNITY SING - SERIES 3 #6	series	COLUMBIA	1938
D-COL-631	COMMUNITY SING - SERIES 3 #4	series	COLUMBIA	1939
D-COL-632	COMMUNITY SING - SERIES 3 #5	series	COLUMBIA	1939
D-COL-635	COMMUNITY SING - SERIES 3 #7	series	COLUMBIA	1939
D-COL-636	COMMUNITY SING - SERIES 3 #10	series	COLUMBIA	1939
D-COL-637	COMMUNITY SING - SERIES 3 #8	series	COLUMBIA	1939
D-COL-638	COMMUNITY SING - SERIES 4 #2	series	COLUMBIA	1939
D-COL-639	COMMUNITY SING - SERIES 3 #9	series	COLUMBIA	1939
D-COL-640	COMMUNITY SING - SERIES 4 #1	series	COLUMBIA	1939
D-COL-646	FOOLS WHO MADE HISTORY-ELIAS HOWE	LEMAN	COLUMBIA	1939
D-COL-647	FOOLS WHO MADE HISTORY-CHARLES GOODYEAR		COLUMBIA	1939
D-COL-655	COMMUNITY SING - SERIES 4 #3	series	COLUMBIA	1939
D-COL-656	COMMUNITY SING - SERIES 4 #4	series	COLUMBIA	1939
D-COL-788	TEXAS	MARSHALL	COLUMBIA	1941
D-COL-889	MUSIC IN MY HEART	SANTLEY	COLUMBIA	1940
D-COL-901	SPIDER'S WEB (SERIAL)	HORNE, TAYLOR	COLUMBIA	1938
D-COL-902	FLYING G-MEN - SERIAL	HORNE, TAYLOR	COLUMBIA	1939
D-COL-903	MANDRAKE THE MAGICIAN - SERIAL	DEMING, NELSON	COLUMBIA	1939
D-COL-908	HOWARDS OF VIRGINIA	LLOYD	COLUMBIA	1940
D-COL-911	ADVENTURE IN WASHINGTON	GREEN	COLUMBIA	1941
D-COL-916	SHE KNEW ALL THE ANSWERS	WALLACE	COLUMBIA	1941
D-COL-931	ADAM HAD FOUR SONS	RATOFF	COLUMBIA	1941
D-COL-949	LADIES IN RETIREMENT	VIDOR	COLUMBIA	1941
D-COL-953	MEN IN HER LIFE	RATOFF	COLUMBIA	1941
D-COL-964	ADVENTURES OF MARTIN EDEN	SALKOW	COLUMBIA	1942
D-COL-982	SOMETHING TO SHOUT ABOUT	RATOFF	COLUMBIA	1943
D-COL-996	COMMANDOES STRIKE AT DAWN	FARROW	COLUMBIA	1942
D-COL-1210	MILITARY ACADEMY	LEDERMAN	COLUMBIA	1940
DCP	DR. CHRISTIAN MEETS THE WOMEN	MCGANN	RKO	1940
DD	ARIZONIAN	VIDOR	RKO	1935
DD	DAN DURYEA	portrait	UNIVERSAL	
DD	DANA DALE	portrait	WARNER BROS	
DD	DANCE CHARLIE DANCE	MCDONALD	WARNER BROS	1937
DD	DANCE OF DEATH (UK)	GILES	PARAMOUNT	1968
DD	DANGER: DIABOLIK	BAVA	PARAMOUNT	1968
DD	DAUGHTERS OF DARKNESS (FR)	KUMEL	MARON FILMS	1971
DD	DAWN OF THE DEAD	ROMERO	UNITED FILM	1978
DD	DAY OF THE DOLPHIN	NICHOLS	AVCO EMBASSY	1973
DD	DEADLY DUO	LE BORG	UNITED ARTISTS	1962
DD	DEANNA DURBIN	portrait	UNIVERSAL	
DD	DENNIS DAY	portrait	RKO	
DD	DENNIS DEVINE	portrait	UNIVERSAL	
DD	DESIRE IN THE DUST	CLAXTON	20th CENTURY FOX	1960
DD	DEVIL DANCER	NIBLO	UNITED ARTISTS	1927
DD	DEVIL DOGS OF THE AIR	BACON	WARNER BROS	1935
DD	DEVIL DOLL (UK)	SHONTEFF	ASSOCIATED	1964
DD	DEVIL'S DAFFODIL (UK)	RATHONYI	GOLDSTONE	1961
DD	DEVIL'S DISCIPLE (UK)	HAMILTON	UNITED ARTISTS	1959
DD	DEVILS OF DARKNESS (UK)	COMFORT	20TH CENTURY FOX	1965
DD	DIANA DORS	portrait	UNIVERSAL	
DD	DIANA DORS	portrait	PARAMOUNT`	
DD	DIE DIE MY DARLING (UK: FANATIC)	NARRIZANO	COLUMBIA	1965
DD	DIRTY DOZEN	ALDRICH	MGM	1967
DD	DOLORES DEL RIO	portrait	RKO	
DD	DON DOUGLAS	portrait	RKO	
DD	DONA DRAKE	portrait	UNIVERSAL	
DD	DONNIE DUNAGAN	portrait	RKO	
DD	DOOR TO DOOR MANIAC (5 MINUTES TO LIVE)	KARN	AIP	1966
DD	DORIS DAWSON	portrait	FN	
DD	DORIS DAY	portrait	UNIVERSAL, WARNER BROS	
DD	DORIS DUDLEY	portrait	RKO	1930s,50s
DD	DOROTHY DARE	portrait	WARNER BROS	
DD	DOROTHY DEVORE	portrait	WARNER BROS	

Movie Still Identification Book Ultimate Edition - Letters

CODE	TITLE/NAME	DIRECTOR/TYPE	STUDIO/DISTRIBUTOR	YEAR
DD	DOROTHY DWAN	portrait	PATHE	
DD	DOUBLE DEAL	BERLIN	RKO	1950
DD	DUEL AT DIABLO	NELSON	UNITED ARTISTS	1966
DD	DUST BE MY DESTINY	SEILER	WARNER BROS	1939
DD	MISTER DRAKE'S DUCK (UK)	GUEST	UNITED ARTISTS	1951
DD	TO THE DEVIL A DAUGHTER (UK)	SYKES	CINE ARTISTES	1976
DD	WE DIVE AT DAWN (UK)	ASQUITH	GFD	1943
DD	YES MY DARLING DAUGHTER	KEIGHLEY	WARNER BROS	1939
DD1	DEVIL'S DAFFODIL (UK)	RATHONYI	GOLDSTONE	1961
DD1	SWING IT SAILOR	CANNON	GRAND	1938
DD397	DANCE OF DEATH	GILES	PARAMOUNT	1968
DDA	DANIELLE DARRIEUX	portrait	UNIVERSAL	
DDA	RAGE OF PARIS	KOSTER	UNIVERSAL	1938
DDF	DON DEFORE	portrait	RKO	
DDF	WOMAN OF THE RIVER	SOLDATI	COLUMBIA	1957
DDS	DRUMS IN THE DEEP SOUTH	MENZIES	RKO	1951
DDW	ALL THAT MONEY CAN BUY (DEVIL AND DANIEL WEBSTER)	DIETERLE	RKO	1941
DE	DALE EVANS	portrait	REPUBLIC	
DE	DEEP END (GER)	SKOLIMOWSKI	PARAMOUNT	1971
DE	DEVIL'S EYE (SWE: DJAVULENS OGA)	BERGMAN	JANUS	1960
DE	DIANE ELLIS	portrait	PATHE	
DE	DICK ERDMAN	portrait	WARNER BROS	
DE	DUMBELLS IN ERMINE	ADOLFI	WARNER BROS	1930
DE	HIDEOUT IN THE ALPS (UK: DUSTY ERMINE)	VORHAUS	GRAND	1937
DE	HUMAN MONSTER (UK: DARK EYES LONDON)	SUMMERS	MONOGRAM	1940
DE	MURDER ON THE ORIENT EXPRESS	LUMET	PARAMOUNT	1974
DE	PRICE OF FOLLY (UK: DOUBLE ERROR*)	SUMMERS	PATHE	1937
DE	RICHARD EGAN	portrait	RKO	
DE	STORY OF DR. EHRLICH'S MAGIC BULLET	DIETERLE	WARNER BROS	1940
DEEP ADV	DEEP ADVENTURE	WELBOURNE	WARNER BROS	1957
DEF	DAY THE EARTH FROZE (RUS)	PTUSHKO	AIP	1963
DEF	DEFIANT ONES	KRAMER	UNITED ARTISTS	1958
DEGRASSE	PIPER'S PRICE	DE GRASSE	UNIVERSAL	1917
DER	SAFECRACKER (UK)	MILLAND	MGM	1958
DF	DEADFALL (UK)	FORBES	20th CENTURY FOX	1968
DF	DELTA FORCE	GOLAN	CANNON	1986
DF	DIAMONDS ARE FOREVER	HAMILTON	UNITED ARTISTS	1971
DF	DICK FORAN	portrait	UNIVERSAL, WARNER BROS	
DF	DOG OF FLANDERS	SLOMAN	RKO	1935
DF	DOG OF FLANDERS	CLARK	20th CENTURY FOX	1959
DF	DOUGLAS FAIRBANKS (SR)	portrait	UNITED ARTISTS	
DF	DOUGLAS FAIRBANKS JR	portrait	FN/WARNER BROS, RKO,	
DF	DOUGLAS FAIRBANKS PRODUCTIONS	studio	UNITED ARTISTS	
DF	DR. FAUSTUS (UK)	BURTON, COGHILL	COLUMBIA	1967
DF	DUSTIN FARNUM	portrait	ROBERTSON-COLE	
DF	FACE OF FU MANCHU (UK)	SHARP	SEVEN ARTS	1965
DF	FOR FREEDOM (UK)	ELVEY, KNIGHT	GFD	1940
DF	MARRIED AND IN LOVE	FARROW	RKO	1940
DF	THERE GOES THE GROOM	SANTLEY	RKO	1937
DF	THREE MUSKETEERS	NIBLO	UNITED ARTISTS	1921
DF-28	AROUND THE WORLD WITH DOUGLAS FAIRBANKS	FLEMING, FAIRBANKS	UNITED ARTISTS	1931
DF-4200	REACHING FOR THE MOON	GOULDING	UNITED ARTISTS	1930
DFB	DETECTIVE (UK: FATHER BROWN)	HAMER	COLUMBIA	1954
DFII	DELTA FORCE 2	NORRIS	CANNON	1990
DFjr	DOUGLAS FAIRBANKS JR	portrait	UNIVERSAL 1930S	
DFM	DESIGN FOR MURDER (UK: TRUNK CRIME)	BOULTING	WORLD	1939
DFO	DUET FOR ONE	KONCHALOVSKI	CANNON	1986
DB	DALTON GANG	BEEBE	LIPPERT	1949
DG	DAVID AND GOLIATH (IT)	BALDI, POTTIER	MONOGRAM	1961
DG	DIANA GIBSON aka ROSEMARY SCHROPP	portrait	RKO	
DG	DOROTHY GULLIVER	portrait		
DG	DRAGON'S GOLD	POLLEXFEN, WISBERG	UNITED ARTISTS	1954
DG	DRAGSTRIP GIRL	CAHN	AIP	1957
DG	SHOOTING STRAIGHT	ARCHAINBAUD	RKO	1930
DG	THANK HEAVEN FOR SMALL FAVORS	MOCKY	20th CENTURY FOX	1963
DG4	GREEN GODDESS	OLCOTT	GOLDWYN (COSMOPOLITAN)	1923
DGL	DRACULA'S GREAT LOVE	AGUIRRE	INT'L AMUSEMENT	1974
DGM	DIRTIEST GIRL I EVER MET (UK: COOL IT CAROL)	WALKER	AIP	1972
DH	DANCE WITH ME, HENRY	BARTON	UNITED ARTISTS	1956
DH	DARK HORSE	GREEN	WARNER BROS	1932

Movie Still Identification Book Ultimate Edition - Letters

CODE	TITLE/NAME	DIRECTOR/TYPE	STUDIO/DISTRIBUTOR	YEAR
DH	DAYS OF HEAVEN	MALICK	PARAMOUNT	1978
DH	DEAN HARENS	portrait	UNIV	
DH	DEATH RIDES A HORSE (IT)	PETRONI	UNITED ARTISTS	1967
DH	DENNIS HOPPER	portrait	WARNER BROS	
DH	DESERT HELL	WARREN	20th CENTURY FOX	1958
DH	DEVIL HORSE	JACKMAN	PATHE	1926
DH	DOLL'S HOUSE (UK)	GARLAND	PARAMOUNT	1973
DH	DORIS HILL	portrait	WARNER BROS	
DH	DOROTHY HART	portrait	UNIVERSAL, WARNER BROS	
DH	DOSS HOUSE (UK)	BAXTER	MGM	1933
DH	DOUBLE HARNESS	CROMWELL	RKO	1933
DH	DOWNHILL (UK)	HITCHCOCK	WARDOUR (UK)	1928
DH2	DIE HARD 2	HARLIN	20th CENTURY FOX	1990
DHB	DIARY OF A HIGH SCHOOL BRIDE	TOPPER	AIP	1959
DHLGH	DAY THE HOT LINE GOT HOT (SP)	PRIER	AIP	1959
DHTF	DANCER HAS TWO FACES	NEWLAND	20th CENTURY FOX	1967
DI	DAMSEL IN DISTRESS	STEVENS	RKO	1937
DI	DEVIL'S ISLAND	CLEMENS	WARNER BROS	1939
DI	I ESCAPED FROM DEVIL'S ISLAND	WITNEY	UNITED ARTISTS	1973
DI	PLAY GIRL	WOODRUFF	RKO	1941
DIL	DILLION PRODUCTIONS	studio		
DIL-6	MAN ABOUT TOWN	DILLION	FOX FILM	1932
DIL-7	CALL HER SAVAGE	DILLION	FOX FILM	1932
DIN	DINGAKA	UYS	EMBASSY	1965
DIS	DIVORCE ITALIAN STYLE	GERMI	EMBASSY	1962
DJ	DAVID JANSSEN	portrait	UNIV	
DJ	DAVID JANSSEN	portrait	PARAMOUNT	
DJ	DEAN JAGGER	portrait	RKO	1930s-40s
DJ	DEAR JOHN (SWE: KARE JOHN)	LINDGREN	SIGMA III	1964
DJ	DESPERATE JOURNEY	WALSH	WARNER BROS	1942
DJ	DON JUAN	CROSLAND	WARNER BROS	1926
DJ	GET ON WITH IT! (UK: DENTIST ON THE JOB)	PENNINGTON-RICHARDS	GOVERNOR	1961
DJ	PASSPORT TO DESTINY	MCCAREY	RKO	1944
DJ	PATTY/PATTI/DIANA HALE (aka DIANA JEANNE)	portrait	WARNER BROS	early 40s
DJ	PRIVATE LIFE OF DON JUAN	KORDA	UNITED ARTISTS	1934
DJX	DOROTHY JORDAN	portrait	MGM	1920s-30s
DK	APPRENTICESHIP OF DUDDY KRAVITZ	KOTCHEFF	PARAMOUNT	1974
DK	DANNY KAYE	portrait	RKO, WARNER BROS	
DK	DAUN KENNEDY	portrait	UNIV	
DK	DEBORAH KERR	portrait	MGM	
DK	DODES KA-DEN	KUROSAWA	JANUS (JAP)	1970
DK	DOROTHEA KENT	portrait	UNIVERSAL	
DL	DARLING LILI	EDWARDS	PARAMOUNT	1970
DL	DAVID LOEW	portrait	RKO	
DL	DEVIL'S SADDLE LEGION	CONNOLLY	WARNER BROS	1937
DL	DIANA LEWIS	portrait	WARNER BROS	
DL	DIANA LYNN	portrait	RKO	
DL	DIOS LOS CRIA (MEX)	SOLARES	PELICULAS MEX	1953
DL	DIRTY LITTLE BILLY	DRAGOTI	COLUMBIA	1972
DL	DISHONORED LADY	STEVENSON	UNITED ARTISTS	1947
DL	DOCTOR IN LOVE (UK)	THOMAS	GOVERNOR	1960
DL	DONNA LEE	portrait	RKO	
DL	DOROTHY LEE	portrait	RKO	1920s-40s
DL	DOROTHY LOVETT	portrait	RKO	
DL	DREAMING LIPS (UK)	CZINNER	UNITED ARTISTS	1937
DLL	DANCE LITTLE LADY (UK)	GUEST	TRANS LUX	1954
DLN	DON'T LOOK NOW	ROEG	PARAMOUNT	1973
DLR	DOWN LIBERTY ROAD	FAIRBANKS	WARNER BROS	1956
DLX	DELLA LIND (aka GRETE NATZLER)	portrait	MGM	
DM	BACHELOR BRIDES	HOWARD	PRODUCERS DIST.	1926
DM	DAISY MILLER	BOGDANOVICH	PARAMOUNT	1974
DM	DAY MARS INVADED EARTH	DEXTER	20th CENTURY FOX	1963
DM	DEMILLE PICTURES	studio	PATHE	
DM	DEMOLITION MAN	BRAMBILLA	WARNER BROS	1993
DM	DENNIS MORGAN	portrait	WARNER BROS	
DM	DEPUTY MARSHALL	BERKE	LIPPERT	1949
DM	DESTINATION MURDER	CAHN	RKO	1950
DM	DEWEY MARTIN	portrait	WARNER BROS, RKO	
DM	DIARY OF A MADMAN	LE BORG	UNITED ARTISTS	1963
DM	DICKIE MOORE	portrait	RKO	

Movie Still Identification Book Ultimate Edition - Letters

CODE	TITLE/NAME	DIRECTOR/TYPE	STUDIO/DISTRIBUTOR	YEAR
DM	DOLORES MORAN	portrait	WARNER BROS	
DM	DONNA MARTEL	portrait	UNIVERSAL	
DM	DORIS MAY	portrait	ROBERTSON-COLE	
DM	DOROTHY MACKAILL	portrait	FN	
DM	DOROTHY MALONE	portrait	UNIVERSAL, WARNER BROS	
DM	DOROTHY MOORE	portrait	RKO	1930s-40s
DM	DOROTHY MORRIS	portrait	UNIV	
DM	DOUBLE MAN (UK)	SCHAFFNER	WARNER BROS	1967
DM	DOUBLE MURDER (IT)	STENO	WARNER BROS	1978
DM	DOUGLASS MONTGOMERY	portrait	UNIV	
DM	DR. MONICA	KEIGHLEY	WARNER BROS	1934
DM	SUICIDE SQUADRON (UK: DANGEROUS MOONLIGHT)	HURST	REPUBLIC	1942
DM1	HELL'S HIGHROAD	JULIAN	PRODUCERS DIST.	1925
DM2	WHITE GOLD	HOWARD	PRODUCERS DIST.	1927
DM3	ANGEL OF BROADWAY	WEBER	PRODUCERS DIST.	1927
DM3	FORBIDDEN WOMAN	STEIN	PATHE EXCHANGE	1927
DM3	LEOPARD LADY	JULIAN	PATHE EXCHANGE	1928
DM3-26	CHICAGO	URSON	PATHE	1927
DM4	WEDDING SONG	HALE	PRODUCERS DIST.	1925
DM7	MADE FOR LOVE	SLOANE	PRODUCERS DIST.	1926
DM9	RED DICE	HOWARD	PRODUCERS DIST.	1926
DMc	DIANE McBAIN	portrait	WARNER BROS	1960s
DMC	DRIVE ME CRAZY	SCHULTZ	20th CENTURY FOX	1999
DMCL	DIRTY MARY CRAZY LARRY	HOUGH	20th CENTURY FOX	1974
DME	DIVORCE MADE EASY	BURNS	PARAMOUNT	1929
DMG	DOROTHY McGUIRE	portrait	RKO	
DMP	DESTINATION MOON	PICHEL	EAGLE LION	1950
DN	DAVID NIVEN	portrait	RKO	
DN	DEAD OF NIGHT (UK)	CAVALCANTI	JANUS	R60
DN	DECAMERON NIGHTS (UK)	FREGONESE	RKO	1953
DN	DR. NO	YOUNG	UNITED ARTISTS	1962
DN	DUDLEY NICHOLS	portrait	RKO	
DN	NIGHT OF PASSION (UK: DURING ONE NIGHT)	FURIE	ASTOR	1960
DN	THEY DRIVE BY NIGHT	WALSH	WARNER BROS	1940
DN1	SOUTH AMERICAN GEORGE (UK)	VARNEL	COLUMBIA	1941
DO	DADDY 'O	PLACE	AIP	1959
DO	DEAD ONE	MAHON	MARDI GRAS	1960
DO	DEAR OCTOPUS (UK)	FRENCH	ENGLISH	1943
DO	DOUGHGIRLS	KERN	WARNER BROS	1944
DO	DREAMING OUT LOUD	YOUNG	RKO	1940
Do.D.	DOROTHY DARRELL	portrait	UNIVERSAL	
DOC	DOC	PERRY	UNITED ARTISTS	1971
DOC	DONALD O'CONNOR	portrait	UNIVERSAL	
DOF	DAY THE FISH CAME OUT	KAKOGIANNIS	20th CENTURY FOX	1967
DOG	SHAGGY DOG	BARTON	BUENA VISTA	1959
DOL	DAY OF THE LOCUST	SCHLESINGER	PARAMOUNT	1975
DON	DEAD OF NIGHT (UK)	CAVALCANTI, CRICHTON	UNIVERSAL	1946
DON	DEATH ON THE NILE	GUILLERMIN	PARAMOUNT	1978
DOS	DAVID O. SELZNICK			
DOS	DEATH OF A SCOUNDREL	MARTIN	RKO	1956
DOT	DAYS OF THUNDER	SCOTT	PARAMOUNT	1990
DOW	FABULOUS WORLD OF JULES VERNE (CZ)	ZEMAN	WARNER BROS	1961
D-OX	OPERATION X (UK: MY DAUGHTER JOY)	RATOFF	COLUMBIA	1950
DP	DANCING PIRATE	CORRIGAN	RKO	1936
DP	DAWN PATROL	HAWKS	WARNER BROS	1930
DP	DAWN PATROL	GOULDING	WARNER BROS	1938
DP	DEATH PARTY		COLUMBIA	1965
DP	DESERT PASSAGE	SELANDER	RKO	1952
DP	DEVIL'S HARBOR (UK: DEVIL'S POINT)	TULLY	20th CENTURY FOX	1954
DP	DEVIL'S PARTNER	RONDEAU	FILM GROUP	1961
DP	DICK POWELL	portrait	RKO	
DP	DICK POWELL	portrait	WARNER BROS	
DP	DOROTHY PROVINE	portrait	WARNER BROS	
DP	DREAM OF PASSION	DASSIN	AVCO EMBASSY	1978
DP	GREAT DAN PATCH	NEWMAN	UNITED ARTISTS	1949
DP	MAN WITH THE GUN (DEADLY PEACEMAKER)	WILSON	UNITED ARTISTS	1955
DP	SECRET INVASION	CORMAN	UNITED ARTISTS	1964
DP	DOWN PERISCOPE	WARD	20th CENTURY FOX	1996
DP-1	GILBERT HARDING SPEAKING OF MURDER (UK)	DICKSON	PARAMOUNT BRITISH	1954
DP3	TALE OF THREE WOMEN (UK)	CONNELL, DICKSON	PARAMOUNT BRITISH	1954

Movie Still Identification Book Ultimate Edition - Letters

CODE	TITLE/NAME	DIRECTOR/TYPE	STUDIO/DISTRIBUTOR	YEAR
DP-21	OPERATION MURDER (UK)	MORRIS	UNITED ARTISTS	1957
DP-62E	DEPRAVED (UK)	DICKSON	UNITED ARTISTS	1957
DP-76E	SON OF A STRANGER (UK)	MORRIS	UNITED ARTISTS	1957
DP78E	WOMAN OF MYSTERY (UK)	MORRIS	UNITED ARTISTS	1958
DP108E	WOMAN POSSESSED (UK)	VARNEL	UNITED ARTISTS	1958
DP122E	MOMENT OF INDISCRETION (UK)	VARNEL	UNITED ARTISTS	1958
DP123E	INNOCENT MEETING (UK)	GRAYSON	UNITED ARTISTS	1959
DP158E	WEB OF SUSPICION (UK)	VARNEL	PARAMOUNT BRITISH	1959
DPBS	DEAD PIGEON ON BEETHOVEN ST.	FULLER	EMERSON	1974
DPC	DRAGON OF PENDRAGON CASTLE (UK)	BAXTER	GFD	1950
DPD	DRACULA: PRINCE OF DARKNESS (UK)	FISHER	20TH CENTURY FOX	1966
DPG	SWEETHEARTS AND WIVES	BADGER	WARNER BROS	1930
DPX1	DORIS KENYON	portrait	DE LUXE PICTURES	
DQ	DEVIL BY THE TAIL (FR)	DE BROCA	LOPERT	1969
DQ	DIAMOND QUEEN	BRAHM	WARNER BROS	1953
DQ	DON Q SON OF ZORRO	CRISP	UNITED ARTISTS	1925
DQ	DON QUIXOTE	NUREYEV	CONTINENTAL	1973
DR	DALE ROBERTSON	portrait	RKO	
DR	DEATH RACE 2000	BARTEL	NEW WORLD	1975
DR	DEBBIE REYNOLDS	portrait	UNIVERSAL	late 50s
DR	DER ROSENKAVALIER (UK)	CZINNER	SCHOENFELD	1962
DR	DESERT RAVEN	LEE	ALLIED ARTISTS	1965
DR	DINNER AT THE RITZ (UK)	SCHUSTER	20TH CENTURY FOX	1937
DR	DONNA REED	portrait	RKO	
DR	DONNA REED	portrait	UNIV	
DR	DOWNHILL RACER	RITCHIE	PARAMOUNT	1969
DR	DRAGSTRIP RIOT	BRADLEY	AIP	1958
DR	DRANGO	BARTLETT, BRICKEN	UNITED ARTISTS	1957
DR	DRIVEN	HARLIN	WARNER BROS	2001
DR	DRUM	CARVER	UNITED ARTISTS	1976
DR	DUNCAN RENALDO	portrait	MGM	
DR	FUGITIVE LADY (UK)	SALKOW	REPUBLIC	1950
DS	DARK OF THE SUN (UK: MERCENARIES)	CARDIFF	MGM	1968
DS	DARK SECRET (UK)	ROGERS	BUTCHER'S	1949
DS	DARK STAR	DWAN	PARAMOUNT	1919
DS	DARK SWAN	WEBB	WARNER BROS	1924
DS	DAUGHTERS OF SATAN	MORSE	UNITED ARTISTS	1972
DS	DEATH SHIP	RAKOFF	AVCO EMBASSY	1980
DS	DESERT SANDS	SELANDER	UNITED ARTISTS	1955
DS	DESERT SONG	DEL RUTH	WARNER BROS	1929
DS	DESERT SONG	FLOREY	WARNER BROS	1944
DS	DINAH SHORE	portrait	RKO	
DS	DOCTOR SYN (UK)	NEILL	GAUMONT BRITISH AMERICA	1937
DS	DON SIEGEL	portrait	UNIV	
DS	DORE SCHARY	portrait	RKO	late 40s
DS	DOROTHY SHAY	portrait	UNIVERSAL	early 50s
DS	DR. SOCRATES	DIETERLE	WARNER BROS	1935
DS	DREAMSCAPE	RUBEN	20th CENTURY FOX	1984
DS	DRIVER'S SEAT	GRIFFI	AVCO EMBASSY	1974
DS	DUCK SOUP	MCCAREY	PARAMOUNT	1933
DS	DUCK YOU SUCKER (IT)	LEONE	UNITED ARTISTS	1971
DS	DUEL IN THE SUN	VIDOR	UNITED ARTISTS	1946
DS	HELL BOUND	HOLE JR.	UNITED ARTISTS	1957
DS	STREET OF SINNERS	BERKE	UNITED ARTISTS	1957
DS	THEY WON'T FORGET	LEROY	WARNER BROS	1937
DS	WHO'LL STOP THE RAIN (DOG SOLDIERS)	REISZ	UNITED ARTISTS	1978
DS6	DEEP STAR SIX	CUNNINGHAM	TRI STAR	1989
DS-600	TOPSY AND EVA	LORD	UNITED ARTISTS	1927
DS-A	WHO'LL STOP THE RAIN (DOG SOLDIERS)	REISZ	UNITED ARTISTS	1978
DS-B	WHO'LL STOP THE RAIN (DOG SOLDIERS)	REISZ	UNITED ARTISTS	1978
DSE	DAY THE SKY EXPLODED (IT/FR: LA MORTE VIENE DALLO	HEUSCH	EXCELSIOR	1961
DSM	DEATH SMILES ON A MURDERER	D'AMATO	AVCO EMBASSY	1974
DSS	DESPERATELY SEEKING SUSAN	SEIDELMAN	ORION	1985
DT	BLOOD ON SATAN'S CLAW/DEVIL'S TOUCH* (UK)	HAGGARD	CANNON	1971
DT	DAY OF THE TRIFFIDS (UK)	SEKELY	ALLIED ARTISTS	1962
DT	DEADLY TRACKERS	SHEAR	WARNER BROS	1973
DT	DEE TURNELL	portrait	RKO	
DT	DESTINATION TOKYO	DAVES	WARNER BROS	1943
DT	DICK TRACY	BERKE	RKO	1946
DT	DISTANT TRUMPET (UK)	FISHER	APEX	1952

Movie Still Identification Book Ultimate Edition - Letters

CODE	TITLE/NAME	DIRECTOR/TYPE	STUDIO/DISTRIBUTOR	YEAR
DT	DOCTOR IN TROUBLE (UK)	THOMAS	HEMISPHERE	1970
DT	DOMESTIC TROUBLES	ENRIGHT	WARNER BROS	1928
DT	DON TERRY	portrait	UNIV	
DT	DON'T TURN 'EM LOOSE	STOLOFF	RKO	1936
DT	DOROTHY TREE	portrait	UNIV	
DT	DOROTHY TREE	portrait	WARNER BROS	
DT	DR. TERROR'S HOUSE OF HORRORS (UK)	FRANCIS	PARAMOUNT	1965
DT	DUMMY TALKS (UK)	MITCHELL	ANGLO-AMERICAN	1943
DT	DYNAMITE PASS	LANDERS	RKO	1952
DT	GIRL WITH AN ITCH	ASHCROFT	HOWCO	1958
DT	MAN WITH TWO FACES	MAYO	WARNER BROS	1934
DT	VACATION IN RENO	GOODWINS	RKO	1946
DT2	DEEP THROAT PART 2	SARNO	DAMIANO	1974
DT-2	DICK TRACY VS. CUEBALL	DOUGLAS	RKO	1946
DT-3	DICK TRACY MEETS GRUESOME	RAWLINS	RKO	1947
DTBB	DOUBLE TAKE	GALLO	TOUCHSTONE	2001
DTC	DICK TRACY'S DILEMMA	RAWLINS	RKO	1947
DTC	RACING LUCK	RAYMAKER	ASSOCIATED EXHIBITORS	1924
DTL	DAYS OF THRILLS AND LAUGHTER	YOUNGSON	20th CENTURY FOX	1961
DTM	BORN TO KILL	WISE	RKO	1947
DTN	COUNT THE HOURS	SIEGEL	RKO	1953
DTOPE	DOIN' TIME ON PLANET EARTH	MATTHAU	CANNON	1987
DTR	DEVIL THUMBS A RIDE	FEIST	RKO	1947
DTW	DEAD TO THE WORLD	WEBSTER	UNITED ARTISTS	1961
DU-1	PARTNERS OF FATE	DURNING	FOX FILM	1921
DUBB	DUETS	PALTROW	BUENA VISTA	2000
DULL-6	BRONCHO TWISTER	DULL	FOX FILM	1927
DUN-21	WHISPERING SAGE	DUNLAP	FOX FILM	1927
DUN-22	GOOD AS GOLD	DUNLAP	FOX	1927
DUNL-8	FORBIDDEN TRAILS	DUNLAP	FOX FILM	1920
DUNLAP-8	FORBIDDEN TRAILS	DUNLAP	FOX FILM	1920
DUR-8	STRANGE IDOLS	DURNING	FOX FILM	1922
DUR-12	ELEVENTH HOUR	DURNING	FOX FILM	1923
DV	ANN DVORAK	portrait	WARNER BROS	1930s-40s
DV	DARK VICTORY	GOULDING	WARNER BROS	1939
DV	DIVA	BEINEIX	UNITED ARTISTS	1981
DV	DOROTHY VERNON OF HADDON HALL	NEILAN	UNITED ARTISTS	1924
DVSF	DRACULA VS. FRANKENSTEIN	ADAMSON	INDEPENDENT INTL	1972
DW	ALLAN DWAN PRODUCTIONS	studio	FOX	
DW	AT DAWN WE DIE (UK: TOMORROW WE LIVE)	KING	REPUBLIC	1945
DW	BEFORE DAWN	PICHEL	RKO	1933
DW	DANA WYNTER	portrait	PARAMOUNT, UNIVERSAL	
DW	DANCES WITH WOLVES	COSTNER	ORION	1990
DW	DEATH WISH	WINNER	PARAMOUNT	1974
DW	DIANA WYNYARD	portrait	MGM	
DW	DOCTOR'S WIVES	SCHAEFER	COLUMBIA	1971
DW	DOGS OF WAR	IRVIN	UNITED ARTISTS	1980
DW	DONALD WOODS	portrait	WARNER BROS	
DW	DON'T WORRY, WE'LL THINK OF A TITLE	JONES	UNITED ARTISTS	1966
DW	DOOMWATCH	SASDY	AVCO EMBASSY	1974
DW	DORIS WESTON	portrait	WARNER BROS	late 30s
DW	DOROTHY WILSON	portrait	RKO	1930s
DW	DOWN TWISTED	PYUN	CANNON	1986
DW	DRY WHITE SEASON	PALCY	MGM	1989
DW	IF IT'S TUESDAY, THIS MUST BE BELGIUM	STUART	UNITED ARTISTS	1969
DW	WELL	ROUSE, POPKIN	UNITED ARTISTS	1951
DW	WOMAN ON THE BEACH	RENOIR	RKO	1946
DW-1	SUMMER BACHELORS	DWAN	FOX FILM	1926
DW-2	MUSIC MASTER	DWAN	FOX FILM	1927
DW3	DEATH WISH 3	WINNER	CANNON	1985
DW-3	JOY GIRL	DWAN	FOX FILM	1927
DW4	DEATH WISH 4	THOMPSON	CANNON	1987
DW-4	EAST SIDE, WEST SIDE	DWAN	FOX FILM	1927
DW-5	FAR CALL	DWAN	FOX FILM	1929
DW-6	FROZEN JUSTICE	DWAN	FOX FILM	1929
DW-7	SOUTH SEA ROSE	DWAN	FOX FILM	1929
DW-8	WICKED	DWAN	FOX FILM	1931
DW-9	WHILE PARIS SLEEPS	DWAN	FOX FILM	1932
DW5084	DEATH WISH	WINNER	PARAMOUNT	1974
DWE	BEWARE MY LOVELY	HORNER	RKO	1952

Movie Still Identification Book Ultimate Edition - Letters

CODE	TITLE/NAME	DIRECTOR/TYPE	STUDIO/DISTRIBUTOR	YEAR
DWE	DAY THE WORLD ENDED (ARC)	CORMAN	AIP	1956
DWG-1100	DRUMS OF LOVE	GRIFFITH	UNITED ARTISTS	1928
DWG-1400	BATTLE OF THE SEXES	GRIFFITH	UNITED ARTISTS	1928
DWG-1600	LADY OF THE PAVEMENTS	GRIFFITH	UNITED ARTISTS	1929
DWG-3800	ABRAHAM LINCOLN	GRIFFITH	UNITED ARTISTS	1930
DWII-85	DEATH WISH II	WINNER	FILMWAYS	1982
DWM	APPOINTMENT WITH MURDER	BERNHARD	FILM CLASSICS	1948
DWR	DEATH WARRANT	SARAFIAN	MGM	1990
DWV	THIRD MAN (UK)	REED	SELZNICK RELEASING	1949
DX	DOCTOR X	CURTIZ	WARNER BROS	1932
DY	DYING YOUNG	SCHUMACHER	20th CENTURY FOX	1991
DYC	MY LOVER MY SON/DON'T YOU CRY* (UK)	NEWLAND	MGM	1970
DZ	DOCTOR ZHIVAGO (UK)	LEAN	MGM	1965
E	ECLIPSE (IT)	ANTONIONI	TIMES FILM	1962
E	ELSTREE STUDIO (UK)			
E	EMIL AND THE DETECTIVES (UK)	ROSMER	OLYMPIC	1935
E	ENCHANTED ISLAND	DWAN	WARNER BROS	1958
E	ESCAPADE (UK)	LEACOCK	DCA	1955
E	ESCAPE	DEAN	RKO	1930
E	ESCAPE ME NEVER (UK)	CZINNER	UNITED ARTISTS	1935
E	EVERYDAY	BRITTON	AMERICAN	1976
E	EVERYTHING YOU ALWAYS WANTED TO KNOW ABOUT SEX	ALLEN	UNITED ARTISTS	1972
E	EVIDENCE	ADOLFI	WARNER BROS	1929
E	EXORCIST 3	BLATTY	20th CENTURY FOX	1990
E	FACE OF EVE/US: EVE (UK)	LYNN, SUMMERS	COMMONWEALTH	1968
E	HAPPY GO LOVELY (UK)	HUMBERSTONE	RKO	1951
E	MY LOVE CAME BACK	BERNHARDT	WARNER BROS	1940
E	PLAYBOY (UK: KICKING THE MOON AROUND)	FORDE	GFD	1938
E	THREE MUSKETEERS	NIBLO	UNITED ARTISTS	1921
E	WOMAN I LOVE	MELFORD	FILM BOOKING OFFICE	1929
E	WOMAN I LOVE	LITVAK	RKO	1937
E1	FATHER STEPS OUT (CITY LIMITS*)	YARBROUGH	MONOGRAM	1941
E-1	HOSS AND HOSS (sh)	(UNFINISHED)	PATHE EXCHANGE	1924
E-1	PICKANINNY (sh)	KERR, PARROTT	PATHE EXCHANGE	1921
E-1	YOU BRING THE DUCKS (sh)	YATES	MGM	1934
E1E	DISK-O-TEK HOLIDAY (UK)	HICKOX, SCARZA	MONOGRAM	1966
E-2	HOT HEELS (sh)	JESKE	PATHE EXCHANGE	1924
E-2	NOSED OUT (sh)	YATES	MGM	1934
E-3	BALLAD OF PADUCAH JAIL (sh)	GRINDE	MGM	1934
E-3	SKY PLUMBER (sh)	DAVISS	PATHE EXCHANGE	1924
E-4	LUCKY BEGINNERS (sh)	DOUGLAS, ROACH	MGM	1935
E-4	UNFINISHED ARTHUR STONE (sh)		PATHE EXCHANGE	1924
E-5	INFERNAL TRIANGLE (sh)	DOUGLAS	MGM	1935
E-5	SHOULD LANDLORDS LIVE? (sh)	BARROWS, DAVIS	PATHE EXCHANGE	1924
E6	HIS MAJESTY, THE AMERICAN	HENABERY	UNITED ARTISTS	1919
E-6	JUST A GOOD GUY (sh)	DEL RUTH	PATHE EXCHANGE	1924
E-6	UNFINISHED ROACH (sh)		PATHE EXCHANGE	1924
E-7	JUST A GOOD GUY (sh)	DEL RUTH	PATHE EXCHANGE	1924
E-8	TAME MEN AND WILD WOMEN (sh)	DE SANO	PATHE EXCHANGE	1925
E-9	COMMAND PERFORMANCE	LANG	TIFFANY	1931
E-9	HARD WORKING LOAFERS (sh)		PATHE EXCHANGE	1925
E-10	CHANGE THE NEEDLE (sh)	ROACH	PATHE EXCHANGE	1925
E-10	HELL BOUND	LANG	TIFFANY	1931
E-11	UNNAMED ARTHUR STONE (sh)		PATHE EXCHANGE	1925
E-12	SHERLOCK SLEUTH (sh)	CEDER	PATHE EXCHANGE	1925
E-12	WOMEN GO ON FOREVER	LANG	TIFFANY	1931
E-13	HARD -BOILED (sh)	MCCAREY	PATHE EXCHANGE	1925
E-14	BAD BOY (sh)	MCCAREY	PATHE EXCHANGE	1925
E-15	LOOKING FOR SALLY (sh)	MCCAREY	PATHE EXCHANGE	1925
E-16	WHAT PRICE GOOFY? (sh)	MCCAREY	PATHE EXCHANGE	1925
E-17	ISN'T LIFE TERRIBLE? (sh)	MCCAREY	PATHE EXCHANGE	1925
E-18	INNOCENT HUSBANDS (sh)	MCCAREY	PATHE EXCHANGE	1925
E-19	NO FATHER TO GUIDE HIM (sh)	MCCAREY	PATHE EXCHANGE	1925
E-31	WHEN MEN DESIRE	EDWARDS	FOX FILM	1919
E-36	WINGS OF THE MORNING	EDWARDS	FOX FILM	1919
E-37	IF I WERE KING	EDWARDS	FOX FILM	1920
E-38	HEART STRINGS	EDWARDS	FOX FILM	1920
E-42	SCUTTLERS	EDWARDS	FOX FILM	1920
E-43	DRAG HARLAN	EDWARDS	FOX FILM	1920
E-44	QUEEN OF SHEBA	EDWARDS	FOX FILM	1921

Movie Still Identification Book Ultimate Edition - Letters

CODE	TITLE/NAME	DIRECTOR/TYPE	STUDIO/DISTRIBUTOR	YEAR
E-45	MURDER! (UK)	HITCHCOCK	BIP	1930
E48-1	MAN ON THE RUN (UK)	HUNTINGTON	STRATFORD	1949
E-48-2	HASTY HEART (UK)	SHERMAN	WARNER BROS	1949
E49-1	LANDFALL (UK)	ANNAKIN	STRATFORD	1949
E49-2	DANCING YEARS (UK)	FRENCH	STRATFORD	1950
E49-3	STAGE FRIGHT (UK)	HITCHCOCK	WARNER BROS.	1950
E49-4	PORTRAIT OF CLARE (UK)	COMFORT	STRATFORD	1950
E49-6	GUILT IS MY SHADOW (UK)	KELLINO	STRATFORD	1950
E49-7	HER PANELLED DOOR (UK: WOMAN WITH NO NAME)	VAJDA	SOUVAINE	1950
E50-4	LAUGHTER IN PARADISE (UK)	ZAMPI	STRATFORD	1951
E50-6	YOUNG WIVES' TALE (UK)	CASS	STRATFORD	1951
E51-2	WOMAN'S ANGLE (UK)	ARLISS	STRATFORD	1952
E51-3	SO LITTLE TIME (UK)	BENNETT	MACDONALD	1952
E51-4	ANGELS ONE FIVE (UK)	O'FERRALL	STRATFORD	1952
E51-6	AFFAIR IN MONTE CARLO (UK: 24 HOURS WOMAN'S LIFE)	SAVILLE	ALLIED ARTISTS	1952
E51-7	CASTLE IN THE AIR (UK)	CASS	STRATFORD	1952
E52-1	FATHER'S DOING FINE (UK)	CASS	STRATFORD	1952
E52-2	GOLDEN MASK (UK: SOUTH OF ALGIERS)	LEE	UNITED ARTISTS	1953
E52-5	UNCLE WILLIE'S BICYCLE SHOP (UK:ISN'T LIFE WONDERFUL!)	FRENCH	STRATFORD	1954
E52-7	VALLEY OF SONG (UK)	GUNN	STRATFORD	1953
E52-8	WILL ANY GENTLEMAN...? (UK)	ANDERSON	STRATFORD	1953
E53-1	HOUSE OF THE ARROW (UK)	ANDERSON	STRATFORD	1953
E53-2	GOOD BEGINNING (UK)	GUNN	STRATFORD	1953
E53-4	YOUNG AND WILLING (UK: WEAK AND THE WICKED)	THOMPSON	ALLIED ARTISTS	1954
E-53-6	DUEL IN THE JUNGLE (UK)	MARSHALL	WARNER BROS	1954
E53-7	TONIGHT'S THE NIGHT (UK: HAPPILY EVER AFTER)	ZAMPI	ALLIED ARTISTS	1954
E54-1	DAM BUSTERS (UK)	ANDERSON	WARNER BROS.	1955
E54-2	COCKTAILS IN THE KITCHEN (UK: FOR BETTER, FOR WORSE)	THOMPSON	STRATFORD	1954
E-54-4	MOBY DICK	HUSTON	UNITED ARTISTS	1954
E54-5	WARRIORS/US: DARK AVENGER (UK)	LEVIN	ALLIED ARTISTS	1955
E55-1	OH... ROSALINDA!! (UK)	POWELL, PRESSBURGER	ASSOCIATED BRITISH-PATHE	1955
E55-3	NOW AND FOREVER (UK)	ZAMPI	STRATFORD	1956
E-55-6	1984 (UK)	ANDERSON	COLUMBIA	1956
E55-7	IT'S GREAT TO BE YOUNG! (UK)	FRANKEL	FINE ARTS	1956
E55-8	IT'S NEVER TOO LATE (UK)	MCCARTHY	STRATFORD	1956
E55-10	TONS OF TROUBLE (UK)	HISCOTT	RENOWN	1956
E56-1	MY WIFE'S FAMILY (UK)	GUNN	ASSOCIATED BRITISH-PATHE	1956
E56-3	GOOD COMPANIONS (UK)	THOMPSON	STRATFORD	1957
E56-12	NO TIME FOR TEARS (UK)	FRANKEL	ASSOCIATED BRITISH-PATHE	1957
E57-1	ACCUSED/US: MARK OF THE HAWK (UK)	AUDLEY	UNIVERSAL	1957
E-57-2	DANGEROUS YOUTH (UK)	WILCOX	WARNER BROS	1957
E-57-3	WOMAN IN A DRESSING GOWN (UK)	THOMPSON	WARNER BROS	1957
E57-6	YOUNG AND THE GUILTY (UK)	COTES	NTA	1958
E57-8	CHASE A CROOKED SHADOW (UK)	ANDERSON	WARNER BROS.	1958
E57-9	MOONRAKER (UK)	MACDONALD	ASSOCIATED BRITISH-PATHE	1958
E57-15	DESERT ATTACK (UK: ICE COLD IN ALEX)	THOMPSON	20TH CENTURY FOX	1958
E57-18	INDISCREET (UK 1957)	DONEN	WARNER BROS	1969
E57-19	WONDERFUL THINGS! (UK)	WILCOX	ASSOCIATED BRITISH-PATHE	1958
E58-5	NO TREES IN THE STREET (UK)	THOMPSON	SEVEN ARTS	1959
E58-10	LADY IS A SQUARE (UK)	WILCOX	ASSOCIATED BRITISH-PATHE	1959
E58-12	ALIVE AND KICKING (UK)	FRANKEL	SEVEN ARTS	1959
E58-16	LOOK BACK IN ANGER (UK)	RICHARDSON	WARNER BROS.	1959
E58-19	OPERATION BULLSHINE (UK)	GUNN	ASSOCIATED BRITISH-PATHE	1959
E59-3	SCHOOL FOR SCOUNDRELS (UK)	HAMER	CONTINENTAL	1960
E59-7	TOMMY THE TOREADOR (UK)	CARSTAIRS	WARNER-PATHE	1959
E59-10	FOLLOW THAT HORSE! (UK)	BROMLY	WARNER BROS.	1960
E59-11	BOTTOMS UP (UK)	ZAMPI	WARNER BROS/7ARTS	1960
E59-12	HELL IS A CITY (UK)	GUEST	COLUMBIA	1960
E60-1	SANDS OF THE DESERT (UK)	CARSTAIRS	WARNER-PATHE	1960
E60-6	JUNGLE FIGHTERS (UK: LONG AND THE SHORT AND THE TALL)	NORMAN	CONTINENTAL	1961
E60-8	CALL ME GENIUS (UK: REBEL)	DAY	CONTINENTAL	1961
E-60-10	CHASE A CROOKED SHADOW (UK)	ANDERSON	WARNER BROS.	1958
E61-3	GO TO BLAZES (UK)	TRUMAN	WARNER-PATHE	1962
E61-4	PETTICOAT PIRATES (UK)	MACDONALD	WARNER-PATHE	1961
E61-6	WONDERFUL TO BE YOUNG! (UK: YOUNG ONES)	FURIE	PARAMOUNT	1961
E61-8	OPERATION SNATCH (UK)	DAY	CONTINENTAL	1962
E61-10	POT CARRIERS (UK)	SCOTT	WARNER-PATHE	1962
E61-11	GUNS OF DARKNESS (UK)	ASQUITH	WARNER BROS.	1962
E62-4	PUNCH AND JUDY MAN (UK)	SUMMERS	WARNER-PATHE	1963
E62-5	WE JOINED THE NAVY (UK)	TOYE	WARNER-PATHE	1962

Movie Still Identification Book Ultimate Edition - Letters

CODE	TITLE/NAME	DIRECTOR/TYPE	STUDIO/DISTRIBUTOR	YEAR
E62-6	SUMMER HOLIDAY (UK)	YATES	AIP	1963
E-62-9	DR. CRIPPEN (UK)	LYNN	WARNER BROS	1964
E63-1	WEST 11 (UK)	WINNER	WARNER-PATHE	1963
E63-3	WORLD TEN TIMES OVER (UK)	RILLA	GOLDSTONE	1963
E63-4	CROOKS IN CLOISTERS (UK)	SUMMERS	WARNER-PATHE	1964
E63-7	FRENCH DRESSING (UK)	RUSSELL	WARNER-PATHE	1964
E63-11	BARGEE (UK)	WOOD	WARNER-PATHE	1964
E64-4	RATTLE OF A SIMPLE MAN (UK)	BOX	CONTINENTAL	1964
E66-5	MISTER TEN PER CENT (UK)	SCOTT	WARNER-PATHE	1967
E67-4	VENGEANCE OF SHE (UK)	OWEN	20TH CENTURY FOX	1968
E67-5	LAST CONTINENT (UK)	CARRERAS	20TH CENTURY FOX	1968
E67-6	DEVIL RIDES OUT (UK: DEVIL'S BRIDE)	FISHER	20TH CENTURY FOX	1968
E-80	CONDORMAN	JARROTT	BUENA VISTA	1981
E3345	GRACE KELLY	portrait	MGM	
E3348	GRACE KELLY	portrait	MGM	
E3349	GRACE KELLY	portrait		
EA	BRITISH INTELLIGENCE	MORSE	WARNER BROS	1940
EA	CRY IN THE DARK (EVIL ANGELS)	SCHEPISI	WARNER BROS	1988
EA	EDDIE ACUFF	portrait	WARNER BROS	
EA	EDDIE ALBERT	portrait	REP,, RKO, UNIV., WARNER	
EA	EDITH ALLEN	portrait	MGM	1920s
EA	EDWARD ARNOLD	portrait	RKO	
EA	ENCHANGED APRIL	BEAUMONT	RKO	1935
EA	EVANGELINE	CAREWE	UNITED ARTISTS	1929
EA	EVE ARDEN	portrait	WARNER BROS	
EA	EVELYN ANKERS	portrait	UNIVERSAL	
EA	EXECUTIVE ACTION	MILLER	NATIONAL GENERAL PICTURES	1973
EA	EXPERIMENT ALCATRAZ	CAHN	RKO	1950
EA	WE STILL KILL THE OLD WAY (IT: A CIASCUNO IL SUO)	PETRI	UNITED ARTISTS	1967
EA1	DECISION AGAINST TIME (UK: MAN IN THE SKY)	CRICHTON	MGM	1957
EAGLE	EAGLE VS DRAGON (DOCUMENTARY FEATURETTE)	THOMA		1944
EAM	STRANGE ONE	GARFEIN	COLUMBIA	1957
EB	EARLY BIRD	HINES	EAST COAST	1925
EB	EDD "KOOKIE" BYRNES	portrait	WARNER BROS	
EB	EDDIE BRACKEN	portrait	RKO	
EB	EDDIE BRACKEN	portrait		
EB	EDGAR BERGEN	portrait	UNIVERSAL	
EB	EDGAR BUCHANAN	portrait	RKO	
EB	EDNA BEST	portrait	RKO	
EB	ELEPHANT BOY	FLAHERTY, KORDA	UNITED ARTISTS	1937
EB	ENID BENNETT	portrait	METRO	
EB	ERIC BLORE	portrait	RKO	
EB	ERNEST BORGNINE	portrait	UNITED ARTISTS	
EB	ETHEL BARRYMORE	portrait	BRITISH LION	
EB	EVELYN BRENT	portrait	RKO	1930s-40s
EB	EXCESS BAGGAGE (UK)	DAVIS	RKO	1933
EB	EXPRESSO BONGO (UK)	GUEST	CONTINENTAL	1959
EBAH	ANNE HEYWOOD	portrait		
EBXX	EDWINA BOOTH	portrait	MGM	
EC	BIG SHOT	SEILER	WARNER BROS	1942
EC	EDDIE CANTOR	portrait	RKO	
EC	EDUARDO CIANNELLI	portrait	RKO	
EC	EL CID	MANN	ALLIED ARTISTS	1961
EC	ELLEN CORBY	portrait	RKO	
EC	EMERGENCY CALL	CAHN	RKO	1933
EC	ENCHANTED COTTAGE	CROMWELL	RKO	1945
EC	ESCAPE FROM CRIME	LEDERMAN	WARNER BROS	1942
EC	ETCHIKA CHOUREAU	portrait	WARNER BROS	
EC	FRIENDS OF EDDIE COYLE	YATES	PARAMOUNT	1973
EC	JANET SHAW aka ELLEN CLANCY	portrait	UNIVERSAL	
ECBB	ERNEST GOES TO CAMP	CHERRY III	BUENA VISTA	1987
ECS	ELIZA COMES TO STAY (UK)	H EDWARDS	TWICKENHAM	1936
ECS	ETHEL CLAYTON	portrait	FBO	
ECX	EDWARD CONNELLY	portrait	MGM	late 20s
ED	EACH DAWN I DIE	KEIGHLEY	WARNER BROS	1939
ED	EDDIE DOWLING	portrait	PARAMOUNT	
ED	EDDY DUCHIN	portrait	MCA RECORDS	
ED	EDGE OF DARKNESS	MILESTONE	WARNER BROS	1943
ED	EDWARD DMYTRYK	portrait	RKO	1930s-40s
ED	ELLEN DREW	portrait	RKO	

Movie Still Identification Book Ultimate Edition - Letters

CODE	TITLE/NAME	DIRECTOR/TYPE	STUDIO/DISTRIBUTOR	YEAR
ED	EVERYBODY DANCE (UK)	REISNER	GAUMONT BRITISH AMERICA	1936
ED	EVERYBODY'S DANCIN'	JASON	LIPPERT	1950
ED	EXECUTIVE DECISION	BAIRD	WARNER BROS	1996
ED	TREASURE OF THE JAMAICA REEF/EVIL IN THE DEEP	STONE		1975
ED	WHERE EAGLES DARE (UK)	HUTTON	MGM	1969
ED1	GIVE US THIS DAY (UK)	DMYTRYK	EAGLE LION	1949
ED-46	NERO	EDWARDS	FOX FILM	1922
ED-49	SILENT COMMAND	EDWARDS	FOX FILM	1923
ED101	WHILE I LIVE (UK)	HARLOW	20TH CENTURY FOX	1947
EDS	EARTH DIES SCREAMING (UK)	FISHER	20th CENTURY FOX	1964
EE	ELIZABETH EARL	portrait	WARNER BROS	
EE	EMPLOYEE'S ENTRANCE	DEL RUTH	WARNER BROS	1933
EE	EVER SINCE EVE	BACON	WARNER BROS	1937
EE	PRIVATE LIVES OF ELIZABETH AND ESSEX	CURTIZ	WARNER BROS	1939
EE	SUPERBEAST	SCHENCK	UNITED ARTISTS	1972
EEH	EDWARD EVERETT HORTON	portrait	RKO, WARNER BROS	
E-EW	HOW TO EDUCATE A WIFE	BELL	WARNER BROS	1924
EF	BREAK TO FREEDOM (UK: ALBERT, R.N.)	GILBERT	UNITED ARTISTS	1953
EF	EDGE OF FURY	LERNER, GURNEY JR.	UNITED ARTISTS	1958
EF	ELINOR/ELEANOR/LENOR FAIR/CROWE	portrait		
EF	ELIZABETH FRASER	portrait	WARNER BROS	
EF	EMERALD FOREST	BOORMAN	EMBASSY	1985
EF	ERROL FLYNN	portrait	WARNER BROS	
EF	ESTHER FERNANDEZ	portrait	RKO	
EF	JEANNIE (UK)	FRENCH	ENGLISH	1941
EF	YOU CAN'T ESCAPE FOREVER	GRAHAM	WARNER BROS	1942
EF-144	NOWHERE TO GO (UK)	HOLT	MGM	1958
EFE	EYE FOR AN EYE	MOORE	EMBASSY	1966
EG	EL GREGO	SALCE	20th CENTURY FOX	1966
EG	ELECTRA GLIDE IN BLUE	GUERCIO	UNITED ARTISTS	1973
EG	ELMER GANTRY	BROOKS	UNITED ARTISTS	1960
EG	ELMER THE GREAT	LEROY	WARNER BROS	1933
EG	EVERY GIRL SHOULD BE MARRIED	HARTMAN	RKO	1948
EG	EVERY TIME WE SAY GOODBYE	MIZRAHI	TRI STAR	1986
EG	EXPLOSIVE GENERATION	KULIK	UNITED ARTISTS	1961
EG	HAPPY GO LOVELY (UK)	HUMBERSTONE	RKO	1951
EG	MAN WITH MY FACE	MONTAGNE	UNITED ARTISTS	1951
EG	ON AGAIN OFF AGAIN	CLINE	RKO	1937
EG-201	SNUFFY SMITH YARDBIRD (PRIVATE SNUFFY SMITH)	CLINE	MONOGRAM	1942
EG-202	HILLBILLY BLITZKRIEG	MACK	MONOGRAM	1942
EGR	EDWARD G ROBINSON	portrait	FN/WARNER BROS	
EGX	EDMUND GOULDING	portrait	MGM	
EGXX	EDMUND GWENN	portrait	MGM	
EH	EILEEN HERLIE	portrait		
EH	ELAINE HAMMERSTEIN	portrait	SELZNICK	
EH	ELEANOR HANSEN	portrait	RKO	late 30s
EH	ELEANOR HOLM	portrait	WARNER BROS	
EH	ELECTRIC HORSEMAN	POLLACK	COLUMBIA	1979
EH1	EMERGENCY HOSPITAL	SHOLEM	UNITED ARTISTS	1956
EH	EMPTY HOLSTERS	EASON	WARNER BROS	1937
EH	ETHEL HAWORTH	portrait	RKO	
EH	EVER IN MY HEART	MAYO	WARNER BROS	1933
EH	EVERY HOME SHOULD HAVE ONE (UK)	CLARK	QUARTET	1970
EH	EXPENSIVE HUSBANDS	CONNOLLY	WARNER BROS	1937
EH	IS EVERYBODY HAPPY?	MAYO	WARNER BROS	1929
EH	MAD MEN OF EUROPE (UK: ENGLISHMAN'S HOME)	DE COURVILLE	COLUMBIA	1940
EI	AMAZON TRADER	MCGOWAN	WARNER BROS	1956
EIE	DISK-O-TEK HOLIDAY (UK: JUST FOR YOU)	HICKOX, SCARZA	ALLIED ARTISTS	1966
EIR	EVERYTHING IS RHYTHM (UK)	GOULDING	ASTOR	1936
EJ	ELSIE JANIS FILMS	portrait		
EJ	EMPEROR JONES	MURPHY	UNITED ARTISTS	1933
EJ	NEW LIFE	ALDA	PARAMOUNT	1988
EK	DEAD HEAT ON A MERRY-GO-ROUND	GIRARD	COLUMBIA	1966
EK	ELKAY PRODUCTIONS	L'ESTRANGE-KAHN (LK)	studio	
EK	ELYSE KNOX	portrait	UNIVERSAL	
EK	ESTHER AND THE KING	BAVA (SH)	20th CENTURY FOX	1960
EK	EVELYN KNAPP	portrait	WARNER BROS	
EK	SISTER KENNY	NICHOLS	RKO	1946
EK1	BUZZY RIDES THE RANGE	KAHN	ELKAY PROD	1940
EK2	BUZZY AND THE PHANTOM PINTO	KAHN	ELKAY PROD	1941

Movie Still Identification Book Ultimate Edition - Letters

CODE	TITLE/NAME	DIRECTOR/TYPE	STUDIO/DISTRIBUTOR	YEAR
EL	EASY LIFE (IT: IL SORPASSO)	RISI	EMBASSY	1962
EL	EASY TO LOVE	KEIGHLEY	WARNER BROS	1934
EL	EDMUND LOWE	portrait	PATHE	
EL	EDMUND LOWE	portrait	MGM	
EL	EL DORADO	HAWKS	PARAMOUNT	1966
EL	ELLA LOGAN	portrait	GOLDWYN/UA	
EL	ELMO LINCOLN	portrait		
EL	ELSA LANCHESTER	portrait	RKO	
EL	END OF THE LINE (UK)	SAUNDERS	EROS	1957
EL	ENTER LAUGHING	REINER	COLUMBIA	1967
EL	ERIC LINDEN	portrait	RKO	
EL	EX-LADY	FLOREY	WARNER BROS	1933
EL1-1	CAVALCADE OF STUFF NO. 1		GRAND NATIONAL	1938
EL1-2	CAVALCADE OF STUFF NO. 2		GRAND NATIONAL	1938
EL-606	REPEAT PERFORMANCE	WEAKER	EAGLE LION	1947
ELV-1	MY HUSBAND'S WIVES	ELVEY	FOX FILM	1924
ELVEY-4	SHE WOLVES	ELVEY	FOX FILM	1925
ELX	ERIC LINDEN	portrait	MGM	
EM	8 MILLION WAYS TO DIE	ASHBY	TRI STAR	1986
EM	EDWARD MONTAGNE	portrait	UNIV	
EM	ELAINE MOREY (aka JANET WARREN)	portrait	UNIVERSAL	1940s
EM	ELEPHANT MAN	LYNCH	PARAMOUNT	1980
EM	ELSA MARTINELLI	portrait	UNIVERSAL	
EM	ENEMY MINE	PETERSEN	20th CENTURY FOX	1985
EM	ESTHER MUIR	portrait	RKO	1930s-40s
EM	EVE MILLER	portrait	WARNER BROS	
EM	EVERETT MARSHALL	portrait	WARNER BROS	mid 30s
EM	EVERYBODY'S DOING IT	CABANNE	RKO	1938
EM	FROM THE EARTH TO THE MOON	HASKIN	WARNER BROS	1958
EM	STORY OF LOUIS PASTEUR	DIETERLE	WARNER BROS	1935
EM-1	MICKEY'S CLEANER (sh)		COLUMBIA	
EM-16	EMMANUELLE II (FR)	GIACOBETTI	PARAMOUNT	1975
EMERALD-2	NOT WANTED	CLIFTON	FILM CLASSICS	1949
EMG	EMIGRANTS (SWE)	TROELL	WARNER BROS	1972
EMO	EDNA MAY OLIVER	portrait	RKO	
EMS	ENTERTAINING MR. SLOANE (UK)	HICKOX	CONTINENTAL	1970
EN	DESERT MICE (UK)	RELPH	RANK	1959
EN	EDWARD/EDDIE NUGENT	portrait	MGM	
ENY	ESCAPE FROM NEW YORK	CARPENTER	AVCO EMBASSY	1981
EO	EVERYTHINGS ON ICE	KENTON	RKO	1939
EOB	EDMOND O'BRIEN	portrait	UNIVERSAL	
EOB	EUGENE O'BRIEN	portrait		
EOK	EAST OF KILIMANJARO (UK)	BELGARD, CAPOLINO	PARADE	1957
EOL	EIGHT ON THE LAM	MARSHALL	UNITED ARTISTS	1967
EOM	ERIN O'BRIEN MOORE	portrait	RKO	
EP	CLAMBAKE	NADEL	UNITED ARTISTS	1967
EP	EAT THE PEACH (UK)	ORMROD	SKOURAS	1986
EP	ELEANOR PARKER	portrait	MGM, WARNER BROS	
EP	ELEANOR POWELL	portrait	MGM	
EP	ELVIS PRESLEY	portrait		
EP	EMORY PARNELL	portrait	RKO	1930s-50s
EP	EXPERIMENT PERILOUS	TOURNEUR	RKO	1945
EP	EXTREME PREJUDICE	HILL	TRI STAR	1987
EP	FIGHTING PIMPERNEL (UK: ELUSIVE PIMPERNEL)	POWELL, PRESSBURGER	CARROLL	1950
EP	NAKED HEART (UK: MARIA CHAPDELAINE)	ALLEGRET	AAP	1950
EP 101	GUN GIRLS	DERTANO	ASTOR	1957
EPA	ESCAPE FROM PLANET OF THE APES	TAYLOR	20th CENTURY FOX	1971
EQ	EQUUS	LUMET	UNITED ARTISTS	1977
ER	EAST OF THE RIVER	GREEN	WARNER BROS	1940
ER	EASY RIDER	HOPPER	COLUMBIA	1969
ER	ELAINE RILEY (aka ELAINE REILLY)	portrait	RKO	1940s-50s
ER	ELIZABETH RUSSELL	portrait	UNIVERSAL	
ER	ELLA RAINES	portrait	UNIVERSAL	
ER	END OF THE ROAD (UK)	RILLA	DCA	1957
ER	END OF THE ROAD	AVAKIAN	ALLIED ARTISTS	1970
ER	ESCAPE FROM RED ROCK	BERNDS	20th CENTURY FOX	1957
ER	ESTHER RALSTON	portrait	MGM et al	
ER	EVA RENZI	portrait	UNIVERSAL	
ER	EVERYTHING'S ROSIE	BRUCKMAN	RKO	1931
ER	WOMAN HATER	FLOOD	WARNER BROS	1925

Movie Still Identification Book Ultimate Edition - Letters

CODE	TITLE/NAME	DIRECTOR/TYPE	STUDIO/DISTRIBUTOR	YEAR
ERB	LOVE, THE MAGICIAN (SP: EL AMOR BRUJO	SAURA	ORION	1986
ERD	ELEONORA ROSSI DRAGO	portrait	ITALIAN FILM EXPORT (IFE)	
ERIC-1	WOMAN FROM HELL	ERICKSON	FOX FILM	1929
ERIC-2	LONE STAR RANGER	ERICKSON	FOX FILM	1930
ERIC-3	ROUGH ROMANCE	ERICKSON	FOX FILM	1930
ERIC-4	UNDER SUSPICION	ERICKSON	FOX FILM	1930
ES	EAST OF SUDAN (UK)	JURAN	COLUMBIA	1964
ES	EDWARD SCISSORHANDS	BURTON	20th CENTURY FOX	1990
ES	EDWARD SMALL PRODUCTIONS	studio		
ES	EDWARD STEVENSON	portrait	RKO	
ES	ELAINE SHEPARD	portrait	RKO	
ES	ELAINE STEWART	portrait	UNIVERSAL	
ES	ENDLESS SUMMER	BROWN	CINEMA V	1966
ES	ENEMY FROM SPACE (UK: QUATERMASS 2)	GUEST	UNITED ARTISTS	1957
ES	ESCAPE FROM NEW YORK	CARPENTER	AVCO EMBASSY	1981
ES	EYES OF A STRANGER	WEIDERHORN	WARNER BROS	1981
ES	RAIDERS OF THE SEVEN SEAS	SALKOW	UNITED ARTISTS	1953
ES	WILD CHILD (FR: L'ENFANT SAUVAGE)	TRUFFAUT	UNITED ARTISTS	1970
ES-15	ABROAD WITH TWO YANKS	DWAN	UNITED ARTISTS	1944
ES-16	BREWSTER'S MILLIONS	DWAN	UNITED ARTISTS	1945
ES-17	GETTING GERTIE'S GARTER	DWAN	UNITED ARTISTS	1945
ES-22	WALK A CROOKED MILE	DOUGLAS	COLUMBIA	1948
ES-23	VALENTINO	ALLEN	COLUMBIA	1951
ES-358	INTERNATIONAL LADY	WHELAN	UNITED ARTISTS	1941
ES-9045	UP IN MABEL'S ROOM	DWAN	UNITED ARTISTS	1944
ES-35900	CORSICAN BROTHERS	RATOFF	UNITED ARTISTS	1941
ES-36000	TWIN BEDS	WHELAN	UNITED ARTISTS	1942
ES-36100	GENTLEMAN AFTER DARK	MARIN	UNITED ARTISTS	1942
ES-36200	FRIENDLY ENEMIES	DWAN	UNITED ARTISTS	1942
ES-36300	MISS ANNIE ROONEY	MARIN	UNITED ARTISTS	1942
ES-C	BLACK MAGIC/CAGLIOSTRO	RATOFF	UNITED ARTISTS	1949
ES-R-7	DAVY CROCKETT, INDIAN SCOUT	LANDERS	UNITED ARTISTS	1950
ESS-6	1984	ANDERSON	COLUMBIA	1956
ET	AS THE EARTH TURNS	GREEN	WARNER BROS	1934
ET	EARTHWORM TRACTORS	ENRIGHT	WARNER BROS	1936
ET	ELIZABETH TAYLOR	portrait	UNIVERSAL	early 40s
ET	ELIZABETH TAYLOR	portrait	UNITED ARTISTS	
ET	ERNEST TORRENCE	portrait	MGM et al	
ET	ESCAPE TO PARADISE	KENTON	RKO	1939
ET	ESTELLE TAYLOR	portrait	UNITED ARTISTS	
ET	MAN ON EIFFEL TOWER	MEREDITH	RKO	1950
ETB	ESCAPE TO BURMA	DWAN	RKO	1955
ETMD	EVIL THAT MEN DO	THOMPSON	TRI STAR	1984
ETR	THUNDERING HOOFS	SELANDER	RKO	1942
EU	GREATEST LOVE (IT: EUROPA '51)	ROSSELLINI	IFE	1952
EV	EASY VIRTUE (UK)	HITCHCOCK	SONO ART	1928
EVD	EAGLE VS DRAGON (documentary featurette)	THOMA		1944
EVES	EVE'S LOVER	DEL RUTH	WARNER BROS	1925
EVS	ERICH VON STROHEIM	portrait		
EW	COWBOY	WILLIAMS	LIPPERT	1954
EW	EARLE WILLIAMS	portrait	METRO	early 20s
EW	EDGE OF THE WORLD (UK)	POWELL	PAX	1937
EW	EDY WILLIAMS	portrait	FOX	1960s-70s
EW	ESCORT WEST	LYON	UNITED ARTISTS	1958
EW	ESTHER WILLIAMS	portrait	UNIVERSAL	late 50s
EW	EVERYBODY WINS	REISZ	ORION	1990
EW	EYES OF THE WORLD	KING	UNITED ARTISTS	1930
EW	LIFE IN EMERGENCY WARD 10 (UK)	DAY	EROS	1959
EW	MY BILL	FARROW	WARNER BROS	1938
EX	EXODUS	PREMINGER	UNITED ARTISTS	1960
EX1	JEANNIE (UK)	FRENCH	ENGLISH	1941
EX2	TALK ABOUT JACQUELINE (UK)	FRENCH, STEIN	MGM	1942
EXA	ELIZABETH ALLAN	portrait	MGM	
EXB	ETHEL BARRYMORE	portrait	MGM	
EXBX	ELEANOR BOARDMAN	portrait	MGM	
EXL-1	MEET ME AT DAWN (UK)	CRESWELL, FREELAND	20TH CENTURY FOX	1947
EXT	EXTERMINATOR	GLICKENHAUS	EMBASSY	1980
EXT2	EXTERMINATOR 2	BUNTZMAN	CANNON	1984
EYC	THOSE ENDEARING YOUNG CHARMS	ALLEN	RKO	1945
EYE	EYE OF THE NEEDLE	MARQUAND	UNITED ARTISTS	1981

Movie Still Identification Book Ultimate Edition - Letters

CODE	TITLE/NAME	DIRECTOR/TYPE	STUDIO/DISTRIBUTOR	YEAR
EYE	REFLECTIONS IN A GOLDEN EYE	HUSTON	WARNER BROS	1967
EYG	BLACK EYE	ARNOLD	WARNER BROS	1974
EZ	EFREM ZIMBALIST, JR	portrait	WARNER BROS	1950s-60s
EZ	LIFE OF EMILE ZOLA	DIETERLE	WARNER BROS	1937
F	8 1/2 (IT)	FELLINI	EMBASSY	1963
F	CURSE OF FRANKENSTEIN (UK)	FISHER	WARNER BROS	1957
F	DECEPTION	SEILER	COLUMBIA	1932
F	DECEPTION	RAPPER	WARNER BROS	1946
F	DESPERATE	MANN	RKO	1947
F	F.I.S.T.	JEWISON	UNITED ARTISTS	1978
F	FANTASIA	ALGAR	BUENA VISTA	R56
F	FANTOMAS [US: LOPERT; UK: UA]	HUNEBELLE	UNITED ARTISTS	1964
F	FAR FROM HOME	BORSOS	20th CENTURY FOX	1995
F	FAR FROM MADDING CROWD	SCHLESINGER	MGM	1968
F	FATHER TAKES A WIFE	HIVELY	RKO	1941
F	FATHOM (UK)	MARTINSON	20TH CENTURY FOX	1967
F	FEARMAKERS	TOURNEUR	UNITED ARTISTS	1958
F	FEMALE	CURTIZ	WARNER BROS	1933
F	FIEND WITHOUT A FACE (UK)	CRABTREE	MGM	1958
F	FIRE DOWN BELOW (UK)	PARRISH	COLUMBIA	1957
F	FIREBIRD	DIETERLE	WARNER BROS	1934
F	FIRST A GIRL (UK)	SAVILLE	GAUMONT BRITISH AMERICA	1935
F	FITZWILLY	MANN	UNITED ARTISTS	1967
F	FIVE ON THE BLACK HAND SIDE	WILLIAMS	UNITED ARTISTS	1973
F	FLY II	WALAS	20th CENTURY FOX	1989
F	FORWARD PASS	CLINE	WARNER BROS	1929
F	FRAMED	ARCHAINBAUD	RKO	1930
F	FRAMED	KARLSON	PARAMOUNT	1975
F	FRECKLES	HAMILTON, KILLY	RKO	1935
F	FRIEDA (UK)	DEARDEN	UNIVERSAL	1947
F	FRIENDS (UK)	GILBERT	PARAMOUNT	1971
F	FRIGHT	COLLINSON	ALLIED ARTISTS	1971
F	FUGITIVE	DAVIS	WARNER BROS	1993
F	FUN AT ST. FANNY'S (UK)	ELVEY	BRITISH LION	1956
F	FURY	DE PALMA	20th CENTURY FOX	1978
F	GENTLEMEN MARRY BRUNETTES	SALE	UNITED ARTISTS	1955
F	I DIDN'T DO IT (UK)	VARNEL	COLUMBIA	1945
F	ROAD GANG	KING	WARNER BROS	1936
F	SAM FULLER PRODUCTIONS	studio		
F	SON OF FLUBBER	STEVENSON	BUENA VISTA	R70
F	STUDY IN TERROR (UK)	HILL	COLUMBIA	1965
F-#-RC	MR. ROBINSON CRUSOE	SUTHERLAND	UNITED ARTISTS	1932
F007	TRUDY MARSHALL	portrait	FOX	
F-1	EASTWARD HO!	FLYNN	FOX FILM	1919
F-1	LETTER	DE LIMUR	PARAMOUNT	1929
F-1	MONTY COLLINS (sh)		COLUMBIA	
F-1	PARDON US	PARROTT	MGM	1931
F-1	ROUGHING IT (sh)	JACKMAN	PATHE EXCHANGE	1923
F-1	SIX GUN RHYTHM	NEWFIELD	GRAND	1939
F-2	HOLE IN THE WALL	FLOREY	PARAMOUNT	1929
F-2	LET'S BUILD (sh)	PEMBROKE	PATHE EXCHANGE	1923
F-2	LINCOLN HIGHWAYMEN	FLYNN	FOX FILM	1919
F-2	PACK UP YOUR TROUBLES (sh)	MARSHALL, MCCAREY	MGM	1932
F-3	DEVIL'S BROTHER	ROACH, ROGERS	MGM	1933
F-3	GENTLEMEN OF THE PRESS	WEBB	PARAMOUNT	1929
F-3	HEAVY SEAS (sh)	GUIOL, HOWE	PATHE EXCHANGE	1923
F3	JOHN BOLES	portrait	FOX	1930s
F3	ROCK AROUND THE WORLD (UK: TOMMY STEELE STORY)	BRYANT	AIP	1957
F-3	SHOD WITH FIRE	FLYNN	FOX FILM	1920
F-4	GREAT OUTDOORS (sh)	GUIOL	PATHE EXCHANGE	1923
F4	JUNE LANG (aka JUNE VLASEK)	portrait	FOX	1935
F4	LEAVE IT TO ME	FLYNN	FOX FILM	1920
F-4	NOTHING BUT THE TRUTH	SCHERTZINGER	PARAMOUNT	1929
F-4	SONS OF THE DESERT	SEITER	MGM	1933
F-5	5 GUNS WEST (ARC)	CORMAN	AIP	1955
F-5	BABES IN TOYLAND (MARCH OF THE WOODEN SOLDIERS)	MEINS, ROGERS	MGM	1934
F5	CLAIRE TREVOR	portrait	FOX	1937
F-5	COCOANUTS	FLOREY, SANTLEY	PARAMOUNT	1929
F-5	CURSE OF A BROKEN HEART (sh)	NEILSON	COLUMBIA	1933
F-5	DARKEST HOUR (sh)	HOWE	PATHE EXCHANGE	1923

Movie Still Identification Book Ultimate Edition - Letters

CODE	TITLE/NAME	DIRECTOR/TYPE	STUDIO/DISTRIBUTOR	YEAR
F-5	MAN WHO DARED	FLYNN	FOX FILM	1920
F-6	JEALOUSY	DE LIMUR	PARAMOUNT	1929
F-6	POLITICAL PULL (sh)	CLEMENTS	PATHE EXCHANGE	1924
F6	SHIRLEY TEMPLE	portrait	FOX	1930's
F-6	VAGABOND LADY	TAYLOR	MGM	1935
F-7	BONNIE SCOTLAND	HORNE	MGM	1935
F-7	HELP ONE ANOTHER (sh)	GUIOL	PATHE EXCHANGE	1924
F-7	LADY LIES	HENLEY	PARAMOUNT	1929
F-8	BOHEMIAN GIRL	HORNE, ROGERS	MGM	1936
F-8	GLORIFYING THE AMERICAN GIRL	WEBB	PARAMOUNT	1929
F-8	HUNTERS BOLD (sh)		PATHE EXCHANGE	1924
F8	JANET GAYNOR	portrait	FOX	1930s
F8	LURE OF JADE	CAMPBELL	ROBERTSON COLE	1921
F-8	SHAME	FLYNN	FOX FILM	1921
F-8	WHAT PRICE INNOCENCE	MACK	COLUMBIA	1933
F-9	APPLAUSE	MAMOULIAN	PARAMOUNT	1929
F9	ASTRID ALLWYN	portrait	FOX	1935
F-9	HIT THE HIGH SPOTS (sh)	GUIOL	PATHE EXCHANGE	1924
F-9	MR. CINDERELLA		MGM	1936
F9	MYRT AND MARGE	BOASBERG	UNIVERSAL	1933
F10	BACHELOR IN PARIS (UK: SONG OF PARIS)	GUILLERMIN	LIPPERT	1952
F-10	BATTLE OF PARIS	FLOREY	PARAMOUNT	1929
F-10	BOTTLE BABIES (sh)	HOWE, PEMBROKE	PATHE EXCHANGE	1924
F-10	KELLY THE SECOND	MEINS	MGM	1936
F10	KETTI GALLIAN	portrait	FOX	1930s
F10	MONTE CRISTO	FLYNN	FOX FILM	1922
F10	OLD MOTHER RILEY MEETS VAMPIRE/VAMPIRE ... LONDON	GILLING	BLUE CHIP	1952
F11	LORETTA YOUNG	portrait	FOX	1936
F-11	OUR RELATIONS	LACHMAN	MGM	1936
F-11	RETURN OF SHERLOCK HOLMES	DEAN	PARAMOUNT	1929
F-11	SECOND HONEYMOON	LANG	20th CENTURY FOX	1937
F-11	SUFFERING SHAKESPEARE (sh)	CEDER	PATHE EXCHANGE	1924
F-12	GENERAL SPANKY	DOUGLAS, NEWMEYER	MGM	1936
F-12	LAUGHING LADY (HUN)	HEGEDUS	PARAMOUNT	1930
F-12	RADIO MAD (sh)	HOWE	PATHE EXCHANGE	1924
F-13	BIG POND	HENLEY	PARAMOUNT	1930
F-13	HARD-BOILED TENDERFOOT (sh)	HOWE	PATHE EXCHANGE	1924
F13	PEGGY FEARS	portrait	FOX	1930s
F-13	UNRELEASED ROACH (sh)		MGM	1936
F13-3D	FRIDAY THE 13TH - 3D	MINER	PARAMOUNT	1982
F-14	ROADHOUSE NIGHTS	HENLEY	PARAMOUNT	1930
F-14	SOUTH O' THE NORTH POLE	HOWE	PATHE EXCHANGE	1924
F-14	WAY OUT WEST (sh)	HORNE	MGM	1937
F15	ALICE FAYE	portrait	FOX	1936
F-15	DANGEROUS NAN MCGREW	ST. CLAIR	PARAMOUNT	1930
F-15	LOST DOG (sh)	HOWE	PATHE EXCHANGE	1924
F-15	PICK A STAR	SEDGWICK	MGM	1937
F-16	HOT STUFF (sh)	HOWE	PATHE EXCHANGE	1924
F-16	NOBODY'S BABY	MEINS	MGM	1937
F-16	YOUNG MAN OF MANHATTAN	BELL	PARAMOUNT	1930
F-17	QUEEN HIGH	NEWMEYER	PARAMOUNT	1930
F17	SPENCER TRACY	portrait	FOX	1930s,60s
F-17	TOPPER (sh)	MCLEOD	MGM	1937
F-18	DEAF, DUMB AND DAFFY (sh)	HOWE	PATHE EXCHANGE	1924
F18	HELEN TWELVETREES	portrait	FOX	1930s
F-18	UPSPECIFIEC TITLE	ROACH	MGM	1937
F-19	ANIMAL CRACKERS	HEERMAN	PARAMOUNT	1930
F-19	LAUGH THAT OFF (sh)	HOWE	PATHE EXCHANGE	1925
F-19	MERRILY WE LIVE	MCLEOD	MGM	1938
F20	ANITA LOUISE	portrait	FOX	1930s
F-20	FOX HUNT (sh)	HOWE	PATHE EXCHANGE	1925
F-20	HEADS UP	SCHERTZINGER	PARAMOUNT	1930
F-20	SWISS MISS	BLYSTONE	MGM	1938
F21	CONCHITA MONTENEGRO	portrait	FOX	1930s
F-21	EXCUSE MY GLOVE (sh)	HOWE	PATHE EXCHANGE	1925
F-21	LAUGHTER	D'ARRAST	PARAMOUNT	1930
F21	NANCY CARROLL	portrait	FOX	1930s
F-21	THERE GOES MY HEART	MCLEOD	UNITED ARTISTS	1938
F22	JAMES DUNN	portrait	FOX	1930s
F-22	BLACK HAND BLUES (BLACK HANDS) (sh)	HOWE	PATHE EXCHANGE	1925

Movie Still Identification Book Ultimate Edition - Letters

CODE	TITLE/NAME	DIRECTOR/TYPE	STUDIO/DISTRIBUTOR	YEAR
F-22	BLOCK-HEADS	BLYSTONE	MGM	1938
F-22	FAST AND LOOSE	MARIN	PARAMOUNT	1930
F22	JAMES DUNN	portrait	FOX	1930s
F-22	MARRIED ALIVE	FLYNN	FOX FILM	1927
F-23	FOLLOW THE LEADER	TAUROG	PARAMOUNT	1930
F-23	ROYAL FOUR-FLUSH (sh)	HOWE	PATHE EXCHANGE	1925
F-23	ZENOBIA	DOUGLAS	UNITED ARTISTS	1939
F-24	ROYAL FAMILY OF BROADWAY	CUKOR, GARDNER	PARAMOUNT	1930
F-24	TOPPER TAKES A TRIP	MCLEOD	UNITED ARTISTS	1939
F-24	WILD PAPA (sh)	BARROWS, HOWE	PATHE EXCHANGE	1925
F-25	CAPTAIN FURY	ROACH	UNITED ARTISTS	1939
F-25	DON KEY (sh)	GUIOL, HORNE	PATHE EXCHANGE	1926
F-25	STOLEN HEAVEN	ABBOTT	PARAMOUNT	1931
F25	WARNER BAXTER	portrait	FOX	1936
F-26	CHUMP AT OXFORD	GOULDING	UNITED ARTISTS	1940
F-26	HONOR AMONG LOVERS	ARZNER	PARAMOUNT	1931
F26	ROCHELLE HUDSON	portrait	FOX	1936
F-27	HOUSEKEEPER'S DAUGHTER	ROACH	UNITED ARTISTS	1939
F-27	TARNISHED LADY	CUKOR	PARAMOUNT	1931
F-28	OF MICE AND MEN	MILESTONE	UNITED ARTISTS	1940
F-28	SMILING LIEUTENANT	LUBITSCH	PARAMOUNT	1931
F-29	NIGHT ANGEL	GOULDING	PARAMOUNT	1931
F-29	SAPS AT SEA	DOUGLAS	UNITED ARTISTS	1940
F30	MONA BARRIE	portrait	FOX	1930s
F-30	ONE MILLION B.C.	ROACH, ROACH,JR.	UNITED ARTISTS	1940
F-30	SECRETS OF A SECRETARY	ABBOTT	PARAMOUNT	1931
F-31	GIRL HABIT	CLINE	PARAMOUNT	1931
F-31	TURNABOUT	ROACH	UNITED ARTISTS	1940
F-32	CAPTAIN CAUTION	WALLACE	UNITED ARTISTS	1940
F-32	PERSONAL MAID	BELL, MENDES	PARAMOUNT	1931
F-33	MY SIN	ABBOTT	PARAMOUNT	1931
F-33	ROAD SHOW	ROACH	UNITED ARTISTS	1941
F-34	BROADWAY LIMITED	DOUGLAS	UNITED ARTISTS	1941
F-34	HIS WOMAN	SLOMAN	PARAMOUNT	1931
F-35	CHEAT	ABBOTT	PARAMOUNT	1931
F-35	TOPPER RETURNS	DEL RUTH	UNITED ARTISTS	1941
F-36	NIAGARA FALLS	DOUGLAS	UNITED ARTISTS	1941
F-36	WAYWARD	SLOMAN	PARAMOUNT	1932
F-37	TANKS A MILLION	GUIOL	UNITED ARTISTS	1941
F-37	WISER SEX	VIERTEL	PARAMOUNT	1932
F-38	ALL AMERICAN CO-ED	PRINZ	UNITED ARTISTS	1941
F-38	MISLEADING LADY	WALKER	PARAMOUNT	1932
F-39	MISS POLLY	GUIOL	UNITED ARTISTS	1941
F-40	FIESTA	PRINZ	UNITED ARTISTS	1941
F40	SIG RUMANN	portrait	FOX	
F-41	HAY FOOT	GUIOL	UNITED ARTISTS	1941
F-42	DUDES ARE PRETTY PEOPLE	ROACH, JR.	UNITED ARTISTS	1942
F42	MADGE BELLAMY	portrait	FOX	1930s
F-43	BROOKLYN ORCHID	NEUMANN	UNITED ARTISTS	1942
F-44	ABOUT FACE	NEUMANN	UNITED ARTISTS	1942
F44	JANE DARWELL	portrait	FOX	1930s
F-45	FLYING WITH MUSIC	ARCHAINBAUD	UNITED ARTISTS	1942
F-46	DEVIL WITH HITLER	DOUGLAS	UNITED ARTISTS	1942
F46	RUTH PETERSON	portrait	FOX	
F-47	MCGUERINS FROM BROOKLYN	NEUMANN	UNITED ARTISTS	1942
F-48	CALABOOSE	ROACH, JR.	UNITED ARTISTS	1943
F-49	FALL IN	NEWMANN	UNITED ARTISTS	1943
F50	ALAN DINEHART	portrait	FOX	1930s
F-50	NAZTY NUISANCE	TRYON	UNITED ARTISTS	1943
F-51	TAXI, MISTER?	NEUMANN	UNITED ARTISTS	1943
F51	THOMAS BECK	portrait	FOX	1930s
F-52	PRAIRIE CHICKENS	ROACH, JR.	UNITED ARTISTS	1943
F52	WARNER OLAND	portrait	FOX	1935
F-53	STERLING HOLLOWAY	portrait	FOX	1934
F-53	YANKS AHOY	NEUMANN	UNITED ARTISTS	1943
F-54	CURLEY: HAL ROACH COMEDY CANRINVAL	CARR, FOSTER	UNITED ARTISTS	1947
F-55	HERE COMES TROUBLE: LAFFTIME	GUIOL	UNITED ARTISTS	1948
F-56	FABULOUS JOE: HAL ROACH COMEDY CANRINVAL	CARR, FOSTER	UNITED ARTISTS	1947
F56	JOHN QUALEN	portrait	FOX	1930s
F-57	WHO KILLED DOC ROBBIN?: LAFFTIME	CARR	UNITED ARTISTS	1948

Movie Still Identification Book Ultimate Edition - Letters

CODE	TITLE/NAME	DIRECTOR/TYPE	STUDIO/DISTRIBUTOR	YEAR
F58	BLANCA VISCHER	portrait	FOX	1930s
F59	JANE WITHERS	portrait	FOX	1936
F62	DOROTHY DEARING	portrait	FOX	1930s
F63	SHIRLEY DEANE	portrait	FOX	1930s
F67	JACK DURANT	portrait	FOX	1930s
F76	JACK HALEY	portrait	FOX	1930s
F79	PAUL MCVEY	portrait	FOX	1930s
F81	FRANCES GRANT	portrait	FOX	1930s
F81/2	8 1/2	FELLINI	EMBASSY	1963
F82	JULIE CABANNE	portrait	FOX	1930s
F84	RITA CANSINO (aka RITA HAYWORTH)	portrait	FOX	1930s
F85	LYNN BARI	portrait	FOX	1930s
F86	PHILIPPA HILBER	portrait	FOX	1936
F95	ESTHER BRODELET	portrait	FOX	1930s-40s
F97	WILLIAM (BILL/BILLY) BENEDICT	portrait	FOX	1930s
F100	ALLAN DWAN	portrait	FOX	1920s-50s
F-101	NAKED KISS (MISTAKE-SEE F-102)	FULLER	ALLIED ARTISTS	1964
F-101	SHOCK CORRIDOR	FULLER	ALLIED ARTISTS	1963
F102	NAKED KISS	FULLER	ALLIED ARTISTS	1964
F113	MADELYN EARL(E)	portrait	FOX	1930s
F117	HENRY FONDA	portrait	FOX	1930s
F122	ROSINA LAWRENCE	portrait	FOX	
F-129	BAD BOY	BLYSTONE	FOX FILM	1935
F129	DOROTHY WILSON	portrait	FOX	1930s
F130	TUTTA ROLF	portrait	FOX	1935
F131	ARLINE JUDGE	portrait	FOX	1936
F137	GIRL LIKE THAT	HENDERSON	PARAMOUNT	1917
F137	ROBERT BARRAT	portrait	FOX	1930s
F138	SLAVE MARKET	FORD	PARAMOUNT	1917
F142	PAUL CAVANAGH (PAUL CAVANAUGH)	portrait	FOX	1930s
F143	BARBARA BLAINE	portrait	FOX	1930s
F143	SAPHO	FORD	PARAMOUNT	1917
F145	SLEEPING FIRES	FORD	PARAMOUNT	1917
F146	VALENTINE GIRL	DAWLEY	PARAMOUNT	1917
F147	HEART'S DESIRE	GRANDON	PARAMOUNT	1917
F147	MARIA GAMBARELLI	portrait	FOX	1935
F159	GENEVIEVE TOBIN	portrait	FOX	1930s
F160	PAUL KELLY	portrait	FOX	1930s
F161	ANNABELLA	portrait	FOX	1930s
F162	IRENE HERVEY	portrait	FOX	mid-30s
F165	BEBE DANIELS	portrait	FOX	1930s
F169	PRICE MARK	NEILL	PARAMOUNT	1917
F172	TOSCA	JOSE	PARAMOUNT	1918
F174	PRUNELLA	TOURNEUR	PARAMOUNT	1918
F177	VIRGINIA BRUCE	portrait	FOX	1935
F179	CESAR ROMERO	portrait	FOX	1940's
F181	UNCLE TOM'S CABIN	DAWLEY	PARAMOUNT	1918
F182	FRED ALLEN	portrait	FOX	1930s
F-182	FRIENDS	GILBERT	PARAMOUNT	1971
F183	ANN DVORAK	portrait	FOX	1930s
F184	DICK POWELL	portrait	FOX	1938
F185	PATSY KELLY	portrait	FOX	1930s
F186	LAWRENCE TIBBETT	portrait	FOX	1930s-40s
F190	MARGARET IRVING	portrait	FOX	
F190	THANKS A MILLION	DEL RUTH	20th CENTURY FOX	1935
F191	JOAN BENNETT	portrait	FOX	
F195	EDWARD NORRIS	portrait	FOX	1930s
F200	GWEN WAKELING	portrait	FOX	1930s-40s
F-201	OH, YOU WOMEN	EMERSON	PARAMOUNT	1919
F202	HELEN WOOD	portrait	FOX	1930s
F-202	ROSE OF GRANADA (IT)	GHIONE	PARAMOUNT	1919
F203	GLORIA STUART	portrait	FOX	1930s
F-203	TEST OF HONOR	ROBERTSON	PARAMOUNT	1919
F-204	COME OUT OF THE KITCHEN	ROBERTSON	PARAMOUNT	1919
F-205	FIRING LINE	MAIGNE	PARAMOUNT	1919
F-206	CAREER OF KATHERINE BUSH	NEILL	PARAMOUNT	1919
F-207	MISLEADING WIDOW	ROBERTSON	PARAMOUNT	1919
F207	SIMONE SIMON	portrait	FOX	1930S
F208	IRVIN S. COBB	portrait	FOX	1935
F-208	TEETH OF THE TIGER	WITHEY	PARAMOUNT	1919

Movie Still Identification Book Ultimate Edition - Letters

CODE	TITLE/NAME	DIRECTOR/TYPE	STUDIO/DISTRIBUTOR	YEAR
F209	DIXIE DUNBAR	portrait	FOX	1930s
F-209	SADIE LOVE	ROBERTSON	PARAMOUNT	1919
F-210	INVISIBLE BOND	MAIGNE	PARAMOUNT	1919
F-211	WANTED A HUSBAND	WINDOM	PARAMOUNT	1919
F-212	COPPERHEAD	MAIGNE	PARAMOUNT	1920
F-213	ON WITH THE DANCE	FITZMAURICE	PARAMOUNT	1920
F-214	EASY TO GET	EDWARDS	PARAMOUNT	1920
F214	EDWARD EVERETT HORTON	portrait	FOX	1930s
F-215	DR. JEKYL AND MR. HYDE	ROBERTSON	PARAMOUNT	1920
F215	MICHAEL WHALEN	portrait	FOX	1936
F-216	COST	KNOLES	PARAMOUNT	1920
F216	DELMA BYRON	portrait	FOX	mid 30s
F-217	AMATEUR WIFE	DILLON	PARAMOUNT	1920
F-219	RIGHT TO LOVE	FITZMAURICE	PARAMOUNT	1920
F-220	HALF AN HOUR	KNOLES	PARAMOUNT	1920
F-221	AWAY GOES PRUDENCE	ROBERTSON	PARAMOUNT	1920
F221	MINNA GOMBELL	portrait	FOX	1930s
F-222	CIVILIAN CLOTHES	FORDE	PARAMOUNT	1920
F-223	GUILTY OF LOVE	KNOLES	PARAMOUNT	1920
F224	ARTHUR TREACHER	portrait	FOX	1930s
F-224	IDOLS OF CLAY	FITZMAURICE	PARAMOUNT	1920
F-226	FRONTIER OF THE STARS	MAIGNE	PARAMOUNT	1921
F-227	FRISKY MRS. JOHNSON	DILLON	PARAMOUNT	1921
F-228	BEHIND MASKS	REICHER	PARAMOUNT	1921
F-229	SENTIMENTAL TOMMY	ROBERTSON	PARAMOUNT	1921
F230	DARRYL F ZANUCK		FOX	1930s,70s
F-230	PAYING THE PIPER	FITZMAURICE	PARAMOUNT	1921
F-231	KENTUCKIANS	MAIGNE	PARAMOUNT	1921
F-232	EDUCATION OF ELIZABETH	DILLON	PARAMOUNT	1921
F232	VIRGINIA FIELD	portrait	FOX	1937
F-233	GILDED LILY	LEONARD	PARAMOUNT	1921
F-234	CITY OF SILENT MEN	FORMAN	PARAMOUNT	1921
F-235	PRICE OF POSSESSION	FORD	PARAMOUNT	1921
F-236	IDOL OF THE NORTH	NEILL	PARAMOUNT	1921
F-237	EXPERIENCE	FITZMAURICE	PARAMOUNT	1921
F237	VICTOR MCLAGLEN	portrait	FOX	1930s
F-238	FOOTLIGHTS	ROBERTSON	PARAMOUNT	1921
F238	ROBERT KENT	portrait	FOX	1930s
F-239	CONQUEST OF CANAAN	NEILL	PARAMOUNT	1921
F239	J. EDWARD BROMBERG	portrait	FOX	1930s
F-240	CAPPY RICKS	FORMAN	PARAMOUNT	1921
F-241	FOREVER	FITZMAURICE	PARAMOUNT	1922
F241	SARA HADEN	portrait	FOX	
F-242	MISSING MILLIONS	HENABERY	PARAMOUNT	1922
F-243	ANNA ASCENDS	FLEMING	PARAMOUNT	1922
F-244	OUTCAST	WITHEY	PARAMOUNT	1922
F-245	BACK HOME AND BROKE	GREEN	PARAMOUNT	1922
F-246	JAVA HEAD	MELFORD	PARAMOUNT	1923
F246	JULIE CARTER	portrait	20th CENTURY FOX	
F-247	DARK SECRETS	FLEMING	PARAMOUNT	1923
F247	SLIM SUMMERVILLE	portrait	FOX	1930's
F-248	BRIAN DONLEVY	portrait	FOX	1930s
F-248	LEOPARDESS	KOLKER	PARAMOUNT	1923
F249	DON AMECHE	portrait	FOX	1930's
F-249	GLIMPSES OF THE MOON	DWAN	PARAMOUNT	1923
F-250	NE'ER DO WELL	GREEN	PARAMOUNT	1923
F250	SONYA MITCHELL	portrait	FOX	1936
F251	JEAN HERSHOLT	portrait	FOX	1936
F-251	YOU CAN'T FOOL YOUR WIFE	MELFORD	PARAMOUNT	1923
F-252	SNOW BRIDE	KOLKER	PARAMOUNT	1923
F-253	FOG BOUND	WILLAT	PARAMOUNT	1923
F253	LYNNE BERKELEY	portrait	FOX	
F-254	EXCITERS	CAMPBELL	PARAMOUNT	1923
F254	LUCILLE MILLER	portrait	FOX	
F-255	LAWFUL LARCENY	DWAN	PARAMOUNT	1923
F-256	HEART RAIDER	RUGGLES	PARAMOUNT	1923
F-257	MORAL SINNER	INCE	PARAMOUNT	1924
F-258	HOMEWARD BOUND	INCE	PARAMOUNT	1923
F-259	ZAZA	DWAN	PARAMOUNT	1923
F-260	HIS CHILDREN'S CHILDREN	WOOD	PARAMOUNT	1923

Movie Still Identification Book Ultimate Edition - Letters

CODE	TITLE/NAME	DIRECTOR/TYPE	STUDIO/DISTRIBUTOR	YEAR
F260	INEZ GORMAN	portrait	FOX	1936
F261	JOHN CARRADINE	portrait	FOX	1937
F-261	WEST OF THE WATER TOWER	STURGEON	PARAMOUNT	1924
F-262	BIG BROTHER	DWAN	PARAMOUNT	1923
F262	DOROTHY L JONES	portrait	FOX	1937
F-263	HUMMING BIRD	OLCOTT	PARAMOUNT	1924
F264	ADOLPHE MENJOU	portrait	FOX	1930s-50s
F-264	PIED PIPER MALONE	GREEN	PARAMOUNT	1924
F-265	SOCIETY SCANDAL	DWAN	PARAMOUNT	1924
F265	TONY MARTIN	portrait	FOX	
F-266	ICEBOUND	W. DE MILLE	PARAMOUNT	1924
F266	TYRONE POWER	portrait	FOX	1936
F-267	CONFIDENCE MAN	HEERMAN	PARAMOUNT	1924
F267	SONJA HENIE	portrait	FOX	1930s
F-268	MONSIERU BEAUCAIRE	OLCOTT	PARAMOUNT	1924
F268	RUTH CHATTERTON	portrait	FOX	1930s
F-269	MANHANDLED	DWAN	PARAMOUNT	1924
F-270	SIDE SHOW OF LIFE	BRENON	PARAMOUNT	1924
F271	KEN/KENNETH HOWELL	portrait	FOX	1930s-40s
F-271	UNGUARDED WOMEN	CROSLAND	PARAMOUNT	1924
F-272	HER LOVE STORY	DWAN	PARAMOUNT	1924
F272	JUNE CARLSON	portrait	FOX	1930s
F-273	STORY WITHOUT A NAME	WILLAT	PARAMOUNT	1924
F-274	GEORGE ERNST ALONE / ENTIRE JONES FAMILY	portrait	FOX	1930s
F-274	SAINTED DEVIL	HENABERY	PARAMOUNT	1924
F-275	SINNERS IN HEAVEN	CROSLAND	PARAMOUNT	1924
F275	SPRING BYINGTON	portrait	FOX	1930s
F-276	DOUGLAS FOWLEY	portrait	FOX	1930s
F-276	WAGES OF VIRTUE	DWAN	PARAMOUNT	1924
F-277	DANGEROUS MONEY	TUTTLE	PARAMOUNT	1924
F278	JAYNE REGAN	portrait	FOX	
F-278	MANHATTAN	BURNSIDE	PARAMOUNT	1924
F-279	TONGUES OF FLAME	HENABERY	PARAMOUNT	1924
F-280	SWAN	BUCHOWETZKI	PARAMOUNT	1925
F-281	SALOME OF THE TENEMENTS	OLCOTT	PARAMOUNT	1925
F282	CONSTANCE BENNETT	portrait	FOX	1930s
F-282	MAN MUST LIVE	SLOANE	PARAMOUNT	1925
F-283	ARGENTINE LOVE	DWAN	PARAMOUNT	1924
F284	HELEN ERICKSON	portrait	FOX	1930s
F-284	MADAME SANS GENE	PERRET	PARAMOUNT	1925
F-285	MISS BLUEBEARD	TUTTLE	PARAMOUNT	1925
F-286	COMING THROUGH	SUTHERLAND	PARAMOUNT	1925
F287	LEAH RAY	portrait	FOX	1937
F-287	TOO MANY KISSES	SLOANE	PARAMOUNT	1925
F288	KATHERINE DEMILLE	portrait	FOX	1930s
F-288	KISS IN THE DARK	TUTTLE	PARAMOUNT	1925
F-289	CROWDED HOUR	HOPPER	PARAMOUNT	1925
F-290	MEN AND WOMEN	W. DE MILLE	PARAMOUNT	1925
F291	JUNE GALE	portrait	FOX	1937
F-291	LITTLE FRENCH GIRL	BRENON	PARAMOUNT	1925
F292	HELEN WESTLEY	portrait	FOX	1930s-40s
F-292	MAN WHO FOUND HIMSELF	GREEN	PARAMOUNT	1925
F-293	SHOCK PUNCH	SLOANE	PARAMOUNT	1925
F-294	OLD HOME WEEK	HEERMAN	PARAMOUNT	1925
F-295	MANICURE GIRL	TUTTLE	PARAMOUNT	1925
F-296	NIGHT LIFE IN NEW YORK	DWAN	PARAMOUNT	1925
F-297	SALLY OF THE SAWDUST	GRIFFITH	PARAMOUNT	1925
F-298	STREET OF FORGOTTEN MEN	BRENON	PARAMOUNT	1925
F-299	LUCKY DEVIL	TUTTLE	PARAMOUNT	1925
F-300	WILD, WILD SUSAN	SUTHERLAND	PARAMOUNT	1925
F-301	THAT ROYLE GIRL	GRIFFITH	PARAMOUNT	1925
F-302	LOVERS IN QUARANTINE	TUTTLE	PARAMOUNT	1925
F-303	KISS FOR CINDERELLA	BRENON	PARAMOUNT	1925
F-304	IRISH LUCK	HEERMAN	PARAMOUNT	1925
F-305	STAGE STRUCK	DWAN	PARAMOUNT	1925
F-306	KING ON MAIN STREET	BELL	PARAMOUNT	1925
F307	JOAN DAVIS	portrait	FOX	1930s
F-307	WOMANHANDLED	LACAVA	PARAMOUNT	1926
F-308	AMERICAN VENUS	TUTTLE	PARAMOUNT	1926
F309	FRANCES DRAKE	portrait	FOX	

Movie Still Identification Book Ultimate Edition - Letters

CODE	TITLE/NAME	DIRECTOR/TYPE	STUDIO/DISTRIBUTOR	YEAR
F-309	SONG AND DANCE MAN	DWAN	PARAMOUNT	1926
F-310	ALOMA OF THE SOUTH SEAS	TOURNEUR	PARAMOUNT	1926
F310	IRVING BERLIN	portrait	FOX	late 30s
F-311	FASCINATING YOUTH	WOOD	PARAMOUNT	1926
F311	PETER LORRE	portrait	FOX	1930s-40s
F-312	DANCING MOTHERS	BRENON	PARAMOUNT	1926
F-313	NEW KLONDIKE	MILESTONE	PARAMOUNT	1926
F-314	NOT MADE		PARAMOUNT	
F315	PAULINE MOORE	portrait	FOX	late 30s
F-315	UNTAMED LADY	TUTTLE	PARAMOUNT	1926
F316	EARL CARROLL	portrait	FOX	1930s
F-316	SOCIAL CELEBRITY	ST. CLAIR	PARAMOUNT	1926
F-317	LET'S GET MARRIED	LA CAVA	PARAMOUNT	1926
F317	WALTER WINCHELL	portrait	FOX	1930s
F318	BEN BERNIE	portrait	FOX	1930s
F-318	TIN GODS	DWAN	PARAMOUNT	1926
F-319	FINE MANNERS	ROSSON	PARAMOUNT	1926
F319	MARJORIE WEAVER	portrait	FOX	1930s
F-320	ELSIE VALENTINE	portrait	FOX	1937
F-320	PALM BEACH GIRL	KENTON	PARAMOUNT	1926
F321	ELSIE ARGALL	portrait	FOX	1937
F-321	SAY IT AGAIN	LA CAVA	PARAMOUNT	1926
F-322	IT'S THE OLD ARMY GAME	SUTHERLAND	PARAMOUNT	1926
F322	MARGARET SKOURAS	portrait	FOX	
F323	SALLY BLANE	portrait	FOX	1930s
F-323	SORROWS OF SATAN	GRIFFITH	PARAMOUNT	1926
F-324	SHOW OFF	ST. CLAIR	PARAMOUNT	1926
F-325	QUARTERBACK	NEWMEYER	PARAMOUNT	1926
F-326	SO'S YOUR OLD MAN	LA CAVA	PARAMOUNT	1926
F327	GRACIE FIELDS	portrait	FOX	1930s
F-327	GREAT GATSBY	BRENON	PARAMOUNT	1926
F-328	ACE OF CADS	REED	PARAMOUNT	1926
F-329	POPULAR SIN	ST. CLAIR	PARAMOUNT	1926
F-330	CANADIAN	BEAUDINE	PARAMOUNT	1926
F-331	GOD GAVE ME TWENTY CENTS	BRENON	PARAMOUNT	1926
F-332	NEW YORK	REED	PARAMOUNT	1927
F-333	LOVE 'EM AND LEAVE 'EM	TUTTLE	PARAMOUNT	1926
F-334	STARK LOVE	BROWN	PARAMOUNT	1927
F-335	AFRAID TO LOVE	GRIFFITH	PARAMOUNT	1927
F-336	POTTERS	NEWMEYER	PARAMOUNT	1927
F-337	LOVE'S GREATEST MISTAKE	SUTHERLAND	PARAMOUNT	1927
F-338	PARADISE FOR TWO	LA CAVA	PARAMOUNT	1927
F-339	NOT MADE		PARAMOUNT	
F-340	BLIND ALLEYS	TUTTLE	PARAMOUNT	1927
F-341	CABARET	VIGNOLA	PARAMOUNT	1927
F-342	RUBBER HEELS	HEERMAN	PARAMOUNT	1927
F-343	MANPOWER	BADGER	PARAMOUNT	1927
F-344	KNOCKOUT REILLY	ST. CLAIR	PARAMOUNT	1927
F-345	TELEPHONE GIRL	BRENON	PARAMOUNT	1927
F-346	RUNNING WILD	LA CAVA	PARAMOUNT	1927
F361	GERMAINE AUSSEY	portrait	FOX	1930s
F362	ROBERT LOWERY	portrait	FOX	1930s
F364	ELIZABETH PALMER	portrait	FOX	1930's
F366	IVA STEWART	portrait	FOX	1930s-40s
F368	ALICE ARMAND	portrait	FOX	1930s
F369	JOAN MARSH	portrait	FOX	1930s
F371	LOUISE HOVICK (aka GYPSY ROSE LEE)	portrait	FOX	1930s
F372	PHYLLIS BROOKS	portrait	FOX	1930s
F373	EDDIE CANTOR	portrait	FOX	1930s
F376	PETER LORRE	portrait	FOX	
F381	GEORGE SANDERS	portrait	FOX	1930s-50s
F384	GEORGE BARBIER	portrait	FOX	1930s
F385	LON CHANEY JR.	portrait	FOX	1930s
F392	DICK BALDWIN	portrait	FOX	1930s
F402	RUTH TERRY	portrait	FOX	
F403	WALLY VERNON	portrait	FOX	1930s,60s
F409	ETHEL MERMAN	portrait	FOX	
F410	ANNABELLA	portrait	FOX	1937
F412	JUNE WILKINS	portrait	FOX	1937
F416	DOLORES DEL RIO	portrait	FOX	1930s

Movie Still Identification Book Ultimate Edition - Letters

CODE	TITLE/NAME	DIRECTOR/TYPE	STUDIO/DISTRIBUTOR	YEAR
F419	CHICK CHANDLER	portrait	FOX	1930s
F421	ALEXANDRIA DEAN	portrait	FOX	1930s
F423	OSA MASSEN	portrait	FOX	
F424	ARLEEN WHELAN	portrait	FOX	1930s
F425	JOANN CASTLE	portrait	FOX	1930s
F429	ROBERT ALLEN	portrait	FOX	1930s
F430	RICHARD GREENE	portrait	FOX	1939
F435	DORRIS BOWDON	portrait	FOX	1930s
F436	MARY HEALY	portrait	FOX	1930s
F438	JEAN ROGERS	portrait	FOX	1930s
F440	AMANDA DUFF	portrait	FOX	1940
F441	JOAN VALERIE	portrait	FOX	1930s-50s
F442	NANCY KELLY	portrait	FOX	1939
F444	BARBARA STANWYCK	portrait	FOX	1930s
F446	KAY GRIFFITH	portrait	FOX	1930s
F449	JEANNE SPITZEL	portrait	FOX	1938
F451	JOSEPH SCHILDKRAUT	portrait	FOX	1938
F454	BINNIE BARNES	portrait	FOX	1930s
F457	SIDNEY TOLER	portrait	FOX	1938
F480	ROBERT SHAW	portrait	FOX	
F484	RUDY VALLEE	portrait	FOX	1930s-40s
F485	KATHARINE/KATHERINE/KAY ALDRIDGE	portrait	FOX	1940s
F486	LINDA DARNELL	portrait	FOX	1940s
F487	BRENDA JOYCE	portrait	FOX	1940s
F490	ANN SOTHERN	portrait	FOX	1940s
F490	HOTEL FOR WOMEN	RATOFF	20th CENTURY FOX	1939
F492	KANE RICHMOND	portrait	FOX	
F493	GLENN FORD	portrait	FOX	1940s
F498	GLADYS GEORGE	portrait	FOX	1940s
F499	GEORGE MONTGOMERY	portrait	FOX	1930s-50s
F504	ELYSE KNOX	portrait	FOX	1940s
F520	MARY BETH HUGHES	portrait	FOX	1940s
F522	JOHN PAYNE	portrait	FOX	
F525	DEAN JAGGER	portrait	FOX	1940s
F528	TED NORTH (aka MICHAEL NORTH)	portrait	FOX	1940s
F534	ANNE BAXTER	portrait	FOX	1940's
F535	GENE TIERNEY	portrait	FOX	1940s
F540	SHEILA RYAN	portrait	FOX	
F542	BETTY GRABLE	portrait	FOX	1940's
F547	JOHN SUTTON	portrait	FOX	1940s
F549	LAIRD CREGAR	portrait	FOX	1940s
F552	DANA ANDREWS	portrait	FOX	1940s
F553	VIRGINIA GILMORE	portrait	FOX	1940s
F554	COBINA WRIGHT, JR.	portrait	FOX	Early 40s
F556	CARMEN MIRANDA	portrait	FOX	1940s
F560	RODDY MCDOWALL	portrait	FOX	1940s
F562	MILTON BERLE	portrait	FOX	1940s
F563	CAROLE LANDIS	portrait	FOX	1940s
F564	ROBERT CORNELL	portrait	FOX	
F566	RICHARD DERR	portrait	FOX	1940s
F570	STANLEY CLEMENTS	portrait	FOX	1940s
F571	SHELDON LEONARD	portrait	FOX	1940s
F573	RITA HAYWORTH / RITA CANSINO	portrait	FOX	
F574	JEAN GABIN	portrait	FOX	1940s
F581	JANIS CARTER	portrait	FOX	
F583	MAUREEN O'HARA	portrait	FOX	1940s
F585	VICTOR MATURE	portrait	FOX	
F587	HELENE REYNOLDS	portrait	FOX	
F594	MARY HOWARD (aka MARY ROGERS)	portrait	FOX	1940s
F598	CORNEL WILDE	portrait	FOX	1940s
F601	DALE EVANS	portrait	FOX	1940s
F604	JOAN FONTAINE	portrait	FOX	1940s
F605	VIVIAN BLAINE	portrait	FOX	
F606	ANTHONY QUINN	portrait	FOX	1940s
F607	TRUDY MARSHALL	portrait	FOX	1940s-50s
F608	VIVIAN BLAINE	portrait	FOX	1940s
F623	DORIS MERRICK	portrait	FOX	1940s
F626	LOIS ANDREWS	portrait	FOX	1940s
F643	JUNE HAVER	portrait	FOX	1940s
F661	MARY ANDERSON	portrait	FOX	1940s

Movie Still Identification Book Ultimate Edition - Letters

CODE	TITLE/NAME	DIRECTOR/TYPE	STUDIO/DISTRIBUTOR	YEAR
F664	WILLIAM EYTHE	portrait	FOX	1940s
F670	JAMES GLEASON	portrait	FOX	1940s
F672	GALE ROBBINS	portrait	FOX	1943
F673	JENNIFER JONES	portrait	FOX	1940s
F674	MADELEINE LEBEAU	portrait	FOX	
F678	CEDRIC HARDWICKE	portrait	FOX	
F680	PEGGY ANN GARNER	portrait	FOX	1940s
F687	JO-CARROLL DENNISON	portrait	FOX	1940s
F690	PAT PATRICK (aka PATRICIA PATRICK)	portrait	FOX	1940s
F694	DOROTHY MCGUIRE	portrait	FOX	1940s-60s
F695	JEANNE CRAIN	portrait	FOX	1940s
F705	EVA GABOR	portrait	FOX	1940s
F708	WILLIAM BENDIX	portrait	FOX	1940s
F719	BRENDA MARSHALL	portrait	FOX	
F720	RICHARD CONTE	portrait	FOX	1940s
F721	PETER VAN EYCK	portrait	FOX	1940s-60s
F722	TONI/TONY EDEN	portrait	FOX	mid-1940s
F723	JOHN HARVEY	portrait	FOX	
F726	LON MCCALLISTER	portrait	FOX	1940s
F727	GEORGE JESSEL	portrait	FOX	1940s-60s
F728	DAVE WILLOCK	portrait	FOX	
F737	JAMES CARDWELL	portrait	FOX	1940s
F740	DICK HAYMES	portrait	FOX	1940s
F751	FAYE MARLOWE	portrait	FOX	1940s-50s
F-754	HONG KONG AFFAIR	HEARD	ALLIED ARTISTS	1958
F755	FRANK LATIMORE	portrait	FOX	1940s
F763	GREGORY PECK	portrait	FOX	1940s-50s
F769	RICHARD JAECKEL	portrait	FOX	1940s-60s
F771	RONALD GRAHAM	portrait	FOX	
F776	GLENN LANGAN	portrait	FOX	
F783	STANLEY PRAGER	portrait	FOX	
F789	MICHAEL O'SHEA	portrait	FOX	1940s-50s
F792	JOAN BLONDELL	portrait	FOX	1940s
F798	JANE BALL	portrait	FOX	1940s
F805	WILLIAM MARSHALL	portrait	FOX	
F814	JEAN WALLACE	portrait	FOX	1940s
F856	CATHY DOWNS	portrait	FOX	1940s
F865	GEORGE MELFORD	portrait	FOX	1940s
F869	COLEEN GRAY (aka COLLEEN GRAY)	portrait	FOX	1940s
F878	HENRY HATHAWAY	portrait	FOX	1940s-60s
F887	MARTHA STEWART	portrait	FOX	1940s
F892	MARK STEVENS	portrait	FOX	1940s
F916	TOM MOORE	portrait	FOX	1940s
F921	KURT KREUGER	portrait	FOX	
F927	BARBARA RUICK	portrait	FOX	1940s
F928	MAE MARSH	portrait	FOX	1940s
F935	PEGGY CUMMINS	portrait	FOX	1940s
F949	REX HARRISON	portrait	FOX	1940s
F955	CELESTE HOLM	portrait	FOX	1940s
F958	CLIFTON WEBB	portrait	FOX	1940s-60s
F959	HELEN WALKER	portrait	FOX	1940s
F962	VANESSA BROWN	portrait	FOX	1940s
F966	JEAN PETERS	portrait	FOX	1940s-50s
F970	ROSSANO BRAZZI	portrait	FOX	1950s
F986	CARRIE MCCORD	portrait	FOX	
F992	DWAYNE HICKMAN	portrait	FOX	1950s
F996	DAN DAILEY	portrait	FOX	1950s
F999	ANTHONY QUINN	portrait	FOX	1950s
F999	MARILYN MONROE	portrait	FOX	1940s-60s
F-999	HOW TO MARRY A MILLIONAIRE	NEGULESCO	20th CENTURY FOX	1953
F1000	LEE MACGREGOR	portrait	FOX	1950s
F1021	COLLEEN TOWNSEND	portrait	FOX	1950
F1022	MARION MARSHALL	portrait	FOX	1950
F1029	NATALIE WOOD	portrait	FOX	1940s-50s
F1034	RICHARD WIDMARK	portrait	FOX	1950s
F-5800	STREET SCENE	VIDOR	UNITED ARTISTS	1931
F-6500	GREEKS HAD A WORD FOR THEM	SHERMAN	UNITED ARTISTS	1932
F-7000	RAIN	MILESTONE	UNITED ARTISTS	1932
F-7100	HALLELUJAH I'M A BUM	MILESTONE	UNITED ARTISTS	1933
F&J	FRANKIE AND JOHNNY	AUER, ERSKINE	REPUBLIC	1936

Movie Still Identification Book Ultimate Edition - Letters

CODE	TITLE/NAME	DIRECTOR/TYPE	STUDIO/DISTRIBUTOR	YEAR
FA	ARSON INC.	BERKE	LIPPERT	1949
FA	FAKE (UK)	GRAYSON	UNITED ARTISTS	1953
FA	FALCON'S ADVENTURE	BERKE	RKO	1947
FA	FALCON'S ALIBI	MCCAREY	RKO	1946
FA	FIFTH AVENUE GIRL	LA CAVA	RKO	1939
FA	FINAL ANALYSIS	JOANOU	WARNER BROS	1992
FA	FOOLIN AROUND	HEFFRON	COLUMBIA	1980
FA	FORT ALGIERS	SELANDER	UNITED ARTISTS	1953
FA	FOURTH ALARM	ROACH	PATHE	1926
FA	FRANCIS OF ASSISI	CURTIZ	20th CENTURY FOX	1961
FA	FRED ASTAIRE	portrait	RKO	
FA	FROZEN ALIVE (UK)	KNOWLES	FEATURE FILM CORP AMERICA	1964
FA-1	SECRET WITNESS	FREELAND	COLUMBIA	1931
FAC	FALCON AND THE COEDS	CLEMENS	RKO	1943
FAL	FUNNY ABOUT LOVE	NIMOY	PARAMOUNT	1990
FAN	FANTASIA (t)	ALGAR, ARMSTRONG	RKO	1940
FAUST	FAUST AND THE DEVIL	GALLONE	COLUMBIA	1948
FB	BAD BLONDE (UK: FLANAGAN BOY)	LE BORG	LIPPERT	1953
FB	DETECTIVE (UK: FATHER BROWN)	HAMER	COLUMBIA	1954
FB	FALCON'S BROTHER	LOGAN	RKO	1942
FB	FANCY BAGGAGE	ADOLFI	WARNER BROS	1929
FB	FANNIE BRICE	portrait	WARNER BROS	
FB	FAY BAINTER	portrait	WARNER BROS	
FB	FIREBRAND	DEXTER	20th CENTURY FOX	1962
FB	FLAME BARRIER	LANDRES	UNITED ARTISTS	1958
FB	FLASHBACK	AMURRI	PARAMOUNT	1990
FB	FLESH & BLOOD (UK)	KIMMINS	SNADER	1951
FB	FLY AWAY BABY	MCDONALD	WARNER BROS	1937
FB	FORT BOWIE	KOCH	UNITED ARTISTS	1958
FB	FOUR BOYS AND A GUN	BERKE	UNITED ARTISTS	1957
FB	FUNERAL IN BERLIN (UK)	HAMILTON	PARAMOUNT	1966
FB	FURY OF THE PAGANS (IT)	MALATESTA	COLUMBIA	1960
FB	FURY ON THE BOSPHORNS		COLUMBIA	1965
FB	HIGH FURY (UK: WHITE CRADLE INN)	FRENCH	UNITED ARTISTS	1947
FB	HIS FIGHTING BLOOD	ENGLISH	AMBASSADOR	1935
FB-3500	BE YOURSELF!	FREELAND	UNITED ARTISTS	1930
FBB	FABULOUS BAKER BOYS	KLOVES	20th CENTURY FOX	1989
FBI	FBI GIRL	BERKE	LIPPERT	1951
FBT	FRANKENSTEIN'S BLOODY TERROR	EGUILEZ	INDEPENDENT INTL	1971
FBX	FREDDIE BARTHOLOMEW	portrait	MGM	
FC	FAMOUS FERGUSON CASE	BACON	WARNER BROS	1932
FC	FANG AND CLAW	BUCK	RKO	1935
FC	FAT CITY	HUSTON	COLUMBIA	1972
FC	FIGHT CLUB	FINCHER	20th CENTURY FOX	1999
FC	FINAL COUNTDOWN	TAYLOR	UNITED ARTISTS	1980
FC	FIVE CAME BACK	FARROW	RKO	1939
FC	FIVE CARD STUD	HATHAWAY	PARAMOUNT	1968
FC	FLYING DEVILS	BIRDWELL	RKO	1933
FC	FORTUNE COOKIE	WILDER	UNITED ARTISTS	1966
FC	FOUR'S A CROWD	CURTIZ	WARNER BROS	1938
FC	FRANK CAPRA	portrait	WARNER BROS	
FC	FRIGHTENED CITY	LEMONT	ALLIED ARTISTS	1961
FC	SIDE STREETS	GREEN	WARNER BROS	1934
FCB	FALCON STRIKES BACK	DMYTRYK	RKO	1943
FCC	FRENCH CAN CAN (ONLY THE FRENCH CAN)	RENOIR	UMPO	1954
FC-CR	FIRST CIRCLE	FORD	PARAMOUNT	1973
FCMC	CATHERINE MCLEOD	portrait		
FCO	FULL CONFESSION	FARROW	RKO	1939
FC-R	FIVE CARD STUD	HATHAWAY	PARAMOUNT	1968
FCS	CRIME IN THE STREETS	SIEGEL	ALLIED ARTISTS	1956
FCW	FRANKENSTEIN CREATED WOMAN (UK)	FISHER	20TH CENTURY FOX	1967
FCWT	FINAL CHAPTER WALKING TALL	STARRETT	AIP	1977
FD	FAITH DOMERGUE	portrait	RKO	
FD	FAITH DORN	portrait	WARNER BROS	
FD	FATAL DESIRE (IT)	GALLONE	ULTRA PICTURES	1963
FD	FEDORA	WILDER	UNITED ARTISTS	1978
FD	FIGHTING FATHER DUNNE	TETZLAFF	RKO	1948
FD	FISTFUL OF DOLLARS (IT: PER UN PUGNO DI DOLLARI)	LEONE	UNITED ARTISTS	1964
FD	FLIGHT THAT DISAPPEARED	LE BORG	UNITED ARTISTS	1961
FD	FLOATING DUTCHMAN (UK)	SEWELL	ALLIED ARTISTS	1952

Movie Still Identification Book Ultimate Edition - Letters

CODE	TITLE/NAME	DIRECTOR/TYPE	STUDIO/DISTRIBUTOR	YEAR
FD	FLOOD (TV)	BELLAMY	WARNER BROS	1976
FD	FLORENTINE DAGGER	FLOREY	WARNER BROS	1935
FD	FLYING DEUCES	SUTHERLAND	RKO	1939
FD	FOLLOW THAT DREAM	DOUGLAS	UNITED ARTISTS	1962
FD	FOOTSTEPS IN THE DARK	BACON	WARNER BROS	1941
FD	FORBIDDEN DESERT	WINTER	WARNER BROS	1957
FD	FORT DEFIANCE	RAWLINS	UNITED ARTISTS	1951
FD	FOUR DESPERATE MEN (UK: SIEGE OF PINCHGUT)	WATT	CONTINENTAL	1959
FD	FRANCES DEE	portrait	RKO	1930s-50s
FD	FRANKENSTEIN MUST BE DESTROYED (UK)	FISHER	WARNER BROS	1969
FD	FROZEN DEAD (UK)	LEDER	WARNER BROS.	1966
FDM	FOR A FEW DOLLARS MORE (IT: PER QUALCHE DOLLARO IN	LEONE	UNITED ARTISTS	1967
FDR	FLYING DOWN TORIO	FREELAND	RKO	1933
FE	FAYE EMERSON	portrait	WARNER BROS	
FE	FIGHTING EDGE	LEHMAN	WARNER BROS	1926
FE	FLIGHT ANGELS	SEILER	WARNER BROS	1940
FE	FOREVER AND A DAY	GOULDING, HARDWICKE	RKO	1943
FE-1	GIRLS DEMAND EXCITEMENT	FELIX	FOX FILM	1931
FE-2	STEPPING SISTERS	FELIX	FOX FILM	1932
FEP	FIVE EASY PIECES	RAFELSON	COLUMBIA	1970
FF	ATTACK	ALDRICH	UNITED ARTISTS	1956
FF	ATTACK!	ALDRICH	UNITED ARTISTS	1956
FF	CAUGHT IN THE FOG	BRETHERTON	WARNER BROS	1928
FF	FACE TO FACE (SWE)	BERGMAN	PARAMOUNT	1976
FF	FEMALE FIENDS (UK: STRANGE AWAKENING)	TULLY	CINEMA ASSOCIATES	1958
FF	FLAMING FRONTIER	NEWFIELD	20TH CENTURY FOX	1958
FF	FLAMING FRONTIER (GER)	VOHRER	WARNER BROS	1968
FF	FLIGHT FROM GLORY	LANDERS	RKO	1937
FF	FLORENCE FAIR	portrait	WARNER BROS	
FF	FLYING FOOL (UK)	SUMMERS	WARDOUR	1931
FF	FOR FREEDOM (UK)	ELVEY, KNIGHT	GFD	1940
FF	FORBIDDEN FRUIT (FR: LE FRUIT DEFENDU)	VERNEUIL	FILMS AROUND THE WORLD	1952
FF	FOUR FLIES ON GREY VELVET (IT)	ARGENTO	PARAMOUNT	1972
FF	FRANCES FARMER	portrait	UNIVERSAL	
FF	FRANCES FARMER	portrait	WARNER BROS	
FF	FUN AND FANCY FREE (t)	KINNEY, LUSKE	RKO	1947
FF	FISTS OF FURY	WEI LO	NATIONAL GENERAL	1973
FF1	CARNEGIE HALL	ULMER	UNITED ARTISTS	1947
FF202	MATTER OF WHO (UK)	CHAFFEY	MGM	1961
FF-508	FOR COUNTRY LIFE		20th CENTURY FOX	1940
FF-508	FORD FAIRLANE	HARLIN	20th CENTURY FOX	1990
FFA	FLIGHT FROM ASHIYA	ANDERSON	UNITED ARTISTS	1964
FFA	LADY TAKES A CHANCE	SEITER	RKO	1943
FF-C	FACE TO FACE (SWE)	BERGMAN	PARAMOUNT	1976
FFC	FALSTAFF'S FUR COAT (UK: TV FEATURETTE)		PARAMOUNT	1954
FFC	FOUR FLIES ON GREY VELVET (IT:4 MOSCHE DI VELLUTO	ARGENTO	PARAMOUNT	1972
FFH	FANNY FOLEY HERSELF	BROWN	RKO	1931
FFPI	STOWAWAY GIRL (UK: MANUELA)	HAMILTON	PARAMOUNT	1957
FG	FAIR GAME	SIPES	WARNER BROS	1995
FG	FARLEY GRANGER	portrait	RKO	
FG	FERNAND GRAVET/GRAVEY	portrait	MGM, WARNER BROS	
FG	FERNGULLY	KROYER	20th CENTURY FOX	1992
FG	FIGHTING GRINGO	HOWARD	RKO	1939
FG	FILE OF THE GOLDEN GOOSE (UK)	WANAMAKER	UNITED ARTISTS	1969
FG	FLAMING GOLD	INCE	RKO	1933
FG	FLESH GORDON	BENVENISTE, ZIEHM	MAMMOTH	1974
FG	FLOWING GOLD	GREEN	WARNER BROS	1940
FG	FLOYD GIBBONS	portrait		
FG	FOREST GUMP	ZEMECKIS	PARAMOUNT	1994
FG	FRONTIER GUN	LANDRES	20TH CENTURY FOX	1958
FG	FUNNY GIRL	WYLER	COLUMBIA	1968
FG	GAUCHO	JONES	UNITED ARTISTS	1927
FG	MAGIC BOX (UK)	BOULTING	MAYER-KINGLSEY	1951
FG	MAN OF EVIL (UK: FANNY BY GASLIGHT)	ASQUITH	UNITED ARTISTS	1945
FG	WINGED DEVILS (IT: FORZA G)	TESSARI	UNITED ARTISTS	1972
FG-4	AFFAIRS OF A ROGUE (UK)	CAVALCANTI	COLUMBIA	1948
FH	AGE OF CONSENT	LA CAVA	RKO	1932
FH	FEVER HEAT	DOUGHTEN JR.	PARAMOUNT	1968
FH	FIELD OF HONOR (FR: CHAMP D'HONNEUR)	DENIS	ORION	1987
FH	FIVE HEARTBEATS	TOWNSEND	20th CENTURY FOX	1991

Movie Still Identification Book Ultimate Edition - Letters

CODE	TITLE/NAME	DIRECTOR/TYPE	STUDIO/DISTRIBUTOR	YEAR
FH	FLOWING GOLD	GREEN	WARNER BROS	1940
FH	FOOTLOOSE HEIRESS	CLEMENS	WARNER BROS	1937
FH	FROM HEADQUARTERS	DIETERLE	WARNER BROS	1933
FH	FRONTIER HELLCAT (GER)	VOHRER	COLUMBIA	1964
FH	GREAT LIE	GOULDING	WARNER BROS	1941
FH	MR. LUCKY	POTTER	RKO	1943
FHC	DOORWAY TO HELL	MAYO	WARNER BROS	1930
FHK	FLIGHT TO HONG KONG	NEWMAN	UNITED ARTISTS	1956
FHL	48 HOURS TO LIVE (UK)	BOURNE	ARCHWAY	1959
FI	FADE IN	TAYLOR	PARAMOUNT	1968
FI	FARMER IN THE DELL	HOLMES	RKO	1936
FI	FIRE AND ICE	BAKSHI	20th CENTURY FOX	1983
FI	FLIGHT OF THE INTRUDER	MILIUS	PARAMOUNT	1991
FI	FLYING IRISHMAN	JASON	RKO	1939
FI	FOREIGN INTRIGUE	REYNOLDS	UNITED ARTISTS	1956
FI	FRIEDA INESCOURT	portrait	RKO	
FID	FALCON IN DANGER	CLEMENS	RKO	1943
FIH	FALCON IN HOLLYWOOD	DOUGLAS	RKO	1945
FIL	TROUBLE AHEAD (UK: FALLING IN LOVE)	BANKS	TIMES	1934
FIM	FALCON IN MEXICO	BERKE	RKO	1944
FIRE	FIRE (tv)	BELLAMY	WARNER BROS	1977
FIT	FALCON OUT WEST	CLEMENS	RKO	1944
FIVE	FIVE	OBOLER	COLUMBIA	1951
FIW	FLESH IS WEAK (UK)	CHAFFEY	DCA	1957
FJ	FOUR IN A JEEP	LINDTBERG	UNITED ARTISTS	1951
FJ	FOUR JACKS AND A JILL	HIVELY	RKO	1942
FJ	FRANKIE AND JOHNNY	DE CORDOVA	UNITED ARTISTS	1966
FJ	FRANKIE AND JOHNNY	MARSHALL	PARAMOUNT	1991
FJ	FUGITIVE FROM JUSTICE	MORSE	WARNER BROS	1940
FJM	FOUR JUST MEN (UK: SECRET FOUR)	FORDE	MONOGRAM	1939
FK	FARGO KID	KILLY	RKO	1940
FK	FATHER IS A PRINCE	SMITH	WARNER BROS	1940
FK	FEAR IS THE KEY	TUCHNER	PARAMOUNT	1973
FK	FINDERS KEEPERS (UK)	HAYERS	UNITED ARTISTS	1966
FK	FIT FOR A KING	SEDGWICK	RKO	1937
FK	FOR KEEPS	AVILDSEN	TRI STAR	1988
FK	FRED KOHLER	portrait		
FK	FRENCH KISS	KASDAN	20th CENTURY FOX	1995
FK	FRISCO KID	BACON	WARNER BROS	1935
FK	FUGITIVE KIND	LUMET	UNITED ARTISTS	1960
FL	FINGERPRINTS DON'T LIE	NEWFIELD	LIPPERT	1951
FL	FIRST LADY	LOGAN	WARNER BROS	1937
FL	FIRST LOVE	DARLING	PARAMOUNT	1977
FL	FLAIRUP	NEILSON	MGM	1970
FL	FLYING LEATHERNECKS	RAY	RKO	1951
FL	FOREVER, LULU	KOLLEK	TRI STAR	1987
FL	FRANCES LANGFORD	portrait	RKO	
FL	FRANCIS LEDERER	portrait	RKO	mid 30s
FL	FRANK LOVEJOY	portrait	WARNER BROS	
FL	FRENCH LEAVE (UK)	LEE	PATHE	1937
FL	FRENCH LINE	BACON	RKO	1954
FL	FRESHMAN LOVE	MCGANN	WARNER BROS	1936
FL	FRIGHTENED LADY (UK: CASE OF THE FRIGHTENED LADY)	KING	HOFFBERG ZIEHM	1940
FL	FROZEN LIMITS (UK)	VARNEL	GFD	1939
FL	FUNNY LADY	ROSS	COLUMBIA	1975
FL	LOVES OF A DICTATOR (UK: DICTATOR)	SAVILLE	GAUMONT BRITISH	1935
FL	SCHOOL FOR LOVE (FR 1955)	ALLEGRET	NTA	1960
FL-1	FIRE OVER AFRICA (MALAGA)	SALE	COLUMBIA	1954
FL-2	FOOTSTEPS IN THE FOG (UK)	LUBIN	COLUMBIA	1955
FL2	REBOUND (UK: VIOLENT MOMENT)	HAYERS	SCHOENFELD	1959
FL2	STRANGE AFFECTION (UK: SCAMP)	RILLA	JOSEPH BRENNER	1957
FL-23	LINCOLN HIGHWAYMEN	FLYNN	FOX FILM	1919
FL-23	VEILED WOMAN	FLYNN	FOX FILM	1929
FLB	FLIGHT OF THE LOST BALLOON	JURAN	AIP	1961
FLEM-1	COMMON CLAY	FLEMING	FOX FILM	1930
FLEM-2	RENEGADES	FLEMING	FOX FILM	1930
FLK	FRONT LINE KIDS (UK)	ROGERS	BUTCHER'S	1942
FLOC-3	JOE MACBETH	HUGHES	COLUMBIA	1955
FLOC-4	SPIN A DARK WEB (UK: SOHO INCIDENT)	SEWELL	COLUMBIA	1956
FLW	FRENCH LIEUTENANT'S WOMAN	REISZ	UNITED ARTISTS	1981

Movie Still Identification Book Ultimate Edition - Letters

CODE	TITLE/NAME	DIRECTOR/TYPE	STUDIO/DISTRIBUTOR	YEAR
FLYNN-15	GERALD CRANSTON'S LADY	FLYNN	FOX FILM	1924
FLYNN-18	EAST LYNNE	FLYNN	FOX FILM	1925
FLYNN-19	YANKEE SENOR	FLYNN	FOX FILM	1926
FM	FACING THE MUSIC (UK)	ROGERS	BUTCHER'S	1941
FM	FAR FROM THE MADDENING CROWD (UK)	SCHLESINGER	MGM	1968
FM	FAY MCKENZIE (aka FAY SHANNON)	portrait	REPUBLIC, UNIVERSAL	1930s-40s
FM	FERRY CROSS THE MERSEY (UK)	SUMMERS	UNITED ARTISTS	1965
FM	FICTION MAKERS (UK)	BAKER		1967
FM	FIGHTING MARINES (serial)	EASON, KANE	REPUBLIC	1935
FM	FIRE MAIDENS FROM OUTER SPACE (UK)	ROTH	TOPAZ	1956
FM	FIRST MEN IN THE MOON (UK)	JURAN	COLUMBIA	1964
FM	FIVE MINUTES TO LIVE	KARN	AIP	1961
FM	FLORENCE MARLY (aka FLORENCE MARLEY)	portrait	RKO	
FM	FOLLOW THAT MAN	EPSTEIN	UNITED ARTISTS	1961
FM	FORBIDDEN MUSIC (UK: LAND WITHOUT MUSIC)	FORDE	WORLD	1936
FM	FORT MASSACRE	NEWMAN	UNITED ARTISTS	1958
FM	FOUR MOTHERS	KEIGHLEY	WARNER BROS	1941
FM	FRANCES MERCER	portrait	RKO	late 30s
FM	FRANCINE LARRIMORE	portrait	MGM	
FM	FRANK MAYO	portrait	RKO	
FM	FRANK MCHUGH	portrait	WARNER BROS	1930s-50s
FM	FRANK MORGAN	portrait	MGM	
FM	FRANKENSTEIN AND MONSTER FROM HELL (UK)	FISHER	PARAMOUNT	1974
FM	FRANKIE MASTERS (& ORCHESTRA)	portrait	MCA	
FM	FRED MACMURRAY	portrait	RKO	
FM	FREDRIC MARCH	portrait	UNIV	
FM	FREDRIC MARCH	portrait	WARNER BROS	
FM	FURY AT SMUGGLER'S BAY (UK)	GILLING	EMBASSY	1961
FM	LADY KILLER	DEL RUTH	WARNER BROS	1933
FM/E	FIRST MEN ON THE MOON (UK)	JURAN	COLUMBIA	1964
FMF	FIFTY MILLION FRENCHMEN	BACON	WARNER BROS	1931
FML	FAREWELL MY LOVELY	RICHARDS	AVCO EMBASSY	1975
FML	MURDER MY SWEET	DMYTRYK	RKO	1945
FMM	FIBBER MCGEE & MOLLY		RKO	
FMO	FOR MEN ONLY (TALL LIE)	HENREID	LIPPERT	1952
FMQ	FOLLOW ME QUIETLY	FLEISCHER	RKO	1949
FMT	FIRST YANK INTO TOKYO	DOUGLAS	RKO	1945
FMY	FIVE MILLION YEARS TO EARTH (UK: QUATERMASS AND THE	BAKER	20th CENTURY FOX	1967
FN	40 NAUGHTY GIRLS	CLINE	RKO	1937
FN	FRANCES NEAL	portrait	RKO	early 40s
FN	FRIENDS AND NEIGHBOURS (UK)	PARRY	SCHOENFELD	1959
FN	FROM NOON TILL THREE	GILROY	UNITED ARTISTS	1976
FN	LOVE HONOR AND BEHAVE	LOGAN	WARNER BROS	1938
FN	MENACE IN THE NIGHT (UK: FACE IN THE NIGHT)	COMFORT	UNITED ARTISTS	1957
FN	WHITE ANGEL	DIETERLE	WARNER BROS	1936
FNX-6	ANITA LOOS	portrait		
FNX-36	POLA NEGRI	portrait		
FO	FATHER O'FLYNN (UK)	NOY, TENNYSON	JH HOFFBERG	1935
FO	FOOD OF THE GODS	GORDON	AIP	1976
FOC	FORTY CARATS	KATSELAS	COLUMBIA	1973
FOF	CAUGHT PLASTERED	SEITER	RKO	1931
FOG	FOG	CARPENTER	AVCO EMBASSY	1980
FOM	FATE OF A MAN (RUS)	BONDARCHUK	UNITED ARTISTS	1959
FOR-1	ABUSED CONFIDENCE	DECOIN	COLUMBIA	1938
FOR-2	LIFE DANCES ON	DUVIVIER	AFE (SIGMA-FR)	1937
FOR-4	ALIBI (FR: L'ALIBI)	CHENAL	COLUMBIA	1939
FOR-10	ABUSED CONFIDENCE	DECOIN	COLUMBIA (BERCHOLZ)	1938
FORD-2	BIG PUNCH	FORD	FOX FILM	1921
FORD-2	JACKIE	FORD	FOX FILM	1921
FORD-4	LITTLE MISS SMILES	FORD	FOX FILM	1922
FORD-5	VILLAGE BLACKSMITH	FORD	FOX FILM	1922
FORD-6	FACE ON BATHROOM FLOOR	FORD	FOX FILM	1923
FORD-7	THREE JUMPS AHEAD	FORD	FOX FILM	1922
FORD-11	IRON HORSE	FORD	FOX FILM	1924
FORD-14	FIGHTING HEART	FORD	FOX FILM	1925
FORD-15	LIGHTNIN'	FORD	FOX FILM	1925
FORD-17	3 BAD MEN	FORD	FOX FILM	1926
FORD-18	SHAMROCK HANDICAP	FORD	FOX FILM	1926
FORD-19	BLUE EAGLE	FORD	FOX FILM	1926
FORD-20	MOTHER MACREE	FORD	FOX FILM	1928

Movie Still Identification Book Ultimate Edition - Letters

CODE	TITLE/NAME	DIRECTOR/TYPE	STUDIO/DISTRIBUTOR	YEAR
FORD-21	UPSTREAM	FORD	FOX FILM	1927
FORD-22	FOUR SONS	FORD	FOX FILM	1928
FORD-23	HANGMAN'S HOUSE	FORD	FOX FILM	1928
FORD-24	RILEY THE COP	FORD	FOX FILM	1928
FORD-26	STRONG BOY	FORD	FOX FILM	1929
FORD-27	BLACK WATCH	FORD	FOX FILM	1929
FORD-28	SALUTE	FORD	FOX FILM	1929
FORD-29	MEN WITHOUT WOMEN	FORD	FOX FILM	1930
FORD-30	BORN RECKLESS	FORD	FOX FILM	1930
FORD-31	UP THE RIVER	FORD	FOX FILM	1930
FORD-32	SEAS BENEATH	FORD	FOX FILM	1931
FORD-33	BRAT	FORD	FOX FILM	1931
FORD-34	PILGRIMAGE	FORD	FOX FILM	1933
FORDE-10	DEVIL'S REWARD	FORDE	FOX FILM	1928
FOT	FINGER ON THE TRIGGER (SP)	PINK	MONOGRAM	1965
FOX	FOX		WARNER BROS	
FOX1	FOXHOLE IN CAIRO (UK)	MOXEY	PARAMOUNT	1960
FP	CAPTURED	DEL RUTH	WARNER BROS	1933
FP	FABIOLA (IT)	BLASETTI	UNITED ARTISTS	1951
FP	FIGHT FOR PEACE	ROSS	MONOGRAM	1938
FP	FIGHTING MAN OF THE PLAINS	MARIN	20th CENTURY FOX	1949
FP	FINGERPRINTS	BACON	WARNER BROS	1927
FP	FLASHPOINT	TANNEN	TRI STAR	1984
FP	FOOTLIGHT PARADE	BERKELEY	WARNER BROS	1933
FP	FOR PETE'S SAKE	YATES	COLUMBIA	1974
FP	FORBIDDEN PARADISE (GER)	BONDY	COLORAMA	1958
FP	FRANKLIN PANGBORN	portrait	RKO	
FP	FRONT PAGE WOMAN	CURTIZ	WARNER BROS	1935
FP	FUZZY PINK NIGHTGOWN	TAUROG	UNITED ARTISTS	1957
FP	INTERNATIONAL SQUADRON	MENDES, SEILER	WARNER BROS	1941
FP1	MAN WITHOUT A BODY (UK)	SAUNDERS, WILDER	BUDD ROGERS	1957
FP2	KILL HER GENTLY (UK)	SAUNDERS	COLUMBIA	1957
FP5	MURDER REPORTED (UK)	SAUNDERS	COLUMBIA	1958
FP-617	STAGECOACH DRIVER	COLLINS	MONOGRAM	1951
FP-618	OKLAHOMA JUSTICE	COLLINS	MONOGRAM	1951
FP-619	WANTED DEAD OR ALIVE	CARR	MONOGRAM	1951
FP-620	LONGHORN	COLLINS	MONOGRAM	1951
FP-621	KANSAS TERRITORY	COLLINS	MONOGRAM	1952
FP-622	TEXAS LAWMEN	COLLINS	MONOGRAM	1951
FP-623	WHISTLING HILLS	ABRAHAMS	MONOGRAM	1951
FP-624	LAWLESS COWBOYS	COLLINS	MONOGRAM	1951
FP-5151	CANYON RAIDERS	COLLINS	MONOGRAM	1951
FP-5152	NEVADA BADMAN	COLLINS	MONOGRAM	1951
FPP	FANTASTIC PLASTIC MACHINE	BLUM, BLUM	CROWN INT'L	1969
FR	FALSE RAPTURE (UK: BLACK EYES)	BRENON	FILM ALLIANCE	1939
FR	FACE IN THE RAIN	KERSHNER	EMBASSY	1963
FR	FIDDLER ON THE ROOF	JEWISON	UNITED ARTISTS	1971
FR	FLORENCE RICE	portrait	RKO	
FR	FRANCES ROBINSON	portrait	UNIVERSAL	
FR	FREELAND PRODUCTIONS	studio	FOX	
FR	QUIET GUN	CLAXTON	20th CENTURY FOX	1957
FR	TORMENT/FRENZY (SWE: HETS)	SJOBERG	LOPERT	1944
FR	VOICE IN THE NIGHT	COLEMAN	COLUMBIA	1934
FR-1	SIX CYLINDER LOVE	FREELAND	FOX FILM	1931
F-RH	ROBIN HOOD	DWAN	UNITED ARTISTS	1922
FRWL	FROM RUSSIA WITH LOVE	YOUNG	UNITED ARTISTS	1963
FS	FAIL SAFE	LUMET	COLUMBIA	1964
FS	FALCON AND THE SNOWMAN	SCHLESINGER	ORION	1985
FS	FAST AND SEXY (IT)	LASTRICATI, DE SICA	COLUMBIA	1958
FS	FATHER'S SON	LEDERMAN	WARNER BROS	1941
FS	FIGHTING 69TH	KEIGHLEY	WARNER BROS	1940
FS	FIGHTING STOCK (UK)	WALLS	GAUMONT BRITISH	1935
FS	FINISHING SCHOOL	NICHOLS JR., TUCHOCK	RKO	1934
FS	FIRESTORM	SEMLER	20th CENTURY FOX	1998
FS	FIRST SPACESHIP VENUS (GER)	MAETZIG	CROWN INT'L	1962
FS	FOOLS FOR SCANDAL	LEROY, CONNOLLY	WARNER BROS	1938
FS	FORTY SECOND STREET	BACON	WARNER BROS	1933
FS	FOUR SKULLS OF JONATHAN DRAKE	CAHN	UNITED ARTISTS	1959
FS	FOURTH SEX (FR: QUATRIEME SEXE)	GIMENO, METZGER	AUDUBON	1962
FS	FRANK SINATRA	portrait	RKO	1940s-50s

Movie Still Identification Book Ultimate Edition - Letters

CODE	TITLE/NAME	DIRECTOR/TYPE	STUDIO/DISTRIBUTOR	YEAR
FS	FRED STONE	portrait	RKO	
FS	FRIENDS OF MR. SWEENEY	LUDWIG	WARNER BROS	1934
FS	FRONTIER UPRISING	CAHN	UNITED ARTISTS	1961
FS	IN THE FRENCH STYLE	PARRISH	COLUMBIA	1963
FS	LUCKY NUMBER (UK)	ASQUITH	IDEAL	1932
FS	MAKE MINE A DOUBLE (UK: NIGHT WE DROPPED A CLANGER)	CONYERS	ELLIS	1961
FS	MURDER OF DR. HARRIGAN	MCDONALD	WARNER BROS	1936
FS	NAKED HILLS	SHAFTEL	ALLIED ARTISTS	1956
FS	QUINCANNON, FRONTIER SCOUT	SELANDER	UNITED ARTISTS	1956
FSC	FIREMAN SAVE MY CHILD	BACON	WARNER BROS	1932
FSC	FOR SINGLES ONLY	DREIFUSS	COLUMBIA	1968
FSF	FALCON IN SAN FRANCISCO	LEWIS	RKO	1945
FSF	FIVE STAR FINAL	LEROY	WARNER BROS	1931
FSM	FRANKENSTEIN MEETS THE SPACE MONSTER	GAFFNEY	ALLIED ARTISTS	1965
FSP	FISH THAT SAVED PITTSBURGH	MOSES	UNITED ARTISTS	1979
FST	FIVE STEPS TO DANGER	KESLER	UNITED ARTISTS	1957
FST	FOUR SIDED TRIANGLE (UK)	FISHER	ASTOR	1953
FSW	FACE OF THE SCREAMING WEREWOLF	SOLARES	ADP	1965
FT	FATHER TAKES A WIFE	HIVELY	RKO	1941
FT	FEMALE TROUBLE	WATERS	NEW LINE CINEMA	1974
FT	FIGHTING TROOPER	TAYLOR	AMBASSADOR	1934
FT	FIVE GUNS TO TOMBSTONE	CAHN	UNITED ARTISTS	1960
FT	FOLLOW THE FLEET	SANDRICH	RKO	1936
FT	FOR THOSE WHO THINK YOUNG	MARTINSON	UNITED ARTISTS	1964
FT	FORBIDDEN TERRITORY (UK)	ROSEN	JH HOFFBERG	1934
FT	FORREST TUCKER	portrait	REPUBLIC	1940s-50s
FT	FRANCHOT TONE	portrait	MGM, RKO, UNIVERSAL	
FT	FRANKIE THOMAS	portrait	WARNER BROS	
FT	FUNNY THING HAPPENED ON WAY TO FORUM (UK)	LESTER	UNITED ARTISTS	1966
FT	KNIGHTS FOR A DAY (UK) FULL TILT*	GINEVER, LEE	PATHE	1937
FT	STOP ME BEFORE I KILL (UK: FULL TREATMENT)	GUEST	COLUMBIA	1960
FT	THUNDERING HOOFS	SELANDER	RKO	1942
FT	WHILE NERO FIDDLED (UK: FIDDLERS THREE)	WATT	BELL	1944
FTB	FOR THE BOYS	RYDELL	20th CENTURY FOX	1991
FTO	FALCON TAKES OVER	REIS	RKO	1942
FTP	FOR THOSE IN PERIL (UK)	CRICHTON	EALING	1944
FTT	FRIDAY THE THIRTEENTH (UK)	SAVILLE	GAUMONT BRITISH AMERICA	1933
FTY	RETURN TO YESTERDAY (UK)	STEVENSON	JH HOFFBERG	1940
FUR-3	COLORADO PLUCK	FURTHMAN	FOX FILM	1923
FV	FOR VALOUR (UK)	WALLS	GFD	1937
FW	CRIME BY NIGHT	CLEMENS	WARNER BROS	1944
FW	FACE AT THE WINDOW (UK)	HISCOTT	RKO	1932
FW	FAMILY WAY (UK)	BOULTING	WARNER BROS	1967
FW	FANGS OF THE WILD (aka FOLLOW THE HUNTER)	CLAXTON	LIPPERT	1954
FW	FARMER'S WIFE (UK)	ARLISS, LEE	PATHE	1941
FW	FAY WRAY	portrait	RKO	1930s-40s
FW	FAY WRAY	portrait	GAUMONT BRITISH	mid 30s
FW	FIREWALKER	THOMPSON	CANNON	1986
FW	FISHERMAN'S WHARF	VORHAUS	RKO	1939
FW	FLIRTATION WALK	BORZAGE	WARNER BROS	1934
FW	FOUR WIVES	CURTIZ	WARNER BROS	1939
FW	FRANCES WILLIAMS	portrait	UNITED ARTISTS	early 30s
FX	FOXES	LYNE	UNITED ARTISTS	1980
FW	I COULD NEVER HAVE SEX WITH ANY MAN WHO ... HUSBAND	MCCARTY	CINEMA 5	1973
FX9	MADGE BELLAMY	portrait	FOX	1920s-30s
FX17	SALLY PHIPPS	portrait	FOX	1920s
FX18	JANET GAYNOR	portrait	FOX	1920s
FX20	LOIS MORAN	portrait	FOX	1920s
FX27	GEORGE O'BRIEN	portrait	FOX	1920s-30s
FX28	OLIVE BORDEN	portrait	FOX	1920s
FX29	WINFIELD SHEEHAN	portrait	FOX	1920s-40s
FX35	GRETA NISSEN	portrait	FOX	1920s
FX37	MARJORIE BEEBE	portrait	FOX	1920s
FX40	MAE BUSCH	portrait	FOX	
FX43	MARY DUNCAN	portrait	FOX	1920's
FX52	LIA TORA	portrait	FOX	1920s-30s
FX61	JAMES HALL	portrait	FOX	late 20s
FX62	NANCY DREXEL (aka DOROTHY KITCHEN)	portrait	FOX	late 20s
FX64	NANCY CARROLL	portrait	FOX	late 1920s-
FX73	MARY ASTOR	portrait	FOX	late 20s

Movie Still Identification Book Ultimate Edition - Letters

CODE	TITLE/NAME	DIRECTOR/TYPE	STUDIO/DISTRIBUTOR	YEAR
FX74	AIDA WILLIAMS/ADA WILLIAMS/ADA INCE	portrait	FOX	1920s-30s
FX75	FLORENCE LAKE	portrait	FOX	
FX76	LOLA LANE	portrait	FOX	
FX77	SHARON LYNN (aka SHARON LYNNE)	portrait	FOX	1920s-30s
FX80	MARCELINE DAY	portrait	FOX	1920s-30s
FX95	HUGH SINCLAIR	portrait	FOX	
FX97	J. HAROLD MURRAY	portrait	FOX	1920s-30s
FX102	KENNETH MACKENNA	portrait	FOX	
FX106	EL BRENDEL	portrait	FOX	
FX111	WARREN HYMER	portrait	FOX	1920s-30s
FX117	EDMUND LOWE	portrait	FOX	1920s
FX129	JOYCE COMPTON	portrait	FOX	1920s
FX131	FIFI D'ORSAY	portrait	FOX	1920s
FX138	JEAN LAVERTY (aka JEAN BARY)	portrait	FOX	1929
FX139	JOHN GARRICK	portrait	FOX	1920s-30s
FX144	GEORGE OLSEN	portrait	FOX	1930's
FX188	ROSE HOBART	portrait	FOX	1930s
FXB	FRANCIS X. BUSHMAN	portrait	UNIVERSAL	
FXS	FRANK SINATRA	portrait	MGM	1940s-70s
FY	FIGHT FOR YOUR LADY	STOLOFF	RKO	1937
FY	FOREVER YOUNG	MINER	WARNER BROS	1992
FY	FORT YUMA	SELANDER	UNITED ARTISTS	1955
FYEO	FOR YOUR EYES ONLY	GLEN	UNITED ARTISTS	1981
FYH	SING YOUR WAY HOME	MANN	RKO	1946
FZ	FUZZ	COLLA	UNITED ARTISTS	1972
FZS	BABY FACE NELSON	SIEGEL	UNITED ARTISTS	1957
G	BORN FOR GLORY (UK: BROWN ON RESOLUTION)	FORDE	MONOGRAM	1935
G	FOUR DIMENSIONS OF GRETA (UK)	WALKER	DIMENSION	1972
G	GALLIPOLI	WEIR	PARAMOUNT	1981
G	GAMBLER	REISZ	PARAMOUNT	1974
G	GAMMA PEOPLE (UK)	GILLING	COLUMBIA	1956
G	GANG WAR (UK)	MARSHALL	UNITED ARTISTS	1962
G	GATE	TAKACS	NEW CENTURY	1986
G	GERONIMO	LAVEN	UNITED ARTISTS	1962
G	GIGOLETTE	LAMONT	RKO	1935
G	GIGOT	KELLY	20th CENTURY FOX	1962
G	GLORY	BUTLER	RKO	1956
G	GODSPELL	GREENE	COLUMBIA	1973
G	GODZILLA, KING OF THE MONSTERS	MORSE-HONDA	TRANSWORLD	1956
G	GOLD IS WHERE YOU FIND IT	CURTIZ	WARNER BROS	1938
G	GOLDFINGER (UK)	HAMILTON	UNITED ARTISTS	1964
G	GOLDIE GETS ALONG	ST. CLAIR	RKO	1933
G	GUENDALINA (IT/FR 1957)	LATTUADA	LOPERT	1958
G	GUERRILLA GIRL	CHRISTIAN	UNITED ARTISTS	1953
G	GUILTY? (UK)	GREVILLE	GRAND NATIONAL	1956
G	GUNSLINGER	CORMAN	AIP	1956
G	HOW TO MURDER A RICH UNCLE	PATRICK	COLUMBIA	1957
G	ROOKIE COP	HOWARD	RKO	1939
G-1	BIG EARS (sh)	MCGOWAN	MGM	1931
G1	POT O' GOLD	MARSHALL	UNITED ARTISTS	1941
G-1	REGULAR PAL (sh)	ROACH	PATHE EXCHANGE	1920
G1	WEB OF CHANCE	GREEN	FOX FILM	1919
G-1	YALE VS. HARVARD (sh)	MCGOWAN	MGM	1927
G 2	GREASE 2	BIRCH	PARAMOUNT	1982
G2	GREMLINS 2	DANTE	WARNER BROS	1990
G-2	MERELY A MAID (sh)	ROACH	PATHE EXCHANGE	1920
G-2	MOUNTAIN WOMAN	GIBLYN	FOX FILM	1921
G-2	OLD WALLOP (sh)	MCGOWAN	MGM	1927
G-2	SAILOR PAPA (sh)	GUIOL, WILDE	PATHE EXCHANGE	1925
G-2	SHIVER MY TIMBERS (sh)	MCGOWAN	MGM	1931
G2	WIFE'S AWAKENING	GASNIER	ROBERTSON COLE	1921
G-3	DOGS IS DOGS (sh)	MCGOWAN	MGM	1931
G-3	HEEBEE JEEBEES (sh)	MCGOWAN, MCGOWAN	MGM	1927
G-3	HELLO UNCLE (sh)	ROACH	PATHE EXCHANGE	1920
G-3	MEET THE MISSUS (sh)	CLEMENTS, GUIOL	PATHE EXCHANGE	1924
G3-2	BRANDY FOR THE PARSON (UK)	ELDRIDGE	MAYER-KINGLSEY	1952
G3-5	BRAVE DON'T CRY (UK)	LEACOCK	MAYER-KINGLSEY	1952
G3-7	ORACLE/US: HORSE'S MOUTH (UK)	PENNINGTON-RICHARDS	MAYER-KINGLSEY	1953
G3-8	SCOTCH ON THE ROCKS (UK: LAXDALE HALL)	ELDRIDGE	KINGSLEY INTERNATIONAL	1953
G3-11	EDGE OF DIVORCE (UK: BACKGROUND)	BIRT	KINGSLEY INTERNATIONAL	1953

Movie Still Identification Book Ultimate Edition - Letters

CODE	TITLE/NAME	DIRECTOR/TYPE	STUDIO/DISTRIBUTOR	YEAR
G3-12	ANGEL WHO PAWNED HER HARP (UK)	BROMLY	AAP	1954
G3-13	DEVIL ON HORSEBACK (UK)	FRANKEL	BRITISH LION	1954
G3-14	CONFLICT OF WINGS (UK)	ELDRIDGE	AAP	1954
G3-15	END OF THE ROAD (UK)	RILLA	DCA	1957
G3-16	ORDERS ARE ORDERS (UK)	PALTENGHI	DCA	1954
G3-17	MAKE ME AN OFFER (UK)	FRANKEL	DOMINANT	1954
G3-18	NAVY HEROES (UK: BLUE PETER)	RILLA	DCDS	1955
G3-19	LOVE MATCH (UK)	PALTENGHI	BRITISH LION	1955
G-4	DOG HEAVEN (sh)	MCGOWAN	MGM	1927
G-4	READIN' AND WRITIN' (sh)	MCGOWAN	MGM	1932
G-4	START THE SHOW (sh)	ROACH	PATHE EXCHANGE	1920
G-4	WAGES OF TIN (sh)	CLEMENTS	PATHE EXCHANGE	1925
G-5	FREE EATS (sh)	MCCAREY	MGM	1932
G-5	SPOOK SPOOFING (sh)	MCGOWAN	MGM	1928
G-5	TELL IT TO A POLICEMAN (sh)	GUIOL	PATHE EXCHANGE	1925
G6	DEBRA PAGET	portrait	FOX	1950s
G-6	HOLD MY BABY - WHOSE BABY ARE YOU? (sh)	HOWE	PATHE EXCHANGE	1925
G-6	RAINY DAYS (sh)	MCGOWAN, OELZE	MGM	1928
G-6	SPANKY (sh)	MCGOWAN	MGM	1932
G-7	CHOO CHOO (sh)	MCGOWAN	MGM	1932
G-7	EDISON, MARCONI & CO. (sh)	MCGOWAN	MGM	1928
G-7	HAUNTED HONEYMOON (sh)	GUIOL, WILDE	PATHE EXCHANGE	1925
G-8	BARNUM & RINGLING INC. (sh)	MCGOWAN	MGM	1928
G-8	POOCH (sh)	MCGOWAN	MGM	1932
G-8	THUNDERING LANDLORDS (sh)	HORNE	PATHE EXCHANGE	1925
G9	BOB/ROBERT PATTEN	portrait	FOX	
G-9	DADDY GOES A' GRUNTING (sh)	HORNE	PATHE EXCHANGE	1925
G-9	FAIR AND MUDDY (sh)	OELZE	MGM	1928
G-9	HOOK AND LADDER (sh)	MCGOWAN	MGM	1932
G-10	CRAZY HOUSE (sh)	MCGOWAN	MGM	1928
G-10	FREE WHEELING (sh)	MCGOWAN	MGM	1932
G-10	MADAME SANS JANE (sh)	HORNE	PATHE EXCHANGE	1925
G-10	STRUGGLE	GRIFFITH	UNITED ARTISTS	1931
G-11	BIRTHDAY BLUES (sh)	MCGOWAN	MGM	1932
G-11	CUCKOO LOVE (sh)	GUIOL	PATHE EXCHANGE	1925
G-11	GROWING PAINS (sh)	MCGOWAN	MGM	1928
G11	KATHLEEN HUGHES	portrait	FOX	1940s-50s
G-12	A LAD AN' A LAMP (sh)	MCGOWAN	MGM	1932
G-12	OL' GRAY HOSS (sh)	MCGOWAN	MGM	1928
G-12	PAPA, BE GOOD! (sh)	GUIOL	PATHE EXCHANGE	1925
G12	VALENTINA CORTESE	portrait	FOX	1950s
G-13	FISH HOOKY (sh)	MCGOWAN	MGM	1933
G-13	SCHOOL BEGINS (sh)	MCGOWAN	MGM	1928
G-14	FORGOTTEN BABIES (sh)	MCGOWAN	MGM	1933
G14	HELEN WESTCOTT	portrait	FOX	1950s
G-14	SPANKING AGE (sh)	MCGOWAN	MGM	1928
G-15	ELECTION DAY (sh)	MCGOWAN	MGM	1929
G-15	KID FROM BORNEO (sh)	MCGOWAN	MGM	1933
G15	SHARI ROBINSON	portrait	FOX	
G-16	MUSH AND MILK (sh)	MCGOWAN	MGM	1933
G-16	NOISY NOISES (sh)	MCGOWAN	MGM	1929
G-17	BEDTIME WORRIES (sh)	MCGOWAN	MGM	1933
G-17	HOLY TERROR (sh)	MCGOWAN	MGM	1929
G17	TYRONE POWER & LINDA CHRISTIAN	portrait	FOX	
G18	DON HICKS	portrait	FOX	1950s
G-18	WIGGLE YOUR EARS (sh)	MCGOWAN	MGM	1929
G-18	WILD POSES (sh)	MCGOWAN	MGM	1933
G-19	FAST FREIGHT (sh)	MACK	MGM	1929
G-19	HI' NEIGHBOR! (sh)	MEINS	MGM	1934
G-20	FOR PETE'S SAKE! (sh)	MEINS	MGM	1934
G-20	LITTLE MOTHER (sh)	MCGOWAN	MGM	1929
G-21	CAT, DOG & CO. (sh)	MCGOWAN	MGM	1929
G-21	FIRST ROUNDUP (sh)	MEINS	MGM	1934
G-22	HONKY DONKEY (sh)	MEINS	MGM	1934
G-22	SATURDAY'S LESSON (sh)	MCGOWAN	MGM	1929
G-23	MIKE FRIGHT (sh)	MEINS	MGM	1934
G-23	SMALL TALK (sh)	MCGOWAN	MGM	1929
G24	PAUL DOUGLAS	portrait	FOX	1950s
G-24	RAILROADIN' (sh)	MCGOWAN	MGM	1929
G-24	WASHEE IRONEE (sh)	PARROTT	MGM	1934

Movie Still Identification Book Ultimate Edition - Letters

CODE	TITLE/NAME	DIRECTOR/TYPE	STUDIO/DISTRIBUTOR	YEAR
G-25	BOXING GLOVES (sh)	MCGOWAN	MGM	1929
G-25	MAMA'S LITTLE PIRATE (sh)	MEINS	MGM	1935
G25	MICHELINE PRESLE	portrait	FOX	
G-26	LAZY DAYS (sh)	MCGOWAN	MGM	1929
G-26	SHRIMPS FOR A DAY (sh)	MEINS	MGM	1935
G26	THELMA RITTER	portrait	FOX	
G-27	ANNIVERSARY TROUBLE (sh)	MEINS	MGM	1935
G-27	BOUNCING BABIES (sh)	MCGOWAN	MGM	1929
G-27	TRAILIN' TROUBLE (GIBSON)	ROSSON	UNIVERSAL	1930
G-28	BEGINNER'S LUCK (sh)	MEINS	MGM	1935
G28	JOYCE MACKENZIE	portrait	FOX	
G-28	MOAN & GROAN INC. (sh)	MCGOWAN	MGM	1929
G-29	SHIVERING SHAKESPEARE (sh)	MCGOWAN	MGM	1930
G-29	TEACHER'S BEAU (sh)	MEINS	MGM	1935
G-30	FIRST SEVEN YEARS (sh)	MCGOWAN	MGM	1930
G-30	SPRUCIN' UP (sh)	MEINS	MGM	1935
G-31	LUCKY CORNER (sh)	MEINS	MGM	1936
G-31	WHEN THE WIND BLOWS (sh)	HORNE	MGM	1930
G-32	BEAR SHOOTERS (sh)	MCGOWAN	MGM	1930
G-32	LITTLE PAPA (sh)	MEINS	MGM	1935
G-33	LITTLE SINNER (sh)	MEINS	MGM	1935
G-33	TOUGH WINTER (sh)	MCGOWAN	MGM	1930
G-34	OUR GANG FOLLIES OF 1936 (sh)	MEINS	MGM	1935
G-34	PUPS IS PUPS (sh)	MCGOWAN	MGM	1930
G-35	PINCH SINGER (sh)	NEWMEYER	MGM	1936
G-35	TEACHER'S PET (sh)	MCGOWAN	MGM	1930
G-36	DIVOT DIGGERS (sh)	MCGOWAN	MGM	1936
G-36	SCHOOL'S OUT (sh)	MCGOWAN	MGM	1930
G-37	HELPING GRANDMA (sh)	MCGOWAN	MGM	1931
G-37	SECOND CHILDHOOD (sh)	MEINS	MGM	1936
G-38	ARBOR DAY (sh)	NEWMEYER	MGM	1936
G-38	LOVE BUSINESS (sh)	MCGOWAN	MGM	1931
G-39	LITTLE DADDY (sh)	MCGOWAN	MGM	1931
G-39	OUR GANG FOLLIES OF 1938 (sh)	DOUGLAS	MGM	1937
G-40	BARGAIN DAY (sh)	MCGOWAN	MGM	1931
G41	BARBARA BATES	portrait	FOX	1950s
G-41	FLY MY KITE (sh)	MCGOWAN	MGM	1931
G-42	FLAME OF LOVE (UK: ROAD TO DISHONOUR)	EICHBERG, SUMMERS	BRITISH INTERNATIONAL	1930
G52	SUSAN HAYWARD	portrait	FOX	
G54	DELMER DAVES	portrait	FOX	
G57	CRAIG HILL	portrait	FOX	1950s
G59	GENE TIERNEY	portrait	FOX	1950s
G60	BETTY GRABLE	portrait	FOX	1950s
G61	JEANNE CRAIN	portrait	FOX	1950s
G63	ANN SHERIDAN	portrait	FOX	
G64	ROBERT WAGNER	portrait	FOX	1950s
G69	MITZI GAYNOR	portrait	FOX	1953
G79	LOUIS JOURDAN	portrait		
G83	DAVID WAYNE	portrait	FOX	1940s-60s
G85	PATRICIA OWENS	portrait	FOX	1950's
G-90	EARTHBOUND	HUNTER	GOLDWYN	1920
G92	JEFFREY HUNTER	portrait	FOX	1950s
G95	GLENN FORD	portrait	FOX	1950s
G103	ANNE FRANCIS	portrait	FOX	1950s
G108	RORY CALHOUN	portrait	FOX	1950s
G110	CHARLOTTE AUSTIN	portrait	FOX	1950s
G115	MICHAEL RENNIE	portrait	FOX	
G-118	GALLIPOLI	WEIR	PARAMOUNT	1981
G119	JOANNE DRU	portrait	FOX	1950s
G126	ANNE BANCROFT	portrait	FOX	1950s
G126	GORILLA AT LARGE	JONES	20th CENTURY FOX	1954
G127	HILDEGARDE NEFF (aka HILDEGARD KNEF)	portrait	FOX	early 50s
G134	CASEY ADAMS (aka MAX SHOWALTER)	portrait	FOX	1950s
G135	GLORIA GORDON	portrait	FOX	1950s
G138	PENNY EDWARDS	portrait	FOX	1950s
G140	CARY GRANT	portrait	FOX	1950s
G142	CAMERON MITCHELL	portrait	FOX	1950s-60s
G145	SCOTT BRADY	portrait	FOX	
G147	MARISA PAVAN	portrait	FOX	
G150	GEORGE WINSLOW	portrait	FOX	1950's

Movie Still Identification Book Ultimate Edition - Letters

CODE	TITLE/NAME	DIRECTOR/TYPE	STUDIO/DISTRIBUTOR	YEAR
G151	TERRY MOORE	portrait	FOX	1950's
G156	RICHARD BURTON	portrait	FOX	1950s
G161	BELLA DARVI	portrait	FOX	1950s
G167	LAUREN BACALL	portrait	FOX	
G168	VIRGINIA LEITH	portrait	FOX	
G169	MAGGIE MCNAMARA	portrait	FOX	
G174	SHEREE NORTH	portrait	FOX	1950's
G176	RITA MORENO	portrait	FOX	1950s
G177	JEAN SIMMONS	portrait	FOX	1950s
G182	LESLIE PARRISH (aka MARJORIE/MARGARET HELLEN)	portrait	FOX	mid-50s
G183	JOAN COLLINS	portrait	FOX	1950's
G183	RALLY 'ROUND THE FLAG, BOYS	MCCAREY	20th CENTURY FOX	1958
G184	RICHARD EGAN	portrait	FOX	1955
G185	HUGH O'BRIAN	portrait	FOX	1950s
G186	BARRY COE	portrait	FOX	1950s
G188	JOANNE WOODWARD	portrait	FOX	1950's
G189	DANA WYNTER	portrait	FOX	1950's
G192	SHIRLEY JONES	portrait	FOX	1950's
G193	KIPP HAMILTON	portrait	FOX	1950s
G196	RUBEN FUENTES	portrait	FOX	1950s
G197	BUDDY ADLER	portrait	FOX	1950s
G201	GUY MADISON	portrait	FOX	1956
G203	RICK JASON	portrait	FOX	1950s
G206	JENNIFER JONES	portrait	FOX	1950s-60s
G207	LILI GENTLE	portrait	FOX	1950s
G208	JANE RUSSELL	portrait	FOX	1950s
G212	JOSHUA LOGAN	portrait	FOX	1950s
G214	BARBARA RUSH	portrait	FOX	
G216	DON MURRAY	portrait	FOX	
G217	GORDON MACRAE	portrait	FOX	
G219	PATRICIA OWENS	portrait	FOX	1950s
G220	JERRY WALD	portrait	FOX	1950s-60s
G222	HOPE LANGE	portrait	FOX	1950s-60s
G225	KENDALL SCOTT	portrait	FOX	late 50s
G231	DIANE JERGENS	portrait	FOX	1950s
G232	JAYNE MANSFIELD	portrait	FOX	1950s
G234	ALENA MURRAY	portrait	FOX	1950's
G237	PATRICIA OWENS	portrait	FOX	1950's
G237	PATRICIA POWELL (SAME # AS PATRICIA OWENS)	portrait	FOX	1950's
G238	DEBORAH KERR	portrait	FOX	1950s
G242	DOLORES MICHAELS	portrait	FOX	1950s-60s
G244	ANNEMARIE DURINGER (aka ANNA DURRINGER)	portrait	FOX	1950s
G248	TAMI CONNER	portrait	FOX	late 50s
G254	MAY BRITT	portrait	FOX	1950s
G255	DAVID HEDISON	portrait	FOX	
G257	SUZY PARKER	portrait	FOX	1950s
G259	STEPHEN BOYD	portrait	FOX	1950s
G261	CHRISTINE CARERE (CARRERE)	portrait	FOX	1950s-60s
G262	TONY RANDAL	portrait		
G263	PAT BOONE	portrait	FOX	1950s
G269	BRADFORD DILLMAN	portrait	FOX	1950's
G274	JUNE BLAIR	portrait	FOX	1959
G275	JO MORROW	portrait	FOX	1950's
G282	KATHLEEN GALLANT	portrait	FOX	1950's
G283	DIANE VARSI	portrait	FOX	
G285	NINA SHIPMAN	portrait	FOX	1950s
G287	DIANE BAKER	portrait	FOX	1950's
G288	ROBERT EVANS	portrait	FOX	1950's
G291	JILL ST JOHN	portrait	FOX	1950's
G294	ROBERT MITCHUM	portrait	FOX	
G295	LEE REMICK	portrait	FOX	1950s
G300	STUART WHITMAN	portrait	FOX	1950's
G301	STELLA STEVENS	portrait	FOX	1950s
G303	CAROL LYNLEY	portrait	FOX	1950s
G306	GARDNER MCKAY	portrait	FOX	1959
G309	TUESDAY WELD	portrait	FOX	1950s-70s
G310	BARBARA EDEN	portrait	FOX	1950s
G313	RICHARD BEYMER	portrait	FOX	1950s
G319	LUCIANA PALUZZI	portrait	FOX	1960
G320	LINDA HUTCHINGS	portrait	FOX	1960s

Movie Still Identification Book Ultimate Edition - Letters

CODE	TITLE/NAME	DIRECTOR/TYPE	STUDIO/DISTRIBUTOR	YEAR
G325	MARTHA HYER	portrait	FOX	1950s-60s
G327	MARGO MOORE	portrait	FOX	1950s-60s
G330	ELANA EDEN	portrait	FOX	1960s
G334	FABIAN	portrait	FOX	
G336	TOM TRYON	portrait	FOX	1960s
G337	DEAN STOCKWELL	portrait	FOX	
G339	ANNE BENTON	portrait	FOX	1960s
G342	CAROL CHRISTENSEN	portrait	FOX	1960s
G344	ANN DEL GUERCIO	portrait	FOX	
G349	BARBARA STEELE	portrait	FOX	1960s
G364	RAFER JOHNSON	portrait	FOX	1960's
G376	ANN-MARGRET	portrait	FOX	1960s
G380	BARRIE CHASE	portrait	FOX	1960s
G382	NANCY PRIEST	portrait	FOX	1960s
G406	PAMELA TIFFIN	portrait	FOX	1960s
G407	DOLORES HART	portrait	FOX	1960s
G412	FRANKLIN J. SCHAFFNER	portrait	FOX	1960s-70s
G428	RAQUEL WELCH	portrait	FOX	
G459	JACQUELINE BISSET	portrait	FOX	1960s
G460	HAMPTON FANCHER	portrait	FOX	
G468	ELAINE DEVRY	portrait	FOX	
GA	GABY ANDRE	portrait	WARNER BROS	
GA	GATOR	REYNOLDS	UNITED ARTISTS	1976
GA	GENE AUTRY	portrait		
GA	GEORGE ARLISS	portrait	WARNER BROS	
GA	GOLDEN ARROW	GREEN	WARNER BROS	1936
GA	GOODBYE AGAIN	CURTIZ	WARNER BROS	1933
GA	GRACIE ALLEN	portrait	RKO	late 30s
GA	GWILI ANDRE	portrait	RKO	
G-AB	ANYBODY'S BLONDE	STRAYER	ACTION	1931
GABY	GABY	MANDOKI	TRI STAR	1987
GAC	GOLDEN AGE OF COMEDY	YOUNGSON	DCA	1958
GAC	GREAT ARMORED CAR SWINDLE (UK: BREAKING POINT)	COMFORT	FALCON	1964
GAL-1	NIX ON DAMES	GALLAHER	FOX FILM	1929
GAN	BADGE OF MARSHALL BRENNAN	GANNAWAY	ALLIED ARTISTS	1957
GANG	GANG WAR	FOWLER	20th CENTURY FOX	1958
GANG	GANG WAR	MARSHALL	UNITED ARTISTS	1962
GAP	40 GUNS TO APACHE PASS	WITNEY	COLUMBIA	1967
GAS	GIRLS AT SEA (UK)	GUNN	SEVEN ARTS	1958
GAY	GAY PUREE (t)	LEVITOW	WARNER BROS	1962
GB	GABY	MANDOKI	TRI STAR	1987
GB	GANGBUSTERS	KARN	VISUAL DRAMA	1954
GB	GENEVIEVE BUJOLD	portrait	UNIVERSAL	
GB	GEORGE BEBAN JR	portrait	UNIVERSAL	
GB	GEORGE BRENT	portrait	UNIVERSAL, WARNER BROS	
GB	GERALDINE BROOKS	portrait	UNIVERSAL, WARNER BROS	
GB	GLORIA BLONDELL	portrait	WARNER BROS	
GB	GLORIOUS BETSY	CROSLAND	WARNER BROS	1928
GB	GO BETWEEN (UK)	LOSEY	COLUMBIA	1970
GB	GRETA BALDWIN	portrait	PARAMOUNT`	
GB	GUNS AT BATASI (UK)	GUILLERMIN	20th CENTURY FOX	1964
GB	HAPPINESS AHEAD	LEROY	WARNER BROS	1934
GB	IT'S TOUGH TO BE FAMOUS	GREEN	WARNER BROS	1932
GB	LOOKING FOR MR. GOODBAR	BROOKS	PARAMOUNT	1977
GB	MILLIONAIRE PLAYBOY	GOODWINS	RKO	1940
GB	TOMORROW AT TEN (UK)	COMFORT	GOVERNOR	1965
GB	WILD HEART (UK: GONE TO EARTH)	POWELL, PRESSBURGER	RKO	1952
GBA	GOODBYE AGAIN	LITVAK	UNITED ARTISTS	1961
GBBB	GUN IN BETTY LOU'S HANDBAG	MOYLE	BUENA VISTA	1992
GBF	GREAT BALLS OF FIRE	MCBRIDE	ORION	1989
GBS	GIRL IN BLACK STOCKINGS	KOCH	UNITED ARTISTS	1957
GC	CAPTAIN THUNDER	CROSLAND	WARNER BROS	1930
GC	GARY CROSBY	portrait	FOX	
GC	GENE CORMAN	portrait	FOX	
GC	GENERAL CRACK	CROSLAND	WARNER BROS	1930
GC	GEORGE CLEVELAND	portrait	RKO	
GC	GEORGE COOPER	portrait	MGM	
GC	GEORGIA CARROLL	portrait	WARNER BROS	
GC	GET CARTER (UK)	HODGES	MGM	1971
GC	GHOST CAMERA (UK)	VORHAUS	OLYMPIC	1933

Movie Still Identification Book Ultimate Edition - Letters

CODE	TITLE/NAME	DIRECTOR/TYPE	STUDIO/DISTRIBUTOR	YEAR
GC	GINGER CROWLEY	portrait	WARNER BROS.	
GC	GIRL CRAZY	SEITER	RKO	1932
GC	GIRL OF THE CANAL (UK: PAINTED BOATS)	CRICHTON	AFE	1945
GC	GLADYS COOPER	portrait	UNITED ARTISTS	
GC	GO CHASE YOURSELF	CLINE	RKO	1938
GC	GOLDEN CIRCLE (YOUNG ACTORS)	portrait	PARAMOUNT	
GC	GOLDEN COCOON	WEBB	WARNER BROS	1925
GC	GOODBYE, COLUMBUS	PEERCE	PARAMOUNT	1969
GC	GRAND CANYON	LANDRES	LIPPERT	1949
GC	GRAND CANYON	KASDAN	20th CENTURY FOX	1991
GC	GREAT CATHERINE (UK)	FLEMYNG	WARNER BROS	1969
GC	GRETA CHRISTENSEN	portrait	RKO	
GC	MIDSHIPMAN JACK	CABANNE	RKO	1933
GC	VALLEY OF THE REDWOODS	WITNEY	20th CENTURY FOX	1960
GD	CHRISTOPHER STRONG	ARZNER	RKO	1933
GD	DARING DESPERADOES (GAY DESPERADO 1936)	MAMOULIAN	FAVORITE FILM	R47
GD	GALLOPING DYNAMITE	FRASER	AMBASSADOR	1937
GD	GAME OF DEATH (HK)	CLOUSE	COLUMBIA	1978
GD	GAY DESPERADO	MAMOULIAN	UNITED ARTISTS	1936
GD	GAY DIVORCEE	SANDRICH	RKO	1934
GD	GAY DOG (UK)	ELVEY	EROS	1954
GD	GEORGE DOLENZ	portrait	UNIVERSAL	
GD	GHOST DIVER	WHITE	20th CENTURY FOX	1957
GD	GILDERSLEEVE'S GHOST	DOUGLAS	RKO	1944
GD	GLORIA DICKSON	portrait	WARNER BROS	
GD	GOLD DUST GERTIE	BACON	WARNER BROS	1931
GD	GOLDDIGGERS		WARNER BROS	1929
GD	GOLDDIGGERS IN PARIS	ENRIGHT	WARNER BROS	1938
GD	GOLDDIGGERS OF 1933	BERKELEY	WARNER BROS	1933
GD	GOLDDIGGERS OF 1935	BERKELEY	WARNER BROS	1935
GD	GOLDDIGGERS OF 1937	BACON	WARNER BROS	1936
GD	GOLDEN DAWN	ENRIGHT	WARNER BROS	1930
GD	GREAT DAY (UK)	COMFORT	RKO	1946
GD	GREAT DICTATOR	CHAPLIN	UNITED ARTISTS	1940
GD	GUESS WHO'S COMING TO DINNER	KRAMER	COLUMBIA	1967
GD	GUN DUEL AT DURANGO	SALKOW	UNITED ARTISTS	1957
GD	GUN THE MAN DOWN	MCLAGLEN	UNITED ARTISTS	1956
GD	GUNGA DIN	STEVENS	RKO	1939
GD	INBETWEEN-AGE (UK: GOLDEN DISC)	SHARP	MONOGRAM	1958
GD	IT'S IN THE BAG (UK)	MASON	BUTCHER'S	1944
GD	LOVE IS A BALL	SWIFT	UNITED ARTISTS	1963
GD	SOME GIRLS DO (UK)	THOMAS	UNITED ARTISTS	1969
GD	WANTED – JANE TURNER	KILLY	RKO	1936
GD II	GODFATHER 2	COPPOLA	PARAMOUNT	1974
GD-3027	GALLOPING THUNDER	NAZARRO	COLUMBIA	1946
GDH	GLORIA DEHAVEN	portrait	UNIVERSAL	
GDM	GREAT DAY IN THE MORNING	TOURNEUR	RKO	1956
GE	GENE EVANS	portrait		
GE	GERALDINE FITZGERALD	portrait	WARNER BROS	
GE	GOLDEN ERA PRODUCTIONS (UK)	studio		
GE	GOLDENEYE	CAMPBELL	UNITED ARTISTS	1995
GE	GREAT ESCAPE	STURGES	UNITED ARTISTS	1963
GE	GREEN EYES	THORPE	CHESTERFIELD	1934
GE3	CHILD IN THE HOUSE (UK)	ENDFIELD	EROS	1956
GEF	WAR IS OVER (FR: GUERRE EST FINIE)	RESNEIS	BRANDON FILMS	1966
GERT	GERTRUDE MICHAEL	portrait	WARNER BROS	
GES	GEORGE E. STONE	portrait	WARNER BROS	
GF	GAY FALCON	REIS	RKO	1941
GF	GERALDINE FITZGERALD	portrait	UNIVERSAL	
GF	GIRL FEVER	PRICE	GENERAL SCREEN	1961
GF	GIRLFRIENDS	WEILL	WARNER BROS	1978
GF	GIRL IN THE FLAT (UK)	DAVIS	PARAMOUNT BRITISH	1934
GF	GLENDA FARRELL	portrait	WARNER BROS	
GF	GODFATHER	COPPOLA	PARAMOUNT	1972
GF	GOLD FEVER	GOODWINS	MONOGRAM	1952
GF	GOODFELLAS	SCORSESE	WARNER BROS	1990
GF	GRACE FORD	portrait	MGM	
GF	GUN FEVER	STEVENS	UNITED ARTISTS	1958
GF	GUNFIGHTERS OF ABILENE	CAHN	UNITED ARTISTS	1960
GF	POSSESSORS (FR: LES GRANDES FAMILIES 1958)	PATELLIERE	LOPERT	1959

Movie Still Identification Book Ultimate Edition - Letters

CODE	TITLE/NAME	DIRECTOR/TYPE	STUDIO/DISTRIBUTOR	YEAR
GF1	WEE GEORDIE (UK: GEORDIE)	LAUNDER	TIMES	1955
GF II	GODFATHER II	COPPOLA	PARAMOUNT	1974
GF-2800	LOCKED DOOR	FITZMAURICE	UNITED ARTISTS	1929
GF-4000	BAD ONE	FITZMAURICE	UNITED ARTISTS	1930
GFD	GIGANTIS THE FIRE MONSTER (JAP)	ODA	WARNER BROS	1959
GFM	GIGANTIS THE FIRE MONSTER	ODA	WARNER BROS	1959
GG	FLIGHT TO NOWHERE	ROWLAND	SCREEN GUILD	1946
GG	GAILY, GAILY	JEWISON	UNITED ARTISTS	1969
GG	GENTLE GIANT	NEILSON	PARAMOUNT	1967
GG	GEORGIE GIRL	NARIZZANO	COLUMBIA	1966
GG	GHOST GOES WEST (UK)	CLAIR	UNITED ARTISTS	1935
GG	GIANT GILA MONSTER	KELLOGG	McLENDON	1959
GG	GIRL GANGS	BROOKS		1952
GG	GLORIA GRAHAME	portrait	RKO	
GG	GLORY GUYS	LAVEN	UNITED ARTISTS	1965
GG	GO-GETTER	BERKELEY	WARNER BROS	1937
GG	GOOSE AND THE GANDER	GREEN	WARNER BROS	1935
GG	GORDON GEBERT	portrait	RKO	
GG	GOVERNMENT GIRL	NICHOLS	RKO	1943
GG	GRANNY GET YOUR GUN	AMY	WARNER BROS	1940
GG	GREAT GABBO	CRUZE	SONO ART (Worldwide Pic)	1929
GG	GREAT GARRICK	WHALE	WARNER BROS	1937
GG	GREAT GATSBY	CLAYTON	PARAMOUNT	1974
GG	GREEN GLOVE (GAUNTLET)	MATE	UNITED ARTISTS	1952
GG	GREEN GODDESS	GREEN	WARNER BROS	1930
GG	GUN TO GUN (sh)	LEDERMAN	WARNER BROS	1944
GG	GYPSY GIRL (UK: SKY WEST AND CROOKED)	MILLS	CONTINENTAL	1965
GG	MAN WITH THE GOLDEN GUN	HAMILTON	UNITED ARTISTS	1974
GG	MILLIONAIRE FOR CHRISTY	MARSHALL	20th CENTURY FOX	1951
GG	PEDRO GONZALEZ GONZALEZ	portrait	WARNER BROS	
GG	PRIDE OF THE BLUEGRASS	MCGANN	WARNER BROS	1939
GG	SCARED TO DEATH	CABANNE	SCREEN GUILD	1947
GG-8	MY DOG SHEP	BEEBE	SCREEN GUILD	1946
GGE	GIRL-GETTERS (UK: SYSTEM)	WINNER	AIP	1964
GGE	GIRL WITH GREEN EYES [US: LOPERT]	DAVIS	UNITED ARTISTS	1964
GGG	GORE GORE GIRLS	LEWIS	LEWIS	1972
GGG	GUNS, GIRLS, AND GANGSTERS	CAHN	UNITED ARTISTS	1959
GGP	GIRL FROM GAY PAREE	GOLDSTONE, GREGOR	TIFFANY	1927
GGW	GIRL OF THE GOLDEN WEST (IT)	KOCH	FIRST NATIONAL	1930
GGW	GOD'S GIFT TO WOMEN	CURTIZ	WARNER BROS	1931
GGX	GRETA GARBO	portrait	MGM	
GH	GALLANT HOURS	MONTGOMERY	UNITED ARTISTS	1960
GH	GAYLE HUNNICUTT	portrait	UNIVERSAL	
GH	GEORGE "GABBY" HAYES	portrait		
GH	GEORGE HOUSTON MOVIES (LONE RIDER series)	portrait	PRC	
GH	GIRL HUNTERS (UK)	ROWLAND	COLORAMA	1963
GH	GLASS HOUSES	SINGER	COLUMBIA	1972
GH	GORDON HART	portrait	WARNER BROS	
GH	LITTLE MISS REBELLION	FAWCETT	PARAMOUNT	1920
GH	MONSTER FROM GREEN HELL	CRANE	DCA	1957
GH-19	LONE RIDER IN CHEYENNE	NEWFIELD	PRC	1942
GH-70	LONE RIDER IN FRONTIER FURY	NEWFIELD	PRC	1941
GH-124	GRASSHOPPER	PARIS	NAT'L GENERAL	1970
GHL-108	IMPORTANT WITNESS	NEWFIELD	CAPITOL (states rights)	1933
GHW	GREAT MR. HANDEL (UK)	WALKER	MIDFILM	1942
GHW3	HARD STEEL (UK)	WALKER	GFD	1942
GI	GRAND ILLUSION (FR)	RENOIR	CONTINENTAL	R56
GI	WHITE HUNTRESS (UK: GOLDEN IVORY)	BREAKSTON	AIP	1954
G-II	GREASE 2	BIRCH	PARAMOUNT	1982
GIJ	G. I. JANE	LE BORG	LIPPERT	1951
GIO	GAME IS OVER (FR)	VADIM	COLUMBIA	1966
GIS	DANCERS	ROSS	CANNON	1987
GIT	GIRL IN TROUBLE	CHASE	MPA	1963
GJ	GENTLEMAN JIM	WALSH	WARNER BROS	1942
GJ	GLORIA JEAN	portrait	UNIVERSAL	1930s-40s
GJ	GREAT JASPER	RUBEN	RKO	1933
GK	CHARLES KORVIN aka GEORGE KORVIN	portrait	UNIV	
GK	DESTINATION 60,000	WAGGNER	ALLIED ARTISTS	1957
GK	FORBIDDEN (UK)	KING	BRITISH LION	1949
GK	GARSON KANIN	portrait	RKO	1930s-40s

Movie Still Identification Book Ultimate Edition - Letters

CODE	TITLE/NAME	DIRECTOR/TYPE	STUDIO/DISTRIBUTOR	YEAR
GK	GENE KELLY	portrait	MGM	
GK	GENE KRUPA	portrait	MCA RECORDS	
GK	GENGHIS KHAN	CONDE, SALVADOR	UNITED ARTISTS	1950
GK	GENGHIS KHAN (UK)	LEVIN	COLUMBIA	1965
GK	GEORGE KENNEDY	portrait	UNIV	
GK	GEORGIA KING aka ANDREA KING	portrait	WARNER BROS	
GK	GUY KIBBEE	portrait	WARNER BROS	
GK	ROMANCE AND RICHES (UK: AMAZING QUEST ERNEST BLISS)	ZEISLER	GRAND NATIONAL	1936
GK1	SHOWTIME (UK: GAIETY GIRLS)	KING, SAGAN	ENGLISH	1946
G-K-3	PLEASURE CRAZED	GALLAHER, KLEIN	FOX FILM	1929
GKA	GEORGE K ARTHUR	portrait	MGM	
GL	ATTACK OF THE GIANT LEECHES	KOWALSKI	AIP	1959
GL	FRONTIER GAMBLER	NEWFIELD	ASSOCIATED FILM RELEASING	1956
GL	GAMBLING LADY	MAYO	WARNER BROS	1934
GL	GASLIGHT (UK)	DICKINSON	COMMERCIAL	1940
GL	GENE LOCKHART	portrait	WARNER BROS	
GL	GIANT LEECHES	KOWALSKI	AIP	1959
GL	GINA LOLLOBRIGIDA	portrait	UNIVERSAL	
GL	GIRL MUST LIVE (UK)	REED	UNIVERSAL	1939
GL	GREEN LIGHT	BORZAGE	WARNER BROS	1937
GL	GREYHOUND LIMITED	BRETHERTON	WARNER BROS	1929
GL	GUN LAW	DE LACEY	RKO	1929
GL	GUN LAW	HOWARD	RKO	1938
GL	GWEN LEE	portrait	MGM	
GL	GWYNETH LLOYD	portrait	GAUMONT BRITISH	
GL	LUCKY PARTNERS	MILESTONE	RKO	1940
GLA	GOD'S LITTLE ACRE	MANN	UNITED ARTISTS	1958
GLC	GREGORY LACAVA	portrait	UNIVERSAL	
GM	GABLES MYSTERY (UK)	HUGHES	MGM	1938
GM	GALLOPING MAJOR (UK)	CORNELIUS	SOUVAINE SELECTIVE	1951
GM	GAR MOORE	portrait	UNIVERSAL	
GM	GARDEN OF THE MOON	BERKELEY	WARNER BROS	1938
GM	GEORGE MINTER PRODUCTIONS (UK)	studio		
GM	GEORGE MURPHY	portrait	RKO	
GM	GERTRUDE MICHAEL	portrait	RKO	
GM	GIRL ON A MOTORCYCLE (UK)	CARDIFF	WARNER BROS	1968
GM	GIVE HER THE MOON (FR)	DE BROCA	UNITED ARTISTS	1970
GM	GLASS MOUNTAIN (UK)	CASS	EAGLE-LION	1949
GM	G-MEN	KEIGHLEY	WARNER BROS	1935
GM	GOLDEN MADONNA (UK)	CARPENTIERI, VAJDA	STRATFORD	1949
GM	GOLDFINGER (UK)	HAMILTON	UNITED ARTISTS	1964
GM	GOOD MORNING, BOYS (UK)	VARNEL	GAUMONT BRITISH	1937
GM	GORDON MACRAE	portrait	WARNER BROS	
GM	GRACE MCDONALD	portrait	UNIVERSAL	
GM	GRACE MOORE	portrait	MGM	
GM	GREEN MAN (UK)	DAY	DCA	1956
GM	GREG MCCLURE	portrait	UNITED ARTISTS	mid 40s
GM	GREGG MARTELL	portrait	UNIVERSAL	
GM	GUNS OF THE MAGNIFICENT SEVEN	WENDKOS	UNITED ARTISTS	1969
GM	GUY MADISON	portrait	RKO, SELZNICK	
GM	GUY MADISON	portrait		
GM	IT'S LOVE I'M AFTER	MAYO	WARNER BROS	1937
GM	OUTLAW'S SON (GAMBLING MAN) (HIS FATHER'S SON)	SELANDER	UNITED ARTISTS	1957
GM	SECOND WIFE	KILLY	RKO	1936
GM	GHOST IN THE MACHINE	TALALAY	20th CENTURY FOX	1993
GM2	IT'S A WONDERFUL WORLD (UK)	GUEST	JOSEPH BRENNER	1956
GMC	GIANNA MARIA CANALE	portrait		
GMc	GRACE MCDONALD	portrait	UNIVERSAL	1940s
GMG	GO MAN GO	HOWE	UNITED ARTISTS	1954
GML	GIRL MOST LIKELY	LEISEN	RKO	1958
GMX	GERTRUDE MICHAEL	portrait	MGM	
GN	GEORGE NADER	portrait	UNIVERSAL	
GN	GERTRUDE NIESEN (aka GERTRUDE NESSEN)	portrait		
GN	GIRL IN THE NEWS (UK)	REED	20TH CENTURY FOX	1940
GN	GUNPLAY	SELANDER	RKO	1951
GN	HANDS OF A STRANGER	ARNOLD	ALLIED ARTISTS	1962
GND	GIRL NEXT DOOR	HONG	COLUMBIA	1978
GO	GERTRUDE OLMSTEAD	portrait	MGM	
GO	GIRLS OF THE NIGHT	CLOCHE	CONTINENTAL	1959
GO	GORDON OLIVER	portrait	WARNER BROS	

- 150 -

Movie Still Identification Book Ultimate Edition - Letters

CODE	TITLE/NAME	DIRECTOR/TYPE	STUDIO/DISTRIBUTOR	YEAR
GO	GORGO (UK)	LOURIE	MGM	1961
GO	GORP	RUBEN	AIP	1980
GO	IMPASSE	BENEDICT	UNITED ARTISTS	1969
GO1	TO HELL WITH HITLER (UK: LET GEORGE DO IT!)	VARNEL	FILM ALLIANCE	1940
GOB	GEORGE O'BRIEN	portrait	RKO	
GOB	GIRL ON THE BOAT (UK)	KAPLAN	UNITED ARTISTS	1961
GOG	GOG	STROCK	UNITED ARTISTS	1954
GOG	GUNMEN OF RIO GRANDE (SP)	DEMICHELI	MONOGRAM	1965
GON	GOLD OF NAPLES (IT: L'ORO DI NAPOLI)	DE SICA	DCA	1954
GOTP	GIRL OF THE PORT	GLENNON	RKO	1929
GOW	GUNS OF HATE	SELANDER	RKO	1948
GP	BREAKFAST IN HOLLYWOOD	SCHUSTER	UNITED ARTISTS	1946
GP	CAESAR AND CLEOPATRA (UK)	PASCAL	UNITED ARTISTS	1945
GP	CANNON FOR CORDOBA	WENDKOS	UNITED ARTISTS	1970
GP	GAIL PATRICK	portrait	RKO	
GP	GALE PAGE	portrait		
GP	GEORGE PEPPARD	portrait	PARAMOUNT`	
GP	GERALDINE PAGE	portrait	PARAMOUNT`	
GP	GIGI PERREAU	portrait	UNIVERSAL	
GP	GIRLS IN PRISON	CAHN	AIP	1956
GP	GIRLS ON PROBATION	MCGANN	WARNER BROS	1938
GP	GOD IS MY PARTNER	CLAXTON	20th CENTURY FOX	1957
GP	GOING PLACES	ENRIGHT	WARNER BROS	1938
GP	GOLDEN PICTURES			
GP	GRAND PRIX	FRANKENHEIMER	MGM	1967
GP	GREEN PASTURES	CONNELLY, KEIGHLEY	WARNER BROS	1936
GP	GREGORY PECK	portrait	RKO, UNIV	
GP	GUEST WIFE	WOOD	UNITED ARTISTS	1945
GP	GUN BROTHERS	SALKOW	UNITED ARTISTS	1956
GP	MONSTER THAT CHALLENGED THE WORLD	LAVEN	UNITED ARTISTS	1957
GP	MY KID OF A FATHER (FR: MON GOSSE DE PERE)	DE LIMUR	CAPITOL	1930
GP	NEW WINE	SCHUNZEL	UNITED ARTISTS	1941
GP	NUN AND THE SERGEANT	ADREON	UNITED ARTISTS	1962
GP	OUT OF THE FOG	LITVAK	WARNER BROS	1941
GP-7	GHOST PATROL	NEWFIELD	PURITAN	1936
GP-101	BREAKFAST IN HOLLYWOOD	SCHUSTER	UNITED ARTISTS	1946
GP/CP	OUTSIDER (UK: GUINEA PIG)	BOULTING	BALLANTINE	1948
GR	GENE RAYMOND	portrait	RKO	
GR	GENERAL DELLA ROVERE (IT: IL GENERALE DELLA ROVERE)	ROSSELLINI	CONTINENTAL	1959
GR	GEORGE RAFT	portrait	UNIV	
GR	GIDGET GOES TO ROME	WENDKOS	COLUMBIA	1963
GR	GILBERT ROLAND	portrait	MGM, RKO	
GR	GINGER ROGERS	portrait	RKO	1930s-40s
GR	GINGER ROGERS	portrait	UNIVERSAL	1930s-50s
GR	GINGER ROGERS	portrait	WARNER BROS	1930s-50s
GR	GIRL RUSH	DOUGLAS	RKO	1945
GR	GOLD RUSH	CHAPLIN	UNITED ARTISTS	1925
GR	GOLDFINGER (UK)	HAMILTON	UNITED ARTISTS	1964
GR	GREASE	KLEISER	PARAMOUNT	1978
GR	GUN SMUGGLERS	MCDONALD	RKO	1949
GR-5201	GREASE	KLEISER	PARAMOUNT	1978
GRA	GRADUATE	NICHOLS	AVCO EMBASSY	1968
GRB	SEPTEMBER STORM	HASKIN	20th CENTURY FOX	1960
GRC	SKY GIANT	LANDERS	RKO	1938
GRH	GIRL WITH THE RED HAIR (NETH)	VERBONG	UNITED ARTISTS	1981
GRI	GRISBI (FR: TOUCHEZ PAS AU GRISBI)	BECKER	UMPO	1954
GRIF-5	DEVILISH ROMEO	GRIFFIN	FOX FILM	1921
GRL	GYPSY ROSE LEE	portrait	AMERICAN INTER'L TV	
GRM	GRUMPIER OLD MEN	DEUTCH	WARNER BROS	1995
GRS	REFORM SCHOOL GIRL	BERNDS	AIP	1957
GS	CAST A GIANT SHADOW	SHAVELSON	UNITED ARTISTS	1966
GS	FOG OVER FRISCO	DIETERLE	WARNER BROS	1934
GS	GALE SONDERGAARD	portrait	WARNER BROS	
GS	GALE STORM	portrait		
GS	GAMBLING ON THE HIGH SEAS	AMY	WARNER BROS	1940
GS	GANG (UK: GANG SHOW)	GOULDING	SYNDICATE	1938
GS	GARDENS OF STONE	COPPOLA	TRI STAR	1987
GS	GAY SISTERS	RAPPER	WARNER BROS	1942
GS	GEORGE SANDERS	portrait	RKO	
GS	GEORGE SEATON	portrait	PARAMOUNT`	

Movie Still Identification Book Ultimate Edition - Letters

CODE	TITLE/NAME	DIRECTOR/TYPE	STUDIO/DISTRIBUTOR	YEAR
GS	GETTING STRAIGHT	RUSH	COLUMBIA	1970
GS	GHOST SHIP	ROBSON	RKO	1943
GS	GIA SCALA	portrait	COL, UNIVERSAL	
GS	GIMME SHELTER	MAYSLES	20th CENTURY FOX	1970
GS	GLORIA STUART	portrait	UNIVERSAL	1930s-40s
GS	GLORIA SWANSON	portrait	RKO, UNITED ARTISTS	
GS	GLORIA SWANSON PRODUCTIONS	studio	UNITED ARTISTS	
GS	GOIN' SOUTH	NICHOLSON	PARAMOUNT	1978
GS	GOOD SAM	MCCAREY	RKO	1948
GS	GOOD SON	RUBEN	20th CENTURY FOX	1993
GS	GRAND SLAM	DIETERLE	WARNER BROS	1933
GS	GRAVEYARD SHIFT	SINGLETON	PARAMOUNT	1990
GS	GREAT SIOUX MASSACRE	SALKOW	COLUMBIA	1965
GS	GREATEST STORY EVER TOLD	STEVENS	UNITED ARTISTS	1965
GS	GUMSHOE	FREARS	COLUMBIA	1971
GS	MUSS 'EM UP	VIDOR	RKO	1936
GS	TAKE A GIANT STEP	LEACOCK	UNITED ARTISTS	1959
GS	TEN DAYS TO TULARA	SHERMAN	UNITED ARTISTS	1958
GS	THERE'S A GIRL IN MY SOUP (UK)	BOULTING	COLUMBIA	1970
GS	THIRD TIME LUCKY (UK)	PARRY	PENTAGON	1949
GS	TOO MANY WIVES	HOLMES	RKO	1937
GS-200	SADIE THOMPSON	WALSH	UNITED ARTISTS	1928
GS-5500	INDISCREET	MCCAREY	UNITED ARTISTS	1931
GS-6700	TONIGHT OR NEVER	LEROY	UNITED ARTISTS	1931
GS-A	QUEEN KELLY (1932)	VON STROHEIM	UNITED ARTISTS (Swanson)	1950
GS-A	TRESPASSER	GOULDING	UNITED ARTISTS	1929
GS-A	WHAT A WIDOW!	DWAN	UNITED ARTISTS	1930
GSH	GHOST OF DRAGSTRIP HOLLOW	HOLE JR.	AIP	1959
GSI	GIANT SPIDER INVASION	REBANE	GROUP 1	1975
GSL	GREAT ST. LOUIS BANK ROBBERY	GUGGENHEIM	UNITED ARTISTS	1959
GSM	GREAT SIOUX MASSACRE	SALKOW	COLUMBIA	1965
GSO	GOOSE STEPS OUT (UK)	DEARDEN, HAY	ABFD	1942
GSP	GAMES SCHOOLGIRLS PLAY (GER)	NACHMANN	SUNSET INT'L	1974
GT	GENE TIERNEY	portrait	WARNER BROS, FOX	
GT	GENEVIEVE TOBIN	portrait	FN/WARNER BROS	
GT	GEORGE TOBIAS	portrait	WARNER BROS	
GT	GHOST TOWN	MINER	UNITED ARTISTS	1956
GT	GHOST TRAIN (UK)	FORDE	GAUMONT BRITISH AMERICA	1931
GT	GHOST TRAIN (UK)	FORDE	GFD	1941
GT	GOLDEN TWENTIES		RKO	1950
GT	GOOD TIME CHARLEY	CURTIZ	WARNER BROS	1927
GT	GRAND JURY	ROGELL	RKO	1936
GT	RIDER FROM TUCSON	SELANDER	RKO	1950
GTR	GREAT TRAIN ROBBERY	CRICHTON	UNITED ARTISTS	1979
GTS-F	GO TELL THE SPARTANS	POST	AVCO EMBASSY	1978
GTT	GOIN' TO TOWN	GOODWINS	RKO	1944
GUB	GOOD, THE BAD AND THE UGLY	LEONE	UNITED ARTISTS	1966
GUM	GIVE US THE MOON (UK)	GUEST	GFD	1944
GUN	GUN RUNNERS	SIEGEL	UNITED ARTISTS	1958
GUN	MY GUN IS QUICK	VICTOR, WHITE	UNITED ARTISTS	1957
GV	GLENN VERNON	portrait	RKO	
GVF	ACT OF LOVE (FR)	LITVAK	UNITED ARTISTS	1953
GVR	GREAT VAN ROBBERY (UK)	VARNEL	UNITED ARTISTS	1959
GVS	GOLDEN VOYAGE OF SINBAD	HESSLER	COLUMBIA	1974
GW	GEORGE WASHINGTON SLEPT HERE	KEIGHLEY	WARNER BROS	1942
GW	GLASS WALL	SHANE	COLUMBIA	1953
GW	GLORIA WARREN	portrait	WARNER BROS	early 40s
GW	GOD'S COUNTRY AND THE WOMAN	KEIGHLEY	WARNER BROS	1937
GW	GOING WILD	SEITER	WARNER BROS	1930
GW	GORDON'S WAR	DAVIS	20th CENTURY FOX	1973
GW	GRANT WILLIAMS	portrait	UNIVERSAL	1950s-60s
GW	GRANT WITHERS	portrait	WARNER BROS	
GW	GREAT WAR		LOPERT	1959
GW	GUY WILLIAMS	portrait	UNIVERSAL	1950s
GW	GUY WILLIAMS	portrait	UNIV	
GW	PAST OF MARY HOLMES	THOMPSON, VORKAPICH	RKO	1932
GW	PULP	HODGES	UNITED ARTISTS	1972
GW	SEALED CARGO	WERKER	RKO	1951
GW1	BEHIND THE MASK (UK)	HURST	SHOWCORPORATION	1958
GW-1	DAMN THE DEFIANT (UK: H.M.S. DEFIANT)	GILBERT	COLUMBIA	1962

Movie Still Identification Book Ultimate Edition - Letters

CODE	TITLE/NAME	DIRECTOR/TYPE	STUDIO/DISTRIBUTOR	YEAR
GW-10	GHOST RIDER	FOX	MONOGRAM	1943
GW-11	STRANGER FROM PECOS	HILLYER	MONOGRAM	1943
GW-12	SIX GUN GOSPEL	HILLYER	MONOGRAM	1943
GW-13	OUTLAWS OF STAMPEDE PASS	FOX	MONOGRAM	1943
GW-14	TEXAS KID	HILLYER	MONOGRAM	1943
GW-15	RAIDERS OF THE BORDER	MCCARTHY	MONOGRAM	1944
GW-16	PARTNERS OF THE TRAIL	HILLYER	MONOGRAM	1944
GW-17	LAW MEN	HILLYER	MONOGRAM	1944
GW-18	RANGE LAW	HILLYER	MONOGRAM	1944
GW-19	WEST OF THE RIO GRANDE	HILLYER	MONOGRAM	1944
GW-20	LAND OF THE OUTLAWS	HILLYER	MONOGRAM	1944
GW-21	LAW OF THE VALLEY	BRETHERTON	MONOGRAM	1944
GW-22	GHOST GUNS	HILLYER	MONOGRAM	1944
GW-23	GUN SMOKE	BRETHERTON	MONOGRAM	1945
GW-24	NAVAJO TRAIL	BRETHERTON	MONOGRAM	1945
GW-25	STRANGER FROM SANTA FE	HILLYER	MONOGRAM	1945
GW-26	FLAME OF THE WEST	HILLYER	MONOGRAM	1945
GW-27	LOST TRAIL	HILLYER	MONOGRAM	1945
GW-28	FRONTIER FEUD	HILLYER	MONOGRAM	1945
GW-29	BORDER BANDITS	HILLYER	MONOGRAM	1946
GW-30	DRIFTING ALONG	ABRAHAMS	MONOGRAM	1946
GW-31	HAUNTED MINE	ABRAHAMS	MONOGRAM	1946
GW-32	UNDER ARIZONA SKIES	HILLYER	MONOGRAM	1946
GW-33	GENTLEMAN FROM TEXAS	HILLYER	MONOGRAM	1946
GW-34	SHADOWS ON THE RANGE	HILLYER	MONOGRAM	1946
GW-35	TRIGGER FINGERS	HILLYER	MONOGRAM	1946
GW-36	SILVER RANGE	HILLYER	MONOGRAM	1946
GW-37	RAIDERS OF THE SOUTH	HILLYER	MONOGRAM	1947
GW-38	VALLEY OF FEAR	HILLYER	MONOGRAM	1947
GW-39	TRAILING DANGER	HILLYER	MONOGRAM	1947
GW-40	LAND OF THE LAWLESS	HILLYER	MONOGRAM	1947
GW-41	LAW COMES TO GUNSIGHT	HILLYER	MONOGRAM	1947
GW-42	CODE OF THE SADDLE	CARR	MONOGRAM	1947
GW-43	FLASHING GUNS	HILLYER	MONOGRAM	1947
GW-44	PRAIRIE EXPRESS	HILLYER	MONOGRAM	1947
GW-45	GUN TALK	HILLYER	MONOGRAM	1947
GW-46	OVERLAND TRAILS	HILLYER	MONOGRAM	1948
GW-47	CROSSED TRAILS	HILLYER	MONOGRAM	1948
GW-48	FRONTIER AGENT	HILLYER	MONOGRAM	1948
GW-49	TRIGGERMAN	BRETHERTON	MONOGRAM	1948
GW-50	BACK TRAIL	CABANNE	MONOGRAM	1948
GW-51	FIGHTING RANGER	HILLYER	MONOGRAM	1948
GW-52	SHERIFF OF MEDICINE BOW	HILLYER	MONOGRAM	1948
GW-53	GUNNING FOR JUSTICE	TAYLOR	MONOGRAM	1948
GW-54	HIDDEN DANGER	TAYLOR	MONOGRAM	1948
GW-55	LAW OF THE WEST	TAYLOR	MONOGRAM	1949
GW-56	TRAILS END	HILLYER	MONOGRAM	1949
GW-57	WEST OF EL DORADO	TAYLOR	MONOGRAM	1949
GW-58	RANGE JUSTICE	TAYLOR	MONOGRAM	1949
GW-59	WESTERN RENEGADES	FOX	MONOGRAM	1949
GW-60	WEST OF WYOMING	FOX	MONOGRAM	1950
GW-61	OVER THE BORDER	FOX	MONOGRAM	1950
GW-62	SIX GUN MESA	FOX	MONOGRAM	1950
GW-63	LAW OF THE PANHANDLE	COLLINS	MONOGRAM	1950
GW-200	HAUNTED TRAILS	HILLYER	MONOGRAM	1949
GW-201	SHADOWS OF THE WEST	TAYLOR	MONOGRAM	1949
GW-203	RIDERS OF THE DUSK	HILLYER	MONOGRAM	1949
GW-204	RANGE LAND	HILLYER	MONOGRAM	1949
GW-206	GUNSLINGERS	FOX	MONOGRAM	1950
GW-300	STAMPEDE	SELANDER	ALLIED ARTISTS	1949
GWCQ	GIRL WHO COULDN'T QUITE (UK)	LEE	CLASSIC	1950
GWH	GREAT WHITE HOPE	HUDLIN	20th CENTURY FOX	1996
GWS	GEORGE WHITE'S SCANDALS	FEIST	RKO	1945
GWWLST	GUESS WHAT WE LEARNED IN SCHOOL TODAY?	AVILDSEN	CANNON	1970
GXG	GLADYS GEORGE	portrait	MGM	
GXGX	GREER GARSON	portrait	MGM	
GXM	GEORGE MURPHY	portrait	MGM	
GXS	GLORIA SWANSON	portrait	MGM	
GY	GIG YOUNG	portrait	WARNER BROS	1940s-50s
GY	QUEEN OF DESTINY (UK: SIXTY GLORIOUS YEARS)	WILCOX	RKO	1938

Movie Still Identification Book Ultimate Edition - Letters

CODE	TITLE/NAME	DIRECTOR/TYPE	STUDIO/DISTRIBUTOR	YEAR
H	FROM HEADQUARTERS	BRETHERTON	WARNER BROS	1929
H	GEORGE HURRELL PORTRAITS	portrait	MGM	
H	HACKERS	SOFTLEY	UNITED ARTISTS	1995
H	HAIR	FORMAN	UNITED ARTISTS	1979
H	HALLOWEEN	CARPENTER	COMPASS INT'L	1978
H	HAMLET (UK)	OLIVIER	UNIVERSAL	1949
H	HAMLET	COLLERAN, GIELGUD	WARNER BROS	1964
H	HAMLET (UK)	RICHARDSON	COLUMBIA	1969
H	HAMMERHEAD (UK)	MILLER	COLUMBIA	1968
H	HEAD	RAFELSON	COLUMBIA	1968
H	HEADLINE (UK)	HARLOW	EALING	1943
H	HEART OF THE NORTH	SEILER	WARNER BROS	1938
H	HEAT	MORRISSEY	LEVITT-PICKMAN	1972
H	HEIDI (GER)	JACOBS	WARNER BROS	1968
H	HELP! (UK)	LESTER	UNITED ARTISTS	1965
H	HERCULES (IT)	FRANCISCI	WARNER BROS	1959
H	HERCULES	COZZI	CANNON	1983
H	HERO AND THE TERROR	TANNEN	CANNON	1988
H	HEROD THE GREAT (IT)	TOURJANSKY	MONOGRAM	1960
H	HIGH FIDELITY	MONICELLI	MAGNA	1965
H	HIGH FLIGHT	GILLING	COLUMBIA	1957
H	HITCHER	HARMON	TRI STAR	1986
H	HOFFA	DEVITO	20th CENTURY FOX	1992
H	HOME TOWNERS	FOY	WARNER BROS	1928
H	HONDO	FARROWE	WARNER BROS	1953
H	HONEYMOON (UK: LUNA DE MIEL)	POWELL, PRESSBURGER	CONTINENTAL	1959
H	HONKY	GRAHAM	JACK HARRIS	1971
H	HOODLUM	NOSSECK	UNITED ARTISTS	1951
H	HOODLUM	DUKE	UNITED ARTISTS	1997
H	HOSPITAL	HILLER	UNITED ARTISTS	1971
H	HOUSEWIFE	GREEN	WARNER BROS	1934
H	HOWCO INTERNATIONAL			
H	HUMONGOUS	LYNCH	EMBASSY	1982
H	HURRICANE (HURRICANE STREETS)	FREEMAN	UNITED ARTISTS	1997
H	HUSTLE	ALDRICH	PARAMOUNT	1975
H	HYSTERIA (UK)	FRANCIS	MGM	1965
H	IS YOUR HONEYMOON REALLY NECESSARY? (UK)	ELVEY	AAP	1953
H	MAYOR'S DILEMMA (FR: LES OTAGES)	BERNARD	FILM ALLIANCE	1939
H	MR. HOBO (UK - GUV'NOR)	ROSMER	GAUMONT BRITISH	1935
H	OLD FAITHFUL (UK: HANSOM*)	ROGERS	RKO	1935
H	ONE ROUND HOGAN	BRETHERTON	WARNER BROS	1927
H	OTHER WOMEN'S HUSBANDS	KENTON	WARNER BROS	1926
H	THREE WHO LOVED	ARCHAINBAUD	RKO	1931
H	TO HAVE AND TO HOLD (UK)	GRAYSON	EXCLUSIVE	1951
H	WE'RE ONLY HUMAN	FLOOD	RKO	1936
H	SUDS	DILLON	UNITED ARTISTS	1920
H#	JACK HOXIE MOVIES		MAJESTIC	
H-1	ALL AT SEA (sh)	CHASE, GOULDING	PATHE EXCHANGE	1919
H-1	BIG TIME	HAWKS	FOX FILM	1929
H-1	FIREBRAND TREVISON	HEFFRON	FOX FILM	1920
H-1	FLAMING FLAPPERS (sh)	GUIOL	PATHE EXCHANGE	1925
H1	LAW AND DISORDER (UK)	CRICHTON	CONTINENTAL	1958
H-1	TUMBLEWEEDS	BAGGOT	UNITED ARTISTS	1925
H-2	BLACK PANTHER	ORMOND	HOWCO	1956
H-2	DEAD LINE	HENDERSON	FOX FILM	1920
H-2	FIG LEAVES	HAWKS	FOX FILM	1926
H-2	HERCULES UNCHAINED (IT)	FRANCISCI	WARNER BROS	1960
H-2	HITLER: BEAST OF BERLIN (BEAST OF BERLIN*)	NEWFIELD	PRC	1939
H-2	LONG PANTS (sh)	GUIOL	PATHE EXCHANGE	1926
H-2	START SOMETHING (sh)	GOULDING	PATHE EXCHANGE	1919
H-2	SUCH MEN ARE DANGEROUS	HAWKS	FOX FILM	1930
H-3	45 MINUTES FROM HOLLYWOOD (sh)	GUIOL	PATHE EXCHANGE	1926
H-3	CALL FOR MR. CAVEMAN (sh)	CHASE	PATHE EXCHANGE	1919
H-3	PAID TO LOVE	HAWKS	FOX FILM	1927
H-4	CRADLE SNATCHERS	HAWKS	FOX FILM	1927
H-4	GIVING THE BRIDE AWAY (sh)	CHASE, ROACH	PATHE EXCHANGE	1919
H-4	HUG BUG (sh)	GUIOL	PATHE EXCHANGE	1926
H-5	FAZIL	HAWKS	FOX FILM	1928
H-5	ORDER IN THE COURT (sh)	CHASE	PATHE EXCHANGE	1919
H-5	UKULELE SHEIKS (sh)	GUIOL	PATHE EXCHANGE	1926

Movie Still Identification Book Ultimate Edition - Letters

CODE	TITLE/NAME	DIRECTOR/TYPE	STUDIO/DISTRIBUTOR	YEAR
H-6	A GIRL IN EVERY PORT	HAWKS	FOX FILM	1928
H-6	IT'S A HARD LIFE (sh)	ROACH	PATHE EXCHANGE	1919
H-6	SAY IT WITH BABIES (sh)	GUIOL	PATHE EXCHANGE	1926
H-7	AIR CIRCUS	HAWKS	FOX FILM	1928
H-7	COW'S KIMONO (sh)	GUIOL, PARROTT	PATHE EXCHANGE	1926
H-7	HOW DRY I AM (sh)	ROACH	PATHE EXCHANGE	1919
H-7	KENTUCKY RIFLE	HITTLEMAN	HOWCO	1955
H-8	ALONG CAME AUNTIE (sh)	GUIOL, WALLACE	PATHE EXCHANGE	1926
H-8	PRIVATE LIFE OF HENRY VIII (UK)	KORDA	UNITED ARTISTS	1933
H-8	UNFINISHED ROACH (sh)		PATHE EXCHANGE	1919
H-9	GETTING HIS GOAT (sh)	CHASE	PATHE EXCHANGE	1920
H9	PUBLIC LIFE OF HENRY THE NINTH (UK)	MAINWARING	MGM	1935
H-9	TRENT'S LAST CASE	HAWKS	FOX FILM	1929
H-9	TWO TIME MAMA (sh)	GUIOL	PATHE EXCHANGE	1927
H-10	ONE HOUR MARRIED (sh)	STRONG, YATES	PATHE EXCHANGE	1927
H-10	TEENAGE THUNDER	HELMICK	HOWCO	1957
H-10	TOUGH LUCK (sh)	CHASE	PATHE EXCHANGE	1919
H-11	CARNIVAL ROCK	CORMAN	HOWCO	1957
H-11	LOOKING FOR TROUBLE (sh)	ROACH	PATHE EXCHANGE	1919
H-11	NICKEL HOPPER (sh)	JONES, YATES	PATHE EXCHANGE	1926
H-12	ANYTHING ONCE! (sh)	JONES, YATES	PATHE EXCHANGE	1927
H-12	BRAIN FROM PLANET AROUS	JURAN (HERTZ)	HOWCO	1957
H-12	FLOOR BELOW (sh)	CHASE, GOULDING	PATHE EXCHANGE	1919
H-13	RED HOT HOTTENTOTS (sh)	CHASE	PATHE EXCHANGE	1920
H-14	WHY GO HOME? (sh)	CHASE	PATHE EXCHANGE	1920
H-15	LOST, LONELY AND VICIOUS	MYERS	HOWCO	1958
H-15	SHOULD MEN WALK HOME? (sh)	MCCAREY	PATHE EXCHANGE	1927
H-15	SLIPPERY SLICKERS (sh)	CHASE	PATHE EXCHANGE	1920
H-16	DIPPY DENTIST (sh)	GOULDING	PATHE EXCHANGE	1920
H-16	JEWISH PRUDENCE (sh)	MCCAREY	PATHE EXCHANGE	1927
H-17	ALL LIT UP (sh)	NEWMEYER	PATHE EXCHANGE	1920
H-17	EVE'S LOVE LETTERS (sh)	MCCAREY	PATHE EXCHANGE	1927
H-18	DON'T TELL EVERYTHING (sh)	MCCAREY	PATHE EXCHANGE	1927
H-18	NIGHT OF LOVE (CONCERT OF INTRIGUE) (IT: TRADITA 1954)	BONNARD	HOWCO	1959
H-18	WALTZ ME AROUND (sh)	CHASE	PATHE EXCHANGE	1920
H-19	RAISE THE RENT (sh)	NEWMEYER	PATHE EXCHANGE	1920
H-19	SHOULD SECOND HUSBANDS COME FIRST? (sh)	MCCAREY	PATHE EXCHANGE	1927
H-20	FIND THE GIRL (sh)	CHASE	PATHE EXCHANGE	1920
H-20	NAKED VENUS	ULMER	HOWCO	1959
H-21	FLAT BROKE (sh)	CHASE	PATHE EXCHANGE	1920
H-22	FRESH PAINT (sh)	CHASE, GOULDING	PATHE EXCHANGE	1920
H-23	CUT THE CARDS (sh)	CHASE	PATHE EXCHANGE	1920
H-24	CRACKED WEDDING BELLS (sh)	LA ROSE	PATHE EXCHANGE	1920
H-25	DINNER HOUR (sh)	CHASE	PATHE EXCHANGE	1920
H-26	SPEED TO SPARE (sh)	CHASE	PATHE EXCHANGE	1920
H-27	SHOOT ON SIGHT (sh)	CHASE	PATHE EXCHANGE	1920
H-28	DON'T WEAKEN (sh)	GOULDING	PATHE EXCHANGE	1920
H-29	DRINK HEARTY (sh)	GOULDING	PATHE EXCHANGE	1920
H-30	TROTTING THROUGH TURKEY (sh)	CHASE	PATHE EXCHANGE	1920
H-31	ALL DRESSED UP (sh)	CHASE	PATHE EXCHANGE	1920
H-32	GRAB THE GHOST (sh)	GOULDING	PATHE EXCHANGE	1920
H-33	YOU'RE PINCHED (sh)	ROACH	PATHE EXCHANGE	1920
H-34	ALL IN A DAY (sh)	CHASE	PATHE EXCHANGE	1920
H-35	ANY OLD PORT (sh)	GOULDING	PATHE EXCHANGE	1920
H-36	DON'T ROCK THE BOAT (sh)	CHASE	PATHE EXCHANGE	1920
H-37	HOME STRETCH (sh)	CHASE	PATHE EXCHANGE	1920
H-38	CALL A TAXI (sh)	CHASE	PATHE EXCHANGE	1920
H-39	LIVE AND LEARN (sh)	CHASE	PATHE EXCHANGE	1920
H-40	RUN 'EM RAGGED (sh)	GOULDING	PATHE EXCHANGE	1920
H-41	LONDON BOBBY (sh)	CHASE	PATHE EXCHANGE	1920
H-42	MONEY TO BURN (sh)	NEWMEYER	PATHE EXCHANGE	1920
H-43	ROCK A BYE BABY (sh)	CHASE	PATHE EXCHANGE	1920
H-44	GO AS YOU PLEASE (sh)	GOULDING	PATHE EXCHANGE	1920
H-45	DOING TIME (sh)	GOULDING	PATHE EXCHANGE	1920
H-46	FELLOW CITIZENS (sh)	GOULDING	PATHE EXCHANGE	1920
H-47	WHEN THE WIND BLOWS (sh)	CHASE	PATHE EXCHANGE	1920
H-48	INSULTING THE SULTAN (sh)	GOULDING	PATHE EXCHANGE	1920
H-49	DEAR DEPARTED (sh)	CHASE	PATHE EXCHANGE	1920
H-50	CASH CUSTOMERS (sh)	GOULDING	PATHE EXCHANGE	1920
H-51	PARK YOUR CAR (sh)	GOULDING	PATHE EXCHANGE	1920

Movie Still Identification Book Ultimate Edition - Letters

CODE	TITLE/NAME	DIRECTOR/TYPE	STUDIO/DISTRIBUTOR	YEAR
H-52	OPEN ANOTHER BOTTLE (sh)	GOULDING	PATHE EXCHANGE	1921
H-53	MORNING AFTER (sh)	GOULDING	PATHE EXCHANGE	1921
H-54	WHIRL OF THE WEST (sh)	BARROWS	PATHE EXCHANGE	1921
H-55	HIS BEST GIRL (sh)	CHASE	PATHE EXCHANGE	1921
H-56	MAKE IT SNAPPY (sh)		PATHE EXCHANGE	1921
H-57	FELLOW ROMANS (sh)	ROACH	PATHE EXCHANGE	1921
H-58	RUSH ORDERS (sh)	CHASE	PATHE EXCHANGE	1921
H-59	BUBBLING OVER (sh)	ROACH	PATHE EXCHANGE	1921
H-60	NO CHILDREN (sh)	GOULDING	PATHE EXCHANGE	1921
H-61	BIG GAME (sh)	GOULDING	PATHE EXCHANGE	1921
H-62	KILLJOYS (BLUE SUNDAY) (sh)	CHASE	PATHE EXCHANGE	1921
H-63	OWN YOUR OWN HOME (sh)	ROACH	PATHE EXCHANGE	1921
H-64	WHERE'S THE FIRE (sh)	ROACH	PATHE EXCHANGE	1921
H-65	HIGH ROLLERS (sh)	GOULDING	PATHE EXCHANGE	1921
H-66	YOU'RE NEXT (sh)	CHASE	PATHE EXCHANGE	1921
H-67	SAVE YOUR MONEY (sh)	ROACH	PATHE EXCHANGE	1921
H-68	BIKE BUG (sh)	ROACH	PATHE EXCHANGE	1921
H-69	NAME THE DAY (sh)	ROACH	PATHE EXCHANGE	1921
H-70	AT THE RING SIDE (sh)	CHASE	PATHE EXCHANGE	1921
H-71	NO STOP-OVER (sh)	ROACH	PATHE EXCHANGE	1921
H-72	LATE LODGERS (sh)	CHASE	PATHE EXCHANGE	1921
H-73	WHAT A WHOPPER (sh)	CHASE	PATHE EXCHANGE	1921
H-74	TEACHING THE TEACHER (sh)	ROACH	PATHE EXCHANGE	1921
H-75	SPOT CASH (sh)	CHASE	PATHE EXCHANGE	1921
H-77	GONE TO THE COUNTRY (sh)	CHASE	PATHE EXCHANGE	1921
H-78	LAW AND ORDER (sh)	CHASE	PATHE EXCHANGE	1921
H-79	FIFTEEN MINUTES (sh)	CHASE	PATHE EXCHANGE	1921
H-80	ON LOCATION (sh)	CHASE	PATHE EXCHANGE	1921
H-81	HOCUS POCUS (sh)	CHASE	PATHE EXCHANGE	1921
H-82	PENNY-IN-THE-SLOT (sh)	CHASE	PATHE EXCHANGE	1921
H-83	JOY RIDER (sh)	ROACH	PATHE EXCHANGE	1921
H-84	HUSTLER (sh)	CHASE	PATHE EXCHANGE	1921
H-85	SINK OR SWIM (sh)	CHASE	PATHE EXCHANGE	1921
H-86	SHAKE 'EM UP (sh)	CHASE	PATHE EXCHANGE	1921
H-87	STONE AGE (sh)	CHASE	PATHE EXCHANGE	1922
H-88	CORNER POCKET (sh)	CHASE	PATHE EXCHANGE	1921
H-89	LOSE NO TIME (sh)	CHASE	PATHE EXCHANGE	1922
H-90	CALL THE WITNESS (sh)	CHASE	PATHE EXCHANGE	1922
H-91	BLOW 'EM UP (sh)	CHASE	PATHE EXCHANGE	1922
H-92	YEARS TO COME (sh)	CHASE	PATHE EXCHANGE	1922
H-93	STAGE STRUCK (sh)	WATSON	PATHE EXCHANGE	1922
H-94	SOME BABY (sh)	CEDER	PATHE EXCHANGE	1922
H-95	DOWN AND OUT (sh)	CEDER	PATHE EXCHANGE	1922
H-96	PARDON ME (sh)	CEDER	PATHE EXCHANGE	1922
H-97	BOW WOWS (sh)	CEDER	PATHE EXCHANGE	1922
H-98	HOT OFF THE PRESS (sh)	CEDER, CHASE	PATHE EXCHANGE	1922
H-99	ANVIL CHORUS (sh)	CEDER	PATHE EXCHANGE	1922
H-100	JUMP YOUR JOB (sh)	CEDER	PATHE EXCHANGE	1922
H-101	KILL THE NERVE (sh)	CEDER	PATHE EXCHANGE	1922
H-102	FULL O' PEP (sh)	CHASE	PATHE EXCHANGE	1922
H-103	DO YOUR DUTY (sh)	CEDER	PATHE EXCHANGE	1926
H-104	DAYS OF OLD (DAYS OF GOLD) (sh)	CHASE	PATHE EXCHANGE	1922
H-105	LIGHT SHOWERS (sh)	CHASE	PATHE EXCHANGE	1922
H-106	DO ME A FAVOR (sh)	CHASE	PATHE EXCHANGE	1922
H-107	PUNCH THE CLOCK (sh)	BEAUDINE	PATHE EXCHANGE	1922
H-108	IN THE MOVIES (sh)	CHASE	PATHE EXCHANGE	1922
H-109	HALE AND HEARTY (sh)	SANTELL	PATHE EXCHANGE	1922
H-110	STRICTLY MODERN (sh)	BEAUDINE	PATHE EXCHANGE	1922
H-111	DUMB BELL (sh)	CHASE	PATHE EXCHANGE	1922
H130	HEADLESS HORSEMAN	VENTURINI	W.W. HODKINSONS	1922
H-3100	SIREN OF ATLANTIS	TALLAS	UNITED ARTISTS	1949
H-5140	HUSTLE	ALDRICH	PARAMOUNT	1975
H7195	JOAN CRAWFORD	portrait	MGM	
H7197	JOAN CRAWFORD	portrait	MGM	
H7200	JOAN CRAWFORD	portrait	MGM	
HA	20 MILLION SWEETHEARTS	ENRIGHT	WARNER BROS	1934
HA	HAMMER	CLARK	UNITED ARTISTS	1972
HA	HANNIBAL (IT)	BRAGAGLIA, ULMER	WARNER BROS	1959
HA	HAPPY ANNIVERSARY	MILLER	UNITED ARTISTS	1959
HA	HARDIE ALBRIGHT	portrait		

Movie Still Identification Book Ultimate Edition - Letters

CODE	TITLE/NAME	DIRECTOR/TYPE	STUDIO/DISTRIBUTOR	YEAR
HA	HAVING WONDERFUL TIME	SANTELL	RKO	1938
HA	HEATHER ANGEL	portrait	RKO	
HA	HEAVENS ABOVE (UK)	BOULTING BROS	JANUS	1963
HA	HELL'S ANGELS	HUGHES	UNITED ARTISTS	1930
HA	HERBERT ANDERSON	portrait	WARNER BROS	1940s-60s
HA	HOME ALONE	COLUMBUS	20th CENTURY FOX	1990
HA	HOME AND AWAY (UK)	SEWELL	EROS	1956
HA	TO HAVE AND TO HOLD (UK)	WISE	ANGLO-AMALGAMATED	1963
HA2	HOME ALONE 2	COLUMBUS	20th CENTURY FOX	1992
HA-103	MAN WITH TWO LIVES	ROSEN	MONOGRAM	1942
HAK	HAKIM BROTHERS PRODUCTION			
HAK	WITHOUT HONOR	PICHEL	UNITED ARTISTS	1949
HAM	HAROLD AND MAUDE	ASHBY	PARAMOUNT	1971
HAS	HALF A SIXPENCE (UK)	SIDNEY	PARAMOUNT	1968
HB	HALF BREED	GILMORE	RKO	1952
HB	HALLIDAY BRAND	LEWIS	UNITED ARTISTS	1957
HB	HANNIBAL BROOKS (UK)	WINNER	UNITED ARTISTS	1969
HB	HARRY BLACK AND THE TIGER (UK: HARRY BLACK)	FREGONESE	20TH CENTURY FOX	1958
HB	HAZEL BROOKS	portrait		
HB	HEARTBEAT	WOOD	RKO	1946
HB	HELEN BAXTER	portrait		
HB	HELEN BRODERICK	portrait	RKO	
HB	HICKEY AND BOGGS	CULP	UNITED ARTISTS	1972
HB	HILLARY BROOKE	portrait	RKO	
HB	HORN BLOWS AT MIDNIGHT	WALSH	WARNER BROS	1945
HB	HORST BUCHHOLZ (aka BUCHOLZ)	portrait		
HB	HOUND OF THE BASKERVILLES (UK)	GUNDREY	FIRST DIVISION	1932
HB	HOUSE THAT DRIPPED BLOOD (UK)	DUFFEL	CINERAMA	1970
HB	HUMPHREY BOGART	portrait	WARNER BROS	
HB	I'VE GOT YOUR NUMBER	ENRIGHT	WARNER BROS	1934
HB	OF HUMAN BONDAGE	CROMWELL	RKO	1934
HB	OF HUMAN BONDAGE (UK)	HUGHES	COLUMBIA	1964
HB	VICE SQUAD	LAVEN	UNITED ARTISTS	1953
HB-1000	SORRELL AND SON (UK)	BRENON	UNITED ARTISTS	1927
HB-2200	LUMMOX	BRENON	UNITED ARTISTS	1930
HB-2800	LUMMOX	BRENON	UNITED ARTISTS	1930
HBD	HELL'S BLOODY DEVILS	ADAMSON	INDEPENDENT INTL	1970
HBG	HAPPY BIRTHDAY, GEMINI	BENNER	UNITED ARTISTS	1980
HBH	HELL BENT FOR HEAVEN	BLACKTON	WARNER BROS	1926
HB MPI	HARRY BLACK AND THE TIGER	FREGONESE	20th CENTURY FOX	1958
HBT	HOLD BACK TOMORROW	HAAS	UNIVERSAL	1955
HBW	HENRY B. WALTHALL	portrait	RKO	1930s
HBW	HENRY B. WALTHALL	portrait	SONO ART-WORLD WIDE	1920s-30s
HBWJ	HAPPY BIRTHDAY WANDA JANE	ROBSON	COLUMBIA	1971
HBX	HOBART BOSWORTH	portrait	MGM	
HBZ	HELL BELOW ZERO (UK)	ROBSON	COLUMBIA	1954
HC	DANGEROUS CARGO (UK: HELL'S CARGO)	HUTH	FILM ALLIANCE	1939
HC	DANGEROUS CARGO (UK)	HARLOW	MONARCH	1954
HC	DEVIL'S PLAYGROUND	ARCHAINBAUD	UNITED ARTISTS	1946
HC	HANNIE CAULDER	KENNEDY	PARAMOUNT	1972
HC	HARD CONTRACT	POGOSTIN	20th CENTURY FOX	1969
HC	HARRY CAREY	portrait	POWERS/FBO, RKO	
HC	HAWAII CALLS	CLINE	RKO	1938
HC	HELENA CARTER	portrait	UNIVERSAL, WARNER BROS	
HC	HELL IS A CITY (UK)	GUEST	COLUMBIA	1960
HC	HIGH COMMAND (UK)	DICKINSON	GRAND NATIONAL	1937
HC	HOAGY CARMICHAEL	portrait	RKO	
HC	HOBART CAVANAUGH	portrait	WARNER BROS	
HC	HOT CARS	MCDOUGALL	UNITED ARTISTS	1956
HC	HOW I GOT INTO COLLEGE	HOLLAND	20th CENTURY FOX	1989
HC	HUE AND CRY (UK)	CRICHTON	FINE ARTS	1947
HC	HURRY CHARLIE HURRY	ROBERTS	RKO	1941
HC	JIMMY THE GENT	CURTIZ	WARNER BROS	1934
HC-1	BELLS OF SAN FERNANDO	MORSE	SCREEN GUILD	1947
HC2	FOOL'S GOLD	ARCHAINBAUD	UNITED ARTISTS	1947
HC3	DANGEROUS VENTURE	ARCHAINBAUD	UNITED ARTISTS	1947
HC-4	UNEXPECTED GUEST	ARCHAINBAUD	UNITED ARTISTS	1947
HC-5	HOPPY'S HOLIDAY	ARCHAINBAUD	UNITED ARTISTS	1947
HC-6	MARAUDERS	ARCHAINBAUD	UNITED ARTISTS	1947
HC-7	SILENT CONFLICT	ARCHAINBAUD	UNITED ARTISTS	1948

Movie Still Identification Book Ultimate Edition - Letters

CODE	TITLE/NAME	DIRECTOR/TYPE	STUDIO/DISTRIBUTOR	YEAR
HC-8	DEAD DON'T DREAM	ARCHAINBAUD	UNITED ARTISTS	1948
HC-9	SINISTER JOURNEY	ARCHAINBAUD	UNITED ARTISTS	1948
HC-10	BORROWED TROUBLE	ARCHAINBAUD	UNITED ARTISTS	1948
HC-11	FALSE PARADISE	ARCHAINBAUD	UNITED ARTISTS	1948
HC-12	STRANGE GAMBLE	ARCHAINBAUD	UNITED ARTISTS	1948
HC-5152	HANNIE CAULDER	KENNEDY	PARAMOUNT	1972
HCA	WORLD OF HANS CHRISTIAN ANDERSEN	KILGORE, McCANN	UNITED ARTISTS	1971
HCG	HAT, COAT, GLOVE	MINER	RKO	1934
HC/HCP	HOPALONG CASSIDY PRODUCTIONS	studio		
HCH	HITLER'S CHILDREN	DMYTRYK	RKO	1943
HCS	HERE COMES THE SUN (UK)	BAXTER	GFD	1946
HCT	CHOSEN (IT/UK)	De MARTINO	WARNER BROS	1978
HCT	TOMCAT (UK: MINI WEEKEND)	ROBIN	JOSEPH BRENNER	1968
HCW	HEAVEN CAN WAIT	BEATTY, HENRY	PARAMOUNT	1978
HD	DANGEROUS	GREEN	WARNER BROS	1935
HD	HEARTS DIVIDED	BORZAGE	WARNER BROS	1936
HD	HEAVENLY DAYS	ESTABROOK	RKO	1944
HD	HELMUT DANTINE	portrait	WARNER BROS	
HD	HILLS OF DONEGAL (UK)	ARGYLE	BUTCHER'S	1947
HD	HOUSE OF THE DAMNED	DEXTER	20th CENTURY FOX	1963
HD	HOUSE OF DARKNESS (UK)	MITCHELL	REALART	1948
HD	HOWARD DUFF	portrait	UNIVERSAL	
HD	HUMAN DUPLICATORS	GRIMALDI	ALLIED ARTISTS	1965
HD	MAN WHO DARED	WILBUR	WARNER BROS	1939
HD	SO DEAR TO MY HEART	SCHUSTER, LUSKE	RKO	1948
HD'A	HELENA D'ALGY	portrait	MGM	
HDD	HI DIDDLE DIDDLE	STONE	UNITED ARTISTS	1943
HDI	HELL ON DEVIL'S ISLAND	NYBY	20th CENTURY FOX	1957
HDN	HARD DAY'S NIGHT (UK)	LESTER	UNITED ARTISTS	1964
HDY	HEROES DIE YOUNG	SHEPARD	ALLIED ARTISTS	1961
HE	HEARTS IN EXILE	CURTIZ	WARNER BROS	1929
HE	HELL BOATS	WENKOS	UNITED ARTISTS	1970
HE	HOWARD'S END	IVORY	SONY PICTURES	1992
HE	SPELLBOUND	HITCHCOCK	UNITED ARTISTS	1945
HE	HOLD EVERYTHING	DEL RUTH	WARNER BROS	1930
HEA	MORE THAN A MIRACLE	ROSI	MGM	1967
HEER-1	LADIES MUST DRESS	HEERMAN	FOX FILM	1927
HEH	HANG 'EM HIGH	POST	UNITED ARTISTS	1968
HEJ	HOLD 'EM JAIL	TAUROG	RKO	1932
HEMI	THUNDERSTORM (UK)	GUILLERMIN	ALLIED ARTISTS	1956
HERB	HUGH HERBERT	portrait	WARNER BROS	
HERC	HERCULES (t)	CLEMENTS	BUENA VISTA	1997
HF	HAZEL FORBES	portrait	RKO	
HF	HELLFIRE CLUB (UK)	BAKER, BERMAN	EMBASSY	1961
HF	HENRY FONDA	portrait	RKO, UNITED ARTISTS	
HF	HENRY FONDA	portrait	UNIV	
HF	HIDDEN FEAR	DE TOTH	UNITED ARTISTS	1957
HF	HIGH FLYERS	CLINE	RKO	1937
HF	HONEYMOON FOR 3	BACON	WARNER BROS	1941
HF	HONOR OF THE FAMILY	BACON	WARNER BROS	1931
HF	HORROR OF FRANKENSTEIN (UK)	SANGSTER	CONTINENTAL	1971
HF	HUCKLEBERRY FINN	THOMPSON	UNITED ARTISTS	1974
HF	HUMAN FACTOR	PREMINGER	UNITED ARTISTS	1979
HF	MERRY FRINKS	GREEN	WARNER BROS	1934
HF	SCREAM OF FEAR (UK: TASTE OF FEAR)	HOLT	COLUMBIA	1961
HF	SMART BLONDE	MCDONALD	WARNER BROS	1937
HF-72	SCREAM OF FEAR (UK)	HOLT	COLUMBIA	1961
HFA	HER FIRST AFFAIRE (UK)	DWAN	STERLING	1932
HFBB	HIGH FIDELITY	FREARS	BUENA VISTA	2000
HFC	DOORWAY TO HELL	MAYO	WARNER BROS	1930
HFH	TAMING OF DOROTHY (UK: HER FAVOURITE HUSBAND)	SOLDATI	EAGLE LION	1950
HFRO	HUNT FOR RED OCTOBER	MCTIERNAN	PARAMOUNT	1990
HFX	HARRISON FORD	portrait	MGM	1920S
HG	GATE OF HELL	KINUGASA	HARRISON (JAP)	1954
HG	HACKERS	SOFTLEY	UNITED ARTISTS	1995
HG	HANSEL AND GRETEL (t)	MYERBERG, PAUL	RKO	1954
HG	HAUNTED GOLD	WRIGHT	WARNER BROS	1932
HG	HEADLESS GHOST (UK)	SCOTT	AIP	1959
HG	HEAVEN'S GATE	CIMINO	UNITED ARTISTS	1980
HG	HELEN GAHAGAN (DOUGLAS)	portrait	RKO	

Movie Still Identification Book Ultimate Edition - Letters

CODE	TITLE/NAME	DIRECTOR/TYPE	STUDIO/DISTRIBUTOR	YEAR
HG	HELLGATE	WARREN	LIPPERT	1952
HG	HI GAUCHO	ATKINS	RKO	1935
HG	HIDDEN GUNS	GANNAWAY	REPUBLIC	1956
HG	HOOKED GENERATION	GREFE	ALLIED ARTISTS	1968
HG	HUNTLY GORDON	portrait	WARNER BROS	
HG	MAIL TRAIN (UK: INSPECTOR HORNLEIGH GOES TO IT)	FORDE	20TH CENTURY FOX	1941
HH	CAPTAIN HORATIO HORNBLOWER	WALSH	WARNER BROS	1951
HH	HALF HUMAN	CRANE, HONDA	DCA	1957
HH	HALFWAY HOUSE (UK)	DEARDEN	AFE	1944
HH	HALLS OF ANGER	BOGART	UNITED ARTISTS	1970
HH	HAPPY HOOKER	SGARRO	CANNON	1975
HH	HARD TO GET	ENRIGHT	WARNER BROS	1938
HH	HARRIET HILLIARD	portrait	RKO, UNIVERSAL	
HH	HARRIET HOCTOR	portrait	RKO	
HH	HARRY HARVEY	portrait	RKO	
HH	HARRY IN YOUR POCKET	GELLER	UNITED ARTISTS	1973
HH	HAUNTED HONEYMOON	WILDER	ORION	1986
HH	HELEN HAYES	portrait	UNIVERSAL	
HH	HELL HARBOR	KING	UNITED ARTISTS	1930
HH	HELL'S HORIZON	GRIES	COLUMBIA	1955
HH	HERE COMES HAPPINESS	SMITH	WARNER BROS	1941
HH	HIDDEN HAND	STOLOFF	WARNER BROS	1942
HH	HIDDEN HOMICIDE	YOUNG	REPUBLIC	1959
HH	HIGHER AND HIGHER	WHELAN	RKO	1943
HH	HIPS HIPS HOORAY	SANDRICH	RKO	1934
HH	HIS AND HERS (UK)	HURST	FAVORITE	1961
HH	HOLLYWOOD HOTEL	BERKELEY	WARNER BROS	1937
HH	HONEYMOON HOTEL (UK: UNDER NEW MANAGEMENT)	BLAKELEY	BUTCHER'S	1946
HH	HORACE HEIDT	portrait	MCA RECORDS	
HH	HORROR HOTEL	HOOPER	MARS	R1980
HH	HORROR HOTEL (UK: CITY OF THE DEAD)	MOXEY	TRANS LUX	1962
HH	HOT HEIRESS	BADGER	WARNER BROS	1931
HH	HUGH HERBERT	portrait	WARNER BROS	
HH	HUNTZ HALL	portrait	WARNER BROS	
HH	LEGEND OF HELL HOUSE	HOUGH	20th CENTURY FOX	1973
HH	MAYBE IT'S LOVE	WELLMAN	WARNER BROS	1930
HH	PEG ENTWHISTLE	portrait	RKO	
HH	YOURS, MINE AND OURS	SHAVELSON	UNITED ARTISTS	1968
HH2	HAPPY HOOKER GOES TO WASHINGTON	LEVEY	CANNON	1977
HHE	HILLS HAVE EYES	CRAVEN	VANGUNITED ARTISTSRD	1978
HHGW	HAPPY HOOKER GOES TO WASHINGTON	LEVEY	CANNON	1977
HHH	HUNDRED HOUR HUNT (UK: EMERGENCY CALL)	GILBERT	ABNER J. GRESHLER	1952
HHR	HOBART HENLEY	portrait	METRO	
HHU	HEAVEN HELP US	DINNER	TRI STAR	1985
HHXX	HARRIET HAMMOND	portrait	MGM	
HI	DANCE GIRL DANCE	ARZNER	RKO	1940
HI	HIDEAWAY	ROSSON	RKO	1937
HI	MIDNIGHT MYSTERY	SEITZ	RKO	1930
HIB	HAPPY IS THE BRIDE (UK)	BOULTING	KASSLER	1958
HILL-5	WAR HORSE	HILLYER	FOX FILM	1927
HILL-6	HILLS OF PERIL	HILLYER	FOX FILM	1927
HILL-7	CHAIN LIGHTNING	HILLYER	FOX FILM	1927
HIM	HONEYMOON	KEIGHLEY	RKO	1947
HIR	HIRELING	BRIDGES	COLUMBIA	1973
HIT	HIT	FURIE	PARAMOUNT	1973
HIT	HITLER: THE LAST TEN DAYS	DE CONCINI	PARAMOUNT	1973
HJ	HIGHJACKED	NEWFIELD	LIPPERT	1950
HJE	HELEN JEROME EDDY	portrait	FBO	
HK	HARDY KRUGER	portrait	PARAMOUNT`	
HK	HELL IN KOREA (UK: HILL IN KOREA)	AMYES	DCA	1956
HK	HENRY KING	portrait	ROBERTSON-COLE	
HK	KILLING	KUBRICK	UNITED ARTISTS	1956
HK	TWELVE HOURS TO KILL	CAHN	20th CENTURY FOX	1960
HK (R5)	KILLING	KUBRICK	UNITED ARTISTS	1956
HKX	HARRY KEATON	portrait	MGM	1920s-30s
HL	BEST HOUSE IN LONDON (UK)	SAVILLE	MGM	1969
HL	HAL LE ROY	portrait	WARNER BROS	1930s
HL	HARMONY LANE	SANTLEY	MASCOT	1935
HL	HARRY LANGDON	portrait		
HL	HARRY LEWIS	portrait	WARNER BROS	

Movie Still Identification Book Ultimate Edition - Letters

CODE	TITLE/NAME	DIRECTOR/TYPE	STUDIO/DISTRIBUTOR	YEAR
HL	HEAT LIGHTING	LEROY	WARNER BROS	1934
HL	HEAT WAVE (UK: HOUSE ACROSS THE LAKE)	HUGHES	LIPPERT	1954
HL	HEDY LAMARR	portrait	UNITED ARTISTS	
HL	HOORAY FOR LOVE	LANG	RKO	1934
HL	MAN OF AFFAIRS (UK: HIS LORDSHIP)	MASON	GAUMONT BRITISH AMERICA	1936
HL1	PROFESSOR BEWARE	NUGENT	PARAMOUNT	1938
HL-101	APACHE	ALDRICH	UNITED ARTISTS	1954
HL-DL	DISHONORED LADY	STEVENSON	UNITED ARTISTS	1947
HLM	HEDY LAMARR	portrait	RKO	
HL&S	HOOK, LINE AND SINKER	CLINE	RKO	1930
HLS	HOOK LINE AND SINKER	MARSHALL	COLUMBIA	1969
HM	BUNKER BEAN	HAMILTON, KILLY	RKO	1936
HM	HALF MARRIAGE	COWEN	RKO	1929
HM	HARVEY MIDDLEMAN-FIREMAN	PINTOFF	COLUMBIA	1965
HM	HATCHET MAN	WELLMAN	WARNER BROS	1932
HM	HEART OF THE MATTER (UK)	O'FERRALL	AAP	1953
HM	HECHT MACARTHUR PRODUCTIONS	studio		
HM	HELEN MACK	portrait	UNIVERSAL	1930s-40s
HM	HELEN MACK	portrait	RKO	
HM	HELEN MORGAN	portrait	WARNER BROS	
HM	HERBERT MARSHALL	portrait	RKO	
HM	HIGH AND THE MIGHTY	WELLMAN	WARNER BROS	1954
HM	H-MAN (JAP)	HONDA	COLUMBIA	1958
HM	HORSE'S MOUTH (UK)	NEAME	UNITED ARTISTS	1958
HM	HOT MILLIONS (UK)	TILL	MGM	1968
HM	SHINE ON HARVEST MOON	BUTLER	WARNER BROS	1944
HM	SORORITY		WARNER BROS	
HMG	HOT MONEY GIRL (UK: TREASURE OF SAN TERESA)	RAKOFF	UNITED PRODUCERS REL.	1959
HML	COMMON-LAW CABIN	MEYER	EVE	1967
HML	HER MAJESTY LOVE	DIETERLE	WARNER BROS	1931
HMM	HOW TO MAKE A MONSTER	STROCK	AIP	1958
HMP	HARRY M. POPKIN PRODUCTIONS			
HMP1	MY DEAR SECRETARY	MARTIN	UNITED ARTISTS	1948
HMP2	IMPACT	LUBIN	UNITED ARTISTS	1949
HMP3	D.O.A.	MATE	UNITED ARTISTS	1950
HMP4	CHAMPAGNE FOR CAESAR	WHORF	UNITED ARTISTS	1950
HMP5	SECOND WOMAN (ELLEN)	KERN	UNITED ARTISTS	1950
HMW	HATCHET MAN	WELLMAN	FIRST NATIONAL	1932
HN	HARLEM NIGHTS	MURPHY	PARAMOUNT	1989
HN	HI NELLIE	LEROY	WARNER BROS	1934
HN	HIGH NOON	ZINNEMANN	UNITED ARTISTS	1952
HN	HILDEGARDE NEFF/HILDEGARD KNEF	portrait		
HN	HIS HOUR OF MANHOOD	CHATTERTON	NEW YORK MOTION PICTURE	1914
HN	HORNET'S NEST	KARLSON	UNITED ARTISTS	1970
HN	IN THE HEAT OF THE NIGHT	JEWISON	UNITED ARTISTS	1967
HN-5	HIGH NOON	ZINNEMANN	UNITED ARTISTS	1952
HNY	HERCULES IN NEW YORK	SEIDELMAN	RAF INDUSTRIES	1970
HO	HANDS OF ORLAC (UK)	GREVILLE	CONTINENTAL	1960
HO	HEAD OFFICE	FINKLEMAN	TRI STAR	1986
HO	HENRY O'NEILL	portrait	WARNER BROS	
HO	HOLE IN THE HEAD	CAPRA	UNITED ARTISTS	1959
HO	HONKERS	IHNAT	UNITED ARTISTS	1972
HO	HOOSIERS	ANSPAUGH	ORION	1986
HO	HOPSCOTCH	NEAME	AVCO EMBASSY	1980
HO	HUGH O'BRIAN	portrait	UNIVERSAL	
HO	HUNCHBACK OF NOTRE DAME	DIETERLE	RKO	1939
HOD	HAND OF DEATH	NELSON	20th CENTURY FOX	1962
HOD	HOUR OF DECISION (UK)	PENNINGTON-RICHARDS	ASTOR	1957
HOD	HOUSE OF DEATH		20th CENTURY FOX	1962
HOH	CHILLY SCENES OF WINTER (HEAD OVER HEELS)	SILVER	UNITED ARTISTS	1979
HONG	HONG KONG CONFIDENTIAL	CAHN	UNITED ARTISTS	1958
HOR	HORROR OF IT ALL (UK)	FISHER	20th CENTURY FOX	1964
HOR-1	DOES IT PAY?	HORAN	FOX FILM	1923
HOUGH-2	GIRL-SHY COWBOY	HOUGH	FOX FILM	1928
HOW-3	RIVER PIRATE	HOWARD	FOX FILM	1928
HOW-4	CHRISTINA	HOWARD	FOX FILM	1929
HOW-5	VALIANT	HOWARD	FOX FILM	1929
HOW-6	LOVE, LIVE AND LAUGH	HOWARD	FOX FILM	1929
HOW-7	GOOD INTENTIONS	HOWARD	FOX FILM	1930
HOW-8	SCOTLAND YARD	HOWARD	FOX FILM	1930

Movie Still Identification Book Ultimate Edition - Letters

CODE	TITLE/NAME	DIRECTOR/TYPE	STUDIO/DISTRIBUTOR	YEAR
HOW-9	DON'T BET ON WOMEN	HOWARD	FOX FILM	1931
HOW-10	TRANSATLANTIC	HOWARD	FOX FILM	1931
HOW-11	SURRENDER	HOWARD	FOX FILM	1931
HOW-12	TRIAL OF VIVIENNE WARE	HOWARD	FOX FILM	1932
HOW-13	FIRST YEAR	HOWARD	FOX FILM	1932
HP	BUG	SZWARC	PARAMOUNT	1975
HP	DAREDEVIL DRIVER	EASON	WARNER BROS	1938
HP	DIVORCE AMONG FRIENDS	DEL RUTH	WARNER BROS	1930
HP	HALPERIN PRODUCTIONS	studio		
HP	HARRIET PARSONS	portrait	RKO	
HP	HEIDI AND PETER	SCHNYDER	UNITED ARTISTS	1955
HP	HELEN PARRISH	portrait	UNIVERSAL	
HP	HERMES PAN	portrait	RKO	
HP	HIGH FLIGHT	GILLING	COLUMBIA	1957
HP	HIGH PRESSURE	LEROY	WARNER BROS	1932
HP	HIGHWAY PICKUP	MARQUAND	TIMES REL	1963
HP	HONEY POT	MANKIEWICZ	UNITED ARTISTS	1967
HP	HOODLUM PRIEST	KERSHNER	UNITED ARTISTS	1961
HP	HOTEL PARADISO (UK)	GLENVILLE	MGM	1966
HP	HUNTING PARTY	MEDFORD	UNITED ARTISTS	1971
HP	IT'S HOT IN PARADISE	BOTTGER	PACEMAKER	1962
HP	WHEN I GROW UP	KANIN	UNITED ARTISTS	1951
HP-1	CLOUDS OVER EUROPE (UK: Q PLANES)	WHELAN, WOODS	COLUMBIA	1939
HP-2	U-BOAT 29 (UK: SPY IN BLACK)	POWELL	COLUMBIA	1939
HP-3	BRIDGE ON THE RIVER KWAI (UK)	LEAN	COLUMBIA	1957
HP-3	MINE OWN EXECUTIONER (UK)	KIMMINS	20TH CENTURY FOX	1947
HP-31-Z	WHITE ZOMBIE	HALPERIN	UNITED ARTISTS	1932
HP 183	PARADISE HAWAIIAN STYLE	MOORE	PARAMOUNT	1966
HP 918-10)	HOODLUM PRIEST	KERSHNER	UNITED ARTISTS	1961
HPM5	THEY MET IN THE DARK (UK)	LAMAC	ENGLISH	1943
HPP	YOU CAN'T TAKE IT WITH YOU	CAPRA	COLUMBIA	1938
HQ2	TIME WITHOUT PITY (UK)	LOSEY	ASTOR	1957
HR	CONFESSION	MAY	WARNER BROS	1937
HR	HAL ROACH PICTURES	studio		
HR	HARDBOILED ROSE	WEIGHT	WARNER BROS	1929
HR	HIT AND RUN	HAAS	UNITED ARTISTS	1957
HR	HOT ROD GIRL	MARTINSON	AIP	1956
HR	HOTEL RESERVE (UK)	COMFORT, GREENBAUM	RKO	1944
HR-3600	PUTTIN' ON THE RITZ	SLOMAN	UNITED ARTISTS	1930
HR A-1	CATCH AS CATCH CAN (sh)	NEILAN	MGM	1931
HR A-1	LUKE RIDES ROUGHSHOD (sh)	ROACH	PATHE EXCHANGE	1916
HR A-1	OUR GANG (sh)	MCGOWAN	PATHE EXCHANGE	1922
HR A-2	FIRE FIGHTERS (sh)	MCGOWAN	PATHE EXCHANGE	1922
HR A-2	LUKE, CRYSTAL GAZER (sh)	ROACH	PATHE EXCHANGE	1916
HR A-2	PAJAMA PARTY (sh)	ROACH	MGM	1931
HR A-3	LUKE'S LOST LAMB (sh)	ROACH	PATHE EXCHANGE	1916
HR A-3	WAR MAMAS (sh)	NEILAN	MGM	1931
HR A-3	YOUNG SHERLOCKS (sh)	MCGOWAN	PATHE EXCHANGE	1922
HR A-4	LUKE DOES THE MIDWAY (sh)	ROACH	PATHE EXCHANGE	1916
HR A-4	ON THE LOOSE (sh)	ROACH	MGM	1931
HR A-4	ONE TERRIBLE DAY (sh)	MCGOWAN	PATHE EXCHANGE	1922
HR A-5	A QUIET STREET (sh)	MCGOWAN	PATHE EXCHANGE	1922
HR A-5	LUKE AND THE BANGTAILS (sh)	ROACH	PATHE EXCHANGE	1916
HR A-5	SEAL SKINS (sh)	LIGHTFOOT	MGM	1932
HR A-6	LUKE JOINS THE NAVY (sh)	ROACH	PATHE EXCHANGE	1916
HR A-6	RED NOSES (sh)	HORNE	MGM	1932
HR A-6	SATURDAY MORNING (sh)	MCGOWAN	PATHE EXCHANGE	1922
HR A-7	BIG SHOW (sh)	MCGOWAN	PATHE EXCHANGE	1923
HR A-7	LUKE AND THE MERMAIDS (sh)	ROACH	PATHE EXCHANGE	1916
HR A-7	STRICTLY UNRELIABLE (sh)	MARSHALL	MGM	1932
HR A-8	COBBLER (sh)	MCNAMARA	PATHE EXCHANGE	1923
HR A-8	LUKE'S SPEEDY CLUB LIFE (sh)	ROACH	PATHE EXCHANGE	1916
HR A-8	OLD BULL (sh)	MARSHALL	MGM	1932
HR A-9	CHAMPEEN (sh)	MCGOWAN	PATHE EXCHANGE	1923
HR A-9	LUKE THE CHAUFFEUR (sh)	ROACH	PATHE EXCHANGE	1916
HR A-9	SHOW BUSINESS (sh)	WHITE	MGM	1932
HR A-10	ALUM AND EVE (sh)	MARSHALL	MGM	1932
HR A-10	BOYS TO BOARD (sh)	MCNAMARA	PATHE EXCHANGE	1923
HR A-10	LUKE'S PREPAREDNESS PREPARATIONS (sh)	ROACH	PATHE EXCHANGE	1916
HR A-11	LUKE THE GLADIATOR (sh)	ROACH	PATHE EXCHANGE	1916

Movie Still Identification Book Ultimate Edition - Letters

CODE	TITLE/NAME	DIRECTOR/TYPE	STUDIO/DISTRIBUTOR	YEAR
HR A-11	PLEASANT JOURNEY (sh)	MCGOWAN	PATHE EXCHANGE	1923
HR A-11	SOILERS (sh)	MARSHALL	MGM	1932
HR A-12	GIANTS VS. YANKS (sh)	MCGOWAN	PATHE EXCHANGE	1923
HR A-12	LUKE, PATIENT PROVIDER (sh)	ROACH	PATHE EXCHANGE	1916
HR A-12	SNEAK EASILY (sh)	MEINS	MGM	1932
HR A-13	ASLEEP IN THE FLEET (sh)	MEINS	MGM	1933
HR A-13	BACK STAGE (sh)	MCGOWAN	PATHE EXCHANGE	1923
HR A-14	DOGS OF WAR (sh)	MCGOWAN	PATHE EXCHANGE	1923
HR A-14	LUKE'S NEWSIE KNOCKOUT (sh)	ROACH	PATHE EXCHANGE	1916
HR A-14	MAIDS A LA MODE (sh)	MEINS	MGM	1933
HR A-15	BARGAIN OF THE CENTURY (sh)	CHASE	MGM	1933
HR A-15	LODGE NIGHT (sh)	MCGOWAN	PATHE EXCHANGE	1923
HR A-15	LUKE'S MOVIE MUDDLE (LUKE'S MODEL MOVIE) (sh)	ROACH	PATHE EXCHANGE	1916
HR A-16	FAST COMPANY (sh)	MCGOWAN	PATHE EXCHANGE	1924
HR A-16	LUKE'S RANK IMPERSONATOR (sh)	ROACH	PATHE EXCHANGE	1916
HR A-16	ONE TRACK MINDS (sh)	MEINS	MGM	1933
HR A-17	BEAUTY AND THE BUS (sh)	MEINS	MGM	1933
HR A-17	LUKE'S FIREWORKS FIZZLE (sh)	ROACH	PATHE EXCHANGE	1916
HR A-17	STAGE FRIGHT (sh)	MCGOWAN	PATHE EXCHANGE	1923
HR A-18	BACK TO NATURE (sh)	MEINS	MGM	1933
HR A-18	JULY DAYS (sh)	MCGOWAN	PATHE EXCHANGE	1923
HR A-18	LUKE LOCATES THE LOOT (sh)	ROACH	PATHE EXCHANGE	1916
HR A-19	AIR FRIGHT (sh)	MEINS	MGM	1933
HR A-19	LUKE'S SHATTERED SLEEP (sh)	ROACH	PATHE EXCHANGE	1916
HR A-19	SUNDAY CALM (sh)	MCGOWAN	PATHE EXCHANGE	1923
HR-A20	BABES IN THE GOODS	MEINS	MGM	1934
HR A-20	LUKE'S LOST LIBERTY (sh)	ROACH	PATHE EXCHANGE	1917
HR A-20	NO NOISE (sh)	MCGOWAN	PATHE EXCHANGE	1923
HR A-21	DERBY DAY (sh)	MCGOWAN	PATHE EXCHANGE	1923
HR A-21	LUKE'S BUSY DAY (sh)	ROACH	PATHE EXCHANGE	1917
HR A-21	SOUP AND FISH (sh)	MEINS	MGM	1934
HR A-22	LUKE'S TROLLEY TROUBLES (sh)	ROACH	PATHE EXCHANGE	1917
HR A-22	MAID IN HOLLYWOOD (sh)	MEINS	MGM	1934
HR A-22	TIRE TROUBLE (sh)	MCGOWAN	PATHE EXCHANGE	1924
HR A-23	BIG BUSINESS (sh)	MCGOWAN	PATHE EXCHANGE	1924
HR A-23	I'LL BE SUING YOU (sh)	MEINS	MGM	1934
HR A-23	LONESOME LUKE, LAWYER (sh)	ROACH	PATHE EXCHANGE	1917
HR A-24	BUCCANEERS (sh)	MCGOWAN, GOLDAINE	PATHE EXCHANGE	1924
HR A-24	LUKE WINS YE LADYE FAIRE (sh)	ROACH	PATHE EXCHANGE	1917
HR A-24	THREE CHUMPS AHEAD (sh)	MEINS	MGM	1934
HR A-25	DONE IN OIL (sh)	MEINS	MGM	1934
HR A-25	LONESOME LUKE'S LIVELY LIFE (sh)	ROACH	PATHE EXCHANGE	1917
HR A-25	SEEIN' THINGS (sh)	MCGOWAN	PATHE EXCHANGE	1924
HR A-26	COMMENCEMENT DAY (sh)	MCGOWAN, GOLDAINE	PATHE EXCHANGE	1924
HR A-26	LONESOME LUKE, MECHANIC (sh)	ROACH	PATHE EXCHANGE	1917
HR A-26	ONE HORSE FARMERS (sh)	MEINS	MGM	1934
HR A-27	IT'S A BEAR (sh)	MCGOWAN	PATHE EXCHANGE	1924
HR A-27	LONESOME LUKE'S HONEYMOON (sh)	ROACH	PATHE EXCHANGE	1917
HR A-27	OPENED BY MISTAKE (sh)	PARROTT	MGM	1934
HR A-28	BUM VOYAGE (sh)	GRINDE	MGM	1934
HR A-28	CRADLE ROBBERS (sh)	MCGOWAN	PATHE EXCHANGE	1924
HR A-28	LONESOME LUKE, PLUMBER (sh)	ROACH	PATHE EXCHANGE	1917
HR A-29	JUBLIO, JR. (sh)	MCGOWAN	PATHE EXCHANGE	1924
HR A-29	STOP! LUKE! LISTEN! (sh)	ROACH	PATHE EXCHANGE	1917
HR A-29	TREASURE BLUES (sh)	PARROTT	MGM	1935
HR A-30	HIGH SOCIETY (sh)	MCGOWAN	PATHE EXCHANGE	1924
HR A-30	LONESOME LUKE'S WILD WOMEN (sh)	ROACH	PATHE EXCHANGE	1917
HR A-30	TIN MAN (sh)	PARROTT	MGM	1935
HR A-31	LONESOME LUKE ON TIN CAN ALLEY (sh)	ROACH	PATHE EXCHANGE	1917
HR A-31	MISSES STOOGE (sh)	PARROTT	MGM	1935
HR A-31	SUN DOWN LIMITED (sh)	MCGOWAN	PATHE EXCHANGE	1924
HR A-32	EVERY MAN FOR HIMSELF (sh)	MCGOWAN	PATHE EXCHANGE	1924
HR A-32	LONESOME LUKE LOSES PATIENTS (sh)	ROACH	PATHE EXCHANGE	1917
HR A-32	SING, SISTER, SING (sh)	PARROTT	MGM	1935
HR A-33	LONESOME LUKE IN LOVE, LAUGHS AND LATHER (sh)	ROACH	PATHE EXCHANGE	1917
HR A-33	MYSTERIOUS MYSTERY! (sh)	MCGOWAN	PATHE EXCHANGE	1924
HR A-33	SLIGHTLY STATIC (sh)	TERHUNE	MGM	1935
HR A-34	BIG TOWN (sh)	MCGOWAN	PATHE EXCHANGE	1925
HR A-34	LONESOME LUKE, MESSENGER (sh)	ROACH	PATHE EXCHANGE	1917
HR A-34	TWIN TRIPLETS (sh)	TERHUNE	MGM	1935

Movie Still Identification Book Ultimate Edition - Letters

CODE	TITLE/NAME	DIRECTOR/TYPE	STUDIO/DISTRIBUTOR	YEAR
HR A-35	CIRCUS FEVER (sh)	MCGOWAN	PATHE EXCHANGE	1925
HR A-35	HOT MONEY (sh)	HORNE	MGM	1935
HR A-35	LONESOME LUKE IN FROM LONDON TO LARAMIE (sh)	ROACH	PATHE EXCHANGE	1917
HR A-36	DOG DAYS (sh)	MCGOWAN	PATHE EXCHANGE	1925
HR A-36	LONESOME LUKE IN BIRDS OF A FEATHER (sh)	ROACH	PATHE EXCHANGE	1917
HR A-36	TOP FLAT (sh)	JEVNE, TERHUNE	MGM	1935
HR A-37	ALL AMERICAN TOOTHACHE (sh)	MEINS	MGM	1936
HR A-37	LOVE BUG (sh)	MCGOWAN	PATHE EXCHANGE	1925
HR A-37	TRUMPS (sh)	ROACH	PATHE EXCHANGE	1917
HR A-38	ASK GRANDMA (sh)	MCGOWAN	PATHE EXCHANGE	1925
HR A-38	LONESOME LUKE IN WE NEVER SLEEP (sh)	ROACH	PATHE EXCHANGE	1917
HR A-38	PAN HANDLERS (sh)	TERHUNE	MGM	1936
HR A-39	AT SEA ASHORE (sh)	TERHUNE	MGM	1936
HR A-39	SHOOTIN' INJUNS (sh)	MCGOWAN	PATHE EXCHANGE	1925
HR A-40	HILL TILLIES (sh)	MEINS	MGM	1936
HR A-40	OFFICIAL OFFICERS (sh)	MCGOWAN	PATHE EXCHANGE	1925
HR A-41	MARY, QUEEN OF TOTS (sh)	MCGOWAN	PATHE EXCHANGE	1925
HR A-42	BOYS WILL BE JOYS (sh)	MCGOWAN	PATHE EXCHANGE	1925
HR A-43	BETTER MOVIES (sh)	MCGOWAN	PATHE EXCHANGE	1925
HR AC-105	UNNAMED DIPPY DOO DADS (sh)		PATHE EXCHANGE	1923
HR AC-113	KNOCKOUT (sh)	POWERS	PATHE EXCHANGE	1923
HR AC-124	BAR-FLY (sh)	POWERS	PATHE EXCHANGE	1924
HR AC-128	MAN PAYS (sh)	POWERS	PATHE EXCHANGE	1924
HR B-1	365 DAYS (sh)	CHASE	PATHE EXCHANGE	1922
HR B-1	CARETAKER'S DAUGHTER (sh)	MCCAREY	PATHE EXCHANGE	1925
HR B-1	GO GET 'EM HUTCH (sh)	SEITZ	PATHE EXCHANGE	1922
HR B-1	MOVIE DAZE (sh)	MEINS	MGM	1934
HR B-1	SCHEMER SKINNY'S SCHEMES (sh)		PATHE EXCHANGE	1917
HR B-2	BEFORE THE PUBLIC (sh)	CHASE	PATHE EXCHANGE	1923
HR B-2	CROOK'S TOUR (sh)	MCGOWAN	MGM	1933
HR B-2	SKINNY'S LOVE TRIANGLE (sh)		PATHE EXCHANGE	1917
HR B-2	UNEASY THREE (sh)	CHASE	PATHE EXCHANGE	1925
HR B-3	HIS WOODEN WEDDING (sh)	MCCAREY	PATHE EXCHANGE	1925
HR B-3	NEWLY RICH (sh)	CHASE	PATHE EXCHANGE	1922
HR B-3	SCHEMER SKINNY'S SCHEMES (sh)		PATHE EXCHANGE	1917
HR B-3	TWIN SCREWS (sh)	PARROTT	MGM	1933
HR B-4	CHARLEY MY BOY (sh)	MCCAREY	PATHE EXCHANGE	1926
HR B-4	DRAMA'S DREADFUL DEAL (sh)		PATHE EXCHANGE	1917
HR B-4	GREEN CAT (sh)	CHASE	PATHE EXCHANGE	1922
HR B-4	MIXED NUTS (sh)	PARROTT	MGM	1934
HR B-5	MAMA BEHAVE (sh)	CHASE	PATHE EXCHANGE	1926
HR B-5	NEXT WEEKEND (sh)	DUNN	MGM	1934
HR B-5	SKINNY GETS A GOAT (sh)	ROACH	PATHE EXCHANGE	1917
HR B-5	WHERE AM I? (sh)	CHASE	PATHE EXCHANGE	1923
HR B-6	CARETAKER'S DAUGHTER (sh)	FRENCH	MGM	1934
HR B-6	DOG SHY (sh)	MCCAREY	PATHE EXCHANGE	1926
HR B-6	OLD SEA DOG (sh)	CHASE	PATHE EXCHANGE	1922
HR B-6	SKINNY'S FALSE ALARM (sh)	ROACH	PATHE EXCHANGE	1917
HR B-7	DIG UP (sh)	HUTCHINSON	PATHE EXCHANGE	1923
HR B-7	MRS. BARNACLE BILL (sh)	FRENCH	MGM	1934
HR B-7	MUM'S THE WORD (sh)	MCCAREY	PATHE EXCHANGE	1926
HR B-7	SKINNY'S SHIP-WRECKED SAND-WITCH (sh)	ROACH	PATHE EXCHANGE	1917
HR B-8	HOOK, LINE AND SINKER (sh)	CHASE	PATHE EXCHANGE	1922
HR B-8	LONG FLIV THE KING (sh)	MCCAREY	PATHE EXCHANGE	1926
HR B-8	SKINNY ROUTS A ROBBER (sh)		PATHE EXCHANGE	1917
HR B8	SPEAKING OF RELATIONS	YATES	MGM	1934
HR B-9	BOARDER BUSTERS (sh)		PATHE EXCHANGE	1917
HR B-9	CALIFORNIA OR BUST (sh)	HUTCHINSON	PATHE EXCHANGE	1923
HR B-9	MIGHTY LIKE A MOOSE (sh)	MCCAREY	PATHE EXCHANGE	1926
HR B-10	CRAZY LIKE A FOX (sh)	MCCAREY	PATHE EXCHANGE	1926
HR B-10	TOUGH WINTER (sh)	CHASE	PATHE EXCHANGE	1923
HR B-11	BROMO AND JULIET (sh)	MCCAREY	PATHE EXCHANGE	1926
HR B-11	IT'S A GIFT (sh)	FAY	PATHE EXCHANGE	1923
HR B-12	SOLD AT AUCTION (sh)	CHASE	PATHE EXCHANGE	1923
HR B-12	TELL 'EM NOTHING (sh)	MCCAREY	PATHE EXCHANGE	1926
HR B-13	BE YOUR AGE (sh)	CHASE	PATHE EXCHANGE	1926
HR B-13	WALKOUT (sh)	JESKE	PATHE EXCHANGE	1923
HR B-13	WHY WORRY? (sh)	TAYLOR, NEWMEYER	PATHE EXCHANGE	1923
HR B-14	MANY SCRAPY RETURNS (sh)	PARROTT	PATHE EXCHANGE	1927
HR B-14	MYSTERY MAN (sh)	FAY	PATHE EXCHANGE	1923

Movie Still Identification Book Ultimate Edition - Letters

CODE	TITLE/NAME	DIRECTOR/TYPE	STUDIO/DISTRIBUTOR	YEAR
HR B-15	JACK FROST (sh)	CHASE	PATHE EXCHANGE	1923
HR B-15	THERE AIN'T NO SANTA CLAUS (sh)	PARROTT	PATHE EXCHANGE	1926
HR B-16	ARE BRUNETTES SAFE? (sh)	PARROTT	PATHE EXCHANGE	1927
HR B-16	COURTSHIP OF MILES SANDWICH (sh)	CHASE	PATHE EXCHANGE	1923
HR B-17	ONE MAMA MAN (sh)	PARROTT	PATHE EXCHANGE	1927
HR B-18	FORGOTTEN SWEETIES (sh)	PARROTT	PATHE EXCHANGE	1927
HR B-19	BIGGER AND BETTER BLONDS (sh)	PARROTT	PATHE EXCHANGE	1927
HR B-20	FLUTTERING HEARTS (sh)	PARROTT	PATHE EXCHANGE	1927
HR B-21	WHAT WOMEN DID FOR ME (sh)	PARROTT	PATHE EXCHANGE	1927
HR B-22	NOW I'LL TELL ONE (sh)	PARROTT	PATHE EXCHANGE	1927
HR B-23	ASSISTANT WIVES (sh)	PARROTT	PATHE EXCHANGE	1927
HR-C	CHARLEY CHASE series at HAL ROACH			
HRC	HERCULES	COZZI	CANNON	1983
HR C-1	HE FORGOT TO REMEMBER (sh)	POWERS, BUCKINGHAM	PATHE EXCHANGE	1926
HR C-1	JUNE MADNESS (sh)	PEMBROKE	PATHE EXCHANGE	1920
HR C-1	LIGHTER THAT FAILED (sh)	PARROTT	MGM	1927
HR C-1	PANIC IS ON (sh)	PARROTT	MGM	1931
HR C-1	UNNAMED ROLIN PROJECT (sh)	WHITING	PATHE EXCHANGE	1915
HR C-2	SANDMAN (sh)	NEWMEYER	PATHE EXCHANGE	1920
HR C-2	SHOULD SAILORS MARRY? (sh)	ROBBINS	PATHE EXCHANGE	1925
HR C-2	SKIP THE MALOO! (sh)	PARROTT	MGM	1931
HR C-2	STING OF STINGS (sh)	PARROTT	MGM	1927
HR C-2	UNNAMED ROLIN PROJECT (sh)	WHITING	PATHE EXCHANGE	1915
HR C-3	ALIAS ALADDIN (sh)	ROACH	PATHE EXCHANGE	1920
HR C-3	MOONLIGHT AND NOSES (sh)	LAUREL, JONES	PATHE EXCHANGE	1925
HR C-3	UNNAMED ROLIN PROJECT (sh)	WHITING	PATHE EXCHANGE	1915
HR C-3	WAY OF ALL PANTS (sh)	JONES, MCCAREY	MGM	1927
HR C-3	WHAT A BOZO (sh)	PARROTT	MGM	1931
HR C-4	HASTY MARRIAGE (sh)	PRATT	MGM	1931
HR C-4	MAMMA'S BOY (sh)	DORAN	PATHE EXCHANGE	1920
HR C-4	UNNAMED ROLIN PROJECT (sh)	WHITING	PATHE EXCHANGE	1915
HR C-4	US (sh)		MGM	1927
HR C-4	WANDERING PAPAS (sh)	LAUREL	PATHE EXCHANGE	1926
HR C-5	NEVER THE DAMES SHALL MEET (sh)	PARROTT	MGM	1927
HR C-5	POWDER MANKEYS (sh)	WHITING	PATHE EXCHANGE	1915
HR C-5	QUEEN'S UP! (sh)	NEWMEYER	PATHE EXCHANGE	1920
HR C-5	STARVATION BLUES (sh)	WALLACE	PATHE EXCHANGE	1925
HR C-5	TABASCO KID (sh)	HORNE	MGM	1932
HR C-6	ALL FOR NOTHING (sh)	PARROTT	MGM	1928
HR C-6	MAN HATERS (sh)	BARROWS	PATHE EXCHANGE	1922
HR C-6	NICKLE NURSER (sh)	DOANE	MGM	1932
HR C-6	WHAT'S THE WORLD COMING TO? (sh)	JONES, WALLACE	PATHE EXCHANGE	1926
HR C-7	GREEK MEETS GREEK (sh)	BARROWS	PATHE EXCHANGE	1920
HR C-7	IN WALKED CHARLEY (sh)	DOANE	MGM	1932
HR C-7	MOVIE NIGHT (sh)	FOSTER	MGM	1929
HR C-7	SCARED STIFF (sh)	HORNE	PATHE EXCHANGE	1926
HR C-8	FAMILY GROUP (sh)	GUIOL, MCCAREY	MGM	1928
HR C-8	FIRST IN WAR (sh)	DOANE	MGM	1932
HR C-8	SLEEPY HEAD (sh)	BARROWS	PATHE EXCHANGE	1920
HR C-8	WIFE TAMERS (sh)	HORNE	PATHE EXCHANGE	1926
HR C-9	ACHING YOUTH (sh)	GUIOL	MGM	1928
HR C-9	BURGLARS BOLD (sh)	BARROWS	PATHE EXCHANGE	1921
HR C-9	GALLOPING GHOSTS (sh)	PARROTT	PATHE EXCHANGE	1928
HR C-9	MERRY WIDOWER (sh)	WALLACE	PATHE EXCHANGE	1926
HR C-9	YOUNG IRONSIDES (sh)	PARROTT	MGM	1932
HR C-10	GIRL GRIEF (sh)	PARROTT	MGM	1932
HR C-10	LIMOUSINE LOVE (sh)	GUIOL	MGM	1928
HR C-10	PINNING IT ON (sh)	BARROWS	PATHE EXCHANGE	1921
HR C-10	SHOULD HUSBANDS PAY? (sh)	JONES, LAUREL	PATHE EXCHANGE	1926
HR C-11	FIGHT PEST (sh)	GUIOL, MCCAREY	MGM	1928
HR C-11	NOW WE'LL TELL ONE (sh)	PARROTT	MGM	1932
HR C-11	OH, PROMISE ME (sh)	BARROWS	PATHE EXCHANGE	1921
HR C-12	IMAGINE MY EMBARRASSMENT (sh)	YATES, MCCAREY	MGM	1928
HR C-12	MR. BRIDE (sh)	PARROTT	MGM	1932
HR C-12	PRINCE PISTACHIO (sh)	BARROWS	PATHE EXCHANGE	1921
HR C-13	FALLEN ARCHES (sh)	MEINS	MGM	1933
HR C-13	IS EVERYBODY HAPPY? (sh)	YATES	MGM	1928
HR C-13	PAINT AND POWDER (sh)	ROACH	PATHE EXCHANGE	1921
HR C-14	BOOSTER (sh)	YATES	MGM	1928
HR C-14	HURRY WEST (sh)	BARROWS	PATHE EXCHANGE	1921

Movie Still Identification Book Ultimate Edition - Letters

CODE	TITLE/NAME	DIRECTOR/TYPE	STUDIO/DISTRIBUTOR	YEAR
HR C-14	NATURE IN THE WRONG (sh)	CHASE	MGM	1933
HR C-15	ALL PARTS (sh)	YATES	MGM	1928
HR C-15	HIS SILENT RACKET (sh)		MGM	1933
HR C-15	RUNNING WILD (sh)	BARROWS	PATHE EXCHANGE	1921
HR C-16	ARABIAN TIGHTS (sh)	ROACH	MGM	1933
HR C-16	CHASING HUSBANDS (sh)	PARROTT	MGM	1928
HR C-16	HOBGOBLINS (sh)	GORDON	PATHE EXCHANGE	1921
HR C-17	LOVE LESSON (sh)	BARROWS	PATHE EXCHANGE	1921
HR C-17	RUBY LIPS (sh)	PARROTT	MGM	1929
HR C-17	SHERMAN SAID IT (sh)	CHASE	MGM	1933
HR C-18	MIDSUMMER MUSH (sh)	CHASE	MGM	1933
HR C-18	NON SKID KID (sh)	GORDON	PATHE EXCHANGE	1922
HR C-18	OFF TO BUFFALO (sh)	HORNE	MGM	1929
HR C-19	LOUD SOUP (sh)	FOSTER	MGM	1929
HR C-19	LUNCHEON AT TWELVE (sh)	CHASE	MGM	1933
HR C-19	STRAIGHT CROOK (sh)	ROACH	PATHE EXCHANGE	1921
HR C-20	CHINK (sh)	BARROWS	PATHE EXCHANGE	1921
HR C-20	CRACKED ICEMAN (sh)	DUNN	MGM	1934
HR C-20	THIN TWINS (sh)	HORNE	MGM	1929
HR C-21	BIG SQUAWK (sh)	DOANE	MGM	1929
HR C-21	FOUR PARTS (sh)	CHASE, DUNN	MGM	1934
HR C-21	LATE HOURS (sh)	BARROWS	PATHE EXCHANGE	1921
HR C-22	I'LL TAKE VANILLA (sh)	DUNN	MGM	1934
HR C-22	LEAPING LOVE (sh)	DOANE	MGM	1929
HR C-22	STOP KIDDING (sh)	KERR, BARROWS	PATHE EXCHANGE	1921
HR C-23	ANOTHER WILD IDEA (sh)	CHASE, DUNN	MGM	1934
HR C-23	GOOD MORNING JUDGE (sh)	ROACH	PATHE EXCHANGE	1922
HR C-23	SNAPPY SNEEZER (sh)	DOANE	MGM	1929
HR C-24	CRAZY FEET (sh)	DOANE	MGM	1929
HR C-24	IT HAPPENED ONE DAY (sh)	DUNN	MGM	1934
HR C-24	LATE LAMENTED (sh)	EDDY	PATHE EXCHANGE	1922
HR C-25	ON THEIR WAY (sh)	BARROWS	PATHE EXCHANGE	1921
HR C-25	SOMETHING SIMPLE (sh)	CHASE, WEEMS	MGM	1934
HR C-25	STEPPING OUT (sh)	DOANE	MGM	1929
HR C-26	GREAT GOBS! (sh)	DOANE	MGM	1929
HR C-26	SWEET BY AND BY (sh)	KERR	PATHE EXCHANGE	1921
HR C-26	YOU SAID A HATFUL! (sh)	CHASE	MGM	1934
HR C-27	FATE'S FATHEAD (sh)	CHASE	MGM	1934
HR C-27	MANY HAPPY RETURNS (sh)	KERR	PATHE EXCHANGE	1922
HR C-27	REAL MCCOY (sh)	DOANE	MGM	1930
HR C-28	ALL TEED UP (sh)	KENNEDY	MGM	1930
HR C-28	BUSY BEES (sh)	KERR	PATHE EXCHANGE	1922
HR C-28	CHASES OF PIMPLE STREET (sh)	CHASE	MGM	1934
HR C-29	HIGH TIDE (sh)	BARROWS	PATHE EXCHANGE	1922
HR C-29	OKAY TOOTS! (sh)	CHASE, TERHUNE	MGM	1935
HR C-29	WHISPERING WHOOPEE (sh)	HORNE	MGM	1930
HR C-30	BETWEEN MEALS (sh)	GREY	PATHE EXCHANGE	1926
HR C-30	FIFTY MILLION HUSBANDS (sh)	HORNE, KENNEDY	MGM	1930
HR C-30	POKER AT EIGHT (sh)	CHASE	MGM	1935
HR C-31	DON'T BUTT IN (ROUSTABOUT) (sh)	GREY	PATHE EXCHANGE	1926
HR C-31	FAST WORK (sh)	HORNE	MGM	1930
HR C-31	SOUTHERN EXPOSURE	CHASE, ROACH	MGM	1935
HR C-32	FOUR STAR BOARDER (sh)	CHASE	MGM	1935
HR C-32	GIRL SHOCK (sh)	HORNE	MGM	1930
HR C-32	TRY, TRY AGAIN (sh)	GREY	PATHE EXCHANGE	1922
HR C-33	DOLLAR DIZZY (sh)	HORNE	MGM	1930
HR C-33	NURSE TO YOU! (sh)	CHASE, MOFFITT	MGM	1935
HR C-33	SOFT PEDAL (sh)	GREY	PATHE EXCHANGE	1926
HR C-34	LOOSER THAN LOOSE (sh)	HORNE	MGM	1930
HR C-34	MANHATTAN MONKEY BUSINESS (sh)	CHASE, LAW	MGM	1935
HR C-35	HIGH C'S (sh)	HORNE	MGM	1930
HR C-35	PAY THE CASHIER (sh)	GREY	PATHE EXCHANGE	1926
HR C-35	PUBLIC GHOST #1 (sh)	CHASE, LAW	MGM	1935
HR C-36	LIFE HESITATES AT 40 (sh)	CHASE, LAW	MGM	1936
HR C-36	SLEUTH (sh)	GREY	PATHE EXCHANGE	1922
HR C-36	THUNDERING TENORS (sh)	HORNE	MGM	1931
HR C-37	COUNT TAKES THE COUNT (sh)	LAW	MGM	1936
HR C-37	ONLY SON (sh)	GREY	PATHE EXCHANGE	1926
HR C-37	PIP FROM PITTSBURGH (sh)	PARROTT	MGM	1931
HR C-38	HIRED AND FIRED (sh)	GREY	PATHE EXCHANGE	1926

Movie Still Identification Book Ultimate Edition - Letters

CODE	TITLE/NAME	DIRECTOR/TYPE	STUDIO/DISTRIBUTOR	YEAR
HR C-38	ROUGH SEAS (sh)	PARROTT	MGM	1931
HR C-38	VAMP TILL READY (sh)	CHASE, LAW	MGM	1936
HR C-39	NEIGHBORHOOD HOUSE (sh)	CHASE, LAW	MGM	1936
HR C-39	ONE OF THE SMITHS (sh)	PARROTT	MGM	1931
HR C-39	RICH MAN, POOR MAN (sh)	CHASE	PATHE EXCHANGE	1922
HR C-40	ON THE WRONG TREK (sh)	CHASE, LAW	MGM	1936
HR C-41	ARE PARENTS PICKLES? (sh)	PRATT	PATHE EXCHANGE	1925
HR C-42	WINNER TAKE ALL (sh)	SANTELL	PATHE EXCHANGE	1923
HR C-43	FRIDAY THE 13TH (sh)	DAVIS	PATHE EXCHANGE	1922
HR C-44	TRUTH JUGGLER (sh)	DAVIS	PATHE EXCHANGE	1922
HR C-45	BED OF ROSES (sh)	HOWE	PATHE EXCHANGE	1922
HR C-46	BRIDE-TO-BE (sh)	DAVIS	PATHE EXCHANGE	1922
HR C-47	TAKE THE NEXT CAR (sh)	HOWE	PATHE EXCHANGE	1922
HR C-48	TOUCH ALL THE BASES (sh)	DAVIS	PATHE EXCHANGE	1922
HR C-49	ROUGH ON ROMEO (sh)	DAVIS	PATHE EXCHANGE	1922
HR C-50	WET WEATHER (sh)	HOWE	PATHE EXCHANGE	1922
HR C-51	OUT ON BAIL (sh)	DAVIS	PATHE EXCHANGE	1922
HR C-52	SHOOT STRAIGHT (sh)	HOWE	PATHE EXCHANGE	1923
HR C-53	LANDLUBBER (sh)	DAVIS	PATHE EXCHANGE	1922
HR C-54	SOAK THE SHEIK (sh)	HOWE	PATHE EXCHANGE	1922
HR C-55	BONE DRY (sh)	CHASE, DAVIS	PATHE EXCHANGE	1922
HR C-56	LOOSE TIGHT WAD (sh)	HOWE	PATHE EXCHANGE	1923
HR C-57	SHINE 'EM UP (sh)	DAVIS	PATHE EXCHANGE	1922
HR C-58	FACE THE CAMERA (sh)	HOWE	PATHE EXCHANGE	1922
HR C-59	GOLF BUG (sh)	DAVIS	PATHE EXCHANGE	1922
HR C-60	UPPERCUT (sh)	HOWE	PATHE EXCHANGE	1922
HR C-61	WHISTLING LIONS (sh)	PARROTT	PATHE EXCHANGE	1925
HR C-62	SHIVER AND SHAKE (sh)	HOWE	PATHE EXCHANGE	1922
HR C-63	HARVEST HANDS (sh)	DAVIS	PATHE EXCHANGE	1922
HR C-64	FLIVVER (sh)	HOWE	PATHE EXCHANGE	1922
HR C-65	I'LL TAKE VANILLA (sh)	DAVIS	PATHE EXCHANGE	1922
HR C-66	WASHED ASHORE (sh)	HOWE	PATHE EXCHANGE	1922
HR C-67	FAIR WEEK (sh)	DAVIS	PATHE EXCHANGE	1922
HR C-68	BLAZE AWAY (sh)	HOWE	PATHE EXCHANGE	1922
HR C-69	FIRE THE FIREMAN (sh)	HOWE	PATHE EXCHANGE	1922
HR C-70	WHITE BLACKSMITH (sh)	JESKE	PATHE EXCHANGE	1922
HR C-71	WATCH YOUR WIFE (sh)	HOWE	PATHE EXCHANGE	1923
HR C-72	PASTE AND PAPER (sh)	JESKE	PATHE EXCHANGE	1923
HR C-73	SPEED THE SWEDE (sh)	HOWE	PATHE EXCHANGE	1923
HR C-74	MR. HYPPO (sh)	JESKE	PATHE EXCHANGE	1923
HR C-75	DON'T SAY DIE (sh)	JESKE	PATHE EXCHANGE	1923
HR C-76	ONCE OVER (sh)	JESKE	PATHE EXCHANGE	1923
HR C-77	JAILED AND BAILED (sh)	HOWE	PATHE EXCHANGE	1923
HR C-78	TIGHT SHOES (sh)	JESKE	PATHE EXCHANGE	1923
HR C-79	DO YOUR STUFF (sh)	HOWE	PATHE EXCHANGE	1923
HR C-80	BOWLED OVER (sh)	JESKE	PATHE EXCHANGE	1923
HR C-81	GET YOUR MAN (sh)	JESKE	PATHE EXCHANGE	1923
HR C-82	FOR SAFE KEEPING (sh)	JESKE	PATHE EXCHANGE	1923
HR C-83	SMILE WINS (sh)	JESKE	PATHE EXCHANGE	1923
HR C-84	DON'T FLIRT (sh)	POWERS	PATHE EXCHANGE	1923
HR C-85	GOOD RIDDANCE (sh)	JESKE	PATHE EXCHANGE	1923
HR C-86	UNDER TWO JAGS (sh)	JESKE	PATHE EXCHANGE	1923
HR C-87	SUNNY SPAIN (sh)	HOWE	PATHE EXCHANGE	1923
HR C-88	WATCH DOG (sh)	POWERS	PATHE EXCHANGE	1923
HR C-89	NOON WHISTLE (sh)	JESKE	PATHE EXCHANGE	1923
HR C-90	FOR ART'S SAKE (sh)	CHASE	PATHE EXCHANGE	1923
HR C-91	WHITE WINGS (sh)	JESKE	PATHE EXCHANGE	1923
HR C-92	PICK AND SHOVEL (sh)	JESKE	PATHE EXCHANGE	1923
HR C-93	FRESH EGGS (sh)	HOWE	PATHE EXCHANGE	1923
HR C-94	BE HONEST (sh)	POWERS	PATHE EXCHANGE	1923
HR C-95	KILL OR CURE (sh)	PEMBROKE	PATHE EXCHANGE	1923
HR C-96	FINGER PRINTS (sh)	CEDER	PATHE EXCHANGE	1923
HR C-97	COLLARS AND CUFFS (sh)	JESKE	PATHE EXCHANGE	1923
HR C-98	LIVE WIRES (sh)	HOWE	PATHE EXCHANGE	1923
HR C-99	GAS AND AIR (sh)	PEMBROKE	PATHE EXCHANGE	1923
HR C-100	POST NO BILLS (sh)	CEDER	PATHE EXCHANGE	1923
HR C-101	FOR GUESTS ONLY (sh)	HOWE	PATHE EXCHANGE	1923
HR C-102	ORANGES AND LEMONS (sh)	JESKE	PATHE EXCHANGE	1923
HR C-103	TAKE THE AIR (sh)	CEDER	PATHE EXCHANGE	1923
HR C-104	SHORT ORDERS (sh)	PEMBROKE	PATHE EXCHANGE	1923

Movie Still Identification Book Ultimate Edition - Letters

CODE	TITLE/NAME	DIRECTOR/TYPE	STUDIO/DISTRIBUTOR	YEAR
HR C-105	UNNAMED DIPPY DOO DADS (sh)		PATHE EXCHANGE	1923
HR C-106	SAVE THE SHIP (sh)	JESKE, ROACH	PATHE EXCHANGE	1923
HR C-107	UNCOVERED WAGON (sh)	HOWE	PATHE EXCHANGE	1923
HR C-109	NO PETS (sh)	HOWE	PATHE EXCHANGE	1923
HR C-110	STEPPING OUT (sh)	POWERS	PATHE EXCHANGE	1923
HR C-112	SCORCHING SANDS (sh)	WILLIAMSON, ROACH	PATHE EXCHANGE	1923
HR C-113	KNOCKOUT (sh)	POWERS	PATHE EXCHANGE	1923
HR C-114	JOIN THE CIRCUS (sh)	JESKE	PATHE EXCHANGE	1923
HR C-115	WHOLE TRUTH (sh)	CEDER	PATHE EXCHANGE	1923
HR C-116	GO WEST (sh)	POWERS	PATHE EXCHANGE	1923
HR C-117	LOVEY-DOVEY (sh)	POWERS	PATHE EXCHANGE	1923
HR C-118	DEAR OLD PAL (sh)		PATHE EXCHANGE	1923
HR C-119	FROZEN HEARTS (sh)	HOWE	PATHE EXCHANGE	1923
HR C-120	GET BUSY (sh)	HAYES	PATHE EXCHANGE	1924
HR C-121	OLD WAR HORSE (sh)	JESKE	PATHE EXCHANGE	1926
HR C-122	AT FIRST SIGHT (sh)	ROACH	PATHE EXCHANGE	1924
HR C-123	IT'S A JOY (IT'S A BOY) (sh)	JESKE	PATHE EXCHANGE	1923
HR C-124	BAR-FLY (sh)	POWERS	PATHE EXCHANGE	1924
HR C-125	FULLY INSURED (sh)	JESKE	PATHE EXCHANGE	1923
HR C-126	FRIEND HUSBAND (WHY MARRY?) (sh)	HOWE	PATHE EXCHANGE	1924
HR C-127	BIG IDEA (sh)	JESKE	PATHE EXCHANGE	1924
HR C-128	MAN PAYS (sh)	POWERS	PATHE EXCHANGE	1924
HR C-129	HARD KNOCKS (sh)	PARROTT	PATHE EXCHANGE	1924
HR C-129	PERFECT LADY (sh)	PARROTT	PATHE EXCHANGE	1924
HR C-130	JUST A MINUTE (sh)	PARROTT	PATHE EXCHANGE	1924
HR C-131	ONE OF THE FAMILY (sh)	PEMBROKE	PATHE EXCHANGE	1924
HR C-132	LOVE'S REWARD (sh)	POWERS	PATHE EXCHANGE	1924
HR C-133	POWDER AND SMOKE (sh)	PARROTT	PATHE EXCHANGE	1924
HR C-134	LOVE'S DETOUR (sh)	PARROTT	PATHE EXCHANGE	1924
HR C-135	OUR LITTLE NELL (sh)	POWERS	PATHE EXCHANGE	1924
HR C-136	HARD KNOCKS (sh)	PARROTT	PATHE EXCHANGE	1924
HR C-137	NORTH OF 50-50 (sh)	POWERS	PATHE EXCHANGE	1924
HR C-138	DON'T FORGET (sh)	PARROTT	PATHE EXCHANGE	1924
HR CA-84	DON'T FLIRT (sh)	POWERS	PATHE EXCHANGE	1923
HR CA-88	WATCH DOG (sh)	POWERS	PATHE EXCHANGE	1923
HR CC-129	HARD KNOCKS (sh)	PARROTT	PATHE EXCHANGE	1924
HR CC-131	ONE OF THE FAMILY (sh)	PEMBROKE	PATHE EXCHANGE	1924
HR D-1	FOR ART'S SAKE (sh)	CHASE	PATHE EXCHANGE	1923
HR D-1	TROLLEY TROUBLES (sh)	GOULDING	PATHE EXCHANGE	1921
HR D-1	UNNAMED ROLIN PROJECT (sh)	WHITING	PATHE EXCHANGE	1915
HR D-1	WHAT EVERY ICEMAN KNOWS (sh)	YATES, MCCAREY	MGM	1927
HR D-2	CALL OF THE CUCKOOS (sh)	BRUCKMAN	MGM	1927
HR D-2	ROUGH SEAS (sh)	GOULDING	PATHE EXCHANGE	1921
HR D-2	UNNAMED ROLIN PROJECT (sh)	WHITING	PATHE EXCHANGE	1915
HR D-2	WHITE WINGS (sh)	JESKE	PATHE EXCHANGE	1923
HR D-3	DODGE YOUR DEBTS (sh)	KENTON	PATHE EXCHANGE	1921
HR D-3	LOVE 'EM AND FEED 'EM (sh)	BRUCKMAN	MGM	1927
HR D-3	PICK AND SHOVEL (sh)	JESKE	PATHE EXCHANGE	1923
HR D-3	UNNAMED ROLIN PROJECT (sh)	WHITING	PATHE EXCHANGE	1915
HR D-4	FIGHTING FATHERS (sh)	GUIOL	MGM	1927
HR D-4	FRESH EGGS (sh)	HOWE	PATHE EXCHANGE	1923
HR D-4	ZERO HERO (sh)	KENTON	PATHE EXCHANGE	1921
HR D-5	KILL OR CURE (sh)	PEMBROKE	PATHE EXCHANGE	1923
HR D-5	LUCKY NUMBER (sh)	KENTON	PATHE EXCHANGE	1921
HR D-5	TELL IT TO THE JUDGE (sh)	MCCAREY, YATES	MGM	1928
HR D-6	FINGER PRINTS (sh)	CEDER	PATHE EXCHANGE	1923
HR D-6	PASS THE GRAVY (sh)	GUIOL, MCCAREY	MGM	1928
HR D-7	COLLARS AND CUFFS (sh)	JESKE	PATHE EXCHANGE	1923
HR D-7	DUMB DADDIES (sh)	YATES	MGM	1928
HR D-8	CAME THE DAWN (sh)	HEATH, MCCAREY	MGM	1928
HR D-8	LIVE WIRES (sh)	HOWE	PATHE EXCHANGE	1923
HR D-9	BLOW BY BLOW (sh)	MCCAREY	MGM	1928
HR D-9	GAS AND AIR (sh)	PEMBROKE	PATHE EXCHANGE	1923
HR D-10	POST NO BILLS (sh)	CEDER	PATHE EXCHANGE	1923
HR D-10	SHOULD WOMEN DRIVE? (sh)	MCCAREY	MGM	1928
HR D-11	FOR GUESTS ONLY (sh)	HOWE	PATHE EXCHANGE	1923
HR D-12	ORANGES AND LEMONS (sh)	JESKE	PATHE EXCHANGE	1923
HR D-13	TAKE THE AIR (sh)	CEDER	PATHE EXCHANGE	1923
HR D-14	SHORT ORDERS (sh)	PEMBROKE	PATHE EXCHANGE	1923
HR D-15	SAVE THE SHIP (sh)	JESKE, ROACH	PATHE EXCHANGE	1923

Movie Still Identification Book Ultimate Edition - Letters

CODE	TITLE/NAME	DIRECTOR/TYPE	STUDIO/DISTRIBUTOR	YEAR
HR D-16	UNCOVERED WAGON (sh)	HOWE	PATHE EXCHANGE	1923
HR D-17	MAN ABOUT TOWN (sh)	JESKE	PATHE EXCHANGE	1923
HR D17	TOPPER (sh)	MCLEOD	MGM	1937
HR D-18	NO PETS (sh)	HOWE	PATHE EXCHANGE	1923
HR D-19	SCORCHING SANDS (sh)	WILLIAMSON, ROACH	PATHE EXCHANGE	1923
HR D-20	KNOCKOUT (sh)	POWERS	PATHE EXCHANGE	1923
HR D-21	JOIN THE CIRCUS (sh)	JESKE	PATHE EXCHANGE	1923
HR D-22	WHOLE TRUTH (sh)	CEDER	PATHE EXCHANGE	1923
HR D-23	GO WEST (sh)	POWERS	PATHE EXCHANGE	1923
HR D-24	DEAR OLD PAL (sh)		PATHE EXCHANGE	1923
HR D-25	LOVEY-DOVEY (sh)	POWERS	PATHE EXCHANGE	1923
HR D-26	GET BUSY (sh)	HAYES	PATHE EXCHANGE	1924
HR D-27	OLD WAR HORSE (sh)	JESKE	PATHE EXCHANGE	1926
HR D-28	AT FIRST SIGHT (sh)	ROACH	PATHE EXCHANGE	1924
HR D-29	IT'S A JOY (IT'S A BOY) (sh)	JESKE	PATHE EXCHANGE	1923
HR D-30	BAR-FLY (sh)	POWERS	PATHE EXCHANGE	1924
HR D-31	FULLY INSURED (sh)	JESKE	PATHE EXCHANGE	1923
HR D-32	FRIEND HUSBAND (WHY MARRY?) (sh)	HOWE	PATHE EXCHANGE	1924
HR D-33	BIG IDEA (sh)	JESKE	PATHE EXCHANGE	1924
HR D-34	MAN PAYS (sh)	POWERS	PATHE EXCHANGE	1924
HR D-35	PERFECT LADY (sh)	PARROTT	PATHE EXCHANGE	1924
HR D-36	POWDER AND SMOKE (sh)	PARROTT	PATHE EXCHANGE	1924
HR D-37	ONE OF THE FAMILY (sh)	PEMBROKE	PATHE EXCHANGE	1924
HR D-38	LOVE'S REWARD (sh)	POWERS	PATHE EXCHANGE	1924
HR D-39	JUST A MINUTE (sh)	PARROTT	PATHE EXCHANGE	1924
HR D-40	LOVE'S DETOUR (sh)	PARROTT	PATHE EXCHANGE	1924
HR D-41	OUR LITTLE NELL (sh)	POWERS	PATHE EXCHANGE	1924
HR D-42	HARD KNOCKS (sh)	PARROTT	PATHE EXCHANGE	1924
HR D-43	NORTH OF 50-50 (sh)	POWERS	PATHE EXCHANGE	1924
HR D-44	DON'T FORGET (sh)	PARROTT	PATHE EXCHANGE	1924
HR D-45	FRAIDY CAT (sh)	PARROTT	PATHE EXCHANGE	1924
HR D-46	UP AND AT 'EM (sh)	POWERS	PATHE EXCHANGE	1924
HR D-47	PUBLICITY PAYS (sh)	MCCAREY	PATHE EXCHANGE	1924
HR D-48	POSITION WANTED (sh)	CEDER	PATHE EXCHANGE	1924
HR D-49	BIG KICK (sh)	GUIOL, ROACH	PATHE EXCHANGE	1925
HR D-50	ONE AT A TIME (sh)	CEDER	PATHE EXCHANGE	1924
HR D-51	BOUNCER (sh)	CEDER, GUIOL	PATHE EXCHANGE	1925
HR D-52	APRIL FOOL (sh)	CEDER	PATHE EXCHANGE	1924
HR D-53	SOLID IVORY (sh)	CEDER	PATHE EXCHANGE	1925
HR D-54	STOLEN GOODS (sh)	MCCAREY	PATHE EXCHANGE	1924
HR D-55	BEFORE TAKING (sh)	CEDER	PATHE EXCHANGE	1924
HR D-56	YOUNG OLDFIELD (sh)	MCCAREY	PATHE EXCHANGE	1924
HR D-57	FAST BLACK (sh)	GARNETT	PATHE EXCHANGE	1924
HR D-58	JEFFRIES JR. (sh)	MCCAREY	PATHE EXCHANGE	1924
HR D-59	RIDER OF THE KITCHEN RANGE (sh)	GARNETT, JESKE	PATHE EXCHANGE	1925
HR D-60	WHY HUSBANDS GO MAD (sh)	MCCAREY	PATHE EXCHANGE	1924
HR D-61	ALL WOOL (sh)	GARNETT	PATHE EXCHANGE	1925
HR D-62	SEEING NELLIE HOME (sh)	MCCAREY	PATHE EXCHANGE	1924
HR D-63	GRIEF OF BAGDAD(SHEIKS IN BAGDAD) (sh)	LEDERMAN	PATHE EXCHANGE	1925
HR D-64	TEN MINUTE EGG (sh)	MCCAREY	PATHE EXCHANGE	1924
HR D-65	ACCIDENTAL ACCIDENTS (sh)	MCCAREY	PATHE EXCHANGE	1924
HR D-66	BIG RED RIDING HOOD (sh)	MCCAREY	PATHE EXCHANGE	1925
HR D-67	WHY MEN WORK (sh)	MCCAREY	PATHE EXCHANGE	1924
HR D-68	SWEET DADDY (sh)	MCCAREY	PATHE EXCHANGE	1924
HR D-69	OUTDOOR PAJAMAS (sh)	MCCAREY	PATHE EXCHANGE	1924
HR D-70	SITTIN' PRETTY (sh)	MCCAREY	PATHE EXCHANGE	1924
HR D-71	TOO MANY MAMMAS (sh)	MCCAREY	PATHE EXCHANGE	1924
HR D-72	BUNGALOW BOOBS (sh)	MCCAREY	PATHE EXCHANGE	1924
HR D-73	ALL WET (sh)	MCCAREY	PATHE EXCHANGE	1924
HR D-74	POOR FISH (sh)	MCCAREY	PATHE EXCHANGE	1924
HR D-75	ROYAL RAZZ (sh)	MCCAREY	PATHE EXCHANGE	1924
HR D-76	RAT'S KNUCKLES (sh)	MCCAREY	PATHE EXCHANGE	1925
HR D-77	HELLO BABY (sh)	MCCAREY	PATHE EXCHANGE	1925
HR D-78	FIGHTING FLUID (sh)	MCCAREY	PATHE EXCHANGE	1925
HR D-79	FAMILY ENTRANCE (sh)	MCCAREY	PATHE EXCHANGE	1925
HR D-80	SHOULD HUSBANDS BE WATCHED? (sh)	MCCAREY	PATHE EXCHANGE	1925
HR D-81	PLAIN AND FANCY GIRLS (sh)	MCCAREY	PATHE EXCHANGE	1925
HR D-82	IS MARRIAGE THE BUNK? (sh)	MCCAREY	PATHE EXCHANGE	1925
HR D-83	HOLD EVERYTHING (sh)	GUIOL, MCCAREY	PATHE EXCHANGE	1925
HR D-84	ARE HUSBANDS HUMAN? (sh)	BARROWS	PATHE EXCHANGE	1925

Movie Still Identification Book Ultimate Edition - Letters

CODE	TITLE/NAME	DIRECTOR/TYPE	STUDIO/DISTRIBUTOR	YEAR
HR D-85	SURE MIKE (sh)	GUIOL	PATHE EXCHANGE	1925
HR D-86	TOL'ABLE ROMEO (sh)	ROBBINS	PATHE EXCHANGE	1925
HR D-87	IN THE GREASE (sh)	HOWE	PATHE EXCHANGE	1925
HR D-88	CHASING THE CHASER (sh)	LAUREL	PATHE EXCHANGE	1925
HR D-89	UNFRIENDLY ENEMIES (sh)	LAUREL	PATHE EXCHANGE	1925
HR D-90	YES, YES NANETTE (sh)	HENNECKE, LAUREL	PATHE EXCHANGE	1925
HR E-1	HOSS AND HOSS (sh)	(UNFINISHED)	PATHE EXCHANGE	1924
HR E-1	PICKANINNY (sh)	KERR, PARROTT	PATHE EXCHANGE	1921
HR E-1	YOU BRING THE DUCKS (sh)	YATES	MGM	1934
HR E-2	HOT HEELS (sh)	JESKE	PATHE EXCHANGE	1924
HR E-2	NOSED OUT (sh)	YATES	MGM	1934
HR E-3	BALLAD OF PADUCAH JAIL (sh)	GRINDE	MGM	1934
HR E-3	SKY PLUMBER (sh)	DAVISS	PATHE EXCHANGE	1924
HR E-4	LUCKY BEGINNERS (sh)	DOUGLAS, ROACH	MGM	1935
HR E-4	UNFINISHED ARTHUR STONE (sh)		PATHE EXCHANGE	1924
HR E-5	INFERNAL TRIANGLE (sh)	DOUGLAS	MGM	1935
HR E-5	SHOULD LANDLORDS LIVE? (sh)	BARROWS, DAVIS	PATHE EXCHANGE	1924
HR E-6	UNFINISHED ROACH (sh)		PATHE EXCHANGE	1924
HR E-6	JUST A GOOD GUY (sh)	DEL RUTH	PATHE EXCHANGE	1924
HR E-7	JUST A GOOD GUY (sh)	DEL RUTH	PATHE EXCHANGE	1924
HR E-8	TAME MEN AND WILD WOMEN (sh)	DE SANO	PATHE EXCHANGE	1925
HR E-9	HARD WORKING LOAFERS (sh)		PATHE EXCHANGE	1925
HR E-10	CHANGE THE NEEDLE (sh)	ROACH	PATHE EXCHANGE	1925
HR E-11	UNNAMED ARTHUR STONE (sh)		PATHE EXCHANGE	1925
HR E-12	SHERLOCK SLEUTH (sh)	CEDER	PATHE EXCHANGE	1925
HR E-13	HARD -BOILED (sh)	MCCAREY	PATHE EXCHANGE	1925
HR E-14	BAD BOY (sh)	MCCAREY	PATHE EXCHANGE	1925
HR E-15	LOOKING FOR SALLY (sh)	MCCAREY	PATHE EXCHANGE	1925
HR E-16	WHAT PRICE GOOFY? (sh)	MCCAREY	PATHE EXCHANGE	1925
HR E-17	ISN'T LIFE TERRIBLE? (sh)	MCCAREY	PATHE EXCHANGE	1925
HR E-18	INNOCENT HUSBANDS (sh)	MCCAREY	PATHE EXCHANGE	1925
HR E-19	NO FATHER TO GUIDE HIM (sh)	MCCAREY	PATHE EXCHANGE	1925
HR F-1	PARDON US	PARROTT	MGM	1931
HR F-1	ROUGHING IT (sh)	JACKMAN	PATHE EXCHANGE	1923
HR F-2	LET'S BUILD (sh)	PEMBROKE	PATHE EXCHANGE	1923
HR F-2	PACK UP YOUR TROUBLES (sh)	MARSHALL, MCCAREY	MGM	1932
HR F-3	DEVIL'S BROTHER	ROACH, ROGERS	MGM	1933
HR F-3	HEAVY SEAS (sh)	GUIOL, HOWE	PATHE EXCHANGE	1923
HR F-4	GREAT OUTDOORS (sh)	GUIOL	PATHE EXCHANGE	1923
HR F4	SONS OF THE DESERT	SEITER	MGM	1933
HR F-5	BABES IN TOYLAND (MARCH OF THE WOODEN SOLDIERS)	MEINS, ROGERS	MGM	1934
HR F-5	DARKEST HOUR (sh)	HOWE	PATHE EXCHANGE	1923
HR F-6	POLITICAL PULL (sh)	CLEMENTS	PATHE EXCHANGE	1924
HR F-6	VAGABOND LADY	TAYLOR	MGM	1935
HR-F7	BONNIE SCOTLAND	HORNE	MGM	1935
HR F-7	HELP ONE ANOTHER (sh)	GUIOL	PATHE EXCHANGE	1924
HR F-8	BOHEMIAN GIRL	HORNE, ROGERS	MGM	1936
HR F-8	HUNTERS BOLD (sh)	ROACH	PATHE EXCHANGE	1924
HR F-9	HIT THE HIGH SPOTS (sh)	GUIOL	PATHE EXCHANGE	1924
HR F-9	MR. CINDERELLA		MGM	1936
HR F-10	BOTTLE BABIES (sh)	HOWE, PEMBROKE	PATHE EXCHANGE	1924
HR F-10	KELLY THE SECOND	MEINS	MGM	1936
HR-F11	NOBODY'S BABY	MEINS	MGM	1937
HR F-11	OUR RELATIONS	LACHMAN	MGM	1936
HR F-11	SUFFERING SHAKESPEARE (sh)	CEDER	PATHE EXCHANGE	1924
HR F-12	GENERAL SPANKY	DOUGLAS, NEWMEYER	MGM	1936
HR F-12	RADIO MAD (sh)	HOWE	PATHE EXCHANGE	1924
HR F-13	HARD-BOILED TENDERFOOT (sh)	HOWE	PATHE EXCHANGE	1924
HR F-13	UNRELEASED ROACH (sh)		MGM	1936
HR F-14	SOUTH O' THE NORTH POLE	HOWE	PATHE EXCHANGE	1924
HR F-14	WAY OUT WEST	HORNE	MGM	1937
HR F-15	LOST DOG (sh)	HOWE	PATHE EXCHANGE	1924
HR F-15	PICK A STAR	SEDGWICK	MGM	1937
HR F-16	HOT STUFF (sh)	HOWE	PATHE EXCHANGE	1924
HR F-16	NOBODY'S BABY	MEINS	MGM	1937
HR F-17	TOPPER (sh)	MCLEOD	MGM	1937
HR F-18	DEAF, DUMB AND DAFFY (sh)	HOWE	PATHE EXCHANGE	1924
HR F-18	UPSPECIFIEC TITLE	ROACH	MGM	1937
HR F-19	LAUGH THAT OFF (sh)	HOWE	PATHE EXCHANGE	1925
HR F-19	MERRILY WE LIVE	MCLEOD	MGM	1938

Movie Still Identification Book Ultimate Edition - Letters

CODE	TITLE/NAME	DIRECTOR/TYPE	STUDIO/DISTRIBUTOR	YEAR
HR F-20	FOX HUNT (sh)	HOWE	PATHE EXCHANGE	1925
HR F-20	SWISS MISS	BLYSTONE	MGM	1938
HR F-21	EXCUSE MY GLOVE (sh)	HOWE	PATHE EXCHANGE	1925
HR F-21	THERE GOES MY HEART	MCLEOD	UNITED ARTISTS	1938
HR F-22	BLACK HAND BLUES (BLACK HANDS) (sh)	HOWE	PATHE EXCHANGE	1925
HR F-22	BLOCK-HEADS	BLYSTONE	MGM	1938
HR F-23	ROYAL FOUR-FLUSH (sh)	HOWE	PATHE EXCHANGE	1925
HR-F23	ZENOBIA	DOUGLAS	UNITED ARTISTS	1939
HR-F24	TOPPER TAKES A TRIP	MCLEOD	UNITED ARTISTS	1938
HR F-24	WILD PAPA (sh)	BARROWS, HOWE	PATHE EXCHANGE	1925
HR F-25	CAPTAIN FURY	ROACH	UNITED ARTISTS	1939
HR F-25	DON KEY (sh)	GUIOL, HORNE	PATHE EXCHANGE	1926
HR F-26	CHUMP AT OXFORD	GOULDING	UNITED ARTISTS	1940
HR F-27	HOUSEKEEPER'S DAUGHTER (see F-31)	ROACH	UNITED ARTISTS	1939
HR F-28	OF MICE AND MEN	MILESTONE	UNITED ARTISTS	1939
HR-F28-H	OF MICE AND MEN	MILESTONE	UNITED ARTISTS	1939
HR-F29	SAPS AT SEA	DOUGLAS	UNITED ARTISTS	1940
HR-F30	ONE MILLION B.C.	ROACH, ROACH JR.	UNITED ARTISTS	1940
HR-F31	HOUSEKEEPER'S DAUGHTER (see F27)	ROACH	UNITED ARTISTS	1940
HR-F31	TURNABOUT	ROACH	UNITED ARTISTS	1940
HR-F32	CAPTAIN CAUTION	WALLACE	UNITED ARTISTS	1940
HR-F33	ROAD SHOW	ROACH	UNITED ARTISTS	1941
HR-F34	BROADWAY LIMITED	DOUGLAS	UNITED ARTISTS	1941
HR-F35	TOPPER RETURNS	RUTH	UNITED ARTISTS	1941
HR-F36	NIAGARA FALLS	DOUGLAS	UNITED ARTISTS	1941
HR-F37	TANKS A MILLION	GUIOL	UNITED ARTISTS	1941
HR-F38	ALL-AMERICAN CO-ED	PRINZ	UNITED ARTISTS	1941
HR-F39	MISS POLLY	GUIOL	UNITED ARTISTS	1941
HR-F40	FIESTA (GAIETY)	PRINZ	UNITED ARTISTS	1941
HR-F41	HAY FOOT	GUIOL	UNITED ARTISTS	1942
HR-F42	DUDES ARE PRETTY PEOPLE	ROACH JR.	UNITED ARTISTS	1942
HR-F43	BROOKLYN ORCHID	NEUMANN	UNITED ARTISTS	1942
HR-F44	ABOUT FACE	NEUMANN	UNITED ARTISTS	1942
HR-F45	FLYING WITH MUSIC	ARCHAINBAUD	UNITED ARTISTS	1942
HR-F46	DEVIL WITH HITLER	DOUGLAS	UNITED ARTISTS	1942
HR-F47	TWO MUGS FROM BROOKLYN	NEUMANN	UNITED ARTISTS	1942
HR-F48	CALABOOSE	ROACH JR.	UNITED ARTISTS	1943
HR-F49	FALL IN	NEUMANN	UNITED ARTISTS	1942
HR-F50	NAZTY NUISANCE (THAT NAZTY NUISANCE)	TRYON	UNITED ARTISTS	1943
HR-F51	TAXI, MISTER	NEUMANN	UNITED ARTISTS	1943
HR-F52	PRAIRIE CHICKENS	ROACH JR.	UNITED ARTISTS	1943
HR-F53	YANKS AHOY	NEUMANN	UNITED ARTISTS	1943
HR-F54	CURLEY	CARR	UNITED ARTISTS	1947
HR-F55	HERE COMES TROUBLE	GUIOL	UNITED ARTISTS	1948
HR-F56	FABULOUS JOE	FOSTER	UNITED ARTISTS	1947
HR-F57	WHO KILLED DOC ROBIN	CARR	UNITED ARTISTS	1948
HRG	HOT ROD GANG	LANDERS	AIP	1958
HR G-1	BIG EARS (sh)	MCGOWAN	MGM	1931
HR G-1	REGULAR PAL (sh)	ROACH	PATHE EXCHANGE	1920
HR G-1	YALE VS. HARVARD (sh)	MCGOWAN	MGM	1927
HR G-2	MERELY A MAID (sh)	ROACH	PATHE EXCHANGE	1920
HR G-2	OLD WALLOP (sh)	MCGOWAN	MGM	1927
HR G-2	SAILOR PAPA (sh)	GUIOL, WILDE	PATHE EXCHANGE	1925
HR G-2	SHIVER MY TIMBERS (sh)	MCGOWAN	MGM	1931
HR G-3	DOGS IS DOGS (sh)	MCGOWAN	MGM	1931
HR G-3	HEEBEE JEEBEES (sh)	MCGOWAN, MCGOWAN	MGM	1927
HR G-3	HELLO UNCLE (sh)	ROACH	PATHE EXCHANGE	1920
HR G-3	MEET THE MISSUS (sh)	CLEMENTS, GUIOL	PATHE EXCHANGE	1924
HR G-4	DOG HEAVEN	MCGOWAN	MGM	1927
HR G-4	READIN' AND WRITIN' (sh)	MCGOWAN	MGM	1932
HR G-4	START THE SHOW	ROACH	PATHE EXCHANGE	1920
HR G-4	WAGES OF TIN	CLEMENTS	PATHE EXCHANGE	1925
HR G-5	FREE EATS (sh)	MCCAREY	MGM	1932
HR G-5	SPOOK SPOOFING	MCGOWAN	MGM	1928
HR G-5	TELL IT TO A POLICEMAN	GUIOL	PATHE EXCHANGE	1925
HR G-6	HOLD MY BABY - WHOSE BABY ARE YOU?	HOWE	PATHE EXCHANGE	1925
HR G-6	RAINY DAYS (sh)	MCGOWAN, OELZE	MGM	1928
HR G-6	SPANKY	MCGOWAN	MGM	1932
HR-G7	CHOO CHOO	MCGOWAN	MGM	1932
HR G-7	EDISON, MARCONI & CO. (sh)	MCGOWAN	MGM	1928

Movie Still Identification Book Ultimate Edition - Letters

CODE	TITLE/NAME	DIRECTOR/TYPE	STUDIO/DISTRIBUTOR	YEAR
HR G-7	HAUNTED HONEYMOON	GUIOL, WILDE	PATHE EXCHANGE	1925
HR G-8	BARNUM & RINGLING INC.	MCGOWAN	MGM	1928
HR G-8	POOCH (sh)	MCGOWAN	MGM	1932
HR G-8	THUNDERING LANDLORDS	HORNE	PATHE EXCHANGE	1925
HR G-9	DADDY GOES A' GRUNTING	HORNE	PATHE EXCHANGE	1925
HR G-9	FAIR AND MUDDY	OELZE	MGM	1928
HR G-9	HOOK AND LADDER (sh)	MCGOWAN	MGM	1932
HR G-10	CRAZY HOUSE (sh)	MCGOWAN	MGM	1928
HR G-10	FREE WHEELING (sh)	MCGOWAN	MGM	1932
HR G-10	MADAME SANS JANE	HORNE	PATHE EXCHANGE	1925
HR G-11	BIRTHDAY BLUES (sh)	MCGOWAN	MGM	1932
HR G-11	CUCKOO LOVE	GUIOL	PATHE EXCHANGE	1925
HR G-11	GROWING PAINS (sh)	MCGOWAN	MGM	1928
HR G-12	A LAD AN' A LAMP (sh)	MCGOWAN	MGM	1932
HR G-12	OL' GRAY HOSS (sh)	MCGOWAN	MGM	1928
HR G-12	PAPA, BE GOOD!	GUIOL	PATHE EXCHANGE	1925
HR G-13	FISH HOOKY (sh)	MCGOWAN	MGM	1933
HR G-13	SCHOOL BEGINS	MCGOWAN	MGM	1928
HR G-14	FORGOTTEN BABIES (sh)	MCGOWAN	MGM	1933
HR G-14	SPANKING AGE (sh)	MCGOWAN	MGM	1928
HR G-15	ELECTION DAY (sh)	MCGOWAN	MGM	1929
HR G-15	KID FROM BORNEO (sh)	MCGOWAN	MGM	1933
HR G-16	MUSH AND MILK (sh)	MCGOWAN	MGM	1933
HR G-16	NOISY NOISES	MCGOWAN	MGM	1929
HR G-17	BEDTIME WORRIES (sh)	MCGOWAN	MGM	1933
HR G-17	HOLY TERROR	MCGOWAN	MGM	1929
HR G-18	WIGGLE YOUR EARS (sh)	MCGOWAN	MGM	1929
HR G-18	WILD POSES (sh)	MCGOWAN	MGM	1933
HR G-19	FAST FREIGHT (sh)	MACK	MGM	1929
HR G-19	HI' NEIGHBOR! (sh)	MEINS	MGM	1934
HR G-20	FOR PETE'S SAKE!	MEINS	MGM	1934
HR G-20	LITTLE MOTHER	MCGOWAN	MGM	1929
HR G-21	CAT, DOG & CO. (sh)	MCGOWAN	MGM	1929
HR G-21	FIRST ROUNDUP (sh)	MEINS	MGM	1934
HR G-22	HONKY DONKEY (sh)	MEINS	MGM	1934
HR G-22	SATURDAY'S LESSON (sh)	MCGOWAN	MGM	1929
HR G-23	MIKE FRIGHT (sh)	MEINS	MGM	1934
HR G-23	SMALL TALK	MCGOWAN	MGM	1929
HR G-24	RAILROADIN' (sh)	MCGOWAN	MGM	1929
HR G-24	WASHEE IRONEE	PARROTT	MGM	1934
HR G-25	BOXING GLOVES (sh)	MCGOWAN	MGM	1929
HR G-25	MAMA'S LITTLE PIRATE	MEINS	MGM	1935
HR G-26	LAZY DAYS (sh)	MCGOWAN	MGM	1929
HR G-26	SHRIMPS FOR A DAY	MEINS	MGM	1935
HR G-27	ANNIVERSARY TROUBLE (sh)	MEINS	MGM	1935
HR G-27	BOUNCING BABIES	MCGOWAN	MGM	1929
HR G-28	BEGINNER'S LUCK (sh)	MEINS	MGM	1935
HR G-28	MOAN & GROAN INC. (sh)	MCGOWAN	MGM	1929
HR G-29	SHIVERING SHAKESPEARE (sh)	MCGOWAN	MGM	1930
HR G-29	TEACHER'S BEAU	MEINS	MGM	1935
HR G-30	FIRST SEVEN YEARS (sh)	MCGOWAN	MGM	1930
HR G-30	SPRUCIN' UP	MEINS	MGM	1935
HR G-31	LUCKY CORNER (sh)	MEINS	MGM	1936
HR G-31	WHEN THE WIND BLOWS (sh)	HORNE	MGM	1930
HR G-32	BEAR SHOOTERS (sh)	MCGOWAN	MGM	1930
HR G-32	LITTLE PAPA (sh)	MEINS	MGM	1935
HR G-33	LITTLE SINNER (sh)	MEINS	MGM	1935
HR G-33	TOUGH WINTER	MCGOWAN	MGM	1930
HR G-34	OUR GANG FOLLIES OF 1936 (sh)	MEINS	MGM	1935
HR G-34	PUPS IS PUPS (sh)	MCGOWAN	MGM	1930
HR G-35	PINCH SINGER (sh)	NEWMEYER	MGM	1936
HR G-35	TEACHER'S PET	MCGOWAN	MGM	1930
HR G-36	DIVOT DIGGERS	MCGOWAN	MGM	1936
HR G-36	SCHOOL'S OUT	MCGOWAN	MGM	1930
HR G-37	HELPING GRANDMA	MCGOWAN	MGM	1931
HR G-37	SECOND CHILDHOOD (sh)	MEINS	MGM	1936
HR G-38	ARBOR DAY (sh)	NEWMEYER	MGM	1936
HR G-38	LOVE BUSINESS	MCGOWAN	MGM	1931
HR G-39	LITTLE DADDY (sh)	MCGOWAN	MGM	1931
HR-G-39	OUR GANG FOLLIES OF 1936 (sh)	MEINS	MGM	1935

Movie Still Identification Book Ultimate Edition - Letters

CODE	TITLE/NAME	DIRECTOR/TYPE	STUDIO/DISTRIBUTOR	YEAR
HR G-40	BARGAIN DAY	MCGOWAN	MGM	1931
HR G-41	FLY MY KITE	MCGOWAN	MGM	1931
HRH	HOT ROD HULLABALOO	NAUD	ALLIED ARTISTS	1966
HR H-1	ALL AT SEA	CHASE, GOULDING	PATHE EXCHANGE	1919
HR H-1	FLAMING FLAPPERS	GUIOL	PATHE EXCHANGE	1925
HR H-2	LONG PANTS	GUIOL	PATHE EXCHANGE	1926
HR H-2	START SOMETHING	GOULDING	PATHE EXCHANGE	1919
HR H-3	45 MINUTES FROM HOLLYWOOD	GUIOL	PATHE EXCHANGE	1926
HR H-3	CALL FOR MR. CAVEMAN	CHASE	PATHE EXCHANGE	1919
HR H-4	GIVING THE BRIDE AWAY	CHASE, ROACH	PATHE EXCHANGE	1919
HR H-4	HUG BUG	GUIOL	PATHE EXCHANGE	1926
HR H-5	ORDER IN THE COURT	CHASE	PATHE EXCHANGE	1919
HR H-5	UKULELE SHEIKS	GUIOL	PATHE EXCHANGE	1926
HR H-6	IT'S A HARD LIFE	ROACH	PATHE EXCHANGE	1919
HR H-6	SAY IT WITH BABIES	GUIOL	PATHE EXCHANGE	1926
HR H-7	COW'S KIMONO	GUIOL, PARROTT	PATHE EXCHANGE	1926
HR H-7	HOW DRY I AM	ROACH	PATHE EXCHANGE	1919
HR H-8	ALONG CAME AUNTIE	GUIOL, WALLACE	PATHE EXCHANGE	1926
HR H-8	UNFINISHED ROACH		PATHE EXCHANGE	1919
HR H-9	GETTING HIS GOAT	CHASE	PATHE EXCHANGE	1920
HR H-9	TWO TIME MAMA	GUIOL	PATHE EXCHANGE	1927
HR H-10	ONE HOUR MARRIED	STRONG, YATES	PATHE EXCHANGE	1927
HR H-10	TOUGH LUCK	CHASE	PATHE EXCHANGE	1919
HR H-11	LOOKING FOR TROUBLE	ROACH	PATHE EXCHANGE	1919
HR H-11	NICKEL HOPPER	JONES, YATES	PATHE EXCHANGE	1926
HR H-12	ANYTHING ONCE!	JONES, YATES	PATHE EXCHANGE	1927
HR H-12	FLOOR BELOW	CHASE, GOULDING	PATHE EXCHANGE	1919
HR H-13	RED HOT HOTTENTOTS	CHASE	PATHE EXCHANGE	1920
HR H-14	WHY GO HOME?	CHASE	PATHE EXCHANGE	1920
HR H-15	SHOULD MEN WALK HOME?	MCCAREY	PATHE EXCHANGE	1927
HR H-15	SLIPPERY SLICKERS	CHASE	PATHE EXCHANGE	1920
HR H-16	DIPPY DENTIST	GOULDING	PATHE EXCHANGE	1920
HR H-16	JEWISH PRUDENCE	MCCAREY	PATHE EXCHANGE	1927
HR H-17	ALL LIT UP	NEWMEYER	PATHE EXCHANGE	1920
HR H-17	EVE'S LOVE LETTERS	MCCAREY	PATHE EXCHANGE	1927
HR H-18	DON'T TELL EVERYTHING	MCCAREY	PATHE EXCHANGE	1927
HR H-18	WALTZ ME AROUND	CHASE	PATHE EXCHANGE	1920
HR H-19	RAISE THE RENT	NEWMEYER	PATHE EXCHANGE	1920
HR H-19	SHOULD SECOND HUSBANDS COME FIRST?	MCCAREY	PATHE EXCHANGE	1927
HR H-20	FIND THE GIRL	CHASE	PATHE EXCHANGE	1920
HR H-21	FLAT BROKE	CHASE	PATHE EXCHANGE	1920
HR H-22	FRESH PAINT	CHASE, GOULDING	PATHE EXCHANGE	1920
HR H-23	CUT THE CARDS	CHASE	PATHE EXCHANGE	1920
HR H-24	CRACKED WEDDING BELLS	LA ROSE	PATHE EXCHANGE	1920
HR H-25	DINNER HOUR	CHASE	PATHE EXCHANGE	1920
HR H-26	SPEED TO SPARE	CHASE	PATHE EXCHANGE	1920
HR H-27	SHOOT ON SIGHT	CHASE	PATHE EXCHANGE	1920
HR H-28	DON'T WEAKEN	GOULDING	PATHE EXCHANGE	1920
HR H-29	DRINK HEARTY	GOULDING	PATHE EXCHANGE	1920
HR H-30	TROTTING THROUGH TURKEY	CHASE	PATHE EXCHANGE	1920
HR H-31	ALL DRESSED UP	CHASE	PATHE EXCHANGE	1920
HR H-32	GRAB THE GHOST	GOULDING	PATHE EXCHANGE	1920
HR H-33	YOU'RE PINCHED	ROACH	PATHE EXCHANGE	1920
HR H-34	ALL IN A DAY	CHASE	PATHE EXCHANGE	1920
HR H-35	ANY OLD PORT	GOULDING	PATHE EXCHANGE	1920
HR H-36	DON'T ROCK THE BOAT	CHASE	PATHE EXCHANGE	1920
HR H-37	HOME STRETCH	CHASE	PATHE EXCHANGE	1920
HR H-38	CALL A TAXI	CHASE	PATHE EXCHANGE	1920
HR H-39	LIVE AND LEARN	CHASE	PATHE EXCHANGE	1920
HR H-40	RUN 'EM RAGGED	GOULDING	PATHE EXCHANGE	1920
HR H-41	LONDON BOBBY	CHASE	PATHE EXCHANGE	1920
HR H-42	MONEY TO BURN	NEWMEYER	PATHE EXCHANGE	1920
HR H-43	ROCK A BYE BABY	CHASE	PATHE EXCHANGE	1920
HR H-44	GO AS YOU PLEASE	GOULDING	PATHE EXCHANGE	1920
HR H-45	DOING TIME	GOULDING	PATHE EXCHANGE	1920
HR H-46	FELLOW CITIZENS	GOULDING	PATHE EXCHANGE	1920
HR H-47	WHEN THE WIND BLOWS	CHASE	PATHE EXCHANGE	1920
HR H-48	INSULTING THE SULTAN	GOULDING	PATHE EXCHANGE	1920
HR H-49	DEAR DEPARTED	CHASE	PATHE EXCHANGE	1920
HR H-50	CASH CUSTOMERS	GOULDING	PATHE EXCHANGE	1920

Movie Still Identification Book Ultimate Edition - Letters

CODE	TITLE/NAME	DIRECTOR/TYPE	STUDIO/DISTRIBUTOR	YEAR
HR H-51	PARK YOUR CAR	GOULDING	PATHE EXCHANGE	1920
HR H-52	OPEN ANOTHER BOTTLE	GOULDING	PATHE EXCHANGE	1921
HR H-53	MORNING AFTER	GOULDING	PATHE EXCHANGE	1921
HR H-54	WHIRL OF THE WEST	BARROWS	PATHE EXCHANGE	1921
HR H-55	HIS BEST GIRL	CHASE	PATHE EXCHANGE	1921
HR H-56	MAKE IT SNAPPY		PATHE EXCHANGE	1921
HR H-57	FELLOW ROMANS	ROACH	PATHE EXCHANGE	1921
HR H-58	RUSH ORDERS	CHASE	PATHE EXCHANGE	1921
HR H-59	BUBBLING OVER	ROACH	PATHE EXCHANGE	1921
HR H-60	NO CHILDREN	GOULDING	PATHE EXCHANGE	1921
HR H-61	BIG GAME	GOULDING	PATHE EXCHANGE	1921
HR H-62	KILLJOYS (BLUE SUNDAY)	CHASE	PATHE EXCHANGE	1921
HR H-63	OWN YOUR OWN HOME	ROACH	PATHE EXCHANGE	1921
HR H-64	WHERE'S THE FIRE	ROACH	PATHE EXCHANGE	1921
HR H-65	HIGH ROLLERS	GOULDING	PATHE EXCHANGE	1921
HR H-66	YOU'RE NEXT	CHASE	PATHE EXCHANGE	1921
HR H-67	SAVE YOUR MONEY	ROACH	PATHE EXCHANGE	1921
HR H-68	BIKE BUG	ROACH	PATHE EXCHANGE	1921
HR H-69	NAME THE DAY	ROACH	PATHE EXCHANGE	1921
HR H-70	AT THE RING SIDE	CHASE	PATHE EXCHANGE	1921
HR H-71	NO STOP-OVER	ROACH	PATHE EXCHANGE	1921
HR H-72	LATE LODGERS	CHASE	PATHE EXCHANGE	1921
HR H-73	WHAT A WHOPPER	CHASE	PATHE EXCHANGE	1921
HR H-74	TEACHING THE TEACHER	ROACH	PATHE EXCHANGE	1921
HR H-75	SPOT CASH	CHASE	PATHE EXCHANGE	1921
HR H-77	GONE TO THE COUNTRY	CHASE	PATHE EXCHANGE	1921
HR H-78	LAW AND ORDER	CHASE	PATHE EXCHANGE	1921
HR H-79	FIFTEEN MINUTES	CHASE	PATHE EXCHANGE	1921
HR H-80	ON LOCATION	CHASE	PATHE EXCHANGE	1921
HR H-81	HOCUS POCUS	CHASE	PATHE EXCHANGE	1921
HR H-82	PENNY-IN-THE-SLOT	CHASE	PATHE EXCHANGE	1921
HR H-83	JOY RIDER	ROACH	PATHE EXCHANGE	1921
HR H-84	HUSTLER	CHASE	PATHE EXCHANGE	1921
HR H-85	SINK OR SWIM	CHASE	PATHE EXCHANGE	1921
HR H-86	SHAKE 'EM UP	CHASE	PATHE EXCHANGE	1921
HR H-87	STONE AGE	CHASE	PATHE EXCHANGE	1922
HR H-88	CORNER POCKET	CHASE	PATHE EXCHANGE	1921
HR H-89	LOSE NO TIME	CHASE	PATHE EXCHANGE	1922
HR H-90	CALL THE WITNESS	CHASE	PATHE EXCHANGE	1922
HR H-91	BLOW 'EM UP	CHASE	PATHE EXCHANGE	1922
HR H-92	YEARS TO COME	CHASE	PATHE EXCHANGE	1922
HR H-93	STAGE STRUCK	WATSON	PATHE EXCHANGE	1922
HR H-94	SOME BABY	CEDER	PATHE EXCHANGE	1922
HR H-95	DOWN AND OUT	CEDER	PATHE EXCHANGE	1922
HR H-96	PARDON ME	CEDER	PATHE EXCHANGE	1922
HR H-97	BOW WOWS	CEDER	PATHE EXCHANGE	1922
HR H-98	HOT OFF THE PRESS	CEDER, CHASE	PATHE EXCHANGE	1922
HR H-99	ANVIL CHORUS	CEDER	PATHE EXCHANGE	1922
HR H-100	JUMP YOUR JOB	CEDER	PATHE EXCHANGE	1922
HR H-101	KILL THE NERVE	CEDER	PATHE EXCHANGE	1922
HR H-102	FULL O' PEP	CHASE	PATHE EXCHANGE	1922
HR H-103	DO YOUR DUTY	CEDER	PATHE EXCHANGE	1926
HR H-104	DAYS OF OLD (DAYS OF GOLD)	CHASE	PATHE EXCHANGE	1922
HR H-105	LIGHT SHOWERS	CHASE	PATHE EXCHANGE	1922
HR H-106	DO ME A FAVOR	CHASE	PATHE EXCHANGE	1922
HR H-107	PUNCH THE CLOCK	BEAUDINE	PATHE EXCHANGE	1922
HR H-108	IN THE MOVIES	CHASE	PATHE EXCHANGE	1922
HR H-109	HALE AND HEARTY	SANTELL	PATHE EXCHANGE	1922
HR H-110	STRICTLY MODERN	BEAUDINE	PATHE EXCHANGE	1922
HR H-111	DUMB BELL	CHASE	PATHE EXCHANGE	1922
HRH-F21	THERE GOES MY HEART	MCLEOD	UNITED ARTISTS	1938
HR J-1	CALL OF THE WILD	JACKMAN	PATHE EXCHANGE	1923
HR J-2	KING OF WILD HORSES	JACKMAN	PATHE EXCHANGE	1924
HR J-3	BLACK CYCLONE	JACKMAN	PATHE EXCHANGE	1925
HR J-4	DEVIL HORSE	JACKMAN	PATHE EXCHANGE	1926
HR J-5	NO MAN'S LAW	JACKMAN	PATHE EXCHANGE	1927
HR K-1	BETTER MOVIES	MCGOWAN	PATHE EXCHANGE	1925
HR K-1	BORED OF EDUCATION	DOUGLAS	MGM	1936
HR K-1	HER DANGEROUS PATH (10 CH series)	CLEMENTS	PATHE EXCHANGE	1923
HR K-2	TWO TOO YOUNG	DOUGLAS	MGM	1936

Movie Still Identification Book Ultimate Edition - Letters

CODE	TITLE/NAME	DIRECTOR/TYPE	STUDIO/DISTRIBUTOR	YEAR
HR K-2	YOUR OWN BACK YARD	MCGOWAN	PATHE EXCHANGE	1925
HR K-3	ONE WILD RIDE	MCGOWAN	PATHE EXCHANGE	1925
HR K-3	PAY AS YOU EXIT	DOUGLAS	MGM	1936
HR K-4	GOOD CHEER	MCGOWAN	PATHE EXCHANGE	1926
HR K-4	SPOOKY HOOKY	DOUGLAS	MGM	1936
HR K-5	BURIED TREASURE	MCGOWAN	PATHE EXCHANGE	1926
HR K-5	REUNION IN RHYTHM	DOUGLAS	MGM	1937
HR K-6	GLOVE TAPS	DOUGLAS	MGM	1937
HR K-6	MONKEY BUSINESS	MCGOWAN	PATHE EXCHANGE	1926
HR K-7	BABY CLOTHES	MCGOWAN	PATHE EXCHANGE	1926
HR K-7	HEARTS ARE THUMPS	DOUGLAS	MGM	1937
HR K-8	THREE SMART BOYS	DOUGLAS	MGM	1937
HR K-8	UNCLE TOM'S UNCLE	MCGOWAN	PATHE EXCHANGE	1926
HR K-9	RUSHIN' BALLET	DOUGLAS	MGM	1937
HR K-9	THUNDERING FLEAS	MCGOWAN	PATHE EXCHANGE	1926
HR K-10	ROAMIN' HOLIDAY	DOUGLAS	MGM	1937
HR K-10	SHIVERING SPOOKS	MCGOWAN	PATHE EXCHANGE	1926
HR K-11	FOURTH ALARM	MCGOWAN	PATHE EXCHANGE	1926
HR K-11	NIGHT 'N' GALES	DOUGLAS	MGM	1937
HR K-12	FISHY TALES	DOUGLAS	MGM	1937
HR K-12	WAR FEATHERS	MCGOWAN, MCGOWAN	PATHE EXCHANGE	1926
HR K-13	FRAMING YOUTH	DOUGLAS	MGM	1937
HR K-13	SEEING THE WORLD	MCGOWAN, MCGOWAN	PATHE EXCHANGE	1927
HR K-14	KWAIDAN (JAP)	KOBAYASHI	CONTINENTAL	1966
HR K-14	PIGSKIN PALOOKA	DOUGLAS	MGM	1937
HR K-14	TELLING WHOPPERS	MCGOWAN, MCGOWAN	PATHE EXCHANGE	1926
HR K-15	BRING HOME THE TURKEY	MCGOWAN, MCGOWAN	PATHE EXCHANGE	1927
HR K-15	MAIL AND FEMALE	NEWMEYER	MGM	1937
HR K-16	CANNED FISHING	DOUGLAS	MGM	1938
HR K-16	TEN YEARS OLD	MCGOWAN	PATHE EXCHANGE	1927
HR K-17	BEAR FACTS	DOUGLAS	MGM	1938
HR K-17	LOVE MY DOG	MCGOWAN	PATHE EXCHANGE	1927
HR K-18	THREE MEN IN A TUB	WATT	MGM	1938
HR K-18	TIRED BUSINESS MEN	MCGOWAN, OELZE	PATHE EXCHANGE	1927
HR K-19	BABY BROTHER	MCGOWAN, OELZE	PATHE EXCHANGE	1927
HR K-19	CAME THE BRAWN	DOUGLAS	MGM	1938
HR K-20	CHICKEN FEED	MCGOWAN, OELZE	PATHE EXCHANGE	1927
HR K-20	FEED 'EM AND WEEP	DOUGLAS	MGM	1938
HR K-21	AWFUL TOOTH	WATT	MGM	1938
HR K-21	OLYMPIC GAMES	MCGOWAN	PATHE EXCHANGE	1927
HR K-22	GLORIOUS FOURTH	MCGOWAN	PATHE EXCHANGE	1927
HR K-22	HIDE AND SHRIEK	DOUGLAS	MGM	1938
HR K-23	SMILE WINS	MCGOWAN	PATHE EXCHANGE	1928
HR K-24	PLAYIN' HOOKEY	MCGOWAN	PATHE EXCHANGE	1928
HR L-1	BUMPING INTO BROADWAY	ROACH	PATHE EXCHANGE	1919
HR L-1	COME CLEAN	HORNE	MGM	1931
HR L-1	OVER THE FENCE	LLOYD, MACDONALD	PATHE EXCHANGE	1917
HR L-1	ROUGHEST AFRICA	CEDER	PATHE EXCHANGE	1923
HR L-2	CAPTAIN KIDD'S KIDS	ROACH	PATHE EXCHANGE	1919
HR L-2	FROZEN HEARTS	HOWE	PATHE EXCHANGE	1923
HR L-2	ONE GOOD TURN	HORNE	MGM	1931
HR L-2	PINCHED	LLOYD, PRATT	PATHE EXCHANGE	1917
HR L-3	BEAU HUNKS	HORNE	MGM	1931
HR L-3	BY THE SAD SEA WAVES	GOULDING	PATHE EXCHANGE	1917
HR L-3	FROM HAND TO MOUTH	GOULDING	PATHE EXCHANGE	1919
HR L-3	SOILERS	CEDER	PATHE EXCHANGE	1923
HR L-4	ANY OLD PORT	HORNE	MGM	1932
HR L-4	HIS ROYAL SLYNESS	ROACH	PATHE EXCHANGE	1920
HR L-4	MOTHER'S JOY	CEDER	PATHE EXCHANGE	1923
HR L-4	RAINBOW ISLAND	GILBERT	PATHE EXCHANGE	1917
HR L-5	BLISS	GOULDING	PATHE EXCHANGE	1917
HR L-5	HAUNTED SPOOKS	ROACH	PATHE EXCHANGE	1920
HR L-5	HELPMATES	PARROTT	MGM	1932
HR L-5	NEAR DUBLIN	CEDER	PATHE EXCHANGE	1924
HR L-6	AN EASTERN WESTERNER	ROACH	PATHE EXCHANGE	1920
HR L-6	FLIRT	GILBERT	PATHE EXCHANGE	1917
HR L-6	MUSIC BOX	PARROTT	MGM	1932
HR L-6	SMITHY	JESKE, ROACH	PATHE EXCHANGE	1924
HR L-7	ALL ABOARD	GOULDING	PATHE EXCHANGE	1917
HR L-7	CHIMP	PARROTT	MGM	1932

Movie Still Identification Book Ultimate Edition - Letters

CODE	TITLE/NAME	DIRECTOR/TYPE	STUDIO/DISTRIBUTOR	YEAR
HR L-7	HIGH AND DIZZY	ROACH	PATHE EXCHANGE	1920
HR L-7	ZEB VS. PAPRIKA	CEDER	PATHE EXCHANGE	1924
HR L-8	COUNTY HOSPITAL	PARROTT	MGM	1932
HR L-8	GET OUT AND GET UNDER	ROACH	PATHE EXCHANGE	1920
HR L-8	MOVE ON	PRATT, GILBERT	PATHE EXCHANGE	1917
HR L-8	POSTAGE DUE	JESKE	PATHE EXCHANGE	1924
HR L-9	BASHFUL	GOULDING	PATHE EXCHANGE	1917
HR L-9	BROTHER UNDER THE CHIN	CEDER	PATHE EXCHANGE	1924
HR L-9	NUMBER, PLEASE?	ROACH	PATHE EXCHANGE	1920
HR L-9	SCRAM!	MCCAREY	MGM	1932
HR L-10	NOW OR NEVER	ROACH	PATHE EXCHANGE	1921
HR L-10	THEIR FIRST MISTAKE	MARSHALL	MGM	1932
HR L-10	TIP	PRATT, GILBERT	PATHE EXCHANGE	1918
HR L-10	WIDE OPEN SPACES	JESKE	PATHE EXCHANGE	1924
HR L-11	AMONG THOSE PRESENT	NEWMEYER	PATHE EXCHANGE	1921
HR L-11	RUPERT OF HEE HAW	PEMBROKE	PATHE EXCHANGE	1924
HR L-11	SHOULD MARRIED MEN GO HOME?	MCCAREY, PARROTT	MGM	1928
HR L-11	STEP LIVELY	GOULDING	PATHE EXCHANGE	1917
HR L-11	TOWED IN A HOLE	MARSHALL	MGM	1932
HR L-12	BIG IDEA	MOHR, PRATT	PATHE EXCHANGE	1918
HR L-12	EARLY TO BED	FLYNN	MGM	1928
HR L-12	I DO	NEWMEYER	PATHE EXCHANGE	1921
HR L-12	SHORT KILTS	JESKE	PATHE EXCHANGE	1924
HR L-12	TWICE TWO	PARROTT	MGM	1933
HR L-13	HELLO TEACHER	ROACH	PATHE EXCHANGE	1918
HR L-13	ME AND MY PAL	ROGERS	MGM	1933
HR L-13	NEVER WEAKEN	NEWMEYER	PATHE EXCHANGE	1921
HR L-13	TWO TARS	PARROTT	MGM	1928
HR L-14	HABEAS CORPUS	PARROTT, MCCAREY	MGM	1928
HR L-14	LAMB (GOAT)	LLOYD, PRATT	PATHE EXCHANGE	1918
HR L-14	MIDNIGHT PATROL	FRENCH	MGM	1933
HR L-14	SAILOR-MADE MAN	NEWMEYER	PATHE EXCHANGE	1921
HR L-15	BUSY BODIES	FRENCH	MGM	1933
HR L-15	GRANDMA'S BOY	NEWMEYER	ASSOC. EXHIBITORS	1922
HR L-15	LET'S GO	GOULDING	PATHE EXCHANGE	1918
HR L-15	WE FAW DOWN	MCCAREY	MGM	1928
HR L-16	BEAT IT	PRATT	PATHE EXCHANGE	1918
HR L-16	DIRTY WORK	FRENCH	MGM	1933
HR L-16	DR. JACK	NEWMEYER	PATHE EXCHANGE	1922
HR L-16	LIBERTY	MCCAREY	MGM	1929
HR L-17	GASOLINE WEDDING	GOULDING	PATHE EXCHANGE	1918
HR L-17	OLIVER THE EIGHTH	FRENCH	MGM	1934
HR L-17	SAFETY LAST!	TAYLOR, NEWMEYER	PATHE EXCHANGE	1923
HR L-17	WRONG AGAIN	MCCAREY	MGM	1929
HR L-18	GOING BYE-BYE!	ROGERS	MGM	1934
HR L-18	HIT HIM AGAIN	PRATT	PATHE EXCHANGE	1918
HR L-18	THAT'S MY WIFE	FRENCH	MGM	1929
HR L-19	BIG BUSINESS	HORNE, MCCAREY	MGM	1929
HR L-19	LOOK PLEASANT, PLEASE	GOULDING	PATHE EXCHANGE	1918
HR L-19	THEM THAR HILLS	ROGERS	MGM	1934
HR L-20	DOUBLE WHOOPEE	FOSTER	MGM	1929
HR L-20	HERE COME THE GIRLS	HIBBARD	PATHE EXCHANGE	1918
HR L-20	LIVE GHOST	ROGERS	MGM	1934
HR L-21	BACON GRABBERS	FOSTER	MGM	1929
HR L-21	ON THE JUMP	GOULDING	PATHE EXCHANGE	1918
HR L-21	TIT FOR TAT	ROGERS	MGM	1935
HR L-22	ANGORA LOVE	FOSTER	MGM	1929
HR-L22	FIXER UPPERS	ROGERS	MGM	1935
HR L-22	HEY THERE!	GOULDING	PATHE EXCHANGE	1918
HR L-23	KICKED OUT	GOULDING	PATHE EXCHANGE	1918
HR L-23	THICKER THAN WATER	HORNE	MGM	1935
HR L-23	UNACCUSTOMED AS WE ARE	FOSTER, ROACH	MGM	1929
HR L-24	BERTH MARKS	FOSTER	MGM	1929
HR L-24	NON STOP KID	PRATT	PATHE EXCHANGE	1918
HR L-25	FOLLOW THE CROWD	GOULDING	PATHE EXCHANGE	1918
HR L-25	MEN O' WAR	FOSTER	MGM	1929
HR L-26	IT'S A WILD LIFE	PRATT	PATHE EXCHANGE	1918
HR L-26	PERFECT DAY	PARROTT	MGM	1929
HR L-27	PIPE THE WHISKERS	GOULDING	PATHE EXCHANGE	1918
HR L-27	THEY GO BOOM	PARROTT	MGM	1929

Movie Still Identification Book Ultimate Edition - Letters

CODE	TITLE/NAME	DIRECTOR/TYPE	STUDIO/DISTRIBUTOR	YEAR
HR L-28	HOOSE-GOW	PARROTT	MGM	1929
HR L-28	SIC 'EM TOWSER	PRATT	PATHE EXCHANGE	1918
HR L-29	NIGHT OWLS	PARROTT	MGM	1930
HR L-29	TWO GUN GUSSIE	GOULDING	PATHE EXCHANGE	1918
HR L-30	BLOTTO	PARROTT	MGM	1930
HR L-30	LOVE'S YOUNG SCREAM	JEFFERSON	PATHE EXCHANGE	1919
HR-L31	BRATS	PARROTT	MGM	1930
HR L-31	FIREMAN SAVE MY CHILD	GOULDING	PATHE EXCHANGE	1918
HR-L32	BELOW ZERO	PARROTT	MGM	1930
HR L-32	CITY SLICKER	PRATT	PATHE EXCHANGE	1918
HR L-33	HOG WILD	PARROTT	MGM	1930
HR L-33	SOMEWHERE IN TURKEY	GOULDING	PATHE EXCHANGE	1918
HR L-34	ARE CROOKS DISHONEST	PRATT	PATHE EXCHANGE	1918
HR L-34	LAUREL-HARDY MURDER CASE	PARROTT	MGM	1930
HR L-35	OZARK ROMANCE	GOULDING	PATHE EXCHANGE	1918
HR L-35	PARDON US	PARROTT	MGM	1930
HR-L36	ANOTHER FINE MESS	PARROTT	MGM	1930
HR L-36	THAT'S HIM	PRATT	PATHE EXCHANGE	1918
HR L-37	BE BIG!	HORNE, PARROTT	MGM	1931
HR L-37	BRIDE AND GLOOM	GOULDING	PATHE EXCHANGE	1918
HR L-38	CHICKENS COME HOME	HORNE	MGM	1931
HR L-38	TWO SCRAMBLED	PRATT	PATHE EXCHANGE	1918
HR L-39	KICKING THE GERM OUT OF GERMANY	GOULDING	PATHE EXCHANGE	1918
HR-L39	LAUGHING GRAVY	HORNE	MGM	1931
HR L-40	BEES IN HIS BONNET	PRATT	PATHE EXCHANGE	1918
HR L-40	OUR WIFE	HORNE	MGM	1931
HR L-41	SWING YOUR PARTNERS	GOULDING	PATHE EXCHANGE	1918
HR L-42	HEAR 'EM RAVE	PRATT	PATHE EXCHANGE	1918
HR L-43	NOTHING BUT TROUBLE	ROACH	PATHE EXCHANGE	1918
HR L-44	WHY PICK ON ME?	ROACH	PATHE EXCHANGE	1918
HR L-45	TAKE A CHANCE	GOULDING	PATHE EXCHANGE	1918
HR L-46	GOING! GOING! GONE!	PRATT	PATHE EXCHANGE	1919
HR L-47	SHE LOVES ME NOT		PATHE EXCHANGE	1918
HR L-48	WANTED $5000	PRATT	PATHE EXCHANGE	1919
HR L-49	I'M ON MY WAY	ROACH	PATHE EXCHANGE	1919
HR L-50	ASK FATHER	ROACH	PATHE EXCHANGE	1919
HR L-51	ON THE FIRE	ROACH	PATHE EXCHANGE	1919
HR L-52	LOOK OUT BELOW!	ROACH	PATHE EXCHANGE	1919
HR L-53	DUTIFUL DUB	GOULDING	PATHE EXCHANGE	1919
HR L-54	NEXT AISLE OVER	ROACH	PATHE EXCHANGE	1919
HR L-55	RING UP THE CURTAIN	GOULDING	PATHE EXCHANGE	1919
HR L-56	JUST DROPPED IN	ROACH	PATHE EXCHANGE	1919
HR L-57	CRACK YOUR HEELS	GOULDING	PATHE EXCHANGE	1919
HR L-58	YOUNG MR. JAZZ	ROACH	PATHE EXCHANGE	1919
HR L-59	SI, SENOR	GOULDING	PATHE EXCHANGE	1919
HR L-60	BEFORWE BREAKFAST	ROACH	PATHE EXCHANGE	1919
HR L-61	MARATHON	GOULDING	PATHE EXCHANGE	1919
HR L-62	BACK TO THE WOODS	ROACH	PATHE EXCHANGE	1919
HR L-63	PISTOLS FOR BREAKFAST	GOULDING	PATHE EXCHANGE	1919
HR L-64	SWAT THE CROOK	ROACH	PATHE EXCHANGE	1919
HR L-65	OFF THE TROLLEY	GOULDING	PATHE EXCHANGE	1919
HR L-66	AT THE OLD STAGE DOOR	ROACH	PATHE EXCHANGE	1919
HR L-67	JAZZED HONEYMOON	ROACH	PATHE EXCHANGE	1919
HR L-68	NEVER TOUCHED ME	GOULDING	PATHE EXCHANGE	1919
HR L-69	BILL BLAZES, ESQ.	ROACH	PATHE EXCHANGE	1919
HR L-70	COUNT YOUR CHANGE	GOULDING	PATHE EXCHANGE	1919
HR L-71	CHOP SUEY AND COMPANY	ROACH	PATHE EXCHANGE	1919
HR L-72	HEAP BIG CHIEF	GOULDING	PATHE EXCHANGE	1919
HR L-73	SAMMY IN SIBERIA	ROACH	PATHE EXCHANGE	1919
HR L-74	DON'T SHOVE	GOULDING	PATHE EXCHANGE	1919
HR L-75	BE MY WIFE	ROACH	PATHE EXCHANGE	1919
HR L-76	RAJAH	ROACH	PATHE EXCHANGE	1919
HR L-77	HE LEADS, OTHERS FOLLOW	ROACH	PATHE EXCHANGE	1919
HR L-78	SOFT MONEY	ROACH	PATHE EXCHANGE	1919
HR L-79	COUNT THE VOTES	ROACH	PATHE EXCHANGE	1919
HR L-80	PAY YOUR DUES	ROACH	PATHE EXCHANGE	1919
HR L-81	HIS ONLY FATHER	ROACH	PATHE EXCHANGE	1919
HR L-82	SPRING FEVER	ROACH	PATHE EXCHANGE	1919
HR L-83	JUST NEIGHBORS	LLOYD, TERRY	PATHE EXCHANGE	1919
HR LC-89	NOON WHISTLE	JESKE	PATHE EXCHANGE	1923

Movie Still Identification Book Ultimate Edition - Letters

CODE	TITLE/NAME	DIRECTOR/TYPE	STUDIO/DISTRIBUTOR	YEAR
HR LC-91	WHITE WINGS	JESKE	PATHE EXCHANGE	1923
HR LC-92	PICK AND SHOVEL	JESKE	PATHE EXCHANGE	1923
HR LC-95	KILL OR CURE	PEMBROKE	PATHE EXCHANGE	1923
HR LC-97	COLLARS AND CUFFS	JESKE	PATHE EXCHANGE	1923
HR LC-99	GAS AND AIR	PEMBROKE	PATHE EXCHANGE	1923
HR LC-102	ORANGES AND LEMONS	JESKE	PATHE EXCHANGE	1923
HR LC-104	SHORT ORDERS	PEMBROKE	PATHE EXCHANGE	1923
HR LC-106	SAVE THE SHIP	JESKE, ROACH	PATHE EXCHANGE	1923
HR LC-112	SCORCHING SANDS	WILLIAMSON, ROACH	PATHE EXCHANGE	1923
HR LC-115	WHOLE TRUTH	CEDER	PATHE EXCHANGE	1923
HR LG-30	LOVE'S YOUNG SCREAM	JEFFERSON	PATHE EXCHANGE	1919
HR M-1	DESERT'S TOLL	SMITH	MGM	1926
HR M-1	ONE AT A TIME	CEDER	PATHE EXCHANGE	1924
HR M-1	RHAPSODY IN BREW	GILBERT	MGM	1934
HR M-2	KEG O' MY HEART	GILBERT	MGM	1933
HR M-2	VALLEY OF HELL	SMITH	MGM	1927
HR M-3	MUSIC IN YOUR HAIR	CHASE	MGM	1934
HR M-4	APPLES TO YOU!	JASON	MGM	1934
HR M-5	ROAMIN' VANDALS	JASON, YATES	MGM	1934
HR M-6	DUKE FOR A DAY	PARROTT	MGM	1934
HR M-7	BENNY, FROM PANAMA	PARROTT	MGM	1934
HR P-1	SPITBALL SADIE	ROACH	PATHE EXCHANGE	1915
HR P-2	TERRIBLY STUCK UP	ROACH	PATHE EXCHANGE	1915
HR P-3	DEVIL'S BROTHER	ROGERS	MGM	1933
HR P-3	RUSES, RHYMES AND ROUGHNECKS	ROACH	PATHE EXCHANGE	1915
HR P-4	MIXUP FOR MAZIE	ROACH	PATHE EXCHANGE	1915
HR P-5	SOME BABY	ROACH	PATHE EXCHANGE	1915
HR P-6	FRESH FROM THE FARM	ROACH	PATHE EXCHANGE	1915
HR P-7	FOOZLE AT THE TEE PARTY	ROACH	PATHE EXCHANGE	1915
HR P-8	GREAT WHILE IT LASTED	ROACH	PATHE EXCHANGE	1915
HR P-9	GIVING THEM FITS	ROACH	PATHE EXCHANGE	1915
HR P-10	TINKERING WITH TROUBLE	ROACH	PATHE EXCHANGE	1915
HR P-11	PECULIAR PATIENTS' PRANKS	ROACH	PATHE EXCHANGE	1915
HR P-12	LONESOME LUKE, SOCIAL GANGSTER	ROACH, MACDONALD	PATHE EXCHANGE	1915
HR P-13	BUGHOUSE BELLHOPS	ROACH	PATHE EXCHANGE	1915
HR P-14	RAGTIME SNAP SHOTS	ROACH	PATHE EXCHANGE	1915
HR P-15	LUKE LUGS LUGGAGE	ROACH	PATHE EXCHANGE	1916
HR P-16	LONESOME LUKE LEANS TO THE LITERARY	ROACH	PATHE EXCHANGE	1916
HR P-17	LONESOME LUKE LOLLS IN LUXURY	ROACH	PATHE EXCHANGE	1916
HR P-17	TOPPER (sh)	MCLEOD	MGM	1937
HR P-18	LUKE FOILS THE VILLAIN	ROACH	PATHE EXCHANGE	1916
HR P-19	LUKE, THE CANDY CUT-UP	ROACH	PATHE EXCHANGE	1916
HR P-20	LUKE AND THE RURAL ROUGHNECKS	ROACH	PATHE EXCHANGE	1916
HR P-21	LUKE PIPES THE PIPPINS	ROACH	PATHE EXCHANGE	1916
HR P-22	THEM WAS THE DAYS	ROACH	PATHE EXCHANGE	1916
HR P-23	LUKE'S DOUBLE	ROACH	PATHE EXCHANGE	1916
HR P-24	LONESOME LUKE, CIRCUS KING	ROACH	PATHE EXCHANGE	1916
HR P-25	LUKE'S LATE LUNCHERS	ROACH	PATHE EXCHANGE	1916
HR P-26	LUKE AND THE BOMB THROWERS	ROACH	PATHE EXCHANGE	1916
HR P-27	LUKE LAUGHS LAST	ROACH	PATHE EXCHANGE	1916
HR P-28	LUKE'S FATAL FLIVVER	ROACH	PATHE EXCHANGE	1916
HR P-29	LUKE'S SOCIETY MIX-UP	ROACH	PATHE EXCHANGE	1916
HR P-30	LUKE'S WASHFUL WAITING	ROACH	PATHE EXCHANGE	1916
HR-P38	ALL AMERICAN CO-ED	PRINZ	UNITED ARTISTS	1941
HR PC-126	FRIEND HUSBAND (WHY MARRY?)	HOWE	PATHE EXCHANGE	1924
HRP-F	BONNIE SCOTLAND	HORNE	MGM	1935
HRP-F21	THERE GOES MY HEART (scenes)	MCLEOD	UNITED ARTISTS	1938
HRP-F24	TOPPER TAKES A TRIP (scenes)	MCLEOD	UNITED ARTISTS	1938
HRP-G	MAMA'S LITTLE PIRATE	MEINS	MGM	1934
HRR	HILLS RUN RED (IT)	LIZZANI	UNITED ARTISTS	1966
HR R-1	DO YOU LOVE YOUR WIFE?	ROACH	PATHE EXCHANGE	1919
HR R-1	JUS PASSIN' THROUGH	ROACH	PATHE EXCHANGE	1923
HR R-1	WHITE EAGLE (15 CH series)	JACKMAN, VAN DYKE	PATHE EXCHANGE	1922
HR R-2	JUST RAMBLING ALONG	ROACH	PATHE EXCHANGE	1918
HR R-2	TIMBER QUEEN (15 CH series)	JACKMAN	PATHE EXCHANGE	1922
HR R-3	HOOT MON!	ROACH	PATHE EXCHANGE	1919
HR R-3	UNCENSORED MOVIES	CLEMENTS	PATHE EXCHANGE	1923
HR R-4	GEE WHIZ, GENEVIEVE	HOWE	PATHE EXCHANGE	1924
HR R-4	NO PLACE LIKE JAIL	TERRY	PATHE EXCHANGE	1918
HR R-5	HUSTLING FOR HEALTH	TERRY	PATHE EXCHANGE	1919

Movie Still Identification Book Ultimate Edition - Letters

CODE	TITLE/NAME	DIRECTOR/TYPE	STUDIO/DISTRIBUTOR	YEAR
HR R-5	TWO WAGONS, BOTH COVERED	WAGNER	PATHE EXCHANGE	1924
HR R-6	COWBOY SHEIK	HOWE	PATHE EXCHANGE	1924
HR R-7	CAKE EATER	HOWE	PATHE EXCHANGE	1924
HR R-8	UNNAMED WILL ROGERS		PATHE EXCHANGE	1924
HR R-9	BIG MOMENTS FROM LITTLE PICTURES	CLEMENTS	PATHE EXCHANGE	1924
HR R-11	GOING TO CONGRESS	WAGNER	PATHE EXCHANGE	1924
HR R-12	DON'T PARK THERE!	GUIOL	PATHE EXCHANGE	1924
HR R-13	OUR CONGRESSMAN	WAGNER	PATHE EXCHANGE	1924
HR R-14	TRUTHFUL LIAR	DEL RUTH	PATHE EXCHANGE	1924
HR S-1	CALL A COP	STEVENS	MGM	1931
HR S-1	DON KEY	GUIOL, HORNE	PATHE EXCHANGE	1926
HR S-1	SUGAR DADDIES	GUIOL, MCCAREY	MGM	1927
HR S-2	MAMA LOVES PAPA	STEVENS	MGM	1931
HR S-2	PUNCH IN THE NOSE	HOWE	PATHE EXCHANGE	1926
HR S-2	SECOND HUNDRED YEARS	GUIOL	MGM	1927
HR S-3	HATS OFF	YATES	MGM	1927
HR S-3	KICKOFF	STEVENS	MGM	1931
HR S-3	SOMEWHERE IN SOMEWHERE	HORNE	PATHE EXCHANGE	1925
HR S-4	LOVE PAINS	ROACH	MGM	1932
HR S-4	PUTTING PANTS ON PHILIP	BRUCKMAN	MGM	1927
HR S-4	THERE GOES THE BRIDE	HORNE	PATHE EXCHANGE	1925
HR S-5	BATTLE OF THE CENTURY	BRUCKMAN	MGM	1927
HR S-5	KNOCKOUT	FRENCH, MCGOWAN	MGM	1932
HR S-5	LAUGHING LADIES	HORNE	PATHE EXCHANGE	1925
HR S-6	LEAVE 'EM LAUGHING	BRUCKMAN	MGM	1928
HR S-6	YOUR HUSBAND'S PAST	GUIOL	PATHE EXCHANGE	1926
HR S-6	YOU'RE TELLING ME	FRENCH, MCGOWAN	MGM	1932
HR S-7	DIZZY DADDIES	WALLACE	PATHE EXCHANGE	1926
HR S-7	FINISHING TOUCH	BRUCKMAN, MCCAREY	MGM	1928
HR S-7	TOO MANY WOMEN	FRENCH, MCGOWAN	MGM	1932
HR S-8	FROM SOUP TO NUTS	KENNEDY	MGM	1928
HR S-8	LET GEORGE DO IT*	KENNEDY	MGM	1928
HR S-8	MADAME MYSTERY	WALLACE, LAUREL	PATHE EXCHANGE	1926
HR S-8	WILD BABIES	FRENCH, MCGOWAN	MGM	1932
HR S-9	NEVER TOO OLD	WALLACE	PATHE EXCHANGE	1926
HR S-9	YOU'RE DARN TOOTIN'	KENNEDY	MGM	1928
HR S-10	MERRY WIDOWER	WALLACE	PATHE EXCHANGE	1926
HR S-10	THEIR PURPLE MOMENT	PARROTT	MGM	1928
HR S-11	RAGGEDY ROSE	WALLACE	PATHE EXCHANGE	1926
HR S-11	THAT NIGHT	HEATH, MCCAREY	MGM	1928
HR S-12	DO GENTLEMEN SNORE?	MCCAREY	MGM	1928
HR S-12	WISE GUYS PREFER BRUNETTES	LAUREL	PATHE EXCHANGE	1926
HR S-13	BOY FRIEND	GUIOL	MGM	1928
HR S-13	GET 'EM YOUNG	GUIOL, LAUREL	PATHE EXCHANGE	1926
HR S-14	DUCK SOUP	GUIOL	PATHE EXCHANGE	1927
HR S-14	FEED 'EM AND WEEP	GUIOL, MCCAREY	MGM	1928
HR S-15	GOING GA GA	MCCAREY	MGM	1929
HR S-15	ON THE FRONT PAGE	PARROTT	PATHE EXCHANGE	1926
HR S-16	PAIR OF TIGHTS	YATES	MGM	1929
HR S-16	WHY GIRLS SAY NO	MCCAREY	PATHE EXCHANGE	1927
HR S-17	HONORABLE MR. BUGGS	JACKMAN	PATHE EXCHANGE	1927
HR S-17	WHEN MONEY COMES	MCCAREY	MGM	1929
HR S-18	SLIPPING WIVES	GUIOL	PATHE EXCHANGE	1927
HR S-18	UNKISSED MAN	ROACH, MCCAREY	MGM	1929
HR S-19	LOVE 'EM AND WEEP	GUIOL, JONES	PATHE EXCHANGE	1927
HR S-19	WHY IS A PLUMBER?	MCCAREY	MGM	1929
HR S-20	THUNDERING TOUPEES	MCGOWAN	MGM	1929
HR S-20	WHY GIRLS LOVE SAILORS	GUIOL	PATHE EXCHANGE	1927
HR-S21	HURDY GURDY	MCCAREY	MGM	1929
HR S-21	WITH LOVE AND HISSES	GUIOL	PATHE EXCHANGE	1927
HR S-22	MADAME "Q"	MCCAREY	MGM	1929
HR S-22	SAILORS, BEWARE!	GUIOL	PATHE EXCHANGE	1927
HR S-23	COWBOYS CRY FOR IT*	GASNIER	PATHE EXCHANGE	1928
HR S-23	DAD'S DAY	MCCAREY	MGM	1929
HR S-23	SHOULD TALL MEN MARRY?	GASNIER	PATHE EXCHANGE	1928
HR S-24	DO DETECTIVES THINK?	GUIOL	PATHE EXCHANGE	1927
HR S-24	HOTTER THAN HOT	FOSTER	MGM	1929
HR S-25	FLAMING FATHERS	LAUREL, MCCAREY	PATHE EXCHANGE	1927
HR S-25	SKY BOY	ROGERS	MGM	1929
HR S-26	FLYING ELEPHANTS	ROACH, BUTLER	PATHE EXCHANGE	1928

Movie Still Identification Book Ultimate Edition - Letters

CODE	TITLE/NAME	DIRECTOR/TYPE	STUDIO/DISTRIBUTOR	YEAR
HR S-26	SKIRT SHY	ROGERS	MGM	1929
HR S-27	HEAD GUY	ROACH	MGM	1930
HR S-28	FIGHTING PARSON	GUIOL, ROGERS	MGM	1930
HR S-29	BIG KICK	DOANE	MGM	1930
HR S-30	SHRIMP	ROGERS	MGM	1930
HR S-31	KING		MGM	1930
HR S-32	DOCTOR'S ORDERS	HEATH	MGM	1930
HR S-33	BIGGER AND BETTER	KENNEDY	MGM	1930
HR S-34	LADIES LAST	STEVENS	MGM	1930
HR S-35	BLOOD AND THUNDER	STEVENS	MGM	1931
HR S-36	LOVE FEVER	MCGOWAN	MGM	1931
HR S-37	HIGH GEAR	STEVENS	MGM	1931
HR S-38	AIR TIGHT	STEVENS	MGM	1931
HR-S39	LET'S DO THINGS	ROACH	MGM	1931
HR T-1	BATTLING ORIOLES	GUIOL, WILDE	PATHE EXCHANGE	1924
HR T-1	MOVIE DUMMY (MOVIE MUMMY)	ROACH	PATHE EXCHANGE	1918
HR T-1	THUNDERING TAXIS	LORD, MEINS	MGM	1933
HR T-2	JUNKMAN	ROACH	PATHE EXCHANGE	1918
HR T-2	WHAT PRICE TAXI	LORD	MGM	1932
HR T-2	WHITE SHEEP	ROACH	PATHE EXCHANGE	1924
HR T-3	STRANGE INNERTUBE	LORD	MGM	1932
HR T-3	TOTO IN FARE PLEASE		PATHE EXCHANGE	1918
HR T-4	HOT SPOT	LORD	MGM	1932
HR T-4	TOTO IN ONE NIGHT ONLY	ROACH	PATHE EXCHANGE	1918
HR T-5	FIRE THE COOK (edited to create T-7)	ROACH	PATHE EXCHANGE	1918
HR T-5	TAXI FOR TWO	LORD	MGM	1932
HR T-6	BRING 'EM BACK A WIFE	LORD	MGM	1933
HR T-6	HIS BUSY DAY	ROACH	PATHE EXCHANGE	1918
HR T-7	DIPPY DAUGHTER	ROACH	PATHE EXCHANGE	1918
HR T-7	WRECKETY WRECKS	LORD	MGM	1933
HR T-8	CLEOPATSY - aka CLEO PROXY	ROACH	PATHE EXCHANGE	1918
HR T-8	TAXI BARONS	MEINS	MGM	1933
HR T-9	CALL HER SAUSAGE	MEINS	MGM	1933
HR T-9	FURNITURE MOVERS	ROACH	PATHE EXCHANGE	1918
HR T-10	CHECK YOUR BAGGAGE	ROACH	PATHE EXCHANGE	1918
HR T-10	RUMMY	LORD	MGM	1933
HR T-11	GREAT WATER PERIL (POOR CLARINE)	ROACH	PATHE EXCHANGE	1918
HR T-12	DO HUSBANDS DECEIVE?	ROACH	PATHE EXCHANGE	1918
HR T-13	BEACH NUTS	ROACH	PATHE EXCHANGE	1918
HR T-14	ENEMY OF SOAP	ROACH	PATHE EXCHANGE	1918
HRX-F24	TOPPER TAKES A TRIP (PUBS)	MCLEOD	UNITED ARTISTS	1938
HRZ	HARD ROCK ZOMBIES	SHAH	CANNON	1986
HS	HARRY SHERMAN PRODUCTIONS	studio	PARAMOUNT	
HS	HAUNTED SUMMER	PASSER	CANNON	1988
HS	HEIDI'S SONG (t)	TAYLOR	PARAMOUNT	1982
HS	HELENE STANLEY	portrait	RKO	
HS	HER HUSBAND'S SECRET	LLOYD	WARNER BROS	1925
HS	HER HUSBAND'S SECRETARY	MCDONALD	WARNER BROS	1937
HS	HERE COMES THE NAVY	BACON	WARNER BROS	1934
HS	HIGH SIERRA	WALSH	WARNER BROS	1941
HS	HIGH SPIRITS	JORDAN	TRI STAR	1988
HS	HIGH STAKES	SHERMAN	RKO	1931
HS	HORSE SOLDIERS	FORD	UNITED ARTISTS	1959
HS	HOT SHOTS	ABRAHAMS	20th CENTURY FOX	1991
HS	HOTEL SAHARA	ANNAKIN	UNITED ARTISTS	1951
HS	HOTEL SPLENDIDE (UK)	POWELL	IDEAL	1932
HS	HOUSE ON 56TH STREET	FLOREY	WARNER BROS	1933
HS	HOW BAXTER BUTTED IN	BEAUDINE	WARNER BROS	1925
HS	PIER 5, HAVANA	CAHN	UNITED ARTISTS	1959
HS	SPIKES GANG	FLEISCHER	UNITED ARTISTS	1974
HS	HERO OF THE BIG SNOWS	RAYMAKER	WARNER BROS	1926
HS 1	HOP ALONG CASSIDY	BRETHERTON	PARAMOUNT	1935
H.S.1	LADY OF BURLESQUE	WELLMAN	UNITED ARTISTS	1943
HS 2	EAGLE'S BROOD	BRETHERTON	PARAMOUNT	1935
HS-2	GUEST IN THE HOUSE	BRAHM	UNITED ARTISTS	1944
HS2	HOT SHOTS! PART DEAUX	ABRAHAMS	20th CENTURY FOX	1993
HS 2A	LLANO KID	VENTURINI	PARAMOUNT	1939
HS 3	BAR 20 RIDS AGAIN	BRETHERTON	PARAMOUNT	1935
HS 3A	ROUNDUP	SELANDER	PARAMOUNT	1941
HS 4	CALL OF THE PRAIRIE	BRETHERTON	PARAMOUNT	1936

Movie Still Identification Book Ultimate Edition - Letters

CODE	TITLE/NAME	DIRECTOR/TYPE	STUDIO/DISTRIBUTOR	YEAR
HS 5	THREE ON THE TRAIL	BRETHERTON	PARAMOUNT	1936
HS 6	HEART OF THE WEST	BRETHERTON	PARAMOUNT	1936
HS 7	HOPALONG CASSIDY RETURNS	WATT	PARAMOUNT	1936
HS 8	TRAIL DUST	WATT	PARAMOUNT	1936
HS 9	BORDERLAND	WATT	PARAMOUNT	1936
HS 10	HILLS OF OLD WYOMING	MACK	PARAMOUNT	1937
HS 11	NORTH OF THE RIO GRANDE	WATT	PARAMOUNT	1937
HS 12	RUSTLER'S VALLEY	WATT	PARAMOUNT	1937
HS 13	HOPALONG RIDES AGAIN	SELANDER	PARAMOUNT	1937
HS 14	TEXAS TRAIL	SELMAN	PARAMOUNT	1937
HS 15	BARRIER	SELANDER	PARAMOUNT	1937
HS 16	PARTNERS OF THE PLAINS	SELANDER	PARAMOUNT	1938
HS 17	CASSIDY OF BAR 20	SELANDER	PARAMOUNT	1938
HS 18	HEART OF ARIZONA	SELANDER	PARAMOUNT	1938
HS 20	PRIDE OF THE WEST	SELANDER	PARAMOUNT	1938
HS 21	IN OLD MEXICO	VENTURINI	PARAMOUNT	1938
HS 22	MYSTERIOUS RIDER	SELANDER	PARAMOUNT	1938
HS 23	SUNSET TRAIL	SELANDER	PARAMOUNT	1938
HS 24	FRONTIERSMAN	SELANDER	PARAMOUNT	1938
HS 25	SILVER ON THE SAGE	SELANDER	PARAMOUNT	1938
HS 26	RENEGADE TRAIL	SELANDER	PARAMOUNT	1939
HS 27	RANGE WAR	SELANDER	PARAMOUNT	1939
HS 28	LAW OF THE PAMPAS	WATT	PARAMOUNT	1939
HS 29	SANTA FE MARSHALL	SELANDER	PARAMOUNT	1940
HS 30	KNIGHTS OF THE RANGE	SELANDER	PARAMOUNT	1940
HS 31	SHOWDOWN	BRETHERTON	PARAMOUNT	1940
HS 32	LIGHT OF WESTERN STARS	SELANDER	PARAMOUNT	1940
HS 33	HIDDEN GOLD	SELANDER	PARAMOUNT	1940
HS 34	STAGECOACH WAR	SELANDER	PARAMOUNT	1940
HS 35	THREE MEN FROM TEXAS	SELANDER	PARAMOUNT	1940
HS 36	DOOMED CARAVAN	SELANDER	PARAMOUNT	1941
HS 37	CHEROKEE STRIP	SELANDER	PARAMOUNT	1940
HS 38	IN OLD COLORADO	BRETHERTON	PARAMOUNT	1941
HS 39	BORDER VIGILANTES	ABRAHAMS	PARAMOUNT	1941
HS 40	PIRATES ON HORSEBACK	SELANDER	PARAMOUNT	1941
HS 41	WIDE OPEN TOWN	SELANDER	PARAMOUNT	1941
HS 42	PARSON OF PANAMINT	MCGANN	PARAMOUNT	1941
HS 43	SECRET OF THE WASTELANDS	ABRAHAMS	PARAMOUNT	1941
HS 44	OUTLAWS OF THE DESERT	BRETHERTON	PARAMOUNT	1941
HS 45	RIDERS OF THE TIMERLAND	SELANDER	PARAMOUNT	1941
HS 46	STICK TO YOUR GUNS	SELANDER	PARAMOUNT	1941
HS 47	TWILIGHT ON THE TRAIL	BRETHERTON	PARAMOUNT	1941
HS 48	TOMBSTONE TOWN TOO TOUGH TO DIE	MCGANN	PARAMOUNT	1942
HS-56	COLT COMRADES	SELANDER	UNITED ARTISTS	1943
HS-57	BAR 20	SELANDER	UNITED ARTISTS	1943
HS-58	KANSAN	ARCHAINBAUD	UNITED ARTISTS	1943
HS-59	FALSE COLORS	ARCHAINBAUD	UNITED ARTISTS	1943
HS-60	RIDERS OF THE DEADLINE	SELANDER	UNITED ARTISTS	1943
HS-61	WOMAN OF THE TOWN	ARCHAINBAUD	UNITED ARTISTS	1943
HS-62	TEXAS MASQUERADE	ARCHAINBAUD	UNITED ARTISTS	1944
HS-63	MYSTERY MAN	ARCHAINBAUD	UNITED ARTISTS	1944
HS-64	LUMBERJACK	SELANDER	UNITED ARTISTS	1944
HS-65	FORTY THIEVES	SELANDER	UNITED ARTISTS	1944
HSAS	HALF SHOT AT SUNRISE	SLOANE	RKO	1930
HSD	HIDEOUS SUN DEMON	CLARKE, BOUTROSS	PACIFIC INT'L	1959
HSH	HER SUMMER HERO	DUGAN	FILM BOOKING OFFICE	1928
HSH	HOME SWEET HOME (UK)	BLAKELEY	BUTCHER'S	1945
HSKB	HONEY I SHRUNK THE KIDS	JOHNSTON	BUENA VISTA	1989
HSM	HELL SHIP MUTINY	SHOLEM, WILLIAMS	REPUBLIC	1957
HT	ALL THIS AND HEAVEN TOO	LITVAK	WARNER BROS	1940
HT	CROSS COUNTRY ROMANCE	WOODRUFF	RKO	1940
HT	DANGER PATROL	LANDERS	RKO	1937
HT	HALLELUJAH TRAIL	STURGES	UNITED ARTISTS	1965
HT	HAMMER THE TOFF (UK)	ROGERS	BUTCHER'S	1952
HT	HAPPY THIEVES	MARSHALL	UNITED ARTISTS	1962
HT	HARD TIMES	HILL	COLUMBIA	1975
HT	HEAT	MANN	WARNER BROS	1995
HT	HELEN TALBOT	portrait		
HT	HELEN TWELVETREES	portrait	RKO	
HT	HEROES Of TELEMARK (UK)	MANN	COLUMBIA	1965

Movie Still Identification Book Ultimate Edition - Letters

CODE	TITLE/NAME	DIRECTOR/TYPE	STUDIO/DISTRIBUTOR	YEAR
HT	HIGH TERRACE (UK)	CASS	ALLIED ARTISTS	1956
HT	HIGH TREASON (UK)	BOULTING	MAYER-KINGLSEY	1951
HT	HURRY UP OR I'LL BE 30	JACOBY	AVCO EMBASSY	1972
HT	KEYSTONE HOTEL	STAUB	WARNER BROS	1935
HT	SHOCK TROOPS (FR)	GAVRAS	UNITED ARTISTS	1967
HTB	HOW TO BEAT THE HIGH COST OF LIVING	SCHEERER	AIP	1980
HTD	HIT THE DECK	REED	RKO	1929
HTMW	HOW TO MURDER YOUR WIFE	QUINE	UNITED ARTISTS	1965
HTP	HARD TIMES FOR PRINCES (IT)	SCOLA	COLUMBIA	1965
HTS	HOW TO SUCCEED IN BUSINESS WITHOUT REALLY TRYING	SWIFT	UNITED ARTISTS	1967
HUD	HUD	RITT	PARAMOUNT	1963
HUP	HUNG UP	LUNTZ	20th CENTURY FOX	1968
HUS	HUSBANDS	CASSAVETES	COLUMBIA	1970
HV	HOLLYWOOD VARIETIES	LANDRES	LIPPERT	1950
HW	HEADLINE WOMAN	NIGH	MASCOT	1935
HW	HEAT WAVE (UK: HOUSE ACROSS THE LAKE)	HUGHES	LIPPERT	1954
HV	HELEN VALKIS	portrait	WARNER BROS	
HV	HELEN VINSON	portrait	WARNER BROS	1930s-40s
HVR	VERA RALSTON	portrait	REP	
HW	HANNA'S WAR	GOLAN	CANNON	1988
HW	HARD WAY	SHERMAN	WARNER BROS	1943
HW	HAVANA WIDOWS	ENRIGHT	FIRST NATIONAL	1933
HW	HAWAII	HILL	UNITED ARTISTS	1966
HW	HE RAN ALL THE WAY	BERRY	UNITED ARTISTS	1951
HW	HEATWAVE (UK)	HUGHES	LIPPERT	1954
HW	HELEN WESTCOTT	portrait	WARNER BROS	
HW	HENRY WADSWORTH	portrait	MGM	
HW	HERE WE GO AGAIN	DWAN	RKO	1942
HW	HIGHWAY WEST	MCGANN	WARNER BROS	1941
HW	HOLIDAY WEEK (UK: HINDLE WAKES)	CRABTREE	MONARCH	1952
HW	THOSE WHO DANCE	BEAUDINE	WARNER BROS	1930
HW	THREE THE HARD WAY	PARKS, JR.	ALLIED ARTISTS	1974
HWC	HAVING WONDERFUL CRIME	SUTHERLAND	RKO	1945
HWH	IN HARM'S WAY	PREMINGER	PARAMOUNT	1975
HWP	HAL WALLIS PRODUCTIONS	studio	PARAMOUNT	
HWW	HOW I WON THE WAR (UK)	LESTER	UNITED ARTISTS	1967
HXCX	HARRY CAREY	portrait	MGM	
HXH	HELEN HAYES	portrait	MGM	
I	EASY LIVING	TOURNEUR	RKO	1949
I	IDOL (UK)	PETRIE	EMBASSY	1966
I	ILLICIT	MAYO	WARNER BROS	1931
I	IMPULSE	GREFE	CAMELOT	1974
I	IMPULSE	BAKER	20th CENTURY FOX	1984
I	IMPULSE	LOCKE	WARNER BROS	1990
I	INFATUATION	CUMMINGS	WARNER BROS	1925
I	INFORMER	FORD	RKO	1935
I	INGA (SWE: JAG - EN OSKULD)	SARNO	CINEMATION	1968
I	INHERITOR (FR)	LABRO	HERA FILMS	1973
I	INNOCENTS (UK)	CLAYTON	20TH CENTURY FOX	1961
I	INTERLUDE	BILLINGTON	COLUMBIA	1968
I	INTERVAL	MANN	AVCO EMBASSY	1973
I	INTRIGUE	MARIN	UNITED ARTISTS	1947
I	IRENE	WILCOX	RKO	1940
I	IRONWEED	BABENCO	TRI STAR	1987
I	ISRAEL		WARNER BROS	1959
I	PICKUP ALLEY (UK: INTERPOL)	GILLING	COLUMBIA	1957
I1	WEDDING REHEARSAL (UK)	KORDA	IDEAL	1932
IA	BACK TO BATAAN	DMYTRYK	RKO	1945
IA	INADMISSABLE EVIDENCE (UK)	PAGE	PARAMOUNT	1968
IA	INDIAN AGENT	SELANDER	RKO	1948
IA	INTERNAL AFFAIRS	FIGGIS	PARAMOUNT	1990
IA	INVISIBLE AVENGER	HOWE, PARKER	REPUBLIC	1958
IA	IRIS ADRIAN	portrait		
IAP	IT'S A PLEASURE	SEITER	RKO	1945
IB	INGRID BERGMAN	portrait	RKO, UA, WARNER BROS	
IB	INNOCENT BLOOD (aka FRENCH VAMPIRE IN AMERICA)	LANDIS	WARNER BROS	1992
IB	INNOCENT BYSTANDERS	COLLINSON	PARAMOUNT	1972
IB	INVISIBLE BOY	HOFFMAN	MGM	1957
IB	IRENE BORDONI	portrait	FN	
IB	IRVING BERLIN	portrait	RKO	

Movie Still Identification Book Ultimate Edition - Letters

CODE	TITLE/NAME	DIRECTOR/TYPE	STUDIO/DISTRIBUTOR	YEAR
IBD	ISLAND OF BURNING DOOMED (UK: NIGHT OF BIG HEAT)	FISHER	MARON	1967
IBS	BEAST (IT/FR: IL BESTIONE)	CORBUCCI	WARNER BROS	1974
IC	ICE CASTLES	WRYE	COLUMBIA	1978
IC	ICHABOD AND MR. TOAD (t)	ALGAR, GERONIMI	RKO	1949
IC	ILKA CHASE	portrait		
IC	ILLUSTRIOUS CORPSES (IT)	ROSI	UNITED ARTISTS	1976
IC	IN COUNTRY	JEWISON	WARNER BROS	1989
IC	INA CLAIRE	portrait	PATHE	
IC	INTERNATIONAL COUNTERFEITERS (GER: ADV BERLIN 1952)	CAP	REPUBLIC	1958
IC	INVESTIGATION OF A CITIZEN ABOVE SUSPICION (IT)	PETRI	COLUMBIA	1970
IC	IRENE CASTLE	portrait	RKO	
IC	IRENE COLEMAN	portrait	WARNER BROS	
IC	IT'S A COP (UK)	ROGERS	UNITED ARTISTS	1934
IC	STORY OF VERNON AND IRENE CASTLE	POTTER	RKO	1939
IC	THIS MARRIAGE BUSINESS	CABANNE	RKO	1938
IC-CX	ILLUSTRIOUS CORPSES (IT)	ROSI	UNITED ARTISTS	1976
ICE	LOVE IS MY PROFESSION (IT)	AUTANT-LARA	UNION FILMS	1959
ICE	ON THIN ICE	ST. CLAIR	WARNER BROS	1925
ICFHW	FIRE MAIDENS OF OUTER SPACE	ROTH	SATURN	1956
ICW	IT COVERED THE WORLD	CORMAN	AIP	1956
ID	I MARRIED A DOCTOR	MAYO	WARNER BROS	1936
ID	IDOL (UK)	PETRIE	PARAMOUNT	1966
ID	INDEPENDENCE DAY	EMMERICH	20th CENTURY FOX	1996
ID	IRENE DELROY	portrait	WARNER BROS	
ID	IRENE DUNNE	portrait	MGM, RKO, UNIVERSAL	
ID	IRINA DEMICH	portrait	FOX	
ID	IRMA LA DOUCE	WILDER	UNITED ARTISTS	1963
IDH	IN THE DOGHOUSE (UK)	CONYERS	SCHOENFELD	1962
IE	ISLE OF ESCAPE	BRETHERTON	WARNER BROS	1930
IE2	IRON EAGLE 2	FURIE	TRI STAR	1988
IF	BLIND ADVENTURE	SCHOEDSACK	RKO	1933
IF	I AM A FUGITIVE FROM A CHAIN GANG	LEROY	WARNER BROS	1932
IF	I WAS FRAMED	LEDERMAN	WARNER BROS	1942
IF	IF (UK)	ANDERSON	PARAMOUNT	1968
IF	INDIAN FIGHTER	DE TOTH	UNITED ARTISTS	1955
IF2	COLDITZ STORY (UK)	HAMILTON	DCA	1955
IFI	INTRUDER (UK)	HAMILTON	AAP	1953
IFM	INVADERS FROM MARS	MENZIES	20th CENTURY FOX	1953
IFM	INVADERS FROM MARS	HOOPER	CANNON	1986
IFT	INN FOR TROUBLE (UK)	PENNINGTON-RICHARDS	EROS	1960
IG	STREET SINGER (UK)	DE MARGUENAT	ABFD	1937
IGY	LUCKY NICK CAIN (UK: I'LL GET YOU FOR THIS)	NEWMAN	20TH CENTURY FOX	1951
IH	ANOTHER FACE	CABANNE	RKO	1935
IH	CHINESE CONNECTION	HONG	NAT'L GENERAL	1973
IH	IAN HUNTER	portrait	WARNER BROS	
IH	INVISIBLE HORROR (INVISIBLE DR. MABUSE)	REINL	THUNDER	R66
IH	IRENE HERVEY	portrait	UNIVERSAL	
IH	IRISH HEARTS	BAKER, MEREDYTH	WARNER BROS	1927
IH	IT HAPPENED HERE (UK) [US: LOPERT]	BROWNLOW, MOLLO	UNITED ARTISTS	1965
IH	IVORY HUNTER (UK: WHERE NO VULTURES FLY)	WATT	UNIVERSAL	1951
IHX	IRENE HERVEY	portrait	MGM	
II	INVISIBLE INVADERS	CAHN	UNITED ARTISTS	1959
II	SUMMER INTERLUDE/ILLICIT INTERLUDE (SWE: SOMMARLEK)	BERGMAN	GASTON HAKIM	1951
IJ	I, THE JURY	HEFFRON	20th CENTURY FOX	1982
IJ	ITALIAN JOB (UK)	COLLINSON	PARAMOUNT	1969
IJL	IMAGINE	SOLT	WARNER BROS	1988
IJ-TD	INDIANA JONES AND THE TEMPLE OF DOOM	SPIELBERG	PARAMOUNT	1984
IK	F. HUGH HERBERT	portrait	RKO	
IK	INTENT TO KILL (UK)	CARDIFF	20TH CENTURY FOX	1958
IL	IDA LUPINO	portrait	RKO, WARNER BROS	
IL	ILA RHODES	portrait	WARNER BROS	late 30s
IL	ILONA MASSEY	portrait	UNIVERSAL, UNITED ARTISTS	
IM	FIRST MAN INTO SPACE (UK)	DAY	MGM	1959
IM	ILONA MASSEY	portrait	MGM	
IM	INDESTRUCTIBLE MAN	POLLEXFEN	ALLIED ARTISTS	1956
IM	IRENE MANNING	portrait	WARNER BROS	
IM	IRON MAJOR	ENRIGHT	RKO	1943
IM	IRON MASK	DWAN	UNITED ARTISTS	1929
IM	LADY CONSENTS	ROBERTS	RKO	1936
IM	PRIVATE IZZY MURPHY	BACON	WARNER BROS	1926

Movie Still Identification Book Ultimate Edition - Letters

CODE	TITLE/NAME	DIRECTOR/TYPE	STUDIO/DISTRIBUTOR	YEAR
IM	WOMAN ON PIER 13 (I MARRIED A COMMUNIST*)	STEVENSON	RKO	1949
IMP-4	ELIZABETH OF LADYMEAD (UK)	WILCOX	BRITISH LION	1948
IMP-107	MAN IN THE DINGHY (UK: INTO THE BLUE)	WILCOX	SNADER	1950
IMP-108	LADY WITH THE LAMP (UK: LADY WITH A LAMP)	WILCOX	CONTINENTAL	1951
IMP-109	DERBY DAY (UK)	WILCOX	AAP	1952
IMP-111	BEGGAR'S OPERA (UK)	BROOK	WARNER BROS	1953
IMP 114	LET'S MAKE UP (UK: LILACS IN THE SPRING)	WILCOX	UNITED ARTISTS	1954
IMP-115	KING'S RHAPSODY (UK)	WILCOX	UNITED ARTISTS	1955
IMW	I MARRIED A WOMAN	KANTER	RKO	1958
IMW	IT'S A MAD MAD MAD MAD WORLD	KRAMER	UNITED ARTISTS	1963
IN	HITTING A NEW HIGH	WALSH	RKO	1937
IN	IN THE NICK (UK)	HUGHES	COLUMBIA	1960
IN	INCHON	YOUNG	MGM/UNITED ARTISTS	1982
IN	INDISCREET (UK)	DONEN	WARNER BROS	1958
IN	INSERTS	BYRUM	UNITED ARTISTS	1974
IN	JAZZ BOAT	HUGHES	COLUMBIA	1960
IN	THEY MEET AGAIN	KENTON	RKO	1941
INS	I NEVER SANG FOR MY FATHER	CATES	COLUMBIA	1970
INT	INTERIORS	ALLEN	UNITED ARTISTS	1978
INT-103	WOMAN IN THE WINDOW	LANG	RKO	1944
INT-9300	CASANOVA BROWN	WOOD	RKO	1944
INT-9500	BELLE OF THE YUKON	SEITER	RKO	1944
INV	INVASION OF THE BODY SNATCHERS	KAUFMAN	UNITED ARTISTS	1978
INV-USA	INVASION U.S.A.	GREEN	COLUMBIA	1952
IO	ISLE OF DESTINY	CLIFTON	RKO	1940
IOD	LITTLE IODINE	LE BORG	UNITED ARTISTS	1946
IOM	DOUBLE DYNAMITE	CUMMINGS	RKO	1951
IOW	TENTH WOMAN	FLOOD	WARNER BROS	1924
IP	IN PERSON	SEITER	RKO	1935
IP	IRENE PURCELL	portrait	MGM	
IP-103	SPRING IN PARK LANE (UK)	WILCOX	EAGLE-LION	1948
IP-107	MAYTIME IN MAYFAIR (UK)	WILCOX	REALART	1949
IPB	IS PARIS BURNING?	CLEMENT	PARAMOUNT	1966
IPL-15	NOTORIOUS GENTLEMAN (UK: RAKE'S PROGRESS)	GILLIAT	UNIVERSAL	1945
IPL-15A	NOTORIOUS GENTLEMAN (UK: RAKE'S PROGRESS)	GILLIAT	UNIVERSAL	1945
IPL-16	ADVENTURESS (UK: I SEE A DARK STRANGER)	LAUNDER	EAGLE-LION	1946
IPL-24	I KNOW WHERE I'M GOING! (UK)	POWELL, PRESSBURGER	UNIVERSAL	1945
IPL-26	BRIEF ENCOUNTER (UK)	LEAN	UNIVERSAL	1945
IPL-111	GREEN FOR DANGER (UK)	GILLIAT	EAGLE-LION	1946
IPW	INCREDIBLE PETRIFIED WORLD	WARREN	GOVERNOR	1959
IR	IRENE RICH	portrait	UNIVERSAL, WARNER BROS	
IR-F-25	CAPTAIN FURY	ROACH	FAVORITE	R46
IRM	I REMEMBER MAMA	STEVENS	RKO	1948
US	I, MONSTER (UK 1971)	WEEKS	CANNON	1973
IS	I START COUNTING	GREENE	UNITED ARTISTS	1969
IS	IF I WERE SINGLE	DEL RUTH	WARNER BROS	1927
IS	INVISIBLE STRIPES	BACON	WARNER BROS	1939
IS	ISLANDS IN THE STREAM	SCHAFFNER	PARAMOUNT	1977
IS	JUDGE STEPS OUT	INGSTER	RKO	1948
IS	LOVE IS ON THE AIR	GRINDE	WARNER BROS	1937
ISC	INCREDIBLY STRANGE CREATURES	STECKLER	FAIRWAY INT'L	1964
ISF	SILENT DUST (UK)	COMFORT	STRATFORD	1949
ISF-4	HIDDEN ROOM (UK: OBSESSION)	DMYTRYK	EAGLE-LION	1949
ISM	INVASION OF THE SAUCER-MEN	CAHN	AIP	1957
ISR	INCREDIBLE SEX REVOLUTION	ZUGSMITH	FAMOUS PLAYERS	1965
IT	I AM A THIEF	FLOREY	WARNER BROS	1934
IT	IN OUR TIME	SHERMAN	WARNER BROS	1944
IT	IT (UK)	LEDER	WARNER BROS	1967
IT	IVAN THE TERRIBLE: PART II	EISENSTEIN	JANUS	1958
ITD	ISLE OF THE DEAD	ROBSON	RKO	1945
ITG	INVITATION TO A GUNFIGHTER	WILSON	UNITED ARTISTS	1964
ITMA	IT'S THAT MAN AGAIN (UK)	FORDE	GFD	1943
ITS	I'LL TAKE SWEDEN	DE CORDOVA	UNITED ARTISTS	1965
ITS	IN THE SOUP (UK)	EDWARDS	TWICKENHAM	1936
ITS	ISLAND IN THE SKY	WELLMAN	WARNER BROS	1953
ITT	IVAN THE TERRIBLE: PART I	EISENSTEIN	ARTKINO	1944
IU	IRISH IN THE U.S.	BACON	WARNER BROS	1935
IV	EAGLE	BROWN	UNITED ARTISTS	1925
IV	INTERVIEW WITH THE VAMPIRE	JORDAN	GEPPEN	1994
IV	YOUNG AND THE PASSIONATE (IT: I VITELLONI)	FELLINI	JANUS	1953

Movie Still Identification Book Ultimate Edition - Letters

CODE	TITLE/NAME	DIRECTOR/TYPE	STUDIO/DISTRIBUTOR	YEAR
IW	I WALKED WITH A ZOMBIE	TOURNEUR	RKO	1943
IW	IMAGENE WILLIAMS	portrait	WARNER BROS	
IW	INHERIT THE WIND	KRAMER	UNITED ARTISTS	1960
IWC	INTERVIEW WITH THE VAMPIRE	JORDAN	GEPPEN	1994
IWH	HAPPENING	SILVERSTEIN	COLUMBIA	1967
IWL	IT'S A WONDERFUL LIFE	CAPRA	RKO	1947
IWTF	I WAS A TEENAGE FRANKENSTEIN	STROCK	AIP	1957
IWTL	I WANT TO LIVE	WISE	UNITED ARTISTS	1958
IY	I THANK YOU (UK)	VARNEL	GFD	1941
IY	IF YOU KNEW SUSIE	DOUGLAS	RKO	1947
IZ	ACTION IN ARABIA	MOGUY	RKO	1944
J	JAMBOREE	LOCKWOOD	WARNER BROS	1957
J	JANIE	CURTIZ	WARNER BROS	1944
J	JAWS OF STEEL	ENRIGHT	WARNER BROS	1927
J	JEREMY	BARRON	UNITED ARTISTS	1973
J	JERICHO (UK)	FREELAND	RECORD	1937
J	JESSICA	NEGULESCO	UNITED ARTISTS	1962
J	JEZEBEL	WYLER	WARNER BROS	1938
J	JINGLE ALL THE WAY	LEVANT	20th CENTURY FOX	1996
J	JOURNEY TOGETHER (UK)	BOULTING	ENGLISH	1945
J	JUAREZ	DIETERLE	WARNER BROS	1939
J	JUDGEMENT AT NUREMBERG	KRAMER	UNITED ARTISTS	1961
J	JUGGERNAUT (UK)	EDWARDS	GRAND	1937
J	JUNGLE	BERKE	LIPPERT	1952
J	LAST MAN TO HANG (UK: AMAZING DAPHNE STROOD)	FISHER	COLUMBIA	1956
J	MOUNTAIN JUSTICE	CURTIZ	WARNER BROS	1937
J#	BOBBY JONES SHORTS	studio	WARNER BROS	
J-1	CALL OF THE WILD	JACKMAN	PATHE EXCHANGE	1923
J-2	KING OF WILD HORSES	JACKMAN	PATHE EXCHANGE	1924
J-2	LINCOLN HIGHWAYMAN	FLYNN	FOX FILM	1919
J-2	TERROR	JACCARD	FOX FILM	1920
J-3	BLACK CYCLONE	JACKMAN	PATHE EXCHANGE	1925
J-4	DEVIL HORSE	JACKMAN	PATHE EXCHANGE	1926
J4	GOODBYE LOVE	HUMBERSTONE	RKO	1933
J-5	NO MAN'S LAW	JACKMAN	PATHE EXCHANGE	1927
J-320	CANDLELIGHT IN ALGERIA (UK)	KING	20TH CENTURY FOX	1944
J-323	YOU CAN'T DO WITHOUT LOVE (UK: ONE EXCITING NIGHT)	FORDE	COLUMBIA	1944
JA	ADVENTURES OF JANE ARDEN	MORSE	WARNER BROS	1939
JA	JAMES ARNESS	portrait	RKO, WARNER BROS	
JA	JANE ADAMS	portrait	UNIVERSAL	
JA	JASON AND THE ARGONAUTS (UK)	CHAFFEY	COLUMBIA	1963
JA	JEAN AMES	portrait	WARNER BROS	
JA	JEAN ARTHUR	portrait	RKO	
JA	JET ATTACK	CAHN	AIP	1958
JA	JOE'S APARTMENT	PAYSON	GEFFEN	1996
JA	JOHN AGAR	portrait	UNIVERSAL	
JA	JOHN ALVIN	portrait	WARNER BROS	1940s-60s
JA	JOHN ARCHER	portrait	RKO	
JA	JOHN ARLEDGE	portrait	RKO	
JA	JOHNNY ANGEL	MARIN	RKO	1945
JA	JOSEPH ANDREWS	RICHARDSON	PARAMOUNT	1977
JA	JOSEPH ANTHONY	portrait	PARAMOUNT	
JA	JUDITH ANDERSON	portrait	UNITED ARTISTS	
JA	JULIE/JULIA ADAMS	portrait	UNIVERSAL	
JA	JUNE ADAMS	portrait	UNIVERSAL	
JA	JUNE ALLYSON	portrait	UNIVERSAL	
JAN	JUDGEMENT AT NUREMBERG	KRAMER	UNITED ARTISTS	1961
JAR	J ARTHUR RANK	studio	UNIVERSAL	
JB	DR. JEKYL AND MR. HYDE	ROBERTSON	PARAMOUNT	1920
JB	HIS JAZZ BRIDE	RAYMAKER	WARNER BROS	1926
JB	JACK AND THE BEANSTALK	YARBROUGH	WARNER BROS	1952
JB	JACK BENNY	portrait		
JB	JACK BEUTEL	portrait	RKO, UNITED ARTISTS	
JB	JACK THE BEAR	HERSKOVITZ	20th CENTURY FOX	1993
JB	JACQUELINE BISSET	portrait	UNIVERSAL	
JB	JAILBREAKERS	GRASSHOFF	AIP	1960
JB	JAMES BELL	portrait	RKO	
JB	JAMES BURKE	portrait	RKO	
JB	JAMES BUSH	portrait	RKO	
JB	JANE BRYAN	portrait	WARNER BROS	

Movie Still Identification Book Ultimate Edition - Letters

CODE	TITLE/NAME	DIRECTOR/TYPE	STUDIO/DISTRIBUTOR	YEAR
JB	JAZZ BOAT (UK)	HUGHES	COLUMBIA	1960
JB	JEAN BROOKS	portrait	RKO	
JB	JESS BARKER	portrait	UNIVERSAL	
JB	JOAN BARCLAY	portrait	RKO	
JB	JOAN BENNETT	portrait	RKO, UNIVERSAL	
JB	JOAN BLONDELL	portrait	UNIVERSAL	
JB	JOAN BROOKS	portrait	WARNER BROS	1930s-40s
JB	JOAN BROOKS aka JOAN LESLIE akaJOAN BRODEL	portrait		
JB	JOE E. BROWN movies		COL, RKO	
JB	JOEY BOY (UK)	LAUNDER	BRITISH LION	1965
JB	JOHN BARRYMORE	portrait	RKO, UNITED ARTISTS,	
JB	JOHN BEAL	portrait	RKO	
JB	JOHN BOLES	portrait	FOX	
JB	JUDITH BLAKE	portrait	RKO	1930s
JB	JUDITH BRAUN	portrait	UNIVERSAL	
JB	JULIE BISHOP (aka JACQUELINE WELLS - DIANE DUVAL)	portrait	WARNER BROS	
JB	JUNIOR BONNER	PECKINPAH	CINERAMA RELEASING	1972
JB	NUMBERED MEN	LEROY	WARNER BROS	1930
JB	PRIME OF MISS JEAN BRODIE (UK)	NEAME	20TH CENTURY FOX	1969
JB	TERROR IN TINY TOWN	BUELL	COLUMBIA	1937
JB-1	LARCENY STREET (UK: SMASH AND GRAB)	WHELAN	FILM ALLIANCE	1937
JB-1	WIDE OPEN FACES (JOE E. BROWN series)	NEUMANN	COLUMBIA	1938
JB-2	GLADIATOR	SEDGWICK	COLUMBIA	1938
JB-2	SKY'S THE LIMIT (UK)	BUCHANAN, GARMES	GFD	1938
JB-4	BREAK THE NEWS (UK)	CLAIR	MONOGRAM	1938
JB-4	ETERNAL MASK (SWIT)	HOCHBAUM	MAYER & BURSTYN	1937
JB-800	TEMPEST	TAYLOR	UNITED ARTISTS	1928
JB-1500	ETERNAL LOVE	LUBITSCH	UNITED ARTISTS	1929
JC	HALF BREED	GILMORE	RKO	1952
JC	JACK CARSON	portrait	WARNER BROS	
JC	JACKIE COOPER	portrait	MONOGRAM, RKO, UNIV.	
JC	JAMES CAGNEY	portrait	WARNER BROS	
JC	JAMES CRAIG	portrait	RKO	
JC	JAMES CRAIG	portrait	WARNER BROS	
JC	JAMES CURTIS/TONY CURTIS	portrait	UNIVERSAL	1948
JC	JANE COWL	portrait		
JC	JANIS CARTER	portrait	RKO, UNITED ARTISTS	
JC	JEAN CAROL	portrait	UNIVERSAL	1930s-40s
JC	JEAN(NE) CAGNEY	portrait	WARNER BROS	
JC	JEANNE CRAIN	portrait	UNIVERSAL	
JC	JEFF CHANDLER	portrait	UNIVERSAL	
JC	JEROME COWAN	portrait	REP	
JC	JEROME COWAN	portrait	RKO, UNITED ARTISTS	
JC	JOAN CARROLL	portrait	RKO, UNITED ARTISTS	
JC	JOAN COLLINS	portrait		
JC	JOAN CRAWFORD	portrait	WARNER BROS	
JC	JOHN CARROLL	portrait	RKO	
JC	JOHN CROMWELL	portrait	RKO	
JC	JOHNNY CONCHO	MCGUIRE	UNITED ARTISTS	1956
JC	JOHNNY COOL	ASHER	UNITED ARTISTS	1963
JC	JOSEPH COTTEN	portrait	RKO, WARNER BROS	
JC	JOSEPH COTTON	portrait	UNIVERSAL, SELZNICK/UA	
JC	JOURNAL OF A CRIME	KEIGHLEY	WARNER BROS	1934
JC	JOYCE COMPTON	portrait	RKO	
JC	JULIE CHRISTIE	portrait	UNIVERSAL	
JC	JUNE CARROLL	portrait	REPUBLIC	1940s
JC	JUNE CLYDE	portrait	UNIVERSAL	
JC	JUNGLE OF CHANG (SWE 1940)	FEJOS, SKOGLUND	RKO	1951
JC	JUST CAUSE	GLIMCHER	WARNER BROS	1995
JCXX	JACKIE COOPER	portrait	MGM	
JD	J.D.'S REVENGE	MARKS	AIP	1976
JD	JACQUELINE DEWIT	portrait	UNIVERSAL	
JD	JAMES DUNN	portrait	FOX	
JD	JANE DARWELL	portrait	RKO	
JD	JEAN DALE	portrait	WARNER BROS	
JD	JEFF DONNELL	portrait	RKO	
JD	JIMMY DURANTE	portrait	UNIVERSAL	
JD	JOAN DOWLING	portrait	ASSOCIATED BRITISH	
JD	JOANNE DRU	portrait	UNITED ARTISTS, UNIVERSAL	
JD	JOHN DARROW	portrait	RKO	

Movie Still Identification Book Ultimate Edition - Letters

CODE	TITLE/NAME	DIRECTOR/TYPE	STUDIO/DISTRIBUTOR	YEAR
JD	JOHNNIE DAVIS	portrait	WARNER BROS	
JD	JOHNNY DANGEROUSLY	HECKERLING	20th CENTURY FOX	1984
JD	JUDGMENT DEFERRED (UK)	BAXTER	ASSOCIATED BRITISH-PATHE	1952
JD	JULIE DUNCAN	portrait	UNIVERSAL	
JD	JUNE DUPREZ	portrait	RKO	
JD	MEET JOHN DOE	CAPRA	WARNER BROS	1940
JD	MIDNIGHT COURT	MCDONALD	WARNER BROS	1937
JD	POSSESSION OF JOEL DELANEY	HUSSEIN	PARAMOUNT	1972
JDEW	WAKING UP THE TOWN	CRUZE	UNITED ARTISTS	1925
JdW	JACQUELINE DeWIT	portrait	UNIV	
JDX	JOSEPHINE DUNN	portrait	MGM	
JE	DAY IN THE DEATH OF JOE EGG	MEDAK	COLUMBIA	1972
JE	JAMES ELLISON	portrait	RKO	
JE	JANE EYRE (R60S tv)	STEVENSON	NTA	1944
JE	JEANNE EAGELS	portrait	MGM	
JE	JOAN EDWARDS	portrait		
JE	JOAN EVANS	portrait	GOLDWYN	
JE	JOHN ELDRIDGE	portrait	WARNER BROS	
JEB	FLIRTING WITH FATE	MCDONALD	MGM	1938
JEB	JOE E BROWN	portrait	WARNER BROS	
JEC	JEAN(NE) CAGNEY	portrait	UNITED ARTISTS	
JEL	JOE E. LEWIS	portrait	UNIV	
JF	JACQUES FRANCOIS	portrait	UNIVERSAL	1940s
JF	JAMES FARENTINO	portrait	UNIVERSAL	
JF	JAMES FOX	portrait	UNIV	
JF	JANE FARRAR	portrait	UNIVERSAL	
JF	JANE FRAZEE	portrait	PARA,, RKO, REP., UNIV.	
JF	JANE FROMAN	portrait	UNITED ARTISTS, WARNER BR.	
JF	JOAN FITZGERALD	portrait	WARNER BROS	
JF	JOAN FONTAINE	portrait	RKO, UNIVERSAL	
JF	JOAN FONTAINE	portrait	UNITED ARTISTS	
JF	JOAN FULTON	portrait	UNIVERSAL	
JF	JOHNNY FRENCHMAN (UK)	FREND	UNIVERSAL	1945
JF	JOYCE REYNOLDS	portrait	WARNER BROS	
JF	JULIA FAYE	portrait		
JF	JUST FOR FUN (UK)	FLEMYNG	COLUMBIA	1963
JF1	PARDON MY FRENCH	VORHAUS	UNITED ARTISTS	1951
JFL-220	FIVE ANGLES ON MURDER (UK: WOMAN IN QUESTION)	ASQUITH	COLUMBIA	1950
JFL-226	BROWNING VERSION (UK)	ASQUITH	UNIVERSAL	1951
JG	JAMES GARNER	portrait	UA, UNIVERSAL, WB	
JG	JAMES GLEASON	portrait	RKO	
JG	JAN GARBER (AND ORCHESTRA)	portrait	MCA MUSIC	
JG	JANE GREER	portrait	RKO, UNIVERSAL	
JG	JETTA GOUDAL	portrait	PATHE-DE MILLE	
JG	JETTA GOUDAL	portrait		
JG	JOHN GARFIELD	portrait	WARNER BROS	
JG	JOHN GAVIN	portrait	UNIVERSAL	
JG	JOHN GIELGUD	portrait	GAUMONT BRITISH	
JG	JOHN GILBERT	portrait	MGM	
JG	JUKE GIRL	BERNHARDT	WARNER BROS	1942
JG	JULIETTE GRECO	portrait	FOX	
JG	LOVES OF JOANNA GODDEN (UK)	FREND	GFD	1947
JG	NINE DAYS A QUEEN (UK: TUDOR ROSE)	STEVENSON	GAUMONT	1936
JG	RACHEL RACHEL	NEWMAN	WARNER BROS	1968
JG	SUPPORT YOUR LOCAL GUNFIGHTER	KENNEDY	UNITED ARTISTS	1971
JG	SUPPORT YOUR LOCAL SHERIFF!	KENNEDY	UNITED ARTISTS	1969
JGXX	JUDY GARLAND	portrait	MGM	
JH	JACK HALEY	portrait	RKO	
JH	JACK HULBERT	portrait	GAUMONT BRITISH	1930s
JH	JAMES HOLDEN	portrait	WARNER BROS	
JH	JANE HAMILTON	portrait	RKO	
JH	JAZZ HEAVEN	BROWN	RKO	1929
JH	JEAN HERSHOLT	portrait	MGM, RKO	
JH	JENNIFER HOLT	portrait	UNIVERSAL	
JH	JOAN HARRISON	portrait		
JH	JOEY HEATHERTON	portrait	PARAMOUNT	
JH	JOHN HALLIDAY	portrait	WARNER BROS	
JH	JOHN HOWARD	portrait	RKO	
JH	JOHNNY HINES	portrait	FN	
JH	JOHNNY HOLIDAY (BOY'S PRISON 1955)	GOLDBECK	UNITED ARTISTS	1949

Movie Still Identification Book Ultimate Edition - Letters

CODE	TITLE/NAME	DIRECTOR/TYPE	STUDIO/DISTRIBUTOR	YEAR
JH	JON HALL	portrait	UNIVERSAL	
JH	JOSEPHINE HUSTON	portrait	FOX	
JH	JOSEPHINE HUTCHINSON	portrait	FN/WARNER BROS	
JH	JOY HODGES	portrait	RKO, UNIVERSAL	
JH	JOYCE HOLDEN	portrait	UNIVERSAL	
JH	JULIE HAYDON	portrait	RKO	
JH	JUNE HAVOC	portrait	RKO	
JH	JUNGLE HEADHUNTERS	ANSEN, LANSBURGH	RKO	1951
JH	JUNGLE HEAT	KOCH	UNITED ARTISTS	1957
JH-1	NORTH OF NOME	NIGH	COLUMBIA	1937
JH-2	TROUBLE IN MOROCCO	SCHOEDSACK	COLUMBIA	1937
JH-3	ROARING TIMBER	ROSEN	COLUMBIA	1937
JH-4	OUTLAWS OF THE ORIENT	SCHOEDSACK	COLUMBIA	1937
JH-5	TRAPPED BY G-MEN	COLLINS	COLUMBIA	1937
JH-6	UNDER SUSPICION	COLLINS	COLUMBIA	1937
JH-7	MAKING THE HEADLINES	COLLINS	COLUMBIA	1938
JH-8	FLIGHT INTO NOWHERE	COLLINS	COLUMBIA	1938
JH-9	CRIME TAKES A HOLIDAY	COLLINS	COLUMBIA	1938
JH-10	REFORMATORY	COLLINS	COLUMBIA	1938
JH-11	STRANGE CASE OF DR. MEADE	COLLINS	COLUMBIA	1938
JH-12	WHISPERING ENEMIES	COLLINS	COLUMBIA	1939
JH-13	TRAPPED IN THE SKY	COLLINS	COLUMBIA	1939
JH-14	HIDDEN POWER	COLLINS	COLUMBIA	1939
JH-15	FUGITIVE AT LARGE	COLLINS	COLUMBIA	1939
JH-16	OUTSIDE THE 3 MILE LIMIT	COLLINS	COLUMBIA	1940
JH-17	PASSPORT TO ALCATRAZ	COLLINS	COLUMBIA	1940
JH-18	FUGITIVE FROM PRISON CAMP	COLLINS	COLUMBIA	1940
JH-19	GREAT PLANE ROBBERY	COLLINS	COLUMBIA	1940
JH-20	GREAT SWINDLE	COLLINS	COLUMBIA	1941
JHB	JIMI HENDRIX	BOYD	WARNER BROS	1973
JH-COL-11	STRANGE CASE OF DR. MEADE	COLLINS	COLUMBIA	1938
JH-COL-15	FUGITIVE AT LARGE	COLLINS	COLUMBIA	1939
JHF-1	MAKE MINE A MILLION (UK)	COMFORT	SCHOENFELD	1959
JH-OR	JEAN HARLOW	portrait	MGM	
JHP	BLUE MURDER AT ST. TRINIAN'S	LAUNDER	CONTINENTAL	1957
JHP	JOHN HARVEL PRODUCTIONS	studio		
JHP-1	SHE PLAYED WITH FIRE (UK: FORTUNE WAS A WOMAN)	GILLIAT	COLUMBIA	1957
JHP-2	BLUE MURDER AT ST. TRINIAN'S (UK)	LAUNDER	CONTINENTAL	1957
JHX	JEAN HARLOW	portrait	MGM	
JIF	JOURNEY INTO FEAR	FOSTER	RKO	1943
JJ	I SHOT JESSE JAMES	FULLER	SCREEN GUILD	1949
JJ	JACK JOHNSON	JACOBS	CONTINENTAL	1970
JJ	JANICE JARRATT	portrait	UNIVERSAL	1930s
JJ	JENNIFER JONES	portrait	SELZNICK	
JJ	JESSE JAMES MEETS FRANKENSTEIN'S DAUGHTER	BEAUDINE	EMBASSY	1965
JJ	JOHN AND JULIE (UK)	FAIRCHILD	DCA	1955
JJ	JULES AND JIM (FR: JULES ET JIM)	TRUFFAUT	JANUS	1961
JJ	JUMPIN' JACK FLASH	MARSHALL	20th CENTURY FOX	1986
JJ	JUSTINE JOHNSTONE	portrait	REALART	
JJ	RETURN OF JESSE JAMES	HILTON	LIPPERT	1950
JJ	RIOT IN JUVENILE PRISON	CAHN	UNITED ARTISTS	1959
JJR	GREAT JESSE JAMES RAID	LE BORG	LIPPERT	1953
JJW	JESSE JAMES' WOMEN	BARRY	UNITED ARTISTS	1954
JK	JACK KELLY	portrait	UNIV	
JK	JACK THE GIANT KILLER	JURAN	UNITED ARTISTS	1962
JK	JAMES KIRKWOOD	portrait		
JK	JEANNE KELLY	portrait	UNIVERSAL	
JK	JEANNE KELLY aka JEAN BROOKS	portrait	UNIV	
JK	JOHN KIRBY (AND HIS ORCHESTRA)	portrait	MCA RECORDS	
JK	JUNE KNIGHT	portrait		
JL	CONDEMNED TO DEATH (UK)	FORDE	FIRST DIVISION	1932
JL	DON'T RAISE THE BRIDGE, LOWER THE RIVER (UK)	PARIS	COLUMBIA	1968
JL	JACKIE LOUGHERY	portrait	UNIV	
JL	JAGUAR LIVES	PINTOFF	AIP	1979
JL	JANET LEIGH	portrait	RKO, UA, WARNER BROS	
JL	JANET LEIGH	portrait	UNIV	
JL	JAY LEWIS PRODUCTIONS (UK)	studio		
JL	JEANETTE LOFF	portrait	PATHE, UNIVERSAL	
JL	JOAN LESLIE	portrait	RKO, WARNER BROS	
JL	JOAN OF ARC	FLEMING	RKO	1948

Movie Still Identification Book Ultimate Edition - Letters

CODE	TITLE/NAME	DIRECTOR/TYPE	STUDIO/DISTRIBUTOR	YEAR
JL	JOHN LITEL	portrait	WARNER BROS	
JL	JOHN LODER	portrait	RKO, UNITED ARTISTS	
JL	JOSEPH LOSEY	portrait	RKO	
JL	JULIE LONDON	portrait	UNIVERSAL	
JL	JUNE LANG	portrait	UNIVERSAL	1930s-40s
JL-216	OPERATION DISASTER (UK: MORNING DEPARTURE)	BAKER	UNIVERSAL	1950
JL-9200	HAIRY APE	SANTELL	UNITED ARTISTS	1944
JLP	FRONT PAGE STORY (UK)	PARRY	AAP	1954
JLP	JAY LEWIS PRODUCTIONS (UK)	studio		
JLS	JOE LOUIS STORY	GORDON	UNITED ARTISTS	1953
JM	JAYNE MANSFIELD	portrait	WARNER BROS	
JM	JAYNE MANSFIELD	portrait		
JM	JEAN MUIR	portrait	FN/WARNER BROS	
JM	JESSE MATTHEWS	portrait	GAUMONT BRITISH	1930s
JM	JOAN MCCRACKEN	portrait	WARNER BROS	
JM	JOANNA MOORE	portrait	UNIVERSAL	
JM	JOCK MAHONEY	portrait	UNIVERSAL	
JM	JOEL MCCREA	portrait	UNIV	
JM	JOHN MILLS	portrait	UNIVERSAL	
JM	JUDI MEREDITH	portrait	UNIVERSAL	1950s-60s
JM	JUNE MARLOWE	portrait	WARNER BROS	
JM	JUNE MARLOWE	portrait	WARNER BROS	
JM	JUNGLE MENACE - SERIAL	FRASER, MELFORD	COLUMBIA	1937
JM-5191	TELL ME THAT YOU LOVE ME, JUNIE MOON	PREMINGER	SIGMA	1970
JMAC	JEANETTE MACDONALD	portrait	MGM	
JMB	JOHNNY MACK BROWN	portrait	MGM, MONOGRAM, UNIV.	
JMC	JOEL MCCREA	portrait	UNIV	
JMcC	JOEL MCCREA	portrait	RKO	
JM-COL-11	STRANGE CASE OF DR. MEADE	COLLINS	COLUMBIA	1938
JMK	JOYCE MACKENZIE	portrait	RKO	
JML	JOAN MARIE LAWES	portrait		
JML	JUST MY LUCK (UK)	RAYMOND	WOOLF & FREEDMAN	1933
JMX	JAMES MURRAY	portrait	MGM	
JN	INNOCENT AFFAIR (DON'T TRUST YOUR HUSBAND)	BACON	UNITED ARTISTS	1948
JN	JEWEL OF THE NILE	TEAGUE	20th CENTURY FOX	1985
JN	JOHNNY NOBODY (UK)	PATRICK	MEDALLION	1961
JN	JUDGEMENT AT NUREMBERG	KRAMER	UNITED ARTISTS	1961
JO	JACK OAKIE	portrait	RKO	
JO	JOAN OF PARIS	STEVENSON	RKO	1942
JO	JOANNA (UK)	SARNE	20TH CENTURY FOX	1968
JO	JOHNNY ONE-EYE	FLOREY	UNITED ARTISTS	1950
JO	JOY OF LIVING	GARNETT	RKO	1938
JOA	JET OVER THE ATLANTIC	HASKIN	INTER-CONTINENT FILM	1959
JOAN.C.	JOAN CRAWFORD	portrait	WARNER BROS	
JOAN W.	JOAN WELDON	portrait	WARNER BROS	1950s
JOAN.C.	JOAN CRAWFORD	portrait	WARNER BROS	
JOE	JOE	AVILDSEN	CANNON	1970
JOHN-1	CONGORILLA	JOHNSON	FOX FILM	1932
JOM	JENNIFER ON MY MIND	BLACK	UNITED ARTISTS	1971
JOS	ALLYN JOSLYN	portrait	WARNER BROS	
JOW	JOAN WINFIELD	portrait	WARNER BROS	
JP	JACK PAAR	portrait	RKO	
JP	JACK PALANCE	portrait	RKO	
JP	JANIS PAIGE	portrait	WARNER BROS	
JP	JEAN PARKER	portrait	MGM, UNIVERSAL	
JP	JEAN PARKER	portrait	MONOGRAM	
JP	JEAN PETERS	portrait		
JP	JET PILOT	VON STERNBERG	UNIVERSAL	1957
JP	JOAN PERRY	portrait	WARNER BROS	
JP	JOE PENNER	portrait	RKO	1930s-40s
JP	JOHN PAYNE	portrait	WARNER BROS	
JP	JUDGEMENT AT NUREMBERG	KRAMER	UNITED ARTISTS	1961
JP	LAST MAN TO HANG	FISHER	COLUMBIA	1956
JPA	JEAN-PIERRE AUMONT	portrait	UNIVERSAL	
JPEW	WAKING UP THE TOWN	CRUZE	UNITED ARTISTS	1925
JQ	JUANITA QUIGLEY	portrait	MGM	
JR	JACK THE RIPPER (UK)	BAKER, BERMAN	PARAMOUNT	1960
JR	JAMES RENNIE	portrait	FN	
JR	JANE RUSSELL	portrait	RKO	
JR	JANICE RULE	portrait		

Movie Still Identification Book Ultimate Edition - Letters

CODE	TITLE/NAME	DIRECTOR/TYPE	STUDIO/DISTRIBUTOR	YEAR
JR	JEAN RENOIR	portrait	RKO	
JR	JEAN ROGERS	portrait	RKO	early 40s
JR	JEAN ROGERS	portrait	UNIVERSAL	1930s
JR	JEWEL ROBBERY	DIETERLE	WARNER BROS	1932
JR	JOAN RICE	portrait	WARNER BROS	
JR	JOHN RIDGELY	portrait	WARNER BROS	
JR-11	RHYTHM RACKETEER (UK)	SEYMOUR	BRITISH INDEPENDENT	1937
JRB-1	JOSEPHINE AND MEN (UK)	BOULTING	CONTINENTAL	1955
JRB-2	PRIVATE'S PROGRESS (UK)	BOULTING	DCA	1956
JRB-3	BROTHERS IN LAW (UK)	BOULTING	CONTINENTAL	1957
JRB-3	MAN IN A COCKED HAT (UK: CARLTON-BROWNE OF THE F.O.)	DELL, BOULTING	SHOWCORPORATION	1959
JRB-4	LUCKY JIM (UK)	BOULTING	KINGSLEY INTERNATIONAL	1957
JRB-5	THE RISK (UK: SUSPECT)	BOULTING, BOULTING	KINGSLEY INTERNATIONAL	1960
JRB-6	FRENCH MISTRESS (UK)	BOULTING	FILMS AROUND THE WORLD	1960
JRP-1	MYSTERIOUS MR. REEDER (UK: MIND OF MR. REEDER)	RAYMOND	GRAND NATIONAL	1939
JS	BUFFALO BILL RIDES AGAIN	RAY	SCREEN GUILD	1947
JS	CAPTAIN JOHN SMITH AND POCAHONTAS	LANDERS	UNITED ARTISTS	1953
JS	JACQUES ("JACK") SERNAS	portrait	WARNER BROS	
JS	JAMES STEWART	portrait	UNIVERSAL	
JS	JAN STERLING	portrait	UNIVERSAL	
JS	JAZZ SINGER	CROSLAND	WARNER BROS	1927
JS	JEAN SEBERG	portrait	COL, UNIV	
JS	JEAN SHRIMPTON	portrait	UNIVERSAL	
JS	JEAN SIMMONS	portrait	RKO, UNIVERSAL	
JS	JEAN SULLIVAN	portrait	WARNER BROS	
JS	JET STORM (UK)	ENDFIELD	UNITED PRODUCERS	1959
JS	JOHN SAXON	portrait	UNIVERSAL	
JS	JOSEPH SCHILDKRAUT	portrait		
JS	JUANITA STARK	portrait	WARNER BROS	1940s
JS	JULIET OF THE SPIRITS (IT)	FELLINI	CINERIZ	1965
JS	JUNE STOREY	portrait		
JS	JUNGLE STREET GIRLS (UK: JUNGLE STREET)	SAUNDERS	AJAY	1960
JS-2	HOLLYWOOD BARN DANCE	RAY	SCREEN GUILD	1947
JSJ	JILL ST JOHN	portrait	UNIVERSAL	
J.ST.	JAMES STEPHENSON	portrait	WARNER BROS	
JT	JEAN TRENT	portrait	UNIVERSAL	1940s
JT	JUNE TRAVIS	portrait	RKO	late 30s
JT	JUNE TRAVIS	portrait	WARNER BROS	late 30s
JT	JUNGLE TREASURE (UK: OLD MOTHER RILEY'S JUNGLE TREAS.)	ROGERS	RENOWN	1951
JT	JUST THE TICKET	WENK	UNITED ARTISTS	1999
JT	TWO OF US (UK: JACK OF ALL TRADES)	HULBERT, STEVENSON	GAUMONT	1936
JTB	JACK THE BEAR	HERSKOVITZ	20th CENTURY FOX	1993
JU	JUDITH	MANN	PARAMOUNT	1966
JU	JUGGERNAUT	LESTER	UNITED ARTISTS	1974
JULIAN-1515	MIDNIGHT MADNESS	JULIAN	UNIVERSAL (Bluebird)	1918
JULIAN-2476	MOTHER O'MINE	JULIAN	UNIVERSAL (Bluebird)	1917
JULIAN-2715	DOOR BETWEEN	JULIAN	UNIVERSAL	1917
JV	JOAN VOHS	portrait	WARNER BROS	1940s-50s
JV	JOSEPH VITALI	portrait	RKO	
JV	JOYCE VANDERVEEN (JOYCE VAN DER VEEN)	portrait	UNIVERSAL	
JV	JUGGERNAUT	LESTER	UNITED ARTISTS	1974
JV	JUNE VINCENT	portrait	UNIVERSAL	1940s
JV	LES MISERABLES	BOLESLAWSKI	PATHE-NATAN	1934
JW	JACK L. WARNER	portrait	WARNER BROS	
JW	JACK WHITING	portrait	WARNER BROS	early 30s
JW	JACQUELINE WHITE	portrait	RKO	1940s-50s
JW	JAMES WARREN	portrait	RKO	
JW	JANE WALSH	portrait	RKO	late 1930s
JW	JANE WINTON	portrait	WARNER BROS	1920s-30s
JW	JANE WYATT	portrait	RKO	1930s-50s
JW	JANE WYMAN	portrait	RKO, WARNER BROS	
JW	JEAN WALLACE	portrait	RKO	late 40s
JW	JESSE WHITE	portrait	UNIVERSAL	1950s-60s
JW	JOAN WELDON	portrait	WARNER BROS	
JW	JOAN WINFIELD	portrait	WARNER BROS	1940s-50s
JW	JOHN WAYNE	portrait	RKO, REPUBLIC, UA, WB	
JW	JOHN WAYNE	portrait	PAR, UNIV	
JW	JOHNNY WEISSMULLER	portrait	MGM	
JW	JULIET WARE (aka JULIETTE WARE)	portrait	WARNER BROS	1930s
JW	JUST LIKE A WOMAN (UK)	FUEST	MONARCH	1967

Movie Still Identification Book Ultimate Edition - Letters

CODE	TITLE/NAME	DIRECTOR/TYPE	STUDIO/DISTRIBUTOR	YEAR
JW1	BIRTHDAY PRESENT (UK)	JACKSON	BRITISH LION	1957
JW1	MAN WHO CHEATED HIMSELF	FEIST	20th CENTURY FOX	1950
JWC	J. W. COOP	ROBERTSON	COLUMBIA	1971
JXB	JOHN BARRYMORE	portrait	MGM	
JXC	JANET CURRIE	portrait	MGM	
JXCX	JOAN CRAWFORD	portrait	MGM	
JXD	JIMMY DURANTE	portrait	MGM	
JXK	JUNE KNIGHT	portrait	MGM	
JXM	JOHN MILJAN	portrait		
JXM	JOHN MILJAN	portrait	MGM	
JXMX	JOAN MARSH	portrait	MGM	
JXS	JAMES STEWART	portrait	MGM	
JY	JUST YOU AND ME KID	STERN	COLUMBIA	1979
JY	MIGHTY JOE YOUNG	SCHOEDSACK	RKO	1948
K	BUSTER KEATON FEATURES		MGM	
K	CACTUS IN THE SNOW	ZWEIBACH	GENERAL FILM	1971
K	I BURY THE LIVING	BAND	UNITED ARTISTS	1958
K	KAGEMUSHA (JAP)	KUROSAWA	20th CENTURY FOX	1980
K	KAMA SUTRA (GER)	JAEGER	AIP	1970
K	KENTUCKIAN	LANCASTER	UNITED ARTISTS	1955
K	KERIMA	portrait	UNITED ARTISTS	
K	KHARTOUM (UK)	DEARDEN, ELISOFON	UNITED ARTISTS	1966
K	KIDNAPPED (UK)	STEVENSON	DISNEY	1960
K	KINDRED	CARPENTER, OBROW	FM ENTERTAINMENT	1987
K	KING KONG	COOPER	RKO	1933
K	KING OF THE DAMNED (UK)	FORDE	GAUMONT BRITISH	1935
K	KISMET	DILLON	WARNER BROS	1930
K	KITCHEN (UK)	HILL	KINGSLEY INTERNATIONAL	1961
K	KLANSMAN	YOUNG	PARAMOUNT	1974
K	KNOCKOUT	CLEMENS	WARNER BROS	1941
K	KRONOS	NEUMANN	20th CENTURY FOX	1957
K	OUTCAST OF THE ISLANDS	REED	LOPERT	1952
K	REMARKABLE MR. KIPPS (UK: KIPPS)	REED	20TH CENTURY FOX	1941
K	STAMBOUL (UK)	BUCHOWETZKI	TOBIS FORENFILMS	1931
K	UNTAMED WOMEN	CONNELL	UNITED ARTISTS	1952
K-1	BETTER MOVIES	MCGOWAN	PATHE EXCHANGE	1925
K-1	BORED OF EDUCATION	DOUGLAS	MGM	1936
K-1	HER DANGEROUS PATH (10 ch. series)	CLEMENTS	PATHE EXCHANGE	1923
K-1	TOLL OF THE DESERT	BERKE	ASTOR	1935
K2	PECOS KID	FRASER	COMMODORE	1935
K-2	TWO TOO YOUNG	DOUGLAS	MGM	1936
K-2	YOUR OWN BACK YARD	MCGOWAN	PATHE EXCHANGE	1925
K-3	ONE WILD RIDE	MCGOWAN	PATHE EXCHANGE	1925
K-3	PAY AS YOU EXIT	DOUGLAS	MGM	1936
K-4	GOOD CHEER	MCGOWAN	PATHE EXCHANGE	1926
K-4	SPOOKY HOOKY	DOUGLAS	MGM	1936
K-5	BURIED TREASURE	MCGOWAN	PATHE EXCHANGE	1926
K-5	REUNION IN RHYTHM	DOUGLAS	MGM	1937
K-6	GLOVE TAPS	DOUGLAS	MGM	1937
K-6	MONKEY BUSINESS	MCGOWAN	PATHE EXCHANGE	1926
K-7	BABY CLOTHES	MCGOWAN	PATHE EXCHANGE	1926
K-7	HEARTS ARE THUMPS	DOUGLAS	MGM	1937
K-8	THREE SMART BOYS	DOUGLAS	MGM	1937
K-8	UNCLE TOM'S UNCLE	MCGOWAN	PATHE EXCHANGE	1926
K-9	RUSHIN' BALLET	DOUGLAS	MGM	1937
K-9	THUNDERING FLEAS	MCGOWAN	PATHE EXCHANGE	1926
K-10	ROAMIN' HOLIDAY	DOUGLAS	MGM	1937
K-10	SHIVERING SPOOKS	MCGOWAN	PATHE EXCHANGE	1926
K-11	FOURTH ALARM	MCGOWAN	PATHE EXCHANGE	1926
K-11	NIGHT 'N' GALES	DOUGLAS	MGM	1937
K-12	FISHY TALES	DOUGLAS	MGM	1937
K-12	WAR FEATHERS	MCGOWAN, MCGOWAN	PATHE EXCHANGE	1926
K-13	FRAMING YOUTH	DOUGLAS	MGM	1937
K-13	SEEING THE WORLD	MCGOWAN, MCGOWAN	PATHE EXCHANGE	1927
K-14	KWAIDAN (JAP)	KOBAYASHI	CONTINENTAL	1966
K-14	PIGSKIN PALOOKA	DOUGLAS	MGM	1937
K-14	TELLING WHOPPERS	MCGOWAN, MCGOWAN	PATHE EXCHANGE	1926
K-15	BRING HOME THE TURKEY	MCGOWAN, MCGOWAN	PATHE EXCHANGE	1927
K-15	MAIL AND FEMALE	NEWMEYER	MGM	1937
K-16	CANNED FISHING	DOUGLAS	MGM	1938

Movie Still Identification Book Ultimate Edition - Letters

CODE	TITLE/NAME	DIRECTOR/TYPE	STUDIO/DISTRIBUTOR	YEAR
K-16	TEN YEARS OLD	MCGOWAN	PATHE EXCHANGE	1927
K-17	BEAR FACTS	DOUGLAS	MGM	1938
K-17	LOVE MY DOG	MCGOWAN	PATHE EXCHANGE	1927
K-18	THREE MEN IN A TUB	WATT	MGM	1938
K-18	TIRED BUSINESS MEN	MCGOWAN, OELZE	PATHE EXCHANGE	1927
K-19	BABY BROTHER	MCGOWAN, OELZE	PATHE EXCHANGE	1927
K-19	CAME THE BRAWN	DOUGLAS	MGM	1938
K-20	CHICKEN FEED	MCGOWAN, OELZE	PATHE EXCHANGE	1927
K-20	FEED 'EM AND WEEP	DOUGLAS	MGM	1938
K-21	AWFUL TOOTH	WATT	MGM	1938
K-21	OLYMPIC GAMES	MCGOWAN	PATHE EXCHANGE	1927
K 21	OUR HOSPITALITY	KEATON	METRO PICTURES (Keaton)	1923
K-22	GLORIOUS FOURTH	MCGOWAN	PATHE EXCHANGE	1927
K-22	HIDE AND SHRIEK	DOUGLAS	MGM	1938
K 22	SHERLOCK JR.	KEATON	METRO PICTURES (Keaton)	1924
K-23	SMILE WINS	MCGOWAN	PATHE EXCHANGE	1928
K-24	PLAYIN' HOOKEY	MCGOWAN	PATHE EXCHANGE	1928
K26	BATTLING BUTLER	KEATON	MGM	1926
K27	GENERAL	BRUCKMAN, KEATON	UNITED ARTISTS	1926
K-28	COLLEGE	HORNE	UNITED ARTISTS	1927
K101	THIEF OF BAGDAD (UK)	BERGER, POWELL	UNITED ARTISTS	1940
K101P	THIEF OF BAGDAD (UK)	BERGER, POWELL, WHALEN	UNITED ARTISTS	1940
K-106	GUSSIE'S DAY OF REST		MUTUAL FILM	1915
K-124	AMBROSE'S FURY	HENDERSON	MUTUAL FILM	1915
K-125	CAUGHT IN THE ACT	JONES	MUTUAL FILM	1915
K-126	SETTLED AT THE SEASIDE	GRIFFIN	MUTUAL FILM	1915
K-129	AMBROSE'S LOFTY PERCH	WRIGHT	MUTUAL FILM	1915
K-130	RENT JUMPERS	GRIFFIN	MUTUAL FILM	1915
K-131	DO-RE-ME-FA	CHASE	MUTUAL FILM	1915
K-132	AMBROSE'S NASTY TEMPER	HENDERSON	MUTUAL FILM	1915
K-139	BEAR AFFAIR	HENDERSON	MUTUAL FILM	1915
K-140	GUSSIE'S BACKWARD WAY		MUTUAL FILM	1915
K-141	CANNON BALL	WRIGHT	MUTUAL FILM	1915
K-144	THEIR SOCIAL SPLASH	GILLSTROM, JONES	MUTUAL FILM	1915
K-145	HUMAN HOUND'S TRIUMPH	HENDERSON	MUTUAL FILM	1915
K-146	HE WOULDN'T STAY DOWN	STERLING	MUTUAL FILM	1915
K-147	THOSE COLLEGE GIRLS	JONES	MUTUAL FILM	1915
K-148	CROSSED LOVE AND SWORDS	GRIFFIN	MUTUAL FILM	1915
K-150	LOVER'S LOST CONTROL	AVERY, CHAPLIN	MUTUAL FILM	1915
K-152	FOR BETTER-BUT WORSE	HENDERSON	MUTUAL FILM	1915
K-153	VERSATILE VILLAIN	GRIFFIN	MUTUAL FILM	1915
K-154	SUBMARINE PIRATE	AVERY, CHAPLIN	TRIANGLE	1915
K-155	LITTLE TEACHER	SENNETT	MUTUAL FILM	1915
K-157	COURT HOUSE CROOKS	STERLING	MUTUAL FILM	1915
K-158	THOSE BITTER SWEETS	HENDERSON	MUTUAL FILM	1915
K-160	WHEN AMBROSE DATED WALRUS		MUTUAL FILM	1915
K-161	HASH HOUSE FRAUD	CHASE	MUTUAL FILM	1915
K-162	HOME BREAKING HOUND	CHASE	MUTUAL FILM	1915
K-163	MERELY A MARRIED MAN	HENDERSON	MUTUAL FILM	1915
K-164	STOLEN MAGIC	SENNETT	TRIANGLE	1915
K-166	DIRTY WORK IN A LAUNDRY	SANTELL	MUTUAL FILM	1915
K-168	FIDO'S TIN-TYPE-TANGLE	ARBUCKLE	MUTUAL FILM	1915
K-169	RASCAL'S WOLFISH WAY	HENDERSON, SENNETT	MUTUAL FILM	1915
K-170	BATTLE OF AMBROSE AND WALRUS	WRIGHT	MUTUAL FILM	1915
K-171	MY VALET	SENNETT	TRIANGLE	1915
K-172	ONLY A MESSENGER BOY	GRIFFIN, STERLING	MUTUAL FILM	1915
K-175	GAME OLD KNIGHT	JONES	TRIANGLE	1915
K-177	FAVORITE FOOL	FRAZEE	TRIANGLE	1915
K-184	FICKLE FATTY'S FALL	ARBUCKLE	TRIANGLE	1915
K-187	MODERN ENOCH ARDEN	BADGER, AVERY	TRIANGLE	1916
K-190	GREAT PEARL TANGLE	HENDERSON	TRIANGLE	1916
K-195	CINDERS OF LOVE	WRIGHT	TRIANGLE	1916
K-197	BETTER LATE THAN NEVER	GRIFFIN	TRIANGLE	1916
K-201	GYPSY JOE	BADGER	TRIANGLE	1916
K-208	JUDGE	JONES	TRIANGLE	1916
K-209	WIFE AND AUTO TROUBLE	HENDERSON, SENNETT	TRIANGLE	1916
K-210	HE DID AND HE DIDN'T	ARBUCKLE	TRIANGLE	1916
K-212	DASH OF COURAGE	PARROTT	TRIANGLE	1916
K-214	HIS LAST LAUGH	WRIGHT	TRIANGLE	1916
K-222	HIS BITTER PILL	FISHBACK	TRIANGLE	1916

Movie Still Identification Book Ultimate Edition - Letters

CODE	TITLE/NAME	DIRECTOR/TYPE	STUDIO/DISTRIBUTOR	YEAR
K-230	BATH TUB PERILS	FRAZEE	TRIANGLE	1916
K-232	LOVE COMET	WRIGHT	TRIANGLE	1916
K-233	AMBROSE'S CUP OF WOE	FISHBACK	TRIANGLE	1916
K-234	SURF GIRL	EDWARDS	TRIANGLE	1916
K-235	PILLS OF PERIL	JONES	TRIANGLE	1916
K-236	HIS LAST SCENT	AVERY, CHAPLIN	TRIANGLE	1916
K-241	HIS LYING HEART	STERLING, AVERY	TRIANGLE	1916
K-243	TUGBOAT ROMEO	CAMPBELL, WILLIAMS	TRIANGLE	1916
K-245	SCOUNDREL'S TOLL	CAVENDER	TRIANGLE	1916
K-250	MAIDEN'S TRUST	HEERMAN	TRIANGLE	1916
K-251	HIS BUSTED TRUST	CLINE	TRIANGLE	1916
K-253	HAYSTACKS AND STEEPLES	BADGER	TRIANGLE	1916
K-255	STARS AND BARS	HEERMAN	TRIANGLE	1917
K-256	BOMBS!	GRIFFIN	TRIANGLE	1916
K-257	AMBROSE'S RAPID RISE	FISHBACK	TRIANGLE	1916
K-258	VILLA OF THE MOVIES	CLINE	TRIANGLE	1917
K-260	HER CIRCUS KNIGHT	WRIGHT	TRIANGLE	1917
K-261	HIS NAUGHTY THOUGHT	FISHBACK	TRIANGLE	1917
K-262	NICK OF TIME BABY	BADGER	TRIANGLE	1917
K-263	MAGGIE'S FIRST FALSE STEP	GRIFFIN	TRIANGLE	1917
K-264	DODGING HIS DOOM	WILLIAMS	TRIANGLE	1917
K-265	SAFETY FIRST AMBROSE	FISHBACK	TRIANGLE	1916
K-266	CACTUS NELL	FISHBACK	TRIANGLE	1917
K-267	HER NATURE DANCE	CAMPBELL	TRIANGLE	1917
K-268	SKIDDING HEARTS	WRIGHT	TRIANGLE	1917
K-269	HER FAME AND SHAME	GRIFFIN	TRIANGLE	1917
K-270	TEDDY AT THE THROTTLE	BADGER	TRIANGLE	1917
K-271	ROYAL ROGUE	KERR, HARTMAN	TRIANGLE	1917
K-272	DOG CATCHER'S LOVE	CLINE	TRIANGLE	1917
K-273	SECRETS OF A BEAUTY PARLOR	WILLIAMS	TRIANGLE	1917
K-274	HER TORPEDOED LOVE	GRIFFIN	TRIANGLE	1917
K-275	PINCHED IN THE FINISH	WRIGHT, WILLIAMS	TRIANGLE	1917
K-276	ORIENTAL LOVE	WRIGHT	TRIANGLE	1917
K-277	THIRST	FISHBACK	TRIANGLE	1917
K-278	WHOSE BABY	BADGER	TRIANGLE	1917
K-279	HULA-HULA LAND	CAMPBELL	TRIANGLE	1917
K-279	SHANGHAIED JONAH	CAMPBELL	TRIANGLE	1917
K-280	BETRAYAL OF MAGGIE	GRIFFIN	TRIANGLE	1917
K-281	DANGERS OF A BRIDE	KERR, HARTMAN	TRIANGLE	1917
K-282	TWO CROOKS	HEERMAN	TRIANGLE	1917
K-283	HIS UNCLE DUDLEY	JONES	TRIANGLE	1917
K-284	SHE NEEDED A DOCTOR	JONES	TRIANGLE	1917
K-285	SULTAN'S WIFE	BADGER	TRIANGLE	1917
K-286	HIS PRECIOUS LIFE	RAYMAKER	TRIANGLE	1917
K-287	PAWNBROKER'S HEART	CLINE	TRIANGLE	1917
K-288	CLEVER DUMMY	RAYMAKER	TRIANGLE	1917
K-289	LATE LAMENTED	WILLIAMS	TRIANGLE	1917
K-292	LOST, A COOK	JONES	TRIANGLE	1917
KA	KATHARINE/KATHERINE/KAY ALDRIDGE	portrait	WARNER BROS	
KA	KATHRYN ADAMS	portrait	UNIVERSAL	
KA	KEITH ANDES	portrait	RKO, UNIVERSAL	
KA	KNIVES OF THE AVENGER (IT)	BAVA	WORLD ENT	1966
KAL	KALEIDESCOPE (UK)	SMIGHT	WARNER BROS	1966
KB	I KILLED THAT MAN	ROSEN	MONOGRAM	1941
KB	KATHLEEN BYRON	portrait	LONDON FILMS	
KB	KAYE BALLARD	portrait	UNIVERSAL	
KB	KEEFE BRASSELLE	portrait	WARNER BROS	
KB	KENNY BAKER	portrait	RKO, WARNER BROS	
KA	KING ARTHUR WAS A GENTLEMAN (UK)	VARNEL	GFD	1942
KB	KICKBOXER	DISALLE	CANNON	1989
KB	KING BROTHERS PRODUCTIONS	studio		
KB	WHEN KNIGHTS WERE BOLD (UK)	RAYMOND	UNITY	1936
KB-2	KLONDIKE FURY	HOWARD	MONOGRAM	1942
KB-4	RUBBER RACKETEERS	YOUNG	MONOGRAM	1942
KB-5	I ESCAPED FROM THE GESTAPO	YOUNG	MONOGRAM	1943
KB-6	UNKNOWN GUEST	NEUMANN	MONOGRAM	1943
KB-7	JOHNNY DOESN'T LIVE HERE ANYMORE	MAY	MONOGRAM	1944
K B-14	KWAIDAN (JAP)	KOBAYASHI	CONTINENTAL	1966
KBC	GAY DIPLOMAT	BOLESLAWSKI	RKO	1931
KBS-111	FALSE FACES	SHERMAN	SONO ART-WORLD WIDE	1932

Movie Still Identification Book Ultimate Edition - Letters

CODE	TITLE/NAME	DIRECTOR/TYPE	STUDIO/DISTRIBUTOR	YEAR
KBS-113	DEATH KISS	MARIN	SONO ART-WORLD WIDE	1932
KBS-116	CONSTANT WOMAN	SCHERTZINGER	SONO ART-WORLD WIDE	1933
KBS-117	STUDY IN SCARLET	MARIN	SONO ART-WORLD WIDE	1933
KC	KATHERINE CORNELL	portrait	UNITED ARTISTS	
KC	KATHRYN CRAWFORD	portrait	UNIVERSAL	
KC	KAY CHRISTOPHER	portrait	RKO	
KC	KEEP IT CLEAN (UK)	PALTENGHI	EROS	1956
KC	KENNEL MURDER CASE	CURTIZ	WARNER BROS	1933
KC	KILL ME QUICK, I'M COLD (IT)	MASELLI	COLUMBIA	1967
KC	KING AND THE CHORUS GIRL	LEROY	WARNER BROS	1937
KC	KING OF COMEDY	SCORSESE	PARAMOUNT	1983
KC	KISS FOR CORLISS	WALLACE	UNITED ARTISTS	1949
KC	KITTY CARLISLE	portrait	UNIVERSAL	
KC	KONA COAST	JOHNSON	WARNER BROS	1968
KC	WHO IS GUILTY? (UK: I KILLED THE COUNT)	ZELNIK	GRAND NATIONAL	1939
KCS	KING OF THE CORAL SEA	ROBINSON	ALLIED ARTISTS	1953
KD	KARL DANE	portrait	MGM	
KD	KILL A DRAGON	MOORE	UNITED ARTISTS	1967
KD	KIM DARBY	portrait	UNIVERSAL	
KD	KING DINOSAUR	GORDON	LIPPERT	1955
KD	KIRK DOUGLAS	portrait	UNIVERSAL, WARNER BROS	
KD	KISS BEFORE DYING	OSWALD	UNITED ARTISTS	1956
KD	KISS ME DEADLY	ALDRICH	UNITED ARTISTS	1955
KE	CARL ESMOND	portrait	RKO	
KE	KILLER ELITE	PECKINPAH	UNITED ARTISTS	1975
KF	FASHIONS OF 1934	DIETERLE	WARNER BROS	1934
KF	KAY FRANCIS	portrait	FN/WARNER BROS,	
KF	KITTY FOYLE	WOOD	RKO	1940
KFC	FARMER'S DAUGHTER	POTTER	RKO	1947
KFL	KNIFE FOR THE LADIES	SPANGLER	WARNER BROS	1974
KF-NY	HORSE'S MOUTH	NEAME	UNITED ARTISTS	1958
KG	KATHRYN GRAYSON	portrait	MGM, WARNER BROS	
KG	KID GALAHAD	CURTIZ	WARNER BROS	1937
KG	KID GALAHAD	KARLSON	UNITED ARTISTS	1962
KG	KIRBY GRANT	portrait	UNIVERSAL	
KGF	KINGS GO FORTH	DAVES	UNITED ARTISTS	1958
KH	KATHARINE HEPBURN	portrait	RKO	
KH	KATHLEEN HUGHES	portrait	UNIVERSAL	
KH	KEPT HUSBANDS	BACON	RKO	1930
KH	KEYSTONE HOTEL (sh)	STAUB	WARNER BROS	1935
KH	KIM HUNTER	portrait	COL, UNIVERSAL	
KH	KING OF HEARTS (FR)	DE BROCA	UNITED ARTISTS	1966
KHG	KILL HER GENTLY	SAUNDERS	COLUMBIA	1957
KI	STRANGE JUSTICE	SCHERTZINGER	RKO	1932
KIDD	ABBOTT AND COSTELLO MEET CAPT. KIDD	LAMONT	WARNER BROS	1952
KIM	KILLER INSIDE ME	KENNEDY	WARNER BROS	1976
KING	KING PRODUCTIONS	studio	FOX	
KING-1	LIGHTNIN'	KING	FOX FILM	1930
KING-2	OVER THE HILL	KING	FOX FILM	1931
KING-3	MERELY MARY ANN	KING	FOX FILM	1931
KING-4	WOMAN IN ROOM 13	KING	FOX FILM	1932
KING-5	STATE FAIR	KING	FOX FILM	1933
KJ	KAREN JENSEN	portrait		
KJ	KAY JOHNSON	portrait	TIFFANY	early 30s
KJ	KAY JOHNSON	portrait	TIFFANY, MGM	
KJ	KENTUCKY JUBILEE	ORMOND	LIPPERT	1951
KJ	KIMBERLEY JIM	NOFAL	EMBASSY	1963
KJ	KINJITE: FORBIDDEN SUBJECTS	THOMPSON	CANNON	1989
KJ	KISS THE GIRLS AND MAKE THEM DIE (IT)	LEVIN, MAIURI	COLUMBIA	1966
KK	CASE OF THE BLACK CAT	MCGANN	WARNER BROS	1936
KK	KAREN KADLER	portrait	UNIVERSAL	
KK	KAY KYSER	portrait	RKO	
KK	KENTUCKY KERNELS	STEVENS	RKO	1934
KK	KES	LOACH	UNITED ARTISTS	1969
KK	KILLER'S KISS	KUBRICK	UNITED ARTISTS	1955
KK	KING KONG	GUILLERMIN	PARAMOUNT	1976
KK	KITTY KELLY	portrait	RKO	
KK	KURT KREUGER	portrait	RKO	
KK	LITA CHEVRET	portrait	RKO	
K/KL	KLANSMAN	YOUNG	PARAMOUNT	1974

Movie Still Identification Book Ultimate Edition - Letters

CODE	TITLE/NAME	DIRECTOR/TYPE	STUDIO/DISTRIBUTOR	YEAR
KL	KAY LESLIE	portrait	UNIVERSAL	
KL	KILLER IS LOOSE	BOETTICHER	UNITED ARTISTS	1956
KL	KIND OF LOVING (UK)	SCHLESINGER	GOVERNOR	1962
KLEIN-1	BLINDFOLD	KLEIN	FOX FILM	1928
KLEIN-2	SIN SISTER	KLEIN	FOX FILM	1929
KM	KAREN MORLEY	portrait	MGM	
KM	KARL MALDEN	portrait	WARNER BROS	
KM	KEN MAYNARD	portrait	GN; FN	1920s-30s
KM	KYLE MACDONNELL	portrait	WARNER BROS	
KM-1	SENOR DAREDEVIL	ROGELL	WARNER BROS	1926
KM-1	TRAILING TROUBLE	ROSSON	GRAND	1937
KM-2	BOOTS OF DESTINY	ROSSON	GRAND	1937
KM-2	UNKNOWN CAVALIER	ROGELL	WARNER BROS	1926
KM-3	OVERLAND STAGE	ROGELL	WARNER BROS	1927
KM-3	WHIRLWIND HORSEMAN	HILL	GRAND	1938
KM-4	SIX SHOOTIN' SHERIFF	FRASER	GRAND	1938
KM-4	SOMEWHERE IN SONORA	ROGELL	WARNER BROS	1927
KM-5	LAND BEYOND THE LAW	BROWN	WARNER BROS	1927
KM-6	DEVIL'S SADDLE	ROGELL	WARNER BROS	1927
KM-7	RED RAIDERS	ROGELL	WARNER BROS	1927
KM-8	GUN GOSPEL	BROWN	WARNER BROS	1927
KM-9	WAGON SHOW	BROWN	WARNER BROS	1928
KM-10	CANYON OF ADVENTURE	ROGELL	WARNER BROS	1928
KM-11	UPLAND RIDER	ROGELL	WARNER BROS	1928
KM-12	CODE OF THE SCARLET	BROWN	WARNER BROS	1928
KM-13	PHANTOM CITY	ROGELL	WARNER BROS	1928
KM-14	GLORIOUS TRAIL	BROWN, ROGELL	WARNER BROS	1928
KM-15	CHEYENNE	ROGELL	WARNER BROS	1929
KM-16	LAWLESS LEGION	BROWN	WARNER BROS	1929
KM-17	CALIFORNIA MAIL	ROGELL	WARNER BROS	1929
KM-18	ROYAL RIDER	BROWN	WARNER BROS	1929
KM-203	SILENT WITNESS	YARBROUGH	MONOGRAM	1943
KMcG	KATHRYN MCGUIRE	portrait	METRO	1920s
KMG	KING OF MARVIN GARDENS	RAFELSON	COLUMBIA	1972
KN	BUSTER KEATON SHORTS	studio	MGM	
KN	KID NIGHTINGALE	AMY	WARNER BROS	1939
KNY	KING IN NEW YORK (UK)	CHAPLIN	ARCHWAY	1957
KO	GRIDIRON FLASH	TRYON	RKO	1934
KOD	KISS OF DEATH	SCHROEDER	20th CENTURY FOX	1995
KOM	KATHLEEN O'MALLEY	portrait	UNIVERSAL	
KOR-1	WOMEN EVERYWHERE	KORDA	FOX FILM	1930
KOR-2	PRINCESS AND THE PLUMBER	KORDA	FOX FILM	1930
KP	KHYBER PATROL	FRIEDMAN	UNITED ARTISTS	1954
KQ	KING AND FOUR QUEENS	WALSH	UNITED ARTISTS	1956
KR	KANE RICHMOND	portrait	MGM	
KR	KAREN RANDLE	portrait	UNIVERSAL	
KR	KATHARINE ROSS	portrait	UNIV	
KR	KING'S ROW	WOOD	WARNER BROS	1942
KR	KNUTE ROCKNE: ALL AMERICAN	BACON	WARNER BROS	1940
KR	LAW OF THE TROPICS	ENRIGHT	WARNER BROS	1941
KR	NIGHT AT THE RITZ	MCGANN	WARNER BROS	1935
KS	KAY SUTTON	portrait	RKO, WARNER BROS	
KS	KINGS OF THE SUN	THOMPSON	UNITED ARTISTS	1963
KS	KISS ME, STUPID [US: LOPERT]	WILDER	UNITED ARTISTS	1964
KS	ONE MINUTE TO ZERO	GARNETT	RKO	1952
KS	KING SISTERS	portrait	UNIV	
KT	KENNETH TOBEY	portrait	RKO	
KT	KITCHEN TOTO	HOOK	CANNON	1987
KT	KONTIKI (NOR)	HEYERDAHL	RKO	1951
KV	KAAREN VERNE (aka KAREN VERNE)	portrait	WARNER BROS	early 40s
KV	KING VIDOR		MGM	1920s-40s
KV	KING'S VACATION	ADOLFI	WARNER BROS	1933
L	DEATH VALLEY	LANDERS	SCREEN GUILD	1946
L	LABYRINTH	HENSON	TRI STAR	1986
L	LADDIE	STEVENS	RKO	1935
L	LADY IN DISTRESS (UK: WINDOW IN LONDON)	MASON	TIMES	1940
L	LAIR OF THE WHITE WORM	RUSSELL	VESTRON	1988
L	LAND OF FURY (UK: SEEKERS)	ANNAKIN	UNIVERSAL	1954
L	LASH (UK)	EDWARDS	RKO	1934
L	LAWMAN	WINNER	UNITED ARTISTS	1971

Movie Still Identification Book Ultimate Edition - Letters

CODE	TITLE/NAME	DIRECTOR/TYPE	STUDIO/DISTRIBUTOR	YEAR
L	LEGERAN PICTURES (UK)			
L	LENNY	FOSSE	UNITED ARTISTS	1974
L	LETTER	WYLER	WARNER BROS	1940
L	LIANNA	SAYLES	UNITED ARTISTS	1983
L	LIBERTINE	CAMPANILE	AUDUBON	1969
L	LIES MY FATHER TOLD ME	KADAR	COLUMBIA	1975
L	LIMELIGHT	CHAPLIN	UNITED ARTISTS	1952
L	LINK	FRANKLIN	CANNON	1986
L	LISA	SHERMAN	UNITED ARTISTS	1990
L	LODGER (UK)	HITCHCOCK	AMERANGLO	1927
L	LOLITA (UK)	KUBRICK	MGM	1962
L	LOOT (UK)	NARIZZANO	CINEVISION	1970
L	LORD OF ILLUSIONS	BARKER	UNITED ARTISTS	1995
L	LORNA	MEYER	EVE	1964
L	ONE BIG AFFAIR	GODFREY	UNITED ARTISTS	1952
L	OUTCASTS OF THE CITY	PETROFF	REPUBLIC	1958
L	PLAYGIRL	ENRIGHT	WARNER BROS	1932
L	SECRETS OF AN ACTRESS	KEIGHLEY	WARNER BROS	1938
L	UNTAMED WOMEN	CONNELL	UNITED ARTISTS	1952
L	VIVACIOUS LADY	STEVENS	RKO	1938
L	YOU LUCKY PEOPLE (UK)	ELVEY	ADELPHI	1955
L1	AUNT CLARA (UK)	KIMMINS	BRITISH LION	1954
L-1	BUMPING INTO BROADWAY	ROACH	PATHE EXCHANGE	1919
L-1	COME CLEAN	HORNE	MGM	1931
L1	OLD BILL AND SON (UK)	DALRYMPLE	GFD	1941
L-1	OVER THE FENCE	LLOYD, MACDONALD	PATHE EXCHANGE	1917
L-1	ROUGHEST AFRICA	CEDER	PATHE EXCHANGE	1923
L1	WEB OF CHANCE	GREEN	FOX FILM	1919
L-2	CAPTAIN KIDD'S KIDS	ROACH	PATHE EXCHANGE	1919
L2	CHARLEY MOON (UK)	HAMILTON	BRITISH LION	1956
L-2	FROZEN HEARTS	HOWE	PATHE EXCHANGE	1923
L-2	ONE GOOD TURN	HORNE	MGM	1931
L-2	PINCHED	LLOYD, PRATT	PATHE EXCHANGE	1917
L-2	TRAIL OF THE MOUNTIES	BRETHERTON	LIPPERT	1947
L-3	A SELF MADE MAN	LEE	FOX FILM	1922
L-3	BEAU HUNKS	HORNE	MGM	1931
L-3	BY THE SAD SEA WAVES	GOULDING	PATHE EXCHANGE	1917
L-3	FROM HAND TO MOUTH	GOULDING	PATHE EXCHANGE	1919
L-3	PLAYGIRL	ENRIGHT	WARNER BROS	1932
L-3	SOILERS	CEDER	PATHE EXCHANGE	1923
L-4	ANY OLD PORT	HORNE	MGM	1932
L-4	HIS ROYAL SLYNESS	ROACH	PATHE EXCHANGE	1920
L-4	MOTHER'S JOY	CEDER	PATHE EXCHANGE	1923
L-4	RAINBOW ISLAND	GILBERT	PATHE EXCHANGE	1917
L-5	BLISS	GOULDING	PATHE EXCHANGE	1917
L-5	HAUNTED SPOOKS	ROACH	PATHE EXCHANGE	1920
L-5	HELPMATES	PARROTT	MGM	1932
L-5	NEAR DUBLIN	CEDER	PATHE EXCHANGE	1924
L-5	QUEEN OF HEARTS	LAWRENCE	FOX FILM	1918
L-5	SHIRLEY OF THE CIRCUS	LEE	FOX FILM	1922
L5	WRATH OF LOVE	VINCENT	FOX FILM	1917
L-6	AN EASTERN WESTERNER	ROACH	PATHE EXCHANGE	1920
L-6	FLIRT	GILBERT	PATHE EXCHANGE	1917
L-6	LOVE AUCTION	LAWRENCE	FOX FILM	1919
L-6	MUSIC BOX	PARROTT	MGM	1932
L-6	SMITHY	JESKE, ROACH	PATHE EXCHANGE	1924
L-7	ALL ABOARD	GOULDING	PATHE EXCHANGE	1917
L-7	CHIMP	PARROTT	MGM	1932
L-7	HIGH AND DIZZY	ROACH	PATHE EXCHANGE	1920
L-7	ZEB VS. PAPRIKA	CEDER	PATHE EXCHANGE	1924
L-8	CHEATING HERSELF	LAWRENCE	FOX FILM	1919
L-8	COUNTY HOSPITAL	PARROTT	MGM	1932
L-8	GET OUT AND GET UNDER	ROACH	PATHE EXCHANGE	1920
L-8	MOVE ON	PRATT, GILBERT	PATHE EXCHANGE	1917
L-8	POSTAGE DUE	JESKE	PATHE EXCHANGE	1924
L-9	BASHFUL	GOULDING	PATHE EXCHANGE	1917
L-9	BROTHER UNDER THE CHIN	CEDER	PATHE EXCHANGE	1924
L-9	NUMBER, PLEASE?	ROACH	PATHE EXCHANGE	1920
L-9	SCRAM!	MCCAREY	MGM	1932
L10	CRASHING HOLLYWOOD	LANDERS	RKO	1938

Movie Still Identification Book Ultimate Edition - Letters

CODE	TITLE/NAME	DIRECTOR/TYPE	STUDIO/DISTRIBUTOR	YEAR
L-10	NOW OR NEVER	ROACH	PATHE EXCHANGE	1921
L-10	THEIR FIRST MISTAKE	MARSHALL	MGM	1932
L-10	TIP	PRATT, GILBERT	PATHE EXCHANGE	1918
L-10	WIDE OPEN SPACES	JESKE	PATHE EXCHANGE	1924
L-11	AMONG THOSE PRESENT	NEWMEYER	PATHE EXCHANGE	1921
L11	OLD HOMESTEAD	NIGH	LIBERTY PICTURES	1935
L-11	RUPERT OF HEE HAW	PEMBROKE	PATHE EXCHANGE	1924
L-11	SHOULD MARRIED MEN GO HOME?	MCCAREY, PARROTT	MGM	1928
L-11	STEP LIVELY	GOULDING	PATHE EXCHANGE	1917
L-11	TOWED IN A HOLE	MARSHALL	MGM	1932
L-11	WHAT WOULD YOU DO?	LAWRENCE	FOX FILM	1920
L-12	BIG IDEA	MOHR, PRATT	PATHE EXCHANGE	1918
L-12	EARLY TO BED	FLYNN	MGM	1928
L-12	I DO	NEWMEYER	PATHE EXCHANGE	1921
L-12	SHORT KILTS	JESKE	PATHE EXCHANGE	1924
L-12	TWICE TWO	PARROTT	MGM	1933
L-13	HELLO TEACHER	ROACH	PATHE EXCHANGE	1918
L-13	ME AND MY PAL	ROGERS	MGM	1933
L-13	NEVER WEAKEN	NEWMEYER	PATHE EXCHANGE	1921
L-13	TWO TARS	PARROTT	MGM	1928
L-14	HABEAS CORPUS	PARROTT, MCCAREY	MGM	1928
L-14	LAMB (GOAT)	LLOYD, PRATT	PATHE EXCHANGE	1918
L-14	MIDNIGHT PATROL	FRENCH	MGM	1933
L-14	SAILOR-MADE MAN	NEWMEYER	PATHE EXCHANGE	1921
L-15	BUSY BODIES	FRENCH	MGM	1933
L-15	GRANDMA'S BOY	NEWMEYER	ASSOC. EXHIBITORS	1922
L-15	LET'S GO	GOULDING	PATHE EXCHANGE	1918
L-15	WE FAW DOWN	MCCAREY	MGM	1928
L-16	BEAT IT	PRATT	PATHE EXCHANGE	1918
L-16	DIRTY WORK	FRENCH	MGM	1933
L-16	DR. JACK	NEWMEYER	PATHE EXCHANGE	1922
L16	FLAME OF THE FLESH	LESAINT	FOX FILM	1920
L-16	LIBERTY	MCCAREY	MGM	1929
L-17	GASOLINE WEDDING	GOULDING	PATHE EXCHANGE	1918
L-17	OLIVER THE EIGHTH	FRENCH	MGM	1934
L-17	SAFETY LAST!	TAYLOR, NEWMEYER	PATHE EXCHANGE	1923
L-17	WRONG AGAIN	MCCAREY	MGM	1929
L-18	GOING BYE-BYE!	ROGERS	MGM	1934
L-18	HIT HIM AGAIN	PRATT	PATHE EXCHANGE	1918
L-18	THAT'S MY WIFE	FRENCH	MGM	1929
L-19	BIG BUSINESS	HORNE, MCCAREY	MGM	1929
L-19	LOOK PLEASANT, PLEASE	GOULDING	PATHE EXCHANGE	1918
L19	ROSE OF NOME	LESAINT	FOX FILM	1920
L-19	THEM THAR HILLS	ROGERS	MGM	1934
L-20	DOUBLE WHOOPEE	FOSTER	MGM	1929
L-20	HERE COME THE GIRLS	HIBBARD	PATHE EXCHANGE	1918
L-20	HOT WATER	NEWMEYER, TAYLOR	PATHE	1924
L-20	LIVE GHOST	ROGERS	MGM	1934
L-21	BACON GRABBERS	FOSTER	MGM	1929
L-21	ON THE JUMP	GOULDING	PATHE EXCHANGE	1918
L-21	TIT FOR TAT	ROGERS	MGM	1935
L-22	ANGORA LOVE	FOSTER	MGM	1929
L-22	FIXER-UPPERS	ROGERS	MGM	1935
L-22	HEY THERE!	GOULDING	PATHE EXCHANGE	1918
L-23	KICKED OUT	GOULDING	PATHE EXCHANGE	1918
L-23	THICKER THAN WATER	HORNE	MGM	1935
L-23	UNACCUSTOMED AS WE ARE	FOSTER, ROACH	MGM	1929
L-24	BERTH MARKS	FOSTER	MGM	1929
L-24	NON STOP KID	PRATT	PATHE EXCHANGE	1918
L-25	FOLLOW THE CROWD	GOULDING	PATHE EXCHANGE	1918
L-25	MEN O' WAR	FOSTER	MGM	1929
L-26	IT'S A WILD LIFE	PRATT	PATHE EXCHANGE	1918
L-26	PERFECT DAY	PARROTT	MGM	1929
L-27	PIPE THE WHISKERS	GOULDING	PATHE EXCHANGE	1918
L-27	THEY GO BOOM	PARROTT	MGM	1929
L-28	HOOSE-GOW	PARROTT	MGM	1929
L-28	SIC 'EM TOWSER	PRATT	PATHE EXCHANGE	1918
L-29	NIGHT OWLS	PARROTT	MGM	1930
L-29	TWO GUN GUSSIE	GOULDING	PATHE EXCHANGE	1918
L-30	BLOTTO	PARROTT	MGM	1930

Movie Still Identification Book Ultimate Edition - Letters

CODE	TITLE/NAME	DIRECTOR/TYPE	STUDIO/DISTRIBUTOR	YEAR
L-30	LOVE'S YOUNG SCREAM	JEFFERSON	PATHE EXCHANGE	1919
L-31	BRATS	PARROTT	MGM	1930
L-31	FIREMAN SAVE MY CHILD	GOULDING	PATHE EXCHANGE	1918
L-32	BELOW ZERO	PARROTT	MGM	1930
L-32	CITY SLICKER	PRATT	PATHE EXCHANGE	1918
L-33	HOG WILD	PARROTT	MGM	1930
L-33	SOMEWHERE IN TURKEY	GOULDING	PATHE EXCHANGE	1918
L-34	ARE CROOKS DISHONEST	PRATT	PATHE EXCHANGE	1918
L-34	LAUREL-HARDY MURDER CASE	PARROTT	MGM	1930
L-35	OZARK ROMANCE	GOULDING	PATHE EXCHANGE	1918
L-35	PARDON US	PARROTT	MGM	1931
L-36	ANOTHER FINE MESS	PARROTT	MGM	1930
L-36	THAT'S HIM	PRATT	PATHE EXCHANGE	1918
L-37	BE BIG!	HORNE, PARROTT	MGM	1931
L-37	BRIDE AND GLOOM	GOULDING	PATHE EXCHANGE	1918
L-38	CHICKENS COME HOME	HORNE	MGM	1931
L-38	TWO SCRAMBLED	PRATT	PATHE EXCHANGE	1918
L-39	KICKING THE GERM OUT OF GERMANY	GOULDING	PATHE EXCHANGE	1918
L-39	LAUGHING GRAVY	HORNE	MGM	1931
L-40	BEES IN HIS BONNET	PRATT	PATHE EXCHANGE	1918
L-40	OUR WIFE	HORNE	MGM	1931
L-41	SWING YOUR PARTNERS	GOULDING	PATHE EXCHANGE	1918
L-42	HEAR 'EM RAVE	PRATT	PATHE EXCHANGE	1918
L-43	NOTHING BUT TROUBLE	ROACH	PATHE EXCHANGE	1918
L-44	WHY PICK ON ME?	ROACH	PATHE EXCHANGE	1918
L-45	TAKE A CHANCE	GOULDING	PATHE EXCHANGE	1918
L-46	GOING! GOING! GONE!	PRATT	PATHE EXCHANGE	1919
L-47	SHE LOVES ME NOT	ROACH	PATHE EXCHANGE	1918
L-48	WANTED $5000	PRATT	PATHE EXCHANGE	1919
L-49	I'M ON MY WAY	ROACH	PATHE EXCHANGE	1919
L-50	ASK FATHER	ROACH	PATHE EXCHANGE	1919
L-51	ON THE FIRE	ROACH	PATHE EXCHANGE	1919
L-52	LOOK OUT BELOW!	ROACH	PATHE EXCHANGE	1919
L-53	DUTIFUL DUB	GOULDING	PATHE EXCHANGE	1919
L-54	NEXT AISLE OVER	ROACH	PATHE EXCHANGE	1919
L-55	RING UP THE CURTAIN	GOULDING	PATHE EXCHANGE	1919
L-56	JUST DROPPED IN	ROACH	PATHE EXCHANGE	1919
L-57	CRACK YOUR HEELS	GOULDING	PATHE EXCHANGE	1919
L-58	YOUNG MR. JAZZ	ROACH	PATHE EXCHANGE	1919
L-59	SI, SENOR	GOULDING	PATHE EXCHANGE	1919
L-60	BEFORWE BREAKFAST	ROACH	PATHE EXCHANGE	1919
L-61	MARATHON	GOULDING	PATHE EXCHANGE	1919
L-62	BACK TO THE WOODS	ROACH	PATHE EXCHANGE	1919
L-63	PISTOLS FOR BREAKFAST	GOULDING	PATHE EXCHANGE	1919
L-64	SWAT THE CROOK	ROACH	PATHE EXCHANGE	1919
L-65	OFF THE TROLLEY	GOULDING	PATHE EXCHANGE	1919
L-66	AT THE OLD STAGE DOOR	ROACH	PATHE EXCHANGE	1919
L-67	JAZZED HONEYMOON	ROACH	PATHE EXCHANGE	1919
L-68	NEVER TOUCHED ME	GOULDING	PATHE EXCHANGE	1919
L-69	BILL BLAZES, ESQ.	ROACH	PATHE EXCHANGE	1919
L-70	COUNT YOUR CHANGE	GOULDING	PATHE EXCHANGE	1919
L-71	CHOP SUEY AND COMPANY	ROACH	PATHE EXCHANGE	1919
L-72	HEAP BIG CHIEF	GOULDING	PATHE EXCHANGE	1919
L-73	SAMMY IN SIBERIA	ROACH	PATHE EXCHANGE	1919
L-74	DON'T SHOVE	GOULDING	PATHE EXCHANGE	1919
L-75	BE MY WIFE	ROACH	PATHE EXCHANGE	1919
L-76	RAJAH	ROACH	PATHE EXCHANGE	1919
L-77	HE LEADS, OTHERS FOLLOW	ROACH	PATHE EXCHANGE	1919
L-78	SOFT MONEY	ROACH	PATHE EXCHANGE	1919
L-79	COUNT THE VOTES	ROACH	PATHE EXCHANGE	1919
L-80	PAY YOUR DUES	ROACH	PATHE EXCHANGE	1919
L-81	HIS ONLY FATHER	ROACH	PATHE EXCHANGE	1919
L-82	SPRING FEVER	ROACH	PATHE EXCHANGE	1919
L-83	JUST NEIGHBORS	LLOYD, TERRY	PATHE EXCHANGE	1919
L266	SECRET GARDEN	SEYFFERTITZ	PARAMOUNT	1919
L282	MEN, WOMEN AND MONEY	MELFORD	PARAMOUNT	1919
L314	SEA WOLF	MELFORD	PARAMOUNT	1920
L325	SINS OF ST. ANTHONY	CRUZE	PARAMOUNT	1920
L348	TRAVELING SALESMAN	HENABERY	PARAMOUNT	1921
L359	TO PLEASE ONE WOMAN	WEBER	PARAMOUNT	1920

Movie Still Identification Book Ultimate Edition - Letters

CODE	TITLE/NAME	DIRECTOR/TYPE	STUDIO/DISTRIBUTOR	YEAR
L367	AFFAIRS OF ANATOL	DEMILLE	PARAMOUNT	1921
L369	WHISTLE	HILLYER	PARAMOUNT	1921
L371	TOO WISE WIVES	WEBER	PARAMOUNT	1921
L373	WHITE AND UNMARRIED	FORMAN	PARAMOUNT	1921
L374	GREAT MOMENT	WOOD	PARAMOUNT	1921
L382	GREAT IMPERSONATION	MELFORD	PARAMOUNT	1921
L383	HELL DIGGERS	URSON	PARAMOUNT	1921
LA	ASTRID ALLWYN	portrait	RKO	
LA	DEAF SMITH & JOHNNY EARS (IT: LOS AMIGOS)	CAVARA	MGM	1973
LA	HEARTBEAT (FR: LA CHAMADE)	CAVALIER	UNITED ARTISTS	1968
LA	IT LIVES AGAIN (IT'S ALIVE 2)	COHEN	WARNER BROS	1978
LA	KAY LINAKER	portrait	WARNER BROS	
LA	L. A. CONFIDENTIAL	HANSON	WARNER BROS	1997
LA	LAVERNE ANDREWS (ANDREWS SISTERS)	portrait	UNIVERSAL	
LA	LAWRENCE OF ARABIA (UK)	LEAN	COLUMBIA	1962
LA	LEON ABRAMS	portrait	MGM	
LA	LEW AYRES	portrait	UNIVERSAL, WARNER BROS	
LA	LI'L ABNER	ROGELL	RKO	1940
LA	LOUISE ALLBRITTON	portrait	UNIVERSAL	
LA	LOVE AFFAIR	MCCAREY	RKO	1939
LA	LOVE IN THE AFTERNOON	WILDER	ALLIED ARTISTS	1957
LA	LUIS CESAR AMADORI	portrait	RKO	
LA	LYONS ABROAD (UK: LYONS IN PARIS)	GUEST	EXCLUSIVE	1955
LA-2	BASHFUL BACHELOR	ST. CLAIR	RKO	1942
LAB	REFLECTION OF FEAR	FRAKER	COLUMBIA	1973
LACH-1	FACE IN THE SKY	LACHMAN	FOX FILM	1933
LAD	LAWRENCE OF ARABIA (UK)	LEAN	COLUMBIA	1962
LADY	LADY & THE TRAMP (t)	GERONIMI	DISNEY	1955
LADY-NY	LADY & THE TRAMP (t)	GERONIMI	DISNEY	R62
LAF	LAWRENCE OF ARABIA	LEAN	COLUMBIA	1962
LAL	LAWRENCE OF ARABIA (UK)	LEAN	COLUMBIA	1962
LAN-1	CHEER UP AND SMILE	LANFIELD	FOX FILM	1930
LAN-3	3 GIRLS LOST	LANFIELD	FOX FILM	1931
LAN-5	DANCE TEAM	LANFIELD	FOX FILM	1932
LAN-5	HUSH MONEY	LANFIELD	FOX FILM	1931
LAN-6	SOCIETY GIRL	LANFIELD	FOX FILM	1932
LAN-7	HAT CHECK GIRL	LANFIELD	FOX FILM	1932
LAN-8	BROADWAY BAD	LANFIELD	FOX FILM	1933
LAT	LIFE AT THE TOP (UK)	KOTCHEFF	COLUMBIA	1965
LAW	MILDRED LAW	portrait	WARNER BROS.	
LB	CHARGE OF THE LIGHT BRIGADE	CURTIZ	WARNER BROS	1936
LB	GRAND OLD GIRL	ROBERTSON	RKO	1935
LB	LAUREN BACALL	portrait	UNIVERSAL, WARNER BROS	
LB	LEATHER BOYS (UK)	FURIE	ALLIED ARTISTS	1964
LB	LEE BOWMAN	portrait	UNIVERSAL	
LB	LESLIE BANNING	portrait	UNIVERSAL	
LB	LEX BARKER	portrait	RKO	
LB	LIFE BEGINS	FLOOD, NUGENT	WARNER BROS	1932
LB	LILIAN/LILLIAN BOND	portrait	FN/WARNER BROS	
LB	LINA BASQUETTE	portrait		
LB	LIONEL BARRYMORE	portrait	MGM	
LB	LOCAL BOY MAKES GOOD	LEROY	WARNER BROS	1931
LB	LONG GOODBYE	ALTMAN	UNITED ARTISTS	1973
LB	LOST BOUNDARIES	WERKER	FILM CLASSICS	1949
LB	LUCILLE BALL	portrait	RKO, UNIVERSAL	
LB	LUCILLE BARKLEY	portrait	UNIVERSAL	
LB	LYNN BARI	portrait	RKO	
LB	LYNN/LYNNE BAGGETT	portrait	WARNER BROS	
LB	MONTY PYTHON'S LIFE OF BRIAN (UK)	JONES	WARNER BROS	1979
LB	POUND	DOWNEY SR.	UNITED ARTISTS	1970
L-BAL	LITTLE BALLERINA (UK)	GILBERT	UNIVERSAL	1948
LBC	LEGEND OF BOGGY CREEK	PIERCE	HOWCO	1972
LBG	LINDA BE GOOD	MCDONALD	EAGLE LION	1948
LBH	LITTLE BIG HORN	WARREN	LIPPERT	1951
LBJ	LEGEND OF BILLIE JEAN	ROBBINS	TRI STAR	1985
LBJ	LIBERATION OF LB JONES	WYLER	COLUMBIA	1970
LBX	LILIAN/LILLIAN BOND	portrait	MGM	
LC	HOT TIP	GLEASON, MCCAREY	RKO	1935
LC	LA CAGE AUX FOLLES 3 (FR)	LAUTNER	TRI STAR	1985
LC	LADY CAROLINE LAMB	BOLT	UNITED ARTISTS	1972

Movie Still Identification Book Ultimate Edition - Letters

CODE	TITLE/NAME	DIRECTOR/TYPE	STUDIO/DISTRIBUTOR	YEAR
LC	LAIRD CREGAR	portrait	RKO	
LC	LAST CONTINENT (UK)	CARRERAS	20TH CENTURY FOX	1968
LC	LEGEND OF NIGGER CHARLEY	GOLDMAN	PARAMOUNT	1972
LC	LEO CARRILLO	portrait	UNIVERSAL	
LC	LESLIE CARON	portrait	UNIVERSAL	
LC	LITTLE CAESAR	LEROY	WARNER BROS	1931
LC	LOIS COLLIER	portrait	UNIVERSAL	
LC	LON CHANEY	portrait	MGM	
LC	LON CHANEY JR.	portrait	UNIVERSAL	
LC	LONESOME COWBOYS	WARHOL	SHERPIX	1968
LC	LOST COMMAND	ROBSON	COLUMBIA	1966
LC	LOST CONTINENT	NEWFIELD	LIPPERT	1951
LC	LOU COSTELLO	portrait	UNIVERSAL	
LC	LOUISE CAMPBELL	portrait	RKO	
LC	LOVE IN THE CITY (IT: L'AMORE IN CITTA)	ANTONIONI, FELLINI	IFE	1953
LC	LUCIA CARROLL	portrait	WARNER BROS	early 40s
LC	QUEST FOR THE LOST CITY	LAMB	RKO	1955
LC-25	ABBOTT AND COSTELLO MEET FRANKENSTEIN	BARTON	UNIVERSAL	1948
LC-89	NOON WHISTLE	JESKE	PATHE EXCHANGE	1923
LC-91	WHITE WINGS	JESKE	PATHE EXCHANGE	1923
LC-92	PICK AND SHOVEL	JESKE	PATHE EXCHANGE	1923
LC-95	KILL OR CURE	PEMBROKE	PATHE EXCHANGE	1923
LC-97	COLLARS AND CUFFS	JESKE	PATHE EXCHANGE	1923
LC-99	GAS AND AIR	PEMBROKE	PATHE EXCHANGE	1923
LC-102	ORANGES AND LEMONS	JESKE	PATHE EXCHANGE	1923
LC-104	SHORT ORDERS	PEMBROKE	PATHE EXCHANGE	1923
LC-106	SAVE THE SHIP	JESKE, ROACH	PATHE EXCHANGE	1923
LC-112	SCORCHING SANDS	WILLIAMSON, ROACH	PATHE EXCHANGE	1923
LC-115	WHOLE TRUTH	CEDER	PATHE EXCHANGE	1923
LCA	LOVE COMES ALONG	JULIAN	RKO	1929
LCD	LLOYD OF THE C.I.D. (UK) (serial)	MACRAE, TAYLOR	UNIVERSAL	1932
LCE	LADIES CRAVE EXCITEMENT	GRINDE	MASCOT	1935
LC-GIJ	STORY OF G.I. JOE	WELLMAN	UNITED ARTISTS	1945
LCH	LOUISE CLOSSER HALE	portrait	MGM	
LCL	LADY CHATTERLEYS LOVER (FR: L'AMANT DI LADY	ALLEGRET	KINGSLEY-INTERNATIONAL	1955
LCL	LADY CHATTERLEY'S LOVER	JAECKIN	CANNON	1981
LCS	LEW CODY	portrait	ROBERTSON COLE	
LCT	LAW COMES TO TEXAS (1939)	LEVERING	ASTOR	R48
LCX	LEW CODY	portrait	MGM	
LD	INCIDENT IN AN ALLEY	CAHN	UNITED ARTISTS	1962
LD	LADIES DAY	GOODWINS	RKO	1943
LD	LARAINE DAY	portrait	RKO	
LD	LAST DAYS OF POMPEII	SCHOEDSACK	RKO	1935
LD	LAST DETAIL	ASHBY	COLUMBIA	1973
LD	LAST DRAGON	SCHULTZ	TRI STAR	1985
LD	LAUGHTER IN THE DARK (UK)	RICHARDSON	UNITED ARTISTS	1969
LD	LAURA DEVON	portrait	UNIVERSAL	
LD	LAURIE DOUGLAS	portrait	UNIVERSAL	
LD	LAW AND DISORDER	PASSER	COLUMBIA	1974
LD	LEE DIXON	portrait	WARNER BROS	
LD	LIFE IN DANGER (UK)	BISHOP	ALLIED ARTISTS	1964
LD	LIGHT OF DAY	SCHRADER	TRI STAR	1987
LD	LILAC DOMINO (UK)	ZELNIK	MAJESTIC FILMS (UK)	1937
LD	LINDA DARNELL	portrait	RKO	
LD	LINDA DOUGLAS/MARY JO TAROLA/GREENBERG	portrait	RKO	
LD	LISA AND THE DEVIL		MONOGRAM	
LD	LITTLE DORRIT	EDZARD	CANNON	1988
LD	LIVE AND LET DIE	HAMILTON	UNITED ARTISTS	1973
LD	LIVING DAYLIGHTS	GLEN	UNITED ARTISTS	1987
LD	LOCK UP YOUR DAUGHTERS (UK)	COE	COLUMBIA	1969
LD	LONG DAY'S DYING (UK)	COLLINSON	PARAMOUNT	1968
LD	LONG DUEL (UK)	ANNAKIN	PARAMOUNT	1967
LD	LOUISE DRESSER	portrait		
LD	LOVE AND DEATH	ALLEN	UNITED ARTISTS	1975
LD	LUCKY DEVILS	INCE	RKO	1932
LD	LULI DESTE	portrait	UNIVERSAL	
LD	PRIVATE DETECTIVE	SMITH	WARNER BROS	1939
LD	TRUTH ABOUT MURDER	LANDERS	RKO	1946
L.D-COL-S-1	SHADOW (serial)	HORNE	COLUMBIA	1940
L.D-COL-S-2	TERRY AND THE PIRATES (serial)	HORNE	COLUMBIA	1940

Movie Still Identification Book Ultimate Edition - Letters

CODE	TITLE/NAME	DIRECTOR/TYPE	STUDIO/DISTRIBUTOR	YEAR
L.D-COL-S-3	DEADWOOD DICK (serial)	HORNE	COLUMBIA	1940
L.D-COL-S-4	GREEN ARCHER (serial)	HORNE	COLUMBIA	1940
L.D-COL-S-5	WHITE EAGLE (serial)	HORNE	COLUMBIA	1941
L.D-COL-S-6	SPIDER RETURNS (serial)	HORNE	COLUMBIA	1941
LD-COL-S-7	IRON CLAW	HORNE	COLUMBIA	1941
L.D-COL-S-8	HOLT OF THE SECRET SERVICE (serial)	HORNE	COLUMBIA	1941
L.D-COL-S-10	PERILS OF THE ROYAL MOUNTED (serial)	HORNE	COLUMBIA	1942
L.D-COL-S-11	SECRET CODE (serial)	BENNET	COLUMBIA	1942
L.D-COL-S-13	BATMAN (serial)	HILLYER	COLUMBIA	1943
LD-F1	NO PLACE FOR A LADY	HOGAN	COLUMBIA	1943
LD-F2	CRIME DOCTOR	GORDON	COLUMBIA	1943
LDH	LONG DARK HALL (UK)	BECK, BUSHELL	UNITED ARTISTS	1951
LDIA	LET'S DO IT AGAIN	POITIER	WARNER BROS	1975
LDR	SIGN OF THE GLADIATOR (IT)	BRIGNONE	AIP	1959
LDV	LA DOLCE VITA (IT)	FELLINI	ASTOR	1960
LD-X	LONG DAY'S JOURNEY INTO NIGHT	LUMET	EMBASSY	1962
LE	LAST EMBRACE	DEMME	UNITED ARTISTS	1979
LE	LAST ESCAPE	GRAUMAN	UNITED ARTISTS	1970
LE	LEON ERROL	portrait	FN, PDC, RKO	
LE	LEON ERROL SERIES OF SHORTS	studio	RKO	
LE	LOVE IN EXILE (UK)	WERKER	CAPITOL-GFD	1936
LE	MEXICAN SPITFIRE'S BABY	GOODWINS	RKO	1941
LEB	OBSESSED (UK: LATE EDWINA BLACK)	ELVEY	UNITED ARTISTS	1951
LED	LORD EDGWARE DIES (UK)	EDWARDS	RKO	1934
LEE-11	SILVER TREASURE	LEE	FOX FILM	1926
LEE-12	SILVER TREASURE	LEE	FOX FILM	1926
LED	LEGEND OF EARL DURAND	PATTERSON	HOWCO	1974
LEE-13	ZOO IN BUDAPEST	LEE	FOX FILM	1933
LEH-6	HOMESICK	LEHRMAN	FOX FILM	1928
LEH-8	NEW YEAR'S EVE	LEHRMAN	FOX FILM	1929
LEHR-8	NEW YEAR'S EVE	LEHRMAN	FOX FILM	1929
LEONARD-2787	HER BODY IN BOND	LEONARD	UNIVERSAL	1918
LEOP	LEOPARD (IT: IL GATTOPARDO)	VISCONTI	TITANUS	1963
LEPKE	LEPKE	GOLAN	WARNER BROS	1974
LEX	ALEXIS SMITH	portrait	WARNER BROS	
LF	EARTH DIES SCREAMING (UK)	FISHER	20TH CENTURY FOX	1964
LF	HOLLYWOOD COWBOY	SCOTT	RKO	1937
LF	LAWMAN	WINNER	UNITED ARTISTS	1971
LF	LEONARD FREEMAN	portrait	UNIVERSAL	early 50s
LF	LESLIE FENTON	portrait		
LF	LET'S MAKE MUSIC	GOODWINS	RKO	1941
LF	LIFEFORCE (SPACE VAMPIRES)	HOOPER	TRI STAR	1985
LF	LITTLE FUGITIVE	ASHLEY/ENGEL	BURNSTYN	1953
LF	LIVING FREE	COUFFER	COLUMBIA	1972
LF	LONDON FILMS			
LF	LORD OF THE FLIES (UK)	BROOK	CONTINENTAL	1963
LF	LOUISE FAZENDA	portrait	FN/WARNER BROS	
LF	LOVING FEELING (UK)	WARREN	U-M	1968
LF	LUCILE (LUCILLE) FAIRBANKS	portrait	WARNER BROS	1930s-40s
LF	MAURICE 'LEFTY' FLYNN	portrait	METRO	
LF	SCOTLAND YARD INSPECTOR (UK: LADY IN THE FOG)	NEWFIELD	LIPPERT	1952
LFB	LOVE AT FIRST BITE	DRAGOTI	AIP	1979
LFD	OVER THE MOON (UK)	FREELAND	UNITED ARTISTS	1939
LFH	LADY REFUSES	ARCHAINBAUD	RKO	1931
LFLS	LIKE FATHER LIKE SON	DANIEL	TRI STAR	1987
LFO	LITTLE FOXES	WYLER	RKO	1941
LFP	LONDON FILM PRODUCTION	studio		
LFP-8	ELEPHANT BOY (UK)	FLAHERTY, KORDA	UNITED ARTISTS	1937
LFP-20	I, CLAUDIUS (UK) (unfinished)	VON STERNBERG		1937
LFP-22	KNIGHT WITHOUT ARMOR (UK)	FEYDER	UNITED ARTISTS (UK)	1936
LFP-23	MURDER ON DIAMOND ROW (UK: SQUEAKER)	HOWARD	UNITED ARTISTS	1937
LFP-24	FIRST AND THE LAST (21 DAYS TOGETHER)	DEAN	LONDON FILM	1940
LFP-25	DRUMS (UK: DRUM)	Z. KORDA	UNITED ARTISTS (UK)	1938
LFP-27	GAIETY GIRLS (UK: PARADISE FOR TWO)	FREELAND	UNITED ARTISTS (UK)	1937
LFP-31	DIVORCE OF LADY X (UK)	WHELAN	UNITED ARTISTS (UK)	1938
LFP-32	OVER THE MOON (UK)	FREELAND	UNITED ARTISTS	1939
LFP-33	REBEL SON aka TARAS BULBA (FR/UK)	BRUNEL, DE COURVILLE		1938
LFP-34	PRISON WITHOUT BARS (UK)	HURST	UNITED ARTISTS (UK)	1938
LFP-35	FOUR FEATHERS (UK)	Z. KORDA	UNITED ARTISTS (UK)	1939
LFP-101	AN IDEAL HUSBAND	KORDA	20th CENTURY FOX	1948

Movie Still Identification Book Ultimate Edition - Letters

CODE	TITLE/NAME	DIRECTOR/TYPE	STUDIO/DISTRIBUTOR	YEAR
LFP-102	ANNA KARENINA (UK)	DUVIVIER	20TH CENTURY FOX	1948
LFP-105	ANGEL WITH THE TRUMPET (UK)	BUSHELL	SNADER	1950
LFP-106	DEEP BLUE SEA (UK)	LITVAK	20TH CENTURY FOX	1955
LFP-106	IF THIS BE SIN (UK: THAT DANGEROUS AGE)	RATOFF	UNITED ARTISTS	1949
LFP-107	SMILEY (UK 1956)	KIMMINS	20th CENTURY FOX	1957
LFS	NIGHT OF TERROR (UK: LOVE FROM A STRANGER)	LEE	UNITED ARTISTS	1937
LFX	ALFRED LUNT LYNN FONTANNE	portrait	MGM	
LG	LADY GANGSTER	FLOREY	WARNER BROS	1942
LG	LEO GORCEY	portrait	WARNER BROS	
LG	LIFEGUARD	PETRIE	PARAMOUNT	1976
LG	LILLIAN GISH	portrait	MGM, UNIVERSAL	
LG	LISA GAYE	portrait	UNIVERSAL	
LG	LITTLE GIANT	DEL RUTH	WARNER BROS	1933
LG	LITTLE GIANTS	DUNHAM	WARNER BROS	1994
LG	LORRAINE/LORAINE GETTMAN (aka LESLIE BROOKS)	portrait	WARNER BROS	
LG	LOVE GODDESSES: HISTORY OF SEX IN CINEMA	TURELL	PARAMOUNT	1965
LG	PAYOFF	SHERMAN	RKO	1930
LG-30	LOVE'S YOUNG SCREAM	JEFFERSON	PATHE EXCHANGE	1919
LG-2500	ONE ROMANTIC NIGHT	STEIN	UNITED ARTISTS	1930
LGB	LOOKING FOR MR. GOODBAR	BROOKS	PARAMOUNT	1977
LGF	LONG GOOD FRIDAY	MCKENZIE	EMBASSY	1982
LGH	LET'S GET HARRY	ROSENBERG (SMITHEE)	TRI STAR	1986
LG/T/15	LEAGUE OF GENTLEMEN (UK)	DEARDEN	KINGSLEY-INTERNATIONAL	1960
LH	BIG FRAME (UK: LOST HOURS)	MACDONALD	RKO	1952
LH	KAY HARDING (NEE JACKIE LOU HARDING)	portrait	UNIVERSAL	
LH	LAURENCE HARVEY	portrait	HAL WALLIS PRODS	
LH	LAW IN HER HANDS	CLEMENS	WARNER BROS	1936
LH	LEILA HYAMS	portrait	WARNER BROS	late 20s
LH	LESLIE HOWARD	portrait	WARNER BROS	
LH	LEWIS HOWARD	portrait	UNIVERSAL	1930s-40s
LH	LEZA HOLLAND	portrait	RKO	late 40s
LH	LILIAN HARVEY	portrait	FOX	
LH	LINDA HAYES	portrait	RKO	
LH	LITTLEST HOBO	RONDEAU	ALLIED ARTISTS	1958
LH	LLOYD HUGHES	portrait	FN	
LH	LOEW-HAKIM PRODUCTIONS	studio		
LH	LONELYHEARTS (MISS LONELYHEART)	DONEHUE	UNITED ARTISTS	1958
LH	LOST HORIZON	JARROTT	COLUMBIA	1973
LH	LOUISIANA HUSSY	SHOLEM	HOWCO	1959
LH	LOVE HAPPY	MILLER	UNITED ARTISTS	1949
LH	LOYAL HEART (UK)	MITCHELL	ANGLO-AMERICAN	1946
LH	SOUTHERNER	RENOIR	UNITED ARTISTS	1945
LH-1	SPITFIRE (UK: FIRST OF THE FEW)	HOWARD	RKO	1943
LHL	LOVERS,HAPPY LOVERS! (UK: LOVER BOY) (KNAVE OF HEARTS)	CLEMENT	AFE	1954
LHX	LARS HANSON	portrait	MGM	
LHXX	LEILA HYAMS	portrait	MGM	
LI	ABE LINCOLN IN ILLINOIS	CROMWELL	RKO	1940
LI	FEMALE AND THE FLESH (FR: LIGHT ACROSS THE STREET)	LACOMBE	UMPO	R60
LI	LIVING ON LOVE	LANDERS	RKO	1937
LI	LOVE-INS	DREIFUSS	COLUMBIA	1967
LIB	LET IT BE (UK)	LINDSAY-HOGG	UNITED ARTISTS	1970
LIB-A	EX-FLAME	HALPERIN	LIBERTY	1930
LIM	LAND OF MINOTAUR	KARAGIANNUS	CROWN INTL	1977
LIP3	BOTH SIDES OF THE LAW (UK: STREET CORNER)	BOX	UNIVERSAL	1953
LIQ	LIQUIDATOR (UK)	CARDIFF	MGM	1965
LIW	LION IN WINTER (UK)	HARVEY	AVCO EMBASSY	1968
LJ	LEATRICE JOY	portrait	UNIVERSAL	
LJ	LEMONADE JOE (CZ)	LIPSKY	MONOGRAM	1967
LJ	LEON JANNEY	portrait	WARNER BROS	
LJ	LES JOHNSON	portrait	WARNER BROS	mid 50s
LJ	LORD JIM (UK)	BROOKS	COLUMBIA	1965
LJ	LOUIS JOURDAN	portrait	SELZNICK, UNIVERSAL	
LJ	LUCKY JIM (UK)	BOULTING	KINGSLEY INTL	1957
LK	LORRAINE KRUEGER	portrait		
LK	LOUISE KING (KING SISTERS)	portrait	UNIV	
L KING-1	ROBBERS ROOST	L KING	FOX FILM	1932
LL	BASTARD (TV)	KATZIN	UNIVERSAL-TV	1978
LL	BLONDE CRAZY	DEL RUTH	WARNER BROS	1931
LL	FAMILY AFFAIR (UK: LIFE WITH THE LYONS)	GUEST	LIPPERT	1954
LL	HE COULDN'T SAY NO	SEILER	WARNER BROS	1938

Movie Still Identification Book Ultimate Edition - Letters

CODE	TITLE/NAME	DIRECTOR/TYPE	STUDIO/DISTRIBUTOR	YEAR
LL	LADIES MUST LIVE	SMITH	WARNER BROS	1940
LL	LADY LIBERTY (IT: MORTADELLA)	MONICELLI	UNITED ARTISTS	1971
LL	LADY LUCK	MARIN	RKO	1946
LL	LADY VANISHES (UK)	HITCHCOCK	GAUMONT PICTURES (UA)	1938
LL	LADYBUG LADYBUG	PERRY	UNITED ARTISTS	1963
LL	LANCASHITE LUCK (UK)	CASS	PARAMOUNT BRITISH	1937
LL	LAUGHING LADY (UK)	STEIN	FOUR CONTINENTS	1946
LL	LAURA LA PLANTE	portrait		
LL	LAWFUL LARCENY	SHERMAN	RKO	1930
LL	LEGEND OF THE LOST	HATHAWAY	UNITED ARTISTS	1957
LL	LENI LYNN	portrait		
LL	LEO AND LOREE	PARIS	UNITED ARTISTS	1980
LL	LESSON IN LOVE (SWE: EN LEKTION IN KARLEK)	BERGMAN	JANUS	1954
LL	LIFE WITH THE LYONS (UK) (FAMILY AFFAIR 1955)	GUEST	LIPPERT	1954
LL	LILA LEE	portrait	WARNER BROS	
LL	LILA LEEDS	portrait		
LL	LITTLE MISS THOROUGHBRED	FARROW	WARNER BROS	1938
LL	LOEW-LEWIN PRODUCTIONS	studio		
LL	LOLA LANE	portrait	TIFFANY, WARNER BROS	
LL	LONELINESS OF THE LONG DISTANCE RUNNER (UK)	RICHARDSON	CONTINENTAL	1962
LL	LORENA LAYSON/DANKER MAYER/LORENA MAYER NIDORF	portrait	WARNER BROS	
LL	LOST LADY	GREEN	FIRST NATIONAL	1934
LL	LOST LAGOON	RAWLINS	UNITED ARTISTS	1958
LL	LOUISE LATIMER	portrait	RKO	
LL	LOVE LINES	AMATEAU	TRI STAR	1984
LL	LUCKY LUCIANO	ROSI	AVCO EMBASSY	1973
LL	LUCKY LUKE (t) (FR)	GOSCINNY, GRUEL	DISNEY	1978
LL	NAUGHTY BUT NICE	ENRIGHT	WARNER BROS	1939
LL	PERSONAL MAID'S SECRET	COLLINS	WARNER BROS	1935
LL	PRIVATE AFFAIRS OF BEL AMI (WOMEN OF PARIS R1953)	LEWIN	UNITED ARTISTS	1947
LL	VOICE OF SCANDAL (HERE COMES CARTER)	CLEMENS	FIRST NATIONAL	1936
LL	WHITE BONDAGE	GRINDE	WARNER BROS	1937
LL	WINE WOMEN AND HORSES	KING	WARNER BROS	1937
LL-16	EAST LYNNE	LLOYD	FOX FILM	1931
LL-17	PASSPORT TO HELL	LLOYD	FOX FILM	1932
LL-18	CAVALCADE	LLOYD	FOX FILM	1933
L.L.101	SO ENDS OUR NIGHT	CROMWELL	UNITED ARTISTS	1941
LL-7301	MOON AND SIXPENCE	LEWIN	UNITED ARTISTS	1942
L-LADY	LOST LADY	BEAUMONT	WARNER BROS	1924
LLD	DANGEROUS LIAISONS	FREARS	WARNER BROS	1988
LLD	LORD LOVE A DUCK	AXELROD	UNITED ARTISTS	1966
LLE	LADIES CRAVE EXCITEMENT	GRINDE	MASCOT	1935
LLF	LONG LOST FATHER	SCHOEDSACK	RKO	1934
LLL	LOVE, LIFE & LAUGHTER (UK)	ELVEY	ABFD	1934
LLOYD	ALMA LLOYD	portrait	WARNER BROS	
LLOYD-1015	LITTLE GIRL OF THE ATTIC	LLOYD	UNIVERSAL	1915
LLX	LOUISE LORRAINE	portrait	MGM	
LM	BACHELOR MOTHER	KANIN	RKO	1939
LM	CAPTIVE HEART (UK)	DEARDEN	UNIVERSAL	1946
LM	DON'T GO NEAR THE WATER	WALTERS	MGM	1957
LM	FILMS LOUIS MERCANTON	studio		
LM	GIRL IN THE STREET (UK: LONDON MELODY)	WILCOX	GAUMONT BRITISH AMERICA	1937
LM	LADY WITH THE RED HAIR	BERNHARDT	WARNER BROS	1941
LM	LAST MILE	KOCH	UNITED ARTISTS	1959
LM	LAST OF THE MOHICANS	MANN	20th CENTURY FOX	1992
LM	LAWYER MAN	DIETERLE	WARNER BROS	1932
LM	LEOPARD MAN	TOURNEUR	RKO	1943
LM	LESLIE MORRIS	portrait	RKO	
LM	LILI MARLEEN (GER)	FASSBINDER	UNITED ARTISTS	1981
LM	LILI MARLENE (UK)	CRABTREE	RKO	1951
LM	LIMPING MAN (UK)	SUMMERS	PATHE	1936
LM	LIMPING MAN (UK)	ENDFIELD	LIPPERT	1953
LM	LINDA MARSH	portrait	WARNER BROS	
LM	LION AND THE MOUSE	BACON	WARNER BROS	1928
LM	LISA MONTELL	portrait	BOGEAS-RKO	
LM	LITTLE MEN	ROSEN	MASCOT	1934
LM	LITTLE MINISTER	WALLACE	RKO	1934
LM	LITTLE MONSTERS	GREENBERG	UNITED ARTISTS	1989
LM	LORRAIN/LORETTA MILLER (aka LORRAINE MICHIE)	portrait	UNIVERSAL	1940s
LM	LOVE MACHINE	HALEY JR.	COLUMBIA	1971

Movie Still Identification Book Ultimate Edition - Letters

CODE	TITLE/NAME	DIRECTOR/TYPE	STUDIO/DISTRIBUTOR	YEAR
LM	LOVIN' MOLLY	LUMET	COLUMBIA	1974
LM	LUBA MOLINA (aka LUBA MALINA)	portrait	UNIVERSAL	late 40s
LM	LUCY MARLOW (aka LUCY ANN MCALEER)	portrait	WARNER BROS	mid 50s
LM	MINOTAUR, THE WILD BEAST OF CRETE	AMADIO	UNITED ARTISTS	1960
LM	NIGHT IN CASABLANCA	MAYO	UNITED ARTISTS	1946
LM	TOP OF THE WORLD	FOSTER	UNITED ARTISTS	1955
LM	UP GOES MAISIE	BEAUMONT	MGM	1946
LM	WEDDING OF LILLI MARLENE (UK)	CRABTREE	MONARCH	1953
LM48	ADA	MANN	MGM	1961
LM228	JOHN HODIAK	portrait	MGM	
LM1046	ANN SOTHERN	portrait	MGM	
LM-1699	RICHARD CARLSON	portrait	MGM	
LM2573	JUNE ALLYSON	portrait	MGM	
LM2797	MAY WHITTY	portrait	MGM	
LM3057	FRANK MORGAN	portrait	MGM	
LM4831	WALTER PIDGEON	portrait	MGM	
LM8471	VAN JOHNSON	portrait	MGM	
LM8587	ELIZABETH TAYLOR	portrait	MGM	
LM8879	RICARDO MONTALBAN	portrait	MGM	
LM9407	JUNE ALLYSON	portrait	MGM	
LM10314	MICKEY ROONEY	portrait	MGM	
LM14363	JOHN HODIAK	portrait	MGM	
LM16391	NANCY DAVIS/REAGAN	portrait	MGM	
LM16511	ARLENE DAHL	portrait	MGM	
LM16512	ARLENE DAHL	portrait	MGM	
LM16695	KATHRYN GRAYSON	portrait	MGM	
LM16965	HOWARD KEEL	portrait	MGM	
LM16965	HOWARD KEEL	portrait	MGM	
LM16966	HOWARD KEEL	portrait	MGM	
LM16966	HOWARD KEEL	portrait	MGM	
LM16967	HOWARD KEEL	portrait	MGM	
LM17140	ELIZABETH TAYLOR	portrait	MGM	
LM17141	ELIZABETH TAYLOR	portrait	MGM	
LM17159	ELIZABETH TAYLOR	portrait	MGM	
LM17671	JUNE ALLYSON	portrait	MGM	
LM17672	JUNE ALLYSON	portrait	MGM	
LM18045	STEWART GRANGER	portrait	MGM	
LM18582	ANN HARDING	portrait	MGM	
LM18658	PIER ANGELI	portrait	MGM	
LM18693	PIER ANGELI	portrait	MGM	
LM18694	PIER ANGELI	portrait	MGM	
LM18696	PIER ANGELI	portrait	MGM	
LM18698	PIER ANGELI	portrait	MGM	
LM18815	MONICA LEWIS	portrait	MGM	
LM19341	DEBBIE REYNOLDS	portrait	MGM	
LM19471	ELIZABETH TAYLOR	portrait	MGM	
LM19622	LANA TURNER	portrait	MGM	
LM19627	ESTHER WILLIAMS	portrait	MGM	
LM19635	KEENAN WYNN	portrait	MGM	
LM19671	LANA TURNER	portrait	MGM	
LM19783	VAN JOHNSON	portrait	MGM	
LM19933	AVA GARDNER	portrait	MGM	
LM20060	LANA TURNER	portrait	MGM	
LM20168	AVA GARDNER	portrait	MGM	
LM20193	DIANA LYNN	portrait	MGM	
LM20363	GENE KELLY	portrait	MGM	
LM20385	FERNANDO LAMAS	portrait	MGM	
LM20567	JANET LEIGH	portrait	MGM	
LM20589	LESLIE CARON	portrait	MGM	
LM22051	DEBBIE REYNOLDS	portrait	MGM	
LM22051	DEBBIE REYNOLDS	portrait	MGM	
LM22674	JANET LEIGH	portrait	MGM	
LM22954	FERNANDO LAMAS	portrait	MGM	
LM25102	ESTHER WILLIAMS	portrait	MGM	
LM25300	JEAN HAGEN	portrait	MGM	
LM25302	JEAN HAGEN	portrait	MGM	
LM25312	ESTHER WILLIAMS	portrait	MGM	
LM25770	DAWN ADDAMS	portrait	MGM	
LM25771	DAWN ADDAMS	portrait	MGM	
LM25912	LESLIE CARON	portrait	MGM	

Movie Still Identification Book Ultimate Edition - Letters

CODE	TITLE/NAME	DIRECTOR/TYPE	STUDIO/DISTRIBUTOR	YEAR
LM26230	ESTHER WILLIAMS	portrait	MGM	
LM26519	LESLIE CARON - LILI	portrait	MGM	
LM26691	JEAN SIMMONS	portrait	MGM	
LM26731	ESTHER WILLIAMS	portrait	MGM	
LM27226	GRACE KELLY	portrait	MGM	
LM27387	ROBERT TAYLOR	portrait	MGM	
LM27392	ROBERT TAYLOR	portrait	MGM	
LM27394	ROBERT TAYLOR	portrait	MGM	
LM27644	GENE TIERNEY	portrait	MGM	
LM27645	ELAINE STEWART	portrait	MGM	
LM27645	ELAINE STEWART	portrait	MGM	
LM28052	DEBBIE REYNOLDS	portrait	MGM	
LM28247	LESLIE CARON - LILI	portrait	MGM	
LM28882	ELAINE STEWART	portrait	MGM	
LM28888	ELAINE STEWART	portrait	MGM	
LM28893	ELAINE STEWART	portrait	MGM	
LM28955	LESLIE CARON	portrait	MGM	
LM29246	LESLIE CARON	portrait	MGM	
LM29421	ANN BLYTH	portrait	MGM	
LM30162	ESTHER WILLIAMS	portrait	MGM	
LM30198	JEAN SIMMONS	portrait	MGM	
LM30382	ELAINE STEWART	portrait	MGM	
LM30410	ELAINE STEWART	portrait	MGM	
LM31865	GENE KELLY	portrait	MGM	
LM32680	JANE POWELL	portrait	MGM	
LM32816	ELEANOR PARKER	portrait	MGM	
LM33056	GENE KELLY	portrait	MGM	
LM33068	GREER GARSON, DONNA CORCORAN, CLAIRE SOMBERT	portrait	MGM	
LM33689	ELAINE STEWART	portrait	MGM	
LM33743	DONNA REED	portrait	MGM	
LM34442	ROBERT TAYLOR	portrait	MGM	
LM34526	ELAINE STEWART	portrait	MGM	
LM35636	JANE POWELL	portrait	MGM	
LM35952	ANNE FRANCIS	portrait	MGM	
LM35952	ANNE FRANCIS	portrait	MGM	
LM35956	ANNE FRANCIS	portrait	MGM	
LM36084	WALTER PIDGEON	portrait	MGM	
LM36087	WALTER PIDGEON	portrait	MGM	
LM36097	WALTER PIDGEON	portrait	MGM	
LM36098	WALTER PIDGEON	portrait	MGM	
LM36818	JANE POWELL	portrait	MGM	
LM37456	CYD CHARISSE	portrait	MGM	
LM37467	LAUREN BACALL	portrait	MGM	
LM37601	LANA TURNER	portrait	MGM	
LM38043	LANA TURNER	portrait	MGM	
LM38061	DARLEEN ENGLE	portrait	MGM	
LM41177	CYD CHARISSE	portrait	MGM	
LM41323	RUBY DEE	portrait	MGM	
LM41543	GRACE KELLY	portrait	MGM	
LM42367	MITZI GAYNOR	portrait	MGM	
LM43154	JEAN SIMMONS	portrait	MGM	
LM43155	JEAN SIMMONS	portrait	MGM	
LM43938	ELIZABETH TAYLOR	portrait	MGM	
LM43979	JEAN SIMMONS	portrait	MGM	
LM44028	SANDRA DEE	portrait	MGM	
LM44035	SANDRA DEE	portrait	MGM	
LM44145	JULIE LONDON	portrait	MGM	
LM44530	LESLIE CARON - GIGI	portrait	MGM	
LM47361	ELIZABETH TAYLOR	portrait	MGM	
LMBB	LITTLE MERMAID	CLEMENTS	BUENA VISTA	1989
LMG	LEE MACGREGOR	portrait	RKO	early 50s
LMN	LITTLE MEN	MCLEOD	RKO	1941
LMS	NIGHT IN CASABLANCA	MAYO	UNITED ARTISTS	1946
LN	I LIKE YOUR NERVE	MCGANN	WARNER BROS	1931
LA	LA NOTTE (IT/FR: 1961)	ANTONIONI	LOPERT	1962
LN	LADIES THEY TALK ABOUT	BRETHERTON	WARNER BROS	1933
LN	LEATHERNECKING	CLINE	RKO	1930
LN	LORI NELSON	portrait	WARNER BROS	
LNPL	LIVE NOW, PAY LATER (UK)	LEWIS	REGAL	1962
LO	DAY OF THE OUTLAW	DE TOTH	UNITED ARTISTS	1959

Movie Still Identification Book Ultimate Edition - Letters

CODE	TITLE/NAME	DIRECTOR/TYPE	STUDIO/DISTRIBUTOR	YEAR
LO	LAST OUTLAW	CABANNE	RKO	1936
LO	LAURENCE OLIVIER	portrait	UNIVERSAL	
LO	LEGION OF THE LAWLESS	HOWARD	RKO	1940
LO	LIFE OF THE PARTY	SEITER	RKO	1937
LO	LITTLE ONES (UK)	O'CONNOLLY	COLUMBIA	1965
LO	LITTLE ORVIE	MCCAREY	RKO	1940
LO	LOTTI LODER	portrait	WARNER BROS	1930s
LO	TRUTH ABOUT MURDER	LANDERS	RKO	1946
LOD	LAST OF THE DESPERADOS	NEWFIELD	ASSOCIATED FILM	1956
LOD	LAUGH IT OFF (UK)	BAXTER, ORTON	ANGLO-AMERICAN	1940
LOD	LOVE ON THE DOLE (UK)	BAXTER	UNITED ARTISTS	1941
LOD	SAVE A LITTLE SUNSHINE (UK)	LEE	PATHE	1938
LOF	LILIES OF THE FIELD	NELSON	UNITED ARTISTS	1963
LOF	LORD OF THE FLIES (UK)	BROOK	CONTINENTAL	1963
LOFTJ	LADIES OF THE JURY	SHERMAN	RKO	1931
LOLA	LOLA	FASSBINDER	UNITED ARTISTS	1981
LON	LEGIONS OF THE NILE	COTTAFAVI	20th CENTURY FOX	1960
LOS	CHEYENNE KID	HILL	RKO	1932
LOT	LAND OF THE OPEN RANGE	KILLY	RKO	1943
LOV	LOVING	KERSHNER	COLUMBIA	1970
LP	FIRST LEGION	SIRK	UNITED ARTISTS	1951
LP	I DREAM TOO MUCH	CROMWELL	RKO	1935
LP	LADY WITH A PAST	GRIFFITH	RKO	1932
LP	LAST DAYS OF POMPEII	BONNARD	UNITED ARTISTS	1959
LP	LAST PAGE/US: MAN BAIT (UK)	FISHER	LIPPERT	1952
LP	LAURA LA PLANTE	portrait	UNIV	
LP	LEE PATRICK	portrait	RKO	
LP	LEE PATRICK	portrait	WARNER BROS	
LP	LILLI PALMER	portrait	WARNER BROS et al	
LP	LILO PULVER	portrait	UNIV	
LP	LILY PONS	portrait	RKO	1930s
LP	LINDA PERRY	portrait	WARNER BROS	
LP	LINDSLEY PARSONS PRODUCTIONS	studio		
LP	LIPSTICK	JOHNSON	PARAMOUNT	1976
LP	LITTLE PRINCE	DONEN	PARAMOUNT	1974
LP	LOST PATROL	FORD	RKO	1933
LP	LUANA PATTEN	portrait	UNIV	
LP	SAY IT WITH SONGS	BACON	WARNER BROS	1929
LP	SING ME A LOVE SONG	ENRIGHT	WARNER BROS	1936
LP	THREE WOMEN	LUBITSCH	WARNER BROS	1924
LP-702	PORTLAND EXPOSE	SCHUSTER	ALLIED ARTISTS	1957
LPS	LAST PICTURE SHOW	BOGDANOVICH	COLUMBIA	1971
LPS	LIPSTICK	JOHNSON	PARAMOUNT	1976
LQ	BURN! (QUEIMADA)	PONTECORVO	UNITED ARTISTS	1969
LR	GUNS OF THE PECOS	SMITH	WARNER BROS	1937
LR	LAST RITES	BELLISARIO	MGM	1988
LR	LET'S ROCK	FOSTER	COLUMBIA	1958
LR	LITTLE ROMANCE	HILL	WARNER BROS	1979
LR	LONG RIDERS	HILL	UNITED ARTISTS	1980
LR	LONG ROPE	WITNEY	20th CENTURY FOX	1961
LR	LONG ROPE (UK: LARGE ROPE)	RILLA	UNITED ARTISTS	1953
LR	LOVE IS A RACKET	WELLMAN	WARNER BROS	1932
LR	LUISE RAINER	portrait	MGM	
LR	ROOKIE	O'HANLON	20th CENTURY FOX	1959
LR	SCOTLAND YARD COMMANDS (UK: LONELY ROAD)	FLOOD	GRAND	1937
LRH	TIME FOR KILLING	KARLSON	COLUMBIA	1967
LR-O	LONE RANGER AND THE LOST CITY OF GOLD	SELANDER	UNITED ARTISTS	1958
LRRH	LITTLE RED RIDING HOOD	RODRIGUEZ	J. GORDON MURRAY	1963
LS	CRIME OF PASSION	OSWALD	UNITED ARTISTS	1957
LS	DESIRABLE	MAYO	WARNER BROS	1934
LS	FLESH IS WEAK (UK)	CHAFFEY	EROS	1957
LS	I COULD GO ON SINGING (UK)	NEAME	UNITED ARTISTS	1963
LS	I DREAM TOO MUCH	CROMWELL	RKO	1935
LS	LADY SCARFACE	WOODRUFF	RKO	1941
LS	LADY SURRENDERS (UK: LOVE STORY)	ARLISS	UNIVERSAL	1944
LS	LANE WATSON	portrait		
LS	LAST SAFARI (UK)	HATHAWAY	PARAMOUNT	1967
LS	LAST SUMMER	PERRY	ALLIED ARTISTS	1969
LS	LEIGH SNOWDEN	portrait	UNIVERSAL	
LS	LEWIS STONE	portrait	MGM	

Movie Still Identification Book Ultimate Edition - Letters

CODE	TITLE/NAME	DIRECTOR/TYPE	STUDIO/DISTRIBUTOR	YEAR
LS	LIGHTNING STRIKES TWICE	HOLMES	RKO	1934
LS	LINDA STERLING	portrait	REPUBLIC	
LS	LION IS IN THE STREETS	WALSH	WARNER BROS	1953
LS	LISBON STORY (UK)	STEIN	FOUR CONTINENTS	1946
LS	LITTLE BIG SHOT	CURTIZ	WARNER BROS	1935
LS	LITTLE SAVAGE	HASKIN	20th CENTURY FOX	1959
LS	LITTLE SHEPHERD OF KINGDOM COME	MCLAGLEN	20th CENTURY FOX	1961
LS	LIZABETH SCOTT	portrait	RKO	
LS	LOAN SHARK	FRIEDMAN	LIPPERT	1952
LS	LONG SHIPS (UK)	CARDIFF	COLUMBIA	1964
LS	LOST SQUADRON	ARCHAINBAUD	RKO	1932
LS	LOUISE STANLEY	portrait	UNIVERSAL	late 30s
LS	LOVE IS A FUNNY THING (FR)	LELOUCH	UNITED ARTISTS	1969
LS	LOVE SPECIALIST	ZAMPA	MEDALLION	1959
LS	LOVE STREAMS	CASSAVETTES	CANNON	1983
LS	LURE OF THE SWAMP	CORNFIELD	20th CENTURY FOX	1957
LS	MISSISSIPPI MERMAID (FR: LA SIRENE DU MISSISSIPPI)	TRUFFAUT	UNITED ARTISTS	1969
LS	TEMPTRESS (UK)	MITCHELL	AMBASSADOR	1949
LS	WHILE LONDON SLEEPS	BRETHERTON	WARNER BROS	1926
LS20	SISTER TO SALOME	LESAINT	FOX FILM	1920
LSB	LADY SINGS THE BLUES	FURIE	PARAMOUNT	1972
LSB-5113	LADY SINGS THE BLUES	FURIE	PARAMOUNT	1972
LSD	LIGHTNING SWORDS OF DEATH (JAP)	MISUMI	COLUMBIA	1972
LSD	SHE DEVIL	NEUMANN	20th CENTURY FOX	1957
LSP	LONE STAR PIONEERS	LEVERING	ASTOR	R48
LSR	L-SHAPED ROOM (UK)	FORBES	COLUMBIA	1962
LSYH	LAST SHOT YOU HEAR (UK)	HESSLER	20TH CENTURY FOX	1969
LT	HOUR OF THE GUN	STURGES	UNITED ARTISTS	1967
LT	LANA TURNER	portrait	UNIVERSAL, WARNER BROS	
LT	LAST ONE		COLUMBIA	
LT	LAST TANGO IN PARIS (IT)	BERTOLUCCI	UNITED ARTISTS	1972
LT	LAST TIME I SAW ARCHIE	WEBB	UNITED ARTISTS	1961
LT	LAURETTE TAYLOR	portrait	MGM	
LT	LAWRENCE TIERNEY	portrait	RKO	1940s-50s
LT	LEE TRACY	portrait	RKO	1930s-40s
LT	LIFE AT THE TOP (UK)	KOTCHEFF	ROYAL	1965
LT	LILLY TURNER	WELLMAN	WARNER BROS	1933
LT	LITTLE TREASURE	SHARP	TRI STAR	1985
LT	LONDON TOWN (UK) (US: MY HEART GOES CRAZY)	RUGGLES	UNITED ARTISTS	1946
LT	LOUISIANA TERRITORY	SMITH	RKO	1953
LT	LOVE BEGINS AT TWENTY	MCDONALD	WARNER BROS	1936
LT	LOVE TEST (UK)	POWELL	FOX	1935
LT	LUDMILLA TCHERINA	portrait	UNIVERSAL	
LT	TERRIBLE BEAUTY	GARNETT	UNITED ARTISTS	1961
LTA	LOSER TAKES ALL (UK)	ANNAKIN	DCA	1956
LTK	LICENCE TO KILL	GLEN	UNITED ARTISTS	1989
LTL	LARGER THAN LIFE	FRANKLIN	UNITED ARTISTS	1996
LTP	UNHOLY WIFE	FARROW	UNIVERSAL	1957
LTX	LAWRENCE TIBBETT	portrait	MGM	
LU	LAUGHTER IN THE DARK (UK)	RICHARDSON	LOPERT	1969
LU	LENORE ULRIC	portrait	MGM	
LUB1	MARRIAGE CIRCLE	LUBITSCH	WARNER BROS	1924
LUPO	LUPO (ISRAEL 1970)	GOLAN	CANNON	1971
LUV	LUV	DONNOR	COLUMBIA	1967
LV	LADY OF VENGEANCE (UK)	BALABAN	UNITED ARTISTS	1957
LV	LAWLESS VALLEY	HOWARD	RKO	1938
LV	LEAVING LAS VEGAS	FIGGIS	UNITED ARTISTS	1995
LV	LESTER VAIL	portrait	MGM	
LV	LEVIATHAN	COSMATOS	MGM	1989
LV	LIVING ON VELVET	BORZAGE	WARNER BROS	1935
LV	LUPE VELEZ	portrait	RKO, UNIVERSAL	
LV	NIGHT IN CASABLANCA	MAYO	UNITED ARTISTS	1946
LVBY	LOVERBOY	SILVER	TRI STAR	1989
LVL	LINDA VAN LOON	portrait	RKO	
LVS	LAS VEGAS STORY	STEVENSON	RKO	1952
LW	LAST WALTZ	SCORSESE	UNITED ARTISTS	1978
LW	LAUGHING WOMAN (IT)	SCHIVAZAPPA	AUDUBON	1969
LW	LAW WEST OF TOMBSTONE	TRYON	RKO	1938
LW	LETHAL WEAPON	DONNOR	WARNER BROS	1987
LW	LITTLE WOMEN	CUKOR	RKO	1933

Movie Still Identification Book Ultimate Edition - Letters

CODE	TITLE/NAME	DIRECTOR/TYPE	STUDIO/DISTRIBUTOR	YEAR
LW	LOIS WILSON	portrait	FN	
LW	LONE WOLF MCQUADE	CARVER	ORION	1983
LW	LONG WAIT	SAVILLE	UNITED ARTISTS	1954
LW2	LETHAL WEAPON 2	DONNOR	WARNER BROS	1989
LW3	LETHAL WEAPON 3	DONNOR	WARNER BROS	1992
LW4	LETHAL WEAPON 4	DONNOR	WARNER BROS	1998
LWD	LADIES WHO DO (UK)	PENNINGTON-RICHARDS	CONTINENTAL	1963
LWF	LADY WINDERMERE'S FAN	LUBITSCH	WARNER BROS	1925
LWFC	LIKE WATER FOR CHOCOLATE (MEX: COMO ... CHOCOLATE)	ARAU	MIRAMAX	1992
LWG	LUDWIG (IT)	VISCONTI	MGM	1972
LWH	LAST OF THE WILD HORSES	LIPPERT	SCREEN GUILD	1948
LWT	LOOK WHO'S LAUGHING	DWAN	RKO	1941
L-X	LUNA (IT)	BERTOLUCCI	20th CENTURY FOX	1979
LXA	LEW AYRES	portrait	MGM	
LXB	LORRAINE BRIDGES	portrait	MGM	
LXBX	LEE BOWMAN	portrait	MGM	
LXC	LYNNE CARVER	portrait	MGM	
LXCX	LEO CARRILLO	portrait	MGM	
LXD	LARAINE DAY	portrait	MGM	
LXGX	LAWRENCE GRAY	portrait	MGM	
LXH	LOTTICE HOWELL	portrait	MGM	early 30s
LXHX	LEILA HYAMS	portrait	MGM	1920s-40s
LXT	LANA TURNER	portrait	MGM	
LXT	LEE TRACY	portrait	MGM	
LXX	I WALKED WITH A ZOMBIE	TOURNEUR	RKO	1943
LY	DOWN TO THEIR LAST YACHT	SLOANE	RKO	1934
LY	LORETTA YOUNG	portrait	COL, UNIVERSAL, WB	
LY	LORETTA YOUNG	portrait	MGM, RKO	
LY	LOYALTIES (UK)	DEAN, DICKINSON	HAROLD AUTEN	1933
LY	SHE HAD TO SAY YES	AMY, BERKELEY	FIRST NATIONAL	1933
LYS	LYA LYS	portrait	WARNER BROS	
LZ	LATITUDE ZERO (JAP)	HONDA	NATIONAL GENERAL PIC.	1969
LZ	LIZZIE	HAAS	MGM	1957
M	200 MOTELS	PALMER, ZAPPA	UNITED ARTISTS	1971
M	ANGEL FACE	PREMINGER	RKO	1953
M	BEYOND MOMBASA (UK)	MARSHALL	COLUMBIA	1956
M	CANDLES AT NINE (UK)	HARLOW	ANGLO-AMERICAN	1944
M	GAMBLER AND THE LADY (UK)	JENKINS	LIPPERT	1952
M	HEART OF MARYLAND	BACON	WARNER BROS	1927
M	HORSE'S MOUTH (UK)	NEAME	UNITED ARTISTS	1958
M	M	LANG	FOREMCO	1933
M	M	LOSEY	COLUMBIA	1951
M	M'LISS	NICHOLS JR.	RKO	1936
M	MACABRE	CASTLE	ALLIED ARTISTS	1958
M	MACAO	VON STERNBERG	RKO	1952
M	MACHETE	NEUMANN	UNITED ARTISTS	1958
M	MADEMOISELLE (UK)	RICHARDSON	UNITED ARTISTS	1966
M	MAHOGANY	GORDY	PARAMOUNT	1975
M	MAMMY	CURTIZ	WARNER BROS	1930
M	MAN INSIDE (UK)	GILLING	COLUMBIA	1958
M	MANIA (UK: FLESH AND THE FIENDS)	GILLING	VALIANT	1960
M	MARGO		RKO	
M	MAROONED	STURGES	COLUMBIA	1969
M	MARTY	MANN	UNITED ARTISTS	1955
M	MASQUERADE (UK)	DEARDEN	UNITED ARTISTS	1965
M	MASSACRE	CROSLAND	WARNER BROS	1934
M	MASSACRE	KING	20th CENTURY FOX	1956
M	MASSACRE AT GRAND CANYON (IT)	BAND, CORBUCCI	COLUMBIA	1965
M	MATCHLESS	LATAUADA	UNITED ARTISTS	1967
M	MATEWAN	SAYLES	CINECOM	1987
M	MATRIMONIAL BED	CURTIZ	WARNER BROS.	1930
M	MAURICE	IVORY	CINECOM	1987
M	MAVERICK	DONNER	WARNER BROS	1994
M	MAYERLING (UK)	YOUNG	MGM	1968
M	MCGUIRE, GO HOME! (UK: HIGH BRIGHT SUN)	THOMAS	CONTINENTAL	1964
M	MELBA (UK)	MILESTONE	UNITED ARTISTS	1953
M	METEOR MAN	TOWNSEND	MGM	1993
M	MIKADO (UK)	SCHERTZINGER	UNIVERSAL	1939
M	MILLENNIUM	ANDERSON	20th CENTURY FOX	1989
M	MILLIE	DILLON	RKO	1930

Movie Still Identification Book Ultimate Edition - Letters

CODE	TITLE/NAME	DIRECTOR/TYPE	STUDIO/DISTRIBUTOR	YEAR
M	MIMI (UK)	STEIN	UNITED ARTISTS	1935
M	MIRACLE ON 34TH STREET	MAYFIELD	UNITED ARTISTS	1994
M	MITCHELL	MCLAGLEN	ALLIED ARTISTS	1975
M	MOONRAKER	GILBERT	UNITED ARTISTS	1979
M	MORALS OF MARCUS (UK)	MANDER	GAUMONT BRITISH	1935
M	MOTHRA (JAP: MOSURA)	HONDA	COLUMBIA	1961
M	MOUTHPIECE	FLOOD, NUGENT	WARNER BROS	1932
M	MOVITA			
M	MOZAMBIQUE (UK)	LYNN	SEVEN ARTS	1965
M	MURDER IN THE BIG HOUSE	EASON	WARNER BROS	1942
M	MURIEL OR TIME OF RETURN (FR: MURIEL OU LE TEMPS D'UN	RESNAIS	LOPERT	1963
M	MURIETTA		WARNER BROS	
M	MUSTANG	GRIES	UNITED ARTISTS	1959
M	MUTATIONS	CARDIFF	COLUMBIA	1974
M	MUTINY	DMYTRYK	UNITED ARTISTS	1952
M	RED RIVER	HAWKS	UNITED ARTISTS	1948
M	ROADHOUSE GIRL (UK: MARILYN)	RILLA	ASTOR	1955
M-1	DESERT'S TOLL	SMITH	MGM	1926
M-1	ONE AT A TIME	CEDER	PATHE EXCHANGE	1924
M 1	PRETTY MRS. SMITH	BOSWORTH	PARAMOUNT	1915
M-1	RHAPSODY IN BREW	GILBERT	MGM	1934
M-1	SUNRISE	MURNAU	FOX FILM	1927
M-2	FIVE GOLDEN HOURS	ZAMPI	COLUMBIA	1961
M-2	FOUR DEVILS	MURNAU	FOX FILM	1928
M 2	HELP WANTED	BOSWORTH	PARAMOUNT	1915
M-2	KEG O' MY HEART	GILBERT	MGM	1933
M-2	SNARES OF PARIS	MITCHELL	FOX FILM	1919
M-2	VALLEY OF HELL	SMITH	MGM	1927
M-3	CITY GIRL	MURNAU	FOX FILM	1930
M-3	MUSIC IN YOUR HAIR	CHASE	MGM	1934
M 3	WILD OLIVE	APFEL	PARAMOUNT	1915
M-4	APPLES TO YOU!	JASON	MGM	1934
M 4	FAITH	MITCHELL	FOX FILM	1920
M 4	KILMENY	APFEL	PARAMOUNT	1915
M4V2	CHANDU THE MAGICIAN	MENZIES, VARNEL	FOX FILM	1932
M-5	BEAST FROM 20,000 FATHOMS	LOURIE	WARNER BROS	1953
M 5	PEER GYNT	APFEL, WALSH	PARAMOUNT	1915
M-5	ROAMIN' VANDALS	JASON, YATES	MGM	1934
M-6	DUKE FOR A DAY	PARROTT	MGM	1934
M 6	JANE	LLOYD	PARAMOUNT	1915
M-7	BENNY, FROM PANAMA	PARROTT	MGM	1934
M 7	MAROC 7 (UK)	O'HARA	PARAMOUNT	1966
M 7	YANKEE GIRL	CLARK	PARAMOUNT	1915
M 8	LOVE'S HARVEST	MITCHELL	FOX FILM	1920
M 8	TONGUES OF MEN	LLOYD	PARAMOUNT	1915
M 9	MADAME LA PRESIDENTE	LLOYD	PARAMOUNT	1916
M 10	CODE OF MARCIA GREY	LLOYD	PARAMOUNT	1916
M-10	HUSBAND HUNTER	MITCHELL	FOX FILM	1920
M 11	PASQUALE	TAYLOR	PARAMOUNT	1916
M-11	WESTERN LIMITED	CABANNE	MONOGRAM	1932
M 12	MAKING OF MADDELENA	LLOYD	PARAMOUNT	1916
M 13	INTERNATIONAL MARRIAGE	LLOYD	PARAMOUNT	1916
M 14	STRONGER LOVE	FLOYD	PARAMOUNT	1916
M 15	HOUSE OF LIES	TAYLOR	PARAMOUNT	1916
M 16	HER FATHER'S SON	TAYLOR	PARAMOUNT	1916
M-17	OVER THE HILL TO THE POORHOUSE	MILLARDE	FOX FILM	1920
M 17	ROAD TO LOVE	SIDNEY	PARAMOUNT	1916
M 18	REDEEMING LOVE	TAYLOR	PARAMOUNT	1916
M 19	HAPPINESS OF THREE WOMEN	TAYLOR	PARAMOUNT	1917
M-21	CRUSADERS	MITCHELL	FOX FILM	1922
M 21	OUT OF THE WRECK	TAYLOR	PARAMOUNT	1917
M 22	GIVING BECKY A CHANCE	ESTABROOK	PARAMOUNT	1917
M 23	MARCELLINI MILLIONS	CRISP	PARAMOUNT	1917
M 24	HIGHWAY OF HOPE	ESTABROOK	PARAMOUNT	1917
M 25	WORLD APART	TAYLOR	PARAMOUNT	1917
M 26	COOK OF CANYON CAMP	CRISP	PARAMOUNT	1917
M 27	BIG TIMBER	TAYLOR	PARAMOUNT	1917
M 28	VARMINT		PARAMOUNT	1917
M 29	JACK AND JILL	TAYLOR	PARAMOUNT	1917
M 31	SPIRIT OF '17	TAYLOR	PARAMOUNT	1917

Movie Still Identification Book Ultimate Edition - Letters

CODE	TITLE/NAME	DIRECTOR/TYPE	STUDIO/DISTRIBUTOR	YEAR
M 32	HIS MAJESTY BUNKER BEAN	TAYLOR	PARAMOUNT	1918
M 33	MILE-A-MINUTE KENDALL	TAYLOR	PARAMOUNT	1918
M 34	UP THE ROAD WITH SALLY	TAYLOR	PARAMOUNT	1918
M 35	GOOD NIGHT PAUL	EDWARDS	PARAMOUNT	1918
M 36	PAIR OF SILK STOCKINGS	EDWARDS	PARAMOUNT	1918
M 37	SAUCE FOR THE GOOSE	EDWARDS	PARAMOUNT	1918
M 38	MRS. LEFFINGWELLS BOOTS	EDWARDS	PARAMOUNT	1918
M 39	MIRANDY SMILES	DE MILLE	PARAMOUNT	1918
M 40	LADY'S NAME	EDWARDS	PARAMOUNT	1918
M 41	YOU NEVER SAW SUCH A GIRL	VIGNOLA	PARAMOUNT	1919
M 42	WHO CARES	EDWARDS	PARAMOUNT	1918
M 43	LITTLE COMRADE	WITHEY	PARAMOUNT	1919
M 44	ROMANCE AND ARABELLA	EDWARDS	PARAMOUNT	1919
M 45	RESCUING ANGEL	EDWARDS	PARAMOUNT	1919
M 46	EXPERIMENTAL MARRIAGE	VIGNOLA	PARAMOUNT	1919
M 47	FINAL CLOSEUP	EDWARDS	PARAMOUNT	1919
M 48	HOME TOWN GIRL	VIGNOLA	PARAMOUNT	1919
M 49	VEILED ADVENTURE	EDWARDS	PARAMOUNT	1919
M 50	INNOCENT ADVENTURESS	VIGNOLA	PARAMOUNT	1919
M 51	HAPPINESS A LA MODE	EDWARDS	PARAMOUNT	1919
M 52	THIRD KISS	VIGNOLA	PARAMOUNT	1919
M 53	GIRLS	EDWARDS	PARAMOUNT	1919
M 53	HIS OFFICIAL FIANCEE	VIGNOLA	PARAMOUNT	1919
M 54	LOUISIANA	VIGNOLA	PARAMOUNT	1919
M 55	WIDOW BY PROXY	EDWARDS	PARAMOUNT	1919
M 56	HUCKLEBERRY FINN	TAYLOR	PARAMOUNT	1920
M 57	LUCK IN PAWN	EDWARDS	PARAMOUNT	1919
M 59	GIRL NAMED MARY	EDWARDS	PARAMOUNT	1920
M 60	ALL-OF-A-SUDDEN PEGGY	EDWARDS	PARAMOUNT	1920
M 61	MORE DEADLY THAN THE MALE	VIGNOLA	PARAMOUNT	1919
M 62	13TH COMMANDMENT	VIGNOLA	PARAMOUNT	1920
M 63	JUDY OF ROGUES HARBOR	TAYLOR	PARAMOUNT	1920
M 64	NURSE MARJORIE	TAYLOR	PARAMOUNT	1920
M 65	JENNY BE GOOD	TAYLOR	PARAMOUNT	1920
M 66	WHAT HAPPENED TO JONES	CRUZE	PARAMOUNT	1920
M 67	MISS HOBBS	CRISP	PARAMOUNT	1920
M 68	FULL HOUSE	CRUZE	PARAMOUNT	1920
M 69	BURGLAR PROOF	CAMPBELL	PARAMOUNT	1920
M 70	FOOD FOR SCANDAL	CRUZE	PARAMOUNT	1920
M 71	AMATEUR DEVIL	CAMPBELL	PARAMOUNT	1920
M 72	HER BELOVED VILLAIN	WOOD	PARAMOUNT	1920
M 73	OH LADY, LADY	CAMPBELL	PARAMOUNT	R
M 74	HER FIRST ELOPEMENT	WOOD	PARAMOUNT	1921
M 75	SHE COULDN'T HELP IT	CAMPBELL	PARAMOUNT	1921
M 76	SNOB	WOOD	PARAMOUNT	1921
M 77	DUCKS AND DRAKES	CAMPBELL	PARAMOUNT	1921
M 78	OUTSIDE WOMAN	BRONSTON	PARAMOUNT	1921
M 79	TWO WEEKS WITH PAY	CAMPBELL	PARAMOUNT	1921
M 80	LITTLE CLOWN	HEFFRON	PARAMOUNT	1921
M 81	PRIVATE SCANDAL	FRANKLIN	PARAMOUNT	1921
M 82	KISS IN TIME	HEFFRON	PARAMOUNT	1921
M 83	MARCH HARE	CAMPBELL	PARAMOUNT	1921
M 84	HER STURDY OAK	HEFFRON	PARAMOUNT	1921
M 85	HER WINNING WAY	HENABERY	PARAMOUNT	1921
M 86	ONE WILD WEEK	CAMPBELL	PARAMOUNT	1921
M 87	HER FACE VALUE	HEFFRON	PARAMOUNT	1921
M 88	SPEED GIRL	CAMPBELL	PARAMOUNT	1921
M 89	LOVE CHARM	HEFFRON	PARAMOUNT	1921
M 90	FIRST LOVE	CAMPBELL	PARAMOUNT	1921
M 91	NANCY FROM NOWHERE	FRANKLIN	PARAMOUNT	1921
M 92	SOUTH OF SUVA	URSON	PARAMOUNT	1922
M 93	TOO MUCH WIFE	HEFFRON	PARAMOUNT	1922
M 94	MIDNIGHT	CAMPBELL	PARAMOUNT	1922
M 95	BOBBED HAIR	HEFFRON	PARAMOUNT	1922
M 96	GAME CHICKEN	FRANKLIN	PARAMOUNT	1922
M 97	TILLIE	URSON	PARAMOUNT	1922
M 98	TRUTHFUL LIAR	HEFFRON	PARAMOUNT	1922
M 99	SLEEPWALKER	LESAINT	PARAMOUNT	1922
M 100	HEART SPECIALIST	URSON	PARAMOUNT	1922
M-392	BOB MATHIAS STORY	LYON	ALLIED ARTISTS	1954

Movie Still Identification Book Ultimate Edition - Letters

CODE	TITLE/NAME	DIRECTOR/TYPE	STUDIO/DISTRIBUTOR	YEAR
M. DE LA M.	MARGUERITE DE LA MOTTE/DE LAMOTTE	portrait	PDC	1925-26
M.CH.	MARGUERITE CHAPMAN	portrait	WARNER BROS	
MA	MAGNIFICENT AMBERSONS	WELLES	RKO	1942
MA	MAIN ATTRACTION (UK)	PETRIE	MGM	1962
MA	MAKE MINE MINK (UK)	ASHER	CONTINENTAL	1960
MA	MALE ANIMAL	NUGENT	WARNER BROS	1942
MA	MAMBO	ROSSEN	PARAMOUNT	1954
MA	MAN ALIVE	ENRIGHT	RKO	1945
MA	MANNEQUIN	GOTTLEIB	20th CENTURY FOX	1987
MA	MARGARET ADAMS	portrait	UNIVERSAL	
MA	MARI ALDON	portrait	WARNER BROS	
MA	MARS ATTACKS!	BURTON	WARNER BROS	1996
MA	MARY ANDERSON	portrait	RKO	ca. 1950
MA	MARY ASTOR	portrait	PATHE, WARNER BROS	
MA	MAURIE	DANIEL MANN	NATIONAL GENERAL	1973
MA	MAXENE ANDREWS (ANDREWS SISTERS)	portrait	UNIVERSAL	
MA	MEET THE MISSUS	SANTLEY	RKO	1937
MA	MEN OF AMERICA	INCE	RKO	1932
MA	MINI-MOB (UK: MINI AFFAIR)	AMRAM	UNITED SCREEN ARTS	1967
MA	MISCHA AUER	portrait	UNIVERSAL	
MA	MURDER BY AN ARISTOCRAT	MCDONALD	WARNER BROS	1936
MAC	MACBETH (UK)	POLANSKI	COLUMBIA	1971
MAC	MAY MCAVOY	portrait	REALART	
MAC2	MAY MCAVOY	portrait	REALART	
MacI 99	PRIVATE SCANDAL	FRANKLIN	REALART	1921
MAD	MAD WOMAN OF CHAILLOT	FORBES	WARNER BROS	1969
M-ADV	M'LISS	NICHOLS JR.	RKO	1936
MAG	MAGUS (UK)	GREEN	20TH CENTURY FOX	1968
MAN	MANIFESTO	MAKAVEJEY	CANNON	1988
MAM	GHOST OF ST. MICHAEL'S (UK)	VARNEL	ABFD	1941
MAR	WILLIAM MARSHALL	portrait	WARNER BROS	
MAR-1	PRAIRIE TRAILS	MARSHALL	FOX FILM	1920
MAR-5	AFTER YOUR OWN HEART	MARSHALL	FOX FILM	1921
MARIS	MARIS WRIXON	portrait	WARNER BROS	1930s-40s
MAS-4	SHADOW OF THE EAGLE (serial)	BEEBE	MASCOT	1932
MAS-5	LAST OF THE MOHICANS (serial)	BEEBE, EASON	MASCOT	1932
MAS-6	HURRICANE EXPRESS (serial)	MCGOWAN, SCHAEFER	MASCOT	1932
MAS-8	DEVIL HORSE (serial)	BROWER	MASCOT	1932
MAS-9	WHISPERING SHADOW (serial)	CLARK, HERMAN	MASCOT	1933
MAS-11	FIGHTING WITH KIT CARSON (RETURN OF KIT CARSON 1947)	CLARK/SCHAEFER	MASCOT	1933
MAS-13	LOST JUNGLE (serial)	HOWARD, SCHAEFER	MASCOT	1934
MAS-18	PHANTOM EMPIRE/GENE AUTRY PHANTOM EMPIRE (serial)	BROWER, EASON	MASCOT	1935
MASK	MASK	ROFFMAN	WARNER BROS	1961
MAW	MEN AT WORK	ESTEVEZ	TRIUMPH	1990
MAY	MAYERLING (UK)	YOUNG	MGM	1968
MB	HERE WE GO ROUND THE MULBERRY BUSH (UK)	DONNER	UNITED ARTISTS	1968
MB	MADAME BUTTERFLY	GALLONE	I.F.E.	1956
MB	MAGIC BOW (UK)	KNOWLES	UNIVERSAL	1947
MB	MAJOR BARBARA (UK)	PASCAL	UNITED ARTISTS	1941
MB	MAN AND BOY aka RIDE A DARK HORSE	SWACKHAMER	LEVITT-PICKMAN	1971
MB	MAN ON THE BOX	REISNER	WARNER BROS	1925
MB	MARI BLANCHARD	portrait	UNIVERSAL, RKO	
MB	MARINA BERTI	portrait	UNIVERSAL	
MB	MARY BOLAND	portrait		
MB	MARY BRODEL	portrait	WARNER BROS	
MB	MASTER OF BALLANTRAE	KEIGHLEY	WARNER BROS	1953
MB	MCKENZIE BREAK (UK)	JOHNSON	UNITED ARTISTS	1970
MB	MEL BERNS	portrait	RKO	1930s-50s
MB	MEMPHIS BELLE	CATON-JONES	WARNER BROS	1990
MB	MILTON BERLE	portrait	RKO	
MB	MIMI BERRY	portrait	RKO	
MB	MISSOURI BREAKS	PENN	UNITED ARTISTS	1976
MB	MONA BARRIE	portrait	RKO	
MB	MONTANA BELLE	DWAN	RKO	1952
MB	MONTE BLUE	portrait	WARNER BROS	
MB	MOTHER'S BOY	BARKER	PATHE	1929
MB	MRS. BROWN, YOU'VE GOT A LOVELY DAUGHTER (UK)	SWIMMER	MGM	1968
MB	MUMMY'S BOYS	GUIOL	RKO	1936
MB	MURDER IS MY BEAT	ULMER	ALLIED ARTISTS	1955
MB-1	FROM BROADWAY TO CHEYENNE	FRASER	MONOGRAM	1932

Movie Still Identification Book Ultimate Edition - Letters

CODE	TITLE/NAME	DIRECTOR/TYPE	STUDIO/DISTRIBUTOR	YEAR
MB-1	FROM HELL IT CAME	MILNER	MONOGRAM	1957
MB-2	MAN FROM ARIZONA	FRASER	MONOGRAM	1932
MB-2	MEATBALLS 2	WIEDERHORN	TRI STAR	1984
MB-3	LUCKY LARRIGAN	MCCARTHY	MONOGRAM	1932
MB-4	DIAMOND TRAIL	FRASER	MONOGRAM	1933
MB-5	CRASHING BROADWAY	MCCARTHY	MONOGRAM	1932
MB-6	FIGHTING TEXAS	SCHAEFER	MONOGRAM	1933
MB-7	FUGITIVE	FRASER	MONOGRAM	1933
MB-8	RAINBOW RANCH	FRASER	MONOGRAM	1933
MB-81	MAD MONSTER	NEWFIELD	PRC	1942
MBB	MR. BLANDINGS BUILDS HIS DREAM HOUSE	POTTER	RKO	1948
MBE	MOURNING BECOMES ELECTRA	NICHOLS	RKO	1947
MBG	MY BEST GIRL	TAYLOR	UNITED ARTISTS	1927
MBH	MAGIC BOY (JP)	DAIKUHARA	MGM	1961
MBH	MY BLUE HEAVEN	ROSS	WARNER BROS	1990
MBS	MAJOR BARBARA	PASCAL	UNITED ARTISTS	1941
MBS	MONSTER FROM THE OCEAN FLOOR	ORDUNG	LIPPERT	1954
MBS	MYSTERY OF THUG ISLAND (IT)	CAPUANO	COLUMBIA	1965
MBX	MAE BUSCH	portrait	MGM	
MC	MACDONALD CAREY	portrait	UNIVERSAL	
MC	MADELEINE CARROLL	portrait	GAUMONT BRITISH	
MC	MADY CHRISTIANS	portrait	MGM	
MC	MAGIC CHRISTIAN (UK)	MCGRATH	COMMONWEALTH UNITED	1969
MC	MAIN CHANCE (UK)	KNIGHT	ANGLO-AMALGAMATED	1964
MC	MAN FROM PLANET X	ULMER	UNITED ARTISTS	1951
MC	MAN WHO LIVED AGAIN (UK: MAN WHO CHANGED MIND)	STEVENSON	GAUMONT	1936
MC	MANCHURIAN CANDIDATE	FRANKENHEIMER	UNITED ARTISTS	1962
MC	MARA CORDAY	portrait	UNIVERSAL	
MC	MARGARET CALLAHAN	portrait	RKO	
MC	MARGUERITE CHAPMAN	portrait	RKO	
MC	MARIANNE KOCH (aka MARIANNE COOK)	portrait	UNIVERSAL	
MC	MARINES ARE COMING	HOWARD	MASCOT	1934
MC	MARRIAGE CIRCLE	LUBITSCH	WARNER BROS	1924
MC	MARY CARLISLE	portrait	MGM, UNIVERSAL	
MC	MARY CASTLE	portrait	UNIVERSAL	
MC	MATING CALL	CRUZE	PARAMOUNT	1928
MC	MELODY CRUISE	SANDRICH	RKO	1933
MC	MICHAEL COLLINS	JORDAN	WARNER BROS	1996
MC	MICHAEL CRAWFORD	portrait	UNIVERSAL	
MC	MICHELINE CHEIREL	portrait	RKO	
MC	MIDNIGHT COWBOY	SCHLESINGER	UNITED ARTISTS	1969
MC	MIKEL CONRAD	portrait	UNIVERSAL	
MC	MILDRED (HARRIS) CHAPLIN	portrait		
MC	MILDRED COLES	portrait	RKO	
MC	MILLER'S CROSSING	COEN BROS	20th CENTURY FOX	1990
MC	MIXED COMPANY	SHAVELSON	UNITED ARTISTS	1974
MC	MONTE CARLO STORY	TAYLOR	UNITED ARTISTS	1957
MC	MORGAN CONWAY	portrait	RKO	
MC	MOTHER CAREY'S CHICKENS	LEE	RKO	1938
MC	MOTHER'S CRY	HENLEY	WARNER BROS	1930
MC	MURDER IN THE CATHEDRAL (UK)	HOELLERING	CLASSIC	1951
MC	MURDER IN THE CLOUDS	LEDERMAN	WARNER BROS	1934
MC	NAUGHTY FLIRT	CLINE	WARNER BROS	1931
MC	PRISONER OF CORBAL (UK: MARRIAGE OF CORBAL)	GRUNE	GFD	1936
MC	PROSPERITY	WOOD	MGM	1932
MC	SECRET OF MONTE CRISTO (UK: TREASURE MONTE CRISTO)	BAKER, BERMAN	MGM	1961
MC	SLASHER (UK: COSH BOY)	GILBERT	LIPPERT	1953
MC	YOUNG SAVAGES	FRANKENHEIMER	UNITED ARTISTS	1961
MC-1	DUGAN OF THE BADLANDS	BRADBURY	MONOGRAM	1931
MC2	MANIA (UK: FLESH AND THE FIENDS)	GILLING	VALIANT	1960
MC-2	MONTANA KID	FRASER	MONOGRAM	1931
MC-3	OKLAHOMA JIM	FRASER	MONOGRAM	1931
MC-4	LAND OF WANTED MEN	FRASER	MONOGRAM	1931
MC-5	GHOST CITY	FRASER	MONOGRAM	1932
MC-6	TEXAS PIONEERS	FRASER	MONOGRAM	1932
MC-7	MASON OF THE MOUNTED	FRASER	MONOGRAM	1932
MC-8	LAW OF THE NORTH	FRASER	MONOGRAM	1932
MC-108	SIEGE OF SIDNEY STREET (UK)	BAKER, BERMAN	UNITED PRODUCERS REL.	1960
MC-2482	HANNIE CAULDER	KENNEDY	PARAMOUNT	1972
MC 3400	GREEN PROMISE	RUSSELL	RKO	1949

Movie Still Identification Book Ultimate Edition - Letters

CODE	TITLE/NAME	DIRECTOR/TYPE	STUDIO/DISTRIBUTOR	YEAR
MCA	MAN CALLED ADAM	PENN	EMBASSY	1966
MCA	MANIAC (UK)	CARRERAS	COLUMBIA	1963
MCC-1	WILD COMPANY	MCCAREY	FOX FILM	1930
MCC-2	PART TIME WIFE	MCCAREY	FOX FILM	1930
MCCL-1	ON YOUR BACK	MCCLINTIC	FOX FILM	1930
MCCL-2	ONCE A SINNER	MCCLINTIC	FOX FILM	1931
MCE	MANIAC (UK)	CARRERAS	COLUMBIA	1963
MCF	BLACK CAMEL	MCFADDEN	FOX FILM	1931
MCF-1	HARMONY AT HOME	MCFADDEN	FOX FILM	1930
MCF-2	CRAZY THAT WAY	MCFADDEN	FOX FILM	1930
MCF-3	ARE YOU THERE?	MCFADDEN	FOX FILM	1930
MCF-4	OH, FOR A MAN!	MCFADDEN	FOX FILM	1930
MCF-6	BLACK CAMEL	MCFADDEN	FOX FILM	1931
MCF-9	SECOND HAND WIFE	MCFADDEN	FOX FILM	1933
MCFAD-4	OH, FOR A MAN!	MCFADDEN	FOX FILM	1930
MCFAD-7	RIDERS OF THE PURPLE SAGE	MCFADDEN	FOX FILM	1931
MCFAD-8	CHEATERS AT PLAY	MCFADDEN	FOX FILM	1932
MCFAD-9	SECOND HAND WIFE	MCFADDEN	FOX FILM	1933
MCFED-7	RIDERS OF THE PURPLE SAGE	MCFADDEN	FOX FILM	1931
MCH	MAN IN A COCKED HAT (UK: CARLTON-BROWNE OF THE F.O.)	BOULTING	BRITISH LION (UK)	1959
MCK	ALWAYS GOODBYE	MCKENNA	FOX FILM	1931
MCKEN-3	GOOD SPORT	MCKENNA	FOX FILM	1931
MCKEN-3	MCKENNA OF THE MOUNTIES	LEDERMAN	COLUMBIA	1932
MCKEN-4	CARELESS LADY	MCKENNA	FOX FILM	1932
MCK-M-1	ALWAYS GOODBYE	MCKENNA, MENZIES	FOX FILM	1931
MCK-M-2	SPIDER	MCKENNA, MENZIES	FOX FILM	1931
MCL	MCLINTOCK	MCLAGLEN	UNITED ARTISTS	1963
MCP	ROARING SIX GUNS	MCGOWEN	CONN PICT (states rights)	1937
MCR	THOSE DARING YOUNG MEN IN THEIR JAUNTING JALOPIES	ANNAKIN	PARAMOUNT	1969
MCR	YOUNG SAVAGES	FRANKENHEIMER	UNITED ARTISTS	1961
MCS	MAN CALLED SARGE	GILLARD	CANNON	1990
MCS	MAN CALLED SLEDGE	MORROW	COLUMBIA	1970
MCT	MARSEILLES CONTRACT (FR/UK: DESTRUCTORS)	PARRISH	WARNER BROS	1974
MCV	MY COUSIN VINNY	LYNN	20th CENTURY FOX	1992
MCW	MAN WHO COULDN'T WALK (UK)	CASS	FALCON	1961
MCX	MADY CHRISTIANS	portrait	MGM	
MD	BLONDE CHEAT	SANTLEY	RKO	1938
MD	EARRINGS OF MADAME DE	OPHULS	ARLAN	1953
MD	HEAVEN, HELL OR HOBOKEN (UK: I WAS MONTY'S DOUBLE)	GUILLERMIN	NTA	1958
MD	MARION DAVIES	portrait	MGM, WARNER BROS	
MD	MARK DANA	portrait	WARNER BROS	
MD	MARKED FOR DEATH	LITTLE	20th CENTURY FOX	1990
MD	MARLENE DIETRICH	portrait	UNIVERSAL	
MD	MARSHAL'S DAUGHTER	BERKE	UNITED ARTISTS	1953
MD	MARY DUNCAN	portrait		
MD	MARTIN'S DAY	GIBSON	MGM/UNITED ARTISTS	1985
MD	MASK OF DIMITRIOS	NEGULESCO	WARNER BROS	1944
MD	MAX DUGAN RETURNS	ROSS	20th CENTURY FOX	1983
MD	MAXINE DOYLE	portrait	FN	1933-34
MD	MEET DR. CHRISTIAN	VORHAUS	RKO	1940
MD	MELVYN DOUGLAS	portrait	RKO	
MD	MIDSUMMER'S NIGHT DREAM	DIETERLE, REINHARDT	WARNER BROS	1935
MD	MOBY DICK	BACON	WARNER BROS	1930
MD	MORE DEAD THAN ALIVE	SPARR	UNITED ARTISTS	1969
MD	MORTON DOWNEY	portrait	CBS RADIO	
MD	MR. DOODLE KICKS OFF	GOODWINS	RKO	1938
MD	MURDER BY DECREE	CLARK	AVCO EMBASSY	1979
MD	MURDER CAN BE DEADLY (UK: PAINTED SMILE)	COMFORT	COLORAMA	1962
MD	MYRNA DELL	portrait	RKO	
MD	MYSTERIOUS DOCTOR	STOLOFF	WARNER BROS	1943
MD	PATIENT VANISHES (UK)	HUNTINGTON	FILM CLASSICS	1941
MD	PEGGY DRAKE (NÉE MARGARET DRAKE)	portrait	RKO	
MD	RACE FOR LIFE (UK: MASK OF DUST)	FISHER	LIPPERT	1954
MD	SIX DAY BIKE RIDER	BACON	FIRST NATIONAL	1934
MD	SMARTEST GIRL IN TOWN	SANTLEY	RKO	1936
MD	UNDER SECRET ORDERS (MADEMOISELLE DOCTEUR)	GREVILLE	UNITED ARTISTS	1937
MD	WIDOW FROM MONTE CARLO	COLLINS	WARNER BROS	1935
MD	MRS. DOUBTFIRE	COLUMBUS	20th CENTURY FOX	1993
MDC	MAD DOG COLL	BALABAN	COLUMBIA	1961
MDD	DIAMOND WIZARD (UK: DIAMOND)	TULLY, O'KEEFE	UNITED ARTISTS	1954

Movie Still Identification Book Ultimate Edition - Letters

CODE	TITLE/NAME	DIRECTOR/TYPE	STUDIO/DISTRIBUTOR	YEAR
MDG	GAME OF DEATH	WISE	RKO	1946
MDG	MOST DANGEROUS GAME	PICHEL, SCHOEDSACK	RKO	1932
MDL	MEN DON'T LEAVE	BRICKMAN	GEFFEN	1989
MDR	MILLION DOLLAR RACKET	HILL	VICTORY (states rights)	1937
MDS	PUBLIC DEFENDER	RUBEN	RKO	1931
MDX	MARCELINE DAY	portrait	MGM	
MDXX	MARY DORAN	portrait	MGM	
ME	MADGE EVANS	portrait	MGM, UNIVERSAL	
ME	MAIN EVENT	ZIEFF	WARNER BROS	1979
ME	MAN OF THE EAST (IT)	BARBONI	UNITED ARTISTS	1972
ME	MANCHU EAGLE MURDER CAPER MYSTERY	HARGOVE	UNITED ARTISTS	1975
ME	MELBA	MILESTONE	UNITED ARTISTS	1953
ME	MEN IN EXILE	FARROW	WARNER BROS	1937
ME	MIDNIGHT EXPRESS	PARKER	COLUMBIA	1978
MED	MEDUSA TOUCH (UK)	GOLD	WARNER BROS	1978
MEM	MARIA ELENA MARQUES	portrait	RKO	
MEN	AFFAIRS OF ANNABELLE	STOLOFF	RKO	1938
MES	AFFAIRS OF MESSALINA	GALLONE	COLUMBIA	1951
MES	MEXICAN SPITFIRE	GOODWINS	RKO	1940
MEX	MURIEL EVANS	portrait	MGM	
MF	AMOROUS ADVENTURES OF MOLL FLANDERS (UK)	YOUNG	PARAMOUNT	1965
MF	BEYOND THE CURTAIN (UK)	BENNETT	RANK	1960
MF	BUONA SERA, MRS. CAMPBELL	FRANK	UNITED ARTISTS	1968
MF	DISPATCH FROM REUTERS	DIETERLE	WARNER BROS	1940
MF	GAMBLING HOUSE	TETZLAFF	RKO	1951
MF	MADEMOISELLE FIFI	WISE	RKO	1944
MF	MAGIC FACE	TUTTLE	COLUMBIA	1951
MF	MAGIC FLAME	KING	UNITED ARTISTS	1927
MF	MALTESE FALCON	DEL RUTH	WARNER BROS	1931
MG	MAN FRIDAY	GOLD	AVCO EMBASSY	1975
MF	MAN OF FLOWERS	COX	INT'L SPECTRAFILM	1984
MG	MAN ON FIRE	CHOURAQUI	TRI STAR	1987
MF	MANFISH	W. WILDER	UNITED ARTISTS	1956
MF	MARINES FLY HIGH	STOLOFF, NICHOLS JR.	RKO	1940
MF	MASCULINE-FEMININE	GODARD	ROYAL FILMS INT'L	1966
MF	MEL FERRER	portrait	RKO	
MF	MEN ARE SUCH FOOLS	BERKELEY	WARNER BROS	1938
MF	MONA FREEMAN	portrait	UNITED ARTISTS, RKO	
MF	MULHOLLAND FALLS	TAMAHORI	MGM	1996
MF	MUSIC FOR MADAME	BLYSTONE	RKO	1937
MF	MY FRIENDS (IT: AMICI MIEI)	MONICELLI	MONOGRAM	1976
MF	STOLEN HOLIDAY	CURTIZ	WARNER BROS	1936
MF-1	13TH GUEST (MYSTERY OF 13TH GUEST)	BEAUDINE	MONOGRAM	1943
MF1	TWIST OF FATE (FR/UK: BEAUTIFUL STRANGER)	MILLER	UNITED ARTISTS	1954
MF-1	VESSEL OF WRATH (UK: BEACHCOMBER)	POMMER	ASSOCIATED BRITISH FILM	1938
MF-2	GIRL FROM CALGARY	WHITMAN	MONOGRAM	1932
MF-2	TOWN ON TRIAL (UK)	GUILLERMIN	COLUMBIA	1957
MF-3	JAMAICA INN (UK)	HITCHCOCK	PARAMOUNT	1939
MF-3	LONG HAUL (UK)	HUGHES	COLUMBIA	1957
MF-3	STRANGE ADVENTURE	DEL RUTH, WHITMAN	MONOGRAM	1932
MF-6	OLIVER TWIST	COWEN	MONOGRAM	1933
MF-7	JUNGLE BRIDE	HOYT, KELLEY	MONOGRAM	1933
MF-8	WEST OF SINGAPORE	RAY	MONOGRAM	1933
MF-9	BLACK BEAUTY	ROSEN	MONOGRAM	1933
MF-10	PHANTOM BROADCAST	ROSEN	MONOGRAM	1933
MF-11	RETURN OF CASEY JONES	MCCARTHY	MONOGRAM	1933
MF-12	SPHYNX	ROSEN	MONOGRAM	1933
MF-13	SKYWAY	COLLINS	MONOGRAM	1933
MF-14	DEVIL'S MATE	ROSEN	MONOGRAM	1933
MF-15	HE COULDN'T TAKE IT	NIGH	MONOGRAM	1933
MFAS	MAN FOR ALL SEASONS	ZINNEMANN	COLUMBIA	1966
MFE	MAN WHO FELL TO EARTH	ROEG	CINEMA 5	1976
MFG	FRANCES GIFFORD (aka MARY GIFFORD)	portrait	RKO	
MFI	TWIST OF FATE (FR/UK: BEAUTIFUL STRANGER)	MILLER	UNITED ARTISTS	1954
MFM	MAID FOR MURDER (UK: SHE'LL HAVE TO GO)	ASHER	JANUS	1962
MFM	MAN FROM MOROCCO (UK)	GREENBAUM	ENGLISH	1945
MFS	MESSAGE FROM SPACE (JAP: UCHU KARA NO MESSEJI)	FUKASAKU	UNITED ARTISTS	1978
MFS	MY FAVORITE SPY	GARNETT	RKO	1942
MFW	MY FAVORITE WIFE	KANIN	RKO	1940
MG	BEAU HUNKS	HORNE	MGM	1931

Movie Still Identification Book Ultimate Edition - Letters

CODE	TITLE/NAME	DIRECTOR/TYPE	STUDIO/DISTRIBUTOR	YEAR
MG	FROM HELL IT CAME	MILNER	ALLIED ARTISTS	1957
MG	MACKENNA'S GOLD	THOMPSON	COLUMBIA	1969
MG	MARGOT GRAHAME	portrait	MGM, RKO	
MG	MERV GRIFFIN	portrait	WARNER BROS	
MG	MICHELE GIRARDON	portrait	PARAMOUNT	
MG	MINNA GOMBELL	portrait	RKO	
MG	MORNING GLORY	SHERMAN	RKO	1933
MG	MOTORCYCLE GANG	CAHN	AIP	1957
MG	MURDER GAME	SALKOW	20TH CENTURY FOX	1965
MG14	GRETA GARBO	portrait	MGM	
MG15	GRETA GARBO	portrait	MGM	
MG23	GRETA GARBO	portrait	MGM	
MG25	GRETA GARBO	portrait	MGM	
MG34	GRETA GARBO	portrait	MGM	
MG972	JOAN CRAWFORD	portrait	MGM	
MG976	JOAN CRAWFORD	portrait	MGM	
MG1040	GRETA GARBO	portrait	MGM	
MG1226	GRETA GARBO	portrait	MGM	
MG1306	ANITA PAGE	portrait	MGM	
MG1323	GRETA GARBO	portrait	MGM	
MG1328	GRETA GARBO	portrait	MGM	
MG1331	GRETA GARBO	portrait	MGM	
MG1336	GRETA GARBO	portrait	MGM	
MG1337	GRETA GARBO	portrait	MGM	
MG1758	GRETA GARBO	portrait	MGM	
MG1895	JACK CONWAY	portrait	MGM	
MG2073	JOAN CRAWFORD	portrait	MGM	
MG2240	BUSTER KEATON	portrait	MGM	
MG2259	RENEE ADOREE	portrait	MGM	
MG2404	BASIL RATHBONE	portrait	MGM	
MG2436	BASIL RATHBONE	portrait	MGM	
MG2444	BASIL RATHBONE	portrait	MGM	
MG2716	MARIE DRESSLER, POLLY MORAN	portrait	MGM	
MG3257	JOAN CRAWFORD	portrait	MGM	
MG3316	JOAN CRAWFORD	portrait	MGM	
MG3332	JOAN CRAWFORD	portrait	MGM	
MG3333	RAMON NAVARRO	portrait	MGM	
MG3333	RAMON NOVARRO	portrait	MGM	
MG3500	NORMA SHEARER	portrait	MGM	
MG3722	LILIAN ROTH	portrait	MGM	
MG4146	SALLY EILERS	portrait	MGM	
MG4251	JOAN CRAWFORD	portrait	MGM	
MG4299	LIONEL BARRYMORE	portrait	MGM	
MG4471	SALLY EILERS	portrait	MGM	
MG4559	REGINALD DENNY	portrait	MGM	
MG4793	NORMA SHEARER	portrait	MGM	
MG5046	GRETA GARBO	portrait	MGM	
MG5102	GRETA GARBO	portrait	MGM	
MG5107	GRETA GARBO	portrait	MGM	
MG5202	GRETA GARBO	portrait	MGM	
MG5211	GRETA GARBO	portrait	MGM	
MG5238	GRETA GARBO	portrait	MGM	
MG5249	GRETA GARBO	portrait	MGM	
MG5337	GRETA GARBO	portrait	MGM	
MG5351	ANITA PAGE & MOTHER	portrait	MGM	
MG5361	GRETA GARBO	portrait	MGM	
MG5380	GAVIN GORDON	portrait	MGM	
MG5578	MARY PICKFORD	portrait	MGM	
MG5609	LILA LEE	portrait	MGM	
MG5617	JOAN CRAWFORD	portrait	MGM	
MG6224	ROBERT MONTGOMERY	portrait	MGM	
MG6354	ANITA PAGE + HER FATHER	portrait	MGM	
MG6374	RAMON NOVARRO	portrait	MGM	
MG6454	GRETA GARBO	portrait	MGM	
MG6476	ROBERT MONTGOMERY	portrait	MGM	
MG6847	JOAN CRAWFORD/XAVIER CUGAT	portrait	MGM	
MG7564	FIFI DORSAY	portrait	MGM	
MG7825	LUPE VELEZ	portrait	MGM	
MG7943	MARIE DRESSLER	portrait	MGM	
MG8153	JOAN CRAWFORD	portrait	MGM	

Movie Still Identification Book Ultimate Edition - Letters

CODE	TITLE/NAME	DIRECTOR/TYPE	STUDIO/DISTRIBUTOR	YEAR
MG8555	WILLIAM BAKEWELL	portrait	MGM	
MG9124	JOAN CRAWFORD	portrait	MGM	
MG9143	JOAN CRAWFORD	portrait	MGM	
MG9436	KAY FRANCIS	portrait	MGM	
MG9492	WALLACE BEERY	portrait	MGM	
MG9592	POLLY MORAN	portrait	MGM	
MG9685	JOAN CRAWFORD	portrait	MGM	
MG9771	WALLACE BEERY	portrait	MGM	
MG9795	MARIE PREVOST	portrait	MGM	
MG9795	MARIE PREVOST	portrait	MGM	
MG9848	MARIE PREVOST	portrait	MGM	
MG10137	HEDDA HOPPER	portrait	MGM	
MG10257	MARJORIE RAMBEAU	portrait	MGM	
MG10632	CONSTANCE BENNETT	portrait	MGM	
MG10634	JOAN CRAWFORD, LESTER VAIL - DANCE FOOLS DANCE	portrait	MGM	
MG10657	BUSTER KEATON, WIFE NATALIE TALMADGE, SONS	portrait	MGM	
MG10848	BUSTER KEATON - SPITE MARRIAGE	portrait	MGM	
MG10938	JOAN CRAWFORD	portrait	MGM	
MG10946	JOAN CRAWFORD	portrait	MGM	
MG10952	JOAN CRAWFORD	portrait	MGM	
MG10957	BUSTER KEATON	portrait	MGM	
MG11201	JOAN CRAWFORD	portrait	MGM	
MG11269	JOAN CRAWFORD	portrait	MGM	
MG11271	JOAN CRAWFORD	portrait	MGM	
MG11283	NORMA SHEARER	portrait	MGM	
MG11418	GRETA GARBO	portrait	MGM	
MG11442	GRETA GARBO	portrait	MGM	
MG11443	GRETA GARBO	portrait	MGM	
MG11448	GRETA GARBO	portrait	MGM	
MG11449	GRETA GARBO	portrait	MGM	
MG11452	GRETA GARBO	portrait	MGM	
MG11453	GRETA GARBO	portrait	MGM	
MG11462	BUSTER KEATON	portrait	MGM	
MG11488	GRETA GARBO	portrait	MGM	
MG11578	JEAN HARLOWE	portrait	MGM	
MG11592	JOAN CRAWFORD	portrait	MGM	
MG11844	GRETA GARBO	portrait	MGM	
MG11890	MARY DUNCAN	portrait	MGM	
MG12384	ANITA PAGE	portrait	MGM	
MG12592	LEILA HYAMS	portrait	MGM	
MG12603	LILIAN BOND	portrait	MGM	
MG12785	HELEN CHANDLER	portrait	MGM	
MG12865	CLARK GABLE, JEAN HARLOW, W. BEERY, M. CARLISLE	portrait	MGM	
MG12964	JOAN CRAWFORD	portrait	MGM	
MG13025	JOAN CRAWFORD	portrait	MGM	
MG13145	NORMA SHEARER	portrait	MGM	
MG13152	NORMA SHEARER	portrait	MGM	
MG13169	NORMA SHEARER	portrait	MGM	
MG13173	NORMA SHEARER	portrait	MGM	
MG13174	NORMA SHEARER	portrait	MGM	
MG13311	ANITA PAGE	portrait	MGM	
MG13541	GRETA GARBO	portrait	MGM	
MG13547	GRETA GARBO	portrait	MGM	
MG13802	JOAN CRAWFORD	portrait	MGM	
MG13895	JOAN CRAWFORD	portrait	MGM	
MG13900	JOAN CRAWFORD	portrait	MGM	
MG13924	JOAN CRAWFORD	portrait	MGM	
MG14100	WARNER BAXTER	portrait	MGM	
MG14264	NORMA SHEARER	portrait	MGM	
MG14477	GRETA GARBO	portrait	MGM	
MG14571	WALLACE BEERY	portrait	MGM	
MG14643	LUPE VELEZ	portrait	MGM	
MG14694	LUPE VELEZ	portrait	MGM	
MG14784	CLARK GABLE	portrait	MGM	
MG15237	ROBERT MONTGOMERY	portrait	MGM	
MG15242	EDWINA BOOTH	portrait	MGM	
MG15437	IRENE DUNN	portrait	MGM	
MG15623	JANET CURRIE	portrait	MGM	
MG16529	JACKIE COOPER	portrait	MGM	
MG16538	JACKIE COOPER	portrait	MGM	

Movie Still Identification Book Ultimate Edition - Letters

CODE	TITLE/NAME	DIRECTOR/TYPE	STUDIO/DISTRIBUTOR	YEAR
MG16555	JOAN CRAWFORD	portrait	MGM	
MG16585	GRETA GARBO	portrait	MGM	
MG16586	GRETA GARBO	portrait	MGM	
MG16610	GRETA GARBO	portrait	MGM	
MG16612	GRETA GARBO	portrait	MGM	
MG16613	GRETA GARBO	portrait	MGM	
MG16614	GRETA GARBO	portrait	MGM	
MG16617	GRETA GARBO	portrait	MGM	
MG16619	GRETA GARBO	portrait	MGM	
MG16621	GRETA GARBO	portrait	MGM	
MG16625	GRETA GARBO	portrait	MGM	
MG16628	GRETA GARBO	portrait	MGM	
MG16629	GRETA GARBO	portrait	MGM	
MG16939	WALLACE BEERY VISITING SET OF FLYING HIGH	portrait	MGM	
MG17057	KAREN MORLEY	portrait	MGM	
MG17342	ANITA PAGE	portrait	MGM	
MG17367	CLARK GABLE	portrait	MGM	
MG17479	ANITA PAGE	portrait	MGM	
MG17804	JOAN CRAWFORD	portrait	MGM	
MG17906	BUSTER KEATON	portrait	MGM	
MG18049	BUSTER KEATON	portrait	MGM	
MG18139	JOAN CRAWFORD	portrait	MGM	
MG18474	JOAN CRAWFORD	portrait	MGM	
MG18700	JOHN BARRYMORE, LIONEL BARRYMORE	portrait	MGM	
MG19015	JOAN MARSH	portrait	MGM	
MG19069	NORMA SHEARER	portrait	MGM	
MG19138	CLARK GABLE	portrait	MGM	
MG19156	ANITA PAGE	portrait	MGM	
MG19182	JOAN CRAWFORD	portrait	MGM	
MG19355	JOAN CRAWFORD	portrait	MGM	
MG19386	GRETA GARBO	portrait	MGM	
MG19387	GRETA GARBO	portrait	MGM	
MG19388	GRETA GARBO	portrait	MGM	
MG19389	GRETA GARBO	portrait	MGM	
MG19390	GRETA GARBO	portrait	MGM	
MG19391	GRETA GARBO	portrait	MGM	
MG19392	GRETA GARBO	portrait	MGM	
MG19393	GRETA GARBO	portrait	MGM	
MG19394	GRETA GARBO	portrait	MGM	
MG19395	GRETA GARBO	portrait	MGM	
MG19396	GRETA GARBO	portrait	MGM	
MG19397	GRETA GARBO	portrait	MGM	
MG19399	GRETA GARBO	portrait	MGM	
MG19404	GRETA GARBO	portrait	MGM	
MG19422	GRETA GARBO	portrait	MGM	
MG19576	GRETA GARBO	portrait	MGM	
MG19579	GRETA GARBO	portrait	MGM	
MG19583	GRETA GARBO	portrait	MGM	
MG19635	JOHNNY WEISSMULLER	portrait	MGM	
MG19673	ANITA PAGE	portrait	MGM	
MG19716	NORMA SHEARER	portrait	MGM	
MG20016	JOAN CRAWFORD	portrait	MGM	
MG20059	WALLACE BEERY	portrait	MGM	
MG20060	JACKIE COOPER	portrait	MGM	
MG20177	JOAN CRAWFORD	portrait	MGM	
MG20286	JOAN CRAWFORD	portrait	MGM	
MG20329	JOAN CRAWFORD	portrait	MGM	
MG20378	JOAN CRAWFORD	portrait	MGM	
MG20381	JOAN CRAWFORD	portrait	MGM	
MG20645	JOAN CRAWFORD	portrait	MGM	
MG20653	WALLACE BEERY	portrait	MGM	
MG20740	JOAN CRAWFORD	portrait	MGM	
MG20810	JOHN BARRYMORE	portrait	MGM	
MG20812	JOAN CRAWFORD	portrait	MGM	
MG20814	JOAN CRAWFORD	portrait	MGM	
MG20972	MARY CARLISLE	portrait	MGM	
MG21026	JOAN CRAWFORD	portrait	MGM	
MG21038	MYRNA LOY	portrait	MGM	
MG21073	LIONEL BARRYMORE	portrait	MGM	
MG21083	DOROTHY JORDAN	portrait	MGM	

Movie Still Identification Book Ultimate Edition - Letters

CODE	TITLE/NAME	DIRECTOR/TYPE	STUDIO/DISTRIBUTOR	YEAR
MG21085	MAUREEN O'SULLIVAN	portrait	MGM	
MG21118	ANITA PAGE	portrait	MGM	
MG21359	NORMA SHEARER	portrait	MGM	
MG21371	JACKIE COOPER	portrait	MGM	
MG21640	WALTER HUSTON	portrait	MGM	
MG21640	WALTER HUSTON - NIGHT COURT	portrait	MGM	
MG21672	LAUREL & HARDY, BUSTER KEATON, JIMMY DURANTE	portrait	MGM	
MG21805	ANITA PAGE	portrait	MGM	
MG22021	MAUREEN O'SULLIVAN	portrait	MGM	
MG22038	ANITA PAGE	portrait	MGM	
MG22143	NORMA SHEARER	portrait	MGM	
MG22160	NORMA SHEARER	portrait	MGM	
MG22161	NORMA SHEARER	portrait	MGM	
MG22240	JOAN CRAWFORD	portrait	MGM	
MG22242	JOAN CRAWFORD	portrait	MGM	
MG22247	JOAN CRAWFORD	portrait	MGM	
MG22249	JOAN CRAWFORD	portrait	MGM	
MG22350	DICKIE MOORE	portrait	MGM	
MG22369	MAUREEN O'SULLIVAN	portrait	MGM	
MG22371	MAUREEN O'SULLIVAN	portrait	MGM	
MG22372	MAUREEN O'SULLIVAN	portrait	MGM	
MG22375	MAUREEN O'SULLIVAN	portrait	MGM	
MG22376	MAUREEN O'SULLIVAN	portrait	MGM	
MG22383	JACKIE COOPER	portrait	MGM	
MG22387	JACKIE COOPER	portrait	MGM	
MG22434	JOAN CRAWFORD	portrait	MGM	
MG22481	JACKIE COOPER	portrait	MGM	
MG22518	MAUREEN O'SULLIVAN	portrait	MGM	
MG22519	MAUREEN O'SULLIVAN	portrait	MGM	
MG22520	MAUREEN O'SULLIVAN	portrait	MGM	
MG22524	JACKIE COOPER	portrait	MGM	
MG22724	GRETA GARBO	portrait	MGM	
MG22725	GRETA GARBO	portrait	MGM	
MG22748	UNA MERKEL	portrait	MGM	
MG22759	JOAN CRAWFORD	portrait	MGM	
MG22760	JOAN CRAWFORD	portrait	MGM	
MG22822	GRETA GARBO	portrait	MGM	
MG22839	GRETA GARBO	portrait	MGM	
MG22843	GRETA GARBO	portrait	MGM	
MG22850	GRETA GARBO	portrait	MGM	
MG22851	GRETA GARBO	portrait	MGM	
MG22861	GRETA GARBO	portrait	MGM	
MG22935	ROBERT YOUNG, KAREN MORLEY	portrait	MGM	
MG22938	CLARK GABLE	portrait	MGM	
MG22958	JOAN CRAWFORD	portrait	MGM	
MG22966	ROBERT YOUNG, KAREN MORLEY	portrait	MGM	
MG22968	ROBERT YOUNG, KAREN MORLEY	portrait	MGM	
MG23089	CLARK GABLE	portrait	MGM	
MG23137	ANITA PAGE	portrait	MGM	
MG23416	THELMA TODD	portrait	MGM	
MG23545	JOHN GILBERT	portrait	MGM	
MG23737	JOHN BARRYMORE, ETHEL BARRYMORE	portrait	MGM	
MG23794	CHESTER MORRIS	portrait	MGM	
MG23833	COLLEEN MOORE	portrait	MGM	
MG23836	COLLEEN MOORE	portrait	MGM	
MG23949	GRETA GARBO	portrait	MGM	
MG24254	JOHN BARRYMORE, DOLORES COSTELLO, JOHN JR	portrait	MGM	
MG24320	JOAN CRAWFORD	portrait	MGM	
MG24336	MAUREEN O'SULLIVAN	portrait	MGM	
MG24349	KAREN MORLEY	portrait	MGM	
MG24352	FREDRIC MARCH, RALPH FORBES	portrait	MGM	
MG24373	MAUREEN O'SULLIVAN	portrait	MGM	
MG24522	KAREN MORLEY	portrait	MGM	
MG24557	GERTRUDE MICHAEL	portrait	MGM	
MG24748	JOHN GILBERT	portrait	MGM	
MG24799	KAREN MORLEY	portrait	MGM	
MG24981	MAUREEN O'SULLIVAN	portrait	MGM	
MG24986	MAUREEN O'SULLIVAN	portrait	MGM	
MG25308	JOAN CRAWFORD	portrait	MGM	
MG25350	CLARK GABLE	portrait	MGM	

Movie Still Identification Book Ultimate Edition - Letters

CODE	TITLE/NAME	DIRECTOR/TYPE	STUDIO/DISTRIBUTOR	YEAR
MG25397	MYRNA LOY	portrait	MGM	
MG25484	LAUREL & HARDY, FRED QUIMBY, FELIX FEIST	portrait	MGM	
MG25621	UNA MERKEL	portrait	MGM	
MG25624	UNA MERKEL	portrait	MGM	
MG25625	UNA MERKEL	portrait	MGM	
MG25626	UNA MERKEL	portrait	MGM	
MG25701	LUPE VELEZ	portrait	MGM	
MG25826	WALLACE BEERY	portrait	MGM	
MG25843	MARY ASTOR	portrait	MGM	
MG26149	WALLACE BEERY	portrait	MGM	
MG26174	UNA MERKEL	portrait	MGM	
MG26238	JOHN BARRYMORE	portrait	MGM	
MG26252	BUSTER KEATON	portrait	MGM	
MG26302	WALLACE BEERY	portrait	MGM	
MG26303	WALLACE BEERY	portrait	MGM	
MG26425	JOAN CRAWFORD	portrait	MGM	
MG26429	JOAN CRAWFORD	portrait	MGM	
MG26458	JOAN CRAWFORD	portrait	MGM	
MG26559	RUTH SELWYN	portrait	MGM	
MG26754	ROBERT MONTGOMERY	portrait	MGM	
MG26787	JOAN CRAWFORD	portrait	MGM	
MG26797	MADGE EVANS	portrait	MGM	
MG27008	JOAN CRAWFORD	portrait	MGM	
MG27193	MAUREEN O'SULLIVAN	portrait	MGM	
MG27317	MYRNA LOY	portrait	MGM	
MG27349	MYRNA LOY	portrait	MGM	
MG27362	MAUREEN O'SULLIVAN	portrait	MGM	
MG27416	JOAN CRAWFORD	portrait	MGM	
MG27455	JOAN CRAWFORD	portrait	MGM	
MG27557	JOAN CRAWFORD	portrait	MGM	
MG27562	JOAN CRAWFORD	portrait	MGM	
MG27599	JOAN CRAWFORD	portrait	MGM	
MG27638	JOAN CRAWFORD	portrait	MGM	
MG27740	MARY CARLISLE	portrait	MGM	
MG27779	NORMA SHEARER	portrait	MGM	
MG28154	JOAN CRAWFORD	portrait	MGM	
MG28294	UNA MERKEL	portrait	MGM	
MG28295	UNA MERKEL	portrait	MGM	
MG28313	MAUREEN O'SULLIVAN	portrait	MGM	
MG28367	JOAN CRAWFORD	portrait	MGM	
MG28731	JOAN CRAWFORD	portrait	MGM	
MG28786	JOAN CRAWFORD	portrait	MGM	
MG28799	UNA MERKEL	portrait	MGM	
MG28947	JOAN CRAWFORD	portrait	MGM	
MG29007	JOHNNY WEISSMULLER	portrait	MGM	
MG29014	JOHNNY WEISSMULLER	portrait	MGM	
MG29053	LEE TRACY	portrait	MGM	
MG29082	JOHNNY WEISSMULLER	portrait	MGM	
MG29161	RAMON NOVARRO	portrait	MGM	
MG29193	MYRNA LOY	portrait	MGM	
MG29277	CLARK GABLE	portrait	MGM	
MG29333	MAUREEN O'SULLIVAN	portrait	MGM	
MG29667	UNA MERKEL	portrait	MGM	
MG29695	UNA MERKEL	portrait	MGM	
MG29780	UNA MERKEL	portrait	MGM	
MG29979	BILLIE BURKE	portrait	MGM	
MG29990	UNA MERKEL	portrait	MGM	
MG29991	UNA MERKEL	portrait	MGM	
MG30319	MARIE DRESSLER, RICHARD BOLESLAVSKY	portrait	MGM	
MG30586	MAUREEN O'SULLIVAN	portrait	MGM	
MG30594	JOAN CRAWFORD	portrait	MGM	
MG30607	MYRNA LOY	portrait	MGM	
MG30667	MYRNA LOY	portrait	MGM	
MG30687	MYRNA LOY	portrait	MGM	
MG30847	MARIE DRESSLER'S HOME	portrait	MGM	
MG31167	JOHN BARRYMORE	portrait	MGM	
MG31281	MADGE EVANS	portrait	MGM	
MG31402	MAUREEN O'SULLIVAN	portrait	MGM	
MG31501	IRVING THALBERG, WIFE NORMA SHEARER	portrait	MGM	
MG31502	IRVING THALBERG, WIFE NORMA SHEARER	portrait	MGM	

Movie Still Identification Book Ultimate Edition - Letters

CODE	TITLE/NAME	DIRECTOR/TYPE	STUDIO/DISTRIBUTOR	YEAR
MG31834	GRETA GARBO	portrait	MGM	
MG32014	UNA MERKEL	portrait	MGM	
MG32016	UNA MERKEL	portrait	MGM	
MG32020	UNA MERKEL	portrait	MGM	
MG32129	GRETA GARBO	portrait	MGM	
MG32190	IRVING THALBERG, WIFE NORMA SHEARER, LOUIS B MAYER	portrait	MGM	
MG32432	MYRNA LOY	portrait	MGM	
MG32439	JOAN CRAWFORD	portrait	MGM	
MG32702	JEANETTE MACDONALD	portrait	MGM	
MG32742	JOAN CRAWFORD	portrait	MGM	
MG32754	JOAN CRAWFORD	portrait	MGM	
MG32822	UNA MERKEL	portrait	MGM	
MG32989	DOROTHY MACKAILL	portrait	MGM	
MG33003	LILLYAN ANDRUS	portrait	MGM	
MG33067	JOAN CRAWFORD	portrait	MGM	
MG33184	LUPE VELEZ	portrait	MGM	
MG33235	WALLACE BEERY	portrait	MGM	
MG33276	JEAN PARKER	portrait	MGM	
MG33329	ROBERT MONTGOMERY	portrait	MGM	
MG33485	MADGE EVANS	portrait	MGM	
MG33493	LUPE VELEZ	portrait	MGM	
MG33536	JOAN CRAWFORD	portrait	MGM	
MG33588	CLARK GABLE	portrait	MGM	
MG33592	CLARK GABLE	portrait	MGM	
MG33650	JEAN PARKER	portrait	MGM	
MG33722	JEAN HARLOW	portrait	MGM	
MG33723	NORMA SHEARER	portrait	MGM	
MG33875	JEANETTE MACDONALD	portrait	MGM	
MG33977	MYRNA LOY	portrait	MGM	
MG33979	MYRNA LOY	portrait	MGM	
MG34335	JOAN CRAWFORD	portrait	MGM	
MG34355	UNA MERKEL	portrait	MGM	
MG34510	JEAN HOWARD	portrait	MGM	
MG34566	JEANETTE MACDONALD	portrait	MGM	
MG34797	UNA MERKEL	portrait	MGM	
MG34864	MYRNA LOY	portrait	MGM	
MG34865	MYRNA LOY	portrait	MGM	
MG34915	MYRNA LOY	portrait	MGM	
MG35645	MAUREEN O'SULLIVAN	portrait	MGM	
MG35679	JOHNNY WEISSMULLER	portrait	MGM	
MG35694	JEAN HOWARD	portrait	MGM	
MG35748	MURIEL EVANS	portrait	MGM	
MG36061	JOAN CRAWFORD	portrait	MGM	
MG36075	JOAN CRAWFORD	portrait	MGM	
MG36201	FRANCHOT TONE	portrait	MGM	
MG36807	NORMA SHEARER	portrait	MGM	
MG36840	NORMA SHEARER	portrait	MGM	
MG36841	NORMA SHEARER	portrait	MGM	
MG37109	JOHNNY WEISMULLER	portrait	MGM	
MG37120	LUPE VELEZ	portrait	MGM	
MG37306	FRANCHOT TONE	portrait	MGM	
MG37310	NORMA SHEARER	portrait	MGM	
MG37488	JOHNNY WEISSMULLER	portrait	MGM	
MG37598	MYRNA LOY	portrait	MGM	
MG37749	MYRNA LOY	portrait	MGM	
MG37749	MYRNA LOY	portrait	MGM	
MG38350	MYRNA LOY	portrait	MGM	
MG38402	MYRNA LOY	portrait	MGM	
MG38406	JOHNNY WEISSMULLER	portrait	MGM	
MG38642	ELIZABETH ALLAN	portrait	MGM	
MG38648	MAE CLARKE	portrait	MGM	
MG38894	JEANETTE MACDONALD	portrait	MGM	
MG38994	NORMA SHEARER	portrait	MGM	
MG39038	JEANETTE MACDONALD	portrait	MGM	
MG39619	CHARLES LAUGHTON	portrait	MGM	
MG39620	CHARLES LAUGHTON	portrait	MGM	
MG39849	KAREN MORLEY	portrait	MGM	
MG39911	MAUREEN O'SULLIVAN	portrait	MGM	
MG39913	MAUREEN O'SULLIVAN	portrait	MGM	
MG39922	MAUREEN O'SULLIVAN	portrait	MGM	

Movie Still Identification Book Ultimate Edition - Letters

CODE	TITLE/NAME	DIRECTOR/TYPE	STUDIO/DISTRIBUTOR	YEAR
MG40147	BRIAN AHERNE	portrait	MGM	
MG40153	WILLIAM POWELL	portrait	MGM	
MG40271	NORMA SHEARER	portrait	MGM	
MG40480	JOAN CRAWFORD	portrait	MGM	
MG40518	JOAN CRAWFORD	portrait	MGM	
MG40528	JOAN CRAWFORD	portrait	MGM	
MG40532	NORMA SHEARER	portrait	MGM	
MG40584	MAURICE CHEVALIER	portrait	MGM	
MG40810	BASIL RATHBONE	portrait	MGM	
MG41026	EVELYN LAYE	portrait	MGM	
MG41053	MICKEY ROONEY	portrait	MGM	
MG41092	GRETA GARBO	portrait	MGM	
MG41093	GRETA GARBO	portrait	MGM	
MG41094	GRETA GARBO	portrait	MGM	
MG41100	GRETA GARBO	portrait	MGM	
MG41101	GRETA GARBO	portrait	MGM	
MG41102	GRETA GARBO	portrait	MGM	
MG41177	GRETA GARBO	portrait	MGM	
MG41187	GRETA GARBO	portrait	MGM	
MG41188	GRETA GARBO	portrait	MGM	
MG41189	GRETA GARBO	portrait	MGM	
MG41195	GRETA GARBO	portrait	MGM	
MG41201	GRETA GARBO	portrait	MGM	
MG41203	GRETA GARBO	portrait	MGM	
MG41204	GRETA GARBO	portrait	MGM	
MG41205	GRETA GARBO	portrait	MGM	
MG41206	GRETA GARBO	portrait	MGM	
MG41207	GRETA GARBO	portrait	MGM	
MG41208	GRETA GARBO	portrait	MGM	
MG41209	GRETA GARBO	portrait	MGM	
MG41211	GRETA GARBO	portrait	MGM	
MG41213	GRETA GARBO	portrait	MGM	
MG41215	GRETA GARBO	portrait	MGM	
MG41216	GRETA GARBO	portrait	MGM	
MG41217	GRETA GARBO	portrait	MGM	
MG41218	GRETA GARBO	portrait	MGM	
MG41219	GRETA GARBO	portrait	MGM	
MG41221	GRETA GARBO	portrait	MGM	
MG41223	GRETA GARBO	portrait	MGM	
MG41226	GRETA GARBO	portrait	MGM	
MG41227	GRETA GARBO	portrait	MGM	
MG41230	GRETA GARBO	portrait	MGM	
MG41233	GRETA GARBO	portrait	MGM	
MG41505	JEANETTE MACDONALD	portrait	MGM	
MG41582	MAUREEN O'SULLIVAN	portrait	MGM	
MG41611	BILLIE BURKE	portrait	MGM	
MG41785	CECILIA PARKER	portrait	MGM	
MG41796	JEAN PARKER	portrait	MGM	
MG41850	CHESTER MORRIS	portrait	MGM	
MG42039	NORMA SHEARER	portrait	MGM	
MG42237	JOAN CRAWFORD	portrait	MGM	
MG42248	JEANETTE MACDONALD	portrait	MGM	
MG42295	JOAN CRAWFORD	portrait	MGM	
MG42379	WILLIAM POWELL	portrait	MGM	
MG42477	WILLIAM POWELL	portrait	MGM	
MG42538	CLARK GABLE	portrait	MGM	
MG42560	KAREN MORLEY	portrait	MGM	
MG42613	JUNE KNIGHT	portrait	MGM	
MG42700	CONSTANCE BENNETT	portrait	MGM	
MG42748	MAUREEN O'SULLIVAN	portrait	MGM	
MG42976	BETTY FURNESS	portrait	MGM	
MG43171	MAUREEN O'SULLIVAN	portrait	MGM	
MG43334	WS VAN DYKE, CECILIA PARKER, I. HERVEY, L. ROSINE	portrait	MGM	
MG43451	ROBERT TAYLOR	portrait	MGM	
MG43455	HELEN HAYES	portrait	MGM	
MG43922	JUNE KNIGHT	portrait	MGM	
MG43928	CORA SUE COLLINS	portrait	MGM	
MG43968	FRANK MORGAN	portrait	MGM	
MG44011	NINA MAE MCKINNEY	portrait	MGM	
MG44076	WALLACE BEERY	portrait	MGM	

Movie Still Identification Book Ultimate Edition - Letters

CODE	TITLE/NAME	DIRECTOR/TYPE	STUDIO/DISTRIBUTOR	YEAR
MG44313	FRANCHOT TONE	portrait	MGM	
MG44333	MAUREEN O'SULLIVAN	portrait	MGM	
MG44360	MAUREEN O'SULLIVAN	portrait	MGM	
MG44446	MAUREEN O'SULLIVAN	portrait	MGM	
MG44507	FREDDIE BARTHOLOMEW	portrait	MGM	
MG44911	FREDDIE BARTHOLOMEW	portrait	MGM	
MG44913	MAUREEN O'SULLIVAN	portrait	MGM	
MG44915	MAUREEN O'SULLIVAN	portrait	MGM	
MG44971	GREER GARSON, HUSBAND RICHARD NEY	portrait	MGM	
MG45068	MYRNA LOY	portrait	MGM	
MG45071	FREDDIE BARTHOLOMEW	portrait	MGM	
MG45082	MYRNA LOY	portrait	MGM	
MG45356	MYRNA LOY AT 3 MONTHS	portrait	MGM	
MG45383	ELEANOR POWELL	portrait	MGM	
MG45539	FREDDIE BARTHOLOMEW	portrait	MGM	
MG45548	NORMA SHEARER	portrait	MGM	
MG45582	JOAN CRAWFORD	portrait	MGM	
MG45972	VIRGINIA BRUCE	portrait	MGM	
MG46033	FREDDIE BARTHOLOMEW	portrait	MGM	
MG46078	WALLACE BEERY	portrait	MGM	
MG46167	NORMA SHEARER	portrait	MGM	
MG46217	JUNE KNIGHT	portrait	MGM	
MG46387	MAUREEN O'SULLIVAN	portrait	MGM	
MG46389	MAUREEN O'SULLIVAN	portrait	MGM	
MG46390	MAUREEN O'SULLIVAN	portrait	MGM	
MG46612	JUNE KNIGHT	portrait	MGM	
MG47020	ELIZABETH ALLAN	portrait	MGM	
MG47321	BRIAN AHERNE	portrait	MGM	
MG47475	LUCILE WATSON	portrait	MGM	
MG47842	THE MARX BROTHERS	portrait	MGM	
MG48052	JOSEPH L MANKIEWICZ	portrait	MGM	
MG48099	JUANITA QUIGLEY	portrait	MGM	
MG48534	UNA MERKEL	portrait	MGM	
MG48539	CECILIA PARKER	portrait	MGM	
MG48893	NORMA SHEARER	portrait	MGM	
MG48894	NORMA SHEARER	portrait	MGM	
MG48950	ROBERT YOUNG	portrait	MGM	
MG48951	JUDY GARLAND	portrait	MGM	
MG49109	JEANETTE MACDONALD	portrait	MGM	
MG49215	CECILIA PARKER	portrait	MGM	
MG49229	NORMA SHEARER	portrait	MGM	
MG49234	NORMA SHEARER	portrait	MGM	
MG49247	NORMA SHEARER	portrait	MGM	
MG49252	NORMA SHEARER	portrait	MGM	
MG49253	NORMA SHEARER	portrait	MGM	
MG49256	NORMA SHEARER	portrait	MGM	
MG49257	NORMA SHEARER	portrait	MGM	
MG49270	NORMA SHEARER	portrait	MGM	
MG49290	MADGE EVANS	portrait	MGM	
MG49351	NORMA SHEARER	portrait	MGM	
MG49469	MAUREEN O'SULLIVAN	portrait	MGM	
MG49601	JEANETTE MACDONALD	portrait	MGM	
MG49664	MAUREEN O'SULLIVAN	portrait	MGM	
MG49671	MAUREEN O'SULLIVAN	portrait	MGM	
MG49762	JEAN PARKER	portrait	MGM	
MG49849	MADGE EVANS	portrait	MGM	
MG50229	LUISE RAINER	portrait	MGM	
MG50232	LUISE RAINER	portrait	MGM	
MG50233	JOAN CRAWFORD	portrait	MGM	
MG50683	MAUREEN O'SULLIVAN	portrait	MGM	
MG50736	ROBERT TAYLOR	portrait	MGM	
MG50739	JEANETTE MACDONALD	portrait	MGM	
MG50742	JEANETTE MACDONALD	portrait	MGM	
MG50839	BETTY FURNESS	portrait	MGM	
MG51109	DARLA HOOD	portrait	MGM	
MG51523	MAUREEN O'SULLIVAN	portrait	MGM	
MG51574	ROBERT TAYLOR	portrait	MGM	
MG51589	ROBERT TAYLOR	portrait	MGM	
MG51717	LUISE RAINER	portrait	MGM	
MG51777	MAUREEN O'SULLIVAN	portrait	MGM	

Movie Still Identification Book Ultimate Edition - Letters

CODE	TITLE/NAME	DIRECTOR/TYPE	STUDIO/DISTRIBUTOR	YEAR
MG52483	FRANCHOT TONE	portrait	MGM	
MG52525	JOAN CRAWFORD	portrait	MGM	
MG53205	FRANK MORGAN	portrait	MGM	
MG53297	JEANETTE MACDONALD	portrait	MGM	
MG53611	NELSON EDDY	portrait	MGM	
MG53820	ELEANOR POWELL	portrait	MGM	
MG54034	ELEANOR POWELL	portrait	MGM	
MG54396	FRANCHOT TONE	portrait	MGM	
MG54538	MYRNA LOY	portrait	MGM	
MG54765	JUNE KNIGHT	portrait	MGM	
MG54874	VIRGINIA GREY	portrait	MGM	
MG55067	MICKEY ROONEY	portrait	MGM	
MG55492	ROBERT YOUNG	portrait	MGM	
MG55516	UNA MERKEL	portrait	MGM	
MG55826	MYRNA LOY	portrait	MGM	
MG55945	MAUREEN O'SULLIVAN	portrait	MGM	
MG56003	UNA MERKEL	portrait	MGM	
MG56006	MAUREEN O'SULLIVAN	portrait	MGM	
MG56231	MAUREEN O'SULLIVAN	portrait	MGM	
MG56310	JOAN CRAWFORD	portrait	MGM	
MG56436	DELLA LIND	portrait	MGM	
MG56707	MAUREEN O'SULLIVAN	portrait	MGM	
MG56743	JAMES STEWART	portrait	MGM	
MG56746	JAMES STEWART	portrait	MGM	
MG56761	CLARK GABLE, WILLAM POWELL, S. TRACY, R. TAYLOR	portrait	MGM	
MG56953	ROBERT YOUNG, DAUGHTER CAROL ANN	portrait	MGM	
MG57004	DOROTHY GISH	portrait	MGM	
MG57075	LUISE RAINER	portrait	MGM	
MG57210	MAUREEN O'SULLIVAN	portrait	MGM	
MG57353	GRETA GARBO	portrait	MGM	
MG57356	GRETA GARBO	portrait	MGM	
MG57357	GRETA GARBO	portrait	MGM	
MG57359	GRETA GARBO	portrait	MGM	
MG57360	GRETA GARBO	portrait	MGM	
MG57362	GRETA GARBO	portrait	MGM	
MG57363	GRETA GARBO	portrait	MGM	
MG57364	GRETA GARBO	portrait	MGM	
MG57365	GRETA GARBO	portrait	MGM	
MG57366	GRETA GARBO	portrait	MGM	
MG57367	GRETA GARBO	portrait	MGM	
MG57368	GRETA GARBO	portrait	MGM	
MG57369	GRETA GARBO	portrait	MGM	
MG57413	ROBERT TAYLOR	portrait	MGM	
MG57449	GRETA GARBO	portrait	MGM	
MG57450	GRETA GARBO	portrait	MGM	
MG57451	GRETA GARBO	portrait	MGM	
MG57452	GRETA GARBO	portrait	MGM	
MG57455	GRETA GARBO	portrait	MGM	
MG57456	GRETA GARBO	portrait	MGM	
MG57457	GRETA GARBO	portrait	MGM	
MG57458	GRETA GARBO	portrait	MGM	
MG57465	GRETA GARBO	portrait	MGM	
MG57468	GRETA GARBO	portrait	MGM	
MG57469	GRETA GARBO	portrait	MGM	
MG57470	GRETA GARBO	portrait	MGM	
MG57471	GRETA GARBO	portrait	MGM	
MG57473	GRETA GARBO	portrait	MGM	
MG57474	GRETA GARBO	portrait	MGM	
MG57475	GRETA GARBO	portrait	MGM	
MG57476	GRETA GARBO	portrait	MGM	
MG57478	GRETA GARBO	portrait	MGM	
MG57479	GRETA GARBO	portrait	MGM	
MG57481	GRETA GARBO	portrait	MGM	
MG57482	GRETA GARBO	portrait	MGM	
MG57483	GRETA GARBO	portrait	MGM	
MG57484	GRETA GARBO	portrait	MGM	
MG57485	GRETA GARBO	portrait	MGM	
MG57486	GRETA GARBO	portrait	MGM	
MG57487	GRETA GARBO	portrait	MGM	
MG57488	GRETA GARBO	portrait	MGM	

Movie Still Identification Book Ultimate Edition - Letters

CODE	TITLE/NAME	DIRECTOR/TYPE	STUDIO/DISTRIBUTOR	YEAR
MG57489	GRETA GARBO	portrait	MGM	
MG57490	GRETA GARBO	portrait	MGM	
MG57492	GRETA GARBO	portrait	MGM	
MG57493	GRETA GARBO	portrait	MGM	
MG57494	GRETA GARBO	portrait	MGM	
MG57495	GRETA GARBO	portrait	MGM	
MG57496	GRETA GARBO	portrait	MGM	
MG57497	GRETA GARBO	portrait	MGM	
MG57499	GRETA GARBO	portrait	MGM	
MG57500	GRETA GARBO	portrait	MGM	
MG57502	GRETA GARBO	portrait	MGM	
MG57503	GRETA GARBO	portrait	MGM	
MG57504	GRETA GARBO	portrait	MGM	
MG57505	GRETA GARBO	portrait	MGM	
MG57506	GRETA GARBO	portrait	MGM	
MG57507	GRETA GARBO	portrait	MGM	
MG57508	GRETA GARBO	portrait	MGM	
MG57509	GRETA GARBO	portrait	MGM	
MG57510	GRETA GARBO	portrait	MGM	
MG57511	GRETA GARBO	portrait	MGM	
MG57512	GRETA GARBO	portrait	MGM	
MG57513	GRETA GARBO	portrait	MGM	
MG57514	GRETA GARBO	portrait	MGM	
MG57516	GRETA GARBO	portrait	MGM	
MG57517	GRETA GARBO	portrait	MGM	
MG57812	LUISE RAINER	portrait	MGM	
MG57888	JOHN BARRYMORE, MARY GARDEN	portrait	MGM	
MG57922	LUISE RAINER	portrait	MGM	
MG58038	BUDDY EBSEN	portrait	MGM	
MG58071	MYRNA LOY	portrait	MGM	
MG58414	WS VAN DYKE, PATIENCE ABBE, JOHN ABBE, RICHARD ABBE	portrait	MGM	
MG58641	LUISE RAINER	portrait	MGM	
MG58646	MAUREEN O'SULLIVAN	portrait	MGM	
MG59620	WS VAN DYKE	portrait	MGM	
MG60537	CECILIA PARKER, LILLIAN ROSINE	portrait	MGM	
MG60654	CECILIA PARKER, LILLIAN ROSINE	portrait	MGM	
MG60659	CECILIA PARKER, LILLIAN ROSINE	portrait	MGM	
MG60778	MYRNA LOY	portrait	MGM	
MG60871	MAUREEN O'SULLIVAN	portrait	MGM	
MG61696	MAUREEN O'SULLIVAN	portrait	MGM	
MG61798	MADGE EVANS	portrait	MGM	
MG61804	MYRNA LOY, DIRECTOR RICHARD THORPE	portrait	MGM	
MG62653	IRENE MANNING	portrait	MGM	
MG63203	ROBERT TAYLOR	portrait	MGM	
MG63232	LUISE RAINER	portrait	MGM	
MG63396	MAUREEN O'SULLIVAN	portrait	MGM	
MG63573	WALLACE BEERY - BAD MAN OF BRIMSTONE	portrait	MGM	
MG63685	ALLAN JONES	portrait	MGM	
MG63867	WALTER PIDGEON	portrait	MGM	
MG63958	GRETA GARBO	portrait	MGM	
MG63961	GRETA GARBO	portrait	MGM	
MG63963	GRETA GARBO	portrait	MGM	
MG63965	GRETA GARBO	portrait	MGM	
MG63966	GRETA GARBO	portrait	MGM	
MG63970	GRETA GARBO	portrait	MGM	
MG63973	GRETA GARBO	portrait	MGM	
MG63974	GRETA GARBO	portrait	MGM	
MG63975	GRETA GARBO	portrait	MGM	
MG63976	GRETA GARBO	portrait	MGM	
MG63977	GRETA GARBO	portrait	MGM	
MG63979	GRETA GARBO	portrait	MGM	
MG63980	GRETA GARBO	portrait	MGM	
MG63981	GRETA GARBO	portrait	MGM	
MG63983	GRETA GARBO	portrait	MGM	
MG63984	GRETA GARBO	portrait	MGM	
MG63986	GRETA GARBO	portrait	MGM	
MG63988	GRETA GARBO	portrait	LMGM	
MG63989	GRETA GARBO	portrait	MGM	
MG63990	GRETA GARBO	portrait	MGM	
MG63994	GRETA GARBO	portrait	MGM	

Movie Still Identification Book Ultimate Edition - Letters

CODE	TITLE/NAME	DIRECTOR/TYPE	STUDIO/DISTRIBUTOR	YEAR
MG63996	GRETA GARBO	portrait	MGM	
MG63997	GRETA GARBO	portrait	MGM	
MG63999	GRETA GARBO	portrait	MGM	
MG64001	GRETA GARBO	portrait	MGM	
MG64007	GRETA GARBO	portrait	MGM	
MG64017	GRETA GARBO	portrait	MGM	
MG64365	MICKEY ROONEY	portrait	MGM	
MG64480	LASZLO WILLINGER	portrait	MGM	
MG64812	FANNY BRICE	portrait	MGM	
MG65054	JOAN CRAWFORD	portrait	MGM	
MG65056	JOAN CRAWFORD	portrait	MGM	
MG65091	JOAN CRAWFORD	portrait	MGM	
MG65093	JOAN CRAWFORD	portrait	MGM	
MG65295	MAUREEN O'SULLIVAN	portrait	MGM	
MG65296	MAUREEN O'SULLIVAN	portrait	MGM	
MG65344	MYRNA LOY	portrait	MGM	
MG65356	FRANK MORGAN	portrait	MGM	
MG65394	CLARK GABLE, MYRNA LOY	portrait	MGM	
MG65586	MICKEY ROONEY	portrait	MGM	
MG65619	MICKEY ROONEY	portrait	MGM	
MG65639	ROSALIND RUSSELL	portrait	MGM	
MG65732	WS VAN DYKE, FRANK MORGAN	portrait	MGM	
MG65823	VIRGINIA GREY	portrait	MGM	
MG66098	GALE SONDERGAARD	portrait	MGM	
MG66116	ROBERT MORLEY	portrait	MGM	
MG66404	GRETA GARBO	portrait	MGM	
MG66580	ELEANOR POWELL	portrait	MGM	
MG66819	WALLACE BEERY	portrait	MGM	
MG66967	JEANETTE MACDONALD	portrait	MGM	
MG67026	LUISE RAINER	portrait	MGM	
MG67152	LUISE RAINER	portrait	MGM	
MG67484	HEDY LAMARR	portrait	MGM	
MG67550	MARGARET SULLAVAN	portrait	MGM	
MG67643	NORMA SHEARER	portrait	MGM	
MG67644	NORMA SHEARER	portrait	MGM	
MG67823	MAUREEN O'SULLIVAN	portrait	MGM	
MG67851	ROSALIND RUSSELL	portrait	MGM	
MG67907	FAY HOLDEN	portrait	MGM	
MG68327	NORMA SHEARER	portrait	MGM	
MG68545	ROBERT MONTGOMERY	portrait	MGM	
MG68547	ROBERT MONTGOMERY	portrait	MGM	
MG68609	UNA MERKEL	portrait	MGM	
MG68922	JANET GAYNOR	portrait	MGM	
MG68957	ELEANOR POWELL	portrait	MGM	
MG69279	TERRY KILBURN	portrait	MGM	
MG69284	UNA MERKEL	portrait	MGM	
MG69287	RUTH HUSSEY	portrait	MGM	
MG69294	ANN MORRISS	portrait	MGM	
MG69418	HEDY LAMARR	portrait	MGM	
MG69489	UNA MERKEL	portrait	MGM	
MG69608	RUTH HUSSEY	portrait	MGM	
MG69656	JOAN CRAWFORD	portrait	MGM	
MG69758	WALTER PIDGEON	portrait	MGM	
MG69936	SARA HADEN	portrait	MGM	
MG69936	SARA HADEN	portrait	MGM	
MG69974	MAUREEN O'SULLIVAN	portrait	MGM	
MG70124	HEDY LAMARR	portrait	MGM	
MG70181	GRETA GARBO	portrait	MGM	
MG70331	JEANETTE MACDONALD	portrait	MGM	
MG70450	JEANETTE MACDONALD	portrait	MGM	
MG70477	LENI LYNN	portrait	MGM	
MG70805	ROBERT BENCHLEY	portrait	MGM	
MG70957	GREER GARSON	portrait	MGM	
MG70962	MICKEY ROONEY	portrait	MGM	
MG71055	GREER GARSON	portrait	MGM	
MG71145	MAUREEN O'SULLIVAN	portrait	MGM	
MG71152	MAUREEN O'SULLIVAN	portrait	MGM	
MG71313	HEDY LAMARR	portrait	MGM	
MG71371	WALTER PIDGEON	portrait	MGM	
MG71379	WALTER PIDGEON	portrait	MGM	

Movie Still Identification Book Ultimate Edition - Letters

CODE	TITLE/NAME	DIRECTOR/TYPE	STUDIO/DISTRIBUTOR	YEAR
MG71380	ROBERT YOUNG	portrait	MGM	
MG71383	FAY HOLDEN	portrait	MGM	
MG71491	RUTH HUSSEY	portrait	MGM	
MG71512	NORMA SHEARER	portrait	MGM	
MG71517	NORMA SHEARER	portrait	MGM	
MG71553	RUTH HUSSEY	portrait	MGM	
MG71554	JUNE PREISSER	portrait	MGM	
MG71555	ROBERT YOUNG	portrait	MGM	
MG71555	ROBERT YOUNG	portrait	MGM	
MG71686	RUTH HUSSEY	portrait	MGM	
MG71687	ROBERT YOUNG	portrait	MGM	
MG71699	MARY HOWARD	portrait	MGM	
MG71786	NORMA SHEARER	portrait	MGM	
MG71856	ELEANOR POWELL	portrait	MGM	
MG71911	JOAN CRAWFORD	portrait	MGM	
MG72008	HEDY LAMARR	portrait	MGM	
MG72080	VIRGINIA GREY	portrait	MGM	
MG72159	VIRGINIA GREY	portrait	MGM	
MG72183	MYRNA LOY	portrait	MGM	
MG72197	MYRNA LOY	portrait	MGM	
MG72200	VIRGINIA GREY	portrait	MGM	
MG72320	ANN RUTHERFORD	portrait	MGM	
MG72357	HEDY LAMARR	portrait	MGM	
MG72518	LANA TURNER	portrait	MGM	
MG72542	LANA TURNER	portrait	MGM	
MG72898	GREER GARSON	portrait	MGM	
MG72947	VIRGINIA WEIDLER	portrait	MGM	
MG73260	ROBERT TAYLOR	portrait	MGM	
MG73296	MAUREEN O'SULLIVAN	portrait	MGM	
MG73371	ELEANOR POWELL	portrait	MGM	
MG73503	GREER GARSON	portrait	MGM	
MG73518	ANN SOTHERN	portrait	MGM	
MG73587	VIRGINIA WEIDLER	portrait	MGM	
MG74342	NORMA SHEARER	portrait	MGM	
MG74497	JOAN CRAWFORD	portrait	MGM	
MG74509	GRETA GARBO	portrait	MGM	
MG74512	GRETA GARBO	portrait	MGM	
MG74514	GRETA GARBO	portrait	MGM	
MG74516	GRETA GARBO	portrait	MGM	
MG74517	GRETA GARBO	portrait	MGM	
MG74523	GRETA GARBO	portrait	MGM	
MG74524	GRETA GARBO	portrait	MGM	
MG74525	GRETA GARBO	portrait	MGM	
MG74562	ILONA MASSEY	portrait	MGM	
MG74580	LANA TURNER	portrait	MGM	
MG74885	GREER GARSON	portrait	MGM	
MG74950	MARSHA HUNT	portrait	MGM	
MG75142	LARAINE DAY	portrait	MGM	
MG75280	LARAINE DAY	portrait	MGM	
MG75341	RUTH HUSSEY	portrait	MGM	
MG75342	RUTH HUSSEY	portrait	MGM	
MG75343	RUTH HUSSEY	portrait	MGM	
MG75352	LANA TURNER	portrait	MGM	
MG75429	GREER GARSON	portrait	MGM	
MG75448	JOAN CRAWFORD	portrait	MGM	
MG75515	GREER GARSON	portrait	MGM	
MG75731	MAUREEN O'SULLIVAN	portrait	MGM	
MG75741	ELEANOR POWELL	portrait	MGM	
MG75796	GRETA GARBO	portrait	MGM	
MG75800	GRETA GARBO	portrait	MGM	
MG75801	GRETA GARBO	portrait	MGM	
MG75802	GRETA GARBO	portrait	MGM	
MG75803	GRETA GARBO	portrait	MGM	
MG75804	GRETA GARBO	portrait	MGM	
MG75805	GRETA GARBO	portrait	MGM	
MG75806	GRETA GARBO	portrait	MGM	
MG75807	GRETA GARBO	portrait	MGM	
MG75809	GRETA GARBO	portrait	MGM	
MG75811	GRETA GARBO	portrait	MGM	
MG75812	GRETA GARBO	portrait	MGM	

Movie Still Identification Book Ultimate Edition - Letters

CODE	TITLE/NAME	DIRECTOR/TYPE	STUDIO/DISTRIBUTOR	YEAR
MG75814	GRETA GARBO	portrait	MGM	
MG75815	GRETA GARBO	portrait	MGM	
MG75817	GRETA GARBO	portrait	MGM	
MG75821	GRETA GARBO	portrait	MGM	
MG75822	GRETA GARBO	portrait	MGM	
MG75823	GRETA GARBO	portrait	MGM	
MG75825	GRETA GARBO	portrait	MGM	
MG75826	GRETA GARBO	portrait	MGM	
MG75827	GRETA GARBO	portrait	MGM	
MG75828	GRETA GARBO	portrait	MGM	
MG75829	GRETA GARBO	portrait	MGM	
MG75830	GRETA GARBO	portrait	MGM	
MG75834	GRETA GARBO	portrait	MGM	
MG75836	GRETA GARBO	portrait	MGM	
MG75898	GRETA GARBO	portrait	MGM	
MG75928	INA CLAIRE	portrait	MGM	
MG75968	JUDY GARLAND	portrait	MGM	
MG76193	ANN RUTHERFORD	portrait	MGM	
MG76243	MICKEY ROONEY	portrait	MGM	
MG76251	WALTER PIDGEON	portrait	MGM	
MG76368	LARAINE DAY	portrait	MGM	
MG76591	FRED ASTAIRE	portrait	MGM	
MG76621	LANA TURNER	portrait	MGM	
MG76867	VIRGINIA WEIDLER	portrait	MGM	
MG76984	MARGARET SULLAVAN	portrait	MGM	
MG76987	MARGARET SULLAVAN	portrait	MGM	
MG77055	FRED ASTAIRE	portrait	MGM	
MG77056	FRED ASTAIRE	portrait	MGM	
MG77057	FRED ASTAIRE	portrait	MGM	
MG77058	FRED ASTAIRE	portrait	MGM	
MG77059	FRED ASTAIRE	portrait	MGM	
MG77502	DIANA LEWIS	portrait	MGM	
MG77761	DIANA LEWIS	portrait	MGM	
MG77805	DIANA LEWIS	portrait	MGM	
MG77805	DIANA LEWIS	portrait	MGM	
MG77880	LANA TURNER	portrait	MGM	
MG77996	MAUREEN O'SULLIVAN	portrait	MGM	
MG77997	MAUREEN O'SULLIVAN	portrait	MGM	
MG78000	ANN RUTHERFORD	portrait	MGM	
MG78004	FAY BAINTER	portrait	MGM	
MG78010	RUTH HUSSEY	portrait	MGM	
MG78014	DIANA LEWIS	portrait	MGM	
MG78031	ROBERT YOUNG	portrait	MGM	
MG78081	MAUREEN O'SULLIVAN	portrait	MGM	
MG78096	HEDY LAMARR	portrait	MGM	
MG78262	DIANA LEWIS, WILLIAM POWELL	portrait	MGM	
MG78264	VIRGINIA WEIDLER	portrait	MGM	
MG7835X	GRETA GARBO	portrait	MGM	
MG7838X	GRETA GARBO	portrait	MGM	
MG7841X	GRETA GARBO	portrait	MGM	
MG78598	RUTH HUSSEY	portrait	MGM	
MG78637	DIANA LEWIS	portrait	MGM	
MG78722	ANN RUTHERFORD	portrait	MGM	
MG78890	LAURENCE OLIVIER	portrait	MGM	
MG78917	SPENCER TRACY + HIS MOTHER	portrait	MGM	
MG78918	SPENCER TRACY	portrait	MGM	
MG79043	VIRGINIA WEIDLER	portrait	MGM	
MG79065	ELEANOR POWELL	portrait	MGM	
MG79069	DIANA LEWIS	portrait	MGM	
MG79075	RUTH HUSSEY	portrait	MGM	
MG79076	DIANA LEWIS	portrait	MGM	
MG79226	LANA TURNER AT 8	portrait	MGM	
MG80224	CLAUDETTE COLBERT	portrait	MGM	
MG80299	VIRGINIA WEIDLER	portrait	MGM	
MG80570	MYRNA LOY	portrait	MGM	
MG80686	KATHARINE HEPBURN	portrait	MGM	
MG80736	LARAINE DAY	portrait	MGM	
MG80969	KATHRYN GRAYSON	portrait	MGM	
MG80971	KATHRYN GRAYSON	portrait	MGM	
MG80974	HEDY LAMARR	portrait	MGM	

Movie Still Identification Book Ultimate Edition - Letters

CODE	TITLE/NAME	DIRECTOR/TYPE	STUDIO/DISTRIBUTOR	YEAR
MG81006	KATHARINE HEPBURN	portrait	MGM	
MG81007	KATHARINE HEPBURN	portrait	MGM	
MG81012	VIRGINIA O'BRIEN	portrait	MGM	
MG81013	VIRGINIA O'BRIEN	portrait	MGM	
MG81032	KATHARINE HEPBURN	portrait	MGM	
MG81063	RUTH HUSSEY	portrait	MGM	
MG81102	RUTH HUSSEY	portrait	MGM	
MG81162	NORMA SHEARER	portrait	MGM	
MG81163	RUTH HUSSEY	portrait	MGM	
MG81173	LANA TURNER	portrait	MGM	
MG81178	ANN RUTHERFORD	portrait	MGM	
MG81180	DIANA LEWIS	portrait	MGM	
MG81239	MARY HOWARD	portrait	MGM	
MG81249	VIRGINIA O'BRIEN	portrait	MGM	
MG81377	ANN SOTHERN	portrait	MGM	
MG81385	RUTH HUSSEY	portrait	MGM	
MG81427	JEANETTE MACDONALD	portrait	MGM	
MG81479	MYRNA LOY	portrait	MGM	
MG81484	MYRNA LOY	portrait	MGM	
MG81514	LARAINE DAY	portrait	MGM	
MG81555	RUTH HUSSEY	portrait	MGM	
MG81560	SARA HADEN	portrait	MGM	
MG81685	NORMA SHEARER	portrait	MGM	
MG81695	SUSAN PETERS	portrait	MGM	
MG81881	MARJORIE MAIN	portrait	MGM	
MG81884	MARJORIE MAIN	portrait	MGM	
MG82098	RED SKELTON	portrait	MGM	
MG82100	RED SKELTON	portrait	MGM	
MG82120	RUTH HUSSEY	portrait	MGM	
MG82122	RUTH HUSSEY, EDWARD G. ROBINSON - BLACKMAIL	portrait	MGM	
MG82255	RUTH HUSSEY	portrait	MGM	
MG82259	HEDY LAMARR	portrait	MGM	
MG82259	HEDY LAMARR	portrait	MGM	
MG82397	RUTH HUSSEY + MOTHER, SISTER BETTY	portrait	MGM	
MG82398	RUTH HUSSEY, ROBERT YOUNG - RICH MAN, POOR GIRL	portrait	MGM	
MG82401	RUTH HUSSEY, CLIFF EDWARDS, ROBERT YOUNG - MAISIE	portrait	MGM	
MG82402	RUTH HUSSEY, MARY BETH HUGHES, NORMA SHEARER	portrait	MGM	
MG82405	RUTH HUSSEY, J. CRAWFORD, R. HOBART - SUSAN & GOD	portrait	MGM	
MG82410	RUTH HUSSEY	portrait	MGM	
MG82509	LANA TURNER	portrait	MGM	
MG82553	NORMA SHEARER	portrait	MGM	
MG82584	NORMA SHEARER	portrait	MGM	
MG82585	NORMA SHEARER	portrait	MGM	
MG82587	RUTH HUSSEY	portrait	MGM	
MG82713	GRETA GARBO	portrait	MGM	
MG82714	KATHARINE HEPBURN	portrait	MGM	
MG82957	MICKEY ROONEY	portrait	MGM	
MG82963	MYRNA LOY	portrait	MGM	
MG83104	ANN SOTHERN	portrait	MGM	
MG83108	ANN SOTHERN	portrait	MGM	
MG83278	LARAINE DAY	portrait	MGM	
MG83281	LARAINE DAY	portrait	MGM	
MG83448	LARAINE DAY	portrait	MGM	
MG83659	ROBERT YOUNG	portrait	MGM	
MG83690	JOAN CRAWFORD	portrait	MGM	
MG83700	JOAN CRAWFORD	portrait	MGM	
MG83949	MYRNA LOY	portrait	MGM	
MG83965	MYRNA LOY	portrait	MGM	
MG83989	JOAN CRAWFORD	portrait	MGM	
MG84057	ANN MORRISS, MARY HOWARD	portrait	MGM	
MG84135	ROBERT YOUNG, WIFE BETTY HENDERSON	portrait	MGM	
MG84138	ANN SOTHERN, HUSBAND ROGER PRYOR	portrait	MGM	
MG84152	ROBERT YOUNG	portrait	MGM	
MG84183	FAY HOLDEN	portrait	MGM	
MG84184	FAY HOLDEN	portrait	MGM	
MG84247	JOAN CRAWFORD	portrait	MGM	
MG84249	JOAN CRAWFORD	portrait	MTGM	
MG84276	LANA TURNER	portrait	MGM	
MG84311	RED SKELTON	portrait	MGM	
MG84312	RED SKELTON	portrait	MGM	

Movie Still Identification Book Ultimate Edition - Letters

CODE	TITLE/NAME	DIRECTOR/TYPE	STUDIO/DISTRIBUTOR	YEAR
MG84316	RED SKELTON	portrait	MGM	
MG84338	VIRGINIA GREY	portrait	MGM	
MG84367	JEANETTE MACDONALD	portrait	MGM	
MG84371	JEANETTE MACDONALD	portrait	MGM	
MG84539	ELEANOR POWELL	portrait	MGM	
MG84540	ELEANOR POWELL	portrait	MGM	
MG84594	LANA TURNER	portrait	MGM	
MG84663	DONALD MEEK	portrait	MGM	
MG84669	JOAN CRAWFORD	portrait	MGM	
MG84696	JOHNNY WEISSMULLER, WIFE BERYL, SON JOHN SCOTT	portrait	MGM	
MG84745	HEDY LAMARR	portrait	MGM	
MG84749	LARAINE DAY	portrait	MGM	
MG84921	GREER GARSON	portrait	MGM	
MG85212	VIRGINIA GREY	portrait	MGM	
MG85219	VIRGINIA GREY	portrait	MGM	
MG85244	GREER GARSON	portrait	MGM	
MG85370	RUTH HUSSEY	portrait	MGM	
MG85381	GREER GARSON	portrait	MGM	
MG85455	DONNA REED	portrait	MGM	
MG85536	ROBERT TAYLOR	portrait	MGM	
MG85679	BARRY NELSON	portrait	MGM	
MG85778	MARSHA HUNT	portrait	MGM	
MG85779	MARSHA HUNT	portrait	MGM	
MG85828	FAY HOLDEN	portrait	MGM	
MG85833	KATHRYN GRAYSON + HUSBAND JOHN SHELTON	portrait	MGM	
MG85852	MAUREEN O'SULLIVAN	portrait	MGM	
MG86066	BARRY NELSON	portrait	MGM	
MG86066	BARRY NELSON	portrait	MGM	
MG86153	NORMA SHEARER	portrait	MGM	
MG86173	NORMA SHEARER	portrait	MGM	
MG86324	HEDY LAMARR	portrait	MGM	
MG86360	RUTH HUSSEY	portrait	MGM	
MG86366	RUTH HUSSEY	portrait	MGM	
MG86382	GRETA GARBO	portrait	MGM	
MG86383	GRETA GARBO	portrait	MGM	
MG86384	GRETA GARBO	portrait	MGM	
MG86393	GRETA GARBO	portrait	MGM	
MG86402	ANN SOTHERN	portrait	MGM	
MG86423	MAUREEN O'SULLIVAN	portrait	MGM	
MG86494	HEDY LAMARR	portrait	MGM	
MG86528	DONNA REED	portrait	MGM	
MG86579	BARRY NELSON	portrait	MGM	
MG86664	RUTH GORDON	portrait	MGM	
MG86677	ANN SOTHERN	portrait	MGM	
MG86679	ANN SOTHERN	portrait	MGM	
MG86803	RUTH HUSSEY	portrait	MGM	
MG86887	HEDY LAMARR	portrait	MGM	
MG86959	WALTER PIDGEON	portrait	MGM	
MG87048	MARSHA HUNT	portrait	MGM	
MG87063	KATHARINE HEPBURN	portrait	MGM	
MG87064	KATHARINE HEPBURN	portrait	MGM	
MG87079	KATHARINE HEPBURN	portrait	MGM	
MG87080	KATHARINE HEPBURN	portrait	MGM	
MG87202	WILLIAM LUNDIGAN	portrait	MGM	
MG87224	RUTH HUSSEY	portrait	MGM	
MG87318	LARAINE DAY	portrait	MGM	
MG87363	LARAINE DAY	portrait	MGM	
MG87377	KATHARINE HEPBURN	portrait	MGM	
MG87431	MARSHA HUNT	portrait	MGM	
MG87818	ANN SOTHERN	portrait	MGM	
MG87833	VIRGINIA O'BRIEN	portrait	MGM	
MG87836	VIRGINIA O'BRIEN	portrait	MGM	
MG87872	MAUREEN O'SULLIVAN	portrait	MGM	
MG87902	ANN SOTHERN	portrait	MGM	
MG87939	JEANETTE MACDONALD	portrait	MGM	
MG87950	JEANETTE MACDONALD	portrait	MGM	
MG87951	JEANETTE MACDONALD	portrait	MGM	
MG87953	JEANETTE MACDONALD	portrait	MGM	
MG87983	RUTH HUSSEY	portrait	MGM	
MG88078	RAGS RAGLAND	portrait	MGM	

Movie Still Identification Book Ultimate Edition - Letters

CODE	TITLE/NAME	DIRECTOR/TYPE	STUDIO/DISTRIBUTOR	YEAR
MG88078	RAGS RAGLAND	portrait	MGM	
MG88087	RED SKELTON	portrait	MGM	
MG88091	RED SKELTON	portrait	MGM	
MG88120	LARAINE DAY	portrait	MGM	
MG88160	DONNA REED AT 7, BROTHER KEITH, SISTER LAVONNE	portrait	MGM	
MG88183	MARJORIE MAIN	portrait	MGM	
MG88184	MARJORIE MAIN	portrait	MGM	
MG88184	MARJORIE MAIN	portrait	MGM	
MG88186	JOHN GARFIELD	portrait	MGM	
MG88186	JOHN GARFIELD	portrait	MGM	
MG88256	BASIL RATHBONE	portrait	MGM	
MG88496	VIRGINIA WEIDLER	portrait	MGM	
MG88657	MYRNA LOY	portrait	MGM	
MG88816	MYRNA LOY	portrait	MGM	
MG88853	VAN HEFLIN	portrait	MGM	
MG88995	DOROTHY MORRIS	portrait	MGM	
MG89131	FRANK MORGAN	portrait	MGM	
MG89177	VIRGINIA O'BRIEN	portrait	MGM	
MG89210	DICK SIMMONS	portrait	MGM	
MG89277	ANN SOTHERN	portrait	MGM	
MG89277	RED SKELTON, WIFE EDNA	portrait	MGM	
MG89362	DONNA REED	portrait	MGM	
MG89393	DONNA REED	portrait	MGM	
MG89395	DONNA REED	portrait	MGM	
MG89589	FAY HOLDEN	portrait	MGM	
MG89612	WILLIAM LUNDIGAN	portrait	MGM	
MG89616	DONNA REED	portrait	MGM	
MG89655	MYRNA LOY, HUSBAND JOHN D. HERTZ, JR	portrait	MGM	
MG89718	WILLIAM POWELL	portrait	MGM	
MG89753	RICHARD NEY	portrait	MGM	
MG89760	LANA TURNER	portrait	MGM	
MG89795	DOROTHY MORRIS	portrait	MGM	
MG89905	LARAINE DAY	portrait	MGM	
MG89956	DONNA REED	portrait	MGM	
MG90111	JEAN-PIERRE AUMONT	portrait	MGM	
MG90323	FAY BAINTER	portrait	MGM	
MG90338	GREER GARSON	portrait	MGM	
MG90369	FRANCES RAFFERTY	portrait	MGM	
MG90411	RUTH HUSSEY + HUSBAND C. ROBERT LONGENECKER	portrait	MGM	
MG90421	SIGNE HASSO	portrait	MGM	
MG90797	HEDY LAMARR	portrait	MGM	
MG90867	SUSAN PETERS	portrait	MGM	
MG90881	GREER GARSON, E. LAWRENCE - STARS OVER AMERICA	portrait	MGM	
MG90962	GREER GARSON, R. COLMAN, H. LAMARR, V. GILMORE	portrait	MGM	
MG91006	SUSAN PETERS	portrait	MGM	
MG91008	SUSAN PETERS	portrait	MGM	
MG91045	MARSHA HUNT	portrait	MGM	
MG91089	LANA TURNER	portrait	MGM	
MG91267	LARAINE DAY	portrait	MGM	
MG91324	NANCY WALKER	portrait	MGM	
MG91332	KATHARINE HEPBURN	portrait	MGM	
MG91553	MARILYN MAXWELL	portrait	MGM	
MG91583	JOAN CRAWFORD	portrait	MGM	
MG91584	SPRING BYINGTON	portrait	MGM	
MG91596	JOAN CRAWFORD	portrait	MGM	
MG91604	MARILYN MAXWELL	portrait	MGM	
MG91612	MARILYN MAXWELL	portrait	MGM	
MG91789	VIRGINIA O'BRIEN	portrait	MGM	
MG91996	RED SKELTON	portrait	MGM	
MG92114	ANN SOTHERN	portrait	MGM	
MG92153	LANA TURNER	portrait	MGM	
MG92169	LANA TURNER	portrait	MGM	
MG92273	GLORIA DE HAVEN	portrait	MGM	
MG92551	SPRING BYINGTON	portrait	MGM	
MG92752	DONNA REED	portrait	MGM	
MG92799	IRENE DUNNE	portrait	MGM	
MG92889	JOAN CRAWFORD	portrait	MGM	
MG93149	DAME MAY WHITTY	portrait	MGM	
MG93179	DONNA REED	portrait	MGM	
MG93538	PAMELA BLAKE	portrait	MGM	

Movie Still Identification Book Ultimate Edition - Letters

CODE	TITLE/NAME	DIRECTOR/TYPE	STUDIO/DISTRIBUTOR	YEAR
MG93796	MARY ASTOR	portrait	MGM	
MG93797	MARY ASTOR	portrait	MGM	
MG93798	MARY ASTOR	portrait	MGM	
MG93799	MARY ASTOR	portrait	MGM	
MG93832	DONNA REED, HUSBAND BILL TUTTLE	portrait	MGM	
MG93863	JOAN CRAWFORD	portrait	MGM	
MG93877	ELEANOR POWELL	portrait	MGM	
MG93879	ELEANOR POWELL	portrait	MGM	
MG93881	ELEANOR POWELL	portrait	MGM	
MG93886	ELEANOR POWELL	portrait	MGM	
MG93924	ANN RICHARDS	portrait	MGM	
MG93940	LAURA LA PLANTE	portrait	MGM	
MG93995	MARY ASTOR	portrait	MGM	
MG94326	MARY ASTOR	portrait	MGM	
MG94377	FRANCES RAFFERTY	portrait	MGM	
MG94594	VIRGINIA WEIDLER	portrait	MGM	
MG94655	SARA HADEN	portrait	MGM	
MG94661	MICKEY ROONEY	portrait	MGM	
MG94661	MICKEY ROONEY	portrait	MGM	
MG94737	MARILYN MAXWELL	portrait	MGM	
MG94910	FRANCES GIFFORD	portrait	MGM	
MG94969	GREER GARSON, HUSBAND RICHARD NEY	portrait	MGM	
MG94984	CONNIE GILCHRIST	portrait	MGM	
MG95005	LARAINE DAY	portrait	MGM	
MG95083	DONNA REED	portrait	MGM	
MG95155	DONNA REED	portrait	MGM	
MG95177	FAY BAINTER	portrait	MGM	
MG95215	TOMMY DIX	portrait	MGM	
MG95312	MARGARET SULLAVAN	portrait	MGM	
MG95386	MARILYN MAXWELL	portrait	MGM	
MG95388	MARILYN MAXWELL	portrait	MGM	
MG95389	MARILYN MAXWELL	portrait	MGM	
MG95390	MARILYN MAXWELL	portrait	MGM	
MG95481	ANN SOTHERN	portrait	MGM	
MG95511	BERT LAHR	portrait	MGM	
MG95629	HEDY LAMARR	portrait	MGM	
MG95719	GREER GARSON	portrait	MGM	
MG95776	GINNY SIMMS	portrait	MGM	
MG95793	ESTHER WILLIAMS	portrait	MGM	
MG95906	FRANCES GIFFORD	portrait	MGM	
MG96092	FRANCES GIFFORD	portrait	MGM	
MG96093	FRANCES GIFFORD	portrait	MGM	
MG96097	FRANCES GIFFORD	portrait	MGM	
MG96108	KATHRYN GRAYSON	portrait	MGM	
MG96304	GREER GARSON	portrait	MGM	
MG96499	LANA TURNER	portrait	MGM	
MG96591	FRANCES GIFFORD	portrait	MGM	
MG96592	FRANCES GIFFORD	portrait	MGM	
MG96622	HEDY LAMARR	portrait	MGM	
MG96626	HEDY LAMARR	portrait	MGM	
MG96684	JUNE LOCKHART	portrait	MGM	
MG96685	LANA TURNER	portrait	MGM	
MG96854	GLORIA DE HAVEN	portrait	MGM	
MG96861	JUNE ALLYSON	portrait	MGM	
MG96872	JOHN HODIAK	portrait	MGM	
MG96872	JOHN HODIAK	portrait	MGM	
MG96873	JOHN HODIAK	portrait	MGM	
MG96874	JOHN HODIAK	portrait	MGM	
MG97091	TOM DRAKE	portrait	MGM	
MG97126	KEENAN WYNN	portrait	MGM	
MG97149	HURD HATFIELD	portrait	MGM	
MG97151	ANN SOTHERN, HUSBAND ROBERT STERLING	portrait	MGM	
MG97191	IRENE DUNNE	portrait	MGM	
MG97192	LARAINE DAY	portrait	MGM	
MG97194	FRANCES GIFFORD	portrait	MGM	
MG97381	GLORIA DE HAVEN	portrait	MGM	
MG97393	FRANCES GIFFORD	portrait	MGM	
MG97487	GINNY SIMMS	portrait	MGM	
MG97522	ANN SOTHERN	portrait	MGM	
MG98088	GLORIA DE HAVEN	portrait	MGM	

Movie Still Identification Book Ultimate Edition - Letters

CODE	TITLE/NAME	DIRECTOR/TYPE	STUDIO/DISTRIBUTOR	YEAR
MG98192	JOHN HODIAK	portrait	MGM	
MG98328	MARY ASTOR	portrait	MGM	
MG98377	LANA TURNER	portrait	MGM	
MG98525	JOHN HODIAK	portrait	MGM	
MG98972	ROBERT WALKER	portrait	MGM	
MGA	MAN WITH THE GOLDEN ARM	PREMINGER	UNITED ARTISTS	1955
MGH	TAMING OF DOROTHY	SOLDATI	LUX	1950
MGK	MACHINE GUN KELLY	CORMAN	AIP	1958
MGLL	SHOW BOAT	WHALE	UNIVERSAL	1936
MGM-1	YANK AT OXFORD (UK)	CONWAY	MGM	1938
MGM-4	HAUNTED HONEYMOON (UK: BUSMAN'S HOLIDAY)	WOODS	MGM	1940
MGM-6	VACATION FROM MARRIAGE (UK: PERFECT STRANGERS)	KORDA	MGM	1945
MGM-8	EDWARD, MY SON (UK)	CUKOR	MGM	1949
MGM-9	CONSPIRATOR (UK)	SAVILLE	MGM	1949
MGM-28	SCAPEGOAT (UK)	HAMER	MGM	1959
MGM-32	INVASION QUARTET (UK)	LEWIS	MGM	1961
MGM-37	MURDER SHE SAID (UK)	POLLOCK	MGM	1961
MGM39	POSTMAN'S KNOCK (UK)	LYNN	MGM-UK	1962
MGM40	VILLAGE OF DAUGHTERS (UK)	POLLOCK	MGM-UK	1962
MGM-44	KILL OR CURE (UK)	POLLOCK	MGM	1962
MGM-46	COME FLY WITH ME (UK)	LEVIN	MGM	1963
MGM48	MURDER AT THE GALLOP (UK)	POLLOCK	MGM-UK	1963
MGM50	CHILDREN OF THE DAMNED (UK)	LEADER	MGM-UK	1964
MGM-52	NIGHT MUST FALL (UK)	REISZ	MGM	1964
MGM54	MURDER MOST FOUL (UK)	POLLOCK	MGM-UK	1964
MGM-57	MURDER AHOY (UK)	POLLOCK	MGM	1964
MGM-59	OPERATION CROSSBOW (UK)	ANDERSON	MGM	1965
MGM-60	ALPHABET MURDERS (UK)	TASHLIN	MGM	1965
MGM-80	SECRET OF MY SUCCESS (UK)	STONE	MGM	1965
MGM85	WHERE THE SPYS ARE (UK)	GUEST	MGM	1961
MGM-287	GRETA GARBO	portrait	MGM	
MGM529	LILLIAN GISH	portrait	MGM	
MGM682	NORMA SHEARER	portrait	MGM	
MGM-895	JOAN CRAWFORD	portrait	MGM	
MGM-965	GRETA GARBO	portrait	MGM	
MGM1076	CLAIRE WINDSOR	portrait	MGM	
MGM1086	CLAIRE WINDSOR	portrait	MGM	
MGM1100	CLAIRE WINDSOR	portrait	MGM	
MGM1123	KING VIDOR, E. BOARDMAN, J. GILBERT - BARDELYS...	portrait	MGM	
MGM-1254	GEORGE K. ARTHUR	portrait	MGM	
MGM-1330	JOAN CRAWFORD	portrait	MGM	
MGM-1657	SALLY O'NEIL	portrait	MGM	
MGM-1704	GRETA GARBO	portrait	MGM	
MGM2336	GWEN LEE	portrait	MGM	
MGM2603	GWEN LEE	portrait	MGM	
MGM-2781	JOAN CRAWFORD	portrait	MGM	
MGM2785	GWEN LEE	portrait	MGM	
MGM-2819	JOAN CRAWFORD	portrait	MGM	
MGM-2967	JOAN CRAWFORD	portrait	MGM	
MGM-3106	JOAN CRAWFORD	portrait	MGM	
MGM3158	CLAIRE WINDSOR, WILLIAM HAINES	portrait	MGM	
MGM4020	NORMA SHEARER	portrait	MGM	
MGM4022	NORMA SHEARER	portrait	MGM	
MGM4115	JOHN GILBERT	portrait	MGM	
MGM-4220	JOAN CRAWFORD	portrait	MGM	
MGM-4254	JOAN CRAWFORD	portrait	MGM	
MGM4385	NORMA SHEARER	portrait	MGM	
MGM4391	CLAIRE WINDSOR	portrait	MGM	
MGM-4398	JOAN CRAWFORD	portrait	MGM	
MGM5511	GWEN LEE	portrait	MGM	
MGM-5795	JOAN CRAWFORD	portrait	MGM	
MGM5826	GWEN LEE	portrait	MGM	
MGM6071	WILLIAM HAINES	portrait	MGM	
MGM6769	GWEN LEE	portrait	MGM	
MGM-6862	JOAN CRAWFORD	portrait	MGM	
MGM-6970	JOAN CRAWFORD	portrait	MGM	
MGM-7125	JOAN CRAWFORD	portrait	MGM	
MGM-7457	JOAN CRAWFORD	portrait	MGM	
MGM8354	GWEN LEE	portrait	MGM	
MGM-8375	MARION DAVIES	portrait	MGM	

Movie Still Identification Book Ultimate Edition - Letters

CODE	TITLE/NAME	DIRECTOR/TYPE	STUDIO/DISTRIBUTOR	YEAR
MGM8377	JOHN GILBERT	portrait	MGM	
MGM-8566	JOAN CRAWFORD	portrait	MGM	
MGM8575	GWEN LEE	portrait	MGM	
MGM8752	NORMA SHEARER	portrait	MGM	
MGM9223	NORMA SHEARER	portrait	MGM	
MGM9358	LON CHANEY	portrait	MGM	1927
MGM9801	GWEN LEE	portrait	MGM	
MGM9805	AILEEN PRINGLE	portrait	MGM	
MGM-9986	JOAN CRAWFORD	portrait	MGM	
MGM-10070	GRETA GARBO	portrait	MGM	
MGM-10544	FLASH, THE WONDER DOG	portrait	MGM	
MGM10573	GWEN LEE	portrait	MGM	
MGM10837	JOAN CRAWFORD	portrait	MGM	
MGM11656	LILLIAN GISH	portrait	MGM	
MGM11827	NORMA SHEARER	portrait	MGM	
MGM-11851X	JOAN CRAWFORD	portrait	MGM	
MGM11891	MARCELINE DAY	portrait	MGM	
MGM-12213	JOAN CRAWFORD	portrait	MGM	
MGM-12214	JOAN CRAWFORD	portrait	MGM	
MGM12235	GWEN LEE	portrait	MGM	
MGM-12384	JOAN CRAWFORD	portrait	MGM	
MGM-13322	JOAN CRAWFORD	portrait	MGM	
MGM13804	STAN LAUREL, DOROTHY COBURN - FLYING ELEPHANTS	portrait	MGM	
MGM13903	LON CHANEY	portrait	MGM	
MGM13991	GWEN LEE	portrait	MGM	
MGM14109	GWEN LEE	portrait	MGM	
MGM14110	GWEN LEE	portrait	MGM	
MGM-14197	ANNA MAY WONG	portrait	MGM	
MGMP	CHASING RAINBOWS	REISNER	MGM	1930
MGMP-746	EVELYN BRENT	portrait	MGM	
MGMP-959	KARL DANE	portrait	MGM	
MGMP-1121	GRETA GARBO	portrait	MGM	
MGMP-1122	GRETA GARBO	portrait	MGM	
MGMP-1134	ANNA MAY WONG	portrait	MGM	
MGMP-1405	JOAN CRAWFORD	portrait	MGM	
MGMP1464	GWEN LEE	portrait	MGM	
MGMP1566	GWEN LEE	portrait	MGM	
MGMP2096	CHARLEY CHASE	portrait	MGM	
MGMP-3375	LILLIAN GISH	portrait	MGM	
MGMP-3404	LILLIAN GISH	portrait	MGM	
MGMP-3612	JOAN CRAWFORD	portrait	MGM	
MGMP4179	ANITA PAGE, USC PRES. R. VON KLEIN, DEAN RAY K. IMMEL	portrait	MGM	
MGMP4593	BUSTER KEATON	portrait	MGM	
MGMP4688	DOROTHY REIVER	portrait	MGM	late 20's
MGMP4923	LAUREL & HARDY, MARION BYRON	portrait	MGM	
MGMP-5167	RAQUEL TORRES, MARIO CALVO - ESTRELLADOS	portrait	MGM	
MGMP-5889	JOAN CRAWFORD	portrait	MGM	
MGMP-5891	JOAN CRAWFORD	portrait	MGM	
MGMP-6092	JOAN CRAWFORD	portrait	MGM	
MGMP-6093	JOAN CRAWFORD	portrait	MGM	
MGMP-6094	JOAN CRAWFORD	portrait	MGM	
MGMP-6095	JOAN CRAWFORD	portrait	MGM	
MGMP-6371	JOAN CRAWFORD	portrait	MGM	
MGMP6877	EVA VON BERNE	portrait	MGM	
MGMP-7359	LILLIAN GISH	portrait	MGM	
MGMP8781	IRVING THALBERG, WIFE NORMA SHEARER	portrait	MGM	
MGMP 8783	CHANNING OF THE NORTHWEST	INCE	MGM (SELECT)	R
MGMP8883	BUSTER KEATON	portrait	MGM	
MGMP-9027	JOAN CRAWFORD	portrait	MGM	
MGMP-9028	JOAN CRAWFORD	portrait	MGM	
MGMP-9029	JOAN CRAWFORD	portrait	MGM	
MGMP-9037	JOAN CRAWFORD	portrait	MGM	
MGMP-9038	JOAN CRAWFORD	portrait	MGM	
MGMP-9048	JOAN CRAWFORD	portrait	MGM	
MGMP-9188	JOAN CRAWFORD	portrait	MGM	
MGMP9202	GWEN LEE	portrait	MGM	
MGMP-9418	ARTHUR FREED/NACIO HERB BROWN	portrait	MGM	
MGMP-9486	JOAN CRAWFORD	portrait	MGM	
MGMP9619	BUSTER KEATON	portrait	MGM	
MGMP-9839	GRETA GARBO	portrait	MGM	

Movie Still Identification Book Ultimate Edition - Letters

CODE	TITLE/NAME	DIRECTOR/TYPE	STUDIO/DISTRIBUTOR	YEAR
MGMP-10382	JOAN CRAWFORD	portrait	MGM	
MGMP-10583	JOAN CRAWFORD	portrait	MGM	
MGMP10590	ANITA PAGE	portrait	MGM	
MGMP-11244	LON CHANEY	portrait	MGM	
MGMP11303	ANITA PAGE	portrait	MGM	
MGMP-11882	JOAN CRAWFORD	portrait	MGM	
MGMP12150	ANITA PAGE	portrait	MGM	
MGMP-12778	BASIL RATHBONE	portrait	MGM	
MGMP-12925	ANITA PAGE	portrait	MGM	
MGMP-13199	BUSTER KEATON	portrait	MGM	
MGMP-14351	GRETA GARBO	portrait	MGM	
MGMP14390	LON CHANEY	portrait	MGM	
MGMP-14538	JOAN CRAWFORD	portrait	MGM	
MGMP-14759	JOAN CRAWFORD	portrait	MGM	
MGMP-14843	GRETA GARBO	portrait	MGM	
MGMP14866	CHARLEY CHASE	portrait	MGM	
MGMP-15147	LAUREL & HARDY	portrait	MGM	
MGMP-15773	NORMA SHEARER	portrait	MGM	
MGMP-15786	JOHN GILBERT	portrait	MGM	
MGMP-15817	ANITA PAGE	portrait	MGM	
MGMP-16417	JOAN CRAWFORD	portrait	MGM	
MGMP-16488	JOAN CRAWFORD	portrait	MGM	
MGMP16623X	NORMA SHEARER	portrait	MGM	
MGMP-17041	GRETA GARBO	portrait	MGM	
MGMP-17064	GRETA GARBO	portrait	MGM	
MGMP17455	LAUREL & HARDY	portrait	MGM	
MGMP-17656	GRETA GARBO	portrait	MGM	
MGMP-17961	GRETA GARBO	portrait	MGM	
MGMP17990	ROBERT MONTGOMERY	portrait	MGM	
MGMP-18015	GRETA GARBO	portrait	MGM	
MGMP18224	ROBERT MONTGOMERY	portrait	MGM	
MGMP-18649	GRETA GARBO	portrait	MGM	
MGMP-18793	AILEEN PRINGLE	portrait	MGM	
MGMP-19599	JOAN CRAWFORD	portrait	MGM	
MGMP19794	ANITA PAGE	portrait	MGM	
MGMP-20126	LAUREL & HARDY	portrait	MGM	
MGMP-20764	JACKIE COOPER	portrait	MGM	
MGMP-21578	ANITA PAGE	portrait	MGM	
MGMP-22006	ANN DVORAK	portrait	MGM	
MGMP-22007	ANN DVORAK	portrait	MGM	
MGMP-22017	ANN DVORAK	portrait	MGM	
MGMP-22022	ANN DVORAK	portrait	MGM	
MGMP-22027	ANN DVORAK	portrait	MGM	
MGMP-22329	JOAN CRAWFORD	portrait	MGM	
MGMP-22360	RAQUEL TORRES	portrait	MGM	
MGMP-22416	JOAN CRAWFORD	portrait	MGM	
MGMP-22438	JOAN CRAWFORD	portrait	MGM	
MGMP22814	JACKIE COOPER	portrait	MGM	
MGMP-22847	JOAN CRAWFORD	portrait	MGM	
MGPG-6187	GRETA GARBO	portrait	MGM	
MGPG-7404	GRETA GARBO	portrait	MGM	
MGPG-7419	GRETA GARBO	portrait	MGM	
MGPG-9301	GRETA GARBO	portrait	MGM	
MGPG-9836	GRETA GARBO	portrait	MGM	
MGPG-9838	GRETA GARBO	portrait	MGM	
MGX1	MILDRED HARRIS	portrait		
MH	MANHATTAN	ALLEN	UNITED ARTISTS	1979
MH	MAN HUNT	LANG	WARNER BROS	1941
MH	MARCIA HENDERSON	portrait	UNIVERSAL	
MH	MARIAN HALL	portrait	WARNER BROS	
MH	MARION HUTTON (aka MARIAN HUTTON)	portrait	UNIVERSAL	1940s
MH	MARSHA HUNT	portrait	RKO	1930s-40s
MH	MARTHA HOLLIDAY	portrait	RKO	
MH	MARTHA HYER	portrait	RKO, UNIVERSAL	
MH	MARY HOWARD	portrait	RKO	1930s-40s
MH	MASTER OF HORROR (ARG)	CARRERAS	US FILMS	1965
MH	MIRIAM HOPKINS	portrait	RKO, WARNER BROS	
MH	MODERN HERO	PABST	WARNER BROS	1934
MH	MONTE HALE	portrait	REP	
MH	MONTE HALE	portrait		

Movie Still Identification Book Ultimate Edition - Letters

CODE	TITLE/NAME	DIRECTOR/TYPE	STUDIO/DISTRIBUTOR	YEAR
MH	MOTEL HELL	CONNOR	UNITED ARTISTS	1980
MH	MOTEL HELL	CONNOR	UNITED ARTISTS	1980
MH	MYRNA HANSEN	portrait	UNIVERSAL	
MH	RETURN OF A MAN CALLED HORSE	KERSHNER	UNITED ARTISTS	1976
MH	SATAN MET A LADY	DIETERLE	WARNER BROS	1936
MHF	WHIP HAND	MENZIES	RKO	1951
MH-INT	MOTEL HELL	CONNOR	UNITED ARTISTS	1980
MHP	MAN WHO HAD POWER OVER WOMEN (UK)	KRISH	AVCO EMBASSY	1970
MI	HEART OF NEW YORK	LEROY	WARNER BROS	1932
MI	HOW TO MURDER YOUR WIFE	QUINE	UNITED ARTISTS	1965
MI	JANET MUNRO	portrait		
MI	MADE IN ITALY		COLUMBIA	1971
MI	MARTY INGELS	portrait	UNIVERSAL	1960s
MI	MATINEE IDOL (UK)	KING	UNITED ARTISTS	1933
MI	MILLIONAIRES IN PRISON	MCCAREY	RKO	1940
MI	MURDER, INC.	BALABAN	20TH CENTURY FOX	1960
MIA	MADE IN AMERICA	BENJAMIN	WARNER BROS	1993
MIA	MISSING IN ACTION	ZITO	CANNON	1984
MIA2	MISSING IN ACTION 2	HOOL	CANNON	1985
MIB	MOON IS BLUE	PREMINGER	UNITED ARTISTS	1953
MIG	MAN IN GREY (UK)	ARLISS	UNIVERSAL	1943
MIL	MAYBE IT'S LOVE	WELLMAN	WARNER BROS	1930
MIL-21	IF WINTER COMES	MILLARDE	FOX FILM	1923
MIL-22	GOVERNOR'S LADY	MILLARDE	FOX FILM	1923
MIL-23	FOOL	MILLARDE	FOX FILM	1925
MILLARDE 10	MY FRIEND THE DEVIL	MILLARDE	FOX FILM	1922
MIM	MAN IN THE IRON MASK	WALLACE	UNITED ARTISTS	1998
MIM	MAN IN THE MIRROR (UK)	ELVEY	GRAND	1937
MIM	MYSTERY IN MEXICO	WISE	RKO	1948
MIM	WINSTON AFFAIR (UK: MAN IN THE MIDDLE)	HAMILTON	20TH CENTURY FOX	1964
MIN	MAN IN THE NET	CURTIZ	UNITED ARTISTS	1959
MIS	MEN OF THE SKY	EASON	WARNER BROS	1942
MITR	MIRACLE IN THE RAIN	MATE	WARNER BROS	1956
MJ	MARGARET JOHNSTON	portrait	BRITISH LION	1940s-50s
MJ	MARTIN (E.) JOHNSON	portrait	METRO	
MJ	MAXINE JENNINGS	portrait	RKO	1930s
MJ	MIRIAM JORDAN	portrait	FOX	
MJ	MISS JULIE	FIGGIS	UNITED ARTISTS	1999
MJ	WOMAN BETWEEN	SCHERTZINGER	RKO	1931
MJH	(MARY) JANE HARKER	portrait		
MJT	MARY JO TAROLA/GREENBERG (aka LINDA DOUGLAS)	portrait	RKO	
ML	MADAME GAMBLES (UK: MADAME LOUISE)	ROGERS	BUTCHER'S	1951
MK	MATCH KING	BRETHERTON, KEIGHLEY	WARNER BROS	1932
MK	MEIN KAMPF (SWE)	LEISER	COLUMBIA	1960
MK-1	KILLER DILL	COLLINS	SCREEN GUILD	1947
MK-102	FOREIGN AGENT	BEAUDINE	MONOGRAM	1942
ML	MACUMBA LOVE	FOWLEY	UNITED ARTISTS	1960
ML	MAGICIAN OF LUBLIN	STALIN	CANNON	1979
ML	MAN OF LA MANCHA	HILLER	UNITED ARTISTS	1972
ML	MANDALAY	CURTIZ	WARNER BROS	1934
ML	MARGARET LANDRY	portrait	RKO	
ML	MARGARET LEIGHTON	portrait		
ML	MARGARET LINDSAY	portrait	RKO, UA, UNIVERSAL, WB	
ML	MARGARET LOCKWOOD	portrait		
ML	MARIA'S LOVERS	KONCHALOVSKY	CANNON	1984
ML	MARJORIE LORD	portrait	UNIV	
ML	MARY HAD A LITTLE... (UK)	BUZZELL	UNITED ARTISTS	1961
ML	MARY LEE	portrait	REPUBLICUBLIC	
ML	MELODY TIME (t)	GERONIMI, JACKSON	RKO	1948
ML	MISS LONDON LTD. (UK)	GUEST	GFD	1943
ML	MISSING LINK	REISNER	WARNER BROS	1927
ML	MOLLY LAMONT	portrait	RKO	
ML	MONTAGU LOVE	portrait	RKO	
ML	MURIEL LAWRENCE	portrait	REP	
ML	MUSIC LAND		RKO	1955
ML	MUSIC LOVERS (UK)	RUSSELL	UNITED ARTISTS	1970
ML	MY LIFE WITH CAROLINE	MILESTONE	RKO	1941
ML	MYRNA LOY	portrait	RKO	
ML	MYRNA LOY	portrait	UNIVERSAL, WARNER BROS	
ML	PURCHASE PRICE	WELLMAN	WARNER BROS	1932

Movie Still Identification Book Ultimate Edition - Letters

CODE	TITLE/NAME	DIRECTOR/TYPE	STUDIO/DISTRIBUTOR	YEAR
ML	THEFT OF MONA LISA	VON BOLVARY	RKO	1932
ML	YELLOW DUST	FOX	RKO	1936
ML	MAJOR LEAGUE	WARD	PARAMOUNT	1989
M-L	SWEET DADDIES	SANTELL	FIRST NATIONAL	1926
ML3	BROADWAY ROSE	LEONARD	METRO PICTURES (Tiffany)	1922
MLB	MADELEINE LE BEAU	portrait	WARNER BROS	
MLC	MARY LOU COOK	portrait	UNIVERSAL	
MLC	MONSTER OF LONDON CITY	DBONEK	PRODUCERS REL	1967
MLF	MY LEARNED FRIEND (UK)	DEARDEN, HAY	EALING	1943
MLM	KISS THE OTHER SHEIK (IT)	DE FILIPPO	MGM	1968
MLP	MAMA LOVES PAPA	STRAYER	RKO	1945
MLSN	MR. LORD SAYS NO (UK: HAPPY FAMILY)	BOX	SOUVAINE SELECTIVE	1952
MLX	MYRNA LOY	portrait	MGM	
MM	CRIMINAL COURT	WISE	RKO	1946
MM	GIRL FROM 10TH AVENUE	GREEN	WARNER BROS	1935
MM	GREAT O'MALLEY	DIETERLE	WARNER BROS	1937
MM	HIS FAMILY TREE	VIDOR	RKO	1935
MM	KISS ME AGAIN	SEITER	WARNER BROS	1931
MM	MAD MAX (AUS)	MILLER	AIP	1980
MM	MAD MISS MANTON	JASON	RKO	1938
MM	MADGE MEREDITH (aka MARJORIE MASSOW)	portrait	RKO	
MM	MAE MURRAY	portrait	METRO, MGM	
MM	MAKE MINE MUSIC (t)	CORMACK, GERONIMI	RKO	1946
MM	MAN FROM MOROCCO (UK)	GREENBAUM	ENGLISH	1945
MM	MAN IN THE MOON (UK)	DEARDEN	TRANS LUX	1960
MM	MAN ON THE PROWL	NAPOLEON	UNITED ARTISTS	1957
MM	MAN WHO COULD WORK MIRACLES (UK)	MENDES	UNITED ARTISTS	1936
MM	MANHATTAN MERRY-GO-ROUND	REISNER	REPUBLIC	1937
MM	MARATHON MAN	SCHLESINGER	PARAMOUNT	1977
MM	MARCY MCGUIRE	portrait	RKO	
MM	MARIA MONTEZ	portrait	UNIVERSAL	
MM	MARIE MCDONALD	portrait	UNITED ARTISTS	
MM	MARILYN MAXWELL	portrait	RKO	
MM	MARILYN MAXWELL	portrait	UNIVERSAL	
MM	MARILYN MILLER	portrait		
MM	MARILYN MONROE	portrait	RKO	1950s
MM	MARION MARTIN	portrait	RKO, UNIVERSAL	
MM	MARION MARTIN	portrait	WARNER BROS	
MM	MARRY ME MARRY ME (FR)	BERRI	MONOGRAM	1969
MM	MARTHA VICKERS (NÉE MARTHA MACVICAR)	portrait	RKO	
MM	MARY MAGUIRE	portrait	RKO, WARNER BROS	
MM	MARY MASON	portrait	RKO	
MM	MATTER OF MORALS	CROMWELL	UNITED ARTISTS	1961
MM	MATTER OF MURDER (UK)	GILLING	GRAND NATIONAL	1949
MM	MERCEDES MCCAMBRIDGE	portrait	WARNER BROS	
MM	MICHELE MORGAN	portrait	RKO	1940s
MM	MICHELE MORGAN	portrait	UNIV, WARNER BROS	
MM	MIKE MAZURKI	portrait	RKO	
MM	MILES MANDER	portrait	RKO	
MM	MISSION TO MOSCOW	CURTIZ	WARNER BROS	1943
MM	MISTER MOSES	NEAME	UNITED ARTISTS	1965
MM	MODEL FOR MURDER (UK)	BISHOP	CINEMA ASSOCIATES	1959
MM	MOLLY MAGUIRES	RITT	PARAMOUNT	1970
MM	MONA MARIS	portrait	RKO	1940s
MM	MONA MARIS	portrait	WARNER BROS	
MM	MR. MAJESTYK	FLEISCHER	UNITED ARTISTS	1974
MM	MR. MOM	DRAGOTI	20th CENTURY FOX	1983
MM	MRS. MIKE	KING	UNITED ARTISTS	1949
MM	MY MAN	MAYO	WARNER BROS	1928
MM	RED PLANET MARS	HORNER	UNITED ARTISTS	1952
MM	YOU HAVE TO RUN FAST/MAN MISSING	CAHN	UNITED ARTISTS	1961
MM-1	SHIPS OF HATE	MCCARTHY	MONOGRAM	1931
MM-3	IN LINE OF DUTY	GLENNON	MONOGRAM	1931
MM-4	FORGOTTEN WOMAN	THORPE	MONOGRAM	1932
MM-6	POLICE COURT	KING	MONOGRAM	1932
MM-7	COUNTY FAIR	KING	MONOGRAM	1932
MM-9	ARM OF THE LAW	KING	MONOGRAM	1932
MM-10	FLAMES	BROWN	MONOGRAM	1932
MM-12	KLONDIKE	ROSEN	MONOGRAM	1932
MM-112	MR. CELEBRITY	BEAUDINE	PRC	1941

Movie Still Identification Book Ultimate Edition - Letters

CODE	TITLE/NAME	DIRECTOR/TYPE	STUDIO/DISTRIBUTOR	YEAR
MM-5157	MARATHON MAN	SCHLESINGER	PARAMOUNT	1977
MMA	MY MAN ADAM	SIMON	TRI STAR	1985
MMAC	MARTHA VICKERS (NÉE MARTHA MACVICAR)	portrait	UNIVERSAL	
MMC	MARIE MCDONALD	portrait	UNIVERSAL	
MMC	MAY MCAVOY	portrait	WARNER BROS	
MMC	MEET MR. CALLAGHAN (UK)	SAUNDERS	EROS	1954
MMD	MAKE MINE A DOUBLE (UK: NIGHT WE DROPPED A CLANGER)	CONYERS	ELLIS	1961
MMM	MARY MILES MINTER	portrait	REALART	
MM-MF	MARATHON MAN	SCHLESINGER	PARAMOUNT	1976
MMP	MAD MONSTER PARTY	BASS	EMBASSY	1967
MMPR	MIGHTY MORPHIN POWER RANGERS	SPICER	20th CENTURY FOX	1995
MMR-130	MAKING MR. RIGHT	SEIDELMAN	ORION	1987
MMS	MR AND MRS. SMITH	HITCHCOCK	RKO	1941
MMX	MARION MARSH	portrait		
MMX	MAY MCAVOY	portrait	MGM	1920s-50s
MN	MAGIC NIGHT (UK: GOOD NIGHT, VIENNA)	WILCOX	UNITED ARTISTS	1932
MN	MIKEY AND NICKY	MAY	PARAMOUNT	1976
MN	MURDER IN THE NIGHT (UK: MURDER IN SOHO)	LEE	FILM ALLIANCE	1939
MN	PARIS DOES STRANGE THINGS (FR: ELENA ET LES HOMMES)	RENOIR	WARNER BROS	1957
MND	MIDSUMMER NIGHT'S DREAM	DIETERLE, REINHARDT	WARNER BROS	1935
MO	IN NAME ONLY (MEMORY OF LOVE*)	CROMWELL	RKO	1939
MO	MAN OUTSIDE (UK)	MARZANO	ALLIED ARTISTS	1965
MO	MARY OF SCOTLAND	FORD	RKO	1936
MO	MAUREEN O'HARA	portrait	UNIV	
MO	MERLE OBERON	portrait	RKO, UNIVERSAL, WARNER	
MO	MICKEY ONE	PENN	COLUMBIA	1965
MO	MONROE OWSLEY	portrait	MGM	
MO	MONSOON (UK)	AMATEAU	UNITED ARTISTS	1952
MO	MUTINY IN OUTER SPACE	GRIMALDI	ALLIED ARTISTS	1965
MO	SPOILERS	ENRIGHT	UNIVERSAL	1942
MOB	MIRACLE OF THE BELLS	PICHEL	RKO	1948
MOC	HARD FAST AND BEAUTIFUL	LUPINO	RKO	1951
MOD	MARTHA O'DRISCOLL	portrait	UNIVERSAL	
MOD	MESSENGER OF DEATH	THOMPSON	CANNON	1988
MOD	MY OLD DUTCH (UK)	HILL	GAUMONT BRITISH	1934
MOF	MILL ON THE FLOSS (UK)	WHELAN	STANDARD	1937
MOFC	MEN OF CHANCE	ARCHAINBAUD	RKO	1931
MOH	MAUREEN O'HARA	portrait	RKO, UNIVERSAL	
MOI	MAN OF IRON (POL)	WAJDA	UNITED ARTISTS	1981
MOL	NIGHT SONG	CROMWELL	RKO	1947
MOM	MARSHAL OF MESA CITY	HOWARD	RKO	1939
MOM	MOST DANGEROUS MAN ALIVE	DWAN	COLUMBIA	1961
MOM	MOUSE ON THE MOON (UK)	LESTER	LOPERT	1963
MOP	TARGET	GILMORE	RKO	1952
MOR-3	JUST OFF BROADWAY	MORTIMER	FOX FILM	1924
MOS	MAUREEN O'SULLIVAN	portrait	MGM	
MP	DAYS OF SIN AND NIGHTS OF NYMPHOMANIA	METZGER	AUDUBON	1965
MP	DOCTOR RHYTHM	TUTTLE	PARAMOUNT	1938
MP	IT'S IN THE BAG!	WALLACE	UNITED ARTISTS	1945
MP	LITTLE LORD FAUNTLEROY	GREEN	UNITED ARTISTS	1921
MP	MAJOR PICTURES - EMANUEL COHEN	portrait	PARAMOUNT	
MP	MALA POWERS	portrait	RKO	
MP	MANHATTAN PARADE	BACON	WARNER BROS	1931
MP	MANHATTAN PROJECT	BRICKMAN	20th CENTURY FOX	1986
MP	MANITOU	GIRDLER	AVCO EMBASSY	1978
MP	MANPOWER	WALSH	WARNER BROS	1941
MP	MARGARET PERRY	portrait	MGM	
MP	MARIA PALMER	portrait	RKO	
MP	MARIA PALMER	portrait	UNIV	
MP	MARIE PREVOST	portrait	WARNER BROS	
MP	MARIE PREVOST	portrait	WARNER BROS	
MP	MARY PICKFORD PRODUCTIONS	studio		
MP	MASTER PLAN (UK)	ENDFIELD	ASTOR	1955
MP	MENACE IN THE NIGHT (UK: FACE IN THE NIGHT)	COMFORT	UNITED ARTISTS	1957
MP	MISS PINKERTON	BACON	WARNER BROS	1932
MP	MONDO CANE	JACOPETTI	CINEMATION IND	1970
MP	MONKEY'S PAW	RUGGLES, SCHOEDSACK	RKO	1932
MP	MOONLIGHT ON THE PRAIRIE	LEDERMAN	WARNER BROS	1935
MP	MYSTERIOUS PILOT (serial)	BENNET	COLUMBIA	1937
MP	ON OUR MERRY WAY (MIRACLE CAN HAPPEN)	FENTON, VIDOR	UNITED ARTISTS	1948

Movie Still Identification Book Ultimate Edition - Letters

CODE	TITLE/NAME	DIRECTOR/TYPE	STUDIO/DISTRIBUTOR	YEAR
MP	POLLYANNA	POWELL	UNITED ARTISTS	1920
MP	SMALL TOWN BOY	TRYON	GRAND	1937
MP	THAT NAUGHTY GIRL	BOISROND	FILMS AROUND WORLD	1956
MP-1	GO WEST YOUNG MAN	HATHAWAY	PARAMOUNT	1936
MP-1	LEGION OF MISSING MEN	MACFADDEN	MONOGRAM	1937
MP1	NEARLY A NASTY ACCIDENT (UK)	CHAFFEY	UNIVERSAL	1961
MP-2	MIND YOUR OWN BUSINESS	MCLEOD	PARAMOUNT	1937
MP 3	HEART O' THE HILLS	GRASSE, FRANKLIN	FIRST NATIONAL (Pickford)	1919
MP 3	LOVE LIGHT	MARION	UNITED ARTISTS	1921
MP-3	OUTCAST	FLOREY	PARAMOUNT	1937
MP-4	GIRL FROM SCOTLAND YARD	VIGNOLA	PARAMOUNT	1937
MP-5	MIDNIGHT MADONNA	FLOOD	PARAMOUNT	1937
MP-6	ON SUCH A-NIGHT	DUPONT	PARAMOUNT	1937
MP-7	LOVE ON TOAST	DUPONT	PARAMOUNT	1937
MP-8	EVERY DAY'S A HOLIDAY	SUTHERLAND	PARAMOUNT	1937
MP-9	DOCTOR RHYTHM	TUTTLE	PARAMOUNT	1938
MP-10	HOODLUM	FRANKLIN	WARNER BROS	1919
MP 101	LITTLE LORD FAUNTLEROY	GREEN	UNITED ARTISTS	1921
MP-309	MAN OF COURAGE	THURN-TAXIS	PRC	1943
MP-3600	OUTPOST IN MOROCCO	FLOREY	UNITED ARTISTS	1949
MP-5400	KIKI	TAYLOR	UNITED ARTISTS	1931
MPC	COQUETTE	TAYLOR	UNITED ARTISTS	1929
MPDV	DOROTHY VERNON OF HADDON HALL	NEILAN	UNITED ARTISTS	1924
MPG	MAN WHO PLAYED GOD	ADOLFI	WARNER BROS	1932
MPGP	LA BOHEME	VIDOR	MGM	1926
MPGP-744	EVELYN BRENT	portrait	MGM	
MPGP2195	JOHN GILBERT	portrait	MGM	
MPGP2198	JOHN GILBERT	portrait	MGM	
MPGP2200	JOHN GILBERT	portrait	MGM	
MPGP2226	JOHN GILBERT	portrait	MGM	
MPGP2227	JOHN GILBERT	portrait	MGM	
MPGP2274	RAMON NOVARRO	portrait	MGM	
MPGP-2619	LON CHANEY	portrait	MGM	1924
MPGP-2620	LON CHANEY	portrait	MGM	1924
MPGP2770	NORMA SHEARER	portrait	MGM	
MPGP-2782	LON CHANEY	portrait	MGM	1924
MPGP2784	NORMA SHEARER	portrait	MGM	
MPGP3230	NORMA SHEARER	portrait	MGM	
MPGP3241	NORMA SHEARER	portrait	MGM	
MPGP3370	LILLIAN GISH	portrait	MGM	
MPGP3375	LILLIAN GISH	portrait	MGM	
MPGP3425	KING VIDOR, MARION DAVIES - ZANDER THE GREAT	portrait	MGM	
MPGP3916	CLAIRE WINDSOR, BERT LYTELL	portrait	MGM	
MPGP5135	NORMA SHEARER	portrait	MGM	
MPGP5260	NORMA SHEARER	portrait	MGM	
MPGP5262	NORMA SHEARER	portrait	MGM	
MPGP6142	RAMON NOVARRO	portrait	MGM	
MPGP6267	NORMA SHEARER	portrait	MGM	
MPGP6268	NORMA SHEARER	portrait	MGM	
MPGP6270	NORMA SHEARER	portrait	MGM	
MPGP6273	NORMA SHEARER	portrait	MGM	
MPGP6662	NORMA SHEARER	portrait	MGM	
MPGP6767	NORMA SHEARER	portrait	MGM	
MPGP7189	LILLIAN GISH	portrait	MGM	
MPGP7467	CLAIRE WINDSOR	portrait	MGM	
MPGP7517	GWEN LEE	portrait	MGM	
MPGP7687	NORMA SHEARER	portrait	MGM	
MPGP7723	GWEN LEE	portrait	MGM	
MPGP7838	GWEN LEE	portrait	MGM	
MPGP8163	CLAIRE WINDSOR	portrait	MGM	
MPGP8356	GERTRUDE OLMSTEAD	portrait	MGM	
MPGP-8588	KARL DANE	portrait	MGM	
MPGP8697	NORMA SHEARER	portrait	MGM	
MPGP8734	GWEN LEE	portrait	MGM	
MPGP8855	NORMA SHEARER	portrait	MGM	
MPGP8975	NORMA SHEARER	portrait	MGM	
MPGP-8989	LILYAN TASHMAN	portrait	MGM	
MPGP9303	NORMA SHEARER	portrait	MGM	
MPGP9452	GWEN LEE	portrait	MGM	
MPGP9736	GWEN LEE	portrait	MGM	

Movie Still Identification Book Ultimate Edition - Letters

CODE	TITLE/NAME	DIRECTOR/TYPE	STUDIO/DISTRIBUTOR	YEAR
MPGP9790	GWEN LEE	portrait	MGM	
MPGP9799	GWEN LEE	portrait	MGM	
MPGP9806	GWEN LEE	portrait	MGM	
MPGP9952	CLAIRE WINDSOR	portrait	MGM	
MPI	HARRY BLACK AND THE TIGER	FREGONESE	20th CENTURY FOX	1958
MPJ/PS	MY BROTHER JONATHAN (UK)	FRENCH	ALLIED ARTISTS	1948
MPM3	LIFE AND DEATH OF COLONEL BLIMP (UK)	POWELL/ PRESSBURGER	GENERAL FILM	1943
MPM-6	SILVER FLEET (UK)	SEWELL, WELLESLEY	PRC	1943
MPOP	LA BOHEME	VIDOR	MGM	1926
MPP	MISS PILGRIM'S PROGRESS (UK)	GUEST	GRAND NATIONAL	1949
MP-S	SECRETS	BORZAGE	UNITED ARTISTS	1933
MP-S	SPARROWS	BEAUDINE	UNITED ARTISTS	1926
MPX1	VIOLA DANA	portrait	METRO	
MPX2	FRANCESCA BERTINI	portrait	METRO	
MPX5	THE DOLLY SISTERS	portrait	METRO	
MPX16	BERT LYTELL	portrait	METRO	
MPX19	ALICE LAKE	portrait	METRO	
MPX33	JOHN INCE	portrait	METRO	1910s-20s
MPX46	ALICE TERRY	portrait	METRO	1923
MPX73	RUDOLPH VALENTINO	portrait	METRO	
MQ	BORDER CAFÉ	LANDERS	RKO	1937
MQ	MIGHTY QUINN	SCHENKEL	MGM	1989
MQ	MOSQUITO SQUADRON (UK)	SAGAL	UNITED ARTISTS	1969
M&R-203	SWAMP WOMAN	CLIFTON	PRC	1941
MR	MAD ROOM	GIRARD	COLUMBIA	1969
MR	MAN FROM DEL RIO	HORNER	UNITED ARTISTS	1956
MR	MARCIA RALSTON	portrait	WARNER BROS	late 30s
MR	MARGARET RUTHERFORD	portrait		
MR	MARINE RAIDERS	SCHUSTER	RKO	1944
MR	MARJORIE RAMBEAU	portrait	PATHE	
MR	MARJORIE REYNOLDS	portrait	MON, RKO, UNIV	
MR	MARJORIE RIORDAN	portrait	WARNER BROS	
MR	MARTHA RAYE	portrait	UNIV	
MR	MARTIN RACKIN	portrait	FOX	
MR	MAY ROBSON	portrait	RKO	
MR	MEG RANDALL	portrait	UNIVERSAL	
MR	MERRY WIVES OF RENO	HUMBERSTONE	WARNER BROS	1934
MR	MICHAEL REDGRAVE	portrait	UNIVERSAL	
MR	MIDNIGHT RIDE	BRALVER	CANNON	1990
MR	MIND READER	DEL RUTH	WARNER BROS	1933
MR	MIRACLE RIDER (serial)	EASON, SCHAEFER	MASCOT	1935
MR	MOONRUNNERS	WALDRON	UNITED ARTISTS	1975
MR	MOULIN ROUGE	HUSTON	UNITED ARTISTS	1952
MR	MURDERER'S ROW	LEVIN	COLUMBIA	1966
MR	MY REPUTATION	BERNHARDT	WARNER BROS	1946
MR	OLD MOTHER RILEY (UK)	MITCHELL	BUTCHER'S	1937
MR	ROOM UPSTAIRS	LACOMBE	LOPERT	1948
MR	SADDLE BUSTER	ALLEN	RKO	1932
MR	SHERLOCK HOLMES MISSING REMBRANDT	HISCOTT	FIRST DIVISION	1932
MR	TARNISHED ANGEL	GOODWINS	RKO	1938
MR-3400	GLORIOUS VAMPS (sh)	DULL	UNITED ARTISTS	1930
MR-4600	WIZARD'S APPRENTICE (sh)	LEVEE	UNITED ARTISTS	1930
MR-5100	ZAMPA (sh)	FORDE	UNITED ARTISTS	1930
MRB	OLD MOTHER RILEY IN BUSINESS (UK)	BAXTER	ANGLO-AMERICAN	1941
MRBB	RUNAWAY BRAIN	BAILEY	BUENA VISTA	1995
MRD	OLD MOTHER RILEY DETECTIVE (UK)	COMFORT	ANGLO-AMERICAN	1943
MRH	OLD MOTHER RILEY AT HOME (UK)	MITCHELL	ANGLO-AMERICAN	1945
MRXX	MAY ROBSON	portrait	MGM	
MS	BEAST FROM 20,000 FATHOMS	LOURIE	WARNER BROS	1953
MS	LITTLE MISS SOMEBODY (UK)	TENNYSON	BUTCHER'S	1937
MS	MACK SENNETT SHORTS	studio	PARAMOUNT	
MS	MADAME (IT/FR: MADAME SANS-GENE 1961)	JAQUE	EMBASSY	1963
MS	MAGNIFICENT SEVEN	STURGES	UNITED ARTISTS	1960
MS	MAID IN SWEDEN	WOLMAN	CANNON	1971
MS	MAIN STREET	BEAUMONT	WARNER BROS	1923
MS	MARAT/SADE (UK)	BROOK	UNITED ARTISTS	1967
MS	MARGARET SHERIDAN	portrait	RKO	
MS	MARGARET SULLAVAN	portrait	UNIVERSAL	
MS	MARGIE STEWART	portrait	RKO	
MS	MARGOT STEVENSON	portrait	WARNER BROS	

Movie Still Identification Book Ultimate Edition - Letters

CODE	TITLE/NAME	DIRECTOR/TYPE	STUDIO/DISTRIBUTOR	YEAR
MS	MARK STEVENS	portrait	RKO	
MS	MARTHA SCOTT	portrait	RKO	
MS	MARY STEVENS, M.D.	BACON	WARNER BROS	1933
MS	MASTER SPY (UK)	TULLY	ALLIED ARTISTS	1964
MS	MAXIMILIAN SCHELL	portrait	UNIV	
MS	MEXICAN SPITFIRE SEES A GHOST	GOODWINS	RKO	1942
MS	MODEL SHOP	DEMY	COLUMBIA	1969
MS	MONROE SALISBURY	portrait	UNIVERSAL	
MS	MONSTER SQUAD	DEKKER	TRI STAR	1987
MS	MOVITA	portrait	MONOGRAM	
MS	MR. SKEFFINGTON	SHERMAN	WARNER BROS	1944
MS	MUMMY'S SHROUD (UK)	GILLING	20TH CENTURY FOX	1967
MS	ON OUR MERRY WAY (MIRACLE CAN HAPPEN)	FENTON, VIDOR	UNITED ARTISTS	1948
MS	SEBASTIAN (UK)	GREENE	PARAMOUNT	1968
MS	SHADOWS ON THE STAIRS	LEDERMAN	WARNER BROS	1941
MS	SOLDIER AND THE LADY	NICHOLS JR.	RKO	1937
MS-1	HIDDEN VALLEY	BRADBURY	MONOGRAM	1932
MS-2	YOUNG BLOOD	ROSEN	MONOGRAM	1932
MS-3	FIGHTING CHAMP	MCCARTHY	MONOGRAM	1932
MS-4	TRAILING NORTH	MCCARTHY	MONOGRAM	1933
MS-5	BREED OF THE BORDER	BRADBURY	MONOGRAM	1933
MS-6	GALLANT FOOL	BRADBURY	MONOGRAM	1933
MS-7	GALLOPING ROMEO	BRADBURY	MONOGRAM	1933
MS-8	MEAN SEASON	BORSOS	ORION	1984
MS-18	SINGING BOXER (sh)	PEARCE	PARAMOUNT	1933
MS-20	LADIES FIRST	GRAINGER	PARAMOUNT (SENNETT)	1918
MS-20	RANGER'S CODE	BRADBURY	MONOGRAM	1933
MS-33	KNOCKOUT KISSES	MARSHALL	PARAMOUNT (SENNETT)	1933
MS-33	NEVER TOO OLD (?)	JONES	PARAMOUNT	1933
MSA	MEXICAN SPITFIRE AT SEA	GOODWINS	RKO	1942
MSA	OH THOSE MOST SECRET AGENTS (IT)	FULCI	MONOGRAM	1964
MSB	MEXICAN SPITFIRE'S BLESSED EVENT	GOODWINS	RKO	1943
MSB	MOSCOW STRIKES BACK	KOPALIN, VARLAMOV	REPUBLIC	1942
MSE	MEXICAN SPITFIRE'S ELEPHANT	GOODWINS	RKO	1942
MSH	MOIRA SHEARER	portrait	UNITED ARTISTS	
M-SK	BOYS OF THE CITY	LEWIS	MONOGRAM	1940
MSM	MADONNA OF THE SEVEN MOONS (UK)	CRABTREE	GUNIVERSAL	1945
MSO	MEXICAN SPITFIRE OUT WEST	GOODWINS	RKO	1940
MSP-1	PARADISE LAGOON (UK: ADMIRABLE CRICHTON)	GILBERT	COLUMBIA	1957
MSPR	TIME TABLE/TIMETABLE	STEVENS	UNITED ARTISTS	1956
MSR	HELL'S CARGO (UK: MCGLUSKY THE SEA ROVER)	SUMMERS	FILM ALLIANCE	1935
MSR	MAGNIFICENT SEVEN RIDE	MCCOWAN	UNITED ARTISTS	1972
MST	MADEMOISELLE STRIPTEASE (FR)	ALLEGRET	DCA	1957
MSV	OLD MOTHER RILEY MEETS THE VAMPIRE/VAMPIRE LONDON	GILLING	BLUE CHIP	1952
MT	ADVENTURES OF MARK TWAIN	RAPPER	WARNER BROS	1944
MT	INSPECTOR MAIGRET (FR: MAIGRET TEND UN PIEGE)	DELANNOY	LOPERT	1958
MT	MAGIC TOWN	WELLMAN	RKO	1947
MT	MAN IN HIDING (UK) (MANTRAP)(WOMAN IN HIDING)	FISHER	UNITED ARTISTS	1953
MT	MAN TROUBLE	RAFELSON	20th CENTURY FOX	1992
MT	MARGARET TALLICHET	portrait	RKO	
MT	MARTA TOREN	portrait	COL, UNIVERSAL	
MT	MARTHA TILTON	portrait		
MT	MARY TREEN	portrait	WARNER BROS	
MT	MELODY FOR TWO	KING	WARNER BROS	1937
MT	MELODY TIME (t)	GERONIMI	RKO	1948
MT	MELODY TRAIL	KANE	REPUBLIC	1935
MT	MIDNIGHT TAXI	ADOLFI	WARNER BROS	1928
MT	MONDO TOPLESS	MEYER	EVE	1966
MT	MONEY TALKS	FUNT	UNITED ARTISTS	1972
MT	NEVER LET GO (UK)	GUILLERMIN	CONTINENTAL	1960
MT	THEY CALL ME MISTER TIBBS!	DOUGLAS	UNITED ARTISTS	1970
MT-1	PARTNERS OF THE TRAIL	FOX	MONOGRAM	1931
MT-2	MAN FROM DEATH VALLEY	NOSLER	MONOGRAM	1931
MT-3	TWO FISTED JUSTICE	DURLAM	MONOGRAM	1931
MT-4	GALLOPING THRU	NOSLER	MONOGRAM	1931
MT-5	SINGLE HANDED SAUNDERS	POST	MONOGRAM	1932
MT-6	MAN FROM NEW MEXICO	MCGOWAN	MONOGRAM	1932
MT-7	VANISHING MEN	FRASER	MONOGRAM	1932
MT-8	HONOR OF THE MOUNTED	FRASER	MONOGRAM	1932
MT-80	AROUND THE WORLD IN EIGHTY DAYS	ANDERSON	UNITED ARTISTS	1956

Movie Still Identification Book Ultimate Edition - Letters

CODE	TITLE/NAME	DIRECTOR/TYPE	STUDIO/DISTRIBUTOR	YEAR
MTD	TEENAGE BAD GIRL (UK: MY TEENAGE DAUGHTER)	WILCOX	DCA	1956
MTG	MAKING THE GRADE	WALKER	CANNON	1984
MTM	MARY TYLER MOORE	portrait	UNIVERSAL	50s-60s
MTM	MISSLE TO THE MOON	CUNHA	ASTOR	1959
MTM	MUPPETS TAKE MANHATTAN	OZ	TRI STAR	1984
MTS	MUCH TOO SHY (UK)	VARNEL	COLUMBIA BRITISH	1942
MU	MAN UPSTAIRS (UK)	CHAFFEY	KINGSLEY-UNION	1958
MU	MASTERS OF THE UNIVERSE	GODDARD	CANNON	1987
MU	MILLIONS LIKE US (UK)	GILLIAT, LAUNDER	GFD	1943
MUL	HERE WE GO ROUND THE MULBERRY BUSH (UK)	DONNER	UNITED ARTISTS	1968
MULAN	MULAN	COOK	BUENA VISTA	1998
MUS	LA MUSICA	DURAS	UNITED ARTISTS	1967
MV	MAN IN THE VAULT	MCLAGLEN	RKO	1956
MV	MARTHA VICKERS	portrait	WARNER BROS	
MV	MEETING VENUS	SZABO	WARNER BROS	1991
MV	MONSIEUR VERDOUX	CHAPLIN	UNITED ARTISTS	1947
MV	TALK OF THE DEVIL (UK)	REED	GAUMONT	1936
MVD	MAMIE VAN DOREN	portrait	UNIVERSAL	
MW	IT'S A MAD, MAD, MAD, MAD WORLD	KRAMER	UNITED ARTISTS	1964
MW	MAD AT THE WORLD	ESSEX	FILMAKERS RELEASING	1955
MW	MAE WEST	portrait	UNIVERSAL	1940
MW	MAGIC WEAVER (USSR)	ROU	MONOGRAM	1965
MW	MAKE A WISH	NEUMANN	RKO	1937
MW	MAN OF THE WEST	MANN	UNITED ARTISTS	1958
MW	MARA OF THE WILDERNESS	MCDONALD	ALLIED ARTISTS	1965
MW	MARIE WILSON	portrait	RKO, WARNER BROS	
MW	MARIE WINDSOR	portrait	RKO, WARNER BROS	
MW	MARIS WRIXON	portrait	WARNER BROS	30s-40s
MW	MARKED WOMAN	BACON	WARNER BROS	1937
MW	MEN IN WAR	MANN	UNITED ARTISTS	1957
MW	MICHAEL WILDING	portrait	WARNER BROS	
MW	MICHAEL WOULFE	portrait	RKO	40s-50s
MW	MIDDLE WATCH (UK)	BENTLEY	PATHE	1940
MW	MIDGE WARE	portrait	UNIVERSAL	
MW	MILLION DOLLAR BABY	BERNHARDT	WARNER BROS	1941
MW	MIRACLE WORKER	PENN	UNITED ARTISTS	1962
MW	MISSING WITNESSES	CLEMENS	WARNER BROS	1937
MW	MONEY AND THE WOMAN	HOWARD	WARNER BROS	1940
MW	MONTY WOOLLEY	portrait	FOX	40s-50s
MW	MURPHY'S WAR (UK)	YATES	PARAMOUNT	1971
MW	NO OTHER WOMAN	RUBEN	RKO	1932
MW	SMUGGLERS (UK)	KNOWLES	EAGLE LION	1948
MW	WOMAN FROM MONTE CARLO	CURTIZ	WARNER BROS	1932
MW-1	RIDERS OF DESTINY	BRADBURY	MONOGRAM	1935
MW-2	SAGEBRUSH TRAIL	SCHAEFER	MONOGRAM	1933
MW-3	WEST OF THE DIVIDE	BRADBURY	MONOGRAM	1933
MW-4	LUCKY TEXAN	BRADBURY	MONOGRAM	1934
MW-5	BLUE STEEL	BRADBURY	MONOGRAM	1934
MW-6	MAN FROM UTAH	BRADBURY	MONOGRAM	1934
MW-7	RANDY RIDES ALONE	FRASER	MONOGRAM	1934
MW-8	STAR PACKER	BRADBURY	MONOGRAM	1934
MW-9	TRAIL BEYOND	BRADBURY	MONOGRAM	1934
MW-10	NEATH ARIZONA SKIES	FRASER	MONOGRAM	1934
MW-11	LAWLESS FRONTIER	BRADBURY	MONOGRAM	1935
MW-11	MARRYING WIDOWS	NEWFIELD	CAPITOL	1934
MW-12	RAINBOW VALLEY	BRADBURY	MONOGRAM	1935
MW-13	TEXAS TERROR	BRADBURY	MONOGRAM	1935
MW-14	DESERT TRAIL	COLLINS	MONOGRAM	1935
MW-15	DAWN RIDER	BRADBURY	MONOGRAM	1935
MW-16	PARADISE CANYON	PIERSON	MONOGRAM	1935
MWC	MAN WITH CONNECTIONS (FR)	BERRI	COLUMBIA	1970
MWD	MORO, WITCH DOCTOR	ROMERO	20th CENTURY FOX	1954
MWFD	MAN WHO FINALLY DIED (UK)	LAWRENCE	GOLDSTONE	1963
MWH	MAN WHO HAUNTED HIMSELF (UK)	DEARDEN	LEVITT-PICKMAN	1970
MWH	MY WIFE'S HUSBAND (FR: LA CUISINE AU BEURRE)	GRANGIER	UNITED ARTISTS	1963
MWL	MY WIFE'S LODGER (UK)	ELVEY	ADELPHI	1952
MWM	DARK HIGHWAY*	RAY	RKO	1952
MWM	ON DANGEROUS GROUND	RAY	RKO	1952
MWR-2	CHEYENNE KID	RAY	MONOGRAM	1940
MWT	MAN WHO WOULDN'T TALK (UK)	WILCOX	SHOWCORPORATION	1958

Movie Still Identification Book Ultimate Edition - Letters

CODE	TITLE/NAME	DIRECTOR/TYPE	STUDIO/DISTRIBUTOR	YEAR
MWU	BAD SISTER (UK: WHITE UNICORN)	KNOWLES	UNIVERSAL	1947
MWU	SMUGGLERS (UK: MAN WITHIN)	KNOWLES	EAGLE LION	1947
MX	MALCOLM X	LEE	WARNER BROS	1992
MXB	MARX BROTHERS	portrait	MGM	
MXC	MAE CLARKE	portrait	MGM	
MXD	MARIE DRESSLER	portrait	MGM	
MXKX	MILIZA KORJUS	portrait	MGM	
MXR	MICKEY ROONEY	portrait	MGM	
MXS	MONA SMITH	portrait	MGM	
MXXD	MELVYN DOUGLAS	portrait	MGM	
MZ	YOUR PAST IS SHOWING (UK: NAKED TRUTH)	ZAMPI	RANK	1957
MZ195	FIVE GOLDEN HOURS (UK)	ZAMPI	COLUMBIA	1961
MZT	MOON ZERO TWO (UK)	BAKER	WARNER BROS.	1969
N	BOYS WILL BE BOYS (UK)	BEAUDINE	GAUMONT	1935
N	CAUGHT PLASTERED	SEITER	RKO	1931
N	FRED NIBLO FILMS	studio	METRO	
N	NADINE	BENTON	TRI STAR	1987
N	NAPOLEON	GANCE	MGM	1929
N	NEGATIVES (UK)	MEDAK	CONTINENTAL	1968
N	NELL	APTED	20th CENTURY FOX	1994
N	NEVADA	KILLY	RKO	1944
N	NIGHT THEY RAIDED MINSKY'S	FRIEDKIN	UNITED ARTISTS	1968
N	NIGHTMARE	SHANE	UNITED ARTISTS	1956
N	NIKKI, WILD DOG OF THE NORTH	COUFFER, HALDANE	BUENA VISTA	1961
N	NORWOOD	HALEY JR.	PARAMOUNT	1970
N	NOTORIOUS	HITCHCOCK	RKO	1946
N	ONE STOLEN NIGHT	DUNLAP	WARNER BROS	1929
N	SEYMOUR NEBENZAL PRODUCTIONS	studio		
N	TANK FORCE (UK: NO TIME TO DIE)	YOUNG	COLUMBIA	1958
N1	DOLLS HOUSE	BRYANT	UNITED ARTISTS	1922
N1	HOT ROD RUMBLE	MARTINSON	ALLIED ARTISTS	1957
N-2	IDOL DANCER	GRIFFITH	WARNER BROS	1920
N-2	UNDERSEA GIRL	PEYSER	ALLIED ARTISTS	1957
N-2100	CHASE	RIPLEY	UNITED ARTISTS	1946
N-2900	HEAVEN ONLY KNOWS	ROGELL	UNITED ARTISTS	1947
NA	GLAD RAG DOLL	CURTIZ	WARNER BROS	1929
NA	NAKED AFRICA	PHOENIX, WORTH	AIP	1957
NA	NAKED AMAZON (BRA)	SULISTROWSKI	TIMES FILM	1955
NA	NICHOLAS AND ALEXANDRA	SCHAFFNER	COLUMBIA	1971
NA	NICK ADAMS	portrait	WARNER BROS	
NA	NILS ASTHER	portrait	MGM	
NA	NOAH'S ARK	CURTIZ	WARNER BROS	1928
NB	NAVY BLUES	BACON	WARNER BROS	1941
NB	NIGHT BOAT TO DUBLIN (UK)	HUNTINGTON	PATHE	1946
NB	NIGHT OF BLOODY HORROR	HOUCK JR	HOWCO	1969
NB	NO BLADE OF GRASS	WILDE	MGM	1971
NB	NOAH BEERY JR	portrait	UNIVERSAL	
NB	NOTHING BUT THE BEST (UK)	DONNOR	COLUMBIA	1964
NB	NOW BARABBAS (UK)	PARRY	WARNER BROS.	1949
NBK	NATURAL BORN KILLERS	STONE, TARANTINO	WARNER BROS	1994
NBL	NONE BUT THE LONELY HEART	ODETS	RKO	1944
NC	CONVICTS AT LARGE	BEAL	PRINCIPAL DIST.	1938
NC	NANCY COLEMAN	portrait	WARNER BROS	
NC	NARROW CORNER	GREEN	WARNER BROS	1933
NC	NARROWING CIRCLE (UK)	SAUNDERS	EROS	1956
NC	NAVY COMES THROUGH	SUTHERLAND	RKO	1943
NC	NIGHT AND THE CITY	WINKLER	20th CENTURY FOX	1992
NC	NIGHTCOMERS	WINNER	AVCO EMBASSY	1972
NC	NIGHT CRY	RAYMAKER	WARNER BROS	1926
NC	QUEEN OF HEARTS		WARNER BROS	
NC	ROCKETSHIP X-M	NEUMANN	LIPPERT	1950
NCM	NORTHVILLE CEMETERY MASSACRE	DEAR	CANNON	1976
ND	NANCY DREW DETECTIVE	CLEMENS	WARNER BROS	1938
ND	NIGHT OF THE LIVING DEAD	ROMERO, RUSSO	CONTINENTAL	1968
ND	NO DEFENSE	BACON	WARNER BROS	1929
ND	NOT SO DUSTY (UK)	ROGERS	EROS	1956
NDB	NIGEL DE BRULIER	portrait	METRO	
NDD	NO MY DARLING DAUGHTER (UK)	THOMAS	ZENITH	1961
NE	BURN, WITCH, BURN	HAYERS	AIP	1962
NE	NAKED EDGE (UK)	ANDERSON	UNITED ARTISTS	1961

Movie Still Identification Book Ultimate Edition - Letters

CODE	TITLE/NAME	DIRECTOR/TYPE	STUDIO/DISTRIBUTOR	YEAR
NE	NELSON EDDY	portrait	MGM	
NE	NO ESCAPE	BENNETT	UNITED ARTISTS	1953
NE	THERE IS NO ESCAPE (UK: DARK ROAD)	GOULDING	LIPPERT	1948
NEC	NURSE EDITH CAVELL	WILCOX	RKO	1939
NEILL-7	BLACK PARADISE	NEILL	FOX FILM	1926
NF	FUGITIVE (UK: ON THE NIGHT OF THE FIRE)	HURST	UNIVERSAL	1939
NF	NANETTE FABRAY (aka NANETTE FABARES)	portrait	WARNER BROS	
NF	NEW FACES OF 1937	JASON	RKO	1937
NF	NIGHT WAS OUR FRIEND (UK)	ANDERSON	MONARCH	1951
NF	NINA FOCH	portrait	WARNER BROS	
NF	SHOT IN THE DARK	MCGANN	WARNER BROS	1941
NF	TRUCK BUSTERS	EASON	WARNER BROS	1943
NF-3	JAMAICA INN (UK)	HITCHCOCK	ASSOCIATED BRITISH FILM	1939
NFH	IRON PETTICOAT (UK)	THOMAS	MGM	1956
NFM	IRON PETTICOAT (UK)	THOMAS	MGM	1956
NFR	NIGHT FULL OF RAIN (CAN/IT)	WERTMULLER	WARNER BROS	1978
NG	NAME OF THE GAME (TV)	WYLIE	NBC-TV	1968
NG	NAN GREY	portrait	UNIVERSAL, WARNER BROS	
NG	NANCY GATES	portrait	RKO	
NG	NANCY GUILD	portrait	UNIVERSAL	
NG	NELL GWYN (UK)	WILCOX	UNITED ARTISTS	1934
NG	NIGHT GAMES	ZETTERLING	MONDIAL FILMS	1966
NG	NIGHT OF THE GRIZZLY	PEVNEY	PARAMOUNT	1966
NG	NOOSE FOR A GUNMAN	CAHN	UNITED ARTISTS	1960
NG	SWINGTIME	STEVENS	RKO	1936
NGL	NICE GIRL LIKE ME (UK)	DAVIS	AVCO EMBASSY	1969
NH	NEIL HAMILTON	portrait	MGM. TIFFANY	
NH	NIGHT OF THE HUNTER	LAUGHTON	UNITED ARTISTS	1955
NHF	NIGHT HEAVEN FELL (FR: LES BIJOUTIERS DU CLAIRE DE LUNE)	VADIM	KINGSLEY INT'L	1958
NI	GREATEST QUESTION	GRIFFITH	WARNER BROS	1919
NIC	NOTHING IN COMMON	MARSHALL	TRI STAR	1986
NIMH	SECRET OF NIMH	BLUTH	UNITED ARTISTS	1982
NIN	REVENGE OF THE NINJA	FIRSTENBERG	CANNON	1983
NJ	NAVAJO JOE	CORBUCCI	UNITED ARTISTS	1966
NJ	NEW JACK CITY	VAN PEEBLES	WARNER BROS	1991
NJ	RUSSIANS ARE COMING THE RUSSIANS ARE COMING	JEWISON	UNITED ARTISTS	1966
NK	NANCY KELLY	portrait	RKO, UNIVERSAL	
NK	NANCY KWAN	portrait	PARAMOUNT`	
NK	NED KELLY (UK)	RICHARDSON	UNITED ARTISTS	1970
NK	NEXT OF KIN (UK)	DICKINSON	UNIVERSAL	1942
NK	NORMAN KERRY	portrait	MGM	
NK	NORMAN KRASNA	portrait	RKO	
NKW	NAMU, THE KILLER WHALE	BENEDEK	UNITED ARTISTS	1966
NL	DON'T BET ON BLONDES	FLOREY	WARNER BROS	1935
NL	NAN LESLIE	portrait	RKO	
NL	NATIONAL LAMPOON'S MOVIE MADNESS	GIRALDI, JAGLOM	UNITED ARTISTS	1982
NL	NAVY LARK (UK)	PARRY	20TH CENTURY FOX	1959
NL	NEVER LET GO (UK)	GUILLERMIN	CONTINENTAL	1960
NL	NIGHT OF LOVE	FITZMAURICE	UNITED ARTISTS	1927
NL	NINA LUNN	portrait	UNIVERSAL	
NL	SWEET DADDIES	SANTELL	WARNER BROS	1926
NLB	NAZI LOVE CAMP 27	CAIANO	GROUP 1 INT'L	1977
NLBB	NOTHING TO LOSE	OEDEKERK	BUENA VISTA	1997
NLC	NIGHTS OF THE LUCRETIA BORGIA (IT)	GRIECO	COLUMBIA	1959
NLG	NIGHT THE LIGHTS WENT OUT IN GEORGIA	MAXWELL	AVCO EMBASSY	1981
NL-R	NEW LEAF	MAYFIELD	PARAMOUNT	1971
NM	NAKED MAJA	KOSTER	UNITED ARTISTS	1958
NM	NEANDERTHAL MAN	DUPONT	UNITED ARTISTS	1953
NM	NEW MEXICO	REIS	UNITED ARTISTS	1951
NM	NEXT MAN	SARAFIAN	ALLIED ARTISTS	1976
NM	NINE MONTHS	COLUMBUS	20th CENTURY FOX	1995
NM	NO MAN'S LAND	WERNER	ORION	1987
NM	NO MERCY	PEARCE	TRI STAR	1986
NM	NOREEN MICHAELS	portrait		
NM	PLATOON LEADER	NORRIS	CANNON	1988
NM	THIS IS MY LOVE	HEISLER	RKO	1954
NMF	NIGHT IS MY FUTURE/MUSIC IN DARKNESS (SWE)	BERGMAN	EMBASSY	1948
NN	GHOSTS OF BERKELEY SQUARE (UK)	SEWELL	PATHE	1947
NN	LIFE AND ADVENTURES OF NICHOLAS NICKLEBY (UK)	CAVALCANTI	UNIVERSAL	1947
NN	NIGHT NURSE	WELLMAN	WARNER BROS	1931

Movie Still Identification Book Ultimate Edition - Letters

CODE	TITLE/NAME	DIRECTOR/TYPE	STUDIO/DISTRIBUTOR	YEAR
NN	NO NO NANETTE	WILCOX	RKO	1940
NN	SAWDUST TINSEL/NAKED NIGHT (SWE: GYCKLARNAS AFTON)	BERGMAN	TIMES	1953
NN	WHILE THE CITY SLEEPS	LANG	RKO	1956
NNT	NEXT TO NO TIME (UK)	CORNELIUS	SHOW CORPORATION	1958
NO	BLUES IN THE NIGHT	LITVAK	WARNER BROS	1941
NO	IN NAME ONLY	CROMWELL	RKO	1939
NO	NANCY OLSON	portrait	WARNER BROS	1950s
NO	NINA ORLA	portrait	UNIV	
NO	NINA ORLA	portrait		
NO	NOCTURNE	MARIN	RKO	1946
NO	SEPTEMBER STORM	HASKIN	20th CENTURY FOX	1960
NOC	NILS OLAF CHRISANDER	portrait	PDC	
NOG	NIGHT OF THE GENERALS	LITVAK	COLUMBIA	1967
NOI	NIGHT OF THE IGUANA	HUSTON	MGM	1964
NOS	NEVER ON SUNDAY (GK: POTE TIN KYRIAKI)	DASSIN	LOPERT	1960
NOW	NUMBER ONE WITH A BULLET	SMIGHT	CANNON	1986
NOW	NURSE ON WHEELS (UK)	THOMAS	JANUS	1963
NP	ESCAPE BY NIGHT (UK)	GILLING	EROS	1953
NP	ESCAPE BY NIGHT (UK: CLASH BY NIGHT)	TULLY	MONOGRAM	1964
NP	MOHAWK	NEUMANN	20th CENTURY FOX	1956
NP	NAKED PARADISE	CORMAN	AIP	1957
NP	NATIONAL PICTURES CORP		FOX	
NP	NATURE'S PARADISE (UK: NUDIST PARADISE)	SAUNDERS	FANFARE	1959
NP	NEUTRAL PORT (UK)	VARNEL	GFD	1940
NP	NIGHT PARADE	ST. CLAIR	RKO	1929
NP	NIGHT PORTER (IT)	CAVANI	AVCO EMBASSY	1974
NP	NOTHING PERSONAL	BLOOMFIELD	AIP	1980
NP	NOVA PILBEAM	portrait	GAUMONT BRITISH	
NP-49	I, MOBSTER	CORMAN	20th CENTURY FOX	1958
NP-110	TRAIL BLAZERS	BARRY	ALLIED ARTISTS	1953
NPA	SMART WOMEN	LA CAVA	RKO	1931
NPT	PAUL TEMPLE'S TRIUMPH (UK)	ROGERS	BUTCHER'S	1950
NPW	NEVER PUT IT IN WRITING (UK)	STONE	ALLIED ARTISTS	1964
NR	NAKED RUNNER	FURIE	WARNER BROS	1967
NR	NIGHT THEY RAIDED BIG BERTHA	KARES	SCOTIA AMERICAN	1975
NR	NO ROAD BACK (UK)	TULLY	RKO	1957
NR	NUNS ON THE RUN	LYNN	20th CENTURY FOX	1990
NR	NURSES REPORT (GER)	BOOS		1977
NRBB	NANCY DREW REPORTER	CLEMENS	WARNER BROS	1939
NRI	NO ROOM AT THE INN	BIRT	UNITED ARTISTS	1948
NRI/PS	NO ROOM AT THE INN (UK)	BIRT	STRATFORD	1948
NRP	NO RESTING PLACE (UK)	ROTHA	LASSIC	1951
NS	92 IN THE SHADE	MCGUANE	UNITED ARTISTS	1975
NS	CONFESSIONS OF A NAZI SPY	LITVAK	WARNER BROS	1939
NS	FOR MEMBERS ONLY: NUDIST STORY	HERRINGTON	ART IN MOTION PICT	1959
NS	LIFE IN HER HANDS (UK)	LEACOCK	UNITED ARTISTS	1951
NS	NAKED IN THE SUN	HUGH	ALLIED ARTISTS	1957
NS	NAKED SEA	MINER	RKO	1955
NS	NARROW STREET	BEAUDINE	WARNER BROS	1925
NS	NATALIE SCHAEFER	portrait	UNITED ARTISTS	
NS	NAUGHTY STEWARDESSES	ADAMSON	INDEPENDENT INT'L PIC.	1975
NS	NEVADA SMITH	HATHAWAY	PARAMOUNT	1966
NS	NIGHT SCHOOL	HUGHES	PARAMOUNT	1981
NS	NORMA SHEARER	portrait	MGM	
NS	NURSE'S SECRET	SMITH	WARNER BROS	1941
NS	OUTRAGE	LUPINO	RKO	1950
NS	WOMAN IN RED	FLOREY	FIRST NATIONAL	1935
NS-137	NAVY SPY	WILBUR	GRAND	1937
NSP1	AVENGERS (UK: DAY WILL DAWN)	FRENCH	PARAMOUNT	1942
NSS	NIGHT OF THE SHOOTING STARS (IT)	TAVIANI	UNITED ARTISTS	1982
NT	BIG CITY		WARNER BROS	
NT	NIGHT TIDE	HARRINGTON	AIP	1963
NT	NO TIME FOR COMEDY	KEIGHLEY	WARNER BROS	1940
NT	NO TIME FOR TEARS (UK)	FRANKEL	PATHE	1957
NT	NORMA TALMADGE FILM CORPORATION		WARNER BROS	
NT	RED HOUSE	DAVES	UNITED ARTISTS	1947
NT	SECRET DOOR (UK)	KAY	ALLIED ARTISTS	1964
N-T-13	PROBATION WIFE	FRANKLIN	SELECT (Talmadge)	1919
NT-16	ISLE OF CONQUEST	JOSE	SELECT	1919
NT-27	ETERNAL FLAME	LLOYD	WARNER BROS	1922

Movie Still Identification Book Ultimate Edition - Letters

CODE	TITLE/NAME	DIRECTOR/TYPE	STUDIO/DISTRIBUTOR	YEAR
NT-29	WITHIN THE LAW	LLOYD	WARNER BROS	1923
NT-31	DUST OF DESIRE	VEKROFF	WARNER BROS	1919
NT-32	SECRETS	BORZAGE	WARNER BROS	1924
NT-33	ONLY WOMAN	OLCOTT	WARNER BROS	1924
NT-34	LADY	BORZAGE	FIRST NATIONAL (Talmadge)	1925
NT-35	GRUSTARK	BUCHOWETZKI	WARNER BROS	1925
NT-36	KIKI	BROWN	FIRST NATIONAL (Talmadge)	1926
NT-37	CAMILLE	NIBLO	WARNER BROS	1926
NT-700	DOVE	WEST	UNITED ARTISTS	1927
NT-1200	WOMAN DISPUTED	H. KING, TAYLOR	UNITED ARTISTS	1928
NT-2700	NEW YORK NIGHTS	MILESTONE	UNITED ARTISTS	1929
NT-4400	DU BARRY, WOMAN OF PASSION	TAYLOR	UNITED ARTISTS	1930
NTC	BASHFUL ELEPHANT	MCGOWAN, MCGOWAN	ALLIED ARTISTS	1962
NTF	NO TIME FOR FLOWERS	SIEGEL	RKO	1953
NTK	NATALIE TALMADGE (KEATON)	portrait	METRO	
NTK	NO TIME TO KILL (UK)	YOUNGER	ADP	1959
NTL	TIME, GENTLEMEN, PLEASE! (UK)	GILBERT	MAYER-KINGLSEY	1952
NTN	NEVER TAKE NO FOR AN ANSWER (UK: SMALL MIRACLE)	CLOCHE, SMART	SOUVAINE SELECTIVE	1951
NTP	NIGHT TRAIN TO PARIS (UK)	DOUGLAS	20TH CENTURY FOX	1964
NV	NASHVILLE	ALTMAN	PARAMOUNT	1975
NV	NEVER PUT IT IN WRITING	STONE	ALLIED ARTISTS	1964
NV	NIGHT VISITOR	HITZIG	UNITED ARTISTS	1989
NV	NOW VOYAGER	RAPPER	WARNER BROS	1942
NV	VAMPIRE	LANDRES	UNITED ARTISTS	1957
NW	NATALIE WOOD	portrait	RKO, WARNER BROS	
NW	NEVER WAVE AT A WAC	MCLEOD	RKO	1953
NW	NIGHT WAITRESS	LANDERS	RKO	1936
NW	NIGHT WATCH	HUTTON	AVCO EMBASSY	1973
NW	NITWITS	STEVENS	RKO	1935
NW	NO PLACE LIKE HOMICIDE! (UK: WHAT A CARVE UP!)	JACKSON	EMBASSY	1961
NW	WINGS OF THE MORNING (UK)	SCHUSTER	20TH CENTURY FOX	1937
NW2	UNDER THE RED ROBE (UK)	SJOSTROM	20TH CENTURY FOX	1937
NW3	GREEN COCKATOO (UK)	MENZIES	20TH CENTURY FOX	1937
NWO	NO WAY OUT	DONALDSON	ORION	1987
NWS	NIGHT WITHOUT STARS (UK)	PELISSIER	RKO	1953
NX	LARCENY, INC.	BACON	WARNER BROS	1942
NY	NED YOUNG (aka NEDRICK YOUNG)	portrait	WARNER BROS	1950s
NY	NEW YORK, NEW YORK	SCORSESE	UNITED ARTISTS	1977
NY	REQUIEM FOR A HEAVYWEIGHT	NELSON	COLUMBIA	1962
NY-670	FLYING DEVILS	BIRDWELL	RKO	1933
NY-695	LITTLE WOMEN	CUKOR	RKO	1933
NY-787	GRIDIRON FLASH	TRYON	RKO	1934
NY-803	ROBERTA	SEITER	RKO	1935
NY-827	LAST DAYS OF POMPEII	SCHOEDSACK	RKO	1935
NYC	NEW YORK CONFIDENTIAL	ROUSE	WARNER BROS	1955
NY-HM	HORSE'S MOUTH	NEAME	UNITED ARTISTS	1958
NYIM	IRON MASK	DWAN	UNITED ARTISTS	1929
NYIN	IRON MASK	DWAN	UNITED ARTISTS	1929
NY-M	HORSE'S MOUTH (UK)	NEAME	UNITED ARTISTS	1958
O	HANNAH LEE (OUTLAW TERRITORY)	GARMES	REALART	1953
O	ODETTE (UK)	WILCOX	LOPERT	1950
O	OLIVER (UK)	REED	COLUMBIA	1968
O	OMOO - OMOO THE SHARK GOD	LEONARD	SCREEN GUILD	1949
O	ORDET (DEN)	DREYER	KINGSLEY INT'L	1955
O	OTHELLO	WELLES	UNITED ARTISTS	1952
O	OTHELLO (UK)	BIRGE	WARNER BROS	1965
O	OTLEY	CLEMENT	COLUMBIA	1968
O	OUTLAW (1943)	HUGHES	UNITED ARTISTS	R46
O	OUTLAWED	FORDE	FBO	1929
O-1	LOVEBOUND	OTTO	FOX FILM	1923
O03	IT'S ALIVE	COHEN	WARNER BROS	1974
O04	A STAR IS BORN	PIERSON	WARNER BROS	1976
O5-B3	ANCIENT MARINER	OTTO, BENNETT	FOX FILM	1925
O08	LISZTOMANIA	RUSSELL	WARNER BROS	1975
O10	SELLOUT (IS)	COLLINSON	WARNER BROS	1976
O12	STRAIGHT TIME	GROSBARD	WARNER BROS	1978
O18	THIEF WHO CAME TO DINNER	YORKIN	WARNER BROS	1973
O19	COME BACK CHARLESTON BLUE	WARREN	WARNER BROS	1972
O20	TRAIN ROBBERS	KENNEDY	WARNER BROS	1973
O25	EXORCIST	FRIEDKIN	WARNER BROS	1973

Movie Still Identification Book Ultimate Edition - Letters

CODE	TITLE/NAME	DIRECTOR/TYPE	STUDIO/DISTRIBUTOR	YEAR
O26	CLASS OF '44	BOGART	WARNER BROS	1973
O27	BLUME IN LOVE	MAZURSKI	WARNER BROS	1973
O28	ROLLOVER	PAKULA	ORION (WARNER BROS)	1981
O28	SCARECROW	SHATZBERG	WARNER BROS	1973
O30	MAME	SAKS	WARNER BROS	1974
O31	CLEOPATRA JONES	STARRETT	WARNER BROS	1973
O32	FREEBIE AND THE BEAN	RUSH	WARNER BROS	1974
O33	BLAZING SADDLES	BROOKS	WARNER BROS	1974
O34	ZANDY'S BRIDE	TROELL	WARNER BROS	1974
O35	MAGNUM FORCE	POST	WARNER BROS	1973
O36	MCQ	STURGES	WARNER BROS	1974
O37	TERMINAL MAN	HODGES	WARNER BROS	1974
O38	NIGHT MOVES	PENN	WARNER BROS	1975
O39	OUR TIME	HYAMS	WARNER BROS	1974
O41	PRISONER OF SECOND AVENUE	FRANK	WARNER BROS	1975
O42	RAFFERTY AND THE GOLD DUST TWINS	RICHARDS	WARNER BROS	1975
O43	DOC SAVAGE: MAN OF BRONZE	ANDERSON	WARNER BROS	1975
O44	ALICE DOESN'T LIVE HERE ANYMORE	SCORSESE	WARNER BROS	1974
O46	TOWERING INFERNO	GUILLERMIN	WARNER BROS	1974
O47	CLEOPATRA JONES & CASINO GOLD	BAIL	WARNER BROS	1975
O48	ULTIMATE WARRIOR	CLOUSE	WARNER BROS	1975
O49	DOG DAY AFTERNOON	LUMET	WARNER BROS	1975
O50	PIECE OF THE ACTION	POITIER	WARNER BROS	1977
O50	SPARKLE	O'STEEN	WARNER BROS	1976
O51	LONG DARK NIGHT (THE PACK)	CLOUSE	WARNER BROS	1977
O55	GUMBALL RALLY	BAIL	WARNER BROS	1976
O56	ST. IVES	THOMPSON	WARNER BROS	1976
O57	EXORCIST II: HERETIC	BOORMAN	WARNER BROS	1977
O59	VIVA KNIEVEL	DOUGLAS	WARNER BROS	1977
O60	ENFORCER	FARGO	WARNER BROS	1976
O64	OH GOD	REINER	WARNER BROS	1977
O65	GAUNTLET	EASTWOOD	WARNER BROS	1977
O66	BLOOD BROTHERS		WARNER BROS	
O67	BIG WEDNESDAY	MILIUS	WARNER BROS	1978
O68	SWARM	ALLEN	WARNER BROS	1978
O70	AGATHA	APTED	WARNER BROS	1979
O71	HOOPER	NEEDHAM	WARNER BROS	1978
O72	EVERY WHICH WAY BUT LOOSE	FARGO	WARNER BROS	1978
O73	TIME AFTER TIME	MEYER	WARNER BROS	1979
O74	FRISCO KID	ALDRICH	WARNER BROS	1979
O75	IN-LAWS	HILLER	WARNER BROS	1979
O76	BEYOND THE POSEIDON ADVENTURE	ALLEN	WARNER BROS	1979
O77	JUST TELL ME WHAT YOU WANT	LUMET	WARNER BROS	1980
O78	WHEN TIME RAN OUT	GOLDSTONE	WARNER BROS	1980
O79	GOING IN STYLE	BREST	WARNER BROS	1979
O80	ALTERED STATES	RUSSELL	WARNER BROS	1980
O82	HONEYSUCKLE ROSE	SCHATZBERG	WARNER BROS	1980
O360	BUT NOT FOR ME	LANG	PARAMOUNT	1959
O5003	FAHRENHEIT 451	TRUFFAUT	UNIVERSAL	1966
OA	LITTLE ORPHAN ANNIE	ROBERTSON	RKO	1932
OA	OLD ACQUAINTANCE	SHERMAN	WARNER BROS	1943
OAT	ODDS AGAINST TOMORROW	WISE	UNITED ARTISTS	1959
OB	BETWEEN TWO WORLDS	BLATT	WARNER BROS	1944
OB	GUN FIGHT	CAHN	UNITED ARTISTS	1961
OB	ON THE BORDER	MCGANN	WARNER BROS	1930
OB	OPERATION BULLSHINE (UK)	GUNN	PATHE	1959
OB	OUR BETTERS	CUKOR	RKO	1932
OB	OUTLAW BLUES	HEFFRON	WARNER BROS	1977
OB	OUTWARD BOUND	MILTON	WARNER BROS	1930
OB	THREE STOPS TO MURDER (UK: BLOOD ORANGE)	FISHER	EXCLUSIVE	1953
OB	TO THE VICTOR (UK: OWD BOB)	STEVENSON	GAUMONT BRITISH AMERICA	1938
O/BS	BLUE SCAR	CRAIGIE	BRITISH LION	1949
OC	DOG'S BEST FRIEND	CAHN	UNITED ARTISTS	1959
OC	ODD COUPLE	SAKS	PARAMOUNT	1968
OC	OIL FOR THE LAMPS OF CHINA	LEROY	WARNER BROS	1935
OC	ONCE A CROOK (UK)	MASON	20TH CENTURY FOX	1941
OC	ONE CROWDED NIGHT	REIS	RKO	1940
OC	OPEN CITY (IT)	ROSSELLINI	MAYER & BURSTYN	1945
OC-1	COLLEEN	O'CONNOR	FOX FILM	1927
OC2	ODD COUPLE II	DEUTCH	PARAMOUNT	1998

Movie Still Identification Book Ultimate Edition - Letters

CODE	TITLE/NAME	DIRECTOR/TYPE	STUDIO/DISTRIBUTOR	YEAR
OD	COTTON COMES TO HARLEM	DAVIS	UNITED ARTISTS	1970
OD	MIDNIGHT ALIBI	CROSLAND	WARNER BROS	1934
OD	ODONGO (UK)	GILLING	COLUMBIA	1956
OD	OH DAD, POOR DAD	QUINE	PARAMOUNT	1967
OD	OLIVIA DE HAVILLAND	portrait	WARNER BROS	
OD	ONCE A DOCTOR	CLEMENS	WARNER BROS	1937
OD	OPERATION DIPLOMAT (UK)	GUILLERMIN	BUTCHER'S	1953
OD	OUTLAWS DAUGHTER	BARRY	20th CENTURY FOX	1954
OD	OWEN DAVIS JR	portrait	RKO	
ODG	ON DEADLY GROUND	SEAGAL	WARNER BROS	1993
ODH	OLD DARK HOUSE	WHALE	UNIVERSAL	1932
OE	OLD ENGLISH	GREEN	WARNER BROS	1930
OEN	NIGHT OF ADVENTURE	DOUGLAS	RKO	1944
OES	ONE EYED SOLDIERS (UK)	AINSWORTH	UNITED ARTISTS	1966
OF	ODESSA FILE	NEAME	COLUMBIA	1974
OF	ONE FLEW OVER THE CUCKOO'S NEST	FORMAN	UNITED ARTISTS	1975
OF	SOME KIND OF A NUT	KANIN	UNITED ARTISTS	1969
OF1	INVADERS (UK: 49th PARALLEL)	POWELL, PRESSBURGER	COLUMBIA	1941
OFD	ONE FINE DAY	HOFFMAN	20th CENTURY FOX	1996
OFL	PLEASE NOT NOW (FR)	AUREL, TROP	INT'L CLASSICS	1961
OFN	ONE FRIGHTENED NIGHT	CABANNE	MASCOT	1935
OG	OFFICER AND A GENTLEMAN	HACKFORD	PARAMOUNT	1981
OG	OLD GUN	ENRICO	SURROGATE	1975
OG	OUTLAW GIRL (IT)	CAMERINI	IFE RELEASING	1955
OGF	ADVENTURES OF SADIE (UK: OUR GIRL FRIDAY)	LANGLEY	20th CENTURY FOX	1955
OH	ONE FOOT IN HEAVEN	RAPPER	WARNER BROS	1941
OH	OPERATION HAYLIFT	BERKE	LIPPERT	1950
OHBP	ON HER MAJESTY'S SECRET SERVICE (UK)	HUNTINGTON	UNITED ARTISTS	1969
OHGW	ON HER MAJESTY'S SECRET SERVICE (UK)	HUNTINGTON	UNITED ARTISTS	1969
OI	RIVER	RENOIR	UNITED ARTISTS	1951
O-J	OLSEN & JOHNSON (OLE OLSEN, CHIC JOHNSON)	portrait	WARNER BROS	early 30s
OK	MEANEST GAL IN TOWN	MACK	RKO	1934
OK	O-KAY FOR SOUND (UK)	VARNEL	GFD	1937
OK	OKLAHOMA KID	BACON	WARNER BROS	1939
OK	OPERATION KID BROTHER (IT: OK CONNERY)	DE MARTINO	UNITED ARTISTS	1967
OK	ORDERS TO KILL (UK)	ASQUITH	UMPO	1958
OK	OTTO KRUGER	portrait	MGM	
OLE	BEYOND LOVE AND EVIL (FR)	SCANDELARI	ALLIED ARTISTS	1971
OLW	OH! WHAT A LOVELY WAR (UK)	ATTENBOROUGH	PARAMOUNT	1969
OM	EXPERT	MAYO	WARNER BROS	1932
OM	LAWLESS RIDER	CANUTT	UNITED ARTISTS	1954
OM	OLD MAID	GOULDING	WARNER BROS	1939
OM	ONA MUNSON	portrait		
OM	ONCE MORE, WITH FEELING! (UK)	DONEN	COLUMBIA	1960
OM	OPERATION MANHUNT	ALEXANDER	UNITED ARTISTS	1954
OM	OSA MASSEN	portrait	RKO	
OM	OUR MAN IN HAVANA (UK)	REED	COLUMBIA	1959
OM	OUTSIDE MAN (FR: UN HOMME EST MORT)	DERAY	UNITED ARTISTS	1972
OM	OWEN MOORE	portrait	MGM	
OM	PERSONALITY KID	CROSLAND	WARNER BROS	1934
OM/A	OUR MAN IN HAVANA	REED	COLUMBIA	1959
OMH	OUR MOTHER'S HOUSE (UK)	CLAYTON	MGM	1967
OMR	OLD MOTHER RILEY JOINS UP (UK)	ROGERS	ANGLO-AMERICAN	1940
OMR	SAID O'REILLY TO MCNAB (UK)	BEAUDINE	GAUMONT BRITISH AMERICA	1937
OMW	MAN AND A WOMAN (FR)	LELOUCH	MONOGRAM	1966
OMW	ONE MAN'S WAY	SANDERS	UNITED ARTISTS	1964
OMWF	ONCE MORE WITH FEELING (UK)	DONEN	COLUMBIA	1960
OMY	ONE MILLION YEARS B.C. (UK)	CHAFFEY	20TH CENTURY FOX	1966
ON	OVER NIGHT (UK: THAT NIGHT IN LONDON)	LEE	PARAMOUNT	1932
ONE	ONCE IS NOT ENOUGH	GREEN	PARAMOUNT	1975
ONS	ONE NIGHT AT SUSIE'S	DILLON	WARNER BROS	1930
OO	DON'T TELL THE WIFE	CABANNE	RKO	1937
OO	ONE AND ONLY	REINER	PARAMOUNT	1978
OP	OH, MR. PORTER!	VARNEL	GFD	1937
OP	ONE WAY PASSAGE	GARNETT	WARNER BROS	1932
OP	OUTCASTS OF POKER FLATS	CABANNE	RKO	1937
OP	OVERLAND PACIFIC (SILVER DOLLAR)	SEARS	UNITED ARTISTS	1954
OP	OWL AND THE PUSSYCAT	ROSS	COLUMBIA	1970
OP1	STOLEN LIFE (UK)	CZINNER	PARAMOUNT	1939
OP2	MOUSE THAT ROARED (UK)	ARNOLD	COLUMBIA	1959

Movie Still Identification Book Ultimate Edition - Letters

CODE	TITLE/NAME	DIRECTOR/TYPE	STUDIO/DISTRIBUTOR	YEAR
OPB	WAY BACK HOME	SEITER	RKO	1931
OPY	OCTOPUSSY	GLEN	UNITED ARTISTS	1983
OQ	PENNY POINT TO PARADISE (UK)	YOUNG	ADELPHI	1951
OR	ORCA	ANDERSON	PARAMOUNT	1977
OR-1	KEY (UK)	REED	COLUMBIA	1958
ORA	ONE RAINY AFTERNOON	LEE	UNITED ARTISTS	1936
ORB	ORGANIZATION	MEDFORD	UNITED ARTISTS	1971
ORG	MURDER BY CONTRACT	LERNER	COLUMBIA	1958
ORG	ORGANIZATION	MEDFORD	UNITED ARTISTS	1971
OS	OLD SAN FRANCISCO	CROSLAND	WARNER BROS	1927
OS	ONCE A SINNER (UK)	GILBERT	J.H. HOFFBERG	1950
OS	OPERATION SNATCH (UK)	DAY	CONTINENTAL	1962
OS	OTHER SIDE OF BONNIE AND CLYDE	BUCHANAN	DAL-ART	1968
OS	OTIS SKINNER	portrait		
OS	SPIES IN THE AIR (UK: SPIES OF THE AIR)	MACDONALD	FILM ALLIANCE	1940
OS	STREET OF SINNERS	BERKE	UNITED ARTISTS	1957
OS	SUMMERTIME (UK: SUMMER MADNESS)	LEAN	UNITED ARTISTS	1955
OSBC	TRAILIN' WEST	SMITH	WARNER BROS	1936
OSD	DOUBLE CONFESSION (UK)	ANNAKIN	STRATFORD	1950
OSF	IN OLD SANTA FE	HOWARD	MASCOT	1934
OSJ	OLGA SAN JUAN	portrait	UNIVERSAL	
OSP	PRINCESS O'HARA	BURTON	UNIVERSAL	1935
OSPC	YOU CAN'T CHEAT AN HONEST MAN	MARSHALL	UNIVERSAL	1939
OSS	ON HER MAJESTY'S SECRET SERVICE (UK)	HUNT	UNITED ARTISTS	1969
OSS	OSS 117 IS NOT DEAD (FR: O.S.S. 117 N'EST PAS MORT 1957)	SACHA	REPUBLIC	1959
OSS	OSS 117: MISSION FOR A KILLER (FR: FURIA A ... OSS 117)	HUNEBELLE	EMBASSY	1966
OSTM	ONE SPY TOO MANY	SARGENT	MGM	1966
OT	BANDIT TRAIL	KILLY	RKO	1941
OT	OKLAHOMA TERRITORY	CAHN	UNITED ARTISTS	1960
OT	OLIVE THOMAS	portrait	SELZNICK/SELECT	
OT	ON TRIAL	MORSE	WARNER BROS	1939
OT	ON YOUR TOES	ENRIGHT	WARNER BROS	1939
OT	ORRIN TUCKER	portrait	MCA MUSIC	
OT	OTHER MRS. BRADFORD (EX-MRS. BRADFORD)	ROBERTS	RKO	1936
OT	OUT OF IT	WILLIAMS	UNITED ARTISTS	1969
OT	OUT-OF-TOWNERS	HILLER	PARAMOUNT	1969
OT	OVER THE WALL	MCDONALD	WARNER BROS	1938
OT	OVERLAND TELEGRAPH	SELANDER	RKO	1951
O-T-7	FLAPPER	CROSLAND	SELZNICK	1920
OTB	ON THE BEACH	KRAMER	UNITED ARTISTS	1959
OTL	ON THE LOOSE	LEDERER	RKO	1951
OTL	ONLY THE LONELY	COLUMBUS	20th CENTURY FOX	1991
OTT	ONE, TWO, THREE	WILDER	UNITED ARTISTS	1961
OTTO-4	FOLLY OF VANITY	OTTO	FOX FILM	1924
OTTO4 ELVEY3	FOLLY OF VANITY	OTTO, ELVEY	FOX FILM	1924
OU	ONCE UPON A HONEYMOON	MCCAREY	RKO	1942
OUF	ONCE UPON A FOREST (t)	GROSVENOR	20th CENTURY FOX	1993
OUW	ONCE UPON A TIME IN THE WEST (IT)	LEONE	PARAMOUNT	1968
OV	RUSTLERS	SELANDER	RKO	1949
OW	MY OFFICIAL WIFE	STEIN	WARNER BROS	1926
OW	OFFICE WIFE	BACON	WARNER BROS	1930
OW	ONCE UPON WHEEL (tv documentary)	WINTERS	SAGGITARIUS	1968
OW	ORSON WELLES	portrait	RKO	
OW	OSCAR WILDE (UK)	RATOFF	FOUR CITY	1960
OW	OSKAR WERNER	portrait	UNIV	
OW	OUTLAW WOMEN	NEWFIELD	LIPPERT	1952
OW	TRIALS OF OSCAR WILDE	HUGHES	UNITED ARTISTS	1960
OW	WILD BEAST AT BAY		COSMOPOLITAN	1947
OWL	ONLY WHEN I LARF (UK)	DEARDEN	PARAMOUNT	1969
OWO	ONE WILD OAT (UK)	SAUNDERS	EROS	1951
OWO	ONE WAY OUT (UK)	SEARLE	RANK	1955
OWP	ONE WAY PENDULUM (UK)	YATES	LOPERT	1964
OWS	ON WITH THE SHOW	CROSLAND	WARNER BROS	1929
OWS	OUR WINNING SEASON	RUBEN	AIP	1978
OX	OPERATION X (UK: MY DAUGHTER JOY)	RATOFF	COLUMBIA	1950
OY	OBLIGING YOUNG LADY	WALLACE	RKO	1942
P	BATTLESHIP POTEMKIN (RUS)	EISENSTEIN	AMKINO	1926
P	CAPTIVE WOMEN	GILMORE	RKO	1952
P	GREAT DICTATOR	CHAPLIN	UNITED ARTISTS	1940
P	MATRIMONIAL BED	CURTIZ	WARNER BROS	1930

Movie Still Identification Book Ultimate Edition - Letters

CODE	TITLE/NAME	DIRECTOR/TYPE	STUDIO/DISTRIBUTOR	YEAR
P	MELODY FOR 3	KENTON	RKO	1941
P	MUPPET MOVIE	HENSON	ASSOCIATED FILM	1979
P	PADDY (IRE)	HALLER	ALLIED ARTISTS	1970
P	PAGEMASTER	HUNT, JOHNSTON	20th CENTURY FOX	1994
P	PAISAN (IT: PAISA)	ROSSELLINI	MAYER & BURSTYN	1946
P	PANORAMIC PRODUCTIONS	studio	FOX	
P	PARACHUTE JUMPER	GREEN	WARNER BROS	1933
P	PARADISE	GILLARD	EMBASSY	1982
P	PARKYAKARKUS (aka HARRY PARKE/EINSTEIN)	portrait	RKO	
P	PASSAGE	THOMPSON	UNITED ARTISTS	1979
P	PASSENGER 57	HOOKS	WARNER BROS	1992
P	PASSING OF THE THIRD FLOOR BACK (UK)	VIERTEL	GAUMONT BRITISH	1935
P	PASSION		RKO	1936
P	PASSION OF ANNA (SWE: EN PASSION 1969)	BERGMAN	UNITED ARTISTS	1970
P	PEARL	FERNANDEZ	RKO	1948
P	PENDULUM	SCHAEFER	COLUMBIA	1969
P	PERSONA	BERGMAN	LOPERT	1967
P	PETRIFIED FOREST	MAYO	WARNER BROS	1936
P	PHANTOM FROM 10,000 LEAGUES	MILNER	AIP	1955
P	PHYSICIAN (UK)	JACOBY	TIFFANY	1928
P	PIRATES	POLANSKI	CANNON	1986
P	POLYESTER	WATERS	NEW LINE CINEMA	1981
P	POSSE	DOUGLAS	PARAMOUNT	1975
P	POWER	LUMET	20th CENTURY FOX	1986
P	PRESTIGE	GARNETT	RKO	1932
P	PROPHECY	FRANKENHEIMER	PARAMOUNT	1979
P	PSYCHE 59 (UK)	SINGER	COLUMBIA	1964
P	STRANGLER (UK: EAST OF PICCADILLY)	HUTH	PRC	1941
P	TOUGHEST GUN IN TOMBSTONE	BELLAMY	UNITED ARTISTS	1958
P	TRAPPED IN PARADISE	GALLO	20th CENTURY FOX	1994
P	YOUNG MR. PITT (UK)	REED	20TH CENTURY FOX	1942
P1	ESCAPE IN THE SUN (UK)	BREAKSTON	PARAMOUNT BRITISH	1956
P-1	I WANT MY MAN	HILLYER	WARNER BROS	1925
P1	MEN OF TOMORROW (UK)	SAGAN	MUNDUA	1932
P1	PACIFIC DESTINY (UK)	RILLA	BRITISH LION	1956
P-1	PROJECT MOONBASE	TALMADGE	LIPPERT	1953
P-1	SPITBALL SADIE	ROACH	PATHE EXCHANGE	1915
P.1	SILVER LINING	CROSLAND	UNITED ARTISTS	1932
P2	MAJOR BARBARA (UK)	PASCAL	UNITED ARTISTS	1941
P2	OVER NIGHT (UK: THAT NIGHT IN LONDON)	LEE	PARAMOUNT	1932
P-2	STRANGE IMPERSONATION	MANN	REPUBLIC	1946
P-2	TERRIBLY STUCK UP	ROACH	PATHE EXCHANGE	1915
P-2	THREE YOUNG TEXANS	LEVIN	20th CENTURY FOX	1954
P-3	RUSES, RHYMES AND ROUGHNECKS	ROACH	PATHE EXCHANGE	1915
P-3	SIEGE AT RED RIVER	MATE	20th CENTURY FOX	1954
P4	COUNSEL'S OPINION (UK)	DWAN	PARAMOUNT BRITISH	1933
P4	GORILLA AT LARGE	JONES	20th CENTURY FOX	1954
P-4	MIXUP FOR MAZIE	ROACH	PATHE EXCHANGE	1915
P5	FOR LOVE OR MONEY (UK: CASH)	KORDA	HOFFBERG, MUNDUS	1933
P-5	MAKING OF O'MALLEY	HILLYER	WARNER BROS	1925
P-5	ROCKET MAN	RUDOLPH	20th CENTURY FOX	1954
P-5	SOME BABY	ROACH	PATHE EXCHANGE	1915
P-6	FRESH FROM THE FARM	ROACH	PATHE EXCHANGE	1915
P6	I MARRIED A SPY (UK: SECRET LIVES)	GREVILLE	GRAND NATIONAL	1937
P6	SCHOOL FOR HUSBANDS (UK)	MARTON	JH HOFFBERG	1937
P7	DANGEROUS SECRETS (UK: BRIEF ECSTASY)	GREVILLE	GRAND NATIONAL	1937
P-7	FOOZLE AT THE TEE PARTY	ROACH	PATHE EXCHANGE	1915
P-7	KNOCKOUT	HILLYER	WARNER BROS	1925
P-7	GAMBLER FROM NATCHEZ	LEVIN	20th CENTURY FOX	1954
P-7	PRINCE OF TEMPTERS	MENDES	WARNER BROS	1926
P-8	CONVOY	BOYLE	WARNER BROS	1927
P-8	GREAT WHILE IT LASTED	ROACH	PATHE EXCHANGE	1915
P-8	PACE THAT THRILLS	CAMPBELL	FIRST NATIONAL	1925
P8	PRISON BREAKER (UK)	BRUNEL	COLUMBIA	1936
P-8	RAID	FREGONESE	20th CENTURY FOX	1954
P-9	GIVING THEM FITS	ROACH	PATHE EXCHANGE	1915
P-10	BROADWAY NIGHTS	BOYLE	WARNER BROS	1927
P-10	SCARLET SAINT	ARCHAINBAUD	FIRST NATIONAL	1925
P-10	TINKERING WITH TROUBLE	ROACH	PATHE EXCHANGE	1915
P-10	WHITE FEATHER	WEBB	20th CENTURY FOX	1955

Movie Still Identification Book Ultimate Edition - Letters

CODE	TITLE/NAME	DIRECTOR/TYPE	STUDIO/DISTRIBUTOR	YEAR
P-11	MEN OF STEEL	ARCHAINBAUD	WARNER BROS	1926
P-11	PECULIAR PATIENTS' PRANKS	ROACH	PATHE EXCHANGE	1915
P-12	CALLING OF DAN MATHEWS	ROSEN	COLUMBIA	1935
P-12	LONESOME LUKE, SOCIAL GANGSTER	ROACH, MACDONALD	PATHE EXCHANGE	1915
P-13	BUGHOUSE BELLHOPS	ROACH	PATHE EXCHANGE	1915
P-13	TOO MUCH MONEY	DILLON	WARNER BROS	1926
P14	MILTON SILLS	portrait	PARAMOUNT	
P-14	PUPPETS	ARCHAINBAUD	WARNER BROS	1926
P-14	RAGTIME SNAP SHOTS	ROACH	PATHE EXCHANGE	1915
P-15	LUKE LUGS LUGGAGE	ROACH	PATHE EXCHANGE	1916
P-15	SAVAGE	NEWMEYER	FIRST NATIONAL	1926
P-16	LONESOME LUKE LEANS TO THE LITERARY	ROACH	PATHE EXCHANGE	1916
P-16	MINE WITH THE IRON DOOR	HOWARD	COLUMBIA	1936
P-17	LONESOME LUKE LOLLS IN LUXURY	ROACH	PATHE EXCHANGE	1916
P-17	LOST WORLD	HOYT	WARNER BROS	1925
P-17	SUBWAY SADIE	SANTELL	WARNER BROS	1926
P18	BETTY BRONSON	portrait	PARAMOUNT	
P-18	LUKE FOILS THE VILLAIN	ROACH	PATHE EXCHANGE	1916
P18	MY AMERICAN WIFE	YOUNG	PARAMOUNT	1936
P-19	LUKE, THE CANDY CUT-UP	ROACH	PATHE EXCHANGE	1916
P-20	DOUBLE EXPOSURE	BERKE	PARAMOUNT	1944
P-20	LUKE AND THE RURAL ROUGHNECKS	ROACH	PATHE EXCHANGE	1916
P-20	PERFECT SAP	HIGGIN	WARNER BROS	1927
P-21	DANGEROUS PASSAGE	BERKE	PARAMOUNT	1944
P-21	LUKE PIPES THE PIPPINS	ROACH	PATHE EXCHANGE	1916
P-22	HIGH POWERED	BERKE	PARAMOUNT	1945
P-22	SINGLE WIVES	ARCHAINBAUD	FIRST NATIONAL	1924
P-22	THEM WAS THE DAYS	ROACH	PATHE EXCHANGE	1916
P-23	LUKE'S DOUBLE	ROACH	PATHE EXCHANGE	1916
P-23	SCARED STIFF	MCDONALD	PARAMOUNT	1945
P-24	LONESOME LUKE, CIRCUS KING	ROACH	PATHE EXCHANGE	1916
P-25	LUKE'S LATE LUNCHERS	ROACH	PATHE EXCHANGE	1916
P-26	LUKE AND THE BOMB THROWERS	ROACH	PATHE EXCHANGE	1916
P-27	LUKE LAUGHS LAST	ROACH	PATHE EXCHANGE	1916
P-28	LUKE'S FATAL FLIVVER	ROACH	PATHE EXCHANGE	1916
P-29	LUKE'S SOCIETY MIX-UP	ROACH	PATHE EXCHANGE	1916
P-29	SO BIG	BRABIN	FIRST NATIONAL	1924
P-30	LUKE'S WASHFUL WAITING	ROACH	PATHE EXCHANGE	1916
P-31	IF I MARRY AGAIN	DILLON	WARNER BROS	1925
P-35	SALLY	GREEN	WARNER BROS	1925
P63	COLLEEN MOORE	portrait	PARAMOUNT	
P65	PRANCER	HANCOCK	ORION	1989
P-73	MUPPET MOVIE	HENSON	ASSOCIATED FILM	1979
P-7S	R.S.V.P.	RAY	WARNER BROS	1921
P-101	TORMENTED	GORDON	ALLIED ARTISTS	1960
P102	CECIL B DEMILLE	portrait	PARAMOUNT	
P104	KATHLYN WILLIAMS	portrait	PARAMOUNT	
P106	VIVIAN MARTIN	portrait	PARAMOUNT`	
P107	ANNA Q. NILSSON	portrait	PARAMOUNT	
P-108	HATS OFF	PETROFF	GRAND	1936
P110	PAULINE FREDERICK	portrait	PARAMOUNT	
P112	MARGUERITE CLARK	portrait	PARAMOUNT	
P115	SESSUE HAYAKAWA	portrait	PARAMOUNT	
P116	ROSCOE "FATTY" ARBUCKLE	portrait	PARAMOUNT	
P120	THEODORE ROBERTS	portrait	PARAMOUNT	
P123	JACK PICKFORD	portrait	PARAMOUNT	
P128	WALLACE REID	portrait	PARAMOUNT	
P-134	OUTCAST	SEITER	FIRST NATIONAL	1928
P135	ADOLPH ZUKOR	portrait	PARAMOUNT	
P138	JESSE L LASKY	portrait	PARAMOUNT	
P143	BUSTER KEATON	portrait	PARAMOUNT	
P144	THOMAS MEIGHAN	portrait	PARAMOUNT	
P-149	SEVEN FOOTPRINTS TO SATAN	CHRISTENSEN	WARNER BROS	1929
P151	BILLIE BURKE	portrait	PARAMOUNT	
P156	WILLIAM S. HART	portrait	PARAMOUNT	
P160	CHARLES RAY	portrait	PARAMOUNT	
P161	ENID BENNETT	portrait	PARAMOUNT	
P163	DOROTHY DALTON	portrait	PARAMOUNT	
P-165	GREAT DICTATOR	CHAPLIN	UNITED ARTISTS	1940
P165	J. STUART BLACKTON	portrait	PARAMOUNT	

Movie Still Identification Book Ultimate Edition - Letters

CODE	TITLE/NAME	DIRECTOR/TYPE	STUDIO/DISTRIBUTOR	YEAR
P166	MARGARET LOOMIS	portrait	PARAMOUNT	
P174	KATHLEEN CLIFFORD	portrait	PARAMOUNT	
P178	JESSE L LASKY; ART LASKY; MAURICE LASKY	portrait	PARAMOUNT	
P181	MARIE PREVOST	portrait	PARAMOUNT	
P184	GLORIA SWANSON	portrait	PARAMOUNT	
P194	LINA CAVALIERI	portrait	PARAMOUNT	
P200	JACK HOLT	portrait	PARAMOUNT	
P208	LILA LEE	portrait	PARAMOUNT	
P211	WANDA HAWLEY	portrait	PARAMOUNT	
P212	BARRIER	SELANDER	PARAMOUNT	1937
P213	DOROTHY GISH	portrait	PARAMOUNT	
P214	LILLIAN GISH	portrait	PARAMOUNT	
P221	BRYANT WASHBURN	portrait	PARAMOUNT	
P222	ETHEL CLAYTON	portrait	PARAMOUNT	
P237	HARRIET HAMMOND	portrait	PARAMOUNT	
P240	CONSTANCE BINNEY	portrait	PARAMOUNT	
P242	ELLIOT DEXTER	portrait	PARAMOUNT`	
P245	MONTE BLUE	portrait	PARAMOUNT	
P246	RICHARD BARTHELMESS	portrait	PARAMOUNT	
P249	JULIA FAYE	portrait	PARAMOUNT	
P252	GEORGE FITZMAURICE	portrait	PARAMOUNT	
P255	IRENE CASTLE	portrait	PARAMOUNT	
P257	HARRY HOUDINI	portrait	PARAMOUNT	
P260	MILTON SILLS	portrait	PARAMOUNT	
P263	DORIS MAY	portrait	PARAMOUNT	
P264	DOUGLAS MACLEAN	portrait	PARAMOUNT`	
P265	SYDNEY CHAPLIN	portrait	PARAMOUNT	
P267	MARION DAVIES	portrait	PARAMOUNT	
P268	VIOLET HEMING	portrait	PARAMOUNT	
P269	BEBE DANIELS	portrait	PARAMOUNT	
P270	BETTY COMPSON	portrait	PARAMOUNT	
P276	DAVID POWELL	portrait	PARAMOUNT	
P282	LOIS WILSON	portrait	PARAMOUNT	
P295	MABEL JULIENNE SCOTT	portrait	PARAMOUNT	
P300	WALTER HIERS	portrait	PARAMOUNT	
P302	HARRISON FORD	portrait	PARAMOUNT	
P-302	MEXICAN MANHUNT	BAILEY	ALLIED ARTISTS	1953
P-303	JACK SLADE	SCHUSTER	ALLIED ARTISTS	1953
P-304	CRY VENGEANCE	STEVENS	ALLIED ARTISTS	1954
P-305	LOOPHOLE	SCHUSTER	ALLIED ARTISTS	1954
P-306	DRAGOON WELLS MASSACRE	SCHUSTER	ALLIED ARTISTS	1957
P318	CLAIRE WINDSOR	portrait	PARAMOUNT	
P319	WILLIAM DE MILLE	portrait	PARAMOUNT	
P320	FORD STERLING	portrait	PARAMOUNT	
P321	JOHN HENRY JR. (aka DON MARION)	portrait	PARAMOUNT	
P327	JEANIE MACPHERSON	portrait	PARAMOUNT	
P335	GEORGE MELFORD	portrait	PARAMOUNT	
P337	OUIDA BERGERE	portrait	PARAMOUNT	
P358	CHARLES OGLE	portrait	PARAMOUNT	
P370	VIORA DANIEL	portrait	PARAMOUNT	
P382	ANN FORREST	portrait	PARAMOUNT	
P393	BETTY ROSS CLARK	portrait	PARAMOUNT	
P394	BETTY FRANCISCO	portrait	PARAMOUNT	
P398	CONRAD NAGEL	portrait	PARAMOUNT	
P-404	FINGERMAN	SCHUSTER	ALLIED ARTISTS	1955
P-405	A DAUGHTER OF LUXURY	POWELL	PARAMOUNT	1922
P405	AGNES AYRES	portrait	PARAMOUNT	
P408	FORREST STANLEY	portrait	PARAMOUNT	
P-408	STRANGE INTRUDER	RAPPER	ALLIED ARTISTS	1956
P409	MAY MCAVOY	portrait	PARAMOUNT	
P415	MARY GLYNNE	portrait	PARAMOUNT	
P423	THEODORE KOSLOFF	portrait	PARAMOUNT	
P432	SIDNEY R. KENT	portrait	PARAMOUNT	
P439	WALTER HIERS	portrait	PARAMOUNT	
P443	ROSE CADE	portrait	PARAMOUNT	
P446	ELINOR GLYN	portrait	PARAMOUNT	
P454	HENRY ARTHUR JONES	portrait	PARAMOUNT	
P470	NADJA OSTROVSKA	portrait	PARAMOUNT	
P-470	NOT OF THIS EARTH	CORMAN	ALLIED ARTISTS	1957
P473	JACQUELINE LOGAN	portrait	PARAMOUNT	

Movie Still Identification Book Ultimate Edition - Letters

CODE	TITLE/NAME	DIRECTOR/TYPE	STUDIO/DISTRIBUTOR	YEAR
P474	JAMES KIRKWOOD	portrait	PARAMOUNT	
P475	GRACE DARMOND	portrait	PARAMOUNT	
P478	NORMAN KERRY	portrait	PARAMOUNT	
P484	NITA NALDI	portrait	PARAMOUNT	
P485	BETTY CARPENTER	portrait	PARAMOUNT	
P491	SEENA OWEN	portrait	PARAMOUNT	
P496	MILDRED HARRIS	portrait	PARAMOUNT	
P-501	COME ON	BIRDWELL	ALLIED ARTISTS	1956
P-502	RETURN OF JACK SLADE	SCHUSTER	ALLIED ARTISTS	1955
P509	CLARENCE BURTON	portrait	PARAMOUNT	
P510	RAYMOND HATTON	portrait	PARAMOUNT`	
P511	RUDOLPH VALENTINO	portrait	PARAMOUNT	
P513	LEATRICE JOY	portrait	PARAMOUNT	
P513	CHANGING HUSBANDS	IRIBE, URSON	PARAMOUNT	1924
P517	POLA NEGRI	portrait	PARAMOUNT	
P519	EDITH ROBERTS	portrait	PARAMOUNT	
P521	T. ROY BARNES	portrait	PARAMOUNT	
P522	MARY MILES MINTER	portrait	PARAMOUNT	
P525	MIA MAY	portrait	PARAMOUNT	
P526	ELINOR GLYN	portrait	PARAMOUNT	
P527	TOM MOORE	portrait	PARAMOUNT	
P529	BERT LYTELL	portrait	PARAMOUNT	
P533	ALLAN DWAN	portrait	PARAMOUNT	
P534	WYNDHAM STANDING	portrait	PARAMOUNT	
P535	SAM WOOD	portrait	PARAMOUNT	
P540	JACQUELINE LOGAN	portrait	PARAMOUNT	
P540	HOLLYWOOD, CITY OF DREAMS	CRONE	UNIVERSAL	1932
P541	ADOLPHE MENJOU	portrait	PARAMOUNT	
P542	MARY MACLAREN	portrait	PARAMOUNT	
P542	MOUNTAINS IN FLAMES (POL)	BATORY, HECHTKOPF	UNIVERSAL	1956
P543	PAULINE GARON	portrait	PARAMOUNT	
P544	J. WARREN KERRIGAN	portrait	PARAMOUNT	
P546	ANTONIO MORENO	portrait	PARAMOUNT	
P547	RAYMOND HATTON	portrait	PARAMOUNT	
P548	LEWIS STONE	portrait	PARAMOUNT	
P551	RICARDO CORTEZ	portrait	PARAMOUNT	
P554	MAURICE COSTELLO	portrait	PARAMOUNT	
P555	RICHARD DIX	portrait	PARAMOUNT	
P557	GLENN HUNTER	portrait	PARAMOUNT	
P558	MARY ASTOR	portrait	PARAMOUNT	20s-1933
P560	CONSTANCE WILSON	portrait	PARAMOUNT	
P564	JOSEPH HENABERY	portrait	PARAMOUNT	
P565	ROBERT AGNEW	portrait	PARAMOUNT	
P567	ALMA BENNETT	portrait	PARAMOUNT	
P571	JAMES CRUZE	portrait	PARAMOUNT	
P573	HERBERT BRENON	portrait	PARAMOUNT	
P575	SIGRID/SIE HOLMQUIST BIE HOLMQUIST	portrait	PARAMOUNT	
P577	ERNEST TORRENCE	portrait	PARAMOUNT	
P578	VERA REYNOLDS	portrait	PARAMOUNT	
P579	ROD LA ROCQUE	portrait	PARAMOUNT	
P582	DOUGLAS FAIRBANKS JR	portrait	PARAMOUNT	
P583	ESTELLE TAYLOR	portrait	PARAMOUNT	
P584	KATHLYN WILLIAMS	portrait	PARAMOUNT	
P585	MARY EATON	portrait	PARAMOUNT	
P587	DOROTHY MACKAILL	portrait	PARAMOUNT	
P590	NOAH BEERY	portrait	PARAMOUNT	
P595	LOUISE DRESSER	portrait	PARAMOUNT	
P598	SAZU PITTS	portrait	PARAMOUNT`	
P600	GEORGE FAWCETT	portrait	PARAMOUNT	
P-601	WOLF LARSEN	JONES	ALLIED ARTISTS	1958
P603	EDWARD EVERETT HORTON	portrait	PARAMOUNT	
P604	LLOYD HUGHES	portrait	PARAMOUNT	
P610	PATSY RUTH MILLER	portrait	PARAMOUNT	
P611	VICTOR VARCONI	portrait	PARAMOUNT	
P613	RAYMOND GRIFFITH	portrait	PARAMOUNT	
P614	BILLIE DOVE	portrait	PARAMOUNT	
P615	IRVIN WILLAT	portrait	PARAMOUNT	
P619	PAUL BERN	portrait	PARAMOUNT	
P621	VICTOR FLEMING	portrait	PARAMOUNT	
P622	BEN LYON, DIMITRI BUCHOWETZKI	portrait	PARAMOUNT	

Movie Still Identification Book Ultimate Edition - Letters

CODE	TITLE/NAME	DIRECTOR/TYPE	STUDIO/DISTRIBUTOR	YEAR
P624	ERNST LUBITSCH	portrait	PARAMOUNT	
P627	PERCY MARMONT	portrait	PARAMOUNT	
P638	VIOLA DANA	portrait	PARAMOUNT	
P639	WILLIAM BOYD	portrait	PARAMOUNT	
P641	JANE WINTON	portrait	PARAMOUNT	
P643	IAN KEITH	portrait	PARAMOUNT	
P644	JETTA GOUDAL	portrait	PARAMOUNT	
P645	HANS DREIER	portrait	PARAMOUNT	
P647	FRANK TUTTLE	portrait	PARAMOUNT	
P648	VIRGINIA LEE CORBIN	portrait	PARAMOUNT	
P652	BETTY BRONSON	portrait	PARAMOUNT	
P653	HELENE CHADWICK	portrait	PARAMOUNT	
P656	MARY BRIAN	portrait	PARAMOUNT	
P657	ESTHER RALSTON	portrait	PARAMOUNT	
P658	WARNER BAXTER	portrait	PARAMOUNT	
P660	FRANCES HOWARD	portrait	PARAMOUNT	
P661	PAULINE STARKE	portrait	PARAMOUNT	
P662	MABEL BALLIN	portrait	PARAMOUNT	
P663	CONSTANCE BENNETT	portrait	PARAMOUNT	
P665	LILYAN TASHMAN	portrait	PARAMOUNT	
P666	GRETA NISSEN	portrait	PARAMOUNT	
P-667	EMERGENCY CALL	CAHN	RKO	1933
P667	RAOUL WALSH	portrait	PARAMOUNT	
P668	MOUNTED STRANGER	ROSSEN	UNIVERSAL	1930
P669	TRAILIN' TROUBLE	ROSSON	UNIVERSAL	1930
P670	CLAIRE ADAMS	portrait	PARAMOUNT	
P670	ROARING RANCH	EASON	UNIVERSAL	1930
P671	ANNA MAY WONG	portrait	PARAMOUNT	
P672	CLARENCE BADGER	portrait	PARAMOUNT	
P672	CONCENTRATIN' KID	ROSSEN	UNIVERSAL	1930
P-672	PROFESSIONAL SWEETHEART	SEITER	RKO	1933
P673	SPURS	EASON	UNIVERSAL	1930
P674	VIOLA DANA	portrait	PARAMOUNT	
P677	ALICE TERRY	portrait	PARAMOUNT	
P678	DOROTHY SEBASTIAN	portrait	PARAMOUNT`	
P680	FLORENCE VIDOR	portrait	PARAMOUNT`	
P681	FLORENCE VIDOR	portrait	PARAMOUNT	
P682	NEIL HAMILTON	portrait	PARAMOUNT	
P684	HAROLD LLOYD	portrait	PARAMOUNT	
P685	ALICE JOYCE	portrait	PARAMOUNT	
P685	MICHAEL AND MARY	SAVILLE	UNIVERSAL	1931
P687	LAWRENCE GRAY	portrait	PARAMOUNT	
P688	MAL ST. CLAIR	portrait	PARAMOUNT	
P689	STREET SINGER	BRICE	UNIVERSAL	1932
P689	WALLACE BEERY	portrait	PARAMOUNT	
P-691	ACE OF ACES	RUBEN	RKO	1933
P693	WILLIAM "BUSTER" COLLIER, JR.	portrait	PARAMOUNT	
P695	KATHRYN CARVER	portrait	PARAMOUNT	
P-696	ANN VICKERS	CROMWELL	RKO	1933
P696	ROME EXPRESS	FORDE	UNIVERSAL	1933
P697	BE MINE TONIGHT	LITVAK	UNIVERSAL	1933
P697	RICHARD ARLEN	portrait	PARAMOUNT	
P699	MONTA BELL	portrait	PARAMOUNT	
P700	MOONLIGHT AND PRETZELS	FREUND	UNIVERSAL	1933
P.701	ETTA LEE	portrait	PARAMOUNT	
P-703	AGGIE APPLEBY MAKER OF MEN	SANDRICH	RKO	1933
P703	LOUISE BROOKS	portrait	PARAMOUNT	
P704	DOUGLAS MACLEAN	portrait	PARAMOUNT	
P704	KING OF THE ARENA	JAMES	UNIVERSAL	1933
P705	FIDDLIN' BUCKAROO	MAYNARD	UNIVERSAL	1933
P705	VIRGINIA VALLI	portrait	PARAMOUNT	
P-706	AFTER TONIGHT	ARCHAINBAUD	RKO	1933
P706	TRAIL DRIVE	JAMES	UNIVERSAL	1933
P708	HARRISON FORD	portrait	PARAMOUNT	
P709	BESSIE LOVE	portrait	PARAMOUNT	
P710	HARRIETT KRAUTH (TILLMANY)	portrait	PARAMOUNT	
P-710	LOST PATROL	FORD	RKO	1933
P711	THELDA KENVIN (aka THELMA KENVIN)	portrait	PARAMOUNT	
P712	DOROTHY NOURSE	portrait	PARAMOUNT	
P713	JOSEPHINE DUNN	portrait	PARAMOUNT	

Movie Still Identification Book Ultimate Edition - Letters

CODE	TITLE/NAME	DIRECTOR/TYPE	STUDIO/DISTRIBUTOR	YEAR
P714	CHARLES BROKAW	portrait	PARAMOUNT	
P714	MYRT AND MARGE	BOASBERG	UNIVERSAL	1933
P-714	OLD MOTHER RILEY, HEADMISTRESS (UK)	HARLOW	RENOWN	1950
P715	LORRAINE EASON	portrait	PARAMOUNT	
P716	ROBERT ANDREWS	portrait	PARAMOUNT	
P717	LINDSAY LA VERNE (aka SHARON LYNN/LYNNE)	portrait	PARAMOUNT	
P718	MONA PALMA (aka MIMI PALMERI)	portrait	PARAMOUNT	
P719	GUN JUSTICE	JAMES	UNIVERSAL	1933
P719	JACK LUDEN	portrait	PARAMOUNT	
P-719-P	SPITFIRE	CROMWELL	RKO	1934
P720	CHARLES "BUDDY" ROGERS	portrait	PARAMOUNT	
P720	LONG LOST FATHER	SCHOEDSACK	RKO	1934
P720	WHEELS OF DESTINY	JAMES	UNIVERSAL	1934
P721	MIDNIGHT	ERSKINE	UNIVERSAL	1934
P721	THELMA TODD	portrait	PARAMOUNT	
P721	TWO ALONE	NUGENT	RKO	1934
P722	IRVING HARTLEY	portrait	PARAMOUNT	
P723	HIPS HIPS HOORAY	SANDRICH	RKO	1934
P723	IVY HARRIS	portrait	PARAMOUNT	
P724	CLAUDE BUCHANAN	portrait	PARAMOUNT	
P726	HONOR OF THE RANGE	JAMES	UNIVERSAL	1934
P730	MARGARET MORRIS	portrait	PARAMOUNT	
P732	ED KING	portrait	PARAMOUNT	
P732	SMOKING GUNS	JAMES	UNIVERSAL	1934
P733	GARNETT WESTON	portrait	PARAMOUNT	
P734	W C FIELDS	portrait	PARAMOUNT	
P735	PIERRE COLLINGS	portrait	PARAMOUNT	
P737	CHARLOTTE/CHARLOT BIRD	portrait	PARAMOUNT	
P738	CAROL DEMPSTER	portrait	PARAMOUNT	
P740	MILDRED DAVIS	portrait	PARAMOUNT	
P741	GERTRUDE ASTOR	portrait	PARAMOUNT	
P741	SECRET OF THE CHATEAU	THORPE	UNIVERSAL	1934
P742	WORLD'S FAIR AND WARMER (sh)	TOWNLEY	UNIVERSAL	1934
P743	HOLLYWOOD TROUBLE	TOWNLEY	UNIVERSAL	1935
P743	IRIS GRAY	portrait	PARAMOUNT	
P-744	COCKEYED CAVALIERS	SANDRICH	RKO	1934
P745	DOLORES COSTELLO	portrait	PARAMOUNT	
P746	LET'S TRY AGAIN	MINER	RKO	1934
P746	MAURICE TOURNEUR	portrait	PARAMOUNT	
P747	WALTER PIDGEON	portrait	PARAMOUNT	
P748	MICHAEL ARLEN	portrait	PARAMOUNT	
P748	ROCKY RHODES	RABOCH	UNIVERSAL	1934
P749	WHEN A MAN SEES RED	JAMES	UNIVERSAL	1934
P750	BLANCHE MEHAFFEY	portrait	PARAMOUNT	
P751	A. EDWARD SUTHERLAND	portrait	PARAMOUNT	
P752	DONALD KEITH	portrait	PARAMOUNT	
P753	GEORGE BANCROFT	portrait	PARAMOUNT	
P755	CLARA BOW	portrait	PARAMOUNT	
P756	ALYCE MILLS	portrait	PARAMOUNT	
P756	RENDEZVOUS AT MIDNIGHT	CABANNE	UNIVERSAL	1935
P757	ARLETTE MARCHAL	portrait	PARAMOUNT	
P-757	HAT, COAT, GLOVE	MINER	RKO	1934
P758	B.P. SCHULBERG	portrait	PARAMOUNT	
P759	FATHER KNOWS BEST (sh)	HORNE	UNIVERSAL	1935
P759	WILLIAM POWELL	portrait	PARAMOUNT	
P760	GILBERT ROLAND	portrait	PARAMOUNT	
P760	STONE OF SILVER CREEK	GRINDE	UNIVERSAL	1935
P761	ELSIE LAWSON	portrait	PARAMOUNT	
P761	OLD AGE PENSIONS (sh)	HORNE	UNIVERSAL	1935
P762	HECTOR TURNBULL	portrait	PARAMOUNT	
P763	NORMAN TREVOR	portrait	PARAMOUNT	
P764	JOBYNA RALSTON	portrait	PARAMOUNT	
P765	BRING 'EM BACK A LIE (sh)	GOULDING	UNIVERSAL	1935
P765	LOIS MORAN	portrait	PARAMOUNT	
P766	GEORGIA HALE	portrait	PARAMOUNT	
P766	WOULD YOU BE WILLING (sh)	GOULDING	UNIVERSAL	1935
P767	BORDER BRIGANDS	GRINDE	UNIVERSAL	1935
P767	IRMA KORNELIA	portrait	PARAMOUNT	
P768	TOWNSEND MARTIN	portrait	PARAMOUNT	
P769	AGNES GRIFFITH	portrait	PARAMOUNT	

Movie Still Identification Book Ultimate Edition - Letters

CODE	TITLE/NAME	DIRECTOR/TYPE	STUDIO/DISTRIBUTOR	YEAR
P769	OUTLAWED GUNS	TAYLOR	UNIVERSAL	1935
P770	E. LLOYD SHELDON	portrait	PARAMOUNT	
P770	HIS LAST FLING (sh)	LAMONT	UNIVERSAL	1935
P771	CHESTER CONKLIN	portrait	PARAMOUNT	
P773	GREAT IDEA (sh)	SCHWARZWALD	UNIVERSAL	1935
P774	LUCIEN HUBBARD	portrait	PARAMOUNT	
P775	THROWBACK	TAYLOR	UNIVERSAL	1935
P775	WILLIAM A WELLMAN	portrait	PARAMOUNT	
P776	FRED WALLER JR (aka FRED WALLER)	portrait	PARAMOUNT	
P777	HARLEM BOUND (sh)	SCHWARZWALD	UNIVERSAL	1935
P777	IMRE FAZEKAS	portrait	PARAMOUNT	
P778	GILDA GRAY	portrait	PARAMOUNT	
P779	RONALD COLMAN	portrait	PARAMOUNT	
P-780	KENTUCKY KERNELS	STEVENS	RKO	1934
P780	VERNE HARDIN PORTER	portrait	PARAMOUNT	
P781	FRANK LLOYD	portrait	PARAMOUNT	
P782	SUNSET OF POWER	TAYLOR	UNIVERSAL	1935
P783	JOHN WATERS	portrait	PARAMOUNT	
P784	RALPH FORBES	portrait	PARAMOUNT	
P784	SILVER SPURS	TAYLOR	UNIVERSAL	1936
P785	FOR THE SERVICE	JONES	UNIVERSAL	1936
P787	LYA DE PUTTI	portrait	PARAMOUNT	
P788	VAUD-O-MAT (sh)	SCHWARZWALD	UNIVERSAL	1936
P789	LITTLE MINISTER	WALLACE	RKO	1934
P789	MARINE FOLLIES (sh)	SCHWARZWALD	UNIVERSAL	1936
P790	IVAN LEBEDEFF	portrait	PARAMOUNT	
P796	BOSS RIDER OF GUN CREEK	SELANDER	UNIVERSAL	1936
P797	SEA SPOILERS	STRAYER	UNIVERSAL	1936
P798	ERICH POMMER	portrait	PARAMOUNT	
P799	CONFLICT	HOWARD	UNIVERSAL	1936
P799	IVORY-HANDLED GUN	TAYLOR	UNIVERSAL	1935
P-800	ENCHANGED APRIL	BEAUMONT	RKO	1935
P801	EMPTY SADDLES	SELANDER	UNIVERSAL	1936
P801	JAMES HALL	portrait	PARAMOUNT	
P802	CHARLES FARRELL	portrait	PARAMOUNT	
P803	DOROTHY HUGHES	portrait	PARAMOUNT	
P804	ARTHUR ROSSON	portrait	PARAMOUNT	
P804	SANDFLOW	SELANDER	UNIVERSAL	1937
P805	JULIEN JOSEPHSON	portrait	PARAMOUNT	
P806	TOM KENNEDY	portrait	PARAMOUNT	
P807	GUNBOAT SMITH (aka EDWARD SMITH - ED SMITH)	portrait	PARAMOUNT	
P807	LEFT-HANDED LAW	SELANDER	UNIVERSAL	1937
P808	AILEEN PRINGLE	portrait	PARAMOUNT	
P809	DOG OF FLANDERS	SLOMAN	RKO	1935
P809	HAZEL FORBES	portrait	PARAMOUNT	
P810	FRED NEWMEYER	portrait	PARAMOUNT	
P812	SMOKE TREE RANGE	SELANDER	UNIVERSAL	1937
P813	CONSTANCE HOWARD	portrait	PARAMOUNT	
P815	ROWLAND V. LEE	portrait	PARAMOUNT	
P-816	BREAK OF HEARTS	MOELLER	RKO	1935
P-816	JEAN HERSHOLT	portrait	RKO	
P-817	INFORMER	FORD	RKO	1935
P818	LAW FOR TOMBSTONE	JONES	UNIVERSAL	1937
P819	SUDDEN BILL DORN	TAYLOR	UNIVERSAL	1937
P819	WILLIAM LEBARON	portrait	PARAMOUNT	
P820	IRIS STUART	portrait	PARAMOUNT	
P-821	SHE	HOLDEN, PICHEL	RKO	1935
P821	SUSAN FLEMING	portrait	PARAMOUNT	
P822	WESTLAND CASE	CABANNE	UNIVERSAL	1937
P823	WILLIAM BEAUDINE	portrait	PARAMOUNT	
P824	HELEN MUNDAY	portrait	PARAMOUNT	
P825	BASS OF LONELY VALLEY	TAYLOR	UNIVERSAL	1937
P825	ELINOR GLYN	portrait	PARAMOUNT	
P826	JOCELYN LEE	portrait	PARAMOUNT	
P827	FAY WRAY	portrait	PARAMOUNT	
P-827	LAST DAYS OF POMPEII	SCHOEDSACK	RKO	1935
P828	COURAGE OF THE WEST	LEWIS	UNIVERSAL	1937
P828	LOUISE LONG	portrait	PARAMOUNT	
P830	MARGARET GUINBY	portrait	PARAMOUNT	
P831	JEANNE NAVELLE	portrait	PARAMOUNT	

Movie Still Identification Book Ultimate Edition - Letters

CODE	TITLE/NAME	DIRECTOR/TYPE	STUDIO/DISTRIBUTOR	YEAR
P831	LET'S MAKE A NIGHT OF IT (UK)	CUTTS	UNIVERSAL	1937
P831	QUIET WEDDING	ASQUITH	UNIVERSAL	1941
P832	JOHN MONK SAUNDERS	portrait	PARAMOUNT	
P832	SINGING OUTLAW	LEWIS	UNIVERSAL	1937
P834	BLACK DOLL	GARRETT	UNIVERSAL	1938
P834	EL BRENDEL	portrait	PARAMOUNT	
P835	GARY COOPER	portrait	PARAMOUNT	
P836	BORDER WOLVES	LEWIS	UNIVERSAL	1938
P836	BRUCE BARTON	portrait	PARAMOUNT	
P837	THEODORE BENDICK	portrait	PARAMOUNT	
P839	HARRY D'ABBADIE D'ARRAST	portrait	PARAMOUNT	
P839	LAST STAND	LEWIS	UNIVERSAL	1938
P840	EDNA KIRBY	portrait	PARAMOUNT	
P840	PRISON BREAK	LUBIN	UNIVERSAL	1938
P842	JOSEPH JACKSON	portrait	PARAMOUNT	
P845	LOTUS THOMPSON	portrait	PARAMOUNT	
P846	WINIFRED DUNN	portrait	PARAMOUNT	
P847	ANDRE/GEORGE BERANGER (aka GEORGE ANDRE)	portrait	PARAMOUNT	
P848	BLANCHE LECLAIRE	portrait	PARAMOUNT	
P849	MONTE BRICE	portrait	PARAMOUNT	
P850	DOROTHY MATHEWS	portrait	PARAMOUNT	
P851	HARRY SIMPSON (aka JOHN DARROW)	portrait	PARAMOUNT	
P852	JAMES ASHMORE CREELMAN	portrait	PARAMOUNT	
P853	LAST EXPRESS	GARRETT	UNIVERSAL	1938
P855	BETTY JEWEL	portrait	PARAMOUNT	
P856	NANCY PHILLIPS	portrait	PARAMOUNT	
P857	ANNE SHERIDAN	portrait	PARAMOUNT	
P858	HOWARD EMMETT ROGERS	portrait	PARAMOUNT	
P859	DOUGLAS GILMORE	portrait	PARAMOUNT	
P860	EMIL JANNINGS	portrait	PARAMOUNT	
P860	LAST WARNING (DEAD DON'T CARE)	ROGELL	UNIVERSAL	1938
P860	TARTUFFE THE HYPOCRITE	MURNAU	UFA - GER	1925
P861	HENRY HERZBRUN	portrait	PARAMOUNT	
P862	DORIS ANDERSON	portrait	PARAMOUNT	
P862	GAMBLING SHIP (LADY LUCK)	SCOTTO	UNIVERSAL	1938
P863	TOM GERAGHTY	portrait	PARAMOUNT	
P864	OWEN DAVIS	portrait	PARAMOUNT	
P865	ED WYNN	portrait	PARAMOUNT	
P865	PHANTOM STAGE	WAGGNER	UNIVERSAL	1939
P866	DOROTHY ARZNER	portrait	PARAMOUNT	
P867	ARCHIE HILL	portrait	PARAMOUNT	
P868	HENRY HATHAWAY	portrait	PARAMOUNT	
P869	MYSTERY OF THE WHITE ROOM	GARRETT	UNIVERSAL	1939
P873	CLIVE BROOK	portrait	PARAMOUNT	
P875	DORIS HILL	portrait	PARAMOUNT	
P876	MIKADO	SCHERTZINGER	UNIVERSAL	1939
P876	SALLY BLANE	portrait	PARAMOUNT	
P877	PHILIP STRANGE	portrait	PARAMOUNT	
P877	WITNESS VANISHES	GARRETT	UNIVERSAL	1939
P878	HALF A SINNER (LADY TAKES A CHANCE)	CHRISTIE	UNIVERSAL	1940
P878	LIL DAGOVER	portrait	PARAMOUNT	
P879	EMANUEL COHEN	portrait	PARAMOUNT	
P880	KARL BROWN	portrait	PARAMOUNT	
P882	DAUGHTER OF SHANGHAI	FLOREY	PARAMOUNT	1934
P882	EVELYN BRENT	portrait	PARAMOUNT	
P883	VERA VERONINA (VORONINA)	portrait	PARAMOUNT	
P885	LARRY SEMON	portrait	PARAMOUNT	
P887	EINAR HANSON (aka HANSEN - HANSSON)	portrait	PARAMOUNT	
P888	EDWARD EVERETT HORTON	portrait	PARAMOUNT	
P890	FRED THOMSON	portrait	PARAMOUNT	
P893	MAY ALLISON	portrait	PARAMOUNT	
P897	ERNEST B. SCHOEDSACK	portrait	PARAMOUNT	
P898	ERICH VON STROHEIM	portrait	PARAMOUNT	
P900	BENJAMIN F. (BARNEY) GLAZER	portrait	PARAMOUNT	
P901	ARNOLD KENT	portrait	PARAMOUNT	
P903	MARIETTA MILLNER	portrait	PARAMOUNT	
P904	FREDERICA SAGOR (aka FREDERICA MAAS)	portrait	PARAMOUNT	
P-905	PURPLE GANG	MCDONALD	ALLIED ARTISTS	1959
P906	VERA STEADMAN	portrait	PARAMOUNT	
P907	BOBBY VERNON	portrait	PARAMOUNT	

Movie Still Identification Book Ultimate Edition - Letters

CODE	TITLE/NAME	DIRECTOR/TYPE	STUDIO/DISTRIBUTOR	YEAR
P908	ANN CHRISTY	portrait	PARAMOUNT	
P909	AL CHRISTIE	portrait	PARAMOUNT	
P911	NEAL BURNS	portrait	PARAMOUNT	
P914	DONALD DAVIS	portrait	PARAMOUNT	
P915	FRANK STRAYER	portrait	PARAMOUNT	
P918	JIMMIE ADAMS	portrait	PARAMOUNT	
P919	JACK DUFFY	portrait	PARAMOUNT	
P920	BILLY DOOLEY	portrait	PARAMOUNT	
P923	WILLIAM J. IRVING	portrait	PARAMOUNT	
P925	FRANCES LEE	portrait	PARAMOUNT	
P926	LINA BASQUETTE	portrait	PARAMOUNT	
P930	LANE CHANDLER	portrait	PARAMOUNT	
P933	SUZY VERNON	portrait	PARAMOUNT	
P935	JOSEF VON STERNBERG	portrait	PARAMOUNT	
P942	DORIS DAWSON	portrait	PARAMOUNT	
P944	FRED KOHLER	portrait	PARAMOUNT	
P946	OLGA BACLANOVA	portrait	PARAMOUNT	
P948	ANITA LOOS	portrait	PARAMOUNT	
P949	MACK GORDON	portrait	PARAMOUNT	
P950	ERNEST W. JOHNSON	portrait	PARAMOUNT	
P951	RUTH TAYLOR	portrait	PARAMOUNT	
P953	WILLIAM AUSTIN	portrait	PARAMOUNT	
P957	WILLIAM DE LIGNEMARE	portrait	PARAMOUNT	
P958	ANNE NICHOLS	portrait	PARAMOUNT	
P959	NANCY CARROLL	portrait	PARAMOUNT	
P960	HOPE LORING	portrait	PARAMOUNT	
P961	WILSON MIZNER	portrait	PARAMOUNT	
P962	KEENE THOMPSON	portrait	PARAMOUNT	
P963	GEORGE MARION JR.	portrait	PARAMOUNT	
P965	VAN NEST POLGLASE	portrait	PARAMOUNT`	
P966	JIM TULLY	portrait	PARAMOUNT	
P967	FRED A. DATIG	portrait	PARAMOUNT	
P968	LOUIS D. LIGHTON	portrait	PARAMOUNT	
P969	DAVID O. SELZNICK	portrait	PARAMOUNT	
P970	PAUL LUKAS	portrait	PARAMOUNT	
P971	LOTHAR MENDES	portrait	PARAMOUNT	
P973	HAROLD ROSSON (aka HAL ROSSON)	portrait	PARAMOUNT	
P974	VIVIAN MOSES	portrait	PARAMOUNT	
P975	JEAN ARTHUR	portrait	PARAMOUNT	
P981	H.G. WELLS	portrait	PARAMOUNT	
P982	CHARLES RIESNER	portrait	PARAMOUNT	
P983	BENJAMIN F. ZEIDMAN (aka B.F. 'BENNIE' ZEIDMAN)	portrait	PARAMOUNT	
P987	RUTH ELDER	portrait	PARAMOUNT	
P989	FRED LEAHY	portrait	PARAMOUNT	
P990	TRAVIS BANTON	portrait	PARAMOUNT	
P991	LUDWIG BERGER	portrait	PARAMOUNT	
P996	LUCY DORAN	portrait	PARAMOUNT	
P1001	JOHN LODER	portrait	PARAMOUNT	
P1006	WALTER RUBEN	portrait	PARAMOUNT	
P1008	JOHN CROMWELL	portrait	PARAMOUNT	
P1010	MAURICE CHEVALIER	portrait	PARAMOUNT	
P1011	JOHN LODER	portrait	PARAMOUNT	
P1014	PHILLIPS HOLMES	portrait	PARAMOUNT	
P1015	JACK OAKIE	portrait	PARAMOUNT	
P1018	RUTH CHATTERTON	portrait	PARAMOUNT	
P1019	GLADYS BELMONT (LATER JULIE CARTER)	portrait	PARAMOUNT	
P1020	OCTAVUS ROY COHEN	portrait	PARAMOUNT	
P1021	RICHARD WALLACE	portrait	PARAMOUNT	
P1022	ROBERT CASTLE (aka FRED/FREDERICK SOLM)	portrait	PARAMOUNT	
P1023	GUY OLIVER	portrait	PARAMOUNT	
P1024	LEONE LANE	portrait	PARAMOUNT	
P1025	JEANNE EAGELS	portrait	PARAMOUNT`	
P1026	BOBBE ARNST	portrait	PARAMOUNT	
P1027	BETTY LAWFORD	portrait	PARAMOUNT	
P1028	TAMARA GEVA	portrait	PARAMOUNT	
P1029	JUNE WALKER	portrait	PARAMOUNT	
P1031	FRANCES WILLIAMS	portrait	PARAMOUNT	
P1032	GEORGIA LIRCH/GEORGIA LERCH	portrait	PARAMOUNT	
P1033	DOROTHY TENNANT	portrait	PARAMOUNT	
P1034	DOROTHY TIERNEY	portrait	PARAMOUNT	

Movie Still Identification Book Ultimate Edition - Letters

CODE	TITLE/NAME	DIRECTOR/TYPE	STUDIO/DISTRIBUTOR	YEAR
P1035	VIVIENNE OSBORNE	portrait	PARAMOUNT	
P1036	ANN FORREST/FORREST	portrait	PARAMOUNT	
P1037	DONALD KIRKE	portrait	PARAMOUNT	
P1039	JIMMY CARR	portrait	PARAMOUNT	
P1040	MARY WILLIAMS	portrait	PARAMOUNT	
P1041	ANN PENNINGTON	portrait	PARAMOUNT	
P1042	MINNIE DUPREE	portrait	PARAMOUNT	
P1043	MABEL SWOR	portrait	PARAMOUNT	
P1044	JEANNE GREENE	portrait	PARAMOUNT	
P1045	DITA PARLO	portrait	PARAMOUNT	
P1046	S.S. VAN DINE	portrait	PARAMOUNT	
P1047	FREDRIC MARCH	portrait	PARAMOUNT	
P1048	LUPE VELEZ	portrait	PARAMOUNT	
P1050	HOWARD ESTABROOK	portrait	PARAMOUNT	
P1051	NORMAN FOSTER	portrait	PARAMOUNT	
P1052	KAY FRANCIS	portrait	PARAMOUNT	
P1053	WALTER HUSTON	portrait	PARAMOUNT	
P1054	ELVIA ENDERS	portrait	PARAMOUNT	
P1056	O.P. HEGGIE	portrait	PARAMOUNT	
P1057	ALBERT DESART	portrait	PARAMOUNT	
P1058	LAWFORD DAVIDSON	portrait	PARAMOUNT	
P1059	DAVID NEWELL	portrait	PARAMOUNT	
P1060	WARNER OLAND	portrait	PARAMOUNT	
P1061	GEORGE ABBOTT	portrait	PARAMOUNT	
P1062	EUGENE PALLETTE	portrait	PARAMOUNT	
P1063	HELEN KANE	portrait	PARAMOUNT	
P1064	JOHN FARROW	portrait	PARAMOUNT	
P1065	ANTHONY BUSHELL	portrait	PARAMOUNT	
P1066	EVELYN KAHN	portrait	PARAMOUNT	
P1067	BEN GRAUMAN KOHN	portrait	PARAMOUNT	
P1069	WALTON BUTTERFIELD	portrait	PARAMOUNT	
P1070	AGNES BRAND LEAHY	portrait	PARAMOUNT	
P1071	HAL SKELLY	portrait	PARAMOUNT	
P1072	ROBERT OREN	portrait	PARAMOUNT	
P1073	JOHN V.A. WEAVER	portrait	PARAMOUNT	
P1075	HUGH HERBERT	portrait	PARAMOUNT	
P1078	FRANK ROSS	portrait	PARAMOUNT	
P1081	ALICE BOULDEN	portrait	PARAMOUNT	
P1082	GLORIA SHEA (aka OLIVE SHEA)	portrait	PARAMOUNT	
P1083	FAY COMPTON	portrait	PARAMOUNT	
P1084	EDDIE/EDWARD DOWLING	portrait	PARAMOUNT	
P1085	REGIS TOOMEY	portrait	PARAMOUNT	
P1086	NINO MARTINI	portrait	PARAMOUNT	
P1087	DR. HUGH J. STRATHEARN	portrait	PARAMOUNT	
P1088	BARTLETT CORMACK (aka BARTLETT MCCORMACK)	portrait	PARAMOUNT	
P1089	JEAN DE LIMUR	portrait	PARAMOUNT	
P1090	CLAUDETTE COLBERT	portrait	PARAMOUNT	
P1091	ROBERT FLOREY	portrait	PARAMOUNT	
P1092	FLORENCE ELDRIDGE	portrait	PARAMOUNT	
P1093	ALBERT A. KAUFMAN	portrait	PARAMOUNT	
P1094	VIRGINIA BRUCE	portrait	PARAMOUNT	
P1095	LEO ROBIN	portrait	PARAMOUNT	
P1096	RICHARD WHITING	portrait	PARAMOUNT	
P1097	PATRICK KEARNEY	portrait	PARAMOUNT	
P1099	CHARLES RUGGLES	portrait	PARAMOUNT	
P1099	WESLEY RUGGLES AND WILLIAM LABARON	portrait	PARAMOUNT`	
P1100	LILLIAN ROTH	portrait	PARAMOUNT	
P1101	MIRIAM SEEGAR	portrait	PARAMOUNT	
P1102	DAN HEALY	portrait	PARAMOUNT	
P1104	DENNIS KING	portrait	PARAMOUNT	
P1105	WILLIAM S. PALEY	portrait	PARAMOUNT	
P1106	GUY BOLTON	portrait	PARAMOUNT	
P1107	E.H. CALVERT	portrait	PARAMOUNT	
P1108	ARCH REEVE	portrait	PARAMOUNT	
P1109	DOROTHY REVIER (aka DOROTHY VALEGRA)	portrait	PARAMOUNT	
P1111	JOHN LANGAN	portrait	PARAMOUNT	
P1114	JEANETTE MACDONALD	portrait	PARAMOUNT	
P1115	HELEN MORGAN	portrait	PARAMOUNT	
P1116	MORGAN FARLEY	portrait	PARAMOUNT	
P1117	GERTRUDE LAWRENCE	portrait	PARAMOUNT	

Movie Still Identification Book Ultimate Edition - Letters

CODE	TITLE/NAME	DIRECTOR/TYPE	STUDIO/DISTRIBUTOR	YEAR
P1118	JUNE COLLYER	portrait	PARAMOUNT	
P1121	CHESTER MORRIS	portrait	PARAMOUNT	
P1122	CHARLES SELLON	portrait	PARAMOUNT	
P1123	HARRY GREEN	portrait	PARAMOUNT	
P1125	SAM COSLOW	portrait	PARAMOUNT	
P1127	RUDY VALLEE	portrait	PARAMOUNT	
P1128	B.P. SCHULBERG	portrait	PARAMOUNT	
P1129	HENRY WADSWORTH	portrait	PARAMOUNT	
P1130	MITZI GREEN	portrait	PARAMOUNT	
P1132	TERRY CARROLL	portrait	PARAMOUNT	
P1134	RICHARD 'SKEETS' GALLAGHER	portrait	PARAMOUNT`	
P1134	SKEETS GALLAGHER	portrait	PARAMOUNT	
P1136	STANLEY SMITH	portrait	PARAMOUNT	
P1138	JOAN PEERS	portrait	PARAMOUNT	
P1139	LOUIS GASNIER	portrait	PARAMOUNT	
P1140	STUART ERWIN	portrait	PARAMOUNT	
P1141	ROBERTA ROBINSON	portrait	PARAMOUNT	
P1143	LADY IN THE DARK	LEISEN	PARAMOUNT	1944
P1144	STANLEY FIELDS	portrait	PARAMOUNT	
P1147	EDWIN CAREWE	portrait	PARAMOUNT	
P1153	BARRY NORTON	portrait	PARAMOUNT	
P1156	PERRY IVINS (aka PERRY IVANS)	portrait	PARAMOUNT	
P1157	THOMAS J. AHEARN	portrait	PARAMOUNT	
P1158	J. AUBREY CLARK	portrait	PARAMOUNT	
P1159	L. WOLFE GILBERT	portrait	PARAMOUNT	
P1160	ABEL BLAIR	portrait	PARAMOUNT	
P1161	WILLIAM SLAVENS MCNUTT	portrait	PARAMOUNT	
P1162	DENISON CLIFF (aka DENISON CLIFT)	portrait	PARAMOUNT	
P1163	HOWARD JACKSON	portrait	PARAMOUNT	
P1164	VICTOR MOORE	portrait	PARAMOUNT	
P1165	GERALD GERAGHTY (aka GERRY GERAGHTY)	portrait	PARAMOUNT	
P1166	GEORGE CUKOR	portrait	PARAMOUNT	
P-1167	BLONDE VENUS	VON STERNBERG	PARAMOUNT	1932
P1168	VICTOR HEERMAN	portrait	PARAMOUNT	
P1169	ZOE AKINS	portrait	PARAMOUNT	
P1170	LEON ERROL	portrait	PARAMOUNT	
P1171	W. FRANKE HARLING (aka FRANK HARLING)	portrait	PARAMOUNT	
P1172	CYRIL GARDNER	portrait	PARAMOUNT	
P1173	NORMAN TAUROG	portrait	PARAMOUNT	
P1174	MARION SHILLING	portrait	PARAMOUNT	
P1175	MARTIN BROWN	portrait	PARAMOUNT	
P1177	DAVID O. SELZNICK	portrait	PARAMOUNT	
P1178	BETTY GARDE	portrait	PARAMOUNT	
P1179	ROSITA MORENO	portrait	PARAMOUNT	
P1180	FRANK MORGAN	portrait	PARAMOUNT	
P1181	EDWARD SLOMAN	portrait	PARAMOUNT	
P1182	MARIE BAUMAN	portrait	PARAMOUNT	
P1183	PAUL CAVANAGH (PAUL CAVANAUGH)	portrait	PARAMOUNT	
P1184	SERGEI M. EISENSTEIN	portrait	PARAMOUNT	
P1185	ROBERTO REY	portrait	PARAMOUNT	
P1186	PRISCILLA DEAN	portrait	PARAMOUNT	
P1187	MARCIA MANNERS	portrait	PARAMOUNT	
P1188	FRANCES DEE	portrait	PARAMOUNT	
P1190	BRUCE ROGERS	portrait	PARAMOUNT	
P1191	JACQUES BATAILLE-HENRI	portrait	PARAMOUNT	
P1192	JACKIE COOGAN	portrait	PARAMOUNT	
P1194	EDMUND GOULDING	portrait	PARAMOUNT	
P1195	CYRIL MAUDE	portrait	PARAMOUNT	
P1196	CHARLES STARRETT	portrait	PARAMOUNT	
P1197	HENRY MYERS	portrait	PARAMOUNT	
P1198	SALISBURY FIELD (aka EDWARD SALISBURY FIELD)	portrait	PARAMOUNT	
P1199	FREDRIC D. ALEXANDROV	portrait	PARAMOUNT	
P1201	ROBERT TERRY SHANNON	portrait	PARAMOUNT	
P1202	CAROLE LOMBARD	portrait	PARAMOUNT	
P1203	YVONNE VALLEE	portrait	PARAMOUNT	
P1204	DAVID BURTON	portrait	PARAMOUNT	
P1205	DASHIELL HAMMETT	portrait	PARAMOUNT	
P1206	MIRIAM HOPKINS	portrait	PARAMOUNT	
P1207	CHARLES FRANCIS COE	portrait	PARAMOUNT	
P1208	JULIETTE COMPTON	portrait	PARAMOUNT	

Movie Still Identification Book Ultimate Edition - Letters

CODE	TITLE/NAME	DIRECTOR/TYPE	STUDIO/DISTRIBUTOR	YEAR
P1210	COURTNEY TERRETT	portrait	PARAMOUNT	
P1211	LOUISE CAMPBELL	portrait	PARAMOUNT	
P1212	URSULA PARROTT	portrait	PARAMOUNT	
P1213	HELEN MORGAN	portrait	PARAMOUNT	
P1215	ARTHUR KOBER	portrait	PARAMOUNT	
P1217	JESSE LASKY JR.	portrait	PARAMOUNT	
P1218	SAMSON RAPHAELSON	portrait	PARAMOUNT	
P1219	MARTIN BURTON	portrait	PARAMOUNT	
P1220	SAMUEL HOFFENSTEIN	portrait	PARAMOUNT	
P1221	HENRIETTA CROSMAN	portrait	PARAMOUNT	
P1222	WALTER WANGER	portrait	PARAMOUNT	
P1223	GEOFFREY SHURLOCK	portrait	PARAMOUNT	
P1224	CARMEN BARNES	portrait	PARAMOUNT	
P1225	JACK KING (VIII)	portrait	PARAMOUNT	
P1226	WYNNE GIBSON	portrait	PARAMOUNT	
P1227	RAMON PEREDA	portrait	PARAMOUNT	
P1228	JUNE MACCLOY	portrait	PARAMOUNT	
P1229	BETTY WHITE	portrait	PARAMOUNT	
P1230	SYLVIA SIDNEY	portrait	PARAMOUNT	
P1231	LLOYD CORRIGAN	portrait	PARAMOUNT	
P1232	JACKIE SEARLE (aka JACKIE SEARL)	portrait	PARAMOUNT	
P1233	EVE UNSELL (aka EVA UNSELL)	portrait	PARAMOUNT	
P1235	HARRY LINSLEY CORT	portrait	PARAMOUNT	
P1236	NORMAN Z. MCLEOD	portrait	PARAMOUNT	
P1237	MARION GERING	portrait	PARAMOUNT	
P1238	EDWARD GOODMAN	portrait	PARAMOUNT	
P1239	VIRGINIA KELLOGG	portrait	PARAMOUNT	
P1240	MAX MARCIN	portrait	PARAMOUNT	
P1242	WILL B. JOHNSTONE	portrait	PARAMOUNT	
P1244	PAUL HERVEY FOX (aka PAUL HERVY FOX)	portrait	PARAMOUNT	
P1246	TALLULAH BANKHEAD	portrait	PARAMOUNT	
P1247	F.W. MURNAU	portrait	PARAMOUNT	
P1248	PHOEBE FOSTER	portrait	PARAMOUNT	
P1249	BERTHOLD VIERTEL	portrait	PARAMOUNT	
P1255	JUDITH WOOD (aka HELEN JOHNSON)	portrait	PARAMOUNT	
P1256	TOM DOUGLAS	portrait	PARAMOUNT	
P1257	ROUBEN MAMOULIAN	portrait	PARAMOUNT	
P1259	WILLIAM 'STAGE' BOYD	portrait	PARAMOUNT	
P1261	CLAIRE DODD	portrait	PARAMOUNT	
P1263	ESTHER HOWARD	portrait	PARAMOUNT	
P1264	JOYCE COMPTON	portrait	PARAMOUNT	
P1265	SID/SIDNEY BROD	portrait	PARAMOUNT	
P1266	EARL MILLER	portrait	PARAMOUNT	
P1267	JOHN WEXLEY	portrait	PARAMOUNT	
P1268	ALBERT HACKETT	portrait	PARAMOUNT	
P1269	VIVIAN WINSTON	portrait	PARAMOUNT	
P1270	IRVING PICHEL	portrait	PARAMOUNT	
P1271	LOUIS WEITZENKORN	portrait	PARAMOUNT	
P1272	GEORGES METAXA	portrait	PARAMOUNT	
P1274	A.A. KLINE	portrait	PARAMOUNT	
P1275	GEOFFREY KERR	portrait	PARAMOUNT	
P1276	ELEANOR BOARDMAN	portrait	PARAMOUNT	
P1277	ROBERT COOGAN	portrait	PARAMOUNT`	
P1278	LARRY KENT	portrait	PARAMOUNT	
P1279	ROBERT LEE	portrait	PARAMOUNT	
P1280	RUTH HALL	portrait	PARAMOUNT	
P1281	PEGGY SHANNON	portrait	PARAMOUNT	
P1282	CHARLES TROWBRIDGE	portrait	PARAMOUNT	
P1283	GEORGE ACKERSON	portrait	PARAMOUNT	
P1284	ALLEN JENKINS	portrait	PARAMOUNT	
P1286	GENE RAYMOND	portrait	PARAMOUNT	
P1287	ELSIE CONDE	portrait	PARAMOUNT	
P1288	TAMARA GEVA	portrait	PARAMOUNT	
P1289	FRANCES MOFFETT	portrait	PARAMOUNT	
P1290	RERI	portrait	PARAMOUNT	
P1291	ALAN DINEHART (aka ALLAN DINEHART)	portrait	PARAMOUNT	
P1292	ARTHUR JOHNSTON	portrait	PARAMOUNT	
P1293	JANE KEITHLEY (aka JANE KEITH)	portrait	PARAMOUNT	
P1294	PATRICIA FARR	portrait	PARAMOUNT	
P1295	BRIAN MARLOW	portrait	PARAMOUNT	

Movie Still Identification Book Ultimate Edition - Letters

CODE	TITLE/NAME	DIRECTOR/TYPE	STUDIO/DISTRIBUTOR	YEAR
P1296	IRA HARDS	portrait	PARAMOUNT	
P1297	RALPH BELLAMY	portrait	PARAMOUNT	
P-1298	DUCK SOUP	MCCAREY	PARAMOUNT	1933
P1299	GROUCHO MARX	portrait	PARAMOUNT	
P1300	DONALD MEEK	portrait	PARAMOUNT	
P1301	MARY BOLAND	portrait	PARAMOUNT	
P1302	VICKI BAUM	portrait	PARAMOUNT	
P1303	CHICO MARX	portrait	PARAMOUNT	
P1304	ZEPPO MARX	portrait	PARAMOUNT	
P1305	SAM HARDY	portrait	PARAMOUNT	
P1306	MARGARET DUMONT	portrait	PARAMOUNT	
P1307	JEROME DALEY	portrait	PARAMOUNT	
P1308	SUE CONROY	portrait	PARAMOUNT	
P1309	LENITA LANE	portrait	PARAMOUNT	
P1310	PAT O'BRIEN	portrait	PARAMOUNT	
P1312	HERBERT MARSHALL	portrait	PARAMOUNT	
P1313	ALLEN VINCENT	portrait	PARAMOUNT	
P1314	MARJORIE RAMBEAU	portrait	PARAMOUNT	
P1315	JOHN BREEDEN	portrait	PARAMOUNT	
P1316	KENT TAYLOR	portrait	PARAMOUNT	
P1317	CHARLES D. BROWN	portrait	PARAMOUNT	
P1319	ADRIENNE AMES	portrait	PARAMOUNT	
P1320	FRANCES DADE	portrait	PARAMOUNT	
P1321	BRAMWELL FLETCHER	portrait	PARAMOUNT	
P1322	ERNEST LAWFORD	portrait	PARAMOUNT	
P1323	HAROLD WINSTON	portrait	PARAMOUNT	
P1324	HARRY DAVENPORT	portrait	PARAMOUNT	
P1325	GEORGE BARBIER	portrait	PARAMOUNT	
P1326	SCOTT KOLK/KOLTON/COLTON	portrait	PARAMOUNT	
P1329	ROY LE MAY	portrait	PARAMOUNT	
P1332	ANNE SUTHERLAND	portrait	PARAMOUNT	
P1333	MINOR WATSON	portrait	PARAMOUNT	
P1334	MARJORIE BEEBE	portrait	PARAMOUNT	
P1335	DOROTHY TREE	portrait	PARAMOUNT	
P1337	JERRY TUCKER	portrait	PARAMOUNT	
P1338	A.E./ALFRED	portrait	PARAMOUNT	
P1339	M.C. LEVEE (aka MIKE LEVEE)	portrait	PARAMOUNT	
P1342	MARJORIE GATESON	portrait	PARAMOUNT	
P1343	DOROTHY SPEARE	portrait	PARAMOUNT	
P1345	DOROTHY JORDAN	portrait	PARAMOUNT	
P1348	JOEL MCCREA	portrait	PARAMOUNT	
P1349	ROBERT AMES	portrait	PARAMOUNT	
P1350	CASEY ROBINSON	portrait	PARAMOUNT	
P1351	ROSE HOBART	portrait	PARAMOUNT	
P1352	JUNIOR DURKIN	portrait	PARAMOUNT	
P1355	RUSS CLARK	portrait	PARAMOUNT	
P1356	ANN ANDREWS	portrait	PARAMOUNT	
P1359	HARVEY STEPHENS/STEVENS	portrait	PARAMOUNT	
P1360	FELIX YOUNG	portrait	PARAMOUNT	
P1361	NED MARIN	portrait	PARAMOUNT	
P1362	KATHERINE DEMILLE	portrait	PARAMOUNT	
P1366	ARTHUR PIERSON	portrait	PARAMOUNT	
P1369	CHARLES WINNINGER	portrait	PARAMOUNT	
P1372	FLORINE MCKINNEY	portrait	PARAMOUNT	
P1373	LEIGH ALLEN	portrait	PARAMOUNT	
P1374	RANDOLPH SCOTT	portrait	PARAMOUNT	
P1378	JACKIE COOPER	portrait	PARAMOUNT	
P1379	RICHARD BENNETT	portrait	PARAMOUNT	
P1381	HARRY TEMPLETON	portrait	PARAMOUNT	
P-1383	DOUBLE OR NOTHING	REED	PARAMOUNT	1937
P-1383	DR. RHYTHM	TUTTLE	PARAMOUNT	1938
P1384	GENEVIEVE TOBIN	portrait	PARAMOUNT	
P1385	ROLAND YOUNG	portrait	PARAMOUNT	
P1388	NED SPARKS	portrait	PARAMOUNT	
P1389	SARI MARITZA	portrait	PARAMOUNT	
P1390	MELVYN DOUGLAS	portrait	PARAMOUNT	
P1391	JOHN LITEL	portrait	PARAMOUNT	
P1392	LYDA ROBERTI	portrait	PARAMOUNT	
P1393	GEORGE SOMNES	portrait	PARAMOUNT	
P1394	JAMES J. GAIN	portrait	PARAMOUNT	

Movie Still Identification Book Ultimate Edition - Letters

CODE	TITLE/NAME	DIRECTOR/TYPE	STUDIO/DISTRIBUTOR	YEAR
P1395	HERMAN MICHELSON	portrait	PARAMOUNT	
P1396	CARY GRANT	portrait	PARAMOUNT	
P1397	OSCAR STRAUS	portrait	PARAMOUNT	
P1398	FRANCHOT TONE	portrait	PARAMOUNT	
P-1400	STOLEN HARMONY	WERKER	PARAMOUNT	1935
P1401	VIVIAN GAYLE	portrait	PARAMOUNT	
P1402	ROSS ALEXANDER	portrait	PARAMOUNT	
P1403	EFFIE SHANNON	portrait	PARAMOUNT	
P1405	LILI DAMITA	portrait	PARAMOUNT	
P1406	IRVING BACON	portrait	PARAMOUNT	
P1407	EDMUND LOWE	portrait	PARAMOUNT	
P1408	HAROLD GOODWIN	portrait	PARAMOUNT	
P1410	HELEN COLLINS	portrait	PARAMOUNT	
P1411	LESLIE FENTON	portrait	PARAMOUNT	
P1412	DUDLEY DIGGES	portrait	PARAMOUNT	
P1413	CORA SUE COLLINS	portrait	PARAMOUNT	
P1414	ALISON SKIPWORTH	portrait	PARAMOUNT	
P1415	CAPTAIN OLIVER C. LE BOUTELLIER	portrait	PARAMOUNT	
P1416	A.C. LE BON TELLIER	portrait	PARAMOUNT	
P1417	HARRY HERVEY	portrait	PARAMOUNT	
P1418	MARTIN FLAVIN	portrait	PARAMOUNT	
P1419	WILLIAM JAMES	portrait	PARAMOUNT	
P1420	ALEXIS DAVIDOFF	portrait	PARAMOUNT	
P1421	EDWARD GROSS	portrait	PARAMOUNT	
P1422	LEE KOHLMAR	portrait	PARAMOUNT	
P1423	STEPHEN ROBERTS	portrait	PARAMOUNT	
P1424	ADRIANNE ALLEN	portrait	PARAMOUNT	
P1425	LOUISE CARTER	portrait	PARAMOUNT	
P1426	FRANK S. HEATH	portrait	PARAMOUNT	
P1428	CHARLES LAUGHTON	portrait	PARAMOUNT	
P1429	MYRNA LOY	portrait	PARAMOUNT	
P1430	GORDON WESTCOTT	portrait	PARAMOUNT	
P1431	GERTRUDE MESSINGER (aka MESSENGER)	portrait	PARAMOUNT	
P1435	CHARLES BUTTERWORTH	portrait	PARAMOUNT	
P1436	NADINE DORE	portrait	PARAMOUNT	
P1437	JOAN BLONDELL	portrait	PARAMOUNT	
P1438	ALEXANDER HALL	portrait	PARAMOUNT	
P1441	GEORGE IRVING	portrait	PARAMOUNT	
P1443	GEORGE M. COHAN	portrait	PARAMOUNT	
P1444	DICKIE MOORE	portrait	PARAMOUNT	
P1445	ELISSA LANDI	portrait	PARAMOUNT	
P1446	BELLE OF THE NINETIES	MCCAREY	PARAMOUNT	1934
P1446	EVERY DAY'S A HOLIDAY	SUTHERLAND	MAJOR	R
P1447	TOM CONLON JR.	portrait	PARAMOUNT	
P1448	LEILA HYAMS	portrait	PARAMOUNT	
P1451	ARNOLD LUCY	portrait	PARAMOUNT	
P1452	BING CROSBY	portrait	PARAMOUNT	
P1454	WILLIAM B. DAVIDSON	portrait	PARAMOUNT	
P-1455	MANY HAPPY RETURNS	MCLEOD	PARAMOUNT	1934
P1456	GRACIE ALLEN, GEORGE BURNS	portrait	PARAMOUNT	
P1457	HELEN HAYES	portrait	PARAMOUNT	
P1458	WALTER 'SPEC' O'DONNELL	portrait	PARAMOUNT	
P1460	THE BOSWELL SISTERS	portrait	PARAMOUNT	
P1462	EDWARD LE SAINT	portrait	PARAMOUNT	
P1464	LILA LEE	portrait	PARAMOUNT	
P1466	SHARON LYNN (aka SHARON LYNNE)	portrait	PARAMOUNT	
P1471	JOYZELLE JOYNER	portrait	PARAMOUNT	
P1472	JANE DARWELL	portrait	PARAMOUNT	
P1473	EDWARD WOODS	portrait	PARAMOUNT	
P1474	LILIAN BOND aka LILLIAN BOND	portrait	PARAMOUNT	
P1476	CHARLES GRAPEWIN	portrait	PARAMOUNT	
P1477	GAIL PATRICK	portrait	PARAMOUNT	
P1478	LILLIAN ELLIOTT	portrait	PARAMOUNT	
P1479	REGINALD BARLOW	portrait	PARAMOUNT	
P1480	CECIL CUNNINGHAM	portrait	PARAMOUNT	
P1481	ROSCOE KARNS	portrait	PARAMOUNT	
P1482	KATHLEEN BURKE	portrait	PARAMOUNT	
P1483	LUCIEN LITTLEFIELD	portrait	PARAMOUNT	
P1485	PHILLIPS SMALLEY	portrait	PARAMOUNT	
P1487	SHIRLEY GREY	portrait	PARAMOUNT	

Movie Still Identification Book Ultimate Edition - Letters

CODE	TITLE/NAME	DIRECTOR/TYPE	STUDIO/DISTRIBUTOR	YEAR
P1488	JAMES BUSH	portrait	PARAMOUNT	
P1490	LUCILLE LA VERNE	portrait	PARAMOUNT	
P1491	KARL STRUSS	portrait	PARAMOUNT	
P1492	ARTHUR HOHL	portrait	PARAMOUNT	
P1493	SIDNEY TOLER	portrait	PARAMOUNT	
P1495	LEW CODY	portrait	PARAMOUNT	
P1496	MAY ROBSON	portrait	PARAMOUNT	
P1497	NOEL FRANCIS	portrait	PARAMOUNT	
P1498	ARIZONA RAIDERS	HOGAN	PARAMOUNT	1936
P1499	HAMAGUCHI SUMOKO	portrait	PARAMOUNT	
P1500	GREGORY RATOFF	portrait	PARAMOUNT	
P1501	PATRICIA FARLEY	portrait	PARAMOUNT	
P1502	DOROTHY MACKAILL	portrait	PARAMOUNT	
P1503	CLARK GABLE	portrait	PARAMOUNT	
P1504	JOHN LODGE	portrait	PARAMOUNT	
P1505	FRANK/FRANKLIN HANSEN	portrait	PARAMOUNT	
P1506	LONA ANDRE	portrait	PARAMOUNT	
P1507	ELIZABETH PATTERSON	portrait	PARAMOUNT	
P1508	MICHIO ITO	portrait	PARAMOUNT	
P1510	TIFFANY THAYER	portrait	PARAMOUNT	
P1511	ROCHELLE HUDSON	portrait	PARAMOUNT	
P1512	HARRY WALLACE	portrait	PARAMOUNT	
P1513	TAMMANY YOUNG	portrait	PARAMOUNT	
P1517	FUZZY KNIGHT	portrait	PARAMOUNT	
P1518	DAVID LANDAU	portrait	PARAMOUNT	
P1522	VERREE TEASDALE (aka VEREE TEASDALE)	portrait	PARAMOUNT	
P1523	ZITA JOHANN	portrait	PARAMOUNT	
P1524	GEORGE BRENT	portrait	PARAMOUNT	
P1525	DOLORES TUMA	portrait	PARAMOUNT	
P1526	POLAN BANKS	portrait	PARAMOUNT	
P1527	ARTHUR BYRON	portrait	PARAMOUNT	
P1528	HARVEY GATES	portrait	PARAMOUNT	
P1529	VERNA HILLIE	portrait	PARAMOUNT	
P1531	DAVID MANNERS	portrait	PARAMOUNT	
P1532	JAMES/JIMMIE EAGLE/EAGLES	portrait	PARAMOUNT	
P1533	HELEN TWELVETREES	portrait	PARAMOUNT	
P1534	SIDNEY BLACKMER	portrait	PARAMOUNT	
P1536	RALPH RAINGER, LEO ROBIN	portrait	PARAMOUNT	
P1537	WESLEY RUGGLES	portrait	PARAMOUNT	
P1538	SAM COSLOW (COMPOSER)	portrait	PARAMOUNT	
P1539	SIR GUY STANDING	portrait	PARAMOUNT	
P1540	JOHN HALLIDAY	portrait	PARAMOUNT	
P1541	PEGGY HOPKINS JOYCE (DORIS KENYON)	portrait	PARAMOUNT	
P1544	BRIAN AHERNE	portrait	PARAMOUNT	
P1545	JACK LARUE	portrait	PARAMOUNT	
P1547	LEAH RAY	portrait	PARAMOUNT	
P1548	HELEN FREEMAN	portrait	PARAMOUNT	
P1549	WILLIAM GARGAN	portrait	PARAMOUNT	
P1551	GLORIA STUART	portrait	PARAMOUNT	
P1552	JOHNNY HINES	portrait	PARAMOUNT	
P1553	STERLING HOLLOWAY	portrait	PARAMOUNT	
P1554	JEAN NEGULESCO	portrait	PARAMOUNT	
P1555	WALTER ABEL	portrait	PARAMOUNT	
P1556	ELIZABETH YOUNG	portrait	PARAMOUNT	
P1557	MITCHELL LEISEN	portrait	PARAMOUNT	
P1559	JUDITH ALLEN	portrait	PARAMOUNT	
P1560	NAT FINSTON (aka NATHANIEL W. FINSTON)	portrait	PARAMOUNT	
P1561	AL LEWIS	portrait	PARAMOUNT	
P1562	HAROLD HURLEY	portrait	PARAMOUNT	
P1564	MARY KORNMAN	portrait	PARAMOUNT	
P1565	DOROTHEA WIECK	portrait	PARAMOUNT	
P1565	WINIFRED SHAW	portrait	PARAMOUNT	
P1566	GRACE BRADLEY	portrait	PARAMOUNT	
P1567	BARTON MACLANE	portrait	PARAMOUNT	
P1568	HARRY REYNOLDS	portrait	PARAMOUNT	
P1569	DONALD COOK	portrait	PARAMOUNT	
P1571	DOROTHY WHITNEY	portrait	PARAMOUNT	
P1572	KEN MURRAY	portrait	PARAMOUNT	
P1573	BRUCE CABOT	portrait	PARAMOUNT	
P1574	FRANCES FULLER	portrait	PARAMOUNT	

Movie Still Identification Book Ultimate Edition - Letters

CODE	TITLE/NAME	DIRECTOR/TYPE	STUDIO/DISTRIBUTOR	YEAR
P1575	ARTHUR VINTON	portrait	PARAMOUNT	
P1576	MORGAN WALLACE	portrait	PARAMOUNT	
P1578	EDDIE NUGENT	portrait	PARAMOUNT	
P1579	OSCAR RUDOLPH	portrait	PARAMOUNT	
P1581	RICHARD CROMWELL	portrait	PARAMOUNT	
P1582	BEN ALEXANDER	portrait	PARAMOUNT	
P1583	BRADLEY PAGE	portrait	PARAMOUNT	
P1584	MARJORIE WHITE	portrait	PARAMOUNT	
P1585	EDWARD ARNOLD	portrait	PARAMOUNT	
P1586	TOBY WING	portrait	PARAMOUNT	
P1587	WILLIAM BAKEWELL	portrait	PARAMOUNT	
P1588	TOM BROWN	portrait	PARAMOUNT	
P1589	HELEN VINSON	portrait	PARAMOUNT	
P1590	ALAN MOWBRAY	portrait	PARAMOUNT	
P1591	FERDINAND GOTTSCHALK	portrait	PARAMOUNT	
P1592	FRED OTT	portrait	PARAMOUNT	
P1593	BILLY GILBERT	portrait	PARAMOUNT	
P1595	FRANK TINNEY JR.	portrait	PARAMOUNT	
P1596	FRED KOHLER JR.	portrait	PARAMOUNT	
P1597	CARLYLE BLACKWELL JR.	portrait	PARAMOUNT	
P1598	NEAL HART JR.	portrait	PARAMOUNT	
P1600	WALLACE REID JR.	portrait	PARAMOUNT	
P1601	ERICH VON STROHEIM JR.	portrait	PARAMOUNT	
P1602	JOAN MARSH	portrait	PARAMOUNT	
P1604	CHARLES BICKFORD	portrait	PARAMOUNT	
P1607	HARDIE ALBRIGHT	portrait	PARAMOUNT	
P1608	PATTERSON MCNUTT	portrait	PARAMOUNT	
P1609	DOUGLAS FAIRBANKS JR.	portrait	PARAMOUNT	
P1612	GEORGE M. ARTHUR	portrait	PARAMOUNT	
P1613	SIDNEY J. TWINING	portrait	PARAMOUNT	
P1614	LOREN L. RYDER	portrait	PARAMOUNT	
P1615	LEO TOVER	portrait	PARAMOUNT	
P1616	MARTIN M. PAGGI	portrait	PARAMOUNT	
P1617	HAROLD C. LEWIS (aka HAL LEWIS)	portrait	PARAMOUNT	
P1618	LORIN GRIGNON	portrait	PARAMOUNT	
P1619	JACK A. GOODRICH (aka JOHN GOODRICH)	portrait	PARAMOUNT	
P1620	HARRY MILLS	portrait	PARAMOUNT	
P1621	CHARLES R. ROGERS	portrait	PARAMOUNT	
P1622	BABY LEROY	portrait	PARAMOUNT	
P1623	WALTER CATLETT	portrait	PARAMOUNT	
P1624	DEL LORD	portrait	PARAMOUNT	
P1625	PAUL SLOANE	portrait	PARAMOUNT	
P1626	PERT KELTON	portrait	PARAMOUNT	
P1627	MINNA GOMBELL	portrait	PARAMOUNT	
P1628	FELIX CLIVE	portrait	PARAMOUNT	
P1630	HARRIETTE HADDON	portrait	PARAMOUNT	
P1631	DORRIS DAXTER	portrait	PARAMOUNT	
P1633	LEO MCCAREY	portrait	PARAMOUNT	
P1634	MARY BLACKWOOD	portrait	PARAMOUNT	
P1635	ALICE LIDDELL HARGREAVES	portrait	PARAMOUNT	
P1636	MURIEL KIRKLAND	portrait	PARAMOUNT	
P1637	JEAN ACKER	portrait	PARAMOUNT	
P1638	PAULINE EASTERDAY	portrait	PARAMOUNT	
P1640	GERTRUDE MICHAEL	portrait	PARAMOUNT	
P1641	EVELYN VENABLE	portrait	PARAMOUNT	
P1642	KITTY KELLY	portrait	PARAMOUNT	
P1643	JULIE HAYDON	portrait	PARAMOUNT	
P1644	DOROTHE DUNCAN	portrait	PARAMOUNT	
P1645	COL. TIMOTHY J. LONERGAN	portrait	PARAMOUNT	
P1646	GREGORIO MARTINEZ SIERRA	portrait	PARAMOUNT	
P1647	ELSIE FERGUSON	portrait	PARAMOUNT	
P1648	MARY FLANNERY	portrait	PARAMOUNT	
P1649	JACQUELINE WELLS (aka JULIE BISHOP)	portrait	PARAMOUNT	
P1651	CLIFFORD JONES	portrait	PARAMOUNT	
P1652	PHILIP STRONG	portrait	PARAMOUNT	
P1653	IDA LUPINO	portrait	PARAMOUNT	
P1654	EVELYN OAKIE (aka MRS. EVELYN OFFIELD OAKIE)	portrait	PARAMOUNT	
P1655	STEPHAN PASTERNACKI	portrait	PARAMOUNT	
P1656	ACHMED ABDULLAH	portrait	PARAMOUNT	
P1657	FRANK BUTLER	portrait	PARAMOUNT	

Movie Still Identification Book Ultimate Edition - Letters

CODE	TITLE/NAME	DIRECTOR/TYPE	STUDIO/DISTRIBUTOR	YEAR
P1658	MANUEL KOMROFF	portrait	PARAMOUNT	
P1659	STEPHEN MOREHOUSE AVERY	portrait	PARAMOUNT	
P1660	CAREY WILSON	portrait	PARAMOUNT	
P1661	PHILEP UGLIE	portrait	PARAMOUNT	
P1662	WILLIAM FRAWLEY	portrait	PARAMOUNT	
P1663	ADDISON RICHARDS	portrait	PARAMOUNT	
P1664	JESS CAVIN	portrait	PARAMOUNT	
P1665	MAXINE DOYLE	portrait	PARAMOUNT	
P1666	HARRY CAREY	portrait	PARAMOUNT	
P1667	MARGUERITE CHURCHILL	portrait	PARAMOUNT	
P1668	JEAN ROUVEROL	portrait	PARAMOUNT	
P1669	CHARLOTTE HENRY	portrait	PARAMOUNT	
P1670	GWEN MONROE (aka GWEN MUNRO)	portrait	PARAMOUNT	
P1671	FRANCES DRAKE	portrait	PARAMOUNT	
P1672	BARBARA ADAMS (aka BARBARA FRITCHIE)	portrait	PARAMOUNT	
P1674	THE PICKENS SISTERS: HELEN, JANE, PATTI	portrait	PARAMOUNT	
P1676	DOUGLASS MONTGOMERY	portrait	PARAMOUNT	
P1677	HARRY LANGDON	portrait	PARAMOUNT	
P1680	MACK GORDON & HARRY REVEL	portrait	PARAMOUNT	
P1681	MILDRED HOLLIS	portrait	PARAMOUNT	
P1682	BETTY GREY	portrait	PARAMOUNT	
P1683	VIOLET FORAN	portrait	PARAMOUNT	
P1684	VIVIEN WARD	portrait	PARAMOUNT	
P1685	HELEN MACK	portrait	PARAMOUNT	
P1686	NELLA WALKER	portrait	PARAMOUNT	
P1687	JACK HALEY	portrait	PARAMOUNT	
P1688	DOROTHY WILSON	portrait	PARAMOUNT	
P1689	NINA MOISE	portrait	PARAMOUNT	
P1690	WILLIAM H. HAZELL	portrait	PARAMOUNT	
P1691	ARTHUR HORNBLOW JR.	portrait	PARAMOUNT	
P1693	DOROTHY DELL	portrait	PARAMOUNT	
P1696	ELDRED/DON TIDBURY (aka DONALD GRAY)	portrait	PARAMOUNT	
P1697	GWENLLIAN GILL	portrait	PARAMOUNT	
P1700	VICTOR MCLAGLEN	portrait	PARAMOUNT	
P1701	COLIN TAPLEY	portrait	PARAMOUNT	
P1702	JULIAN MADISON	portrait	PARAMOUNT	
P1703	ANN SHERIDAN	portrait	PARAMOUNT	
P1705	JAY HENRY	portrait	PARAMOUNT	
P1706	LANNY ROSS	portrait	PARAMOUNT	
P1707	SAM HELLMAN	portrait	PARAMOUNT	
P1708	SALLY EILERS	portrait	PARAMOUNT	
P1709	HARRY JOE BROWN	portrait	PARAMOUNT	
P1710	SAM JAFFE	portrait	PARAMOUNT	
P1711	ETHEL MERMAN	portrait	PARAMOUNT	
P1712	WINNIE FLINT (aka WINIFRED FLINT)	portrait	PARAMOUNT	
P1713	CARL BRISSON	portrait	PARAMOUNT	
P1714	ANN SOTHERN	portrait	PARAMOUNT`	
P1715	ADOLPH ZUKOR	portrait	PARAMOUNT	
P1715	WILLIAM S. HART	portrait	PARAMOUNT	
P1716	VIRGINIA HAMMOND	portrait	PARAMOUNT	
P1717	EARL CARROLL	portrait	PARAMOUNT	
P1718	KITTY CARLISLE	portrait	PARAMOUNT	
P1719	TOM W. BAILEY	portrait	PARAMOUNT	
P1720	HENRY WILCOXON	portrait	PARAMOUNT	
P1721	JOE MORRISON	portrait	PARAMOUNT	
P1722	THE GALE SISTERS: JUNE, JOAN & JANE	portrait	PARAMOUNT	
P1723	JACK DENNIS (EDITOR)	portrait	PARAMOUNT	
P1724	3 CHEERS FOR LOVE	MCCAREY	PARAMOUNT	1936
P1724	ARTHUR COOPER	portrait	PARAMOUNT	1936
P1724	BIG BROADCAST OF 1937*	LEISEN	PARAMOUNT	1936
P1724	COLLEGE HOLIDAY	TUTTLE	PARAMOUNT	1936
P1724	DOROTHY LAMOUR LLOYD NOLAN & OTHERS*	portrait	PARAMOUNT	
P1724	EDDIE FOY JR	portrait	PARAMOUNT	
P1724	LUBITSCH PARTY FOR PAR PRES JOHN E OTTERSON	portrait	PARAMOUNT	
P1724	MAKE WAY FOR TOMORROW	MCCAREY	PARAMOUNT	1937
P1724	MAURICE COSTELLO ON THE SET OF HOTEL IMPERIAL	portrait	PARAMOUNT	
P1724	MAX FLEISCHER, DAVE FLEISCHER	portrait	PARAMOUNT	
P1724	NY GOV LEHMAN, AND OTHERS*	portrait	PARAMOUNT	
P1724	PARAMOUNT FUTURE STARLETS OF 1934	portrait	PARAMOUNT	
P1724	PARAMOUNT STARLETS, C.1936	portrait	PARAMOUNT	

Movie Still Identification Book Ultimate Edition - Letters

CODE	TITLE/NAME	DIRECTOR/TYPE	STUDIO/DISTRIBUTOR	YEAR
P1724	PENNY GILL	portrait	PARAMOUNT	1939
P1724	TEXANS	HOGAN	PARAMOUNT	1938
P1724	VENICE PIER FUN HOUSE PARTY	portrait	PARAMOUNT	1935
P1724	WAMPAS BABY STARS OF 1935	portrait	PARAMOUNT	1935
P1726	RAY MILLAND	portrait	PARAMOUNT	
P1726	RETURN OF SOPHIE LANG	ARCHAINBAUD	PARAMOUNT	1936
P1727	HOWARD WILSON	portrait	PARAMOUNT	
P1728	JOSEPH GALLANT	portrait	PARAMOUNT	
P1729	MARY MORRIS	portrait	PARAMOUNT	
P1730	BARBARA SLATER	portrait	PARAMOUNT	
P1730	BEULAH MACDONALD, KAY GORDON & OTHERS*	portrait	PARAMOUNT	
P1730	COLLEGE SWING (1938)*	WALSH	PARAMOUNT	1938
P1730	COLLEGIATE (1936)*	MURPHY	PARAMOUNT	1936
P1730	EARL CARROLL SHOWGIRLS,	portrait	PARAMOUNT	
P1730	MARIE MOSQUINI (aka DE FOREST)	portrait	PARAMOUNT	
P1730	MURDER AT THE VANITIES (1934)*	LEISEN	PARAMOUNT	1934
P1731	JEAN CHATBURN	portrait	PARAMOUNT	
P1732	SHIRLEY TEMPLE	portrait	PARAMOUNT	
P1733	MERRY FAHRNEY MARY FAHRNEY	portrait	PARAMOUNT	
P1734	BEN BERNIE	portrait	PARAMOUNT	
P1735	ALFRED WERKER	portrait	PARAMOUNT	
P1736	JUNE BREWSTER	portrait	PARAMOUNT	
P1737	LYNNE OVERMAN	portrait	PARAMOUNT	
P1738	JOHNNY MACK BROWN	portrait	PARAMOUNT	
P1739	JULIA GRAHAM	portrait	PARAMOUNT	
P1741	GUY LOMBARDO	portrait	PARAMOUNT	
P1742	HAROLD WALDRIDGE	portrait	PARAMOUNT	
P1743	LILLIAN MOORE	portrait	PARAMOUNT	
P1744	RALPH MURPHY	portrait	PARAMOUNT	
P1745	LEROY PRINZ	portrait	PARAMOUNT	
P1750	VELOZ & YOLANDA: FRANK VELOZ, YOLANDA VELOZ	portrait	PARAMOUNT	
P1752	JOHN MILJAN	portrait	PARAMOUNT	
P1753	ROGER PRYOR	portrait	PARAMOUNT	
P1754	BETTY BRYSON	portrait	PARAMOUNT	
P1755	MARY WALLACE	portrait	PARAMOUNT	
P1756	JEAN GALE	portrait	PARAMOUNT	
P1757	LUCILLE LUND	portrait	PARAMOUNT	
P1758	HAZEL HAYES	portrait	PARAMOUNT	
P1759	JUDITH ARLEN	portrait	PARAMOUNT	
P1760	JEAN CARMEN (aka JULIA THAYER)	portrait	PARAMOUNT	
P1761	HELEN E. COHAN	portrait	PARAMOUNT	
P1762	LU ANN MEREDITH	portrait	PARAMOUNT	
P1763	ANN HOVEY	portrait	PARAMOUNT	
P1764	KATHERINE WILLIAMS	portrait	PARAMOUNT	
P1765	MARGERIE BONNER (aka MARJORIE BONNER)	portrait	PARAMOUNT	
P1766	ARLINE JUDGE	portrait	PARAMOUNT	
P1767	CHARLES W. GORMAN	portrait	PARAMOUNT	
P1768	MONA MARIS	portrait	PARAMOUNT	
P1769	JUNE GRABINER (aka TRAVIS)	portrait	PARAMOUNT	
P1770	PATRICIA ELLIS	portrait	PARAMOUNT	
P1771	ISABEL JEWELL	portrait	PARAMOUNT	
P1772	GRACE DURKIN	portrait	PARAMOUNT	
P1774	GIGI PARRISH	portrait	PARAMOUNT	
P1776	FRED MACMURRAY	portrait	PARAMOUNT	
P1777	FLORENCE LAWRENCE	portrait	PARAMOUNT	
P1778	RUTH MARION	portrait	PARAMOUNT	
P1780	OPAL SORNES	portrait	PARAMOUNT	
P1781	BOGART ROGERS	portrait	PARAMOUNT	
P1782	NYDIA WESTMAN	portrait	PARAMOUNT	
P1783	DEAN JAGGER	portrait	PARAMOUNT	
P1784	HELENA PHILLIPS EVANS (aka HELENE P. EVANS)	portrait	PARAMOUNT	
P1785	LEE TRACY	portrait	PARAMOUNT	
P1788	LOUISE SWIFT	portrait	PARAMOUNT	
P1789	PAULINE LORD	portrait	PARAMOUNT	
P1791	DIANA LEWIS	portrait	PARAMOUNT	
P1792	JUNE DEVANI	portrait	PARAMOUNT	
P1803	CHARLOTTE GRANVILLE	portrait	PARAMOUNT	
P1805	PEGGY GRAVES	portrait	PARAMOUNT	
P1808	BILLY LEE (CHILD ACTOR)	portrait	PARAMOUNT	
P1814	DAVID HOLT	portrait	PARAMOUNT	

Movie Still Identification Book Ultimate Edition - Letters

CODE	TITLE/NAME	DIRECTOR/TYPE	STUDIO/DISTRIBUTOR	YEAR
P1815	FRANCIS LEDERER (aka FRANZ LEDERER)	portrait	PARAMOUNT	
P1815	PARADISE	WILLAT	FIRST NATIONAL	1926
P1816	ARTHUR JACOBSON	portrait	PARAMOUNT	
P1817	JOAN BENNETT	portrait	PARAMOUNT	
P1818	PAULINE LAURETTA	portrait	PARAMOUNT	
P1819	VIRGINIA RENDELL	portrait	PARAMOUNT	
P1820	JANET EASTMAN	portrait	PARAMOUNT	
P1822	BARBARA BARONDESS	portrait	PARAMOUNT	
P1823	MARIAN MANSFIELD	portrait	PARAMOUNT	
P1826	ANNE BAUCHENS	portrait	PARAMOUNT	
P1827	JOE PENNER	portrait	PARAMOUNT	
P1828	CARMENCITA JOHNSON (aka CARMEN ROBERTSON)	portrait	PARAMOUNT	
P1830	RALPH REMLEY	portrait	PARAMOUNT	
P1831	PAUL GERRITS	portrait	PARAMOUNT	
P1832	MICHELETTE BURANI (aka MADAME BURANI)	portrait	PARAMOUNT	
P1833	HAL RAYNOR	portrait	PARAMOUNT	
P1834	HAROLD LAMB	portrait	PARAMOUNT	
P1835	LLOYD NOLAN	portrait	PARAMOUNT	
P1836	LORRAINE BRIDGES	portrait	PARAMOUNT	
P1837	ALAN CAMPBELL	portrait	PARAMOUNT	
P1838	ALAN CAMPBELL	portrait	PARAMOUNT	
P1839	QUEENIE SMITH	portrait	PARAMOUNT	
P1840	ROBERT KENT (aka DOUGLAS BLACKLEY/BLECKLEY)	portrait	PARAMOUNT	
P1842	PEGGY CONKLIN	portrait	PARAMOUNT	
P1843	NANCI LYON (NANCY LYON)	portrait	PARAMOUNT	
P1844	BEN BRYANT	portrait	PARAMOUNT	
P1845	VIRGINIA WEIDLER	portrait	PARAMOUNT	
P1846	CONRAD NAGEL	portrait	PARAMOUNT	
P1847	MARGOT SAGE	portrait	PARAMOUNT	
P1848	H.T. ROBINSON	portrait	PARAMOUNT	
P1851	NITA PIKE (aka ANITA PIKE)	portrait	PARAMOUNT	
P1852	MARTY MALONE (aka MARTIN T. MALONE)	portrait	PARAMOUNT	
P1853	JOHN HOWARD	portrait	PARAMOUNT	
P1854	CHRIS ADRIAN	portrait	PARAMOUNT	
P1854	IRIS ADRIAN	portrait	PARAMOUNT	
P1855	RAY WALKER	portrait	PARAMOUNT	
P1856	JEANIE MACPHERSON	portrait	PARAMOUNT	
P1857	H.B. WARNER	portrait	PARAMOUNT	
P1858	MONROE OWSLEY	portrait	PARAMOUNT	
P1861	PLUMA NOISOM	portrait	PARAMOUNT	
P1862	EDDIE CRAVEN (aka EDWARD CRAVEN)	portrait	PARAMOUNT	
P1863	LILLIAN KILGANNON	portrait	PARAMOUNT	
P1864	ROSALIND JAFFE	portrait	PARAMOUNT	
P1865	MARGARET STAGG	portrait	PARAMOUNT	
P1866	J.P./JOHN/JOSEPH MCEVOY	portrait	PARAMOUNT	
P1867	LOIS MAYBELL	portrait	PARAMOUNT	
P1868	LEON GORDON	portrait	PARAMOUNT	
P1871	JEANNETTE WARREN	portrait	PARAMOUNT	
P1872	DIANE WARFIELD	portrait	PARAMOUNT	
P1873	FRANCES WAVERLY (STAND-IN)	portrait	PARAMOUNT	
P1875	CHARLES 'CHIC' SALE	portrait	PARAMOUNT	
P1876	WILLIE FUNG (aka WILLY FUNG)	portrait	PARAMOUNT	
P1877	GEORGE F. MARION (aka GEORGE FRANCIS MARION)	portrait	PARAMOUNT	
P1878	MARY ELLIS (aka MAY BELLE ELSAS)	portrait	PARAMOUNT	
P1879	MRS. LESLIE CARTER	portrait	PARAMOUNT	
P1880	LILLIAN LAMONTE	portrait	PARAMOUNT	
P1881	JACK HUTCHISON	portrait	PARAMOUNT	
P1882	MARGO	portrait	PARAMOUNT	
P1886	DOLORES CASEY	portrait	PARAMOUNT	
P1890	MARINA KOSHETZ (aka MARINA SCHUBERT)	portrait	PARAMOUNT	
P1894	HOWARD ESTABROOK	portrait	PARAMOUNT	
P1898	FRANK CRAVEN	portrait	PARAMOUNT	
P1901	JAN KIEPURA	portrait	PARAMOUNT	
P1904	CHARLES BARTON	portrait	PARAMOUNT	
P1905	DIXIE LEE	portrait	PARAMOUNT	
P1907	WENDY BARRIE	portrait	PARAMOUNT	
P1908	CHARLES LANG	portrait	PARAMOUNT	
P1909	ROAD TO DENVER	KANE	REPUBLIC	1955
P1909	WALTER C KELLY	portrait	PARAMOUNT	
P1910	ANDY CLYDE	portrait	PARAMOUNT	

Movie Still Identification Book Ultimate Edition - Letters

CODE	TITLE/NAME	DIRECTOR/TYPE	STUDIO/DISTRIBUTOR	YEAR
P1912	ELLIOT NUGENT	portrait	PARAMOUNT	
P1914	ANDY DEVINE	portrait	PARAMOUNT	
P1918	CHARLES BOYER	portrait	PARAMOUNT	
P1919	FRED STONE	portrait	PARAMOUNT	
P1920	TULLIO CARMINATI	portrait	PARAMOUNT	
P1921	4 HOURS TO KILL	LEISEN	PARAMOUNT	1935
P1921	RICHARD BARTHELMESS	portrait	PARAMOUNT`	
P1926	ROSALIND KEITH (aka ROSALIND CULLI)	portrait	PARAMOUNT	
P1929	I DREAM OF JEANNIE	DWAN	REPUBLIC	1952
P1932	DOROTHY THOMPSON (aka DOROTHY WARD)	portrait	PARAMOUNT	
P1933	MAXINE REINER	portrait	PARAMOUNT	
P1936	FRANK PANGBORN	portrait	PARAMOUNT	
P1950	AL SANTELL	portrait	PARAMOUNT	
P1951	FERDINAND GOTTSCHALK	portrait	PARAMOUNT	
P1954	JOHNNY DOWNS	portrait	PARAMOUNT	
P1955	TRIXIE FRIGANZA	portrait	PARAMOUNT	
P1957	LORETTA YOUNG	portrait	PARAMOUNT	
P1957	SHANGHAI	FLOOD	PARAMOUNT	1935
P1959	GLADYS SWARTHOUT	portrait	PARAMOUNT	
P1961	SAMUEL S. HINDS (aka SAM HINDS)	portrait	PARAMOUNT	
P1962	FRANK LLOYD	portrait	PARAMOUNT	
P1963	CLYDE BRUCKMAN	portrait	PARAMOUNT	
P1964	HENRY WADSWORTH	portrait	PARAMOUNT	
P1966	ASTRID ALLWYN	portrait	PARAMOUNT	
P1967	HOLMES HERBERT	portrait	PARAMOUNT	
P1969	CLAUDE RAINS	portrait	PARAMOUNT	
P1970	SUZANNE EMERY	portrait	PARAMOUNT	
P1972	MARGARET SULLAVAN	portrait	PARAMOUNT	
P1973	ANN HARDING	portrait	PARAMOUNT	
P1974	ERNEST COSSART	portrait	PARAMOUNT	
P1979	WILLIE HOWARD	portrait	PARAMOUNT	
P1980	BETTY HOLT	portrait	PARAMOUNT	
P1981	BILL "BOJANGLES" ROBINSON	portrait	PARAMOUNT	
P1982	FRANCES LANGFORD	portrait	PARAMOUNT	
P1983	PATSY KELLY	portrait	PARAMOUNT	
P1985	MARSHA HUNT	portrait	PARAMOUNT	
P1987	LEIF/GLENN ERICKSON/ERIKSON	portrait	PARAMOUNT	
P1990	BETTY JANE RHODES (aka BETTY/JANE RHODES)	portrait	PARAMOUNT	
P1993	ROBERT CUMMINGS	portrait	PARAMOUNT	
P2000	JOHN BOLES	portrait	PARAMOUNT	
P2001	BETTY GRABLE	portrait	PARAMOUNT	
P2001	GIVE ME A SAILOR	NUGENT	PARAMOUNT	1938
P2003	ADMIRAL RICHARD E. BYRD	portrait	PARAMOUNT	
P2005	COLLEGE HOLIDAY	TUTTLE	PARAMOUNT	1936
P2005	ELEANORE WHITNEY	portrait	PARAMOUNT	
P2007	BETTY BURGESS	portrait	PARAMOUNT	
P2008	ALAN BAXTER	portrait	PARAMOUNT	
P2009	ADRIENNE MARDEN	portrait	PARAMOUNT	
P2010	PHYLLIS LOUGHTON	portrait	PARAMOUNT	
P2013	BRIAN DONLEVY	portrait	PARAMOUNT	
P2015	MONTE BLUE	portrait	PARAMOUNT	
P2017	LIONEL STANDER	portrait	PARAMOUNT	
P2018	CATHERINE DOUCET	portrait	PARAMOUNT	
P2020	OLYMPE BRADNA	portrait	PARAMOUNT	
P2021	BENNY/BENNIE BARTLETT	portrait	PARAMOUNT	
P2022	FRANCES FARMER	portrait	PARAMOUNT	
P2024	AKIM TAMIROFF	portrait	PARAMOUNT	
P2025	ROBERT YOUNG	portrait	PARAMOUNT	
P2027	PHILLIP BAKER	portrait	PARAMOUNT	
P2029	HENRY FONDA	portrait	PARAMOUNT	
P2034	HENRY ARTHUR	portrait	PARAMOUNT	
P2035	JIMMIE ALLEN	portrait	PARAMOUNT	
P2036	MYRA MARSH	portrait	PARAMOUNT	
P2037	RAOUL WALSH	portrait	PARAMOUNT	
P2039	REGINALD DENNY	portrait	PARAMOUNT	
P2040	ROD LA ROCQUE	portrait	PARAMOUNT	
P2041	FRANK FOREST	portrait	PARAMOUNT	
P2043	IRENE BENNETT	portrait	PARAMOUNT	
P2046	GAIL SHERIDAN	portrait	PARAMOUNT	
P2049	HENRY BRANDON	portrait	PARAMOUNT	

Movie Still Identification Book Ultimate Edition - Letters

CODE	TITLE/NAME	DIRECTOR/TYPE	STUDIO/DISTRIBUTOR	YEAR
P2050	SMITH BALLEW	portrait	PARAMOUNT	
P2051	WILMA FRANCIS	portrait	PARAMOUNT	
P2052	ANN EVERS	portrait	PARAMOUNT	
P2053	LOUISE SMALL	portrait	PARAMOUNT	
P2054	PORTER HALL	portrait	PARAMOUNT	
P2055	JILL DEEN	portrait	PARAMOUNT	
P2056	CHARLES BUTTERWORTH/WINNINGER	portrait	PARAMOUNT	
P2057	JAMES ELLISON	portrait	PARAMOUNT	
P2058	LESTER MATTHEWS	portrait	PARAMOUNT`	
P2059	DORIS LLOYD	portrait	PARAMOUNT	
P2066	BUSTER PHELPS	portrait	PARAMOUNT	
P2068	MADELEINE CARROLL	portrait	PARAMOUNT	
P2069	PAT PATERSON	portrait	PARAMOUNT	
P2070	CHLOE DOUGLAS	portrait	PARAMOUNT	
P2073	ELIZABETH RUSSELL	portrait	PARAMOUNT	
P2075	CHARLES QUIGLEY	portrait	PARAMOUNT`	
P2077	LOUIS DAPRON	portrait	PARAMOUNT	
P2078	TED TETZLAFF	portrait	PARAMOUNT	
P2079	RA HOULD (aka RON/RONALD SINCLAIR)	portrait	PARAMOUNT	
P2082	HELEN HOLMES	portrait	PARAMOUNT	
P2083	WILLIAM/WOLF HOPPER (aka DEWOLF HOPPER JR)	portrait	PARAMOUNT	
P2084	TERRY WALKER	portrait	PARAMOUNT	
P2090	HARRY SHERMAN	portrait	PARAMOUNT	
P2095	BORIS MORROS	portrait	PARAMOUNT	
P2098	JAMES HOGAN	portrait	PARAMOUNT	
P2099	WILLIAM SHEA	portrait	PARAMOUNT	
P2100	LOUISE STUART	portrait	PARAMOUNT	
P2101	VEDA ANN BORG	portrait	PARAMOUNT	
P2106	LOUISE STANLEY	portrait	PARAMOUNT	
P2107	BOB BURNS	portrait	PARAMOUNT	
P2109	LYNN BAILEY	portrait	PARAMOUNT	
P2110	MARTHA RAYE	portrait	PARAMOUNT	
P2112	JOHN E. OTTERSON	portrait	PARAMOUNT	
P2113	KAY GRIFFITH	portrait	PARAMOUNT	
P2115	KETTI GALLIAN	portrait	PARAMOUNT	
P2117	ELLEN DREW (aka TERRY RAY)	portrait	PARAMOUNT	
P2117	GOLDEN CIRCLE (PROMO OF YOUNG STARS)*	portrait	PARAMOUNT	1939
P2118	PURNELL PRATT	portrait	PARAMOUNT	
P2120	JEAN PARKER	portrait	PARAMOUNT	
P2126	HOWARD ESTABROOK	portrait	PARAMOUNT	
P2132	HELEN BURGESS	portrait	PARAMOUNT	
P2133	JACK CHAPIN	portrait	PARAMOUNT	
P2135	BETTY COMPSON	portrait	PARAMOUNT	
P2139	KITTY MCHUGH	portrait	PARAMOUNT	
P2142	LEW AYRES	portrait	PARAMOUNT	
P2144	GLADYS GEORGE	portrait	PARAMOUNT	
P2145	JACKIE MORAN	portrait	PARAMOUNT	
P2149	VIRGINIA VAN UPP	portrait	PARAMOUNT	
P2150	EDITH HEAD	portrait	PARAMOUNT	
P2156	DOROTHY LAMOUR	portrait	PARAMOUNT	
P-2156	BIG BROADCAST OF 1938	LEISEN	PARAMOUNT	1937
P2158	FAY HOLDEN	portrait	PARAMOUNT	
P2159	JACK BENNY	portrait	PARAMOUNT	
P2161	LEE BOWMAN	portrait	PARAMOUNT	
P2162	PRISCILLA LAWSON	portrait	PARAMOUNT	
P2163	LOUISE BEAVERS	portrait	PARAMOUNT	
P2165	SHIRLEY ROSS	portrait	PARAMOUNT	
P2165	WAIKIKI WEDDING	TUTTLE	PARAMOUNT	1937
P2170	LARRY ADLER	portrait	PARAMOUNT	
P2171	BENNY FIELDS	portrait	PARAMOUNT	
P2173	RUTH COLEMAN	portrait	PARAMOUNT	
P2176	LEOPOLD STOKOWSKI	portrait	PARAMOUNT	
P2181	GENE LOCKHART	portrait	PARAMOUNT	
P2183	ANTHONY NACE	portrait	PARAMOUNT	
P2184	BERNADENE HAYES (BERNADINE HAYES)	portrait	PARAMOUNT	
P2185	MARIE DEFORREST	portrait	PARAMOUNT	
P2188	DORIS KENYON	portrait	PARAMOUNT	
P2189	WARREN WILLIAM	portrait	PARAMOUNT	
P2191	GALE SONDERGAARD	portrait	PARAMOUNT	
P2192	JUNE MARTEL	portrait	PARAMOUNT	

Movie Still Identification Book Ultimate Edition - Letters

CODE	TITLE/NAME	DIRECTOR/TYPE	STUDIO/DISTRIBUTOR	YEAR
P2199	EUGENE PALLETTE	portrait	PARAMOUNT	
P2200	NATALIE VISART	portrait	PARAMOUNT	
P2202	RICHARD CARLE	portrait	PARAMOUNT	
P2204	LYLE TALBOT	portrait	PARAMOUNT`	
P2211	KAREN MORLEY	portrait	PARAMOUNT	
P2215	FRANCINE LARRIMORE	portrait	PARAMOUNT	
P2216	JOHN TRENT	portrait	PARAMOUNT	
P2217	FRANCISKA GAAL	portrait	PARAMOUNT	
P2222	IRENE DUNNE	portrait	PARAMOUNT	
P2224	BEN BLUE	portrait	PARAMOUNT	
P2227	BEULAH BONDI	portrait	PARAMOUNT	
P2228	BARBARA STANWYCK	portrait	PARAMOUNT	
P2230	ANTHONY QUINN	portrait	PARAMOUNT	
P2232	ORIEN HEYWARD	portrait	PARAMOUNT	
P2233	THOMAS MITCHELL	portrait	PARAMOUNT	
P2234	BARBARA READ	portrait	PARAMOUNT	
P2235	GRANT RICHARDS	portrait	PARAMOUNT	
P2237	VICTOR YOUNG	portrait	PARAMOUNT	
P2238	FAY BAINTER	portrait	PARAMOUNT	
P2241	JOHN PATTERSON	portrait	PARAMOUNT	
P2244	VINA DELMAR	portrait	PARAMOUNT	
P2246	RUFE DAVIS	portrait	PARAMOUNT	
P2252	PHIL HARRIS	portrait	PARAMOUNT	
P2259	JUDY CANOVA	portrait	PARAMOUNT	
P2262	LOUISE CAMPBELL	portrait	PARAMOUNT	
P2266	WILLIAM ROBERTS	portrait	PARAMOUNT	
P2268	JOHN PAYNE	portrait	PARAMOUNT	
P2269	FANCHON ROYER	portrait	PARAMOUNT	
P2271	FIBBER MCGEE & MOLLY	portrait	PARAMOUNT	
P2274	MARIAN MARSH	portrait	PARAMOUNT	
P2278	SANDRA STORME	portrait	PARAMOUNT	
P2280	LAURIE LANE	portrait	PARAMOUNT`	
P2281	ANDRE KOSTELANETZ	portrait	PARAMOUNT	
P2282	OSCAR HOMOLKA	portrait	PARAMOUNT	
P2284	LUIS ALBERNI	portrait	PARAMOUNT	
P2286	BARLOWE BORLAND	portrait	PARAMOUNT	
P2288	MARY LIVINGSTON	portrait	PARAMOUNT	
P2289	RAY MIDDLETON	portrait	PARAMOUNT	
P2290	JINX FALKENBERG	portrait	PARAMOUNT	
P2291	KATHRYN KANE (aka SUGAR CANE)	portrait	PARAMOUNT	
P2297	MARY DEES	portrait	PARAMOUNT	
P2298	JOHN BARRYMORE	portrait	PARAMOUNT	
P2299	BARRY FITZGERALD	portrait	PARAMOUNT	
P2300	ARCHIE TWITCHELL	portrait	PARAMOUNT	
P2301	EVELYN KEYES	portrait	PARAMOUNT	
P2307	JANE DEWEY	portrait	PARAMOUNT	
P2308	COLLEGE SWING STARLETS*	portrait	PARAMOUNT	
P2311	SUZANNE RIDGEWAY	portrait	PARAMOUNT	
P2313	WILLIAM H PINE	portrait	PARAMOUNT	
P2341	GEORGES RIGAUD	portrait	PARAMOUNT	
P2342	1938 STARLETS*	portrait	PARAMOUNT	
P2343	RICHARD DENNING	portrait	PARAMOUNT	
P2346	THEODORE/TED REED (aka J./JAY THEODORE REED)	portrait	PARAMOUNT	
P2347	HEDDA HOPPER, JACKIE COOPER	portrait	PARAMOUNT	
P2349	JACK HUBBARD ADD: aka JOHN HUBBARD	portrait	PARAMOUNT`	
P2354	MURIEL HUTCHISON	portrait	PARAMOUNT	
P2361	TROPIC HOLIDAY	REED	PARAMOUNT	1938
P2362	MORIA DORAY (aka BOSY ROTH)	portrait	PARAMOUNT	
P2364	UNA MERKEL	portrait	PARAMOUNT	
P2365	ADVENTURE IN DIAMONDS	FITZMAURICE	PARAMOUNT	1940
P2367	MICHAEL BROOKE	portrait	PARAMOUNT	
P2370	NORAH GALE	portrait	PARAMOUNT	
P2375	YVONNE DUVAL	portrait	PARAMOUNT	
P2377	BOB HOPE	portrait	PARAMOUNT	
P2380	KIRSTEN FLAGSTAD	portrait	PARAMOUNT	
P2381	MARIE BURTON (aka CATHERINE COTTER)	portrait	PARAMOUNT	
P2383	EDGAR KENNEDY	portrait	PARAMOUNT	
P2384	LEW FIELDS (OF WEBER & FIELDS)	portrait	PARAMOUNT	
P2385	JOE WEBER (OF WEBER & FIELDS)	portrait	PARAMOUNT	
P2386	SHEP FIELDS	portrait	PARAMOUNT	

Movie Still Identification Book Ultimate Edition - Letters

CODE	TITLE/NAME	DIRECTOR/TYPE	STUDIO/DISTRIBUTOR	YEAR
P2388	CLAIRE DODD	portrait	PARAMOUNT	
P2389	DOROTHY WHITE	portrait	PARAMOUNT	
P2390	LOLA JENSEN & BEBE DANIELS	portrait	PARAMOUNT	
P2391	AL SIEGAL CLAIRE DODD	portrait	PARAMOUNT	
P2395	AGUSTIN/AUGUSTIN LARA	portrait	PARAMOUNT	
P2396	PATRICIA WILDER	portrait	PARAMOUNT	
P2398	BEATRICE LILLIE	portrait	PARAMOUNT	
P2401	SHEILA DARCY (aka REBECCA WASSEM)	portrait	PARAMOUNT	
P2402	TITO GUIZAR	portrait	PARAMOUNT	
P2403	COLLEGE SWING	WALSH	PARAMOUNT	1938
P2403	FLORENCE GEORGE	portrait	PARAMOUNT	
P2404	NELL KELLY	portrait	PARAMOUNT	
P2406	DOROTHY DAYTON	portrait	PARAMOUNT	
P2408	PHYLLIS WELCH (aka PHYLIS WELCH)	portrait	PARAMOUNT	
P2416	MARY LOU LENDER	portrait	PARAMOUNT	
P2419	DAVID NIVEN	portrait	PARAMOUNT	
P2420	JERRY COLONNA	portrait	PARAMOUNT	
P2424	ANDREW STONE	portrait	PARAMOUNT	
P2427	GLENDA FARRELL	portrait	PARAMOUNT	
P2428	COCOANUT GROVE	SANTELL	PARAMOUNT	1938
P2429	RUSSELL HAYDEN	portrait	PARAMOUNT	
P2437	HARRIET HILLIARD (aka HARRIET NELSON)	portrait	PARAMOUNT	
P2438	HOAGY CARMICHAEL	portrait	PARAMOUNT	
P2441	J CARROL NAISH	portrait	PARAMOUNT	
P2442	FRITZ LANG	portrait	PARAMOUNT	
P2444	CAMPUS CONFESSIONS, 1938	ARCHAINBAUD	PARAMOUNT	1938
P2445	ZOE DELL LANTIS	portrait	PARAMOUNT	
P2446	BINNIE BARNES	portrait	PARAMOUNT	
P2447	MARIAN WELDON	portrait	PARAMOUNT`	
P2448	EVE ARDEN	portrait	PARAMOUNT	
P2452	CLAIRE JAMES	portrait	PARAMOUNT	
P2456	JOHN HART	portrait	PARAMOUNT	
P2460	ROBERTO SOTO	portrait	PARAMOUNT	
P2462	LOUISE PLATT	portrait	PARAMOUNT	
P2464	DONALD O'CONNOR	portrait	PARAMOUNT	
P2468	TY HUNGERFORD	portrait	PARAMOUNT	
P2472	MARY (PUNKIN/PUNKINS) PARKER	portrait	PARAMOUNT	
P2473	JACK WHITING	portrait	PARAMOUNT	
P2476	LINDA YALE	portrait	PARAMOUNT	
P2477	BASIL RATHBONE	portrait	PARAMOUNT	
P2480	HEATHER ANGEL	portrait	PARAMOUNT	
P2484	BING CROSBY'S SONS: PHILLIP, GARY, DENNIS, LINDSAY	portrait	PARAMOUNT	
P2485	DOROTHY WRIGHT	portrait	PARAMOUNT	
P2486	JEAN FENWICK	portrait	PARAMOUNT	
P2488	DENNIS MORGAN (aka RICHARD STANLEY)	portrait	PARAMOUNT	
P2491	GOLDEN CIRCLE (PROMO OF YOUNG STARS)*	portrait	PARAMOUNT	1939
P2491	ROBERT PRESTON	portrait	PARAMOUNT	
P2493	CLIFF NAZARRO GLADYS SHEPPARD	portrait	PARAMOUNT	
P2494	JAN/JANE CLAYTON	portrait	PARAMOUNT	
P2496	JUDITH KING	portrait	PARAMOUNT	
P2508	BILLY COOK	portrait	PARAMOUNT	
P2512	JUDITH BARRETT	portrait	PARAMOUNT	
P2515	JOHN BEAL	portrait	PARAMOUNT	
P2518	VIRGINIA DABNEY	portrait	PARAMOUNT	
P2519	WILLIAM FARNUM	portrait	PARAMOUNT	
P2520	ANN GILLIS	portrait	PARAMOUNT	
P2526	PATRICIA MORISON	portrait	PARAMOUNT	
P2527	WILLIAM THOMAS	portrait	PARAMOUNT	
P2530	MICHEL WERBOFF	portrait	PARAMOUNT	
P2532	WILLIAM HENRY	portrait	PARAMOUNT	
P2533	LUANA WALTERS/JUNE WALTERS/SUSAN WALTERS	portrait	PARAMOUNT	
P2536	JOHN HARTLEY	portrait	PARAMOUNT	
P2537	RUDOLPH FORSTER	portrait	PARAMOUNT	
P2538	LUCIUS BEEBE	portrait	PARAMOUNT	
P2539	EDWARD H. GRIFFITH (E.W. GRIFFITH)	portrait	PARAMOUNT	
P2541	ELAINE BARRIE	portrait	PARAMOUNT	
P2542	BUCK JONES	portrait	PARAMOUNT	
P2543	PATSY MACE	portrait	PARAMOUNT	
P2545	DON AMECHE	portrait	PARAMOUNT	
P2548	MARY ASTOR 1939-1947	portrait	PARAMOUNT	

Movie Still Identification Book Ultimate Edition - Letters

CODE	TITLE/NAME	DIRECTOR/TYPE	STUDIO/DISTRIBUTOR	YEAR
P2550	JANICE LOGAN	portrait	PARAMOUNT	
P2552	MELVILLE COOPER	portrait	PARAMOUNT	
P2553	GOLDEN CIRCLE (PROMO OF YOUNG STARS)*- 13 ACTORS	portrait	PARAMOUNT	1939
P2553	SUSAN HAYWARD	portrait	PARAMOUNT	
P2558	EDDIE "ROCHESTER" ANDERSON	portrait	PARAMOUNT	
P2559	GENE KRUPA	portrait	PARAMOUNT	
P2561	MARION MARTIN	portrait	PARAMOUNT	
P2563	STEFFI DUNA	portrait	PARAMOUNT	
P2565	JOSEPH ALLEN (aka JOSEPH ALLEN JR.)	portrait	PARAMOUNT	
P2566	WILLIAM HAADE	portrait	PARAMOUNT	
P2569	MARK SANDRICH	portrait	PARAMOUNT	
P2570	JAMES STEWART	portrait	PARAMOUNT	
P2572	LINDA WARE	portrait	PARAMOUNT	
P2574	PAULETTE GODDARD	portrait	PARAMOUNT	
P2577	WILLIAM HOLDEN	portrait	PARAMOUNT	
P2579	SUSAN PALEY	portrait	PARAMOUNT	
P2580	BETTY FIELD	portrait	PARAMOUNT	
P2581	SHEILA RYAN (aka BETTY MCLAUGHLIN)	portrait	PARAMOUNT	
P2583	ERIC BLORE	portrait	PARAMOUNT	
P2585	WILLIAM WALLING	portrait	PARAMOUNT	
P2586	MURIEL ANGELUS	portrait	PARAMOUNT	
P2589	MARGARET LOCKWOOD	portrait	PARAMOUNT	
P2592	VAUGHN/VAUGHAN GLASER/GLAZER	portrait	PARAMOUNT	
P2593	PRESTON FOSTER	portrait	PARAMOUNT	
P2596	JANE WEBB	portrait	PARAMOUNT	
P2597	THOMAS COLEY	portrait	PARAMOUNT	
P2600	PETER LIND HAYES	portrait	PARAMOUNT	
P2601	DOROTHEA KENT	portrait	PARAMOUNT`	
P2604	REGINALD GARDINER	portrait	PARAMOUNT	
P2605	CAROLYN LEE	portrait	PARAMOUNT	
P2608	VIRGINIA DALE	portrait	PARAMOUNT	
P2610	ALBERT DEKKER	portrait	PARAMOUNT	
P2611	WALTER DAMROSCH	portrait	PARAMOUNT	
P2614	BETTY MORAN	portrait	PARAMOUNT	
P2617	OSA MASSEN	portrait	PARAMOUNT	
P2623	ALLAN JONES	portrait	PARAMOUNT	
P2625	SUSANNA FOSTER	portrait	PARAMOUNT	
P2630	MAUREEN O'HARA	portrait	PARAMOUNT	
P2631	ALAN LADD	portrait	PARAMOUNT	
P2632	WANDA MCKAY	portrait	PARAMOUNT	
P2633	MARY MARTIN	portrait	PARAMOUNT	
P2634	ROBERT PAIGE	portrait	PARAMOUNT	
P2637	BEBE DANIELS, BEN LYON	portrait	PARAMOUNT	
P2638	HOPE HAMPTON	portrait	PARAMOUNT	
P2646	NORMA NELSON	portrait	PARAMOUNT	
P2647	JEAN(NE) CAGNEY	portrait	PARAMOUNT	
P2648	JEROME COWAN	portrait	PARAMOUNT	
P2649	JOHN GARRICK	portrait	PARAMOUNT	
P2650	WALTER CONNOLLY, WILLIAM LEBARON	portrait	PARAMOUNT	
P2657	LOVEY WARNER, GULLIVER'S TRAVELS	portrait	PARAMOUNT	
P2659	JAMES SEAY	portrait	PARAMOUNT	
P2663	ROBERT RYAN	portrait	PARAMOUNT	
P2665	JOHN LAIRD	portrait	PARAMOUNT	
P2666	BONITA GRANVILLE	portrait	PARAMOUNT	
P2667	BARBARA BURKE	portrait	PARAMOUNT	
P2668	LILLIAN CORNELL	portrait	PARAMOUNT	
P2670	KAY STEWART	portrait	PARAMOUNT	
P2672	JEAN PHILLIPS	portrait	PARAMOUNT	
P2677	PRESTON STURGES	portrait	PARAMOUNT	
P2685	HELEN MACK	portrait	PARAMOUNT	
P2687	EVA GABOR	portrait	PARAMOUNT	
P2689	BLANCHE YURKA	portrait	PARAMOUNT	
P2690	EDDIE BRACKEN	portrait	PARAMOUNT	
P2693	KAY LINAKER	portrait	PARAMOUNT	
P2694	LEILA ERNST	portrait	PARAMOUNT	
P2695	RICHARD CARLSON	portrait	PARAMOUNT	
P2697	GLORIA DICKSON	portrait	PARAMOUNT	
P2698	DICK POWELL	portrait	PARAMOUNT	
P2702	GRACE MCDONALD	portrait	PARAMOUNT	
P2709	SAM WOOD	portrait	PARAMOUNT	

Movie Still Identification Book Ultimate Edition - Letters

CODE	TITLE/NAME	DIRECTOR/TYPE	STUDIO/DISTRIBUTOR	YEAR
P2710	ROD CAMERON	portrait	PARAMOUNT	
P2712	FRANK FAY	portrait	PARAMOUNT	
P2714	CAROLE LANDIS	portrait	PARAMOUNT	
P2716	BETTY BREWER	portrait	PARAMOUNT	
P2717	ELLA NEAL	portrait	PARAMOUNT`	
P2718	OSCAR LEVANT	portrait	PARAMOUNT	
P2719	STANLEY CLEMENTS	portrait	PARAMOUNT`	
P2724	MARGARET WYCHERLY	portrait	PARAMOUNT	
P2725	STERLING HAYDEN	portrait	PARAMOUNT	
P2728	WAYNE MORRIS	portrait	PARAMOUNT	
P2730	MARGARET LINDSAY	portrait	PARAMOUNT	
P2741	BURGESS MEREDITH	portrait	PARAMOUNT	
P2743	MERRY MACS: JOE, TED, JUDD MCMICHAEL, H. CARROLL	portrait	PARAMOUNT	
P2744	ARTIE SHAW	portrait	PARAMOUNT	
P2745	VERONICA LAKE	portrait	PARAMOUNT	
P2747	DON CASTLE	portrait	PARAMOUNT	
P2748	MARGARET MAGGIE HAYNES (DANA DALE)	portrait	PARAMOUNT	
P2749	MARIE WILSON	portrait	PARAMOUNT	
P2750	DIANA LYNN	portrait	PARAMOUNT`	
P2751	PHILLIP TERRY	portrait	PARAMOUNT	
P2752	THERESA HARRIS	portrait	PARAMOUNT	
P2753	CONSTANCE MOORE	portrait	PARAMOUNT	
P2754	BONNIE BAKER	portrait	PARAMOUNT	
P2756	ORRIN TUCKER (ORIN TUCKER)	portrait	PARAMOUNT	
P2757	ESTHER FERNANDEZ	portrait	PARAMOUNT	
P2758	JOHN WAYNE	portrait	PARAMOUNT	
P2759	MARTHA O'DRISCOLL	portrait	PARAMOUNT	
P2761	RICHARD WEBB	portrait	PARAMOUNT	
P2762	WILLIAM DEMAREST	portrait	PARAMOUNT	
P2763	TOMMY DORSEY	portrait	PARAMOUNT	
P2764	PHIL REGAN	portrait	PARAMOUNT	
P2765	BERT WHEELER	portrait	PARAMOUNT	
P2766	ELEANOR STEWART	portrait	PARAMOUNT	
P2767	FRANCES GIFFORD	portrait	PARAMOUNT	
P2768	CATHERINE/KATHERINE CRAIG	portrait	PARAMOUNT	
P2770	KEITH RICHARDS	portrait	PARAMOUNT	
P2771	HANK LADD	portrait	PARAMOUNT	
P2772	CHARLES COBURN	portrait	PARAMOUNT	
P2775	PHYLLIS RUTH	portrait	PARAMOUNT	
P2777	ANNE SHIRLEY	portrait	PARAMOUNT	
P2779	K.T. STEVENS (aka KATHARINE STEVENS)	portrait	PARAMOUNT	
P2780	NILS ASTHER	portrait	PARAMOUNT	
P2782	WILLIAM CABANNE (aka BILL CABANNE)	portrait	PARAMOUNT	
P2783	OLIVIA DE HAVILLAND	portrait	PARAMOUNT	
P2784	JUNE PREISSER	portrait	PARAMOUNT	
P2786	BARBARA BRITTON	portrait	PARAMOUNT	
P2790	KARIN/KATHARINE/KATHERINE BOOTH	portrait	PARAMOUNT	
P2791	JIMMY LYDON	portrait	PARAMOUNT	
P2792	MARY ANDERSON	portrait	PARAMOUNT	
P2793	HELEN GILBERT	portrait	PARAMOUNT	
P2794	JACK TEAGARDEN	portrait	PARAMOUNT	
P2796	HARRY ROSENTHAL	portrait	PARAMOUNT	
P2797	DONA DRAKE	portrait	PARAMOUNT	
P2800	MACDONALD CAREY	portrait	PARAMOUNT	
P2801	VERA ZORINA	portrait	PARAMOUNT	
P2803	DARRYL HICKMAN	portrait	PARAMOUNT	
P2805	JEAN WALLACE	portrait	PARAMOUNT	
P2807	FRANK ALBERTSON	portrait	PARAMOUNT	
P2808	REBEL RANDALL (aka ALAINE BRANDES)	portrait	PARAMOUNT	
P2809	RICHARD DENNING	portrait	PARAMOUNT	
P2810	BARBARA SLATER	portrait	PARAMOUNT	
P2812	LOUIS BROMFIELD	portrait	PARAMOUNT	
P2815	LYNDA GREY (aka LINDA GREY - TILLIE GREY)	portrait	PARAMOUNT	
P2817	HAPPY GO LUCKY	BERNHARDT	PARAMOUNT	1943
P2817	LOUISE LA PLANCHE	portrait	PARAMOUNT`	
P2820	BETTY HUTTON	portrait	PARAMOUNT	
P2822	CASS DALEY	portrait	PARAMOUNT	
P2823	GIL LAMB	portrait	PARAMOUNT	
P2824	LAURA LEE	portrait	PARAMOUNT	
P2826	TEALA LORING (aka JUDITH GIBSON)	portrait	PARAMOUNT	

Movie Still Identification Book Ultimate Edition - Letters

CODE	TITLE/NAME	DIRECTOR/TYPE	STUDIO/DISTRIBUTOR	YEAR
P2830	ANN MILLER	portrait	PARAMOUNT	
P2832	JAMES BROWN	portrait	PARAMOUNT	
P2834	MARJORIE REYNOLDS	portrait	PARAMOUNT	
P2835	JOHNNY JOHNSTON/JOHNSTONE/JOHNSTON	portrait	PARAMOUNT	
P2836	ROBERT BENCHLEY	portrait	PARAMOUNT	
P2837	ROSALIND RUSSELL	portrait	PARAMOUNT	
P2838	BILL GEORGE	portrait	PARAMOUNT	
P2839	CLAIRE TREVOR	portrait	PARAMOUNT	
P2842	RITA QUIGLEY	portrait	PARAMOUNT	
P2843	RITA JOHNSON	portrait	PARAMOUNT	
P2844	DONIVEE LEE	portrait	PARAMOUNT	
P2845	EDDIE ALBERT	portrait	PARAMOUNT	
P2847	ANN/ANNE ROONEY	portrait	PARAMOUNT	
P2848	PRISCILLA LANE	portrait	PARAMOUNT	
P2849	LELA ROGERS	portrait	PARAMOUNT	
P2850	LORRAINE MILLER	portrait	PARAMOUNT	
P2851	HELEN WALKER	portrait	PARAMOUNT	
P2852	BILL GOODWIN	portrait	PARAMOUNT	
P2853	WILLIAM BENDIX	portrait	PARAMOUNT	
P2855	KATINA PAXINOU	portrait	PARAMOUNT	
P2856	JUNE HAVOC	portrait	PARAMOUNT	
P2857	GAIL RUSSELL	portrait	PARAMOUNT	
P2858	ILKA CHASE	portrait	PARAMOUNT	
P2859	INGRID BERGMAN	portrait	PARAMOUNT	
P2860	MARIE MCDONALD	portrait	PARAMOUNT	
P2861	VIRGINIA FIELD/FIELDS	portrait	PARAMOUNT	
P2862	BARRY SULLIVAN	portrait	PARAMOUNT	
P2864	FREDERIC HENRY	portrait	PARAMOUNT	
P2866	BILLY DE WOLFE	portrait	PARAMOUNT	
P2867	MABEL PAIGE	portrait	PARAMOUNT	
P2868	ARTURO DE CORDOVA	portrait	PARAMOUNT	
P2870	MIMI CHANDLER	portrait	PARAMOUNT	
P2871	AMELITA WARD (aka LITA WARD)	portrait	PARAMOUNT	
P2872	SONNY TUFTS	portrait	PARAMOUNT	
P2873	GEORGE REEVES	portrait	PARAMOUNT	
P2878	ANNE BAXTER	portrait	PARAMOUNT	
P2879	BILLY WILDER	portrait	PARAMOUNT	
P2880	LUISE RAINER	portrait	PARAMOUNT	
P2884	NANCY BRINCKMAN	portrait	PARAMOUNT	
P2890	RUTH HUSSEY	portrait	PARAMOUNT	
P2891	HEDY LAMARR	portrait	MGM	
P2892	JOAN FONTAINE	portrait	PARAMOUNT	
P2893	LARAINE DAY	portrait	PARAMOUNT	
P2894	NOEL NEILL	portrait	PARAMOUNT	
P2895	JULIE GIBSON (aka JULIE BRIGGS)	portrait	PARAMOUNT	
P2897	OLGA SAN JUAN	portrait	PARAMOUNT	
P2898	HILLARY BROOKE	portrait	PARAMOUNT	
P2899	CAROL THURSTON	portrait	PARAMOUNT	
P2900	RISE STEVENS	portrait	PARAMOUNT	
P2901	RENNY MCEVOY	portrait	PARAMOUNT	
P2904	SIGNE HASSO	portrait	PARAMOUNT	
P2908	MARY BETH HUGHES	portrait	PARAMOUNT	
P2909	POLI DUR/POLDY DUR/ELISABETH HANDL/LISL HANDL	portrait	PARAMOUNT	
P2910	BILL EDWARDS	portrait	PARAMOUNT	
P2911	PHYLLIS BROOKS	portrait	PARAMOUNT	
P2912	MAXINE FIFE	portrait	PARAMOUNT	
P2913	YVONNE DE CARLO	portrait	PARAMOUNT	
P2914	ANN DORAN	portrait	PARAMOUNT	
P2915	MARY TREEN	portrait	PARAMOUNT	
P2916	ROBERT LOWERY	portrait	PARAMOUNT	
P2917	STANLEY CLEMENTS	portrait	PARAMOUNT	
P2918	SIDNEY LANFIELD	portrait	PARAMOUNT`	
P2919	BYRON BARR	portrait	PARAMOUNT	
P2920	MONA FREEMAN	portrait	PARAMOUNT	
P2924	JOAN CAULFIELD	portrait	PARAMOUNT	
P2925	DEREK COOPER	portrait	PARAMOUNT	
P2926	ANN RICHARDS	portrait	PARAMOUNT	
P2928	ANN SAVAGE	portrait	PARAMOUNT	
P2929	JOHNNY COY	portrait	PARAMOUNT	
P2932	JOSEPH COTTEN	portrait	PARAMOUNT	

Movie Still Identification Book Ultimate Edition - Letters

CODE	TITLE/NAME	DIRECTOR/TYPE	STUDIO/DISTRIBUTOR	YEAR
P2933	CHARLES QUIGLEY	portrait	PARAMOUNT`	
P2934	JENNIFER JONES	portrait	PARAMOUNT	
P2935	LIZABETH SCOTT	portrait	PARAMOUNT	
P2936	ROBERT SULLY	portrait	PARAMOUNT	
P2937	VIRGINIA WELLES	portrait	PARAMOUNT	
P2938	DON DEFORE	portrait	PARAMOUNT	
P2940	JANE WYMAN	portrait	PARAMOUNT	
P2944	ANDY RUSSELL	portrait	PARAMOUNT	
P2948	JOHN LUND	portrait	PARAMOUNT	
P2949	TERESA WRIGHT	portrait	PARAMOUNT	
P2952	PEGGY WOOD	portrait	PARAMOUNT	
P2955	PATRIC KNOWLES	portrait	PARAMOUNT	
P2956	KIRK DOUGLAS	portrait	PARAMOUNT	
P2957	VAN HEFLIN	portrait	PARAMOUNT	
P2958	CHARLES BRACKETT	portrait	PARAMOUNT	
P2962	DOUGLAS DICK	portrait	PARAMOUNT	
P2964	BETSY DRAKE	portrait	PARAMOUNT	
P2965	BURT LANCASTER	portrait	PARAMOUNT	
P2966	GERALDINE FITZGERALD	portrait	PARAMOUNT	
P2967	ARLEEN WHELAN	portrait	PARAMOUNT	
P2968	FRANK FAYLEN	portrait	PARAMOUNT	
P2969	WANDA HENDRIX	portrait	PARAMOUNT	
P2970	KAY SCOTT	portrait	PARAMOUNT`	
P2971	DEFOREST KELLEY	portrait	PARAMOUNT	
P2972	KRISTINE MILLER	portrait	PARAMOUNT	
P2974	JEAN RUTH	portrait	PARAMOUNT	
P2975	JANE WITHERS	portrait	PARAMOUNT	
P2979	SALLY RAWLINSON	portrait	PARAMOUNT	
P2981	WENDELL COREY	portrait	PARAMOUNT	
P2984	JOHN HODIAK	portrait	PARAMOUNT	
P2985	MURVYN VYE (aka MERVYN VYE)	portrait	PARAMOUNT	
P2987	JOHNNY SANDS	portrait	PARAMOUNT	
P2991	JUNE HARRIS	portrait	PARAMOUNT	
P2992	MARY HATCHER	portrait	PARAMOUNT	
P2993	ANN TODD	portrait	PARAMOUNT	
P2994	PHYLLIS CALVERT	portrait	PARAMOUNT	
P2995	MAUREEN O'SULLIVAN	portrait	PARAMOUNT	
P2996	CORINNE CALVET	portrait	PARAMOUNT	
P2997	BRENDA MARSHALL	portrait	PARAMOUNT	
P2998	JANE RUSSELL	portrait	PARAMOUNT	
P2999	MARY KAY DODSON	portrait	PARAMOUNT	
P3001	MARGARET FIELD	portrait	PARAMOUNT	
P3003	DONNA REED	portrait	PARAMOUNT	
P3006	CEDRIC HARDWICKE	portrait	PARAMOUNT	
P3007	RHONDA FLEMING	portrait	PARAMOUNT	
P3008	FLORENCE MARLY	portrait	PARAMOUNT	
P3009	JOHN BROMFIELD	portrait	PARAMOUNT	
P3010	SUZANNE DALBERT	portrait	PARAMOUNT	
P3012	SHELLEY WINTERS	portrait	PARAMOUNT	
P3013	LUCILLE BALL	portrait	PARAMOUNT	
P3014	ROBERT STACK	portrait	PARAMOUNT	
P3015	DOROTHY STICKNEY	portrait	PARAMOUNT	
P3016	MARY JANE/JAYNE SAUNDERS	portrait	PARAMOUNT	
P3017	AUDREY TOTTER	portrait	PARAMOUNT	
P3021	JERRY LEWIS	portrait	PARAMOUNT	
P3022	DEAN MARTIN (ALSO MARTIN & LEWIS)	portrait	PARAMOUNT	
P3023	MONTGOMERY CLIFT	portrait	PARAMOUNT	
P3024	ANN BLYTH	portrait	PARAMOUNT	
P3026	JANE NIGH	portrait	PARAMOUNT	
P3027	NANCY OLSON	portrait	PARAMOUNT	
P3028	VICTOR MATURE	portrait	PARAMOUNT	
P3031	COLEEN GRAY (aka COLLEEN GRAY)	portrait	PARAMOUNT	
P3033	LYLE BETTGER	portrait	PARAMOUNT	
P3035	WILLIAM WYLER	portrait	PARAMOUNT	
P3036	MARI BLANCHARD	portrait	PARAMOUNT	
P3037	LAURA ELLIOT	portrait	PARAMOUNT	
P3038	JAN STERLING	portrait	PARAMOUNT	
P3039	DOROTHY KIRSTEN	portrait	PARAMOUNT	
P3041	ELIZABETH TAYLOR	portrait	PARAMOUNT	
P3042	ALLENE ROBERTS	portrait	PARAMOUNT	

Movie Still Identification Book Ultimate Edition - Letters

CODE	TITLE/NAME	DIRECTOR/TYPE	STUDIO/DISTRIBUTOR	YEAR
P3043	CHARLTON HESTON	portrait	PARAMOUNT	
P-3043	DARK CITY	DIETERLE	PARAMOUNT	1950
P3045	BARBARA RUSH	portrait	PARAMOUNT	
P3046	VIVECA LINDFORS	portrait	PARAMOUNT	
P3047	GLENN FORD	portrait	PARAMOUNT	
P3049	ELLEN DREW	portrait	PARAMOUNT	
P3050	ANNE REVERE	portrait	PARAMOUNT	
P3052	GENE TIERNEY	portrait	PARAMOUNT	
P3053	MARILYN MAXWELL	portrait	PARAMOUNT	
P3055	POLLY BERGEN	portrait	PARAMOUNT	
P3056	MARY MURPHY	portrait	PARAMOUNT	
P3058	JOHN IRELAND	portrait	PARAMOUNT	
P3059	ARTHUR KENNEDY	portrait	PARAMOUNT	
P3060	LAURENCE OLIVIER	portrait	PARAMOUNT	
P3061	GLORIA GRAHAME	portrait	PARAMOUNT	
P3062	CORNEL WILDE	portrait	PARAMOUNT	
P3064	MARION MARSHALL	portrait	PARAMOUNT	
P3065	JOAN TAYLOR	portrait	PARAMOUNT	
P3068	ALEXIS SMITH	portrait	PARAMOUNT	
P3069	RICHARD STAPLEY	portrait	PARAMOUNT	
P3070	PETER HANSON/HANSEN (aka PEDER HANSEN)	portrait	PARAMOUNT	
P3071	CATHY O'DONNELL	portrait	PARAMOUNT	
P3074	ELEANOR PARKER	portrait	PARAMOUNT	
P3075	FRANK MCHUGH	portrait	PARAMOUNT	
P3076	SUSAN MORROW	portrait	PARAMOUNT	
P3078	DEBORAH KERR	portrait	PARAMOUNT	
P3079	ADELE JERGENS	portrait	PARAMOUNT	
P3080	DINAH SHORE	portrait	PARAMOUNT	
P3081	ROBERT MERRILL	portrait	PARAMOUNT	
P3083	VINCE 'VINCENT' EDWARDS	portrait	PARAMOUNT	
P3084	NANCY GATES	portrait	PARAMOUNT	
P3086	PETER BALDWIN	portrait	PARAMOUNT	
P3089	JOSE FERRER	portrait	PARAMOUNT	
P3090	FRANCA FALDINI	portrait	PARAMOUNT	
P3092	MARISA PAVAN	portrait	PARAMOUNT	
P3094	ELAINE STEWART	portrait	PARAMOUNT	
P3095	ARLENE DAHL	portrait	PARAMOUNT	
P3096	CAROLYN JONES	portrait	PARAMOUNT	
P3097	GENE BARRY	portrait	PARAMOUNT	
P3098	GEORGE STEVENS	portrait	PARAMOUNT	
P3099	RALPH MEEKER	portrait	PARAMOUNT	
P4000	JAY LIVINGSTON	portrait	PARAMOUNT	
P4002	ETHEL BARRYMORE	portrait	PARAMOUNT	
P4003	ROBERT STRAUSS	portrait	PARAMOUNT	
P4004	TOM MORTON	portrait	PARAMOUNT	
P4006	PATRICIA MEDINA	portrait	PARAMOUNT	
P4007	ANNA MARIA ALBERGHETTI	portrait	PARAMOUNT	
P4008	MARY SINCLAIR	portrait	PARAMOUNT	
P4009	SUZANNE CLOUTIER	portrait	PARAMOUNT	
P4013	DON TAYLOR	portrait	PARAMOUNT	
P4014	TERRY MOORE	portrait	PARAMOUNT	
P4016	RICHARD JAECKEL	portrait	PARAMOUNT	
P4017	ESTELITA (aka ESTELITA RODRIGUEZ)	portrait	PARAMOUNT	
P4018	SHIRLEY BOOTH	portrait	PARAMOUNT	
P4021	ROSEMARY CLOONEY	portrait	PARAMOUNT	
P4022	TONY CURTIS	portrait	PARAMOUNT	
P-4023	DOCTOR AT SEA	THOMAS	REPUBLIC	1956
P4027	JOANNE GILBERT	portrait	PARAMOUNT	
P4029	KATY JURADO	portrait	PARAMOUNT	
P4030	JANET LEIGH	portrait	PARAMOUNT	
P4031	MARLA ENGLISH	portrait	PARAMOUNT	
P4034	NICOLE MAUREY	portrait	PARAMOUNT	
P4035	PAT/PATRICIA CROWLEY	portrait	PARAMOUNT	
P4036	TONY MARTIN	portrait	PARAMOUNT	
P4037	FERNANDO LAMAS	portrait	PARAMOUNT	
P4038	BARBARA BATES	portrait	PARAMOUNT	
P4039	AUDREY HEPBURN	portrait	PARAMOUNT	
P4040	MARA CORDAY	portrait	PARAMOUNT	
P4041	GUY MITCHELL	portrait	PARAMOUNT	
P4042	DANA ANDREWS	portrait	PARAMOUNT	

Movie Still Identification Book Ultimate Edition - Letters

CODE	TITLE/NAME	DIRECTOR/TYPE	STUDIO/DISTRIBUTOR	YEAR
P4043	TERESA BREWER	portrait	PARAMOUNT	
P4044	PETER FINCH	portrait	PARAMOUNT	
P4045	MAI ZETTERLING	portrait	PARAMOUNT	
P4046	JACK PALANCE	portrait	PARAMOUNT	
P4047	DANNY KAYE	portrait	PARAMOUNT	
P4048	BUDDY EBSEN	portrait	PARAMOUNT	
P4052	SHEREE NORTH	portrait	PARAMOUNT	
P4054	YMA SUMAC	portrait	PARAMOUNT	
P4055	MARTHA HYER	portrait	PARAMOUNT	
P4056	GRACE KELLY	portrait	PARAMOUNT	
P4058	VERA ELLEN	portrait	PARAMOUNT	
P4060	JUNE ALLYSON	portrait	PARAMOUNT	
P4063	JOANNE DRU	portrait	PARAMOUNT	
P4065	GLORIA TALBOTT	portrait	PARAMOUNT	
P4067	BRIAN DONLEVY	portrait	PARAMOUNT	
P4069	JOHN DEREK	portrait	PARAMOUNT	
P4070	FRANCES LANSING	portrait	PARAMOUNT	
P4071	ALDO RAY	portrait	PARAMOUNT	
P4073	MILLY VITALE	portrait	PARAMOUNT	
P4074	DONNA PERCY	portrait	PARAMOUNT`	
P4075	JOHN FORSYTHE	portrait	PARAMOUNT	
P4076	MITZI MCCALL	portrait	PARAMOUNT	
P4077	ZIZI JEANMAIRE/JEANMAIRE/JEANMARIE	portrait	PARAMOUNT	
P4078	JEANETTE MILLER	portrait	PARAMOUNT	
P4079	MARTHA SCOTT	portrait	PARAMOUNT	
P4080	SHIRLEY MACLAINE	portrait	PARAMOUNT	
P4082	ANNA MAGNANI	portrait	PARAMOUNT	
P4085	GLYNIS JOHNS	portrait	PARAMOUNT	
P4086	GLORIA DEHAVEN	portrait	PARAMOUNT	
P4087	ORESTE KIRKOP	portrait	PARAMOUNT	
P4088	RITA MORENO	portrait	PARAMOUNT	
P4090	KATHRYN GRAYSON	portrait	PARAMOUNT	
P4091	LARRY PENNELL	portrait	PARAMOUNT	
P4092	CAROL OHMART	portrait	PARAMOUNT	
P4093	ANGELA LANSBURY	portrait	PARAMOUNT	
P4094	MITZI GAYNOR	portrait	PARAMOUNT	
P4095	ANITA EKBERG	portrait	PARAMOUNT	
P4097	DEBRA PAGET	portrait	PARAMOUNT	
P4098	TOM TRYON	portrait	PARAMOUNT	
P4099	GEORGE CHAKIRIS	portrait	PARAMOUNT	
P4100	YUL BRYNNER	portrait	PARAMOUNT	
P4101	JODY LAWRENCE	portrait	PARAMOUNT	
P4102	JACQUELINE BEER	portrait	PARAMOUNT`	
P4103	GEORGE GOBEL	portrait	PARAMOUNT	
P4104	ELAINE STRITCH	portrait	PARAMOUNT`	
P4105	JAMES GREGORY	portrait	PARAMOUNT	
P4111	VALERIE ALLEN	portrait	PARAMOUNT	
P4112	DANIEL GELIN	portrait	PARAMOUNT`	
P4113	JOHN CARRADINE	portrait	PARAMOUNT	
P4115	DEWEY MARTIN	portrait	PARAMOUNT	
P4117	OLIVE DEERING	portrait	PARAMOUNT	
P4119	EVA MARIE SAINT	portrait	PARAMOUNT	
P4120	BARBARA DARROW	portrait	PARAMOUNT	
P4121	NAT KING COLE	portrait	PARAMOUNT	
P4122	THELMA RITTER	portrait	PARAMOUNT	
P4127	GEORGE SANDERS	portrait	PARAMOUNT	
P4129	SPENCER TRACY	portrait	PARAMOUNT	
P4131	ROBERT WAGNER	portrait	PARAMOUNT	
P4132	JACKIE LOUGHERY	portrait	PARAMOUNT	
P4133	LORI NELSON	portrait	PARAMOUNT	
P4134	ANTHONY PERKINS	portrait	PARAMOUNT	
P4137	CLINT WALKER	portrait	PARAMOUNT	
P4137	MARLON BRANDO	portrait	PARAMOUNT	
P4140	ELAINE AIKEN	portrait	PARAMOUNT	
P4141	JEAN ENGSTROM	portrait	PARAMOUNT	
P4142	DOVIMA	portrait	PARAMOUNT	
P4143	MARGARET/MAGGIE HAYES (DANA DALE)	portrait	PARAMOUNT	
P4145	KENNETH TOBEY	portrait	PARAMOUNT	
P4146	MICHAEL RENNIE	portrait	PARAMOUNT	
P4147	ELVIS PRESLEY	portrait	PARAMOUNT	

Movie Still Identification Book Ultimate Edition - Letters

CODE	TITLE/NAME	DIRECTOR/TYPE	STUDIO/DISTRIBUTOR	YEAR
P4149	JO VAN FLEET	portrait	PARAMOUNT	
P4150	RICHARD ANDERSON	portrait	PARAMOUNT	
P4151	STANLEY DONEN	portrait	PARAMOUNT	
P4156	NORMA MOORE	portrait	PARAMOUNT	
P4157	KARL MALDEN	portrait	PARAMOUNT	
P4158	KATHARINE HEPBURN	portrait	PARAMOUNT	
P4159	LLOYD BRIDGES	portrait	PARAMOUNT	
P4160	PERRY WILSON	portrait	PARAMOUNT`	
P4162	VERA MILES	portrait	PARAMOUNT	
P4164	KAY THOMPSON	portrait	PARAMOUNT	
P4166	ROBERT IVERS	portrait	PARAMOUNT	
P4167	CARMEN SEVILLA	portrait	PARAMOUNT	
P4170	BETSY PALMER	portrait	PARAMOUNT	
P4173	JEANNE CRAIN	portrait	PARAMOUNT	
P4175	EARL HOLLIMAN	portrait	PARAMOUNT	
P4176	ANNA KASHFI	portrait	PARAMOUNT	
P4177	DOLORES HART	portrait	PARAMOUNT	
P4178	INGER STEVENS	portrait	PARAMOUNT	
P4179	CLINT KIMBROUGH	portrait	PARAMOUNT	
P4181	GEORGANN JOHNSON	portrait	PARAMOUNT	
P4183	WILLIAM BISHOP	portrait	PARAMOUNT	
P4184	SOPHIA LOREN	portrait	PARAMOUNT	
P4189	MAMIE VAN DOREN	portrait	PARAMOUNT	
P4191	ANTHONY/TONY FRANCIOSA	portrait	PARAMOUNT	
P4193	MERRY ANDERS	portrait	PARAMOUNT	
P4197	KIM NOVAK	portrait	PARAMOUNT	
P4198	ROBERT MORSE	portrait	PARAMOUNT	
P4201	HARRY GUARDINO	portrait	PARAMOUNT	
P4202	MIMI GIBSON	portrait	PARAMOUNT	
P4205	BARBARA BEL GEDDES	portrait	PARAMOUNT	
P4208	PAUL FORD	portrait	PARAMOUNT	
P4218	CONNIE STEVENS	portrait	PARAMOUNT	
P4219	ABBE LANE	portrait	PARAMOUNT	
P4220	THEODORA DAVITT	portrait	PARAMOUNT	
P4221	CLAIRE BLOOM	portrait	PARAMOUNT	
P4223	NOBU MCCARTHY	portrait	PARAMOUNT	
P4225	ROBERT TAYLOR	portrait	PARAMOUNT	
P4226	FESS PARKER	portrait	PARAMOUNT	
P4227	TINA LOUISE	portrait	PARAMOUNT	
P4228	CARROLL BAKER	portrait	PARAMOUNT	
P4229	DIANA SPENCER	portrait	PARAMOUNT	
P4230	DINA MERRILL	portrait	PARAMOUNT	
P4233	BARBARA NICHOLS	portrait	PARAMOUNT	
P4235	MICKEY SHAUGHNESSY	portrait	PARAMOUNT	
P4236	JACK LORD	portrait	PARAMOUNT	
P4238	DONNA DOUGLAS	portrait	PARAMOUNT	
P4239	JOAN BLACKMAN	portrait	PARAMOUNT	
P4240	TUESDAY WELD	portrait	PARAMOUNT	
P4241	LEE J. COBB	portrait	PARAMOUNT	
P4242	LILLI PALMER	portrait	PARAMOUNT	
P4243	PINA PELLICER	portrait	PARAMOUNT	
P4244	JOI LANSING	portrait	PARAMOUNT	
P4245	BARRY COE	portrait	PARAMOUNT	
P4246	JEFF CHANDLER	portrait	PARAMOUNT	
P4247	STEVE FORREST	portrait	PARAMOUNT	
P4248	PAUL FORD	portrait	PARAMOUNT`	
P4249	MARGARET O'BRIEN	portrait	PARAMOUNT	
P4250	STELLA STEVENS	portrait	PARAMOUNT	
P4253	JULIE NEWMAR	portrait	PARAMOUNT	
P4254	PETER PALMER	portrait	PARAMOUNT	
P4255	LESLIE PARRISH	portrait	PARAMOUNT	
P4256	BARBARA LAWSON	portrait	PARAMOUNT	
P4267	DEBBIE REYNOLDS	portrait	PARAMOUNT	
P4270	ED WYNN	portrait	PARAMOUNT	
P4271	JOHN GAVIN	portrait	PARAMOUNT	
P4273	MEL TORME	portrait	PARAMOUNT	
P4275	JAMES SHIGETA	portrait	PARAMOUNT	
P4276	JOHN ERICSON	portrait	PARAMOUNT	
P4278	JULIET PROWSE	portrait	PARAMOUNT	
P4279	SAL MINEO	portrait	PARAMOUNT	

Movie Still Identification Book Ultimate Edition - Letters

CODE	TITLE/NAME	DIRECTOR/TYPE	STUDIO/DISTRIBUTOR	YEAR
P4280	LEE MARVIN	portrait	PARAMOUNT	
P4281	ELSA MARTINELLI	portrait	PARAMOUNT	
P4282	GABRIELLA PALLOTTA/PALLOTTI	portrait	PARAMOUNT	
P4283	MADLYN RHUE	portrait	PARAMOUNT	
P4284	NITA TALBOT	portrait	PARAMOUNT	
P4286	STEVE MCQUEEN	portrait	PARAMOUNT	
P4288	LEE PATRICK	portrait	PARAMOUNT	
P4290	JILL ST. JOHN	portrait	PARAMOUNT	
P4291	BARBARA RUSH	portrait	PARAMOUNT	
P4292	GLYNIS JOHNS	portrait	PARAMOUNT	
P4293	ELIZABETH ALLEN	portrait	PARAMOUNT	
P4295	ELIZABETH MONTGOMERY	portrait	PARAMOUNT	
P4297	VAN JOHNSON	portrait	PARAMOUNT	
P4301	EDIE ADAMS	portrait	PARAMOUNT	
P4303	ELIZABETH ASHLEY	portrait	PARAMOUNT	
P4304	CARROLL BAKER	portrait	PARAMOUNT	
P4305	RALPH TAEGER	portrait	PARAMOUNT	
P4307	PAUL MANTEE	portrait	PARAMOUNT	
P4308	JOEY HEATHERTON	portrait	PARAMOUNT	
P4314	SUSAN OLIVER	portrait	PARAMOUNT	
P4318	CHARLENE HOLT	portrait	PARAMOUNT	
P4320	GEORGE GRIZZARD	portrait	PARAMOUNT	
P4321	KAZ GARAS	portrait	PARAMOUNT	
P-10058	SHANE	STEVENS	PARAMOUNT	1953
P-10059	ROMAN HOLIDAY	WYLER	PARAMOUNT	1953
P-10106	SEVEN LITTLE FOYS	SHAVELSON	PARAMOUNT	1955
P-10201	DARK CITY	DIETERLE	PARAMOUNT	1950
P-10202	RED MOUNTAIN	DIETERLE	PARAMOUNT	1951
P-10203	PEKING EXPRESS	DIETERLE	PARAMOUNT	1951
P-10204	COME BACK LITTLE SHEBA	MANN	PARAMOUNT	1952
P10205	ABOUT MRS. LESLIE	MANN	PARAMOUNT	1954
P-10206	THREE RING CIRCUS	PEVNEY	PARAMOUNT	1954
P-10207	ROSE TATTOO	MANN	PARAMOUNT	1955
P-10208	ARTISTS AND MODELS	TASHLIN	PARAMOUNT	1955
P-10209	GUNFIGHT AT THE OK CORRAL	STURGES	PARAMOUNT	1957
P-10210	HOLLYWOOD OR BUST	TASHLIN	PARAMOUNT	1956
P-10211	RAINMAKER	ANTHONY	PARAMOUNT	1956
P-10212	LOVING YOU	KANTER	PARAMOUNT	1957
P-10213	HOT SPELL	MANN	PARAMOUNT	1958
P-10214	SAD SACK	MARSHALL	PARAMOUNT	1957
P-10215	WILD IS THE WIND	CUKOR	PARAMOUNT	1957
P-10216	KING CREOLE	CURTIZ	PARAMOUNT	1958
P-10217	LAST TRAIN FROM GUN HILL	STURGES	PARAMOUNT	1959
P-10218	DON'T GIVE UP THE SHIP	TAUROG	PARAMOUNT	1959
P-10219	CAREER	ANTHONY	PARAMOUNT	1959
P-10220	VISIT TO A SMALL PLANET	TAUROG	PARAMOUNT	1960
P10221	ALL IN A NIGHT'S WORK	ANTHONY	PARAMOUNT	1961
P-10222	G. I. BLUES	TAUROG	PARAMOUNT	1960
P-10225	GIRL NAMED TAMIKO	STURGES	PARAMOUNT	1962
P-10226	GIRLS, GIRLS, GIRLS	TAUROG	PARAMOUNT	1962
P-10227	FUN IN ACAPULCO	THORPE	PARAMOUNT	1963
P-10228	WIVES AND LOVERS	RICH	PARAMOUNT	1963
P-10230	ROUSTABOUT	RICH	PARAMOUNT	1964
P-10231	SONS OF KATIE ELDER	HATHAWAY	PARAMOUNT	1965
P-10232	BOEING BOEING	RICH	PARAMOUNT	1965
P-10233	PARADISE HAWAIIAN STYLE	MOORE	PARAMOUNT	1966
P-10234	EASY COME EASY GO	RICH	PARAMOUNT	1967
P-10320	CADDY	TAUROG	PARAMOUNT	1954
P-10321	LIVING IT UP	TAUROG	PARAMOUNT	1954
P-10323	PARDNERS	TAUROG	PARAMOUNT	1956
P-10323	YOU'RE NEVER TOO YOUNG	TAUROG	PARAMOUNT	1955
P-10324	DELICATE DELINQUENT	MCGUIRE	PARAMOUNT	1957
P-10325	ROCK-A-BYE BABY	TASHLIN	PARAMOUNT	1958
P-10326	GEISHA BOY	TASHLIN	PARAMOUNT	1958
P-10330	KNOCK ON WOOD	FRANK, PANAMA	PARAMOUNT	1954
P-10331	REAR WINDOW	HITCHCOCK	PARAMOUNT	1954
P-10332	TROUBLE WITH HARRY	HITCHCOCK	PARAMOUNT	1955
P-10333	COURT JESTER	FRANK, PANAMA	PARAMOUNT	1955
P-10334	GIRL RUSH	PIROSH	PARAMOUNT	1955
P-10335	ANYTHING GOES	MILESTONE	PARAMOUNT	1956

Movie Still Identification Book Ultimate Edition - Letters

CODE	TITLE/NAME	DIRECTOR/TYPE	STUDIO/DISTRIBUTOR	YEAR
P-10336	MAN WHO KNEW TOO MUCH	HITCHCOCK	PARAMOUNT	1956
P-10337	BIRDS AND THE BEES	TAUROG	PARAMOUNT	1956
P-10338	THAT CERTAIN FEELING	FRANK, PANAMA	PARAMOUNT	1956
P-10340	BUSTER KEATON STORY	SHELDON	PARAMOUNT	1957
P-10341	BEAU JAMES	SHAVELSON	PARAMOUNT	1957
P-10342	JOKER IS WILD	VIDOR	PARAMOUNT	1957
P-10343	TIN STAR	MANN	PARAMOUNT	1957
P-10344	VERTIGO	HITCHCOCK	PARAMOUNT	1958
P-10345	TEACHER'S PET	SEATON	PARAMOUNT	1957
P-10346	DEVIL'S HAIRPIN	WILDE	PARAMOUNT	1957
P-10348	HEAR ME GOOD	MCGUIRE	PARAMOUNT	1957
P-10349	MATCHMAKER	ANTHONY	PARAMOUNT	1958
P-10350	HOUSEBOAT	SHAVELSON	PARAMOUNT	1958
P-10351	MARACAIBO	WILDE	PARAMOUNT	1958
P-10352	SPACE CHILDREN	ARNOLD	PARAMOUNT	1958
P-10353	COLOSSUS OF NEW YORK	LOURIE	PARAMOUNT	1958
P-10354	AS YOUNG AS WE ARE	GIRARD	PARAMOUNT	1958
P-10355	FIVE PENNIES	SHAVELSON	PARAMOUNT	1959
P-10356	PARTY CRASHERS	GIRAD	PARAMOUNT	1958
P-10357	TRAP	PANAMA	PARAMOUNT	1959
P-10358	ONE EYED JACKS	BRANDO	PARAMOUNT	1961
P-10359	JAYHAWKERS	FRANK	PARAMOUNT	1959
P-10360	BUT NOT FOR ME	LANG	PARAMOUNT	1959
P-10361	IT STARTED IN NAPLES	SHAVELSON	PARAMOUNT	1960
P-10363	LI'L ABNER	FRANK	PARAMOUNT	1959
P-10364	RAT RACE	MULLIGAN	PARAMOUNT	1960
P-10365	CINDERFELLA	TASHLIN	PARAMOUNT	1960
P-10366	PLEASURE OF HIS COMPANY	SEATON	PARAMOUNT	1961
P-10367	WORLD OF SUZIE WONG	QUINE	PARAMOUNT	1961
P-10368	BELLBOY	LEWIS	PARAMOUNT	1960
P-10369	COUNTERFEIT TRAITOR	SEATON	PARAMOUNT	1962
P-10370	MY GEISHA	CARDIFF	PARAMOUNT	1962
P-10371	HATARI	HAWKS	PARAMOUNT	1962
P-10372	BREAKFAST AT TIFFANY'S	EDWARDS	PARAMOUNT	1961
P-10374	LADIES MAN	CORNU	PARAMOUNT	1961
P-10375	LOVE IN A GOLDFISH BOWL	SHER	PARAMOUNT	1961
P-10376	ERRAND BOY	LEWIS	PARAMOUNT	1961
P-10377	MAN WHO SHOT LIBERTY VALANCE	FORD	PARAMOUNT	1962
P-10378	PIGEON THAT TOOK ROME	SHAVELSON	PARAMOUNT	1962
P-10379	WHO'S GOT THE ACTION	MANN	PARAMOUNT	1963
P-10380	IT'S ONLY MONEY	TASHLIN	PARAMOUNT	1962
P-10381	PARIS WHEN IT SIZZLES	QUINE	PARAMOUNT	1964
P-10382	HUD	RITT	PARAMOUNT	1963
P-10384	DONOVAN'S REEF	FORD	PARAMOUNT	1963
P-10385	COME BLOW YOUR HORN	YORKIN	PARAMOUNT	1963
P-10386	NUTTY PROFESSOR	LEWIS	PARAMOUNT	1963
P-10387	NEW KIND OF LOVE	SHAVELSON	PARAMOUNT	1963
P-10388	WHO'S BEEN SLEEPING IN MY BED?	MANN	PARAMOUNT	1963
P-10389	WHO'S MINDING THE STORE?	TASHLIN	PARAMOUNT	1964
P-10390	LADY IN A CAGE	GRAUMAN	PARAMOUNT	1964
P-10391	LOVE WITH THE PROPER STRANGER	MULLIGAN	PARAMOUNT	1963
P-10392	SEVEN DAYS IN MAY	FRANKENHEIMER	PARAMOUNT	1964
P-10394	PATSY	LEWIS	PARAMOUNT	1964
P-10395	DISORDERLY ORDERLY	TASHLIN	PARAMOUNT	1964
P-10396	SYLVIA	DOUGLAS	PARAMOUNT	1965
P-10398	NAKED PREY	WILDE	PARAMOUNT	1966
P-10400	SITUATION HOPELESS NOT SERIOUS	REINHARDT	PARAMOUNT	1965
P-10401	CARIBBEAN		PARAMOUNT	1952
P-10402	TROPIC ZONE	FOSTER	PARAMOUNT	1953
P-10403	VANQUISHED	LUDWIG	PARAMOUNT	1953
P-10404	JAMAICA-RUN	FOSTER	PARAMOUNT	1953
P-10405	SANGAREE	LUDWIG	PARAMOUNT	1953
P-10406	THOSE REDHEADS FROM SEATTLE	FOSTER	PARAMOUNT	1953
P-10407	JIVARO	LUDWIG	PARAMOUNT	1954
P-10408	RUN FOR COVER	RAY	PARAMOUNT	1954
P-10409	HELL'S ISLAND	KARLSON	PARAMOUNT	1954
P-10410	FAR HORIZONS	MATE	PARAMOUNT	1954
P-10411	LUCY GALLANT	PARRISH	PARAMOUNT	1955
P-10412	FAMILY JEWELS	LEWIS	PARAMOUNT	1965
P-10413	RED LINE 700	HAWKS	PARAMOUNT	1965

Movie Still Identification Book Ultimate Edition - Letters

CODE	TITLE/NAME	DIRECTOR/TYPE	STUDIO/DISTRIBUTOR	YEAR
P-10416	SECONDS	FRANKENHEIMER	PARAMOUNT	1966
P-10422	NIGHT OF THE GRIZZLY	PEVNEY	PARAMOUNT	1966
P-10423	EL DORADO	HAWKS	PARAMOUNT	1966
P-10424	LAST OF THE SECRET AGENTS	ABBOTT	PARAMOUNT	1966
P-10426	SWINGER	SIDNEY	PARAMOUNT	1966
P-10428	WARNING SHOT	KULIK	PARAMOUNT	1968
P-10430	SPIRIT IS WILLING	CASTLE	PARAMOUNT	1968
P-10431	RED TOMAHAWK	SPRINGSTEEN	PARAMOUNT	1968
P-10432	CAPER OF THE GOLDEN BULLS	ROUSE	PARAMOUNT	1967
P-10433	FORT UTAH	SELANDER	PARAMOUNT	1968
P-10435	BUSY BODY	CASTLE	PARAMOUNT	1968
P-10437	GUNN	EDWARDS	PARAMOUNT	1968
P-10439	PROJECT X	CASTLE	PARAMOUNT	1968
P-10440	PRESIDENT'S ANALYST	FLICKER	PARAMOUNT	1968
P-10443	NO WAY TO TREAT A LADY	SMIGHT	PARAMOUNT	1968
P-10444	ROSEMARY'S BABY	POLANSKI	PARAMOUNT	1968
P-10449	BUCKSKIN	MOORE	PARAMOUNT	1968
P-11002	LOVE LETTERS	DIETERLE	PARAMOUNT	1945
P-11003	YOU CAME ALONG	FARROW	PARAMOUNT	1945
P-11004	STRANGE LOVE OF MARTHA IVERS	MILESTONE	PARAMOUNT	1946
P-11005	SEARCHING WIND	DIETERLE	PARAMOUNT	1946
P-11006	PERFECT MARRIAGE	ALLEN	PARAMOUNT	1947
P-11007	DESERT FURY	ALLEN	PARAMOUNT	1947
P-11394	MISS SUSSIE SLAGLE'S	BERRY	PARAMOUNT	1945
P-11395	DUFFY'S TAVERN	WALKER	PARAMOUNT	1945
P-11396	VIRGINIAN	GILMORE	PARAMOUNT	1946
P-11397	LOST WEEKEND	WILDER	PARAMOUNT	1945
P-11398	HOLD THAT BLONDE	MARSHALL	PARAMOUNT	1945
P-11399	MASQUERADE IN MEXICO	LEISEN	PARAMOUNT	1945
P-11400	CROSS MY HEART	BERRY	PARAMOUNT	1946
P-11401	WELL GROOMED BRIDE	LANFIELD	PARAMOUNT	1946
P-11402	OUR HEARTS WERE GROWING UP	RUSSELL	PARAMOUNT	1946
P-11403	BLUE DAHLIA	MARSHALL	PARAMOUNT	1946
P-11404	TROUBLE WITH WOMEN	LANFIELD	PARAMOUNT	1947
P-11405	TO TEACH HIS OWN	LEISEN	PARAMOUNT	1946
P-11406	CALCUTTA	FARROW	PARAMOUNT	1947
P-11407	BLUE SKIES	HEISLER	PARAMOUNT	1946
P-11408	BRIDE WORE BOOTS	PICHEL	PARAMOUNT	1946
P-11409	IMPERFECT LADY	ALLEN	PARAMOUNT	1947
P-11410	MONSIEUR BEAUCAIRE	MARSHALL	PARAMOUNT	1946
P-11411	CALIFORNIA	FARROW	PARAMOUNT	1946
P-11412	EASY COME EASY GO	FARROW	PARAMOUNT	1947
P-11413	LADIES MAN	RUSSELL	PARAMOUNT	1947
P-11414	O.S.S.	PICHEL	PARAMOUNT	1946
P-11415	SUDDENLY IT'S SPRING	LEISEN	PARAMOUNT	1947
P-11416	PERILS OF PAULINE	MARSHALL	PARAMOUNT	1947
P-11417	WELCOME STRANGER	NUGENT	PARAMOUNT	1947
P-11418	WHERE THERE'S LIFE	LANFIELD	PARAMOUNT	1947
P-11419	EMPEROR WALTZ	WILDER	PARAMOUNT	1946
P-11420	UNCONQUERED	DEMILLE	PARAMOUNT	1947
P-11421	WILD HARVEST	GARNETT	PARAMOUNT	1947
P-11422	GOLDEN EARRINGS	LEISEN	PARAMOUNT	1947
P-11423	DEAR RUTH	RUSSELL	PARAMOUNT	1947
P-11424	VARIETY GIRL	MARSHALL	PARAMOUNT	1947
P-11425	BLAZE OF NOON	FARROW	PARAMOUNT	1947
P-11426	SAIGON	FENTON	PARAMOUNT	1948
P-11427	BIG CLOCK	FARROW	PARAMOUNT	1948
P-11428	MY OWN TRUE LOVE	BENNETT	PARAMOUNT	1948
P-11429	WHISPERING SMITH	FENTON	PARAMOUNT	1948
P-11430	DREAM GIRL	LEISEN	PARAMOUNT	1948
P-11431	NIGHT HAS A THOUSAND EYES	FARROW	PARAMOUNT	1948
P-11432	PALEFACE	MCLEOD	PARAMOUNT	1948
P-11433	CONNECTICUT YANKEE KING ARTHUR'S COURT	GARNETT	PARAMOUNT	1949
P-11434	BEYOND GLORY	FARROW	PARAMOUNT	1948
P-11435	SAINTED SISTERS	RUSSELL	PARAMOUNT	1948
P-11436	HAZARD	MARSHALL	PARAMOUNT	1948
P-11437	FOREIGN AFFAIR	WILDER	PARAMOUNT	1948
P-11438	SEALED VERDICT	ALLEN	PARAMOUNT	1948
P-11439	SONG OF SURRENDER	LEISEN	PARAMOUNT	1949
P-11440	ISN'T IT ROMANTIC	MCLEOD	PARAMOUNT	1948

Movie Still Identification Book Ultimate Edition - Letters

CODE	TITLE/NAME	DIRECTOR/TYPE	STUDIO/DISTRIBUTOR	YEAR
P-11441	GREAT GATSBY	NUGENT	PARAMOUNT	1949
P-11442	MISS TATLOCK'S MILLIONS	HAYDN	PARAMOUNT	1948
P-11443	SORROWFUL JONES	LANFIELD	PARAMOUNT	1949
P-11444	ACCUSED	DIETERLE	PARAMOUNT	1948
P-11445	ALIAS NICK BEAL	FARROW	PARAMOUNT	1949
P-11446	PAID IN FULL	DIETERLE	PARAMOUNT	1950
P-11447	STREETS OF LAREDO	FENTON	PARAMOUNT	1949
P-11448	CHICAGO DEADLINES	ALLEN	PARAMOUNT	1949
P-11449	SAMSON AND DELILAH	DEMILLE	PARAMOUNT	1950
P-11450	BRIDE OF VENGEANCE	LEISEN	PARAMOUNT	1949
P-11451	RED, HOT AND BLUE	FARROW	PARAMOUNT	1949
P-11452	DEAR WIFE	HAYDN	PARAMOUNT	1950
P-11453	CAPTAIN CAREY USA	LEISEN	PARAMOUNT	1950
P-11454	SUNSET BOULEVARD	WILDER	PARAMOUNT	1950
P-11455	COPPER CANYON	FARROW	PARAMOUNT	1950
P-11456	NO MAN OF HER OWN	LEISEN	PARAMOUNT	1950
P-11457	LET'S DANCE	MCLEOD	PARAMOUNT	1950
P-11458	APPOINTMENT WITH DANGER	ALLEN	PARAMOUNT	1951
P-11459	FANCY PANTS	MARSHALL	PARAMOUNT	1950
P-11460	SEPTEMBER AFFAIR	DIETERLE	PARAMOUNT	1950
P-11461	UNION STATION	MATE	PARAMOUNT	1950
P-11462	MR. MUSIC	HAYDN	PARAMOUNT	1950
P-11463	BRANDED	MATE	PARAMOUNT	1950
P-11464	REDHEAD AND THE COWBOY	FENTON	PARAMOUNT	1950
P-11465	MATING SEASON	LEISEN	PARAMOUNT	1951
P-11466	ACE IN THE HOLE (BIG CARNIVAL)	WILDER	PARAMOUNT	1951
P-11467	MOLLY (GOLDBERGS)	HART	PARAMOUNT	1951
P-11468	DEAR BRAT	SEITER	PARAMOUNT	1951
P-11469	HERE COMES THE GROOM	CAPRA	PARAMOUNT	1951
P-11470	DARLING HOW COULD YOU	LEISEN	PARAMOUNT	1951
P-11471	WHEN WORLDS COLLIDE	MATE	PARAMOUNT	1951
P-11472	SUBMARINE COMMAND	FARROW	PARAMOUNT	1951
P-11473	GREATEST SHOW ON EARTH	DEMILLE	PARAMOUNT	1951
P-11474	MY FAVORITE SPY	MCLEOD	PARAMOUNT	1951
P-11475	THUNDER IN THE EAST	VIDOR	PARAMOUNT	1953
P-11476	RHUBARB	LUBIN	PARAMOUNT	1951
P-11477	AARON SLICK FROM PUNKIN CRICK	BINYON	PARAMOUNT	1952
P-11478	SILVER CITY	HASKIN	PARAMOUNT	1951
P-11479	SAVAGE	MARSHALL	PARAMOUNT	1952
P-11480	ANYTHING CAN HAPPEN	SEATON	PARAMOUNT	1952
P-11481	DENVER AND RIO GRANDE	HASKIN	PARAMOUNT	1952
P-11482	SOMEBODY LOVES ME	BRECHER	PARAMOUNT	1952
P-11483	TURNING POINT (THIS IS DYNAMITE*)	DIETERLE	PARAMOUNT	1952
P-11484	ATOMIC CITY	HOPPER	PARAMOUNT	1952
P-11485	JUST FOR YOU	NUGENT	PARAMOUNT	1952
P-11486	STARS ARE SINGING	TAUROG	PARAMOUNT	1953
P-11487	BOTANY BAY	FARROW	PARAMOUNT	1953
P-11488	OFF LIMITS	MARSHALL	PARAMOUNT	1953
P-11489	WAR OF THE WORLDS	HASKIN	PARAMOUNT	1953
P-11490	STALAG 17	WILDER	PARAMOUNT	1953
P-11491	HURRICANE SMITH	HOPPER	PARAMOUNT	1953
P-11492	GIRLS OF PLEASURE ISLAND	GANZER, HERBERT	PARAMOUNT	1953
P-11493	PONY EXPRESS	HOPPER	PARAMOUNT	1953
P-11494	LITTLE BOY LOST	SEATON	PARAMOUNT	1953
P-11495	HOUDINI	MARSHALL	PARAMOUNT	1953
P-11496	FOREVER FEMALE	RAPPER	PARAMOUNT	1953
P-11497	ARROWHEAD	WARREN	PARAMOUNT	1953
P-11498	ELEPHANT WALK	DIETERLE	PARAMOUNT	1954
P-11499	RED GARTERS	MARSHALL	PARAMOUNT	1953
P-11500	SECRET OF THE INCAS	HOPPER	PARAMOUNT	1954
P-11501	FLIGHT TO TANGIER	WARREN	PARAMOUNT	1953
P-11502	NAKED JUNGLE	HASKIN	PARAMOUNT	1954
P-11503	CASANOVA'S BIG NIGHT	MCLEOD	PARAMOUNT	1954
P-11504	ALASKA SEAS	HOPPER	PARAMOUNT	1954
P-11505	WHITE CHRISTMAS	CURTIZ	PARAMOUNT	1954
P-11506	SABRINA	WILDER	PARAMOUNT	1954
P-11507	CONQUEST OF SPACE	HASKIN	PARAMOUNT	1955
P-11508	BRIDGES AT TOKO-RI	ROBSON	PARAMOUNT	1955
P-11509	COUNTRY GIRL	SEATON	PARAMOUNT	1954
P-11510	STRATEGIC AIR COMMAND	MANN	PARAMOUNT	1955

Movie Still Identification Book Ultimate Edition - Letters

CODE	TITLE/NAME	DIRECTOR/TYPE	STUDIO/DISTRIBUTOR	YEAR
P-11511	TO CATCH A THIEF	HITCHCOCK	PARAMOUNT	1955
P-11512	WE'RE NO ANGELS	CURTIZ	PARAMOUNT	1955
P-11513	DESPERATE HOURS	WYLER	PARAMOUNT	1955
P-11514	VAGABOND KING	CURTIS	PARAMOUNT	1956
P-11515	TEN COMMANDMENTS	DEMILLE	PARAMOUNT	1956
P-11516	SCARLET HOUR	CURTIZ	PARAMOUNT	1956
P-11517	PROUD AND THE PROFANE	SEATON	PARAMOUNT	1956
P-11518	MOUNTAIN	DMYTRYK	PARAMOUNT	1956
P-11519	LEATHER SAINT	GANZER	PARAMOUNT	1956
P-11520	FUNNY FACE	DONEN	PARAMOUNT	1957
P-11521	THREE VIOLENT PEOPLE	MATE	PARAMOUNT	1957
P-11522	OMAR KHAYYAM	DIETERLE	PARAMOUNT	1957
P-11523	LONELY MAN	LEVIN	PARAMOUNT	1957
P-11524	SEARCH FOR BRIDEY MURPHY	LANGLEY	PARAMOUNT	1957
P-11525	FEAR STRIKES OUT	MULLIGAN	PARAMOUNT	1957
P-11526	SHORT CUT TO HELL	CAGNEY	PARAMOUNT	1957
P-11527	BUCCANEER	QUINN	PARAMOUNT	1958
P-11528	ST. LOUIS BLUES	REISNER	PARAMOUNT	1958
P-11529	BLACK ORCHID	RITT	PARAMOUNT	1959
P-11530	I MARRED MONSTER FROM OUTER SPACE	FOWLER JR.	PARAMOUNT	1958
P-11531	THAT KIND OF WOMAN	LUMET	PARAMOUNT	1959
P-11532	YOUNG CAPTIVES	KERSHNER	PARAMOUNT	1959
P-11533	HANGMAN	CURTIZ	PARAMOUNT	1959
P-11535	BREATH OF SCANDAL	CURTIZ	PARAMOUNT	1960
P-11536	WALK LIKE A DRAGON	CLAVELL	PARAMOUNT	1960
P-11537	BLUEPRINT FOR ROBBERY	HOPPER	PARAMOUNT	1961
P-11538	MAN-TRAP	O'BRIEN	PARAMOUNT	1961
P-11539	TOO LATE BLUES	CASSAVETES	PARAMOUNT	1962
P-11540	HELL IS FOR HEROES	SIEGEL	PARAMOUNT	1962
P-11543	MY SIX LOVES	CHAMPION	PARAMOUNT	1963
P-11544	CARPETBAGGERS	DMYTRYK	PARAMOUNT	1964
P-11545	WHERE LOVE HAS GONE	DMYTRYK	PARAMOUNT	1964
P-11547	SLENDER THREAD	POLLACK	PARAMOUNT	1966
P-11548	NEVADA SMITH	HATHAWAY	PARAMOUNT	1966
P-11550	CHUKA	DOUGLAS	PARAMOUNT	1968
P-11551	BAREFOOT IN THE PARK	SAKS	PARAMOUNT	1967
P-11553	WILL PENNY	GRIES	PARAMOUNT	1968
P-14412	CHINATOWN	POLANSKI	PARAMOUNT	1974
P-19347	DESIRE UNDER THE ELMS	MANN	PARAMOUNT	1958
P-21019	SO EVIL MY LOVE	ALLEN	PARAMOUNT	1948
P&P	PRINCE AND THE PAUPER	GEISINGER	CHILDHOOD PROD.	1969
PA	DOUBLE DANGER	LANDERS	RKO	1938
PA	MADE FOR EACH OTHER (UK)	CROMWELL	UNITED ARTISTS	1939
PA	PAM AUSTIN	portrait	UNIVERSAL	
PA	PAN AMERICANA	AUER	RKO	1945
PA	PAPILLON	SCHAFFNER	ALLIED ARTISTS	1973
PA	PARISIENNE (FR)	BOISROND	UNITED ARTISTS	1957
PA	PASSION	GODARD	UNITED ARTISTS	1982
PA	PATRICIA ALPHIN	portrait	UNIVERSAL	
PA	PATTY ANDREWS (ANDREWS SISTERS)	portrait	UNIVERSAL	1940s
PA	PAUL ANKA	portrait	FOX	1960s-70s
PA	PONI ADAMS (aka JANE ADAMS)	portrait	UNIVERSAL	
PA	POSTMARK FOR DANGER (UK: PORTRAIT OF ALISON)	GREEN	RKO	1955
PA	PRIVATE ANGELO (UK)	ANDERSON, USTINOV	PATHE	1949
PA	SHADOWS OF THE ORIENT	LYNWOOD	MONOGRAM	1935
PA2	RUTHLESS	ULMER	EAGLE LION	1948
PA-121	PLANET OF THE APES	SCHAFFNER	20th CENTURY FOX	1968
PAD	PROMISE AT DAWN	DASSIN	AVCO EMBASSY	1970
PAG	CLOWN MUST LAUGH (UK: PAGLIACCI)	GRUNE	GAUMONT BRITISH	1936
PAR-1	HAPPY BIRTHDAY	PARROTT	FOX FILM	1929
PAR-BR1	HATTER'S CASTLE (UK)	COMFORT	PARAMOUNT	1942
PAS	PLAY IT AGAIN SAM	ROSS	PARAMOUNT	1972
PB	PARIS BLUES	RITT	UNITED ARTISTS	1961
PB	PATTI BRADY	portrait	WARNER BROS	1940s
PB	PATTI BRILL	portrait	RKO	
PB	PAUL BROOKS (NEE PAUL BRINKMAN)	portrait	WARNER BROS	1940s
PB	PAYMENT IN BLOOD (IT)	CASTELLARI	COLUMBIA	1968
PB	PECK'S BAD BOY WITH THE CIRCUS	CLINE	RKO	1938
PB	PETER BROWN	portrait	WARNER BROS	
PB	PHYLLIS BROOKS	portrait	RKO	

Movie Still Identification Book Ultimate Edition - Letters

CODE	TITLE/NAME	DIRECTOR/TYPE	STUDIO/DISTRIBUTOR	YEAR
PB	PHYLLIS BROOKS	portrait	UNIV	
PB	PLEASURE BUYERS	WITHEY	WARNER BROS	1925
PB	POINT BREAK	BIGELOW	20th CENTURY FOX	1991
PB	POSSE	DOUGLAS	PARAMOUNT	1975
PB	POWDER MY BACK	DEL RUTH	WARNER BROS	1928
PB	PRINCESS BABA (aka PRINCESS BAIGUM)	portrait		late 30s
PB	PRIVATE BENJAMIN	ZIEFF	WARNER BROS	1980
PB-2	SPY FOR A DAY (UK)	ZAMPI	PARAMOUNT BRITISH	1940
PB-3	FRENCH WITHOUT TEARS (UK)	ASQUITH	PARAMOUNT	1941
PBA	PARACHUTE BATALLION	GOODWINS	RKO	1941
PBF	FOREMAN WENT TO FRANCE (SOMEWHERE IN FRANCE)	FREND	UNITED ARTISTS	1942
PC	ALEXANDRA (UK: PRINCESS CHARMING)	ELVEY	GAUMONT	1934
PC	LURED (PERSONAL COLUMN)	SIRK	UNITED ARTISTS	1947
PC	PAT CLARK	portrait	WARNER BROS	
PC	PAT CROWLEY	portrait	UNIV	
PC	PATTI CHANDLER	portrait	AIP	1960s
PC	PAULA/PAULE CROSET (aka PAULA/RITA CORDAY)	portrait	UNIVERSAL	1940s-50s
PC	PEGGIE/PEGGY CASTLE	portrait	UNIVERSAL	
PC	PETER COE	portrait	UNIVERSAL	
PC	PETULA CLARK	portrait		
PC	PHANTOM OF CRESTWOOD	RUBEN	RKO	1932
PC	PHAROAH'S CURSE	SHOLEM	UNITED ARTISTS	1957
PC	PHILIP CAREY	portrait	COL, WARNER BROS	
PC	PHYLLIS CALVERT	portrait	UNIVERSAL	1940s
PC	PHYLLIS COATES	portrait	WARNER BROS	
PC	PLAY IT COOL (UK)	WINNER	ALLIED ARTISTS	1962
PC	POOR COW (UK)	LOACH	NATIONAL GENERAL	1967
PC	PRODUCERS CORPORATION OF AMERICA		UNITED ARTISTS	
PC	SILVER LODE	DWAN	RKO	1954
PC-126	FRIEND HUSBAND (WHY MARRY?)	HOWE	PATHE EXCHANGE	1924
PC-9000	KNICKERBOCKER HOLIDAY	BROWN	UNITED ARTISTS	1944
PCA-1	POWER DRIVE	HOGAN	PARAMOUNT	1941
PCA-2	FORCED LANDING	WILES	PARAMOUNT	1941
PCA-3	FLYING BLIND	MCDONALD	PARAMOUNT	1941
PCA-4	NO HANDS ON THE CLOCK	MCDONALD	PARAMOUNT	1942
PCA-5	TORPEDO BOAT	RAWLINS	PARAMOUNT	1942
PCA-6	I LIVE ON DANGER	WHITE	PARAMOUNT	1942
PCA-7	WILDCAT	MCDONALD	PARAMOUNT	1942
PCA-8	WRECKING CREW	MCDONALD	PARAMOUNT	1943
PCA-9	SUBMARINE ALERT	MCDONALD	PARAMOUNT	1943
PCA-10	HIGH EXPLOSIVE	MCDONALD	PARAMOUNT	1943
PCA-11	AERIAL GUNNER	PINE	PARAMOUNT	1943
PCA-12	TORNADO	BERKE	PARAMOUNT	1943
PCA-13	MINDSWEEPER	BERKE	PARAMOUNT	1943
PCA-14	TIMBER QUEEN	MCDONALD	PARAMOUNT	1944
PCA-15	NAVY WAY	BERKE	PARAMOUNT	1944
PCA-16	TAKE IT BIG	MCDONALD	PARAMOUNT	1944
PCA-17	GAMBLER'S CHOICE	MCDONALD	PARAMOUNT	1944
PCA-18	ONE BODY TOO MANY	MCDONALD	PARAMOUNT	1945
PCA-80	ALASKA-HIGHWAY	MCDONALD	PARAMOUNT	1943
PCH	PORK CHOP HILL	MILESTONE	UNITED ARTISTS	1959
PCU	PCU	BOCHNER	20th CENTURY FOX	1994
PCY	PERCY (UK)	THOMAS	MGM	1970
PD	PAINTED DESERT	HOWARD	RKO	1938
PD	PAUL DOUGLAS	portrait	RKO	1950s
PD	PAULA DREW	portrait	UNIVERSAL	1940s
PD	PAULETTE DUVAL	portrait	MGM	
PD	PEG OF OLD DRURY (UK)	WILCOX	PARAMOUNT	1935
PD	PEGGY DIGGINS	portrait	WARNER BROS	early 40s
PD	PEGGY DOW	portrait	UNIVERSAL	
PD	PHILIP DORN	portrait	RKO, REPUBLIC, WARNER	
PD	PHILIP DORN	portrait	UNIV	
PD	PIPE DREAMS	VERONA	AVCO EMBASSY	1976
PD	PIT OF DARKNESS (UK)	COMFORT	BUTCHER'S	1961
PD	PLAY DIRTY (UK)	DE TOTH	UNITED ARTISTS	1969
PD	POACHER'S DAUGHTER (UK: SALLY'S IRISH ROGUE)	POLLOCK	SHOWCORPORATION	1958
PD	POLICE DOG STORY	CAHN	UNITED ARTISTS	1961
PD	PRISCILLA DEAN	portrait	UNIVERSAL	1910s-20s
PD	PRIVATE DETECTIVE	SMITH	WARNER BROS	1939
PD	PROMISES IN THE DARK	HELLMAN	ORION	1979

Movie Still Identification Book Ultimate Edition - Letters

CODE	TITLE/NAME	DIRECTOR/TYPE	STUDIO/DISTRIBUTOR	YEAR
PD-1	FIRE OVER ENGLAND (UK)	HOWARD	UNITED ARTISTS (UK)	1937
PD2	TROOPSHIP (UK: FAREWELL AGAIN)	WHELAN	UNITED ARTISTS	1937
PDL	GATES OF PARIS (FR: PORTE DES LILAS)	CLAIR	LOPERT	1957
PDL	PEG OF OLD DRURY (UK)	WILCOX	UNITED ARTISTS	1935
PE	COHENS AND KELLYS IN HOLLYWOOD	DILLON	UNIVERSAL	1932
PE	PATRICIA ELLIS	portrait	WARNER BROS	
PE	PENNY EDWARDS	portrait	WARNER BROS	
PE	PEOPLE'S ENEMY (RACKETEERS R1947)	WILBUR	RKO	1935
PE	PUBLIC ENEMY	WELLMAN	WARNER BROS	1931
PE	PUMPKIN EATER (UK)	CLAYTON	COLUMBIA	1964
PE6	FACES IN THE DARK (UK)	EADY	SCHOENFELD	1960
PEER	TOUGHEST GUN IN TOMBSTONE	BELLAMY	UNITED ARTISTS	1958
PEK	55 DAYS AT PEKING	RAY	ALLIED ARTISTS	1963
PEL	PETTICOAT LARCENY	HOLMES	RKO	1943
PER	PERFORMANCE (UK)	CAMMELL, ROEG	WARNER BROS	1970
PET	PETULIA	LESTER	WARNER BROS	1968
PEWE	PERC WESTMORE	portrait	WARNER BROS	1920s-50s
PF	FEMALE FIENDS (UK: STRANGE AWAKENING)	TULLY	CINEMA ASSOCIATES	1958
PF	HIGH FURY (UK: WHITE CRADLE INN)	FRENCH	UNITED ARTISTS	1947
PF	MRS. FITZHERBERT (UK)	TULLY	STRATFORD	1947
PF	PAULINE FREDERICK	portrait	ROBERTSON-COLE, WARNER	
PF	PERFECT FRIDAY (UK)	HALL	CHEVRON	1970
PF	PHYLLIS FRASER	portrait		
PF	PRESTON FOSTER	portrait	FN, RKO	
pf	THEY RAID BY NIGHT	BENNET	PRC	1942
PF	WOLVES OF THE UNDERWORLD (PUPPETS OF FATE)	COOPER	UNITED ARTISTS	1933
PF1	PYGMALION (UK)	ASQUITH, HOWARD	MGM	1938
PF4	COHEN AND KELLY'S IN TROUBLE	STEVENS	UNIVERSAL	1933
PF4	DO YOU KNOW THIS VOICE? (UK)	NESBITT	COLUMBIA	1964
PF8	HAIR OF THE DOG (UK)	BISHOP	RANK	1962
PF-437	PARIS FOLLIES OF 1956	GOODWINS	ALLIED ARTISTS	1955
PFL	PLACE FOR LOVERS	DESICA	MGM	1969
PFR	PISTOL FOR RINGO	TESSARI	EMBASSY	1966
PFX	PHOEBE FOSTER	portrait	RKO	
PG	PAGE MISS GLORY	LEROY	WARNER BROS	1935
PG	PAPER GALLOWS (UK: TORMENT)	GUILLERMIN	EAGLE-LION	1950
PG	PATHS OF GLORY	KUBRICK	UNITED ARTISTS	1957
PG	PETER GRAVES	portrait		
PG	PLEASURE GIRLS (UK)	O'HARA	TIMES	1965
PG	PRIZE OF GOLD (UK)	ROBSON	COLUMBIA	1955
PG	PROBLEM GIRLS	DUPONT	COLUMBIA	1953
PGP	SONG OF SONGS	MAMOULIAN	PARAMOUNT	1933
PH	PACIFIC HEIGHTS	SCHLESINGER	20th CENTURY FOX	1990
PH	PARIS HOLIDAY	OSWALD	UNITED ARTISTS	1958
PH	PARTY HUSBAND	BADGER	WARNER BROS	1931
PH	PASSPORT FROM HONG KONG	LEDERMAN	WARNER BROS	1941
PH	PASTOR HALL (UK)	BOULTING	UNITED ARTISTS	1940
PH	PATRICIA HALL	portrait	UNIVERSAL	
PH	PATTY HALE (aka DIANA HALE/JEANNE)	portrait	WARNER BROS	early 40s
PH	PAUL HARTMAN	portrait	RKO	
PH	PAUL HENREID	portrait	RKO, WARNER BROS	
PH	PEGGY HYLAND	portrait		
PH	PENTHOUSE (UK)	COLLINSON	PARAMOUNT	1967
PH	PHAEDRA	DASSIN	LOPERT	1962
PH	PHIL HARRIS	portrait	MCA RECORDS	
PH	PHIL HARVEY	portrait	UNIVERSAL	
PH	PHYLLIS HAVER	portrait	PDC, PATHE	
PH	PHYLLIS HAVER	portrait	MGM	
PH	PISTOL HARVEST	SELANDER	RKO	1951
PH	PLACES IN THE HEART	BENTON	TRI STAR	1984
PH	PRIVATE HELL 36	SIEGEL	FILMAKERS	1954
PHA	PROMISE HER ANYTHING (UK)	HILLER	PARAMOUNT	1965
PH-IV	PHASE IV	BASS	PARAMOUNT	1974
PH-M	PIRATES OF THE HALF MOON		COLUMBIA	1972
PHST	PURE HELL OF ST. TRINIAN'S (UK)	LAUNDER	CONTINENTAL	1961
PHX	PHILLIPS HOLMES	portrait	MGM	
PI	I WANT MY MAN	HILLYER	WARNER BROS	1925
PI	LURE OF THE WASTELAND	FRASER	MONOGRAM	1939
PI	PRESUMED INNOCENT	PAKULA	WARNER BROS	1990
PI	PRIVATE INFORMATION (UK)	MCDONELL	MONARCH	1952

Movie Still Identification Book Ultimate Edition - Letters

CODE	TITLE/NAME	DIRECTOR/TYPE	STUDIO/DISTRIBUTOR	YEAR
PII	PENITENTIARY II	FANAKA	UNITED ARTISTS	1982
PIN	PINOCCHIO (t)	FERGUSON, HEE	RKO	1940
PIP	PRETTY IN PINK	DEUTCH	PARAMOUNT	1986
PISK	PITFALL	DE TOTH	UNITED ARTISTS	1948
PIT	PARTNERS IN TIME	NIGH	RKO	1946
PIT	PITFALL	DE TOTH	UNITED ARTISTS	1948
PIT	TERROR IN THE CITY	BARON	ALLIED ARTISTS	1964
PI-YC	YELLOW CARGO	WILBUR	GRAND	1936
PJ	DEVIL'S IMPOSTER (UK: POPE JOAN)	ANDERSON	COLUMBIA	1972
PJ	PHANTOM JUSTICE	THOMAS	FBO	1924
PJ	POLO JOE	MCGANN	WARNER BROS	1936
PJ	PORTRAIT OF JENNIE	DIETERLE	SELZNICK	1948
PJB	PRIME OF MISS JEAN BRODIE (UK)	NEAME	20TH CENTURY FOX	1969
PK	FIVE DAYS/US: PAID TO KILL (UK)	TULLY	LIPPERT	1954
PK	MR. PEEK-A-BOO	BOYER	UNITED ARTISTS	1951
PK	PAID TO KILL (UK: FIVE DAYS)	TULLY	LIPPERT	1954
PK	PATRIC KNOWLES	portrait	RKO, UNIV	
PK	PATRIC KNOWLES	portrait	WARNER BROS	
PK	PATSY KELLY	portrait	MGM	
PK	PAUL KELLY	portrait	RKO	
PK	PEGGY KNUDSEN	portrait	WARNER BROS	
PK	PERCY KILBRIDE	portrait	UNIV	
PK	PERT KELTON	portrait	RKO	
PK	PHYLLIS KIRK	portrait	WARNER BROS	
PK	PRELUDE TO A KISS	RENE	20th CENTURY FOX	1992
P-K	PORKY'S	CLARK	20th CENTURY FOX	1982
PL	DAUGHTER OF DR. JEKYLL	ULMER	ALLIED ARTISTS	1957
PL	I, THE JURY	ESSEX	UNITED ARTISTS	1953
PL	PACIFIC LINER	LANDERS	RKO	1939
PL	PALMER LEE	portrait	UNIV	
PL	PAPER LION	MARCH	UNITED ARTISTS	1968
PL	PARK AVENUE LOGGER	HOWARD	RKO	1937
PL	PARK LANE PRODUCTIONS	studio		
PL	PAULA LANE	portrait	PARAMOUNT	
PL	PEGGY LEE	portrait	WARNER BROS	
PL	PHANTOM LIGHT (UK)	POWELL	GAUMONT BRITISH	1935
PL	PIPER LAURIE	portrait	UNIVERSAL	
PL	PLATOON	STONE	ORION	1986
PL	PLEASURE LOVERS (UK: NAKED FURY)	SAUNDERS	JOSEPH BRENNER	1959
PL	POMMER-LAUGHTON PRODUCTIONS	studio	PARAMOUNT	
PL	PRIDE AND THE PASSION	KRAMER	UNITED ARTISTS	1957
PL	PRISCILLA LANE	portrait	FN/WARNER BROS,	
PL-1	BEACHCOMBER (UK: VESSEL OF WRATH)	POMMER	PARAMOUNT	1938
PL-2	JAMAICA INN (UK)	HITCHCOCK	PARAMOUNT	1939
PL-3	SIDEWALKS OF LONDON (UK: ST. MARTIN'S LANE)	WHELAN	PARAMOUNT	1939
PLA	PLAYMATES	BUTLER	RKO	1941
PLH	PETER LIND HAYES	portrait	RKO, UNIVERSAL	
PLX	COSMIC MONSTER (UK: STRANGE WORLD OF PLANET X)	GUNN	DCA	1958
PM	10:30 P.M. SUMMER	DASSIN	LOPERT	1966
PM	DANGEROUS CARGO (UK)	HARLOW	MONARCH	1954
PM	PANDEMONIUM	SOLE	UNITED ARTISTS	1982
PM	PAPER MOON	BOGDANOVICH	PARAMOUNT	1973
PM	PARIS MODEL	GREEN	COLUMBIA	1953
PM	PASSAGE TO MARSEILLE	CURTIZ	WARNER BROS	1944
PM	PATRICE MUNSEL	portrait	UNITED ARTISTS	
PM	PATRICIA MEDINA	portrait	UNIV (40S-50S)	
PM	PATRICIA MORISON	portrait	UNIV	
PM	PATTERNS	COOK	UNITED ARTISTS	1956
PM	PAUL AND MICHELLE	GILBERT	PARAMOUNT	1974
PM	PAUL MUNI	portrait	WARNER BROS	
PM	PEACEMAKER	POST	UNITED ARTISTS	1956
PM	PEGGY MORAN	portrait	UNIVERSAL, WARNER BROS	
PM	PENGUIN POOL MURDER	ARCHAINBAUD	RKO	1932
PM	PETER MANN	portrait	UNIV	
PM	PICTURE MOMMY DEAD	GORDON	EMBASSY	1966
PM	POCKETFUL OF MIRACLES	CAPRA	UNITED ARTISTS	1961
PM	SMALL CHANGE (FR)	TRUFFANT	NEW WORLD PICTURES	1976
PM1	MOONLIGHT SONATA (UK)	MENDES	UNITED ARTISTS	1937
PMC	PANDA AND THE MAGIC SERPENT (t) (JAP)	OKABE	GLOBE	1958
PMC	PATTI MCCARTY	portrait		

Movie Still Identification Book Ultimate Edition - Letters

CODE	TITLE/NAME	DIRECTOR/TYPE	STUDIO/DISTRIBUTOR	YEAR
PMP	PARDON MY PAST	FENTON	COLUMBIA	1945
PMX	POLLY MORAN	portrait	MGM	
PN	GIVE ME THE STARS (UK)	ROGERS	ANGLO-AMERICAN	1945
PN	PAUL NEWMAN	portrait	UNIV	
PN	POLICE NURSE	DEXTER	20th CENTURY FOX	1963
PN	PRIVATE NAVY OF SGT. O'FARRELL	TASHLIN	UNITED ARTISTS	1968
PN	PROM NIGHT	LYNCH	AVCO EMBASSY	1980
PND	PEOPLE NEXT DOOR	GREENE	AVCO EMBASSY	1970
PNP	PANIC IN NEEDLE PARK	SCHATZBERG	20th CENTURY FOX	1971
PO	MURDER ON A BRIDLE PATH	HAMILTON, KILLY	RKO	1936
PO	PAT O'BRIEN	portrait	WARNER BROS	
PO	PIRATES OF THE PRAIRIE	BRETHERTON	RKO	1942
PO	PLACE OF ONE'S OWN (UK)	KNOWLES	EAGLE-LION	1945
PO	PRINCESS O'ROURKE	KRASNA	WARNER BROS	1943
PO	WOMAN REBELS	SANDRICH	RKO	1936
POA	POSTMARK FOR DANGER (UK: PORTRAIT OF ALISON)	GREEN	RKO	1956
POB	PAT O'BRIEN	portrait	RKO	1940s
POC	PATSY O'CONNOR	portrait	UNIV	
POC	PIRATES OF CAPRI	ULMER	UNITED ARTISTS	1949
POC	PIRATES OF THE COAST	PAOLELLA	SEVEN ARTS	1960
POC	PORT OF CALL (SWE: HAMNSTAD)	BERGMAN	JANUS	1948
POH	PURSUIT OF HAPPINESS	MULLIGAN	COLUMBIA	1971
POJ	PHANTOM OF THE JUNGLE	BENNET	LIPPERT	1955
POL	POLLYANNA	SWIFT	BUENA VISTA	1960
POM	PAT O'MALLEY	portrait	METRO	1910s-50s
POR	PEACH-O-RENO	SEITER	RKO	1931
POS	PHANTOM OF SOHO (GER)	GOTTLIEB	COLUMBIA	1964
PP	BEHOLD THE MAN! (UK)	RILLA	PHILOMENA	1951
PP	COURAGEOUS MR.PENN (UK: PENN OF PENNSYLVANIA)	COMFORT	JH HOFFBERG	1942
PP	CROSSED SWORDS	FLEISCHER	WARNER BROS	1977
PP	GIRL ON THE PIER (UK)	COMFORT	APEX	1953
PP	HUK!	BARWELL	UNITED ARTISTS	1956
PP	PAPILLON	SCHAFFNER	COLUMBIA	R
PP	PATHER PANCHALI (IND)	RAY	EDWARD HARRISON	1955
PP	PENNY POOL (UK)	BLACK	MACUNIAN	1937
PP	PETER PAN	GERONIMI, JACKSON	RKO	1953
PP	PEYTON PLACE - TV SERIES	VARIOUS	20th CENTURY FOX	1964
PP	PICKWICK PAPERS (UK)	LANGLEY	MAYER-KINGSLEY	1952
PP	POISON PEN (UK)	STEIN	REPUBLIC	1941
PP	POPI	ARKIN	UNITED ARTISTS	1969
PP	PRESSURE POINT	CORNFIELD	UNITED ARTISTS	1962
PP	PRIDE AND THE PASSION	KRAMER	UNITED ARTISTS	1957
PP	PRIMROSE PATH	LA CAVA	RKO	1940
PP	PRINCE AND THE PAUPER	KEIGHLEY	FIRST NATIONAL	1937
PP	PRIVATE PROPERTY	STEVENS	CITATION	1960
PP	PRIVATE'S PROGRESS (UK)	BOULTING	DCA	1956
PP	PROMISES! PROMISES!	DONOVAN	NTD	1963
PP	PUBLIC PIGEON NO. 1	MCLEOD	RKO	1956
PP102	IDOL OF PARIS (UK)	ARLISS	WARNER BROS	1948
PP-B	POUND PUPPIES LEGEND OF BIG PAW (t)	DECELLES	CAROLCO, TRI STAR	1988
PPM	PENGUIN POOL MURDER	ARCHAINBAUD	RKO	1932
PPSA	PINK PANTHER STRIKES AGAIN	EDWARDS	UNITED ARTISTS	1976
PPX1	MARTHA MANSFIELD	portrait	PYRAMID PICTURES	
PQ	PIRATES OF THE PRAIRIE	BRETHERTON	RKO	1942
PR	AFTER THE BALL (UK)	BENNETT	IFD	1957
PR	GREAT PLANE ROBBERY	CAHN	UNITED ARTISTS	1950
PR	I PROMISED TO PAY (UK: PAYROLL)	HAYERS	MONOGRAM	1961
PR	PARK ROW	FULLER	UNITED ARTISTS	1952
PR	PATRICIA ROC	portrait	RKO	
PR	PATRICIA ROC	portrait	UNIVERSAL	
PR	PEGGY RYAN	portrait	UNIVERSAL	
PR	PLUNDER ROAD	CORNFIELD	20th CENTURY FOX	1957
PR	POWDERSMOKE RANGE	FOX	RKO	1935
PR	PRIDE AND THE PASSION	KRAMER	UNITED ARTISTS	1957
PR	PRISCILLA ROSE	portrait	UNIVERSAL	
PR	PRUDENCE AND THE PILL	NEAME	20th CENTURY FOX	1968
PR1	NOVEL AFFAIR (UK: PASSIONATE STRANGER)	BOX	CONTINENTAL	1957
PRC-101	PRISONER OF JAPAN	RIPLEY	PRC	1942
PRC-114	VALLEY OF VENGEANCE	NEWFIELD	PRC	1944
PRC-115	FUZZY SETTLES DOWN	NEWFIELD	PRC	1944

Movie Still Identification Book Ultimate Edition - Letters

CODE	TITLE/NAME	DIRECTOR/TYPE	STUDIO/DISTRIBUTOR	YEAR
PRC-119	OATH OF VENGEANCE	NEWFIELD	PRC	1944
PRC-120	HIS BROTHER'S GHOST	NEWFIELD	PRC	1945
PRC-122	SHADOWS OF DEATH	NEWFIELD	PRC	1945
PRC-123	GANGSTER'S DEN	NEWFIELD	PRC	1945
PRC-126	STAGECOACH OUTLAWS	NEWFIELD	PRC	1945
PRC-127	BORDER BADMEN	NEWFIELD	PRC	1945
PRC-128	FIGHTING BILL CARSON	NEWFIELD	PRC	1945
PRC-130	PRAIRIE RUSTLERS	NEWFIELD	PRC	1945
PRC-131	LIGHTNING RAIDERS	NEWFIELD	PRC	1946
PRC-133	TERRORS ON HORSEBACK	NEWFIELD	PRC	1946
PRC-134	GENTLEMEN WITH GUNS	NEWFIELD	PRC	1946
PRC-135	LARCENY IN HER HEART	NEWFIELD	PRC	1946
PRC-136	GHOST OF HIDDEN VALLEY	NEWFIELD	PRC	1946
PRC-138	PRAIRIE BADMEN	NEWFIELD	PRC	1946
PRC-139	OVERLAND RIDERS	NEWFIELD	PRC	1946
PRC-140	OUTLAWS OF THE PLAINS	NEWFIELD	PRC	1946
PRC-163	LONE RIDER RIDES ON	NEWFIELD	PRC	1941
PRC-177	SWING HOSTESS	NEWFIELD	PRC	1944
PRC-218	BOMBS OVER BURMA	LEWIS	PRC	1942
PRC-221	YANK IN LIBYA	HERMAN	PRC	1942
PRC-354	BORDER BUCKAROOS	DRAKE	PRC	1943
PRC-407	DANGER! WOMEN AT WORK	NEWFIELD	PRC	1943
PRC-411	HARVEST MELODY	NEWFIELD	PRC	1943
PRC-412	GIRL FROM MONTERREY	FOX	PRC	1943
PRC-417	DIXIE JAMBOREE	CABANNE	PRC	1944
PRC-418	LADY IN THE DEATH HOUSE	SEKELY	PRC	1944
PRC-423	SEVEN DOORS TO DEATH	CLIFTON	PRC	1944
PRC-428	ENCHANTED FOREST	LANDERS	PRC	1945
PRC-443	APOLOGY FOR MURDER	NEWFIELD	PRC	1945
PRC-444	QUEEN OF BURLESQUE	NEWFIELD	PRC	1946
PRC-445	DANNY BOY	MORSE	PRC	1946
PRC-446	MASK OF DIIJON	LANDERS	PRC	1946
PRC-451	DEVIL BAT'S DAUGHTER	WISBAR	PRC	1946
PRC-452	WIFE OF MONTE CRISTO	ULMER	PRC	1946
PRC-456	SPOOK TOWN	CLIFTON	PRC	1944
PRC-477	BLUEBEARD	ULMER	PRC	1944
PRC-479	WHEN THE LIGHTS GO ON AGAIN	HOWARD	PRC	1944
PRC-480	TOWN WENT WILD	MURPHY	PRC	1944
PRC-481	GREAT MIKE	FOX	PRC	1944
PRC-484	MAN WHO WALKED ALONE	CABANNE	PRC	1945
PRC-485	CRIME INC aka GANGSTER KELLY	LANDERS	PRC	1945
PRC-489	PHANTOM OF 42ND STREET	HERMAN	PRC	1945
PRC-493	DETOUR	ULMER	PRC	1945
PRC-501	GANGSTERS OF THE FRONTIER	CLIFTON	PRC	1944
PRC-502	DEAD OR ALIVE	CLIFTON	PRC	1945
PRC-503	WHISPERING SKULL	CLIFTON	PRC	1944
PRC-518	TOO MANY WINNERS	BEAUDINE	PRC	1947
PRC-519	LAW OF THE LASH	TAYLOR	PRC	1947
PRC-520	BORDER FEUD	TAYLOR	PRC	1947
PRC-524	RETURN OF THE LASH	TAYLOR	PRC	1947
PRC-525	WEST TO GLORY	TAYLOR	PRC	1947
PRC-526	BIG FIX	FLOOD	PRC	1947
PRC-528	GHOST TOWN RENEGADES	TAYLOR	PRC	1947
PRC-529	PIONEER JUSTICE	TAYLOR	PRC	1947
PRC-530	CHEYENNE TAKES OVER	TAYLOR	PRC	1947
PRC-534	HEARTACHES	WRANGELL	PRC	1947
PRC-535	CHECK YOUR GUNS	TAYLOR	PRC	1947
PRC-536	BLACK HILLS	TAYLOR	PRC	1947
PRC-537	WESTWARD TRAIL	TAYLOR	PRC	1947
PRC-538	SHADOW VALLEY	TAYLOR	PRC	1947
PRC-540	TIOGA KID	TAYLOR	PRC	1947
PRC-553	WHY GIRLS LEAVE HOME	BERKE	PRC	1945
PRC-555	STRANGLER OF THE SWAMP	WISBAR	PRC	1946
PRC-557	HER SISTER'S SECRET	ULMER	PRC	1946
PRC-562	ROMANCE OF THE WEST	TANSEY as EMMETT	PRC	1946
PRC-563	NAVAJO KID	FRASER	PRC	1945
PRC-564	SIX GUN MAN	FRASER	PRC	1946
PRC-566	CARAVAN TRAILS (aka CARAVAN TRAIL)	TANSEY as EMMETT	PRC	1946
PRC-569	AMBUSH TRAIL	FRASER	PRC	1946
PRC-570	THUNDER TOWN	FRASER	PRC	1946

Movie Still Identification Book Ultimate Edition - Letters

CODE	TITLE/NAME	DIRECTOR/TYPE	STUDIO/DISTRIBUTOR	YEAR
PRC-574	COLORADO SERENADE	TANSEY	PRC	1946
PRC-575	DOWN MISSOURI WAY	BERNE	PRC	1946
PRC-578	PHILO VANCE RETURNS	BEAUDINE	PRC	1947
PRC-587	GAS HOUSE KIDS	NEWFIELD	PRC	1946
PRC-589	LADY CHASER	NEWFIELD	PRC	1946
PRC-593	DRIFTIN' RIVER	TANSEY	PRC	1946
PRC-595	STARS OVER TEXAS	TANSEY	PRC	1946
PRC-599	DON RICARDO RETURNS	MORSE	PRC	1946
PRC-603	DEVIL ON WHEELS	WILBUR	PRC	1947
PRC-605	ACCOMPLICE	COLMES	PRC	1946
PRC-663	CHEYENNE TAKES OVER	TAYLOR	PRC	1947
PRG	UNDER 18	MAYO	WARNER BROS	1931
PRL	PRAIRIE LAW	HOWARD	RKO	1940
PRM	PATSY RUTH MILLER	portrait	WARNER BROS	
PRO	HEART OF A SIREN	ROSEN	FIRST NATIONAL	1925
PRO	NUMBER ONE	GRIES	UNITED ARTISTS	1969
PRO	PRODUCERS	BROOKS	EMBASSY	1967
PRO	SHADOW OF THE EAGLE (UK)	SALKOW	UNITED ARTISTS	1950
PROD	HELLIONS	ALLEN, ANNAKIN	COLUMBIA	1961
PS	BEHIND CLOSED DOORS		RKO	1931
PS	EXPENSIVE WOMAN	HENLEY	WARNER BROS	1931
PS	MY PAL WOLF	WERKER	RKO	1944
PS	NO MARRIAGE TIES	RUBEN	RKO	1933
PS	PASSPORT TO SHAME (UK) (ROOM 43)	RAKOFF	BRITISH LION	1959
PS	PAULA STONE	portrait	WARNER BROS	1930s
PS	PAULINE STARKE	portrait	MGM	
PS	PEGGY SUE GOT MARRIED	COPPOLA	TRI STAR	1986
PS	PENNY SINGLETON	portrait	WARNER BROS	late 30s
PS	PENROD AND SAM	BEAUDINE	WARNER BROS	1931
PS	PENROD AND SAM	MCGANN	WARNER BROS	1937
PS	PERFECT SPECIMEN	CURTIZ	WARNER BROS	1937
PS	PHANTOM SHIP (UK: MYSTERY OF THE MARIE CELESTE)	CLIFT	GUARANTEED	1935
PS	PICTURE SNATCHER	BACON	WARNER BROS	1933
PS	PORT SINISTER (BEAST OF PARADISE R1957)	DANIELS	RKO	1953
PS	PRICE OF SILENCE (UK)	TULLY	EXCLUSIVE INTL	1959
PS	PRISON SHADOWS	HILL	MERCURY (states rights)	1936
PS	PRIVATE SECRETARY (UK)	EDWARDS	TWICKENHAM	1935
PS	PUTNEY SWOPE	DOWNEY SR.	CINEMA V	1969
PS	ROOM 43 (UK: PASSPORT TO SHAME)	RAKOFF	CORY	1958
PS	SIN OF HAROLD DIDDLEBOCK	STURGES	UNITED ARTISTS	1947
PS	STEEL TRAP	STONE	20th CENTURY FOX	1952
PS	WHILE THE PATIENT SLEPT	ENRIGHT	WARNER BROS	1935
PS	WICKED AS THEY COME (UK)	HUGHES	COLUMBIA	1956
PS	WICKED DREAMS OF PAULA SCHULTZ	MARSHALL	UNITED ARTISTS	1968
PS	WOMEN WITHOUT MEN (UK)	WILLIAMS, GLAZER	ASSOCIATED	1956
PS	SAN QUENTIN	DOUGLAS	RKO	1946
PS1 (E15)	WHO IS NUMBER ONE? EPISODE 15	BERTRAM	PARAMOUNT	1917
PS99	PARENTS WANTED (sh)	GUIOL	RKO PATHE	1931
PS101	PARADING PAJAMAS (sh)	FOX	RKO PATHE	1931
PS107	STAGE STRUCK (sh)	RAY	RKO PATHE	1931
PS111	WHAT A TIME (sh)	GREEN	RKO PATHE	1931
PS113	HOT WIRES (sh)	SWEET	RKO PATHE	1931
PS115	ROUGH HOUSE RHYTHM (sh)	SWEET	RKO PATHE	1931
PS116	TWISTED TALES (sh)	FOX	RKO PATHE	1931
PS117	OPENING HOUSE (sh)	FRASER	RKO PATHE	1931
PS120	THREE WISE CLUCKS (sh)	FOX	RKO PATHE	1931
PS121	NOT SO LOUD (sh)	SWEET	RKO PATHE	1931
PS123	NIGHT CLASS (sh)	FRASER	RKO PATHE	1931
PS191	STOUT HEARTS AND WILLING HANDS (sh)	FOY	RKO PATHE	1931
PS192	THAT'S NEWS TO ME (sh)	GILLSTROM	RKO PATHE	1931
PS193	SHE SNOOPS TO CONQUER (sh)	GUIOL	RKO PATHE	1931
PS194	THAT'S MY LINE (sh)	ARBUCKLE as GOODRICH	RKO PATHE	1931
PS195	LEMON MERINGUE (sh)	SWEET	RKO PATHE	1931
PS196	OH! OH! CLEOPATRA (sh)	SANTLEY	RKO PATHE	1931
PS197	MESSENGER BOY (sh)	LUDWIG	RKO PATHE	1931
PS198	OH! MARRY ME (sh)	WATSON	RKO PATHE	1931
PS201	THANKS AGAIN (sh)	SWEET	RKO PATHE	1931
PS204	TAKE 'EM AND SHAKE 'EM (sh)	ARBUCKLE as GOODRICH	RKO PATHE	1931
PS205	WHERE CANARIES SING BASS (sh)	GREEN	RKO PATHE	1931
PS206	HOT SPOT (sh)	GALLAHER	RKO PATHE	1931

Movie Still Identification Book Ultimate Edition - Letters

CODE	TITLE/NAME	DIRECTOR/TYPE	STUDIO/DISTRIBUTOR	YEAR
PS211	SLOW POISON (sh)	SWEET	RKO PATHE	1931
PS214	SELLING SHORTS (sh)	EDWARDS	RKO PATHE	1931
PS215	ONLY MEN WANTED (sh)	CEDER	RKO PATHE	1931
PS218	STOP THAT RUN (sh)	BRETHERTON	RKO PATHE	1931
PS220	PROMOTER (sh)	CEDER	RKO PATHE	1931
PS222	WIDE OPEN SPACES (sh)	ROSSON	RKO PATHE	1931
PS223	NEWS HOUNDS (sh)		RKO PATHE	1931
PS225	PERFECT 36	CEDER	RKO PATHE	1931
PS227	NIAGARA FALLS (sh)	ARBUCKLE as GOODRICH	RKO PATHE	1931
PS228	MOTHER-IN-LAW'S DAY (sh)	SWEET	RKO PATHE	1932
PS229	WINNER TAKES ALL (sh)		RKO PATHE	1932
PS230	STEALIN' HOME (sh)	SWEET	RKO PATHE	1932
PS231	PETE BURKE, REPORTER (sh)		RKO PATHE	1932
PS232	RULE 'EM AND WEEP (sh)	SWEET	RKO PATHE	1932
PSD	MAD WEDNESDAY (SINS OF HAROLD DIDDLEBOCK 1947)	STURGES	RKO	R50
PSGM	PEGGY SUE GOT MARRIED	COPPOLA	TRI STAR	1986
PSP	PEARL OF THE SOUTH PACIFIC	DWAN	RKO	1955
PSV	VENDETTA	FERRER	RKO	1950
PSW	PINK STRING AND SEALING WAX (UK)	HAMER	PENTAGON	1945
PT	BOMBAY WATERFRONT (UK: PAUL TEMPLE RETURNS)	ROGERS	BUTCHER'S	1952
PT	MURDER ON A HONEYMOON	CORRIGAN	RKO	1935
PT	PAMELA TIFFIN	portrait	PARAMOUNT	
PT	PEEPING TOM (UK)	POWELL	ASTOR	1960
PT	PENROD AND HIS TWIN BROTHER	MCGANN	WARNER BROS	1938
PT	PHILLIP TERRY	portrait	RKO	1940s
PT	PHYLLIS THAXTER	portrait	WARNER BROS	
PT	POWDER TOWN	LEE	RKO	1942
PT	PRAIRIE THUNDER	EASON	WARNER BROS	1937
PT2	CALLING PAUL TEMPLE (UK)	ROGERS	BUTCHER'S	1948
PT-163	ANTIQUE SHOP	COZINE	PARAMOUNT	1931
PT-185	SINGAPORE SUE (LA)	ROBINSON	PARAMOUNT	1932
PTP	FINGER OF GUILT (UK: INTIMATE STRANGER)	SNOWDEN	RKO	1956
PTP	PINE-THOMAS PRODUCTIONS	studio	PARAMOUNT	
PTS	PICCADILLY THIRD STOP (UK)	RILLA	GOLDSTONE	1960
PTS	PLUNDER OF THE SUN	FARROW	WARNER BROS	1953
PU	52 PICKUP	FRANKENHEIMER	CANNON	1986
PU	PERFECT UNDERSTANDING (UK)	GARDNER	UNITED ARTISTS	1933
PU	PICKUP	HAAS	COLUMBIA	1951
PU	PUSSYCAT, PUSSYCAT, I LOVE YOU	AMATEAU	UNITED ARTISTS	1970
PV	CALLING PHILO VANCE	CLEMENS	WARNER BROS	1940
PV	PARALLAX VIEW	PAKULA	PARAMOUNT	1974
PW	PAINT YOUR WAGON	LOGAN	PARAMOUNT	1969
PW	PATRICE WYMORE	portrait	WARNER BROS	
PW	PATRICIA WILDERS	portrait	RKO	1930s
PW	PERFECT WEAPON	DISALLE	PARAMOUNT	1991
PW	PERFECT WORLD	EASTWOOD	WARNER BROS	1993
PW	POLLY WALTERS	portrait	WARNER BROS	
PW	PREHISTORIC WOMEN	TALLAS	EAGLE LION	1950
PW	PREHISTORIC WOMEN (UK: SLAVE GIRLS)	CARRERAS	20TH CENTURY FOX	1967
PW	PUBLIC ENEMY'S WIFE	GRINDE	WARNER BROS	1936
PW	ST. LOUIS KID	ENRIGHT	WARNER BROS	1934
PW	TEENAGE CAVEMAN	CORMAN	AIP	1958
PWBB	PRETTY WOMAN	MARSHALL	TOUCHSTONE	1990
PWR	PAINT YOUR WAGON	LOGAN	PARAMOUNT	1969
PX	PROJECT X	KAPLAN	20th CENTURY FOX	1987
PX1	LOUISE GLAUM	portrait		
PZ	PLAGUE OF THE ZOMBIES (UK)	GILLING	20th CENTURY FOX	1966
Q	FIVE OF A KIND	LEEDS	20th CENTURY FOX	1938
Q	THE DIONNE QUINTUPLETS	portrait	FOX	
Q	QUADROON	JANNEKE, JR.	CONSOLIDATED	1971
Q	QUERY (UK: MURDER IN REVERSE)	TULLY	FOUR CONTINENTS	1945
Q-403	DIARY OF ANNE FRANK	STEVENS	UNIVERSAL	R64
QA	QUESTION OF ADULTERY (UK)	CHAFFEY	EROS	1958
QA	QUIET AMERICAN	MANKIEWICZ	UNITED ARTISTS	1958
QA-M	QUIET AMERICAN	MANKIEWICZ	UNITED ARTISTS	1958
QD	QUEEN FOR A DAY	LUBIN	UNITED ARTISTS	1951
QE	CREEPING UNKNOWN (UK: QUATERMASS XPERIMENT)	GUEST	UNITED ARTISTS	1955
QF	QUILLAN FAMILY i.e. EDDIE QUILLAN & FAMILY	portrait	PATHE	
QFD	AND QUIET FLOWS THE DON (RUS)	GERASIMOV	UNITED ARTISTS	1957
QG	QUEEN FOR A DAY	LUBIN	UNITED ARTISTS	1951

Movie Still Identification Book Ultimate Edition - Letters

CODE	TITLE/NAME	DIRECTOR/TYPE	STUDIO/DISTRIBUTOR	YEAR
QH	QUEEN FOR A DAY	LUBIN	UNITED ARTISTS	1951
QK	JOEL KUPPERMAN (7-year-old 'Quiz Kid')	portrait	UNIV	
QM	QUIET WOMAN (UK)	GILLING	EROS	1951
QM	QUILLER MEMORANDUM	ANDERSON	20th CENTURY FOX	1966
QM	SMASHING THE MONEY RING	MORSE	WARNER BROS	1939
Q OF S	QUEEN OF SPADES (UK)	DICKINSON	MONOGRAM	1949
QOJ	TIGER AND THE FLAME (IND: JHANSI KI RANI)	MODI	UNITED ARTISTS	1952
QOS	QUEEN OF SHEBA (IT: LA REGINA DI SABA)	FRANCISCI	LIPPERT	1952
QP	FIVE MILLION YEARS TO EARTH	BAKER	20th CENTURY FOX	1967
QP	QUEEN OF THE PIRATES (IT)	COSTA	COLUMBIA	1960
QP	QUIET PLACE IN THE COUNTRY	PETRI	UNITED ARTISTS	1969
QR	QUEEN FOR A DAY	LUBIN	UNITED ARTISTS	1951
QS	QUALITY STREET	STEVENS	RKO	1937
QV	QUO VADIS (IT)	D'ANNUNZIO, JACOBY	WARNER BROS	1925
QW	QUIET WEEKEND (UK)	FRENCH	DISTINGUISHED	1946
QWE	QUIET WEEKEND (UK)	FRENCH	DISTINGUISHED	1946
R	ADVENTURES OF ROBIN HOOD	CURTIZ, KEIGHLEY	WARNER BROS	1938
R	BEST OF ENEMIES (IT)	HAMILTON	COLUMBIA	1962
R	BLACK DOLL	GARRETT	UNIVERSAL	1937
R	DIPLOMANIACS	SEITER	RKO	1933
R	GENTLEMEN MARRY BRUNETTES	SALE	UNITED ARTISTS	1955
R	KEEP 'EM ROLLING	ARCHAINBAUD	RKO	1934
R	KING'S ROW	WOOD	WARNER BROS	1942
R	MURPHY'S LAW	THOMPSON	CANNON	1986
R	RACHEL AND THE STRANGER	FOSTER	RKO	1948
R	RAGE: CARRIE 2	SHEA	UNITED ARTISTS	1999
R	RAMROD	DE TOTH	UNITED ARTISTS	1947
R	RASPUTIN, THE MAD MONK	SHARP	SEVEN ARTS	1966
R	RAT (UK)	RAYMOND	RKO	1937
R	RAVAGERS	COMPTON	COLUMBIA	1979
R	RECKONING	GOLD	COLUMBIA	1969
R	RED HOT TIRES	LEDERMAN	WARNER BROS	1935
R	REINCARNATION OF PETER PROUD	THOMPSON	AIP	1975
R	RELIANCE PICTURES		UNITED ARTISTS	
R	RENDEZ-VOUS	TECHINE	INT'L SPECTRAFILM	1986
R	RENO	FARROW	RKO	1939
R	RICHARD III	LONCRAINE	UNITED ARTISTS	1995
R	RIMFIRE	EASON	LIPPERT	1949
R	RING	NEWMANN	UNITED ARTISTS	1952
R	RIOT	KULIK	PARAMOUNT	1969
R	RITUAL/RITE (SWE: RITEN)	BERGMAN	JANUS	1969
R	ROADIE	RUDOLPH	UNITED ARTISTS	1980
R	ROB ROY	CATON-JONES	UNITED ARTISTS	1995
R	ROBERTA	SEITER	RKO	1935
R	ROCKABYE	CUKOR	RKO	1932
R	RODAN (JAP)	HONDA	KING BROTHERS	1957
R	ROLLERBALL	JEWISON	UNITED ARTISTS	1975
R	ROME, OPEN CITY (IT: ROMA CITTA APERTA)	ROSSELLINI	MAYER & BURSTYN	1945
R	RONIN	FRANKENHEIMER	UNITED ARTISTS	1998
R	ROOM TO LET (UK)	GRAYSON	EXCLUSIVE	1950
R	ROSE	RYDELL	20th CENTURY FOX	1979
R	ROSEBUD	PREMINGER	UNITED ARTISTS	1975
R	ROSHOMON (JAP)	KUROSAWA	RKO	1952
R	ROSSITER CASE (UK)	SEARLE	EXCLUSIVE	1951
R	RUMPLESTILTSKIN	IRVING	CANNON	1987
R	RUNAWAY	CRICHTON	TRI STAR	1984
R	SCARLET DAWN	DIETERLE	WARNER BROS	1932
R	SCARLET SPEAR	BREAKSTON	UNITED ARTISTS	1954
R	SHOOTING OF DAN MCGREW	BADGER	METRO	1924
R	SO YOUNG SO BAD	VORHAUS	UNITED ARTISTS	1950
R	SONG OF THE WEST	ENRIGHT	WARNER BROS	1930
R	SUSPECT/US: RISK (UK)	BOULTING, BOULTING	KINGSLEY INTERNATIONAL	1960
R&B	LAUGH AND GET RICH	LA CAVA	RKO	1931
R-1	BILLY THE KID RETURNS	KANE	REPUBLIC	1938
R-1	DO YOU LOVE YOUR WIFE?	ROACH	PATHE EXCHANGE	1919
R-1	JUS PASSIN' THROUGH	ROACH	PATHE EXCHANGE	1923
R-1	SKY PATROL	BRETHERTON	MONOGRAM	1939
R-1	WHITE EAGLE (15 ch. series)	JACKMAN, VAN DYKE	PATHE EXCHANGE	1922
R1/AB-1	SINNERS	WEBB	PARAMOUNT	1920
R1A	WE'RE IN THE LEGION NOW	WILBUR	GRAND	1936

Movie Still Identification Book Ultimate Edition - Letters

CODE	TITLE/NAME	DIRECTOR/TYPE	STUDIO/DISTRIBUTOR	YEAR
R-2	COME ON RANGERS	KANE	REPUBLIC	1938
R-2	FIGHTING MAD	NEWFIELD	MONOGRAM	1939
R-2	JUST RAMBLING ALONG	ROACH	PATHE EXCHANGE	1918
R-2	TIMBER QUEEN (15 ch. series)	JACKMAN	PATHE EXCHANGE	1922
R2A	CAPTAIN CALAMITY	REINHARDT	GRAND	1936
R2/CB-1	ERSTWHILE SUSAN (LA)	ROBERTSON	PARAMOUNT	1919
R-3	CRASHING THRU	CLIFTON	MONOGRAM	1939
R-3	HOOT MON!	ROACH	PATHE EXCHANGE	1919
R3	RAMBO 3	MACDONALD	TRI STAR	1988
R-3	SHINE ON HARVEST MOON	KANE	REPUBLIC	1938
R-3	UNCENSORED MOVIES	CLEMENTS	PATHE EXCHANGE	1923
R3A	DEVIL ON HORSEBACK	FRANKEL	GRAND	1936
R3/MMM-1	ANNE OF GREEN GABLES	TAYLOR	PARAMOUNT	1919
R-4	GEE WHIZ, GENEVIEVE	HOWE	PATHE EXCHANGE	1924
R4	I AM GUILTY	NELSON	ASSOCIATED PRODUCERS	1921
R-4	MURDER ON THE YUKON	GASNIER	MONOGRAM	1940
R-4	NO PLACE LIKE JAIL	TERRY	PATHE EXCHANGE	1918
R-4	ROUGH RIDERS ROUND-UP	KANE	REPUBLIC	1939
R-4	SOLDIERS OF FORTUNE	DWAN	REALART	1919
R4/AB-2	FEAR MARKET	WEBB	PARAMOUNT	1920
R-5	ARIZONA KID	KANE	REPUBLIC	1939
R-5	HUSTLING FOR HEALTH	TERRY	PATHE EXCHANGE	1919
R5	NEW ORLEANS	LUBIN	UNITED ARTISTS	1947
R5	EVERYTHING IS RHYTHM (UK)	GOULDING	ASTOR	1936
R-5	TWO WAGONS, BOTH COVERED	WAGNER	PATHE EXCHANGE	1924
R-5	YUKON FLIGHT	STAUB	MONOGRAM	1940
R5/AB-3	DARK LANTERN	ROBERTSON	PARAMOUNT	1920
R-6	COWBOY SHEIK	HOWE	PATHE EXCHANGE	1924
R-6	DANGER AHEAD	STAUB	MONOGRAM	1940
R6	MAN BEHIND THE MASK (UK)	POWELL	MGM	1936
R-6	SOUTHWARD HO	KANE	REPUBLIC	1939
R6/CB-2	STOLEN KISS	WEBB	PARAMOUNT	1920
R-7	CAKE EATER	HOWE	PATHE EXCHANGE	1924
R-7	FRONTIER PONY EXPRESS	KANE	REPUBLIC	1939
R-7	SKY BANDITS	STAUB	MONOGRAM	1940
R7/JJ-1	BLACKBIRDS	DILLON	PARAMOUNT	1920
R-8	IN OLD CALIENTE	KANE	REPUBLIC	1939
R-8	UNNAMED WILL ROGERS		PATHE EXCHANGE	1924
R8/CB-3	39 EAST	ROBERTSON	PARAMOUNT	1920
R-9	BIG MOMENTS FROM LITTLE PICTURES	CLEMENTS	PATHE EXCHANGE	1924
R-9	WALL STREET COWBOY	KANE	REPUBLIC	1939
R9/AB-4	NEW YORK IDEA	BLACHE	PARAMOUNT	1920
R-10	TEXAN	REYNOLDS	FOX FILM	1920
R10/CB-4	SOMETHING DIFFERENT	NEILL	PARAMOUNT	1920
R-11	GOING TO CONGRESS	WAGNER	PATHE EXCHANGE	1924
R11/AB-5	OUT OF THE CHORUS	BLACHE	PARAMOUNT	1921
R-12	DON'T PARK THERE!	GUIOL	PATHE EXCHANGE	1924
R12/JJ-2	PLAYTHING OF BROADWAY	DILLON	PARAMOUNT	1921
R-13	OUR CONGRESSMAN	WAGNER	PATHE EXCHANGE	1924
R13/CB-5	MAGIC CUP	ROBERTSON	PARAMOUNT	1921
R-14	TRUTHFUL LIAR	DEL RUTH	PATHE EXCHANGE	1924
R14/AB-6	HUSH MONEY	MAIGNE	PARAMOUNT	1921
R15/JJ-3	SHELTERED DAUGHTERS	DILLON	PARAMOUNT	1921
R16/AB-7	LAND OF HOPE	GRIFFITH	PARAMOUNT	1921
R17/CB-6	SUCH A-LITTLE QUEEN	FAWCETT	PARAMOUNT	1921
R18/JJ-4	HEART TO LET	DILLON	PARAMOUNT	1921
R19/AB-8	LITTLE ITALY	TERWILLIGER	PARAMOUNT	1921
R20/CB-7	ROOM AND BOARD	CROSLAND	PARAMOUNT	1921
R21/CB-8	CASE OF BECKY	FRANKLIN	PARAMOUNT	1921
R22/AB-9	DAWN OF THE EAST	GRIFFITH	PARAMOUNT	1921
R-23	CASE OF BECKY	FRANKLIN	PARAMOUNT	1921
R-40	WEST SIDE STORY	ROBBINS, WISE	UNITED ARTISTS	1961
R-71	WEST SIDE STORY	ROBBINS, WISE	UNITED ARTISTS	1961
R101	PANDORA AND THE FLYING DUTCHMAN	LEWIN	MGM	1951
R-101	PERSUADER	ROSS	ALLIED ARTISTS	1957
R114	AFRICAN QUEEN	HUSTON	UNITED ARTISTS	1951
R122	INNOCENTS IN PARIS (UK)	PARRY	TUDOR	1953
R-123	BEAT THE DEVIL (UK)	HUSTON	UNITED ARTISTS	1953
R125	GOOD DIE YOUNG (UK)	GILBERT	UNITED ARTISTS	1954
R128	COURT MARTIAL (UK: CARRINGTON V.C.)	ASQUITH	KINGSLEY INTERNATIONAL	1954

Movie Still Identification Book Ultimate Edition - Letters

CODE	TITLE/NAME	DIRECTOR/TYPE	STUDIO/DISTRIBUTOR	YEAR
R133	I AM A CAMERA (UK)	CORNELIUS	DCA	1955
R-135	STORY OF ESTHER COSTELLO (UK)	MILLER	COLUMBIA	1957
R141	PANIC IN THE PARLOR (UK: SAILOR BEWARE)	PARRY	DCA	1956
R142	DRY ROT (UK)	ELVEY	IFD	1956
R146	THREE MEN IN A BOAT (UK)	ANNAKIN	HAL ROACH	1956
R156	ROOM AT THE TOP (UK)	CLAYTON	CONTINENTAL	1959
R-205	ROCKING HORSE WINNER	PELISSIER	UNIVERSAL	1950
R-300	COUNT OF MONTE CRISTO	LEE	UNITED ARTISTS	1934
R-400	TRANSATLANTIC MERRY-GO-ROUND	STOLOFF	UNITED ARTISTS	1934
R-494	NEVER LOVE A STRANGER	STEVENS	ALLIED ARTISTS	1958
R-500	LET 'EM HAVE IT	WOOD	UNITED ARTISTS	1935
R-600	RED SALUTE	LANFIELD	UNITED ARTISTS	1935
R-700	MELODY LINGERS ON	BURTON	UNITED ARTISTS	1935
R-800	LAST OF THE MOHICANS	SEITZ	UNITED ARTISTS	1936
R 810	LADDIE	STEVENS	RKO	1935
R-7900	I COVER THE WATERFRONT	CRUZE	UNITED ARTISTS	1933
R-8200	PALOOKA	STOLOFF	UNITED ARTISTS	1934
RA	BIMBO THE GREAT (GER)	PHILIPP	WARNER BROS	1961
RA	MEN AGAINST THE SKY	GOODWINS	RKO	1939
RA	RAISING ARIZONA	COEN	20th CENTURY FOX	1987
RA	RAMSBOTTOM RIDES AGAIN (UK)	BAXTER	BRITISH LION	1956
RA	RAMSEY AMES	portrait	RKO, UNIVERSAL	
RA	REALART PICTURES	portrait		
RA	RENEE ADOREE	portrait	MGM	
RA	REPENT AT LEISURE	WOODRUFF	RKO	1941
RA	RETURN FROM THE ASHES (UK)	THOMPSON	UNITED ARTISTS	1965
RA	REVENGE	CAREWE	UNITED ARTISTS	1928
RA	REX ALLEN	portrait	REPUBLIC	
RA	RICHARD ANDERSON	portrait	RKO	
RA	RICHARD ARLEN	portrait	UNIVERSAL	
RA	ROAD AGENT	SELANDER	RKO	1952
RA	ROBERT ALDA	portrait	WARNER BROS	
RA	ROBERT ARMSTRONG	portrait	RKO	
RA	ROSCOE "FATTY" ARBUCKLE	portrait	PARAMOUNT	
RA	ROSCOE ATES	portrait		
RA	ROSS ALEXANDER	portrait	WARNER BROS	
RA	RUNAWAY (UK)	YOUNG	COLUMBIA	1963
RA	RUSSELL ARMS	portrait	WARNER BROS	
RA	TRAIL GUIDE	SELANDER	RKO	1952
RA1	ANGRY SILENCE (UK)	GREEN	VALIANT	1961
RA-1	UNKNOWN RANGER	BENNET	COLUMBIA	1936
RA-2	RANGER COURAGE	GORDON	COLUMBIA	1936
RA-3	RIO GRANDE RANGER (BOB ALLEN series)	BENNET	COLUMBIA	1936
RA-4	LAW OF THE RANGER (BOB ALLEN series)	BENNET	COLUMBIA	1937
RA-5	RECKLESS RANGER	BENNET	COLUMBIA	1937
RA-6	RANGERS STEP IN	BENNET	COLUMBIA	1937
RAB	RABBIT TEST	RIVERS	AVCO EMBASSY	1978
RAC	RATS ARE COMING, WEREWOLVES ARE HERE	MILLIGAN	MISHKIN	1972
RA-COL-1	UNKNOWN RANGER	BENNET	COLUMBIA	1936
RA-COL-2	RANGER COURAGE	GORDON	COLUMBIA	1936
RA-COL-3	RIO GRANDE RANGER (BOB ALLEN series)	BENNET	COLUMBIA	1936
RA-COL-4	LAW OF THE RANGER (BOB ALLEN series)	BENNET	COLUMBIA	1937
RA-COL-5	RECKLESS RANGER	BENNET	COLUMBIA	1937
RA-COL-6	RANGERS STEP IN	BENNET	COLUMBIA	1937
RAN	ROCK ALL NIGHT	CORMAN	AIP	1957
RAR-1	CHEERS FOR MISS BISHOP	GARNETT	UNITED ARTISTS	1941
RATH	BASIL RATHBONE	portrait	WARNER BROS	
RAW	RICH ARE ALWAYS WITH US	GREEN	WARNER BROS	1932
RAY-16	PUBLICITY MADNESS	RAY	FOX FILM	1927
RB	ABDULLAH'S HAREM (UK: ABDULLA THE GREAT)	RATOFF	20TH CENTURY FOX	1955
RB	RACING BLOOD	BARRY	20th CENTURY FOX	1954
RB	RACKET BUSTERS	BACON	WARNER BROS	1938
RB	RAGING BULL	SCORSESE	UNITED ARTISTS	1980
RB	RALPH BELLAMY	portrait	RKO, UNIVERSAL	
RB	RAY BOLGER	portrait	RKO, WARNER BROS	
RB	RAYMOND BURR	portrait	RKO, UNIVERSAL	
RB	REMBRANDT (UK)	KORDA	UNITED ARTISTS	1936
RB	RESTLESS BREED	DWAN	20th CENTURY FOX	1957
RB	RHAPSODY IN BLUE	RAPPER	WARNER BROS	1945
RB	RICHARD BARTHELMESS	portrait	FN, WARNER BROS	

Movie Still Identification Book Ultimate Edition - Letters

CODE	TITLE/NAME	DIRECTOR/TYPE	STUDIO/DISTRIBUTOR	YEAR
RB	RICHARD BASEHART	portrait		
RB	RICHARD BENJAMIN	portrait	UNIVERSAL	
RB	RICHARD BEYMER	portrait	FOX	
RB	RICHARD BURTON	portrait		
RB	RIVER BEAT (UK)	GREEN	LIPPERT	1954
RB	ROAD BLOCK	DANIELS	RKO	1951
RB	ROBERT BARRAT	portrait	UNITED ARTISTS	
RB	ROCKABILLY BABY	CLAXTON	20th CENTURY FOX	1957
RB	ROSEMARY'S BABY	POLANSKI	PARAMOUNT	1968
RB	ROSSANO BRAZZI	portrait	SELZNICK, UNIVERSAL	
RB	TOAST OF NEW YORK	LEE	RKO	1937
RB	TWO GROOMS FOR A BRIDE (UK: RELUCTANT BRIDE)	CASS	20TH CENTURY FOX	1955
RB-1	RANGE BUSTERS	LUBY	MONOGRAM	1940
RB-1	WAR DOGS	LUBY	MONOGRAM	1942
RB-2	TRAILING DOUBLE TROUBLE	LUBY	MONOGRAM	1940
RB-3	WEST OF PINTO BASIN	LUBY	MONOGRAM	1940
RB-4	TRAIL OF THE SILVER SPURS	LUBY	MONOGRAM	1941
RB-5	KID'S LAST RIDE	LUBY	MONOGRAM	1941
RB-6	TUMBLE DOWN RANCH IN ARIZONA	LUBY	MONOGRAM	1941
RB-7	WRANGLER'S ROOSE	LUBY	MONOGRAM	1941
RB-8	FUGITIVE VALLEY	LUBY	MONOGRAM	1941
RB-8	GIRL FROM OUTSIDE	BARKER	GOLDWYN	1919
RB-9	SADDLE MOUNTAIN ROUNDUP	LUBY	MONOGRAM	1941
RB-9	SILVER HORDE	LLOYD	GOLDWYN	1920
RB-10	TONTO BASIN OUTLAWS	LUBY	MONOGRAM	1941
RB-11	UNDERGROUND RUSTLERS	LUBY	MONOGRAM	1941
RB-12	THUNDER RIVER FEUD	LUBY	MONOGRAM	1942
RB-13	ROCK RIVER RENEGADES	LUBY	MONOGRAM	1942
RB-14	BOOTHILL BANDITS	LUBY	MONOGRAM	1942
RB-15	TEXAS TROUBLE SHOOTERS	LUBY	MONOGRAM	1942
RB-16	ARIZONA STAGECOACH	LUBY	MONOGRAM	1942
RB-17	TEXAS TO BATAAN	TANSEY	MONOGRAM	1942
RB-18	TRAIL RIDERS	TANSEY	MONOGRAM	1942
RB-19	TWO FISTED JUSTICE	TANSEY	MONOGRAM	1943
RB-20	HAUNTED RANCH	TANSEY	MONOGRAM	1943
RB-21	LAND OF HUNTED MEN	LUBY	MONOGRAM	1943
RB-22	COWBOY COMMANDOES	LUBY	MONOGRAM	1943
RB-23	BLACK MARKET RUSTLERS	LUBY	MONOGRAM	1943
RB-24	BULLETS AND SADDLES	MARSHALL	MONOGRAM	1943
RB-131	ROSEMARY'S BABY	POLANSKI	PARAMOUNT	1968
RB-A	ABDULLAH'S HAREM	RATOFF	20th CENTURY FOX	1956
RBD	RETURN OF BULLDOG DRUMMOND (UK)	SUMMERS	MUNDUS	1934
RBM	RETURN OF THE BADMEN	ENRIGHT	RKO	1948
RB-R	ROSEMARY'S BABY	POLANSKI	PARAMOUNT	1968
RBS	RAIDERS FROM BENEATH THE SEA	DEXTER	20th CENTURY FOX	1964
RBW	RING OF BRIGHT WATER (UK)	COUFFER	CINERAMA	1969
RC	ADVENTURES OF ROBINSON CRUSOE	BUNUEL	UNITED ARTISTS	1954
RC	CROWD ROARS	HAWKS	WARNER BROS	1932
RC	FRONTIER GAL	LAMONT	UNIVERSAL	1945
RC	HEAVEN IS ROUND THE CORNER (UK)	ROGERS	ANGLO-AMERICAN	1944
RC	RADIO CITY REVELS	STOLOFF	RKO	1938
RC	REGAN CALLAIS	PORT	RKO	
RC	RENEGADE RANGER	HOWARD	RKO	1938
RC	REPORT TO THE COMMISSIONER	KATSELAS	UNITED ARTISTS	1975
RC	RICARDO CORTEZ	portrait		
RC	RICHARD CARLSON	portrait		
RC	RICHARD CLAYTON	portrait	WARNER BROS	
RC	RICHARD CONTE	portrait	UNIVERSAL, FOX	
RC	RIDE HIM COWBOY	ALLEN	WARNER BROS	1932
RC	RITA HAYWORTH (CANSINO)	portrait	RKO	
RC	RITA/PAULA CORDAY (aka PAULA/PAULE CROSET)	portrait	RKO	
RC	ROARING CITY	BERKE	LIPPERT	1951
RC	ROBERT CLARKE	portrait	RKO	
RC	ROBERT CUMMINGS	portrait	UNIVERSAL, WARNER BROS	
RC	ROBINSON CRUSOE AND THE TIGER (MEX)	CARDONA JR	AVCO EMBASSY	1972
RC	ROBINSON CRUSOELAND (FR)	JOANNON	FRANCO LONDON (UK)	1951
RC	ROD CAMERON	portrait	UNIVERSAL	
RC	RONALD COLMAN	portrait	RKO, UNIVERSAL	
RC	RORY CALHOUN	portrait	RKO, UNIVERSAL	
RC	ROTTEN TO THE CORE (UK)	BOULTING	CINEMA V	1965

Movie Still Identification Book Ultimate Edition - Letters

CODE	TITLE/NAME	DIRECTOR/TYPE	STUDIO/DISTRIBUTOR	YEAR
RC	RULING CLASS [US: AVCO EMBASSY]	MEDAK	UNITED ARTISTS (UK)	1972
RC	RUTH CHATTERTON	portrait	FN/WARNER BROS	
R-C	ROBERTSON-COLE	portrait		
RC1	NIGHT WE GOT THE BIRD (UK)	CONYERS	BRITISH LION	1961
RC-33	THREE SMART GIRLS GROW UP	KOSTER	UNIVERSAL	1940
RCB	RACE FOR YOUR LIFE, CHARLIE BROWN (t)	MELENDEZ, ROMAN	PARAMOUNT	1977
RCI	RIX-CONYERS PRODUCTIONS (UK)	studio		
RCL	RULING CLASS [US: AVCO EMBASSY]	MEDAK	UNITED ARTISTS (UK)	1972
RCU	OLD MOTHER RILEY'S GHOSTS (UK)	BAXTER	ANGLO-AMERICAN	1941
RD	RANCHO DELUXE	PERRY	UNITED ARTISTS	1975
RD	RAY DANTON	portrait	UNIVERSAL, WARNER BROS	
RD	RED DAWN	MILLIUS	MGM	1984
RD	RED DESERT	BEEBE	LIPPERT	1949
RD	RED DESERT (IT: IL DESERTO ROSSO)	ANTONIONI	RIZZOLI	1964
RD	RED DRAGON	HOFBAUER	WOOLNER BROS	1961
RD	REGINALD DENNY	portrait	MGM	
RD	RELUCTANT DRAGON (t)	WERKER, LUSKE	RKO	1941
RD	RETURN OF DR. X	SHERMAN	WARNER BROS	1939
RD	RICHARD DAVIES	portrait	UNIVERSAL	
RD	RICHARD DENNING	portrait	RKO	
RD	RICHARD DIX	portrait	RKO	
RD	ROBERT DONAT	portrait	LONDON FILMS	
RD	ROBERT DOUGLAS	portrait		
RD	ROBERT DUVALL	portrait	UNIVERSAL	
RD	ROGER DANIEL	portrait	RKO	
RD	ROSEMARY DECAMP	portrait	WARNER BROS	
RD	RUNAWAY DAUGHTERS	CAHN	AIP	1956
RD	RUTH DONNELLY	portrait	WARNER BROS	
RD	RYAN'S DAUGHTER (UK)	LEAN	MGM	1970
RD	YOUNG, WILLING AND EAGER (UK: RAG DOLL)	COMFORT	MANSON	1961
RD1	CURE FOR LOVE (UK)	DONAT	BRITISH LION	1949
RDB	RETURN OF DANIEL BOONE	HILLYER	COLUMBIA	1941
RDC	ROSEMARY DECAMP	portrait	UNIVERSAL	
RDH	RIDER ON A DEAD HORSE	STROCK	ALLIED ARTISTS	1962
RDI	ROBERT DONAT PRODUCTIONS (UK)	studio	at Isleworth Studio	
RE	BRIDGE AT REMAGEN	GUILLERMIN	UNITED ARTISTS	1969
RE	DAYS OF GLORY	TOURNEUR	RKO	1944
RE	REPULSION (UK)	POLANSKI	COLUMBIA	1965
RE	RICHARD EGAN	portrait	UNIV	
RE	RIVER'S EDGE	DWAN	20th CENTURY FOX	1957
RE	RIVER'S END	CURTIZ	WARNER BROS	1930
RE	RIVER'S END	ENRIGHT	WARNER BROS	1940
RE	ROBERT EVANS	portrait		
REC	RECOMPENSE	BEAUMONT	WARNER BROS	1945
Rex Beach 8	GIRL FROM OUTSIDE	BARKER	GOLDWYN	1919
Rex Beach 9	SILVER HORDE	LLOYD	GOLDWYN	1920
REY-14	BIG TIME ROUND-UP	REYNOLDS	FOX FILM	1921
REY-15	TRAILIN'	REYNOLDS	FOX FILM	1921
REY-23	LAST OF THE DUANES	REYNOLDS	FOX FILM	1924
REYN-25	RIDERS OF THE PURPLE SAGE	REYNOLDS	FOX FILM	1925
RF	NOBODY HOME (UK: RETURN OF THE FROG)	ELVEY	SELECT ATTRACTIONS	1938
RF	RHONDA FLEMING	portrait	UNIVERSAL, RKO	
RF	ROBERT FRAZER	portrait	METRO	
RF	ROSEMARY FORSYTH	portrait	UNIVERSAL	
RF	THREE RUSSIAN GIRLS	OTSEP	UNITED ARTISTS	1943
RF1	FALLEN IDOL (UK)	REED	SELZNICK RELEASING	1948
RF2	THIRD MAN (UK)	REED	SELZNICK RELEASING	1949
RFI	FALLEN IDOL (UK)	REED	BRITISH LION (UK)	1948
RFL	REVOLT AT FORT LARAMIE	SELANDER	UNITED ARTISTS	1957
RFS	RUN FOR THE SUN	BOULTING	UNITED ARTISTS	1956
RFTR	RISE AND FALL OF THE THIRD REICH	KAUFMAN	ABC-TV	1968
RF-X	RHONDA FLEMING (SPELLBOUND ONLY)	portrait	VANGUARD	
RG	AFFAIR IN HAVANA	BENEDEK	ALLIED ARTISTS	1957
RG	PARSON AND THE OUTLAW	DRAKE	COLUMBIA	1957
RG	RACE GENTRY	portrait	UNIVERSAL	
RG	REAL GENIUS	COOLIDGE	TRI STAR	1985
RG	REGINALD GARDINER	portrait	RKO	
RG	RITA GAM	portrait	FOX	
RG	ROAD GAMES	FRANKLIN	AVCO EMBASSY	1980
RG	ROBERT GOULET	portrait	UNIVERSAL	

Movie Still Identification Book Ultimate Edition - Letters

CODE	TITLE/NAME	DIRECTOR/TYPE	STUDIO/DISTRIBUTOR	YEAR
RG	ROGUE'S GALLERY	HORN	PARAMOUNT	1968
RG	ROSE GARDEN	RADEMAKERS	CANNON	1989
RG	ROY D'ARCY (NÉE ROY GIUSTI)	portrait	MGM	1920s
RG	RUBY GENTRY	VIDOR	20th CENTURY FOX	1953
RG	RUTH GORDON	portrait	RKO	early 40s
RG	SAM WHISKEY	LAVEN	UNITED ARTISTS	1969
RG	UFO (UNIDENTIFIED FLYING OBJECTS)	JONES	UNITED ARTISTS	1956
RG	UNIDENTIFIED FLYING OBJECTS	JONES	UNITED ARTISTS	1956
RGP	RIO GRANDE PATROL	SELANDER	RKO	1950
RH	CHALLENGE FOR ROBIN HOOD (UK)	PENNINGTON-RICHARDS	20TH CENTURY FOX	1967
RH	I LIVE FOR LOVE	BERKELEY	WARNER BROS	1935
RH	RAY HEATHERTON (AND HIS ORCHESTRA)	portrait	MCA RECORDS	
RH	RAYMOND HATTON	portrait	METRO	
RH	RED HEAT	HILL	TRI STAR	1988
RH	RELUCTANT HEROES (UK)	RAYMOND	ASSOCIATED BRITISH-PATHE	1951
RH	RENATE HOY (aka RENATE HUY)	portrait	UNIVERSAL	early 50s
RH	REQUIEM FOR A HEAVYWEIGHT	NELSON	COLUMBIA	1962
RH	REX HARRISON	portrait		
RH	RHONDO HATTON	portrait	UNIVERSAL	
RH	RITA HAYWORTH	portrait	WARNER BROS	
RH	ROAD HOUSE	HERRINGTON	UNITED ARTISTS	1989
RH	ROAD HUSTLERS	JACKSON	AIP	1968
RH	ROBIN HOOD	DWAN	UNITED ARTISTS	1922
RH	ROBIN HOOD: MEN IN TIGHTS	BROOKS	20th CENTURY FOX	1993
RH	ROBIN HOOD: PRINCE OF THIEVES	REYNOLDS	WARNER BROS	1991
RH	ROBOT VS AZTEC MUMMY (MEX)	PORTILLO	YOUNG AMERICA	1959
RH	ROCHELLE HUDSON	portrait		
RH	ROCK HUDSON	portrait	UNIVERSAL	
RH	ROCKY HORROR PICTURE SHOW	SHARMAN	20th CENTURY FOX	1975
RH	ROMANCE OF A HORSE THIEF (YUGO)	POLONSKY	MONOGRAM	1971
RH	ROSE HOBART	portrait	UNIVERSAL	
RH	ROSS HUNTER	portrait	UNIV	
RH	RUTH HALL	portrait	WARNER BROS	
RH	RUTH HAMPTON	portrait	UNIVERSAL	
RH	RUTH HUSSEY	portrait	RKO	1940s
RH	STORY OF ROBIN HOOD (UK)	ANNAKIN	RKO	1952
RH	TALES OF ROBIN HOOD	TINLING	LIPPERT	1951
RH-EX	ROSS HUNTER	portrait	UNIVERSAL	1950s-70s
RHI	RIDE THE HIGH IRON	WEIS	COLUMBIA	1956
RHK	ROAD TO HONG KONG	PANAMA	UNITED ARTISTS	1962
RHL	LAST OF THE RED HOT LOVERS	SAKS	PARAMOUNT	1972
RHM	HE SNOOPS TO CONQUER (UK)	VARNEL	COLUMBIA BRITISH	1944
RHT	RED HOT TIRES	LEDERMAN	WARNER BROS	1935
RI	MILLIE	DILLON	RKO	1930
RI	RAVISHING IDIOT (FR) (AGENT 38-24-36)	MOLINARO	SEVEN ARTS	1964
RI	REX INGRAM	portrait	METRO	
RIB	ROOKIES IN BURMA	GOODWINS	RKO	1943
RII	ROCKY II	STALLONE	UNITED ARTISTS	1979
RIII	ROCKY III	STALLONE	MGM/UNITED ARTISTS	1982
RIO	DOLORES DEL RIO	portrait	WARNER BROS	
RIT	REBEL IN TOWN	WERKER	UNITED ARTISTS	1956
RJ	RITA JOHNSON	portrait	MGM, UNIVERSAL	
RJ	ROMEO AND JULIET (UK)	CASTELLANI	UNITED ARTISTS	1954
RJ	ROMEO AND JULIET (UK)	CZINNER	RANK	1966
RJ	ROMEO AND JULIET (UK)	ZEFFIRELLI	PARAMOUNT	1968
RJ	WHITE GODDESS	FOX	LIPPERT	1953
RJ-1027	ROMEO AND JULIET	ZEFFIRELLI	PARAMOUNT	1968
RJSS	RUNNING, JUMPING AND STANDING STILL (UK)	LESTER, SELLERS	BRITISH LION (UK)	1959
RK	RICH KIDS	YOUNG	UNITED ARTISTS	1979
RK	ROBERT KENT	portrait	UNIV	
RK	RUBY KEELER	portrait	WARNER BROS	
RKO-5	SQUADRON LEADER X (UK)	COMFORT	RKO	1943
RKO-6	ESCAPE TO DANGER (UK)	COMFORT, HANBURY	RKO	1945
RKO-9	GREAT DAY (UK)	COMFORT	RKO	1945
RL	LOVIN' THE LADIES	BROWN	RKO	1930
RL	RAGE TO LIVE	GRAUMAN	UNITED ARTISTS	1965
RL	RED LIGHT	DEL RUTH	UNITED ARTISTS	1949
RL	RICHARD LONG	portrait	UNIV	
RL	RIGHT TO LIVE	KEIGHLEY	WARNER BROS	1935
RL	ROSEMARY LANE	portrait	UNIVERSAL, WARNER BROS	

Movie Still Identification Book Ultimate Edition - Letters

CODE	TITLE/NAME	DIRECTOR/TYPE	STUDIO/DISTRIBUTOR	YEAR
RL	WOMEN ARE LIKE THAT	LOGAN	WARNER BROS	1938
R-L	ADVENTURES OF ROBIN HOOD	CURTIZ, KEIGHLEY	WARNER BROS	1938
R.La.R.	RITA LA ROY	portrait	PATHE	
RLD	RETURN OF THE LIVING DEAD	O'BANNON	ORION	1985
RLR	ROD LA ROCQUE	portrait		
RLS	RALPH LEWIS	portrait	FBO	
RM	I LOVED A WOMAN	GREEN	WARNER BROS	1933
RM	PAYOFF	FLOREY	WARNER BROS	1935
RM	RAY MILLAND	portrait	WARNER BROS	
RM	RAY MONTGOMERY	portrait	WARNER BROS.	
RM	RAYMOND MASSEY	portrait	WARNER BROS	
RM	REAL MEN	FELDMAN	UNITED ARTISTS	1987
RM	REMEMBER MY NAME	RUDOLPH	COLUMBIA	1978
RM	RENFREW OF THE ROYAL MOUNTED	HERMAN	GRAND	1937
RM	ROADHOUSE MURDER	RUBEN	RKO	1932
RM	ROBERT MITCHUM	portrait	COL, RKO	
RM	ROBERT MONTGOMERY	portrait	MGM, UNIVERSAL, WARNER	
RM	ROMANCE IN MANHATTAN	ROBERTS	RKO	1934
RM	ROOM 43 (UK: PASSPORT TO SHAME)	RAKOFF	CORY FILM	1959
RM	ROSALIND MARQUIS	portrait	WARNER BROS	
RM	RUDOLPH MATE	portrait	UNIV	
RM	RUNNING MAN	REED	COLUMBIA	1963
RM	RUNNING MAN	GLASER	TRI STAR	1987
RM	YOU CAN'T FOOL YOUR WIFE	MCCAREY	RKO	1940
RM	RIVER AND DEATH (MEX)	BUNUEL	CLASA	1955
RM-3	HAWAIIAN HOLIDAY (t)	SHARPSTEIN	RKO	1937
RM-10	DONALD'S NEPHEWS (t)	KING	RKO	1938
RM-19	POINTER (t)	GERONIMI	RKO	1939
RM-22	BEACH PICNIC (t)	GERONIMI	RKO	1939
RM-39	MR MOUSE TAKES A TRIP (t)	GERONIMI	RKO	1940
RM-41	FIRE CHIEF (t)	KING	RKO	1940
RM-55	ART OF SKIING (t)	KINNEY	RKO	1941
RM-73	NEW SPIRIT (t)	JACKSON	RKO	1942
RM-93	FLYING JALOPY (t)	LUNDY	RKO	1943
RMH	RETURN OF A MAN CALLED HORSE	KERSHNER	UNITED ARTISTS	1976
RMM	RETURN OF MR. MOTO (UK)	MORRIS	20TH CENTURY FOX	1965
RMP	OLD MOTHER RILEY, MP (UK)	MITCHELL	BUTCHER'S	1939
RM(PK)	RAIN MAN	LEVINSON	UNITED ARTISTS	1988
RMV	RUSS MEYER'S VIXEN	MEYER	EVE	1968
RN	MARRIAGE	NEILL	FOX FILM	1927
RN	RAMON NOVARRO	portrait	MGM, RKO	
RN	RAY NOBLE	portrait	RKO	
RN	REGISTERED NURSE	FLOREY	WARNER BROS	1934
RN	REVENGE OF THE NERDS	KANEW	20th CENTURY FOX	1984
RN	SANDY THE RELUCTANT NATURE GIRL (UK)	PELC	PRC	1966
RN-10	MARRIAGE	NEILL	FOX FILM	1927
RNBB	RENAISSANCE MAN	MARSHALL	BUENA VISTA	1994
RNP	RIVER NIGER	SHAH	CINE ARTIST	1976
RO	OLD MOTHER RILEY OVERSEAS (UK)	MITCHELL	ANGLO-AMERICAN	1943
RO	PLOT THICKENS	HOLMES	RKO	1936
RO	RACKETEERS OF THE RANGE	LEDERMAN	RKO	1939
RO	RITA OEHMEN	portrait	RKO	
RO	ROMA	FELLINI	UNITED ARTISTS	1972
RO-101	ISLE OF MISSING MEN	OSWALD	MONOGRAM	1942
ROB	ROBBERY (UK)	YATES	EMBASSY	1967
ROC	RAIDERS OF OLD CALIFORNIA	GANNAWAY	REPUBLIC	1957
ROC	ROCKULA	BERCOVICI	CANNON	1989
ROC	ROSE OF CIMARRON	KELLER	20th CENTURY FOX	1952
ROD	RIVER OF DEATH	CARVER	CANNON	1989
ROD	ROAR OF THE DRAGON	RUGGLES	RKO	1932
RO-F	FELLINI'S ROMA	FELLINI	UNITED ARTISTS	1972
ROH	REBELLION OF THE HANGED	FERNANDEZ	UNITED ARTISTS	1954
ROJ	RETURN OF THE JEDI	MARQUAND	20th CENTURY FOX	1983
ROL	ROLLER BOOGIE	LESTER	UNITED ARTISTS	1979
RON	DANGEROUS MISSION	KING	RKO	1954
ROP	REVENGE OF THE PINK PANTHER	EDWARDS	UNITED ARTISTS	1978
ROR	MYSTERIOUS DESPERADO	SELANDER	RKO	1949
RORY	ROSSANA RORY	portrait		
ROS	REVOLT OF THE SLAVES	MALASOMMA	UNITED ARTISTS	1960
ROS	ROSALIND RUSSELL	portrait	WARNER BROS	

Movie Still Identification Book Ultimate Edition - Letters

CODE	TITLE/NAME	DIRECTOR/TYPE	STUDIO/DISTRIBUTOR	YEAR
ROS-1	WIZARD	R. ROSSEN	FOX FILM	1927
RP	10 RILLINGTON PLACE (UK)	FLEISCHER	COLUMBIA	1971
RP	ALOHA	ROGELL	TIFFANY	1931
RP	CREEPER	YARBROUGH	20th CENTURY FOX	1948
RP	DICK PURCELL (NÉE RICHARD PURCELL)	portrait	FN	
RP	IROQUOIS TRAIL	KARLSON	UNITED ARTISTS	1950
RP	MASSACRE HARBOR	PEYSER	UNITED ARTISTS	1968
RP	MILLIONAIRE	ADOLFI	WARNER BROS	1931
RP	PIRATES OF BLOOD RIVER (UK)	GILLING	COLUMBIA	1962
RP	RAMROD	DETOTH	UNITED ARTISTS	1947
RP	RETURN OF RIN-TIN-TIN	NOSSECK	PRODUCERS RELEASING	1947
RP	RIKKY AND PETE	TASS	UNITED ARTISTS	1988
RP	ROBERT PAIGE/PAGE DAVID CARLYLE/NEWELL	portrait	WARNER BROS	late 30s
RP	ROBERT PAIGE/PAGE DAVID CARLYLE/NEWELL	portrait	UNIVERSAL	1930s-50s
RP	ROSAMOND PINCHOT	portrait	RKO	mid 30s
RP	ROSSANA PODESTA	portrait	WARNER BROS	
RP	UNCENSORED (UK)	ASQUITH	20TH CENTURY FOX	1942
RP-1	CHALLENGE	GILLING	20th CENTURY FOX	1948
RP-2	13 LEAD SOLDIERS	MACDONALD	20th CENTURY FOX	1948
RP-314	BEHIND PRISON WALLS	SEKELY	PRC	1943
RPC-4	ALICE BRADY	portrait	REALART	early 20s
RPC-7	JUSTINE JOHNSTONE	portrait	REALART	early 20s
RPM	R.P.M.	KRAMER	COLUMBIA	1970
RPP	RETURN OF THE PINK PANTHER	EDWARDS	UNITED ARTISTS	1975
RR	CUCKOOS	SLOANE	RKO	1930
RR	DANGER LIGHTS	SEITZ	RKO	1930
RR	HOT LEAD	GILMORE	RKO	1951
RR	HOUSE OF BLACKMAIL (UK)	ELVEY	MONARCH	1956
RR	RADAR SECRET SERVICE	NEWFIELD	LIPPERT	1950
RR	RAFTER ROMANCE	SEITER	RKO	1933
RR	RAGGEDY ROSE	WALLACE	PATHE EXCHANGE	1926
RR	RAINBOW ON THE RIVER	NEUMANN	RKO	1936
RR	REMEDY FOR RICHES	KENTON	RKO	1940
RR	RICHIE RICH	PETRIE	WARNER BROS	1994
RR	RIDE OUT FOR REVENGE	GIRARD	UNITED ARTISTS	1957
RR	RIFFRAFT	TETZLAFF	RKO	1946
RR	RINTY OF THE DESERT	LEDERMAN	WARNER BROS	1928
RR	RIO RITA	REED	RKO	1929
RR	RIVERBOAT RHYTHM	GOODWINS	RKO	1946
RR	ROB ROY (UK)	FRENCH	RKO	1954
RR	ROBBERS ROOST	SALKOW	UNITED ARTISTS	1955
RR	ROBERT RYAN	portrait	RKO	
RR	ROGUE RIVER	RAWLINS	EAGLE LION	1950
RR	RONALD REAGAN	portrait	WARNER BROS	
RR	ROSALIND RUSSELL	portrait	RKO, WARNER BROS	
RR	ROSANNA RORY	portrait	UNITED ARTISTS	
RR	ROY ROGERS	portrait		
RR	RUSSIAN ROULETTE	LOMBARDO	AVCO EMBASSY	1975
RR	RUTH ROMAN	portrait	WARNER BROS	
RRBB	WHO FRAMED ROGER RABBIT	ZAMECKIS	BUENA VISTA	1988
RRR	ROCK, ROCK, ROCK	PRICE	DCA	1956
RS	FACE BEHIND THE SCAR (UK: RETURN OF A STRANGER)	HANBURY	FILM ALLIANCE	1937
RS	MAYOR OF HELL	MAYO	WARNER BROS	1933
RS	PORTRAIT OF A SINNER (UK: ROUGH AND THE SMOOTH)	SIODMAK	AIP	1959
RS	QUICKSAND	PICHEL	UNITED ARTISTS	1950
RS	RANDOLPH SCOTT	portrait	RKO, WB, UA, UNIVERSAL	
RS	RED SNOW	PETROFF	COLUMBIA	1952
RS	RED SONJA	FLEISCHER	MGM/UNITED ARTISTS	1985
RS	REDEEMING SIN	BRETHERTON	WARNER BROS	1928
RS	RETURN OF SABATA (IT)	PAROLINI	UNITED ARTISTS	1971
RS	RETURN OF THE SEVEN	KENNEDY	UNITED ARTISTS	1966
RS	RING OF TREASON (UK: RING OF SPIES)	TRONSON	PARAMOUNT	1964
RS	RINGSIDE	MCDONALD	LIPPERT	1949
RS	RISING SUN	KAUFMAN	20th CENTURY FOX	1993
RS	ROAD TO SALINA	LAUTNER	AVCO EMBASSY	1970
RS	ROBERT STACK	portrait	UNIVERSAL	
RS	ROMANCING THE STONE	ZEMECKIS	20th CENTURY FOX	1984
RS	ROMY SCHNEIDER	portrait	DISNEY	
RS	ROOM SERVICE	SEITER	RKO	1938
RS	ROSS-STILLMAN PRODUCTIONS	studio		

Movie Still Identification Book Ultimate Edition - Letters

CODE	TITLE/NAME	DIRECTOR/TYPE	STUDIO/DISTRIBUTOR	YEAR
RS	ROUGHSHOD	ROBSON	RKO	1949
RS	RUNNING SCARED	HYAMS	MGM	1986
RS	SHOOT FIRST (UK: ROUGH SHOOT)	PARRISH	UNITED ARTISTS	1953
RS	UNDER THE RED SEA	HASS	RKO	1952
RS1	LADY SAYS NO	ROSS	UNITED ARTISTS	1952
RS-4	PRACTICAL PIG (t)	RICKARD	RKO	1939
RS 5	FARMYARD SYMPHONY (t)	CUTTING	RKO	1938
RS-7	UGLY DUCKLING (t)	CUTTING	RKO	1939
RS-10	MERBABIES (t)	STALLINGS	RKO	1938
RS-101	HELL IS SOLD OUT (UK)	ANDERSON	REALART	1951
RS 666	BADLANDS OF MONTANA (REGAL)	ULLMAN	20th CENTURY FOX	1957
RSM	RATTLE OF A SIMPLE MAN (UK)	BOX	CONTINENTAL	1964
RSMS	ROMAN SPRING OF MRS. STONE	QUINTERO	WARNER BROS	1961
RSP	RADIO STARS ON PARADE	GOODWINS	RKO	1945
RSR	RUN SILENT RUN DEEP	WISE	UNITED ARTISTS	1958
RST	RACE STREET	MARIN	RKO	1948
RT	DANGEROUSLY THEY LIVE	FLOREY	WARNER BROS	1941
RT	HE WHO RIDES THE TIGER (UK)	CRICHTON	SIGMA III	1965
RT	RABBIT TRAP	LEACOCK	UNITED ARTISTS	1959
RT	RAGTIME	FORMAN	PARAMOUNT	1981
RT	RED TERROR (GERMAN - GPU 1942)	RITTER	HOFFBERG PROD (UFA)	1960
RT	REGIS TOOMEY	portrait	RKO	
RT	RETURN OF THE TERROR	BRETHERTON	WARNER BROS	1934
RT	RICHARD TAYLOR aka JEFF RICHARDS	portrait		
RT	RICHARD THOMAS	portrait	UNIV	
RT	RICHARD TODD	portrait	WARNER BROS	1940s-60s
RT	RICHARD TRAVIS	portrait	WARNER BROS	1940s
RT	RICHARD TUCKER	portrait		
RT	RITA TUSHINGHAM	portrait		
RT	ROARING TWENTIES	WALSH	WARNER BROS	1939
RT	ROBBERS OF THE RANGE	KILLY	RKO	1941
RT	ROOM AT THE TOP (UK)	CLAYTON	COLUMBIA	1959
RT	ROSELLA TOWNE	portrait	WARNER BROS	1930s-40s
RT	RUTH TERRY	portrait	UNIV	
RTP	RETURN TO PARADISE	ROBSON	UNITED ARTISTS	1953
RTR	DAUGHTERS OF TODAY (UK)	KRAEMER	UNITED ARTISTS	1933
RTS	RIDERS TO THE STARS (scenes)	CARLSON	UNITED ARTISTS	1954
RTT	RIN-TIN-TIN		WARNER BROS	
RTW	RIDING ON THE WIND	KILLY	RKO	1942
RTX	ROBERT TAYLOR	portrait	MGM	
RU	GEORGE IN CIVVY STREET (UK)	VARNEL	COLUMBIA	1946
RU1	GLORY AT SEA (UK: GIFT HORSE)	BENNETT	SOUVAINE SELECTIVE	1952
RV	RETURN OF THE VIKINGS (UK)	FREND	ABFD	1945
RV	ROCKS OF VALPRE (UK)	EDWARDS	OLYMPIC	1935
RV	ROCKY V	AVILDSEN	UNITED ARTISTS	1990
RV	ROYAL JOURNEY (CAN)	BAIRSTOW, BLAIS	UNITED ARTISTS	1951
RV	RUDY VALLEE	portrait	WARNER BROS	
RVM	RIDE A VIOLENT MILE	WARREN	20th CENTURY FOX	1957
RW	RALPH WALSH	portrait	FOX	
RW	READY WILLING AND ABLE	ENRIGHT	WARNER BROS	1937
RW	RED WAGON (UK)	STEIN	WARDOUR	1934
RW	RETURN OF WILDFIRE	TAYLOR	SCREEN GUILD	1948
RW	RICH ARE ALWAYS WITH US	GREEN	WARNER BROS	1932
RW	RICHARD WIDMARK	portrait	UA, WB, UNIVERSAL	
RW	RIGHT OF WAY		WARNER BROS	1931
RW	ROBERT WAGNER	portrait	UNIV	
RW	ROBERT WILCOX	portrait	UNIVERSAL	1930s-40s
RW	ROBERT WOOLSEY	portrait	RKO	1920s-30s
RW	ROSE OF THE WORLD	BEAUMONT	WARNER BROS	1925
RW	ROSEWOOD	SINGLETON	WARNER BROS	1996
RW	RUNAWAY	CRICHTON	TRI STAR	1984
RW	RUTH WARRICK	portrait	RKO	
RW	STORM OVER WYOMING	SELANDER	RKO	1950
RW	THEY LIVE BY NIGHT	RAY	RKO	1949
RW	TWISTED ROAD	RAY	RKO	1949
RW-20	WHAT PRICE GLORY?	WALSH	FOX FILM	1926
RW-21	MONKEY TALKS	WALSH	FOX FILM	1927
RW-22	LOVE OF CARMEN	WALSH	FOX FILM	1927
RW-23	RED DANCE	WALSH	FOX FILM	1928
RW-24	ME, GANGSTER	WALSH	FOX FILM	1928

Movie Still Identification Book Ultimate Edition - Letters

CODE	TITLE/NAME	DIRECTOR/TYPE	STUDIO/DISTRIBUTOR	YEAR
RW-2300	ALIBI	WEST	UNITED ARTISTS	1929
RW-5000	BAT WHISPERS	WEST	UNITED ARTISTS	1930
RW-5700	CORSAIR	WEST	UNITED ARTISTS	1931
RXB	RAY BOLGER	portrait	MGM	
RXC	RUTH CHANNING	portrait	MGM	
RXCX	RUTH CHATTERTON	portrait	MGM	
RXFX	RALPH FORBES	portrait	MGM	
RXHX	RAYMOND HACKETT	portrait	MGM	
RXL	ROSINA LAWRENCE	portrait	MGM	
RXO	REGINALD OWEN	portrait	MGM	
RXR	ROSALIND RUSSELL	portrait	MGM	
RXSX	RED SKELTON	portrait	MGM	
RY	REVOLUTIONARY	WILLIAMS	UNITED ARTISTS	1970
RY	ROGUE'S YARN (UK)	SEWELL	EROS	1957
RY	ROBERT YOUNG	portrait	RKO	1930s-50s
RY	ROCKY	AVILDSEN	UNITED ARTISTS	1977
RY	ROLAND YOUNG	portrait	MGM	
RY	ROOKIE OF THE YEAR	STERN	20th CENTURY FOX	1993
RYX	ROBERT YOUNG	portrait	MGM	
S	39 STEPS (UK)	HITCHCOCK	GAUMONT BRITISH AMERICA	1935
S	AMATEUR GENTLEMAN (UK)	FREELAND	UNITED ARTISTS	1936
S	B. P. SCHULBERG PRODUCTIONS	studio	PARAMOUNT	
S	CHRISTMAS CAROL (UK: SCROOGE)	HURST	UNITED ARTISTS	1951
S	CIRCUS CLOWN	ENRIGHT	WARNER BROS	1934
S	COVER UP	GREEN	UNITED ARTISTS	1949
S	CROSSED SWORDS (IT: IL MAESTRO DI DON GIOVANNI)	KRIMS	UNITED ARTISTS	1954
S	FABULOUS SUZANNE	SEKELY	REPUBLIC	1946
S	GOLD RUSH	CHAPLIN	UNITED ARTISTS	R41
S	LAND OF FURY (UK: SEEKERS)	ANNAKIN	UNIVERSAL	1955
S	LIFE OF JIMMY DOLAN	MAYO	WARNER BROS	1933
S	MAN WHO TALKED TOO MUCH	SHERMAN	WARNER BROS	1940
S	SABAKA	FERRIN	UNITED ARTISTS	1954
S	SABATA (IT)	PAROLINI	UNITED ARTISTS	1969
S	SABRE JET	KING	UNITED ARTISTS	1953
S	SABU	portrait	UNIVERSAL	
S	SADIST	LANDIS	FAIRWAY INT'L	1963
S	SAFARI (UK)	YOUNG	COLUMBIA	1956
S	SAILOR'S SWEETHEART	BACON	WARNER BROS	1927
S	SALOME	D'ANNA	CANNON	1986
S	SALUTOS AMIGOS (t)	JACKSON, KINNEY	RKO	1943
S	SCALPHUNTERS	POLLACK	UNITED ARTISTS	1968
S	SEARCHERS	FORD	WARNER BROS	1956
S	SEBASTIAN (UK)	GREENE	PARAMOUNT	1968
S	SECONDS	FRANKENHEIMER	PARAMOUNT	1966
S	SECRET OF STAMBOUL (UK)	MARTON	WORLD	1936
S	SECRET SERVICEOF THE AIR	SMITH	WARNER BROS	1939
S	SERENGETTI SHALL NOT DIE (GER)	GRZIMEK	MONOGRAM	1960
S	SERGEANTS 3	STURGES	UNITED ARTISTS	1962
S	SERVANT (UK)	LOSEY	LANDAU RELEASING	1963
S	SHADOWLANDS	ATTENBOROUGH	SAVOY	1993
S	SHALAKO (UK)	DMYTRYK	CINERAMA	1968
S	SHAME (SWE: SKAMMEN)	BERGMAN	LOPERT	1968
S	SHE	HOLDEN, PICHEL	RKO	1935
S	SHIPBUILDERS (UK)	BAXTER	ANGLO-AMERICAN	1943
S	SHOOT	HART	AVCO EMBASSY	1976
S	SILKWOOD	NICHOLS	20th CENTURY FOX	1983
S	SINGAPORE WOMAN	NEGULESCO	WARNER BROS	1941
S	SISTERS		WARNER BROS	
S	SKULL (UK)	FRANCIS	PARAMOUNT	1965
S	SLEEP WITH ME	KELLY	UNITED ARTISTS	1994
S	SLIM	ENRIGHT	WARNER BROS	1937
S	SLIVER	NOYCE	PARAMOUNT	1993
S	SMALL WORLD OF SAMMY LEE (UK)	HUGHES	BRYANSTON	1963
S	SNOWFIRE	MCGOWAN, MCGOWAN	ALLIED ARTISTS	1958
S	SORCERERS (UK)	REEVES	MONOGRAM	1967
S	SPACEWAYS (UK)	FISHER	LIPPERT	1953
S	SPEECHLESS	UNDERWOOD	MGM	1994
S	SPEED	DE BONT	20th CENTURY FOX	1994
S	SPEED 2: CRUISE CONTROL	DE BONT	20th CENTURY FOX	1997
S	SPELLBINDER	HIVELY	RKO	1939

Movie Still Identification Book Ultimate Edition - Letters

CODE	TITLE/NAME	DIRECTOR/TYPE	STUDIO/DISTRIBUTOR	YEAR
S	SPRINGTIME (UK: SPRING SONG)	TULLY	ANGLO-AMERICAN	1946
S	SPY IN THE SKY (UK)	WILDER	ALLIED ARTISTS	1958
S	SQUEEZE	YOUNG	TRI STAR	1987
S	STARDUST	APTED	COLUMBIA	1974
S	STEAMING (UK)	LOSEY	COLUMBIA	1985
S	STINGAREE	WELLMAN	RKO	1934
S	STRANDED	BORZAGE	WARNER BROS	1935
S	STRIPORAMA	INTRATOR	FINE ARTS	1953
S	SUBMARINE D-1	BACON	WARNER BROS	1937
S	SUBTERFUGE (UK)	SCOTT	COMMONWEALTH	1968
S	SUNDOWN	HOYT, TRIMBLE	ASSOCIATED FIRST NATIONAL	1924
S	SUNNY	SEITER	WARNER BROS	1930
S	SUNSET	EDWARDS	TRI STAR	1988
S	SUPERMAN	DONNER	WARNER BROS	1978
S	SUSPECT	YATES	TRI STAR	1987
S	SVENGALI	MAYO	WARNER BROS	1931
S	SWEEPINGS	CROMWELL	RKO	1932
S	SWIMMER	PERRY	COLUMBIA	1968
S	SYNCOPATION	DIETERLE	RKO	1942
S	TERROR IN A TEXAS TOWN	LEWIS	UNITED ARTISTS	1958
S	TWO LOST WORLDS	DAWN	EAGLE LION	1951
S	UP JUMPED A SWAGMAN (UK)	MILES	WARNER-PATHE	1965
S-1	CALL A COP	STEVENS	MGM	1931
S-1	DON KEY	GUIOL, HORNE	PATHE EXCHANGE	1926
S-1	GHOST VALLEY RAIDERS	SHERMAN	REPUBLIC	1940
S-1	QUEEN OF THE AMAZON	FINNEY	SCREEN GUILD	1947
S-1	SHADOWS*		COLUMBIA	
S1	SHEPPERTON STUDIO	studio		
S-1	SPOILERS	HILLYER	GOLDWYN	1923
S-1	SUGAR DADDIES	GUIOL, MCCAREY	PATHE EXCHANGE , MGM	1927
S-1	TEXAS CITY	COLLINS	MONOGRAM	1952
S-1	TWO GUNS AND A BADGET	COLLINS	ALLIED ARTISTS	1954
S-1	WEDDING PRESENT	WALLACE	PARAMOUNT	1936
S-2	BORROWED HERO	COLLINS	MONOGRAM	1941
S-2	DESPERADO	CARR	ALLIED ARTISTS	1954
S-2	JOHN MEADE'S WOMAN	WALLACE	PARAMOUNT	1937
S-2	MAMA LOVES PAPA	STEVENS	MGM	1931
S-2	NIGHT RAIDERS	BRETHERTON	MONOGRAM	1952
S-2	ONE MAN'S LAW	SHERMAN	REPUBLIC	1940
S-2	PUNCH IN THE NOSE	HOWE	PATHE EXCHANGE	1926
S-2	SECOND HUNDRED YEARS	GUIOL	MGM	1927
S2	SMOKEY TRAILS	RAY	METROPOLITAN	1939
S-2	TERRY AND THE PIRATES	HORNE	COLUMBIA	1940
S-3	DEADWOOD DICK	HORNE	COLUMBIA	1940
S-3	DOCTOR'S DIARY	VIDOR	PARAMOUNT	1937
S-3	HATS OFF	YATES	MGM	1927
S-3	KICKOFF	STEVENS	MGM	1931
S-3	SOMEWHERE IN SOMEWHERE	HORNE	PATHE EXCHANGE	1925
S-3	STAGE TO BLUE RIVER	COLLINS	MONOGRAM	1951
S-3	TEXAS TERRORS	SHERMAN	REPUBLIC	1940
S-4	GREEN ARCHER	HORNE	COLUMBIA	1940
S-4	HER HUSBAND LIES	LUDWIG	PARAMOUNT	1937
S-4	LOVE PAINS	ROACH	MGM	1932
S-4	OBEY THE LAW	STOLOFF	COLUMBIA	1933
S-4	ONE THRILLING NIGHT	BEAUDINE	MONOGRAM	1942
S-4	PUTTING PANTS ON PHILIP	BRUCKMAN	MGM	1927
S-4	THERE GOES THE BRIDE	HORNE	PATHE EXCHANGE	1925
S-4	TULSA KID	SHERMAN	REPUBLIC	1940
S-5	BATTLE OF THE CENTURY	BRUCKMAN	MGM	1927
S-5	FRONTIER VENGEANCE	WATT	REPUBLIC	1940
S-5	GREAT GAMBINI	VIDOR	PARAMOUNT	1937
S-5	KNOCKOUT	FRENCH, MCGOWAN	MGM	1932
S-5	LAUGHING LADIES	HORNE	PATHE EXCHANGE	1925
S-5	MAN FROM THE BLACK HILLS	CARR	MONOGRAM	1952
S-5	WHITE EAGLE	HILLYER	COLUMBIA	1932
S-6	39 STEPS	HITCHCOCK	GAUMONT	1935
S-6	DEAD MAN'S TRAIL	COLLINS	MONOGRAM	1952
S-6	GUNMAN	COLLINS	MONOGRAM	1952
S-6	LEAVE 'EM LAUGHING	BRUCKMAN	MGM	1928
S-6	SECRET OF TREASURE ISLAND	CLIFTON	COLUMBIA	1938

Movie Still Identification Book Ultimate Edition - Letters

CODE	TITLE/NAME	DIRECTOR/TYPE	STUDIO/DISTRIBUTOR	YEAR
S-6	SHE'S NO LADY	VIDOR	PARAMOUNT	1937
S-6	SWELL HEAD	STOLOFF	COLUMBIA	1935
S-6	TWO GUN SHERIFF	SHERMAN	REPUBLIC	1941
S-6	YOUR HUSBAND'S PAST	GUIOL	PATHE EXCHANGE	1926
S-6	YOU'RE TELLING ME	FRENCH, MCGOWAN	MGM	1932
S-7	BLOSSOMS ON BROADWAY	WALLACE	PARAMOUNT	1937
S-7	DIZZY DADDIES	WALLACE	PATHE EXCHANGE	1926
S7	FINISHING TOUCH	BRUCKMAN, MCCAREY	MGM	1928
S-7	GUNMAN	COLLINS	MONOGRAM	1952
S-7	IRON CLAW	HORNE	COLUMBIA	1941
S-7	TOO MANY WOMEN	FRENCH, MCGOWAN	MGM	1932
S-7	WYOMING WILDCAT	SHERMAN	REPUBLIC	1941
S-8	FARGO	COLLINS	MONOGRAM	1952
S8	FROM SOUP TO NUTS	KENNEDY	MGM	1928
S-8	HOLT OF THE SECRET SERVICE	HORNE	COLUMBIA	1941
S-8	LET GEORGE DO IT*	KENNEDY	MGM	1928
S-8	MADAME MYSTERY	WALLACE, LAUREL	PATHE EXCHANGE	1926
S-8	PHANTOM COWBOY	SHERMAN	REPUBLIC	1941
S-8	WILD BABIES	FRENCH, MCGOWAN	MGM	1932
S-9	CAPTAIN MIDNIGHT	HORNE	COLUMBIA	1942
S-9	DESERT BANDIT	SHERMAN	REPUBLIC	1941
S-9	MAVERICK	CARR	ALLIED ARTISTS	1952
S-9	NEVER TOO OLD	WALLACE	PATHE EXCHANGE	1926
S-9	YOU'RE DARN TOOTIN'	KENNEDY	MGM	1928
S-10	KANSAS CYCLONE	SHERMAN	REPUBLIC	1941
S-10	MERRY WIDOWER	WALLACE	PATHE EXCHANGE	1926
S-10	MONTANA INCIDENT	COLLINS	MONOGRAM	1952
S-10	PERILS OF THE ROYAL MOUNTED	HORNE	COLUMBIA	1942
S-10	THEIR PURPLE MOMENT	PARROTT	MGM	1928
S-11	APACHE KID	SHERMAN	REPUBLIC	1941
S-11	RAGGEDY ROSE	WALLACE	PATHE EXCHANGE	1926
S-11	SECRET CODE	BENNET	COLUMBIA	1942
S-11	SHOULD MARRIED MEN GO HOME?	MCCAREY, PARROTT	MGM	1928
S-11	THAT NIGHT	HEATH, MCCAREY	MGM	1928
S-11	WYOMING ROUNDUP	CARR	MONOGRAM	1952
S-12	CANYON AMBUSH	COLLINS	MONOGRAM	1952
S-12	DEATH VALLEY OUTLAWS	SHERMAN	REPUBLIC	1941
S-12	DO GENTLEMEN SNORE?	MCCAREY	MGM	1928
S-12	EARLY TO BED	FLYNN	MGM	1928
S-12	VALLEY OF VANISHING MEN (serial)	BENNET	COLUMBIA	1942
S-12	WISE GUYS PREFER BRUNETTES	LAUREL	PATHE EXCHANGE	1926
S-13	BATMAN	HILLYER	COLUMBIA	1943
S-13	BOY FRIEND	GUIOL	MGM	1928
S-13	GET 'EM YOUNG	GUIOL, LAUREL	PATHE EXCHANGE	1926
S-13	HOMESTEADERS	COLLINS	ALLIED ARTISTS	1953
S-13	MISSOURI OUTLAW	SHERMAN	REPUBLIC	1941
S13	TWO TARS	PARROTT	MGM	1928
S-14	DUCK SOUP	GUIOL	PATHE EXCHANGE	1927
S-14	FEED 'EM AND WEEP	GUIOL, MCCAREY	MGM	1928
S-14	HABEAS CORPUS	MCCAREY, PARROTT	MGM	1928
S-14	JESSE JAMES JR.	SHERMAN	REPUBLIC	1942
S-14	REBEL CITY	CARR	ALLIED ARTISTS	1953
S-15	ARIZONA TERRORS	SHERMAN	REPUBLIC	1942
S-15	DESERT HAWK	EASON	COLUMBIA	1944
S-15	GOING GA GA	MCCAREY	MGM	1929
S-15	ON THE FRONT PAGE	PARROTT	PATHE EXCHANGE	1926
S-15	WE FAW DOWN	MCCAREY	MGM	1928
S-16	PAIR OF TIGHTS	YATES	MGM	1929
S-16	STAGECOACH EXPRESS	SHERMAN	REPUBLIC	1942
S-16	WHY GIRLS SAY NO	MCCAREY	PATHE EXCHANGE	1927
S-17	HONORABLE MR. BUGGS	JACKMAN	PATHE EXCHANGE	1927
S-17	WHEN MONEY COMES	MCCAREY	MGM	1929
S-18	CYCLONE KID	MCGOWAN	REPUBLIC	1942
S-18	SLIPPING WIVES	GUIOL	PATHE EXCHANGE	1927
S-18	UNKISSED MAN	ROACH, MCCAREY	MGM	1929
S-19	LOVE 'EM AND WEEP	GUIOL, JONES	PATHE EXCHANGE	1927
S-19	SOMBRERO KID	SHERMAN	REPUBLIC	1942
S-19	WHY IS A PLUMBER?	MCCAREY	MGM	1929
S-20	OUTLAWS OF PINE RIDGE	WITNEY	REPUBLIC	1942
S-20	THUNDERING TOUPEES	MCGOWAN	MGM	1929

Movie Still Identification Book Ultimate Edition - Letters

CODE	TITLE/NAME	DIRECTOR/TYPE	STUDIO/DISTRIBUTOR	YEAR
S-20	WHY GIRLS LOVE SAILORS	GUIOL	PATHE EXCHANGE	1927
S-21	HURDY GURDY	ROACH	MGM	1929
S-21	SUNDOWN KID	CLIFTON	REPUBLIC	1942
S-21	WITH LOVE AND HISSES	GUIOL	PATHE EXCHANGE	1927
S-22	DEAD MAN'S GULCH	ENGLISH	REPUBLIC	1943
S-22	MADAME "Q"	MCCAREY	MGM	1929
S-22	SAILORS, BEWARE!	GUIOL	PATHE EXCHANGE	1927
S-23	CARSON CITY CYCLONE	BRETHERTON	REPUBLIC	1943
S-23	COWBOYS CRY FOR IT*	GASNIER	PATHE EXCHANGE	1928
S-23	DAD'S DAY	MCCAREY	MGM	1929
S-23	SHOULD TALL MEN MARRY?	GASNIER	PATHE EXCHANGE	1928
S-24	DAYS OF OLD CHEYENNE	CLIFTON	REPUBLIC	1943
S-24	DO DETECTIVES THINK?	GUIOL	PATHE EXCHANGE	1927
S-24	HOTTER THAN HOT	FOSTER	MGM	1929
S-25	FLAMING FATHERS	LAUREL, MCCAREY	PATHE EXCHANGE	1927
S-25	FUGITIVE FROM SONORA	BRETHERTON	REPUBLIC	1943
S-25	SKY BOY	ROGERS	MGM	1929
S-26	BLACK HILL EXPRESS	ENGLISH	REPUBLIC	1943
S-26	FLYING ELEPHANTS	ROACH, BUTLER	PATHE EXCHANGE	1928
S-26	SKIRT SHY	ROGERS	MGM	1929
S-27	HEAD GUY	ROACH	MGM	1930
S-27	MAN FROM RIO GRANDE	BRETHERTON	REPUBLIC	1943
S-28	FIGHTING PARSON	GUIOL, ROGERS	MGM	1930
S-29	BIG KICK	DOANE	MGM	1930
S-29	CALIFORNIA JOE	BENNET	REPUBLIC	1943
S-30	CANYON CITY	BENNET	REPUBLIC	1943
S-30	SHRIMP	ROGERS	MGM	1930
S-31	KING		MGM	1930
S-31	OUTLAWS OF SANTA FE	BRETHERTON	REPUBLIC	1944
S-31	WHY MEN LEAVE HOME		WARNER BROS	
S-32	DOCTOR'S ORDERS	HEATH	MGM	1930
S-33	BIGGER AND BETTER	KENNEDY	MGM	1930
S-34	LADIES LAST	STEVENS	MGM	1930
S-35	BLOOD AND THUNDER	STEVENS	MGM	1931
S-36	LOVE FEVER	MCGOWAN	MGM	1931
S-37	HIGH GEAR	STEVENS	MGM	1931
S-38	AIR TIGHT	STEVENS	MGM	1931
S-39	LET'S DO THINGS	ROACH	MGM	1931
S-98	ACCIDENTS WILL HAPPEN	BLUMENSTOCK	PARAMOUNT	1930
S-102	DOUBLE TROUBLE	WEST	MONOGRAM	1941
S-112	SOMETHING TO SING ABOUT	SCHERTZINGER	GRAND NATIONAL	1937
S-320	SUBMARINE BASE	KELLEY	PRC	1943
S-543	SECONDS	FRANKENHEIMER	PARAMOUNT	1966
S-601	FABULOUS SUZANNE	SEKELY	REPUBLIC	1946
S1000	PIGSKIN CHAMPIONS (sh)	CLARKE	MGM	1937
S1002	MARRIED BEFORE BREAKFAST	MARIN	MGM	1937
S1003	THIRTEENTH CHAIR	SEITZ	MGM	1937
S1005	LONDON BY NIGHT	THIELE	MGM	1937
S1006	BETWEEN TWO WOMEN	SEITZ	MGM	1937
S1007	LIVE, LOVE AND LEARN	FITZMAURICE	MGM	1937
S1008	SPORTING BLOOD	SIMON	MGM	1940
S1010	BIG CITY	BORZAGE	MGM	1937
S1011	ROSALIE	VAN DYKE	MGM	1937
S1012	BAD GUY	CAHN	MGM	1937
S1013	MADAME X	WOOD	MGM	1937
S1014	WOMEN MEN MARRY	TAGGART	MGM	1937
S1015	MY DEAR MISS ALDRICH	SEITZ	MGM	1937
S1016	LAST GANGSTER	LUDWIG	MGM	1937
S1017	BAD MAN OF BRIMSTONE	RUBEN	MGM	1937
S1018	NAVY BLUE AND GOLD	WOOD	MGM	1937
S1020	EVERYBODY SING	MARIN	MGM	1938
S1021	MANNEQUIN	BORZAGE	MGM	1938
S1022	THOROUGHBREDS DON'T CRY	GREEN	MGM	1937
S1023	MAN-PROOF	THORPE	MGM	1937
S1024	YOU'RE ONLY YOUNG ONCE	SEITZ	MGM	1937
S1025	GIRL OF THE GOLDEN WEST	LEONARD	MGM	1938
S1026	OF HUMAN HEARTS	BROWN	MGM	1938
S1027	TEST PILOT	FLEMING	MGM	1938
S1028	BEG, BORROW OR STEAL	THIELE	MGM	1937
S1029	PORT OF THE SEVEN SEAS	WHALE	MGM	1938

Movie Still Identification Book Ultimate Edition - Letters

CODE	TITLE/NAME	DIRECTOR/TYPE	STUDIO/DISTRIBUTOR	YEAR
S1030	MARIE ANTOINETTE	VAN DYKE	MGM	1938
S1032	ARSENE LUPIN RETURNS	FITZMAURICE	MGM	1938
S1033	PARADISE FOR THREE	BUZZELL	MGM	1938
S1034	LOVE IS A HEADACHE	THORPE	MGM	1938
S1035	FIRST HUNDRED YEARS	THORPE	MGM	1938
S1036	THREE COMRADES	BORZAGE	MGM	1938
S1037	JUDGE HARDY'S CHILDREN	SEITZ	MGM	1938
S1039	LORD JEFF	WOOD	MGM	1938
S1040	TOY WIFE	THORPE	MGM	1938
S1041	YELLOW JACK	SEITZ	MGM	1938
S1042	SHOPWORN ANGEL	POTTER	MGM	1938
S1043	HOLD THAT KISS	MARIN	MGM	1938
S1044	NORTHWEST PASSAGE	VIDOR	MGM	1940
S1045	SEA OF GRASS	KAZAN	MGM	1947
S1046	TOO HOT TO HANDLE	CONWAY	MGM	1938
S1047	WOMAN AGAINST WOMAN	SINCLAIR	MGM	1938
S1048	HONOLULU	BUZZELL	MGM	1939
S1049	CROWD ROARS	THORPE	MGM	1938
S1049	VIC DAMONE	portrait	MGM	
S1050	LOVE FINDS ANDY HARDY	SEITZ	MGM	1938
S1051	FAST COMPANY	BUZZELL	MGM	1938
S1052	THREE LOVES HAS NANCY	THORPE	MGM	1938
S1053	LISTEN, DARLING	MARIN	MGM	1938
S1054	BOYS TOWN	TAUROG	MGM	1938
S1055	SWEETHEARTS	VAN DYKE	MGM	1938
S1056	IDIOT'S DELIGHT	BROWN	MGM	1939
S1057	CHASER	MARIN	MGM	1938
S1058	RICH MAN, POOR GIRL	SCHUNZEL	MGM	1938
S1059	STABLEMATES	WOOD	MGM	1938
S1060	WIZARD OF OZ	FLEMING	MGM	1939
S1061	OUT WEST WITH THE HARDYS	SEITZ	MGM	1938
S1062	VACATION FROM LOVE	FITZMAURICE	MGM	1938
S1063	SHINING HOUR	BORZAGE	MGM	1938
S1064	DRAMATIC SCHOOL	SINCLAIR	MGM	1938
S1065	STAND UP AND FIGHT	VAN DYKE	MGM	1939
S1066	ICE FOLLIES OF 1939	SCHUNZEL	MGM	1939
S1067	YOUNG DR. KILDARE	BUCQUET	MGM	1938
S1068	CHRISTMAS CAROL	MARIN	MGM	1938
S1069	SPRING MADNESS	SIMON	MGM	1938
S1070	I TAKE THIS WOMAN	VAN DYKE	MGM	1940
S1071	GIRL DOWNSTAIRS	TAUROG	MGM	1938
S1072	BURN 'EM UP O'CONNOR	SEDGWICK	MGM	1939
S1073	ADVENTURES OF HUCKLEBERRY FINN	THORPE	MGM	1939
S1074	BROADWAY SERENADE	LEONARD	MGM	1939
S1075	LET FREEDOM RING	CONWAY	MGM	1939
S1076	FOUR GIRLS IN WHITE	SIMON	MGM	1939
S1077	TARZAN FINDS A SON	THORPE	MGM	1939
S1078	FAST AND LOOSE	MARIN	MGM	1939
S1079	KID FROM TEXAS	SIMON	MGM	1939
S1080	WITHIN THE LAW	MACHATY	MGM	1939
S1081	SERGEANT MADDEN	VON STERNBERG	MGM	1939
S1082	HARDYS RIDE HIGH	SEITZ	MGM	1939
S1083	IT'S A WONDERFUL WORLD	VAN DYKE	MGM	1939
S1085	CALLING DR. KILDARE	BUCQUET	MGM	1939
S1086	SOCIETY LAWYER	MARIN	MGM	1939
S1087	TELL NO TALES	FENTON	MGM	1939
S1088	BABES IN ARMS	BERKELEY	MGM	1939
S1089	FLORIAN	MARIN	MGM	1940
S1090	ON BORROWED TIME	BUCQUET	MGM	1939
S1091	WOMEN	CUKOR	MGM	1939
S1092	6,000 ENEMIES	SEITZ	MGM	1939
S1093	BALALAIKA	SCHUNZEL	MGM	1939
S1094	MAISIE	MARIN	MGM	1939
S1095	ANDY HARDY GETS SPRING FEVER	VAN DYKE	MGM	1939
S1096	STRONGER THAN DESIRE	FENTON	MGM	1939
S1097	LADY OF THE TROPICS	CONWAY	MGM	1939
S1098	BLACKMAIL	POTTER	LMGM	1939
S1099	AT THE CIRCUS	BUZZELL	MGM	1939
S1100	NINOTCHKA	LUBITSCH	MGM	1939
S1101	MIRACLES FOR SALE	BROWNING	MGM	1939

Movie Still Identification Book Ultimate Edition - Letters

CODE	TITLE/NAME	DIRECTOR/TYPE	STUDIO/DISTRIBUTOR	YEAR
S1102	THUNDER AFLOAT	SEITZ	MGM	1939
S1103	THESE GLAMOUR GIRLS	SIMON	MGM	1939
S1104	HENRY GOES ARIZONA	MARIN	MGM	1940
S1105	THEY ALL COME OUT	TOURNEUR	MGM	1939
S1106	DANCING CO-ED	SIMON	MGM	1939
S1107	ANOTHER THIN MAN	VAN DYKE	MGM	1939
S1108	REMEMBER?	MCLEOD	MGM	1940
S1110	FAST AND FURIOUS	BERKELEY	MGM	1939
S1111	BROADWAY MELODY OF 1940	TAUROG	MGM	1940
S1112	BAD LITTLE ANGEL	THIELE	MGM	1939
S1113	JOE & ETHEL TURP CALL ON PRESIDENT	SINCLAIR	MGM	1939
S1114	JUDGE HARDY AND SON	SEITZ	MGM	1939
S1115	NICK CARTER, MASTER DETECTIVE	TOURNEUR	MGM	1939
S1116	SECRET OF DR. KILDARE	BUCQUET	MGM	1939
S1117	STRANGE CARGO	BORZAGE	MGM	1940
S1118	EARL OF CHICAGO	THORPE	MGM	1940
S1119	CONGO MAISIE	POTTER	MGM	1940
S1120	GO WEST	BUZZELL	MGM	1940
S1121	SHOP AROUND THE CORNER	LUBITSCH	MGM	1940
S1122	NEW MOON	LEONARD	MGM	1940
S1123	YOUNG TOM EDISON	TAUROG	MGM	1940
S1124	MAN FROM DAKOTA	FENTON	MGM	1940
S1125	EDISON THE MAN	BROWN	MGM	1940
S1126	FORTY LITTLE MOTHERS	BERKELEY	MGM	1940
S1127	20 MULE TEAM	THORPE	MGM	1940
S1128	GHOST COMES HOME	THIELE	MGM	1940
S1130	WATERLOO BRIDGE	LEROY	MGM	1940
S1131	SUSAN AND GOD	CUKOR	MGM	1940
S1133	TWO GIRLS ON BROADWAY	SIMON	MGM	1940
S1135	MORTAL STORM	BORZAGE	MGM	1940
S1136	PRIDE AND PREJUDICE	LEONARD	MGM	1940
S1137	AND ONE WAS BEAUTIFUL	SINCLAIR	MGM	1940
S1138	BOOM TOWN	CONWAY	MGM	1940
S1139	ANDY HARDY MEETS DEBUTANTE	SEITZ	MGM	1940
S1140	WE WHO ARE YOUNG	BUCQUET	MGM	1940
S1141	STRIKE UP THE BAND	BERKELEY	MGM	1940
S1142	I LOVE YOU AGAIN	VAN DYKE	MGM	1940
S1143	PHANTOM RAIDERS	TOURNEUR	MGM	1940
S1144	CAPTAIN IS A LADY	SINCLAIR	MGM	1940
S1145	GOLD RUSH MAISIE	MARIN	MGM	1940
S1146	ESCAPE	LEROY	MGM	1940
S1147	WYOMING	THORPE	MGM	1940
S1148	GOLDEN FLEECING	FENTON	MGM	1940
S1149	DULCY	SIMON	MGM	1940
S1150	FLIGHT COMMAND	BORZAGE	MGM	1940
S1151	BITTER SWEET	VAN DYKE	MGM	1940
S1152	PHILADELPHIA STORY	CUKOR	MGM	1940
S1153	LITTLE NELLIE KELLY	TAUROG	MGM	1940
S1155	THIRD FINGER LEFT HAND	LEONARD	MGM	1940
S1156	SKY MURDER	SEITZ	MGM	1940
S1158	HULLABALOO	MARIN	MGM	1940
S1159	COMRADE X	VIDOR	MGM	1940
S1161	GALLANT SONS	SEITZ	MGM	1941
S1162	COME LIVE WITH ME	BROWN	MGM	1941
S1163	WILD MAN OF BORNEO	SINCLAIR	MGM	1941
S1165	ZIEGFELD GIRL	LEONARD, BERKELEY	MGM	1941
S1166	KEEPING COMPANY	SIMON	MGM	1941
S1167	MAISIE WAS A LADY	MARIN	MGM	1941
S1168	BOYS TOWN	TAUROG	MGM	1938
S1168	MEN OF BOYS TOWN	TAUROG	MGM	1941
S1169	BAD MAN	THORPE	MGM	1941
S1170	BLONDE INSPIRATION	BERKELEY	MGM	1941
S1172	BILLY THE KID	MILLER	MGM	1941
S1173	FREE AND EASY	SIDNEY	MGM	1941
S1174	ANDY HARDY'S PRIVATE SECRETARY	SEITZ	MGM	1941
S1175	TRIAL OF MARY DUGAN	MCLEOD	MGM	1941
S1176	PENALTY	BUCQUET	MGM	1941
S1177	WOMAN'S FACE	CUKOR	MGM	1941
S1178	DR. JEKYLL AND MR HYDE	FLEMING	MGM	1941
S1179	BLOSSOMS IN THE DUST	LEROY	MGM	1941

Movie Still Identification Book Ultimate Edition - Letters

CODE	TITLE/NAME	DIRECTOR/TYPE	STUDIO/DISTRIBUTOR	YEAR
S1180	LOVE CRAZY	CONWAY	MGM	1941
S1181	THEY MET IN BOMBAY	BROWN	MGM	1941
S1182	LADY BE GOOD	MCLEOD	MGM	1941
S1183	WASHINGTON MELODRAMA	SIMON	MGM	1941
S1184	PEOPLE VS. DR. KILDARE	BUCQUET	MGM	1941
S1185	I'LL WAIT FOR YOU	SINCLAIR	MGM	1941
S1186	YEARLING	BROWN	MGM	1946
S1187	BIG STORE	REISNER	MGM	1941
S1187	PETER LAWFORD	portrait	MGM	
S1188	SMILIN' THROUGH	BORZAGE	MGM	1941
S1189	GET-AWAY	BUZZELL	MGM	1941
S1190	TWO-FACED WOMAN	CUKOR	MGM	1941
S1191	BARNACLE BILL	THORPE	MGM	1941
S1192	TARZAN'S SECRET TREASURE	THORPE	MGM	1941
S1193	LIFE BEGINS FOR ANDY HARDY	SEITZ	MGM	1941
S1194	UNHOLY PARTNERS	LEROY	MGM	1941
S1195	RINGSIDE MAISIE	MARIN	MGM	1941
S1196	WHEN LADIES MEET	LEONARD	MGM	1941
S1197	HONKY TONK	CONWAY	MGM	1941
S1199	CHOCOLATE SOLDIER	DEL RUTH	MGM	1941
S1201	WHISTLING IN THE DARK	SIMON	MGM	1941
S1202	MARRIED BACHELOR	BUZZELL	MGM	1941
S1203	FEMININE TOUCH	VAN DYKE	MGM	1941
S1204	BABES ON BROADWAY	BERKELEY	MGM	1941
S1205	PANAMA HATTIE	MCLEOD	MGM	1941
S1206	H. M. PULHAM, ESQ.	VIDOR	MGM	1941
S1207	KATHLEEN	BUCQUET	MGM	1941
S1208	SHADOW OF THE THIN MAN	VAN DYKE	MGM	1941
S1209	WOMAN OF THE YEAR	STEVENS	MGM	1942
S1210	DESIGN FOR SCANDAL	TAUROG	MGM	1941
S1211	BUGLE SOUNDS	SIMON	MGM	1942
S1212	JOHNNY EAGER	LEROY	MGM	1942
S1213	VANISHING VIRGINIAN	BORZAGE	MGM	1942
S1214	WE WERE DANCING	LEONARD	MGM	1942
S1215	I MARRIED AN ANGEL	VAN DYKE	MGM	1942
S1217	MR. AND MRS. NORTH	SINCLAIR	MGM	1941
S1218	BORN TO SING	LUDWIG	MGM	1942
S1219	JOE SMITH AMERICAN	THORPE	MGM	1942
S1220	YANK ON THE BURMA ROAD	SEITZ	MGM	1942
S1221	MRS. MINIVER	WYLER	MGM	1942
S1222	RIO RITA	SIMON	MGM	1942
S1223	SHIPS AHOY	BUZZELL	MGM	1942
S1224	NAZI AGENT	DASSIN	MGM	1942
S1225	TORTILLA FLAT	FLEMING	MGM	1942
S1226	THIS TIME FOR KEEPS	REISNER	MGM	1942
S1227	KID GLOVE KILLER	ZINNEMANN	MGM	1942
S1228	TARZAN'S NEW YORK ADVENTURE	THORPE	MGM	1942
S1229	SOMEWHERE I'LL FIND YOU	RUGGLES	MGM	1942
S1230	COURTSHIP OF ANDY HARDY	SEITZ	MGM	1942
S1232	FINGERS AT THE WINDOW	LEDERER	MGM	1942
S1233	JACKASS MAIL	MCLEOD	MGM	1942
S1234	SUNDAY PUNCH	MILLER	MGM	1942
S1236	CALLING DR. GILLESPIE	BUCQUET	MGM	1942
S1237	STAND BY FOR ACTION	LEONARD	MGM	1943
S1238	APACHE TRAIL	THORPE	MGM	1942
S1239	CROSSROADS	CONWAY	MGM	1942
S1240	GRAND CENTRAL MURDER	SIMON	MGM	1942
S1241	PACIFIC RENDEZVOUS	SIDNEY	MGM	1942
S1242	AFFAIRS OF MARTHA	DASSIN	MGM	1942
S1243	MAISIE GETS HER MAN	RUTH	MGM	1942
S1244	FOR ME AND MY GAL	BERKELEY	MGM	1942
S1245	PIERRE OF THE PLAINS	SEITZ	MGM	1942
S1246	SEVEN SWEETHEARTS	BORZAGE	MGM	1943
S1247	YANK AT ETON	TAUROG	MGM	1942
S1248	CAIRO	VAN DYKE	MGM	1942
S1249	RANDOM HARVEST	LEROY	MGM	1942
S1250	TISH	SIMON	MGM	1942
S1251	OMAHA TRAIL	BUZZELL	MGM	1942
S1252	WAR AGAINST MRS. HADLEY	BUCQUET	MGM	1942
S1253	EYES IN THE NIGHT	ZINNEMANN	MGM	1942

Movie Still Identification Book Ultimate Edition - Letters

CODE	TITLE/NAME	DIRECTOR/TYPE	STUDIO/DISTRIBUTOR	YEAR
S1254	WHITE CARGO	THORPE	MGM	1942
S1255	NORTHWEST RANGERS	NEWMAN	MGM	1942
S1256	KEEPER OF THE FLAME	CUKOR	MGM	1943
S1257	TENNESSEE JOHNSON	DIETERLE	MGM	1943
S1258	ANDY HARDY'S DOUBLE LIFE	SEITZ	MGM	1943
S1259	WHISTLING IN DIXIE	SIMON	MGM	1943
S1260	JOURNEY FOR MARGARET	VAN DYKE	MGM	1943
S1261	LASSIE COME HOME	WILCOX	MGM	1943
S1262	REUNION IN FRANCE	DASSIN	MGM	1943
S1263	PILOT NO. 5	SIDNEY	MGM	1943
S1264	PRESENTING LILY MARS	TAUROG	MGM	1943
S1266	DU BARRY WAS A LADY	DEL RUTH	MGM	1943
S1267	CABIN IN THE SKY	MINNELLI	MGM	1943
S1268	ASSIGNMENT IN BRITTANY	CONWAY	MGM	1943
S1269	HUMAN COMEDY	BROWN	MGM	1943
S1270	THREE HEARTS FOR JULIA	THORPE	MGM	1943
S1271	SLIGHTLY DANGEROUS	RUGGLES	MGM	1943
S1272	SALUTE TO THE MARINES	SIMON	MGM	1943
S1273	GENTLE ANNIE	MARTON	MGM	1945
S1274	THOUSANDS CHEER	SIDNEY	MGM	1943
S1275	AMERICAN ROMANCE	VIDOR	MGM	1944
S1276	YOUNGEST PROFESSION	BUZZELL	MGM	1943
S1277	HARRIGAN'S KID	REISNER	MGM	1943
S1278	ABOVE SUSPICION	THORPE	MGM	1943
S1279	STRANGER IN TOWN	ROWLAND	MGM	1943
S1280	BATAAN	GARNETT	MGM	1943
S1282	AIR RAID WARDENS	SEDGWICK	MGM	1943
S1283	CHRIS NOEL	portrait	MGM	
S1283	I DOOD IT	MINNELLI	MGM	1943
S1284	BEST FOOT FORWARD	BUZZELL	MGM	1943
S1285	GIRL CRAZY	TAUROG, BERKELEY	MGM	1943
S1286	SWING FEVER	WHELAN	MGM	1944
S1287	SWING SHIFT MAISIE	MCLEOD	MGM	1943
S1288	YOUNG IDEAS	DASSIN	MGM	1943
S1289	MARRIAGE IS A PRIVATE AFFAIR	LEONARD	MGM	1944
S1290	MADAME CURIE	LEROY	MGM	1943
S1291	GUY NAMED JOE	FLEMING	MGM	1944
S1292	MAN FROM DOWN UNDER	LEONARD	MGM	1943
S1293	SONG OF RUSSIA	RATOFF	MGM	1944
S1294	HITLER'S MADMAN	SIRK	MGM	1943
S1295	WHISTLING IN BROOKLYN	SIMON	MGM	1943
S1296	LOST ANGEL	ROWLAND	MGM	1943
S1298	CROSS OF LORRAINE	GARNETT	MGM	1944
S1299	CRY HAVOC	THORPE	MGM	1944
S1300	HEAVENLY BODY	HALL	MGM	1944
S1301	WHITE CLIFFS OF DOVER	BROWN	MGM	1944
S1302	MEET THE PEOPLE	REISNER	MGM	1944
S1303	BROADWAY RHYTHM	DEL RUTH	MGM	1944
S1304	SEE HERE, PRIVATE HARGROVE	RUGGLES	MGM	1944
S1305	DRAGON SEED	BUCQUET, CONWAY	MGM	1944
S1306	ANDY HARDY'S BLONDE TROUBLE	SEITZ	MGM	1944
S1307	RATIONING	GOLDBECK	MGM	1944
S1308	BATHING BEAUTY	SIDNEY	MGM	1944
S1309	KISMET	DIETERLE	MGM	1944
S1310	CANTERVILLE GHOST	DASSIN	MGM	1944
S1311	GASLIGHT	CUKOR	MGM	1944
S1312	QUO VADIS	LEROY	MGM	1951
S1313	TWO GIRLS AND A SAILOR	THORPE	MGM	1944
S1314	SEVENTH CROSS	ZINNEMANN	MGM	1944
S1315	NATIONAL VELVET	BROWN	MGM	1945
S1316	THIRTY SECONDS OVER TOKYO	LEROY	MGM	1944
S1317	MEET ME IN ST. LOUIS	MINNELLI	MGM	1944
S1318	THREE MEN IN WHITE	GOLDBECK	MGM	1944
S1319	PICTURE OF DORIAN GRAY	LEWIN	MGM	1945
S1320	THIS MAN'S NAVY	WELLMAN	MGM	1945
S1321	MRS. PARKINGTON	GARNETT	MGM	1944
S1323	MAISIE GOES TO RENO	BEAUMONT	MGM	1944
S1324	BARBARY COAST GENT	DEL RUTH	MGM	1944
S1325	ZIEGFELD FOLLIES	MINNELLI	MGM	1946
S1326	LOST IN A HAREM	REISNER	MGM	1945

Movie Still Identification Book Ultimate Edition - Letters

CODE	TITLE/NAME	DIRECTOR/TYPE	STUDIO/DISTRIBUTOR	YEAR
S1327	SON OF LASSIE	SIMON	MGM	1945
S1328	THIN MAN GOES HOME	THORPE	MGM	1945
S1329	MUSIC FOR MILLIONS	KOSTER	MGM	1945
S1330	LOVE LAUGHS AT ANDY HARDY	GOLDBECK	MGM	1946
S1331	CLOCK	MINNELLI	MGM	1945
S1332	NOTHING BUT TROUBLE	TAYLOR	MGM	1945
S1333	ANCHORS AWEIGH	SIDNEY	MGM	1945
S1334	BLONDE FEVER	WHORF	MGM	1945
S1335	BETWEEN TWO WOMEN	GOLDBECK	MGM	1945
S1337	THRILL OF A ROMANCE	THORPE	MGM	1945
S1338	KEEP YOUR POWER DRY	BUZZELL	MGM	1945
S1339	COURAGE OF LASSIE	WILCOX	MGM	1946
S1340	WITHOUT LOVE	BUCQUET	MGM	1945
S1341	VALLEY OF DECISION	GARNETT	MGM	1945
S1342	OUR VINES HAVE TENDER GRAPES	ROWLAND	MGM	1945
S1343	WEEK-END AT THE WALDORF	LEONARD	MGM	1945
S1344	TWICE BLESSED	BEAUMONT	MGM	1945
S1345	HIDDEN EYE	WHORF	MGM	1946
S1346	HER HIGHNESS AND THE BELLBOY	THORPE	MGM	1945
S1347	YOLANDA AND THE THIEF	MINNELLI	MGM	1945
S1348	HARVEY GIRLS	SIDNEY	MGM	1946
S1349	THEY WERE EXPENDABLE	FORD	MGM	1945
S1350	DANGEROUS PARTNERS	CAHN	MGM	1945
S1351	EASY TO WED	BUZZELL	MGM	1946
S1352	ADVENTURE	FLEMING	MGM	1946
S1353	SAILOR TAKES A WIFE	WHORF	MGM	1946
S1354	ABBOTT & COSTELLO IN HOLLYWOOD	SYLVAN	MGM	1945
S1355	POSTMAN ALWAYS RINGS TWICE	BARNETT	MGM	1946
S1356	SHE WENT TO THE RACES	GOLDBECK	MGM	1946
S1357	TWO SISTERS FROM BOSTON	KOSTER	MGM	1946
S1358	LETTER FOR EVIE	DASSIN	MGM	1946
S1359	BAD BASCOMB	SIMON	MGM	1946
S1360	HOLIDAY IN MEXICO	SIDNEY	MGM	1946
S1361	HOODLUM SAINT	TAUROG	MGM	1946
S1363	BOYS' RANCH	ROWLAND	MGM	1946
S1364	UP GOES MAISIE	BEAUMONT	MGM	1946
S1365	GREEN YEARS	SAVILLE	MGM	1946
S1366	NO LEAVE, NO LOVE	MARTIN	MGM	1946
S1367	TWO SMART PEOPLE	DASSIN	MGM	1946
S1368	GALLANT BESS	MARTON	MGM	1946
S1369	TILL THE CLOUDS ROLL BY	WHORF	MGM	1947
S1370	LITTLE MR. JIM	ZINNEMANN	MGM	1947
S1371	FIESTA	THORPE	MGM	1947
S1371	PEARLS AND DEVIL-FISH	AUSTIN	MGM	1931
S1371	SHARKS AND SWORDFISH	SMITH	MGM	1931
S1372	THREE WISE FOOLS	BUZZELL	MGM	1946
S1373	FAITHFUL IN MY FASHION	SALKOW	MGM	1946
S1374	COCKEYED MIRACLE	SIMON	MGM	1946
S1375	INSIDE STRAIGHT	MAYER	MGM	1951
S1376	UNDERCURRENT	MINNELLI	MGM	1946
S1377	BEGINNING OR THE END	TAUROG	MGM	1947
S1378	SHOW-OFF	BEAUMONT	MGM	1946
S1379	TENTH AVENUE ANGEL	ROWLAND	MGM	1948
S1380	MY BROTHER TALKS TO HORSES	ZINNEMANN	MGM	1947
S1380	WHIPPET RACING (sh)	WING	MGM	1931
S1381	DESIRE ME	CONWAY, CUKOR	MGM	1947
S1382	MIGHTY MCGURK	WATERS	MGM	1947
S1383	LADY IN THE LAKE	MONTGOMERY	MGM	1947
S1384	SECRET HEART	LEONARD	MGM	1946
S1385	HIGH BARBAREE	CONWAY	MGM	1947
S1386	SUMMER HOLIDAY	MAMOULIAN	MGM	1948
S1387	UNFINISHED DANCE	KOSTER	MGM	1947
S1388	IT HAPPENED IN BROOKLYN	WHORF	MGM	1947
S1389	THIS TIME FOR KEEPS	THORPE	MGM	1947
S1390	ROMANCE OF ROSY RIDGE	ROWLAND	MGM	1947
S1391	ARNELO AFFAIR	OBOLER	MGM	1947
S1392	LIVING IN A BIG WAY	LA CAVA	MGM	1947
S1393	MERTON OF THE MOVIES	ALTON	MGM	1947
S1394	GREEN DOLPHIN STREET	SAVILLE	MGM	1947
S1396	THREE DARING DAUGHTERS	WILCOX	MGM	1948

Movie Still Identification Book Ultimate Edition - Letters

CODE	TITLE/NAME	DIRECTOR/TYPE	STUDIO/DISTRIBUTOR	YEAR
S1397	DARK DELUSION	GOLDBECK	MGM	1947
S1398	SONG OF LOVE	BROWN	MGM	1947
S1399	UNDERCOVER MAISIE	BEAUMONT	MGM	1947
S1400	PIRATE	MINNELLI	MGM	1948
S1401	HUCKSTERS	CONWAY	MGM	1947
S1402	SONG OF THE THIN MAN	BUZZELL	MGM	1947
S1403	CASS TIMBERLANE	SIDNEY	MGM	1948
S1404	GOOD NEWS	WALTERS	MGM	1947
S1405	ALIAS A GENTLEMAN	BEAUMONT	MGM	1948
S1406	KISSING BANDIT	BENEDEK	MGM	1949
S1407	IF WINTER COMES	SAVILLE	MGM	1948
S1408	KILLER MCCOY	ROWLAND	MGM	1948
S1409	HIGH WALL	BERNHARDT	MGM	1948
S1410	BRIDGE GOES WILD	TAUROG	MGM	1948
S1411	ON AN ISLAND WITH YOU	THORPE	MGM	1948
S1412	LUXURY LINER	WHORF	MGM	1948
S1413	HOMECOMING	LEROY	MGM	1948
S1414	STATE OF THE UNION	CAPRA	MGM	1948
S1415	HILLS OF HOME	WILCOX	MGM	1948
S1416	B.F.'S DAUGHTER	LEONARD	MGM	1948
S1417	BIG CITY	TAUROG	MGM	1948
S1418	EASTER PARADE	WALTERS	MGM	1948
S1419	DATE WITH JUDY	THORPE	MGM	1948
S1420	THREE MUSKETEERS	SIDNEY	MGM	1948
S1421	SECRET LAND (documentary)		MGM	1948
S1422	JULIA MISBEHAVES	CONWAY	MGM	1948
S1423	SOUTHERN YANKEE	SEDGWICK	MGM	1948
S1424	STRATTON STORY	WOOD	MGM	1949
S1425	COMMAND DECISION	WOOD	MGM	1948
S1426	SUN COMES UP	THORPE	MGM	1949
S1427	WORDS AND MUSIC	TAUROG	MGM	1949
S1428	ACT OF VIOLENCE	ZINNEMANN	MGM	1949
S1429	NEPTUNE'S DAUGHTER	BUZZELL	MGM	1949
S1430	LITTLE WOMEN	LEROY	MGM	1949
S1431	BRIBE	LEONARD	MGM	1949
S1432	TAKE ME OUT TO THE BALLGAME	BERKELEY	MGM	1949
S1433	BARKLEYS OF BROADWAY	WALTERS	MGM	1949
S1435	SECRET GARDEN	WILCOX	MGM	1949
S1436	BIG JACK	THORPE	MGM	1949
S1437	GREAT SINNER	SIODMAK	MGM	1949
S1438	THAT FORSYTE WOMAN	BENNETT	MGM	1950
S1439	RED DANUBE	SIDNEY	MGM	1950
S1440	IN THE GOOD OLD SUMMERTIME	LEONARD	MGM	1949
S1441	MADAME BOVARY	MINNELLI	MGM	1949
S1442	CHALLENGE TO LASSIE	THORPE	MGM	1950
S1443	THAT MIDNIGHT KISS	TAUROG	MGM	1949
S1444	ANY NUMBER CAN PLAY	LEROY	MGM	1949
S1445	EDWARD, MY SON (UK)	CUKOR	MGM	1949
S1447	SCENE OF THE CRIME	ROWLAND	MGM	1949
S1448	BORDER INCIDENT	MANN	MGM	1949
S1449	MALAYA	THORPE	MGM	1950
S1450	ANNIE GET YOUR GUN	SIDNEY	MGM	1950
S1451	INTRUDER IN THE DUST	BROWN	MGM	1949
S1452	BATTLEGROUND	WELLMAN	MGM	1949
S1453	ON THE TOWN	DONEN, KELLY	MGM	1949
S1455	SHADOW ON THE WALL	JACKSON	MGM	1950
S1456	DOCTOR AND THE GIRL	BERNHARDT	MGM	1949
S1457	ADAM'S RIB	CUKOR	MGM	1950
S1458	TENSION	BERRY	MGM	1950
S1459	STARS IN MY CROWN	TOURNEUR	MGM	1950
S1460	AMBUSH	WOOD	MGM	1950
S1461	NANCY GOES TO RIO	LEONARD	MGM	1950
S1462	PLEASE BELIEVE ME	TAUROG	MGM	1950
S1463	KEY TO THE CITY	SIDNEY	MGM	1950
S1464	EAST SIDE, WEST SIDE	LEROY	MGM	1949
S1466	BLACK HAND	THORPE	MGM	1950
S1467	KING SOLOMON'S MINES	BENNETT	MGM	1950
S1468	DEVIL'S DOORWAY	MANN	MGM	1950
S1469	OUTRIDERS	ROWLAND	MGM	1950
S1470	BIG HANGOVER	KRASNA	MGM	1950

Movie Still Identification Book Ultimate Edition - Letters

CODE	TITLE/NAME	DIRECTOR/TYPE	STUDIO/DISTRIBUTOR	YEAR
S1471	YELLOW CAB MAN	DONOHUE	MGM	1950
S1472	MINIVER STORY	POTTER	MGM	1950
S1473	HAPPY YEARS	WELLMAN	MGM	1950
S1474	REFORMER AND THE REDHEAD	FRANK, PANAMA	MGM	1950
S1476	KIM	SAVILLE	MGM	1951
S1477	SUMMER STOCK	WALTERS	MGM	1950
S1478	LADY WITHOUT A PASSPORT	LEWIS	MGM	1950
S1479	ASPHALT JUNGLE	HUSTON	MGM	1950
S1480	SKIPPER SURPRISED HIS WIFE	NUGENT	MGM	1950
S1481	MYSTERY STREET	STURGES	MGM	1950
S1482	THREE LITTLE WORDS	THORPE	MGM	1950
S1483	TOAST OF NEW ORLEANS	TAUROG	MGM	1950
S1484	FATHER OF THE BRIDE	MINNELLI	MGM	1950
S1485	LIFE OF HER OWN	CUKOR	MGM	1950
S1486	CRISIS	BROOKS	MGM	1950
S1487	RIGHT CROSS	STURGES	MGM	1950
S1488	NEXT VOICE YOU HEAR	WELLMAN	MGM	1950
S1489	PAGAN LOVE SONG	ALTON	MGM	1950
S1490	DIAL 1119	MAYER	MGM	1950
S1491	TWO WEEKS WITH LOVE	ROWLAND	MGM	1950
S1492	RED HOT WHEELS (TO PLEASE A LADY 1950)	BROWN	MGM	R62
S1492	TO PLEASE A LADY	BROWN	MGM	1950
S1494	CAUSE FOR ALARM	GARNETT	MGM	1951
S1495	GROUNDS FOR MARRIAGE	LEONARD	MGM	1951
S1496	VENGEANCE VALLEY	THORPE	MGM	1951
S1497	WATCH THE BIRDIE	DONOHUE	MGM	1951
S1498	IT'S A BIG COUNTRY (INTERRUPTIONS episode)		MGM	1952
S1499	IT'S A BIG COUNTRY (CENSUS TAKER episode)		MGM	1952
S1500	IT'S A BIG COUNTRY (FOUR EYES episode)		MGM	1952
S1501	IT'S A BIG COUNTRY (ROSIKA episode)		MGM	1952
S1502	ROYAL WEDDING	DONEN	MGM	1951
S1503	MRS. O'MALLEY AND MR. MALONE	TAUROG	MGM	1951
S1504	PAINTED HILLS	KRESS	MGM	1951
S1505	IT'S A BIG COUNTRY (LOAD episode)		MGM	1952
S1506	MAGNIFICENT YANKEE	STURGES	MGM	1950
S1507	AMERICAN IN PARIS	MINNELLI	MGM	1951
S1508	ACROSS THE WIDE MISSOURI	WELLMAN	MGM	1951
S1509	THREE GUYS NAMED MIKE	WALTERS	MGM	1951
S1510	IT'S A BIG COUNTRY (MINISTER IN WASH episode)		MGM	1952
S1510	SHOWBOAT	SIDNEY	MGM	1951
S1511	MR. IMPERIUM	HARTMAN	MGM	1951
S1512	RED BADGE OF COURAGE	HUSTON	MGM	1951
S1513	CALLING BULLDOG DRUMMOND	SAVILLE	MGM	1951
S1514	GREAT CARUSO	THORPE	MGM	1951
S1515	IT'S A BIG COUNTRY (TEXAS episode)		MGM	1951
S1516	GO FOR BROKE	PIROSH	MGM	1951
S1517	SOLDIERS THREE	GARNETT	MGM	1951
S1518	EXCUSE MY DUST	ROWLAND	MGM	1951
S1519	FATHER'S LITTLE DIVIDEND	MINNELLI	MGM	1951
S1520	SHOW BOAT	SIDNEY	MGM	1951
S1521	KIND LADY	STURGES	MGM	1951
S1522	RICH, YOUNG AND PRETTY	TAUROG	MGM	1951
S1523	NIGHT INTO MORNING	MARKEL	MGM	1951
S1524	LOVE IS BETTER THAN EVER	DONEN	MGM	1952
S1525	IT'S A BIG COUNTRY (LETTER FROM KOREA episode)		MGM	1952
S1526	NO QUESTIONS ASKED	KRESS	MGM	1951
S1527	TALL TARGET	MANN	MGM	1951
S1528	STRIP	KARDOS	MGM	1951
S1529	UNKNOWN MAN	THORPE	MGM	1951
S1530	STRICTLY DISHONORABLE	FRANK, PANAMA	MGM	1951
S1531	LAW AND THE LADY	KNOPF	MGM	1951
S1532	TEXAS CARNIVAL	WALTERS	MGM	1951
S1533	SCARAMOUCHE	SIDNEY	MGM	1952
S1534	PEOPLE AGAINST O'HARA	STURGES	MGM	1951
S1535	WILD NORTH	MARTON	MGM	1952
S1536	WESTWARD THE WOMEN	WELLMAN	MGM	1951
S1537	ANGELS IN THE OUTFIELD	BROWN	MGM	1951
S1538	SHADOW IN THE SKY	WILCOX	MGM	1952
S1539	BANNERLINE	WEIS	MGM	1951
S1540	LIGHT TOUCH	BROOKS	MGM	1952

Movie Still Identification Book Ultimate Edition - Letters

CODE	TITLE/NAME	DIRECTOR/TYPE	STUDIO/DISTRIBUTOR	YEAR
S1541	TOO YOUNG TO KISS	LEONARD	MGM	1951
S1542	CALLAWAY WENT THATAWAY	FRANK, PANAMA	MGM	1952
S1544	MAN WITH A CLOAK	MARKLE	MGM	1951
S1545	BELLE OF NEW YORK	WALTERS	MGM	1952
S1546	SINGIN' IN THE RAIN	DONEN, KELLY	MGM	1952
S1548	WHEN IN ROME	BROWN	MGM	1952
S1549	IVANHOE (UK)	THORPE	MGM	1952
S1550	JUST THIS ONCE	WEIS	MGM	1952
S1551	SELLOUT	MAYER	MGM	1952
S1552	PLYMOUTH ADVENTURE	BROWN	MGM	1952
S1553	BECAUSE YOU'RE MINE	HALL	MGM	1952
S1554	TALK ABOUT A STRANGER	BRADLEY	MGM	1952
S1555	LOVELY TO LOOK AT	LEROY	MGM	1952
S1556	SKIRTS AHOY	LANFIELD	MGM	1952
S1557	MERRY WIDOW	BERNHARDT	MGM	1952
S1559	YOUNG MAN WITH IDEAS	LEISEN	MGM	1952
S1560	HOUR OF 13	FRENCH	MGM	1952
S1561	GIRL IN WHITE	STURGES	MGM	1952
S1564	GLORY ALLEY	WALSH	MGM	1952
S1565	CARBINE WILLIAMS	THORPE	MGM	1952
S1566	PAT AND MIKE	CUKOR	MGM	1952
S1567	MILLION DOLLAR MERMAID	LEROY	MGM	1952
S1568	WASHINGTON STORY	PIROSH	MGM	1952
S1569	DEVIL MAKES THREE	MARTON	MGM	1952
S1570	HOLIDAY FOR SINNERS	MAYER	MGM	1952
S1571	STORY OF THREE LOVES (EQUILIBRIUM episode)	MINNELLI, REINHARDT	MGM	1953
S1572	STORY OF THREE LOVES (MADEMOISELLE episode)	MINNELLI, REINHARDT	MGM	1953
S1573	FEARLESS FAGAN	DONEN	MGM	1952
S1574	ABOVE AND BEYOND	FRANK, PANAMA	MGM	1953
S1576	EVERYTHING I HAVE IS YOURS	LEONARD	MGM	1952
S1577	STORY OF THREE LOVES (BALLERINA episode)	MINNELLI, REINHARDT	MGM	1953
S1578	MY MAN AND I	WELLMAN	MGM	1952
S1579	PRISONER OF ZENDA	THORPE	MGM	1952
S1580	YOU FOR ME	WEIS	MGM	1952
S1581	BAD AND THE BEAUTIFUL	MINNELLI	MGM	1952
S1582	TERROR ON A TRAIN (TIME BOMB)	TETZLAFF	MGM	1953
S1583	SKY FULL OF MOON	FOSTER	MGM	1952
S1584	I LOVE MELVIN	WEIS	MGM	1953
S1585	ROGUE'S MARCH	DAVIS	MGM	1953
S1586	NAKED SPUR	MANN	MGM	1953
S1587	APACHE WAR SMOKE	KRESS	MGM	1952
S1588	SOMBRERO	FOSTER	MGM	1953
S1589	SMALL TOWN GIRL	WELLMAN	MGM	1953
S1590	DESPERATE SEARCH	LEWIS	MGM	1953
S1591	SCANDAL AT SCOURIE	NEGULESCO	MGM	1953
S1592	CONFIDENTIALLY CONNIE	BUZZELL	MGM	1953
S1593	NEVER LET ME GO	DAVES	MGM	1953
S1594	JEOPARDY	STURGES	MGM	1953
S1595	BATTLE CIRCUS	BROOKS	MGM	1953
S1596	STUDENT PRINCE	THORPE	MGM	1954
S1597	RIDE, VAQUERO	FARROW	MGM	1953
S1598	GIRL WHO HAD EVERYTHING	THORPE	MGM	1953
S1599	JULIUS CAESAR	MANKIEWICZ	MGM	1953
S1600	BRIGHT ROAD	MAYER	MGM	1953
S1601	STORY OF THREE LOVES	MINNELLI, REINHARDT	MGM	1953
S1602	DANGEROUS WHEN WET	WALTERS	MGM	1953
S1603	CRY OF THE HUNTED	LEWIS	MGM	1953
S1604	YOUNG BESS	SIDNEY	MGM	1953
S1605	INVITATION TO THE DANCE	KELLY	MGM	1957
S1606	HOAXTERS (documentary)	HOFFMAN	MGM	1953
S1607	DREAM WIFE	SHELDON	MGM	1953
S1608	GIVE A GIRL A BREAK	DONEN	MGM	1954
S1609	CODE TWO	WILCOX	MGM	1953
S1610	BAND WAGON	MINNELLI	MGM	1953
S1611	CLOWN	LEONARD	MGM	1953
S1612	REMAINS TO BE SEEN	WEIS	MGM	1953
S1613	FAST COMPANY	STURGES	LETGM	1953
S1614	ALL THE BROTHERS WERE VALIANT	THORPE	MGM	1953
S1616	MOGAMBO	FORD	MGM	1953
S1617	ACTRESS	CUKOR	MGM	1953

Movie Still Identification Book Ultimate Edition - Letters

CODE	TITLE/NAME	DIRECTOR/TYPE	STUDIO/DISTRIBUTOR	YEAR
S1618	LATIN LOVERS	LEROY	MGM	1953
S1619	SLIGHT CASE OF LARCENY	WEIS	MGM	1953
S1620	GREAT DIAMOND ROBBERY	LEONARD	MGM	1954
S1621	EASY TO LOVE	WALTERS	MGM	1954
S1622	SAADIA	LEWIN	MGM	1954
S1623	TAKE THE HIGH GROUND	BROOKS	MGM	1953
S1624	AFFAIRS OF DOBIE GILLIS	WEIS	MGM	1953
S1625	BIG LEAGUER	ALDRICH	MGM	1953
S1626	ARENA	FLEISCHER	MGM	1953
S1627	ESCAPE FROM FORT BRAVO	STURGES	MGM	1953
S1628	RHAPSODY	VIDOR	MGM	1954
S1629	KISS ME KATE	SIDNEY	MGM	1953
S1630	HALF A HERO	WEIS	MGM	1953
S1631	TORCH SONG	WALTERS	MGM	1953
S1632	LONG, LONG TRAILER	MINNELLI	MGM	1954
S1634	KNIGHTS OF THE ROUND TABLE	THORPE	MGM	1953
S1635	FLAME AND THE FLESH	BROOKS	MGM	1954
S1636	TENNESSEE CHAMP	WILCOX	MGM	1954
S1637	ROSE MARIE	LEROY	MGM	1954
S1638	GYPSY COLT	MARTON	MGM	1954
S1639	HER TWELVE MEN	LEONARD	MGM	1954
S1640	EXECUTIVE SUITE	WISE	MGM	1954
S1641	MEN OF THE FIGHTING LADY	MARTON	MGM	1954
S1642	VALLEY OF THE KINGS	PIROSH	MGM	1954
S1643	SEVEN BRIDES FOR SEVEN BROTHERS	DONEN	MGM	1954
S1644	BAD DAY AT BLACK ROCK	STURGES	MGM	1955
S1645	BRIGADOON	MINNELLI	MGM	1954
S1646	BETRAYED	REINHARDT	MGM	1954
S1647	BEAU BRUMMEL (UK)	BERNHARDT	MGM	1954
S1648	PRISONER OF WAR	MARTON	MGM	1954
S1649	LAST TIME I SAW PARIS	BROOKS	MGM	1954
S1650	ATHENA	THORPE	MGM	1954
S1651	GREEN FIRE	MARTON	MGM	1955
S1652	JUPITER'S DARLING	SIDNEY	MGM	1955
S1653	ROGUE COP	ROWLAND	MGM	1954
S1654	DEEP IN MY HEART	DONEN	MGM	1954
S1655	GLASS SLIPPER	WALTERS	MGM	1955
S1656	MANY RIVERS TO CROSS	ROWLAND	MGM	1955
S1657	INVITATION TO THE DANCE	KELLY	MGM	1957
S1658	PRODIGAL	THORPE	MGM	1955
S1659	HIT THE DECK	ROWLAND	MGM	1955
S1660	MOONFLEET	LANG	MGM	1955
S1661	INTERRUPTED MELODY	BERNHARDT	MGM	1955
S1662	BEDEVILLED	LEISEN	MGM	1955
S1663	IT'S ALWAYS FAIR WEATHER	DONEN, KELLY	MGM	1955
S1664	MARAUDERS	MAYER	MGM	1955
S1665	SCARLET COAT	STURGES	MGM	1955
S1666	BLACKBOARD JUNGLE	BROOKS	MGM	1955
S1667	COBWEB	MINNELLI	MGM	1955
S1668	LOVE ME OR LEAVE ME	VIDOR	MGM	1955
S1669	KING'S THIEF	LEONARD	MGM	1955
S1670	IT'S A DOG'S LIFE	HOFFMAN	MGM	1955
S1671	FORBIDDEN PLANET	WILCOX	MGM	1956
S1672	BHOWANI JUNCTION	CUKOR	MGM	1956
S1673	TRIBUTE TO A BADMAN	WISE	MGM	1956
S1674	QUENTIN DURWARD (UK)	THORPE	MGM	1955
S1675	DIANE	MILLER	MGM	1956
S1676	KISMET	MINNELLI	MGM	1955
S1677	TRIAL	ROBSON	MGM	1955
S1678	LAST HUNT	BROOKS	MGM	1956
S1679	I'LL CRY TOMORROW	MANN	MGM	1955
S1680	MEET ME IN LAS VEGAS	ROWLAND	MGM	1956
S1681	TENDER TRAP	WALTERS	MGM	1955
S1682	LUST FOR LIFE	MINNELLI	MGM	1956
S1683	GABY	BERNHARDT	MGM	1956
S1684	SWAN	VIDOR	MGM	1956
S1685	RANSOM	SEGAL	MGM	1956
S1686	RACK	LAVEN	MGM	1956
S1687	CATERED AFFAIR	BROOKS	MGM	1956
S1688	OPPOSITE SEX	MILLER	MGM	1956

Movie Still Identification Book Ultimate Edition - Letters

CODE	TITLE/NAME	DIRECTOR/TYPE	STUDIO/DISTRIBUTOR	YEAR
S1689	FASTEST GUN ALIVE	ROUSE	MGM	1956
S1690	HIGH SOCIETY	WALTERS	MGM	1956
S1691	SOMEBODY UP THERE LIKES ME	WISE	MGM	1956
S1692	RAINTREE COUNTY	DMYTRYK	MGM	1957
S1693	TEAHOUSE OF THE AUGUST MOON	MANN	MGM	1956
S1694	TEA AND SYMPATHY	MINNELLI	MGM	1956
S1695	52 MILES TO TERROR (HOT RODS TO HELL)	BRAHM	MGM	1967
S1696	THESE WILDER YEARS	ROWLAND	MGM	1956
S1697	POWER AND THE PRIZE	KOSTER	MGM	1956
S1698	BARRETTS OF WIMPOLE STREET	FRANKLIN	MGM	1957
S1699	GREAT AMERICAN PASTIME	HOFFMAN	MGM	1956
S1700	SOMETHING OF VALUE	BROOKS	MGM	1957
S1701	WINGS OF EAGLES	FORD	MGM	1957
S1702	VINTAGE	HAYDEN	MGM	1957
S1703	HOT SUMMER NIGHT	FRIEDKIN	MGM	1957
S1704	SLANDER	ROWLAND	MGM	1957
S1705	TEN THOUSAND BEDROOMS	THORPE	MGM	1957
S1706	DESIGNING WOMAN	MINNELLI	MGM	1957
S1707	LES GIRLS	CUKOR	MGM	1957
S1708	THIS COULD BE THE NIGHT	WISE	MGM	1957
S1709	SILK STOCKINGS	MAMOULIAN	MGM	1957
S1710	SEVENTH SIN	NEAME	MGM	1957
S1711	GUN GLORY	ROWLAND	MGM	1957
S1712	UNTIL THEY SAIL	WISE	MGM	1957
S1713	MAN ON FIRE	MACDOUGALL	MGM	1957
S1714	HOUSE OF NUMBERS	ROUSE	MGM	1957
S1715	DON'T GO NEAR THE WATER	WALTERS	MGM	1957
S1716	TIP ON A DEAD JOCKEY	THORPE	MGM	1957
S1718	MERRY ANDREW	KIDD	MGM	1958
S1719	JAILHOUSE ROCK	THORPE	MGM	1957
S1720	BROTHERS KARAMAZOV	BROOKS	MGM	1958
S1721	SADDLE THE WIND	PARRISH	MGM	1958
S1722	HIRED GUN	NAZARRO	MGM	1957
S1723	GIGI	MINNELLI	MGM	1958
S1724	BEN-HUR	WYLER	MGM	1959
S1725	HIGH COST OF LOVING	FERRER	MGM	1958
S1726	SHEEPMAN	MARSHALL	MGM	1958
S1727	HANDLE WITH CARE	FRIEDKIN	MGM	1958
S1728	LAW AND JAKE WADE	STURGES	MGM	1958
S1729	TUNNEL OF LOVE	KELLY	MGM	1958
S1730	RELUCTANT DEBUTANTE	MINNELLI	MGM	1958
S1731	IMITATION GENERAL	MARSHALL	MGM	1958
S1732	BADLANDERS	DAVES	MGM	1958
S1733	HIGH SCHOOL CONFIDENTIAL	ARNOLD	MGM	1958
S1734	GREEN MANSIONS	FERRER	MGM	1959
S1735	CAT ON A HOT TIN ROOF	BROOKS	MGM	1958
S1737	WORLD, FLESH AND THE DEVIL	MACDOUGALL	MGM	1958
S1738	TORPEDO RUN	PEVNEY	MGM	1958
S1739	ANDY HARDY COMES HOME	KOCH	MGM	1958
S1740	WATUSI	NEUMANN	MGM	1959
S1741	SOME CAME RUNNING	MINNELLI	MGM	1959
S1742	COUNT YOUR BLESSINGS	NEGULESCO	MGM	1959
S1743	NORTH BY NORTHWEST	HITCHCOCK	MGM	1959
S1744	NIGHT OF THE QUARTER MOON	HAAS	MGM	1959
S1746	BEAT GENERATION	HAAS	MGM	1959
S1747	ASK ANY GIRL	WALTERS	MGM	1959
S1748	NEVER SO FEW	STURGES	MGM	1959
S1749	BIG OPERATOR	HAAS	MGM	1959
S1750	WRECK OF THE MARY DEARE	ANDERSON	MGM	1959
S1751	IT STARTED WITH A KISS	MARSHALL	MGM	1959
S1752	TARZAN THE APE MAN	NEWMAN	MGM	1959
S1753	GIRLS TOWN	HAAS	MGM	1960
S1754	HOME FROM THE HILL	MINNELLI	MGM	1960
S1755	TIME MACHINE	PAL	MGM	1960
S1756	PLEASE DON'T EAT THE DAISIES	WALTERS	MGM	1960
S1757	SUBTERRANEANS	MACDOUGALL	MGM	1960
S1758	GAZEBO	MARSHALL	MGM	1959
S1759	KEY WITNESS	KARLSON	MGM	1960
S1760	BELLS ARE RINGING	MINNELLI	MGM	1960
S1761	ADVENTURES OF HUCKLEBERRY FINN	CURTIZ	MGM	1960

Movie Still Identification Book Ultimate Edition - Letters

CODE	TITLE/NAME	DIRECTOR/TYPE	STUDIO/DISTRIBUTOR	YEAR
S1762	PLATINUM HIGH SCHOOL	HAAS	MGM	1960
S1763	CIMARRON	MANN	MGM	1960
S1764	ALL THE FINE YOUNG CANNIBALS	ANDERSON	MGM	1960
S1765	BUTTERFIELD 8	MANN	MGM	1960
S1766	GO NAKED IN THE WORLD	MACDOUGALL	MGM	1961
S1767	ATLANTIS, THE LOST CONTINENT	PAL	MGM	1961
S1768	WHERE THE BOYS ARE	LEVIN	MGM	1960
S1769	MUTINY ON THE BOUNTY	MILESTONE	MGM	1962
S1770	TWO LOVES	WALTERS	MGM	1961
S1771	FOUR HORSEMEN OF THE APOCALYPSE	MINNELLI	MGM	1962
S1773	ADA	MANN	MGM	1961
S1774	HONEYMOON MACHINE	THORPE	MGM	1961
S1775	THUNDER OF DRUMS	NEWMAN	MGM	1961
S1776	HOW THE WEST WAS WON	FORD, HATHAWAY	MGM	1963
S1777	HOW THE WEST WAS WON	FORD, HATHAWAY	MGM	1963
S1778	HOW THE WEST WAS WON	FORD, HATHAWAY	MGM	1963
S1779	HOW THE WEST WAS WON	FORD, HATHAWAY	MGM	1963
S1780	HOW THE WEST WAS WON	FORD, HATHAWAY	MGM	1963
S1781	HOW THE WEST WAS WON	FORD, HATHAWAY	MGM	1963
S1782	HOW THE WEST WAS WON	FORD, HATHAWAY	MGM	1963
S1783	BACHELOR IN PARADISE	ARNOLD	MGM	1961
S1784	SWEET BIRD OF YOUTH	BROOKS	MGM	1962
S1785	WONDERFUL WORLD OF BROTHERS GRIMM (t)	LEVIN, PAL	MGM	1962
S1789	WONDERFUL WORLD OF BROTHERS GRIMM (t)	LEVIN, PAL	MGM	1962
S1790	WONDERFUL WORLD OF BROTHERS GRIMM (t)	LEVIN, PAL	MGM	1962
S1791	ALL FALL DOWN	FRANKENHEIMER	MGM	1962
S1792	HORIZONTAL LIEUTENANT	THORPE	MGM	1962
S1793	RIDE THE HIGH COUNTRY	PECKINPAH	MGM	1962
S1794	TWO WEEKS IN ANOTHER TOWN	MINNELLI	MGM	1962
S1795	BOYS' NIGHT OUT	GORDON	MGM	1962
S1796	BILLY ROSES' JUMBO	WALTERS	MGM	1962
S1797	PERIOD OF ADJUSTMENT	HILL	MGM	1962
S1798	HOOK	SEATON	MGM	1963
S1801	COURTSHIP OF EDDIE'S FATHER	MINNELLI	MGM	1963
S1802	IT HAPPENED AT THE WORLD'S FAIR	TAUROG	MGM	1963
S1803	DRUMS OF AFRICA	CLARK	MGM	1963
S1804	TICKLISH AFFAIR	SIDNEY	MGM	1963
S1805	WHEELER DEALERS	HILLER	MGM	1963
S1806	TWILIGHT OF HONOR	SAGAL	MGM	1963
S1807	SUNDAY IN NEW YORK	TEWKSBURY	MGM	1964
S1808	PRIZE	ROBSON	MGM	1963
S1809	GLOBAL AFFAIR	ARNOLD	MGM	1964
S1810	ADVANCE TO THE REAR	MARSHALL	MGM	1964
S1811	7 FACES OF DR. LAO	PAL	MGM	1964
S1812	VIVA LAS VEGAS	SIDNEY	MGM	1964
S1813	MAIL ORDER BRIDE	KENNEDY	MGM	1964
S1814	HOOTENANNY HOOT	NELSON	MGM	1963
S1815	UNSINKABLE MOLLY BROWN	WALTERS	MGM	1963
S1816	HONEYMOON HOTEL	LEVIN	MGM	1964
S1817	LOOKING FOR LOVE	WEIS	MGM	1964
S1818	SIGNPOST TO MURDER	ENGLUND	MGM	1965
S1819	KISSIN' COUSINS	NELSON	MGM	1964
S1820	AMERICANIZATION OF EMILY	HILLER	MGM	1964
S1823	OUTRAGE	RITT	MGM	1964
S1824	QUICK, BEFORE IT MELTS	MANN	MGM	1965
S1825	ROUNDERS	KENNEDY	MGM	1965
S1826	36 HOURS	SEATON	MGM	1965
S1827	YOUR CHEATIN' HEART	NELSON	MGM	1965
S1828	JOY IN THE MORNING	SEGAL	MGM	1965
S1829	GIRL HAPPY	SAGAL	MGM	1965
S1830	GET YOURSELF A COLLEGE GIRL	MILLER	MGM	1964
S1831	SANDPIPER	MINNELLI	MGM	1965
S1832	ONCE A THIEF	NELSON	MGM	1965
S1833	CINCINNATI KID	JEWISON	MGM	1965
S1834	MONEY TRAP	KENNEDY	MGM	1966
S1835	7 WOMEN	FORD	MGM	1966
S1836	MISTER BUDDWING	MANN	MGM	1966
S1837	PATCH OF BLUE	GREEN	MGM	1965
S1838	HARUM SCARUM	NELSON	MGM	1965
S1839	MADE IN PARIS	SAGAL	MGM	1966

Movie Still Identification Book Ultimate Edition - Letters

CODE	TITLE/NAME	DIRECTOR/TYPE	STUDIO/DISTRIBUTOR	YEAR
S1840	ICE STATION ZEBRA	STURGES	MGM	1968
S1841	WHEN THE BOYS MEET THE GIRLS	GANZER	MGM	1965
S1842	GLASS BOTTOM BOAT	TASHLIN	MGM	1966
S1843	SINGING NUN	KOSTER	MGM	1966
S1844	HOLD ON!	LUBIN	MGM	1966
S1845	SPINOUT	TAUROG	MGM	1966
S1846	DOCTOR, YOU'VE GOT TO BE KIDDING	TEWKSBURY	MGM	1967
S1847	VENETIAN AFFAIR	THORPE	MGM	1967
S1848	PENELOPE	HILLER	MGM	1967
S1851	FASTEST GUITAR ALIVE	MOORE	MGM	1967
S1852	LAST CHALLENGE	THORPE	MGM	1967
S1853	POINT BLANK	BOORMAN	MGM	1967
S1854	GUNS FOR SAN SEBASTIAN	VERNEUIL	MGM	1968
S1855	EXTRAORDINARY SEAMAN	FRANKENHEIMER	MGM	1969
S1856	POWER	HASKINS	MGM	1968
S1857	SOL MADRID	HUTTON	MGM	1968
S1858	PHANTOM TOLLBOOTH (t)	JONES, LEVITOW	MGM	1970
S1859	LEGEND OF LYLAH CLARE	ALDRICH	MGM	1968
S1860	SPEEDWAY	TAUROG	MGM	1968
S1861	WHERE WERE YOU WHEN LIGHTS WENT OUT	AVERBACK	MGM	1968
S1862	DAY OF THE EVIL GUN	THORPE	MGM	1968
S1863	IMPOSSIBLE YEARS	GORDON	MGM	1969
S1864	STAY AWAY, JOE	TEWKSBURY	MGM	1968
S1866	TIME TO SING	DREIFUSS	MGM	1968
S1867	SPLIT	FLEMYNG	MGM	1968
S1868	LIVE A LITTLE, LOVE A LITTLE	TAUROG	MGM	1968
S1869	HEAVEN WITH A GUN	KATZIN	MGM	1969
S1870	YOUNG RUNAWAYS	DREIFUSS	MGM	1968
S1871	GYPSY MOTHS	FRANKENHEIMER	MGM	1969
S1872	MARLOWE	BOGART	MGM	1969
S1873	ZABRISKIE POINT	ANTONIONI	MGM	1970
S1875	TROUBLE WITH GIRLS	TEWKSBURY	MGM	1969
S1876	MALTESE BIPPY	PANAMA	MGM	1969
S1877	TICK ... TICK ... TICK	NELSON	MGM	1970
S1878	MAGIC GARDEN STANLEY SWEETHEART	HORN	MGM	1970
S1879	MOONSHINE WAR	QUINE	MGM	1970
S1880	ZIGZAG	COLLA	MGM	1970
S1881	STRAWBERRY STATEMENT	HAGMANN	MGM	1970
S1884	DIRTY DINGUS MAGEE	KENNEDY	MGM	1970
S1885	TRAVELING EXECUTIONER	SMIGHT	MGM	1970
S1886	HOUSE OF DARK SHADOWS	CURTIS	MGM	1970
S1887	ALEX IN WONDERLAND	MAZURSKY	MGM	1970
S1888	BREWSTER MCCLOUD	ALTMAN	MGM	1971
S1889	ELVIS- THAT'S THE WAY IT IS – DOCU.	SANDERS	MGM	1970
S1890	PRETTY MAIDS ALL IN A ROW	VADIM	MGM	1971
S1891	CORKY	HORN	MGM	1973
S1892	BELIEVE IN ME	HAGMANN	MGM	1971
S1893	FORTUNE AND MEN'S EYES	HART	MGM	1971
S1894	WILD ROVERS	EDWARDS	MGM	1971
S1895	SHAFT	PARKS	MGM	1971
S1896	NIGHT OF DARK SHADOWS	CURTIS	MGM	1971
S1897	GANG THAT COULDN'T SHOOT STRAIGHT	GOLDSTONE	MGM	1971
S1898	GOING HOME	LEONARD	MGM	1971
S1899	EVERY LITTLE CROOK AND NANNY	HOWARD	MGM	1972
S1901	WRATH OF GOD	NELSON	MGM	1972
S1902	CAREY TREATMENT	EDWARDS	MGM	1971
S1903	ONE IS A LONELY NUMBER (TWO IS A HAPPY NUMBER)	STUART	MGM	1972
S1904	NIGHTMARE HONEYMOON	SILVERSTEEN	MGM	1973
S1906	SKYJACKED	GUILLERMIN	MGM	1972
S1907	NIGHT OF THE LEPUS	CLAXTON	MGM	1972
S1908	SHAFT'S BIG SCORE	PARKS	MGM	1972
S1909	MELINDA	ROBERTSON	MGM	1972
S1910	THEY ONLY KILL THEIR MASTERS	GOLDSTONE	MGM	1972
S1911	ELVIS ON TOUR (DOCUMENTARY)	ABEL, ADIDGE	MGM	1972
S1912	LOLLY-MADONNA XXX	SARAFIAN	MGM	1973
S1914	WICKED, WICKED	BARE	MGM	1973
S1915	SOYLENT GREEN	FLEISCHER	MGM	1973
S1916	PAT GARRETT AND BILLY THE KID	PECKINPAH	MGM	1973
S1917	SHAFT IN AFRICA	GUILLERMIN	MGM	1973
S1918	MAN WHO LOVED CAT DANCING	SARAFIAN	MGM	1973

Movie Still Identification Book Ultimate Edition - Letters

CODE	TITLE/NAME	DIRECTOR/TYPE	STUDIO/DISTRIBUTOR	YEAR
S1919	TRADER HORN	BADIYI	MGM	1973
S1921	WESTWORLD	CRICHTON	MGM	1973
S1924	THAT'S ENTERTAINMENT	HALEY JR.	MGM	1974
S1926	HEARTS OF THE WEST	ZIEFF	MGM	1975
S1927	SUNSHINE BOYS	ROSS	MGM	1975
S1928	THAT'S ENTERTAINMENT, PART 2	KELLY	MGM	1976
S1933	DEMON SEED	CAMMELL	MGM	1977
S1938	COMA	CRICHTON	MGM	1978
S1939	CORVETTE SUMMER	ROBBINS	MGM	1978
S1941	CHAMP	ZEFFIRELLI	MGM	1979
S1942	HIDE IN PLAIN SIGHT	CAAN	MGM	1980
S1947	WHY WOULD I LIE?	PEERCE	MGM	1980
S1948	FORMULA	AVILDSEN	MGM	1980
S1950	RICH AND FAMOUS	CUKOR	MGM	1981
S1952	BUDDY EBSEN	portrait	MGM	
S1953	PENNIES FROM HEAVEN	ROSS	MGM	1981
S1954	WHOSE LIFE IS IT ANYWAY?	BADHAM	MGM	1982
S1956	BUDDY, BUDDY	WILDER	MGM	1981
S2045	I LOVE MY HUSBAND BUT …	O'BRIEN	MGM	1946
S2056	NOSTRADAMUS SAYS SO	LANDAU	MGM	1953
S2078	DENISE DARCEL	portrait	MGM	
S2501	ROMANCE OF RADIUM	TOURNEUR	MGM	1937
S2502	EQUESTRIAN ACROBATICS	MILLER	MGM	1937
S2504	CARNIVAL IN PARIS	THIELE	MGM	1937
S2505	SONG OF REVOLT	ROWLAND	MGM	1937
S2506	IT MAY HAPPEN TO YOU	BUCQUET	MGM	1937
S2507	HAVE COURAGE	SHERMAN	MGM	1937
S2508	DECATHLON CHAMPION	FEIST	MGM	1937
S2509	HOW TO START THE DAY	ROWLAND	MGM	1937
S2510	SOAK THE POOR	BUCQUET	MGM	1937
S2511	BOSS DIDN'T SAY GOOD MORNING	TOURNEUR	MGM	1937
S2512	GIVE TILL IT HURTS	FEIST	MGM	1937
S2513	KING WITHOUT A CROWN	TOURNEUR	MGM	1937
S2514	JUNGLE JUVENILES #1	HAESELER	MGM	1937
S2515	FRIEND INDEED	ZINNEMANN	MGM	1938
S-2516	CANDID CAMERAMANIACS	YATES	MGM	1937
S2517	BEHIND THE CRIMINAL	BUCQUET	MGM	1937
S2518	MAN IN THE BARN	TOURNEUR	MGM	1937
S2518	NIGHT AT THE MOVIES	ROWLAND	MGM	1937
s2521	CANARY COMES ACROSS	JASON	MGM	1938
S2524	LA SAVATE	MILLER	MGM	1938
S2525	PENNY'S PARTY	MILLER	MGM	1938
S2526	CAPTAIN KIDD'S TREASURE	FENTON	MGM	1938
S2528	THREE ON A ROPE	VAN DER VEER	MGM	1938
S2529	SURF HEROES	TREGO	MGM	1938
S2530	JUNGLE JUVENILES #2	HAESELER	MGM	1938
S2531	STORY OF DR. CARVER	ZINNEMANN	MGM	1938
S2532	WHAT PRICE SAFETY		MGM	1918
S2533	LIFE IN SOMETOWN U.S.A.	KEATON	MGM	1938
S2534	SHIP THAT DIED	TOURNEUR	MGM	1938
S2536	MODELING FOR MONEY	MILLER	MGM	1938
S2537	OPTICAL POEM (t)	FISCHINGER	MGM	1938
S2538	FACE BEHIND THE MASK	TOURNEUR	MGM	1938
S2540	SNOW GETS IN YOUR EYES	JASON	MGM	1938
S2541	MIRACLE MONEY	FENTON	MGM	1938
S2542	MUSIC MADE SIMPLE	ROWLAND	MGM	1938
S2543	EVENING ALONE	ROWLAND	MGM	1938
S2544	HOT ON ICE	LIEB, VAN DER VEER	MGM	1938
S2545	BILLY ROSE'S CASE MANANA REVUE	SIDNEY	MGM	1938
S2546	POETRY OF NATURE	FREEMAN	MGM	1939
S2547	THAT MOTHERS MIGHT LIVE	ZINNEMANN	MGM	1938
S2549	COME ACROSS	BUCQUET	MGM	1938
S2550	TUPAPAOO	TOURNEUR	MGM	1938
S2551	MAGICIAN'S DAUGHTER	FEIST	MGM	1938
S2552	TRACKING THE SLEEPING DEATH	ZINNEMANN	MGM	1938
S2553	JOAQUIN MURIETTA	WILCOX	MGM	1938
S2554	ANAESTHESIA	JASON	MTGM	1938
S2554	ANESTHESIA	JASON	MGM	1938
S2555	IT'S IN THE STARS	MILLER	MGM	1938
S2556	CRIMINAL IS BORN	FENTON	MGM	1938

Movie Still Identification Book Ultimate Edition - Letters

CODE	TITLE/NAME	DIRECTOR/TYPE	STUDIO/DISTRIBUTOR	YEAR
S2557	STRANGE GLORY	TOURNEUR	MGM	1938
S2558	HOLLYWOOD HANDICAP	KEATON	MGM	1938
S2559	HOW TO RAISE A BABY	ROWLAND	MGM	1938
S2560	FOLLOW THE ARROW	FEIST	MGM	1938
S2561	BRAVEST OF THE BRAVE	CAHN	MGM	1938
S2562	COURTSHIP OF THE NEWT	ROWLAND	MGM	1938
S2564	MIRACLE OF SALT LAKE	WRANGELL	MGM	1938
S2565	FISTICUFFS	MILLER	MGM	1938
S2566	LITTLE RANGER	DOUGLAS	MGM	1938
S2567	HOW TO READ	ROWLAND	MGM	1938
S2568	PARTY FEVER	SIDNEY	MGM	1938
S2570	MAN ON THE ROCK	CAHN	MGM	1938
S2571	FOOTBALL THRILLS	SMITH	MGM	1938
S2572	THEY'RE ALWAYS CAUGHT	BUCQUET	MGM	1938
S2573	ALADDIN'S LANTERN	DOUGLAS	MGM	1938
S2574	GRID RULES	CAHN	MGM	1938
S2575	THINK IT OVER	TOURNEUR	MGM	1938
S2576	NOSTRADAMUS	MILLER	MGM	1938
S2577	STREAMLINED SWING	KEATON	MGM	1938
S2578	UNSEEN GUARDIANS	WRANGELL	MGM	1939
S2579	HOW TO WATCH FOOTBALL	ROWLAND	MGM	1938
S2580	MEN IN FRIGHT	SIDNEY	MGM	1938
S2581	CITY OF LITTLE MEN	LOUD	MGM	1938
S2582	PENNY'S PICNIC	JASON	MGM	1938
S2583	THEY LIVE AGAIN	ZINNEMANN	MGM	1938
S2584	OPENING DAY	ROWLAND	MGM	1938
S2585	ALICE WEAVER	portrait	MGM	
S2585	MAN'S GREATEST FRIEND	NEWMAN	MGM	1938
S2586	MEN OF STEEL	LEE	MGM	1938
S2587	DOUBLE DIVING	FEIST	MGM	1939
S2588	ONCE OVER LIGHTLY	JASON	MGM	1938
S2589	FOOTBALL ROMEO	SIDNEY	MGM	1938
S2590	GREAT HEART	MILLER	MGM	1938
S2593	MENTAL POISE	ROWLAND	MGM	1938
S2594	STORY OF ALFRED NOBEL	NEWMAN	MGM	1939
S2595	PRACTICAL JOKERS	SIDNEY	MGM	1938
S2596	WRONG WAY OUT	MACHATY	MGM	1938
S2597	HOUR FOR LUNCH	ROWLAND	MGM	1939
S2598	HOW TO SUBLET	ROWLAND	MGM	1939
S2599	WEATHER WIZARDS	ZINNEMANN	MGM	1939
S2600	ALFALFA'S AUNT	SIDNEY	MGM	1939
S2602	HAPPILY BURIED	FEIST	MGM	1939
S2603	HEROES AT LEISURE	TREGO	MGM	1939
S2604	MARINE CIRCUS	FITZPATRICK	MGM	1939
S2605	ANGEL OF MERCY	CAHN	MGM	1939
S2606	TINY TROUBLES	SIDNEY	MGM	1939
S2607	DREAM OF LOVE	FITZPATRICK	MGM	1939
S2609	SOMEWHAT SECRET	LEE	MGM	1939
S2610	DUEL PERSONALITIES	SIDNEY	MGM	1939
S2611	MONEY TO LOAN	NEWMAN	MGM	1939
S2612	RADIO HAMS	FEIST	MGM	1939
S2613	CLOWN PRINCES	SIDNEY	MGM	1939
S2614	WHILE AMERICA SLEEPS	ZINNEMANN	MGM	1939
S2615	ICE ANTICS	MILLER	MGM	1939
S2616	GIANT OF NORWAY	CAHN	MGM	1939
S2617	PROPHET WITHOUT HONOR	FEIST	MGM	1939
S2618	COUSSIN WILBUR	SIDNEY	MGM	1939
S2619	STORY THAT COULDN'T BE PRINTED	NEWMAN	MGM	1939
S2622	SKI BIRDS	TREGO	MGM	1939
S2623	YANKEE DOODLE GOES TO WAR		MGM	1939
S2624	HOLLYWOOD HOBBIES	SIDNEY	MGM	1939
S2625	HELP WANTED	ZINNEMANN	MGM	1939
S2626	HOW TO EAT	ROWLAND	MGM	1939
S2627	HOME EARLY	ROWLAND	MGM	1939
S2628	DARK MAGIC	ROWLAND	MGM	1939
S2629	CULINARY CARVING	FEIST	MGM	1939
S2629	IT CAN'T BE DONE		MGM	1948
S2630	JOY SCOUTS	CAHN	MGM	1939
S2631	DOG DAZE	SIDNEY	MGM	1939
S2632	AUTO ANTICS	CAHN	MGM	1939

Movie Still Identification Book Ultimate Edition - Letters

CODE	TITLE/NAME	DIRECTOR/TYPE	STUDIO/DISTRIBUTOR	YEAR
S2633	ONE AGAINST THE WORLD	ZINNEMANN	MGM	1939
S2634	TAKE A CUE	FEIST	MGM	1939
S2636	FOOTBALL THRILLS OF 1938	SMITH	MGM	1939
S2637	SEE YOUR DOCTOR	WRANGELL	MGM	1939
S2638	DAY OF REST	WRANGELL	MGM	1939
S2639	THINK FIRST	ROWLAND	MGM	1939
S2640	CAPTAIN SPANKY'S SHOW BOAT	CAHN	MGM	1939
S2641	LET'S TALK TURKEY	FEIST	MGM	1939
S2642	FAILURE AT FIFTY	JASON	MGM	1939
S2644	MIRACLE AT LOURDES	DUNN	MGM	1939
S2645	CHARLTON HESTON	portrait	MGM	
S2645	DAD FOR A DAY	CAHN	MGM	1939
S2646	SET 'EM UP	FEIST	MGM	1939
S2647	RHUMBA RHYTHM HOLLYWOOD LA CONGO	LEE	MGM	1939
S2648	DRUNK DRIVING	MILLER	MGM	1939
S2649	GOODBYE, MISS TURLOCK	CAHN	MGM	1948
S2649	ROMANCE OF THE POTATO	LEE	MGM	1939
S2652	FORGOTTEN VICTORY	ZINNEMANN	MGM	1939
S2653	MAINTAIN THE RIGHT	NEWMAN	MGM	1940
S2654	THAT INFERIOR FEELING	WRANGELL	MGM	1940
S2655	TIME OUT FOR LESSONS	CAHN, MURRAY	MGM	1939
S2656	ALFALFA'S DOUBLE	CAHN	MGM	1940
S2657	MENDELSSOHN'S WEDDING MARCH	FITZPATRICK	MGM	1939
S2658	FLAG SPEAKS	MILLER	MGM	1940
S2659	POUND FOOLISH	FEIST	MGM	1939
S2660	STUFFIE	ZINNEMANN	MGM	1940
S2661	WHERE TURF MEETS SURF	LEE	MGM	1940
S2662	THIRD DIMENSIONAL MURDER	SIDNEY	MGM	1941
S2663	KNOW YOUR MONEY	NEWMAN	MGM	1940
S2664	OLD SOUTH (TRAILER FOR GONE WITH THE WIND)	ZINNEMANN	MGM	1940
S2665	TRIFLES OF IMPORTANCE	WRANGELL	MGM	1940
S2667	NORTHWARD HO	LOUD	MGM	1940
S2668	BUBBLING TROUBLES	CAHN	MGM	1940
S2669	BIG PREMIERE	CAHN	MGM	1940
S2670	CAT COLLEGE	NEWMAN	MGM	1940
S2671	DOMINEERING MALE	HINES	MGM	1940
S2672	JACK POT	ROWLAND	MGM	1940
S2673	WHAT'S YOUR I.Q.		MGM	1940
S2674	ALL ABOUT HASH	CAHN	MGM	1940
S2675	HIDDEN MASTER	LEE	MGM	1940
S2676	XXX MEDICO	WRANGELL	MGM	1940
S2677	NEW PUPIL	CAHN	MGM	1940
S2678	SERVANT OF MANKIND (trailer for EDISON THE MAN)		MGM	1940
S2679	SPOTS BEFORE OUR EYES	HINES	MGM	1940
S2680	GOIN' FISHIN'	CAHN	MGM	1940
S2681	WAY IN THE WILDERNESS	ZINNEMANN	MGM	1940
S2682	WHAT'S YOUR I.Q. #2	SIDNEY	MGM	1940
S2683	FOOTBALL THRILLS OF 1939	SMITH	MGM	1940
S2684	GOOD BAD BOYS (1940)	CAHN	MGM	R54
S2685	WOMEN IN HIDING	NEWMAN	MGM	1940
S2686	WALDO'S LAST STAND	CAHN	MGM	1940
S2687	KIDDIE KURE	CAHN	MGM	1940
S2688	SOCIAL SEA LIONS	HINES	MGM	1940
S2689	RODEO DOUGH	LEE	MGM	1940
S2690	EYES OF THE NAVY		MGM	1940
S2691	BUYER BEWARE	NEWMAN	MGM	1940
S2692	QUICKER'N A WINK	SIDNEY	MGM	1940
S2693	SOAK THE OLD	LEE	MGM	1940
S2694	PLEASE ANSWER (WHAT'S YOUR I.Q. #3)	ROWLAND	MGM	1940
S2695	UTOPIA OF DEATH		MGM	1940
S2696	FIGHTIN' FOOLS	CAHN	MGM	1941
S2697	GREAT MEDDLER	ZINNEMANN	MGM	1940
S2698	DREAMS	FEIST	MGM	1940
S2698	FAMILY TROUBLES	GLAZER	MGM	1943
S2699	BARON AND THE ROSE	WRANGELL	MGM	1940
S2700	MORE ABOUT NOSTRADAMUS	MILLER	MGM	1941
S2701	WEDDING BILLS	MACK	MGM	1940
S2702	AMERICAN SPOKEN HERE	WRANGELL	MGM	1940
S2703	HAPPIEST MAN ON EARTH	MILLER	MGM	1940
S2704	YOU, THE PEOPLE	ROWLAND	MGM	1940

Movie Still Identification Book Ultimate Edition - Letters

CODE	TITLE/NAME	DIRECTOR/TYPE	STUDIO/DISTRIBUTOR	YEAR
S2705	SEA FOR YOURSELF	TREGO	MGM	1940
S2706	BABY BLUES	CAHN	MGM	1941
S2707	AMERICAN SPOKEN HERE	WRANGELL	MGM	1940
S2707	PENNY TO THE RESCUE	JASON	MGM	1941
S2708	RESPECT THE LAW	NEWMAN	MGM	1941
S2709	WHISPERS	WRANGELL	MGM	1941
S2710	1-2-3- GO	CAHN	MGM	1941
S2711	FORBIDDEN PASSAGE	ZINNEMANN	MGM	1941
S2712	QUIZ BIZ (WHAT'S YOUR I.Q. #4)	JASON	MGM	1941
S2713	LIONS ON THE LOOSE	FREEMAN	MGM	1941
S2714	OUT OF DARKNESS	LEE	MGM	1941
S2716	YE OLDE MINSTRELS	CAHN	MGM	1941
S2717	MEMORY TRICKS	JASON	MGM	1941
S2719	THIS IS THE BOWERY	VON FRITSCH	MGM	1941
S2720	COME BACK MISS PIPPS	CAHN	MGM	1941
S2721	GREENER HILLS	LEE	MGM	1939
S2721	MAN WHO CHANGED THE WORLD	LEE	MGM	1941
S2722	AERONAUTICS	CORBY, HARRISON	MGM	1941
S2723	CUBAN RHYTHM	JASON	MGM	1941
S2724	TRIUMPH WITHOUT DRUMS	NEWMAN	MGM	1941
S2725	LISTEN, BOYS	FRITSCH	MGM	1942
S2726	COFFINS ON WHEELS	NEWMAN	MGM	1941
S2727	ARMY CHAMPIONS (PETE SMITH series)	VOGEL	MGM	1941
S2728	WILLIE AND THE MOUSE	SIDNEY	MGM	1941
S2729	BATTLE (sh)		MGM	1941
S2730	YOUR LAST ACT	ZINNEMANN	MGM	1941
S2731	GHOST TREASURE	JASON	MGM	1941
S2732	ROBOT WRECKS	CAHN	MGM	1941
S2733	FOOTBALL THRILLS OF 1940	SMITH	MGM	1941
S2734	WATER BUGS	JASON	MGM	1941
S2735	STROKE OF GENIUS	ROSS	MGM	1938
S2735	SUCKER LIST	ROWLAND	MGM	1941
S2736	TELL TALE HEART	DASSIN	MGM	1941
S2738	HOW TO HOLD YOUR HUSBAND BACK	HINES	MGM	1941
S2739	MAIN STREET ON THE MARCH	CAHN	MGM	1942
S2740	FANCY ANSWER (WHAT'S YOUR I.Q. #5)	WRANGELL	MGM	1941
S2741	MEMORIES OF EUROPE	FITZPATRICK	MGM	1941
S2742	HOBBIES	LABROUSSE	MGM	1941
S2743	CHANGED IDENTITY	ROWLAND	MGM	1941
S2745	FLICKER MEMORIES	SIDNEY	MGM	1941
S2746	SOARING STARS	WRANGELL	MGM	1942
S2747	STRANGE TESTAMENT	LEE	MGM	1941
S2748	WE DO IT BECAUSE	WRANGELL	MGM	1942
S2750	GREENIE	ZINNEMANN	MGM	1942
S2751	WEDDING WORRIES	CAHN	MGM	1941
S2753	VIVA MEXICO	LEWYN	MGM	1941
S2754	AQUA ANTICS	LEWYN	MGM	1942
S2755	MELODIES OLD AND NEW	CAHN	MGM	1942
S2756	WHAT ABOUT DADDY?	JASON	MGM	1942
S2757	LADY OR THE TIGER?	ZINNEMANN	MGM	1942
S2758	GOING TO PRESS	CAHN	MGM	1942
S2760	FILM THAT WAS LOST	LEE	MGM	1942
S2762	FLAG OF MERCY	CAHN	MGM	1942
S2763	VICTORY QUIZ (WHAT'S YOUR I.Q. #6)	JASON	MGM	1942
S2764	ACRO-BATTY	LEWYN	MGM	1942
S2765	FURTHER PROPHECIES OF NOSTRADAMS	MILLER	MGM	1942
S2766	PETE SMITH SCRAPBOOK	SMITH	MGM	1942
S2767	BARBEE-CUES	JASON	MGM	1942
S2768	WOMAN IN THE HOUSE	LEE	MGM	1942
S2769	INCREDIBLE STRANGER	TOURNEUR	MGM	1942
S2770	SURPRISED PARTIES	CAHN	MGM	1942
S2771	DOIN' THEIR BIT	GLAZER	MGM	1942
S2773	MR. BLABBERMOUTH	WRANGELL	MGM	1942
S2774	GOOD JOB		MGM	1942
S2775	FOOTBALL THRILLS OF 1941	SMITH	MGM	1942
S2776	VENDETTA	NEWMAN	MGM	1942
S2777	FOR THE COMMON DEFENSE	KENWARD	MGM	1942
S2778	IT'S A DOG'S LIFE	WOHLMUTH	MGM	1942
S2779	VICTORY VITTLES	JASON	MGM	1942
S2780	ROVER'S BIG CHANCE	GLAZER	MGM	1942

Movie Still Identification Book Ultimate Edition - Letters

CODE	TITLE/NAME	DIRECTOR/TYPE	STUDIO/DISTRIBUTOR	YEAR
S2781	SELF DEFENSE	ANDERSON	MGM	1942
S2783	MIGHTY LAK A GOAT	GLAZER	MGM	1942
S2784	MAGIC ALPHABET	TOURNEUR	MGM	1942
S2785	A.T.C.A.		MGM	1942
S2787	PORTRAIT OF A GENIUS	LEE	MGM	1943
S2789	GREATEST GIFT	DANIELS	MGM	1942
S2790	BRIEF INTERVAL	LEE	MGM	1943
S2791	FAMOUS BONERS	FOSTER	MGM	1942
S2792	MADERO OF MEXICO	CAHN	MGM	1942
S2793	CALLING ALL PA'S	JASON	MGM	1942
S2794	UNEXPECTED RICHES	GLAZER	MGM	1942
S2795	BENJAMIN FRANKLIN, JR.	GLAZER	MGM	1943
S2796	KEEP 'EM SAILING	WRANGELL	MGM	1942
S2797	INCA GOLD	JASON	MGM	1943
S2799	THAT'S WHY I LEFT YOU	CAHN	MGM	1943
S2800	LAST LESSON	KENWARD	MGM	1942
S2801	JOURNEY TO YESTERDAY	DANIELS	MGM	1943
S2804	TRIFLES THAT WIN WARS	DANIELS	MGM	1943
S2805	ELECTION DAZE	GLAZER	MGM	1943
S2806	FIRST AID	JASON	MGM	1943
S2807	PLAN FOR DESTRUCTION	CAHN	MGM	1943
S2809	HERE AT HOME	HART	MGM	1943
S2810	CALLING ALL KIDS	BAERWITZ	MGM	1943
S2813	HOLLYWOOD DAREDEVILS	LEWYN	MGM	1943
S2815	WHO'S SUPERSTITIOUS	LEE	MGM	1943
S2816	DOG HOUSE (t)	HANNA, BARBERA	MGM	1943
S-2816	DOG-HOUSE	WOHLMUTH	MGM	1943
S2818	INFLATION	ENDFIELD	MGM	1943
S2819	FARM HANDS	GLAZER	MGM	1943
S2820	MARINES IN THE MAKING	POLESIE	MGM	1942
S2821	FORGOTTEN TREASURE	LEE	MGM	1943
S2825	SKY SCIENCE	JASON	MGM	1943
S2825	WILD HORSES		MGM	1943
S2826	FALA	VON FRITSCH	MGM	1943
S2827	NURSERY RHYME MYSTERIES	CAHN	MGM	1943
S2828	PEOPLE OF RUSSIA		MGM	1942
S2829	HEAVENLY MUSIC	BERNE	MGM	1943
S2830	LITTLE MISS PINKERTON	GLAZER	MGM	1943
S2831	SEEING HANDS	VON FRITSCH	MGM	1943
S2832	WOOD GOES TO WAR		MGM	1943
S2833	STORM	BURNFORD	MGM	1943
S2834	ODE TO VICTORY	CAHN	MGM	1943
S2835	SHOE SHINE BOY	HART	MGM	1943
S2838	TO MY UNBORN SON	KARDOS	MGM	1943
S2840	NOSTRADAMUS IV	BURNFORD, ENDFIELD	MGM	1944
S2841	FIRST AID	JASON	MGM	1943
S2841	SEVENTH COLUMN	JASON	MGM	1943
S2842	FIXIN' TRICKS	JASON	MGM	1943
S2844	THREE SMART GUYS	CAHN	MGM	1943
S2845	FOOTBALL THRILLS OF 1942	SMITH	MGM	1943
S2846	THIS IS TOMORROW	NESBITT	MGM	1943
S2848	SCRAP HAPPY	JASON	MGM	1943
S2849	MEMORIES OF AUSTRALIA		MGM	1943
S2854	KID IN UPPER FOUR		MGM	1943
S2855	PRACTICAL JOKER	JASON	MGM	1944
S2856	TIPS ON TRIPS (WHAT'S YOUR I.Q. #7)	JASON	MGM	1943
S2857	NO NEWS IS GOOD NEWS	JASON	MGM	1943
S2858	SOMEWHERE U.S.A.	KNOX, VON FRITSCH	MGM	1944
S2859	MY TOMATO	JASON	MGM	1943
S2860	RADIO BUGS	ENDFIELD	MGM	1944
S2861	DANCING ROMEO	ENDFIELD	MGM	1944
S2862	WATER WISDOM	SMITH	MGM	1943
S2863	IMPORTANT BUSINESS	JASON	MGM	1944
S2864	WHY DADDY?	JASON	MGM	1944
S2866	TALE OF A DOG (OUR GANG series)	ENDFIELD	MGM	1944
S2867	HOME MAID	JASON	MGM	1944
S2868	RETURN FROM NOWHERE	BURNFORD	MGM	1944
S2869	EASY LIFE	HART	MGM	1944
S2870	HOLLYWOOD SCOUT	ANSEN	MGM	1945
S2871	MAIN STREET TODAY	CAHN	MGM	1944

Movie Still Identification Book Ultimate Edition - Letters

CODE	TITLE/NAME	DIRECTOR/TYPE	STUDIO/DISTRIBUTOR	YEAR
S2873	GROOVIE MOVIE	JASON	MGM	1944
S2874	PATROLLING THE ETHER	BURNFORD	MGM	1944
S2875	SPORTSMAN'S MEMORIES		MGM	1944
S2876	GREAT DAY'S COMING	ELWYN	MGM	1944
S2877	IMMORTAL BLACKSMITH	LEE	MGM	1944
S2878	GRANDPA CALLED IT ART	HART	MGM	1944
S2879	LADY FIGHTS BACK		MGM	1944
S2884	SAFETY SLEUTH	JASON	MGM	1944
S2885	MOVIE PESTS	JASON	MGM	1944
S2886	DARK SHADOWS	BURNFORD, HART	MGM	1944
S2888	STRANGE DESTINY	BURNFORD	MGM	1945
S2889	FOOTBALL THRILLS OF 1943	SMITH	MGM	1944
S2891	SPORTS QUIZ (WHAT'S YOUR I.Q. #8)		MGM	1944
S2892	SPREADIN' THE JAM	WALTERS	MGM	1945
S2893	LAST INSTALLMENT	HART	MGM	1945
S2894	SEESAW AND THE SHOES	FOSTER	MGM	1945
S2895	GETTIN' GLAMOUR	ANDERSON	MGM	1946
S2900	PHANTOMS	YOUNG	MGM	1945
S2901	LITTLE WHITE LIE	BURNFORD	MGM	1945
S2902	MUSICAL MASTERPIECES	PYE	MGM	1946
S2903	MIRACLE IN A CORNFIELD	NESBITT	MGM	1947
S2906	GUEST PESTS	JASON	MGM	1945
S2907	TRACK AND FIELD QUIZ (WHAT'S YOUR I.Q. #9)		MGM	1945
S2909	FALL GUY	BURNFORD	MGM	1945
S2910	GREAT AMERICAN MUG	ENDFIELD	MGM	1945
S2912	FALA AT HYDE PARK	VON FRITSCH	MGM	1946
S2913	BADMINTON	ANDERSON	MGM	1945
S2915	GOLDEN HUNCH		MGM	1945
S2917	FOOTBALL THRILLS OF 1944	SMITH	MGM	1945
S2918	MAGIC ON A STICK	ENDFIELD	MGM	1946
S2920	PEOPLE ON PAPER	MORGAN	MGM	1945
S2921	OUR OLD CAR	ENDFIELD	MGM	1946
S2922	GUN IN HIS HAND	LOSEY	MGM	1945
S2923	STUDIO VISIT	SMITH	MGM	1946
S2924	STAIRWAY TO LIGHT	LEE	MGM	1945
S2925	SPORTS STICKLERS (WHAT'S YOUR I.Q. #10)	O'BRIEN	MGM	1946
S2926	PURITY SQUAD	KRESS	MGM	1945
S2928	BUS PESTS	REISNER	MGM	1945
S2929	EQUESTRIAN QUIZ (WHAT'S YOUR I.Q. #11)		MGM	1946
S2929	WRONG SON	VON FRITSCH	MGM	1950
S2932	TREASURES FROM TRASH	O'BRIEN	MGM	1946
S2933	FOOTBALL THRILLS #9	SMITH	MGM	1946
S2935	PLAYING BY EAR	O'BRIEN	MGM	1946
S2936	SURFBOARD RHYTHM	O'BRIEN	MGM	1947
S2937	SURE CURES	O'BRIEN	MGM	1946
S2938	BIKINI, THE ATOM ISLAND	WILSON	MGM	1946
S2939	NEIGHBOR PESTS	O'BRIEN	MGM	1947
S2941	DIAMOND DEMON	O'BRIEN	MGM	1947
S2943	ATHLETIQUIZ (WHAT'S YOUR I.Q. #12)		MGM	1947
S2944	EARLY SPORTS QUIZ (WHAT'S YOUR I.Q. #13)		MGM	1947
S2945	I LOVE MY HUSBAND, BUT	O'BRIEN	MGM	1946
S2946	REALLY IMPORTANT PERSON	WRANGELL	MGM	1947
S2947	LUCKIEST GUY IN THE WORLD	NEWMAN	MGM	1947
S2948	I LOVE MY WIFE BUT ...	O'BRIEN	MGM	1947
S2949	GOODBYE, MISS TURLOCK	CAHN	MGM	1948
S2950	SCIENTIFIQUIZ (WHAT'S YOUR I.Q. #15)		MGM	1949
S2951	WHAT D'YA KNOW (WHAT'S YOUR I.Q.)	O'BRIEN	MGM	1947
S2952	AMAZING MR. NORDILL	NEWMAN	MGM	1947
S2953	PET PEEVES	O'BRIEN	MGM	1947
S2954	THOSE GOOD OLD DAYS	O'BRIEN	MGM	1949
S2956	FOOTBALL THRILLS #10	O'BRIEN	MGM	1947
S2958	I LOVE MY MOTHER-IN-LAW BUT ...	O'BRIEN	MGM	1948
S2960	HAVE YOU EVER WONDERED	O'BRIEN	MGM	1947
S-2961	FISHING FOR FUN	OSSI	MGM	1949
S2962	MY OLD TOWN	NESBITT	MGM	1948
S2963	NOW YOU SEE IT	CASSELL	MGM	1948
S2964	BOWLING TRICKS	O'BRIEN	MGM	1948
S2965	YOU CAN'T WIN	O'BRIEN	MGM	1948
S2966	TENNIS IN RHYTHM	MURRAY	MGM	1949
S2967	GIVE US THE EARTH	VON FRITSCH	MGM	1947

Movie Still Identification Book Ultimate Edition - Letters

CODE	TITLE/NAME	DIRECTOR/TYPE	STUDIO/DISTRIBUTOR	YEAR
S2968	SPORTS ODDITIES		MGM	1949
S2969	IT CAN'T BE DONE		MGM	1948
S2975	JUST SUPPOSE	O'BRIEN	MGM	1948
S2976	LET'S COGITATE	O'BRIEN	MGM	1948
S2977	TEX BENEKE		MGM	1948
S2978	CITY OF CHILDREN	NESBITT	MGM	1949
S2983	PEST CONTROL	O'BRIEN	MGM	1950
S2984	FABULOUS FRAUD	CAHN	MGM	1948
S2985	SOUVENIRS OF DEATH	CAHN	MGM	1948
S2988	WHY IS IT?	O'BRIEN	MGM	1948
S2991	FOOTBALL THRILLS #11	SMITH	MGM	1948
S2992	PIGSKIN SKILL	DUDLEY	MGM	1948
S2993	CRASHING THE MOVIES	ANSEN	MGM	1950
S2995	ICE ACES	O'BRIEN	MGM	1948
S2996	SUPER CUE MEN	ANSEN	MGM	1949
S2997	WHAT I WANT NEXT	O'BRIEN	MGM	1949
S2998	SCREEN ACTORS		MGM	1950
S3000	WATER TRIX	TREGO	MGM	1949
S3001	GOING TO BLAZES	VON FRITSCH	MGM	1948
S3002	CLUES TO ADVENTURE	NESBITT	MGM	1949
S3003	DID' JA KNOW	O'BRIEN	MGM	1950
S3004	HOW COME	O'BRIEN	MGM	1949
S3005	ANNIE WAS A WONDER	CAHN	MGM	1949
S3006	STUFF FOR STUFF		MGM	1949
S3007	WE CAN DREAM, CAN'T WE	O'BRIEN	MGM	1949
S3008	TABLE TOPPERS	O'BRIEN	MGM	1950
S3009	MR. WHITNEY HAD A NOTION	MAYER	MGM	1949
S3010	FOOTBALL THRILLS #12	SMITH	MGM	1949
S3011	THAT'S HIS STORY	O'BRIEN	MGM	1950
S3012	CURIOUS CONTESTS		MGM	1950
S3013	THAT'S WHAT YOU THINK	O'BRIEN	MGM	1951
S3014	MUSIQUIZ (WHAT'S YOUR I.Q. #16)	O'BRIEN	MGM	1952
S3015	CAMERA SLEUTH	O'BRIEN	MGM	1951
S3016	MOMENTS IN MUSIC		MGM	1950
S3017	HEART TO HEART	VON FRITSCH	MGM	1949
S3018	FIXIN' FOOL	O'BRIEN	MGM	1951
S3019	IN CASE YOU'RE CURIOUS	O'BRIEN	MGM	1951
S3020	I LOVE CHILDREN, BUT	O'BRIEN	MGM	1952
S3021	WIFE'S LIFE	O'BRIEN	MGM	1950
S3022	SKY SKIERS	TREGO	MGM	1951
S3023	SWEET MEMORIES	O'BRIEN	MGM	1952
S3024	FOOTBALL THRILLS #13	SMITH	MGM	1950
S3025	WANTED: ONE EGG	O'BRIEN	MGM	1950
S3027	WRONG WAY BUTCH	O'BRIEN	MGM	1950
S3028	MEALTIME MAGIC	O'BRIEN	MGM	1952
S3028	TRAVEL QUIZ (WHAT'S YOUR I.Q. #17)		MGM	1953
S3029	BARGAIN MADNESS	O'BRIEN	MGM	1951
S3030	BANDAGE BAIT	O'BRIEN	MGM	1951
S3031	IT COULD HAPPEN TO YOU	O'BRIEN	MGM	1952
S3033	AIN'T IT AGGRAVATIN'	O'BRIEN	MGM	1954
S3034	ANCIENT CURES (PETE SMITH series)		MGM	1953
S3035	REDUCING	O'BRIEN	MGM	1952
S3037	FOOTBALL THRILLS #14	SMITH	MGM	1951
S3038	MEALTIME MAGIC	O'BRIEN	MGM	1952
S3039	FISHING FEATS	TREGO	MGM	1951
S3041	THIS IS A LIVING?	SMITH	MGM	1953
S3042	DO SOMEONE A FAVOR	O'BRIEN	MGM	1954
S3043	GYMNASTIC RHYTHM	O'BRIEN	MGM	1952
S3044	PEDESTRIAN SAFETY	O'BRIEN	MGM	1952
S3047	LANDLORDING IT	O'BRIEN	MGM	1953
S3048	MOSCONI STORY	O'BRIEN	MGM	1953
S3049	FILM ANTICS	O'BRIEN	MGM	1954
S3051	AQUATIC KIDS		MGM	1953
S3052	KEEP IT CLEAN	O'BRIEN	MGM	1952
S3053	FOOTBALL THRILLS #15	SMITH	MGM	1952
S3054	IT WOULD SERVE 'EM RIGHT	O'BRIEN	MGM	1953
S3055	OUT FOR FUN	O'BRIEN	MGM	1954
S3056	NOSTRADAMUS SAYS SO	LANDAU	MGM	1953
S3058	DOGS 'N DUCKS	BEEBEM WRIGHT	MGM	1953
S3062	POSTMAN		MGM	1953

Movie Still Identification Book Ultimate Edition - Letters

CODE	TITLE/NAME	DIRECTOR/TYPE	STUDIO/DISTRIBUTOR	YEAR
S3063	CASH STASHERS	O'BRIEN	MGM	1953
S3066	FISH TALES	DUDLEY	MGM	1954
S3068	NOSTRADAMUS AND THE QUEEN (1942)		MGM	R53
S3069	THINGS WE CAN DO WITHOUT	O'BRIEN	MGM	1953
S3070	SAFE AT HOME	O'BRIEN	MGM	1954
S3072	MERRY WIVES OF WINDSOR		MGM	1954
S3073	POET AND PEASANT OVERTURE		MGM	1954
S3075	MGM JUBILEE		MGM	1954
S3109	IN CASE YOU'RE CURIOUS	O'BRIEN	MGM	1951
S3602	LITTLE JOURNEY	LEONARD	MGM	1927
S3699	MITCHELL BROTHER	portrait	MGM	
S3700	MITCHELL BROTHER	portrait	MGM	
S3701	MITCHELL BROTHER	portrait	MGM	
S3702	MITCHELL BROTHER	portrait	MGM	
S4001	CAPITAL CITY, WASHINGTON D.C.	FITZPATRICK	MGM	1940
S4002	CATERED AFFAIR	BROOKS	MGM	1956
S4002	CAVALCADE OF SAN FRANCISCO	FITZPATRICK	MGM	1940
S4003	OLD NEW MEXICO	FITZPATRICK	MGM	1940
S4004	BEAUTIFUL BALI	FITZPATRICK	MGM	1940
S4005	OLD NEW ORLEANS	FITZPATRICK	MGM	1940
S4006	MEDITERRANEAN PORTS OF CALL	FITZPATRICK	MGM	1941
S4007	RED MEN ON PARADE	FITZPATRICK	MGM	1941
S4008	ALLURING ALASKA	FITZPATRICK	MGM	1941
S4009	GLIMPSES OF KENTUCKY	FITZPATRICK	MGM	1941
S4010	YOSEMITE THE MAGNIFICENT	FITZPATRICK	MGM	1941
S4011	GLIMPSES OF WASHINGTON STATE	FITZPATRICK	MGM	1941
S4012	HAITI, LAND OF DARK MAJESTY	FITZPATRICK	MGM	1941
S4013	GLIMPSES OF FLORIDA	FITZPATRICK	MGM	1941
S4014	INSIDE PASSAGE	FITZPATRICK	MGM	1941
S4015	GEORGETOWN, PRIDE OF PENANG	FITZPATRICK	MGM	1941
S4016	SCENIC GRANDEUR	FITZPATRICK	MGM	1941
S4017	MINNESOTA, LAND OF PLENTY	FITZPATRICK	MGM	1942
S4018	HISTORIC MARYLAND	FITZPATRICK	MGM	1941
S4019	WEST POINT ON THE HUDSON	FITZPATRICK	MGM	1942
S4020	COLORFUL NORTH CAROLINA	FITZPATRICK	MGM	1942
S4021	LAND OF THE QUINTUPLETS	FITZPATRICK	MGM	1942
S4022	GLACIER PARK AND WATERTON LAKES	FITZPATRICK	MGM	1942
S4023	PICTURESQUE PATZCUARO	FITZPATRICK	MGM	1942
S4024	EXOTIC MEXICO	FITZPATRICK	MGM	1942
S4025	PICTURESQUE MASSACHUSETTS	FITZPATRICK	MGM	1942
S4026	MODERN MEXICO CITY	FITZPATRICK	MGM	1942
S4027	GLIMPSES OF ONTARIO	FITZPATRICK	MGM	1942
S4028	LAND OF ORIZABA	FITZPATRICK	MGM	1943
S4029	MIGHTY NIAGARA	FITZPATRICK	MGM	1943
S4030	MEXICAN POLICE ON PARADE	FITZPATRICK	MGM	1943
S4031	MOTORING IN MEXICO	FITZPATRICK	MGM	1943
S4032	ON THE ROAD TO MONTEREY	FITZPATRICK	MGM	1943
S4033	ROMANTIC NEVADA	FITZPATRICK	MGM	1943
S4034	SCENIC OREGON	FITZPATRICK	MGM	1943
S4035	GLIMPSES OF MEXICO	FITZPATRICK	MGM	1943
S4036	OVER THE ANDES	FITZPATRICK	MGM	1943
S4037	THROUGH THE COLORADO ROCKIES	FITZPATRICK	MGM	1943
S4038	GRAND CANYON, PRIDE OF CREATION	FITZPATRICK	MGM	1943
S4039	DAY IN DEATH VALLEY	FITZPATRICK	MGM	1944
S4040	SALT LAKE DIVERSIONS	FITZPATRICK	MGM	1943
S4041	MACKINAC ISLAND	FITZPATRICK	MGM	1944
S4042	VISITING ST. LOUIS	FITZPATRICK	MGM	1944
S4043	ALONG THE CACTUS TRAIL	FITZPATRICK	MGM	1944
S4044	ROAMING THROUGH ARIZONA	FITZPATRICK	MGM	1944
S4045	COLORFUL COLORADO	FITZPATRICK	MGM	1944
S4046	CITY OF BRIGHAM YOUNG	FITZPATRICK	MGM	1944
S4047	MONUMENTAL UTAH	FITZPATRICK	MGM	1944
S4048	WANDERING HERE AND THERE	FITZPATRICK	MGM	1944
S4049	SEEING EL SALVADOR	FITZPATRICK	MGM	1945
S4051	LAND OF THE MAYAS	FITZPATRICK	MGM	1946
S4052	MERIDA AND CAMPECHE	FITZPATRICK	MGM	1945
S4053	MODERN GUATEMALA CITY	FITZPATRICK	LMGM	1945
S4054	WHERE TIME STANDS STILL	FITZPATRICK	MGM	1945
S4055	GLIMPSES OF GUATEMALA	FITZPATRICK	MGM	1946
S4056	VISITING VERA CRUZ	FITZPATRICK	MGM	1946

Movie Still Identification Book Ultimate Edition - Letters

CODE	TITLE/NAME	DIRECTOR/TYPE	STUDIO/DISTRIBUTOR	YEAR
S4057	MISSION TRAIL	FITZPATRICK	MGM	1946
S4058	CALLING ON COSTA RICA	FITZPATRICK	MGM	1947
S4059	GLIMPSES OF CALIFORNIA	FITZPATRICK	MGM	1946
S4060	AROUND THE WORLD IN CALIFORNIA	FITZPATRICK	MGM	1947
S4061	ON THE SHORES OF NOVA SCOTIA	FITZPATRICK	MGM	1947
S4062	LOOKING AT LONDON	FITZPATRICK	MGM	1946
S4063	VISITING VIRGINIA	SMITH	MGM	1947
S4064	CRADLE OF A NATION	SMITH	MGM	1947
S4065	CAPE BRETON ISLAND	FITZPATRICK	MGM	1948
S4066	GLIMPSES OF NEW SCOTLAND	FITZPATRICK	MGM	1947
S4067	OVER THE SEAS TO BELFAST	FITZPATRICK	MGM	1946
S4068	WANDERING THROUGH WALES	FITZPATRICK	MGM	1948
S4069	FROM LIVERPOOL TO STRATFORD	DONALDSON	MGM	1949
S4070	SCHOLASTIC ENGLAND	FITZPATRICK	MGM	1948
S4071	GLIMPSES OF OLD ENGLAND	FITZPATRICK	MGM	1949
S4072	ROAMING THROUGH NORTHERN IRELAND	FITZPATRICK	MGM	1949
S4073	TO THE COAST OF DEVON	FITZPATRICK	MGM	1950
S4074	LAND OF TRADITION	FITZPATRICK	MGM	1950
S4075	WEE BIT OF SCOTLAND	FITZPATRICK	MGM	1949
S4076	TOURING NORTHERN ENGLAND	FITZPATRICK	MGM	1950
S4077	LAND OF AULD LANG SYNE	FITZPATRICK	MGM	1950
S4078	LIFE ON THE THAMES	FITZPATRICK	MGM	1950
S4079	PASTORAL PANORAMAS	FITZPATRICK	MGM	1950
S4080	CHICAGO THE BEAUTIFUL	FITZPATRICK	MGM	1948
S4081	NIGHT LIFE IN CHICAGO	FITZPATRICK	MGM	1948
S4082	CALLING ON MICHIGAN	FITZPATRICK	MGM	1949
S4083	MIGHTY MANHATTAN, NEW YORK'S WONDER CITY	SMITH	MGM	1949
S4084	QUEBEC IN SUMMERTIME	FITZPATRICK	MGM	1949
S4085	ONTARIO, LAND OF LAKES	FITZPATRICK	MGM	1949
S4086	PLAYLANDS OF MICHIGAN	FITZPATRICK	MGM	1949
S4087	ROAMING THROUGH MICHIGAN	FITZPATRICK	MGM	1950
S4088	IN OLD AMSTERDAM	DONALDSON	MGM	1949
S4089	COLORFUL HOLLAND	DONALDSON	MGM	1950
S4090	LAND OF THE ZUIDER ZEE	FITZPATRICK	MGM	1951
S4091	SPRINGTIME IN THE NETHERLANDS	FITZPATRICK	MGM	1951
S4092	VOICES OF VENICE	FITZPATRICK	MGM	1951
S4093	EGYPT SPEAKS	FITZPATRICK	MGM	1951
S4094	WORD FOR THE GREEKS	FITZPATRICK	MGM	1951
S4095	ROMANTIC RIVIERA	FITZPATRICK	MGM	1951
S4096	GLIMPSES OF MOROCCO & ALGIERS	FITZPATRICK	MGM	1951
S4097	VISITING ITALY	FITZPATRICK	MGM	1951
S4098	GLIMPSES OF ARGENTINA	FITZPATRICK	MGM	1951
S4099	BEAUTIFUL BRAZIL	FITZPATRICK	MGM	1951
S4100	PICTURESQUE NEW ZEALAND	FITZPATRICK	MGM	1952
S4101	LIFE IN THE ANDES	FITZPATRICK	MGM	1952
S4102	LAND OF THE TAJ MAHAL	FITZPATRICK	MGM	1952
S4103	SEEING CEYLON	FITZPATRICK	MGM	1952
S4104	JASPER NATIONAL PARK	FITZPATRICK	MGM	1952
S4105	ANCIENT INDIA	FITZPATRICK	MGM	1952
S4106	PRETORIA TO DURBAN	FITZPATRICK	MGM	1952
S4107	IN THE LAND OF DIAMONDS	FITZPATRICK	MGM	1952
S4108	CALLING ON CAPETOWN	FITZPATRICK	MGM	1952
S4110	LAND OF THE UGLY DUCKING	FITZPATRICK	MGM	1953
S4111	JOHANNESBURG – CITY OF GOLD	FITZPATRICK	MGM	1953
S4112	DELIGHTFUL DENMARK	FITZPATRICK	MGM	1953
S4113	COPENHAGEN, CITY OF TOWERS	FITZPATRICK	MGM	1953
S4114	SEEING SPAIN	FITZPATRICK	MGM	1953
S4115	IN THE VALLEY OF THE RHINE	FITZPATRICK	MGM	1953
S4116	LOOKING AT LISBON	FITZPATRICK	MGM	1953
S4117	GLIMPSES OF WESTERN GERMANY	FITZPATRICK	MGM	1954
S4660	RAGS RAGLAND	portrait	MGM	
S4662	RAGS RAGLAND	portrait	MGM	
S4744	PETER LAWFORD	portrait	MGM	
S4804	HOLLYWOOD PARTY (1934) SHOWGIRLS	portrait	MGM	
S4813	HOLLYWOOD PARTY (1934) SHOWGIRLS	portrait	MGM	
S4925	HURD HATFIELD	portrait	MGM	
S5033	VILLAGE OF THE DAMNED	RILLA	MGM	1960
S5047	SECRET PARTNER	DEARDEN	MGM	1961
S5061	VERY PRIVATE AFFAIR	MALLE	MGM	1962
S5074	CAPTAIN SINBAD	HASKIN	MGM	1963

Movie Still Identification Book Ultimate Edition - Letters

CODE	TITLE/NAME	DIRECTOR/TYPE	STUDIO/DISTRIBUTOR	YEAR
S5075	TARZAN GOES TO INDIA	GUILLERMIN	MGM	1962
S5170	GONE WITH THE WIND (1939)	FLEMING	MGM	R68
S5174	GONE WITH THE WIND (1939)	FLEMING	MGM	R68
S5233	SHOOT THE MOON	PARKER	MGM	1982
S5302	IN THE COOL OF THE DAY	STEVENS	MGM	1963
S5303	HAUNTING	WISE	MGM	1963
S5308	RHINO!	TORS	MGM	1964
S5309	V.I.P.'S	ASQUITH	MGM	1963
S5587	ELISABETH MUELLER	portrait	MGM	
S5593	WHERE THE BOYS ARE	LEVIN	MGM	1960
S5710	PETER LAWFORD	portrait	MGM	
S6025	KARATE KILLERS	SHEAR	MGM	1967
S6050	HOT RODS TO HELL	BRAHM	MGM	1967
S6400	RAGS RAGLAND	portrait	MGM	
S7004	SING AND BE HAPPY	KEMP	UNIVERSAL	1946
S7005	SING AND BE HAPPY	KEMP	UNIVERSAL	1946
S7006	SIX GUN MUSIC	WATT	UNIVERSAL	1948
S7007	CHEYENNE COWBOY	WATT	UNIVERSAL	1948
S7009	TED WEEMS	portrait	MGM	
S7011	WEST OF LARAMIE	COWAN	UNIVERSAL	1948
S7012	PRAIRIE PIRATES	COWAN	UNIVERSAL	1948
S7015	DUKE ELLINGTON	portrait	MGM	
S7018	SILVER BUTTE	COWAN	UNIVERSAL	1948
S7019	NEVADA TRAIL	MARTELL	UNIVERSAL	1948
S7020	PECOS PISTOL (GIRL FROM GUNSIGHT)	COWAN	UNIVERSAL	1948
S7022	TED FRENTA	portrait	MGM	
S7023	DEL COURTNEY	portrait	MGM	
S7025	SPADE COOLEY	portrait	MGM	
S7027	WESTERN COURAGE	COWAN	UNIVERSAL	1949
S7034	COYOTE CANYON	COWAN	UNIVERSAL	1949
S7035	FARGO PHANTOM	COWAN	UNIVERSAL	1949
S7036	GOLD STRIKE	COWAN	UNIVERSAL	1949
S7037	RUSTLER'S RANSOM	COWAN	UNIVERSAL	1949
S7045	CACTUS CARAVAN/READY TO RIDE	COWAN	UNIVERSAL	1949
S7755	HOW GRINCH STOLE CHRISTMAS (t)	JONES	MGM	1966
S9433	IT'S A WISE CHILD	LEONARD	MGM	1931
S9676	HURD HATFIELD	portrait	MGM	
SA	FELLINI SATYRICON (IT)	FELLINI	UNITED ARTISTS	1969
SA	GIVE ME YOUR HEART	MAYO	WARNER BROS	1936
SA	I SELL ANYTHING	FLOREY	WARNER BROS	1934
SA	SAINTS AND SINNERS (UK)	ARLISS	LOPERT	1949
SA	SAY ANYTHING	CROWE	20th CENTURY FOX	1989
SA	SCATTERGOOD RIDES HIGH	CABANNE	RKO	1942
SA	SECRETS OF AN ACTRESS	KEIGHLEY	WARNER BROS	1938
SA	SHOOT TO KILL	BERKE	SCREEN GUILD	1947
SA	SILKEN AFFAIR (UK)	KELLINO	DCA	1956
SA	SPECIAL AGENT	KEIGHLEY	WARNER BROS	1935
SA	SPY 77 (UK: ON SECRET SERVICE)	WOODS	FIRST DIVISION	1933
SA	STEPPING ALONG	HINES	FIRST NATIONAL	1926
SA	STRANGE AFFAIR (UK)	GREEN	PARAMOUNT	1968
SA	STRANGE ALIBI	LEDERMAN	WARNER BROS	1941
SA	STRANGERS ALL	VIDOR	RKO	1935
SA	WARRIOR EXPRESS	FRANCISCI	COLUMBIA	1961
SAC	SPARE A COPPER (UK)	CARSTAIRS	ABFD	1940
SAE	SIN OF ADAM AND EVE (MEX: PECADO D ADAN Y EVA 1969)	ZACHARY	DEMENSION	1972
SAF	SAFARI 300	HURWITZ	UNITED ARTISTS	1982
SAH	SAHARA	MCLAGLEN	CANNON	1983
SAL	SONS AND LOVERS (UK)	CARDIFF	20TH CENTURY FOX	1960
SAM	SUPERMAN AND THE MOLE MEN	SHOLEM	LIPPERT	1951
SAN	SANDWICH MAN (UK)	HARTFORD-DAVIS	RANK	1966
SAN-2	ROMANCE OF THE RIO GRANDE	SANTELL	FOX FILM	1929
SAN-3	ARIZONA KID	SANTELL	FOX FILM	1930
SAN-4	SEA WOLF	SANTELL	FOX FILM	1930
SAN-5	BODY AND SOUL	SANTELL	FOX FILM	1931
SAN-6	DADDY LONG LEGS	SANTELL	FOX FILM	1931
SAN-7	SOB SISTER	SANTELL	FOX FILM	1931
SAN-8	REBECCA OF SUNNYBROOK FARM	SANTELL	FOX FILM	1932
SAN-9	TESS OF THE STORM COUNTRY	SANTELL	FOX FILM	1932
SAN-10	BONDAGE	SANTELL	FOX FILM	1933
SAS	ALIAS FRENCH GERTI	ARCHAINBAUD	RKO	1930

Movie Still Identification Book Ultimate Edition - Letters

CODE	TITLE/NAME	DIRECTOR/TYPE	STUDIO/DISTRIBUTOR	YEAR
SAS	SAY AMEN, SOMEBODY	NIERENBERG	UNITED ARTISTS	1982
SAS	SOLOMON AND SHEBA	VIDOR	UNITED ARTISTS	1959
SAS	SOLOMON AND SHEBA	VIDOR	UNITED ARTISTS	1959
SAU	SEA AROUND US	CARSON	RKO	1953
SAW	STRANGE BARGAIN	PRICE	RKO	1949
SAWM	SING ALONG WITH ME (UK)	SCOTT	BRITISH LION	1952
SB	BORN TO WIN	PASSER	UNITED ARTISTS	1971
SB	FUN ON A WEEK-END (STRANGE BEDFELLOWS)	STONE	UNITED ARTISTS	1947
SB	LAST FLIGHT	DIETERLE	WARNER BROS	1931
SB	MEET SEXTON BLAKE (UK)	HARLOW	ANGLO-AMERICAN	1945
SB	PANIC IN THE PARLOR (UK: SAILOR BEWARE)	PARRY	DCA	1956
SB	SABINA BETHMANN	portrait	UNIVERSAL	
SB	SALOON BAR (UK)	FORDE	ABFD	1940
SB	SATAN BUG	STURGES	UNITED ARTISTS	1965
SB	SCOTT BRADY	portrait	UNIVERSAL	
SB	SEA BEAST	WEBB	WARNER BROS	1926
SB	SECOND BUREAU (UK)	HANBURY	RKO	1936
SB	SHE BEAST (UK)	REEVES		1966
SB	SIDNEY BLACKMER	portrait	FN, RKO	
SB	SIERRA BARON	CLARK	20th CENTURY FOX	1958
SB	SILVER BULLET	ATTAIS	PARAMOUNT	1985
SB	SITTING BULL	SALKOW	UNITED ARTISTS	1954
SB	SLEEPING BEAUTY (t)	GERONIMI	BUENA VISTA	R70S
SB	SMILEY BURNETTE	portrait	REPUBLIC	
SB	SMITH BALLEW	portrait	RKO	
SB	SMOKE BELLEW	DUNLAP	FIRST DIVISION	1929
SB	SO BIG	BRABIN	FIRST NATIONAL	1924
SB	SO BIG	WELLMAN	WARNER BROS	1932
SB	SONNY BOY	MAYO	WARNER BROS	1929
SB	SPIDER AND THE FLY (UK)	HAMER	UNIVERSAL	1949
SB	SPRING BYINGTON	portrait	RKO	
SB	ST. BENNY THE DIP	ULMER	UNITED ARTISTS	1951
SB	STARS OVER BROADWAY	KEIGHLEY	WARNER BROS	1935
SB	STEEL BAYONET (UK)	CARRERAS	UNITED ARTISTS	1957
SB	STEPHANIE BACHELOR	portrait		
SB	STEPHEN BROOKS	portrait	WARNER BROS-TV	
SB	STEVE BRODIE	portrait	RKO	
SB	STORM BOUND (IT)	CAPUANO	REPUBLIC	1951
SB	STRAWBERRY BLONDE	WALSH	WARNER BROS	1941
SB	SUICIDE BATTALION	CAHN	AIP	1958
SB	SUSAN BLAKELY	portrait	UNITED ARTISTS	
SB	SUZAN BALL (SUSAN BALL)	portrait	UNIVERSAL	
SB	UNDERCOVERS HERO (UK: SOFT BEDS, HARD BATTLES)	BOULTING	UNITED ARTISTS	1974
SB	VILLAGE SQUIRE (UK)	DENHAM	PARAMOUNT BRITISH	1935
SB-1	SCATTERGOOD BAINES	CABANNE	RKO	1941
SB-4	SCATTERGOOD SURVIVES A MURDER	CABANNE	RKO	1942
SB-8900	JACK LONDON	SANTELL	UNITED ARTISTS	1943
SBA	SINK THE BISMARCK (UK)	GILBERT	20th CENTURY FOX	1960
SB-C	SLEEPING BEAUTY (t)	GERONIMI	BUENA VISTA	1959
SBD	SWEET BODY OF DEBORAH (IT)	GUERRIERI	WARNER BROS	1969
SBM	RAGE AT DAWN	WHELAN	RKO	1955
SBS	2ND BEST SECRET AGENT IN WHOLE WIDE WORLD (UK)	SHONTEFF	EMBASSY	1965
SBS	STEP BY STEP	ROSEN	RKO	1946
SBS	SUNDAY BLOODY SUNDAY	SCHLESINGER	UNITED ARTISTS	1971
SBT	FLIGHT FOR FREEDOM	MENDES	RKO	1943
SBU	FOOTLIGHT FEVER	REIS	RKO	1941
SBV	BELOVED VAGABOND (UK)	BERNHARDT	COLUMBIA	1936
SC	7TH COMMANDMENT	BERWICK	CROWN INTERNATIONAL	1961
SC	EDUCATION OF SONNY CARSON	CAMPUS	PARAMOUNT	1973
SC	FURY AT SHOWDOWN	OSWALD	UNITED ARTISTS	1957
SC	HAND IN HAND (UK)	LEACOCK	COLUMBIA	1960
SC	MAN FROM CAIRO (UK: CRIME SQUAD)	ANTON, ENRIGHT	LIPPERT	1953
SC	MORGAN! (UK: MORGAN: A SUITABLE CASE FOR TREATMENT)	REISZ	CINEMA V	1966
SC	SANTA CLAUS THE MOVIE	SZWARC	TRI STAR	1985
SC	SATAN'S CRADLE	BEEBE	UNITED ARTISTS	1949
SC	SATURDAY'S CHILDREN	SHERMAN	WARNER BROS	1940
SC	SCORPIO	WINNER	UNITED ARTISTS	1973
SC	SEA CREATURE	CAHN	AIP	1956
SC	SEAN CONNERY	portrait	UNIVERSAL	
SC	SECOND CHANCE	MATE	RKO	1953

Movie Still Identification Book Ultimate Edition - Letters

CODE	TITLE/NAME	DIRECTOR/TYPE	STUDIO/DISTRIBUTOR	YEAR
SC	SECOND CHOICE	BRETHERTON	WARNER BROS	1930
SC	SECRET CHOICE		WARNER BROS	1929
SC	SERIOUS CHARGE (UK)	YOUNG	GOVERNOR	1959
SC	SHE CREATURE	CAHN	AIP	1956
SC	SHORT CIRCUIT	BADHAM	TRI STAR	1986
SC	SHIRLEY CHAMBERS	portrait	FN/WARNER BROS	
SC	SILENT CALL	BUSHELMAN	20th CENTURY FOX	1961
SC	SILVER CHORD	CROMWELL	RKO	1933
SC	SIN SHIP	WOLHEIM	RKO	1930
SC	SNOW CREATURE	WILDER	UNITED ARTISTS	1954
SC	SOMETHING IN THE CITY (UK)	ROGERS	BUTCHER'S	1950
SC	SOMEWHERE IN CAMP (UK)	BLAKELEY	BUTCHER'S	1942
SC	SOMEWHERE IN CIVVIES (UK)	ROGERS	BUTCHER'S	1943
SC	SPACE COWBOYS	EASTWOOD	WARNER BROS	2000
SC	STEEL CAGE	DONIGER	UNITED ARTISTS	1954
SC	STERILE CUCKOO	PAKULA	PARAMOUNT	1969
SC	STEVE COCHRAN	portrait	WARNER BROS	
SC	STOCK CAR (UK)	RILLA	BUTCHER'S	1955
SC	STRANGERS CAME (UK: YOU CAN'T FOOL AN IRISHMAN)	TRAVERS	BELL	1949
SC	STREETCAR NAMED DESIRE	KAZAN	WARNER BROS	R93
SC	SUCCESSFUL CALAMITY	ADOLFI	WARNER BROS	1932
SC	SUGAR COOKIES	GERSHUNY	GENERAL	1972
SC	SUSAN CABOT	portrait	UNIVERSAL	
SC	SUZI CRANDALL	portrait	RKO, WARNER BROS	
SC	SWORD OF THE CONQUEROR (IT)	CAMPOGALLIANI	UNITED ARTISTS	1961
SC	SYD CHAPLIN	portrait		
SC	TEAR GAS SQUAD	MORSE	WARNER BROS	1940
SCA	SCALAWAG	DOUGLAS	PARAMOUNT	1973
SCA	SCANNERS	CRONENBERG	AVCO EMBASSY	1981
SCDF	STRANGE CASE OF DR. MANNING (UK: MORNING CALL)	CRABTREE	REPUBLIC	1957
SCDM	STRANGE CASE OF DR. MANNING (UK: MORNING CALL)	CRABTREE	REPUBLIC	1957
SCF	SMALL CIRCLE OF FRIENDS	COHEN	UNITED ARTISTS	1980
SCH 2	THUNDER MOUNTAIN	SCHERTZINGER	FOX FILM	1925
SCH7	STAGE MADNESS	SCHERTZINGER	FOX FILM	1927
SCH8	HEART OF SALOME	SCHERTZINGER	FOX FILM	1927
SCH-GG	GREAT GADSBY	CLAYTON	PARAMOUNT	1974
SCK-5	MEN	ZINNEMANN	UNITED ARTISTS	1950
SCM	SLEEPING CAR MURDER (FR: COMPARTIMENT TUEURS)	GAVRAS	SEVEN ARTS	1966
SCN	SPY WITH A COLD NOSE (UK)	PETRIE	EMBASSY	1966
SCT	CRY TERROR	STONE	MGM	1958
SD	MALA HEMBRA	DELGADO	MAYA	1950
SD	SAN DEMETRIO LONDON (UK)	FREND	20TH CENTURY FOX	1943
SD	SANDRA DEE	portrait	UNIVERSAL	
SD	SAVAGE DRUMS	BERKE	LIPPERT	1951
SD	SCARS OF DRACULA (UK)	BAKER	CONTINENTAL	1971
SD	SCHOOL FOR DANGER (UK) [US: ENGLISH FILMS]	BAIRD	UNITED ARTISTS	1947
SD	SHE DEMONS	CUNHA	ASTOR	1958
SD	SHOT IN THE DARK (UK)	EDWARDS	UNITED ARTISTS	1964
SD	SHOUT AT THE DEVIL	HUNT	AIP	1976
SD	SILVER DARLINGS (UK)	ELDER	PATHE	1947
SD	SILVER DOLLAR	GREEN	WARNER BROS	1932
SD	SIN & DESIRE	ROZIER	ATLANTIS	1960
SD	SKIN DEEP	ENRIGHT	WARNER BROS	1929
SD	SKY DEVILS	SUTHERLAND	UNITED ARTISTS	1932
SD	SLOW DANCING IN THE BIG CITY	AVILDSEN	UNITED ARTISTS	1978
SD	SNOW DAY	KOCH	PARAMOUNT	2000
SD	SOAP DISH	HOFFMAN	PARAMOUNT	1991
SD	SON OF DRACULA	FRANCIS	CINEMATION	1974
SD	SPECIAL DELIVERY		AIP	1957
SD	SPECIAL DELIVERY (GER)	BRAHM	COLUMBIA	1955
SD	SPLIT DECISIONS	DRURY	NEW CINEMA	1988
SD	SPOOK WHO SAT BY THE DOOR	DIXON	UNITED ARTISTS	1973
SD	STAGE DOOR	LA CAVA	RKO	1937
SD	STEFFI DUNA	portrait	RKO	
SD	STRANGE DECEPTION (IT: IL CRISTO PROIBITO)	MALAPARTE	CASINO	1951
SD	SUZANNE DALBERT (DELBERT)	portrait	WARNER BROS	
SD	SWEET DREAMS	REISZ	TRI STAR	1985
SDC	STAGE DOOR CANTEEN	BORZAGE	UNITED ARTISTS	1943
SDD	DING DON WILLIAMS	BERKE	RKO	1946
SDER	SAFECRACKER (UK)	MILLAND	MGM	1958

Movie Still Identification Book Ultimate Edition - Letters

CODE	TITLE/NAME	DIRECTOR/TYPE	STUDIO/DISTRIBUTOR	YEAR
SDJ	SQUARE DANCE JUBILEE	LANDRES	LIPPERT	1949
SDL	SEVEN DAYS ASHORE	AUER	RKO	1944
SDS	DUEL IN THE SUN	VIDOR	SELZNICK	1947
SDSN	SHE DIDN'T SAY NO! (UK)	FRANKEL	SEVEN ARTS	1958
SDT	SAINTS DOUBLE TROUBLE	HIVELY	RKO	1940
SDT	STRANGER ON THE 3RD FLOOR	INGSTER	RKO	1940
SDW	SHE-DEVILS ON WHEELS	LEWIS	MAYFLOWER	1968
SE	SALLY EILERS	portrait	RKO, UNIVERSAL	
SE	SCATTERGOOD MEETS BROADWAY	CABANNE	RKO	1941
SE	SECRET ENEMIES	STOLOFF	WARNER BROS	1942
SE	SERPENT'S EGG	BERGMAN	PARAMOUNT	1978
SE	SILK EXPRESS	ENRIGHT	WARNER BROS	1933
SE	SO EVIL, SO YOUNG (UK)	GRAYSON	UNITED ARTISTS	1961
SE	SOMEWHERE IN ENGLAND (UK)	BLAKELEY	BUTCHER'S	1940
SE	STARS IN YOUR EYES (UK)	ELVEY	BRITISH LION	1956
SE	STREAMLINE EXPRESS	FIELDS	MASCOT	1935
SE	STUART ERWIN	portrait	GRAND NATIONAL	
SE	STUART ERWIN	portrait	MGM	
SE	SWORD OF SHERWOOD FOREST	FISHER	COLUMBIA	1960
SE	WITHOUT ORDERS	LANDERS	RKO	1936
SE5	DANCING WITH CRIME (UK)	CARSTAIRS	PARAMOUNT BRITISH	1947
SEA	DECKS RAN RED	STONE	MGM	1958
SEA	GHOST OF THE CHINA SEA	SEARS	COLUMBIA	1958
SEA	SEA GYPSIES	RAFFILL	WARNER BROS	1978
SEDG-7	DO AND DARE	SEDGWICK	FOX FILM	1922
SEI-1	BLACK MAGIC	SEITZ	FOX FILM	1929
SEI-23	GREAT K & A TRAIN ROBBERY	SEILER	FOX FILM	1926
SEI-24	LAST TRAIL	SEILER	FOX FILM	1927
SEI-25	OUTLAWS OF RED RIVER	SEILER	FOX	1927
SEI-26	TUMBLING RIVER	SEILER	FOX FILM	1927
SEI-27	WOLF FANGS	SEILER	FOX FILM	1927
SEI-30	GIRLS GONE WILD	SEILER	FOX FILM	1929
SEI-31	A SONG OF KENTUCKY	SEILER	FOX FILM	1929
SEK	MEN	ZINNEMANN	UNITED ARTISTS	1950
SEK	STANLEY KRAMER PRODUCTIONS	studio		
SEL	FRANK SELTZER PRODUCTIONS	studio		
SEL	SELENA	NAVA	WARNER BROS	1997
SEPT	SEPARATE TABLES	MANN	UNITED ARTISTS	1958
SES	PANAMA LADY	HIVELY	RKO	1939
SF	DAY THEY ROBBED THE BANK OF ENGLAND (UK)	GUILLERMIN	MGM	1960
SF	LISTEN, LET'S MAKE LOVE (IT)	CAPRIOLI	UNITED ARTISTS	1967
SF	MEN ARE SUCH FOOLS	NIGH	RKO	1932
SF	MEN OF SHERWOOD FOREST (UK: 1954)	GUEST	ASTOR	1956
SF	ROCK 'N ROLL REVUE	KOHN	STUDIO FILMS	1955
SF	SACRED FLAME	MAYO	WARNER BROS	1929
SF	SALLY FORREST	portrait	RKO	
SF	SAN FRANCISCO STORY	PARRISH	WARNER BROS	1952
SF	SANTA FE TRAIL	CURTIZ	WARNER BROS	1940
SF	SCARFACE	HAWKS	UNITED ARTISTS	1932
SF	SCOTT FORBES	portrait		
SF	SECOND FIDDLE (UK)	ELVEY	BRITISH LION	1957
SF	SHARKFIGHTERS	HOPPER	UNITED ARTISTS	1956
SF	SHEP FIELDS	portrait	MCA RECORDS	
SF	SIDNEY FOX	portrait	RKO, UNIVERSAL	
SF	SKI FEVER	SIODMAK	ALLIED ARTISTS	1966
SF	SOUND OF FURY	ENDFIELD	UNITED ARTISTS	1950
SF	SPACEFLIGHT IC-1 (UK)	KNOWLES	LIPPERT	1965
SF	STAGE FRIGHT (UK)	HITCHCOCK	WARNER BROS	1950
SF	STEVE FORREST	portrait	WARNER BROS	
SF	STEVEN FLAGG/MICHAEL ST. ANGEL/MICHAEL HAWKS	portrait	RKO	
SF	STOLEN FACE (UK)	FISHER	LIPPERT	1952
SF	SUDDEN FEAR	MILLER	RKO	1952
SF	SUED FOR LIBEL	GOODWINS	RKO	1939
SF	SUPER FLY, T.N.T.	O'NEAL	PARAMOUNT	1973
SF	SUSANNA FOSTER	portrait	UNIVERSAL	
SF	THREE SONS	HIVELY	RKO	1939
SF.1	SUBWAY IN THE SKY (UK)	BOX	UNITED ARTISTS	1959
SFB1	OPERATION SNAFU (UK: ON THE FIDDLE)	FRANKEL	AIP	1961
SFH	SECRET FILE HOLLYWOOD	CUSUMANO	CROWN INTERNATIONAL	1961
SFM	SHIELD FOR MURDER	KOCH, O'BRIEN	UNITED ARTISTS	1954

Movie Still Identification Book Ultimate Edition - Letters

CODE	TITLE/NAME	DIRECTOR/TYPE	STUDIO/DISTRIBUTOR	YEAR
SFP	SECRETS OF THE FRENCH POLICE	SUTHERLAND	RKO	1932
SFS	SCHOOL FOR SEX (UK)	WALKER	PAUL MART	1969
SFT	SEVEN FROM TEXAS		COLUMBIA	1962
SG	3 SONS 'O GUNS	BACON	WARNER BROS	1936
SG	JONATHAN LIVINGSTON SEAGULL	BARTLETT	PARAMOUNT	1973
SG	LET'S TRY AGAIN	MINER	RKO	1934
SG	MAGIC SWORD (UK: ST. GEORGE AND THE DRAGON)	GORDON	UNITED ARTISTS	1962
SG	RUNNING TARGET	WEINSTEIN	UNITED ARTISTS	1956
SG	SAILOR FROM GIBRALTAR (UK) [US: LOPERT]	RICHARDSON	UNITED ARTISTS	1967
SG	SAMUEL GOLDWYN PICTURES		RKO, UNITED ARTISTS	
SG	SEVEN GUNS FOR MACGREGORS	GIRALDI	COLUMBIA	1966
SG	SHE'S GOT EVERYTHING	SANTLEY	RKO	1937
SG	SHOWGIRLS	VERHOEVEN	UNITED ARTISTS	1995
SG	SIGRID GURIE	portrait	UNIVERSAL	
SG	SIX GUN GOLD	HOWARD	RKO	1941
SG	SMARTEST GIRL IN TOWN	SANTLEY	RKO	1936
SG	SMILING GHOST	SEILER	WARNER BROS	1941
SG	SODOM AND GOMORRAH	ALDRICH	20th CENTURY FOX	1963
SG	SON OF A SAILOR	BACON	FIRST NATIONAL	1933
SG	SUPERGIRL	SZWARC	TRI STAR	1984
SG	SYDNEY GREENSTREET	portrait	WARNER BROS	
SG	THAT GIRL FROM PARIS	JASON	RKO	1937
SG	WHITE FIRE (UK: THREE STEPS TO THE GALLOWS)	GILLING	LIPPERT	1953
SG-16	AWAKENING	FLEMING	UNITED ARTISTS	1928
SG-17	RESCUE	BRENON	UNITED ARTISTS	1929
SG-18	THIS IS HEAVEN	SANTELL	UNITED ARTISTS	1929
SG-19	BULLDOG DRUMMOND	JONES	UNITED ARTISTS	1929
SG-20	CONDEMNED	RUGGLES	UNITED ARTISTS	1929
SG-200	WEDDING NIGHT	VIDOR	UNITED ARTISTS	1935
SG-700	KID FROM BROOKLYN	MCLEOD	RKO	1946
SG-1000	DARK ANGEL	FRANKLIN	UNITED ARTISTS	1935
SG-1100	STRIKE ME PINK	TAUROG	UNITED ARTISTS	1936
SG-1200	BARBARY COAST	HAWKS	UNITED ARTISTS	1935
SG-1400	SPLENDOR	NUGENT	UNITED ARTISTS	1935
SG-1600	THESE THREE	MENZIES	UNITED ARTISTS	1936
SG-1800	BEST YEARS OF OUR LIVES	WYLER	RKO	1946
SG-1900	COME AND GET IT	HAWKS, ROSSON	UNITED ARTISTS	1936
SG-2000	DODSWORTH	WYLER	UNITED ARTISTS	1936
SG-2000	SECRET LIFE OF WALTER MITTY	MCLEOD	RKO	1946
SG-2100	BELOVED ENEMY	POTTER	UNITED ARTISTS	1936
SG-2200	WOMAN CHASES MAN	BLYSTONE	UNITED ARTISTS	1937
SG-2300	HURRICANE	FORD	UNITED ARTISTS	1937
SG-2700	DEAD END	WYLER	UNITED ARTISTS	1937
SG-2800	STELLA DALLAS	VIDOR	UNITED ARTISTS	1937
SG-3000	BISHOP'S WIFE	KOSTER	RKO	1947
SG-3100	ADVENTURES OF MARCO POLO	MAYO	UNITED ARTISTS	1938
SG-3200	GOLDWYN FOLLIES	MARSHALL	UNITED ARTISTS	1938
SG-3200	SONG IS BORN	HAWKS	RKO	1948
SG-3500	ENCHANTMENT	REIS	RKO	1948
SG-3800	COWBOY AND THE LADY	POTTER	UNITED ARTISTS	1938
SG-3800	ROSEANNA MCCOY	REIS	RKO	1949
SG-3900	REAL GLORY	HATHAWAY	UNITED ARTISTS	1939
SG-4000	MY FOOLISH HEART	ROBSON	RKO	1949
SG-4100	OUR VERY OWN	MILLER	RKO	1950
SG-4200	EDGE OF DOOM	ROBSON	RKO	1950
SG-4200	WUTHERING HEIGHTS	WYLER	UNITED ARTISTS	1939
SG-4300	RAFFLES	FITZMAURICE	UNITED ARTISTS	1930
SG-4500	WHOOPEE!	FREELAND	UNITED ARTISTS	1930
SG-4600	THEY SHALL HAVE MUSIC	MAYO	UNITED ARTISTS	1939
SG-4700	RAFFLES	WOOD	UNITED ARTISTS	1939
SG-4900	ONE HEAVENLY NIGHT	FITZMAURICE	UNITED ARTISTS	1931
SG-5300	DEVIL TO PAY!	FITZMAURICE	UNITED ARTISTS	1930
SG-5400	I WANT YOU	ROBSON	RKO	1952
SG-5600	WESTERNER	WYLER	UNITED ARTISTS	1940
SG-6200	PALMY DAYS	SUTHERLAND	UNITED ARTISTS	1931
SG-6300	UNHOLY GARDEN	FITZMAURICE	UNITED ARTISTS	1931
SG-6400	ARROWSMITH	FORD	UNITED ARTISTS	1931
SG-6800	HANS CHRISTIAN ANDERSON	VIDOR	RKO	1953
SG-7200	MASQUERADER	WALLACE	UNITED ARTISTS	1933
SG-7300	KID FROM SPAIN	MCCAREY	UNITED ARTISTS	1932

Movie Still Identification Book Ultimate Edition - Letters

CODE	TITLE/NAME	DIRECTOR/TYPE	STUDIO/DISTRIBUTOR	YEAR
SG-7400	GUYS AND DOLLS	MANKIEWICZ	MGM	1955
SG-7500	BALL OF FIRE	HAWKS	RKO	1942
SG-7600	CYNARA	VIDOR	UNITED ARTISTS (Goldwyn)	1932
SG-8000	ROMAN SCANDALS	TUTTLE	UNITED ARTISTS (Goldwyn)	1933
SG-8100	NANA	ARZNER, FITZMAURICE	UNITED ARTISTS	1934
SG-8100	PRIDE OF THE YANKEES	WOOD	RKO	1943
SG-8200	THEY GOT ME COVERED	BUTLER	RKO	1943
SG-8500	NORTH STAR	MILESTONE	RKO	1943
SG-8700	UP IN ARMS	NUGENT	RKO	1944
SG-9100	BELOVED ENEMY	POTTER	GOLDWYN	1936
SG-9400	PRINCESS AND THE PIRATE	BUTLER	RKO	1944
SG-9600	WONDER MAN	HUMBERSTONE	RKO	1945
SG-9700	NANA	ARZNER, FITZMAURICE	UNITED ARTISTS	1934
SG-9700	WE LIVE AGAIN	MAMOULIAN	UNITED ARTISTS	1934
SG-9800	KID MILLIONS	DEL RUTH	UNITED ARTISTS	1934
SGF	SUCH GOOD FRIENDS	PREMINGER	PARAMOUNT	1972
SGG	SMILEY GETS A GUN	KIMMINS	20th CENTURY FOX	1959
SGO	GORGO	LOURIE	MGM	1961
SGPB	PORGY AND BESS	PREMINGER, MAMOULIAN	COLUMBIA	1959
SGSR	SHE GODS OF SHARK REEF	CORMAN	AIP	1958
SGT	SERGEANT	FLYNN	WARNER BROS	1968
SH	BABY SANDY (aka SANDRA LEE HENVILLE)	portrait	UNIVERSAL	
SH	GREAT MR. NOBODY	STOLOFF	WARNER BROS	1941
SH	HOME, SWEET HOME (UK)	COOPER	RKO	1933
SH	PRIVATE LIFE OF SHERLOCK HOLMES	WILDER	UNITED ARTISTS	1970
SH	SAD HORSE	CLARK	20th CENTURY FOX	1959
SH	SAFE AT HOME	DONIGER	COLUMBIA	1962
SH	SAFE IN HELL	WELLMAN	WARNER BROS	1931
SH	SAM HARDY	portrait	FN	
SH	SATURDAY'S HEROES	KILLY	RKO	1937
SH	SAVAGE HARVEST	COLLINS	UNITED ARTISTS	1981
SH	SCRATCH HARRY	MATTER	CANNON	1969
SH	SEA HAWK	CURTIZ	WARNER BROS	1940
SH	SECRET OF DEEP HARBOR	CAHN	UNITED ARTISTS	1961
SH	SESSUE HAYAKAWA	portrait	ROBERTSON-COLE	
SH	SHADOW OF THE HAWK	MCGOWAN	COLUMBIA	1976
SH	SHAKE HANDS WITH THE DEVIL	ANDERSON	UNITED ARTISTS	1959
SH	SHAKESPEARE WALLAH (IND)	IVORY	CONTINENTAL	1965
SH	SHALAKO (UK)	DMYTRYK	CINERAMA	1968
SH	SHAMPOO	ASHBY	COLUMBIA	1975
SH	SHANKS	CASTLE	PARAMOUNT	1974
SH	SHARON HUGUENY	portrait	WARNER BROS	
SH	SHE HAD TO SAY YES	LIGHTNER	WARNER BROS	1933
SH	SHEMP HOWARD	portrait	UNIVERSAL	early 40s
SH	SHOOTIST	SIEGEL	PARAMOUNT	1976
SH	SIGNE HASSO	portrait	RKO, UNIVERSAL	
SH	SKIP HOMEIER (aka SKIPPY HOMEIER)	portrait	UNITED ARTISTS	
SH	SONJA HENIE	portrait	UNIVERSAL	
SH	SONNIE HALE	portrait		
SH	SORORITY HOUSE	FARROW	RKO	1939
SH	STAY HUNGRY	RAFELSON	UNITED ARTISTS	1976
SH	STEEL HELMET	FULLER	LIPPERT	1951
SH	STRANGER'S HAND (UK)	SOLDATI	DCA	1954
SH	SURRENDER HELL	BARNWELL	ALLIED ARTISTS	1959
SH	SUSAN HARRISON	portrait	UNITED ARTISTS	
SH	SUSAN HAYWARD	portrait	RKO, UNIVERSAL	
SH-5025	SHOOTIST	SIEGEL	PARAMOUNT	1976
SHB	SHOW BUSINESS	MARIN	RKO	1944
SHD	SHAKE HANDS WITH THE DEVIL	ANDERSON	UNITED ARTISTS	1959
SHD	SWEET HEARTS DANCE	GREENWALD	TRI STAR	1988
SHE	SHE (UK)	DAY	MGM	1965
SHE	SPELLBOUND	HITCHCOCK	UNITED ARTISTS	1945
SHH	SWEDEN HEAVEN AND HELL (IT: SVEZIA, INFERNO E	SCATTINI	AVCO EMBASSY	1969
SHM	SHE SHALL HAVE MURDER (UK)	BIRT	IFD	1950
SHY	SAY HELLO TO YESTERDAY (UK)	RAKOFF	CINERAMA	1970
SI	ISLAND OF DESIRE (UK: SATURDAY ISLAND)	HEISLER	UNITED ARTISTS	1951
SI	SAINT IN NEW YORK	HOLMES	RKO	1938
SI	SAINT IN PALM SPRINGS	HIVELY	RKO	1941
SI	SATURDAY ISLAND (UK) (US: ISLAND OF DESIRE)	HEISLER	UNITED ARTISTS	1952
SI	SCANDAL, INC.	MANN	REPUBLIC	1956

Movie Still Identification Book Ultimate Edition - Letters

CODE	TITLE/NAME	DIRECTOR/TYPE	STUDIO/DISTRIBUTOR	YEAR
SI	SPECIAL INVESTIGATOR	KING	RKO	1936
SI	STAR OF INDIA (UK)	LUBIN	UNITED ARTISTS	1954
SI547	LONE STAR	SHERMAN	MGM	1951
SIG	BANDIT RANGER	SELANDER	RKO	1942
SIG	MAN ABOUT TOWN (FR)	CLAIR	RKO	1947
SIG	SIGRID GURIE	portrait	GOLDWYN	
SIH	COP-OUT (UK: STRANGER IN THE HOUSE)	ROUVE	CINERAMA	1967
SII	SUPERMAN II	LESTER	WARNER BROS	1981
SIL-3	FOX MOVIETONE FOLLIES OF 1929	SILVER	FOX FILM	1929
SIL-3	WORDS AND MUSIC	SILVER	FOX FILM	1929
SIL-4	MARRIED IN HOLLYWOOD	SILVER	FOX FILM	1929
S-IM	MAN IN THE IRON MASK	WHALE	UNITED ARTISTS	1939
SIN	IF THIS BE SIN (UK: THAT DANGEROUS AGE)	RATOFF	UNITED ARTISTS	1949
SIN	RUNAWAY BUS (UK)	GUEST	KRAMER-HYAMS	1954
SIN	SINFUL DAVEY (UK)	HUSTON	UNITED ARTISTS	1969
SING	SING	BASKIN	TRI STAR	1989
SINL	SINNERS IN LOVE	MELFORD	FILM BOOKING OFFICES	1928
SIP	SELZNICK INTERNATIONAL PICTURES	studio		
SIP-100	LITTLE LORD FAUNTLEROY	CROMWELL	UNITED ARTISTS	1936
SIP-101	GARDEN OF ALLAH	BOLESLAWSKI	UNITED ARTISTS (Selznick)	1936
SIP-102	STAR IS BORN	WELLMAN	UNITED ARTISTS (Selznick)	1937
SIP-103	PRISONER OF ZENDA	CROMWELL	UNITED ARTISTS	1937
SIP-104	NOTHING SACRED	WELLMAN	UNITED ARTISTS (Selznick)	1937
SIP-105	ADVENTURES OF MARCO POLO	MAYO	UNITED ARTISTS	1938
SIP-105	ADVENTURES OF TOM SAWYER	TAUROG	UNITED ARTISTS (Selznick)	1938
SIP-106	YOUNG IN HEART	WALLACE	UNITED ARTISTS	1938
SIP-107	MADE FOR EACH OTHER	CROMWELL	UNITED ARTISTS	1939
SIP-108	GONE WITH THE WIND	FLEMING	UNITED ARTISTS (Selznick)	1939
SIP-108	REBECCA (see SIP-110 - mistake)	HITCHCOCK	UNITED ARTISTS (Selznick)	1940
SIP-109	INTERMEZZO	RATOFF	UNITED ARTISTS	1939
SIP-110	REBECCA	HITCHCOCK	UNITED ARTISTS (Selznick)	1940
SIP-TS	ADVENTURES OF TOM SAWYER	TAUROG	UNITED ARTISTS (Selznick)	1938
SIT	STRANGER IN TOWN (UK)	POLLOCK	ASTOR	1957
SITC	SUNDAY IN THE COUNTRY (CINERAMA)	TRENT	AIP	1975
SITN	SKIMPY IN THE NAVY (UK)	DICKENS	ADELPHI	1949
SJ	DAVID JANSSEN	portrait	UNIVERSAL	1950s-70s
SJ	PASSING STRANGER (UK)	ARNOLD	CONTINENTAL	1954
SJ	SAINT JOAN (UK)	PREMINGER	UNITED ARTISTS	1957
SJ	SHERRY JACKSON	portrait	WARNER BROS	early 50s
SJ	SINS OF JEZEBEL	LE BORG	LIPPERT	1953
SJ	SISTER TO JUDAS	HOPPER	MAYFAIR	1932
SJ	SPACE JAM	PYTKA	WARNER BROS	1996
SJ	SYBIL JASON	portrait	WARNER BROS	
SJ -2	HAPPY PEST	HARTMAN	FOX FILM	1921
SK	CAPTAIN KIDD AND THE SLAVE GIRL	LANDERS	UNITED ARTISTS	1954
SK	CHAMPION	ROBSON	UNITED ARTISTS	1949
SK	CORPSE VANISHES	FOX	FAVORITE FILM	R49
SK	KISSES FOR BREAKFAST	SEILER	WARNER BROS	1941
SK	NOT AS A STRANGER	KRAMER	UNITED ARTISTS	1955
SK	SAM KATZMAN PRODUCTIONS	studio		
SK	SAMMY KAYE & HIS ORCHESTRA	portrait	MCA RECORDS	
SK	SANDS OF THE KALAHARI (UK)	ENDFIELD	PARAMOUNT	1965
SK	SEVEN KEYS TO BALDPATE	HAMILTON, KILLY	RKO	1935
SK	SHAKEDOWN (UK)	LEMONT	UNIVERSAL	1960
SK	SHIRLEY KNIGHT	portrait		
SK	SINGING KID	KEIGHLEY	WARNER BROS	1936
SK	SKIDOO	PREMINGER	PARAMOUNT	1968
SK	SKULL (UK)	FRANCIS	PARAMOUNT	1965
SK	SOMEBODY KILLER HER HUSBAND	JOHNSON	COLUMBIA	1978
SK	SON OF KONG	SCHOEDSACK	RKO	1933
SK	STANLEY KRAMER PRODUCTIONS	studio		
SK	STONE KILLER	WINNER	COLUMBIA	1973
SK	SUZANNE KAAREN	portrait	GRAND NATIONAL, RKO	
SK	SYLVA KOSCINA	portrait	UNIVERSAL	
SK	SKULL	FRANCIS	PARAMOUNT	1965
SK-2	THAT GANG OF MINE	LEWIS	MONOGRAM	1940
SK3	YELLOW TOMAHAWK	SELANDER	UNITED ARTISTS	1954
SK-3	PRIDE OF THE BOWERY	LEWIS	MONOGRAM	1940
SK-4	FLYING WILD	WEST	MONOGRAM	1941
SK-6	INVISIBLE GHOST	LEWIS	MONOGRAM	1941

Movie Still Identification Book Ultimate Edition - Letters

CODE	TITLE/NAME	DIRECTOR/TYPE	STUDIO/DISTRIBUTOR	YEAR
SK-7	BOWERY BLITZKRIEG	FOX	MONOGRAM	1941
SK-8	SPOOKS RUN WILD	ROSEN	MONOGRAM	1941
SK9	STEEL KEY (UK)	BAKER	EROS	1953
SK-9	ZIS BOOM BAH	NIGH	MONOGRAM	1941
SK-10	MR. WISE GUY	NIGH	MONOGRAM	1942
SK-11	BLACK DRAGONS	NIGH	MONOGRAM	1942
SK-12	CORPSE VANISHES	FOX	MONOGRAM	1942
SK-13	LET'S GET TOUGH	FOX	MONOGRAM	1942
SK-14	CORPSE VANISHES	FOX	MONOGRAM	1942
SK-15	SMART ALECKS	FOX	MONOGRAM	1942
SK-110	JUNIOR PROM	DREIFUSS	MONOGRAM	1946
SK-206	BOWERY AT MIDNIGHT	FOX	MONOGRAM	1942
SK-207	NEATH BROOKLYN BRIDGE	FOX	MONOGRAM	1942
SK-208	KID DYNAMITE	FOX	MONOGRAM	1943
SK-209	APE MAN	BEAUDINE	MONOGRAM	1943
SK-210	CLANCY STREET BOYS	BEAUDINE	MONOGRAM	1943
SK-211	GHOSTS ON THE LOOSE	BEAUDINE	MONOGRAM	1943
SK-212	SPOTLIGHT ON SCANDAL (SPOTLIGHT REVUE)	BEAUDINE	MONOGRAM	1943
SK-213	FOLLOW THE LEADER	BEAUDINE	MONOGRAM	1944
SK-214	MR. MUGGS STEPS OUT	BEAUDINE	MONOGRAM	1943
SK-215	MILLION DOLLAR KID	FOX	MONOGRAM	1944
SK-216	RETURN OF THE APE MAN	ROSEN	MONOGRAM	1944
SK-217	VOODOO MAN	BEAUDINE	MONOGRAM	1944
SK-218	BLOCK BUSTERS	FOX	MONOGRAM	1944
SK-219	THREE OF A KIND	LEDERMAN	MONOGRAM	1944
SK-220	BOWERY CHAMPS	BEAUDINE	MONOGRAM	1944
SK-221	CRAZY KNIGHTS	BEAUDINE	MONOGRAM	1944
SK-222	DOCKS OF NEW YORK	FOX	MONOGRAM	1945
SK-223	MR. MUGGS RIDES AGAIN	FOX	MONOGRAM	1945
SK-224	COME OUT FIGHTING	BEAUDINE	MONOGRAM	1945
SK-225	TROUBLE CHASERS	LANDERS	MONOGRAM	1945
SKB	SEVEN KEYS TO BALDPATE	LANDERS	RKO	1946
SKB	SWEET KITTY BELLAIRS	GREEN	WARNER BROS	1930
SKC	CYRANO DE BERGERAC	GORDON	UNITED ARTISTS	1950
SKC	KIT CARSON	SEITZ	UNITED ARTISTS	1940
SKC	WHO IS KILLING THE GREAT CHIEFS OF EUROPE?	KOTCHEFF	WARNER BROS	1978
SKH-5124	SOME KIND OF HERO	PRESSMAN	PARAMOUNT	1981
SK-R	CHAMPION	KRAMER	UNITED ARTISTS	1955
SK-S	NOT AS A STRANGER	LARDNER	UNITED ARTISTS	1949
S-KT	KING OF THE TURF	GREEN	UNITED ARTISTS	1939
SL	DR. STRANGELOVE	KUBRICK	COLUMBIA	1964
SL	ONE MORE TIME	LEWIS	UNITED ARTISTS	1970
SL	SADDLE LEGION	SELANDER	RKO	1951
SL	SAINT IN LONDON	CARSTAIRS	RKO	1939
SL	SANDLOT	EVANS	20th CENTURY FOX	1993
SL	SANDRA	SAWYER	FIRST NATIONAL	1924
SL	SHAMELESS OLD LADY	ALLIO	RANK	1966
SL	SHEILA LEVINE IS DEAD AND LIVING IN NEW YORK	FURIE	PARAMOUNT	1975
SL	SILENCE OF THE LAMBS	DEMME	ORION	1991
SL	SLEEPER	ALLEN	UNITED ARTISTS	1973
SL	SO LONG LETTY	BACON	WARNER BROS	1929
SL	SOME LIKE IT HOT	WILDER	UNITED ARTISTS	1959
SL	SONS OF LIBERTY (sh)	CURTIZ	WARNER BROS	1939
SL	STEEL LADY	DUPONT	UNITED ARTISTS	1953
SL	STEP LIVELY	WHELAN	RKO	1944
SL	STUDS LONIGAN	LERNER	UNITED ARTISTS	1960
SL	SUDDENLY	ALLEN	UNITED ARTISTS	1954
SL	SWAN LAKE (RUS: 1957)	TULUBYEVA	COLUMBIA	1960
SL	SWING YOUR LADY	ENRIGHT	WARNER BROS	1938
SL	THIS SPORTING LIFE (UK)	ANDERSON	CONTINENTAL	1963
SL	THREE IS A FAMILY	LUDWIG	UNITED ARTISTS	1944
SL	TOO BAD SHE'S BAD	BLASETTI	GETZ-KINGSLEY	1955
SL-16	SILENCE OF THE LAMBS	DEMME	ORION	1991
SL-5900	OUR TOWN	WOOD	UNITED ARTISTS	1940
SL-6400	THAT UNCERTAIN FEELING	LUBITSCH	UNITED ARTISTS	1941
SLBB	SCARLET LETTER	JOFFE	BUENA VISTA	1995
SLC	SOME LIKE IT COOL (UK)	WINNER	JANUS	1961
SLD	STARS LOOK DOWN (UK)	REED	MGM	1940
SLH	SOME LIKE IT HOT	WILDER	UNITED ARTISTS	1959
SLO-2	THREE SISTERS	SLOANE	FOX FILM	1930

Movie Still Identification Book Ultimate Edition - Letters

CODE	TITLE/NAME	DIRECTOR/TYPE	STUDIO/DISTRIBUTOR	YEAR
SLOANE-1	HEARTS IN DIXIE	SLOANE	FOX FILM	1929
SLS	SUDDENLY LAST SUMMER	MANKIEWICZ	COLUMBIA	1959
SLU	SPIES LIKE US	LANDIS	WARNER BROS	1985
SLW	DR. STRANGELOVE (UK)	KUBRICK	COLUMBIA	1964
SM	CODE OF THE SECRET SERVICE	SMITH	WARNER BROS	1939
SM	DENNIS MORGAN / STANLEY MORNER	portrait	MGM	
SM	I'M STILL ALIVE	REIS	RKO	1940
SM	SAL MINEO	portrait	WARNER BROS	
SM	SCENES FROM A MARRIAGE (SWE: SCENER … AKTENSKAP)	BERGMAN	CINEMA 5	1973
SM	SECOND MATE (UK)	BAXTER	ASSOCIATED BRITISH-PATHE	1950
SM	SEVEN MINUTES	MEYER	20th CENTURY FOX	1971
SM	SGT. MURPHY	portrait	WARNER BROS	
SM	SHADOW MAN (UK: STREET OF SHADOWS)	VERNON	LIPPERT	1953
SM	SHIRLEY MACLAINE	portrait	UNIV	
SM	SHIRLEY MASON	portrait	FOX	
SM	SILVANA MANGANO	portrait	PARAMOUNT`	
SM	SINGING MARINE	ENRIGHT	WARNER BROS	1937
SM	SKY ABOVE - MUD BELOW (FR)	GAISSEAU	EMBASSY	1960
SM	SLIGHT CASE OF MURDER	BACON	WARNER BROS	1938
SM	SMILE	RITCHIE	UNITED ARTISTS	1975
SM	SOUTHERN MAID (UK)	HUGHES	WARDOUR	1933
SM	SPACE MASTER X-7	BERNDS	20th CENTURY FOX	1958
SM	SPANISH MAIN	BORZAGE	RKO	1945
SM	STAR OF MIDNIGHT	ROBERTS	RKO	1935
SM	STARDUST MEMORIES	ALLEN	UNITED ARTISTS	1980
SM	STARK MAD	BACON	WARNER BROS	1929
SM	STEPHEN MCNALLY	portrait		
SM	STRANGLER'S MORGUE (UK: CURSE OF THE WRAYDONS)	GOVER	JH HOFFBERG	1946
SM	SUICIDE MISSION (UK)	FORLONG	COLUMBIA	1954
SM	SWEET MAMA	CLINE	FIRST NATIONAL	1930
SM	SWEET MUSIC	GREEN	WARNER BROS	1943
SM	THOMAS CROWN AFFAIR	JEWISON	UNITED ARTISTS	1968
SM	TIL WE MEET AGAIN	GOULDING	WARNER BROS	1940
SM223	MR. MUGGS RIDES AGAIN	FOX	MONOGRAM	1945
SMC	SWORD OF THE MONTE CRISTO	GERAGHTY	20th CENTURY FOX	1951
SMF	7 MILES FROM ALCATRAZ	DMYTRYK	RKO	1943
SML	SLEEP, MY LOVE	SIRK	UNITED ARTISTS	1948
SMS	MY SON, MY SON!	VIDOR	UNITED ARTISTS	1940
SMT	SAINT MEETS TIGER	STEIN	REPUBLIC	1943
SMW	DANGEROUS MILLIONS	TINLING	20th CENTURY FOX	1946
SMW	SHE'S MY WEAKNESS	BROWN	RKO	1930
SMW	SOL M. WURTZEL PRODUCTIONS	studio	FOX	
SMW	SPIRAL STAIRCASE	SIODMAK	RKO	1946
SMW 1	RENDEZVOUS 24	TINLING	20th CENTURY FOX	1946
SMW2	DEADLINE FOR MURDER	TINLING	20th CENTURY FOX	1946
SMW 4	DANGEROUS MILLIONS	TINLING	20th CENTURY FOX	1946
SMW 5	BACKLASH	FORDE	20th CENTURY FOX	1946
SMW 7	CRIMSON KEY	FORDE	20th CENTURY FOX	1947
SMW 8	SECOND CHANCE	TINLING	20th CENTURY FOX	1947
SMW-10	ROSES ARE RED	TINLING	20th CENTURY FOX	1947
SMW-11	DANGEROUS YEARS	PIERSON	20th CENTURY FOX	1947
SMW-13	ARTHUR TAKES OVER	ST. CLAIR	20th CENTURY FOX	1948
SMW-14	FIGHTING BACK	ST. CLAIR	20th CENTURY FOX	1948
SMW-18	MISS MINK OF 1949	TRYON	20th CENTURY FOX	1949
SN	SATURDAY NIGHT & SATURDAY MORNING (UK)	REISZ	CONTINENTAL	1961
SN	SATURDAY NIGHT FEVER	BADHAM	PARAMOUNT	1977
SN	SECRET OF NIHM	BLUTH	MGM/UNITED ARTISTS	1982
SN	SECRET OF NIMH (t)	BLUTH	MGM/UNITED ARTISTS	1982
SN	SHE COULDN'T SAY NO	BACON	WARNER BROS	1930
SN	SNORKEL (UK)	GREEN	COLUMBIA	1958
SN	STUDENT NURSES	ROTHMAN	NEW WORLD PICTURES	1970
SNBB	SHANGHAI NOON	DEY	BUENA VISTA	2000
SNC	SOUL OF NIGGER CHARLEY	SPANGLER	PARAMOUNT	1973
SND	OH SAILOR BEHAVE	MAYO	WARNER BROS	1930
SNDN	SILENT NIGHT DEADLY NIGHT	SELLIER JR	TRI STAR	1984
SNE	SEE NO EVIL (UK: BLIND TERROR)	FLEISCHER	COLUMBIA	1971
SNE	SEE NO EVIL, HEAR NO EVIL	HILLER	TRI STAR	1989
SNO	SATURDAY NIGHT OUT (UK)	HARTFORD-DAVIS	CAMEO	1964
SO	SAINT TAKES OVER	HIVELY	RKO	1940
SO	SH! THE OCTOPUS	MCGANN	WARNER FILM	1937

Movie Still Identification Book Ultimate Edition - Letters

CODE	TITLE/NAME	DIRECTOR/TYPE	STUDIO/DISTRIBUTOR	YEAR
SO	SMILES OF A SUMMER NIGHT (SWE: SOMMARNATTENS...)	BERGMAN	RANK FILMS OF AMERICA	1955
SOA	SIGN OF AQUARIUS (GHETTO FREAKS, LOVE COMMUNE)	EMERY	CINAR PROD	1970
SOB	SON OF BLOB (BEWARE! THE BLOB)	HAGMAN	HARRIS ENT.	1972
SOD	PAYMENT ON DEMAND	BERNHARDT	RKO	1951
SOD	STREET OF DARKNESS	WALKER	REPUBLIC	1958
SOE	SHADOW OF THE EAGLE (UK)	SALKOW	UNITED ARTISTS	1950
SOH	7 DAYS LEAVE	WHELAN	RKO	1942
SOH	STRANGER ON HORSEBACK	TOURNEUR	UNITED ARTISTS	1955
SOLO	TO TRAP A SPY	MEDFORD	MGM	1966
SOM	AT SWORD'S POINT	ALLEN	RKO	1952
SON	SALLY O'NEIL (SALLY O'NEILL)	portrait	MGM	late 20s
SON	SPY OF NAPOLEON (UK)	ELVEY	GRAND NATIONAL	1936
SONY	SLAVES OF NEW YORK	IVORY	TRI STAR	1989
SOP	STRANGER ON THE PROWL	LOSEY	UNITED ARTISTS	1952
SOR	SCOTCH ON THE ROCKS (UK: LAXDALE HALL)	ELDRIDGE	KINGSLEY INTERNATIONAL	1953
SOR	SINS OF ROME	FREDA	RKO	1954
SOR	SONG OF THE OPEN ROAD	SIMON	UNITED ARTISTS	1944
SOS	FIGHTING FRONTIER	HILLYER	RKO	1943
SOS	SON OF SINBAD	TETZLAFF	RKO	1955
SOS	SOS PACIFIC (UK)	GREEN	UNIVERSAL	1959
SOUV	SUMMER WISHES WINTER DREAMS	CATES	COLUMBIA	1973
SP	CHASING YESTERDAY	NICHOLS JR.	RKO	1935
SP	CHRISTMAS CAROL	HURST	UNITED ARTISTS	1951
SP	CURSE OF THE DEMON (UK: NIGHT OF THE DEMON)	TOURNEUR	COLUMBIA	1957
SP	DEBT OF HONOUR (UK)	WALKER	GFD	1936
SP	DON Q, SON OF ZORRO	CRISP	UNITED ARTISTS	1925
SP	HOME OF THE BRAVE	ROBSON	UNITED ARTISTS	1949
SP	I FOUND STELLA PARRISH	LEROY	WARNER BROS	1935
SP	LI'L ABNER	FRANK	PARAMOUNT	1959
SP	PRINCE AND THE SHOWGIRL	OLIVIER	WARNER BROS	1957
SP	SALT AND PEPPER	DONNER	UNITED ARTISTS	1968
SP	SCANDALS OF PARIS (UK: THERE GOES SUSIE)	HANBURY, STAFFORD	REGAL	1934
SP	SCARLET PIMPERNEL (UK)	YOUNG	UNITED ARTISTS	1934
SP	SCATTERGOOD PULLS THE STRINGS	CABANNE	RKO	1941
SP	SEA PIRATE (SP)	BERGONZELLI, ROWLAND	PARAMOUNT	1967
SP	SECRET OF THE PURPLE REEF	WITNEY	20th CENTURY FOX	1960
SP	SEPARATE PEACE	PEERCE	PARAMOUNT	1972
SP	ABOUT LAST NIGHT (SEXUAL PERVERSITY IN CHICAGO*)	ZWICK	TRI STAR	1986
SP	SHY PEOPLE	KONCHALOVSKY	CANNON	1987
SP	SLIME PEOPLE	HUTTON	HANSEN ENT	1963
SP	SO THIS IS NEW YORK	FLEISCHER	UNITED ARTISTS	1948
SP	SOME PEOPLE (UK)	DONNER	AAIP	1962
SP	SPACE: 1999 (tv)	various	ITC	1975
SP	SPARROWS CAN'T SING (UK)	LITTLEWOOD	JANUS	1963
SP	SPETTERS (NETH)	VERHOEVEN	SAMUEL GOLDWYN	1981
SP	SPHERE	LEVINSON	WARNER BROS	1998
SP	SPORT PARADE	MURPHY	RKO	1932
SP	SPY WHO CAME IN FROM THE COLD (UK)	RITT	PARAMOUNT	1965
SP	SUNSET PASS	BERKE	RKO	1946
SP	SURF PARTY	DEXTER	20th CENTURY FOX	1964
SP	SUSPECTED PERSON (UK)	HUNTINGTON	PRC	1942
SP	SUZANNE PLESHETTE	portrait	UNIV	
SP	TWO LIVING, ONE DEAD (UK)	ASQUITH	BRITISH LION	1961
SP	WILD PARTY	HORNER	UNITED ARTISTS	1956
SP	SPECIES II	MEDAK	MGM	1998
SP-1	GO TELL THE SPARTANS	POST	AVCO EMBASSY	1978
SP1	TWO WAY STRETCH (UK)	DAY	SHOWCORPORATION	1960
SP-1A	FEDERAL AGENT	NEWFIELD	REPUBLIC	1936
SP-2	GO TELL THE SPARTANS	POST	AVCO EMBASSY	1978
SP2	ROAD TO THE BIG HOUSE	COLMES	SCREEN GUILD	1947
SP-2AS	BURNING GOLD	NEWFIELD	REPUBLIC	1935
SP-3A	GO GET EM HAINES	NEWFIELD	REPUBLIC	1936
SP-101	GENTLE GANGSTER	ROSEN	REPUBLIC	1943
SP-105	PHANTOM KILLER	BEAUDINE	MONOGRAM	1942
SP-106	LIVING GHOST	BEAUDINE	MONOGRAM	1942
SP-AD-A	PRINCE AND THE SHOWGIRL	OLIVIER	WARNER BROS	1957
SPC	SERPICO	LUMET	PARAMOUNT	1973
SPC-5064	SERPICO	LUMET	PARAMOUNT	1973
S-PJ	PORTRAIT OF JENNIE (1948)	DIETERLE	SELZNICK	R56
SPL	AMATEUR GENTLEMAN	FREELAND	UNITED ARTISTS	1936

Movie Still Identification Book Ultimate Edition - Letters

CODE	TITLE/NAME	DIRECTOR/TYPE	STUDIO/DISTRIBUTOR	YEAR
SPL	SPY WHO LOVED ME	GILBERT	UNITED ARTISTS	1977
SPP	SOUTH OF PAGO PAGO	GREEN	UNITED ARTISTS	1940
SP-P-A	PRINCE AND THE SHOWGIRL	OLIVIER	WARNER BROS	1957
SPRA-1	NOT DAMAGED	SPRAGUE	FOX FILM	1930
SPRA-2	DANCERS	SPRAGUE	FOX FILM	1930
SPRA-3	THEIR MAD MOMENT	SPRAGUE, MCFADDEN	FOX FILM	1931
SP-S	KILLERS OF THE SEA	FRIEDGEN	GRAND	1937
SQ	633 SQUADRON (UK)	GRAUMAN	UNITED ARTISTS	1964
SQ	SAN QUENTIN	BACON	WARNER BROS	1937
SQ	SQUEEZE	APTED	WARNER BROS	1977
SR	DAY MARS INVADED EARTH	DEXTER	20th CENTURY FOX	1963
SR	SAINT'S GIRL FRIDAY	FRIEDMAN	RKO	1954
SR	SECRETS OF THE REEF	LERNER	MARINE STUDIOS	1956
SR	SHARK RIVER	RAWLINS	UNITED ARTISTS	1953
SR	SHIRLEY ROSS	portrait	MUT. UA, BROADCASTING	radio
SR	SHUTTERED ROOM (UK)	GREENE	WARNER BROS.	1967
SR	SKIPALONG ROSENBLOOM	NEWFIELD	UNITED ARTISTS	1951
SR	SNIPER'S RIDGE	BUSHELMAN	20th CENTURY FOX	1961
SR	SONG OF THE ROAD (UK)	BAXTER	SELECT ATTRACTIONS	1937
SR	SPRING REUNION	PIROSH	UNITED ARTISTS	1957
SR	STORM RIDER	BERNDS	20th CENTURY FOX	1957
SR	STRYKER OF THE YARD (UK)	CRABTREE	REPUBLIC	1953
SR	SWORD AND THE ROSE (UK)	ANNAKIN	RKO	1953
SR	SUMMER TO REMEMBER (IT)	MARTINO	TITANUS	1974
SRK	SIDNEY R. KENT	portrait	FOX	
SR-P8	SAINT'S GIRL FRIDAY (SAINT'S RETURN)	FRIEDMAN	RKO	1954
SRR	SHAKE, RATTLE AND ROCK	CAHN	AIP	1956
SS	BACKSTAGE (UK: LIMELIGHT) STREET SINGER'S SERENADE*	WILCOX	GAUMONT BRITISH AMERICA	1937
SS	GREAT MANHUNT (UK: STATE SECRET)	GILLIAT	BRITISH LION	1950
SS	S.Z. SAKALL	portrait	WARNER BROS	
SS	SAINT STRIKES BACK	FARROW	RKO	1939
SS	SAINTLY SINNERS	YARBROUGH	UNITED ARTISTS	1962
SS	SALLY STARR	portrait	MGM	
SS	SAM SMALL LEAVES TOWN	GOULDING	BRITISH SCREEN SERVICE	1937
SS	SATCHMO THE GREAT	MURROW	UNITED ARTISTS	1957
SS	SATIN IN SABLES	FLOOD	WARNER BROS	1925
SS	SAVAGE SPLENDOR	COTLOW, DENIS	RKO	1949
SS	SAVANNAH SMILES	DE MORO	GOLD COAST	1982
SS	SCREAMING SKULL	NICOL	AIP	1958
SS	SEASIDE SWINGERS (UK: EVERY DAY'S A HOLIDAY)	HILL	EMBASSY	1964
SS	SECRET SERVICE		RKO	1931
SS	SEVENTH SEAL (SWED)	BERGMAN	JANUS	1957
SS	SEVENTH SIGN	SCHULTZ	TRI STAR	1988
SS	SH! THE OCTOPUS	MCGANN	WARNER BROS	1937
SS	SHADOW MAN (UK: STREET OF SHADOWS)	VERNON	LIPPERT	1953
SS	SHIPYARD SALLY (UK)	BANKS	20TH CENTURY FOX	1939
SS	SHOESHINE (IT: SCIUSCIA 1946)	DE SICA	LOPERT	1947
SS	SIDE SHOW	DEL RUTH	WARNER BROS	1931
SS	SIDE STREET	ST. CLAIR	RKO	1929
SS	SIEGE OF THE SAXONS (UK)	JURAN	COLUMBIA	1963
SS	SILKEN SHACKLES	MOROSCO	WARNER BROS	1926
SS	SILVER SLAVE	BRETHERTON	WARNER BROS	1927
SS	SILVER STAR	BARLETT	LIPPERT	1955
SS	SILVER STREAK	ATKINS	RKO	1934
SS	SIMONE SIGNORET	portrait	UNIV	
SS	SIMONE SIMON	portrait	RKO	early 40s
SS	SIMONE SIMON	portrait	FOX	late 30s
SS	SING AND SWING (UK: LIVE IT UP!)	COMFORT	UNIVERSAL	1963
SS	SLIGHTLY SCARLET	DWAN	RKO	1956
SS	SOLOMON AND SHEBA	VIDOR	UNITED ARTISTS	1959
SS	SOMEWHERE IN SONORA	WRIGHT	WARNER BROS	1933
SS	SON OF SAMSON	CAMPOGALLIANI	MEDALLION	1962
SS	SORRELL AND SON	BRENON	UNITED ARTISTS	1927
SS	SORRELL AND SON (UK)	RAYMOND	UNITED ARTISTS	1933
SS	SOUL SOLDIER (RED, WHITE AND BLACK 1970)	CARDOS	FANFARE	1972
SS	SOUTH OF SUEZ	SEILER	WARNER BROS	1940
SS	SOUTHERN STAR	HAYERS	COLUMBIA	1969
SS	SPLIT SECOND	POWELL	RKO	1953
SS	STELLA STEVENS	portrait		
SS	STOWAWAY IN THE SKY (FR: LE VOYAGE EN BALLOON 1960)	LAMORISSE	LOPERT	1962

Movie Still Identification Book Ultimate Edition - Letters

CODE	TITLE/NAME	DIRECTOR/TYPE	STUDIO/DISTRIBUTOR	YEAR
SS	STREET SMART	SCHATZBERG	CANNON	1986
SS	STREET SONG (UK)	VORHAUS	RKO	1935
SS	STREETS OF SHANGHAI	GASNIER	TIFFANY	1927
SS	SUCCESS AT ANY PRICE	RUBEN	RKO	1934
SS	SUPER SLEUTH	STOLOFF	RKO	1937
SS	SUSAN SLEPT HERE (LA)	TASHLIN	RKO	1954
SS	SWEET SMELL OF SUCCESS	MACKENDRICK	UNITED ARTISTS	1957
SS	SYLVIA SCARLET	CUKOR	RKO	1935
SS1	SEPARATE TABLES	MANN	UNITED ARTISTS	1958
SS3	LADY FROM LISBON (UK)	HISCOTT	ANGLO-AMERICAN	1942
SS-231	SEPTEMBER STORM	HASKIN	20th CENTURY FOX	1960
SS/C	CODE SCOTLAND YARD (UK: SHOP AT SLY CORNER)	KING	REPUBLIC	1948
SSCT	CHINATOWN	POLANSKI	PARAMOUNT	1974
SSD	SEASON OF PASSION (SUMMER OF THE 17TH DOLL)	NORMAN	UNITED ARTISTS	1959
SSE	GIRL IN EVERY PORT	ERSKINE	RKO	1952
SSF	STREETS OF SAN FRANCISCO (tv series)	VARIOUS	WARNER BROS TV	1972
SSF	SWORD OF SHERWOOD FOREST (UK)	FISHER	COLUMBIA	1960
SS-F	ADIOS SABATA (IT)	PAROLINI	UNITED ARTISTS	1971
SSI	CINDERELLA SWINGS IT	CABANNE	RKO	1943
SSI	STARSHIP INVASIONS	HUNT	WARNER BROS	1977
SSM	SHE SHALL HAVE MUSIC (UK)	HISCOTT	IMPERIAL	1935
SSM	SYMPHONY OF 6 MILLION	LA CAVA	RKO	1932
SSOE	BIG TIME OPERATORS (UK: SMALLEST SHOW ON EARTH)	DEARDEN	TIMES	1957
SSP	HIGHWAYS BY NIGHT	GODFREY	RKO	1942
SSS	GUNSIGHT RIDGE	LYON	UNITED ARTISTS	1957
SSS	SIEGE OF SIDNEY STREET (UK)	BAKER, BERMAN	UNITED PRODUCERS REL.	1960
SSS	STATE STREET SADIE	MAYO	WARNER BROS	1928
SSS	STATION SIX SAHARA (UK)	HOLT	MONOGRAM	1962
SST	CINDERELLA SWINGS IT	CABANNE	RKO	1943
ST	BLONDE BLACKMAILER (UK: STOLEN TIME)	DEANE	ALLIED ARTISTS	1955
ST	BRIGHTHAVEN EXPRESS (UK: SALUTE THE TOFF)	ROGERS	BUTCHER'S	1952
ST	CLIMAX (IT: L'IMMORALE)	GERMI	LOPERT	1967
ST	PARIS EXPRESS (UK: MAN WHO WATCHED TRAINS GO BY)	FRENCH	MACDONALD	1952
ST	SARATOGA TRUNK	WOOD	WARNER BROS	1945
ST	SCARLET THREAD (UK)	GILBERT	REALART	1951
ST	SECRET TUNNEL (UK)	HAMMOND	GFD	1948
ST	SEMI-TOUGH	RITCHIE	UNITED ARTISTS	1977
ST	SHARKS' TREASURE	WILDE	UNITED ARTISTS	1975
ST	SHEILA TERRY	portrait	WARNER BROS	
ST	SHINING THROUGH	SELTZER	20th CENTURY FOX	1992
ST	SHIRLEY TEMPLE	portrait	WARNER BROS	1930s-40s
ST	SHIRLEY TEMPLE	portrait	RKO	late 40s
ST	SHORT TIME	CHAMPION	20th CENTURY FOX	1990
ST	SINBAD AND THE EYE OF THE TIGER	WANAMAKER	COLUMBIA	1977
ST	SIT TIGHT	BACON	WARNER BROS	1931
ST	SLAUGHTER TRAIL	LOSEY (HANBURY)	ASTOR	1954
ST	SLEEPING TIGER	ALLEN	RKO	1951
ST	SLEEPING TIGER (UK)	LOSEY	ASTOR	1954
ST	SLENDER THREAD	POLLACK	PARAMOUNT	1966
ST	SMASHING THE RACKETS	LANDERS	RKO	1938
ST	SMASHING TIME (UK)	DAVIS	PARAMOUNT	1967
ST	SMOOTH TALK	CHOPRA	INT'L SPECTRAFILM	1985
ST	SOMETHING TO TALK ABOUT	HALSTROM	WARNER BROS	1995
ST	SPEED TRAP	BELLAMY	FIRST ARTISTS	1977
ST	SPENCER TRACY	portrait	MGM	
ST	STAGE TO CHINO	KILLY	RKO	1940
ST	STORK TALK (UK)	FORLONG	PARADE RELEASING	1962
ST	STORM OVER TIBET	MARTON	COLUMBIA	1952
ST	STORYVILLE	FROST	20th CENTURY FOX	1992
ST	STREAMERS	ALTMAN	UNITED ARTISTS	1983
ST	SUNDOWN TRAIL	HILL	RKO	1932
ST	SUNRISE TRAIL	MCCARTHY	TIFFANY	1931
ST	SURE THING	REINER	EMBASSY	1985
ST	SWAMP THING	CRAVEN	EMBASSY	1982
ST	THREE COCKEYED SAILORS (UK: SAILORS THREE)	FORDE	UNITED ARTISTS	1940
ST-1	LET'S GO PLACES	STRAYER	FOX FILM	1930
ST2	STAR TREK: WRATH OF KHAN	MEYER	PARAMOUNT	1982
ST3	STAR TREK III	NIMOY	PARAMOUNT	1984
ST4	HEADIN' NORTH	MCCARTHY	TIFFANY	1930
ST4	STAR TREK IV	NIMOY	PARAMOUNT	1986

Movie Still Identification Book Ultimate Edition - Letters

CODE	TITLE/NAME	DIRECTOR/TYPE	STUDIO/DISTRIBUTOR	YEAR
ST5	STAR TREK V	SHATNER	PARAMOUNT	1989
STB	STILL OF THE NIGHT	BENTON	MGM/UNITED ARTISTS	1982
STC	SAVE THE CHILDREN	LATHAN	PARAMOUNT	1973
STC	STAIRCASE (UK)	DONEN	20th CENTURY FOX	1969
STC	STOP THAT CAB	DE LIGUORO	LIPPERT	1951
STF	STAGECOACH TO FURY	CLAXTON	LIPPERT	1956
STH	STOLEN HOURS (UK) (US: SUMMER FLIGHT)	PETRIE	UNITED ARTISTS	1963
STN-101	QUEEN OF BROADWAY	NEWFIELD	PRC	1942
STO	SHE'S THE ONE	BURNS	20th CENTURY FOX	1996
STO	STOLOFF PRODUCTIONS	studio	FOX	
STO-6	GOODBYE GIRLS	STORM	FOX FILM	1923
STO-20	CANYON OF LIGHT	STOLOFF	FOX FILM	1926
STO-21	GAY RETREAT	STOLOFF	FOX FILM	1927
STO-22	CIRCUS ACE	STOLOFF	FOX	1927
STO-23	SILVER VALLEY	STOLOFF	FOX FILM	1927
STO-28	SPEAKEASY	STOLOFF	FOX FILM	1928
STO-30	GIRL FROM HAVANA	STOLOFF	FOX FILM	1929
STO-31	HAPPY DAYS	STOLOFF	FOX FILM	1929
STO-32	FOX MOVIETONE FOLLIES OF 1929	STOLOFF	FOX FILM	1930
STO-32	JUST LIKE HEAVEN	NEILL	TIFFANY	1930
STO-33	SOUP TO NUTS	STOLOFF	FOX FILM	1930
STO-34	THREE ROGUES	STOLOFF	FOX FILM	1931
STO-35	GOLDIE	STOLOFF	FOX FILM	1931
STORM-4	ST. ELMO	STORM	FOX FILM	1923
STS	SANDY THE SEAL (UK)	LYNN	TIGON	1968
STS	SEVEN TIMES SEVEN (IT)	LUPO	MONOGRAM	1969
STS	SINBAD THE SAILOR	WALLACE	RKO	1947
STS	SMALL TOWN STORY (UK)	TULLY	GFD	1953
STS	STUDY THE SEAL (GER)		WARNER BROS	1965
STT	SAVE THE TIGER	AVILDSEN	PARAMOUNT	1973
STVI	STAR TREK VI	MEYER	PARAMOUNT	1991
SU	2 THOROUGHBREDS	HIVELY	RKO	1939
SU	FLESH AND THE SPUR	CAHN	AIP	1957
SU	SETUP	WISE	RKO	1949
SU	SEVEN-UPS	D'ANTONI	20th CENTURY FOX	1974
SU	SNOWED UNDER	ENRIGHT	WARNER BROS	1936
SU	SWEET ECSTASY	PECAS	AUDUBON	1962
SUB	SUBMARINE X-1 (UK)	GRAHAM	UNITED ARTISTS	1968
SUBC	STAND UP AND BE COUNTED	COOPER	COLUMBIA	1972
SUPER-E	SUPERMAN AND THE JUNGLE DEVIL	BLAIR, CARR	20th CENTURY FOX	1954
SV	7TH VICTIM	ROBSON	RKO	1943
SV	KING OF HOCKEY	SMITH	WARNER BROS	1936
SV	SAINT'S VACATION	FENTON	RKO	1941
SV	SECRET OF SANTA VITTORIA	KRAMER	UNITED ARTISTS	1969
SV	SEVENTH VEIL (UK)	BENNETT	UNIVERSAL	1945
SV	STRANGE VOYAGE	ALLEN	MONOGRAM	1946
SV	SUPER VIXEN	MEYER	R.M. FILMS	1975
SV	SURVIVE (MEX)	CORDONA	PARAMOUNT	1976
SV	SUZY VERNON	portrait		
SW	BIG SHOW OFF	BRETHERTON	REPUBLIC	1945
SW	BOY SLAVES	WOLFSON	RKO	1939
SW	HUNT THE MAN DOWN	portrait	WARNER BROS	1940s
SW	JANE WYMAN	ARCHAINBAUD	RKO	1950
SW	SALLY WADSWORTH	portrait	RKO	
SW	SEA WIFE (UK)	MCNAUGHT	20th CENTURY FOX	1957
SW	SEA WOLF	CURTIZ	WARNER BROS	1941
SW	SHELLEY WINTERS	portrait	RKO, UNIVERSAL	
SW	SHOCK WAVES	WIEDERHORN	JOSEPH BRENNER ASSOC	1977
SW	SILENT WORLD (FR)	COUSTEAU, MALLE	COLUMBIA	1956
SW	SOMETHING WILD	GARFEIN	UNITED ARTISTS	1961
SW	SOMETHING WILD	DEMME	ORION	1986
SW	SPIDER'S WEB (UK)	GRAYSON	UNITED ARTISTS	1960
SW	STATION WEST	LANFIELD	RKO	1948
SW	STEPFORD WIVES	FORBES	COLUMBIA	1975
SW	STRANGE WOMAN	ULMER	UNITED ARTISTS	1946
SW	STRANGE WORLD (GER: GOTTIN VOM RIO BENI)	EICHHORN	UNITED ARTISTS	1951
SW	STREET OF WOMEN	MAYO	WARNER BROS	1932
SW	SWEEPSTAKES WINNER	MCGANN	WARNER BROS	1939
SW	SWITCHING CHANNELS	KOTCHEFF	TRI STAR	1987
SW	WINGS FOR THE EAGLE	BACON	WARNER BROS	1942

Movie Still Identification Book Ultimate Edition - Letters

CODE	TITLE/NAME	DIRECTOR/TYPE	STUDIO/DISTRIBUTOR	YEAR
SW1	STAR WARS PHANTOM MENACE	LUCAS	20th CENTURY FOX	1999
SW-2	LAST STRAW	SWICKARD	FOX FILM	1920
SW-C	SWORD AND THE STONE (t)	REITHERMAN	BUENA VISTA	1964
SWE	SLEEPING WITH THE ENEMY	RUBEN	20th CENTURY FOX	1991
SWF	SAY IT WITH FLOWERS (UK)	BAXTER	RKO	1934
SWFH	SEVEN WOMEN FROM HELL	WEBB	20th CENTURY FOX	1961
SWG	HIS KIND OF WOMAN	FARROW	RKO	1951
SWG	SWIMMING POOL	DERAY	AVCO EMBASSY	1970
SWI	SOMMERSBY	AMIEL	WARNER BROS	1993
SWL	SPY WHO LOVED ME	GILBERT	UNITED ARTISTS	1977
SWR	SO WELL REMEMBERED (UK)	DMYTRYK	RKO	1947
SWR	SWISS FAMILY ROBINSON	LUDWIG	RKO	1940
SWS	SIN WITH A STRANGER (FR)	GOBBI	FILMS DISTRIBUTING	1969
SWS	SNOW WHITE AND THE 7 DWARFS (t)	COTTRELL, HAND	RKO	1938
SWW	SHIPS WITH WINGS (UK)	NOLBANDOV	UNITED ARTISTS	1941
SWY	SHE WORE A YELLOW RIBBON	FORD	RKO	1949
SX	SEX OF ANGELS (IT)	LIBERATORE	LOPERT	1968
SXT	SOPHIE TUCKER	portrait	MGM	
SXTX	SHIRLEY TEMPLE	portrait	MGM	1940s
SY	SERGEANT YORK	HAWKS	WARNER BROS	1941
SY	SUNNY	WILCOX	RKO	1941
SYM	LIVING DEAD (UK: SCOTLAND YARD MYSTERY)	BENTLEY	FIRST DIVISION	1934
SYW	SING YOUR WORRIES AWAY	SUTHERLAND	RKO	1942
T	BATTLE TAXI	STROCK	UNITED ARTISTS	1955
T	ADVENTURES OF ICHOBOD AND MR. TOAD	GERONIMI	RKO	1949
T	KID COMES BACK	EASON	WARNER BROS	1938
T	KING OF THE LUMBERJACKS	CLEMENS	WARNER BROS	1940
T	LADY CRAVED EXCITEMENT (UK)	GRAYSON, SEARLE	EXCLUSIVE	1950
T	LORD OF ILLUSIONS	BARKER	UNITED ARTISTS	1995
T	MR. ACE	MARIN	UNITED ARTISTS	1946
T	NARROW MARGIN	FLEISCHER	RKO	1952
T	PARIS EXPRESS (UK: MAN WHO WATCHED TRAINS GO BY)	FRENCH	MACDONALD	1952
T	PLAYGIRL AFTER DARK	YOUNG	TOPAZ	1962
T	PROUD VALLEY (UK)	TENNYSON	SUPREME	1940
T	RIDERS TO THE STARS (portraits)	CARLSON	UNITED ARTISTS	1954
T	RING-A-DING RHYTHM (UK: IT'S TRAD, DAD!)	LESTER	COLUMBIA	1962
T	SPITFIRE	CROMWELL	RKO	1934
T	T.A.M.I. SHOW	BINDER	AIP	1964
T	TAFFY AND THE JUNGLE HUNTER	MORSE	ALLIED ARTISTS	1965
T	TAKE MY TIP (UK)	MASON	GFD	1937
T	TAMAHINE	LEACOCK	ASSOC. BRITISH	1964
T	TANK GIRL	TALALAY	UNITED ARTISTS	1995
T	TAP	CASTLE	TRI STAR	1989
T	TEMPO		RKO	1952
T	TENDERFOOT	ENRIGHT	WARNER BROS	1932
T	TENDERLOIN	CURTIZ	WARNER BROS	1928
T	TERMINATOR	CAMERON	ORION	1984
T	TERROR	CORMAN	AIP	1963
T	THAT MAN FROM TANGIER	DELGADO, ELWYN	UNITED ARTISTS	1953
T	THE TOY	DONNOR	COLUMBIA	1982
T	THREAT	FEIST	RKO	1949
T	THUMBELINA (t)	BLEUTH	WARNER BROS	1994
T	THUNDERBALL	YOUNG	UNITED ARTISTS	1965
R	TOKOLOSHE: THE EVIL SPIRIT	PROWSE	ARTISTS INT'L	1971
T	TOM THUMB (UK)	PAL	MGM	1958
T	TOMMY	RUSSELL	COLUMBIA	1975
T	TOPAZE		RKO	1937
T	TOPKAPI	DASSIN	UNITED ARTISTS	1964
T	TORERO	VELO	COLUMBIA	1957
T	TORMENT (SWE: HETS 1944)	SJOBERG	LOPERT	1947
T	TORSO (IT)	MARTINO	JOSEPH BRENNER	1973
T	TOUCH	SCHRADER	UNITED ARTISTS	1997
T	TOVARICH	LITVAK	WARNER BROS	1937
T	TOYS	LEVINSON	20th CENTURY FOX	1992
T	TRANS-ATLANTIC TUNNEL (UK: TUNNEL)	ELVEY	GAUMONT BRITISH AMERICA	1935
T	TROJAN BROTHERS (UK)	ROGERS	ANGLO-AMERICAN	1946
T	TROUBLE (UK)	ROGERS	UNITED ARTISTS	1933
T	TRUNK (UK)	WINTER	COLUMBIA	1961
T	TWONKY	OBOLER	UNITED ARTISTS	1953
T1	TYCOON	WALLACE	RKO	1946

Movie Still Identification Book Ultimate Edition - Letters

CODE	TITLE/NAME	DIRECTOR/TYPE	STUDIO/DISTRIBUTOR	YEAR
T	YOU SAID A MOUTHFUL	BACON	FN, WARNER	1932
T-1	BATTLING ORIOLES	GUIOL, WILDE	PATHE EXCHANGE	1924
T1	LAST OF THE MOHICANS (GER)	WELLIN	ASSOCIATED PRODUCERS	1920
T-1	MOVIE DUMMY (MOVIE MUMMY)	ROACH	PATHE EXCHANGE	1918
T-1	MY VALET	SENNETT	TRIANGLE	1915
T-1	THUNDERING TAXIS	LORD, MEINS	MGM	1933
T1	TARZAN THE FEARLESS	HILL	PRINCIPAL	1933
T-2	GAME OLD KNIGHT	JONES	TRIANGLE	1915
T-2	JUNKMAN		PATHE EXCHANGE	1918
T-2	WHAT PRICE TAXI	LORD	MGM	1932
T-2	WHITE SHEEP	ROACH	PATHE EXCHANGE	1924
T-3	FARE PLEASE		PATHE EXCHANGE	1918
T-3	HER PAINTED HERO	JONES	TRIANGLE	1915
T3	SHOD WITH FIRE	FLYNN	FOX FILM	1920
T-3	STRANGE INNERTUBE	LORD	MGM	1932
T-4	FAVORITE FOOL	FRAZEE	TRIANGLE	1915
T-4	HOT SPOT	LORD	MGM	1932
T-4	TOTO IN ONE NIGHT ONLY	ROACH	PATHE EXCHANGE	1918
T-5	FIRE THE COOK (edited to create T-7)	ROACH	PATHE EXCHANGE	1918
T-5	STOLEN MAGIC	SENNETT	TRIANGLE	1915
T-5	TAXI FOR TWO	LORD	MGM	1932
T-6	BRING 'EM BACK A WIFE	LORD	MGM	1933
T-6	GETAWAY	PECKINPAH	WARNER BROS	1972
T-6	HIS BUSY DAY	ROACH	PATHE EXCHANGE	1918
T-7	DIPPY DAUGHTER	ROACH	PATHE EXCHANGE	1918
T-7	FICKLE FATTY'S FALL	ARBUCKLE	TRIANGLE	1915
T-7	WRECKETY WRECKS	LORD	MGM	1933
T-8	CLEOPATSY (CLEO PROXY)	ROACH	PATHE EXCHANGE	1918
T-8	NAMELESS MEN	CABANNE	TIFFANY	1928
T-8	TAXI BARONS	MEINS	MGM	1933
T-9	CALL HER SAUSAGE	MEINS	MGM	1933
T-9	CALL HER SAUSAGE	MEINS	MGM	1933
T-9	FURNITURE MOVERS	ROACH	PATHE EXCHANGE	1918
T-10	CHECK YOUR BAGGAGE	ROACH	PATHE EXCHANGE	1918
T-10	JANITOR'S WIFE'S TEMPTATION	HENDERSON	TRIANGLE	1915
T-10	RUMMY	LORD	MGM	1933
T-11	GREAT WATER PERIL (POOR CLARINE)	ROACH	PATHE EXCHANGE	1918
T-11	SUBMARINE PIRATE	AVERY, CHAPLIN	TRIANGLE	1915
T-12	DO HUSBANDS DECEIVE?	ROACH	PATHE EXCHANGE	1918
T-13	BEACH NUTS	ROACH	PATHE EXCHANGE	1918
T-14	CROOKED TO THE END	FRAZEE, REED	TRIANGLE	1915
T-14	ENEMY OF SOAP	ROACH	PATHE EXCHANGE	1918
T-15	FATTY AND THE BROADWAY STARS	ARBUCKLE	TRIANGLE	1915
T-16	HUNT	STERLING, PARROTT	TRIANGLE	1915
T-17	DIZZY HEIGHTS AND DARING HEARTS	WRIGHT	TRIANGLE	1916
T-19	GREAT PEARL TANGLE	HENDERSON	TRIANGLE	1916
T19	MAN IN THE MOON (UK)	DEARDEN	TRANS LUX	1960
T-20	FATTY AND MABEL ADRIFT	ARBUCKLE	TRIANGLE	1916
T-21	BECAUSE HE LOVED HER	HENDERSON	TRIANGLE	1916
T-22	MODERN ENOCH ARDEN	BADGER, AVERY	TRIANGLE	1916
T22	WATCH YOUR STERN (UK)	THOMAS	ANGLO AMALGAMATED (UK)	1960
T24	BEWARE OF CHILDREN (UK: NO KIDDING)	THOMAS	AIP	1961
T-24	MOVIE STAR	CLINE	TRIANGLE	1916
T-26	HE DID AND HE DIDN'T	ARBUCKLE	TRIANGLE	1916
T27	CARRY ON REGARDLESS (UK)	THOMAS	GOVERNOR	1961
T-27	HIS HEREAFTER	JONES	TRIANGLE	1916
T-28	FIDO'S FATE	GRIFFIN	TRIANGLE	1916
T28	VICTIM (UK)	DEARDEN	ASTOR	1961
T-29	BETTER LATE THAN NEVER	GRIFFIN	TRIANGLE	1916
T29	WHISTLE DOWN THE WIND (UK)	FORBES	ASTOR	1961
T30	HIS AUTO RUINATION	FISHBACK	TRIANGLE	1916
T30	ROOMMATES (UK: RAISING THE WIND)	THOMAS	HERTS-LION	1961
T-32	CINDERS OF LOVE	WRIGHT	TRIANGLE	1916
T32	WHAT A WHOPPER (UK)	GUNN	REGAL	1961
T-33	JUDGE	JONES	TRIANGLE	1916
T34	WALTZ OF THE TOREADORS (UK)	GUILLERMIN	CONTINENTAL	1962
T-35	WIFE AND AUTO TROUBLE	HENDERSON, SENNETT	TRIANGLE	1916
T36	TWICE ROUND THE DAFFODILS (UK)	THOMAS	ANGLO-AMALGAMATED	1962
T-38	GYPSY JOE	BADGER	TRIANGLE	1916
T-39	BY STORK DELIVERY	FISHBACK	TRIANGLE	1916

Movie Still Identification Book Ultimate Edition - Letters

CODE	TITLE/NAME	DIRECTOR/TYPE	STUDIO/DISTRIBUTOR	YEAR
T39	CARRY ON CRUISING (UK)	THOMAS	ANGLO-AMALGAMATED	1962
T-40	LOVE RIOT	JONES	TRIANGLE	1916
T40	PLAY IT COOL (UK)	WINNER	ALLIED ARTISTS	1962
T-41	OILY SCOUNDREL	FRAZEE	TRIANGLE	1916
T-42	HIS LAST LAUGH	WRIGHT	TRIANGLE	1916
T-43	HIS WIFE'S MISTAKE	ARBUCKLE	TRIANGLE	1916
T-44	SWINGIN' MAIDEN (UK: IRON MAIDEN)	THOMAS	COLUMBIA	1962
T-46	BUCKING SOCIETY	CAMPBELL	TRIANGLE	1916
T46	MIND BENDERS (UK)	DEARDEN	AIP	1963
T49	CALL ME BWANA (UK)	DOUGLAS	UNITED ARTISTS	1963
T-49	HIS BITTER PILL	FISHBACK	TRIANGLE	1916
T-50	DASH OF COURAGE	PARROTT	TRIANGLE	1916
T50	NURSE ON WHEELS (UK)	THOMAS	JANUS	1963
T-53	BATH TUB PERILS	FRAZEE	TRIANGLE	1916
T-54	LOVE COMET	WRIGHT	TRIANGLE	1916
T55	SÉANCE ON A WET AFTERNOON (UK)	FORBES	ARTIXO	1964
T-57	AMBROSE'S CUP OF WOE	FISHBACK	TRIANGLE	1916
T57	THIS IS MY STREET (UK)	HAYERS	PATHE	1964
T59	CARRY ON JACK (UK)	THOMAS	ANGLO-AMALGAMATED	1963
T68	CARRY ON CLEO (UK)	THOMAS	GOVERNOR	1964
T-71	HIS LYING HEART	STERLING, AVERY	TRIANGLE	1916
T72	THREE HATS FOR LISA (UK)	HAYERS	ANGLO-AMALGAMATED	1966
T-73	RECKLESS ROMEO	ARBUCKLE	TRIANGLE	1916
T79	CARRY ON COWBOY (UK)	THOMAS	ANGLO-AMALGAMATED	1965
T-79	SCOUNDREL'S TOLL	CAVENDER	TRIANGLE	1916
T-81	AMBROSE'S RAPID RISE	FISHBACK	TRIANGLE	1916
T-82	HIS BUSTED TRUST	CLINE	TRIANGLE	1916
T-83	HAYSTACKS AND STEEPLES	BADGER	TRIANGLE	1916
T-84	TUGBOAT ROMEO	CAMPBELL, WILLIAMS	TRIANGLE	1916
T-85	BOMBS!	GRIFFIN	TRIANGLE	1916
T85	CARRY ON SCREAMING! (UK)	THOMAS	SIGMA III	1966
T-86	HONEST THIEVES	MATTHEWS	TRIANGLE	1917
T-88	HIS LAST SCENT	AVERY, CHAPLIN	TRIANGLE	1916
T-89	HEART STRATEGY	MACDONALD	TRIANGLE	1917
T-93	BLACK EYES AND BLUE	KERR	TRIANGLE	1916
T-96	SAFETY FIRST AMBROSE	FISHBACK	TRIANGLE	1916
T99	CARRY ON PIMPERNEL (UK: DON'T LOSE YOUR HEAD)	THOMAS	RANK	1966
T-100	HER CIRCUS KNIGHT	WRIGHT	TRIANGLE	1917
T-101	TELEPHONE BELLE	RAYMAKER	TRIANGLE	1917
T-103	BACHELOR'S FINISH	DILLION	TRIANGLE	1917
T-105	DONE IN OIL	AVERY	TRIANGLE	1917
T-106	STONE AGE	HARTMAN	TRIANGLE	1917
T-107	FILM EXPOSURE	MCCOY	TRIANGLE	1917
T108	CARRY ON IN THE LEGION (UK: FOLLOW THAT CAMEL)	THOMAS	SCHOENFELD	1967
T-108	DODGING HIS DOOM	WILLIAMS	TRIANGLE	1917
T-109	VILLA OF THE MOVIES	CLINE	TRIANGLE	1917
T-110	HOBBLED HARTS	DILLION	TRIANGLE	1917
T-111	HER FAME AND SHAME	GRIFFIN	TRIANGLE	1917
T112	CARRY ON DOCTOR (UK)	THOMAS	RANK	1967
T-114	HER CANDY KID	AVERY	TRIANGLE	1917
T-115	FINISHED PRODUCT	MORRIS	TRIANGLE	1917
T117	CARRY ON... UP THE KHYBER (UK)	THOMAS	RANK	1968
T-117	TUNER OF NOTE	MCCOY	TRIANGLE	1917
T-123	DOG'S OWN TALE	RAYMAKER	TRIANGLE	1917
T-131	HER NATURE DANCE	CAMPBELL	TRIANGLE	1917
T-134	HIS ONE NIGHT STAND	MCCOY	TRIANGLE	1917
T-137	HIS SOCIAL RISE	MORRIS	TRIANGLE	1917
T-141	MAIDEN'S TRUST	HEERMAN	TRIANGLE	1916
T-146	HIS MARRIAGE FAILURE	RAYMAKER	TRIANGLE	1917
T-147	HIS BITTER FATE	WILLIAMS	TRIANGLE	1917
T-149	JANITOR'S VENGEANCE	AVERY	TRIANGLE	1917
T-151	AIRED IN COURT	DILLION	TRIANGLE	1917
T-152	HIS PERFECT DAY	MCCOY	TRIANGLE	1917
T-154	HIS THANKLESS JOB	MORRIS	TRIANGLE	1917
T-155	DAD'S DOWNFALL	RAYMAKER	TRIANGLE	1917
T-156	CACTUS NELL	FISHBACK	TRIANGLE	1917
T-158	HIS SUDDEN RIFVAL	DILLION	TRIANGLE	1917
T-159	TOY OF FATE	MCCOY	TRIANGLE	1917
T-160	INNOCENT VILLAIN	WILLIAMS	TRIANGLE	1917
T-162	HIS WIDOW'S MIGHT	KERNAN	TRIANGLE	1917

Movie Still Identification Book Ultimate Edition - Letters

CODE	TITLE/NAME	DIRECTOR/TYPE	STUDIO/DISTRIBUTOR	YEAR
T-164	HIS FATAL MOVE	MORRIS	TRIANGLE	1917
T-166	HIS COOL NERVE	MCCOY	TRIANGLE	1917
T-167	MATRIMONIAL ACCIDENT	AVERY	TRIANGLE	1917
T168	CARRY ON CLEO	THOMAS	ANGLO AMALGAMATED	1964
T-168	HIS HIDDEN TALENT (UK)	MORRIS	TRIANGLE	1917
T-169	LOVE CASE	KERNAN	TRIANGLE	1917
T-170	DOG CATCHER'S LOVE	CLINE	TRIANGLE	1917
T-172	HOTEL DISGRACE	DILLION	TRIANGLE	1917
T-173	HER DONKEY LOVE	AVERY	TRIANGLE	1917
T-175	HIS FOOT-HILL FOLLY	MORRIS	TRIANGLE	1917
T-176	FALLEN STAR	MCCOY	TRIANGLE	1917
T-177	DANGERS OF A BRIDE	KERR, HARTMAN	TRIANGLE	1917
T-178	DARK ROOM SECRET	KERNAN	TRIANGLE	1917
T-179	WARM RECEPTION	DILLION	TRIANGLE	1917
T-180	HIS BABY DOLL	WILLIAMS	TRIANGLE	1917
T-181	HIS UNCONSCIOUS CONSCIENCE	AVERY	TRIANGLE	1917
T-182	CLEVER DUMMY	RAYMAKER	TRIANGLE	1917
T-417	THUNDERSTORM (UK)	GUILLERMIN	ALLIED ARTISTS	1956
T&theGL	TARZAN AND THE GOLDEN LION	MCGOWAN	RKO	1927
TA	ABYSS	CAMERON	20th CENTURY FOX	1989
TA	ALAMO	WAYNE	UNITED ARTISTS	1960
TA	AMBUSHERS	LEVIN	COLUMBIA	1967
TA	ANNIVERSARY (UK)	BAKER	20TH CENTURY FOX	1968
TA	CAPTAIN TUGBOAT ANNIE	ROSEN	REPUBLIC	1945
TA	FACTS OF LIFE	FRANK	UNITED ARTISTS	1960
TA	SHIRLEY O'HARA	portrait		
TA	TANGIER ASSIGNMENT (UK)	ARDAVIN, LEVERSUCH	AAP	1955
TA	TARZAN AND THE AMAZONS	NEUMANN	RKO	1945
TA	TEENAGERS FROM OUTER SPACE	GRAEFF	WARNER BROS	1959
TA	THAT'S MY BABY	BERKE	REPUBLIC	1944
TA	THE ADVENTURER	CHAPLIN	RKO	R32
TA	THEY ALL DIED LAUGHING (UK: JOLLY BAD FELLOW)	CHAFFEY	CONTINENTAL	1964
TA	THIS IS THE ARMY	CURTIZ	WARNER BROS	1943
TA	TOUGH ASSIGNMENT	BEAUDINE	SCREEN GUILD	1949
TA	TOYS IN THE ATTIC	HILL	UNITED ARTISTS	1963
TA	TWO IN REVOLT	TRYON	RKO	1936
TA L	THE APARTMENT (pre-prod -see APT)	WILDER	UNITED ARTISTS	1960
TA-1	SKYLINE	TAYLOR	FOX FILM	1931
TA-2	AMBASSADOR BILL	TAYLOR	FOX FILM	1931
TA-3	DEVIL'S LOTTERY	TAYLOR	FOX FILM	1932
TAD	TARZAN'S MAGIC FOUNTAIN	SHOLEM	RKO	1949
TAH	WHAT PRICE HOLLYWOOD?	CUKOR	RKO	1932
TAL	THEY ALL LAUGHED	BOGDANOVICH	MOON	1981
TAM	12 ANGRY MEN	LUMET	UNITED ARTISTS	1957
TAM	THANKS A MILLION	DEL RUTH	20th CENTURY FOX	1935
TAM	TWELVE ANGRY MEN	LUMIT	UNITED ARTISTS	1957
TAR	ARIZONA RANGER	RAWLINS	RKO	1948
TAS	TARZAN'S DESERT MYSTERY	THIELE	RKO	1943
TAT	TENSION AT TABLE ROCK	WARREN	RKO	1956
TAWM	THEY'RE A WEIRD MOB (UK)	POWELL	RANK	1966
TB	BETRAYAL (IT: FRAULEIN DOKTOR)	LATTUADA	PARAMOUNT	1969
TB	BLOB	RUSSELL	TRI STAR	1988
TB	BORROWER	MCNAUGHTON	CANNON	1991
TB	BROADWAY MUSKETEERS	FARROW	WARNER BROS	1938
TB	NIGHT FIGHTERS (UK: TERRIBLE BEAUTY)	GARNETT	UNITED ARTISTS	1960
TB	SPY TRAIN (TIME BOMB)*	YOUNG	MONOGRAM	
TB	T BIRD GANG	HARBINGER	FILM GROUP	1959
TB	TALA BIRELL	portrait	UNIVERSAL	
TB	TARAS BULBA	THOMPSON	UNITED ARTISTS	1962
TB	TERMINAL BLISS	ALAN	CANNON	1992
TB	THEATER OF BLOOD	HICKOX	UNITED ARTISTS	1973
TB	THIEF OF BAGDAD	WALSH	UNITED ARTISTS	1924
TB	THOMASINE AND BUSHROD	PARKS	COLUMBIA	1974
TB	THUNDERBIRDS ARE GO (UK)	LANE	UNITED ARTISTS (UK)	1966
TB	TIGER BAY (UK)	WILLS	ABFD	1934
TB	TIGER BAY (UK)	THOMPSON	CONTINENTAL	1959
TB	TIMBUKTU	TOURNEUR	UNITED ARTISTS	1959
TB	TIME BANDITS (UK)	GILLIAM	EMBASSY	1981
TB	TO BEAT THE BAND	STOLOFF	RKO	1935
TB	TOD BROWNING	portrait	MGM	

Movie Still Identification Book Ultimate Edition - Letters

CODE	TITLE/NAME	DIRECTOR/TYPE	STUDIO/DISTRIBUTOR	YEAR
TB	TOGETHER BROTHERS	GRAHAM	20TH CENTURY FOX	1974
TB	TOM BROWN	portrait	RKO	
TB	TOM BROWN'S SCHOOL DAYS	STEVENSON	RKO	1940
TB	TOP BANANA	GREEN	UNITED ARTISTS	1954
TB	TRAVIS BANTON	portrait	UNIVERSAL	1930s-40s
TB	TROUBLE BREWING (UK)	KIMMINS	ABFD	1939
TB	TUGBOAT ANNIE SALES AGAIN	SEILER	WARNER BROS	1940
TB	TURHAN BEY	portrait	UNIVERSAL	
TB-1	WILD HORSE STAMPEDED	JAMES	MONOGRAM	1943
TB-2	LAW RIDES AGAIN	JAMES	MONOGRAM	1943
TB-3	BLAZING GUNS	TANSEY	MONOGRAM	1943
TB-4	DEATH VALLEY RANGERS	TANSEY	MONOGRAM	1943
TB-5	WESTWARD BOUND	TANSEY	MONOGRAM	1944
TB-6	ARIZONA WHIRLWIND	TANSEY	MONOGRAM	1944
TB-7	OUTLAW TRAIL	TANSEY	MONOGRAM	1944
TBB	BANK RAIDERS (UK)	MUNDEN	RANK	1958
TBC	BIG CITY (INDIA: MAHANAGAR)	RAY	EDWARD HARRISON	1963
TBC	BIG DIAMOND ROBBERY	CONNOR	WARNER BROS	1976
TBC	TRIAL BY COMBAT	CONNOR	WARNER BROS	1976
T-BDR	TRIAL BY COMBAT (UK)(DIRTY KNIGHT'S WORK)	FORDE	FILM BOOKING (RKO)	1929
TBFL4	CARRY ON TEACHER (UK)	THOMAS	GOVERNOR	1959
TBG	IRON SHERIFF	SALKOW	UNITED ARTISTS	1957
TBH	TEXAS, BROOKLYN & HEAVEN	CASTLE	UNITED ARTISTS	1948
TBL	THREE BLONDS IN HIS LIFE	CHOOLUCK	CINEMA ASSOCIATES	1960
TBM	BEASTMASTER	COSCARELLI	MGM	1982
TBM	BEST MAN	SCHAFFNER	UNITED ARTISTS	1964
TBM	BIG MOUTH	LEWIS	COLUMBIA	1967
TBM	BLACK MARBLE	BECKER	AVCO EMBASSY	1980
TBM	CRY OF BATTLE	LERNER	ALLIED ARTISTS	1963
TBM	TARAS BULBA	THOMPSON	UNITED ARTISTS	1962
TBR	BROTHER		WARNER BROS	
TBS	BIG SKY	HAWKS	RKO	1952
TBS	BIG SLEEP	WINNER	UNITED ARTISTS	1978
TBS	BIG STEAL	SIEGEL	RKO	1949
TBS	BIG STREET	REIS	RKO	1942
TBS	BRIGHTON STRANGLER	NOSSECK	RKO	1945
TBS	THREE BAD SISTERS	KAY	UNITED ARTISTS	1956
TBS	TWO IF BY SEA (STOLEN HEARTS*)	BENNETT	WARNER BROS	1996
TC	3 CABALLEROS (t)	FERGUSON, GERONIMI	RKO	1945
TC	3 CHEERS FOR THE IRISH	BACON	WARNER BROS	1940
TC	BIG CHASE	HILTON	LIPPERT	1954
TC	CANADIANS	KENNEDY	20th CENTURY FOX	1961
TC	CARDINAL	PREMINGER	COLUMBIA	1963
TC	CARETAKERS	BARTLETT	UNITED ARTISTS	1963
TC	CHAIRMAN (UK)	THOMPSON	20TH CENTURY FOX	1969
TC	CHALLENGE	FRANKENHEIMER	EMBASSY	1982
TC	CHEAT		PARAMOUNT	1915
TC	CONQUEROR	POWELL	RKO	1956
TC	CONSPIRATORS	NEGULESCO	WARNER BROS	1944
TC	CROONER	BACON	WARNER BROS	1932
TC	MURDER GO ROUND (FR/IT: UN CONDE)	BOISSET	AUDUBON	1973
TC	NIGHT OF THE EXECUTIONER (SP)	NASCHY	AUDUBON	1992
TC	STORY OF VERNON AND IRENE CASTLE	POTTER	RKO	1939
TC	TANIS CHANDLER	portrait	RKO	
TC	TENDER COMRADE	DMYTRYK	RKO	1944
TC	THE CLOWNS (IT)	FELLINI	LEVITT-PICKMAN	1971
TC	THOUSAND CLOWNS	COE	UNITED ARTISTS	1965
TC	THREE'S COMPANY (tv)	VARIOUS	ABC-TV	1976
TC	THUNDER IN CAROLINA	HELMICK	HOWCO	1960
TC	THURSDAY'S CHILD (UK)	ACKLAND	ABPC-PATHE	1943
TC	TOM CONWAY	portrait	RKO	
TC	TONY CURTIS	portrait	UNIVERSAL	1953-60s
TC	TORCHY BLANE IN CHINATOWN	BEAUDINE	WARNER BROS	1939
TC	TRIPLE CROSS (UK)	YOUNG	WARNER BROS	1967
TC	TRUE CONFESSIONS	GROSBARD	UNITED ARTISTS	1981
TC	TWELVE CHAIRS	BROOKS	UNITED ARTISTS	1970
TC	TWO CITIES (UK PRODUCTION CO.)	studio		
TC-1	LADY LET'S DANCE	WOODRUFF	MONOGRAM	1944
TC-6	UNPUBLISHED STORY (UK)	FRENCH	COLUMBIA	1942
TC-7	IN WHICH WE SERVE (UK)	LEAN	UNITED ARTISTS	1942

Movie Still Identification Book Ultimate Edition - Letters

CODE	TITLE/NAME	DIRECTOR/TYPE	STUDIO/DISTRIBUTOR	YEAR
TC-8	ADVENTURE FOR TWO (UK: DEMI-PARADISE)	ASQUITH	UNIVERSAL	1943
TC-9	GENTLE SEX (UK)	HOWARD	GFD	1943
TC-10	FLEMISH FARM (UK)	DELL	GFD	1943
TC-16	LAMP STILL BURNS (UK)	ELVEY	GFD	1943
TC-17	MEN OF TWO WORLDS (UK: WITCH DOCTOR)	DICKINSON	INTERNATIONAL RELEASING	1946
TC-18	HENRY V (UK)	OLIVIER	UNITED ARTISTS	1944
TC-19	TAWNY PIPIT (UK)	MILES, SAUNDERS	UNIVERSAL	1944
TC-20	HER MAN GILBEY (UK: ENGLISH WITHOUT TEARS)	FRENCH	UNIVERSAL	1944
TC-21	WAY AHEAD (UK)	REED	20TH CENTURY FOX	1944
TC 22	MR. EMMANUEL (UK)	FRENCH	UNITED ARTISTS	1944
TC 24	BLITHE SPIRIT (UK)	LEAN	UNITED ARTISTS	1945
TC-27	DON'T TAKE IT TO HEART (UK)	DELL	EAGLE-LION	1944
TC 30	JOHNNY IN THE CLOUDS (UK: WAY TO THE STARS)	ASQUITH	UNITED ARTISTS	1945
TC-30A	JOHNNY IN THE CLOUDS (UK: WAY TO THE STARS)	ASQUITH	UNITED ARTISTS	1945
TC-33	CARNIVAL (UK)	HAYNES	GFD	1946
TC-34	BEWARE OF PITY (UK)	ELVEY	EAGLE-LION	1946
TC-107	WAY WE LIVE (UK)	CRAIGIE	GFD	1946
TC-110	HUNGRY HILL (UK)	HURST	UNIVERSAL	1947
TC112	ODD MAN OUT (UK)	REED	UNIVERSAL	1947
TC-120	FAME IS THE SPUR (UK)	BOULTING	TOXFORD	1947
TC-124	INHERITANCE (UK: UNCLE SILAS)	FRANK	FINE ARTS	1947
TC-126	OCTOBER MAN (UK)	BAKER	EAGLE LION	1947
TC-131	VICE VERSA (UK)	USTINOV	GFD	1948
TC-132	MARK OF CAIN (UK)	HURST	GFD	1947
TC-133	HAMLET (UK)	OLIVIER	UNIVERSAL	1949
TC-142	ONE NIGHT WITH YOU (UK)	YOUNG	UNIVERSAL	1948
TC-142	THIS HAPPY BREED (UK)	LEAN	UNIVERSAL	1944
TC-159	MR. PERRIN AND MR. TRAILL (UK)	HUNTINGTON	EAGLE-LION	1948
TC-160	SLEEPING CAR TO TRIESTE (UK)	CARSTAIRS	EAGLE-LION	1948
TC-164	WOMAN HATER (UK)	YOUNG	UNIVERSAL	1948
TC-168	WEAKER SEX (UK)	BAKER	EAGLE-LION	1948
TC-172	HISTORY OF MR. POLLY (UK)	PELISSIER	INTERNATIONAL RELEASING	1949
TC-183	CARDBOARD CAVALIER (UK)	FORDE	GFD	1949
TC-185	THE GAY LADY (UK: TROTTIE TRUE)	HURST	EAGLE-LION	1949
TC-188	ADAM AND EVALYN (UK: ADAM AND EVELYNE)	FRENCH	UNIVERSAL	1949
TC-193	MADNESS OF THE HEART (UK)	BENNETT	UNIVERSAL	1949
TC-196	PERFECT WOMAN (UK)	KNOWLES	EAGLE-LION	1949
TC-199	AMAZING MR. BEECHAM (UK: CHILTERN HUNDREDS)	CARSTAIRS	EAGLE-LION	1949
TC 203	THEY WERE NOT DIVIDED (UK)	YOUNG	UNITED ARTISTS	1950
TC-205	ROCKING HORSE WINNER (UK)	PELISSIER	UNIVERSAL	1949
TC-209	PRELUDE TO FAME (UK)	MCDONNELL	UNIVERSAL	1950
TC-223	HIGHLY DANGEROUS (UK)	BAKER	LIPPERT	1950
TC-233	ENCORE (UK)	FRENCH, JACKSON. PELISSIER	PARAMOUNT	1951
TCA	THOMAS CROWN AFFAIR	MCTIERNAN	MGM	1999
TCC	THEY CAME TO A CITY (UK)	DEARDEN	AFE	1944
TCF1	WE'RE GOING TO BE RICH (UK)	BANKS	20TH CENTURY FOX	1938
TCG	TERROR CREATURES FROM GRAVE	ZUCKER	PACEMAKER	1967
TCH	12 CROWDED HOURS	LANDERS	RKO	1939
TCH	CHAIRMAN (UK)	THOMPSON	20th CENTURY FOX	1969
TCK	INSIDE THE MAFIA	CAHN	UNITED ARTISTS	1959
TCM	TEXAS CHAINSAW MASSACRE	HOOPER	BRYANSTON	1974
TCM	THERE WAS A CROOKED MAN (UK)	BURGE	UNITED ARTISTS	1960
TCM2	TEXAS CHAINSAW MASSACRE 2	HOOPER	CANNON	1986
TCP-4	INSPECTOR HORNLEIGH (UK)	FORDE	20TH CENTURY FOX	1939
TCS	THEY CALL IT SIN	FREELAND	WARNER BROS	1932
TD	BLOOD FIEND (UK: THEATRE OF DEATH)	GALLU	HEMISPHERE	1967
TD	DEERSLAYER	NEUMANN	20TH CENTURY FOX	1957
TD	DELINQUENTS	ALTMAN	UNITED ARTISTS	1957
TD	DOVE	JARROTT	PARAMOUNT	1974
TD	GIRL AND THE GAMBLER	LANDERS	RKO	1939
TD	GIRL OF THE RIO	BRENON	RKO	1931
TD	GLORIA DICKSON (NÉE THAIS DICKERSON)	portrait	WARNER BROS	
TD	HITCH-HIKER	LUPINO	RKO	1953
TD	MAN WHO CAME TO DINNER	KEIGHLEY	WARNER BROS	1942
TD	ONE MAN'S JOURNEY	ROBERTSON	RKO	1933
TD	POLYESTER	WATERS	NEW LINE CINEMA	1981
TD	SCARF	DUPONT	UNITED ARTISTS	1951
TD	TAD DEVINE	portrait	UNIVERSAL	
TD	TAMARA DESNI	portrait	GAUMONT BRITISH	
TD	TAXI DRIVER	SCORSESE	COLUMBIA	1976

Movie Still Identification Book Ultimate Edition - Letters

CODE	TITLE/NAME	DIRECTOR/TYPE	STUDIO/DISTRIBUTOR	YEAR
TD	THE DISH	SITCH	WARNER BROS	2000
TD	THREE DESPERATE MEN	NEWFIELD	LIPPERT	1951
TD	TILL DEATH US DO PART (UK)	COHEN	SHERPIX	1969
TD	TILL THE END OF TIME	DMYTRYK	RKO	1946
TD	TOM D'ANDREA	portrait	WARNER BROS	
TD	TOM DRAKE	portrait	UNIVERSAL	
TD	TOMMY DORSEY	portrait	MCA RECORDS	
TD	TONY DEVLIN	portrait	EDWARD SMALL	
TD	TRACKDOWN	HEFFRON	UNITED ARTISTS	1976
TD	TROY DONAHUE	portrait	UNIVERSAL	
TD	TURKISH DELIGHT (NETH: TURKS FRUIT 1973) (SENSUALIST)	VERHOEVEN	CINEMATION	1974
TD4	TWO DAUGHTERS	RAY	JANUS	1963
TDA	DEVIL AND MISS JONES	WOOD	RKO	1941
TDG	DALTON GIRLS	LE BORG	UNITED ARTISTS	1957
TDH	12 DESPERATE HOURS (UK: THE EXTRA DAY)	FAIRCHILD	UNITED ARTISTS	1956
TDH	TOM, DICK AND HARRY	KANIN	RKO	1941
TDM	POP ALWAYS PAYS	GOODWINS	RKO	1940
TDO	DEVIL'S OWN	FRANKEL	20th CENTURY FOX	1967
TDR	DELIGHTFUL ROGUE	SHORES, PEARCE	RKO	1929
TDT	DAY THE BOOKIES WEPT	GOODWINS	RKO	1939
TE	20,000 EYES	LEEWOOD	20TH CENTURY FOX	1961
TE	BELOVED BRAT	LUBIN	WARNER BROS	1938
TE	BEST OF ENEMIES (IT)	HAMILTON	COLUMBIA	1961
TE	DANGER ROUTE (UK)	HOLT	UNITED ARTISTS	1967
TE	END	REYNOLDS	UNITED ARTISTS	1978
TE	ENTERTAINER (UK)	RICHARDSON	CONTINENTAL	1960
TE	ISLE OF DESTINY		WARNER BROS	
TE	KILLERS FROM SPACE	WILDER	RKO	1954
TE	TANGLED EVIDENCE (UK)	COOPER	RKO	1934
TE	TEOREMA	PASOLINI	CONTINENTAL	1969
TE	THIS ENGLAND (UK)	MACDONALD	WORLD	1941
TE	THUNDER IN THE EAST (UK: THE BATTLE)	FARKAS	UNITED ARTISTS	1935
TEL	SUSIE STEPS OUT (LA)	LE BORG	UNITED ARTISTS	1946
TER	TERESA	ZINNEMANN	MGM	1951
TER	TERRORNAUTS (UK)	TULLY	EMBASSY	1967
TEX	LONE TEXAN	LANDRES	20TH CENTURY FOX	1959
TF	BACHELOR OF HEARTS (UK)	RILLA	CONTINENTAL	1958
TF	FIGHTER	KLINE	UNITED ARTISTS	1952
TF	FORTUNE	NICHOLS	COLUMBIA	1975
TF	FROG (UK)	RAYMOND	20TH CENTURY FOX	1937
TF	FUGITIVE	FORD	RKO	1947
TF	HEROES OF THE ALAMO	FRASER	COLUMBIA	1937
TF	SAILOR BE GOOD	CRUZE	RKO	1933
TF	THE RACKET	CROMWELL	RKO	1951
TF	THORNTON FREELAND FILMS		SCHENCK-UNITED ARTISTS	
TF	TIME FLIES (UK)	FORDE	GFD	1944
TF	TOKYO FILE-212	MCGOWAN	RKO	1951
TF	TONGFATHER	TIEN	SINO-AMERICAN	1974
TF	TRYGON FACTOR (UK)	FRANKEL	WARNER BROS	1969
TF	WINGS AND THE WOMAN (UK: THEY FLEW ALONE)	WILCOX	RKO	1942
TF 1	TOM BROWN'S SCHOOLDAYS	PARRY	UNITED ARTISTS	1951
TF-2900	THREE LIVE GHOSTS	FREELAND	UNITED ARTISTS	1929
TFA-ADV	FALCON'S ALIBI	MCCAREY	RKO	1946
TFB	STOP TRAIN 349 (FR)	HADRICH	MONOGRAM	1964
TFE	3 FACES EAST	DEL RUTH	WARNER BROS	1930
TFG	FALL GUY	PEARCE	RKO	1930
TFL	TALENT FOR LOVING (UK)	QUINE	PARAMOUNT	1969
TFM	TO FIND A MAN	KULIK	COLUMBIA	1972
TFP	FINGER POINTS	DILLON	WARNER BROS	1931
TFR	TWO FOR THE ROAD (UK)	DONEN	20th CENTURY FOX	1967
TFS	FALLEN SPARROW	WALLACE	RKO	1943
TFU	DANCING SWEETIES	ENRIGHT	WARNER BROS	1930
TFW	TALE OF FIVE WOMEN (UK: TALE OF FIVE CITIES)	TULLY	UNITED ARTISTS	1951
TG	GAMBLERS	CURTIZ	WARNER BROS	1929
TG	GAUCHO	JONES	UNITED ARTISTS	1927
TG	GETAWAY	PECKINPAH	NATIONAL GENERAL	1972
TG	GRADUATE [US: EMBASSY; UK, FR, GER: UA]	NICHOLS	UNITED ARTISTS	1967
TG	GREAT MAN VOTES	KANIN	RKO	1939
TG	GROUP	LUMET	UNITED ARTISTS	1966
TG	GUEST (UK: CARETAKER)	DONNER	JANUS	1963

Movie Still Identification Book Ultimate Edition - Letters

CODE	TITLE/NAME	DIRECTOR/TYPE	STUDIO/DISTRIBUTOR	YEAR
TG	LAST GRENADE (UK)	FLEMYNG	CINERAMA	1970
TG	MAD GENIUS	CURTIZ	WARNER BROS	1931
TG	MAGIC WORLD OF TOPO GIGIO	CALDURA, DE RICO	COLUMBIA	1961
TG	MUSIC BOX KID	CAHN	UNITED ARTISTS	1960
TG	STRANGE LOVE OF MOLLY LOUVAIN	CURTIZ	WARNER BROS	1932
TG	THERE GOES MY GIRL	HOLMES	RKO	1937
TG	THOMAS GOMEZ	portrait	UNIVERSAL	
TG	TITO GUIZAR	portrait	REPUBLIC	
TG	TOP GUN	NAZARRO	UNITED ARTISTS	1955
TG	TOP GUN	SCOTT	PARAMOUNT	1986
TG	TORTURE GARDEN (UK)	FRANCIS	COLUMBIA	1967
TG	TOUCH AND GO	MANDEL	TRI STAR	1986
TG	TRAITOR'S GATE (UK)	FRANCIS	COLUMBIA	1964
TG	TRUE GLORY	KANIN	COLUMBIA	1945
TG	TRUE GRIT	HATHAWAY	PARAMOUNT	1969
TG	TUNES OF GLORY (UK)	NEAME	UNITED ARTISTS	1960
TG	TWO GALS AND A GUY	GREEN	UNITED ARTISTS	1951
TG	WITHOUT RESERVATIONS	LEROY	RKO	1946
TGA	GIRL, GUY AND A GOB	WALLACE	RKO	1941
TGBB	TIGGER MOVIE (t)	FALKENSTEIN	BUENA VISTA	2000
TGD	THROUGH A GLASS DARKLY (SWE: SASOM I EN SPEGEL)	BERGMAN	JANUS	1961
TGDD	TOUGH GUYS DON'T DANCE	MAILER	CANNON	1987
TGF	GIRL FROM MEXICO	GOODWINS	RKO	1939
TGG	BATTLE HELL (UK: YANGTSE INCIDENT)	ANDERSON	DCA	1957
TGG	GREAT GILDERSLEEVE	DOUGLAS	RKO	1943
TGG	THAT'S A GOOD GIRL (UK)	BUCHANAN	UNITED ARTISTS	1933
TGIK	NAME OF THE GAME IS KILL	HELLSTROM	FANFARE	1968
TGO	THUNDERBIRDS ARE GO	LANE	UNITED ARTISTS	1966
TGS	THERE'S A GIRL IN MY SOUP	BOULTING	COLUMBIA	1970
TGT	GLASS TOMB (UK: GLASS CAGE)	TULLY	LIPPERT	1955
TGU	TAKE A GIRL LIKE YOU	MILLER	COLUMBIA	1970
TH	3 MEN ON A HORSE		WARNER BROS	1936
TH	BEHIND THE HEADLINES	ROSSON	RKO	1937
TH	HAWAIIANS	GRIES	UNITED ARTISTS	1970
TH	HEAD	TRIVAS	TRANSLUX	1962
TH	HERO (UK: BLOOMFIELD 1971)	HARRIS	AVCO EMBASSY	1972
TH	HILL (UK)	LUMET	MGM	1965
TH	HOSTAGE (UK)	HUTH	EROS	1956
TH	HOWLING	DANTE	AVCO EMBASSY	1981
TH	I'LL GET YOU (UK: ESCAPE ROUTE)	FRIEDMAN, SCOTT	LIPPERT	1952
TH	TAB HUNTER	portrait	WARNER BROS	1950s
TH	TARZAN AND THE HUNTRESS	NEUMANN	RKO	1947
TH	TASTE OF HONEY (UK)	RICHARDSON	CONTINENTAL	1961
TH	TEDDY HART	portrait	WARNER BROS	
TH	TEMPTATION HARBOR (UK: TEMPTATION HARBOUR)	COMFORT	MONOGRAM	1947
TH	THE HUNTER	KULIK	PARAMOUNT	1980
TH	THIEF	MANN	UNITED ARTISTS	1981
TH	TIM HOLT	portrait	RKO	
TH	TIM HOVEY	portrait	UNIVERSAL	
TH	TIPPI HEDREN	portrait	UNIVERSAL	
TH	TO HAVE AND HAVE NOT	HAWKS	WARNER BROS	1944
TH	TOP HAT	SANDRICH	RKO	1935
TH	TRAVELING HUSBANDS	SLOANE	RKO	1931
TH	TREASURE HUNT (UK)	CARSTAIRS	CARDINAL	1952
TH	TROOPER HOOK	WARREN	UNITED ARTISTS	1957
TH	TWILIGHT HOUR (UK)	STEIN	ANGLO-AMERICAN	1945
TH	TY HARDIN	portrait	WARNER BROS	
TH-4	SAGEBRUSH LAW	NELSON	RKO	1942
THE	HAPPY ENDING	BROOKS	UNITED ARTISTS	1969
THE MEDIUM	MEDIUM	MENOTTI	LOPPERT	1951
THG	BRIDE BY MISTAKE	WALLACE	RKO	1944
THH	HANOI HILTON	CHETWYND	CANNON	1987
THI	12 DESPERATE HOURS (UK: THE EXTRA DAY)	FAIRCHILD	UNITED ARTISTS	1956
THJ	TARZAN'S HIDDEN JUNGLE	SCHUSTER	RKO	1955
THN	THINGS HAPPEN AT NIGHT (UK)	SEARLE	RENOWN	1948
THUNDERBOLT	THUNDERBOLT	STURGES	MONOGRAM	1947
TI	HARD TO HANDLE	LEROY	WARNER BROS	1933
TI	IDOLMAKER	HACKFORD	UNITED ARTISTS	1980
TI	IMPERSONATOR (UK)	SHAUGHNESSY	CONTINENTAL	1961
TI	RETURN TO TREASURE ISLAND	DUPONT	UNITED ARTISTS	1954

Movie Still Identification Book Ultimate Edition - Letters

CODE	TITLE/NAME	DIRECTOR/TYPE	STUDIO/DISTRIBUTOR	YEAR
TI	SMART MONEY	GREEN	WARNER BROS	1931
TI	TALL IN THE SADDLE	MARIN	RKO	1944
TI	THERESE AND ISABELLE	METZGER	AUDUBON	1968
TI	THOMAS INCE PRODUCTIONS	studio		
TI	THUNDER ISLAND	LEEWOOD	20th CENTURY FOX	1963
TI	VISCOUNT (FR: LE VICOMTE REGLE SES COMPTES)	CLOCHE	WARNER BROS	
TI-51	WHAT EVERY WOMAN LEARNS	NIBLO	PARAMOUNT	1919
TI-55	HIS WIFE'S FRIEND	DE GRASSE	PARAMOUNT	1919
TIF	TOMORROW IS FOREVER	PICHEL	RKO	1946
TIME	VALLEY OF THE GWANGI	O'CONNOLLY	WARNER BROS	1969
TIML	THIS IS MY LIFE	EPHRON	20th CENTURY FOX	1992
TIN-4	TRUE HEAVEN	TINLING	FOX FILM	1929
TIN-5	EXALTED FLAPPER	TINLING	FOX FILM	1929
TIN-6	WORDS AND MUSIC	TINLING	FOX FILM	1929
TIN-7	ONE MAD KISS	TINLING	FOX FILM	1930
TING	TINLING PRODUCTIONS	studio	FOX	
TING-1	VERY CONFIDENTIAL	TINLING	FOX FILM	1927
TIT	TRAPPED IN TANGIER	FREDA	20th CENTURY FOX	1960
TJ	TERROR IN THE JUNGLE	DESIMONE	CROWN INT'L	1968
TJ	TOM JONES [US: LOPERT; UK: UA]	RICHARDSON	UNITED ARTISTS	1963
TJ	TRIPLE JUSTICE	HOWARD	RKO	1940
TJ	VOYAGE (IT: IL VIAGGIO) (UK: THE JOURNEY)	DE SICA	UNITED ARTISTS	1974
TJA	JAZZ AGE	SHORES	RKO	1929
TJ-R	THUNDERING JETS	DANTINE	20TH CENTURY FOX	1958
TK	KEY	CURTIZ	WARNER BROS	1934
TK	KEYHOLE	CURTIZ	WARNER BROS	1933
TK	KID	CHAPLIN	FIRST NATIONAL	1921
TK	KNACK... AND HOW TO GET IT [US: LOPERT; UK: UA]	LESTER	UNITED ARTISTS	1965
TK	SACRED KNIVES OF VENGEANCE (HK: DA SHA SHOU)	CHOR	WARNER BROS	1972
TK	KEEP	MANN	PARAMOUNT	1983
TK	KISS	DENSHAM	TRI STAR	1988
TK	THEY KNEW WHAT THEY WANTED	KANIN	RKO	1940
TK	TOM KEENE	portrait		
TK	WHEN A MAN LOVES	CROSLAND	WARNER BROS	1927
TK-1	WANDERERS OF THE WEST	HILL	MONOGRAM	1941
TK-2	DYNAMITE CANYON	TANSEY	MONOGRAM	1941
TK-3	DRIFTIN' KID	TANSEY	MONOGRAM	1941
TK-4	RIDIN' THE SUNSET TRAIL	TANSEY	MONOGRAM	1941
TK-5	LONE STAR LAW MEN	TANSEY	MONOGRAM	1941
TK-6	WESTERN MAIL	TANSEY	MONOGRAM	1942
TK-7	ARIZONA ROUNDUP	TANSEY	MONOGRAM	1942
TK-8	WHERE TRAILS END	TANSEY	MONOGRAM	1942
TKG	THAT KIND OF GIRL (UK)	O'HARA	TOPAZ	1963
TKH	THREE KINDS OF HEAT	STEVENS	CANNON	1987
TL	HERO'S ISLAND (LAND WE LOVE)	STEVENS	UNITED ARTISTS	1962
TL	IN THIS OUR LIFE	HUSTON	WARNER BROS	1942
TL	LANDLORD	ASHBY	UNITED ARTISTS	1970
TL	TANNED LEGS	GERAGHTY	RKO	1929
TL	TEN LITTLE INDIANS (UK)	POLLOCK	SEVEN ARTS	1965
TL	TEXAS LADY	WHELAN	RKO	1955
TL	THANK YOU ALL VERY MUCH (UK: TOUCH OF LOVE)	HUSSEIN	COLUMBIA	1969
TL	THELMA AND LOUISE	SCOTT	MGM	1991
TL	THELMA LEEDS	portrait	RKO	
TL	THINGS OF LIFE	SAUTET	COLUMBIA	1970
TL	THIS LAND IS MINE	RENOIR	RKO	1943
TL	THUNDERBOLT AND LIGHTFOOT	CIMINO	UNITED ARTISTS	1974
TL	TILT	DURAND	WARNER BROS	1979
TL	TIME LIMIT	MALDEN	UNITED ARTISTS	1957
TL	TIME LOCK (UK)	THOMAS	DCA	1957
TL	TIME LOST AND TIME REMEMBERED (UK: I WAS HAPPY HERE)	DAVIS	CONTINENTAL	1966
TL	TINA LOUISE	portrait		
TL	TO BE A LADY (UK)	KING	PARAMOUNT BRITISH	1934
TL	TOWER OF LONDON	CORMAN	UNITED ARTISTS	1962
TL	TRUE LIES	CAMERON	20th CENTURY FOX	1994
TL	TRUE LOVE	SAVOCA	UNITED ARTISTS	1989
TL	WHERE THE HOT WIND BLOWS (FR/IT: LA LEGGE)	DASSIN	MGM	1960
TL-12	TARZAN AND THE LOST SAFARI (UK)	HUMBERSTONE	MGM	1957
TLB	TWO LITTLE BEARS	HOOD	20th CENTURY FOX	1961
TLBB	THREE MEN AND A LITTLE LADY	ARDOLINO	BUENA VISTA	1990
TLD	WOMAN'S SECRET		RKO	1934

Movie Still Identification Book Ultimate Edition - Letters

CODE	TITLE/NAME	DIRECTOR/TYPE	STUDIO/DISTRIBUTOR	YEAR
TLM	LAST METRO (FR)	TRUFFAUT	UNITED ARTISTS	1980
TLM	THUNDER MOUNTAIN	LANDERS	RKO	1949
TLOD	TWO LIVING, ONE DEAD (UK)	ASQUITH	BRITISH LION	1961
TLP	TO LIVE IN PEACE (IT: VIVERE IN PACE)	ZAMPA	TIMES	1947
TLT	TOO LATE FOR TEARS (KILLER BAIT)	HASKIN	UNITED ARTISTS	1949
TLTE	THOSE LIPS, THOSE EYES	PRESSMAN	UNITED ARTISTS	1980
TLW	LAST WINTER	NISSIMOFF	TRI STAR	1984
TLW	TARZAN AND THE LEOPARD WOMAN	NEUMANN	RKO	1946
TM	12 ANGRY MEN	LUMET	UNITED ARTISTS	1957
TM	3 MUSKETEERS	LEEWOOD	RKO	1935
TM	MAGICIAN (SWE: ANSIKTET)	BERGMAN	JANIS	1958
TM	MAN FROM BLANKLEYS	GREEN	WARNER BROS	1930
TM	MARK (UK)	GREEN	CONTINENTAL	1961
TM	MAYOR OF 44TH STREET	GREEN	RKO	1942
TM	MECHANIC	WINNER	UNITED ARTISTS	1972
TM	MERCENARY (IT: REVENGE OF A GUNFIGHTER)	CORBUCCI	UNITED ARTISTS	1968
TM	MISFITS	HUSTON	UNITED ARTISTS	1961
TM	MOLESTERS	SCHNYDER	ARISTOCRAT	1964
TM	MOONLIGHTER	ROWLAND	WARNER BROS	1953
TM	MUGGER	BERKE	UNITED ARTISTS	1958
TM	NORTHERN PURSUIT	WALSH	WARNER BROS	1943
TM	SHOW GOES ON (UK: THREE MAXIMS)	WILCOX	GAUMONT BRITISH AMERICA	1936
TM	TARZAN AND THE MERMAIDS	FLOREY	RKO	1948
TM	TARZAN THE MAGNIFICENT (UK)	DAY	PARAMOUNT	1960
TM	TEENAGE MILLIONAIRE	DOHENY	UNITED ARTISTS	1961
TM	TERRY MOORE	portrait	RKO	
TM	THAT MAN FROM RIO	DE BROCA	UNITED ARTISTS	1964
TM	THEY MADE HER A SPY	HIVELY	RKO	1939
TM	THIRD OF A MAN	LEWIN	UNITED ARTISTS	1962
TM	THIS TIME I'LL MAKE YOU RICH (IT)	PAROLINI	AVCO EMBASSY	1974
TM	THREE ON A MATCH	LEROY	WARNER BROS	1932
TM	THROW MAMA FROM THE TRAIN	DEVITO	ORION	1987
TM	TICKLE ME	TAUROG	ALLIED ARTISTS	1965
TM	TIM MCCOY	portrait		
TM	TOM MOORE	portrait	METRO	1920s-50s
TM	TONY MARTIN	portrait	RKO	
TM	TORCHY GETS HER MAN	BEAUDINE	WARNER BROS	1938
TM	TORCHY RUNS FOR MAYOR	MCCAREY	WARNER BROS	1939
TM	UNDER A TEXAS MOON	CURTIZ	WARNER BROS	1930
TM2	TEENAGE MUTANT NINJA TURTLES 2	PRESSMAN	20th CENTURY FOX	1991
TMAG	GAY ADVENTURE (UK: GOLDEN ARROW)	PARRY	UNITED ARTISTS	1949
TMC	TOO MANY COOKS	SEITER	RKO	1931
TMCJ	TEXAN MEETS CALAMITY JANE	LAMB	COLUMBIA	1950
TMG	THAT MAN GEORGE - FR –	DERAY	ALLIED ARTISTS	1967
TMG	TOO MANY GIRLS	ABBOTT	RKO	1940
TMI	THEY MET IN ARGENTINA	GOODWINS, HIVELY	RKO	1941
TM-K	THIS TIME I'LL MAKE YOU RICH (IT/GER: QUESTA VOLTA	KRAMER (PAROLINI)	AVCO EMBASSY	1975
TMM	GENIUS AT WORK	GOODWINS	RKO	1946
TMM	LUSTY MEN		RKO	1946
TMO	MAYOR OF 44TH STREET	GREEN	RKO	1942
TMO	TIGER MAKES OUT	HILLER	COLUMBIA	1967
T-MP	TESS OF THE STORM COUNTRY	ROBERTSON	UNITED ARTISTS	1922
TMR	MASTER RACE	BIBERMAN	RKO	1944
TN	BUTLER'S DILEMMA (UK)	HISCOTT	ANGLO-AMERICAN	1943
TN	NANNY (UK)	HOLT	20TH CENTURY FOX	1965
TN	NATURAL	LEVINSON	TRI STAR	1984
TN	THREE STEPS NORTH	W. WILDER	UNITED ARTISTS	1951
TN	TRACKED IN THE SNOW COUNTRY	RAYMAKER	WARNER BROS	1925
TN	TWISTED NERVE (UK)	BOULTING	NATIONAL GENERAL	1968
TNC	TRANSGRESSION	BRENON	RKO	1931
TNT2	BIG TNT SHOW	PEERCE	AIP	1966
TO	DEADFALL (UK)	FORBES	20TH CENTURY FOX	1968
TO	OFFENCE	LUMET	UNITED ARTISTS	1973
TO	OPTOMISTS	SIMMONS	PARAMOUNT	1973
TO	OUTLAW (1943)	HUGHES	RKO	R50
TO	DEADFALL (UK)	WATT	UNIVERSAL	1946
TO	THIEVES FALL OUT	ENRIGHT	WARNER BROS	1941
TO	TOKYO OLYMPIAD	ICHIKAWA	AIP	1966
TO	TOUCHABLES (UK)	FREEMAN	20TH CENTURY FOX	1968
TO	TUTTLES OF TAHITI	VIDOR	RKO	1942

Movie Still Identification Book Ultimate Edition - Letters

CODE	TITLE/NAME	DIRECTOR/TYPE	STUDIO/DISTRIBUTOR	YEAR
TO	TWO IN THE DARK	STOLOFF	RKO	1936
TOB	THIEF OF BAGDAD (IT)	LUBIN	MGM	1961
TOC	TWO O'CLOCK COURAGE	MANN	RKO	1945
TOE	TERMS OF ENDEARMENT	BROOKS	PARAMOUNT	1983
TOF	ONION FIELD	BECKER	AVCO EMBASSY	1979
TOL	BORDER TREASURE	ARCHAINBAUD	RKO	1950
TOL	OTHER LOVE	DE TOTH	UNITED ARTISTS	1947
TOS	SEA DEVILS	WALSH	RKO	1953
TOS	TAMING OF THE SHREW	ZEFFIRELLI	COLUMBIA	1967
TOS	THUNDER OVER SANGOLAND	NEWFIELD	LIPPERT	1955
TOT	THUNDER OVER TANGIER (UK: MAN FROM TANGIER)	COMFORT	REPUBLIC	1957
TOT	TRACK OF THUNDER	KANE	UNITED ARTISTS	1967
TP	FOUR FACES WEST	GREEN	UNITED ARTISTS	1948
T-P	MR. ACE	MARIN	UNITED ARTISTS	1946
TP	PARTY	EDWARDS	UNITED ARTISTS	1968
TP	PINK PANTHER	EDWARDS	UNITED ARTISTS	1963
TP	PRESS FOR TIME (UK)	ASHER	RANK	1966
TP	PRINCIPAL	CAIN	TRI STAR	1987
TP	PRISONER (UK)	GLENVILLE	COLUMBIA	1955
TP	PSYCHOPATH (UK)	FRANCIS	PARAMOUNT	1966
TP	PUSHER	MILFORD	UNITED ARTISTS	1960
TP	SHE LOVED A FIREMAN	FARROW	WARNER BROS	1937
TP	STORM FEAR	WILDE	UNITED ARTISTS	1955
TP	TAKING OF PELHAM ONE TWO THREE	SARGENT	UNITED ARTISTS	1974
TP	TALES OF PARIS	ALLEGRET, BARMA	TIMES FILM	1962
TP	TARZAN'S PERIL	HASKIN	RKO	1951
TP	TAXI	DEL RUTH	WARNER BROS	1932
TP	TEENAGE PLAYMATES (GER)	HOFBAUER	HEMISPHERE	1974
TP	THE PRINCIPAL	CAIN	TRI STAR	1987
TP	THIS WAS PARIS (UK)	HARLOW	WARNER BROS	1942
TP	THOSE PEOPLE NEXT DOOR (UK)	HARLOW	EROS	1953
TP	THREE PASSIONS	INGRAM	UNITED ARTISTS	1928
TP	THUNDER PASS	MCDONALD	LIPPERT	1954
TP	TRACKED BY THE POLICE	ENRIGHT	WARNER BROS	1927
TP	TURNING POINT	ROSS	20th CENTURY FOX	1977
TP	TWILIGHT PEOPLE	ROMERO	DIMENSION	1972
TP	TYRONE POWER	portrait	UNIVERSAL	
TP-7	OUTLAW ROUNDUP	FRASER	PRC	1944
TP-106	UNDER CAPRICORN (UK)	HITCHCOCK	WARNER BROS	1949
TPG	TIME PLACE AND THE GIRL	BRETHERTON	WARNER BROS	1929
TPH	PURPLE HILLS	DEXTER	20th CENTURY FOX	1961
TPO	PARTY'S OVER (UK)	BEHM	MONOGRAM	1965
TPR	BIG DEADLY GAME (UK: THIRD PARTY RISK)	BIRT	LIPPERT	1954
TPR	FORCE OF EVIL	POLONSKY	MGM	1948
TPROC	THE PURPLE ROSE OF CAIRO	ALLEN	ORION	1985
TPV	TREASURE OF PANCHO VILLA	SHERMAN	RKO	1955
TQ	QUEENS (IT)	BOLOGNINI, MONICELLI	COLUMBIA	1966
TQ	RUNAWAY QUEEN (UK: THE QUEEN'S AFFAIR)	WILCOX	UNITED ARTISTS	1934
TQM	20 QUESTIONS MURDER MYSTERY (UK)	STEIN	GRAND NATIONAL	1950
TR	CAPTIVE CITY	WISE	UNITED ARTISTS	1952
TR	LAWYER	FURIE	PARAMOUNT	1970
TR	NEXT TIME I MARRY	KANIN	RKO	1938
TR	RAINMAKERS	GUIOL	RKO	1935
TR	REPTILE (UK)	GILLING	20TH CENTURY FOX	1966
TR	SHE'S IN THE ARMY	YARBROUGH	MONOGRAM	1942
TR	TEX RITTER MOVIES		GRAND NATIONAL	
TR	THEATRE ROYAL (UK)	BAXTER	ANGLO-AMERICAN	1943
TR	THELMA RITTER	portrait	FOX	
TR	THREE (UK)	SLATER	UNITED ARTISTS	1969
TR	THUNDER ROAD	RIPLEY	UNITED ARTISTS	1958
TR	THUNDER ROCK (UK)	BOULTING	ENGLISH	1942
TR	THUNDER RUN	HUDSON	CANNON	1986
TR	TIGER ROSE	FITZMAURICE	WARNER BROS	1929
TR	TONY RANDALL	portrait	UNIV	
TR	TRAITORS (UK)	TRONSON	UNIVERSAL	1962
TR	TRAPEZE	REED	UNITED ARTISTS	1956
TR	TREASURE ISLAND	HASKIN	RKO	1950
TR	TRILOGY	PERRY	MONOGRAM	1969
TR-1	STARLIGHT OVER TEXAS	HERMAN	MONOGRAM	1938
TR-1	TEX RIDES WITH THE BOY SCOUTS	TAYLOR	GRAND	1937

Movie Still Identification Book Ultimate Edition - Letters

CODE	TITLE/NAME	DIRECTOR/TYPE	STUDIO/DISTRIBUTOR	YEAR
TR-2	FRONTIER TOWN	TAYLOR	GRAND	1938
TR-2	WHERE THE BUFFALO ROAM	HERMAN	MONOGRAM	1938
TR-3	SONG OF THE BUCKAROO	HERMAN	MONOGRAM	1938
TR-4	SUNDOWN ON THE PRAIRIE	HERMAN	MONOGRAM	1939
TR-5	ROLLIN' WESTWARD	HERMAN	MONOGRAM	1939
TR-11	RHYTHM OF THE RIO GRANDE	HERMAN	MONOGRAM	1940
TR-13	COWBOY FROM SUNDOWN	BENNET	MONOGRAM	1940
TR-15	RAINBOW OVER THE RANGE	HERMAN	MONOGRAM	1940
TR-16	ARIZONA FRONTIER	HERMAN	MONOGRAM	1940
TR-17	TAKE ME BACK TO OKLAHOMA	HERMAN	MONOGRAM	1940
TR-18	ROLLIN' HOME TO TEXAS	HERMAN	MONOGRAM	1940
TR-19	RIDIN' THE CHEROKEE TRAIL	BENNET	MONOGRAM	1941
TR-20	PIONEERS	HERMAN	MONOGRAM	1941
TR-113	BLONDE COMET	BEAUDINE	PRC	1941
TRA	TRAMPLERS (IT/FR: GLI UOMINI DAL PASSO PESANTE 1965)	BAND	EMBASSY	1966
TRB	RIDE BACK (WAY BACK)	MINER	UNITED ARTISTS	1957
TRB	ROYAL BED	SHERMAN	RKO	1930
TRH	TOM THUMB AND LITTLE RED RIDING HOOD (MEX)	RODRIGUEZ	K. GORDON MURRAY	1962
TRI-122	GOOD-TIME GIRL (UK)	MACDONALD	EAGLE-LION	1948
TRI-154	ONCE UPON A DREAM (UK)	THOMAS	EAGLE-LION	1949
TRI-198	DON'T EVER LEAVE ME (UK)	CRABTREE	TRITON-GFD	1949
TRL	THIN RED LINE	MARTON	ALLIED ARTISTS	1964
TRP	10 RILLINGTON PLACE (UK)	FLEISCHER	COLUMBIA	1971
TRT	MASKED RAIDERS	SELANDER	RKO	1949
TRY	THAT'S RIGHT YOU'RE WRONG	BUTLER	RKO	1939
TS	BIG SHAKEDOWN	DILLON	WARNER BROS	1934
TS	FIRST TRAVELING SALESLADY	LUBIN	RKO	1956
TS	INDESCRETION OF AN AMERICAN WIFE (IT: STAZIONE	DE SICA	COLUMBIA	1953
TS	MANSTER	BREAKSTON	UNITED ARTISTS	1959
TS	SAP	MAYO	WARNER BROS	1929
TS	SEDUCTION	SCHMOELLER	AVCO EMBASSY	1982
TS	SENDER	CHRISTIAN	PARAMOUNT	1982
TS	SHADOW (UK)	COOPER	GLOBE	1933
TS	SILENCE (SWE: TYSTNADEN)	BERGMAN	JANUS	1963
TS	SKY'S THE LIMIT	GRIFFITH	RKO	1943
TS	STAR	HEISLER	20th CENTURY FOX	1953
TS	STRANGER	WELLES	RKO	1946
TS	STRANGERS IN THE CITY	CARRIER	EMBASSY	1962
TS	SVENGALI (UK)	LANGLEY	MGM	1954
TS	TALENT SCOUT	CLEMENS	WARNER BROS	1937
TS	TAMARIND SEED	EDWARDS	AVCO EMBASSY	1974
TS	TERROR SHIP (UK: DANGEROUS VOYAGE)	SEWELL	LIPPERT	1954
TS	TEXAS STEER	WALLACE	WARNER BROS	1927
TS	THANK YOUR LUCKY STARS	BUTLER	WARNER BROS	1943
TS	THIS SPORTING LIFE (UK)	ANDERSON	CONTINENTAL	1963
TS	THRILL SEEKERS (YELLOW TEDDY BEARS)	HARTFORD-DAVIS	TOPAZ FILMS	1964
TS	TIFFANY STAHL PRODUCTIONS	studio		
TS	TIGER SHARK	HAWKS	WARNER BROS	1932
TS	TIMBER STAMPEDE	HOWARD	RKO	1939
TS	TIMES SQUARE	MOYLE	ASSOCIATED FILM	1980
TS	TISHA STERLING	portrait		
TS	TOM SAWYER	TAYLOR	UNITED ARTISTS	1973
TS	TOMMY SANDS	portrait	FOX	
TS	TOP SECRET	ABRAHAMS, ZUCKER	PARAMOUNT	1984
TS	TOP SPEED	LEROY	WARNER BROS	1930
TS	TORSO MURDER MYSTERY (UK: TRAITOR SPY)	SUMMERS	ARTHUR ZIEHM	1939
TS	TRAIL STREET	ENRIGHT	RKO	1947
TS	TRAIN TO TOMBSTONE	BERKE	LIPPERT	1950
TS	TRAVELING SALESLADY	ENRIGHT	WARNER BROS	1935
TS	TRIO (UK)	ANNAKIN, FRENCH	PARAMOUNT	1950
TS	TROUBLE IN SUNDOWN	HOWARD	RKO	1939
TS	TWO FOR THE SEESAW	WISE	UNITED ARTISTS	1962
TS	TWO SECONDS	LEROY	WARNER BROS	1932
TS2	DUKE WORE JEANS (UK)	THOMAS	ALLIED ARTISTS	1958
TS5	DEVIL'S SKIPPER	ADOLFI	TIFFANY	1928
TS-15	PEACOCK ALLEY	DE SANO	TIFFANY	1930
TS-17	TOILERS	BARKER	TIFFANY	1928
TS-19	MARRIAGE BY CONTRACT	FLOOD	TIFFANY	1928
TS-26	PROWLERS OF THE SEA	ADOLFI	TIFFANY	1928
TS-28	GRAIN OF DUST	ARCHAINBAUD	TIFFANY	1928

Movie Still Identification Book Ultimate Edition - Letters

CODE	TITLE/NAME	DIRECTOR/TYPE	STUDIO/DISTRIBUTOR	YEAR
TS-32	LUCKY BOY	TAUROG, WILSON	TIFFANY	1928
TS-34	MEDICINE MAN	PEMBROKE	TIFFANY	1930
TS-44	MIDSTREAM	FLOOD	TIFFANY	1929
TS-47	PAINTED FACES	ROGELL	TIFFANY	1929
TS-49	MOLLY AND ME	RAY	TIFFANY	1929
TS-54	LOST ZEPPELIN	SLOMAN	TIFFANY	1929
TS-75	HIGH TREASON	ELVEY	TIFFANY	1929
TS-82	UTAH KID	THORPE	TIFFANY	1930
TS-89	BORDER ROMANCE	THORPE	TIFFANY	1929
TS-93	HOT CURVES	TAUROG	TIFFANY	1930
TSD	SHE GOT WHAT SHE WANTED	CRUZE	TIFFANY	1930
TSD	TARZAN AND THE SHE-DEVIL	NEUMANN	RKO	1953
TSD	THREE STEPS IN THE DARK (UK)	BIRT	PATHE	1953
TSF	SINGING FOOL	BACON	WARNER BROS	1928
TSG	TARZAN AND THE SLAVE GIRL	SHOLEM	RKO	1950
TSH	SILVER HORDE	ARCHAINBAUD	RKO	1930
TSHS	SPHYNX		RKO	1931
TSK	SORCERER	FRIEDKIN	FILM PROPERTIES	1977
TSK	STAGECOACH KID	LANDERS	RKO	1949
TSKY	THIS STUFF'LL KILL YA	LEWIS	ULTIMA	1971
TSML	TO SIR WITH LOVE	CLAVELL	COLUMBIA	1967
TSN	DEAD BY MORNING (UK: MISS TULIP STAYS THE NIGHT)	ARLISS	ADELPHI	1955
TS-PF	TAMING OF THE SHREW	TAYLOR	UNITED ARTISTS	1929
TS-PF-101	TAMING OF THE SHREW	TAYLOR	UNITED ARTISTS	1929
TSS	FACE TO FACE	BRAHM, WINDUST	RKO	1952
TSS	TREAD SOFTLY STRANGER (UK)	PARRY	ATLANTIC	1958
TSV	HIDEOUT (UK: SMALL VOICE)	MCDONELL	SNADER	1948
TSX-1	WOMAN TO WOMAN	SAVILLE	TIFFANY-STAHL	1929
TT	ALIAS JOHN PRESTON (UK)	MACDONALD	AAP	1955
TT	BIG SHOT	KILLY	RKO	1937
TT	CRAZY FOR LOVE	NORMAND	ELLIS FILM	1960
TT	GASBAGS (UK)	FORDE, VARNEL	GFD	1941
TT	GREAT ST. TRINIAN'S TRAIN ROBBERY (UK)	GILLIAT, LAUNDER	GARY DARTNELL	1966
TT	GUN BELT	NAZARRO	UNITED ARTISTS	1953
TT	LAW OF THE BADLANDS	SELANDER	RKO	1950
TT	MY SON, THE HERO (IT) (TITANS) (SONS OF THUNDER)	TESSARI	UNITED ARTISTS	1962
TT	TALL TEXAN	WILLIAMS	LIPPERT	1953
TT	TAMARA TOUMANOVA	portrait	RKO	mid 40s
TT	TARZAN TRIUMPHS	THIELE	RKO	1943
TT	TELEGRAPH TRAIL	WRIGHT	WARNER BROS	1933
TT	THAT THING YOU DO	HANKS	20th CENTURY FOX	1996
TT	THELMA TODD	portrait		
TT	THIEF	ROUSE	UNITED ARTISTS	1952
TT	THING	NYBY	RKO	1951
TT	THREAT	RONDEAU	WARNER BROS	1960
TT	TIGER BY THE TAIL	SPRINGSTEEN	AIP	1970
TT	TOMAHAWK TRAIL	SELANDER	UNITED ARTISTS	1957
TT	TOMBSTONE TERROR	BRADBURY	STEINER (states rights)	1935
TT	TOWER OF TERROR (UK)	HUNTINGTON	MONOGRAM	1941
TT	TRAIN	FRANKENHEIMER	UNITED ARTISTS	1964
TT	TRAIN	FRANKENHEIMER	UNITED ARTISTS	1965
TT	TRAP (UK)	HAYERS	CONTINENTAL	1966
TT	TROJAN BROTHERS (UK)	ROGERS	ANGLO-AMERICAN	1946
TT	TRUCK TURNER	KAPLAN	AIP	1974
TT	TUMBLIN TUMBLEWEED	KANE	REPUBLIC	1935
TTB	TWO TICKETS TO BROADWAY	KERN	RKO	1951
TTH	TARZAN'S SAVAGE FURY	ENDFIELD	RKO	1952
TTH	TELL-TALE HEART (UK)	MORRIS	DANBRIGADIER	1960
TTH	TICKET TO HEAVEN	THOMAS	UNITED ARTISTS	1981
TTJ	TAKE THIS JOB AND SHOVE IT	TRIKONIS	AVCO EMBASSY	1981
TTK	LONG NIGHT	LITVAK	RKO	1946
TTL	THIRD TIME LUCKY (UK)	FORDE	WOOLF & FREEDMAN	1931
TTP	SANDRA		COLUMBIA	
TTP	TWO TICKETS TO PARIS	GARRISON	COLUMBIA	1962
TTS	TATTOOED STRANGER	MONTAGNE	RKO	1950
TTS	THIRD SECRET (UK)	CRICHTON	20th CENTURY FOX	1964
TTT	FOR THEM THAT TRESPASS (UK)	CAVALCANTI	ASSSTRATFORD	1949
TTT	QUICK MONEY	KILLY	RKO	1937
TTT	TWICE-TOLD TALES	SALKOW	UNITED ARTISTS	1963
TTW	TALL WOMEN (SP)	PAROLINI, PINK	ALLIED ARTISTS	1967

Movie Still Identification Book Ultimate Edition - Letters

CODE	TITLE/NAME	DIRECTOR/TYPE	STUDIO/DISTRIBUTOR	YEAR
TU	SHIRLEY TEMPLE	portrait	FOX	
TU	THIEVES LIKE US	ALTMAN	UNITED ARTISTS	1974
TU	TUCKER: THE MAN AND HIS DREAM	COPPOLA	PARAMOUNT	1988
TU	UNDEAD	CORMAN	AIP	1957
TUL	TULIPS	BROMFIELD	AVCO EMBASSY	1981
TUN	GHOST GOES WEST (UK)	CLAIR	UNITED ARTISTS	1935
TUV	AND NOW MY LOVE	LELOUCH	AVCO EMBASSY	1974
TV	10TH VICTIM	LEVINE	EMBASSY	1965
TV	LONESOME WOMEN (BRA)	KHOURI	JACK ALEXANDER	1959
TV	MAN AND THE MOON	KIMBALL	DISNEY - TV	1955
TV	MAN IN SPACE	KIM	BUENA VISTA	1956
TV	THIRD VOICE	CORNFIELD	20th CENTURY FOX	1960
TV	VALIANT (UK)	BAKER	UNITED ARTISTS	1962
TV	VIKINGS	NEWLAND	RKO	1957
TV	VIOLATORS	FLEISCHER	UNITED ARTISTS	1958
TV	VISITORS	KAZAN	UNITED ARTISTS	1972
TV	VOYAGE (IT) (UK: JOURNEY)	DE SICA	UNITED ARTISTS	1974
TW	20,000 LEAGUES UNDER THE SEA	FLEISCHER	DISNEY	R63
TW	29TH STREET	GALLO	20th CENTURY FOX	1991
TW	TERESA WRIGHT	portrait	PARA., RKO, UNIV.	
TW	THAT CERTAIN WOMAN	GOULDING	WARNER BROS	1937
TW	THEY WANTED TO MARRY	LANDERS	RKO	1937
TW	THREE WARRIORS	MERRILL	UNITED ARTISTS	1977
TW	THREE WOMEN	ALTMAN	20TH CENTURY FOX	1977
TW	TOMORROW, THE WORLD!	FENTON	UNITED ARTISTS	1944
TW	TUESDAY WELD	portrait	PARAMOUNT	
TW	TWIST OF SAND	CHAFFEY	UNITED ARTISTS	1968
TW	TWO AGAINST THE WORLD	MAYO	FIRST NATIONAL	1932
TW	TWO AGAINST THE WORLD	MCGANN	WARNER BROS	1936
TW	TWO THOUSAND WOMEN (UK)	LAUNDER	ELLIS	1944
TW	TWO WEEKS TO LIVE	ST. CLAIR	RKO	1943
TW	VILLAIN STILL PURSUED HER	CLINE	RKO	1940
TW	WALK A TIGHTROPE (UK)	NESBITT	PARAMOUNT	1965
TW	WINDOW	TETZLAFF	RKO	1949
TW	WITCHES (IT: LE STREGHE)	DE SICA, PASOLINI	UNITED ARTISTS	1967
TW	WORLD IS NOT ENOUGH	APTED	MGM	1999
TW-200	CRASHING THRU	TAYLOR	MONOGRAM	1949
TW-205	FENCE RIDERS	FOX	MONOGRAM	1950
TW-206	GUNSLINGERS	FOX	MONOGRAM	1950
TW-4942	ARIZONA TERRITORY	FOX	MONOGRAM	1950
TW-4943	SILVER RAIDERS	FOX	MONOGRAM	1950
TW-4944	CHEROKEE UPRISING	COLLINS	MONOGRAM	1950
TW-4945	OUTLAWS OF TEXAS	CARR	MONOGRAM	1950
TW-4946	ABILENE TRAIL	COLLINS	MONOGRAM	1951
TW-4954	OUTLAW GOLD	FOX	MONOGRAM	1950
TW-4955	COLORADO AMBUSH	COLLINS	MONOGRAM	1951
TW-5141	MAN FROM SONORA	COLLINS	MONOGRAM	1951
TW-5142	BLAZING BULLETS	FOX	MONOGRAM	1951
TW-5143	MONTANA DESPERADO	FOX	MONOGRAM	1951
TWB	THEY WON'T BELIEVE ME	PICHEL	RKO	1946
TWC	20,000 LEAGUES UNDER THE SEA	FLEISCHER	DISNEY	R63
TWC	WINNERS CIRCLE	FEIST	20th CENTURY FOX	1948
TWGM	ADVENTURES OF WILL BILL HICKOK (tv series)	VARIOUS		1951-58
TWO	CITY AFTER MIDNIGHT (UK: THAT WOMAN OPPOSITE)	BENNETT	RKO	1957
TWO	WAY OUT (UK: DIAL 999)	TULLY	RKO	1956
TWP	TOWN WITHOUT PITY	TULLY	RKO	1956
TWP	TOWN WITHOUT PITY	REINHARDT	UNITED ARTISTS	1961
TWS	THEY WERE SISTERS (UK)	CRABTREE	UNIVERSAL	1945
TWS	THREE WEIRD SISTERS (UK)	BIRT	PATHE	1948
TWS	TWO WEEKS IN SEPTEMBER	BOURGUIGNON	PARAMOUNT	1967
TWW	THAT'S THE WAY OF THE WORLD	SHORE	UNITED ARTISTS	1975
TWW	WAY WEST	MCLAGLEN	UNITED ARTISTS	1967
TX-2	JOURNEY'S END (UK)	WHALE	TIFFANY	1930
TXH	TED HEALY	portrait	MGM	
TY	CASTLE ON THE HUDSON	LITVAK	WARNER BROS	1940
TY	THEY WERE SO YOUNG	NEUMANN	LIPPERT	1953
TYL	2000 YEARS LATER	TENZER	WARNER BROS	1969
TYOF	THIRTY YEARS OF FUN	YOUNGSON	20th CENTURY FOX	1963
TY T	TYPHOON TREASURE (AUS)	MONKMAN	UNITED ARTISTS	1938
TZ	TORRID ZONE	KEIGHLEY	WARNER BROS	1940

Movie Still Identification Book Ultimate Edition - Letters

CODE	TITLE/NAME	DIRECTOR/TYPE	STUDIO/DISTRIBUTOR	YEAR
U	KING OF THE UNDERWORLD	SEILER	WARNER BROS	1939
U	ULYSSES	STRICK	CONTINENTAL	1967
U	UNDERGROUND	SHERMAN	WARNER BROS	1941
U	UNDERGROUND	NADEL	UNITED ARTISTS	1970
U	UNFAITHFULS (IT: LE INFEDELI)	MONTICELLO	MONOGRAM	1953
U	UNTIL THE END OF THE WORLD (GER/FR: BIS ANS ... WELT)	WINDERS	WARNER BROS	1991
U	URUBU	BREAKSTON, COPLEN	UNITED ARTISTS	1948
U1	WAY DOWN EAST	GRIFFITH	UNITED ARTISTS	1920
U2	DREAM STREET	GRIFFITH	UNITED ARTISTS	1921
U3	ORPHANS OF THE STORM	GRIFFITH	UNITED ARTISTS	1921
U4	ONE EXCITING NIGHT	GRIFFITH	UNITED ARTISTS	1922
U7	AMERICA	GRIFFITH	UNITED ARTISTS	1924
UA	BULLETS OR BALLOTS	KEIGHLEY	WARNER BROS	1936
UA3	RISE OF CATHERINE THE GREAT	CZINNER	UNITED ARTISTS	1934
UA-12	I STAND CONDEMNED (UK: MOSCOW NIGHTS)	ASQUITH	UNITED ARTISTS	1935
UA-12A	I STAND CONDEMNED (UK: MOSCOW NIGHTS)	ASQUITH	UNITED ARTISTS	1935
UA-18	FOREVER YOURS (UK: FORGET ME NOT)	KORDA	GRAND NATIONAL	1936
UARR5	SON OF THE RENEGADE	BROWNE	UNITED ARTISTS	1953
UAS	WESTERN HERITAGE	GRISSELL	RKO	1947
UBW	A MAN, A WOMAN AND A BANK	BLACK	EMBASSY	1979
UC	UMBRELLAS OF CHERBOURG	DEMI	LRO	1964
UC	UNDER COVER	STOCKWELL	CANNON	1987
UC	UNDERGROUND GUERRILLAS (UK: UNDERCOVER)	NOLBANDOV	COLUMBIA	1943
UC	URBAN COWBOY	BRIDGES	PARAMOUNT	1980
UCA	ANDALUSIAN DOG (FR: UN CHIEN ANDALOU) (sh)	BUNUEL		1929
UD	UNEARTHLY	PETROFF	REPUBLIC	1957
UD	UNION DEPOT	GREEN	WARNER BROS	1932
UE	UNEXPECTED UNCLE	GODFREY	RKO	1941
UE	UNLAWFUL ENTRY	KAPLAN	20th CENTURY FOX	1992
UE	UP TO HIS EARS	DE BROCA	UNITED ARTISTS	1965
UF	UNDER FIRE	CLARK	20th CENTURY FOX	1957
UF	UNFORGIVEN	EASTWOOD	WARNER BROS	1992
UF	UNHOLY FOUR (UK: STRANGER CAME HOME)	FISHER	LIPPERT	1954
UFC	UP FOR THE CUP (UK)	RAYMOND	ASSOCIATED BRITISH-PATHE	1950
UG	UNCERTAIN GLORY	WALSH	WARNER BROS	1944
UG	UPTURNED GLASS (UK)	HUNTINGTON	RANK (UK) (UNIVERSAL)	1947
UI	INFORMERS (UK) (US: UNDERWORLD INFORMERS)	ANNAKIN	CONTINENTAL	1963
UIS	UP IN SMOKE	ADLER	PARAMOUNT	1978
UJ	UNCLE JOE SHANNON	HANWRIGHT	UNITED ARTISTS	1978
UJ	UP THE JUNCTION	COLLINSON	PARAMOUNT	1968
UK	UP THE JUNCTION (UK)	COLLINSON	PARAMOUNT	1968
UL	ULYSSES	CAMARINI	PARAMOUNT	1955
UM	UNA MERKEL	portrait	MGM, UNIVERSAL	
UMM	MAN WHO COULD WORK MIRACLES	MENDES	UNITED ARTISTS	1936
UN	UNA MERKEL	portrait		
UN	UNCHAINED	BARTLETT	WARNER BROS	1955
UN	UNEARTHLY	PETROFF	AB-PT	1957
UNBB	UNBREAKABLE	SHYAMALAN	BUENA VISTA	2000
UNF	UNFORGIVEN	HUSTON	UNITED ARTISTS	1960
UNS	UN SOIR ... UN TRAIN	DELVANX	20th CENTURY FOX	1968
UP	MRS. POLLIFAX-SPY	MARTINSON	UNITED ARTISTS	1971
UP	NINE MEN (UK)	WATT	UNITED ARTISTS	1943
UP	OFF THE RECORD	FLOOD	WARNER BROS	1939
UPT	UPTOWN SATURDAY NIGHT	POITIER	WARNER BROS	1974
UR	SONG OF THE SOUTH (t)	FOSTER, JACKSON	RKO	1946
US	NIGHT BEFORE CHRISTMAS (t)	JACKSON	UNITED ARTISTS	1933
US	UNFINISHED SYMPHONY (UK)	ASQUITH, FORST	GAUMONT BRITISH	1934
UT	UNKNOWN TERROR	WARREN	20th CENTURY FOX	1957
UT	URSULA THIESS	portrait	RKO	
UT/PS	UNEASY TERMS (UK)	SEWELL	PATHE	1948
UU	RULING VOICE	LEE	WARNER BROS	1931
UV	UNCLE VANYA (UK)	BURGE	ARTHUR CANTOR	1963
UV	UNCOMMON VALOR	KOTCHEFF	PARAMOUNT	1983
UWS	WOMAN HUNGRY	BADGER	WARNER BROS	1931
UWZ	UNMAN, WITTERING AND ZIGO	MACKENZIE	PARAMOUNT	1971
UX	UNTAMED WOMEN	CONNELL	UNITED ARTISTS	1952
V	NOTHING BUT TROUBLE	AKYROYD	WARNER BROS	1991
V	OUR DAILY BREAD	VIDOR	UNITED ARTISTS	1934
V	OUR VIRGIN ISLAND (UK: VIRGIN ISLAND)	JACKSON	FILMS AROUND THE WORLD	1959
V	SINCE YOU WENT AWAY	CROMWELL	UNITED ARTISTS	1944

Movie Still Identification Book Ultimate Edition - Letters

CODE	TITLE/NAME	DIRECTOR/TYPE	STUDIO/DISTRIBUTOR	YEAR
V	VALENTINO	RUSSELL	UNITED ARTISTS	1977
V	VALERIE	OSWALD	UNITED ARTISTS	1957
V	VAULT OF HORROR	BAKER	CINERAMA	1973
V	VENUS	MERCANTON	UNITED ARTISTS	1929
V	VERBOTEN	FULLER	COLUMBIA	1959
V	VICTORIA THE GREAT (UK)	WILCOX	RKO	1937
V	VICTORS (UK)	FOREMAN	COLUMBIA	1963
V	VICTORY (ESCAPE TO VICTORY)	HUSTON	PARAMOUNT	1981
V	VILLA	CLARK	20th CENTURY FOX	1958
V	VIRILITY (IT: VIRILITA)	CAVARA	COLISEUM	1974
V	VOLTAIRE	ADOLFI	WARNER BROS	1933
V	VOLUNTEERS	MEYER	TRI STAR	1985
V	VORTEX	BRUNEL	WOOLF & FREEDMAN (UK)	1928
V	YOUNG BRIDE	SEITER	RKO	1932
V1	MISSILES FROM HELL (UK: BATTLE OF THE V1)	SEWELL	EROS	1958
V2	LEFT RIGHT AND CENTRE (UK)	GILLIAT	BCG	1959
V-21	TALES OF UGETSU (JAP)	MIZOGUCHI	EDWARD HARRISON (DAIEI)	1954
V32	SON OF THE SHEIK	FITZMAURICE	UNITED ARTISTS	1926
V-89	GUNFIRE AT INDIAN GAP	KANE	REPUBLIC	1957
V-91	PANAMA SAL	WITNEY	REPUBLIC	1957
V-1253	ALLISON HAYES	portrait	UNIVERSAL	Spanish
VA	VIVIAN AUSTIN (aka TERRY AUSTIN)	portrait	UNIVERSAL	
VAB	VEDA ANN BORG	portrait	WARNER BROS	
VAC	CARAVAN TO VACCARES		WARNER BROS	
VAL	VALERIE	OSWALD	UNITED ARTISTS	1957
VAM	VAMPIRE'S COFFIN (MEX: ATAUD DEL VAMPIRO 1957)	MENDEZ	YOUNG AMERICA PROD.	1964
VAR-3	INFERNAL MACHINE	VARNEL	FOX FILM	1933
VAS	VICTORY AT SEA	KLEINERMAN	UNITED ARTISTS	1954
VB	FAST LADY (UK)	ANNAKIN	CONTINENTAL	1962
VB	VAMPIRE AND THE BALLERINA	POLSELLI	UNITED ARTISTS	1960
VB	VAMPIRE AND THE BALLERINA	POLSELLI	UNITED ARTISTS	1962
VB	VANESSA BROWN	portrait		
VB	VILMA BANKY	portrait	MGM	
VB	VIRGINIA BELMONT	portrait	RKO	
VB	VIRGINIA BRUCE	portrait	REP	
VB	VIRGINIA BRUCE	portrait	UNIVERSAL	
VB	VIVIAN BLAINE	portrait	FOX	1940s
VC	CASE OF THE VELVET CLAWS	CLEMENS	WARNER BROS	1936
VC	JIGSAW	MARKLE	UNITED ARTISTS	1949
VC	VERA CRUZ	ALDRICH	UNITED ARTISTS	1954
VC	VERA CRUZ	portrait	UNITED ARTISTS	1955
VC	VICTOR CUTLER (aka VICTOR CENTRER)	portrait	RKO	mid-40s
VC	VIRGINIA CHRISTINE	portrait	WARNER BROS	
VC	VIRGINIA CITY	CURTIZ	WARNER BROS	1940
VC	VISIT TO A CHIEF'S SON	JOHNSON	UNITED ARTISTS	1974
VCH	MATTER OF RESISTANCE (FR: LA VIE DE CHATEAU)	RAPPENEAU	ROYAL	1966
V-CH	VIVA CHIHUAHUA	SOLARES	PEL MEX	1961
VD	VIOLA DANA	portrait	MGM	
VDF	I'LL BE SEEING YOU	DIETERLE	UNITED ARTISTS	1944
VDF	I'LL BE SEEING YOU	DIETERLE	UNITED ARTISTS	1944
VE	VERA ELLEN	portrait	RKO	
VE	VERY EDGE (UK)	FRANKEL	BRITISH LION	1963
VE	VICTORY AT ENTEBBE (tv movie)	CHOMSKY	WARNER BROS	1976
VE	VIOLA ESSEN	portrait		
VE	VIRGINIA ENGELS	portrait	UNIVERSAL	
VER	VERDICT (FR/IT) (JURY OF ONE)	CAYATTE	WARNER BROS	1975
VF	VENUS IN FURS (UK: PAROXISMUS)	FRANCO	AIP	1970
VF	VICTOR FRANCEN	portrait		
VF	VIGILANTE FORCE	ARMITAGE	UNITED ARTISTS	1976
VF	VIRGINIA FIELD	portrait	UNIVERSAL	
VF-3	PURE HELL OF ST. TRINIAN'S (UK)	LAUNDER	CONTINENTAL	1960
VF-4	ONLY TWO CAN PLAY (UK)	GILLIAT	COLUMBIA	1962
VFM	VENGEANCE OF FU MANCHU (UK)	SUMMERS	WARNER BROS.	1967
VG	GUN STREET	CAHN	UNITED ARTISTS	1961
VG	VILLAGE OF THE GIANTS	GORDON	EMBASSY	1965
VG	VIRGIN AND THE GYPSY (UK)	MILES	CHEVRON	1970
VG	VIRGINIA GIBSON	portrait	WARNER BROS	
VG	VIRGINIA GREY	portrait	MGM, RKO	
VH	VALERIE HOBSON	portrait	UNIVERSAL	
VH	VAN HEFLIN	portrait	RKO, UNIV	

Movie Still Identification Book Ultimate Edition - Letters

CODE	TITLE/NAME	DIRECTOR/TYPE	STUDIO/DISTRIBUTOR	YEAR
VH	VAN HEFLIN	portrait		
VH	VIRGINIA HUSTON	portrait	RKO	1940s-50s
V-H-1	SILENT WITNESS	VARNEL, HOUGH	FOX FILM	1932
VHR	VERA RALSTON	portrait	REP	
VI	VIGIL IN THE NIGHT	STEVENS	RKO	1940
VI	VOODOO ISLAND	LE BORG	UNITED ARTISTS	1957
VI	VOODOO ISLAND	LELEBORG	UNITED ARTISTS	1957
VI-1	ONE WOMAN IDEA	VIERTEL	FOX FILM	1929
VIE-2	SEVEN FACES	VIERTEL	FOX FILM	1929
VIE-3	MAN TROUBLE	VIERTEL	FOX FILM	1930
VIE-4	SPY	VIERTEL	FOX FILM	1931
VIK	STORY OF VICKIE	MARISCHKA	BUENA VISTA	1958
VIL	VILLAGE (SWIT: SIE FANDEN EINE HEIMAT)	LINDTBERG	UNITED ARTISTS	1953
VK	FEARLESS VAMPIRE KILLERS	POLANSKI	MGM	1967
VKC	VIOLET KEMBLE COOPER	portrait	RKO	
VL	VALDEZ IS COMING	SHERIN	UNITED ARTISTS	1971
VL	VARIETY LIGHTS (IT: LUCI DEL VARIETA)	FELLINI, LATTUADA	PATHE CONTEMPORARY	1950
VL	VICKIE LESTER (aka VICKI LESTER)	portrait	RKO	
VL	VIRGINIA LEITH	portrait	US	
VL	VIVACIOUS LADY	STEVENS	RKO	1938
VL	VIVECA LINDFORS	portrait	WARNER BROS	
VM	VERA MILES	portrait	WARNER BROS	
VM	VICTOR MATURE	portrait	RKO	
VM	VICTOR MOORE	portrait	RKO	
VM	VIRGINIA MAYO	portrait	RKO, UNIVERSAL, WARNER	
VM	VIVA MARIA!	MALLE	UNITED ARTISTS	1965
VM-10	MURDER WILL OUT (UK: VOICE OF MERRILL)	GILLING	KRAMER-HYAMS	1952
VMN	VIRGEN DE MEDIA NOCHE	GALINDO	MUNDIAL	1942
VN	HORROR CASTLE (IT: VERGINE DE NORIMBERGA 1963)	DAWSON (MARGHERITI)	ZODIAC	1964
VN	VIENNESE NIGHTS	CROSLAND	WARNER BROS	1930
VO	VALLEY OF THE SUN	MARSHALL	RKO	1942
VOB	VICAR OF BRAY (UK)	EDWARDS	ABFD	1937
VOF	TRIUMPH OF SHERLOCK HOLMES (UK)	HISCOTT	OLYMPIC	1935
VOL	THIEF OF PARIS (FR: LE VOLEUR)	MALLE	UNITED ARTISTS	1967
VOL	VOLCANO (IT: VULCANO)	DIETERLE	UNITED ARTISTS	1950
VOP	VARIETIES ON PARADE	ORMOND	LIPPERT	1951
VOS	IT! THE TERROR FROM BEYOND SPACE	CAHN	UNITED ARTISTS	1958
VP	EAGLE	BROWN	UNITED ARTISTS	1925
VP	SINCE YOU WENT AWAY	CROMWELL	UNITED ARTISTS	1944
VP	VALACCI PAPERS	YOUNG	COLUMBIA	1972
VP	VANISHING PRAIRIE	ALGAR	BUENA VISTA	1954
VP	VICTIMAS DEL PICADO	EERNANDEZ	PELICULAS MEX.	1951
VP	VINCENT PRICE	portrait	UNIVERSAL	
VP	VINCENT PRICE	portrait	WARNER BROS	
VP	VIRGINIA PINE	portrait	WARNER BROS	
VP1	LET'S GET MARRIED (UK)	SCOTT	EROS	1960
VPV	LIVE FOR LIFE (FR: VIVRE POUR VIVRE)	LELOUCH	UNITED ARTISTS	1967
VQ	VIKING QUEEN (UK)	CHAFFEY	20TH CENTURY FOX	1967
VR	VERA RALSTON	portrait	REPUBLIC	
VR	VERA REYNOLDS	portrait	PATHE	
VR	VIKINGS	FLEISCHER	UNITED ARTISTS	1958
VR	VON RICHTOFEN AND BROWN	CORMAN	UNITED ARTISTS	1971
VRI	GENTLEMEN MARRY BRUNETTES	SALE	UNITED ARTISTS	1955
V+S	VAN AND SCHENCK (GUS VAN, JOE SCHENCK)	portrait	MGM	1929-30
VS	SUICIDE LEGION (UK: SUNSET IN VIENNA)	WALKER	FILM ALLIANCE	1940
VS	VARSITY SHOW	KEIGHLEY	WARNER BROS	1937
VS	VENETIA STEVENSON	portrait		
VS	VENGEANCE OF SHE (UK)	OWEN	20TH CENTURY FOX	1968
VS	VICE SQUAD	SHERMAN	AVCO EMBASSY	1982
VS	VIRGIN SOLDIERS (UK)	DEXTER	COLUMBIA	1969
VS	VIRGIN SPRING	BERGMAN	JANUS	1960
VS	VITAL SIGNS	SILVER	20th CENTURY FOX	1990
VS	VIVIENNE SEGAL	portrait	WARNER BROS	1930s
VS-1	HELLO SISTER!	VON STROHEIM	FOX FILM	1933
VS-1A	DARK JOURNEY (UK)	SAVILLE	UNITED ARTISTS	1937
VS-2A	STORM IN A TEACUP (UK)	DALRYMPLE, SAVILLE	UNITED ARTISTS	1937
V-S-3	ACTION FOR SLANDER (UK)	WHELAN	UNITED ARTISTS	1937
VS-4	SOUTH RIDING (UK)	SAVILLE	UNITED ARTISTS	1938
VT	FOOTLIGHT VARIETIES	GRIFFITH, STOLOFF	RKO	1951
VT	MAYA	BERRY	MGM	1966

Movie Still Identification Book Ultimate Edition - Letters

CODE	TITLE/NAME	DIRECTOR/TYPE	STUDIO/DISTRIBUTOR	YEAR
VT	VARIETY TIME	YATES	RKO	1948
VT	VELVET TOUCH	GAGE	RKO	1948
VT	VERREE/VEREE TEASDALE	portrait	WARNER BROS	
VT	VERY THOUGHT OF YOU	DAVES	WARNER BROS	1944
VUK	INTERVIEW WITH THE VAMPIRE	JORDAN	GEPPEN	1994
VUL	VULTURE (UK)	HUNTINGTON	PARAMOUNT	1966
VV	ANITA LOUISE	portrait	WARNER BROS	1930s
VV	VELVET VAMPIRE	ROTHMAN	NEW WORLD	1971
VV	VERONIKA VOSS	FASSBINDER	UNITED ARTISTS	1982
VV	VICTOR VARCONI	portrait		
VV	VIRGINIA VALE	portrait	RKO	1930s-40s
VVK	FEARLESS VAMPIRE KILLERS (UK: DANCE OF THE VAMPIRES)	POLANSKI	MGM	1967
VW	BEACHCOMBER (UK: VESSEL OF WRATH 1938)	POMMER	VERITY FILMS	R49
VW	LIFE OF VIRGIE WINTERS	SANTELL	RKO	1934
VW	VIRGINIA WEIDLER	portrait	RKO	
VW	VOODOO WOMAN	CAHN	AIP	1957
VX10	CORINNE GRIFFITH	portrait	VITAGRAPH	
VX15	LARRY SEMON	portrait	VITAGRAPH	
VX29	CATHERINE CALVERT	portrait	VITAGRAPH	1920s
VX4	EARLE WILLIAMS	portrait	VITAGRAPH	1910s-20s
VX5	BESSIE LOVE	portrait	VITAGRAPH	
VX9	ALICE JOYCE	portrait	VITAGRAPH	1910s-20s
VXB	VIRGINIA BRUCE	portrait	MGM	
VY	CROOK (FR: SIMON, THE SWISS)	LELOUCH	UNITED ARTISTS	1970
VZ	VERA ZORINA	portrait	UNIVERSAL	
W	DON'T TELL THE WIFE	STEIN	WARNER BROS	1927
W	FIGHTING MUSTANG	DRAKE	ASTOR	1948
W	FRONTIER SCOUT	NEWFIELD	GRAND	1938
W	GEORGE WALSH	portrait	FOX	1910s-30s
W	MARY JANE'S PA	KEIGHLEY	WARNER BROS	1935
W	MYSTERY AT THE BURLESQUE (UK: MURDER AT WINDMILL)	GUEST	MONOGRAM	1949
W	ON THE WATERFRONT	KAZAN	COLUMBIA	1954
W	RAY WHITLEY SHORTS	studio	RKO	
W	WARREN'S OF VIRGINIA	DEMILLE	PARAMOUNT (Lasky)	1915
W	WARREN'S OF VIRGINIA	CLIFTON	FOX FILM	1924
W	WEAPON (UK)	GUEST	REPUBLIC	1956
W	WHAT THE BUTLER SAW (UK)	GRAYSON	EXCLUSIVE	1950
W	WILLOW	HOWARD	MGM	1988
W	WINDOWS	WILLIS	UNITED ARTISTS	1980
W	WINTERSET	SANTELL	RKO	1936
W	WIZARDS	BAKSHI	20th CENTURY FOX	1977
W	WOMAN	ROSSELLINI	CANTON-WEINER	1950
W	WOMAN OF ROME	ZAMPA	DCA	1956
W	WOMEN THEY TALK ABOUT	BACON	WARNER BROS	1928
W 1	AFFAIRS OF SUSAN	SEITER	PARAMOUNT	1945
W-1	MARKSMAN	COLLINS	ALLIED ARTISTS	1953
W1	SEE HOW THEY RUN (UK)	ARLISS	BRITISH LION	1955
W-2	STAR OF TEXAS	CARR	ALLIED ARTISTS	1953
W-3	HER GOLDEN CALF	WEBB	FOX FILM	1930
W-3	VIGILANTE TERROR	COLLINS	ALLIED ARTISTS	1953
W-3	WATERHOLE #3	GRAHAM	PARAMOUNT	1968
W-4	TOPEKA	CARR	MONOGRAM	1953
W-5	TEXAS BAD MAN	COLLINS	MONOGRAM	1953
W-6	FIGHTING LAWMAN	CARR	ALLIED ARTISTS	1953
W-7	BITTER CREEK	CARR	ALLIED ARTISTS	1954
W-8	FORTY NINERS	CARR	ALLIED ARTISTS	1954
W-15	EVERY MOTHER'S SON	WALSH	FOX FILM	1918
W-17	EVANGELINE	WALSH	FOX FILM	1919
W-18	FROM NOW ON	WALSH	FOX FILM	1920
W-25-C-9	IN OLD ARIZONA	WALSH, CUMMINGS	FOX FILM	1928
W49-1	NO PLACE FOR JENNIFER (UK)	CASS	STRATFORD	1950
W49-2	LAST HOLIDAY (UK)	CASS	STRATFORD	1950
W49-3	CAIRO ROAD (UK)	MACDONALD	REALART	1950
W50-1	MURDER WITHOUT CRIME (UK)	THOMPSON	STRATFORD	1950
W50-2	FRANCHISE AFFAIR (UK)	HUNTINGTON	STRATFORD	1951
W50-3	TALK OF A MILLION (UK)	CARSTAIRS	STRATFORD	1951
W-117	WITNESS	WEIR	PARAMOUNT	1985
W-328	WARRIORS (DARK AVENGERS)	LEVIN	MONOGRAM	1955
W515	BLUEBEARD'S 10 HONEYMOONS (UK)	WILDER	ALLIED ARTISTS	1960
WA	FIXER DUGAN	LANDERS	RKO	1939

Movie Still Identification Book Ultimate Edition - Letters

CODE	TITLE/NAME	DIRECTOR/TYPE	STUDIO/DISTRIBUTOR	YEAR
WA	TWO WHO DARED	FRENKE	GRAND	1937
WA	WALTER ABEL	portrait		
WA	WARLORDS OF ATLANTIS	CONNOR	COLUMBIA	1978
WA	WE ARE NOT ALONE	GOULDING	WARNER BROS	1939
WA	WILD AFFAIR (UK)	KRISH	GOLDSTONE	1963
WA	WINNER TAKE ALL	DEL RUTH	WARNER BROS	1932
WA	WOMAN ALONE (UK) (US: TWO WHO DARED)	FRENKE	UNITED ARTISTS	1936
WA	WOMEN AREN'T ANGELS (UK)	HUNTINGTON	PATHE	1943
WA	WRONG ARM OF THE LAW (UK)	OWEN	CONTINENTAL	1963
WAC	RUNAROUND	CRAFT	RKO	1931
WAD	WEEKEND AT DUNKIRK	VERNEUIL	20th CENTURY FOX	1964
WAF	WHERE ANGELS GO-TROUBLE FOLLOWS	NEILSON	COLUMBIA	1968
WAK	WAKAMBA	QUEENY	RKO	1955
WAL	WILD GIRL	WALSH	FOX FILM	1932
WAL-24	COCK-EYED WORLD	WALSH	FOX FILM	1929
WAL-25	HOT FOR PARIS	WALSH	FOX FILM	1929
WAL-26	BIG TRAIL	WALSH	FOX FILM	1930
WAL-26	COCK-EYED WORLD (SOUND)	WALSH	FOX FILM	1929
WAL-27	COCK-EYED WORLD (SILENT)	WALSH	FOX FILM	1929
WAL-27	MAN WHO CAME BACK	WALSH	FOX FILM	1931
WAL-27	WOMEN OF ALL NATIONS	WALSH	FOX FILM	1931
WAL-28	WOMEN OF ALL NATIONS	WALSH	FOX FILM	1931
WAL-29	YELLOW TICKET	WALSH	FOX FILM	1931
WAL-30	WILD GIRL	WALSH	FOX FILM	1932
WAL-31	ME AND MY GAL	WALSH	FOX FILM	1932
WAL-32	SAILOR'S LUCK	WALSH	FOX FILM	1933
WAP-2	MARK OF THE LASH	TAYLOR	SCREEN GUILD	1948
WAP-5	SON OF BILLY THE KID	TAYLOR	SCREEN GUILD	1949
WAP-6	SON OF A BADMAN	TAYLOR	SCREEN GUILD	1949
WAP-10	VANISHING OUTPOST	ORMOND	SCREEN GUILD	1951
WATT	WATTSTAX	STUART	COLUMBIA	1973
WB	TWO ALONE	NUGENT	RKO	1934
WB	WALLY BROWN	portrait	RKO	
WB	WALTER BRENNAN	portrait	UNIV	
WB	WARREN BEATTY	portrait	WARNER BROS	
WB	WEEKEND AT BERNIE'S	KOTCHEFF	20th CENTURY FOX	1989
WB	WENDY BARRIE	portrait	RKO	
WB	WESLEY BARRY	portrait	WARNER BROS	
WB	WHITE BANNERS	GOULDING	WARNER BROS	1938
WB	WHITE BUFFALO	THOMPSON	UNITED ARTISTS	1977
WB	WHITNEY BOURNE	portrait	RKO	
WB	WIDE BOY (UK)	HUGHES	REALART	1952
WB	WILD BILL HICKOK RIDES	ENRIGHT	WARNER BROS	1942
WB	WILD BOY (UK)	DE COURVILLE	GAUMONT BRITISH	1934
WB	WILDCAT BUS	WOODRUFF	RKO	1940
WB	WILLIAM BENDIX	portrait	RKO	
WB	WILLIAM BOYD	portrait	PATHÉ	1920s-30s
WB	WILLIE BEST	portrait	RKO	
WB	WONDER BAR	BACON	WARNER BROS	1934
WB	WRONG BOX	FORBES	COLUMBIA	1966
WB-9	MY FAIR LADY	CUKOR	WARNER BROS	1964
WBA	WHERE THE BOYS ARE	AVERBACK	TRI STAR	1984
WBF-IV	MAN OF THE MOMENT (UK)	BANKS	WARNER BROS.	1935
WBH	ADVENTURES OF WILL BILL HICKOK (tv series)	VARIOUS		1951-58
WBP	WAR BETWEEN THE PLANETS	MARGHERITI	FANFARE FILM	1971
WBX	WALLACE BEERY	portrait	MGM	
WC	CAUGHT	OPHULS	MGM	1949
WC	VICE RAID	CAHN	UNITED ARTISTS	1960
WC	WAITING FOR CAROLINE	KELLY	LOPERT	1969
WC	WARE CASE (UK)	STEVENSON	20TH CENTURY FOX	1938
WC	WE WANT A CHILD (DEN: VI VIL HA' ET BARN)	LAURITZEN	LIPPERT	1949
WC	WHEATON CHAMBERS	portrait	RKO	
WC	WHITE COCKATOO	CROSLAND	WARNER BROS	1935
WC	WICKED CITY (FR: HANS LE MARIN)	VILLIERS	UNITED ARTISTS	1949
WC	WIDOW FROM CHICAGO	CLINE	WARNER BROS	1930
WC	WILBY CONSPIRACY	NELSON	UNITED ARTISTS	1975
WC	WILD CARGO	DENIS	RKO	1934
WC	WILLIAM CAMPBELL	portrait	UNIVERSAL	
WC	WILLIAM CHING (aka WILLIAM BROOKS CHING)	portrait	UNIVERSAL	
WC	WITCHCRAFT	SHARP	20th CENTURY FOX	1964

Movie Still Identification Book Ultimate Edition - Letters

CODE	TITLE/NAME	DIRECTOR/TYPE	STUDIO/DISTRIBUTOR	YEAR
WC	WITNESS CHAIR	NICHOLS, JR.	RKO	1936
WC	WOMAN COMMANDS	STEIN	RKO	1932
WC	WOMAN COMMANDS	STEIN	RKO	1932
WC	WONDERFUL COUNTRY	PARRISH	UNITED ARTISTS	1959
WC	WORLD CHANGES	LEROY	WARNER BROS	1933
WC	WRECKING CREW	MCDONALD	COLUMBIA	1942
WC	YESTERDAY'S CHILD		RKO	1934
WC	WARE CASE	HAYNES	FIRST NATIONAL	1928
WC-103	IDENTITY UNKNOWN	COLMES	REPUBLIC	1945
WC-104	WOMAN WHO CAME BACK	COLMES	REPUBLIC	1945
W.C.8600	JOHNNY COME LATELY	HOWARD	UNITED ARTISTS	1943
WCB	WAR OF THE COLOSSAL BEAST	GORDON	AIP	1958
WCF	W.C. FIELDS	portrait	UNIVERSAL	
WCK	WHEN COMEDY WAS KING	YOUNGSON	20th CENTURY FOX	1960
WD	DR. WHO AND THE DALEKS (UK)	FLEMYNG	CONTINENTAL	1966
WD	WALKING DEAD	CURTIZ	WARNER BROS	1936
WD	WALL OF DEATH (UK: THERE IS ANOTHER SUN)	GILBERT	REALART	1951
WD	WALT DISNEY	portrait		
WD	WAR DRUMS	LE BORG	UNITED ARTISTS	1957
WD	WARM DECEMBER (UK)	POITIER	NATIONAL GENERAL	1973
WD	WARREN DOANE PRODUCTIONS	studio		
WD	WAY DOWN SOUTH	GOODWINS, VORHAUS	RKO	1939
WD	WEB OF EVIDENCE (UK: BEYOND THIS PLACE)	CARDIFF	ALLIED ARTISTS	1959
WD	WHAT DID YOU DO IN THE WAR, DADDY?	EDWARDS	UNITED ARTISTS	1966
WD	WICKED DIE SLOW	HENNIGAR	CANNON	1968
WD	WOLF DOG	NEWFIELD	LIPPERT	1958
WD	WOMAN IN THE DARK	ROSEN	RKO	1934
WD	WOMAN IN THE DUNES	TESHIGAHARA	PATHE CONTEMPORARY	1964
WDIH	WHERE DOES IT HURT?	AMATEAU	CINERAMA RELEASING	1972
WE	GERT AND DAISY'S WEEKEND (UK)	ROGERS	BUTCHERS'	1942
WE	VERA ENGELS	portrait		
WE	WAITING TO EXHALE	WHITAKER	20th CENTURY FOX	1995
WE	WEB OF EVIDENCE (UK: BEYOND THIS PLACE)	CARDIFF	ALLIED ARTISTS	1959
WE	WEEK END	GODARD	GROVE PRESS	1968
WE	WELCOME TO THE CLUB	SHENSON	COLUMBIA	1971
WE	WEST 11 (UK)	WINNER	PATHE	1963
WE	WINK OF AN EYE	JONES	UNITED ARTISTS	1958
WE	WOMAN EATER (UK)	SAUNDERS	COLUMBIA	1958
WEF	WHISTLE AT EATON FALLS	SIODMAK	COLUMBIA	1951
WEL	ROBERT E. WELSH PRODUCTIONS/WELSHAY	studio		
WEL	WEEKEND WITH LULU (UK)	CARSTAIRS	COLUMBIA	1961
WEL-1	GAME OF DANGER (UK: BANG! YOU'RE DEAD)	COMFORT	AAP	1954
WELL	CIRCUS COWBOY	WELLMAN	FOX FILM	1924
WEOB	WALK EAST ON BEACON	WERKER	COLUMBIA	1952
WER	WERKER PRODUCTIONS	studio	FOX	
WER-2	DOUBLE CROSS ROADS	WERKER	FOX FILM	1930
WER-3	LAST OF THE DUANES	WERKER	FOX FILM	1930
WER-4	FAIR WARNING	WERKER	FOX FILM	1931
WER-5	ANNABELLE'S AFFAIRS	WERKER	FOX FILM	1931
WER-6	HEARTBREAK	WERKER	FOX FILM	1931
WER-8	BACHELOR'S AFFAIRS	WERKER	FOX FILM	1932
WER-9	RACKETY RAX	WERKER	FOX FILM	1932
WES	DORIS WESTON	portrait	WARNER BROS	late 30s
WES	SUBMARINE D-1	BACON	FIRST NATIONAL	1937
WES	WESSEX FILMS			
WES-19	RAISING A RIOT (UK)	TOYE	CONTINENTAL	1955
WEST-1	RIDERS OF THE DAWN	DRAKE	MONOGRAM	R45
WEST-2	GOD'S COUNTRY AND THE MAN	MCCARTHY	MONOGRAM	1931
WEV	WORM'S EYE VIEW (UK)	RAYMOND	ASSOCIATED BRITISH-PATHE	1951
WF	99 RIVER STREET	KARLSON	UNITED ARTISTS	1953
WF	MY WIFE'S FAMILY (UK)	MYCROFT	ABPC-PATHE	1941
WF	WALLACE FORD	portrait	RKO	
WF	WEEKEND FOR THREE	REIS	RKO	1941
WF	WHERE'S THAT FIRE? (UK)	VARNEL	20TH CENTURY FOX	1940
WF-1	PARATROOPER (UK: RED BERET)	YOUNG	COLUMBIA	1953
WFP-5	COCKLESHELL HEROES (UK)	FERRER	COLUMBIA	1955
WFP7	KILLERS OF KILIMANJARO (UK)	THORPE	COLUMBIA	1959
WFX	OUTBACK (AUS: WAKE IN FRIGHT)	KOTCHEFF	UNITED ARTISTS	1971
WG	AFTER TONIGHT	ARCHAINBAUD	RKO	1933
WG	FIGHTING WOMAN		MONOGRAM	

Movie Still Identification Book Ultimate Edition - Letters

CODE	TITLE/NAME	DIRECTOR/TYPE	STUDIO/DISTRIBUTOR	YEAR
WG	SECRETS OF A WINDMILL GIRL (UK)	MILLER	COMPTON-CAMEO	1966
WG	WAR GAME (UK)	WATKINS	PATHE CONTEMPORARY	1965
WG	WAR OF THE GARGANTUAS	HONDA	UPA	
WG	WAR OF THE GARGANTUAS-MONSTER ZERO - COMBO	HONDA	UPA	1966
WG	WHY GIRLS GO BACK HOME	FLOOD	WARNER BROS	1926
WG	WILD GUITAR	STECKLER	FAIRWAY INT'L	1962
WG	WILLIAM GARGAN	portrait	RKO, WARNER BROS	
WGG	WHAT'S GOOD FOR THE GOOSE (UK)	GOLAN	NATIONAL SHOWMANSHIP	1969
WGI	INSPECTOR CALLS (UK)	HAMILTON	AAP	1954
WGI	SAFECRACKER (UK)	MILLAND	MGM	1958
WGI	WATERGATE PRODUCTIONS (UK)	studio		
WGI	WYNNE GIBSON	portrait	RKO	
WGL	WIFE OF GENERAL LING (UK)	VAJDA	GAUMONT BRITISH AMERICA	1937
WH	CIRCLE OF DANGER (UK)	TOURNEUR	UNITED ARTISTS	1951
WH	HE WAS HER MAN	BACON	WARNER BROS	1934
WH	WALTER HAMPDEN	portrait	UNIVERSAL	
WH	WALTER HUSTON	portrait	UNITED ARTISTS, WARNER	
WH	WANDA HAWLEY	portrait	REALART	
WH	WANDA HENDRIX	portrait	UNIVERSAL	
WH	WANDA HENDRIX	portrait	WARNER BROS	
WH	WAR HUNT	SANDERS	UNITED ARTISTS	1962
WH	WAR IS HELL	TOPPER	ALLIED ARTISTS	1963
WH	WARREN HULL (aka J. WARREN - JOHN HULL)	portrait	WARNER BROS	1930s
WH	WHISPERERS (UK)	FORBES	UNITED ARTISTS	1967
WH	WILLIAM HAINES	portrait	MGM	
WH	WILLIAM HOLDEN	portrait	WARNER BROS	
WH	WISE GIRL	JASON	RKO	1937
WH	WHITE HUNTER BLACK HEART	EASTWOOD	WARNER BROS	1990
WH	WOMAN HUNT	DEXTER	20TH CENTURY FOX	1962
WHC	WHO'S HARRY CRUMB?	FLAHERTY	TRI STAR	1989
WHM	WILD HORSE MESA	GRISSELL	RKO	1947
WHO	MATTER OF WHO	CHAFFEY	MGM	1961
WHP-7	KILLERS OF KILIMINJARO	THORPE	COLUMBIA	1959
WIC	SIN OF NORA MORAN	GOLDSTONE	MAJESTIC	1934
WID	LOVE AND PAIN AND THE WHOLE DAMN THING	PAKULA	COLUMBIA	1973
WIH	WALK INTO HELL (AUS: WALK INTO PARADISE)	ROBINSON	PATRIC	1957
WII	WILLIAM COMES TO TOWN	GUEST	UNITED ARTISTS	1948
WITD	WHISPERS IN THE DARK	CROWE	PARAMOUNT	1992
WIW	WEDDING IN WHITE	FRUET	AVCO EMBASSY	1973
WJ	WALLABY JIM OF THE ISLANDS	LAMONT	GRAND	1937
WJ	WHERE'S JACK? (UK)	CLAVELL	PARAMOUNT	1969
WJ	WILLARD JILLSON/JIELSON (aka STEVE DUNHILL)	portrait	SELZNICK	1940s
WJ	WINDJAMMER	SCOTT	RKO	1937
WI	WOMEN IN LOVE (UK)	RUSSELL	UNITED ARTISTS	1969
WII	WILLIAM COMES TO TOWN (UK)	GUEST	UNITED ARTISTS	1948
WJ	WANDERING JEW (UK)	ELVEY	OLYMPIC	1933
WJ-P	WALLABY JIM OF THE ISLANDS	LAMONT	GRAND	1937
WK	SAVAGE WEEKEND	PAULSEN	CANNON	1979
WK	WAKE UP AND KILL (IT)	LIZZANI	CINEMATION	1966
WK	WILD FOR KICKS (UK: BEAT GIRL)	GREVILLE	TIMES	1960
WK	WINTER KILLS	RICHERT	AVCO EMBASSY	1979
WK-2	WHERE TRAILS DIVIDE	BRADBURY	MONOGRAM	1937
WK-3	ROMANCE OF THE ROCKIES	BRADBURY	MONOGRAM	1937
WL	WALTER LANTZ	portrait	UNIV	
WL	WAR LOVER	LEACOCK	COLUMBIA	1962
WL	WATERFRONT LADY	SANTLEY	REPUBLIC	1935
WL	WATERLOO	BONDERCHUK	PARAMOUNT	1970
WL	WEST OF SHANGHAI	FARROW	WARNER BROS	1937
WL	WICKED LADY (UK)	ARLISS	UNIVERSAL	1945
WL	WICKED LADY	WINNER	COLUMBIA	1983
WL	WILLARD LEWIS	portrait	WARNER BROS	
WL	WILLIAM LUNDIGAN	portrait	UNIV	
WL	WIND AND THE LION	MILIUS	MGM	1975
WL	WINNIE LIGHTNER	portrait	FN/WARNER BROS	
WL	WINNIE LIGHTNER	portrait		
WL	WINTER LIGHT (SWE: NATTVARDSGASTERNA)	BERGMAN	JANUS	1963
WL	WOMEN IN LOVE (UK)	RUSSELL	UNITED ARTISTS	1969
WLA	WELCOME TO L.A.	RUDOLPH	UNITED ARTISTS	1976
WLA	WICKED LADY (UK)	ARLISS	UNIVERSAL	1945
WLB	WHERE THE LILIES BLOOM	GRAHAM	UNITED ARTISTS	1974

Movie Still Identification Book Ultimate Edition - Letters

CODE	TITLE/NAME	DIRECTOR/TYPE	STUDIO/DISTRIBUTOR	YEAR
WLD	WALK WITH LOVE AND DEATH	HUSTON	20th CENTURY FOX	1969
WLW	VICIOUS CIRCLE	WILDER	UNITED ARTISTS	1948
WLW-510	ONCE A THIEF	WILDER	UNITED ARTISTS	1950
WM	AND WOMEN SHALL WEEP (UK)	LEMONT	RANK	1960
WM	MAN WHO FOUND HIMSELF	LANDERS	RKO	1937
WM	MYSTERY OF THE WAX MUSEUM	CURTIZ	WARNER BROS	1933
WM	PIECES OF DREAMS	HALLER	UNITED ARTISTS	1970
WM	THINGS TO COME (UK)	MENZIES	UNITED ARTISTS	1936
WM	WAGON MASTER	FORD	RKO	1950
WM	WARN THAT MAN (UK)	HUNTINGTON	ABPC-PATHE	1943
WM	WAYNE MORRIS	portrait	WARNER BROS	
WM	WE'RE IN THE MONEY	ENRIGHT	WARNER BROS	1935
WM	WHEN WE ARE MARRIED (UK)	COMFORT	ANGLO-AMERICAN	1943
WM	WICKER MAN (UK-1973)	HARDY	WARNER BROS	1975
WM	WILLIAM CAMERON MENZIES	portrait		
WmB	LOST MISSILE	BERKE	UNITED ARTISTS	1958
WMCJ	WHITE MEN CAN'T JUMP	SHELTON	20th CENTURY FOX	1992
WMM	WHO'S MINDING THE MINT?	MORRIS	COLUMBIA	1967
WMP	WICKER MAN (UK-1973)	HARDY	WARNER BROS	1975
WN	WANDA NEVADA	FONDA	UNITED ARTISTS	1979
WN	WAY WE LIVE NOW	BROWN	UNITED ARTISTS	1970
WN	WHITE NIGHTS (IT: LE NOTTI DI BIANCHI)	VISCONTI	UMPO	1957
WN	WINGS OF THE NAVY	BACON	WARNER BROS	1939
WN	WORLD BY NIGHT NO. 2	PROJA	WARNER BROS	1961
WNA	WE'RE NO ANGELS	JORDAN	PARAMOUNT	1989
WND	WOMAN NEXT DOOR (FR: LA FEMME D'A COTE)	TRUFFAUT	UNITED ARTISTS	1981
WNM	WALK SOFTLY STRANGER	STEVENSON	RKO	1950
WNP	WHAT'S NEW PUSSYCAT	DONNER	UNITED ARTISTS	1965
WNW	LOCKET	BRAHM	RKO	1947
WO	COMPANY SHE KEEPS	CROMWELL	RKO	1950
WO	WARNER OLAND	portrait		
WO	WHITE ORCHID (MEX) (CREATURES OF THE JUNGLE 1957)	LE BORG	UNITED ARTISTS	1954
WO	WIDE OPEN	MAYO	WARNER BROS	1930
WO	WILLIAM ORR	portrait	WARNER BROS	
WO	WITHOUT ORDERS	LANDERS	RKO	1936
WOA	WORLD OF APU (IND: APUR SANSAR)	RAY	EDWARD HARRISON	1959
WOB	WILD ON THE BEACH	DEXTER	20th CENTURY FOX	1965
WOF	HOUR OF THE WOLF (SWE: VARGTIMMEN)	BERGMAN	LOPERT	1968
WOHO	WORLD OF HENRY ORIENT	HILL	UNITED ARTISTS	1964
WON	WEST OF NEVADA	HILL	COLONY*	1936
WOOD	WOODSTOCK	WADLEIGH	WARNER BROS	1970
WOP	WEST OF THE PECOS	KILLY	RKO	1945
WOR	WAR OF THE ROSES	DEVITO	20th CENTURY FOX	1989
WOS	WOMAN OF STRAW (UK)	DEARDEN	UNITED ARTISTS	1964
WOZ	WEST OF ZANZIBAR (UK)	WATT	UNIVERSAL	1954
WP	CAPTAIN'S KID	GRINDE	WARNER BROS	1936
WP	DUKE OF WEST POINT	GREEN	UNITED ARTISTS	1938
WP	FORT APACHE	FORD	RKO	1948
WP	MARRY ME AGAIN	TASHLIN	RKO	1953
WP	TEENAGE DOLL `	CORMAN	ALLIED ARTISTS	1957
WP	WALTER PIDGEON	portrait	UNIVERSAL	
WP	WAR PAINT	SELANDER	UNITED ARTISTS	1953
WP	WAR PARTY	SELANDER	20th CENTURY FOX	1965
WP	WESTERN PACIFIC AGENT	NEWFIELD	LIPPERT	1950
WP	WHERE'S POPPA?	REINER	UNITED ARTISTS	1970
WP	WHILE PARENTS SLEEP (UK)	BRUNEL	UNITED ARTISTS	1935
WP	WILD PUSSYCAT (GR)	DADIRAS	CROWN INTERNATIONAL	1969
WP	WILLIAM PERLBERG	portrait	PARAMOUNT`	
WP	WILLIAM POWELL	portrait	UNIV	
WP	WILLIAM POWELL	portrait	MGM	
WP	WITHOUT PITY (IT: SENZA PIETA)	LATTUADA	LUX	1948
WP	WITNESS FOR THE PROSECUTION	WILDER	UNITED ARTISTS	1957
WP	WOMEN OF PITCAIRN ISLAND	YARBROUGH	20th CENTURY FOX	1956
WP	W-PLAN	SAVILLE	RKO	1930
WP-6	IDOL ON PARADE (UK)	GILLING	COLUMBIA	1959
WPC	WILLIAM T. CARLETON	portrait	MGM	
WPP	WOMEN OF THE PREHISTORIC PLANET	PIERCE	REALART	1966
WPS	WAR AND PEACE	VIDOR	PARAMOUNT	1956
WR	ENEMY OF WOMEN (MAD LOVER)	ZEISLER	MONOGRAM	1944
WR	WARD RAMSEY	portrait	UNIVERSAL	early 60s

Movie Still Identification Book Ultimate Edition - Letters

CODE	TITLE/NAME	DIRECTOR/TYPE	STUDIO/DISTRIBUTOR	YEAR
WR	WATCH ON THE RHINE	SHUMLIN	WARNER BROS	1943
WR	WEDDING REHEARSAL (UK)	KORDA	IDEAL	1932
WR	WHERE DANGER LIVES	FARROW	RKO	1950
WR	WILD BOYS OF THE ROAD	WELLMAN	WARNER BROS	1933
WR	WILLIAM REYNOLDS	portrait	UNIV	
WR	WOMAN IN RED	WILDER	ORION	1984
WR	YOUNG BILLY YOUNG	KENNEDY	UNITED ARTISTS	1969
WR-1	RIDERS OF THE DAWN	BRADBURY	MONOGRAM	1937
WR-2	STARS OVER ARIZONA	BRADBURY	MONOGRAM	1937
WR-3	DANGER VALLEY	BRADBURY	MONOGRAM	1937
WR-4	GATEWAY OF THE MOON	WRAY	FOX FILM	1928
WR-5	SINGED	WRAY	FOX FILM	1927
WR-6	RIDERS FROM NOWHERE	RAY	MONOGRAM	1940
WR-7	WILD HORSE RANGE	RAY	MONOGRAM	1940
WR-379	WORLD FOR RANSOM	HARDY	ALLIED ARTISTS	1954
WRAY-2	GUILDED BUTTERFLY	WRAY	FOX FILM	1926
WRP	SONG FOR MISS JULIE	ROWLAND	REPUBLIC	1945
WS	ACTORS AND SIN	GARMES, HECHT	UNITED ARTISTS	1952
WS	FEMALE (FR: LA FEMME ET LE PANTIN 1959)	DUVIVIER	LOPERT	1960
WS	SHALL WE DANCE	SANDRICH	RKO	1937
WS	WALK IN THE SHADOW (UK: LIFE FOR RUTH)	DEARDEN	CONTINENTAL	1962
WS	WALKING STICK (UK)	TILL	MGM	1970
WS	WALTER SODERLING	portrait	RKO	
WS	WHAT DO YOU SAY TO A NAKED LADY?	FUNT	UNITED ARTISTS	1970
WS	WINDBAG THE SAILOR (UK)	BEAUDINE	GAUMONT BRITISH	1936
WS	WHISPERING SMITH VS. SCOTLAND YARD (UK)	SEARLE	RKO	1952
WS	WHISTLE STOP	MOGUY	UNITED ARTISTS	1946
WS	WHITE SHEIK (IT: LO SCEICCO BIANCO)	FELLINI	JANUS	1952
WS	WHITE SHOULDERS	BROWN	RKO	1931
WS	WHITE SISTER	KING	METRO PICTURES	1923
WS	WILD STRAWBERRIES (SWE: SMULTRONSTALLET 1957)	BERGMAN	JANIS	1959
WS	WINI (WINIFRED) SHAW	portrait	WARNER BROS	
WS	WOMAN LIKE SATAN	DUVIVIER	LOPERT	1959
WS	WONDERFUL STORY (UK)	FOGWELL	STERLING	1932
WSH	WILLIAM S. HART	portrait		
WSR	WHO'LL STOP THE RAIN/DOG SOLDIERS	REISZ	UNITED ARTISTS	1978
WSR	WORLD SEX REPORT (GER)	RIMMEL	WHITE	1971
WSS	WEST SIDE STORY	ROBBINS, WISE	UNITED ARTISTS	1961
WSS	WHILE THE SUN SHINES (UK)	ASQUITH	STRATFORD	1947
WSY	WITH SIX YOU GET EGGROLL	MORRIS	NATIONAL GENERAL	1968
WT	COMPROMISED	ADOLFI	WARNER BROS	1931
WT	TWILIGHT WOMEN (UK: WOMEN OF TWILIGHT)	PARRY	LIPPERT	1952
WT	WAGON TRAIN	KILLY	RKO	1940
WT	WALK TALL	DEXTER	20th CENTURY FOX	1960
WT	WALTZ OF THE TOREADORS (UK)	GUILLERMIN	CONTINENTAL	1962
WT	WALTZ TIME (UK)	THIELE	GAUMONT	1933
WT	WALTZ TIME (UK)	STEIN	FOUR CONTINENTS	1945
WT	WE'RE ON THE JURY	HOLMES	RKO	1937
WT	WHERE IT'S AT	KANIN	UNITED ARTISTS	1969
WT	WHITE TOWER	TETZLAFF	RKO	1950
WT	WHOLE TRUTH (UK)	GUILLERMIN	COLUMBIA	1958
WTC	UP THE CREEK (UK)	GUEST	DOMINANT	1958
WTM	WITNESS TO MURDER	ROWLAND	UNITED ARTISTS	1954
WTO	TRUTH ABOUT YOUTH	SEITER	WARNER BROS	1930
WTO	WORLD TEN TIMES OVER (UK)	RILLA	GOLDSTONE	1963
WTS	WOMAN TIMES SEVEN	DE SICA	EMBASSY	1967
WTT	WAVELL'S 30,000 (UK)	MONCK	MGM	1942
WTW	PASSION	DWAN	RKO	1954
WV	SHINING VICTORY	RAPPER	WARNER BROS	1941
WV	STRAUSS' GREAT WALTZ (UK: WALTZES FROM VIENNA)	HITCHCOCK	GAUMONT BRITISH	1934
WVD	W S VAN DYKE	portrait	MGM	1920s-40s
WW	3 MURDERESS (FR)	BOISROND	20th CENTURY FOX	1960
WW	AMAZONS OF ROME (IT: LE VERGININ DI ROMA)	COTTAFAVI	UNITED ARTISTS	1961
WW	CRIMES AT THE DARK HOUSE (UK)	KING	EXPLOITATION	1940
WW	HAL TALIAFERRO aka WALLY WALES	portrait		
WW	INVISIBLE MENACE	FARROW	WARNER BROS	1938
WW	MAN WANTED	DIETERLE	WARNER BROS	1932
WW	MURDER ON THE WATERFRONT	EASON	WARNER BROS	1943
WW	SILLY BILLIES	GUIOL	RKO	1936
WW	WAITING WOMEN (SWE: KVINNORS VANTAN)	BERGMAN	JANUS	1952

Movie Still Identification Book Ultimate Edition - Letters

CODE	TITLE/NAME	DIRECTOR/TYPE	STUDIO/DISTRIBUTOR	YEAR
WW	WALTER WANGER	portrait		
WW	WALTER WANGER PRODUCTIONS	studio	PARAMOUNT	
WW	WANDERS OF THE WASTELAND	GRISSELL, KILLY	RKO	1945
WW	WARREN WILLIAM	portrait	WARNER BROS	
WW	WATERFRONT WOMEN (UK: WATERFRONT)	ANDERSON	BELL	1950
WW	WHEELER & WOOLSEY: BERT & ROBERT	portrait	RKO	1920s-30s
WW	WHITE WARRIOR	FREDA	WARNER BROS	1961
WW	WICKED WIFE (UK: GRAND NATIONAL NIGHT)	MCNAUGHT	ALLIED ARTISTS	1953
WW	WICKED WOMAN	ROUSE	UNITED ARTISTS	1953
WW	YOUNG AND WILLING (UK: WEAK AND THE WICKED)	THOMPSON	ALLIED ARTISTS	1954
WW-1	PRESIDENT VANISHES	WELLMAN	PARAMOUNT	1935
WW-2	PRIVATE WORLDS	LA CAVA	PARAMOUNT	1935
WW-3	SHANGHAI	FLOOD	PARAMOUNT	1935
WW-4	EVERY NIGHT AT EIGHT	WALSH	PARAMOUNT	1935
WW-5	SMART GIRL	SCOTTO	PARAMOUNT	1935
WW-6	MARY BURNS, FUGITIVE	HOWARD	PARAMOUNT	1935
WW-7	TRAIL OF THE LONESOME PINE	HATHAWAY	PARAMOUNT	1936
WW-8	HER MASTER'S VOICE	SANTLEY	PARAMOUNT	1936
WW-9	PALM SPRINGS	SCOTTO	PARAMOUNT	1936
WW-10	MOON'S OUR HOME	SEITER	PARAMOUNT	1936
WW-11	FATAL LADY	LUDWIG	PARAMOUNT	1936
WW-12	BIG BROWN EYES	WALSH	PARAMOUNT	1936
WW-13	CASE AGAINST MRS. AMES	SEITER	PARAMOUNT	1936
WW.14	PICCADILLY (UK)	DUPONT	SONO ART-WORLD WIDE	1929
WW-14	SPENDTHRIFT	WALSH	PARAMOUNT	1936
WW24	CANNONBALL EXPRESS	FOX	SONO ART WORLD	1932
WW93	CAIRO ROAD (UK - 1950)	MACDONALD	REALART	1952
WW-435	WICKED WIFE (UK: GRAND NATIONAL NIGHT)	MCNAUGHT	ALLIED ARTISTS	1955
WW-2500	YOU ONLY LIVE ONCE	LANG	UNITED ARTISTS	1937
WW-2600	HISTORY IS MADE AT NIGHT	BORZAGE	UNITED ARTISTS	1937
WW-3000	VOGUES OF 1938	CUMMINGS	UNITED ARTISTS	1937
WW-3300	52ND STREET	YOUNG	UNITED ARTISTS	1937
WW-3400	I MET MY LOVE AGAIN	LOGAN, RIPLEY	UNITED ARTISTS	1938
WW-3500	STAND-IN	GARNETT	UNITED ARTISTS	1937
WW-3600	BLOCKADE	KIETERLE	UNITED ARTISTS	1938
WW-3700	ALGIERS	CROMWELL	UNITED ARTISTS	1938
WW-4500	WINTER CARNIVAL	REISNER	UNITED ARTISTS	1939
WW-4800	ETERNALLY YOURS	GARNETT	UNITED ARTISTS	1939
WW-5000	SLIGHTLY HONORABLE	GARNETT	UNITED ARTISTS	1939
WW-5100	HOUSE ACROSS THE BAY	MAYO	UNITED ARTISTS	1940
WW-6000	FOREIGN CORRESPONDENT	HITCHCOCK	UNITED ARTISTS	1940
WW-6200	LONG VOYAGE HOME	FORD	UNITED ARTISTS	1940
WW-7200	SUNDOWN	HATHAWAY	UNITED ARTISTS	1941
WWL	WEEKEND WITH LULU (UK)	CARSTAIRS	COLUMBIA	1961
WWN	WOMEN WITHOUT NAMES (IT: DONNE SENZA NOME 1950)	RADVANYI	LOPERT	1951
WWS	WORLD WITHOUT SHAME (UK)	WINTER	GALAXY	1962
WWS	WORLD WITHOUT SUN	COUSTEAU	COLUMBIA	1964
WWS12	WINE, WOMEN AND SONG	BRENON	CHADWICK	1933
WWW	WAY WE WERE	POLLACK	COLUMBIA	1973
WWW	WILD WILD WORLD	SOKOLER	SOKOLER FILM	1965
WXBX	WILLIAM BAKEWELL	portrait	MGM	
WXP	WALTER PIDGEON	portrait	MGM	
WY	I'LL WALK BESIDE YOU (UK)	ROGERS	BUTCHER'S	1943
WY	WHAT'S YOUR BIRTHDAY	BEAUMONT	RKO	1937
WY	WILD YOUTH	SCHREYER	CINEMA ASSOC	1960
WYCH	WHEN YOU COME HOME (UK)	BAXTER	BUTCHER'S	1948
WYL	YOUNG LAND	TETZLAFF	COLUMBIA	1959
X	ACROSS THE PACIFIC	DEL RUTH	WARNER BROS	1926
X	CARETAKERS	BARTLETT	UNITED ARTISTS	1963
X	FASHION		FIRST NATIONAL	
X	KANGAROO KID (UK)	SELANDER	EAGLE-LION	1950
X	SCARLET SPEAR	BREAKSTON	UNITED ARTISTS	1954
X	X-15	DONNER	UNITED ARTISTS	1961
X-1	LOVE UNDER COVER	MACDONALD	TRIANGLE	1917
X-2	PIPE OF DISCONTENT	MATTHEWS	TRIANGLE	1917
X-3	HEART STRATEGY	MACDONALD	TRIANGLE	1917
X-4	HONEST THIEVES	MATTHEWS	TRIANGLE	1917
X-5	NOBLE FRAUD	WILLIAMS	TRIANGLE	1917
X-6	MALE GOVERNESS	DILLION	TRIANGLE	1917
X-7	WON BY A FOOT	FAY	TRIANGLE	1917

Movie Still Identification Book Ultimate Edition - Letters

CODE	TITLE/NAME	DIRECTOR/TYPE	STUDIO/DISTRIBUTOR	YEAR
X-8	BLACK EYES AND BLUE	KERR	TRIANGLE	1916
X-9	ROAD AGENT		TRIANGLE	1917
X-10	GRAB BAG BRIDE	HARTMAN	TRIANGLE	1917
X-11	DONE IN OIL	AVERY	TRIANGLE	1917
X-12	TELEPHONE BELLE	RAYMAKER	TRIANGLE	1917
X-13	HIS DEADLY UNDERTAKING	MCCOY	TRIANGLE	1917
X-14	WHEN HEARTS COLLIDE	KERR	TRIANGLE	1917
X-15	STONE AGE	HARTMAN	TRIANGLE	1917
X-16	BACHELOR'S FINISH	DILLION	TRIANGLE	1917
X-17	FILM EXPOSURE	MCCOY	TRIANGLE	1917
X-18	CAUGHT WITH THE GOODS	KAUFMAN	TRIANGLE	1917
X-19	INNOCENT SINNERS	RAYMAKER	TRIANGLE	1917
X-20	HOBBLED HARTS	DILLION	TRIANGLE	1917
X-21	HER CANDY KID	AVERY	TRIANGLE	1917
X-22	FINISHED PRODUCT	MORRIS	TRIANGLE	1917
X-23	SELF-MADE HERO	HARTMAN	TRIANGLE	1917
X-24	HIS RISE AND TUMBLE	MCCOY	TRIANGLE	1917
X-25	BERTH SCANDAL	DILLION	TRIANGLE	1917
X-26	BOOKWORM TURNS	AVERY	TRIANGLE	1917
X-27	TUNER OF NOTE	MCCOY	TRIANGLE	1917
X-28	DOG'S OWN TALE	RAYMAKER	TRIANGLE	1917
X-29	WINNING LOSER	HARTMAN	TRIANGLE	1917
X-30	PETTICOAT PERILS	MORRIS	TRIANGLE	1917
X-31	HIS PARLOR ZOO	MCCOY	TRIANGLE	1917
X-32	HER BIRTHDAY KNIGHT	AVERY	TRIANGLE	1917
X-33	HER FINISHING TOUCH	DILLION	TRIANGLE	1917
X-34	LOVE AND FISH	MORRIS	TRIANGLE	1917
X-35	LAUNDRY CLEAN-UP	HARTMAN	TRIANGLE	1917
X-36	CAMERA CURE	RAYMAKER	TRIANGLE	1917
X-37	HIS ONE NIGHT STAND	MCCOY	TRIANGLE	1917
X-38	DISHONEST BURGLAR	DILLION	TRIANGLE	1917
X-39	SKIRT STRATEGY	AVERY	TRIANGLE	1917
X-40	HIS SOCIAL RISE	MORRIS	TRIANGLE	1917
X-41	TWIN TROUBLES	DILLION	TRIANGLE	1917
X-42	GIRL AND THE RING	AVERY	TRIANGLE	1917
X-43	HIS CRIMINAL CAREER	HARTMAN	TRIANGLE	1917
X-44	HIS MARRIAGE FAILURE	RAYMAKER	TRIANGLE	1917
X-45	PERILS OF THE BAKERY	MCCOY	TRIANGLE	1917
X-46	WHEELS AND WOE	DILLION	TRIANGLE	1917
X-47	HIS SPEEDY FINISH	MORRIS	TRIANGLE	1917
X-48	JANITOR'S VENGEANCE	AVERY	TRIANGLE	1917
X-49	THEIR WEAK MOMENTS	MCCOY	TRIANGLE	1917
X-50	HIS BITTER FATE	WILLIAMS	TRIANGLE	1917
X-51	AIRED IN COURT	DILLION	TRIANGLE	1917
X-52	DAD'S DOWNFALL	RAYMAKER	TRIANGLE	1917
X-53	HIS PERFECT DAY	MCCOY	TRIANGLE	1917
X-54	HIS THANKLESS JOB	MORRIS	TRIANGLE	1917
X-55	HOUSE OF SCANDAL	AVERY	TRIANGLE	1917
X-56	HIS SUDDEN RIFVAL	DILLION	TRIANGLE	1917
X-57	INNOCENT VILLAIN	WILLIAMS	TRIANGLE	1917
X-58	HIS WIDOW'S MIGHT	KERNAN	TRIANGLE	1917
X-59	SOLE MATES	RAYMAKER	TRIANGLE	1917
X-60	TOY OF FATE	MCCOY	TRIANGLE	1917
X-61	HIS FATAL MOVE	MORRIS	TRIANGLE	1917
X-62	MATRIMONIAL ACCIDENT	AVERY	TRIANGLE	1917
X-63	LOVE CASE	KERNAN	TRIANGLE	1917
X-64	HIS COOL NERVE	MCCOY	TRIANGLE	1917
X-65	HOTEL DISGRACE	DILLION	TRIANGLE	1917
X-66	HIS HIDDEN TALENT	MORRIS	TRIANGLE	1917
X-67	THEIR DOMESTIC DECEPTION	WILLIAMS	TRIANGLE	1917
X-68	CLEVER DUMMY	RAYMAKER	TRIANGLE	1917
X-69	HER DONKEY LOVE	AVERY	TRIANGLE	1917
X-70	FALLEN STAR	MCCOY	TRIANGLE	1917
X-71	HIS FOOT-HILL FOLLY	MORRIS	TRIANGLE	1917
X-72	HIS BABY DOLL	WILLIAMS	TRIANGLE	1917
X-73	DARK ROOM SECRET	KERNAN	TRIANGLE	1917
X-74	WARM RECEPTION	DILLION	TRIANGLE	1917
X-75	HIS UNCONSCIOUS CONSCIENCE	AVERY	TRIANGLE	1917
X-76	HIS SAVING GRACE	MCCOY	TRIANGLE	1917
X-77	HIS TAKING WAYS	DILLION	TRIANGLE	1917

Movie Still Identification Book Ultimate Edition - Letters

CODE	TITLE/NAME	DIRECTOR/TYPE	STUDIO/DISTRIBUTOR	YEAR
X-78	HALF AND HALF	MORRIS	TRIANGLE	1917
X-79	HER FICKLE FORTUNE	KERNAN	TRIANGLE	1917
X-80	CAUGHT IN THE END	AVERY	TRIANGLE	1917
X-81	ALL AT SEA		TRIANGLE	1917
X-82	THEIR LOVE LESSON		TRIANGLE	1917
X-83	PRAIRIE HEIRESS		TRIANGLE	1917
X-84	HIS BUSY DAY		TRIANGLE	1917
X-85	MODERN SHERLOCK		TRIANGLE	1917
X-86	THEIR HUSBAND		TRIANGLE	1917
X-118	COUNTERFEIT SCENT	MORRIS	TRIANGLE	1917
X537	GEOGRAPHY LESSON (sh) (# 538 crossed out and X537		MGM	1931
X696	HANDLEBARS (sh)	WHITE	MGM	1933
XBA	GEORGE BURNS & GRACIE ALLEN	portrait		
XBL	BEN LYON	portrait	MGM	
XC	XAVIER CUGAT	portrait	MCA RECORDS	
XDM	DIARY OF A MADMAN	LE BORG	UNITED ARTISTS	1963
XHL	HEDY LAMARR	portrait	MGM	
XJC	JEAN CHATBURN	portrait	MGM	
XLD	INCIDENT IN AN ALLEY	CAHN	UNITED ARTISTS	1962
XLH	LESLIE HOWARD	portrait	MGM	1930s-40s
XLXB	LUCILLE BREMER	portrait	MGM	
XMS	MARGARET SULLAVAN	portrait	MGM	
XRH	RUTH HUSSEY	portrait	MGM	
XU	X - THE UNKNOWN (UK)	NORMAN	WARNER BROS	1957
XW	THIS MAN IS MINE (UK)	VARNEL	COLUMBIA BRITISH	1946
XX	HAL ROACH PORTRAIT SERIES	portrait		
XXC	TWENTIETH CENTURY (BEFORE MERGER WITH FOX)			
XXC-100	MIGHTY BARNUM	LANG	UNITED ARTISTS	1934
XXC-500	CALL OF THE WILD	WELLMAN	UNITED ARTISTS	1935
XXC-600	CLIVE OF INDIA	BOLESLAWSKI	UNITED ARTISTS	1935
XXC-700	FOLIES BERGERE	DEL RUTH	UNITED ARTISTS	1935
XXC-800	CARDINAL RICHELIEU	LEE	UNITED ARTISTS	1935
XXC-900	LES MISERABLES	BOLESLAWSKI	UNITED ARTISTS	1935
XXC-5800	BORN TO BE BAD	SHERMAN	20th CENTURY	1934
XXC-8300	BOWERY	WALSH	UNITED ARTISTS	1933
XXC-8400	BLOOD MONEY	BROWN	UNITED ARTISTS	1933
XXC-8500	BROADWAY THROUGH A KEYHOLE	SHERMAN	UNITED ARTISTS	1933
XXC-8600	ADVICE TO THE LOVELORN	WERKER	20th CENTURY	1933
XXC-8700	MOULIN ROUGE	LANFIELD	UNITED ARTISTS	1934
XXC-8800	BORN TO BE BAD	SHERMAN	UNITED ARTISTS	1934
XXC-8900	LOOKING FOR TROUBLE	WELLMAN	UNITED ARTISTS	1934
XXC-9000	GALLANT LADY	LA CAVA	UNITED ARTISTS	1933
XXC-9200	HOUSE OF ROTHSCHILD	WERKER	UNITED ARTISTS	1934
XXC-9400	AFFAIRS OF CELLINI	LA CAVA	UNITED ARTISTS	1934
XXC-9500	BULLDOG DRUMMOND STRIKES BACK	DEL RUTH	UNITED ARTISTS	1934
XXC-9600	LAST GENTLEMAN	LANFIELD	UNITED ARTISTS	1934
XXJC	JOSEPH CALLEIA	portrait	MGM	
XXLH	LOUISE HENRY	portrait	MGM	
XYZ	X, Y AND Z	HUTTON	COLUMBIA	1972
Y	YANKS	SCHLESINGER	UNITED ARTISTS	1979
Y166	NEVER MENTION MURDER (UK)	NELSON-BURTON	ANGLO-AMALGAMATED	1964
YA	FOR YOU ALONE (UK)	FAITHFULL	BUTCHER'S	1945
YA	YOU'RE IN THE ARMY NOW	SEILER	WARNER BROS	1941
YA	YOUNG AMERICANS	GRASSHOFF	COLUMBIA	1967
YAD	YOUNG AND DANGEROUS	CLAXTON	20TH CENTURY FOX	1957
YAI	BARGAIN	MILTON	WARNER BROS	1931
YB	MAKE YOUR OWN BED	GODFREY	WARNER BROS	1944
YB	YEARS BETWEEN (UK)	BENNETT	UNIVERSAL	1946
YB	YELLOW BALLOON (UK)	THOMPSON	ALLIED ARTISTS	1953
YB	YOUNG AND BEAUTIFUL	SANTLEY	MASCOT	1934
YBN	YOU'RE A BIG BOY NOW	COPPOLA	WARNER BROS	1966
YC	YELLOW CANARY (UK)	WILCOX	RKO	1944
YC	YOU CAN'T BEAT LOVE	CABANNE	RKO	1937
YC	YOUNG CASSIDY (UK)	CARDIFF	MGM	1965
YD	GO INTO YOUR DANCE	MAYO	WARNER BROS	1935
YD	YANKEE DOODLE DANDY	CURTIZ	WARNER BROS	1942
YD	YOUNG DILLINGER	MORSE	ALLIED ARTISTS	1965
YD	YOUNG DOCTORS	KARLSON	UNITED ARTISTS	1961
YD	YUKON PATROL	ENGLISH, WITNEY	REPUBLIC	1942
YD	YVETTE DUGAY (aka YVETTE DUGUAY)	portrait	UNIVERSAL	1940s-50s

Movie Still Identification Book Ultimate Edition - Letters

CODE	TITLE/NAME	DIRECTOR/TYPE	STUDIO/DISTRIBUTOR	YEAR
YDC	YVONNE DE CARLO	portrait	UNIVERSAL	
YE	YANK IN ERMINE (UK)	PARRY	M&A ALEXANDER	1955
YE	YOUNG EINSTEIN	SERIOUS	WARNER BROS	1989
YF	WHEN THE CLOCK STRIKES	CAHN	UNITED ARTISTS	1961
YF	YOU'LL FIND OUT	BUTLER	RKO	1941
YG	YOUNG GUNS OF TEXAS	DEXTER	20th CENTURY FOX	1962
YG2	YOUNG GUNS 2	MURPHY	20th CENTURY FOX	1990
YJ	YOU MUST BE JOKING (UK)	WINNER	COLUMBIA	1965
YJJ	YOUNG JESSE JAMES	CLAXTON	20TH CENTURY FOX	1960
YLM	YOU MADE ME LOVE YOU (UK)	BANKS	MAJESTIC	1933
YLT	YOU ONLY LIVE TWICE (UK)	GILBERT	UNITED ARTISTS	1967
YM	YOU SAID A MOUTHFUL	BACON	FN, WARNER	1932
YM	YOUR MONEY OR YOUR WIFE (UK)	SIMMONS	ELLIS	1960
YM	YVES MONTAND	portrait	PARAMOUNT	1960s-70s
YMB	YES, MR. BROWN (UK)	BUCHANAN, WILCOX	WOOLF & FREEDMAN	1933
YMF	YOUNG MAN'S FANCY (UK)	STEVENSON	ABFD	1939
YMM	YOU MUST GET MARRIED (UK)	PEARCE	GFD	1936
YN	BLONDE SINNER (UK: YIELD TO THE NIGHT)	THOMPSON	ALLIED ARTISTS	1957
YO	WONDERFUL TO BE YOUNG! (UK: YOUNG ONES)	FURIE	PARAMOUNT	1961
YR	YELLOW ROLLS ROYCE (UK)	ASQUITH	MGM	1965
YRC	YELLOW ROLLS ROYCE (UK)	ASQUITH	MGM	1965
YRC	YOUNG REBEL	SHERMAN	AIP	1969
YS	YELLOW SUBMARINE	DUNNING	UNITED ARTISTS	1968
YSH	YOUNG SHERLOCK HOLMES	LEVINSON	PARAMOUNT	1985
YSW	YOU CAN'T WIN 'EM ALL	COLLINSON	COLUMBIA	1970
YT	YANK IN VIETNAM	THOMPSON	ALLIED ARTISTS	1964
YT	YESTERDAY AND TODAY	WEATHERWAX	UNITED ARTISTS	1953
YTT	YESTERDAY, TODAY AND TOMORROW	DE SICA	EMBASSY	1964
YW	YOUNG WIDOW	MARIN	UNITED ARTISTS	1946
YW	YOUNG WINSTON	ATTENBOROUGH	COLUMBIA	1972
YW	YOUNG WORLD (IT: UN MONDE NOUVEAU)	DE SICA	LOPERT	1966
YWE	YOUNG, WILLING AND EAGER (UK: RAG DOLL)	COMFORT	MANSON	1961
Z	VERA ZORINA	portrait	UNIVERSAL	
Z	WEST OF ZANZIBAR (UK)	WATT	UNIVERSAL	1954
Z	ZAMBOANGA	DE CASTRO	GRAND	1937
Z	ZAPPED	ROSENTHAL	EMBASSY	1982
Z	ZARAK (UK)	YOUNG	COLUMBIA	1956
Z	ZORRO (IT)	TESSARI	ALLIED ARTISTS	1976
Z	ZORRO GAY BLADE	MEDAK	20th CENTURY FOX	1981
Z	ZACHARIAH	ENGLUND	CINERAMA REL.	1971
Z	ZULU (UK)	ENDFIELD	EMBASSY	1964
Z-601	HELL CANYON OUTLAWS	LANDRES	REPUBLIC	1957
ZANRA	FOREVER DARLING	HALL	MGM	1956
ZEX	ELECTRONIC MONSTER (UK: ESCAPEMENT)	TULLY, PALTENGHI	COLUMBIA	1958
ZH	ZERO HOUR	BARTLETT	PARAMOUNT	1957
ZK	ZENA KEEFE MOVIES		SELZNICK	
ZOB	ZOMBIES ON BROADWAY	DOUGLAS	RKO	1945
ZP	WALKING TARGET	CAHN	UNITED ARTISTS	1960
ZP	ZASU PITTS	portrait	MGM	
ZP1	FRIGHTENED CITY (UK)	LEMONT	RANK	1961
ZRA	ZORRO RIDES AGAIN	ENGLISH, WHITNEY	REPUBLIC	1959
ZS	ZACHARY SCOTT	portrait	WARNER BROS	
ZU	ZULU	ENDFIELD	EMBASSY	1964
ZZ	DESERT PATROL (UK: SEA OF SAND)	GREEN	UNIVERSAL	1958

ADDITIONS

TITLE/NAME	DIRECTOR/TYPE	STUDIO/DISTRIBUTOR	YEAR

ADDITIONS

TITLE/NAME	DIRECTOR/TYPE	STUDIO/DISTRIBUTOR	YEAR

ADDITIONS

TITLE/NAME	DIRECTOR/TYPE	STUDIO/DISTRIBUTOR	YEAR

ADDITIONS

TITLE/NAME	DIRECTOR/TYPE	STUDIO/DISTRIBUTOR	YEAR

ADDITIONS

TITLE/NAME	DIRECTOR/TYPE	STUDIO/DISTRIBUTOR	YEAR

ADDITIONS

TITLE/NAME	DIRECTOR/TYPE	STUDIO/DISTRIBUTOR	YEAR

ADDITIONS

TITLE/NAME	DIRECTOR/TYPE	STUDIO/DISTRIBUTOR	YEAR

ADDITIONS

TITLE/NAME	DIRECTOR/TYPE	STUDIO/DISTRIBUTOR	YEAR

ADDITIONS

TITLE/NAME	DIRECTOR/TYPE	STUDIO/DISTRIBUTOR	YEAR

ADDITIONS

TITLE/NAME	DIRECTOR/TYPE	STUDIO/DISTRIBUTOR	YEAR

ADDITIONS

TITLE/NAME	DIRECTOR/TYPE	STUDIO/DISTRIBUTOR	YEAR

LAMP SPONSORS

Backing to the Future – 378
Bags Unlimited – 377
Best Little Film House – xxxiii
Bonhams Auctions – xxxii
Channing Posters – xxxiii, 376
Cinema Retro – x
Conway's Vintage Treasures – x
Dominique Besson – ii
eMoviePoster.com – i
Ewbank's Auction – xxxiii
Femme, Fatales and Fantasies – xxxv
Film Art Gallery – xxxv, 377
Four Color Comics – xxxiv
French Movie Poster – xxxv
Heritage Auctions – back cover, xii
Hollywood Poster Frames – xxvii, 376
Illustraction Gallery – xxviii
KinoArt – vi

L'Imagerie Gallery – xxviii, 375
Last Moving Picture Show – ix
Limited Runs – ix
Movie Art GmbH – ix
Movie Art of Austin – xi
Movie Poster Page – vi
Movie Poster Works – xiv
Original Poster – xxxii
Past Posters – ix
Poster Conservation – xxxiv
Poster Planet – xxxiv, 377
Posteropolis – x
Simon Dwyer – x
Spotlight Displays – xxvii, 376
Unshredded Nostalgia – 379
Vintage Movie Memorabilia – vi
Vintage Movie Posters – v
Yazoo Mills – v

Please take time to notice the ads throughout this book and support these wonderful people as they have invested financially in YOUR education by sponsoring this book.

L'Imagerie Gallery
- ORIGINAL VINTAGE MOVIE POSTERS
- RARE FILM POSTERS BOUGHT AND SOLD
- LINENBACKING AND RESTORATION SERVICES
- EXPERT CUSTOM FRAMING

L'IMAGERIE ART GALLERY
In Business Since 1973

www.limageriegallery.com

PHONE: 818-762-8488   FAX: 818-762-8499   EMAIL: limageriegallery@gmail.com

10555 Victory Boulevard – North Hollywood, CA 91606
Tuesday through Saturday from 11:30 to 6:00

Movie Poster Frames
Direct from Studio Supplier

Specializing in framing your collectibles since 1984

Made to order custom frames
At Wholesale Prices
~ Delivered to your door ~

www.hollywoodposterframes.com
(800) 463-2994

9260 Deering Ave
Chatsworth, CA 91311

Open to public:
Thur-Fri: 10-5 p.m.
Sat: 9-2 p.m.

channingposters

**ORIGINAL
MOVIE POSTERS,
LOBBY CARDS, AND
AUTOGRAPHED ITEMS**

**CHANNING THOMSON
P. O. BOX 330232
SAN FRANCISCO, CA 94133-0232**

Email: channinglylethomson@att.net
ebay: http://stores.ebay.com/CHANNINGPOSTERS

GOT POSTERS?

SPOTLIGHTDISPLAYS.COM

FILM/ART
Original Film Posters

Hollywood, CA

323.363.2969

filmartgallery.com

Movie Posters ~ Music Posters
TV Posters ~ Celebrity Posters
Star Wars & James Bond
Harry Potter

Collectormania
17892 Cottonwood Dr
Parker, CO 80134

1-866-630-1648

questions@posterplanet.net
posterplanetfile@aol.com

FILM/VIDEO/DVD SUPPLIES

- DVD Storage Boxes
- VERSApak Cases for 7 to 10 DVDs
- Video Cases
- Movie Reel Canisters
- Poster Bins
- Archival Storage Boxes
- Rolled Poster Mailers
- Rolled Poster Storage
- Lobby Card Products

THE COLLECTION PROTECTION SUPPLY COMPANY

BAGS Unlimited INC
since 1976

7 Canal St. Rochester, NY 14608
www.BagsUnlimited.com

FREE CATALOG
1-800-767-2247

BACKING TO THE FUTURE

MOVIE POSTER RESTORATION SERVICES, LINEN BACKING AND SHRINK WRAP FRAMING

www.backingtothefuture.com

The FIRST EVER ...

Silent Studio Directory

During the silent era, the film industry was BOOMING, AND, it was simple to get into the film industry. NO sound equipment, NO studio and NO experience were needed. Scrape up enough money for a camera and cameraman and you were in business. THOUSANDS jumped aboard trying to make their fortune in this new fledgling industry. As talent emerged and the industry stabilized, studios and distributors changed rapidly.

It has been declared that only 10% of the silent feature films made in the U.S. still exist. Unfortunately, documentaries, shorts and regionals weren't even addressed in the statistics.

Documentation during the silent era is a historians' nightmare. Whether you are preparing material for an auction, cataloguing for an archive, adding to your collection, speculating on a possible piece of historical treasure, or doing film research, you want to be able to find information as quickly as possible.

In this first edition, we tackle what was previously considered impossible – the recreating of lost film history - **358 pages and 667 illustrations** - thousands of silent era production and distribution companies from around the world with dates, principles, and hundreds of logs and tags.

Best of all – IT'S ONLY $24.95 + $5 US Shipping

Here's how to get your copy:

On the Web

Learn About Movie Posters Book Store
www.LearnAboutMoviePosters.com

or

Amazon
www.Amazon.com

By mail:

Send $29.95 to:

Ed Poole
P. O. Box 3181
Harvey, LA 70059-3181

(504) 298-5267

www.ingramcontent.com/pod-product-compliance
Lightning Source LLC
Chambersburg PA
CBHW080723230426
43665CB00020B/2592